I0801385

Koren Talmud Bavli

THE NOÉ EDITION

GITTIN

Steinsaltz Center

KOREN

תלמוד בבלי

KOREN TALMUD BAVLI

THE NOÉ EDITION

גיטין

GITTIN

Daf 67b through Daf 90b

COMMENTARY BY

Rabbi Adin Even-Israel Steinsaltz

EDITOR-IN-CHIEF

Rabbi Dr Tzvi Hersh Weinreb

SENIOR CONTENT EDITOR

Rabbi Dr Shalom Z Berger

EXECUTIVE EDITOR

Rabbi Joshua Schreier

•

STEINSALTZ CENTER

KOREN PUBLISHERS JERUSALEM

Supported by the Matanel Foundation

Koren Talmud Bavli, The Noe Edition
Vol. 19d: Tractate Gittin, Daf 67b through Daf 90b
Paperback, ISBN, 978-965-7765-89-0

First Hebrew/English paperback edition, 2021

Koren Publishers Jerusalem Ltd.
PO Box 4044, Jerusalem 91040, ISRAEL
PO Box 8531, New Milford, CT 06776, USA
www.korenpub.com

Steinsaltz Center

Steinsaltz Center is the parent organization of institutions established by Rabbi Adin Even-Israel Steinsaltz

PO Box 45187, Jerusalem 91450 ISRAEL
Telephone: +972 2 646 0900, Fax +972 2 624 9454
www.steinsaltz-center.org

Talmud Commentary © 1965, 2012 Adin Steinsaltz and Steinsaltz Center
Talmud Translation © 2012 Steinsaltz Center
Vocalization and punctuation of the Hebrew/Aramaic text © 2012 Steinsaltz Center
Koren Tanakh & Siddur Fonts © 1962, 1981, 2021 Koren Publishers Jerusalem Ltd.
Talmud Design © 2012 Koren Publishers Jerusalem Ltd.
Original Illustrations © 1965, 2012 Steinsaltz Center
Revised Illustrations © 2012 Koren Publishers Jerusalem Ltd. (except as noted)

This book was published in cooperation with the Israel Institute for Talmudic Publications.
All rights reserved for Rabbi Adin Even-Israel Steinsaltz and Milta Management Ltd.

Considerable research and expense have gone into the creation of this publication. Unauthorized copying may be considered *geneivat da'at* and breach of copyright law.

No part of this publication (content or design, including use of the Talmud translations and Koren fonts) may be reproduced, stored in a retrieval system or transmitted in any form or by any means electronic, mechanical, photocopying or otherwise, without the prior written permission of the publisher, except in the case of brief quotations embedded in critical articles or reviews.

הִנֵּה יָמִים בָּאִים, נְאֻם אֲדֹנָי יֱהוִה, וְהִשְׁלַחְתִּי רָעָב בָּאָרֶץ,
לֹא־רָעָב לַלֶּחֶם וְלֹא־צָמָא לַמַּיִם, כִּי אִם־לִשְׁמֹעַ אֵת דִּבְרֵי יהוה.

Behold, days are coming – says the Lord God – I will send a hunger to the land, not a hunger for bread nor a thirst for water, but to hear the words of the Lord. (AMOS 8:11)

The Noé edition of the Koren Talmud Bavli
with the commentary of Rabbi Adin Even-Israel Steinsaltz
is dedicated to all those who open its covers
to quench their thirst for Jewish Knowledge,
in our generation of Torah renaissance.

This beautiful edition is for the young, the aged,
the novice and the savant alike,
as it unites the depth of Torah knowledge
with the best of academic scholarship.

Within its exquisite and vibrant pages,
words become worlds.

It will claim its place in the library of classics,
in the bookcases of the Beit Midrash,
the classrooms of our schools,
and in the offices of professionals and business people
who carve out precious time to grapple with its timeless wisdom.

For the Student and the Scholar

DEDICATED BY LEO AND SUE NOÉ

Steinsaltz Center

Executive Director, Steinsaltz Center

Rabbi Meni Even-Israel

Managing Editor

Rabbi Jason Rappoport

Senior Content Editor

Rabbi Dr. Shalom Z. Berger

Editors

Rabbi Dr. Joshua Amaru, *Coordinating Editor*
Rabbi Avishai Magence, *Content Curator*
Menucha Chwat
Rabbi Yehoshua Duker
Betzalel Philip Edwards
Rabbi Yonatan Shai Freedman
Nechama Greenberg
Rabbi Adin Krohn
Sholom Licht
Elisha Loewenstern
Sally Mayer
Rafi Miller
Rabbi David Sedley
Shira Shmidman
Avi Steinhart
Rabbi David Strauss

Language Consultants

Dr. Stephanie E. Binder, *Greek & Latin*
Rabbi Yaakov Hoffman, *Arabic*
Dr. Shai Secunda, *Persian*
Shira Shmidman, *Aramaic*

Copy Editors

Aliza Israel, *Coordinator*
Bracha Hermon
Ita Olesker
Debbie Ismailoff
Shira Finson
Ilana Sobel
Deena Nataf
Eliana Kurlantzick Yorav
Erica Hirsch Edvi
Nava Wieder

KOREN

Design & Typesetting

Dena Landowne Bailey, *Typesetting*
Tani Bayer, *Jacket Design*
Raphaël Freeman, *Design & Typography*

Images

Eliahu Misgav, *Illustration & Image Acquisition*
Daniel Gdalevich, *Illustration & Image Acquisition*

Introduction by the Publisher

The Talmud has sustained and inspired Jews for thousands of years. Throughout Jewish history, an elite cadre of scholars has absorbed its learning and passed it on to succeeding generations. The Talmud has been the fundamental text of our people.

Beginning in the 1960s, Rabbi Adin Even-Israel Steinsaltz שליט״א created a revolution in the history of Talmud study. His translation of the Talmud, first into modern Hebrew and then into other languages, as well the practical learning aids he added to the text, have enabled millions of people around the world to access and master the complexity and context of the world of Talmud.

It is thus a privilege to present the *Koren Talmud Bavli*, an English translation of the talmudic text with the brilliant elucidation of Rabbi Steinsaltz. The depth and breadth of his knowledge are unique in our time. His rootedness in the tradition and his reach into the world beyond it are inspirational.

Working with Rabbi Steinsaltz on this remarkable project has been not only an honor, but a great pleasure. Never shy to express an opinion, with wisdom and humor, Rabbi Steinsaltz sparkles in conversation, demonstrating his knowledge (both sacred and worldly), sharing his wide-ranging interests, and, above all, radiating his passion. I am grateful for the unique opportunity to work closely with him, and I wish him many more years of writing and teaching.

Our intentions in publishing this new edition of the Talmud are threefold. First, we seek to fully clarify the talmudic page to the reader – textually, intellectually, and graphically. Second, we seek to utilize today's most sophisticated technologies, both in print and electronic formats, to provide the reader with a comprehensive set of study tools. And third, we seek to help readers advance in their process of Talmud study.

To achieve these goals, the *Koren Talmud Bavli* is unique in a number of ways:

- The classic *tzurat hadaf* of Vilna, used by scholars since the 1800s, has been reset for great clarity, and opens from the Hebrew "front" of the book. Full *nikkud* has been added to both the talmudic text and Rashi's commentary, allowing for a more fluent reading with the correct pronunciation; the commentaries of *Tosafot* have been punctuated. Upon the advice of many English-speaking teachers of Talmud, we have separated these core pages from the translation, thereby enabling the advanced student to approach the text without the distraction of the translation. This also reduces the number of volumes in the set. At the bottom of each *daf*, there is a reference to the corresponding English pages. In addition, the Vilna edition was read against other manuscripts and older print editions, so that texts which had been removed by non-Jewish censors have been restored to their rightful place.
- The English translation, which starts on the English "front" of the book, reproduces the *menukad* Talmud text alongside the English translation (in bold) and commentary and explanation (in a lighter font). The Hebrew and Aramaic text is presented in logical paragraphs. This allows for a fluent reading of the text for the non-Hebrew or non-Aramaic reader. It also allows for the Hebrew reader to refer easily to the text alongside. Where the original text features dialogue or poetry, the English text is laid out in a manner appropriate to the genre. Each page refers to the relevant *daf*.

- Critical contextual tools surround the text and translation: personality notes, providing short biographies of the Sages; language notes, explaining foreign terms borrowed from Greek, Latin, Persian, or Arabic; and background notes, giving information essential to the understanding of the text, including history, geography, botany, archaeology, zoology, astronomy, and aspects of daily life in the talmudic era.
- Halakhic summaries provide references to the authoritative legal decisions made over the centuries by the rabbis. They explain the reasons behind each halakhic decision as well as the ruling's close connection to the Talmud and its various interpreters.
- Photographs, drawings, and other illustrations have been added throughout the text – in full color in the Standard and Electronic editions, and in black and white in the Daf Yomi edition – to visually elucidate the text.

This is not an exhaustive list of features of this edition, it merely presents an overview for the English-speaking reader who may not be familiar with the "total approach" to Talmud pioneered by Rabbi Steinsaltz.

Several professionals have helped bring this vast collaborative project to fruition. My many colleagues are noted on the Acknowledgments page, and the leadership of this project has been exceptional.

RABBI MENACHEM EVEN-ISRAEL, DIRECTOR OF THE STEINSALTZ CENTER, was the driving force behind this enterprise. With enthusiasm and energy, he formed the happy alliance with Koren and established close relationships among all involved in the work.

RABBI DR. TZVI HERSH WEINREB שליט״א, EDITOR-IN-CHIEF, brought to this project his profound knowledge of Torah, intellectual literacy of Talmud, and erudition of Western literature. It is to him that the text owes its very high standard, both in form and content, and the logical manner in which the beauty of the Talmud is presented.

RABBI JOSHUA SCHREIER, EXECUTIVE EDITOR, assembled an outstanding group of scholars, translators, editors, and proofreaders, whose standards and discipline enabled this project to proceed in a timely and highly professional manner.

RABBI MEIR HANEGBI, EDITOR OF THE HEBREW EDITION OF THE STEINSALTZ TALMUD, lent his invaluable assistance throughout the work process, supervising the reproduction of the Vilna pages.

RAPHAËL FREEMAN, EXECUTIVE EDITOR OF KOREN, created this Talmud's unique typographic design which, true to the Koren approach, is both elegant and user friendly.

It has been an enriching experience for all of us at Koren Publishers Jerusalem to work with the Steinsaltz Center to develop and produce the *Koren Talmud Bavli*. We pray that this publication will be a source of great learning and, ultimately, greater *avodat Hashem* for all Jews.

Matthew Miller, Publisher
Koren Publishers Jerusalem
Jerusalem 5772

Contents

For the vocalized Vilna Shas layout, please open as a Hebrew book.

Introduction to **Perek VII**

This chapter addresses two main topics. First, it continues the discussion from the previous chapter that focused on one who instructs others to give his wife a bill of divorce on his behalf. The remainder of the chapter is devoted to the issue of a conditional bill of divorce.

A husband may instruct an agent to give his wife a bill of divorce. If he is not mentally competent, his instructions are not reliable. This chapter discusses to what degree his instructions with regard to a bill of divorce are valid. Similarly explored is the case of one who is unable to verbally express his intent, and to what extent his written instructions or actions express his will.

A husband may give his wife a conditional bill of divorce. Sometimes he is concerned that he might die and leave his wife with a levirate bond, or he might be traveling to a far-off place and be concerned that he will not return, leaving her a deserted wife. Under such circumstances the husband may give a bill of divorce that will take effect only once a certain period of time has passed or a specific condition has been fulfilled. There are also cases in which the husband wishes to receive some benefit from his wife in exchange for the giving of the bill of divorce, such as a monetary payment or service. There are other instances where he intends to cause her suffering by imposing a burdensome condition upon her.

The discussion of conditions in general, and whether the conditions for a bill of divorce are unique, continues in the following chapters. Also enumerated is the requirement for a compound condition, specifying both what happens if the condition is fulfilled and what happens if it is not fulfilled. There is also discussion with regard to whether the condition follows the husband's words or his intent. Furthermore, since a bill of divorce may not be given after the husband's death, it is essential to ascertain, from the language and intent of the condition, when the document takes effect.

This chapter also explores the status of the wife who has received a conditional bill of divorce, from the time she receives the document until the condition is fulfilled.

Included in the chapter is a considerable amount of aggadic material, primarily the listing of remedies for various maladies that proved effective during the talmudic era.

מתני׳ מִי שֶׁאֲחָזוֹ קוֹרְדְיָיקוֹס, וְאָמַר ״כִּתְבוּ גֵּט לְאִשְׁתִּי״ – לֹא אָמַר כְּלוּם. אָמַר ״כִּתְבוּ גֵּט לְאִשְׁתִּי״ וַאֲחָזוֹ קוֹרְדְיָיקוֹס, חָזַר וְאָמַר ״לֹא תִּכְתְּבוּ״ – אֵין דְּבָרָיו הָאַחֲרוֹנִים כְּלוּם.

MISHNA In the case of **one who was afflicted with** temporary **insanity** [*kordeyakos*][HL] **and said: Write a bill of divorce for my wife, he said nothing,** because he was not lucid at the time. If **he said: Write a bill of divorce for my wife,** when he was lucid, **and was** then **afflicted with** temporary **insanity**[H] **and he retracted** his previous statement **and said: Do not write it, his latter statement** is considered to be **nothing,** i.e., it is not halakhically valid.

נִשְׁתַּתֵּק, וְאָמְרוּ לוֹ ״נִכְתּוֹב גֵּט לְאִשְׁתְּךָ״ וְהִרְכִּין בְּרֹאשׁוֹ, בּוֹדְקִין אוֹתוֹ שָׁלֹשׁ פְּעָמִים, אִם אָמַר עַל לָאו לָאו וְעַל הֵן הֵן – הֲרֵי אֵלּוּ יִכְתְּבוּ וְיִתְּנוּ.

The mishna continues: In a case where the husband **became mute, and** two people **said to him:**[HN] Shall **we write a bill of divorce for your wife, and he nodded his head** indicating his agreement, **they examine him** with various questions **three times. If he responded to** questions that have **a negative** answer: **No, and** responded **to** questions that have **a positive** answer: **Yes,** indicating his competence, **they shall write** the bill of divorce **and give** it to his wife based on the nod of his head.

גמ׳ מַאי קוֹרְדְיָיקוֹס? אָמַר שְׁמוּאֵל: דְּנָכְתֵיהּ חַמְרָא חַדְתָּא דְּמַעַצַרְתָּא. וְלִיתְנֵי: מִי שֶׁנְּשָׁכוֹ יַיִן חָדָשׁ! הָא קָא מַשְׁמַע לַן, דְּהַאי רוּחָא קוֹרְדְיָיקוֹס שְׁמָהּ.

GEMARA The Gemara asks: **What is** the nature of the temporary **insanity** mentioned in the mishna? **Shmuel said:** The reference is to one **who was afflicted** by drinking **new wine that** came directly **from the winepress.** The Gemara asks: **And let** the *tanna* of the mishna then **teach** explicitly: With regard to **one who was afflicted by** drinking **new wine.** The Gemara answers: **This teaches us that the name of the demon** that causes this insanity **is *Kordeyakos*.**

לְמַאי נָפְקָא מִינָּהּ? לְקָמֵיעָא. מַאי אָסוּתֵיהּ? בִּישְׂרָא סוּמָּקָא אַגּוּמְרֵי, וְחַמְרָא מַרְקָא.

The Gemara asks: **What difference is there?** The Gemara answers: The difference is with regard **to writing an amulet** to prevent harm caused by the demon. The amulet must include the name of the demon. The Gemara asks: **What is the remedy** for that illness? The Gemara responds: The afflicted person should eat **red meat** roasted **over coals and** drink **wine diluted** [*marka*][L] with a large amount of water.

אָמַר אַבָּיֵי, אֲמַרָה לִי אֵם: לְשִׁימְשָׁא בַּת יוֹמָא – כּוּזָא דְּמַיָּא; בַּת תְּרֵי יוֹמֵי – סִיכּוּרֵי; בַּת תְּלָתָא יוֹמֵי – בִּשְׂרָא סוּמָּקָא אַגּוּמְרֵי, וְחַמְרָא מַרְקָא. לְשִׁימְשָׁא עַתִּיקָתָא – לַיְתֵי תַּרְנְגוֹלְתָּא אוּכַּמְתִּי וְלִיקְרְעָהּ שְׁתִי וָעֵרֶב, וְלִיגַלְּחֵיהּ לִמְצִיעָתָא דְּרֵישֵׁיהּ וְלוֹתְבֵיהּ עִילָּוֵיהּ, וְנִנְחֵיהּ עִילָּוֵיהּ עַד דְּמִיסְרַךְ,

Abaye said: My mother told me[N] that the remedy **for a day-old fever,** i.e., one contracted that day, is drinking **a jug** [*kuza*][L] **of water.** The remedy for a fever **two days old is bloodletting** [*sikurei*].[L] The remedy for a fever **three days old** is eating **red meat** roasted **over coals and drinking diluted wine. For an old fever** that lasts for an extended period of time, the remedy is **to bring a black hen, tear it lengthwise and widthwise, shave the middle of** the sufferer's **head, and place** the hen **upon it, and leave** the hen **upon him until** it **adheres to his** head due to the blood.

וְלִינְחוֹת וְלֵיקוּם בְּמַיָּא עַד צַוָּארֵיהּ עַד דְּחָלִישׁ עָלְמָא עִילָּוֵיהּ, וְלֵימוּד וְלִסְלֵיק וְלֵיתֵיב. וְאִי לָא, לֵיכוּל כָּרָתֵי, וְלִינְחוֹת וְלֵיקוּם בְּמַיָּא עַד צַוָּארֵיהּ עַד דְּחָלִישׁ עָלְמָא עִילָּוֵיהּ, וְלֵימוּד וְלִסְלֵיק וְלֵיתֵיב.

And let him descend into the water **and let him stand in the water up to his neck until the world** appears **faint for him,** i.e., he feels faint. **And let him submerge** himself in the water, **and emerge** from the water **and sit** and rest. **And if** he is **not** able to undergo this process, **let him eat leeks, and descend** into the water, **and stand in the water up to his neck until the world** appears **faint for him. And let him submerge** himself in the water, **and emerge** from the water **and sit** and rest.

HALAKHA

One who was afflicted with temporary insanity – מִי שֶׁאֲחָזוֹ קוֹרְדְיָיקוֹס: If someone is afflicted with mental illness and says: Write a bill of divorce for my wife, his statement is ignored because his mind is not lucid. In such a case any investigation into his intent is not effective. If the court nevertheless followed his instructions, the bill of divorce is void (Rambam *Sefer Nashim, Hilkhot Geirushin* 2:14; *Shulḥan Arukh, Even HaEzer* 121:1 and *Beit Shmuel* there).

He said write…and was then afflicted with insanity, etc. – אָמַר כִּתְבוּ...וַאֲחָזוֹ קוֹרְדְיָיקוֹס וכו׳: If a healthy individual said: Write and give a bill of divorce to my wife, but subsequently was afflicted with mental illness, the court must wait until he recovers. Upon his recovery the bill of divorce can be given to his wife, and there is no need to go back and confirm his original intent. If he gave instructions not to write the bill of divorce while he was not lucid, the court ignores his statement (Rambam *Sefer Nashim, Hilkhot Geirushin* 2:15; *Shulḥan Arukh, Even HaEzer* 121:2, and in the comment of Rema).

Became mute and they said to him – נִשְׁתַּתֵּק וְאָמְרוּ לוֹ: One who is unable to speak but is of sound mind may be asked: Should we write a bill of divorce for your wife? If he nods his head the court must investigate his intent another three times. If he answers yes or no appropriately the court writes a bill of divorce and gives it to his wife. He must be checked thoroughly in case he is no longer lucid (Rambam *Sefer Nashim, Hilkhot Geirushin* 2:16; *Shulḥan Arukh, Even HaEzer* 121:5).

NOTES

Became mute and they said to him – נִשְׁתַּתֵּק וְאָמְרוּ לוֹ: Rashi explains that this is a general statement. The court checks him in this manner in every case in which he cannot speak, regardless of the cause. The Jerusalem Talmud indicates that there is a difference with regard to a case of one who was apparently healthy but suddenly became mute. In such a case the court must be concerned that he is no longer lucid, and consequently must investigate his intent and mental health more thoroughly. By contrast, in a case where one lost his ability to speak due to an illness the court may assume that he is unable to speak only because he is weak, and therefore is not required to investigate as carefully. In practice, the halakhic authorities do not mention this distinction (see *Penei Yehoshua*).

My mother told me – אֲמַרָה לִי אֵם: Abaye quotes the wisdom of his mother, citing her advice for daily life throughout the Gemara. It should be noted that this woman to whom he is referring as his mother was not his biological mother. Abaye was an orphan, and his biological mother died as she gave birth to him. The woman he is referring to as his mother was probably the wife of his uncle, Rabba bar Naḥmani, who raised him.

LANGUAGE

Temporary insanity [*kordeyakos*] **– קוֹרְדְיָיקוֹס:** From the Greek καρδιακός, *kardiakos*, meaning pertaining to the heart, or heart disease. According to both the Sages and the ancient Greeks, the heart was the seat of human intellect. Therefore, the term: Heart disease, was used to describe mental illness.

Diluted [*marka*] **– מַרְקָא:** While some claim that this word derives from the Latin meracum, this seems to be incorrect, as that term means strong, undiluted wine. It is more likely that this word relates to *marak*, the Hebrew word for soup. It follows, then, that the phrase literally means a kind of wine soup, i.e., wine diluted with a lot of water.

Jug [*kuza*] **– כּוּזָא:** Apparently from Middle Persian kūz, meaning a jug.

Bloodletting [*sikurei*] **– סִיכּוּרֵי:** Based on manuscripts, the correct version of the text reads *sivorei*. Accordingly, this is the term for the knife used in bloodletting.

לְשִׁימְשָׁא – בִּישְׂרָא סוּמָּקָא אַגּוּמְרֵי, וְחַמְרָא מַרְקָא. לְתַלְגָּא – בִּישְׂרָא שְׁמִינָא אַגּוּמְרֵי, וְחַמְרָא חַיָּיא.

The remedy **for a fever** is eating **red meat** that was roasted **over coals and** drinking **diluted wine.** A remedy **for the chills** is eating **fatty meat**[B] that was roasted **over coals and** drinking **undiluted wine.**

רַב עַמְרָם חֲסִידָא כִּי הֲוָה מְצָעֲרִין לֵיהּ בֵּי רֵישׁ גָּלוּתָא, הָווּ מַגְנוּ לֵיהּ אַתַּלְגָּא, לְמָחָר אֲמַרוּ לֵיהּ: מַאי נִיחָא לֵיהּ לְמָר דְּלַיְיתוּ לֵיהּ? אֲמַר: הָנֵי כָּל דְּאָמִינָא לְהוּ מֵיפַּךְ אַפְּכִי, אֲמַר לְהוּ: בִּישְׂרָא סוּמָּקָא אַגּוּמְרֵי וְחַמְרָא מַרְקָא, אַיְיתוּ לֵיהּ אִינְהוּ בִּישְׂרָא שְׁמִינָא אַגּוּמְרֵי וְחַמְרָא חַיָּיא;

It was related: **When the** members **of the Exilarch's**[B] **house would afflict Rav Amram the pious they would** make **him lie down** to sleep all night **on the snow. The next day they would say to him: What is preferable for the Master,** i.e., Rav Amram, **for us to bring him** to eat? Rav Amram **said** to himself: **Anything I say to them,** they will do **the opposite. He said to them:** Bring me **red meat** roasted **over coals and diluted wine. They brought him fatty meat** roasted **over coals and undiluted wine** instead, which is what Rav Amram had intended, because this is the remedy for one who suffers from the chills.

שָׁמְעָה יַלְתָּא וּמְעַיְּילָה לֵיהּ לְבֵי מַסּוּתָא, וּמוֹקְמֵי לֵיהּ בְּמַיָּא דְּבֵי מַסּוּתָא עַד דְּמִהַפְּכִי מַיָּא דְּבֵי מַסּוּתָא וְהָווּ דָּמָא, וְקָאֵי בִּישְׂרֵיהּ פְּשִׁיטֵי פָּשֵׁיט.

Yalta,[P] Rav Naḥman's wife, **heard** what the members of the Exilarch's house did, and that Rav Amram was suffering from the chills. **And she brought him to the bathhouse, and placed him in the water of the bathhouse until the water of the bathhouse turned** red like **blood. And his flesh became** covered with spots that looked like **coins** [*peshitei*].[L]

רַב יוֹסֵף אִיעֲסַק בְּרֵיחַיָא. רַב שֵׁשֶׁת אִיעֲסַק בְּכַשּׁוּרֵי, אֲמַר: גְּדוֹלָה מְלָאכָה שֶׁמְּחַמֶּמֶת אֶת בְּעָלֶיהָ.

It is related: When **Rav Yosef** suffered from the cold he **would work** by grinding with **millstones** in order to keep warm. When **Rav Sheshet**[P] suffered from the cold **he would work** by lifting **beams. He said: Great is labor,**[H] **as it warms its master.**

אֲמַר לֵיהּ רֵישׁ גָּלוּתָא לְרַב שֵׁשֶׁת: מַאי טַעֲמָא לָא סָעֵיד מָר גַּבָּן? אֲמַר לֵיהּ: דְּלָא מְעַלּוּ עַבְדֵּי, דַּחֲשִׁידִי אַאֵבֶר מִן הַחַי. אֲמַר לֵיהּ: מִי יֵימַר? אֲמַר לֵיהּ: הָשְׁתָּא מַחֲוֵינָא לָךְ. אֲמַר לֵיהּ לְשַׁמָּעֵיהּ: זִיל גְּנוֹב, אַיְיתֵי לִי חֲדָא כַּרְעָא מֵחֵיוָתָא,

§ The Gemara relates another incident of the house of the Exilarch: **The Exilarch said to Rav Sheshet: What is the reason that the Master,** i.e., Rav Sheshet, **does not eat with us? He said to him: Because the slaves** do not act **according to a high standard,** as they are **suspected** of transgressing the prohibition against eating **a limb** severed **from a living** animal. The Exilarch **said to him: Who says** that this is so? Rav Sheshet **said to him: I will now show you.** Rav Sheshet **said to his servant: Go steal one leg from the animal** that the servants of the Exilarch's house slaughtered for a meal **and bring** it **to me.**

אַיְיתֵי לֵיהּ. אֲמַר לְהוּ: אַהֲדָמוּ לִי הַדְמֵי דְּחֵיוָתָא, אַיְיתוּ תְּלָת כַּרְעֵי אוֹתִיבוּ קַמֵּיהּ. אֲמַר לְהוּ: הָא בַּעֲלַת שָׁלֹשׁ רַגְלַיִם הֲוַאי? פְּסוּק אַיְיתוּ חֲדָא מֵעָלְמָא, אוֹתִיבוּ קַמֵּיהּ. אֲמַר לֵיהּ לְשַׁמָּעֵיהּ: אוֹתְבֵיהּ נַמִי לְהָךְ דִּידָךְ, אוֹתְבָהּ. אֲמַר לְהוּ: הַאי בַּת חָמֵשׁ רַגְלַיִם הֲוַאי?

Rav Sheshet's servant **brought** one leg **to him** and afterward Rav Sheshet **said to** the servants of the Exilarch's household: **Set out the portions of the animal for me. They brought him** only **three legs and placed them before him,** because the fourth leg had been stolen. Rav Sheshet **said to them: Did this** animal **have** only **three legs?** When the servants heard this **they cut one** leg **from** another living animal and **they brought** it and **placed** it **before** Rav Sheshet. Rav Sheshet **said to his servant: Bring** out **this** leg **of yours,** i.e., that you stole, **as well. He placed** that leg on the table **and** Rav Sheshet **said to them: Did this** animal **have five legs?**

BACKGROUND

For the chills, fatty meat – לְתַלְגָּא בִּישְׂרָא שְׁמִינָא: One who is exposed to the cold for a dangerously long time must be quickly supplied with enough caloric intake for his body to function properly and to overcome the effects of hypothermia. Fatty meat and undiluted wine are sources of ready energy as they are digested more quickly than foods which are high in fiber such as vegetables. Even in later periods of history people suffering from the cold were given liquids with a high concentration of alcohol for this very purpose.

Exilarch – רֵישׁ גָּלוּתָא: The Exilarch, who descended from the house of David, was recognized by the Jews as the heir to the scepter of Judah and entrusted with broad official powers. He was the leader of the Jews of the Persian Empire and their representative to the gentile authorities, who regarded him as a member of a royal dynasty. Consequently, the Exilarch enjoyed a lofty position within the Persian court. During various periods, he was even considered third in the royal hierarchy. The Exilarch was responsible for the collection of a major portion of the government taxes from the Jewish community, and he could appoint leaders and judges whose powers included the imposition of corporal, and sometimes capital, punishment.

Adjacent to the Exilarch's home was a special rabbinical court appointed by him to deal with cases involving money, and property in particular. He also apparently had the authority to make certain appointments within the Jewish community throughout the country, although most of these were performed in consultation with the heads of the great academies. The Exilarchs were referred to in the Talmud by the honorific title Mar before or after their name, and they were devoted to the Torah. Some of them were indeed notable scholars in their own right.

LANGUAGE

Coins [*peshitei*] – פְּשִׁיטֵי: From the Middle Persian pišīz, meaning a small copper coin.

HALAKHA

Great is labor – גְּדוֹלָה מְלָאכָה: A general principle with regard to one's physical health is that as long as he exercises and exerts himself in physical labor he will not fall ill (Rambam *Sefer HaMadda*, *Hilkhot Deot* 4:14).

PERSONALITIES

Yalta – יַלְתָּא: Yalta was Rav Naḥman's wife and the daughter of the Exilarch. The Talmud records several exchanges between her, Rav Naḥman, and several other Sages of her generation.

The Gemara also relates certain actions that Yalta was permitted to perform out of respect for her position as a member of the Exilarch's family, and even tells of her many clever questions showing her extensive knowledge of the Torah. Although she had a quick temper and was very concerned for her honor, her status did not prevent her from turning to the Sages with questions. She even went out of her way to offer them assistance in times of need.

While the name Yalta became almost synonymous with a wealthy and pampered woman, opinions differ with regard to the derivation of the name. Some assert that it is a shortened form of Ayalta or Ya'alta, known in Modern Hebrew as *ayala* or *ya'ela*, a female deer. In the Mandaic language, an Aramaic dialect, the word *yalta* means a young girl, which could be the source of her name.

Rav Sheshet – רַב שֵׁשֶׁת: A prominent third-generation Babylonian *amora*, Rav Sheshet was the foremost student of Rav Huna, although he also served and studied under the other Sages of that generation. Rav Sheshet was famous for his unsurpassed expertise in *baraitot*. Many of the Sages of the generation came to learn from him, as they knew that his statements were always based on early sources.

Rav Sheshet lost his eyesight later in life. He remained involved in all aspects of community life and was a frequent guest in the house of the Exilarch. He was characterized as extremely forceful and hard as steel, and he did not defer even to eminent world leaders. He was apparently a garment merchant by trade.

אמר ליה: אי הכי, ליעבדו קמיה (שמעיה) דמר וליכול, אמר ליה: לחיי. קריבו תכא קמייהו, ואייתו קמיה בישרא ואותיבו קמיה ריסתנא דחנקא חמתא, גששיה ושקלה, כרכה בסודריה.

The Exilarch realized that he could not rely on his servants. **He said to** Rav Sheshet: **If so, they should prepare** the meat **in the presence of** my **Master's servant and** then you can **eat** without concern. Rav Sheshet **said to him: Very well. They brought a table before them, and they brought** the **meat before him. And** the servants **placed a small** bone in the meat **before him so that** it **would cause** Rav Sheshet to **choke.** Since Rav Sheshet was blind, they thought that he would be unable to notice the bone. **He felt it, took** the entire piece of meat and **wrapped it in his scarf** [*sudarei*][NL] out of concern that he would be hurt by the small bones that he could not see.

לבתר דאכיל, אמרי ליה:

After he ate, the servants realized what he had done and they wanted to show the Exilarch that Rav Sheshet did not eat the meat that was given to him. Therefore, the servants **said to** the Exilarch:

NOTES

He wrapped it in his scarf – כרכה בסודריה: Rashi explains that Rav Sheshet wrapped the meat in his scarf because he wanted to show the Exilarch that they had given him something dangerous. *Tosafot* explain that Rav Sheshet understood that this piece of meat was dangerous because he tasted it. When he realized that the animal was infected with leprosy he placed the meat in his scarf so that no one else would eat it (see *Iyyun Ya'akov*).

LANGUAGE

Scarf [*sudara*] – סודרא: From the Greek σουδάριον, *sudarion*, or alternatively the Latin sudarium, both of which mean a towel or napkin. The Sages used it to mean a band of simple cloth that was used for several purposes, among them as a scarf and a turban, especially for married Torah scholars. It was a symbol of their special status. In fact, the Sages taught (*Shabbat* 77b) that the word is an acronym for the letters of the verse: "The counsel of the Lord is with those that fear Him" [*sod Adonai lireiav*] (Psalms 25:14).

Perek **VII**
Daf **68** Amud **a**

איגניב לן כסא דכספא! בהדי דקא מעייני ואתי, אשכחוה דכרוכה בסודריה,

A silver cup was stolen from us, and they searched everyone for it. **When they were checking they found** the piece of meat **wrapped in his scarf.**

אמרי ליה: חזי מר, דלא מיכל קא בעי אלא לצעורן! אמר להו: אנא מיכל אכלי, וטעמי ביה טעמא דחיורא. אמרי ליה: חיורא לא עביד לן האידנא. אמר להו: בדקו בדוכתיה; דאמר רב חסדא: אוכמא בחיורא וחיורא באוכמתא – לקותא היא; בדוק אשכחוה.

The Exilarch's servants **said to** the Exilarch: **See Master,** i.e., the Exilarch, Rav Sheshet **does not desire to eat, rather** he wishes only **to afflict us.** Even after everything that was done for him he did not eat from the Exilarch's meal. Rav Sheshet **said to them: I ate and I tasted the taste of white** leprous spots **in** the meat and therefore I did not eat it. **They said to** the Exilarch: **We did not prepare** an animal with **white** spots **today.** Rav Sheshet **said to them: Check the** skin **in the place** of the portion that I was given. He issued this instruction in accordance with the statement of Rav Ḥisda, **as Rav Ḥisda said: Black** spots **within white** skin **and white** spots **within black** skin **are an affliction** and a sign of disease. **They checked** and **found** that the animal was afflicted in this manner, and the Exilarch's servants became even angrier with him.

כי קא נפיק, כרו ליה בירא ושדו ליה ציפתא עילויה, ואמרי ליה: ליתי מר לינח, נחר ליה רב חסדא מאחוריה. אמר ליה לינוקא: פסוק לי פסוקיך, אמר ליה: "נטה לך על ימינך או על שמאלך" אמר ליה לשמעיה: מאי קא חזית? אמר ליה: ציפיתא דשדיא, אמר ליה: הדר מינה.

When Rav Sheshet **was exiting** the house of the Exilarch the servants **dug a pit and placed a reed mat** [*tzifta*][L] **on top of it** so that the pit would not be noticed. **And they said to** Rav Sheshet: **The Master,** i.e., Rav Sheshet, **should come and rest** for a short time, and they intended for him to fall and be hurt. **Rav Ḥisda,** who was also present, **snorted** [*neḥar*][L] **to him**[N] **from behind** in order to signal to him. Rav Sheshet **said to a child** who was there: **Recite your verse for me**[H] that you studied today. The child **said to him: "Turn to your right or to your left"** (II Samuel 2:21). Rav Sheshet, who was blind, **said to his servant: What do you see?** His servant **said to him:** I see **a mat that** has been **placed** on the ground. Rav Sheshet **said to him: Turn away from it** and we will go around it.

לבתר דנפק, אמר ליה רב חסדא: מנא הוה ידע מר? אמר ליה: חדא, דנחר לי מר; ועוד, דפסק לי ינוקא פסוקא; ועוד, דחשידי עבדי דלא מעלו.

After Rav Sheshet **left** the Exilarch's house, **Rav Ḥisda said to him: From where did the Master,** i.e., Rav Sheshet, **know** that the servants had dug a pit in that place? Rav Sheshet **said to him:** There were several matters that raised my suspicions. **One, that the Master,** i.e., Rav Ḥisda, **snorted to me** to signal that I should beware. **And additionally, when the child recited the verse** for me it alluded to this matter. **And additionally, servants are suspect of not** acting **according to a high standard,** and I suspected that they would attempt to cause me harm.

LANGUAGE

Mat [*tzifta*] – ציפתא: An Aramaic word meaning a mat or a kind of bedding.

Snorted [*neḥar*] – נחר: The root of this word also means snore, and refers to any noise made with the nostrils or an undefined breathing sound.

NOTES

Rav Ḥisda snorted to him, etc. – נחר ליה רב חסדא וכו׳: The Maharsha explains that Rav Ḥisda made a noise so that Rav Sheshet would ask him why he did so. Rav Sheshet deduced on his own that there was a trap laid for him. Therefore, Rav Ḥisda asked Rav Sheshet afterward how he knew about the trap. The *Iyyun Ya'akov* explains that Rav Ḥisda did not know about the trap either but just happened to make a noise, and Rav Sheshet understood this as a sign that he should be careful.

HALAKHA

Recite your verse for me – פסוק לי פסוקיך: One may ask a child what verse he is studying and interpret a verse of blessing as a good sign. This does not fall under the prohibition against fortunetelling because one does not act based on the verse, but merely views it as a good sign. The Rema writes that it is permitted to ask a child: Read your verse for me, in order to find out what will happen in the future. The *Shakh* writes that one may act based on the verse recited *ab initio* because it is a minor form of prophecy (Rambam *Sefer HaMadda, Hilkhot Avoda Zara* 11:5; *Shulḥan Arukh, Yoreh De'a* 179:4, and in the comment of Rema).

״עָשִׂיתִי לִי שָׁרִים וְשָׁרוֹת וְתַעֲנוּגוֹת בְּנֵי הָאָדָם שִׁדָּה וְשִׁדּוֹת״, ״שָׁרִים וְשָׁרוֹת״ – אֵלּוּ מִינֵי זֶמֶר, ״וְתַעֲנוּגוֹת בְּנֵי הָאָדָם״ – אֵלּוּ בְּרֵיכוֹת וּמֶרְחֲצָאוֹת, ״שִׁדָּה וְשִׁדּוֹת״ – הָכָא תַּרְגִּימוּ: שִׁידָּה וְשִׁידְּתִין, בְּמַעַרְבָא אָמְרִי: שִׁידְּתָא.

§ After mentioning the spirit named *kordeyakos* on the previous *daf* the Gemara relates other matters connected to spirits and demons. It is written: **"I got myself *sharim* and *sharot*, and human pleasures, *shidda* and *shiddot*"** (Ecclesiastes 2:8). The Gemara explains: ***"Sharim* and *sharot*": These are types of musical** instruments.[N] **"And human pleasures": These are pools and bathhouses. *"Shidda* and *shiddot*": Here,** in Babylonia, **they interpreted** these words in the following manner: **Male demons** [*shidda*] **and female demons** [*shiddetin*]. **In the West,** Eretz Yisrael, **they said** that these words are referring to **carriages** [*shiddeta*].

אָמַר רַבִּי יוֹחָנָן: שְׁלֹשׁ מֵאוֹת מִינֵי שֵׁדִים הָיוּ בְּשִׁיחִין, וְשִׁידָּה עַצְמָהּ אֵינִי יוֹדֵעַ מַה הִיא.

Rabbi Yoḥanan says: There were three hundred types of demons in a place named **Shiḥin, but I do not know** what the form or nature of **a demon itself is.**

אָמַר מָר, הָכָא תַּרְגִּימוּ: שִׁידָּא וְשִׁידְּתִין. שִׁידָּה וְשִׁידְּתִין לְמַאי אִיבָּעֵי לֵיהּ? דִּכְתִיב: ״וְהַבַּיִת בְּהִבָּנֹתוֹ אֶבֶן שְׁלֵמָה מַסָּע נִבְנָה״ וגו׳, אֲמַר לְהוּ לְרַבָּנַן: הֵיכִי אַעֲבֵיד? אֲמַרוּ לֵיהּ: אִיכָּא שָׁמִירָא דְּאַיְיתֵי מֹשֶׁה לְאַבְנֵי אֵפוֹד.

The Master said: Here they interpreted it: **Male demons and female demons.** The Gemara asks: **Why was it necessary for** Solomon, the author of Ecclesiastes, to have **male demons and female demons?** The Gemara answers: **As it is written** with regard to the building of the Temple: **"For the house, when it was being built, was built of stone made ready at the quarry;** and there was neither hammer nor axe nor any tool of iron heard in the house, while it was being built" (1 Kings 6:7). Solomon **said to the sages: How shall I make** it so that the stone will be precisely cut without using iron? **They said to him: There is a** creature called **a *shamir*[B]** that can cut the stones, **which Moses brought** and used to cut **the stones of the ephod.**[N]

אֲמַר לְהוּ: הֵיכָא אִישְׁתַּכַּח? אֲמַרוּ לֵיהּ: אַיְיתֵי שִׁידָּה וְשִׁידְּתִין כָּבְשִׁינְהוּ אַהֲדָדֵי, אֶפְשָׁר דְּיָדְעִי וּמְגַלּוּ לָךְ. אַיְיתֵי שִׁידָּה וְשִׁידְּתִין כָּבְשִׁינְהוּ אַהֲדָדֵי, אָמְרִי: אֲנַן לָא יָדְעִינַן, דִּילְמָא אַשְׁמְדַאי מַלְכָּא דְּשֵׁידֵי יָדַע.

Solomon **said to them: Where is it found? They said to him: Bring a male demon and a female demon and torment them together. It is possible that they know** where, and due to the suffering **they will reveal** the place **to you.** Solomon **brought a male demon and a female demon and tormented them together,** and **they said: We do not know** where to find the *shamir*. **Perhaps Ashmedai,**[L] **king of the demons,**[N] **knows.**

אֲמַר לְהוּ: הֵיכָא אִיתֵיהּ? אָמְרִי לֵיהּ: אִיתֵיהּ בְּטוּרָא פְּלָן; כְּרָיָא לֵיהּ בֵּירָא וּמַלְיָא לֵיהּ מַיָּא וּמִיכַּסְיָא בְּטִינָּרָא וְחַתְמֵיהּ בְּגוּשְׁפַּנְקֵיהּ, וְכָל יוֹמָא סָלֵיק לָרְקִיעַ וְגָמַר מְתִיבְתָּא דִּרְקִיעָא, וְנָחֵית לְאַרְעָא וְגָמַר מְתִיבְתָּא דְּאַרְעָא, וְאָתֵי סָיֵיר לֵיהּ לְגוּשְׁפַּנְקֵיהּ וּמְגַלֵּי לֵיהּ וְשָׁתֵי, וּמְכַסֵּי לֵיהּ וְחָתֵים לֵיהּ וְאָזֵיל.

Solomon **said to them: Where is** Ashmedai? **They said to him: He is on such-and-such a mountain. He has dug a pit for himself** there, **and filled it with water, and covered it with a rock, and sealed it with his seal. And every day he ascends to Heaven and studies in the heavenly study hall and he descends to the earth and studies in the earthly study hall. And he comes and checks his seal** to ensure that nobody has entered his pit, and then **he uncovers it and drinks** from the water in the pit. **And** then **he covers it and seals it** again **and goes.**

שַׁדְרֵיהּ לִבְנָיָהוּ בֶּן יְהוֹיָדָע, יְהַב לֵיהּ שׁוֹשִׁילְתָּא דַּחֲקִיק עֲלָהּ שֵׁם וְעִזְקְתָא דַּחֲקִיק עֲלָהּ שֵׁם, וְגִבְבֵי דְּעַמְרָא וְזִיקֵי דְּחַמְרָא. אֲזַל כְּרָא בֵּירָא מִתַּתַּאי, וְשָׁפִינְהוּ לְמַיָּא וּסְתַמִינְהוּ בְּגִבְבֵי דְּעַמְרָא, וּכְרָא בֵּירָא מֵעִילָּאֵי וּשְׁפָכִינְהוּ לְחַמְרָא וְטָמִינְהוּ, סָלֵיק יָתֵיב בְּאִילָנָא.

Solomon **sent for Benayahu, son of Jehoiada,** a member of the royal entourage, **and gave him a chain onto which** a sacred **name** of God **was carved, and a ring**[N] **onto which** a sacred **name** of God **was carved, and fleeces of wool and wineskins of wine.** What did Benayahu do? **He went and dug a pit lower** down the mountain, below the pit dug by Ashmedai, **drained the water, and plugged it with the fleeces of wool** so that Ashmedai's pit was emptied. **And he dug a pit higher** up the mountain, above Ashmedai's pit. **And he poured the wine** into it so that the wine filled Ashmedai's pit, **and he plugged** the lower and upper pits that he dug. **He climbed up and sat in a tree.**

כִּי אֲתָא סָיְירֵיהּ לְגוּשְׁפַּנְקָא, גַּלְיֵיהּ אַשְׁכְּחֵיהּ חַמְרָא, אֲמַר, כְּתִיב: ״לֵץ הַיַּיִן הוֹמֶה שֵׁכָר וְכָל שֹׁגֶה בּוֹ לֹא יֶחְכָּם״, וּכְתִיב: ״זְנוּת וָיַיִן וְתִירוֹשׁ יִקַּח לֵב״, לָא אִישְׁתֵּי. כִּי צָחֵי, לָא סַגְיָא לֵיהּ, אִישְׁתֵּי רָוָה וּגְנָא.

When Ashmedai **came he checked his seal, opened** the pit, **and found it to be filled with wine. He said** that **it is written: "Wine is a mocker, strong drink is riotous; and whosoever wallows in it is not wise"** (Proverbs 20:1), **and it is written: "Harlotry,**[N] **wine, and new wine take away the heart"** (Hosea 4:11). He concluded: **I will not drink** this wine. Eventually, **when he became thirsty, he was unable to** resist the wine and **he drank, became intoxicated, and fell asleep.**

NOTES

Types of musical instruments – **מִינֵי זֶמֶר**: The Maharsha writes that the reason why these terms for musical instruments are gendered is that certain musical instruments are normally played by men while others are normally played by women.

Which Moses brought for the stones of the ephod – **דְּאַיְיתֵי מֹשֶׁה לְאַבְנֵי אֵפוֹד**: The names of the tribes of Israel were carved on the stones of the ephod, and Moses used the *shamir* to carve out the names. Elsewhere (*Sota* 48b) the Gemara explains that the *shamir* was able to engrave the stone without removing any of it. The Rashash, citing Ramban's Commentary on the Torah, claims that the ephod stones could be carved, and the reference here is to the stones of the breastplate which had to be engraved without removing any of the stone. This is because the Torah states that they must remain: "In their fullness" (Exodus 28:20).

Ashmedai, king of the demons – **אַשְׁמְדַאי מַלְכָּא דְּשֵׁידֵי**: *Midrash Shlomo* explains that this lengthy story of Solomon and Ashmedai symbolizes Solomon's lifelong struggles pursuing worldly knowledge. Although Solomon's initial intent was to enhance his understanding of the mitzvot, in the end his quest resulted in his succumbing to the temptations to which he was exposed. Ashmedai, then, is not actually a demon, but a metaphor for these pursuits. Solomon's struggles are recorded in a different form in the book of Ecclesiastes.

And a ring, etc. – **וְעִזְקְתָא וכו׳**: The commentaries ask: Why did Benayahu need this ring if he had a chain on which God's name was written? They answer that he used the chain to bind Ashmedai, but the ring was meant for Benayahu to protect himself from Ashmedai. Although the demon was bound, he had the ability to cause damage and could have injured Benayahu (Maharsha; Riaf). Others write that this ring had the power to control the demon (*Iyyun Ya'akov*).

And it is written harlotry, etc. – **וּכְתִיב זְנוּת וכו׳**: *Tosafot* point out that this verse was said by the prophet Hosea, who lived long after Solomon. There are numerous similar instances in the Talmud where people cite verses that were not yet written during their lifetimes. *Tosafot* explain that these verses were known earlier by tradition, even though they were recorded in the Bible only at a later date.

BACKGROUND

Shamir – **שָׁמִירָא**: The *shamir* is a worm that was utilized in a miraculous fashion. As the Gemara indicates, Moses used it to cut the gems for the High Priest's ephod. Solomon used it as well in order to cut the stones for the Temple. Since it was prohibited to cut those stones with any metal utensil, he had to resort to this method. The Mishna (*Avot* 5:6) lists the *shamir* as one of the ten items that God created during twilight on the sixth day of Creation. The Mishna (*Sota* 48a) records that after the destruction of the Temple, the *shamir* was no longer used. According to the *Midrash Shlomo*, the *shamir* should be understood metaphorically, as a means by which one accomplished certain difficult tasks.

LANGUAGE

Ashmedai – **אַשְׁמְדַאי**: Derived from the name of a Zoroastrian evil spirit, perhaps the Parthian išm(a)dēw, evil god of wrath. Some have nevertheless asserted that the name is derived from the Aramaic form of the Hebrew root *shin*, *mem*, *dalet*, meaning desolation and destruction, just as the word for demon, *shed*, is derived from the word meaning destroy, *shadad*. In *Bereshit Rabba* (36:3), he is called Shmadon.

נחית, אתא, שדא ביה שושילתא, סתמיה. כי אתער הוה קא מיפרזל, אמר ליה: שמא דמרך עלך! שמא דמרך עלך!

Benayahu **descended** from the tree, **came,** and **threw the chain around** Ashmedai, and **enclosed him** within it. **When** Ashmedai **awoke he struggled** to remove the chain. Benayahu **said to him: The name of your Master is upon you,**[N] **the name of your Master is upon you,** do not tear the chain. God's name is written on this chain, and it is forbidden to destroy it.

כי נקיט ליה ואתי, מטא דיקלא חף ביה שדייה, מטא לביתא שדייה, מטא גבי כובא דההיא ארמלתא, נפקא

When Benayahu **took** Ashmedai **and came** to Jerusalem **he reached a palm tree** and Ashmedai **rubbed against it** and **knocked it down. He reached a house** and **knocked it down. He reached a small shack** [*kuva*][L] **belonging to a certain widow.** This widow **emerged,**

NOTES

The name of your Master is upon you – שמא דמרך עלך: The fact that Ashmedai was unable to destroy the name of God demonstrates the fundamental belief that even powers which appear to be evil, such as demons, ultimately derive their power from God, are subject to divine law, and are part of the divine plan.

LANGUAGE

Shack [*kuva*] – כובא: There is a version of the text which reads *kukha*, which is similar to the Hebrew word *kukh*, meaning digging or a room dug into the earth, and by extension a small, windowless room.

Perek **VII**
Daf **68** Amud **b**

איחננא ליה, כפא לקומתיה מיניה איתבר ביה גרמא, אמר, היינו דכתיב: "ולשון רכה תשבר גרם".

and **she begged him** not to knock down the house. **He bent** his body away **from her,** to the other side, and **broke one of his bones. He said:** This is as it is written: **"Soft speech can break a bone"** (Proverbs 25:15).

חזא סמיא דהוה קא טעי באורחא, אסקיה לאורחיה. חזא רויא דהוה קא טעי באורחא, אסקיה לאורחיה. חזא חדוותא דהוו קמחדי לה, בכה. שמעיה לההוא גברא דהוה קאמר לאושכפא: עביד לי מסאני לשב שני, אחיך. חזא ההוא קסמא דהוה קסים, אחיך.

Ashmedai **saw a blind man who was lost on the road** and **he brought him to the** correct **road. He saw a drunk who was lost on the road** and **he brought him to the correct road. He saw the joy** of a wedding celebration **in which they were celebrating,** and **he cried. He heard a certain man say to a shoemaker** [*ushkafa*]:[L] **Make me shoes** that will last **for seven years,** and **he laughed. He saw a certain sorcerer performing magic,** and **he laughed.**

כי מטא להתם, לא עיילוה לגביה דשלמה עד תלתא יומי. יומא קמא אמר להו: אמאי לא קא בעי לי מלכא לגביה? אמרו ליה: אנסיה מישתיא; שקל לבינתא אותיב אחברתה. אתו אמרו ליה לשלמה, אמר להו, הכי אמר לכו: הדור אשקיוה.

When Ashmedai **arrived there,** in Jerusalem, **they did not bring him before Solomon until three days** had passed. On **the first day he said to them: Why doesn't the king want me** to come **to him? They said to him:** He drank too much and was **overcome** by **drink.** Ashmedai **took a brick** and **placed** it **on** top **of another** brick. The servants **came and told Solomon** what he had done. Solomon interpreted the action and **said to them: This is what he said to you** through this allusion: **Return** and **give** the king more to **drink.**

למחר אמר להו: ואמאי לא קא בעי לי מלכא לגביה? אמרו ליה: אנסיה מיכלא; שקל לבינתא מחברתה אותבה אארעא. אתו אמרו ליה לשלמה, אמר להו, הכי אמר לכו: נגידו מיניה מיכליה.

The following day Ashmedai **said to them: And why doesn't the king want me** to come **to him? They said to him:** He ate too much and was **overcome** by **food.** Ashmedai **took the brick off the other** brick and **placed it on the ground.** The servants **came** and **told Solomon** what Ashmedai had done. **He** interpreted Ashmedai's actions and **said to them: This is what he said to you** through this allusion: **Take his food away from him.**

לסוף תלתא יומי עייל לקמיה; שקל קניא ומשח ארבעה גרמידי ושדא קמיה. אמר ליה: מכדי כי מיית ההוא גברא לית ליה בהדין עלמא אלא ארבעה גרמידי, השתא כבשתיה לכולי עלמא ולא שבעת עד דכבשת נמי לדידי?

At the end of three days Ashmedai **came before** Solomon. Ashmedai **took a reed and measured four cubits** [*garmidei*],[L] **and threw it before him. He said to** Solomon: **See, when that man,** Solomon, **dies, he will have nothing in this world except the four cubits** of his grave. **Now you have conquered the entire world and** yet **you are not satisfied until you also conquer me?**

אמר ליה: לא קא בעינא מינך מידי, בעינא דאיבנייה לבית המקדש וקא מיבעי לי שמירא. אמר ליה: לדידי לא מסיר לי, לשרא דימא מסיר ליה, ולא יהיב ליה אלא לתרנגולא ברא דמהימן ליה אשבועתיה.

Solomon **said to him: I need nothing from you. I want to build the Temple and I need the** ***shamir*** for this. Ashmedai **said to him:** The *shamir* **was not given to me,** but **it was given to the** angelic **minister of the sea. And he gives it only to the wild rooster,** also known as the *dukhifat* or the hoopoe, **whom he trusts by** the force of **his oath** to return it.

LANGUAGE

Shoemaker [*ushkafa*] – אושכפא: From the Babylonian language, this word is also found with the same meaning in Syriac. In Arabic it is إسكاف, *'iskāf*.

Cubits [*garmidei*] – גרמידי: *Garmida* is the Aramaic word for the middle finger, and by extension it also means the measurement of a cubit, which is the distance from the elbow to the end of the middle finger. This word appears, with a slightly different spelling, in the Bible: "And Ehud made him a sword which had two edges, of a cubit [*gomed*] length" (Judges 3:16). In its Aramaic form it has an added letter, *reish*.

וּמַאי עָבֵד בֵּיהּ? מַמְטֵי לֵיהּ לְטוּרֵי דְּלֵית בְּהוּ יִשּׁוּב, וּמַנַּח לָהּ אַשִּׁינָּא דְּטוּרָא וּפָקַע טוּרָא, וּמַנְקִיט מַיְיתֵי בִּיזְרָנֵי מֵאִילָנֵי וְשָׁדֵי הָתָם וְהָוֵי יִשּׁוּב. וְהַיְינוּ דְּמְתַרְגְּמִינַן: נַגָּר טוּרָא.

And what does the wild rooster **do with it? He brings it to mountains that are not fit for habitation,**[N] **and he places** the *shamir* **on the craggy rock and the mountain splits. And he takes** and **brings seeds of trees, throws them there, and it becomes** fit for **habitation. And this is why we interpret** the word *dukhifat* as **a cutter of mountains** [*naggar tura*],[L] i.e., the Aramaic translation of the word *dukhifat* in the Bible is *naggar tura,* cutter of mountains.

בָּדְקוּ קִינָּא דְּתַרְנְגוֹלָא בָּרָא דְּאִית לֵיהּ בְּנֵי, וְחַפּוּיָהּ לְקִינֵּיהּ זוּגִיתָא חִיוּרְתֵּי. כִּי אֲתָא בָּעֵי לְמֵיעַל וְלָא מָצֵי, אֲזַל אַיְיתֵי שָׁמִירָא וְאוֹתְבֵיהּ עִלָּוֵיהּ; רְמָא בֵּיהּ קָלָא, שָׁדְיֵיהּ, שְׁקַלֵיהּ, אֲזַל חֲנַק נַפְשֵׁיהּ אַשְּׁבוּעֲתֵיהּ.

They investigated **and found the nest of a wild rooster in which there were chicks, and he covered its nest with translucent glass. When** the rooster **came it wanted to enter** the nest **but was unable** to do so. **It went and brought the** *shamir* **and placed it on top** to crack the glass. Solomon's servant **threw a clump** of dirt **at** the rooster and the rooster **knocked over** the *shamir.* The man **took it** and the wild rooster **went** and **strangled itself over** the fact that it had not kept **its oath,** by not returning the *shamir.*

אֲמַר לֵיהּ בְּנָיָהוּ: מַאי טַעְמָא כִּי חֲזִיתֵיהּ לְהַהוּא סַמְיָא דַּהֲוָה קָא טָעֵי בְּאוֹרְחָא, אַסִּיקְתֵּיהּ לְאוֹרְחֵיהּ? אֲמַר לֵיהּ: מַכְרְזֵי עֲלֵיהּ בִּרְקִיעָא דְּצַדִּיק גָּמוּר הוּא, וּמַאן דְּעָבַד לֵיהּ נַיְחָא נַפְשֵׁיהּ זָכֵי לְעָלְמָא דְּאָתֵי.

Later, **Benayahu said to** Ashmedai: **What is the reason** that **when you saw that blind man who was lost on the road you brought him to the** correct **road?** Ashmedai **said to him: They proclaim about him in heaven that he is a completely righteous man, and anyone who does good for his soul shall merit** to enter **the World-to-Come.**

וּמַאי טַעְמָא כִּי חֲזִיתֵיהּ לְהַהוּא רַוְיָא דְּקָטָעֵי בְּאוֹרְחָא, אַסִּיקְתֵּיהּ לְאוֹרְחֵיהּ? אֲמַר לֵיהּ: מַכְרְזֵי עֲלֵיהּ בִּרְקִיעָא דְּרָשָׁע גָּמוּר הוּא, וַעֲבַדִי לֵיהּ נַיְחָא נַפְשֵׁיהּ כִּי הֵיכִי דְּלֵיכְלֵיהּ לְעָלְמָא.

Then Benayahu asked: **And what is the reason** that **when you saw the drunk man who was lost on the road you brought him to the** correct **road?** Ashmedai **said to him: They proclaim about him in heaven that he is a completely wicked man. And I did good for his soul so that he will consume** his reward **in this world** and not have any reward in the World-to-Come.

מַאי טַעְמָא כִּי חֲזִיתֵיהּ לְהַהוּא חֶדְוְותָא, בְּכֵית? אֲמַר לֵיהּ: בָּעֵי מֵימַת גַּבְרָא בְּגוֹ תְּלָתִין יוֹמִין, וּבָעֲיָא מִינְטַר לְיָבָם קָטָן תְּלֵיסְרֵי שְׁנִין.

Benayahu continued and asked him: **What is the reason** that **when you saw that joy** of the wedding **you cried?** Ashmedai **said to him:** I knew that this **man will die within thirty days. And** his wife **is required to wait for the** *yavam,* the husband's brother, who is **a minor,** to reach the age of **thirteen years,** the age of majority, so that he can release her through *ḥalitza,* the ritual through which the *yavam* frees the *yevama* of her levirate bonds.

מַאי טַעְמָא כִּי שְׁמַעְתֵּיהּ לְהַהוּא גַּבְרָא דַּאֲמַר לֵיהּ לְאוּשְׁכָּפָא: עֲבֵיד לִי מְסָאנֵי לְשַׁב שְׁנִין, אַחֵיכְתְּ? אֲמַר לֵיהּ: הַהוּא שִׁבְעָה יוֹמֵי לֵית לֵיהּ, מְסָאנֵי לְשַׁב שְׁנִין בָּעֵי?!

In addition, he asked: **What is the reason** that **when you heard that man say to a shoemaker: Make me shoes** that will last **for seven years, you laughed?** Ashmedai **said to him: That** man **does not have seven days** to live; **does he need shoes** that will last **for seven years?**

מַאי טַעֲמָא כִּי חֲזִיתֵיהּ לְהַהוּא קָסְמָא דַּהֲוָה קָסֵים, אַחֵיכְתְּ? אֲמַר לֵיהּ: דַּהֲוָה יָתֵיב אַבֵּי גַּזָּא דְּמַלְכָּא, לִקְסוֹם מַאי דְּאִיכָּא תּוּתֵיהּ.

Benayahu then asked: **What is the reason** that **when you saw that sorcerer performing magic you laughed?** Ashmedai **said to him: Because he was sitting on the king's treasury** [*bei gaza*].[L] **Let him use his magic** to know **what there is** buried **underneath him.**

תַּרְחֵיהּ גַּבֵּיהּ עַד דְּבָנְיֵיהּ לְבֵית הַמִּקְדָּשׁ. יוֹמָא חַד הֲוָה קָאֵי לְחוּדֵיהּ, אֲמַר לֵיהּ, כְּתִיב: ״כְּתוֹעֲפוֹת רְאֵם לוֹ״, וְאָמְרִינַן: ״כְּתוֹעֲפוֹת״ – אֵלּוּ מַלְאֲכֵי הַשָּׁרֵת, ״רְאֵם״ – אֵלּוּ הַשֵּׁדִים, מַאי רְבוּתַיְיכוּ מִינַּן?

Solomon **kept** Ashmedai **with him until** he completed **building the Temple. One day he stood** with Ashmedai **alone. He said** to Ashmedai: **It is written: "For him like the lofty horns of the wild ox"** (Numbers 24:8), **and** the Sages **say** in explanation of the verse: **"Like the lofty horns"; these are the ministering angels. "The wild ox"; these are the demons.** In **what way are you greater**[N] **than us?** Why does the verse praise your abilities and powers over those of human beings?

אֲמַר לֵיהּ: שְׁקוֹל שׁוֹשִׁילְתָּא מִינַּאי וְהַב לִי עִיזְקָתָךְ, וְאַחֲוֵי לָךְ רְבוּתַאי. שְׁקַלֵיהּ לְשׁוֹשִׁילְתָּא מִינֵּיהּ וְיָהֵיב לֵיהּ עִיזְקָתֵיהּ, בְּלָעֵיהּ, אוֹתְבֵיהּ לְחַד גַּפֵּיהּ בִּרְקִיעָא וּלְחַד גַּפֵּיהּ בְּאַרְעָא, פַּתְקֵיהּ אַרְבַּע מְאָה פַּרְסֵי. עַל הַהִיא שַׁעְתָּא אֲמַר שְׁלֹמֹה: ״מַה יִּתְרוֹן לָאָדָם בְּכָל עֲמָלוֹ שֶׁיַּעֲמֹל תַּחַת הַשָּׁמֶשׁ״.

Ashmedai **said to him: Take the chain** engraved with God's name **off me and give me your ring** with God's name engraved on it, **and I will show you my strength.** Solomon **took the chain off him and he gave him his ring.** Ashmedai **swallowed** the ring and grew until **he placed one wing in the heaven and one wing on the earth. He threw** Solomon a distance of **four hundred parasangs. With regard to that moment Solomon said: "What profit is there for a person through all of his toil under the sun?"** (Ecclesiastes 1:3). With Solomon deposed from the throne, Ashmedai took his place.

NOTES

Not fit for habitation, etc. – לֵית בְּהוּ יִשּׁוּב וכו׳: The wild rooster takes the *shamir* to the mountains so that he can help make the land fit for habitation so that he will eventually have food with which to sustain himself. People will settle where trees are growing, and eventually the wild rooster will be able to scavenge for food.

In what way are you greater – מַאי רְבוּתַיְיכוּ: The commentaries write that Solomon knew that demons have abilities that human beings lack. Why, then, do the explanations of the Sages mention both angels and demons? All the powers that the demons possess are presumably possessed by angels as well. Through his actions, Ashmedai demonstrated to Solomon that in certain respects demons have more power than angels, and they are able to make use of powers that the ministering angels cannot (*Iyyun Ya'akov*).

LANGUAGE

Cutter of mountains [*naggar tura*] – נַגָּר טוּרָא: According to Onkelos, this is the Aramaic translation of the biblical word for the hoopoe bird, *dukhifat* (Leviticus 11:19).

Treasury [*bei gaza*] – בֵּי גַּזָּא: Derived from the Persian word ganz, meaning treasury. It appears in the Bible with an extra *nun* as *ginzei hamelekh*, "the king's treasuries" (Esther 3:9), and *ginzayya di-malka*, "the king's treasure house" (Ezra 5:17).

"וזה היה חלקי מכל עמלי" מאי "וזה"? רב ושמואל, חד אמר: מקלו, וחד אמר: גונדו. היה מחזר על הפתחים, כל היכא דמטא אמר: "אני קהלת הייתי מלך על ישראל בירושלים". כי מטא גבי סנהדרין, אמרו רבנן: מכדי שוטה בחדא מילתא לא סריך, מאי האי?

With regard to the verse: **"And this was my portion from all of my toil"** (Ecclesiastes 2:10), the Gemara asks: **What** is the meaning of the expression: **"And this"?** This expression is always an allusion to an item that is actually in his hand or can be shown. **Rav and Shmuel** disagree with regard to the meaning of this phrase. **One said:** This is referring to Solomon's **staff** that remained in his hand. **And one said:** This is referring to **his cloak.** Solomon **circulated from door to door** collecting charity, and **wherever he arrived he would say: "I, Ecclesiastes, was king over Israel in Jerusalem"** (Ecclesiastes 1:12). **When he** finally **arrived at the Sanhedrin** in Jerusalem **the sages said: Now, an imbecile does not fixate on one matter** all of the time, so **what is this** matter? Is this man perhaps telling the truth that he is Solomon?

אמרו ליה לבניהו: קא בעי לך מלכא לגביה? אמר להו: לא. שלחו להו למלכוותא: קאתי מלכא לגבייכו? שלחו להו: אין, קאתי. שלחו להו: בידקו בכרעיה, שלחו להו: במוקי קאתי,

The sages **said to Benayahu:**[N] **Does the king require you** to be **with him?** Benayahu **said to them: No. They sent to the queens** and asked: Does **the king come** to be **with you?** The queens **sent** a response **to them: Yes, he comes. They sent** a request **to** the queens: **Check his feet** to see if they are human feet. The queens **sent** a response **to** the sages: **He** always **comes in socks** [***bemokei***],[L] and it is not possible to see his feet.

וקא תבע להו בנידותייהו, וקא תבע לה נמי לבת שבע אימיה. אתיוה לשלמה והבו ליה עזקתא ושושילתא דחקוק עליה שם, כי עייל חזייה, פרח.

The queens continued discussing the king's behavior: **And he demands of them,** i.e., the queens, to engage in sexual intercourse **when they are menstruating. And he also demands** that **Bathsheba his mother** engage in sexual intercourse with him. Once the Sanhedrin heard this they understood that this was an imposter and not actually Solomon. **They brought Solomon, gave him a ring and the chain on which the name** of God **was carved. When** Solomon **entered,** Ashmedai **saw him** and **fled.**

ואפילו הכי הוה ליה ביעתותא מיניה, והיינו דכתיב: "הנה מטתו שלשלמה ששים גבורים סביב לה מגבורי ישראל כולם אחוזי חרב מלומדי מלחמה איש חרבו על ירכו מפחד בלילות".

The Gemara adds: **And even so,** although Ashmedai fled, Solomon **was fearful of him, and this is as it is written: "Behold the bed of Solomon surrounded by sixty strong men from the warriors of Israel. All of them holding swords and trained in war, each man with his sword on his thigh from fear in the nights"** (Song of Songs 3:7–8).

רב ושמואל, חד אמר: מלך והדיוט, וחד אמר: מלך והדיוט ומלך.

Rav and Shmuel disagreed with regard to this story of Solomon. **One said:** He was **a king and** afterward he became **a commoner,**[N] and never returned to his position as king. **And one said:** He was **a king, and** became **a commoner, and a king,** as ultimately he returned to his throne and defeated Ashmedai.

לדמא דרישא – ליתי שורבינא וביניא ואסא דרא, וזיתא וחילפא, וחילפי דימא ויבלא, ולישלוקינהו בהדי הדדי, ולנטול תלת מאה כסי אהאי גיסא דרישא, ותלת מאה כסי אהאי גיסא דרישא.

§ The Gemara returns to the discussion concerning the different remedies with which the chapter began: As a remedy **for** a headache caused by excessive **blood in the head,**[N] **let him bring cypress** [***shurvina***],[L] **willow, fresh myrtle** [***asa dara***],[L] **olive, poplar, sea willow,**[B] **and cynodon grass and boil them together. And he should pour three hundred cups** of this liquid **on one side of his head and three hundred cups on this,** the other **side of his head.**

LANGUAGE

Socks [*mokei*] – מוקי: Derived from the Persian mōk. According to the *Arukh*, it refers to a shoe with a wooden sole and leather upper. By contrast, Rashi asserts that it is a shoe made from cloth.

Cypress [*shurvina*] – שורבינא: This Aramaic word is the translation of the Hebrew word *te'ashur* (see Isaiah 41:19), and similarly appears in Arabic as شربين, *sharbīn*, or cypress. Accordingly, the name *berosh* mentioned in the verse in Isaiah is obviously a different tree from that which is described by the same word in modern Hebrew.

Fresh myrtle [*asa dara*] – אסא דרא: Rashi explains that *asa* is a myrtle, and that *dara* refers to the way in which the leaves grow from one side of the stem, in a row, rather than indicating fresh. By contrast, in tractate *Pesaḥim* (56a) and elsewhere, Rashi and the *Arukh* explain that it means fresh myrtle. Some say that it derives from the Greek διερός, *dieros*, meaning alive or wet. Another version of the text in the *Arukh* reads *asa rada*, meaning a myrtle whose leaves are flat or flattened.

BACKGROUND

Sea willow [*ḥilfei yam*] – חילפי ים: According to some, *ḥilfei yam* is camel grass, *Cymbopogen schoenathos* (*Ardropogon*), a perennial grass from the Poaceae family that reaches about 60 cm in height. Growing primarily in arid regions, it is used as camel fodder. It has a pleasant fragrance, and its flowers are processed to produce an aromatic oil used both as a medicine and a perfume.

NOTES

They said to Benayahu, etc. – אמרו ליה לבניהו וכו׳: The reason that Ashmedai did not call for Benayahu, even though Ashmedai did make use of the rest of Solomon's servants, was because of the ring he wore, on which God's name was written (Maharsha).

A king and a commoner – מלך והדיוט: The commentaries write that this cannot be understood literally, as how can Rav or Shmuel claim that Solomon never actually returned to serve as king when the Bible records the years of his rule in Jerusalem, his death, and his burial? Rather, it means that he did not return to the same level of authority that he previously enjoyed (Ya'avetz). Alternatively, as the Maharshal writes, Solomon initially ruled over the upper and lower worlds, and afterward he did not rule over the celestial world (see *Megilla* 11b).

Blood in the head, etc. – דמא דרישא וכו׳: The Gemara continues to identify many remedies and supernatural cures for various diseases. The *ge'onim* write that people should not rely on these remedies in practice, and they may not be used unless they have been thoroughly checked by expert doctors and found to not cause any harm to the patient.

Later authorities actually prohibited using these remedies, because the exact ingredients are not known, nor is the way in which they work. Likewise, the precise details and nature of these diseases is not known. These authorities were concerned that perhaps by using such remedies people would come to mock the words of the Gemara.

LANGUAGE

Rose [*varda*] – וַרְדָּא: From the Middle Iranian vard, meaning the rose plant and flower. In talmudic Aramaic and similarly in the parallel word in Greek, it is also a general term for the color red.

וְאִי לָא, לֵיתֵי וַרְדָּא חִיוָּרָא דְּקָאֵי בְּחַד דָּרָא, וְלִישַׁלְקֵיהּ, וְלִינְטוֹל שִׁיתִּין כָּסֵי אַהַאי גִּיסָּא דְּרֵישָׁא, וְשִׁיתִּין כָּסֵי אַהַאי גִּיסָּא דְּרֵישָׁא.

And if it is **not** effective or he is unable to obtain all of these ingredients then **let him bring a white rose** [*varda*][L] **that stands in one row,** meaning that it was growing alone, **and he should boil it. And he should pour sixty cups on this side of** his **head and sixty cups on this side of** his **head.**

לְצִלִּיחְתָּא – לֵיתֵי תַּרְנְגוֹלָא בָּרָא, וְלִישַׁחְטֵיהּ בְּזוּזָא חִיוָּרָא אַהַהוּא גִּיסָּא דְּכָיֵיב לֵיהּ, וְנִזְדַּהַר מִדָּמֵיהּ דְּלָא לְסַמְיִנְהוּ לְעֵינֵיהּ, וְלִיתְלְיֵיהּ בְּסִיפָּא דְּבָבָא, דְּכִי עָיֵיל חָיֵיף בֵּיהּ, וְכִי נָפֵיק חָיֵיף בֵּיהּ.

As a remedy **for a migraine,**[B] **let him bring a wild rooster**[B] **and** slaughter it using **a silver dinar,** so that the blood flows **over the** side of his head **that hurts him. And he should be careful of its blood so as not to blind his eye. And he should hang it on the** doorpost of his house, **so that when he enters he rubs against it and when he exits he rubs against it.**

BACKGROUND

Migraine [*tziliḥta*] – צְלִיחְתָּא: According to all commentaries, the *tziliḥta* mentioned here is what is today called a migraine headache; a sharp, unilateral pain affecting half of the head.

Wild rooster – תַּרְנְגוֹלָא בָּרָא: Based on the continuation of the Gemara, it seems that the bird mentioned here is the hoopoe [*dukhifat*]. Apparently, it was referred to as the wild rooster because the sprouting plumage on its head resembles the crest of a rooster. The identification of the wild rooster with the hoopoe became so engrained that there were Karaite sages who prohibited eating chicken, as they believed that it was the *dukhifat* mentioned in the Torah.

Hoopoe

Perek **VII**
Daf **69** Amud **a**

NOTES

Seven-colored scorpion – עַקְרַבָּא דְּשַׁב חוּמְרֵי: Rashi explains that the scorpion has seven colors, as it is very old and its coloring has many shades. The *Arukh* explains that this is instead referring to seven vertebrae-like rings in the scorpion's tail.

And let him place three eyebrushes full – וְלִימְלֵי תְּלָתָא מַכְחָלֵי: The application of mascara or any medicinal substance in the eye is called filling in Aramaic, because even by placing a small amount in one's eye it is as though he fills his entire eye.

לִבְרוֹקְתִּי – לֵיתֵי עַקְרַבָּא דְּשַׁב חוּמְרֵי וְנַיְיבְּשֵׁיהּ בְּטוּלָּא, וְנִישְׁחוֹק תַּרְתֵּי מְנָתָא כּוּחְלָא וַחֲדָא מְנָתָא מִינֵּיהּ, וְלִימְלֵי תְּלָתָא מַכְחָלֵי בְּהַאי עֵינָא וּתְלָתָא מַכְחָלֵי בְּהַאי עֵינָא, טְפֵי לָא לִימְלֵי, דְּאִי לָא – פָּקַע עֵינֵיהּ.

§ As a remedy **for eye disease** [*beroketi*],[B] **let him bring the body of a seven-colored scorpion,**[NB] **dry it in the shade, and grind** together **two portions of stibium**[B] **and one portion of** the dried scorpion. **And let him place three eyebrushes full**[N] **in this eye, and three eyebrushes full in that eye. But he should not place more, as if** he does **not** heed this advice and he does place more, **his eye will burst.**

LANGUAGE

Rope of hair [*shudra barka*] – שׁוּדְרָא בַּרְקָא: The origin of the word *shudra* is related to the Hebrew word *shazar*, meaning interwoven, like strands of rope twisted together or a chain. Some commentaries explain that the word *barka* means hair, but its source is unclear.

לְשַׁבְרִירֵי דְּלֵילְיָא – נֵיתֵי שׁוּדְרָא בַּרְקָא וְנֵיסַר חֲדָא כַּרְעָא מִינֵּיהּ וַחֲדָא כַּרְעָא מִכַּלְבָּא, וְנִיטְרְפוּ יָנוּקֵי חַסְפָּא אַבַּתְרֵיהּ, וְלֵימְרוּ לֵיהּ: "אָסָא כַּלְבָּא אַכְסָא תַּרְנְגוֹלָא", וְלִיגְבֵּי שַׁב אוּמְצֵי מִשִּׁבְעָה בָּתֵּי וְלֵיתְבִינְהוּ נִיהֲלֵיהּ בְּצִינּוֹרָא דְּדַשָּׁא, וְנֵיכְלִינְהוּ בְּקִלְקוּלֵי דְּמָתָא. בָּתַר הָכִי לִפְשׁוֹט שׁוּדְרָא בַּרְקָא וְנֵימְרוּ הָכִי: "שַׁבְרִירֵי דִּפְלוֹנִי בַּר פְּלוֹנִיתָא שַׁבְקִינְהוּ לִפְלוֹנִי בַּר פְּלוֹנִיתָא וְלִיחֲרוּ לְכַלְבָּא בְּבָבִיתָא דְּעֵינֵיהּ".

As a remedy **for night blindness,**[B] **he should bring a rope of** animal hair [*shudra barka*],[L] **and he should tie one of** his **legs and one leg of a dog** together with the rope. **And let children throw** pottery **shards behind him, and let them say to him: The dog is old and the rooster is foolish. And let him take seven** pieces of **raw meat from seven houses and let him leave them** for him **in the socket of the door.**[B] **And let him** then **eat them in the junkyard**[B] **of the city. Afterward, he should untie the rope of hair and say as follows: The blindness of so-and-so, son of so-and-so; leave so-and-so, son of so-and-so;** and then they say: **Let them blow into the dog's eye.**

BACKGROUND

Eye disease [*beroketi*] – בְּרוֹקְתִּי: Some have identified this illness with glaucoma, where at first one feels sparks or flashes, similar to the word lightning [*barak*], in his eyes, and it is sometimes accompanied by an infection. According to Rashi this is referring to a cataract, which is a film deposited on the lens of the eye. Some authorities identify this as an evil spirit that afflicts the eye (*Arukh*).

Seven-colored scorpion – עַקְרַבָּא דְּשַׁב חוּמְרֵי: The *Arukh* explains that this is a scorpion with seven links to its tail. Even the stinger is counted, as the tail of a scorpion has only six links. Alternatively, if this is referring to the links on a scorpion's stomach, all scorpions have seven links on their stomach.

Stibium – כּוּחְלָא: Stibium is a dark blue or black color that was extracted from the mineral stibnite, or antimonite, Sb_2S_3. The crystals of the mineral were ground and used by women to paint their eyes, accenting them and giving the impression that their eyes were larger.

Night blindness – שַׁבְרִירֵי דְּלֵילְיָא: This is the Aramaic translation of the word biblical word blind, *sanverim* (Genesis 19:11). It means blurring of the vision to the extent of partial blindness. There are two types of sensory cells in the retina of the human eye; cones, which are used for day vision, and rods, which work in lower levels of light, and are important for night vision. There are diseases which affect only one or the other type of cell, leading either to night blindness or day blindness.

Socket of the door – צִינּוֹרָא דְּדַשָּׁא: The socket of the door was the hole in the doorsill in which a pivot attached to the door was placed. In order to make it easy to install and remove the door, there was a small space next to this hole through which one could insert small objects.

Junkyard [*kilkulei*] – קִלְקוּלֵי: Another version of the text reads *kikli*. It is an Aramaic word meaning garbage or a place to discard items. Each city had a lot within or near it that was usually used to discard junk, as opposed to waste, and for this reason people would occasionally be found there.

לשברירי דימממא – ליתי שבעה סומקי מגווא דחיותא וניטוינהו אחספא דאומנא, וליתיב איהו מגואי ואיניש אחרינא מאבראי, ונימא ליה: "עוירא, הב לי דאיכול", ונימא ליה האיך: "פתיחא, סב איכול", ובתר דאכיל ליתבריה לחספא, דאי לא – הדרי עילויה.

As a remedy **for day blindness,** hemeralopia, which is the inability to see clearly in bright light, **let him bring seven animal spleens,**[N] **and let** the patient **roast them on the** pottery **shard of a bloodletter. And let** the patient **sit on the inside** of the house **and** let **another person sit on the outside, and** let the patient **say** to himself: **Blind man, give me** something **to eat, and let the other** one **say to** the patient: **Seeing man, take and eat. And after** the patient **eats, let him break the shard, as if not,** the blindness **will follow him.**

לדמא דאתי מנחירא – ליתי גברא כהן דשמיה לוי, וליכתוב ליה לוי למפרע. ואי לא, ליתי איניש מעלמא, וניכתוב ליה: "אנא פפי שילא בר סומקי" למפרע.

As a remedy **for a nosebleed, let** the patient **bring a man named Levi** who is **a priest,** and that man **should write for** the patient the name **Levi, backward. And if** the patient is **not** able do this **let him bring an ordinary man, and let** that man **write for** the patient the following expression: **I am Pappi Sheila bar Summakei.** And that man should also write this **backward.**

ואי לא, ניכתוב ליה הכי: "טעם דלי במי כסף טעם דלי במי פגם". ואי לא, ליתי עיקרא דאספסתא, ואשלא דפורייא עתיקא, וקורטסא, ומוריקי וסומקא דלוליבא, ונקלינהו בהדי הדדי, וליתי גבבא דעמרא וניגדול תרתי פתילתא, ולטמיש בחלא וניגדבל בקיטמא הדין, וניתיב בנחיריה.

And if he is **not** able to do this **let** that man **write for** the patient **like this: Taste from a bucket in silver water, taste from a bucket in tainted water. And if** the patient is **not** able to do this **let him bring the root of fodder** [*aspasta*],[L] **rope** [*ashla*][L] **from an old bed, and paper** [*kurtesa*],[L] **and saffron, and the red** portion **of a palm branch, and let him burn them with each other. And let** the patient **bring a fleece of wool and spin** it **into two strings, and let him soak** [*litmish*][L] **them in vinegar, roll them in this ash** of the burned materials, **and place** them **in his nostrils.**

ואי לא, ליחזי אמת המים דאזלת במזרח כלפי מערב, ונפסע וניקום חד כרעא להאי גיסא וחד כרעא להאי גיסא, ונישקול טינא בידיה דימינא מתותי כרעא דשמאליה, ובידיה דשמאלא מתותי כרעא דימיניה, וניגדול תרתי פתילתא דעמרא וניטמיש בטינא, וניתיב בנחיריה.

And if the patient is **not** able to do this **let him look at a stream of water flowing from the east toward the west, and let him spread** his legs **and stand with one foot on this side and one foot on that side. And let him take clay in his right hand from under his left foot, and** let him take clay **with his left hand from under his right foot. And let him spin two strings of wool, soak** them **in the clay, and place them in his nostrils.**

ואי לא, ליתיב תותי מרזבא ונייתו מיא ולישדו עליה, ולימרו: "כי היכי דפסקי הני מיא, ליפסוק דמיה דפלניא בר פלניתא".

And if the patient is **not** able to do this **let him sit under the gutter and let them bring water and pour it on him. And let them say: Just as the water has ceased, let the blood of so-and-so, son of so-and-so, cease.**

לדמא דאתי מפומא – בדקינן ליה בגילא דחיטתא, אי סריך – מריאה קאתי ואית ליה תקנתא, ואי לא – מכבדא קאתי ולית ליה תקנתא.

As a remedy **for blood that comes from the mouth**[B] **we check** the patient **with a straw of wheat. If** the blood **sticks** to the straw then it comes **from his lungs and it has a remedy. But if** the blood does **not** stick to the straw, it means that the blood **comes from the liver and it has no remedy.**

אמר ליה רב אמי לרב אשי, והאנן איפכא תנן: ניטל הכבד ולא נשתייר הימנה כלום, הריאה שניקבה או שחסרה! אמר ליה: כיון דמפומיה קאתי, אימר איתמוחי איתמח.

Rav Ami said to Rav Ashi: But didn't we learn the opposite in a mishna (*Ḥullin* 42a): **If the liver was** completely **removed**[H] **and none of it remains,** then it is considered to be an animal with a condition that will cause it to die within twelve months [*tereifa*]. But in the case of **a lung that is punctured**[H] **or missing,** the animal is considered to be a *tereifa*, even it is has not been completely removed. This indicates that damage to the lung is more serious than damage to the liver. Rav Ashi **said to him: Since** the blood **comes out from** this person's **mouth,** one must **say that** the liver has **dissolved** and he will not survive.

NOTES

Spleens – סוּמָּקֵי: Rashi explains that this is referring to spleens, while others explain that it refers to red meat from an animal (*Ge'onim*; the Rabbis of Mainz).

LANGUAGE

Fodder [*aspasta*] – אַסְפַּסְתָּא: From the Middle Persian aspast, which is derived from the Old Persian words aspa, meaning horse, and asti, meaning fodder.

Rope [*ashla*] – אַשְׁלָא: This word is found in Aramaic and in a similar form in Arabic, as أشل, *'ashl*. Apparently, it derives from the Assyrian word ašlu, meaning rope. This word is often used to mean specifically a measuring rope.

Paper [*kurtesa*] – קוּרְטְסָא: From the Greek χάρτης, *khartēs*, meaning paper, papyrus, or a roll of paper. Rashi provides a similar definition.

Soak [*litmish*] – לִטְמִישׁ: From the Aramaic root *tamash*, meaning to immerse or to submerge something in water. It appears in the Aramaic translations of the Bible, e.g., "And the priest shall dip his finger in the blood" (Leviticus 4:6). The word dip is translated in *Targum Yonatan* as *vitamash*.

BACKGROUND

Blood that comes from the mouth – דְּמָא דְּאָתֵי מִפּוּמָא: When blood comes out of the mouth and is not the result of a localized injury it is a sign of an internal illness. Such an illness could be connected to the digestive system, from an ulcer in the duodenum or the stomach, from cancerous growths in various organs, or from cirrhosis of the liver which could cause esophageal bleeding or serious decay of the liver. Blood coming from the mouth may also result from damage to the respiratory system, tuberculosis, or lung cancer.

HALAKHA

The liver was removed, etc. – נִיטַּל הַכָּבֵד וכו׳: If the entire liver was removed from an animal it is considered to be a *tereifa*. If there remains at least an olive-bulk-sized piece of the liver in the place where it is attached and another olive-bulk-sized piece on the side of the gallbladder then it is permitted, as explained in tractate *Ḥullin*. If the liver has dissolved, meaning that blood has emerged from the organ, then the animal is considered to be a *tereifa* (Rambam *Sefer Kedusha, Hilkhot Sheḥita* 8:21; *Shulḥan Arukh, Yoreh De'a* 41:1, 3, and in the comment of Rema).

A lung that is punctured, etc. – הָרֵיאָה שֶׁנִּיקְּבָה וכו׳: There are two membranes protecting the lungs. If one of the membranes was punctured then it the animal is still kosher, but if both of them were punctured then the animal is a *tereifa*, as explained in tractate *Ḥullin* (Rambam *Sefer Kedusha, Hilkhot Sheḥita* 7:1; *Shulḥan Arukh, Yoreh De'a* 36:1).

אָמַר מָר: אִי מֵרֵיאָה קָאָתֵי אִית לֵיהּ תַּקַּנְתָּא. מַאי תַּקַּנְתֵּיהּ? לֵיתֵי שִׁבְעָה כּוּנֵי מִפִּירְמָא דְּסִילְקָא, וְשִׁבְעָה כּוּנֵי פִּירְמָא דְּכַרְתֵּי, וַחֲמִשָּׁה כּוּנֵי פְּרִידָא, וּתְלָתָא כּוּנֵי דְּטַלְפְּחֵי, וְכוּנָא דְּכַמּוֹנָא וְכוּנָא דְּחַבְלֵי, וּכְנֶגְדָּן כַּנְתָּא פְּטִירְתָּא, וְלִיבְשִׁיל וְלֵיכוּל, וְלִישְׁתֵּי אַבַּתְרֵיהּ שִׁיכְרָא חֲרִיפָא דְּטֵבֵת.

The Master said: If the blood comes from the lungs then **it has a remedy.** The Gemara asks: **What is its remedy?** The Gemara answers: **Let him bring seven fistfuls of sliced beets,**[B] **and seven fistfuls of sliced leek, and five fistfuls of *perida***[BN] grass, **and three fistfuls of lentils, and a fistful of cumin, and a fistful of ropes, and a corresponding** amount **of the intestines of a firstborn animal.**[N] **And let him cook** all of it together **and let him eat** everything **and afterward let him drink good, strong beer.**

לְכָכָא – אֲמַר רַבָּה בַּר רַב הוּנָא: לֵיתֵי תּוּמָא יְחִידָאָה וְנִימְרְסֵיהּ בְּמִישְׁחָא וּמִילְחָא, וְנֵיתְבֵיהּ אַטּוּפְרַאי דְּאַלְיוֹנָא דְּהַהוּא גִּיסָא דְּכָיֵיב לֵיהּ, וְנֶהֱדַר לֵיהּ גַּדְנְפָא דְּלִישָׁא, וְנִיזְדַּהַר לְבִישְׂרֵיהּ דְּקָשֵׁי לְחִיוָּרָא.

With regard to the remedy **for** pain in one's **teeth** [*lekhakha*],[L] **Rabba bar Rav Huna said: Let him bring an individual garlic** that grew as a single clove **and grind it with oil and salt. And let him place it on the thumbnail of the side that hurts him, and let him surround it** with a rim [*gedanpa*][L] **of dough. And he should take care** that it does not touch **his flesh** because it is **harmful** and can cause **boils.**

לְחִינְּכֵי – אֲמַר רַבִּי יוֹחָנָן: חוּמְתִּי כִּי מַמְרוּ, וְעִיקָּרָא דְּחוּמְתִּי עָדִיף מִמַּמְרוּ, וְנִינְקוֹט בְּפוּמֵּיהּ; הָנֵי לְאוֹקוֹמֵי. לְבַשּׁוֹלֵי – לַיְיתֵי פָּארֵי דְּרֵישׁ נָפְיָא, וְטַלְפְּחֵי בְּעַפְרַיְיהוּ, וְשׁוּבְלִילְתָּא וְחוּמְרְתָּא דִּכְשׁוּתָא, וְנִינְקוֹט כְּאַמְגוּזָא בְּפוּמֵּיהּ.

With regard to the remedy **for gums,**[B] **Rabbi Yoḥanan said: The Spanish chamomile** [*ḥomti*][L] plant **is like the *mamru***[L] plant, **and the root of the Spanish chamomile is preferable to *mamru*, and let him take it in his mouth. This** is meant **to stabilize** the illness so that it does not intensify. **To boil them,** meaning to cause the wounds to open so that the pus can be removed from them, **let him bring the coarsest bran** found **at the upper portion of the sifter, and lentils in their dirt, and fenugreek** [*shuvlilta*],[L] **and the flower of the hop** plant. **And let him take** an amount **about** the size of a **nut in his mouth.**

לְאִיפְתּוּחֵי – לִינְפַּח לֵיהּ חַבְרֵיהּ תַּחְלֵי חִיוָּרְתָּא בְּגִילָא דְּחִיטְּתָא. לְאַסּוּקֵי – לֵיתֵי עַפְרָא מִטּוּלָּא דְּבֵית הַכִּסֵּא, וְנִיגְבּוֹל בְּדוּבְשָׁא וְנֵיכוּל, דְּמַעֲלֵי לֵיהּ.

In order **to open** the blisters to remove the pus, **let his friend blow white cress** into his mouth **with a straw of wheat.** And if he wishes **to heal** the blisters **let him bring dirt** found **in the shade of the bathroom and knead it with honey and eat it, as this is effective** for curing the blisters.

לְבַרְסָם – לֵיתֵי כִּי פִּיסְתְּקָא דְּנִישְׁדּוֹר, וְכִי אַמְגוּזָא דְּחֶלְבְּנִיתָא דּוּבְשָׁנִיתָא, וּמְלֵי תַּרְוָודָא דּוּבְשָׁא חִיוָּרָא, וּמְלֵי נַטְלָא בַּת מְחוֹזָא חַמְרָא נְקִידָא, וְנִישְׁלוֹקִינְהוּ בַּהֲדֵי הֲדָדֵי, וְכִי בָּשֵׁיל נִשְׁדּוֹר בָּשֵׁיל לֵיהּ כּוּלֵּיהּ. וְאִי לָא, לֵיתֵי רְבִיעֲתָא דַּחֲלָבָא דְּעִיזָּא חִיוַּרְתִּי

For a bronchial infection [*levarsam*], [L] **let him bring a nut-sized** amount **of ammonia** [*nishdor*][L] water **and a nut-sized** amount **of sweet galbanum,**[B] **and a large spoonful of white honey,**[B] **a vessel from Meḥoza,** i.e., one that holds a quarter-*log* of liquid, **full of clear** [*nekida*][L] **wine, and let him boil them together. And once the ammonia is cooked everything will have cooked. And** if he is **not** able to do this **let him bring a quarter-*log* of milk from a white goat,**

BACKGROUND

Beets – סִילְקָא: Beets, *Beta vulgaris cicla*, are a common, garden-variety vegetable from the Chenopodiaceae family. Growing annually, their large, succulent leaves which grow from 15 to 20 cm in length are eaten cooked and taste similar to spinach. Each time beet leaves are trimmed they grow back larger.

Perida – פְּרִידָא: The nature of this plant remains unclear. Some assert that it is a fruit. According to Rashi's second explanation it is a kind of cherry, while others say it is a kind of plum. Others say it is a type of vegetable, possibly a cauliflower or leek.

Gums – חִינְּכֵי: This is a reference to an infection that causes an abscess in the gums. Such an infection may be the result of a wound, and here the Gemara deals with the different stages of its healing process. The first stage is to stabilize the infection in order to stop it from spreading to other teeth. The next stage is to boil the wound so that the abscess becomes more liquid and can be more easily removed. The next stage is to open the abscess in order to drain the pus. Finally, the sufferer must heal the gums and close the open wound by growing new skin.

Sweet galbanum – חֶלְבְּנִיתָא דּוּבְשָׁנִיתָא: This is a plant of the Ferula family found throughout the Middle East. Some of these plants produce a sap that is used as an ingredient in various perfumes, including the galbanum that was used in the incense mixture in the Temple, as well as for medicinal purposes. Here the Gemara is referring to a sweet variety, unlike the normal kind which has a sharp taste and an unpleasant odor.

White honey – דּוּבְשָׁא חִיוָּרָא: The color of honey varies according to the type of flowers from which the bees made the honey and to a certain extent according to the seasons of the year. Alongside dark honey, which comes from certain wildflowers there is a very light-colored honey, such as citrus flower honey. The term white honey apparently refers to these varieties.

NOTES

Perida – פְּרִידָא: In his first explanation, Rashi writes that this refers to a type of grass. He also cites others who claim that it is a type of berry. The *ge'onim* explain that it refers to dried pomegranate seeds.

Intestines of a firstborn animal – כַּנְתָּא פְּטִירְתָּא: Rashi explains that this refers to a portion of a firstborn animal's intestines. The *ge'onim* maintain that this term refers to a loaf of unleavened bread.

LANGUAGE

Teeth [*kakha*] – כָּכָא: According to most commentaries this Aramaic word refers specifically to a molar.

Rim [*gedanpa*] – גַּדְנְפָא: From the Aramaic root *gapa*, meaning side or wing, this word means a frame.

Spanish chamomile [*ḥomti*] – חוּמְתִּי: This plant was given its name, which is related to the word for heat, because one senses a feeling of heat when tasting it. There are parallel forms in other languages. The plant, identified as the *Anacyclus pyrethrrun*, usually grows wild, but it is also cultivated for its medicinal properties. Its root contains an alkaloid which is used in various pain-relief medicines, usually for soothing gum pain.

Mamru – מַמְרוּ: Some say that *mamru* is the same as the Greek μαμιρά, *mamira*. It refers to the root of a certain plant that was used for medicinal purposes.

Fenugreek [*shuvlilta*] – שׁוּבְלִילְתָּא: This is referring to the same plant called elsewhere by the name *tiltan* (see *Kilayim* 2:5). In English it is called fenugreek, whose scientific name is *Trigonella foenum graecum*. The source of the word is apparently the Syrian Aramaic *sam baliltu*.

Bronchial infection [*barsam*] – בַּרְסָם: From the Persian term barsām, meaning an infection (sām) of the chest (bar).

Ammonia [*nishdor*] – נִישְׁדּוֹר: This word also appears in other languages, such as Syriac, as nashdor or anodshdar. In Persian it is called anasadur. All of these words mean ammonia. Nashdor is the liquid solution of ammonium, or NH_4OH. It is used today as a base for various cleaning and disinfecting materials.

Clear [*nekida*] – נְקִידָא: From the Aramaic root *neked*, meaning to be clean. In this context it means clean or clear wine.

וְנִיטַיְּיפֵיהּ אַתְּלָת קִלְחֵי כְּרָבָא, וְנִיבְחֲשֵׁיהּ בְּגַוְוזָא דְּמַרְמְהִין, וְכִי בָּשֵׁיל גַּוְוזָא בְּמַרְמְהִין בָּשֵׁיל לֵיהּ כּוּלֵּיהּ. וְאִי לָא, לֵיתֵי נִפְקֵי דְּכַלְבָּא חִיוָּרָא וְנִיגְבּוֹל בְּנַטְפָּא, וְכַמָּה דְּאֶפְשָׁר נִפְקָא לָא נֵיכוּל, דִּמְפָרֵיק.

and let him drip it on three stalks of cabbage and stir it with a sprig from a marjoram bush. And when the sprig of marjoram is boiled all of it will be boiled. And if he is not able to do that, let him take the feces of a white dog[B] and let him mix it with balm. And as much as possible let him not eat the feces because it causes the separation of the limbs.[N]

לְגִירָא – לֵיתֵי גִּירָא דְּלֵילְתָא וְנֵיפְכֵיהּ, וְנִשְׁדֵּי מַיָּא עִלָּוֵיהּ וְנִשְׁתֵּי. וְאִי לָא, לֵיתֵי מִמַּיָּא דְּאִישְׁתֵּי מִינַּיְיהוּ כַּלְבָּא בְּלֵילְיָא, וְנִיזְדַּהַר מִגִּילּוּיָא. לְגִילּוּיָא – אַנְפָּקָא דְּחַמְרָא חַיָּיא.

With regard to a remedy for a stinging pain [*gira*],[NL] let him bring a stone called an arrow of Lilith,[N] and let him turn it upside down. And let him pour water on it and drink it. And if he is not able to do that, let him bring water from which a dog drank at night, and let him be careful about leaving the water uncovered[H] at night, in case a snake drank from it and left its venom in the water. A remedy for drinking uncovered[B] water is to drink a quarter-*log* [*anpaka*][L] of undiluted wine.

לְמוּרְסָא – אַנְפָּקָא דְּחַמְרָא בְּאַהֲלָא תּוּלָאנָא.

As a remedy for a pus-filled wound, one should drink a quarter-*log* of wine steeped in red ice plant.

לְפִירְחָא דְּלִיבָּא – לֵיתֵי תְּלָת בְּרוּשְׁיָיאתָא דְּשַׂעֲרֵי וְנִשְׁטְרִינְהוּ בְּכַמְכָּא דְּלָא עָבַר עִילָּוֵיהּ אַרְבְּעִין יוֹמִין, וְנֵיכוּל, וְנִשְׁתֵּי אַבַּתְרַיְיהוּ חַמְרָא מַרְקָא. אֲמַר לֵיהּ רַב אַחָא מִדִּיפְתִּי לְרָבִינָא: וְכָל שֶׁכֵּן דְּפָרַח לִיבֵּיהּ! אֲמַר לֵיהּ: אֲנָא – לְיוּקְרָא דְּלִיבָּא אֲמַרִי.

As a remedy for palpitations of the heart, i.e., if his heart is beating too fast, let him bring three loaves of barley, and soak them in *kamka*[L] from which forty days have not yet passed since being made. And let him eat the loaves and drink diluted wine after consuming them. Rav Aḥa of Difti said to Ravina: All the more so his heart will palpitate from these foods. Ravina said to him: You misheard what I had said; I said this as a remedy for heaviness of the heart.

לְפִירְחָא דְּלִיבָּא – לֵיתֵי תְּלָת בְּרוּשְׁיָיאתָא דְּחִיטֵּי וְנִישְׁטְרִינְהוּ בְּדוּבְשָׁא וְנֵיכוּל, וְנִישְׁתֵּי אַבַּתְרַיְיהוּ חַמְרָא חַיָּיא.

As a remedy for palpitations of the heart, let him bring three loaves of wheat, soak them in honey, and eat them. And let him drink undiluted wine after them.

לְצַרְחָא דְּלִיבָּא – לֵיתֵי תְּלָת בֵּיעֵי נִינְיָיא וּבֵיעֲתָא דְּכַמּוֹנָא וּבֵיעֲתָא דְּשׁוּמְשְׁמֵי וְלֵיכוּל.

As a remedy for heart pain, let him bring three egg-bulks of mint,[NB] and an egg-bulk of cumin, and an egg-bulk of sesame seeds, and let him eat them together.

לְכְאֵב מֵעֵי – לֵיתֵי תְּלָת מְאָה פִּלְפְּלֵי אֲרִיכָתָא, וְכָל יוֹמֵי נִשְׁתֵּי מְאָה מִינַּיְיהוּ בְּחַמְרָא. רָבִין דְּמִן נֶרֶשׁ עֲבַד לָהּ לִבְרַתֵּיהּ דְּרַב אַשִׁי מְאָה וְחַמְשִׁין מֵהָנֵי דִּידַן, וְאִתַּסְיָא.

As a remedy for pain of the intestines, let him bring three hundred long peppers, and every day let him drink one hundred of them with wine. It is told: Ravin of the city of Neresh prepared one hundred and fifty of our, i.e., Babylonian, peppers for the daughter of Rav Ashi, who had this illness, and she was healed.

NOTES

The separation [*mefarek*] of the limbs – דִּמְפָרֵיק: This is Rashi's version of the text, and it means that eating the feces can cause the separation of the limbs. The *Arukh* has a version of the text which reads *mefaresh*, meaning that eating the feces can cause infertility. The *ge'onim* have the same version as that of the *Arukh*, but they explain it differently, and maintain that it means to distinguish. This remedy distinguished between one who is dangerously ill, as it will cause him to die, and one whose condition is improving, as it speeds up his healing.

Stinging pain – גִּירָא: Rashi explains that this is an illness that includes a sharp pain. Others explain that this is referring to a wound caused by an arrow (Rav Sherira Gaon).

Arrow of Lilith – גִּירָא דְּלֵילְתָא: Rashi and the *Arukh* explain that this means a stone that looks like an arrow that fell with hail.

Three egg-bulks of mint – תְּלָת בֵּיעֵי נִינְיָיא: This is Rashi's version of the text. The *Arukh* had a version of the text which states that he should take three eggs and eat the other foods with the eggs (see *Migdal David*).

LANGUAGE

Stinging pain [*gira*] – גִּירָא: From the Aramaic word meaning arrow. It describes the pain felt when stabbed with an arrow. The pain stems from an infection or local damage to one of the nerves of the body.

Quarter-*log* [*anpaka*] – אַנְפָּקָא: The source of this word is unclear, but it appears to be related to the Armenian empak, meaning a drinking vessel.

***Kamka* – כַּמְכָּא:** Apparently derived from the Middle Iranian word kāmak, meaning a kind of seasoned sauce.

HALAKHA

And let him be careful about leaving the water uncovered – וְנִיזְדַּהַר מִגִּילּוּיָא: One should not drink water which has been left uncovered in case a snake or other poisonous animal drank from it and left poison in it. In locations where such animals are not found, the custom is to not be careful about this (Rambam *Sefer Nezikin*, *Hilkhot Rotze'aḥ UShmirat HaNefesh* 11:6; *Shulḥan Arukh*, *Yoreh De'a* 116:1).

BACKGROUND

Feces of a…dog – נִפְקֵי דְּכַלְבָּא: Dog feces include, among other things, certain enzymes that break down proteins, which is why it was used in the process of tanning hides. For this reason, ingesting it could cause lesions and ulcers in the stomach and the intestines. In addition to this, there are several parasites in dog excrement that could cause serious damage if passed through the human body.

Uncovered – גִּילּוּיָא: In the time of the Talmud people were very suspicious about foods that were left uncovered, especially liquids, as sometimes poisonous snakes would drink from the liquid and leave some of their venom in the remainder. Some types of snake venom act directly on the nerves and some are dangerous when they come into contact with open wounds, which would pose a danger to a person with any type of lesion in his mouth.

Mint – נִינְיָיא: Rashi and many others identify *ninya* with the mint plant, genus *Mentha*, of the Lamiaceae family. It is known as نعناع, *na'nā'*, in Arabic, and is used as a flavoring for drinks and food. Some say that *ninya* is different from mint, identified as a species of the genus *Ammi*, commonly known as the toothpick weed, from the Apiaceae family.

לְכִירְצָא – אַנְפָּקָא דְּחַמְרָא בְּאַטְרְפָא
דְּעַרְאָה. לְכִירְצָא חִיוָּרָא – לֵיתֵי בִּיזְרָא
גַּלְגִּילָא וְנִיצַיְּירָה בְּשִׁיסְתַּג, וְנִיתַיְּירֵיהּ
בְּמַיָּא וְנִשְׁתֵּיהּ, וְנִזְדַּהַר מִבִּינְתָא, דְּאִי לָא –
מְנַקְבָא לֵהּ לְמַעְיָינֵיהּ.

As a remedy **for roundworm,** he should drink **a quarter-*log* of wine steeped in laurel leaves.** As a remedy **for white worm,**[B] **let him bring cress**[B] **and tie it with a piece of woven cloth. And let him soak it in water and drink it. And let him be careful with the seed, as if** he is **not** careful enough there is a danger that it will grow inside him **and puncture his intestines.**

לְמֵיסַר – סִיסִין רְטִיבָא בְּמַיָּא; לְמִישְׁרָא –
יְבֵישְׁתָּא בְּמַיָּא, וְסִימָנָךְ: אִיצָא רְטִיבָא
דְּסָכַר נַהֲרָא.

The remedy **to bind** the bowels, i.e., to cure diarrhea, is to consume the **chamomile** [*sisin*][B] plant when it is **wet with water.** And the remedy **to relax** the bowels and relieve constipation is to drink **dry** chamomile soaked **in water,** which acts as a laxative. **And your mnemonic** so as not to confuse these remedies is as follows: **Wet grass** [*itza*][B] **that is used to dam rivers,** and through this he will remember that moist chamomile is used to stop diarrhea.

לְטְחָלָא – לֵיתֵי שַׁב בִּינֵּי דְּמַיָּא וְנִיבַּבְשִׁינְהוּ
בְּטוּלָּא, וְכָל יוֹמָא נִישְׁתֵּי תַּרְתֵּי וּתְלָתָא
בְּחַמְרָא. וְאִי לָא, לֵיתֵי טְחָלָא דְּצִיפַּרְתָּא
דְּלָא אִיפַּתַּח וְנִטַּחְיָא בְּתַנּוּרָא, וְנוֹקֵי
לַהֲדֵיהּ וְנֵימָא: "כִּי הֵיכִי דְּיָבֵישׁ הַאי טְחָלָא,
נֵיבַשׁ טְחַלְיָא דִּפְלוֹנִי בַּר פְּלוֹנִיתָא".

As a remedy for illness of **the spleen,**[B] **let him bring seven leeches,**[NHB] **dry them in the shade, and every day drink two or three** of them **with wine. And if** he is **not** able to do this, **let him bring the spleen of a female goat**[N] **that has not given birth, and place it in the oven, and stand across from it, and let him say: Just as this spleen is dried, so shall the spleen of so-and-so, son of so-and-so, be dried.**

וְאִי לָא, נִיטַּחְיֵיהּ בֵּינֵי אוּרְבֵּי דְּבֵיתָא
חֲדַתָּא, וְנֵימָא הָכִי. וְאִי לָא, לִיבְּקֵי שַׁכְבָּא
דִּשְׁכִיב בְּשַׁבְּתָא, וְנִישְׁקְלֵיהּ לְיָדֵיהּ וְנוֹתְבָהּ
אַטְּחָלֵיהּ, וְנֵימָא: כִּי הֵיכִי דְּיָבֵישׁ הָא יָדָא,
נֵיבַשׁ טְחַלְיָא דִּפְלוֹנִי בַּר פְּלוֹנִיתָא.

And if he is **not** able to do this, **let him place** the goat spleen **between the bricks of a new house, and let him say this** same statement. **And if not, let him search for someone who died on Shabbat and let him take the hand** of the deceased, **and let him place it on his spleen and say: Just as the hand of so-and-so was dried,** so too, **the spleen of so-and-so, the son of so-and-so, should be dried.**

NOTES

Seven leeches – שַׁב בִּינֵּי דְּמַיָּא: Some have asked how it is permitted to drink the leeches with wine, since they are in the category of creeping animals and therefore not kosher. They answer that it is permitted because this illness is life threatening. Furthermore, since the leeches are first dried, perhaps they are permitted even if the case is not life threatening (*Eshel Avraham*).

The spleen of a female goat – טְחָלָא דְּצִיפַּרְתָּא: This is based on Rashi's explanation of the text. The *Arukh* explains that it refers to fat birds that have never laid eggs, and the *ge'onim* understand it to be a type of locust called *tzipporet keramim*.

HALAKHA

Seven leeches – שַׁב בִּינֵּי דְּמַיָּא: It is permitted to burn a creeping animal and to consume it for medicinal purposes, even if the patient is not critically ill. This is on the condition that it is a known and tested medicinal remedy, or based on the advice of an expert. If there is an alternative cure it is not permitted, even if the kosher cure will take longer (*Shulḥan Arukh, Yoreh De'a* 84:17, 155:3, and in the comment of Rema).

BACKGROUND

Worm – כִּירְצָא: From the context it appears that this is a reference to parasitic worms found in the intestines and at times in other places in the body. It could be a tapeworm or *Taenia saginata*, a species of flatworm that can grow to over 10 m in length. Alternatively, it could possibly refer to the hookworm or *Ascaris sedocoirbmul*, which is found across the globe.

Cress – גַּלְגִּילָא: According to the commentaries this is referring to cress, commonly known as the rocket or roquette (*Eruca sativa*), which grows annually to a height of 15–60 cm. Its leaves are eaten raw as a salad. Flowers of the cress are yellowish with purple veins. It is cultivated and also grows wild along roadsides in all parts of Eretz Yisrael, especially in the Negev. In the talmudic era its fruits were used as a substitute for pepper.

Chamomile [*sisin*] – סִיסִין: According to the *ge'onim*, *sisin* refers to the two-colored chamomile plant *Matricaria chamomilla*, or *Matricaria recutita*, from the Asteraceae family, which still grows wild in Eretz Yisrael. It is an annual plant whose leaves split into multiple lobes. Its flowers are arranged in a circle, such that the outer petals are white while those in the center are yellow. This plant is still used medicinally, prepared as a tea to alleviate digestive ailments and colds, as well as to heal various external wounds.

Chamomile

Grass [*itza*] – אִיצָא: Based on its similarity to Greek words, some identify this with the willow or with the chaste tree, also known as the vitex plant. From the context it appears that the Gemara is referring to a kind of grass which is capable of damming up rivers when wet. It is likely a variety of the Poaceae family that commonly grows by riverbanks. It seems to have been used to dam rivers by throwing piles of it into the water.

Chaste tree

Spleen – טְחָלָא: A swollen or enlarged spleen can result from a severe infection such as malaria or typhus. When the spleen swells to a certain size it creates a feeling of pressure and pain at times of exertion.

Leeches [*binnei demayya*] – בִּינֵּי דְּמַיָּא: According to Rashi this is a reference to leeches. *Binnei demayya* can be translated as water threads, and leeches are threadlike in appearance.

וְאִי לָא, נֵיתֵי בִּינִיתָא וְנִיטְוְוייַהּ בֵּי נַפָּחָא, וְנֵיכְלֵיהּ בְּמַיָּא דְּבֵי נַפָּחָא וְנִישְׁתֵּי מִמַּיָּא דְּבֵי נַפָּחָא. הַהִיא עִיזָּא דַּהֲוַת שָׁתְיָא מַיָּא דְּבֵי נַפָּחָא, אִישְׁתְּחִיט וְלָא אִישְׁתַּכַּח לָהּ טְחָלָא.

And if he is not able to do this, let him take a fish[B] and roast it in the house of a blacksmith. And let him eat it with the water from the blacksmith's house in which the red-hot metal is cooled. And let him drink water from the blacksmith's house. The Gemara brings corroborative evidence to this remedy: A certain goat drank water from the blacksmith's house, and when it was slaughtered there was no spleen found inside it.

וְאִי לָא, לִיפְתַּח חָבִיתָא דְּחַמְרָא לִשְׁמֵיהּ. אֲמַר לֵיהּ רַב אַחָא בְּרֵיהּ דְּרָבָא לְרַב אַשִׁי: אִי אִית לֵיהּ חָבִיתָא דְּחַמְרָא, לָא אָתֵי לְקַמֵּיהּ דְּמָר! אֶלָּא, מַרְגַּל בְּפַת שַׁחֲרִית, דִּמְעַלְיָא לְכוּלֵּי גּוּפֵיהּ.

And if he is not able to do this, let him open a barrel of wine for his sake, i.e., let him drink a large amount of wine. Rav Aḥa, son of Rava, said to Rav Ashi: If he has a barrel of wine he will not come before my Master for a remedy, as the wine will already have healed him. Rather, what should he do to maintain his health? Let him become accustomed to eat bread in the morning,[H] because it benefits his entire body.

לְרוּשְׁחַתָּא – לֵיתֵי אַקִיקָא וְאִילְוָוא, וְאַסְפִּירְכָא וּמַרְתְּכָא, וְחוּמְרְתָא דְּפִילוֹן וְשִׁיאֲפָא דְּחֲמִימְתָא, וְנִינְקַט בְּשַׁחֲקֵי דְּכִיתָנָא בְּקַיְיטָא וְדַעֲמַר גּוּפְנָא בְּסִיתְוָא. וְאִי לָא, לִישְׁתֵּי שִׁיכְרָא מַרְקָא.

As a remedy for hemorrhoids,[N] let him bring acacia [*akika*],[L] and aloe [*ilava*],[L] and mercury,[N] and silver dross, and a bundle [*ḥumreta*][L] of fragrant herbs [*defilon*],[L] and feces of pigeons [*ḥamimta*].[L] And let him take it in linen bags in the summer, or cotton bags in the winter, and place them on the afflicted area. And if he is not able to do that, let him drink diluted beer.

לְשִׁיגְרוֹנָא – לֵיתֵי פַּתְיָא דְּמוֹנִינֵי, וְנִיגַנְדְּרֵיהּ שִׁיתִּין זִימְנֵי אַהָא מְטַחְתֵּיהּ, וְשִׁיתִּין זִימְנֵי אַהָא מְטַחְתֵּיהּ.

For rheumatism [*shigrona*],[NL] let him bring a vessel full of brine from small fish [*moninei*][L] and roll it sixty times on this thigh and sixty times on that thigh.

לִצְמִירְתָא – נֵיתֵי תְּלָת נִיטוּפַיְיתָא מִישְׁחָא דְּכוּפְרָא, וּתְלָת נִיטוּפַיְיתָא אִיצְרָא דִּכְרָתֵי, וּתְלָת נִיטוּפַיְיתָא דְּחַמְרָא נְקִידָא, וְלִישְׁדֵי לֵיהּ לְאִישׁ בָּאַמָּה וּלְאִשָּׁה בְּאוֹתוֹ מָקוֹם.

As a remedy for a bladder stone [*litzmireta*],[NL] let him bring three drops of tar oil, which is oil that emerges from burning wood, three drops from the squeezing [*itzra*][L] of leeks, and three drops of clean wine, and place this mixture, for a man on the penis, and for a woman on that place, i.e., her genital area.

BACKGROUND

Fish – בִּינִיתָא: Close to the Arabic بنى, *bunnā*, this is apparently referring to the barbel.

Barbel

HALAKHA

Bread in the morning – פַּת שַׁחֲרִית: One should set aside time to eat a morning meal, as it is very beneficial to the body (*Shulḥan Arukh, Oraḥ Ḥayyim* 155:2).

NOTES

For hemorrhoids [*lerushḥata*] – לְרוּשְׁחַתָּא: Rashi explains that this refers to hemorrhoids. Others have a version of the text that reads *leshiḥata*, meaning wounds (*Otzar HaGe'onim*).

Mercury – אַסְפִּירְכָא: Rashi explains that this refers to quicksilver, or mercury. In *Otzar HaGe'onim* it is explained that it refers to a type of lime or plaster, and both explanations are mentioned in the *Arukh*.

Rheumatism – שִׁיגְרוֹנָא: Rashi explains that this refers to a pain in the thighs or hipbone. *Otzar HaGe'onim* maintains that it refers to weakness of the thighs. The *Arukh* identifies this condition as gout.

Bladder stone – צְמִירְתָא: Rashi explains that this is a stone in the urinary tract, while others hold it is a disease that causes one to leak urine (*Otzar HaGe'onim*).

LANGUAGE

Acacia [*akika*] – אַקִיקָא: According to the *Arukh*, this word is derived from the Greek ἀκακία, *akakia*, meaning acacia tree. The reference in the Gemara is to the sap that flows from this kind of tree.

Aloe [*ilava*] – אִילְוָוא: This is a reference to the aloe vera plant, similarly called ἀλόη, *aloe*, in Greek, Latin, and other languages. The plant, which is from the Xanthorrhoeaceae family, has green, succulent leaves that when torn exude a sap whose extract is used for medicinal purposes such as healing dry skin and burns.

Aloe vera

Bundle [*ḥumreta*] – חוּמְרְתָא: This word, depending on its context, is used to reference various round objects such as a ball, a ring, or a loop, and similarly a button or a bead. It is apparently close to the Middle Persian muhr, meaning seal. Here it seems to be referring to a small ball of fragrant herbs which were worn on a chain around the neck. This word is also used for the buds of flowers that have not yet opened and other round protuberances.

Fragrant herbs [*pilon*] – פִּילוֹן: Early commentaries explain *pilon* as a form of the Aramaic *pila*, meaning mixture, yet it appears that its source is the Greek φύλλον, *fullon*, meaning a plant or leaf, or φυλλεῖον, *fuleyon*, meaning small, green herbs such as mint and parsley.

Pigeons [*ḥamimta*] – חֲמִימְתָא: Meaning pigeon in Aramaic. As it sounds like *ḥom*, the word for heat, some assert that the pigeon is called this because its normal body temperature is much higher than that of other animals.

Rheumatism [*shigrona*] – שִׁיגְרוֹנָא: Although some derive this word from the Aramaic, others say its source is the Greek ἰσχιάς, *iskhias*, which is a general term for illness of the thighs, especially for sciatica, an inflammation of the sciatic nerve. This is a very painful condition, sometimes preventing one from walking.

Brine from small fish [*moninei*] – מוֹנִינֵי: The *ge'onim* explain this word as a form of *mei nunei*, literally water of fish or fish brine (*Otzar HaGe'onim*).

Bladder stone [*tzemireta*] – צְמִירְתָא: A similar form of this word is found in the Syrian Aramaic *tzamra*, meaning a urinary blockage. Apparently, the root *tzadi, mem, reish* is akin to the Hebrew and Aramaic root *samekh, mem, reish*, meaning to contract or become hard. Similar to this are the terms *tzimra bara* and *tzimra gavna*, the first meaning an inner blockage of the urinary tract close to the bladder and the second being an outside blockage at the end of the urethra. Such a condition is a result of bladder stones; the smaller stones exit with the urine and the larger ones block the urinary tract and cause pain.

The squeezing [*itzra*] – אִיצְרָא: The meaning of this word, which begins with the letter *alef*, is similar to *itzra* beginning with the letter *ayin*, something squeezed from fruit or vegetables.

וְאִי לָא, לֵיתֵי אוּנָא דְּזִיקָא, וְלִתְלֵי לֵיהּ לְאִישׁ בָּאַמָּה וּלְאִשָּׁה בַּדַּדִּין. וְאִי לָא, לֵיתֵי חוּטָא דִּזְהוֹרִיתָא דִּשְׁדַתֵּיהּ דּוּמָה בַּת דּוּמָה, וְלִיתְלֵי לֵיהּ לְאִישׁ בָּאַמָּה וּלְאִשָּׁה בַּדַּדִּין.

And if he is **not** able to do this, **let him bring the ear,** i.e., handle, **of a wine sac and suspend it, for a man from** his **penis, and for a woman from** her **breasts. And if** he is **not** able to do this, **let him bring a crimson string spun by** a woman **suspected** of prostitution who is also **the daughter of a suspected** woman, **and let him suspend it, for a man from** his **penis and for a woman from** her **breasts.**

וְאִי לָא, לֵיתֵי כִּינָּה דְּזָכָר וּנְקֵבָה, וְלִיתְלֵי לֵיהּ לְאִישׁ בָּאַמָּה וּלְאִשָּׁה בְּאוֹתוֹ מָקוֹם, וְכִי מַשְׁתִּין – נַשְׁתִּין אַסִּיסְנָא יְבֵישְׁתָּא בְּצִינּוֹרָא דְּדַשָּׁא; וּנְעַיֵּין בְּחוּמַרְתָּא דְּנָפְקָא מִינֵּיהּ, דִּמְעַלְיָא לְכוּלְּהוּ צִימְרָא.

And if not, let him bring a louse from a male and a louse from **a female,**[N] **and suspend it, for a man from his penis, and for a woman on that place,** i.e., her genital area. **And when he urinates let him urinate on a dry branch** [*sisna*][L] **by the door pivot. And let him examine**[N] **the bladder stone that comes out of him** with the urine, **as it is effective** as a remedy **for any** illness accompanied by **a fever** [*tzimra*][L] if he grinds it and uses it.

לְצִימְרָא בָּרָא – לֵיתֵי תְּלָתָא גְּרִיבֵי סוּפְלֵי וּתְלָתָא גְּרִיבֵי אַטְרָף אַדְּרָא, וְנִישְׁלוֹקִינְהוּ כָּל חַד לְחוּדֵיהּ וְלֵיתֵיב בֵּינַיְיהוּ, וְלִתְבִינְהוּ בְּתַרְתֵּי מְשִׁיכְלֵי וְנֵיתֵי פָּתוֹרָא וּנְנַח עִילָּוֵיהּ, וְנֵיקוּם מֵעִילָּוֵי הַאי וְלוֹתִיב עִילָּוֵי הַאי, וּמֵעִילָּוֵי הַאי וְלוֹתִיב עִילָּוֵי הַאי, עַד דְּנֵיסַק בֵּיהּ הַבְלָא, וְלִסְחֵי מִינַּיְיהוּ. וְכִי שָׁתֵי, מִמַּיָּא דְּאַדְּרָא לִישְׁתֵּי, מִמַּיָּא דְּסוּפְלֵי לָא לִישְׁתֵּי, מִשּׁוּם דִּמְיַעַקְרֵי.

As a remedy **for an external fever,**[N] **let him bring three** *se'a* **of date pits** [*suflei*],[L] **and three** *se'a* [*gerivei*][L] **of leaves of an** *eder* tree.[L] **Let him cook each one individually and sit between them. And let him place them in two basins, and bring a table and place it over him. And let him stand up from over this** basin **and sit over this** basin, and then **let him stand up from over this** basin **and sit over this** basin, **until the heat rises on him** and he becomes very hot. **And let him wash from the** water of both basins, **and when** he **drinks, let him drink from the** basin containing the *eder* water. But do **not let him drink from** the basin containing **the date water, because** it **causes infertility.**

לְצִימְרָא גַּוָּונָא – לֵיתֵי שַׁבְעָה בּוּנֵי דְּסִילְקָא מִשַּׁב מְשָׁארֵי, וְנִישְׁלוֹקִינְהוּ בְּעַפְרַיְיהוּ וְנֵיכוּל, וְנִישְׁתֵּי אַטְרָף אַדְּרָא בְּשִׁיכְרָא אוֹ

As a remedy **for an internal fever, let him bring seven handfuls of beet leaves from seven furrows. And let him cook them with their dirt and eat** them. **And let him drink** from *eder* leaves mixed **with beer or**

NOTES

A louse from a male and a female – **כִּינָּה דְּזָכָר וּנְקֵבָה:** This means a louse taken from the body of a man and a louse taken from the body of a woman. According to *Otzar HaGe'onim* it refers to the lice themselves, i.e., that one should take a male louse and a female louse.

And let him examine – **וּנְעַיֵּין:** In other words, after passing the bladder stone he should keep it, since it is effective in treating all types of illness when ground up, mixed with liquid, and consumed.

External fever – **צִימְרָא בָּרָא:** Rashi writes that this is an illness accompanied by a fever. In *Otzar HaGe'onim* it is identified as a bladder stone. Furthermore, it is written there that the Gemara differentiates between an outer stone, which is in the urethra, and an inner stone, which is close to the bladder.

LANGUAGE

Branch [*sisna*] – **סִיסְנָא:** *Sisnei* are baskets woven from palm leaves. The word is related to *sansan*, which appears in the verse: "I will climb up into the palm tree, I will take hold of its branches [*sansinav*]" (Song of Songs 7:9).

Fever [*tzimra*] – **צִימְרָא:** Meaning heat, or according to Rashi, a fever. As a verb it connotes something heated by fire. Some understand it to mean shaking or shivering, similar to the Hebrew *tzemarmoret*, chills, which is one of the side effects of a fever.

Date pits [*suflei*] – **סוּפְלֵי:** The *ge'onim* explain *suflei* as date pits and husks. Some see a relationship between this word and the word *shafel*, low; in other words, the least desirable part of the dates.

***Se'a* [*gerivei*]** – **גְּרִיבֵי:** This word also appears in Syrian Aramaic as *griva* and in the Arabic as جريب, *jarīb*, meaning a dry measure. The talmudic Sages commonly refer to this measurement as a *se'a*.

***Eder* tree** – **אַדְּרָא:** The exact identity of this tree is unclear. Some derive its name from Greek and say it is another name for a cedar tree, a kind of oak, or even a species of fig tree. Some derive it from the Hebrew word *adir*, which means large or mighty, referring to a large tree. Nowadays the name is used for the *Acer* genus of trees.

עִנְבֵי תָּאלָא בְּמַיִם.

grapes grown by trellising the vine on **a palm tree** soaked **in water.**

לַחֲזָזִיתָא – לֵיתֵי שַׁב חִיטֵּי אַרְזַנְיָיתָא וְנִיקְלִינְהוּ אַמָּרָא חֲדַתָּא, וְנָפֵיק מִשְׁחָא מִינַּיְיהוּ וְנֵישׁוּף. רַב שִׁימִי בַּר אַשִׁי עֲבַד לֵיהּ לְהַהוּא גּוֹי לְדָבָר אַחֵר, וְאִיתַּסֵּי.

As a remedy **for lichen planus** [*ḥazazita*][L] on one's skin, **let him bring seven large wheat kernels** [*arzanayata*][LN] **and** let him **roast them over** a fire on the blade of **a new hoe. And** let him **extract oil**[B] **from** the wheat **and rub** it into his skin. It is told: **Rav Shimi bar Ashi used this** remedy **for a certain gentile** who had **something else,** i.e., leprosy, **and he was healed.**

אֲמַר שְׁמוּאֵל: הַאי מַאן דְּמָחוּ לֵיהּ בְּאַלוּנְכֵי דְּפַרְסָאֵי מִיחֲיָיא לָא חַיֵּי, אַדְּהָכִי וְהָכִי נִיסְפּוּ לֵיהּ בִּשְׂרָא שְׁמִינָא אַגּוּמְרֵי וְחַמְרָא חַיָּיא, אֶפְשָׁר דְּחַיֵּי פּוּרְתָּא וּמְפַקֵּיד אַבֵּיתֵיהּ.

Shmuel said: One who is struck with Persian spears [*alunkei*][L] **will not live** long afterward, as he will certainly die from this wound. **In the meantime, they should force-feed him fatty meat** that was roasted **over coals, and undiluted wine.** If they do this, it is **possible that he will live for a little bit** longer **and** have time to **instruct his household** with regard to what they should do after his death.

אֲמַר רַב אִידִי בַּר אָבִין: הַאי מַאן דְּבָלַע זִיבּוּרָא מִיחֲיָיא לָא חַיֵּי, אַדְּהָכִי וְהָכִי נַשְׁקֵיהּ רְבִיעֲתָא דְּחַלָּא שַׁמְזָג, אֶפְשָׁר דְּחַיֵּי פּוּרְתָּא וּמְפַקֵּיד לְבֵיתֵיהּ.

Similarly, **Rav Idi bar Avin said: One who swallowed a hornet**[B] **will not live. In the meantime they should give him a quarter-***log* **of sharp** [*shamzag*][L] **vinegar**[N] **to drink.** If they do this, **it is possible that he will live for a little bit** longer **and** have time to **instruct his household** with regard to what they should do after his death.

אָמַר רַבִּי יְהוֹשֻׁעַ בֶּן לֵוִי: אָכַל בְּשַׂר שׁוֹר בְּלֶפֶת, וְלָן בַּלְּבָנָה בְּלֵילֵי אַרְבָּעָה עָשָׂר אוֹ חֲמִשָּׁה עָשָׂר בִּתְקוּפַת תַּמּוּז – אֲחָזַתּוּ אַחִילוּ.

§ **Rabbi Yehoshua ben Levi says:** If one **ate ox meat with a turnip, and slept** by the light of **the moon on the night of the fourteenth or the fifteenth** of the month **in the season of Tammuz,** i.e., summer, he will be **afflicted with** ***aḥilu,***[B] a severe fever.

תָּנָא: וְהַמְמַלֵּא כְּרֵיסוֹ מִכׇּל דָּבָר – אֲחָזַתּוּ אַחִילוּ. אֲמַר רַב פַּפָּא: אֲפִילּוּ מִתַּמְרֵי. פְּשִׁיטָא! סָלְקָא דַּעְתָּךְ אָמִינָא, הוֹאִיל וְאָמַר מָר: תַּמְרֵי – מַשְׂבְּעָן וּמְשַׁחְנָן וּמְשַׁלְשְׁלָן וּמְאַשְּׁרָן וְלָא מְפַנְקָן, אֵימָא לָא, קָא מַשְׁמַע לַן.

A Sage **taught: And one who fills his stomach with anything,**[N] meaning that he eats too much, will be **afflicted with** ***aḥilu.*** **Rav Pappa said: Even** if he fills his stomach **with dates.** The Gemara asks: Isn't this **obvious,** as Rabbi Yehoshua ben Levi explicitly mentioned if one fills his stomach with anything. The Gemara answers: **It might enter your mind to say** that **since the Master said** the following in praise of dates: **Dates satisfy**[B] the body, **warm** it up, **act as a laxative, strengthen** the body, **and do not spoil** it, one might **say** that as dates are beneficial, he would **not** be harmed by eating too many. Nevertheless, it **teaches us** that they can also cause harm when eaten in excess.

מַאי אַחִילוּ? אָמַר רַבִּי אֶלְעָזָר: אֵשׁ שֶׁל עֲצָמוֹת. מַאי אֵשׁ שֶׁל עֲצָמוֹת? אֲמַר אַבַּיֵי: אֵשׁ גַּרְמֵי.

The Gemara asks: **What is** the affliction ***aḥilu*** mentioned here? **Rabbi Elazar says: A fire of the bones.** The Gemara asks: **What is a fire of the bones? Abaye said:** This is what is called ***esh garmei*** in Aramaic.

מַאי אָסוּתֵיהּ? אֲמַר אַבַּיֵי, אֲמַרָה לִי אֵם: כּוּלְּהוּ שְׁקָיֵינֵי – תְּלָתָא וְשִׁבְעָא וּתְרֵיסַר, וְהַאי – עַד דְּמִתַּסֵּי;

What is its remedy? Abaye said: My mother told me that **any drink** consumed for medicinal purposes should be taken for either **three or seven or twelve** days, depending on what is necessary for that specific ailment. **And** if **this** is taken to treat *aḥilu* then he must drink it **until he is healed.**

כּוּלְּהוּ שְׁקָיֵינֵי – אַלִּיבָּא רֵיקָנָא, וְהַאי – בָּתַר דְּאָכַל וְשָׁתֵי וְעָיֵיל לְבֵית הַכִּסֵּא וְנָפֵיק וּמָשֵׁי יְדֵיהּ, וּמַיְיתוּ לֵיהּ בּוּנָא דִּשְׁתִיתָא דְּטַלְפְּחֵי וּבוּנָא דְּחַמְרָא עַתִּיקָא, וְנִיגַבְּלִינְהוּ בַּהֲדֵי הֲדָדֵי וְנֵיכוּל, וְנִיכְרוֹךְ בִּסְדִינֵיהּ וְנִיגְנֵיהּ, וְלֵיכָּא דְּנוֹקְמֵיהּ עַד דְּקָאֵי מִנַּפְשֵׁיהּ, וְכִי קָאֵי לִישְׁקְלֵיהּ לִסְדִינֵיהּ מִינֵּיהּ, וְאִי לָא – הָדַר עִילָּוֵיהּ.

Any drink consumed for medicinal purposes should be consumed **with an empty heart,** i.e., without eating first. **And** for **this** disease of *aḥilu* he consumes the medicine **after he eats and drinks and enters the bathroom, and exits and washes his hands, and they bring him a fistful of** ***shetita,***[B] a type of food made **from lentils,**[N] **and a fistful of aged wine. And let him mix them together and let him eat** this mixture. **And let him wrap himself with his sheet and sleep. And let there be no one who will awaken him until he awakens on his own. And when he awakens let him remove the sheet from himself. And if** he does **not** do this then the illness **will return to him.**

LANGUAGE

Lichen planus [*ḥazazita*] – חֲזָזִיתָא: This is a skin disease which causes flakes and growths on the skin.

Large…kernels [*arzanayata*] – אַרְזַנְיָיתָא: Some explain that this word is derived from the Hebrew word *orez,* rice. In fact, it is probably from the Akkadian arsānu.

Spears [*alunkei*] – אַלוּנְכֵי: Apparently an extended form of the Greek λόγχη, *lonkhē,* meaning spear. According to Rashi, the Persians would smear their weapons with poison to make them more effective against the enemy.

Sharp [*shamzag*] – שַׁמְזָג: Although its source is unclear, the *ge'onim* claim that this is a Persian word meaning strong or spicy.

NOTES

Large wheat kernels – חִיטֵּי אַרְזַנְיָיתָא: Rashi explains this as large wheat kernels, but the *ge'onim* hold that it refers to a unique species of wheat.

Sharp vinegar – חַלָּא שַׁמְזָג: According to Rashi, this refers to a strong vinegar. Similarly, the *ge'onim* explain that it refers to a strong and sharp vinegar used to produce Persian salt.

With anything – מִכׇּל דָּבָר: Rashi explains that this refers to any enjoyable food. The danger is that he may overeat due to his desire for this food. Others explain the words literally, i.e., that with regard to this issue it makes no difference if what he is eating is of high or low quality, as in any case one who fills his stomach will become ill.

***Shetita* from lentils – שְׁתִיתָא דְּטַלְפְּחֵי:** Rashi writes that this a porridge of flour mixed with salt, and in this particular case he should make it with lentil flour. The *ge'onim* explain the word as a mixture of wheat and lentil flour.

BACKGROUND

Extract oil – נָפֵיק מִשְׁחָא: Whenever plants of this type are processed in this manner, they exude oily substances.

Swallowed a hornet – בָּלַע זִיבּוּרָא: The Gemara is talking about a case where someone swallowed a live hornet which stung him while it was in his throat. At times the sting is so severe that it causes the throat to swell, blocking the windpipe and causing the victim to suffocate. Additionally, some people are allergic to the venom of bees, wasps, or hornets, and can die from a sting even without swallowing the insect. A hornet, unlike a bee, can sting several times, and thereby discharge a large amount of venom.

***Aḥilu* – אַחִילוּ:** This seems to be referring to a kind of inflammation of the joints. The afflicted individual feels heat in the affected joints as well as sharp pains, but the illness is not always accompanied by a general fever.

Dates satisfy – תַּמְרֵי מַשְׂבְּעָן: Dates are high in calories; 100 g have approximately 270 calories, most of which are in the form of sugars that digest very quickly. Consequently, eating dates satisfies hunger and warms the body. In addition, due to their high fiber content, dates also act as a laxative. The feelings of satiation and a light stomach also cause a general feeling of relaxation.

***Shetita* – שְׁתִיתָא:** This is a kind of porridge that was usually made from parched grains, i.e., wheat or barley that was picked before ripening and heated in fire until sweet. It was then mixed together with some vinegar. A similar food was sometimes made from lentils.

אֲמַר לֵיהּ אֵלִיָּהוּ לְרַבִּי נָתָן: אֱכוֹל שְׁלִישׁ וּשְׁתֵה שְׁלִישׁ וְהַנַּח שְׁלִישׁ, לִכְשֶׁתִּכְעוֹס תַּעֲמוֹד עַל מִילוּאֲךָ.

§ **Elijah** the prophet **said to Rabbi Natan: Eat a third**[H] of your fill, **and drink a third** of your fill, **and leave a third** of your fill, so that **when you become angry** you will **become full.** If you do this, there will be room, as it were, for the anger. If you become angry when your stomach is full you will be harmed.

תָּנֵי רַבִּי חִיָּיא: הָרוֹצֶה שֶׁלֹּא יָבֹא לִידֵי חוֹלִי מֵעַיִים, יְהֵא רָגִיל בְּטִיבּוּל קַיִץ וָחוֹרֶף, סְעוּדָתְךָ שֶׁהֲנָאָתְךָ מִמֶּנָּה מְשׁוֹךְ יָדְךָ הֵימֶנָּה, וְאַל תַּשְׁהֶה עַצְמְךָ בְּשָׁעָה שֶׁאַתָּה צָרִיךְ לִנְקָבֶיךָ.

Rabbi Ḥiyya teaches: One who does not want to come to a situation whereby he contracts **intestinal disease** should **become accustomed to dipping** his food in wine or vinegar, both in the **summer** and in the **winter.** He also teaches: **You should remove your hand,** i.e., stop eating, **from a meal that you enjoy**[H] so that you do not overeat. **And do not delay yourself at the time when it is necessary to relieve yourself.**[H]

אֲמַר מָר עוּקְבָא: הַאי מַאן דְּשָׁתֵי טִילְיָא חִיוָּרָא – אָחַזְתּוֹ וִיתַק. אֲמַר רַב חִסְדָּא: שִׁיתִּין מִינֵי חַמְרָא הָווּ, מַעַלְיָא דְּכוּלְּהוּ – סוּמָּקָא רֵיחָתָנָא, גְּרִיעָא דְּכוּלְּהוּ – טִילְיָא חִיוָּרָא.

Mar Ukva said: This one who drinks inferior white wine [*tilya*][L] will be **afflicted with weakness** [*vitak*].[L] **Rav Ḥisda said: There are sixty types of wine. The best of them all is red, fragrant** wine. **The worst of them all** is **inferior white wine.**

אֲמַר רַב יְהוּדָה: הַאי מַאן דְּיָתֵיב בְּצַפְרְנֵי נִיסָן גַּבֵּי נוּרָא, וְשָׁיֵיף מִשְׁחָא וְנָפֵיק וְיָתֵיב בְּשִׁמְשָׁא – אָחַזְתּוֹ וִיתַק.

Rav Yehuda said: This one who sits near the fire during the mornings in the month of **Nisan and rubs** himself **with oil** and then **goes out and sits in the sun** will be **afflicted with weakness.**

תָּנוּ רַבָּנַן: הִקִּיז דָּם וְשִׁימֵּשׁ מִטָּתוֹ – הָוְיָין לוֹ בָּנִים וִיתָּקִין, הִקִּיזוּ שְׁנֵיהֶם וְשִׁימְּשׁוּ – הָוְיָין לָהֶן בָּנִים בַּעֲלֵי רָאֲתָן. אֲמַר רַב פָּפָּא: לָא אֲמָרַן אֶלָּא דְּלָא טָעֵים מִידֵּי, אֲבָל טָעֵים מִידֵּי לֵית לָן בָּהּ.

The Sages taught: One who **let blood and** afterward **engaged in sexual intercourse has weak children** conceived from those acts of intercourse. If **both of them,** husband and wife, **let blood and engaged in sexual intercourse they will have children** afflicted with a disease known as *ra'atan*.[B] **Rav Pappa said: We** said this **only** if **he did not taste anything** after letting blood. **But if he tasted something** then **we have no** problem **with it.**

אֲמַר רַבָּה בַּר רַב הוּנָא: בָּא מִן הַדֶּרֶךְ וְשִׁימֵּשׁ מִטָּתוֹ – הָוְיָין לוֹ בָּנִים וִיתָּקִין. תָּנוּ רַבָּנַן: הַבָּא מִבֵּית הַכִּסֵּא, אַל יְשַׁמֵּשׁ מִטָּתוֹ עַד שֶׁיִּשְׁהֶה שִׁיעוּר חֲצִי מִיל, מִפְּנֵי שֶׁשֵּׁד בֵּית הַכִּסֵּא מְלַוֶּה עִמּוֹ, וְאִם שִׁימֵּשׁ – הָוְיָין לוֹ בָּנִים נִכְפִּים.

Rabba bar Rav Huna says: One who **came back from** traveling on **the road**[H] **and engaged in sexual intercourse** immediately **has weak children** conceived from those acts of intercourse. **The Sages taught:** With regard to **one who comes** in **from the bathroom,** he should **not engage in sexual intercourse until he waits the measure of** time it takes to walk **half a** *mil* **because the demon of the bathroom accompanies him. And if he engaged in sexual intercourse** without waiting this measure of time, **he has children** who are **epileptic.**

תָּנוּ רַבָּנַן: הַמְשַׁמֵּשׁ מִטָּתוֹ מְעוּמָּד – אוֹחַזְתּוֹ עֲוִית, מְיוּשָּׁב – אוֹחַזְתּוֹ דַּלְרִיָּא, הִיא מִלְמַעְלָה וְהוּא מִלְּמַטָּה – אוֹחַזְתּוֹ דַּלְרִיָּא.

The Sages taught: One who engages in sexual intercourse while **standing** will be **afflicted by spasms.** One who engages in sexual intercourse while **sitting** will be **afflicted with** *dalarya*. **If she,** the woman, is **above and he,** the husband, is **below** during sexual intercourse, then he will be **afflicted with** ***dalarya***.

HALAKHA

Eat a third, etc. – אֱכוֹל שְׁלִישׁ וכו׳: One should not eat until his stomach is filled. Rather, he should stop when he is one-quarter away from being satiated (Rambam *Sefer HaMadda*, *Hilkhot Deot* 4:2).

A meal that you enjoy, etc. – סְעוּדָתְךָ שֶׁהֲנָאָתְךָ מִמֶּנָּה וכו׳: Excessive eating is as harmful to the body as the elixir of death (Rambam *Sefer HaMadda*, *Hilkhot Deot* 4:15).

And do not delay…when it is necessary to relieve yourself – וְאַל תַּשְׁהֶה...שֶׁאַתָּה צָרִיךְ לִנְקָבֶיךָ: It is prohibited for one to delay relieving himself, when he needs to either urinate or defecate, and anyone who does this is considered to soil his soul, in addition to all of the illnesses that he may cause himself (Rambam *Sefer HaMadda*, *Hilkhot Deot* 4:1 and *Sefer Kedusha*, *Hilkhot Ma'akhalot Assurot* 17:31; *Shulḥan Arukh*, *Oraḥ Ḥayyim* 3:17).

One who came back from the road, etc. – בָּא מִן הַדֶּרֶךְ וכו׳: One should not engage in sexual intercourse while standing or sitting. Nor should one engage in it on the day that he lets blood, or on the day that he returns from traveling. Nor should one engage in sexual intercourse on the days preceding or following any of these days (Rambam *Sefer HaMadda*, *Hilkhot Deot* 4:19; *Shulḥan Arukh*, *Oraḥ Ḥayyim* 240:15).

LANGUAGE

Inferior…wine [*tilya*] – טִילְיָא: From the Arabic طلاء, *ṭilā'*, meaning strong wine.

Weakness [*vitak*] – וִיתַק: The source of this word and its meaning remain unclear. According to Rabbi Binyamin Musafya, it derives from the Greek φθισικός, *phthisikos*, meaning afflicted with a degenerative illness, particularly tuberculosis. Some assert that it comes from the Greek ἑκτικός, *hektikos*, which, among other things, means seriously ill.

BACKGROUND

Ra'atan – רָאֲתָן: This disease, mentioned in the Talmud and in various *midrashim*, is not precisely identified. There are several theories as to its nature. It may be referring to Hansen's disease, more commonly known as leprosy. This disease takes on several forms, but one of them highly resembles the descriptions of *ra'atan* in the Talmud. In addition to severe toughening of the skin which causes a loss of feeling in that area or in the entire limb, leprosy also causes a great deal of mucus to flow from the nose. In later stages leprosy causes more serious wounds, including the eventual rotting of the external limbs.

מַאי דַּלְרְיָא? אֲמַר רַבִּי יְהוֹשֻׁעַ בֶּן לֵוִי: סַם דַּלְרְיָא – דַּרְדְּרָא. מַאי דַּרְדְּרָא? אֲמַר אַבָּיֵי: מוֹרִיקָא דְּחוֹחֵי. רַב פַּפָּא אָלֵיס וּבָלַע לֵיהּ; רַב פַּפִּי אָלֵיס וְשָׁדֵי לֵיהּ.

The Gemara asks: **What is** ***dalarya*****?**[L] **Rabbi Yehoshua ben Levi said: The remedy for** ***dalarya*** **is** ***dardara*****.**[B] The Gemara asks: **What is** ***dardara*****? Abaye said: Saffron of thorns.**[N] **Rav Pappa** would **chew** [*aleis*][L] **and swallow** this remedy. **Rav Pappi** would **chew and spit it** out.

אָמַר אַבָּיֵי: מִי שֶׁאֵינוֹ בָּקִי בְּדֶרֶךְ אֶרֶץ, לֵיתֵי שְׁלֹשָׁה קְפִיזֵי קוֹרְטְמֵי דְּחוֹחֵי, וְנִידוֹקִינְהוּ וְנִישְׁלִיקִינְהוּ בְּחַמְרָא וְנִישְׁתֵּי. אָמַר רַבִּי יוֹחָנָן: הֵן הֵן הֶחֱזִירוּנִי לְנַעֲרוּתִי.

Abaye says: As a remedy for **one who is not an expert,** i.e., does not have strength, **in the way of the world,** i.e., in sexual intercourse, **let him bring three vessels** [*kefizei*],[L] each containing three-quarters of a *log* of **safflower thorns. And let him grind them, and boil them in wine, and drink** the mixture. **Rabbi Yoḥanan says: These are** the remedies that **return me to my youth** with regard to sexual intercourse.

שְׁלֹשָׁה דְּבָרִים מַכְחִישִׁים כֹּחוֹ שֶׁל אָדָם, וְאֵלּוּ הֵן: פַּחַד, דֶּרֶךְ, וְעָוֹן. פַּחַד, דִּכְתִיב: ״לִבִּי סְחַרְחַר עֲזָבַנִי כֹחִי״; דֶּרֶךְ, דִּכְתִיב: ״עִנָּה בַדֶּרֶךְ כֹּחִי״; עָוֹן, דִּכְתִיב: ״כָּשַׁל בַּעֲוֹנִי כֹּחִי״.

§ **Three things diminish a person's strength, and they are: Fear,**[N] traveling on **the road, and sin.**[N] The Gemara explains: **Fear, as it is written: "My heart flutters, my strength fails me"** (Psalms 38:11). Traveling on **the road, as it is written: "He has weakened my strength on the road"** (Psalms 102:24). **Sin, as it is written: "My strength fails because of my sin"** (Psalms 31:11).

שְׁלֹשָׁה דְּבָרִים מַתִּיזִין גּוּפוֹ שֶׁל אָדָם, וְאֵלּוּ הֵן: אָכַל מְעוּמָּד, וְשָׁתָה מְעוּמָּד, וְשִׁימֵּשׁ מִטָּתוֹ מְעוּמָּד.

Three things break a person's body, and they are: If he **ate** while **standing,**[HB] if he **drank** while **standing, and** if he **engaged in sexual intercourse** while **standing.**

חֲמִשָּׁה קְרוֹבִין לְמִיתָה יוֹתֵר מִן הַחַיִּים. וְאֵלּוּ הֵן: אָכַל וְעָמַד, שָׁתָה וְעָמַד, הִקִּיז דָּם וְעָמַד, יָשַׁן וְעָמַד, שִׁימֵּשׁ מִטָּתוֹ וְעָמַד.

There are **five** actions that bring one **closer to death than to life, and they are:** If he **ate and stood**[NH] up immediately, if he **drank and stood** up immediately, if he **let blood and stood**[H] up immediately, if he **slept and stood** up immediately, and if he **engaged in sexual intercourse and stood** up immediately.

BACKGROUND

Dardara – דַּרְדְּרָא: The *ge'onim* explain this as a variety of the cynara plant, perhaps *Cynara syriaca*, also called the wild artichoke, which is a thorny plant with purple flowers. Its petals were eaten like artichokes, another species of cynara. The word appears in the Torah in the verse: "Thorns also and thistles [*dardar*] shall it bring forth to you" (Genesis 3:18).

Despite this, based on the talmudic definition: Saffron of thorns, it seems that it is a species of what is called in Hebrew *kortam*, perhaps the *Carthamus tenuis*, a common thorny plant with pink or purple flowers. Its common name is slender safflower, and its leaves were used to make paint and its seeds were pressed for oil.

Wild artichoke

Ate while standing – אָכַל מְעוּמָּד: The common denominator between the actions listed here is the exertion of standing while doing something else. This could be dangerous, especially for those suffering from heart conditions and the like.

Slender safflower

LANGUAGE

Dalarya – דַּלְרְיָא: There are several opinions as to the correct meaning of this word. Some derive it from the Latin dolor, meaning pain or illness. Others have the version *darariya* and claim that it is derived from the Greek διάρροια, *diarroia*, or diarrhea. According to the *Arukh*, *dalarya* appears to be a disease that causes shortness of breath.

Chew [*aleis*] – אָלֵיס: The root *alef, lamed, samekh*, sometimes written with an *ayin* instead of an *alef*, is the same as the root *lamed, ayin, samekh*, meaning to chew. There are several words in which the letters are occasionally reversed, e.g., the word for sheep, which is spelled either as *keves* or as *kesev*.

Vessels [*kefizei*] – קְפִיזֵי: This refers specifically to a vessel which contains three-quarters of a *log* of liquid. It is derived from the Middle Persian kabīz, a measurement of volume.

NOTES

Saffron of thorns – מוֹרִיקָא דְּחוֹחֵי: Rashi and the *Arukh* explain that this is referring to saffron that grows between thorns. However, in *Otzar HaGe'onim* it is explained that is a type of thistle called cynara, or wild artichoke.

Fear – פַּחַד: Rashi explains that this does not refer to a sudden fear, i.e., shock, but rather to a state of continuous anxiety.

And sin – וְעָוֹן: *Tosafot* explain that this is referring to worries about sins that one has transgressed, or about the punishment that he will receive for sin.

He ate and stood, etc. – אָכַל וְעָמַד וכו׳: There is a version of Rashi which states that these actions, like the list that appears afterward, bring one closer to death only when all of them are performed. However, this is not the opinion of *Tosafot* (*Migdal David*).

HALAKHA

He ate while standing – אָכַל מְעוּמָּד: One should always eat when sitting or reclining, and should never eat while standing (Rambam *Sefer HaMadda, Hilkhot Deot* 4:3).

He ate and stood – אָכַל וְעָמַד: One should neither go for a walk nor perform any other strenuous activity until the food in his stomach is digested. Anyone who does go for a walk or performs other strenuous activity after eating will cause himself to become ill (Rambam *Sefer HaMadda, Hilkhot Deot* 4:3).

He let blood and stood – הִקִּיז דָּם וְעָמַד: One should let blood only when it is very necessary for him to do so, and he should not let blood and bathe on the same day. Furthermore, he should not let blood and set out on a journey on the same day. Rather, he should rest on the day of bloodletting (Rambam *Sefer HaMadda, Hilkhot Deot* 4:18).

שִׁשָּׁה הָעוֹשֶׂה אוֹתָן – מִיָּד מֵת, וְאֵלּוּ הֵן: הַבָּא בַּדֶּרֶךְ וְנִתְיַיגַּע, הִקִּיז דָּם, וְנִכְנַס לְבֵית הַמֶּרְחָץ, וְשָׁתָה וְנִשְׁתַּכֵּר, וְיָשַׁן עַל גַּבֵּי קַרְקַע, וְשִׁימֵּשׁ מִטָּתוֹ. אָמַר רַבִּי יוֹחָנָן: וְהוּא שֶׁעֲשָׂאָן כְּסִידְרָן.

With regard to **one who performs** the following acts, if he performs the **six of them** consecutively **he dies immediately, and they are:** If **one came** back **from** a journey **on the road and was exhausted, let blood, and entered the bathhouse, and drank and became intoxicated, and slept on the ground, and engaged in sexual intercourse,** then he will die. **Rabbi Yoḥanan says: But he** will die for certain only in the case **where he performs them in this order.**

אֲמַר אַבַּיֵי: כְּסִידְרָן – מֵת, שֶׁלֹּא כְּסִידְרָן – חָלֵישׁ. אִינִי? וְהָא מְעוֹרֶת עָבְדָה לֵיהּ לְעַבְדָּהּ תְּלָת מִינַּיְיהוּ וּמִית! הַהוּא כָּחוּשׁ הֲוָה.

Abaye said: If he performs these actions **in this order he will die.** But if he performs them **out of order he will become weak.** The Gemara asks: **Is that so? But didn't** a woman named **Me'oret make her slave** perform **three of these** actions **and he died** as a result? The Gemara answers: **That** slave **was weak,** which is why he died. But an ordinary individual would die only upon performing all of these acts in the previously mentioned order.

שְׁמוֹנָה רוּבָּן קָשֶׁה וּמִיעוּטָן יָפֶה, וְאֵלּוּ הֵן: דֶּרֶךְ, וְדֶרֶךְ אֶרֶץ, עוֹשֶׁר, וּמְלָאכָה, יַיִן, וְשֵׁינָה, חַמִּין, וְהַקָּזַת דָּם.

Eight actions are **difficult** for the body and the soul to handle **in large** amounts **and** are **beneficial in small** amounts, **and they are:** Traveling on the **road,** engaging in the **way of the world,** i.e., engaging in sexual intercourse, having **wealth, work,** drinking **wine, sleep, hot water, and bloodletting.**[B]

שְׁמוֹנָה מְמַעֲטִים אֶת הַזֶּרַע, וְאֵלּוּ הֵן: הַמֶּלַח, וְהָרָעָב, וְהַנֶּתֶק, בְּכִיָּה, וְשֵׁינָה עַל גַּבֵּי קַרְקַע, וְגַדְגְּדָנִיּוֹת, וּכְשׁוּת שֶׁלֹּא בִּזְמַנָּהּ, וְהַקָּזַת דָּם לְמַטָּה – כִּפְלַיִם.

Eight actions or illnesses **decrease the semen, and they are: Salt, hunger,** a skin disease called ***netek*****, crying, sleeping on the ground,** the **melilot**[B] plant, **and dodder**[B] eaten **not in its time,** i.e., before it is ripe. **And bloodletting** performed **below,** on the lower portion of the body, causes **twice** as much harm as the other actions mentioned.

תָּנָא: כְּשֵׁם שֶׁקָּשָׁה לְמַטָּה כִּפְלַיִם, כָּךְ יָפָה לְמַעְלָה כִּפְלַיִם. אֲמַר רַב פַּפָּא:

The Sage **taught: Just as** bloodletting **below** causes **twice** as much harm, **so too,** bloodletting **above,** on the upper portion of the body, is **twice** as **effective. Rav Pappa said:**

BACKGROUND

Bloodletting – הַקָּזַת דָּם: For many generations doctors thought that bloodletting was an effective treatment, either as a cure for certain illnesses or to maintain one's health. People would often undergo bloodletting as a way of strengthening their body. Nevertheless, they also knew that letting blood would weaken the body and could at times be dangerous. For this reason the Sages provided a whole list of different foods intended to supply quick energy after bloodletting.

Melilot – גַּדְגְּדָנִיּוֹת: Most of the commentaries identify this as a species of the genus *Melilotus*, which can be annual or perennial depending on the species. These rather tall plants grow wild, and have clover-like leaves and fruits that grow a husk containing one or two seeds. The plant is usually used as food for animals, but its seeds are suitable for human consumption. It was also used for medicinal purposes.

Sweet clover, a species of *Melilotus*

Dodder – כְּשׁוּת: Dodder is a variety of the species *Cuscuta*, from the Convolvulaceae family. There are several different types of dodder, which are parasitic and wind themselves around other plants to feed off their nutrients. Dodder has fine stalks and is leafless, sucking its food by means of tendrils or roots that penetrate into the stalk of its host plant. The plant is generally cultivated annually in small bushes. It is mostly used for the production of beer. At a certain point in the fermentation process dodder is added in order to give beer its distinctive bitter taste. Inferior-quality dodder can add an unpleasantly bitter taste to a beverage.

Dodder wrapped around stinging nettle

לְמַטָּה – לְמַטָּה מִן הַבֵּיצִים, לְמַעְלָה – לְמַעְלָה מִן הַבֵּיצִים.

When the Gemara mentioned letting blood from **below** it meant **below the testicles,** and when it mentioned letting blood from **above** it meant **above the testicles.**

וּכְשׁוּת שֶׁלֹּא בִּזְמַנָּהּ. תָּנָא: כְּשֵׁם שֶׁקָּשָׁה שֶׁלֹּא בִּזְמַנָּהּ, כָּךְ יָפָה בִּזְמַנָּהּ. אֲמַר רַב פַּפָּא: זְמַנָּהּ – תַּמּוּז, שֶׁלֹּא בִּזְמַנָּהּ – טֵבֵת, יוֹמֵי נִיסָן וְיוֹמֵי תִּשְׁרֵי – לָא מַעֲלוּ וְלָא קָשׁוּ.

It was taught: **And dodder** eaten **not in its time,** before it is ripe, causes harm. The Gemara explains: A Sage **taught: Just as** eating dodder **not in its time is harmful** to the body, **so too,** eating it **in its time,** when it is ripe, is **good** for the body. **Rav Pappa said: Its time is Tammuz,** in the summer, and **not in its time is Tevet,** in the winter. And during **the days of Nisan,** spring, **and the days of Tishrei,** autumn, **they neither help nor harm.**

אָמַר ״כִּתְבוּ גֵּט לְאִשְׁתִּי״ וַאֲחָזוֹ קוֹרְדְיָיקוֹס וְחָזַר וְאָמַר ״אַל תִּכְתְּבוּ״ – אֵין דְּבָרָיו הָאַחֲרוֹנִים כְּלוּם. אֲמַר רַבִּי שִׁמְעוֹן בֶּן לָקִישׁ: כּוֹתְבִין וְנוֹתְנִין גֵּט לְאַלְתַּר, וְרַבִּי יוֹחָנָן אָמַר: אֵין כּוֹתְבִין אֶלָּא לִכְשֶׁיִּשְׁתַּפֶּה.

§ The Gemara returns to its discussion of the *halakhot* mentioned in the mishna. The mishna teaches: If **he said: Write a bill of divorce for my wife,** when he was lucid, **and was** then **afflicted with** temporary **insanity and he retracted** his previous statement **and said: Do not write it, his latter statement** is considered to be **nothing,** i.e., it is not halakhically valid. The Gemara comments on this that **Rabbi Shimon ben Lakish says:** In that case the court **writes and gives the bill of divorce immediately,** because even though he is insane, the court does not wait for him to return to his senses. **And Rabbi Yoḥanan says:** They **write** this bill of divorce based on his instructions **only once he is healed**[H] and returns to a sound state of mind.

מַאי טַעֲמָא דְּרֵישׁ לָקִישׁ? דְּקָתָנֵי: אֵין בִּדְבָרָיו הָאַחֲרוֹנִים כְּלוּם. וְרַבִּי יוֹחָנָן אָמַר לָךְ: אֵין בִּדְבָרָיו הָאַחֲרוֹנִים כְּלוּם – דִּלְכִי מִתְצִיל לָא צָרִיךְ לְמִיהֲדַר אִימְּלוֹכֵי בֵּיהּ, וּלְעוֹלָם אֵין כּוֹתְבִין אֶלָּא לִכְשֶׁיִּשְׁתַּפֶּה.

The Gemara elaborates: **What is the reason** for the opinion **of Reish Lakish? As it teaches** in the mishna: **His final statement** is considered to be **nothing,**[N] which indicates that his initial statement stands and the court should act in accordance with his instructions. By contrast, **Rabbi Yoḥanan** could have **said to you** as follows: When the mishna said that **his final statement** is considered to be **nothing** it means **that when** his mind **becomes lucid** it is **not necessary** for the court **to return and confirm** his instructions; rather, they rely on his statement. **But** the court **actually writes** the bill of divorce **only once he is healed.**

בְּמַאי קָמִיפַּלְגִי? רֵישׁ לָקִישׁ מְדַמֵּי לֵיהּ לְיָשֵׁן, וְרַבִּי יוֹחָנָן מְדַמֵּי לֵיהּ לְשׁוֹטֶה.

The Gemara asks: **With regard to what** principle **do** Reish Lakish and Rabbi Yoḥanan **disagree? Reish Lakish compares** one afflicted with temporary insanity **to one who is sleeping.** If one said to write a bill of divorce and went to sleep then the court may write it without waiting for him to awaken. **And Rabbi Yoḥanan compares him to an imbecile:** When he is afflicted with temporary insanity he is not of sound mind and is therefore unfit to give a bill of divorce.

HALAKHA

They write only once he is healed – אֵין כּוֹתְבִין אֶלָּא לִכְשֶׁיִּשְׁתַּפֶּה: If someone was healthy when he instructed others to write a bill of divorce for his wife and afterward became afflicted with mental illness, the court may not write the bill of divorce until he recovers. If they wrote it and gave it to her while he was still mentally ill, the status of the document depends on the nature of his illness. If there is a remedy for it, then the bill of divorce is invalid by rabbinic law. If there is no remedy then the bill of divorce has no validity at all, in accordance with the opinion of Rabbi Yoḥanan.

The *Baḥ* and the Gra hold that this distinction between whether or not there is a remedy for the illness applies only according to the opinion of Reish Lakish. According to Rabbi Yoḥanan the document has no validity regardless of the nature of the illness (Rambam *Sefer Nashim, Hilkhot Geirushin* 2:15; *Shulḥan Arukh, Even HaEzer* 121:2).

NOTES

His final statement is nothing – אֵין בִּדְבָרָיו הָאַחֲרוֹנִים כְּלוּם: *Tosafot* write that Reish Lakish derives this from the wording of the mishna, as it could have stated the more open-ended statement: They shall write the bill of divorce and give it to his wife, which would not indicate when it should be given. The Rashba writes this is derived from the fact that rather than the expression: He said nothing, the expression: His final statement is nothing, is used. This wording indicates that his initial statement is entirely valid.

NOTES

Slit the two pipes, etc. – **שָׁחַט בּוֹ שְׁנַיִם וכו׳**: The early commentaries write that it is clear that one's strength ebbs immediately prior to death so that his mind is not clear, and at this time he is comparable to someone afflicted with temporary insanity (Ramban). This is explicitly stated in the Jerusalem Talmud when it challenges this *baraita*: And it is not possible that his mind was not confused at that time.

He signaled and stated, write, etc. – **וְרָמַז וְאָמַר כִּתְבוּ וכו׳**: In other words, this is a case where others asked him: Shall we write a bill of divorce for your wife? And the husband signaled his assent (*Tosafot*).

Severed [*meguyyad*] – **מְגוּיָּד**: Rashi explains this version of the text to mean that his limbs were severed. Others have a version of the text that reads *meguyyar*, meaning that he has been shot with arrows (Meiri).

They may testify with regard to him – **מְעִידִין עָלָיו**: This indicates that the witnesses may testify immediately that he is dead, without concern that his death was delayed (*Tosefot HaRosh*).

וְרַבִּי יוֹחָנָן נַמִי לִידַמֵּיהּ לְיָשֵׁן! יָשֵׁן לָא מְחוּסַּר מַעֲשֶׂה, הַאי מְחוּסַּר מַעֲשֶׂה.

The Gemara asks: **And Rabbi Yoḥanan also could compare him to one who is sleeping**, so why does he not do so? The Gemara answers: **One who is sleeping is not lacking an action,** meaning that no action is needed in order to awaken him, and he can awaken on his own. **This** one, who is afflicted with temporary insanity, is **lacking an action** by not taking the remedy mentioned earlier.

וְרֵישׁ לָקִישׁ נַמִי נִידַמְּיֵיהּ לְשׁוֹטֶה! שׁוֹטֶה לָא סַמֵּיהּ בְּיָדָן, הַאי סַמֵּיהּ בְּיָדָן, בִּישְׂרָא סוּמָּקָא אַגּוּמְרֵי וְחַמְרָא מַרְקָא.

The Gemara asks: **And Reish Lakish could also compare him to an imbecile,** so why does he not do so? The Gemara answers: There is a difference, as **there is no remedy in our possession** that can cure **an imbecile.** And since there is no remedy, a bill of divorce may not be written on his behalf. By contrast, for **this** one, who is afflicted with temporary insanity, **there is a remedy in our possession.** As the Gemara explained (67b): The remedy for this disease is for the afflicted person to eat lean **red meat** roasted **over coals and** drink **wine** that has been **diluted** with a large amount of water.

וּמִי אֲמַר רַבִּי יוֹחָנָן הָכִי? וְהָאָמַר רַב יְהוּדָה אָמַר שְׁמוּאֵל: שָׁחַט בּוֹ שְׁנַיִם אוֹ רוֹב שְׁנַיִם, וְרָמַז וְאָמַר ״כִּתְבוּ גֵּט לְאִשְׁתִּי״ – הֲרֵי אֵלּוּ יִכְתְּבוּ וְיִתְּנוּ.

The Gemara asks: **But did Rabbi Yoḥanan** actually **say this,** that the court must wait for him to regain his mental capabilities? **But didn't Rav Yehuda say** that **Shmuel says:** If one was attacked by another who **slit** his throat and severed the **two** pipes,[NHB] his trachea and esophagus, **or the majority** of the **two** pipes, **and** the dying man **signaled and** thereby **stated** through his gestures: **Write**[N] **a bill of divorce for my wife,** then **those** present **should write and give** a bill of divorce to his wife?

וְתַנְיָא: רָאוּהוּ מְגוּיָּד אוֹ צָלוּב עַל הַצְּלִיבָה, וְרָמַז וְאָמַר ״כִּתְבוּ גֵּט לְאִשְׁתִּי״ – הֲרֵי אֵלּוּ יִכְתְּבוּ וְיִתְּנוּ!

And it was similarly **taught** in a *baraita*: If **they saw** a man whose limbs had been **severed**[N] **or crucified**[B] **on a cross, and he signaled and** thereby **stated: Write a bill of divorce for my wife,** then **those** present **should write and give** the document to his wife. This teaches that it is permitted to write a bill of divorce even on behalf of one who cannot be cured and will certainly die. If so, why does Rabbi Yoḥanan claim that a bill of divorce may be written for someone afflicted with temporary insanity only once he has been cured?

הָכִי הָשְׁתָּא?! הָתָם דַּעְתָּא צִילוּתָא הִיא, וּכְחִישׁוּתָא הוּא דְּאַתְחִילָה בֵּיהּ, הָכָא דַּעְתָּא שְׁגִישְׁתָּא הִיא.

The Gemara rejects this: **How can** these cases **be compared? There,** after his throat was slit or he was crucified, **his mind is lucid, but he has begun** to feel **weakness** and will die very soon. Consequently, he cannot speak, but his intellectual capabilities are assumed to be intact. But **here,** in the case of one afflicted with temporary insanity, **his mind is confused,** and he is not lucid enough to act with intent.

וּמִי אֲמַר שְׁמוּאֵל הָכִי? וְהָאָמַר רַב יְהוּדָה אָמַר שְׁמוּאֵל: שָׁחַט בּוֹ שְׁנַיִם אוֹ רוֹב שְׁנַיִם וּבָרַח – מְעִידִין עָלָיו; וְאִי סָלְקָא דַּעְתָּךְ חַי הוּא, אַמַּאי מְעִידִין עָלָיו?

The Gemara asks: **But did Shmuel** actually **say this,** that someone whose throat has been slit is treated as though he is alive, and he can give a bill of divorce? **But didn't Rav Yehuda** say that **Shmuel says:** If someone **slit** the **two** pipes **in** his throat **or the majority of** the **two** pipes **and** the victim **fled**[H] without the witnesses seeing what ultimately happened to him, then **they may testify with regard to him**[N] that he is dead? **And if it enters your mind** to say that one whose throat has been slit **is alive** and able to instruct others to write a bill of divorce for his wife, then **why can** witnesses **testify with regard to him** that he is dead?

HALAKHA

Slit the two pipes, etc. – **שָׁחַט בּוֹ שְׁנַיִם וכו׳**: If someone was cut in pieces, crucified, had the majority of his trachea and esophagus slit, or was being devoured by an animal, and he said or signaled to others that they should write a bill of divorce for his wife, then they should write it and give it to her before he dies (Rambam *Sefer Nashim, Hilkhot Geirushin* 2:13; *Shulḥan Arukh, Even HaEzer* 121:8).

Slit…and fled, etc. – **שָׁחַט...וּבָרַח וכו׳**: If a man's trachea and esophagus were entirely slit or the majority was slit, then one can testify that the victim has died, as he will certainly die within a very short period of time. The same applies to anyone who will certainly not live for more than a very short period of time (Rambam *Sefer Nashim, Hilkhot Geirushin* 13:17; *Shulḥan Arukh, Even HaEzer* 17:30).

BACKGROUND

Slit the two pipes – **שָׁחַט בּוֹ שְׁנַיִם**: Slitting the trachea and the esophagus will not in itself cause a quick death. Nevertheless, when an animal is slaughtered according to kosher practice or a man is killed in this way it will sever the carotid arteries which supply blood to the brain. When the blood flow to the brain ceases death comes very rapidly.

Crucified – **צָלוּב**: One of the Roman methods of execution was crucifixion. This form of punishment, which was uncommonly cruel and painful, was used normally for rebellious slaves and captives. Crucifixion consisted of nailing the victim to a wooden cross by his hands and feet. This itself did not kill the victim; death resulted from loss of blood and dehydration, which took a long time. There are recorded cases of individuals who were removed from the cross and discovered to have survived the ordeal.

אָמְרִי: חַי הוּא וְסוֹפוֹ לָמוּת.

The Gemara **says** in response to this that **he is** currently **alive** and on account of this he can give a bill of divorce to his wife, **but ultimately** he will certainly **die**[H] within a short period of time. Consequently, it is possible to testify with certainty that he died later on.

אֶלָּא מֵעַתָּה, יְהֵא גּוֹלֶה עַל יָדוֹ! אַלְמָה תַּנְיָא: שָׁחַט בּוֹ שְׁנַיִם אוֹ רוֹב שְׁנַיִם – הֲרֵי זֶה אֵינוֹ גּוֹלֶה?

The Gemara asks: **If that is so,** that he is assumed to have ultimately died, then the one who slit his throat **should be exiled on his account** if he did so unintentionally. Exile is the punishment for unintentionally killing another. If so, **why is it taught** in a *baraita*: If **he** unintentionally **slit** the **two** pipes **in** his throat **or the majority of** the **two,** for example if one dropped a knife and accidentally cut another's trachea and esophagus, then **this one is not exiled?**[HN]

הָא אִיתְּמַר עֲלַהּ, אָמַר רַבִּי הוֹשַׁעְיָא: חָיְישִׁינַן שֶׁמָּא הָרוּחַ בִּלְבַּלְתּוֹ; אִי נַמִי, הוּא קֵירֵב אֶת מִיתָתוֹ.

The Gemara answers: **Wasn't it stated with regard to that** *baraita* that **Rabbi Hoshaya says: We are concerned that perhaps the wind made him senseless,** and it was not only the one who dropped the knife who caused this man's death, but also the wind or some other factor. One who only partially causes the death of another is not exiled. **Or also** perhaps **he,** the one who had his throat slit, **brought his death closer** through his convulsions and his death throes.

מַאי בֵּינַיְיהוּ? אִיכָּא בֵּינַיְיהוּ, דְּשַׁחֲטֵיהּ בְּבֵיתָא דְּשֵׁישָׁא וּפִירְכֵּס; אִי נַמִי, דְּשַׁחֲטֵיהּ בְּבָרָא וְלָא פִּירְכֵּס.

What is the difference **between** the first and second explanations with regard to why the killer is not exiled? The difference **between them is if he slit his** throat **in a marble house and** the victim **convulsed.** In such a case the death cannot be attributed to the wind, so according to the first explanation the killer would be exiled. Rather, his death can be attributed to his convulsions, so according to the latter explanation the killer would not be exiled. **Alternatively, he slit his** throat **outside and** the victim **did not convulse.** In such a case the death can be attributed to the wind, so according to the first explanation the killer would not be exiled. Since it cannot be attributed to his convulsions, according to the latter explanation the killer would be exiled.

״נִשְׁתַּתֵּק, וְאָמְרוּ לוֹ נִכְתּוֹב גֵּט לְאִשְׁתְּךָ״ כּוּ׳. וְלֵיחוּשׁ דִּלְמָא שִׁיחָיָא דְּ״לָאו לָאו״ נַקְטֵיהּ, אִי נַמִי שִׁיחָיָא דְּ״הֵין הֵין״ נַקְטֵיהּ!

§ The mishna teaches: In a case where the husband **became mute, and** the members of the court **said to him:** Shall **we will write a bill of divorce for your wife?** And he nodded his head as a signal, and then the court checked his intent three times with different questions; if he said no, shaking his head to questions to which he should have answered no, and yes to questions to which he should have answered yes, this demonstrates that he understands the questions and his intent is clear. The Gemara asks: **But let** there be **a concern that perhaps the** involuntary **movement of: No, no, took hold of him,**[B] and he continuously nods his head as if he were signaling no, even though he does not intend it? **Alternatively,** perhaps **the** involuntary **movement of: Yes, yes, took hold of him?**

אָמַר רַב יוֹסֵף בַּר מִנְיוּמִי אָמַר רַב נַחְמָן: דְּאָמְרִינַן לֵיהּ בְּסֵירוּגִין.

Rav Yosef bar Minyumi says that **Rav Naḥman says:** The meaning of the mishna is **that we,** the court, **say alternating**[N] questions **to him,** switching between asking him questions to which he must answer yes and questions to which he must answer no.

וְלֵיחוּשׁ דִּלְמָא שִׁיחָיָא דְּסֵירוּגִין נַקְטֵיהּ! דְּאָמְרִינַן לֵיהּ חַד לָאו וּתְרֵין הֵין, וּתְרֵין לָאו וְחַד הֵין.

The Gemara asks: **But let** there be **a concern that perhaps alternating** involuntary **movements took hold of him,** such that he switches between nodding his head yes and nodding his head no. The Gemara answers: The meaning of the mishna is **that we,** the court, **say to him** questions to which he must answer **no once and yes twice,**[H] **and twice no and one** time **yes.** If he nevertheless answers each question correctly there is no concern that his movements were involuntary.

BACKGROUND

The involuntary movement of no, no, took hold of him – שִׁיחָיָא דְּלָאו לָאו נַקְטֵיהּ: There are neurological conditions which can cause uncontrolled motion in different parts of the body, including the head. Someone suffering from such a disorder may shake his head involuntarily, which may appear as if he intends to signal no or yes. It is possible that one may combine involuntary motions, alternately implying yes and no.

HALAKHA

He is alive but ultimately he will die – חַי הוּא וְסוֹפוֹ לָמוּת: If one's trachea and esophagus were slit then he does not impart ritual impurity until he actually dies, based on the Gemara here (Rambam *Sefer Tahara, Hilkhot Tumat Met* 1:15; *Shulḥan Arukh, Yoreh De'a* 370:1).

This one is not exiled – הֲרֵי זֶה אֵינוֹ גּוֹלֶה: One who unintentionally kills another is exiled only if the victim dies immediately. Even if the wound is serious enough that it is assumed the victim will die as a result, the killer is not exiled. Nevertheless, if the victim did not convulse at all and was in a place where there is no wind, the killer is exiled even if the victim dies later. The Ra'avad maintains that convulsions and wind apply only in a case where the killer unintentionally slit the trachea and esophagus of the victim, but not to another type of manslaughter (Rambam *Sefer Nezikin, Hilkhot Rotze'aḥ UShmirat HaNefesh* 5:2).

No once and yes twice, etc. – חַד לָאו וּתְרֵין הֵן וכו׳: If one became mute and others asked him if he wants them to write a bill of divorce for his wife, and he nodded his head, then they must check his mental state with alternating questions. First they ask him a question to which he must answer yes and then they ask him two questions to which he must answer no. This is followed by one question to which he must answer no and two more to which he must answer yes. If he answers all of these questions correctly then they should write the bill of divorce and give it to his wife. He must be checked thoroughly so that the court can be certain that he is still coherent. The Rema, citing the Rif and the Rosh, writes that some say they check him with questions with regard to seasonal fruit that are not available at the present time (Rambam *Sefer Nashim, Hilkhot Geirushin* 2:16; *Shulḥan Arukh, Even HaEzer* 121:5 and *Beur HaGra* there).

NOTES

This one is not exiled – הֲרֵי זֶה אֵינוֹ גּוֹלֶה: *Tosafot* write that this concept of the wind or the victim's convulsions contributing to his death if he does not die immediately is applied only with regard to the exile of one who kills unintentionally. One who murders another is liable for punishment even if the victim does not die immediately. The reason for this distinction is that with regard to one who unintentionally kills the verse states: "If he thrust him suddenly without enmity, or hurled upon him anything without lying in wait, or with any stone, whereby a man may die, without seeing him, and cast it upon him, so that he died" (Numbers 35:22–23). This teaches that the killer is liable only if the death of the victim occurs immediately following the blow or a short time thereafter (*Tosafot*; *Tosefot HaRosh*). Others write that since he acted unintentionally the Torah is lenient with regard to his punishment, and he is punished with exile only when it is clear beyond any doubt that the blow he delivered was the direct cause of the victim's death (Meiri).

The Ra'avad explains that the concern about other factors causing the victim's death applies only when the victim's trachea and esophagus were slit. When the victim was killed in a different manner one does not assume that either the wind or convulsions contributed to his death. The Meiri holds that a distinction should be made between a case where the assessment is that the victim will die immediately, for which the killer is punished with exile even if he does not die immediately, and a case in which the initial assessment was that he will not die, where the killer is liable only when it is clear that no other factor contributed to the victim's death.

Alternating [*serugin*] – בְּסֵירוּגִין: Rashi explains here, and in other places, that this term means that the court does not simply ask him immediately, but rather, waits a period of time and then asks him again. Most of the commentaries do not accept this explanation. Instead, they understand the word *serugin* to mean that the court alternates its questions between those to which he must answer yes and those to which he must answer no. The *Beit Yosef* and *Shulḥan Arukh* and their commentaries discuss whether both explanations apply in terms of *halakha* or not.

NOTES

The school of Rabbi Yishmael taught – דְּבֵי רַבִּי יִשְׁמָעֵאל תָּנָא: *Tosafot* explain that the school of Rabbi Yishmael does not disagree with the mishna; rather, it presents an alternate method of checking the mental state of the husband, which the school considers preferable (see *Beit Yosef*).

Let there be a concern that perhaps he has the chills – וְלֵיחוּשׁ דִּלְמָא קוּרָא אַחֲדֵיהּ: *Tosefot HaRosh* and *Tosafot* explain that this does not mean that there is room to be lenient and assume that his bill of divorce is valid. Rather, since this line of questioning does not lead to a clear conclusion, it is preferable to confirm his mental state in a different manner so that there is no doubt that he is lucid.

דְּבֵי רַבִּי יִשְׁמָעֵאל תָּנָא: אוֹמְרִים לוֹ דְּבָרִים שֶׁל יְמוֹת הַחַמָּה בִּימוֹת הַגְּשָׁמִים, וְשֶׁל יְמוֹת הַגְּשָׁמִים בִּימוֹת הַחַמָּה.

The school of Rabbi Yishmael taught:[N] The court **says to him** questions concerning **matters of the summer in the rainy season, and** concerning matters **of the rainy season in the summer,** in order to check if he is answering coherently.

מַאי נִיהוּ? אִילֵימָא גְּלוֹפְקְרֵי וּסְדִינֵי – לֵיחוּשׁ דִּלְמָא קוּרָא אַחֲדֵיהּ, אִי נַמִּי חַמָּה אַחֲדֵיהּ!

The Gemara asks: **What are these** matters that the court asks him? **If we say** that the court asks him if he wants a warm **coat** in the summer or a thin **sheet** in the rainy season, and he answers that he does, this cannot serve as proof of his intellectual capabilities, as the following is possible: **Let** there be **a concern** that **perhaps he has the chills**[N] even though it is the summer and needs a warm coat. **Alternatively,** that **the heat afflicted him** during the rainy season and he requires a thin sheet, in which case his response does not demonstrate a lack of comprehension.

Perek **VII**
Daf **71** Amud **a**

NOTES

With produce – בְּפֵירֵי: According to Rashi, the court asks him if he wants to eat produce that is not currently in season in this location. *Tosafot* add that they must also ask him if he wants the produce fresh from the tree, since perhaps he thought he would be given preserved or dried fruit. The Ramah adds that the court must check that he answers no correctly, i.e., with surprise. If he simply says that he doesn't want any, his answer does not attest to his lucidity, because perhaps he does not wish to eat this type of fruit at the present time.

And this and that are like halakhically competent people – וְזֶה וָזֶה הֲרֵי הֵן כְּפִקְּחִין: The Rambam writes that a deaf person who can speak is considered like a deaf-mute, and his transactions are not valid by Torah law (*Sefer Kinyan*, *Hilkhot Mekhira* 29:1). The *Kesef Mishne* and the *Derisha* attempt to resolve the Rambam's opinion with the Gemara's statement. The *Derisha* explains that the Rambam may have had a different text of the Gemara and that the phrase: This and that, is not referring to a deaf person and a mute, but to a mute from birth and one who has lost the ability to speak. By contrast, the Maharam Schick explains that when the Rambam is referring to a deaf person he is not referring to a deaf person who can speak, but to a deaf person who can produce certain sounds, but who cannot be understood. Rav Hai Gaon, in *Sefer HaMikkaḥ VehaMimkar*, makes a similar distinction.

אֶלָּא בְּפֵירֵי.

Rather, it means that the court asks him questions **with** regard to **produce**[N] that is not found during that season.

אָמַר רַב כָּהֲנָא אָמַר רַב: חֵרֵשׁ שֶׁיָּכוֹל לְדַבֵּר מִתּוֹךְ הַכְּתָב, כּוֹתְבִין וְנוֹתְנִין גֵּט לְאִשְׁתּוֹ. אֲמַר רַב יוֹסֵף: מַאי קָא מַשְׁמַע לַן? תְּנֵינָא: נִשְׁתַּתֵּק, וְאָמְרוּ לוֹ ״נִכְתּוֹב גֵּט לְאִשְׁתְּךָ״ וְהִרְכִּין בְּרֹאשׁוֹ, בּוֹדְקִין אוֹתוֹ שְׁלֹשָׁה פְּעָמִים, אִם אָמַר עַל לָאו לָאו וְעַל הֵן הֵן – הֲרֵי אֵלּוּ יִכְתְּבוּ וְיִתְּנוּ!

Rav Kahana says that **Rav says:** With regard to **a deaf-mute who can express** himself **through writing,**[H] the judges of the court may **write and give a bill of divorce to his wife** based on his written instructions. **Rav Yosef said: What is he teaching us? We** already **learned** in the mishna: In a case where the husband **became mute, and** the members of the court **said to him:** Shall **we write a bill of divorce for your wife, and he nodded his head** indicating his agreement, **they examine him** with various questions **three times. If he responded to** questions that have **a negative** answer: **No, and** responded **to** questions that have **a positive** answer: **Yes,** indicating his competence, **they shall write** the bill of divorce **and give** it to his wife based on the nod of his head.

אֲמַר לֵיהּ רַבִּי זֵירָא: אִלֵּם קָאָמְרַתְּ? שָׁאנֵי אִלֵּם, דְּתַנְיָא: מְדַבֵּר וְאֵינוֹ שׁוֹמֵעַ – זֶהוּ חֵרֵשׁ, שׁוֹמֵעַ וְאֵינוֹ מְדַבֵּר – זֶהוּ אִלֵּם, וְזֶה וָזֶה הֲרֵי הֵן כְּפִקְּחִין לְכָל דִּבְרֵיהֶם.

Rabbi Zeira said to him: A mute, you say? Is your challenge based on the mishna which discusses one who is mute? **A mute is different** because it is clear that his mind is intact. **As it is taught** in a *baraita* (*Tosefta*, *Terumot* 1:2): With regard to one **who speaks but cannot hear, this** individual is categorized as **a deaf person.** With regard to one **who hears but cannot speak,**[H] **this** individual **is** categorized as **a mute person, and** both **this** one **and that** one **are** considered to be **like** halakhically **competent** people[N] **with regard to all their matters.** Rav Kahana stated his ruling with regard to one who can neither hear nor speak. This goes beyond the *halakha* of the mishna, as Rav Kahana says that the written statement of a deaf-mute is an indication of his mental competence.

HALAKHA

Who can express himself through writing – שֶׁיָּכוֹל לְדַבֵּר מִתּוֹךְ הַכְּתָב: Even if a man gave written instructions to a scribe and witnesses that they should write and sign a bill of divorce, they may not do so until they receive verbal instructions from him. This is true regardless of whether he can speak or not. This is in accordance with the statement of Rabbi Yoḥanan (71b). The Rashba, the Rosh, the Mordekhai, the *Smag*, and the *Smak* all rule accordingly.

There are those who rule that the bill of divorce may be written and signed based on written instructions in the case of a mute whose intellectual capabilities remain intact, in accordance with the opinion of Rabbi Zeira. This is also the opinion of the Rambam and *Sefer HaIttur*. The *Beit Shmuel*, citing *Darkhei Moshe*, states that in a case where the woman would be unable to remarry it is preferable to rely on the lenient opinion, but the matter requires further investigation (Rambam *Sefer Nashim*, *Hilkhot Geirushin* 2:16, 17; *Shulḥan Arukh*, *Even HaEzer* 120:5).

One who hears but cannot speak, etc. – שׁוֹמֵעַ וְאֵינוֹ מְדַבֵּר וכו׳: The business transactions of one who can hear but cannot speak or one who temporarily became mute are valid, both with regard to movable property and land, provided the court first checks his mental state as they would in the case of a bill of divorce, or if he issues written instructions. One who is hard of hearing but can hear when spoken to loudly is considered to be halakhically competent (Rambam *Sefer Kinyan*, *Hilkhot Mekhira* 29:3; *Shulḥan Arukh*, *Ḥoshen Mishpat* 235:18–19).

ומנא דמדבר ואינו שומע זהו חרש, שומע ואינו מדבר זהו אלם? דכתיב: "ואני כחרש לא אשמע וכאלם לא יפתח פיו". ואי בעית אימא, כדאמרי אינשי: אישתקיל מילוליה.

The Gemara asks: **And from where** do we learn **that** one **who speaks but cannot hear, this** individual **is** categorized as **a deaf person,** and that with regard to one **who hears but cannot speak, this** individual is categorized as **a mute person? As it is written: "And I am like a deaf man, I do not hear, and like the mute man who will not open his mouth"** (Psalms 38:14). **And if you wish, say as people say:** The word for a mute [*ilem*] is a contraction of the expression **his speech has been taken** [*ishtakil millulei*].

אמר רבי זירא: אי קשיא לי הא קשיא לי, דתניא: "אם לא יגיד" – פרט לאלם שאינו יכול להגיד; אמאי? הא יכול להגיד מתוך הכתב!

Rabbi Zeira said: If Rav Kahana's statement is **difficult for me,**[N] **this is difficult for me, as it is taught** in a *baraita* with regard to the punishment of one who was called to testify and failed to do so: **"If he does not utter** his testimony then he shall bear his iniquity" (Leviticus 5:1). The Sages derive from this that the verse serves **to exclude a mute**[H] **who is unable to utter** his testimony, and he is exempt from bringing the offering of one who refuses to testify. And it is possible to raise the following question: **Why** is he exempt from bringing the offering; **but he is able to utter** his testimony **through writing?** Apparently, written testimony is not valid testimony.

אמר ליה אביי: עדות קאמרת? שאני עדות, דרחמנא אמר: מפיהם – ולא מפי כתבם.

Abaye said to him: You say testimony? Testimony is different, as **the Merciful One states: "From their mouths"** (Deuteronomy 17:6), which emphasizes that testimony must come from the witnesses' mouths **and not from their writing.**[NH]

מיתיבי: כשם שבודקין אותו לגיטין, כך בודקין אותו למשאות ולמתנות, ולעדיות ולירושות; קתני מיהת עדיות!

The Gemara raises an objection to this based on that which is taught in a *baraita* (*Tosefta* 7:1): **Just as** the judges of the court **investigate him,** one who lost his ability to speak, **with regard to bills of divorce, so too,** the judges **investigate him with regard to business** transactions, **testimonies, and inheritances. In any event it teaches: Testimonies,** which proves that even one unable to speak can give testimony.

אמר רב יוסף בר מניומי אמר רב ששת: בעדות אשה, דאקילו בה רבנן.

Rav Yosef bar Minyumi said that **Rav Sheshet said:** This is not referring to testimony in general. Rather, it is referring **to testimony** with regard to **a woman** whose husband died,[NH] **as the Sages were lenient with her** and allowed testimony that would normally not be accepted, in order to permit her to remarry.

והא קתני ירושות! אמר רבי אבהו: ירושת בנו הבכור.

The Gemara challenges: **But isn't it** also **taught: Inheritances.** This seems to be referring to monetary matters, where proper testimony is required. **Rabbi Abbahu said:** The *baraita* is referring to **the inheritance of his** own **firstborn son,**[NH] meaning that he is not testifying about other people's property but testifying which one of his sons is the firstborn. Since this testimony is merely considered to be a division of the property that belongs to him, the testimony of one who is unable to speak is valid.

קתני מיהת למשאות ולמתנות, מאי לאו לעלמא? לא, לדידיה.

The Gemara continues to challenge: **In any event it teaches** in the *baraita*: **With regard to business** transactions, **what, does it not** mean that a mute may testify with regard to business transactions **for everyone** else? The Gemara answers: **No,** he may testify **for himself** only. The *baraita* is saying that when a mute conducts business the court must first check if he is mentally capable.

NOTES

If it is difficult for me, etc. – אי קשיא לי וכו׳: This appears to be a challenge to the statement by Rav Kahana where he cites Rav. Why is it not also a challenge to the mishna itself, which states that one who becomes mute can also give a bill of divorce based on non-verbal signals? *Tosafot* answer that this *baraita* is not a challenge to the mishna because perhaps it is referring to a deaf-mute, whereas the mishna is referring only to one who can hear but is unable to speak. Alternatively, this *baraita* does not contradict the mishna because when giving a bill of divorce there is no requirement of speech, and clear intent is sufficient. Rav Kahana goes further and states that writing is equivalent to speech, in which case written testimony should also be valid.

From their mouths and not from their writing – מפיהם ולא מפי כתבם: Rashi asks: If testimony can be delivered only orally, then why does the court rely on written documents? The early commentaries add that documents have the same validity as verbal testimony, based on the term: "Deed of purchase" (Jeremiah 32:11; see *Kiddushin* 26a). The Rid and the Ritva explain that a signed document is valid only if the witnesses themselves are able to testify orally. Their signatures on the document represent their verbal testimony, in accordance with the Gemara's statement that the witnesses on the document are considered to be like those whose testimony was investigated by the court (*Gittin* 3a).

Testimony with regard to a woman whose husband died – עדות אשה: In order for a widow to remarry, her husband's death must be attested to. Those whose testimony is not accepted in other circumstances are permitted to testify for this purpose, including, *inter alia*, a lone witness, a witness providing secondhand testimony, certain relatives, women, slaves, and a non-Jew who mentions it incidentally. With regard to the reason for this leniency, Rashi, in his commentary on *Shabbat* 145b, where he explains that there are two elements. One is that the Sages desired to avoid the situation of a woman being unable to marry due to uncertainty whether or not her husband is alive. The second is that the Sages have special power to regulate matters of marriage (see 73a). The Rambam explains that since testimony enabling a woman to remarry establishes a fact rather than attests to an action, and since if the testimony is false the lie is likely to be exposed, it is not considered testimony in the formal, legal sense of the term.

The inheritance of his firstborn son – ירושת בנו הבכור: Rashi explains that this is referring to one who instructs that his firstborn son should not receive the double portion to which he is entitled, but rather, should inherit the same share of his father's estate as his brothers. Although one may not contradict the Torah's laws of inheritance, as long as the father is alive he can divide his property as he wishes, as a gift, and not according to the laws of inheritance. Others explain that it is referring to the ability of the father to identify one of his sons as the firstborn (*Tosafot*; Ritva).

HALAKHA

To exclude a mute, etc. – פרט לאלם וכו׳: A deaf-mute is disqualified to serve as a witness. Moreover, even one who can speak and not hear or hear and not speak is disqualified to serve as a witness, since the verse states that testimony must be verbal and the one who testifies must also be able to hear the words of the judges (Rambam *Sefer Shofetim*, *Hilkhot Edut* 9:11; *Shulḥan Arukh*, *Ḥoshen Mishpat* 35:11).

From their mouths and not from their writing – מפיהם ולא מפי כתבם: Written testimony of witnesses is not valid in court, based on the opinion of Abaye. The *Sma* writes that the court may rely on the later ruling of Rabbeinu Tam, who maintains that such testimony is valid if the witnesses are able to testify verbally. Such testimony is valid when given by a Torah scholar (Rambam *Sefer Shofetim*, *Hilkhot Edut* 3:4; *Shulḥan Arukh*, *Ḥoshen Mishpat* 28:11).

Testimony with regard to a woman whose husband died – עדות אשה: The court accepts testimony in writing that a woman's husband died from one who can speak but cannot hear. The Sages were lenient in such a case in order to prevent her from remaining a deserted wife (Rambam *Sefer Shofetim*, *Hilkhot Edut* 9:11; *Shulḥan Arukh*, *Ḥoshen Mishpat* 35:11).

The inheritance of his firstborn son – ירושת בנו הבכור: If a father lost his ability to speak then the court checks his mental state. If he signaled or wrote that one of his sons is the firstborn then that son receives a double portion of the inheritance, in accordance with the opinion of Rabbi Abbahu (Rambam *Sefer Mishpatim*, *Hilkhot Naḥalot* 2:15; *Shulḥan Arukh*, *Ḥoshen Mishpat* 277:14).

מֵיתִיבִי: חֵרֵשׁ, לֹא הָלְכוּ בּוֹ אַחַר רְמִיזוֹתָיו וְאַחַר קְפִיצוֹתָיו וְאַחַר כְּתַב יָדוֹ אֶלָּא בְּמִטַּלְטְלִין, אֲבָל לֹא לְגִיטִּין!

The Gemara raises an objection from a *baraita*: With regard to a **deaf-mute,** the judges of the court **follow his signals, and follow the movement** of his lips, **and follow his handwriting only** for matters of buying and selling **movable property but not for bills of divorce.** This appears to contradict Rav Kahana's statement that it is permitted for a deaf-mute husband to give written instructions to divorce his wife.

תַּנָּאֵי הִיא; דְּתַנְיָא, אָמַר רַבָּן שִׁמְעוֹן בֶּן גַּמְלִיאֵל: בַּמֶּה דְּבָרִים אֲמוּרִים – בְּחֵרֵשׁ מֵעִיקָּרוֹ, אֲבָל פִּיקֵּחַ וְנִתְחָרֵשׁ – הוּא כּוֹתֵב וְהֵן חוֹתְמִין.

The Gemara answers: **It is** a dispute between ***tanna'im*****, as it is taught** in a *baraita* (*Tosefta, Terumot* 1:1) that **Rabban Shimon ben Gamliel said: In what** case **is this statement** that the court may not rely on the written testimony of a deaf-mute with regard to a bill of divorce **said?** Only **in** the case **of a deaf-mute** who was deaf **from the outset,**[N] i.e., from birth. But if he had been halakhically **competent,** i.e., he could previously hear, **but became a deaf-mute** later, then **he may write** instructions to give his wife a bill of divorce **and they,** the witnesses, should **sign,** in accordance with the opinion of Rav Kahana.

וְחֵרֵשׁ מֵעִיקָּרוֹ לָא? כְּשֵׁם שֶׁכּוֹנְסָהּ בִּרְמִיזָה כָּךְ מוֹצִיאָהּ בִּרְמִיזָה!

The Gemara asks: **And** one who is a **deaf-mute from the outset cannot** give written instructions with regard to a bill of divorce? Isn't it true that **just as he marries her with intimation,**[H] i.e., without speaking, **so too, he divorces her with intimation.**

אִי בְּאִשְׁתּוֹ הָכִי נַמִי, הָכָא בְּמַאי עָסְקִינַן – בִּיבִמְתּוֹ.

The Gemara answers: **If** the *baraita* is referring **to his wife, indeed** this would be the case and he could divorce her through intimations, because such a marriage is not a fully valid marriage by Torah law. But **with what are we dealing here? With his** ***yevama*****,**[N] his sister-in-law whose husband, his brother, died childless to whom he performed levirate marriage, and whom he subsequently wishes to divorce. This marriage is a fully valid marriage.

יְבִמְתּוֹ מִמַּאן? אִילֵּימָא דְּנָפְלָה לֵיהּ מֵאָחִיו חֵרֵשׁ? כְּשֵׁם שֶׁכְּנִיסָתָהּ בִּרְמִיזָה כָּךְ יְצִיאָתָהּ בִּרְמִיזָה! אֶלָּא דְּנָפְלָה לֵיהּ מֵאָחִיו פִּיקֵּחַ.

The Gemara asks: **His** ***yevama*** **from whom? If we say that she fell to him from his brother** who was also **a deaf-mute,** then **just as her marriage** to the brother was **through intimation,**[N] **so too, her divorce** from the *yavam* can be **through intimation. Rather,** it must be **that she fell to him from his** halakhically **competent brother.** Consequently, the bond of the levirate marriage is by Torah law, whereas the deaf-mute man's intimations that he desires to divorce her are valid only by rabbinic law.

וְאִיבָּעֵית אֵימָא: לְעוֹלָם דְּנָפְלָה לֵיהּ מֵאָחִיו חֵרֵשׁ, וּגְזֵירָה אָחִיו חֵרֵשׁ אַטּוּ אָחִיו פִּיקֵּחַ.

And if you wish, say instead: **Actually,** explain **that she fell to him from his deaf-mute brother, and** the Sages instituted a rabbinic **decree** with regard to a woman bound in a levirate marriage **from his deaf-mute brother due to** the death of **his** halakhically **competent brother.**

אִי הָכִי, אִשְׁתּוֹ נַמִי! יְבִמְתּוֹ בִּיבִמְתּוֹ מִיחַלְּפָא, אִשְׁתּוֹ בִּיבִמְתּוֹ לָא מִיחַלְּפָא.

The Gemara challenges: **If so,** and the Sages made such a decree with regard to a case where a deaf-mute brother died due to the case where a brother who is halakhically competent died, then with regard to **his** own **wife as well,** they should have made a decree that a deaf-mute husband cannot divorce her with a bill of divorce if he married her as a deaf-mute. The Gemara answers: **His** ***yevama*** who was married to his halakhically competent brother might **be confused with his** ***yevama*** who was married to his deaf-mute brother. But people **would not confuse his** own **wife with his** ***yevama*****.** Therefore, there was no need to institute such a decree.

וּמִי גָּזְרִינַן חֵרֵשׁ אַטּוּ פִּיקֵּחַ?

The Gemara asks: **And do we,** the Sages, **decree** with regard to his **deaf-mute** brother **due to** confusion between him and his halakhically **competent** brother?

NOTES

In the case of a deaf-mute from the outset – **בְּחֵרֵשׁ מֵעִיקָּרוֹ:** There is a halakhic presumption that one who is deaf from birth lacks mental competence, and his written instructions cannot overturn that assumption. It is possible that he learned to write without awareness of the meaning of his actions. By contrast, one who was born hearing and became deaf later is presumed to be mentally competent, and his writing demonstrates that he still retains that status (Rashi; Rid).

His ***yevama*** – **יְבִמְתּוֹ:** Levirate marriage is a continuation of the marriage to the deceased brother. Since that marriage was by Torah law, once the deaf-mute brother performs levirate marriage the *yevama* is married to him also by Torah law. Therefore, the deaf-mute brother who is now her husband is unable to give her a bill of divorce, as a divorce given based on his non-verbal communication would be valid only by rabbinic law, and cannot sever a marriage that is valid by Torah law.

Just as her marriage was through intimation, etc. – **כְּשֵׁם שֶׁכְּנִיסָתָהּ בִּרְמִיזָה וכו׳:** Since levirate marriage is performed though sexual intercourse and is valid even without intent, why does the Gemara claim that the marriage was through intimation, and does not have full validity from the Torah? The answer is that when one acquires a woman through levirate marriage it is considered as a continuation of the marriage performed by his brother. Since in this case the initial marriage was through intimation, the levirate marriage is also considered to have been performed through intimation, and the *yavam* can also divorce his *yevama* through non-verbal communication (*Ma'adannei Melekh*).

HALAKHA

Just as he marries her with intimation – **כְּשֵׁם שֶׁכּוֹנְסָהּ בִּרְמִיזָה:** If a deaf-mute man marries a woman, the marriage is valid by rabbinic law. In the event that he wants to divorce her, just as he married her via non-verbal communication, he may also divorce her in a similar manner (Rambam *Sefer Nashim, Hilkhot Geirushin* 2:17; *Shulḥan Arukh, Even HaEzer* 121:6).

וְהָתְנַן: שְׁנֵי אַחִין חֵרְשִׁין נְשׂוּאִין שְׁתֵּי אֲחָיוֹת פִּיקְחוֹת, אוֹ שְׁתֵּי אֲחָיוֹת חֵרְשׁוֹת, אוֹ שְׁתֵּי אֲחָיוֹת אַחַת פִּיקַּחַת וְאַחַת חֵרֶשֶׁת, וְכֵן שְׁתֵּי אֲחָיוֹת חֵרְשׁוֹת נְשׂוּאוֹת לִשְׁנֵי אַחִין פִּקְחִין, אוֹ לִשְׁנֵי אַחִין חֵרְשִׁין, אוֹ לִשְׁנֵי אַחִין אֶחָד פִּיקֵּחַ וְאֶחָד חֵרֵשׁ – הֲרֵי אֵלּוּ פְּטוּרוֹת מִן הַחֲלִיצָה וּמִן הַיִּבּוּם,

But didn't we learn in a mishna (*Yevamot* 112b): In a case where there were **two deaf-mute brothers,**[H] whose marriage is valid by rabbinic law, **married to two** halakhically **competent sisters, or to two deaf-mute sisters, or to two sisters, one** of whom was halakhically **competent and one** of whom was **a deaf-mute; and similarly,** if there were **two deaf-mute sisters,** whose marriage is valid by rabbinic law, **married to two** halakhically **competent brothers, or to two deaf-mute brothers, or to two brothers, one** of whom was halakhically **competent and one** of whom was **a deaf-mute;** and in each case one brother dies without children, then all **these** women **are exempt**[N] **from *ḥalitza***[B] **and from levirate marriage.**[B] Each sister is exempt, as she is the sister of the wife of the *yavam*.

וְאִם הָיוּ נָכְרִיּוֹת – יִכְנְסוּ. וְאִם רָצוּ לְהוֹצִיאָן – יוֹצִיאוּ!

And if they were unrelated women the men **may marry them** in levirate marriage, **and if they wanted to divorce them** later via a bill of divorce **they may divorce** them. Since this is stated as a general *halakha* it indicates that the deaf-mute brother can also give a bill of divorce to his *yevama* who was previously married to his deaf-mute brother, and the Sages did not institute a decree in order not to create confusion with the similar case of a deceased halakhically competent brother.

אֶלָּא, מְחַוַּורְתָּא כִּדְשַׁנִּין מֵעִיקָּרָא.

Rather, it is clear as we initially answered,[H] that it is referring to a *yevama*, previously married to a halakhically competent brother, who fell before a *yavam* who was a deaf-mute from birth. The alternative answer given on the previous *amud* is rejected.

אָמַר רַבִּי יוֹחָנָן: חֲלוּקִין עָלָיו חֲבֵירָיו עַל רַבָּן שִׁמְעוֹן בֶּן גַּמְלִיאֵל.

Rabbi Yoḥanan says: The colleagues of Rabban Shimon ben Gamliel disagree with him, and hold that written instructions from a deaf-mute have no halakhic validity.

אֲמַר אַבַּיֵי, אַף אֲנַן נַמִי תָּנֵינָא: נִישְׁטֵית – לֹא יוֹצִיא, נִתְחָרֵשׁ הוּא אוֹ נִשְׁתַּטָּה – לֹא יוֹצִיא עוֹלָמִית; מַאי "עוֹלָמִית"? לָאו אַף עַל גַּב דְּיָכוֹל לְדַבֵּר מִתּוֹךְ הַכְּתָב?

Abaye said that **we, too, learn** in the mishna (*Yevamot* 112b) that non-verbal instructions are insufficient to initiate a divorce even for one who was born with the ability to hear and subsequently became a deaf-mute: If a woman **became an imbecile** after her wedding the Sages instituted that the husband **must not divorce** her.[H] If the husband **became a deaf-mute or an imbecile he can never divorce her,** as he does not have the legal competence to grant a bill of divorce. Abaye explains: **What** is the reason that the mishna emphasizes that he can **never** divorce her? **Isn't** this teaching that **even though he can communicate through writing,** he is unable to divorce her?

NOTES

These are exempt, etc. – הֲרֵי אֵלּוּ פְּטוּרוֹת וכו׳: The obligation of levirate marriage does not override any other relationship forbidden by Torah law. Since the *yavam* is already married to the sister of his *yevama* it is prohibited for him to perform levirate marriage with her. In this case, even though the marriage of a deaf-mute is valid only by rabbinic law and not by Torah law, since the marriage of his deaf-mute brother was also valid only by rabbinic law, levirate marriage does not override the prior marriage to the sister of his *yevama*.

BACKGROUND

Ḥalitza – חֲלִיצָה: *Ḥalitza* is the ceremony that frees the widow of a man who died without children and allows her to remarry (see Deuteronomy 25:7–10). The term *ḥalitza*, which literally means removal, is derived from the central element of this ceremony, where the widow removes the shoe from the foot of one the brothers of her deceased husband, described in the verse with the words "*veḥaletza na'alo*" (Deuteronomy 25:9). *Ḥalitza* must be performed before a rabbinical court. The *halakhot* governing this ceremony are discussed in detail in tractate *Yevamot*.

Levirate marriage – יִבּוּם: A man whose brother died without children is obliged by Torah law to either marry his deceased brother's widow or free her via the *ḥalitza* ceremony (see Deuteronomy 25:5–10). As long as neither levirate marriage nor *ḥalitza* has taken place, it is prohibited for her to marry another man. According to the Torah, levirate marriage is effected by the act of sexual intercourse. The Sages instituted the practice of *ma'amar*, corresponding to the stage of betrothal in a standard marriage. Sexual intercourse consummates the marriage between the deceased's brother and the widow and she is thereafter considered his wife in all respects. A bill of divorce is necessary if they wish to divorce.

Today, levirate marriage is not practiced, and the brother-in-law is required to free his brother's widow of her obligation through *ḥalitza*.

HALAKHA

Two deaf-mute brothers, etc. – שְׁנֵי אַחִין חֵרְשִׁין וכו׳: If two deaf-mute brothers were married to two sisters, or two deaf-mute sisters were married to two brothers, and one of the brothers died without children, his wife is exempt from levirate marriage because her *yavam* is married to her sister. If the two women were unrelated, then the surviving brother can enter into levirate marriage and afterward divorce her with a bill of divorce (Rambam *Sefer Nashim*, *Hilkhot Yibbum VaḤalitza* 7:16; *Shulḥan Arukh*, *Even HaEzer* 175:13).

It is clear as we initially answered, etc. – מְחַוַּורְתָּא כִּדְשַׁנִּין בְּעִיקָּרָא וכו׳: A deaf-mute may not perform *ḥalitza*, but he can consummate the levirate marriage. If a deaf-mute consummates the levirate marriage with the wife of a brother who was mentally competent, he can never divorce her. If she was the wife of a deaf-mute brother, he can divorce her with a bill of divorce (*Shulḥan Arukh*, *Even HaEzer* 172:12).

She became an imbecile, he must not divorce her, etc. – נִישְׁטֵית לֹא יוֹצִיא וכו׳: A woman who becomes an imbecile may not be divorced unless she regains halakhic competence. This rabbinic decree was instituted so that she will not be treated like ownerless property. Despite this decree, if her husband did divorce her it is valid, as long as she is capable of guarding her bill of divorce.

The Rema disagrees with this, and writes that even after the fact she is not considered to be divorced. He adds that in such a case the decree of Rabbeinu Gershom Meor HaGola forbidding a man from marrying more than one wife does not apply. Consequently, he may remarry, though he first requires the signatures of one hundred rabbis (Rambam *Sefer Nashim*, *Hilkhot Geirushin* 10:23; *Shulḥan Arukh*, *Even HaEzer* 119:6, 1:10 and *Beit Shmuel* there).

אָמַר רַב פָּפָּא: אִי לָאו דְּאַשְׁמוֹעִינַן רַבִּי יוֹחָנָן, הֲוָה אָמֵינָא, רַבָּן שִׁמְעוֹן בֶּן גַּמְלִיאֵל לְפָרוֹשֵׁי טַעְמָא דְּתַנָּא קַמָּא הוּא דַּאֲתָא, וּמַאי ״עוֹלָמִית״? אַף עַל גַּב דְּחָזֵינָא לֵיהּ דְּחָרִיף.

Rav Pappa said: **If not** for the fact that **Rabbi Yoḥanan teaches us** that there is a dispute between Rabban Shimon ben Gamliel and the Rabbis, then **I would say** that **Rabban Shimon ben Gamliel comes** only **to explain the reason of the first** ***tanna***, not to disagree with him. If that were so, all agree that one who was born with the ability to hear and subsequently became a deaf-mute can issue written instructions to write and give a bill of divorce for his wife. **And** according to this explanation, **what** is the meaning of the word **never?** It is not referring to issuing written instructions. It means that **even though** I **see that he is sharp** by means of examining his gestures, these indications are not sufficient to warrant the giving of a bill of divorce. Despite this, if he were to issue written instructions to divorce his wife, they would be followed.

אִי נַמִּי, לְכִדְרַבִּי יִצְחָק, דְּאָמַר רַבִּי יִצְחָק: דְּבַר תּוֹרָה שׁוֹטָה מִתְגָּרֶשֶׁת, מִידֵּי דַּהֲוָה אַפִּיקַּחַת בְּעַל כָּרְחָהּ.

Alternatively, the mishna emphasized that the only situation where the husband can never divorce his wife is where her husband became a deaf-mute or an imbecile, but not if the husband remained healthy and the wife became a deaf-mute or imbecile, **in accordance with** the opinion **of Rabbi Yitzḥak, as Rabbi Yitzḥak says: By Torah law** a woman who is **an imbecile may be divorced**[N] even though she is unable to give her consent, **just as it is** permitted to divorce a halakhically **competent woman against her will.**

וּמָה טַעַם אָמְרוּ אֵינָהּ מִתְגָּרֶשֶׁת? שֶׁלֹּא יִנְהֲגוּ בָּהּ מִנְהַג הֶפְקֵר.

And what is the reason that the Rabbis **said she may not be divorced?** So **that she will not be treated as ownerless property.** If she has no husband to protect her, and she is unable to protect herself, she may be treated as ownerless property by anyone who wishes to engage in sexual intercourse with her. By contrast, if the husband is a deaf-mute or an imbecile then he cannot divorce her by Torah law. This is why the mishna stresses only that the husband may never divorce his wife in the case where he becomes halakhically incompetent, but not when it is the wife who becomes a deaf-mute or an imbecile, in order to demonstrate the difference between the two cases in terms of Torah law.

מתני׳ אָמְרוּ לוֹ ״נִכְתּוֹב גֵּט לְאִשְׁתְּךָ?״ וְאָמַר לָהֶן ״כְּתוֹבוּ״, אָמְרוּ לַסּוֹפֵר וְכָתַב וְלָעֵדִים וְחָתְמוּ, אַף עַל פִּי שֶׁכְּתָבוּהוּ וַחֲתָמוּהוּ וּנְתָנוּהוּ לוֹ וְחָזַר וּנְתָנוֹ לָהּ – הֲרֵי הַגֵּט בָּטֵל, עַד שֶׁיֹּאמַר לַסּוֹפֵר ״כְּתוֹב״ וְלָעֵדִים ״חֲתוֹמוּ״.

MISHNA If people **said to** the husband: **Shall we write**[H] **a bill of divorce for your wife? And he said to them: Write** the document, and those people **told the scribe** to write it, **and he wrote** it **and** instructed **the witnesses** to sign it, **and they signed** it; **even if they wrote it, and signed it, and gave it to him, and he then gave it to** his wife, **the bill of divorce is void unless he** himself **says to the scribe: Write** the document, **and** he himself **says to the witnesses: Sign** the document.

גמ׳ טַעְמָא דְּלָא אָמַר ״תְּנוּ״, הָא אָמַר ״תְּנוּ״ – נוֹתְנִין, מַנִּי? רַבִּי מֵאִיר הִיא, דְּאָמַר: מִילֵּי מִימְּסְרָן לְשָׁלִיחַ.

GEMARA The Gemara infers from the mishna: **The reason** that the bill of divorce is void is **because** he told the people only to write the document, but **he did not say: Give** a bill of divorce to my wife. **But if he said** to them: **Give** a bill of divorce to my wife, and they told the scribe to write the document and the witnesses to sign it, those people **give** the document to his wife and it is valid. In accordance with **whose** opinion is this statement? **It is** in accordance with the opinion of **Rabbi Meir, who says:** Verbal **directives can be delegated to an agent.** Everyone agrees that an agent can be appointed to perform an action on behalf of another, but Rabbi Meir holds that an agent can be appointed to give instructions to others on behalf of another.

אֵימָא סֵיפָא: עַד שֶׁיֹּאמַר לַסּוֹפֵר ״כְּתוֹב״ וְלָעֵדִים ״חֲתוֹמוּ״, אֲתָאן לְרַבִּי יוֹסֵי, דְּאָמַר: מִילֵּי לָא מִימְּסְרָן לְשָׁלִיחַ.

The Gemara comments: **Say the latter clause** of the mishna: The bill of divorce is void **unless he** himself **says to the scribe: Write** the document, **and** he himself says **to the witnesses: Sign** the document. In the latter clause of the mishna, **we arrive at** the opinion of **Rabbi Yosei, who said:** Verbal **directives cannot be delegated to an agent.**

רֵישָׁא רַבִּי מֵאִיר וְסֵיפָא רַבִּי יוֹסֵי? אִין, רֵישָׁא רַבִּי מֵאִיר וְסֵיפָא רַבִּי יוֹסֵי.

The Gemara asks: Is that to say that **the first clause** of the mishna is in accordance with the opinion of **Rabbi Meir and the latter clause** is in accordance with the opinion of **Rabbi Yosei?** The Gemara answers: **Yes, the first clause** is in accordance with the opinion of **Rabbi Meir and the latter clause** is in accordance with the opinion of **Rabbi Yosei.** Although unusual, it is possible for a single mishna to represent two contrary opinions.

NOTES

By Torah law an imbecile may be divorced – דְּבַר תּוֹרָה שׁוֹטָה מִתְגָּרֶשֶׁת: The Meiri explains, based on the discussion in tractate *Yevamot*, that there are two different cases here: If the wife became an imbecile but is able to take care that men will not take advantage of her sexually and she is able guard her bill of divorce, then her husband may divorce her. If she is unable to guard her bill of divorce and does not understand at all what is happening, she cannot be divorced, even by Torah law. The reason is that the Torah requires that the husband: "Sends her out of his house" (Deuteronomy 24:1), but this woman will not realize that she has been sent away and will keep returning. The statement of Rabbi Yitzḥak applies to a woman who knows how to guard her bill of divorce, and understands that she was divorced, but who is not capable of taking care that men will not take advantage of her sexually. In this case, it is forbidden for her husband to divorce her.

HALAKHA

They said to him, shall we write, etc. – אָמְרוּ לוֹ נִכְתּוֹב וכו׳: If a husband told others to write a bill of divorce for his wife, but they told the scribe to write it and the witnesses to sign it, even if the husband himself gave this bill of divorce to his wife it is not valid because the husband himself did not issue the instructions directly to the scribe and the witnesses (Rambam *Sefer Nashim, Hilkhot Geirushin* 2:5; *Shulḥan Arukh, Even HaEzer* 120:4).

אַבַּיֵי אֲמַר: כּוּלָּהּ רַבִּי מֵאִיר הִיא, וְהָכָא בְּמַאי עָסְקִינַן – דְּלָא אֲמַר ״תְּנוּ״. אִי הָכִי, ״עַד שֶׁיֹּאמַר תְּנוּ״ מִיבָּעֵי לֵיהּ!

Abaye said: Actually, the mishna in **its entirety is** in accordance with the opinion of **Rabbi Meir. And with what are we dealing here?** With a situation **whereby** the husband **did not say: Give** the bill of divorce to my wife, but said only to write it. In that case he must instruct the scribe and the witnesses directly. If he issued instructions to give the bill of divorce, it would also have been effective. The Gemara asks: **If so,** the mishna **should have** said: The bill of divorce is void **unless he says: Give** the bill of divorce to my wife.

אֶלָּא הָכָא בְּמַאי עָסְקִינַן – דְּלָא אֲמַר לְבֵי תְּלָתָא. אִי הָכִי, ״עַד שֶׁיֹּאמַר לִשְׁלֹשָׁה״ מִיבָּעֵי לֵיהּ!

Rather, with what are we dealing here? With a situation **whereby** the husband **did not say** his instructions **to three** people, who constitute a court with the authority to appoint others to write a bill of divorce. Rather, he instructed two people, who do not constitute a court, and therefore do not have the authority to appoint others to write a bill of divorce, even if the husband told them to give the bill of divorce to his wife. Witnesses may only write and give the document themselves. The Gemara challenges: **If so,** the mishna **should have said: Unless he says** his instructions **to three** people.

אֶלָּא כּוּלָּהּ רַבִּי יוֹסֵי הִיא, וְהָכָא בְּמַאי עָסְקִינַן – דְּלָא אֲמַר ״אִמְרוּ״.

Rather, the mishna in **its entirety is** in accordance with the opinion of **Rabbi Yosei, and with what are we dealing here?** With a situation **whereby** the husband **did not** explicitly **say** to his agents: **Say** my instructions to the scribe to write the document.

אִי הָכִי, ״עַד שֶׁיֹּאמַר אִמְרוּ״ מִיבָּעֵי לֵיהּ!

The Gemara challenges: **If so,** the expression: **Until he says** to the scribe, is imprecise. Rather, the mishna **should have** said: Until the husband instructs the agents to **tell.**

וְעוֹד, מִי מוֹדֶה רַבִּי יוֹסֵי בְּאוֹמֵר ״אִמְרוּ״? וְהָתְנַן: כְּתַב סוֹפֵר וְעֵד – כָּשֵׁר, וַאֲמַר רַבִּי יִרְמְיָה: חֲתַם סוֹפֵר שָׁנִינוּ, וַאֲמַר רַב חִסְדָּא: מַתְנִיתִין מַנִּי?

And does Rabbi Yosei concede in the case of **one who says: Tell** another to write it? **But didn't we learn** in a mishna (87b): If a bill of divorce has **the writing of a scribe,** and the scribe identifies his handwriting, **and** one **witness** verifies his signature, it is **valid** as though two witnesses testified to ratify their signatures. **And Rabbi Yirmeya said: We learned** in the mishna that this is the *halakha* with regard to **the scribe's signature** and not the scribe's writing. **And Rav Ḥisda said: Whose** opinion is expressed in the **mishna?**

Perek **VII**
Daf **72** Amud **a**

רַבִּי יוֹסֵי הִיא, דְּאָמַר: מִילֵּי לָא מִימְסְרָן לְשָׁלִיחַ;

It is the opinion of **Rabbi Yosei, who says:** Verbal **directives cannot be delegated to an agent,** and there is no concern that the scribe signed the document without the husband instructing him to do so.

וְאִי סָלְקָא דַּעְתָּךְ מוֹדֶה רַבִּי יוֹסֵי בְּאוֹמֵר ״אִמְרוּ״, נָפֵיק מִינָּהּ חוּרְבָּא, דְּזִימְנִין דַּאֲמַר לְהוּ לִשְׁנַיִם ״אִמְרוּ לַסּוֹפֵר וְיִכְתּוֹב וְלִפְלוֹנִי וּפְלוֹנִי וְיַחְתְּמוּ״, וּמִשּׁוּם כִּיסּוּפָא דְּסוֹפֵר חָיְישֵׁי וּמַחְתְּמֵי לֵיהּ, וּבַעַל לָא אֲמַר הָכִי!

And if it enters your mind to say that **Rabbi Yosei concedes in** the case of one who **says: Tell** another to write it, **a pitfall will result from it. As sometimes,** it happens **that one said to two** people: **Tell a scribe and he will write** the document **and** tell **so-and-so and so-and-so and they will sign it. And due to the shame of the scribe,** who asks: Don't you consider me a sufficiently upright person to sign the document as a witness, the agents **are concerned** to avoid that disgrace **and** they will **have one of those witnesses and the scribe sign together with him, and the husband did not say** to do **so.** This bill of divorce is invalid because it was signed contrary to the husband's instructions, and the agents will mistakenly think it is valid.

אֶלָּא מְחַוַּורְתָּא, רֵישָׁא רַבִּי מֵאִיר וְסֵיפָא רַבִּי יוֹסֵי.

The reason that this is not a concern must be because Rabbi Yosei holds that even if the husband says to the agents: Tell the scribe to write, the bill of divorce is not valid. **Rather, it is clear that the first clause** of the mishna is in accordance with the opinion of **Rabbi Meir and the latter clause** is in accordance with the opinion of **Rabbi Yosei.**

רַב אַשִׁי אֲמַר: כּוּלָּהּ רַבִּי יוֹסֵי הִיא, וְלָא מִיבַּעְיָא קָאָמַר; לָא מִבַּעְיָא הֵיכָא דְּלָא אֲמַר "תְּנוּ", אֶלָּא אֲפִילּוּ אֲמַר "תְּנוּ" – לָא; וְלָא מִיבַּעְיָא הֵיכָא דְּלָא אֲמַר לְבֵי תְּלָתָא, אֶלָּא אֲפִילּוּ אֲמַר לְבֵי תְּלָתָא – לָא; וְלָא מִיבַּעְיָא הֵיכָא דְּלָא אֲמַר "אִמְרוּ", אֶלָּא אֲפִילּוּ אֲמַר "אִמְרוּ" – נַמִּי לָא.

Rav Ashi said an alternative explanation of the attribution of the mishna: The mishna in **its entirety is** in accordance with the opinion of **Rabbi Yosei,** who said that verbal directives cannot be delegated to an agent, **and it is speaking** utilizing the style of: **It is not necessary,** as follows: **It is not necessary** to state that the bill of divorce is not valid in a case **where he did not say** to the agents: **Give** the document to my wife; **rather, even if he said** to the agents: **Give** the bill of divorce to my wife, the document is **not** valid. **And it is not necessary** to state the *halakha* in a case **where** the husband **did not say** his instructions **to three** people; **rather, even if he said** his instructions **to three** people, כ, the bill of divorce is not valid. **And it is not necessary** to state the *halakha* in a case **where** the husband **did not say** to the agents: **Say** my instructions to a scribe, **but even if he said: Say**[H] my instructions to a scribe, the bill of divorce is **also not** valid.

תַּנְיָא כְּוָותֵיהּ דְּרַב אַשִׁי: כָּתַב סוֹפֵר לִשְׁמָהּ וְחָתְמוּ עֵדִים לִשְׁמָהּ, אַף עַל פִּי שֶׁכְּתָבוּהוּ וַחֲתָמוּהוּ וּנְתָנוּהוּ לוֹ וּנְתָנוֹ לָהּ – הֲרֵי הַגֵּט בָּטֵל, עַד שֶׁיִּשְׁמְעוּ קוֹלוֹ שֶׁיֹּאמַר לַסּוֹפֵר "כְּתוֹב" וְלָעֵדִים "חֲתוֹמוּ";

The Gemara notes: It **is taught** in a *baraita* (*Tosefta* 2:7–8) **in accordance with** the opinion **of Rav Ashi** that Rabbi Yosei validated the bill of divorce even if the husband said: Tell my instructions to a scribe, as it is taught: If **the scribe wrote** the bill of divorce **for her sake and the witnesses signed it for her sake** then **even though they wrote it, and they signed it, and they gave it to the** husband **and he gave it to** his wife, **the bill of divorce is void until they hear** the husband's **voice when he says to the scribe: Write** the document for the sake of my wife, **and to the witnesses: Sign** the document for the sake of my wife.

יִשְׁמְעוּ – לְאַפּוּקֵי מִמַּאן דַּאֲמַר: מוֹדֶה רַבִּי יוֹסֵי בְּאוֹמֵר "אִמְרוּ"; קוֹלוֹ – לְאַפּוּקֵי מִדְּרַב כָּהֲנָא אָמַר רַב.

The inference from the *baraita* is that it uses the term: Until they **hear,** serves **to exclude** the opinion of **the one who said: Rabbi Yosei concedes in** a case where the husband **says: Say** my instructions to the scribe; because the scribe and the witnesses must hear the husband themselves. Furthermore, the *baraita* uses the term: **His voice, to exclude that which Rav Kahana says** that **Rav says,** that a husband may issue written instructions to the scribe and witnesses. According to the *baraita* the instructions must be verbal.

מתני׳ "זֶה גִּיטֵּיךְ אִם מַתִּי", "זֶה גִּיטֵּיךְ מֵחוֹלִי זֶה", "זֶה גִּיטֵּיךְ לְאַחַר מִיתָה" – לֹא אָמַר כְּלוּם; "מֵהַיּוֹם אִם מַתִּי", "מֵעַכְשָׁיו אִם מַתִּי" – הֲרֵי זֶה גֵּט;

MISHNA If one says to his wife: **This is your bill of divorce if I die,**[HN] or: **This is your bill of divorce** if I die **from this illness,** or: **This is your bill of divorce after** my **death,** then it is as if **he said nothing,** since a bill of divorce is valid only if it takes effect before the husband's death. But if the husband said to his wife: This is your bill of divorce **from today if I die,**[H] or: This is your bill of divorce **from now if I die,** then **this is** a valid **bill of divorce,** because once he dies, the bill of divorce retroactively applies from when he made this statement.

"מֵהַיּוֹם וּלְאַחַר מִיתָה" – גֵּט וְאֵינוֹ גֵּט, וְאִם מֵת – חוֹלֶצֶת וְלֹא מִתְיַיבֶּמֶת.

If the husband says to his wife: This is your bill of divorce **from today and after my death,**[H] then it is uncertain whether his primary intention was for the bill of divorce to take effect that day, in which case it is a valid bill of divorce, or if his primary intention was that it should take effect after his death and is therefore not valid. The *halakha* is that there is uncertainty whether it is a valid **bill of divorce or not** a valid **bill of divorce. And if he dies** without children his wife must **perform *ḥalitza,*** since perhaps the bill of divorce is not valid and she is bound by the levirate bond and may not remarry without first performing *ḥalitza.* **But she may not enter into levirate marriage,** since perhaps the bill of divorce is valid, and it is prohibited for a divorcée to marry her brother-in-law.

"זֶה גִּיטֵּיךְ מֵהַיּוֹם אִם מַתִּי מֵחוֹלִי זֶה", וְעָמַד וְהָלַךְ בַּשּׁוּק וְחָלָה וּמֵת, אוֹמְדִין אוֹתוֹ, אִם מֵחֲמַת חוֹלִי הָרִאשׁוֹן מֵת – הֲרֵי זֶה גֵּט, וְאִם לָאו – אֵינוֹ גֵּט.

If he said: **This is your bill of divorce from today if I die from this illness,**[H] and he recovered, **and he arose and walked in the market, but** then **became ill** again **and died,** the court **assesses him. If he died because of the first illness** then **this is** a valid **bill of divorce,** as his conditional statement was fulfilled, **but if not,** i.e., if he was cured from the first illness and died from another illness, then **it is not** a valid **bill of divorce.**

HALAKHA

Even if he said: Say – אֲפִילּוּ אֲמַר אִמְרוּ: Even if the husband said: Say to the scribe to write and the witnesses to sign, the scribe should not write and the witnesses should not sign the bill of divorce unless they hear the instructions directly from the husband, in accordance with Rav Ashi's statement. The Rema writes that if the scribe and witnesses acted based on the husband's instructions to the agents, it is uncertain whether the divorce is valid. It is unclear whether Rav Ashi was giving a halakhic ruling or only offering an explanation (Rambam *Sefer Nashim, Hilkhot Geirushin* 2:6; *Shulḥan Arukh, Even HaEzer* 120:4).

This is your bill of divorce if I die, etc. – זֶה גִּיטֵּיךְ אִם מַתִּי וכו׳: If a husband says to his wife: This is your bill of divorce if I die, or: This is your bill of divorce if I die from this illness, or: This is your bill of divorce after my death, the bill of divorce is not valid, in accordance with the unattributed opinion of the mishna. The Ramban and the Ran say that it is uncertain if the bill of divorce is valid, as it is not clear whether the *halakha* is in accordance with the opinion of Rabbi Yosei. Therefore, one should act stringently (Rambam *Sefer Nashim, Hilkhot Geirushin* 9:12; *Shulḥan Arukh, Even HaEzer* 145:1).

From today if I die – מֵהַיּוֹם אִם מַתִּי: If a husband said to his wife: This is your bill of divorce if I die, or: From now if I die, the bill of divorce is valid, and if he dies she is divorced (Rambam *Sefer Nashim, Hilkhot Geirushin* 9:13; *Shulḥan Arukh, Even HaEzer* 145:2).

From today and after my death – מֵהַיּוֹם וּלְאַחַר מִיתָה: If a husband said to his wife: This is your bill of divorce from today and after my death, or: From now and after my death, it is uncertain whether or not she is divorced (Rambam *Sefer Nashim, Hilkhot Geirushin* 9:14; *Shulḥan Arukh, Even HaEzer* 145:3).

From today if I die from this illness – מֵהַיּוֹם אִם מַתִּי מֵחוֹלִי זֶה: If a husband said to his wife: This is your bill of divorce from today if I die from this illness, and he was healed, went to the market, became ill again and died, then the court assesses whether his death was caused by the initial illness, in which case she is divorced, or by a different illness, in which case she is not divorced (Rambam *Sefer Nashim, Hilkhot Geirushin* 9:18; *Shulḥan Arukh, Even HaEzer* 145:7).

NOTES

If I die – אִם מַתִּי: The *ge'onim* write that the expression: If I die, should not be understood as a condition. Rather, it is the establishment of a time for the matter. By contrast, the expressions: From now, or: On the condition, are certainly conditions.

גמ׳ אַלְמָא ״אִם מֵתִּי״ כִּ״לְאַחַר מִיתָה״ דָּמֵי; וַהֲדַר תָּנֵי ״מֵהַיּוֹם אִם מַתִּי״ ״מֵעַכְשָׁיו אִם מַתִּי״, אַלְמָא ״אִם מַתִּי״ לָאו כִּ״לְאַחַר מִיתָה״ דָּמֵי!

GEMARA The mishna teaches: If one says to his wife: This is your bill of divorce if I die, then it is as if he said nothing. The Gemara deduces: **Apparently,** the formulation: **If I die,** is **considered** to be **like** the formulation: The bill of divorce will be valid only **after** my **death. And afterward** the mishna **teaches:** If he said: This is your bill of divorce **from today if I die,** or: This is your bill of divorce **from now if I die,** then this is a valid bill of divorce. **Apparently,** the formulation: **If I die,** is **not considered** to be **like** the formulation: The bill of divorce will be valid only **after** my **death.** As explained previously in the mishna, a bill of divorce which takes effect only after the husband's death is not a valid bill of divorce. There is an apparent contradiction as to the meaning of the term: If I die.

אֲמַר אַבַּיֵי: ״אִם מַתִּי״ – שְׁתֵּי לְשׁוֹנוֹת מַשְׁמַע, מַשְׁמַע כִּ״מֵעַכְשָׁיו״ וּמַשְׁמַע כִּ״לְאַחַר מִיתָה״;

Abaye said: The expression: **If I die, indicates two** different **meanings.** It **indicates** the same meaning **as** one who says: **From now,** i.e., that the bill of divorce will take effect after death retroactively from now. **And** it **indicates** the same meaning **as** one who says: **After** my **death,** i.e., that the bill of divorce will take effect only after his death.

אֲמַר לָהּ ״מֵהַיּוֹם״ – כְּמַאן דְּאָמַר לָהּ ״מֵעַכְשָׁיו״ דָּמֵי, לָא אֲמַר לָהּ ״מֵהַיּוֹם״ – כְּמַאן דְּאָמַר לָהּ ״לְאַחַר מִיתָה״ דָּמֵי.

If the husband **said to** his wife: **From today** if I die, it is **considered** to be **like one who says to her: From now,** conditional upon my death. But if **he did not say to her: From today,** it is **considered** to be **like one who says to her: After** my **death,** and the bill of divorce is void because it takes effect only after his death.

״זֶה גִּיטֵּךְ אִם מַתִּי – לֹא אָמַר כְּלוּם״. אָמַר רַב הוּנָא: וְחוֹלֶצֶת.

§ The mishna teaches that if one says to his wife: **This is your bill of divorce if I die,** then it is as if **he said nothing. Rav Huna says: But** if her husband died without children this woman must **perform *ḥalitza*** and not enter into a levirate marriage because perhaps it is a valid bill of divorce.

וְהָא ״לֹא אָמַר כְּלוּם״ קָתָנֵי! לֹא אָמַר כְּלוּם, דַּאֲסִירָא לְעָלְמָא, וּלְיָבָם נַמִי אֲסִירָא.

The Gemara raises a challenge: **But isn't** the expression: It is as if **he said nothing, taught** in the mishna? The Gemara answers: The mishna means that it is as if **he said nothing** with regard to the fact that **she is** still **forbidden to everyone** after the death of her husband, and is bound by a levirate bond. **And she is also forbidden to the *yavam*** because perhaps the bill of divorce was valid, in which case she has no levirate bond.

וְהָא מִדְּסֵיפָא חוֹלֶצֶת, מִכְּלָל דְּרֵישָׁא יַבּוּמֵי נַמִי מְיַבְּמָה! מַתְנִיתִין כְּרַבָּנַן,

The Gemara raises a challenge: **But since the latter clause** of the mishna teaches that in those cases of uncertainty **she** must **perform *ḥalitza*, by inference** it appears **that** in the cases of **the first clause she may also enter into levirate marriage,** indicating that in those cases the bill of divorce is definitely not valid. The Gemara answers: This is not a challenge to Rav Huna's opinion, as **the mishna is in accordance** with the opinion of **the Rabbis** that this kind of conditional bill of divorce is invalid and she may enter into levirate marriage.

וְרַב הוּנָא דַּאֲמַר – כְּרַבִּי יוֹסֵי, דְּאָמַר: זְמַנּוֹ שֶׁל שְׁטָר מוֹכִיחַ עָלָיו.

But Rav Huna was not explaining the words of the mishna; the statement **that he said is in accordance with** the opinion of **Rabbi Yosei, who says** as a principle: **The date** written **in a document proves** when **it** takes effect.[H] Therefore, since the bill of divorce bears that day's date, it takes effect immediately, even though it is not stated explicitly.

אִי רַבִּי יוֹסֵי, חֲלִיצָה נַמִי לָא תִּיבָּעֵי! וְכִי תֵּימָא, מְסַפְּקָא לֵיהּ לְרַב הוּנָא אִי הִלְכְתָא כְּרַבִּי יוֹסֵי אוֹ אֵין הֲלָכָה כְּרַבִּי יוֹסֵי – וּמִי מְסַפְּקָא לֵיהּ?

The Gemara challenges: **If** Rav Huna's statement is in accordance with the opinion of **Rabbi Yosei** then the woman **should also not require *ḥalitza*,** as in his opinion the bill of divorce is entirely valid and there is no levirate bond at all. **And if you would say** that **Rav Huna is uncertain if the *halakha* is in accordance with** the opinion of **Rabbi Yosei or** if **the *halakha* is not in accordance with** the opinion of **Rabbi Yosei,** and on account of this he was stringent in accordance with both opinions, i.e., the one which requires *ḥalitza* and the one which forbids levirate marriage, this also presents a difficulty. **But is** Rav Huna in fact **uncertain?**

HALAKHA

The date written in a document proves when it takes effect – זְמַנּוֹ שֶׁל שְׁטָר מוֹכִיחַ עָלָיו: A document of gift dated in the lifetime of the giver is effective, even if it states that the transfer of the property in question shall occur only after the giver's death. This is because the date indicates that formal ownership of the gift was transferred during the giver's lifetime. Even if the document does not explicitly state: From today and after my death, the gift is acquired after the giver's death. This is in accordance with Rabbi Yosei's opinion in the mishna of *Bava Batra* 136a (Rambam *Sefer Kinyan, Hilkhot Zekhiya UMattana* 12:15; *Shulḥan Arukh, Ḥoshen Mishpat* 258:1).

PERSONALITIES

Rabba bar Avuh – רַבָּה בַּר אֲבוּהּ: Rabba bar Avuh was a second-generation Babylonian *amora*. He was a close student of Rav, whose teachings he often quotes. He lived and taught in the city of Meḥoza. According to many, his student, Rav Naḥman, became his son-in-law, and taught much of what he learned from his father-in-law. Although Rabba bar Avuh was a member of the Exilarch's family, he remained poor throughout his life, as he did not want to profit from his Torah knowledge. There are a number of stories in the Talmud that describe his interactions with Elijah the prophet and the questions that he posed to him. Rabba bar Avuh's son Rav Ḥama was one of the greatest Sages of his generation, and his descendants, Rav Sherira and Rav Hai Gaon, became the great *ge'onim* of Babylonia.

NOTES

Ask of him, Rabba bar Avuh – בְּעִי מִינֵּיה מֵרַבָּה בַּר אֲבוּהּ: Even though Rav Naḥman was much younger than Rav Huna and was his student, since Rabba bar Avuh was ill Rav Huna did not want to ask him the question. Therefore, he asked Rav Naḥman, who was loved by Rabba bar Avuh and may even have been his son-in-law, to ask the question instead.

וְהָא רַבָּה בַּר אֲבוּהּ חֲלַשׁ, עוּל לְגַבֵּיהּ רַב הוּנָא וְרַב נַחְמָן; אֲמַר לֵיהּ רַב הוּנָא לְרַב נַחְמָן: בְּעִי מִינֵּיה מֵרַבָּה בַּר אֲבוּהּ, הֲלָכָה כְּרַבִּי יוֹסֵי אוֹ אֵין הֲלָכָה? אֲמַר לֵיהּ: טַעְמָא דְּרַבִּי יוֹסֵי לָא יָדַעְנָא, הֲלָכָה אִיבָּעֵי מִינֵּיה? אֲמַר לֵיהּ: אַתְּ בְּעִי מִינֵּיה הֲלָכָה, וְטַעְמֵיהּ דְּרַבִּי יוֹסֵי אֲנָא אֵמֵינָא לָךְ;

But when Rabba bar Avuh[P] was ill Rav Huna and Rav Naḥman entered to visit him. Rav Huna said to Rav Naḥman: Ask of him, Rabba bar Avuh:[N] Is the *halakha* in accordance with the opinion of Rabbi Yosei or is the *halakha* not in accordance with his opinion? Rav Naḥman said to Rav Huna: I do not know the reason for the opinion held by Rabbi Yosei, and you ask me to ask Rabba bar Avuh the *halakha*? Rav Huna said to Rav Naḥman: You ask him the *halakha*, and I will tell you the reason for the opinion held by Rabbi Yosei afterward.

בְּעִי מִינֵּיה. אֲמַר לֵיהּ, הָכִי אָמַר רַב: הֲלָכָה כְּרַבִּי יוֹסֵי; לְבָתַר דִּנְפַק אֲמַר לֵיהּ: הַיְינוּ טַעְמָא דְּרַבִּי יוֹסֵי, דְּקָסָבַר: זְמַנּוֹ שֶׁל שְׁטָר מוֹכִיחַ עָלָיו! אֶלָּא מְסַפְּקָא לֵיהּ

Rav Naḥman asked of Rabba bar Avuh what the *halakha* is. Rabba bar Avuh said to him: So said Rav: The *halakha* is in accordance with the opinion of Rabbi Yosei. After he left Rav Huna said to Rav Naḥman: This is the reason for the opinion of Rabbi Yosei, as he holds: The date written in a document proves when it takes effect. From this incident it is clear that Rav Huna holds that the *halakha* is in accordance with Rabbi Yosei, as Rav Huna certainly accepted the opinion that Rabba bar Avuh said in the name of Rav. Rather, it is necessary to say that Rav Huna is uncertain

Perek **VII**
Daf **72** Amud **b**

NOTES

The court that permitted oil – בֵּי דִינָא דִּשְׁרוּ מִישְׁחָא: This decree dates back at least to the Second Temple period. Many generations later, when the Sages became aware that the decree was not observed by a majority of the people, it was repealed. Although initially the Sages were hesitant about instituting this leniency, it was eventually adopted as normative *halakha* (see *Avoda Zara* 35b).

Apparently, it was the court of Rabbi Yehuda Nesia, the grandson of Rabbi Yehuda HaNasi, during the first generation of *amora'im*, that repealed the decree prohibiting the use of the oil of a gentile (see Rashi on *Avoda Zara* 35b). His is the court referred to in the Gemara here as: And our Rabbis permitted her to marry. Some explain that any time the term: Our Rabbis, is used, the reference is to the court of Rabbi Yehuda Nesia.

אִי אָמַר רַבִּי יוֹסֵי בְּעַל פֶּה אִי לָא אָמַר.

if Rabbi Yosei says that the date on which a document is written proves when it takes effect even when the husband stated a verbal condition as he handed it over, or if Rabbi Yosei does not say his principle in such a case.

וּמִי מְסַפְּקָא לֵיהּ? וְהָתְנַן: ״הֲרֵי זֶה גִּיטֵּךְ אִם לֹא בָּאתִי מִכָּאן וְעַד שְׁנֵים עָשָׂר חֹדֶשׁ״, וּמֵת בְּתוֹךְ שְׁנֵים עָשָׂר חֹדֶשׁ – אֵינוֹ גֵּט; וְתָנֵי עֲלַהּ: רַבּוֹתֵינוּ הִתִּירוּהָ לְהִינָּשֵׂא;

The Gemara asks: But is Rav Huna uncertain with regard to this matter? But didn't we learn in a mishna (76b): If one says to his wife: This is hereby your bill of divorce if I have not come back here from now until the conclusion of twelve months, and he died within twelve months, then it is not a valid bill of divorce because the bill of divorce does not take effect until the end of twelve months, which is after the husband's death? As a result, she is bound by a levirate bond if her husband has no children. And it is taught with regard to that mishna: Our Rabbis disagree, and they rendered it permitted for her to marry, because they are of the opinion that there is no levirate bond in this case.

וְאָמְרִינַן: מַאן רַבּוֹתֵינוּ? אָמַר רַב יְהוּדָה אָמַר שְׁמוּאֵל: בֵּי דִינָא דִּשְׁרוּ מִשְׁחָא, וְסָבְרִי לַהּ כְּרַבִּי יוֹסֵי, דְּאָמַר: זְמַנּוֹ שֶׁל שְׁטָר מוֹכִיחַ עָלָיו!

And we say: Who represents the opinion cited as our Rabbis? Rav Yehuda says that Shmuel says: It is the court that permitted the consumption of oil[N] manufactured by gentiles, and they hold in accordance with the opinion of Rabbi Yosei, who says: The date written in a document proves when it takes effect. Evidently, according to Rabbi Yosei this principle applies even when the husband made a verbal condition with regard to the bill of divorce.

אֶלָּא מְסַפְּקָא לֵיהּ אִי הֲלָכָה כְּרַבִּי יוֹסֵי בְּעַל פֶּה אוֹ אֵין הֲלָכָה.

Rather, it is necessary to say as follows: Rav Huna is uncertain if the *halakha* is in accordance with the opinion of Rabbi Yosei when the husband adds a verbal condition when giving the document, or if the *halakha* is not in accordance with Rabbi Yosei's opinion in such a case.

וּמִי מְסַפְּקָא לֵיהּ? וְהָאָמַר רָבָא: ״הֲרֵי זֶה גִּיטֵּיךְ אִם מַתִּי״ וְ״שֶׁאֲנִי מֵת״ – הֲרֵי זֶה גֵּט, ״כְּשֶׁאָמוּת״ וּ״לְאַחַר מִיתָה״ – אֵין זֶה גֵּט;

The Gemara asks: But is Rav Huna uncertain with regard to this matter? But didn't Rava say: If one says to his wife: This is hereby your bill of divorce if I die, or: "This is your bill of divorce when I am dead, then this is a valid bill of divorce? If he said to her: When I die, or: After my death, then this is not a valid bill of divorce.

הֵיכִי דָּמֵי? אִילֵימָא דְּאָמַר לָהּ "מֵהַיּוֹם" וְרַבָּנַן, צְרִיכָא לְמֵימַר? וְהָתְנַן: "מֵהַיּוֹם אִם מַתִּי" – הֲרֵי זֶה גֵּט! וְאֶלָּא לָאו דְּלָא אֲמַר לָהּ "מֵהַיּוֹם" וְרַבִּי יוֹסֵי, שְׁמַע מִינַּהּ הֲלָכָה כְּרַבִּי יוֹסֵי!

The Gemara clarifies: **What are the circumstances? If we say that he said to her:** This is your bill of divorce **from today** if I die, **and** Rava's statement is in accordance with opinion of **the Rabbis,** which is the unattributed opinion of the mishna, is it **necessary** that this *halakha* **be said by Rava,** an *amora*? **But didn't we learn** explicitly in the mishna that if he said: This is your bill of divorce **from today if I die,** then **it is** a valid **bill of divorce? But rather, is it not** speaking about a case **where he did not say** the term: **From today,** when he gave the bill of divorce, **and** Rava's statement is in accordance with the opinion of **Rabbi Yosei? Conclude from it** that the ***halakha*** **is in accordance with** the opinion of **Rabbi Yosei.**

לְרָבָא פְּשִׁיטָא לֵיהּ, לְרַב הוּנָא מְסַפְּקָא לֵיהּ.

The Gemara answers: **It is obvious to Rava** that the *halakha* is in accordance with the opinion of Rabbi Yosei even when the husband added a verbal condition. **But** according **to Rav Huna,** it **is uncertain** whether or not this is the *halakha*.

וְאִיבָּעֵית אֵימָא: לְעוֹלָם דְּאָמַר לָהּ "מֵהַיּוֹם" וְרַבָּנַן, וְהָנֵי לִישָּׁנֵי אִיצְטְרִיכִי לֵיהּ, "שֶׁאֲנִי מֵת" כְּ"אִם מַתִּי" דָּמֵי, "כְּשֶׁאָמוּת" כִּ"לְאַחַר מִיתָה" דָּמֵי.

And if you wish, say instead: **Actually,** Rava's statement is referring to a case **where he said to her:** This is your bill of divorce **from today, and** it is in accordance with opinion of **the Rabbis. And it was necessary for** Rava to state his ruling to teach the *halakha* of **these expressions** not stated in the mishna: First, the husband saying: **When I am dead,** is **considered** to be **like** the expression: **If I die.** Second, the husband saying: **When I die,** is **considered** to be **like** the expression: **After** my **death.**

וְאִיכָּא דְּמַתְנֵי לָהּ אַסֵּיפָא: "זֶה גִּיטֵּךְ לְאַחַר מִיתָה" – לֹא אָמַר כְּלוּם; אָמַר רַב הוּנָא: וּלְדִבְרֵי רַבִּי יוֹסֵי חוֹלֶצֶת.

§ **And there are those who teach** this statement of Rav Huna **with regard to the latter clause** of the mishna, which states that if the husband said: **This is your bill of divorce after** my **death,** then the bill of divorce is invalid and it is as though **he said nothing. Rav Huna says: But** according **to the statement of Rabbi Yosei she must** nevertheless **perform *ḥalitza*,** as it is uncertain if the bill of divorce takes effect from the day the bill of divorce was given when the date is supplied verbally.

פְּשִׁיטָא, מִדְּסֵיפָא לְרַבָּנַן חוֹלֶצֶת, רֵישָׁא נַמִי לְרַבִּי יוֹסֵי חוֹלֶצֶת!

The Gemara questions this version of Rav Huna's statement: This **is obvious. Since** it was taught **in the latter clause** of the mishna, in a case where he explicitly stated: From today, that **according to** the opinion of **the Rabbis she must perform *ḥalitza*** due to the uncertainty as to when the bill of divorce takes effect, in **the first clause as well,** when he did not add: From today, it is obvious that **according to** the opinion of **Rabbi Yosei she must perform *ḥalitza*** due to the uncertainty. The dispute between Rabbi Yosei and the Rabbis concerns only whether the husband needs to add the term: From today.

מַהוּ דְּתֵימָא, רַבִּי יוֹסֵי בְּהָא כְּרַבִּי סְבִירָא לֵיהּ, דְּאָמַר: גִּיטָּא מְעַלְּיָא הָוֵי, וַחֲלִיצָה נַמִי לָא תִּיבָּעֵי, קָא מַשְׁמַע לַן, דְּלָא רַבִּי סָבַר לָהּ כְּרַבִּי יוֹסֵי וְלָא רַבִּי יוֹסֵי סָבַר לָהּ כְּרַבִּי;

The Gemara answers: His statement necessary, **lest you say** that **with regard to this, Rabbi Yosei holds in accordance with the** opinion of **Rabbi** Yehuda HaNasi, **who says: It is a proper bill of divorce, and she is not even required to perform *ḥalitza*.** Therefore, Rav Huna **teaches us that Rabbi** Yehuda HaNasi **does not hold in accordance with** the opinion of **Rabbi Yosei and Rabbi Yosei does not hold in accordance with** the opinion of **Rabbi** Yehuda HaNasi. Each has a unique, albeit similar, opinion.

רַבִּי לָא סָבַר לָהּ כְּרַבִּי יוֹסֵי, דְּקָתָנֵי "כָּזֶה גֵּט" לְמַעוּטֵי דְּרַבִּי יוֹסֵי; וְרַבִּי יוֹסֵי לָא סָבַר לָהּ כְּרַבִּי, דְּקָתָנֵי "כָּזֶה גֵּט" לְמַעוּטֵי דְּרַבִּי.

The Gemara explains: **Rabbi** Yehuda HaNasi **does not hold in accordance with** the opinion of **Rabbi Yosei,**[N] **as it teaches** in a *baraita*: If the husband said: This is your bill of divorce from today and after my death, Rabbi Yehuda HaNasi says: A case **like this** is a valid **bill of divorce** and there is no need for the wife to perform *ḥalitza*. By emphasizing the term: Like this, Rabbi Yehuda HaNasi intends **to exclude** the opinion **of Rabbi Yosei,** who is uncertain with regard to the matter. **And** similarly, **Rabbi Yosei did not hold in accordance with** the opinion of **Rabbi** Yehuda HaNasi, **as it teaches** in a mishna: Rabbi Yosei says: A case **like this** is a valid **bill of divorce, to exclude** the opinion **of Rabbi** Yehuda HaNasi.

NOTES

Rabbi Yehuda HaNasi does not hold in accordance with the opinion of Rabbi Yosei – **רַבִּי לָא סָבַר לָהּ כְּרַבִּי יוֹסֵי:** Rabbi Yehuda HaNasi considers the bill of divorce to be valid if the husband explicitly stated: From today, but he does not hold that the date written on a bill of divorce proves when it takes effect if the husband explicitly states that it will be valid only after his death (Ritva).

רַבִּי מַאי הִיא? דְּתַנְיָא: ״מֵהַיּוֹם וּלְאַחַר מִיתָה״ – גֵּט וְאֵינוֹ גֵּט, דִּבְרֵי חֲכָמִים, רַבִּי אוֹמֵר: כָּזֶה גֵּט.

The Gemara cites the *baraita* and mishna that demonstrate the difference of opinion between Rabbi Yehuda HaNasi and Rabbi Yosei. **What is** the opinion of **Rabbi** Yehuda HaNasi? **As it is taught** in a *baraita*: If a husband says to his wife: This is your bill of divorce **from today and after** my **death,** then there is uncertainty whether **it is a bill of divorce or** whether **it is not a bill of divorce,** and the wife must perform *ḥalitza*. This is **the statement of the Rabbis. Rabbi** Yehuda HaNasi disagrees and **says:** A case **like this** is a valid **bill of divorce** without any uncertainty, and there is no need for the wife to perform *ḥalitza*.

רַבִּי יוֹסֵי מַאי הִיא? דִּתְנַן: ״כִּתְבוּ וּתְנוּ גֵּט לְאִשְׁתִּי אִם לֹא בָּאתִי מִיכָּן וְעַד שְׁנֵים עָשָׂר חֹדֶשׁ״, כְּתָבוּהוּ בְּתוֹךְ שְׁנֵים עָשָׂר חֹדֶשׁ וְנָתְנוּ לְאַחַר שְׁנֵים עָשָׂר חֹדֶשׁ – אֵינוֹ גֵּט, רַבִּי יוֹסֵי אוֹמֵר: כָּזֶה גֵּט.

What is the opinion of **Rabbi Yosei? As we learned** in a mishna (76b): If one says: **Write and give a bill of divorce to my wife if I have not come from now until** the conclusion of **twelve months,** and the court **wrote** the bill of divorce **within twelve months and gave** it to the wife **after twelve months, it is not** a valid **bill of divorce. Rabbi Yosei** disagrees and **says: A case like this** is a valid **bill of divorce.**

״זֶה גִּיטֵּיךְ מֵהַיּוֹם אִם מַתִּי מֵחוֹלִי זֶה, וְעָמַד וְהָלַךְ בַּשּׁוּק״ כו׳.

§ The mishna teaches: If one says to his wife: **This is your bill of divorce from today if I die from this illness,** and he recovered, **and he arose and walked in the market** and became ill again and died, then it must be assessed whether he died from the first illness and it is therefore a valid bill of divorce. But if he did not die from this illness then it is not a valid bill of divorce.

אֲמַר רַב הוּנָא: גִּיטּוֹ כְּמַתְּנָתוֹ, מַה מַּתְּנָתוֹ אִם עָמַד חוֹזֵר, אַף גִּיטּוֹ אִם עָמַד חוֹזֵר;

Rav Huna said: With regard to a person on his deathbed, the *halakhot* of **his bill of divorce** are the same **as** the *halakhot* of **his gift.** The Sages instituted that when a person on his deathbed gives a gift, no formal act of acquisition is required. **Just as** with regard to **his gift, if he arose** and was cured from his illness the gift he granted while on his deathbed is **retracted,**[H] as he gave it only based on the assumption that he was about to die, **so too,** with regard to **his bill of divorce, if he arose** and was cured from his illness, the bill of divorce is **retracted** and nullified, as he gave his wife her bill of divorce only because he thought he was about to die and he wanted to exempt her from a levirate bond.

וּמַה גִּיטּוֹ אַף עַל גַּב דְּלָא פָּרֵישׁ, כֵּיוָן דַּאֲמַר ״כְּתוֹבוּ״ – אַף עַל גַּב דְּלָא אֲמַר ״תְּנוּ״, אַף מַתְּנָתוֹ כֵּיוָן דַּאֲמַר ״תְּנוּ״ – אַף עַל גַּב דְּלָא קָנוּ מִינֵּיהּ.

Rav Huna continues: **And just as** in the case of **his bill of divorce,** where, **even though he did not explicitly say** his full intention, **once he said: Write** the bill of divorce,[H] his statement is interpreted to mean that the court should give the bill of divorce to his wife **even though he did not say: Give** the bill of divorce to my wife, which a healthy man would need to state, **so too,** this is the *halakha* with regard to **his gift. Once he said: Give**[H] the gift, then **even though** the recipients **did not acquire** it **from him,** which finalizes a gift from a healthy person, because he is dying the *halakha* takes into account his intention without all the necessary legal requirements.

תְּנַן: ״זֶה גִּיטֵּךְ מֵהַיּוֹם אִם מַתִּי מֵחוֹלִי זֶה״, וְעָמַד וְהָלַךְ בַּשּׁוּק וְחָלָה וּמֵת, אוֹמְדִים אוֹתוֹ, אִם מֵחֲמַת חוֹלִי הָרִאשׁוֹן מֵת – הֲרֵי זֶה גֵּט, אִם לָאו – אֵינוֹ גֵּט; וְאִי אָמְרַתְּ אִם עָמַד חוֹזֵר, לָמָּה לִי אוּמְדָּנָא? הֲרֵי עָמַד!

The Gemara challenges: **We learned** in the mishna: If a man said: **This is your bill of divorce from today if I die from this illness,** and he recovered, **and he arose and walked in the market, but** then **became ill** again **and died,** the court **assesses him. If he died because of the first illness** then **this is** a valid **bill of divorce,** but **if not** then it is **not** a valid **bill of divorce. And if you say** that **if he arose** and was cured of his illness the bill of divorce is **retracted,** then **why do I need assessment** at all? **He arose** from his sickbed, so the bill of divorce should automatically be nullified.

אָמַר מָר בְּרֵיהּ דְּרַב יוֹסֵף מִשְּׁמֵיהּ דְּרָבָא: שֶׁנִּיתַּק מֵחוֹלִי לְחוֹלִי.

Mar, son of Rav Yosef, says in the name of Rava: This is referring to a case **where,** instead of recovering completely, **he proceeded from** one **illness** immediately **to** another **illness,** and the assessment is to ascertain whether he died from the first illness or from the second one.

וְהָא ״עָמַד״ קָתָנֵי! עָמַד מֵחוֹלִי זֶה וְנָפַל לְחוֹלִי אַחֵר. וְהָא ״הָלַךְ בַּשּׁוּק״ קָתָנֵי! הָלַךְ עַל מִשְׁעַנְתּוֹ.

The Gemara challenges: **But isn't it taught** in the mishna: **He arose** from his illness, which indicates that he was completely cured? The Gemara answers: No, it means that he **arose from this illness but fell into another illness.** The Gemara challenges: **But isn't it** also **taught** in the mishna: **He walked in the market?** The Gemara answers: This means that **he walked with his staff** for support, meaning that he was not fully recovered from his illness but was able to walk only with assistance.

HALAKHA

With regard to his gift, if he arose from his illness the gift is retracted – מַתְּנָתוֹ אִם עָמַד חוֹזֵר: If a person on his deathbed wrote a deed of gift for all his property and left nothing remaining, and then recovered from his illness, he can retract everything he wrote (Rambam *Sefer Kinyan, Hilkhot Zekhiya UMattana* 8:14; *Shulḥan Arukh, Ḥoshen Mishpat* 250:2).

His bill of divorce…once he said write – גִּיטּוֹ...כֵּיוָן דַּאֲמַר כְּתוֹבוּ: If one suddenly became dangerously ill or traveled to a dangerous place and said to others: Write a bill of divorce for my wife, and did not add: Give the bill of divorce to my wife, they should write and give it on his behalf, as his intention is clear (Rambam *Sefer Nashim, Hilkhot Geirushin* 2:12; *Shulḥan Arukh, Even HaEzer* 141:16).

Once he said give – כֵּיוָן דַּאֲמַר תְּנוּ: If a person on his deathbed says: Give, it is as though he had put this in writing and performed an act of acquisition (Rambam *Sefer Kinyan, Hilkhot Zekhiya UMattana* 8:2; *Shulḥan Arukh, Ḥoshen Mishpat* 250:1).

וְהָא קָא מַשְׁמַע לַן, דְּהָלַךְ עַל מִשְׁעַנְתּוֹ הוּא דְּבָעֵינַן אוּמְדָּנָא, אִידַּךְ – אוּמְדָּנָא נָמֵי לָא בָּעֵינַן.

And this teaches us that we require assessment only in a case **where he walked with his staff.**[N] But in **another** case, where he did not arise from his illness and walk but immediately became ill again, **we do not even require assessment,**[H] as it is clear that his death from the second illness was a result of the first illness.

שְׁמַעַתְּ מִינָּהּ: שְׁכִיב מְרַע שֶׁנִּיתַּק מֵחוֹלִי לְחוֹלִי – מַתְּנָתוֹ מַתָּנָה? אִין, דְּאָמַר רַבִּי אֶלְעָזָר מִשְּׁמֵיהּ דְּרַב: שְׁכִיב מְרַע שֶׁנִּיתַּק מֵחוֹלִי לְחוֹלִי – מַתְּנָתוֹ מַתָּנָה.

The Gemara asks: Can you **conclude from it** that in the case of a **person on his deathbed who proceeded from** one **illness** immediately **to** another **illness, his gift** is a valid **gift,**[H] as he ultimately died as a result of the first illness? The Gemara answers: **Yes, as Rabbi Elazar says in the name of Rav:** In the case of **a person on his deathbed who proceeded from** one **illness** immediately **to** another **illness, his gift** is a valid **gift.**

רַבָּה וְרָבָא לָא סְבִירָא לְהוּ הָא דְּרַב הוּנָא, גְּזֵירָה שֶׁמָּא יֹאמְרוּ יֵשׁ גֵּט לְאַחַר מִיתָה.

The Gemara notes: **Rabba and Rava do not hold** in accordance with **this** *halakha* stated **by Rav Huna,** that if the husband was healed of his illness then the bill of divorce is nullified even if did not specify such a condition. They hold that there is a rabbinic **decree** in place **lest** people **say**[H] that **there** can be a valid **bill of divorce** given **after death.** Since people will see that in this case the bill of divorce took effect only once the husband died, in the future they may mistakenly consider a bill of divorce to be valid even though the husband explicitly made a condition that it would take effect only after his death.

וּמִי אִיכָּא מִידֵּי, דְּמִדְּאוֹרָיְיתָא לָא הָוֵי גִּיטָּא, וּמִשּׁוּם גְּזֵירָה שָׁרֵינַן אֵשֶׁת אִישׁ לְעָלְמָא?

The Gemara asks: **And is there anything that by Torah law is not** a valid **bill of divorce, but due to** a rabbinic **decree we permit a married woman to** marry **anyone,** even though by Torah law she remains married to her husband? Both Rabba and Rava agree that by Torah law the bill of divorce is nullified once the husband is healed from his illness, yet they treat the bill of divorce as valid. How can this be?

אִין, כׇּל דִּמְקַדֵּשׁ אַדַּעְתָּא דְרַבָּנַן מְקַדֵּשׁ, וְאַפְקְעִינְהוּ רַבָּנַן לְקִדּוּשִׁין מִינֵּיהּ.

The Gemara answers: **Yes,** the Sages have the ability to nullify even a marriage that took effect by Torah law, because **anyone who betroths** a woman[N] **betroths** her contingent **upon the will of the Sages, and** when one fails to conform to their will in matters of marriage and divorce **the Sages expropriated his betrothal from him**[N] retroactively. Consequently, it is permitted for the woman to remarry.

אֲמַר לֵיהּ רָבִינָא לְרַב אָשֵׁי: תֵּינַח דְּקַדֵּישׁ בְּכַסְפָּא, קַדֵּישׁ בְּבִיאָה מַאי אִיכָּא לְמֵימַר? אֲמַר לֵיהּ: שַׁוְּיוּהּ רַבָּנַן לִבְעִילָתוֹ בְּעִילַת זְנוּת.

Ravina said to Rav Ashi: This **works out well** in a case **where he betrothed** his wife **with money,** as it is possible to say that the Sages expropriated the money used for the betrothal from the possession of its owner, resulting in a retroactive cancellation of the betrothal. But if **he betrothed** her **by means of sexual intercourse** then **what is there to say?** Rav Ashi **said to him: The Sages declared his sexual intercourse** to be **licentious sexual intercourse,** which does not create a bond of betrothal.

HALAKHA

We do not even require assessment – **אוּמְדָּנָא נָמֵי לָא בָּעֵינַן**: If an ill man gives his wife a bill of divorce with the condition: If I die from this illness, and proceeds from one illness immediately to another illness without arising and walking in the marketplace after the first illness, this is a valid bill of divorce. There is no need for assessment in such a case (Rambam *Sefer Nashim, Hilkhot Geirushin* 9:18; *Shulḥan Arukh, Even HaEzer* 145:7).

Who proceeded from illness to illness, his gift is a valid gift – **שֶׁנִּיתַּק מֵחוֹלִי לְחוֹלִי מַתְּנָתוֹ מַתָּנָה**: In the case of one who gives a gift while on his deathbed, and who proceeded from one illness to another illness, his gift is valid provided he did not arise and walk, even with the aid of a staff, in the marketplace, in accordance with the opinion of Rabbi Elazar. If he recovered completely between one illness and the next, and he walked outside with a staff, then doctors must assess whether he died on account of the first illness, in which case his gift is valid, or from the second, in which case the gift is nullified. If he was well enough between illnesses to go out to the marketplace without a staff then he does not need assessment and his gift is nullified (Rambam *Sefer Kinyan, Hilkhot Zekhiya UMattana* 8:25; *Shulḥan Arukh, Ḥoshen Mishpat* 250:2).

Decree lest people say, etc. – **גְּזֵירָה שֶׁמָּא יֹאמְרוּ וכו׳**: If one says: This is a bill of divorce if I die from this illness, and he recovered enough to go out to the marketplace, then became ill and died, then the court assesses whether he died from the first illness, in which case his bill of divorce is valid, or not, in which case the bill of divorce is invalid, in accordance with the opinions of Rabba and Rava (Rambam *Sefer Nashim, Hilkhot Geirushin* 9:18; *Shulḥan Arukh, Even HaEzer* 145:7).

NOTES

He walked with his staff – **הָלַךְ עַל מִשְׁעַנְתּוֹ**: The Ramah writes that it is specifically when he walked with his staff in the market that an assessment is required. If he walked only inside his house, even without a staff, then there is no need for assessment. One goes to the market only once he thinks he is healthy.

Anyone who betroths a woman, etc. – **כׇּל דִּמְקַדֵּשׁ וכו׳**: Anyone who betroths a woman does so on condition that the Sages confirm his betrothal. In certain cases the Sages used their authority to cancel that betrothal retroactively (Ritva; see also 33a).

The Sages expropriated his betrothal from him – **אַפְקְעִינְהוּ רַבָּנַן לְקִדּוּשִׁין מִינֵּיהּ**: This *halakha* that the Sages can retroactively expropriate the betrothal is applied only in a few specific cases throughout the Talmud, and is not a panacea to be applied in every case where a problem arises, even if the problem is a severe one, e.g., a deserted wife.

Many early commentaries state that this solution is applied only in cases where there is a bill of divorce of some kind (Ramban; Rashba; Ra'ah). The Meiri demonstrates that in certain cases, when halakhic problems arise with regard to the betrothal itself, the Sages used this procedure to expropriate it.

תָּנוּ רַבָּנַן: ״זֶה גִּיטֵּיךְ מֵהַיּוֹם אִם מַתִּי מֵחוֹלִי זֶה״, וְנָפַל הַבַּיִת עָלָיו אוֹ הִכִּישׁוֹ נָחָשׁ – אֵינוֹ גֵּט; ״אִם לֹא אֶעֱמוֹד מֵחוֹלִי זֶה״, וְנָפַל עָלָיו בַּיִת אוֹ הִכִּישׁוֹ נָחָשׁ – הֲרֵי זֶה גֵּט;

§ The Sages taught (*Tosefta* 7:2): If a husband says to his wife: **This is your bill of divorce from today if I die from this illness, and the house collapsed on him**[H] **or a snake bit him,** then **it is not** a valid **bill of divorce.** But if he said: This is your bill of divorce **if I will not arise** healthy **from this illness, and the house collapsed on him or a snake bit him,** then **this is** a valid **bill of divorce.**

מַאי שְׁנָא רֵישָׁא וּמַאי שְׁנָא סֵיפָא?

The Gemara asks: **What is different in the first clause**[N] such that the bill of divorce is not valid **and what is different in the latter clause** that the bill of divorce is valid? In neither case did he die from the illness. The Gemara gives no answer to this question.

שְׁלַחוּ מִתָּם: אֲכָלוֹ אֲרִי, אֵין לָנוּ.

They sent a ruling to Babylonia **from there,** from Eretz Yisrael: If the husband said: This is your bill of divorce if I am not healed from this illness, and **a lion ate him,** then **we do not** need to be concerned about this bill of divorce, for it is certainly not valid.

הַהוּא גַּבְרָא דִּזְבִין אַרְעָא לְחַבְרֵיהּ, קַבֵּיל עֲלֵיהּ כָּל אוֹנְסָא דְּמִתְיְלִיד, לְסוֹף אַפִּיקוּ בָּהּ נַהֲרָא;

It is related: There was **a certain man who sold land to another,** and he **accepted upon himself** the responsibility for **any unavoidable accident that may happen** to the land. In such a case he would reimburse the buyer for the damage. **In the end they diverted a river into it,**[B] meaning the government decided to make a new canal through the land that he sold.

אֲתָא לְקַמֵּיהּ דְּרָבִינָא, אֲמַר לֵיהּ: זִיל שַׁפִּי לֵיהּ, דְּהָא קַבֵּילְתְּ עֲלָךְ כָּל אוֹנְסָא דְּמִתְיְלִיד. אֲמַר לֵיהּ רַב אַחָא בַּר תַּחְלִיפָא לְרָבִינָא: אוֹנְסָא דְּלָא שְׁכִיחַ הוּא!

The buyer **came before Ravina** to lodge a claim. Ravina **said to** the seller: **Go pacify him,** i.e., reimburse him, **as you accepted upon yourself** responsibility for **any unavoidable accident that might happen. Rav Aḥa bar Taḥalifa** disagreed and **said to Ravina: It is an uncommon, unavoidable accident,**[H] and the condition of the sale should not apply in such a case.

אִיגַּלְגַּל מִילְּתָא וּמְטָא לְקַמֵּיהּ דְּרָבָא, אֲמַר לְהוּ: אוֹנְסָא דְּלָא שְׁכִיחַ הוּא. אֵיתִיבֵיהּ רָבִינָא לְרָבָא: ״אִם לֹא אֶעֱמוֹד מֵחוֹלִי זֶה״, וְנָפַל עָלָיו בַּיִת אוֹ הִכִּישׁוֹ נָחָשׁ – הֲרֵי זֶה גֵּט!

The matter was circulated, as this ruling was never finalized, **and it came before Rava. He said to them: It is an uncommon, unavoidable accident,** and the seller should not have to pay. **Ravina raised an objection to Rava:** Isn't it taught that if the husband said: This is your bill of divorce **if I am not healed from this illness, and the house collapsed on him or a snake bit him** then it is a valid **bill of divorce?** These cases are both uncommon, unavoidable accidents, yet the bill of divorce is valid.

אֲמַר לֵיהּ רָבָא: וְאֵימָא מֵרֵישָׁא: אֵינוֹ גֵּט.

Rava said to him: But you can **say** an opposite inference **from the first clause:** If a husband says: This is your bill of divorce from today if I die from this illness, and the house collapsed on him or a snake bit him, then **it is not** a valid **bill of divorce.** Apparently, an uncommon, unavoidable accident is not included within his condition. If so, the inference from first clause of the *baraita* contradicts the inference from latter clause and it cannot be used to prove either opinion.

אֲמַר לֵיהּ רַב אַחָא מִדִּפְתִּי לְרָבִינָא: וּמִשּׁוּם דְּקַשְׁיָא רֵישָׁא אַסֵּיפָא, לָא מוֹתְבִינַן תְּיוּבְתָּא מִינַּהּ?

Rav Aḥa of Difti said to Ravina: And because there is **a difficulty** presented by the contradiction between **the first clause** of the *baraita* **and the latter clause, can we no** longer **raise an objection from it?** Seemingly, the challenge raised by Ravina from the latter clause of the *baraita* is still valid.

אֲמַר לֵיהּ: אִין, כֵּיוָן דְּקַשְׁיָא רֵישָׁא אַסֵּיפָא – לָא אִיתְּמַר בֵּי מִדְרְשָׁא, וּמְשַׁבַּשְׁתָּא הִיא, זִיל בָּתַר סְבָרָא.

Ravina **said to him: Yes,** Rava was correct. **Since** there is **a difficulty** presented by the contradiction between **the first clause** of the *baraita* **and the latter clause,** this *baraita* **was never stated** in **the study hall and it is corrupted.** As it is not possible to rely on this *baraita* one must **follow reason,** and the most reasonable interpretation is that his condition would not include an uncommon and unavoidable accident.

רַב פָּפָּא וְרַב הוּנָא בְּרֵיהּ דְּרַב יְהוֹשֻׁעַ זְבַן שׁוּמְשְׁמֵי אַגִּידָא דִּנְהַר מַלְכָּא, אֲגוּר מַלָּחֵי לְעַבּוּרִינְהוּ, קַבִּילוּ עֲלַיְיהוּ כָּל אוֹנְסָא דְּמִתְיְלִיד, לְסוֹף אִיסְתְּכַר נְהַר מַלְכָּא,

It is related that **Rav Pappa and Rav Huna, son of Rav Yehoshua, purchased sesame on the bank of the Malka River.**[B] **They hired sailors to cross them** to the other side of the river, and the sailors **accepted upon themselves** responsibility for **any unavoidable accident that might occur. In the end the Malka River was dammed** so that the merchandise could not be transported by river.

HALAKHA

The house collapsed on him, etc. – **נָפַל הַבַּיִת עָלָיו וכו׳**: If an ill man said to his wife: This is your bill of divorce from today if I die from this illness, and a house collapsed on him, or he was bitten by a snake, or he was eaten by a lion, the bill of divorce is not valid. If he said: This is your bill of divorce from today if I am not healed from this illness, and one of these unforeseeable events occurred, then it is uncertain if this is a valid bill of divorce. This is in accordance with the explanation offered by many of the early commentaries, and in accordance with the Rambam's ruling (Rambam *Sefer Nashim, Hilkhot Geirushin* 9:17–18; *Shulḥan Arukh, Even HaEzer* 145:6).

An uncommon, unavoidable accident – **אוֹנְסָא דְּלָא שְׁכִיחַ**: One who sells land to another and accepts liability even for an unavoidable accident that occurs to the land is required to pay the new owner under such circumstances, even if a gentile came and stole the land from him. But if the river that irrigated his field was diverted or dried up, or an earthquake destroyed the field, then he is not liable, because he did not even consider such rare, unavoidable circumstances, and he did not accept liability for this. The principle for any condition in monetary law is that the court assesses the intention of the one who made the condition (Rambam *Sefer Kinyan, Hilkhot Mekhira* 19:5–7; *Shulḥan Arukh, Ḥoshen Mishpat* 225:3–4).

NOTES

What is different in the first clause – **מַאי שְׁנָא רֵישָׁא**: *Tosafot* cite the Jerusalem Talmud, in which it is written that when the husband says: If I die from this illness, he intends to make the bill of divorce dependent on this specific illness. Consequently, if something else caused his death it is not a valid bill of divorce. But if he said: If I am not healed from this illness, his intention was that the bill of divorce will not be valid if he remains alive. Since he died it is a valid bill of divorce. *Tosafot* claim that this distinction is ignored in the Babylonian Talmud because it assumes that the essence of the two conditions is identical.

BACKGROUND

They diverted a river into it – **אַפִּיקוּ בָּהּ נַהֲרָא**: The land of Babylonia relies mainly on irrigation from its many large rivers. Even in ancient times the central authorities initiated projects to dig large irrigation canals, some of which were the size of small rivers, especially when they brought water directly from the Tigris or Euphrates. Some of these canals were large enough to accommodate boats. Any field that had a canal diverted through it could no longer be used for agriculture.

Malka River – **נְהַר מַלְכָּא**: The Malka River was one of the largest canals ever built in Babylonia, connecting the Tigris with the Euphrates. It was called a river due to its size, and as it was built by the king it was called the Royal [*Malka*] River. It was used for irrigation as well as for transporting goods and food by boat. Damming such an important waterway was without question a rare event.

Location of the Malka River

אֲמַרוּ לְהוּ: אֲגוּרוּ חֲמָרֵי אַפְקַעִינְהוּ נִיהֲלָן, דְּהָא קַבֵּילְתּוּ עֲלַייכוּ כָּל אוּנְסָא דְּמִיתְלִיד;

The two Sages **said to them: Hire donkeys and release them to us** in order to transport the sesame, **as you accepted upon yourself** responsibility for **any unavoidable accident that might arise.**

אָתוּ לְקַמֵּיהּ דְּרָבָא, אֲמַר לְהוּ: קָאקֵי חִיוָּרֵי מַשְׁלְחֵי גְּלִימֵי דְּאֱינָשֵׁי, אוּנְסָא דְּלָא שְׁכִיחַ הוּא.

The two Sages **came** to court **before Rava and he said to** them: **You white geese** [***kakei ḥivarei***],[L] referring to their long, white beards, **who strip men of their cloaks.** You are acting unfairly with the sailors. **It is an uncommon, unavoidable accident** for the Malka River to be dammed, and the sailors did not accept responsibility for this case.

מתני׳ לֹא תִּתְיַיחֵד עִמּוֹ אֶלָּא בִּפְנֵי עֵדִים,

MISHNA If a woman's ill husband gave her a bill of divorce, and made a condition that it should take effect from today if he dies from his illness, then **she may be secluded with him only in the presence of two witnesses,**[NH] lest they end up engaging in sexual intercourse.

אֲפִילּוּ עַל פִּי עֶבֶד אֲפִילּוּ עַל פִּי שִׁפְחָה, חוּץ מִשִּׁפְחָתָהּ, מִפְּנֵי שֶׁלִּבָּהּ גַּס בָּהּ בְּשִׁפְחָתָהּ.

This applies to being secluded in the presence of not only valid witnesses; it is permitted for her to be secluded with him **even in the presence of a slave or even in the presence of a maidservant, except for** the wife's personal **maidservant.** And it is prohibited for the wife to be secluded in the presence of the latter **because she is accustomed to her maidservant,** and there is concern that she will engage in sexual intercourse with her husband even though the maidservant is present.

מַה הִיא בְּאוֹתָן הַיָּמִים? רַבִּי יְהוּדָה אוֹמֵר:

What is the halakhic status of the wife **during these days** between when the bill of divorce was given but before the condition has been fulfilled with the death of the husband? **Rabbi Yehuda says:** She is

LANGUAGE

White geese [*kakei ḥivarei*] – קָאקֵי חִיוָּרֵי: Rashi translates *kakei* as geese. The *Targum Yonatan* in Deuteronomy 14:17 translates the non-kosher bird called *ka'at* as *kaka ḥivarta*. There are various opinions as to the identification of the *ka'at*. Some translate it as a pelican, while others claim that it is an owl.

NOTES

She may be secluded with him only in the presence of two witnesses – לֹא תִּתְיַיחֵד עִמּוֹ אֶלָּא בִּפְנֵי עֵדִים: Even though he is ill, there is still concern that perhaps his inclination will overcome him and they will engage in sexual intercourse. Rashi explains that if there were witnesses that they were secluded there is concern that they had a second betrothal after the bill of divorce, in which case the wife would be bound by the levirate bond after the husband's death, provided that the husband died childless. Alternatively, if the bill of divorce was valid his wife has the status of a single woman, and the Sages decreed that it is prohibited for a man to be secluded with a single woman. The Rambam explains that the concern is that perhaps he will engage in sexual intercourse with her, and out of affection for her he will cancel the bill of divorce (see Meiri).

HALAKHA

She may be secluded with him only in the presence of two witnesses – לֹא תִּתְיַיחֵד עִמּוֹ אֶלָּא בִּפְנֵי עֵדִים: With regard to one who divorces his wife with a bill of divorce that is valid, upon fulfillment of a condition, from the time it is given, it is prohibited for the husband to be secluded with his wife until the condition is fulfilled, except in the presence of at least one witness. Even one slave or maidservant is considered sufficient as a witness, but not the wife's personal maidservant or a young child, as the wife will not be embarrassed to engage in sexual intercourse in their presence (Rambam *Sefer Nashim, Hilkhot Geirushin* 8:2; *Shulḥan Arukh, Even HaEzer* 148:2).

Perek **VII**
Daf **73** Amud **b**

כְּאֵשֶׁת אִישׁ לְכָל דְּבָרֶיהָ, רַבִּי יוֹסֵי אוֹמֵר: מְגוֹרֶשֶׁת וְאֵינָהּ מְגוֹרֶשֶׁת.

like a married woman with regard to all of her matters, and she remains forbidden to other men. **Rabbi Yosei says:** It is uncertain whether **she is divorced or** whether **she is not divorced.**

גמ׳ תָּנוּ רַבָּנַן: רָאוּהָ שֶׁנִּתְיַיחֲדָה עִמּוֹ בַּאֲפֵילָה, אוֹ שֶׁיְּשֵׁנָה עִמּוֹ תַּחַת מַרְגְּלוֹת הַמִּטָּה – אֵין חוֹשְׁשִׁין שֶׁמָּא נִתְעַסְּקוּ בְּדָבָר אַחֵר; וְחוֹשְׁשִׁין מִשּׁוּם זְנוּת וְאֵין חוֹשְׁשִׁין מִשּׁוּם קִדּוּשִׁין, רַבִּי יוֹסֵי בְּרַבִּי יְהוּדָה אוֹמֵר: אַף חוֹשְׁשִׁין מִשּׁוּם קִידּוּשִׁין.

GEMARA The Sages taught in a *baraita* (*Tosefta* 7:4): If, after the giving of this bill of divorce witnesses **saw that she secluded herself**[H] **with** her husband **in the dark, or that she slept with him under the foot of the bed, one is not concerned** that **perhaps they were engaged in another matter,** i.e., sexual intercourse. **And one is concerned due to** their action of **licentiousness but one is not concerned** that **due to** their actions they performed **a betrothal. Rabbi Yosei, son of Rabbi Yehuda, says: One is also concerned** that **due to** their actions they performed **a betrothal.**

מַאי קָאָמַר? אָמַר רַב נַחְמָן אָמַר רַבָּה בַּר אֲבוּהּ, הָכִי קָאָמַר: רָאוּהָ שֶׁנִּבְעֲלָה – חוֹשְׁשִׁין מִשּׁוּם קִידּוּשִׁין, נָתַן לָהּ כְּסָפִים – חוֹשְׁשִׁין מִשּׁוּם זְנוּת, דְּאָמְרִינַן: בְּאֶתְנַנָּהּ נָתַן לָהּ, וְאֵין חוֹשְׁשִׁין מִשּׁוּם קִידּוּשִׁין, רַבִּי יוֹסֵי בְּרַבִּי יְהוּדָה אוֹמֵר: אַף בְּזוֹ חוֹשְׁשִׁין מִשּׁוּם קִידּוּשִׁין.

The Gemara asks: **What is** the *baraita* **saying? Rav Naḥman said** that **Rabba bar Avuh said: This is what** the *baraita* **is saying:** If **they saw that she engaged in sexual intercourse** with her husband, then **there one is concerned** that **due to** their actions there was **a betrothal** and perhaps through this act he intended to remarry her. If **he gave her money** immediately following the sexual intercourse **one is concerned due to licentiousness,**[N] **wherein we say:** He gave this money **as hire for a prostitute, but one is not concerned** that **due to** their actions they performed **a betrothal. Rabbi Yosei, son of Rabbi Yehuda, says: Even in this** case **one is concerned** that **due to** their actions they performed **a betrothal,** i.e., one is concerned that he gave her the money as betrothal.

HALAKHA

They saw that she secluded herself, etc. – רָאוּהָ שֶׁנִּתְיַיחֲדָה וכו׳: If a husband divorced his wife and afterward two witnesses saw him secluded with her, then if the divorce occurred after marriage rather than after betrothal then there is concern that they engaged in sexual intercourse, and therefore she requires another bill of divorce due to uncertainty. If she was divorced from betrothal, meaning they were never fully married, there is no concern that they engaged in sexual intercourse with the intention to remarry. This is in accordance with the opinion of Rabbi Yosei, son of Rabbi Yehuda, and in accordance with the opinion of Beit Hillel, according to the Gemara's conclusion on 81b (Rambam *Sefer Nashim, Hilkhot Geirushin* 10:18; *Shulḥan Arukh, Even HaEzer* 149:2).

NOTES

One is concerned due to licentiousness – חוֹשְׁשִׁין מִשּׁוּם זְנוּת: Rashi explains that the language used here is not precise, as it is not merely a concern due to licentiousness. The Gemara used this wording only in order to parallel the expression: One is concerned with regard to betrothal. In this case there is no uncertainty but a definite assumption of licentious sexual intercourse, and as a result of this assumption the woman does not become forbidden at all.

כְּמַאן אָזְלָא הָא דְּאָמַר רַבָּה בַּר בַּר חָנָה אָמַר רַבִּי יוֹחָנָן: מַחֲלוֹקֶת – כְּשֶׁרָאוּהָ שֶׁנִּבְעֲלָה, אֲבָל לֹא רָאוּהָ שֶׁנִּבְעֲלָה – דִּבְרֵי הַכֹּל אֵין צְרִיכָה הֵימֶנּוּ גֵּט שֵׁנִי, כְּמַאן?

Based on this explanation of the *baraita*, **in accordance with whose** opinion **is that which Rabba bar bar Ḥana says** that **Rabbi Yoḥanan says,** that **the dispute** between Beit Shammai and Beit Hillel (81a) is relevant only **when they saw that she engaged in sexual intercourse** with her husband, but if **they did not see that she engaged in sexual intercourse** with him, **everyone agrees that she does not require a second bill of divorce from him?** In the case of a divorced woman who was secluded with her husband after the divorce, Beit Shammai are of the opinion that she does not require a second bill of divorce, while Beit Hillel are of the opinion that she does. **In accordance with whose** opinion mentioned in the *baraita* is this?

כְּדִבְרֵי הַכֹּל.

The Gemara explains: It is **in accordance with everyone.** It is in accordance with the opinion of both the first *tanna* and Rabbi Yosei, son of Rabbi Yehuda, who hold that when they did not see that she engaged in sexual intercourse one is not concerned that they are betrothed, and she does not need a second bill of divorce.

מַתְקִיף לַהּ אַבַּיֵי: מִידֵּי כְּסָפִים קָתָנֵי?

Abaye objects to this understanding of the *baraita*, according to which the first *tanna* and Rabbi Yosei, son of Rabbi Yehuda, disagree about a case where he gave her money after they engaged in sexual intercourse: **Is anything** with regard to **money taught**[N] in the *baraita*?

אֶלָּא אָמַר אַבַּיֵי, הָכִי קָאָמַר: רָאוּהָ שֶׁנִּבְעֲלָה – חוֹשְׁשִׁין מִשּׁוּם זְנוּת וְאֵין חוֹשְׁשִׁין מִשּׁוּם קִידּוּשִׁין, רַבִּי יוֹסֵי בְּרַבִּי יְהוּדָה אוֹמֵר: אַף חוֹשְׁשִׁין מִשּׁוּם קִידּוּשִׁין.

Rather, Abaye said: This is what the *baraita* **is saying:** If **they saw that she engaged in sexual intercourse**[H] **one is concerned due to licentiousness, but one is not concerned** that due to their actions there was **a betrothal. Rabbi Yosei, son of Rabbi Yehuda, says: One is also concerned** that **due to** their actions there was **a betrothal.**

כְּמַאן אָזְלָא הָא דְּאָמַר רַבָּה בַּר בַּר חָנָה אָמַר רַבִּי יוֹחָנָן: מַחֲלוֹקֶת – כְּשֶׁרָאוּהָ שֶׁנִּבְעֲלָה, אֲבָל לֹא רָאוּהָ שֶׁנִּבְעֲלָה – דִּבְרֵי הַכֹּל אֵין צְרִיכָה הֵימֶנּוּ גֵּט שֵׁנִי, כְּמַאן?

If so, **in accordance with whose** opinion **is that which Rabba bar bar Ḥana says** that **Rabbi Yoḥanan says: The dispute** between Beit Shammai and Beit Hillel applies only **when they saw that she engaged in sexual intercourse** with him. **But** if **they did not see that she engaged in sexual intercourse** with him then **everyone agrees that she does not require a second bill of divorce from him.** In accordance **with whose** opinion is this statement?

כְּרַבִּי יוֹסֵי בְּרַבִּי יְהוּדָה.

It is **in accordance with** the opinion of **Rabbi Yosei, son of Rabbi Yehuda,** as he holds in accordance with Beit Hillel, that if they saw that she engaged in sexual intercourse one is concerned that she may be betrothed to him and she requires a second bill of divorce. By contrast, according to the first *tanna*, even when they saw that she engaged in sexual intercourse one is not concerned that she may be betrothed.

מַתְקִיף לַהּ רָבָא: אִם כֵּן, מַאי "אַף"?

Rava objects to this: If so, what is the meaning of the expression used by Rabbi Yosei, son of Rabbi Yehuda: There is **also**[N] concern that due to their actions they performed a betrothal? If there is concern about betrothal there should be no concern with regard to licentiousness.

אֶלָּא אָמַר רָבָא, הָכִי קָאָמַר: רַבִּי יוֹסֵי בַּר רַבִּי יְהוּדָה אוֹמֵר: אַף לֹא רָאוּהָ שֶׁנִּבְעֲלָה – חוֹשְׁשִׁין מִשּׁוּם קִידּוּשִׁין.

Rather, Rava said that **this is** what the *baraita* **is saying: Rabbi Yosei, son of Rabbi Yehuda, says: Even if they did not see that she engaged in sexual intercourse, one is concerned** that **due** to their actions they performed **a betrothal.**

כְּמַאן אָזְלָא הָא דְּאָמַר רַבָּה בַּר בַּר חָנָה אָמַר רַבִּי יוֹחָנָן: מַחֲלוֹקֶת – כְּשֶׁרָאוּהָ שֶׁנִּבְעֲלָה, אֲבָל לֹא רָאוּהָ שֶׁנִּבְעֲלָה – דִּבְרֵי הַכֹּל אֵינָהּ צְרִיכָה הֵימֶנּוּ גֵּט, כְּמַאן?

And if so, **in accordance with whose** opinion **is that which Rabba bar bar Ḥana says** that **Rabbi Yoḥanan says: The dispute** between Beit Shammai and Beit Hillel applies only **where they saw that she engaged in sexual intercourse** with him. **But** if **they did not see that she engaged in intercourse** with him, then **everyone agrees that she does not require** a second **bill of divorce from him.** In accordance **with whose** opinion is this statement?

NOTES

Is anything with regard to money taught – מִידֵּי כְּסָפִים קָתָנֵי: Even though there are many cases in which the Sages of the Talmud interpreted tannaitic statements in a way that would limit their applicability to specific circumstances, which implies that the *tanna* omitted details, it is difficult to understand how the *tanna* would leave out this detail when it is a fundamental component of the discussion.

If so what is the meaning of also – אִם כֵּן מַאי אַף: Rashi explains that the statement: One is concerned due to licentiousness, is a leniency, since by assuming her sexual intercourse was licentious, she is not considered to be a married woman. Therefore, the phrase: There is also concern, is not appropriate, as this is not akin to the first concern of betrothal. By contrast, *Tosafot* explain the question as follows: Since the concerns of betrothal and licentiousness are mutually exclusive, as the sexual intercourse was either for the purpose of betrothal or was licentious, the phrase: There is also concern, which indicates that the second concern is in addition to the first, is not appropriate, as there cannot be both concerns.

HALAKHA

They saw that she engaged in sexual intercourse, etc. – רָאוּהָ שֶׁנִּבְעֲלָה וכו׳: In the case of one who divorced his wife and subsequently engaged in sexual intercourse with her in the presence of two witnesses, it is assumed that the intercourse was intended for the sake of betrothal, regardless of whether he had been married to her or was only betrothed to her. Consequently, she requires a second bill of divorce from him. This is in accordance with the opinion of Beit Hillel, and in accordance with the conclusion on 81b. Even if the witnesses saw that the husband gave the wife money, the assumption is that he gave it to her for the sake of betrothal (Rambam *Sefer Nashim, Hilkhot Geirushin* 10:17 and *Maggid Mishne* there; *Shulḥan Arukh, Even HaEzer* 149:1).

דְּלָא כְּחַד.

This is **not in accordance with** any **one** of the *tanna'im*, for according to Rava the first *tanna* is not concerned about betrothal even when they saw that she engaged in sexual intercourse, and Rabbi Yosei, son of Rabbi Yehuda, is concerned even when they did not witness that she engaged in sexual intercourse.

״מַה הִיא בְּאוֹתָן הַיָּמִים? רַבִּי יְהוּדָה אוֹמֵר: כְּאֵשֶׁת אִישׁ לְכָל דְּבָרֶיהָ, רַבִּי יוֹסֵי אוֹמֵר: מְגוֹרֶשֶׁת וְאֵינָהּ מְגוֹרֶשֶׁת״.

§ The mishna teaches: **What is** her status **during these days? Rabbi Yehuda says:** She is **like a married woman with regard to all of her matters. Rabbi Yosei says:** It is uncertain whether **she is divorced or** whether **she is not divorced.**

תָּנָא: וּבִלְבַד שֶׁיָּמוּת. וְלִכִי מָיֵית הָוֵי גִּיטָּא? וְהָא קַיְימָא לַן דְּאֵין גֵּט לְאַחַר מִיתָה! אָמַר רַבָּה: בְּאוֹמֵר ״מֵעֵת שֶׁאֲנִי בָּעוֹלָם״.

The Sages **taught** in reference to the opinions of Rabbi Yehuda and Rabbi Yosei stated in the *baraita*: Their dispute with regard to her status in the interim is stated **provided that he dies.** The Gemara clarifies: **And when he dies,** is this a valid **bill of divorce?**[N] Do they hold that the bill of divorce takes effect after the husband's death? **But don't we maintain that there is no bill of divorce after death? Rabba says** that this is referring to a case **where** the husband **says:** This should be a valid bill of divorce **from the** last **moment that I am in the world,**[N] meaning that it should take effect a moment before he dies.

תָּנוּ רַבָּנַן: יָמִים שֶׁבֵּינְתַיִם – בַּעְלָהּ זַכַּאי בִּמְצִיאָתָהּ וּבְמַעֲשֵׂה יָדֶיהָ וּבַהֲפָרַת נְדָרֶיהָ, וְיוֹרְשָׁהּ,

The Sages taught (*Tosefta* 7:4): In a case where the husband said: This is your bill of divorce from now if I die from this illness, **during the days between,** before he dies, **her husband is entitled to** anything that **she finds,** i.e., any lost item that cannot be returned to its owner, in accordance with the rabbinic principle that any lost item found by a wife belongs to her husband. **And** he is entitled to the profits from **her earnings, and** he is entitled to **annul her vows** (see Numbers 30:7–9), **and he inherits** from **her** if she predeceases him,

NOTES

And when he dies is this a valid bill of divorce – וְלִכִי מָיֵית הָוֵי גִּיטָּא: Rashi explains the question as follows: The dispute in the mishna appears to be that while Rabbi Yehuda holds that the expression: From today if I die, is not a condition but a retraction of his first statement, Rabbi Yosei is uncertain whether it is a condition or a retraction. According to both opinions the bill of divorce is not valid from the time that it is given. Therefore, the challenge is: How can this become a valid bill of divorce at the moment he dies? See also the Rid.

Where the husband says: From the last moment that I am in the world – בְּאוֹמֵר מֵעֵת שֶׁאֲנִי בָּעוֹלָם: Rashi explains that this answer rejects the previous understanding of the final clause of the mishna. Accordingly, the final passage of the mishna: What is the halakhic status of the wife during these days, does not refer to *halakhot* that were stated beforehand. Instead, it begins a new topic: If a husband said to his wife that her bill of divorce will be valid from the last moment that he is in the world, then what is her status before he dies?

Other early commentaries raise many challenges to Rashi's explanation. Consequently, they prefer Rabbeinu Ḥananel's version of the text, which reads: Like one who says: From the last moment that I am in the world, meaning that the mishna continues the discussion of the previous topic, and is teaching that when he says: From today if I die from this illness, it is considered to be as though he said: From the last moment that I am in the world if I die from this illness (see *Tosafot*). Others write that this is the meaning even without changing the text (see Ramban). According to these explanations Rabbi Yehuda holds that the bill of divorce certainly takes effect immediately before the husband's death. Rabbi Yosei is uncertain whether the *halakha* is in accordance with the opinion of Rabbi Yehuda or in accordance with Rabbi Meir (74a), the latter of whom says that the bill of divorce takes effect immediately once it has been given (Rabbeinu Yitzḥak of Dampierre and Rivam in *Tosafot*).

Perek **VII**
Daf **74** Amud **a**

וּמִטַּמֵּא לָהּ. כְּלָלוֹ שֶׁל דָּבָר: הֲרֵי הִיא כְּאִשְׁתּוֹ לְכָל דָּבָר – אֶלָּא שֶׁאֵינָהּ צְרִיכָה הֵימֶנּוּ גֵּט שֵׁנִי, דִּבְרֵי רַבִּי יְהוּדָה:

and he becomes ritually impure for her if he is a priest. **The principle of the matter** is as follows: At that time **she is like his wife in every sense, but she does not require a second bill of divorce from him** when he dies. This is **the statement of Rabbi Yehuda.**

רַבִּי מֵאִיר אוֹמֵר: בְּעִילָתָהּ תְּלוּיָה; רַבִּי יוֹסֵי אוֹמֵר: בְּעִילָתָהּ סָפֵק; וַחֲכָמִים אוֹמְרִים: מְגוֹרֶשֶׁת וְאֵינָהּ מְגוֹרֶשֶׁת, וּבִלְבַד שֶׁיָּמוּת.

Rabbi Meir says: If she engages in sexual intercourse with another man, the legal status of **her sexual intercourse depends** on whether or not her husband dies from this illness. If he dies, she is considered to have been divorced from the time the bill of divorce was given, and her sexual intercourse is not deemed adulterous. **Rabbi Yosei says: Her sexual intercourse** has an **uncertain** status. **And the Rabbis say:**[N] There is uncertainty whether **she is divorced or** whether **she is not divorced,**[H] and this is an uncertainty **provided that he dies** from this illness. If he does not, they are certainly not divorced.

HALAKHA

There is uncertainty whether she is divorced or she is not divorced – מְגוֹרֶשֶׁת וְאֵינָהּ מְגוֹרֶשֶׁת: The Rambam rules that from the time the bill of divorce was given until the husband dies and the condition is fulfilled, the woman is considered to be fully divorced, provided she is never secluded with him. This is based on the version of the Gemara text of the Rif and the *Halakhot Gedolot*, according to which the Rabbis say that she is considered to be divorced with regard to all matters. The *Tur* rules in accordance with the standard version of the text, which states that there is uncertainty whether she is divorced or not.

The *Shulḥan Arukh* rules that if the husband gave his wife a bill of divorce with a condition, he may not annul her vows during the period before the condition has been fulfilled. The *Shakh* adds that if he did annul her vows and subsequently the condition was not fulfilled, the annulment is effective after the fact (Rambam *Sefer Nashim*, *Hilkhot Geirushin* 9:19; *Tur*, *Even HaEzer* 148; *Shulḥan Arukh*, *Yoreh De'a* 234:3).

NOTES

And the Rabbis say, etc. – וַחֲכָמִים אוֹמְרִים וכו׳: This is the version of the text possessed by Rashi and the Ashkenazic sages. Rabbeinu Ḥananel, the Rif, and the early Sephardic commentaries had another version, according to which the Rabbis say: She is divorced with regard to every matter, as long as he dies (see Ramah; Rashba; Rabbeinu Crescas Vidal).

LANGUAGE

Coat [*itztalit*] – אִיצְטָלִית: From the Greek στολή, *stolē*, meaning a garment or coat.

מַאי אִיכָּא בֵּין רַבִּי מֵאִיר לְרַבִּי יוֹסֵי?

The Gemara clarifies: **What** difference **is there between** the opinion of **Rabbi Meir,** who says that the status of her sexual intercourse depends on whether or not her husband dies from his illness, **and** the opinion of **Rabbi Yosei,** who says that the status of her sexual intercourse is uncertain?

אָמַר רַבִּי יוֹחָנָן: אָשָׁם תָּלוּי אִיכָּא בֵּינַיְיהוּ, לְרַבִּי מֵאִיר לָא מַיְיתֵי אָשָׁם תָּלוּי, וּלְרַבִּי יוֹסֵי מַיְיתֵי אָשָׁם תָּלוּי.

Rabbi Yoḥanan said: The practical difference **between them is** with regard to the bringing of **a provisional guilt-offering,** which is brought by one who is uncertain as to whether he committed a sin that requires a sin-offering. **According to** the opinion of **Rabbi Meir,** the paramour **does not bring a provisional guilt-offering** (see Leviticus 5:17–19), because, although there was uncertainty at the time of the act of sexual intercourse, the matter will eventually be clarified once the husband either dies or recovers from his illness. If the husband survives her paramour must bring a sin-offering, and if the husband dies the other man is exempt from bringing any offering. **And according to** the opinion of **Rabbi Yosei** her status is uncertain, and even if the husband dies from this illness Rabbi Yosei is uncertain when the bill of divorce took effect. Therefore, her paramour must **bring a provisional guilt-offering.**

״וַחֲכָמִים אוֹמְרִים: מְגוֹרֶשֶׁת וְאֵינָהּ מְגוֹרֶשֶׁת״. חֲכָמִים הַיְינוּ רַבִּי יוֹסֵי – אִיכָּא בֵּינַיְיהוּ דְּרַבִּי זֵירָא, דְּאָמַר רַבִּי זֵירָא אָמַר רַבָּה בַּר יִרְמְיָה אָמַר שְׁמוּאֵל: כׇּל מָקוֹם שֶׁאָמְרוּ חֲכָמִים ״מְגוֹרֶשֶׁת וְאֵינָהּ מְגוֹרֶשֶׁת״ – בַּעְלָהּ חַיָּיב בִּמְזוֹנוֹתֶיהָ.

The *baraita* taught: **And the Rabbis say:** There is uncertainty whether **she is divorced or** whether **she is not divorced.** The Gemara comments: Apparently, the opinion of **the Rabbis is** the same as the opinion of **Rabbi Yosei.** Why are they recorded as having a dispute? The Gemara answers: **There is** a practical difference **between them** with regard to the halakhic ruling transmitted **by Rabbi Zeira. As Rabbi Zeira says** that **Rabba bar Yirmeya says** that **Shmuel says: Wherever the Sages said:** There is uncertainty whether **she is divorced or** whether **she is not divorced,**[H] **her husband is obligated to provide her** with **sustenance.** This formulation is stated only by the Rabbis, and Rabbi Zeira's *halakha* would apply only according to them, not according to Rabbi Yosei.

מתני׳ ״הֲרֵי זֶה גִּיטֵּךְ עַל מְנָת שֶׁתִּתְּנִי לִי מָאתַיִם זוּז״ – הֲרֵי זוֹ מְגוֹרֶשֶׁת, וְתִתֵּן.

MISHNA If a husband says to his wife: **This is your bill of divorce on the condition that you will give me two hundred dinars,** then **she is divorced and must give** two hundred dinars in order to fulfill the condition of the bill of divorce.

״עַל מְנָת שֶׁתִּתְּנִי לִי מִיכָּן וְעַד שְׁלֹשִׁים יוֹם״, אִם נָתְנָה לוֹ בְּתוֹךְ שְׁלֹשִׁים יוֹם – מְגוֹרֶשֶׁת, וְאִם לָאו – אֵינָהּ מְגוֹרֶשֶׁת.

If a husband says to his wife: This is your bill of divorce **on the condition that you will give me** money **from now**[H] **until** the conclusion of **thirty days, if she gives** the money **to him within thirty days she is divorced. And if not she is not divorced.**

אָמַר רַבָּן שִׁמְעוֹן בֶּן גַּמְלִיאֵל: מַעֲשֶׂה בְּצַיְדָּן, בְּאֶחָד שֶׁאָמַר לְאִשְׁתּוֹ ״הֲרֵי זֶה גִּיטֵּךְ עַל מְנָת שֶׁתִּתְּנִי לִי אִיצְטְלִיתִי״ וְאָבְדָה אִיצְטְלִיתוֹ, וְאָמְרוּ חֲכָמִים: תִּתֵּן לוֹ אֶת דָּמֶיהָ.

Rabban Shimon ben Gamliel said: There was **an incident in** the city of **Tzaidan involving one who said to his wife: This is your bill of divorce on the condition that you will give me my coat** [*itztaliti*],[L] **and she lost his coat,** so that she could not give it to him. **And the Rabbis said** that **she must give him the value** of the coat, and by doing so she fulfills the condition and is divorced.

HALAKHA

Wherever…there is uncertainty whether she is divorced or not she is divorced – כׇּל מָקוֹם...מְגוֹרֶשֶׁת וְאֵינָהּ מְגוֹרֶשֶׁת: If it is uncertain whether or not a wife was divorced, her husband is required to provide her with sustenance during his lifetime until she is fully divorced. She is not sustained from his property after his death, as in a case of uncertainty the heirs are not required to pay (Rambam *Sefer Nashim, Hilkhot Ishut* 18:25; *Shulḥan Arukh, Even HaEzer* 93:2).

On the condition that you will give me from now, etc. – עַל מְנָת שֶׁתִּתְּנִי לִי מִכָּאן וכו׳: If a husband said to his wife: This is your bill of divorce on the condition that you will give me two hundred dinars from now until the conclusion of thirty days, and she paid him within thirty days, then she is divorced. But if she did not pay within this time frame she is not divorced (Rambam *Sefer Nashim, Hilkhot Geirushin* 8:21).

גמ׳ מַאי ״וְתִתֵּן״? רַב הוּנָא אָמַר: וְהִיא תִּתֵּן, רַב יְהוּדָה אָמַר: לִכְשֶׁתִּתֵּן.

GEMARA The mishna teaches: She is divorced and must give the money. The Gemara asks: **What is** the meaning of: **And must give? Rav Huna says:** She is divorced immediately, once the bill of divorce has been given over to her, **and she must give**[H] him the money subsequently in order to fulfill the condition. The bill of divorce takes effect retroactively, from the time when it was given, after she gives the money. **Rav Yehuda says:** She is divorced only **when she gives** him this sum.

מַאי בֵּינַיְיהוּ? אִיכָּא בֵּינַיְיהוּ, שֶׁנִּתְקָרַע הַגֵּט אוֹ שֶׁאָבַד; רַב הוּנָא אָמַר וְהִיא תִּתֵּן – אֵינָהּ צְרִיכָה הֵימֶנּוּ גֵּט שֵׁנִי, רַב יְהוּדָה אָמַר לִכְשֶׁתִּתֵּן – צְרִיכָה הֵימֶנּוּ גֵּט שֵׁנִי.

The Gemara asks: **What is** the difference **between** the opinion of Rav Huna and the opinion of Rav Yehuda? The Gemara answers: **There is** a difference **between them if the bill of divorce was torn or lost** after she received it but before she gave the money. According to the opinion of **Rav Huna,** who **says: And she must give** but the bill of divorce takes effect retroactively, if it was torn or lost then **she does not require a second bill of divorce from him.** By contrast, **Rav Yehuda says** that the divorce takes effect only **when she gives** him the sum. Therefore, if the document is torn or lost **she requires a second bill of divorce from him,** as in his opinion it is not yet a valid bill of divorce until she has given him the money.

וּתְנַן נַמִי גַּבֵּי קִידּוּשִׁין כִּי הַאי גַּוְונָא, דִּתְנַן: הָאוֹמֵר לְאִשָּׁה ״הֲרֵי אַתְּ מְקוּדֶּשֶׁת לִי עַל מְנָת שֶׁאֶתֵּן לָךְ מָאתַיִם זוּז״ – הֲרֵי הִיא מְקוּדֶּשֶׁת, וְיִתֵּן; וְאִיתְּמַר: מַאי ״וְיִתֵּן״? רַב הוּנָא אָמַר: וְהוּא יִתֵּן, רַב יְהוּדָה אָמַר: לִכְשֶׁיִּתֵּן.

The Gemara comments: **And it was also taught** in the mishna **with regard to betrothal** that Rav Huna and Rav Yehuda also disagreed about **a case like this, as we learned** in a mishna (*Kiddushin* 60a): **If one says to a woman: You are hereby betrothed to me on the condition**[H] **that I will give you two hundred dinars,** then **she is betrothed, and he must give** the sum. **And it was stated** that Rav Huna and Rav Yehuda disagreed with regard to **what** is the meaning of: **And he must give. Rav Huna says: And he must give,** meaning that she is betrothed immediately, provided that the husband gives what he promised. **Rav Yehuda says:** She is betrothed only **when he gives.**

מַאי בֵּינַיְיהוּ? אִיכָּא בֵּינַיְיהוּ, שֶׁפָּשְׁטָה יָדָהּ וְקִיבְּלָה קִידּוּשִׁין מֵאַחֵר, רַב הוּנָא אָמַר וְהוּא יִתֵּן, תְּנָאָה בְּעָלְמָא הוּא, מְקַיֵּים תְּנָאֵיהּ וְאָזֵיל; רַב יְהוּדָה אָמַר לִכְשֶׁיִּתֵּן, לְכִי יָהֵיב לָהּ הוּא דְּהָווּ קִידּוּשִׁין, הַשְׁתָּא לָא הָווּ קִידּוּשִׁין.

The Gemara asks: **What is** the difference **between them?** The Gemara answers: **There is** a difference **between them** in a case **where she extended her hand and received**[N] **betrothal from another** man before the first man gave her the money that he promised. **Rav Huna says: And he must give,** meaning that **it is merely a condition** that he accepted upon himself. **He fulfills his condition and moves on,** and the woman is betrothed to him immediately. Therefore, her betrothal to the second man has no validity. **Rav Yehuda says: When he gives,** which means that **when he gives her** the money **it will be** a valid **betrothal.** But **now it is not** a valid **betrothal** and therefore the betrothal from the second man takes effect.

וּצְרִיכָא; דְּאִי אַשְׁמְעִינַן גַּבֵּי קִידּוּשִׁין, בְּהָא קָאָמַר רַב הוּנָא וְהוּא יִתֵּן, מִשּׁוּם דִּלְקָרוֹבַהּ קָאָתֵי, אֲבָל גַּבֵּי גֵּירוּשִׁין דִּלְרַחוֹקַהּ קָאָתֵי – אֵימָא מוֹדֶה לֵיהּ לְרַב יְהוּדָה;

The Gemara comments: **And** it is **necessary** to mention this dispute in both the case of divorce and the case of betrothal. **As if it would have taught us** their opinions only **with regard to betrothal,** then one may think that it is specifically **with regard to this** case that **Rav Huna says: And he should give, because he comes to draw her close** in marriage. Consequently, he does this willingly, and therefore there is an assumption that his intention was for the betrothal to take effect immediately. **But with regard to divorce, where he comes to distance her,** there is an assumption that he does so unwillingly, so that he makes the divorce dependent on a condition in order to delay the matter. Therefore, **say** that Rav Huna **concedes to Rav Yehuda** that the divorce does not take effect until the condition has been fulfilled.

וְאִי אַשְׁמְעִינַן גַּבֵּי גֵּירוּשִׁין, בְּהָא קָאָמַר רַב הוּנָא וְהִיא תִּתֵּן, מִשּׁוּם דְּלָא כְּסִיף לְמִיתְבְּעָהּ, אֲבָל גַּבֵּי קִידּוּשִׁין דִּכְסִיפָא לְמִיתְבְּעֵיהּ – אֵימָא מוֹדֵי לֵיהּ לְרַב יְהוּדָה;

And if it would have taught us their opinions only **with regard to divorce,** then one may think that it is specifically **with regard to this** case that **Rav Huna says: And she must give, because he is not embarrassed to demand**[N] the money **from her** afterward to fulfill the condition of the bill of divorce, and his intent was to divorce her immediately. **But with regard to betrothal, where she is embarrassed to demand** the money that he promised would come **from him,** she may not agree to be betrothed to him until she actually receives the money. Therefore, you might **say** that Rav Huna **concedes to Rav Yehuda** that the betrothal is valid only once he gives her the money.

HALAKHA

And she must give, etc. – וְהִיא תִּתֵּן וכו׳: If a husband gave his wife a conditional bill of divorce, employing the language: On the condition, once the condition is fulfilled she is retroactively divorced from the time that the bill of divorce reached her hand. Even if the document was torn or lost between the time when she received it and the time when the condition was fulfilled it is still valid, in accordance with the opinion of Rav Huna. Other authorities rule that even if he employs the language: On the condition, the bill of divorce is valid only if he also said: From now (Rambam *Sefer Nashim, Hilkhot Geirushin* 8:1; *Shulḥan Arukh, Even HaEzer* 143:2 and *Beit Shmuel* there).

You are hereby betrothed to me on the condition, etc. – הֲרֵי אַתְּ מְקוּדֶּשֶׁת לִי עַל מְנָת וכו׳: If one gave a woman one *peruta* and said to her: You are betrothed to me with this on the condition that I will do such and such a thing for you, e.g., that I will give you one hundred dinars, the betrothal retroactively takes effect from the time he gave her the *peruta*, once he has fulfilled the condition, in accordance with the opinion of Rav Huna. Therefore, if she accepted a betrothal from another man before the condition was fulfilled, then once the condition is fulfilled the betrothal to the second is disregarded (Rambam *Sefer Nashim, Hilkhot Ishut* 6:17–18; *Shulḥan Arukh, Even HaEzer* 38:6).

NOTES

She extended her hand and received, etc. – פָּשְׁטָה יָדָהּ וְקִיבְּלָה וכו׳: Many early commentaries hold that also with regard to the *halakha* of a divorced woman, there is a difference between Rav Huna and Rav Yehuda. If she extended her hand and received betrothal from another man, then according to Rav Huna, after she gives the money this betrothal is valid. According to Rav Yehuda, the bill of divorce is never valid (*Tosafot*; Ritva; Rashba; Rabbeinu Crescas Vidal). *Tosefot HaRosh* disagrees and explains that Rav Yehuda is adding a stringency. Therefore, he would also agree that even if she accepted betrothal from another man she may not remain married to the first husband until the other man gives her a bill of divorce.

Because he is not embarrassed to demand – דְּלָא כְּסִיף לְמִיתְבְּעָהּ: This is not referring to a demand made in court, as the wife is not liable to pay, and she has the choice as to whether or not to fulfill the condition. The same holds true with regard to betrothal, since the husband is not liable to pay. It means that if the husband wants the money, he will not be embarrassed to demand that his wife fulfill the condition. Therefore, his intent is that the divorce will be valid immediately, since he is not concerned that he will not receive the money in the future.

By contrast, with regard to betrothal, since the wife does not wish to cause a fight with her husband, she will not rely on being able to demand the money later. On account of this she may not want the betrothal to take effect until she actually receives the money (Rabbeinu Crescas Vidal).

וְאִי אַשְׁמְעִינַן גַּבֵּי קִידּוּשִׁין, בְּהָא קָאָמַר רַב יְהוּדָה לִכְשֶׁיִּתֵּן, מִשּׁוּם דִּכְסִיפָא לְמִיתְבְּעֵיהּ, אֲבָל גַּבֵּי גֵּירוּשִׁין דְּלָא כָּסֵיף לְמִיתְבְּעָהּ – אֵימָא מוֹדֶה לֵיהּ לְרַב הוּנָא;

And furthermore, **if it would have taught us** their opinions only **with regard to betrothal,** then one may think that it is specifically **with regard to this** case **that Rav Yehuda says** that the betrothal is valid only **when he gives** her the money, **because she is embarrassed to demand it from him** if he does not give it to her. Therefore, her intention is that she will be betrothed only once the condition is fulfilled. **But with regard to divorce, where** the husband **is not embarrassed to demand** the money **from her,** you might **say that** Rav Yehuda **concedes to Rav Huna** that the bill of divorce takes effect immediately.

וְאִי אַשְׁמְעִינַן גַּבֵּי גֵּירוּשִׁין, בְּהָא קָאָמַר רַב יְהוּדָה לִכְשֶׁתִּתֵּן, מִשּׁוּם דִּלְרַחוּקָהּ קָאָתֵי, אֲבָל גַּבֵּי קִידּוּשִׁין דִּלְקָרוּבָהּ קָאָתֵי – אֵימָא מוֹדֶה לֵיהּ לְרַב הוּנָא, צְרִיכָא.

And furthermore, **if it would have taught us** only **with regard to** the case of **divorce,** then one may think that it is specifically **with regard to this** case **that Rav Yehuda says** that the divorce is valid only **when she gives** him the money, **because** the husband **comes to distance her. But with regard to betrothal, where he comes to draw her close,** you might **say** that Rav Yehuda **concedes to Rav Huna.** Therefore, it is **necessary** to state this dispute in both cases.

מֵיתִיבִי: ״הֲרֵי זֶה גִּיטֵּךְ עַל מְנָת שֶׁתִּתְּנִי לִי מָאתַיִם זוּז״, אַף עַל פִּי שֶׁנִּקְרַע הַגֵּט אוֹ שֶׁנֶּאֱבַד – מְגוֹרֶשֶׁת, וּלְאַחֵר לֹא תִּנָּשֵׂא עַד שֶׁתִּתֵּן;

The Gemara raises an objection based on what was taught in a *baraita* (*Tosefta* 7:5): If one says to a woman: **This is your bill of divorce on the condition that you will give me two hundred dinars,** then **even though the bill of divorce was torn or lost she is divorced. And she may not marry another man**[NH] **until she gives** her first husband the money.

וְעוֹד תַּנְיָא: ״הֲרֵי זֶה גִּיטֵּךְ עַל מְנָת שֶׁתִּתְּנִי לִי מָאתַיִם זוּז״ וּמֵת, נָתְנָה – אֵינָהּ זְקוּקָה לְיָבָם, לֹא נָתְנָה – זְקוּקָה לְיָבָם. רַבָּן שִׁמְעוֹן בֶּן גַּמְלִיאֵל אוֹמֵר: נוֹתֶנֶת לְאָבִיו אוֹ לְאָחִיו אוֹ לְאֶחָד מִן הַקְּרוֹבִים;

And it is taught further in that same *baraita*: If one says to his wife: **This is your bill of divorce on the condition that you will give two hundred dinars to me, and** the husband **died**[H] childless, if she had already **given** him the money, then **she is not bound** with a levirate bond **to the** *yavam* because she was already divorced from her husband through the bill of divorce that he gave her. But if **she had not given** him the money, then **she is bound** with a levirate bond **to the** *yavam* because the bill of divorce did not take effect and she is a widow. **Rabban Shimon ben Gamliel says: She should give** the money **to** her late husband's **father, or to his brother, or to one of the relatives** who inherit from him, and by doing so she fulfills the condition and is released from the levirate bond.

עַד כָּאן לָא פְּלִיגִי, אֶלָּא דְּמָר סָבַר: לִי – וְלֹא לְיוֹרְשַׁי, וּמָר סָבַר: לִי – וַאֲפִילּוּ לְיוֹרְשַׁי, וְכוּלֵּי עָלְמָא מִיהָא תְּנָאָה הָוֵי, תְּיוּבְתָּא דְּרַב יְהוּדָה!

The Gemara notes: The first *tanna* and Rabban Shimon ben Gamliel **disagree only with regard to** the meaning of the condition. **One Sage,** the first *tanna,* **holds** that when the husband said: On the condition that she will give **to me,** he meant: To me specifically **and not to my heirs.** Consequently, she cannot fulfill the condition by giving the money to his heirs. **And one Sage,** Rabban Shimon ben Gamliel, **holds** that when the husband said that she will give the money **to me,** he meant **and even to my heirs. But in any event, everyone** agrees that this **is** a valid **condition,** yet its fulfillment does not change the date that the bill of divorce takes effect. This is **a conclusive refutation** of the opinion **of Rav Yehuda,** who said that the bill of divorce takes effect only when she gives.

NOTES

And she may not marry another man – וּלְאַחֵר לֹא תִּנָּשֵׂא: The reason for this is that if she does not give him the money, the bill of divorce will not take effect (Rashi). According to the Ritva, the concern is that one of them may die before the condition has been fulfilled.

Rabbeinu Crescas Vidal writes in the name of the Ra'ah that this principle applies with regard to any condition that requires an action. Even if the husband employed the language: On the condition, which is valid immediately according to *halakha*, the condition should nevertheless be fulfilled as soon as possible.

With regard to any condition that is referring to refraining from an action, e.g., when the husband gives a bill of divorce contingent upon the woman not drinking wine for thirty days, she is not required to wait until the end of this thirty-day period, but may remarry immediately. In this case there is no concern that the condition will not be fulfilled. The Rambam writes that even with regard to a condition that requires an action, provided it is dependent solely on her, she can remarry even before the condition is fulfilled. Most other authorities disagree with this.

HALAKHA

And she may not marry another man – וּלְאַחֵר לֹא תִּנָּשֵׂא: If a husband gave his wife a conditional bill of divorce, she may not remarry until the condition has been fulfilled. If she did remarry, the second husband must separate from her until the condition has been fulfilled. In a case where she had the ability to fulfill the condition, or it was a condition that required her to refrain from a certain action for an amount of time, she is permitted to remarry immediately. This is in accordance with the opinion stated in the *baraita* (Ramah; Ramban; Rashba; Ran). The Rambam permits her to remarry in any case, regardless of the nature of the condition (Rambam *Sefer Nashim, Hilkhot Geirushin* 8:1; *Shulḥan Arukh, Even HaEzer* 143:2).

On the condition that you will give…to me, and the husband died, etc. – עַל מְנָת שֶׁתִּתְּנִי לִי...וּמֵת וכו׳: If a man gives his wife a bill of divorce conditional upon her giving him two hundred dinars within thirty days, and he died during that time frame, then, since she was unable to fulfill the condition, even if she gave the money to his heirs, the bill of divorce is invalid (Rambam *Sefer Nashim, Hilkhot Geirushin* 8:21–22; *Tur, Even HaEzer* 143; *Shulḥan Arukh, Even HaEzer* 143:3).

אָמַר לָךְ רַב יְהוּדָה: הָא מַנִּי? רַבִּי הִיא, דְּאָמַר רַב הוּנָא אָמַר רַבִּי: כׇּל הָאוֹמֵר ״עַל מְנָת״ כְּאוֹמֵר ״מֵעַכְשָׁיו״ דָּמֵי, וּפְלִיגִי רַבָּנַן עֲלֵיהּ, וַאֲנָא דַּאֲמַרִי – כְּרַבָּנַן.

The Gemara answers: **Rav Yehuda** could have **said to you:** In accordance with **whose** opinion **is this** *baraita*? **It is** the opinion of **Rabbi** Yehuda HaNasi. **As Rav Huna says that Rabbi** Yehuda HaNasi **says: Anyone who states** a condition employing the language: **On the condition,** is **like** one who **states:** The agreement will take effect retroactively **from now,** even though the condition is fulfilled only later on. **And the Rabbis disagree with him. And I say** my ruling **in accordance with** the opinion of **the Rabbis.**

וְאָמַר רַבִּי זֵירָא: כִּי הֲוֵינַן בְּבָבֶל, אָמְרִינַן, הָא דְּאָמַר רַב הוּנָא אָמַר רַבִּי כׇּל הָאוֹמֵר ״עַל מְנָת״ כְּאוֹמֵר ״מֵעַכְשָׁיו״ דָּמֵי – פְּלִיגִי רַבָּנַן עֲלֵיהּ. כִּי סְלִיקִי, אַשְׁכַּחְתֵּיהּ לְרַבִּי אַסִּי דְּיָתֵיב וְקָאָמַר מִשְּׁמֵיהּ דְּרַבִּי יוֹחָנָן: הַכֹּל מוֹדִים בְּאוֹמֵר ״עַל מְנָת״ כְּאוֹמֵר ״מֵעַכְשָׁיו״ דָּמֵי, לֹא נֶחְלְקוּ אֶלָּא בְּ״מֵהַיּוֹם וּלְאַחַר מִיתָה״.

And Rabbi Zeira says: When we were in Babylonia we would **say** with regard to **this** following statement **that Rav Huna says** that **Rabbi** Yehuda HaNasi **says: Anyone who states** a condition employing the language: **On the condition,** is **like** one who **states:** The agreement will take effect retroactively **from now,**[H] even though the condition is fulfilled only later on; we would say that **the Rabbis disagree with him. When I ascended** to Eretz Yisrael **I found Rabbi Asi, who was sitting and saying in the name of Rabbi Yoḥanan: Everyone concedes that with regard to** anyone who **states** a condition employing the language: **On the condition,** he is **like** one who **states:** The agreement will take effect retroactively **from now;** and the Rabbis **disagreed** with Rabbi Yehuda HaNasi **only in** a case where the bill of divorce included the condition: **From today and after** my **death.**

HALAKHA

Anyone who states, on the condition, is like one who states, the agreement will take effect retroactively from now – כׇּל הָאוֹמֵר עַל מְנָת כְּאוֹמֵר מֵעַכְשָׁיו דָּמֵי: One who makes a condition employing the language: On the condition, is considered as if he had stated explicitly that it should take effect retroactively from that moment once the condition is fulfilled. This is in accordance with the statements of Rabbi Yehuda HaNasi and Rav Huna (Rambam *Sefer Nashim, Hilkhot Geirushin* 9:19 and *Sefer Kinyan, Hilkhot Zekhiya UMattana* 3:8; *Shulḥan Arukh, Even HaEzer* 38:6 and *Ḥoshen Mishpat* 197:7).

Perek **VII**
Daf **74** Amud **b**

וְהָתַנְיָא: ״מֵהַיּוֹם וּלְאַחַר מִיתָה״ – גֵּט וְאֵינוֹ גֵּט, דִּבְרֵי חֲכָמִים, רַבִּי אוֹמֵר: כָּזֶה גֵּט.

And it is taught in a *baraita*: If a husband says to his wife: This is your bill of divorce **from today and after** my **death,** then this is both a valid **bill of divorce and not** a valid **bill of divorce.** This is **the statement of the Rabbis. Rabbi** Yehuda HaNasi disagrees and **says:** A case **like this** is a valid **bill of divorce** without any uncertainty. This teaches that Rabbi Yehuda HaNasi and the Rabbis disagree only in this case, but everyone agrees that when he employed the language: On the condition, it is as though he stipulated: From now.

וּלְרַב יְהוּדָה דַּאֲמַר: בְּ״עַל מְנָת״ פְּלִיגִי, אַדְּמִיפַּלְגִי בְּ״מֵהַיּוֹם וּלְאַחַר מִיתָה״, לִיפַלְגֵי בְּ״עַל מְנָת״! לְהוֹדִיעֲךָ כֹּחוֹ דְּרַבִּי.

The Gemara asks: **And according to Rav Yehuda, who said** that Rabbi Yehuda HaNasi and the Rabbis **disagree about** one who employs the language: **On the condition, rather than disagreeing with regard to** the case where the husband said: **From today and after** my **death, let them disagree with regard to** the case where the husband said: **On the condition.** The Gemara answers that the *baraita* uses this case **to inform you about the far-reaching nature** of the opinion **of Rabbi** Yehuda HaNasi, who is certain that the bill of divorce is valid.

וְלִיפַלְגוּ בְּ״עַל מְנָת״ וּלְהוֹדִיעֲךָ כֹּחָן דְּרַבָּנַן! כֹּחַ דְּהֶיתֵּירָא עָדִיף לֵיהּ.

The Gemara challenges: **And let them disagree about: On the condition, to convey to you the far-reaching nature** of the opinion **of the Rabbis,** who do not hold that the phrase: On the condition, is considered to be like the phrase: From now, as this ruling is a more general matter. The Gemara answers: It is **preferable** to emphasize **the power of leniency,**[N] and therefore it is preferable to teach the degree to which Rabbi Yehuda HaNasi is lenient.

NOTES

It is preferable to emphasize the power of leniency – כֹּחַ דְּהֶיתֵּירָא עָדִיף לֵיהּ: Rashi explains in tractate *Beitza* (2b) that ruling stringently does not require such great knowledge, as in cases of uncertainty one would rule stringently. One who rules leniently, by contrast, must do so based on his reasoning, and only once the matter is clear to him.

״עַל מְנָת שֶׁתִּתְּנִי לִי מִכָּאן וְעַד שְׁלֹשִׁים יוֹם״ וכו׳. פְּשִׁיטָא! מַהוּ דְּתֵימָא: קְפֵידֵיהּ לָאו קְפֵידָא וּלְזָרְזָהּ קָאָתֵי, קָא מַשְׁמַע לַן.

§ The mishna teaches: If a husband said to his wife: This is your bill of divorce **on the condition that you will give me** money **from now until** the conclusion of **thirty days,** if she gives the money to him within thirty days she is divorced, and if not she is not divorced. The Gemara asks: **Isn't** that **obvious,** since everything depends on whether or not the condition was fulfilled? The Gemara answers: No, the *halakha* that the divorce does not take effect unless she gives the money by that time needs to be said, **lest you say** that **the concern** of the husband that his wife will give him the money within a specific time frame **is not** a real **concern,** and he **comes** only **to galvanize her.** Although he wishes to receive this money as soon as possible, in truth he does not care if he receives it later. Therefore, **it teaches us** that his statement is a valid condition, and if she does not fulfill it then it is not a valid bill of divorce.

״אָמַר רַבָּן שִׁמְעוֹן בֶּן גַּמְלִיאֵל: מַעֲשֶׂה בְּצַיְדָן״ כו׳. מַאי תְּנָא דְּקָתָנֵי מַעֲשֶׂה?

§ The mishna teaches that **Rabban Shimon ben Gamliel said:** There was **an incident in** the city of **Tzaidan** involving one who said to his wife: This is your bill of divorce on the condition that you will give me my coat, and she lost his coat. And the Rabbis said that she should give him the value of that coat, and by doing so she fulfills the condition and is divorced. The Gemara asks: **What** did Rabban Shimon ben Gamliel **teach** before, such **that he** now **teaches** and cites **an incident** which is similar to it? This incident does not seem to be referring to what was stated immediately before in the mishna.

חַסּוּרֵי מִיחַסְּרָא וְהָכִי קָתָנֵי: אִם אָמַר לָהּ ״עַל מְנָת שֶׁתִּתְּנִי לִי אִיצְטְלִיתִי״ וְאָבְדָה אִיצְטְלִיתוֹ, אִיצְטְלִיתִי דַּוְקָא קָאָמַר לָהּ. רַבָּן שִׁמְעוֹן בֶּן גַּמְלִיאֵל אוֹמֵר: תִּתֵּן לוֹ אֶת דָּמֶיהָ; וְאָמַר רַבָּן שִׁמְעוֹן בֶּן גַּמְלִיאֵל: מַעֲשֶׂה נַמִי בְּצַיְדָן, בְּאֶחָד שֶׁאָמַר לְאִשְׁתּוֹ ״הֲרֵי זֶה גִּיטֵּךְ עַל מְנָת שֶׁתִּתְּנִי לִי אִצְטְלִיתִי״ וְאָבְדָה אִצְטְלִיתוֹ, וְאָמְרוּ חֲכָמִים: תִּתֵּן לוֹ אֶת דָּמֶיהָ.

The Gemara answers: The mishna **is incomplete and this is what it is teaching: If** the husband **said to** his wife: This is your bill of divorce **on the condition that you will give me my coat,**[H] **and she lost his coat,** then since **he specifically stated to her:** Give me **my coat,** she cannot give him its value instead. And since she has lost the coat, the bill of divorce is not valid; this is the opinion of the Rabbis. **Rabban Shimon ben Gamliel says:** In such a case **she can give him its value. And Rabban Shimon ben Gamliel said** in support of his statement: There was **an incident also in** the city **of Tzaidan involving one who said to his wife: This is your bill of divorce on the condition that you will give me my coat, and she lost his coat. And the Rabbis said** that **she should give him its value.**

בְּעָא מִינֵּיהּ רַבִּי אַסִּי מֵרַבִּי יוֹחָנָן: ״הֲרֵי זֶה גִּיטֵּךְ עַל מְנָת שֶׁתִּתְּנִי לִי מָאתַיִם זוּז״, וְחָזַר וְאָמַר לָהּ ״מְחוּלִים לָךְ״, מַהוּ?

Rabbi Asi raised a dilemma before Rabbi Yoḥanan: If a man says to his wife: **This is your bill of divorce on the condition that you will give me two hundred dinars, and** afterward **he returned and said to her: It is waived for you,**[HN] then **what is the** *halakha*?

תִּיבָּעֵי לְרַבָּנַן, תִּיבָּעֵי לְרַבָּן שִׁמְעוֹן בֶּן גַּמְלִיאֵל;

He explained his question in detail: **Let the dilemma be raised according to** the opinion of **the Rabbis,** and **let the dilemma be raised according to** the opinion of **Rabban Shimon ben Gamliel.**

HALAKHA

On the condition that you will give me my coat, etc. – עַל מְנָת שֶׁתִּתְּנִי לִי אִיצְטְלִיתִי וכו׳: If a husband gave his wife a bill of divorce and said to her: This is your bill of divorce on the condition that you will give me a specific utensil or garment, and she lost that item or it was destroyed, she cannot give him its value instead; in accordance with the opinion of the first *tanna* the bill of divorce is not valid. The Rosh holds that if the husband then agrees to accept the value of the item in lieu of it, the bill of divorce is valid. According to others the bill of divorce is valid only if the husband nullifies the condition and says to his wife: This is your unconditional bill of divorce (Rambam *Sefer Nashim, Hilkhot Geirushin* 8:23; *Shulḥan Arukh, Even HaEzer* 143:6).

It is waived for you – מְחוּלִים לָךְ: If a husband said to his wife: This is your bill of divorce on the condition that you give me two hundred dinars within thirty days, and subsequently, within the thirty days, he said to her: I waive payment of the money for you, she is not divorced because the condition was not fulfilled, in accordance with the opinion of Rabbi Yoḥanan. Some say that this applies even if he merely said to her: They are waived for you. The Rashba writes that if he said: This should be your unconditional bill of divorce, she is divorced (Rambam *Sefer Nashim, Hilkhot Geirushin* 8:21; *Shulḥan Arukh, Even HaEzer* 143:5 and *Beit Shmuel* there).

NOTES

And said to her: It is waived for you – וְאָמַר לָהּ מְחוּלִים לָךְ: When one forgives a debt he considers it as though he already received the payment; therefore, it is as if the condition were fulfilled. According to the opinion of Rabban Shimon ben Gamliel, the husband intends to receive something of value. Consequently, waiving the debt would perhaps not be sufficient, unless the husband receives something in exchange (see Rashi).

תִּיבָּעֵי לְרַבָּנַן: עַד כָּאן לָא קָאָמְרִי רַבָּנַן הָתָם – אֶלָּא דְּלָא אַחְלַהּ גַּבַּהּ, אֲבָל הָכָא – הָא קָאָמַר לַהּ "מְחוּלִים לָךְ". אוֹ דִּלְמָא אֲפִילּוּ רַבָּן שִׁמְעוֹן בֶּן גַּמְלִיאֵל לָא קָאָמַר אֶלָּא דְּקָא מְפַיְּיסָה לֵיהּ בְּדָמֵי, אֲבָל לְגַמְרֵי – לָא? אֲמַר לֵיהּ: אֵינָהּ מְגוֹרֶשֶׁת.

Let the dilemma be raised according to the opinion of **the Rabbis:** One can say that **only there do the Rabbis state** their opinion that she is not divorced if the condition is not fulfilled and she gives him his coat, because **he did not waive** his claim to it; **but here he says to her: It is waived for you,** so they are divorced. **Or perhaps** one can say that **even Rabban Shimon ben Gamliel states** that she can be divorced even if he does not receive the coat **only there, as she appeases him by** giving him **money,** i.e., the condition is considered to be fulfilled due to the fact that he received the value of the coat; **but** in a case where he waives the condition **entirely, no,** because he does not receive anything from her. Rabbi Yoḥanan **said to him** in response: **She is not divorced,**[N] because the condition has not been fulfilled.

אֵיתִיבֵיהּ: הָאוֹמֵר לַחֲבֵירוֹ "קוֹנָם שֶׁאַתָּה נֶהֱנֶה לִי אִם אִי אַתָּה נוֹתֵן לִבְנִי כּוֹר אֶחָד שֶׁל חִטִּין וּשְׁתֵּי חָבִיּוֹת שֶׁל יַיִן", רַבִּי מֵאִיר אוֹמֵר: אָסוּר עַד שֶׁיִּתֵּן, וַחֲכָמִים אוֹמְרִים: אַף זֶה יָכוֹל לְהַתִּיר אֶת נִדְרוֹ שֶׁלֹּא עַל פִּי חָכָם, וְאוֹמֵר: הֲרֵינִי כְּאִילּוּ הִתְקַבַּלְתִּי!

He raised an objection to his opinion from a mishna (*Nedarim* 63b): In the case of **one who says to another: Benefiting from me is** ***konam***[B] **for you,** meaning it is prohibited for you to derive benefit from me, **if you do not give my son one** ***kor***[B] **of wheat and two barrels of wine** as a wedding gift, **Rabbi Meir says:** It is **prohibited** for this other person to benefit from the person who took the vow **until he gives** his son the gift. **And the Rabbis say: Even this** individual who took the vow **can dissolve his vow without** the **consent of a halakhic authority, and** he does this by **saying: I hereby** consider it **as though I have received** the gift from you.[H] Based on this mishna, it would seem that if the husband forgives his wife the money that she owes him, it should be considered as if he received it, and the bill of divorce should be valid.

הָכִי הַשְׁתָּא?! הָתָם לְצַעוּרַהּ קָא מְכַוֵּין וְלָא צַיְּירַהּ, הָכָא מִשּׁוּם הַרְוָוחָה הוּא וְהָא לָא אִיצְטְרִיךְ!

The Gemara rejects this: **How can these cases be compared? There,** in the case of a bill of divorce, **he intends to vex her, and** until she pays him **he did not vex her.** If he forgives this condition, his initial intention has not been fulfilled. **Here,** in the case of the vow, the reason the father took the vow is **for the sake of profit;** he wants his son to receive a valuable gift, **but** subsequently the one who took the vow decides that **it was not necessary.**[H] Therefore, he can waive his claim.

הַהוּא גַּבְרָא דַּאֲמַר לֵיהּ לַאֲרִיסֵיהּ: כּוּלֵּי עָלְמָא דָּלוּ תְּלָת דַּלְוָותָא וְאָכְלִי רִיבְעָא, אַתְּ דְּלֵי אַרְבְּעָה וֶאֱכוֹל תִּילְתָּא. לְסוֹף אֲתָא מִיטְרָא.

The Gemara relates an incident of **a certain man who said to his sharecropper: Everyone waters** the field **three times**[B] during the season, **and they consume,** i.e., receive as payment, **one quarter** of the crops from the field. Will **you water four times and consume** as your payment **one-third** of the produce? **Ultimately, rain came** when the sharecropper would have needed to water a fourth time, and so he did not need to water the field a fourth time. The question was presented to the Sages: Is the sharecropper still entitled to receive one-third of the produce since he was prepared to water the field four times, although ultimately it was not necessary to do so?

אֲמַר רַב יוֹסֵף: הָא לָא דְּלָה. רַבָּה אָמַר: הָא לָא אִיצְטְרִיכָא.

Rav Yosef said: But he did not water the field a fourth time, so the condition was not fulfilled. Consequently, he deserves the same as the other sharecroppers, and receives only one quarter of the produce. **Rabba said: But it was not necessary** to water the field the fourth time because the rain fell to the benefit of the sharecropper, and therefore he should receive one-third of the produce.

לֵימָא, רַב יוֹסֵף דַּאֲמַר כְּרַבָּנַן, וְרַבָּה דַּאֲמַר כְּרַבָּן שִׁמְעוֹן בֶּן גַּמְלִיאֵל?

The Gemara asks: **Shall we say that Rav Yosef said** his ruling **in accordance** with the opinion of **the Rabbis,** who require that the condition of the bill of divorce be fulfilled, **and that Rabba said** his ruling **in accordance with** the opinion of **Rabban Shimon ben Gamliel,** that it is not the fulfillment of the specifics of the condition that matter but the fulfillment of the intent of the condition?

וְתִסְבְּרָא? וְהָא קַיְימָא לַן הִילְכְתָא כְּווֹתֵיהּ דְּרַבָּה, וּבְהָא אֵין הֲלָכָה כְּרַבָּן שִׁמְעוֹן בֶּן גַּמְלִיאֵל!

The Gemara asks: **And** how can **you understand** it in this way? **But don't we maintain** that in all of their disputes **the** ***halakha*** is **in accordance with** the opinion **of Rabba** when he disagrees with Rav Yosef? **And with regard to this** *halakha* we maintain that the ***halakha*** **is not in accordance with** the opinion of **Rabban Shimon ben Gamliel.** If so, this presents a contradiction between one *halakha* and another.

NOTES

Rabbi Yoḥanan said to him, she is not divorced – אֲמַר לֵיהּ אֵינָהּ מְגוֹרֶשֶׁת: According to the continuation of the Gemara, the essence of the dispute between the Rabbis and Rabban Shimon ben Gamliel is the intent of the husband when he makes this condition. According to the Rabbis, his goal is to vex his wife, while Rabban Shimon ben Gamliel holds that his intention is to receive benefit. Some explain that Rabbi Yoḥanan's answer is in accordance with the opinion of the Rabbis, which is ultimately the *halakha*. Since the husband intended to vex his wife, and in this case he did not vex her, she cannot fulfill the condition, even if he waives the debt. As Rabban Shimon ben Gamliel is of the opinion that the husband's intention was to receive benefit, if he waives his right to this benefit the condition is fulfilled (Ritva).

The Rashba holds that Rabbi Yoḥanan is answering in accordance with the opinion of both the Rabbis and Rabban Shimon ben Gamliel. He explains that although Rabban Shimon ben Gamliel holds that the primary reason for the husband's condition is to benefit, he also intends to vex his wife, and on account of this the condition is not canceled through waiving alone.

BACKGROUND

***Konam* – קוֹנָם:** A *konam* is a type of vow whose *halakhot* are explained at length in tractate *Nedarim*. The word *konam* is a term referring to an offering. When one vows using this word, in effect he renders something forbidden to himself as though it were an offering. One of the basic principles of a *konam* is that it cannot apply to an action or an abstract state but only to an item that can be consecrated.

***Kor* – כּוֹר:** A *kor* is a measure of volume equaling thirty *se'a*, which is approximately 250 ℓ according to the opinion of Rabbi Ḥayyim Na'e and 430 ℓ according to the opinion of the Ḥazon Ish.

Waters three times – דָּלוּ תְּלָת דַּלְוָותָא: This is referring to grain, whose main irrigation comes from rain and groundwater, as opposed to vegetables, which require constant watering. In addition, especially in the flatlands and arid climate of Babylonia, the crops were given extra irrigation in order to hasten the initial growth of the grain until it developed a branched root system that could sustain itself from the groundwater. As additional watering hastens the growth of the plants and increases the yield, it is worthwhile for a landowner to increase the percentage of the produce he gives to a tenant farmer for extra watering, since it will lead to a higher yield.

HALAKHA

I hereby consider it is as though I have received the gift from you – הֲרֵינִי כְּאִילּוּ הִתְקַבַּלְתִּי: If one individual says to another: If you do not give a specific item to my son then I vow that you may not derive benefit from me, he may annul his vow without the consent of a halakhic authority by saying to him: I consider it as though I received this item from you. The Rema writes that the father can say this only if the son is financially dependent on his father. If the son is financially independent, then he must make this statement himself (Rambam *Sefer Hafla'a, Hilkhot Nedarim* 8:14; *Shulḥan Arukh, Yoreh De'a* 232:20).

It was not necessary – הָא לָא אִיצְטְרִיךְ: If one makes a condition with his sharecropper that if he waters the field more than is ordinarily done then the sharecropper will receive more than the standard share, and rain came so that that sharecropper did not need to water the field, the landowner is required to give the sharecropper the agreed-upon amount, in accordance with the opinion of Rabba (Rambam *Sefer Mishpatim, Hilkhot Sekhirut* 9:6; *Shulḥan Arukh, Ḥoshen Mishpat* 334:3).

HALAKHA

Hillel the Elder instituted, etc. – הִתְקִין הִלֵּל הַזָּקֵן וכו׳: If one sold his house in a walled city, and the final day of redemption, at the conclusion of twelve months, arrives, but the purchaser cannot be found, the redeemer may deposit his money with the court, break down the door, and enter his house, in accordance with the ordinance of Hillel the Elder (Rambam *Sefer Zera'im*, *Hilkhot Shemitta VeYovel* 12:7).

LANGUAGE

Deposit [*ḥolesh*] – חוֹלֵשׁ: Literally, to throw or cast. A similar word appears in the phrase *metilin ḥalashin* in tractate *Shabbat* (148b), where it means drawing lots for offerings. Often, when casting lots, items such as stones or dice are thrown, and therefore the root has adopted the latter meaning as well.

אֶלָּא לְעוֹלָם כְּרַבָּנַן, רַב יוֹסֵף כְּרַבָּנַן, וְרַבָּה אָמַר לָךְ: אֲנָא דַּאֲמַרִי אֲפִילּוּ לְרַבָּנַן, עַד כָּאן לָא קָאָמְרִי רַבָּנַן הָתָם – אֶלָּא דִּלְצַעוּרַהּ קָא מִיכַּוֵּין, אֲבָל הָכָא מִשּׁוּם הַרְוָוחָה הוּא, וְהָא לָא אִיצְטְרִיךְ.

Rather, according to both opinions, this dispute is **actually in accordance with** the opinion of **the Rabbis. Rav Yosef** clearly rules **in accordance with the Rabbis. And Rabba** could have **said to you: I was saying** my statement **even according to** the opinion of **the Rabbis,** as **the Rabbis are saying there** that she is not divorced if she does not return the coat itself **only when** the husband **intends to vex her,** and if she does not need to give the coat itself she will not be vexed, as it is not difficult for her to give him its value. But **here,** in the case of watering the field, the reason the owner is making the condition **is** only **for the sake of** increasing his **profit, and it was not necessary** to actually water the field.

תְּנַן הָתָם: בָּרִאשׁוֹנָה הָיָה נִטְמָן יוֹם שְׁנֵים עָשָׂר חֹדֶשׁ, כְּדֵי שֶׁיְּהֵא חָלוּט לוֹ, הִתְקִין הִלֵּל הַזָּקֵן שֶׁיְּהֵא חוֹלֵשׁ אֶת מָעוֹתָיו לַלִּשְׁכָּה, וִיהֵא שׁוֹבֵר אֶת הַדֶּלֶת וְנִכְנָס, וְאֵימָתַי שֶׁיִּרְצֶה הַלָּה יָבוֹא וְיִטּוֹל אֶת מָעוֹתָיו.

§ With regard to the redemption of houses in walled cities, **we learned elsewhere** in a mishna (*Arakhin* 31b) that if a house was sold and not redeemed by its owners within twelve months it remains permanently in the possession of the purchaser. The Gemara describes this: **At first** the purchaser **would hide** for all of the final **day of the twelfth month so that** the house would be **confirmed** as **his** (see Leviticus 25:29–30). Because the purchaser was in hiding, the seller would be unable to redeem the house from him. **Hillel the Elder instituted**[H] an ordinance **whereby** the seller **may deposit [*ḥolesh*]**[L] his redemption **money in the** Temple treasury **chamber, and** then **he may break the door** of his house **and enter** and take possession. **And when that** purchaser **wishes, he should come and take his money** from the Temple treasury.

וְאָמַר רָבָא: מִתַּקָּנָתוֹ שֶׁל הִלֵּל נִשְׁמַע: ״הֲרֵי זֶה גִּיטֵּךְ עַל מְנָת שֶׁתִּתְּנִי לִי מָאתַיִם זוּז״, וְנָתְנָה לוֹ מִדַּעְתּוֹ – מְגוֹרֶשֶׁת, עַל כּוֹרְחוֹ – אֵינָהּ מְגוֹרֶשֶׁת;

And Rava says: From the ordinance of Hillel we learn that if one says to his wife: **This is your bill of divorce on the condition that you will give me two hundred dinars, and she gave him** the money **with his consent,** then she is **divorced.** If she gave it to him **against his will** then **she is not divorced.**

מִדְּאִיצְטְרִיךְ לֵיהּ לְהִלֵּל לְתַקּוּנֵי נְתִינָה בְּעַל כּוֹרְחֵיהּ דְּהָוְיָא לַהּ נְתִינָה,

How does Rava prove this? **From** the fact **that** it **was necessary for Hillel to institute** a unique ordinance in the case of houses in walled cities whereby **giving against the will** of the receiver **is** considered **giving.**

Perek **VII**
Daf **75** Amud **a**

NOTES

By inference that generally, etc. – מִכְּלָל דִּבְעָלְמָא וכו׳: Rashi explains that Hillel instituted his ordinance only with regard to monetary law, but not in the case of a bill of divorce, which involves a prohibition. Other early commentaries hold that Hillel instituted his ordinance specifically for redeeming a house in a walled city, and it does not even apply to other cases of monetary law.

HALAKHA

And she gave it to him…against his will – וְנָתְנָה לוֹ...בְּעַל כָּרְחוֹ: If one said to his wife: This is hereby your bill of divorce on the condition that you will give me two hundred dinars within thirty days, and she gave the money to him within this time period but without his consent, the bill of divorce is invalid. Nevertheless, if she subsequently remarried, her new husband need not divorce her. The *halakha* is in accordance with the second formulation of Rava's statement and Rav Pappa's objection with regard to what is done after the fact, although it follows Rav Pappa's opinion *ab initio* (Gra). According to the Rashba and the Rosh it is uncertain whether or not she is divorced, as it is not clear which formulation is accepted (*Beit Shmuel*). This principle applies only if she gave him the money against his will but in his presence. If she left it for him when he was not present, it is not valid (Rambam *Sefer Nashim*, *Hilkhot Geirushin* 8:21; *Shulḥan Arukh*, *Even HaEzer* 143:4 and *Beit Shmuel* there).

מִכְּלָל דִּבְעָלְמָא נְתִינָה בְּעַל כָּרְחֵיהּ לָא הָוְיָא נְתִינָה.

This proves **by inference that generally,**[N] **giving against** the recipient's **will is not** considered valid **giving,** as if it were, then Hillel would not have needed to institute this ordinance.

מַתְקִיף לַהּ רַב פַּפָּא, וְאִיתֵּימָא רַב שִׁימִי בַּר אַשִׁי: וְדִלְמָא כִּי אִצְטְרִיךְ לֵיהּ לְתַקּוּנֵי – שֶׁלֹּא בְּפָנָיו, אֲבָל בְּפָנָיו – בֵּין מִדַּעְתּוֹ בֵּין בְּעַל כָּרְחוֹ הָוְיָא נְתִינָה!

Rav Pappa objects to this, and some say it was **Rav Shimi bar Ashi** who raises this objection: **And perhaps when it was necessary** for Hillel **to institute** an ordinance allowing the seller to repay the money against the will of the purchaser it was specifically in a case **where** he gives the money **not in the presence** of the purchaser. **But** when he repays him **in his presence, whether** the recipient was **willing** or **whether** it was **against his will, it is** considered valid **giving.** Accordingly, one cannot apply Hillel's ordinance to the case of conditional bills of divorce.

וְאִיכָּא דְּאָמְרִי, אָמַר רָבָא: מִתַּקָּנָתוֹ שֶׁל הִלֵּל, ״הֲרֵי זֶה גִּיטֵּךְ עַל מְנָת שֶׁתִּתְּנִי לִי מָאתַיִם זוּז״, וְנָתְנָה לוֹ – בֵּין מִדַּעְתּוֹ וּבֵין בְּעַל כָּרְחוֹ הָוְיָא נְתִינָה; וְכִי אִיצְטְרִיךְ לֵיהּ לְהִלֵּל לְתַקּוּנֵי – שֶׁלֹּא בְּפָנָיו, אֲבָל בְּפָנָיו – בֵּין מִדַּעְתּוֹ בֵּין בְּעַל כָּרְחוֹ הָוְיָא נְתִינָה.

And there are those **who say** a different version of this discussion. **Rava says: From the ordinance of Hillel** it can be inferred that if one says to his wife: **This is your bill of divorce on the condition that you will give me two hundred dinars, and she gave it to him, whether** it was **with his consent or whether** it was **against his will,**[H] **it is** valid **giving. And** the case **where it was necessary for Hillel to institute** his ordinance was **when** the giving of the money **was not in his presence. But** if the repayment was **in his presence, whether** it was **with his consent** or **whether** it was **against his will, it is** considered valid **giving.**

מַתְקִיף לַהּ רַב פָּפָּא, וְאִיתֵּימָא רַב שִׁימִי בַּר אַשִׁי: וְדִלְמָא אֲפִילּוּ בְּפָנָיו נַמִי – מִדַּעְתּוֹ אִין, עַל כָּרְחוֹ לָא, וְהִלֵּל מַאי דְּאִיצְטְרִיךְ לֵיהּ תַּקִּין!

Rav Pappa objects to this, and some say it was **Rav Shimi bar Ashi** who raises this objection: **And perhaps even** in a case where she gives him the money **in his presence,** if she gives it **with his consent, yes,** it is valid. If she gives it **against his will, no,** it is not considered to be valid giving. **And Hillel** specifically **instituted what was necessary,** because in the case of a house in a walled city the purchaser would hide, and therefore that ordinance was necessary there.

אָמַר רַבָּה בַּר בַּר חָנָה אָמַר רַבִּי יוֹחָנָן: כָּל מָקוֹם שֶׁשָּׁנָה רַבָּן שִׁמְעוֹן בֶּן גַּמְלִיאֵל בְּמִשְׁנָתֵינוּ – הֲלָכָה כְּמוֹתוֹ, חוּץ מֵעָרֵב, וְצַיְדָּן,

§ **Rabba bar bar Ḥana says that Rabbi Yoḥanan says:** In **every place where Rabban Shimon ben Gamliel taught** a *halakha* **in our** body of **Mishna, the** *halakha* **is in accordance with** his opinion, even though it is cited as an individual opinion, **except** for three cases. With regard to the *halakha* of **a guarantor** (*Bava Batra* 173b), if the creditor stipulated that he can collect his debt from either the debtor or the guarantor, according to the Rabbis he can collect from the guarantor's property even if the debtor has available property. Rabban Shimon ben Gamliel holds that the creditor can collect the debt only from the debtor. **And** likewise the *halakha* is not like Rabban Shimon ben Gamliel with regard to the case mentioned here concerning the incident that occurred in **Tzaidan.**

וּרְאָיָה אַחֲרוֹנָה.

And similarly, the *halakha* is not in accordance with the opinion of Rabban Shimon ben Gamliel concerning the dispute with regard to **evidence** in the **final** disagreement (*Sanhedrin* 31a), where the Rabbis hold that if one claims that he has no evidence or witnesses, but subsequently brings evidence to court, the judges do not accept it. According to the opinion of Rabban Shimon ben Gamliel they can accept it.

תָּנוּ רַבָּנַן: "הֲרֵי זֶה גִּיטֵּיךְ וְהַנְּיָיר שֶׁלִּי" – אֵינָהּ מְגוֹרֶשֶׁת, "עַל מְנָת שֶׁתַּחֲזִירִי לִי אֶת הַנְּיָיר" – מְגוֹרֶשֶׁת.

§ **The Sages taught** in a *baraita*: If the husband said to his wife: **Behold this is your bill of divorce,** but **the paper** on which it is written **is** still **mine,**[H] then **she is not divorced,** as he must give her the actual bill of divorce in order for the divorce to take effect. Since the paper still belongs to him, it is as if he had given her only the writing. But if he said to her: Behold this is your bill of divorce **on the condition that you return the paper to me,** then **she is divorced.** The bill of divorce belongs entirely to her, and the returning of the paper is only a stipulation that must be fulfilled later.

מַאי שְׁנָא רֵישָׁא וּמַאי שְׁנָא סֵיפָא? אָמַר רַב חִסְדָּא: הָא מַנִּי? רַבָּן שִׁמְעוֹן בֶּן גַּמְלִיאֵל הִיא, דְּאָמַר: תִּתֵּן לוֹ אֶת דָּמֶיהָ, הָכָא נַמִי אֶפְשָׁר דִּמְפַיְּיסָה לֵיהּ בְּדָמֵי.

The Gemara asks: **What is different** in **the first clause** of the *baraita* **and what is different in the latter clause?** In neither case does she have ownership of the bill of divorce. **Rav Ḥisda said:** In accordance with **whose** opinion **is this** *baraita*? **It is** in accordance with the opinion of **Rabban Shimon ben Gamliel, who says** with regard to his coat that **she** can **give him its value** and does not need to give the item itself in order to fulfill the condition. **Here also,** since **it is possible for her to appease him with money** and she may give him the value of the paper, therefore it is considered as though she received the paper.

מַתְקִיף לַהּ אַבָּיֵי: אֵימוּר דְּאָמַר רַבָּן שִׁמְעוֹן בֶּן גַּמְלִיאֵל – הֵיכָא דְּלֵיתֵיהּ בְּעֵינֵיהּ, הֵיכָא דְּאִיתֵיהּ בְּעֵינֵיהּ מִי אָמַר?

Abaye objects to this answer: **Say that Rabban Shimon ben Gamliel says** that it is acceptable to give the value instead of the item itself **when** the item **is not extant,** because it is lost. But in a case **where it is extant,** such as the paper in this case, **did** Rabban Shimon ben Gamliel actually **say** that giving the value of the item is sufficient?

אֶלָּא אָמַר אַבָּיֵי: הָא מַנִּי? רַבִּי מֵאִיר הִיא, דְּאָמַר: בָּעֵינַן תְּנַאי כָּפוּל, וְהָכָא הָא לָא כַּפְלֵיהּ לִתְנָאֵיהּ.

Rather, Abaye said: In accordance with **whose** opinion **is this** *baraita*? **It is** in accordance with the opinion of **Rabbi Meir, who says: We require** any stipulated condition to be structured as a **compound condition**[H] describing both outcomes, meaning that the condition must mention what will happen both if the condition is fulfilled and if it is not fulfilled. **And here he did not compound his condition.** The husband said only: This is your bill of divorce on the condition that you return the paper to me. He did not specify that it will not be a valid bill of divorce if she does not return it.

HALAKHA

This is your bill of divorce but the paper is mine – זֶה גִּיטֵּיךְ וְהַנְּיָיר שֶׁלִּי: If a husband said to his wife: This is your bill of divorce but the paper is mine, she is not divorced. If he said: On the condition that you return the paper to me, she is divorced, and she should return the paper (Rambam *Sefer Nashim, Hilkhot Geirushin* 8:14; *Shulḥan Arukh, Even HaEzer* 143:11).

We require a compound condition – בָּעֵינַן תְּנַאי כָּפוּל: A valid condition must follow the following four principles: It must be a compound condition, the positive must precede the negative, the condition must precede the consequence, and the condition should be about something that is possible to fulfill. If any one of these elements is missing the condition is invalid. The *Tur* writes that according to some commentaries this applies only to prohibitions, but with regard to monetary law any condition is valid even without these factors (Rif; Ramban; Rashba). Some say that requiring these four factors for this to be a valid condition is a stringency, but a case where requiring them would lead to a leniency, e.g., with regard to betrothal and divorce, the *halakha* considers the condition to be possibly valid.

The Rema writes that according to some commentaries, if one stated that the condition should be like that of the sons of Gad and Reuben then it is a considered to be a valid condition, even without explicitly following all of the requirements (*Ḥelkat Meḥokek*; *Beit Shmuel*). The Rema cites other authorities who rule that it is also necessary for the condition to be about one matter and the action with regard to another matter. If not, the condition is invalid, in accordance with the opinion of Rav Ada bar Ahava (Rosh; *Tur*). One should follow this opinion and act stringently (Rambam *Sefer Nashim, Hilkhot Ishut* 6:1–2; *Shulḥan Arukh, Even HaEzer* 38:2–4).

מַתְקִיף לַהּ רָבָא: טַעְמָא דְּלָא כַּפְלֵיהּ לִתְנָאֵיהּ, הָא כַּפְלֵיהּ לִתְנָאֵיהּ לָא הָוֵי גִּיטָּא? מִכְּדֵי כָּל תְּנַאי מֵהֵיכָא גָּמְרִינַן לְהוּ – מִתְּנַאי בְּנֵי גָד וּבְנֵי רְאוּבֵן;

Rava objects to this explanation: According to Abaye **the reason** the bill of divorce is valid **is that** the husband **did not compound his condition, but if** the husband did **compound his condition** then it **would not be** a valid **bill of divorce. Now, from where do we learn** the *halakhot* of **all conditions?** They are derived **from the condition of the children of Gad and the children of Reuben.** Moses stipulated with them that if they fight the battles with the Jewish people in Eretz Yisrael, they will inherit the land of Gilead in the Transjordan, as they requested; but if they do not fight the battles with the Jewish people in Eretz Yisrael, they will not inherit that land (see Numbers, chapter 32).

מַה הָתָם תְּנַאי קוֹדֵם לְמַעֲשֶׂה, אַף כָּל תְּנַאי קוֹדֵם לְמַעֲשֶׂה, לְאַפּוּקֵי הָכָא דְּמַעֲשֶׂה קוֹדֵם לִתְנַאי!

Just as there, in the conditions that Moses made, the language of the **condition precedes the** consequent **action,** for he first stated the condition and afterward he described the result if they fulfill the condition: "And you shall give them the land of Gilead as an inheritance" (Numbers 32:29), **so too, any condition** is valid only when it is stated **before the** resultant **action.** And this serves **to exclude** the case mentioned **here, where the** resultant **action** of the giving of the bill of divorce **precedes the condition.** Consequently, according to Rabbi Meir this bill of divorce would not be valid, even if the husband had compounded the condition.

אֶלָּא אָמַר רָבָא: מִשּׁוּם דְּמַעֲשֶׂה קוֹדֵם לִתְנַאי.

Rather, Rava said: The condition does not apply and the woman is divorced **because** the **action** of giving the bill of divorce **precedes** the **condition.**

מַתְקִיף לַהּ רַב אַדָּא בַּר אַהֲבָה: טַעְמָא דְּמַעֲשֶׂה קוֹדֵם לִתְנַאי, הָא תְּנַאי קוֹדֵם לְמַעֲשֶׂה לָא הָוֵי גִּיטָּא? מִכְּדֵי כָּל תְּנָאֵי מֵהֵיכָא גָּמְרִינַן לְהוּ – מִתְּנַאי בְּנֵי גָד וּבְנֵי רְאוּבֵן; מַה הָתָם תְּנַאי בְּדָבָר אֶחָד וּמַעֲשֶׂה בְּדָבָר אַחֵר, אַף כֹּל, לְאַפּוּקֵי הָכָא

Rav Adda bar Ahava objects to this explanation: **The reason** that the bill of divorce is valid is **that the action precedes the condition,** and the condition does not take effect. **But if the condition** were to **precede the action** then it would **not be** a valid **bill of divorce. Now, from where do we learn all** the *halakhot* of **conditions?** They are derived **from the condition of the children of Gad and the children of Reuben. Just as there** it is **a condition with regard to one matter,** i.e., that they should fight along with the rest of the Jewish people, **and** a resultant **action with regard to another matter,** i.e., that they would receive the land of Gilead, **so too, every** other condition must follow this pattern. This serves **to exclude** the case mentioned **here,**

Perek **VII**
Daf **75** Amud **b**

NOTES

Because the condition and the action are about the same matter – דְּתְנַאי וּמַעֲשֶׂה בְּדָבָר אֶחָד: Rashi explains that in this case the action is giving the bill of divorce, and the condition is that the wife must return the bill of divorce to the husband. *Tosafot* suggest an alternative explanation, that the problem with this case is that the condition and action contradict one another. The bill of divorce is not valid until the wife has returned it to her husband, at which point it is no longer in her hand.

Anyone who states: On the condition – כָּל הָאוֹמֵר עַל מְנָת: Many early commentaries (Rif; Rambam; Rav Hai Gaon) hold that when one uses the expression: On the condition, then even according to Rabbi Meir a condition that was not compounded is valid. Similarly, the other factors normally required are unnecessary (Rabbeinu Crescas Vidal; Ramah). The Ramban raises numerous challenges to this opinion, and does not offer any solution.

דִּתְנַאי וּמַעֲשֶׂה בְּדָבָר אֶחָד! אֶלָּא אָמַר רַב אַדָּא בַּר אַהֲבָה: מִשּׁוּם דִּתְנַאי וּמַעֲשֶׂה בְּדָבָר אֶחָד.

where the condition and the action are about the same matter, the giving of the bill of divorce. Accordingly, the condition would not be valid even if one were to disregard the concern of the action preceding the condition. **Rather, Rav Adda bar Ahava said** that this condition is void **because the condition and the action are about the same matter,**[N] and therefore the bill of divorce is valid even without fulfillment of the condition.

רַב אַשִׁי אָמַר: הָא מַנִּי? רַבִּי הִיא, דְּאָמַר רַב הוּנָא אָמַר רַב: כָּל הָאוֹמֵר "עַל מְנָת" כְּאוֹמֵר "מֵעַכְשָׁיו" דָּמֵי.

Rav Ashi said: In accordance with **whose** opinion **is this** *baraita*? **It is** in accordance with the opinion of **Rabbi** Yehuda HaNasi, **as Rav Huna says** that **Rav says: Anyone who states** a condition employing the language: **On the condition,**[N] **is like** one who **states:** The agreement will take effect retroactively **from now,** even though the condition is fulfilled only later on. Consequently, the bill of divorce is effective immediately, even if the woman will later be required to return the document itself to him.

אַתְקֵין שְׁמוּאֵל בְּגִיטָּא דִשְׁכִיב מְרַע: ״אִם לֹא מַתִּי לֹא יְהֵא גֵּט, וְאִם מַתִּי יְהֵא גֵּט״.

§ With regard to conditions in a bill of divorce, **Shmuel instituted** that **in a bill of divorce of a person on his deathbed** the following expression should be written: **If I do not die**[H] **this will not be** a valid **bill of divorce, and if I die it will be** a valid **bill of divorce.**

וְלֵימָא: אִם מַתִּי יְהֵא גֵּט, וְאִם לֹא מַתִּי לֹא יְהֵא גֵּט! לָא מַקְדִּים אִינִישׁ פּוּרְעָנוּתָא לְנַפְשֵׁיהּ.

The Gemara asks about the wording used here: **But let us say** this statement in a more intuitive order: **If I die it will be** a valid **bill of divorce, and if I do not die this will not be** a valid **bill of divorce.** The Gemara explains: **A person does not hasten a calamity upon himself.** Consequently, he does not wish to mention his death first.

וְלֵימָא: לֹא יְהֵא גֵּט אִם לֹא מַתִּי! בָּעֵינַן תְּנַאי קוֹדֵם לְמַעֲשֶׂה.

The Gemara asks: Why did Shmuel use this phrasing? **But let us** say the condition using the following formulation: **It will not be** a valid **bill of divorce if I do not die,** and it will be a valid bill of divorce if I do die. The Gemara asks: When stipulating a condition, **we require the condition** to come **before the action,** but in this formulation the resultant action, that the bill of divorce is valid, precedes the condition, if I do not die.

מַתְקִיף לָהּ רָבָא: מִכְּדִי כָּל תְּנַאי מֵהֵיכָא גָּמְרִינַן? מִתְּנַאי בְּנֵי גָד וּבְנֵי רְאוּבֵן, מַה הָתָם ״הֵן״ קוֹדֵם לְ״לָאו״, אַף כֹּל, לְאַפּוּקֵי הָכָא דְּ״לָאו״ קוֹדֵם לְ״הֵן״!

Rava objects to this explanation: **Now, from where do we learn** the principles of **all conditions?** They are derived **from the condition of the children of Gad and the children of Reuben. Just as there, the affirmative precedes the negative,**[N] meaning that the positive portion that speaks about what will occur if the condition is fulfilled appears before the negative portions that describe what will exist if the condition is not fulfilled, **so too, all** conditions must be formulated in this manner. This serves **to exclude** the case **here,** instituted by Shmuel, **where the negative precedes the affirmative.**

אֶלָּא אָמַר רָבָא: ״אִם לֹא מַתִּי לֹא יְהֵא גֵּט, אִם מַתִּי יְהֵא גֵּט, אִם לֹא מַתִּי לֹא יְהֵא גֵּט״;

Rather, Rava said that the condition in the bill of divorce of a dying man should be worded in the following manner: **If I do not die this will not be a bill of divorce. If I die this will be a bill of divorce,** and **if I do not die this will not be a bill of divorce.**

״אִם לֹא מַתִּי לֹא יְהֵא גֵּט״ – לָא מַקְדִּים אִינִישׁ פּוּרְעָנוּתָא לְנַפְשֵׁיהּ, ״אִם מַתִּי יְהֵא גֵּט, אִם לֹא מַתִּי לֹא יְהֵא גֵּט״ – בָּעֵינַן ״הֵן״ קוֹדֵם לְ״לָאו״.

The Gemara explains the necessity for such a formulation: The husband first says: **If I do not die this will not be a bill of divorce,** because **a person does not hasten a calamity upon himself.** Therefore, he first mentions the possibility that he will not die. Then he states the compound condition in the following order: **If I die this will be a bill of divorce,** and **if I do not die this will not be a bill of divorce.** This is because **we require** that **the affirmative precedes the negative.**

מתני׳ ״הֲרֵי זֶה גִּיטֵּיךְ עַל מְנָת שֶׁתְּשַׁמְּשִׁי אֶת אַבָּא״, ״עַל מְנָת שֶׁתָּנִיקִי אֶת בְּנִי״, כַּמָּה הִיא מֵנִיקָתוֹ? שְׁתֵּי שָׁנִים, רַבִּי יְהוּדָה אוֹמֵר: שְׁמוֹנָה עָשָׂר חֹדֶשׁ; מֵת הַבֵּן אוֹ שֶׁמֵּת הָאָב – הֲרֵי זֶה גֵּט.

MISHNA If a husband says to his wife: **This is your bill of divorce on the condition that you will serve** my **father,**[N] or: **On the condition that you will nurse,** i.e., breastfeed, **my son,** without specifying a time period, **how long** is **she** required **to nurse him**[HB] in order to fulfill the condition? She is required to nurse the baby for **two years**[H] from his birth, which is the length of time generally designated for nursing. **Rabbi Yehuda says:** The time for nursing is only **eighteen months. If the** baby **son died**[N] **or the** husband's **father died, this is** a valid **bill of divorce,** even though the condition was not fulfilled.

BACKGROUND

How long is she required to nurse him – **כַּמָּה הִיא מֵנִיקָתוֹ:** There were several reasons for this period of nursing. One was the difficulty of finding and preparing food for small children that was an adequate substitute for mother's milk. It seems that not every family was able to prepare such substitutes, whose expense was often beyond the family's means. A longer nursing period could also prevent pregnancy, although the effectiveness of this method of prevention was limited.

HALAKHA

If I do not die, etc. – **אִם לֹא מַתִּי וכו׳:** If a person on his deathbed wishes to exempt his wife from the obligations of a levirate marriage or *ḥalitza* but does not wish to divorce her at that time and wants to remain married if he is healed, then he should say to her as he gives her the bill of divorce: If I do not die this will not be a valid bill of divorce; and if I die this will be a valid bill of divorce from now; and if I do not die this will not be a valid bill of divorce. This ruling is in accordance with the opinion of Rava (Rambam *Sefer Nashim, Hilkhot Geirushin* 9:20; *Shulḥan Arukh, Even HaEzer* 145:5).

How long is she required to nurse him – **כַּמָּה הִיא מֵנִיקָתוֹ:** The time required for nursing is twenty-four months, excluding the day on which the baby was born, in accordance with the unattributed opinion of the mishna (Rambam *Sefer Nashim, Hilkhot Geirushin* 8:19, 11:26, and *Hilkhot Ishut* 21:3; *Shulḥan Arukh, Even HaEzer* 13:11, 143:8).

On the condition that you will serve…that you will nurse…two years – **עַל מְנָת שֶׁתְּשַׁמְּשִׁי...שֶׁתָּנִיקִי...שְׁתֵּי שָׁנִים:** If a husband said to his wife: This is your bill of divorce on the condition that you will nurse my son for two years, or: On the condition that you will serve my father for two years, then she must do so for the time stipulated. If the son or father died within that time, or the father said that he does not want her to serve him, then the bill of divorce is invalid, in accordance with the unattributed opinion of the mishna (Rif; Rambam; Ramban). Others (Rabbeinu Tam; Rabbeinu Yitzḥak; Rosh) hold that if the obstacle to her fulfilling the condition is not due to her then it is a valid bill of divorce, in accordance with the opinion of Rabban Shimon ben Gamliel. The Rema writes that one should be stringent, in accordance with the first opinion (Rambam *Sefer Nashim, Hilkhot Geirushin* 8:20; *Shulḥan Arukh, Even HaEzer* 143:8).

NOTES

The affirmative precedes the negative – **הֵן קוֹדֵם לְלָאו:** The Ran in tractate *Kiddushin* explains the rationale for this: One's final statement shows his intent, so in order for the action to not take effect the final statement must be under what conditions it will not take effect. By contrast, Rabbi Yom Tov Algazi writes simply that normally people state the affirmative before the negative, and one who deviates from the accepted practice is not concerned about the fulfillment of the condition.

That you will serve my father, etc. – **שֶׁתְּשַׁמְּשִׁי אֶת אַבָּא וכו׳:** Rashi explains that this means she should serve him for the rest of the father's life. The *Ḥatam Sofer* writes that since he stated both conditions together, i.e., that she should serve his father and nurse his son, it is assumed that he had the same two-year period in mind for both.

The son died, etc. – **מֵת הַבֵּן וכו׳:** Rashi and the Ramah explain that this means she already began serving the father or nursing the son before they died, but if they died before she began, then it is not a valid bill of divorce. *Tosafot* and the Rashba hold that it is immaterial whether they died before or after she began performing these actions. In either case the bill of divorce is valid.

The Rashba adds that there is a dispute between *amora'im* in the Jerusalem Talmud with regard to this matter. Some explain that if the father and baby are alive, then the condition is fulfilled only if she serves them as much as they require. If they died, it is sufficient if she had served them for a minimal amount of time. Some say that if they are alive she must serve them for a minimal amount of time, and if they died then the bill of divorce is valid even though she did nothing.

״הֲרֵי זֶה גִּיטֵּיךְ עַל מְנָת שֶׁתְּשַׁמְּשִׁי אֶת אַבָּא שְׁתֵּי שָׁנִים״, ״עַל מְנָת שֶׁתָּנִיקִי אֶת בְּנִי שְׁתֵּי שָׁנִים״, מֵת הַבֵּן, אוֹ שֶׁאָמַר הָאָב ״אִי אֶפְשִׁי שֶׁתְּשַׁמְּשֵׁנִי״, שֶׁלֹּא בְּהַקְפָּדָה – אֵינוֹ גֵּט,

But if the husband said to his wife: **This is your bill of divorce on the condition that you will serve** my **father for two years,** or: **On the condition that you will nurse my son for two years,** and **the son died** before she nursed him for two years, **or the father said: I do not want you to serve me,** then even if the father **did not** say this **in anger**[N] and she did everything she was expected to do, it **is not** a valid **bill of divorce** because the condition was not fulfilled.

רַבָּן שִׁמְעוֹן בֶּן גַּמְלִיאֵל אוֹמֵר: כָּזֶה גֵּט. כְּלָל אָמַר רַבָּן שִׁמְעוֹן בֶּן גַּמְלִיאֵל: כׇּל עַכָּבָה שֶׁאֵינָהּ הֵימֶנָּה – הֲרֵי זֶה גֵּט.

Rabban Shimon ben Gamliel says: In a case **like this** it is a valid **bill of divorce. Rabban Shimon ben Gamliel stated a principle:** If there is **any hindrance** to the fulfillment of the condition **that does not** result **from her,**[N] then **it is** a valid **bill of divorce.**

גמ׳ וּמִי בָּעֵינַן כּוּלֵּי הַאי? וּרְמִינְהִי: שִׁמְּשַׁתּוּ יוֹם אֶחָד, הֵנִיקַתּוּ יוֹם אֶחָד – הֲרֵי זֶה גֵּט!

GEMARA But **do we require** that she serve the father or nurse the son for **all of this** time that was stipulated? **And** the Gemara **raises a contradiction** based on what was taught in a *baraita* (*Tosefta, Nidda* 2:2): If **she served** the father for **one day** or **she nursed** the son for **one day it is** a valid **bill of divorce.**

אָמַר רַב חִסְדָּא, לָא קַשְׁיָא: הָא רַבָּנַן וְהָא רַבָּן שִׁמְעוֹן בֶּן גַּמְלִיאֵל,

Rav Ḥisda said that this is **not difficult: This** *baraita* is in accordance with the opinion of **the Rabbis, and this** mishna is in accordance with the opinion of **Rabban Shimon ben Gamliel,** who disagreed in the previous mishna (74a) with regard to a coat that was lost. According to the opinion of the Rabbis there, if there is no possibility that the wife can fulfill the condition by returning the coat, as it was lost, the bill of divorce is not valid. According to the opinion of Rabban Shimon ben Gamliel there, she can give the husband the coat's value and the bill of divorce is valid.

מַתְנִיתִין רַבָּן שִׁמְעוֹן בֶּן גַּמְלִיאֵל וּבָרַיְיתָא רַבָּנַן.

The Gemara explains: **The mishna** is in accordance with the opinion of **Rabban Shimon ben Gamliel,** who claims that the wife can give the husband the equivalent of the stipulated item to render the bill of divorce valid, as the primary factor is his receiving the benefit he intended when stating his condition. Therefore, she must nurse the child for the standard length of time, as that is the benefit he intended when stating his condition, or else the bill of divorce is not valid. **And the** ***baraita*** is in accordance with the opinion of **the Rabbis,** who hold that the wife must fulfill the literal terms of the condition. If she nurses the baby for even one day, or serves the father for a single day, the literal terms of the condition have been fulfilled.

הָא מִדְּסֵיפָא רַבָּן שִׁמְעוֹן בֶּן גַּמְלִיאֵל הָוֵי, מִכְּלָל דְּרֵישָׁא לָאו רַבָּן שִׁמְעוֹן בֶּן גַּמְלִיאֵל! אֶלָּא, בָּרַיְיתָא רַבָּן שִׁמְעוֹן בֶּן גַּמְלִיאֵל הִיא דְּמֵיקֵל בִּתְנָאֵי, מַתְנִיתִין רַבָּנַן.

The Gemara challenges: Is this explanation possible? **But from** the fact that **the latter clause** of the mishna **is** attributed to **Rabban Shimon ben Gamliel,** it can be derived **by inference that the first clause** is **not** in accordance with the opinion of **Rabban Shimon ben Gamliel. Rather,** the ***baraita*** **is** in accordance with the opinion of **Rabban Shimon ben Gamliel, who is lenient with regard to a condition,** and interprets it so that it can be fulfilled. **The mishna** is in accordance with the opinion of **the Rabbis,** who interpret the condition in an expanded manner.

רָבָא אָמַר, לָא קַשְׁיָא: כָּאן בִּסְתָם, כָּאן בִּמְפָרֵשׁ.

Rava offered an alternative explanation and **said** that the apparent contradiction **is not difficult: Here,** in the mishna, where the husband spoke **without specification** and did not set a time, the Sages assigned what they understand to be the standard time for the stipulated action. **There,** in the *baraita*, it is referring to where the husband said **explicitly**[NH] that she should perform the action for only one day.

רַב אַשִׁי אָמַר: כׇּל סְתָם נָמֵי כִּמְפָרֵשׁ יוֹם אֶחָד דָּמֵי.

Rav Ashi offered a different alternative explanation and **said: Any unspecified** statement is **also considered** to be **as though** he **explicitly said**[N] **one day.**[H] Since the husband did not mention a specific amount of time in which to perform the action, one day should be sufficient.

NOTES

Not in anger – שֶׁלֹּא בְּהַקְפָּדָה: The *Tosefta* explains that the bill of divorce is also invalid if the father said in anger that he does not want her to serve him. The *Tosefta* explains further that Rabban Shimon ben Gamliel also disagrees with the Rabbis in the cases of the first clause of the mishna, where the man did not specify an amount of time (see *Tosefot Ḥadashim*).

Any hindrance that does not result from her – כׇּל עַכָּבָה שֶׁאֵינָהּ הֵימֶנָּה: *Tosafot* distinguish between this case, where the husband's intent is to gain benefit, and the case mentioned earlier (74b) with regard to the wife giving money without the consent of the husband. In that case the husband's intent is to cause his wife to suffer.

There explicitly – כָּאן בִּמְפָרֵשׁ: If the husband stated the duration explicitly, what is novel in this *halakha*? *Tosafot* explain that the mishna is teaching that if she is unable to nurse the baby at all before he died, the bill of divorce is invalid. One might have thought that since the husband stated explicitly that he wanted her to nurse for only one day, his intent was to be lenient on her, and even less would be sufficient, in the event that the baby died. The Ramah writes that because the husband used the expression: One day, this teaches that the nursing must be from one night until the following night, and not simply for any twenty-four-hour block of time.

Any unspecified statement is also considered to be as though he explicitly said – כׇּל סְתָם נָמֵי כִּמְפָרֵשׁ: Rashi writes that Rav Ashi does not intend to explain the contradiction between the mishna and the *baraita*. Rather, he is referring to the *halakha* in the mishna.

HALAKHA

Here without specification, there explicitly – כָּאן בִּסְתָם, כָּאן בִּמְפָרֵשׁ: If a husband gave his wife a bill of divorce that was conditional upon her performing a specific action but he did not specify a time frame, it is sufficient for her to perform the action for only one day, in accordance with the opinion of Rav Ashi. Some say that if the condition was that his wife must serve his father, she must do so for the rest of the father's life (Ramah; Ramban; Rosh). If the condition was to nurse his son, she must do so for twenty-four months. If the father or son died after she fulfilled the condition for even one day, it is a valid bill of divorce, in accordance with the opinion of Rava. The *Beit Shmuel* writes, based on the Rashba and the Ran, that this applies only with regard to bills of divorce. In general, a condition applies for the rest of the life of the one served (Rambam *Sefer Nashim*, *Hilkhot Geirushin* 8:19; *Shulḥan Arukh*, *Even HaEzer* 143:8).

As though he explicitly said one day – כִּמְפָרֵשׁ יוֹם אֶחָד: *Tosafot* say that if the husband specified in his condition that his wife serve for one day, even a single hour is enough. According to the Ramah, one day means from one night to the next (*Shulḥan Arukh*, *Even HaEzer* 143:9 and *Beit Shmuel* there).

תְּנַן: כַּמָּה הִיא מֵנִיקָתוֹ? שְׁתֵּי שָׁנִים, רַבִּי יְהוּדָה אוֹמֵר: שְׁמוֹנָה עָשָׂר חֹדֶשׁ; בִּשְׁלָמָא לְרָבָא נִיחָא, אֶלָּא לְרַב אַשִׁי, לָמָּה לִי שְׁתֵּי שָׁנִים? לָמָּה לִי שְׁמוֹנָה עָשָׂר חֹדֶשׁ? בְּיוֹם אֶחָד סַגִּי!

The Gemara challenges Rav Ashi's explanation: **We learned** in the mishna: **How long** is **she** required **to nurse him** in order to fulfill the condition? She is required to nurse the baby for **two years** from his birth. **Rabbi Yehuda says:** The time for nursing is only **eighteen months. Granted, according to** the opinion of **Rava,** it **works out well** that if the husband does not specify the length of time, the wife must nurse the baby for the generally accepted time. **But according to** the opinion of **Rav Ashi, why do I** need her to nurse the baby for **two years** or **why do I** need her to nurse him for **eighteen months? One day** should **suffice** to fulfill the husband's condition.

הָכִי קָאָמַר: יוֹם אֶחָד מִשְּׁתֵּי שָׁנִים – לְאַפּוּקֵי לְאַחַר שְׁתֵּי שָׁנִים, דְּלָא; יוֹם אֶחָד מִשְּׁמוֹנָה עָשָׂר חֹדֶשׁ – לְאַפּוּקֵי לְאַחַר שְׁמוֹנָה עָשָׂר חֹדֶשׁ, דְּלָא.

The Gemara answers: **This is what** the mishna **is saying** according to the opinion of Rav Ashi: How long is the wife required to nurse the baby? **One day from** within the **two years** of the baby's birth, **to exclude** the case where the one day that she nursed him occurred **after** he was **two years** old, in which case the husband's condition would **not** be fulfilled, for that is the accepted length of time for a mother to nurse a baby. Or according to Rabbi Yehuda **one day from** within the **eighteen months** of the baby's birth, **to exclude** the case where the one day that she nursed him occurred after he was she nursed him occurred **after** he was **eighteen months** old, in which case the bill of divorce would not be valid.

מֵיתִיבִי: "הֲרֵי זֶה גִּיטֵּיךְ עַל מְנָת שֶׁתְּשַׁמְּשִׁי אֶת אַבָּא שְׁתֵּי שָׁנִים", "עַל מְנָת שֶׁתָּנִיקִי אֶת בְּנִי שְׁתֵּי שָׁנִים", מֵת הַבֵּן, אוֹ שֶׁאָמַר הָאָב "אִי אֶפְשִׁי שֶׁתְּשַׁמְּשֵׁנִי", שֶׁלֹּא בְּהַקְפָּדָה – אֵינוֹ גֵּט;

The Gemara **raises an objection** to the opinion of Rav Ashi from the latter clause of the mishna: If a husband said to his wife: **This is your bill of divorce on the condition that you will serve** my **father** for **two years,** or: This is your bill of divorce **on the condition that you will nurse my son** for **two years,** and **the son died or the father said: I do not want you to serve me,** then even though the father **did not** say this **in anger,** it **is not** a valid **bill of divorce.**

Perek **VII**
Daf **76** Amud **a**

בִּשְׁלָמָא לְרָבָא, רֵישָׁא בִּדְלָא פָּרֵישׁ סֵיפָא דְּפָרֵישׁ,

Granted, according to the opinion of **Rava, the first clause** in the mishna is speaking **about** when the husband **did not explicitly mention** a period of time, and **the latter clause** is referring to when he did **explicitly mention** a period of two years.

אֶלָּא לְרַב אַשִׁי, מַאי שְׁנָא רֵישָׁא וּמַאי שְׁנָא סֵיפָא? קַשְׁיָא.

But according to the opinion of **Rav Ashi,** who holds that when the husband does not mention a period of time the wife can fulfill her obligation by performing the action for even a single day, it is necessary to explain that the first clause in the mishna is referring to when she did fulfill the condition for even one day. And therefore, **what is different** in **the first clause and what is different** in **the latter clause?** The Gemara states: According to Rav Ashi's opinion this **is difficult.**

תָּנוּ רַבָּנַן: "הֲרֵי זֶה גִּיטֵּךְ עַל מְנָת שֶׁתְּשַׁמְּשִׁי אֶת אַבָּא שְׁתֵּי שָׁנִים", וְ"עַל מְנָת שֶׁתָּנִיקִי אֶת בְּנִי שְׁתֵּי שָׁנִים", אַף עַל פִּי שֶׁלֹּא נִתְקַיֵּים הַתְּנַאי – הֲרֵי זֶה גֵּט, לְפִי שֶׁלֹּא אָמַר לָהּ "אִם תְּשַׁמְּשִׁי" "אִם לֹא תְּשַׁמְּשִׁי", "אִם תָּנִיקִי" וְ"אִם לֹא תָּנִיקִי", דִּבְרֵי רַבִּי מֵאִיר;

§ **The Sages taught** (*Tosefta* 7:6): If a husband said to his wife: **This is your bill of divorce on the condition that you will serve** my **father for two years, or** he said: This is your bill of divorce **on the condition that you will nurse my son** for **two years, even if the condition was not fulfilled it is** a valid **bill of divorce because he did not say to her: If you will serve** my father then this will be a valid bill of divorce, and **if you will not serve** him it will not be a valid bill of divorce, or: **If you will nurse** my son then this will be a valid bill of divorce, **and if you will not nurse** him it will not be a valid bill of divorce. And if he did not state his condition as a compound condition, stipulating both positive and negative outcomes, the condition is void and the bill of divorce is valid. This is **the statement of Rabbi Meir.**

וַחֲכָמִים אוֹמְרִים: נִתְקַיֵּים הַתְּנַאי – הֲרֵי זֶה גֵּט, וְאִם לָאו – אֵינוֹ גֵּט; רַבָּן שִׁמְעוֹן בֶּן גַּמְלִיאֵל אוֹמֵר: אֵין לְךָ תְּנַאי בַּכְּתוּבִים שֶׁאֵינוֹ כָּפוּל.

And the Rabbis say: The condition is valid even if it the husband does not stipulate both positive and negative outcomes. Consequently, if **the condition was fulfilled this is** a valid **bill of divorce, and if** it was **not** fulfilled **this is not** a valid **bill of divorce. Rabban Shimon ben Gamliel says: You do not have a condition in the Bible that is not compounded.**

אִיכָּא דְּאָמְרִי: לְרַבִּי מֵאִיר קָאָמַר לֵיהּ, וְאִיכָּא דְּאָמְרִי: לְרַבָּנַן קָאָמַר לְהוּ; אִיכָּא דְּאָמְרִי לְרַבִּי מֵאִיר קָאָמַר לֵיהּ, וְהָכִי קָאָמַר לֵיהּ: אֵין לְךָ תְּנַאי בַּכְּתוּבִים שֶׁאֵינוֹ כָּפוּל, וְהָווּ לְהוּ שְׁנֵי כְתוּבִים הַבָּאִין כְּאֶחָד, וְכָל שְׁנֵי כְתוּבִים הַבָּאִין כְּאֶחָד אֵין מְלַמְּדִין.

To which side of the dispute is Rabban Shimon ben Gamliel's statement referring? **There are those who say: He is speaking to Rabbi Meir. And there are those who say: He is speaking to the Rabbis.** The Gemara explains: **There are those who say** that this means **he is speaking to Rabbi Meir and this is what he is saying to him: You do not have a condition in the Bible that is not compounded,** and therefore the compound conditions mentioned in the Torah **have** the status of **two verses that come as one,**[N] i.e., to teach the same matter. **And any two verses that come as one do not teach** about other cases. Consequently, one cannot derive from them that every condition must be compounded.

אִיכָּא דְּאָמְרִי לְרַבָּנַן קָאָמַר לְהוּ, וְהָכִי קָאָמַר לְהוּ: אֵין לְךָ תְּנַאי בַּכְּתוּבִים שֶׁאֵינוֹ כָּפוּל, וְגָמְרִינַן מִינַּיְיהוּ.

There are those **who say: He is saying** this **to the Rabbis, and this is what he is saying to them: There is no condition in the Bible that is not compounded, and we learn from** the conditions written in the Bible[N] that a condition is not valid unless it is compounded.

וּרְמִינְהוּ: ״הֲרֵי זֶה גִּיטֵּיךְ עַל מְנָת שֶׁתְּשַׁמְּשִׁי אֶת אַבָּא שְׁתֵּי שָׁנִים״, ״עַל מְנָת שֶׁתֵּנִיקִי אֶת בְּנִי שְׁתֵּי שָׁנִים״, מֵת הָאָב אוֹ מֵת הַבֵּן – אֵינוֹ גֵּט, דִּבְרֵי רַבִּי מֵאִיר;

And the Gemara **raises a contradiction** based on what was taught in a *baraita* (*Tosefta* 7:6): If a husband said to his wife: **This is your bill of divorce on the condition that you will serve** my **father for two years,** or he said to her: This is your bill of divorce **on the condition that you will nurse my son for two years, and the father died or the son died,** then **it is not** a valid **bill of divorce,** as its condition was not fulfilled. This is **the statement of Rabbi Meir.**

וַחֲכָמִים אוֹמְרִים: אַף עַל פִּי שֶׁלֹּא נִתְקַיֵּים הַתְּנַאי – הֲרֵי זֶה גֵּט, יְכוֹלָה הִיא שֶׁתֹּאמַר לוֹ: תֵּן לִי אָבִיךָ וַאֲשַׁמְּשֶׁנּוּ, תֵּן לִי בִּנְךָ וַאֲנִיקֶנּוּ;

And the Rabbis say: Even though the condition was not fulfilled it is a valid **bill of divorce,** as **she could have said to him: Give me your father and I will serve him,** or: **Give me your son and I will nurse him.**

קַשְׁיָא דְּרַבִּי מֵאִיר אַדְּרַבִּי מֵאִיר, קַשְׁיָא דְּרַבָּנַן אַדְּרַבָּנַן!

It is **difficult** to reconcile one statement **of Rabbi Meir with** the other statement made by **Rabbi Meir,** for the second *baraita* indicates that the husband's condition does not need to be compounded. And it is **difficult** to reconcile one statement **of the Rabbis with** the other statement of **the Rabbis,** for in the second *baraita* they say that if the condition was fulfilled it is a valid bill of divorce, and if it was not fulfilled it is not a valid bill of divorce.

דְּרַבִּי מֵאִיר אַדְּרַבִּי מֵאִיר לָא קַשְׁיָא, הָתָם בְּדְלָא כַּפְלֵיהּ לִתְנָאֵיהּ, הָכָא בְּדְכַפְלֵיהּ לִתְנָאֵיהּ;

The Gemara answers: It is **not difficult** to reconcile one statement **of Rabbi Meir with** the other statement **of Rabbi Meir,** as **there,** in the case where the bill of divorce is valid, it is referring to **when he did not compound his condition. Here,** where the bill of divorce is valid, it is referring to **when he did compound his condition,** but the *tanna* of the *baraita* did not mention that fact explicitly.

וְרַבָּנַן אַדְּרַבָּנַן לָא קַשְׁיָא, מַאן חֲכָמִים דְּהָכָא? רַבָּן שִׁמְעוֹן בֶּן גַּמְלִיאֵל הִיא, דְּאָמַר: כָּל עַכָּבָה שֶׁאֵינָהּ הֵימֶנָּה – הֲרֵי זֶה גֵּט.

And it is **not difficult** to reconcile one statement **of the Rabbis with** the other statement **of the Rabbis,** because **whose** is the opinion mentioned **here** anonymously as **the Rabbis? It is** the opinion of **Rabban Shimon ben Gamliel, who says:** If there is **any hindrance** to fulfilling the condition **that is not from her, it is** a valid **bill of divorce.**

תָּנוּ רַבָּנַן: אָמַר לָהּ בִּפְנֵי שְׁנַיִם – ״הֲרֵי זֶה גִּיטֵּיךְ עַל מְנָת שֶׁתְּשַׁמְּשִׁי אֶת אַבָּא שְׁתֵּי שָׁנִים״, וְחָזַר וְאָמַר לָהּ בִּפְנֵי שְׁנַיִם ״הֲרֵי זֶה גִּיטֵּיךְ עַל מְנָת שֶׁתִּתְּנִי לִי מָאתַיִם זוּז״ – לֹא בִּיטֵּל דְּבָרָיו הָאַחֲרוֹן אֶת הָרִאשׁוֹן, רָצְתָה – מְשַׁמַּשְׁתּוֹ, רָצְתָה – נוֹתֶנֶת לוֹ מָאתַיִם זוּז;

§ The Gemara continues discussing a conditional bill of divorce. **The Sages taught** (*Tosefta* 6:6): If a husband **said to** his wife **in the presence of two**[H] people: **This is your bill of divorce on the condition that you will serve** my **father for two years, and** afterward **he returned and said to her in the presence of two** other people: **This is your bill of divorce on the condition that you will give me two hundred dinars, the latter statement does not nullify the first** statement. Rather, he is giving her the choice, and if she fulfills either one of the conditions, the bill of divorce is valid. If **she wishes,** she **serves** his father and is divorced, or if **she wishes, she gives him two hundred dinars** and is divorced.

NOTES

Two verses that come as one – שְׁנֵי כְתוּבִים הַבָּאִין כְּאֶחָד: A *halakha* written in one context may serve as a general model for many other contexts, in the absence of a restriction limiting the *halakha* to that context. This is the hermeneutical technique called analogy [*binyan av*]. An exception to this is if the same *halakha* appears in two different contexts. As the Torah wrote it in the second context, it is apparent that it cannot have been derived from the first context by way of analogy. Therefore, it cannot be derived by way of analogy to other contexts either. If it is possible to explain why the analogy could not have been applied specifically to the second context, thereby necessitating the writing of the halakha there, the analogy can be applied to other contexts.

Some *tanna'im* maintain that even two verses that teach the same matter can teach their shared *halakha* in other contexts, as the repetition merely serves to emphasize the general *halakha*. Even these *tanna'im* agree that three verses that teach the same matter cannot teach their shared *halakha* with regard to other contexts (see *Yad Malakhi*).

And we learn from them – וְגָמְרִינַן מִינַּיְיהוּ: Rashi explains in tractate *Kiddushin* (61b) that although there are more than three examples of compound conditions in the Bible, each needed to be stated in its own context, so one can learn by analogy that a compound condition is required in all contexts. *Tosafot* note that the Gemara in *Kiddushin* does not explicitly prove that each of them is necessary in its own context, but the Sages had a tradition that this is so.

HALAKHA

Said to his wife in the presence of two, etc. – אָמַר לָהּ בִּפְנֵי שְׁנַיִם וכו׳: If a husband gives a bill of divorce to his wife on the condition that she will give him two hundred dinars, and he subsequently made another condition in the presence of two other witnesses, then the latter condition does not cancel the first. His wife may fulfill whichever condition she prefers. If he made a condition with her that she would give him two hundred dinars and subsequently made a condition in the presence of other witnesses that she must give him three hundred dinars, then only the second condition applies. The Rema, citing the Ran, writes that some say this applies only if he gives her the bill of divorce after he stated both conditions in the presence of two groups of witnesses, but if he gave it to her when he stated either the first or the second condition, then he specifically requires that condition (Rambam *Sefer Nashim*, *Hilkhot Geirushin* 8:18; *Shulḥan Arukh*, *Even HaEzer* 143:10 and *Beit Shmuel* there).

אֲבָל אָמַר לָהּ בִּפְנֵי שְׁנַיִם ״הֲרֵי זֶה גִּיטֵּךְ עַל מְנָת שֶׁתִּתְּנִי לִי מָאתַיִם זוּז״, וְחָזַר וְאָמַר לָהּ בִּפְנֵי שְׁנַיִם ״הֲרֵי זֶה גִּיטֵּךְ עַל מְנָת שֶׁתִּתְּנִי לִי שְׁלֹשׁ מֵאוֹת זוּז״ – בִּיטֵּל דִּבְרֵי הָאַחֲרוֹן אֶת הָרִאשׁוֹן. וְאֵין אֶחָד מִן הָרִאשׁוֹנִים וְאֶחָד מִן הָאַחֲרוֹנִים מִצְטָרְפִין.

But if **he said to her in the presence of two** people: **This is your bill of divorce on the condition that you will give me two hundred dinars,** and afterward **he returned and said to her in the presence of two** other people: **This is your bill of divorce on the condition that you will give me three hundred dinars,** then **the latter statement nullifies the first** statement, and she is not divorced unless she gives him three hundred dinars. **And one of the first** pair of witnesses **and** one **of the last** pair of witnesses **cannot**[N] **combine** their testimonies concerning the condition.

אַהַיָּיא? אִילֵימָא אַסֵּיפָא – הֲרֵי בָּטֵל! אֶלָּא אַרֵישָׁא.

The Gemara asks: **To which** clause of the *baraita* is the statement that the witnesses cannot combine their testimonies referring? **If we say** that it is referring to **the latter clause,** where the husband demanded an additional one hundred dinars, then it already said that the first condition **is nullified.** It is unnecessary to mention that the two pairs of witnesses cannot combine their testimonies, since the condition witnessed by the first witnesses no longer exists. **Rather,** it is referring **to the first clause.**

פְּשִׁיטָא! מַהוּ דְּתֵימָא: כֹּל לְקִיּוּמָא תְּנָאֵי מִצְטָרְפִין, קָא מַשְׁמַע לַן.

But **isn't** it **obvious** that these two pairs of witnesses cannot combine their testimonies, since each of them are testifying about a different condition? The Gemara answers: **Lest you say** that **all** of those who testify **to the existence of conditions can combine** their testimonies to testify that a bill of divorce was given with a condition, it **teaches us** that this is not the case.

מתני׳ ״הֲרֵי זֶה גִּיטֵּךְ אִם לֹא בָּאתִי מִכָּאן עַד שְׁלֹשִׁים יוֹם״, וְהָיָה הוֹלֵךְ מִיהוּדָה לַגָּלִיל, הִגִּיעַ לְאַנְטִיפְרַס וְחָזַר – בָּטֵל תְּנָאוֹ.

MISHNA If a resident of the region of Judea intending to embark on a journey to the Galilee said to his wife: **This is your bill of divorce if I do not come** back **from now until** the conclusion of **thirty days, and** when **he was going from Judea to the Galilee** he **reached Antipatris**[B] **and he returned** immediately, **his condition is void** and his wife is not divorced, even if he subsequently returns to the Galilee for longer than thirty days. The reason for this is because he reached the Galilee and returned to Judea within the time he had allotted.

״הֲרֵי זֶה גִּיטֵּךְ אִם לֹא בָּאתִי מִכָּאן עַד שְׁלֹשִׁים יוֹם״, וְהָיָה הוֹלֵךְ מִגָּלִיל לִיהוּדָה, וְהִגִּיעַ לִכְפַר עוֹתְנַאי וְחָזַר – בָּטֵל תְּנָאוֹ.

Similarly, if a resident of the region of the Galilee intending to embark on a journey to Judea said to his wife: **This is your bill of divorce if I do not come** back **from now until** the conclusion of **thirty days, and he was going from the Galilee to Judea, and he reached Kefar Otnai**[B] **and returned** immediately, **his condition is void** and his wife is not divorced, even if he subsequently returns to Judea for longer than thirty days.

״הֲרֵי זֶה גִּיטֵּךְ אִם לֹא בָּאתִי מִכָּאן עַד שְׁלֹשִׁים יוֹם״, וְהָיָה הוֹלֵךְ לִמְדִינַת הַיָּם, וְהִגִּיעַ לְעַכּוֹ וְחָזַר – בָּטֵל תְּנָאוֹ.

Similarly, if a resident of Eretz Yisrael intending to embark on a journey to a country overseas said to his wife: **This is your bill of divorce if I do not come** back **from now until** the conclusion of **thirty days, and he was going to a country overseas, and he reached Akko and returned** immediately, **his condition is void** and his wife is not divorced, even if he subsequently travels to a country overseas for longer than thirty days.

״הֲרֵי זֶה גִּיטֵּךְ כׇּל זְמַן שֶׁאֶעֱבוֹר מִכְּנֶגֶד פָּנַיִךְ שְׁלֹשִׁים יוֹם״, הָיָה הוֹלֵךְ וּבָא הוֹלֵךְ וּבָא, הוֹאִיל וְלֹא נִתְיַיחֵד עִמָּהּ – הֲרֵי זֶה גֵּט.

If a husband said to his wife: **This is your bill of divorce** if at **any time I will depart from your presence** for **thirty** consecutive **days,** then even if **he was** continually **going and coming, going and coming, since he was not secluded with her during these thirty days, this is** a valid **bill of divorce.**

NOTES

And one of the first…cannot – וְאֵין אֶחָד מִן הָרִאשׁוֹנִים: If the wife claims that there was never any condition on the bill of divorce, or that there was a different condition, one of the witnesses to the first condition may not combine his testimony with that of a witness to the second condition.

Rabbeinu Crescas Vidal explains that this is referring not to witnesses to the condition but rather to witnesses to the fulfillment of the condition. Each one testifies that the wife fulfilled a condition, but since they were different conditions, they may not combine their testimonies to form a pair of witnesses.

BACKGROUND

Antipatris – אַנְטִיפְרַס: Antipatris was built, or at least renovated and fortified, by King Herod and named for his father, Antipater. The city was located close to the source of the Yarkon River, near the modern-day town of Rosh HaAyin. It served as a landmark as the northernmost point in Judea, with Samaria continuing to the north.

Fortress at Antipatris

Kefar Otnai – כְּפַר עוֹתְנַאי: This is a village located in the south of the Jezreel Valley, a few kilometers north of the modern-day town of Ein Ganim. It was considered the southernmost point of the Galilee. Kefar Otnai was apparently a mixed community of Samaritans and Jews.

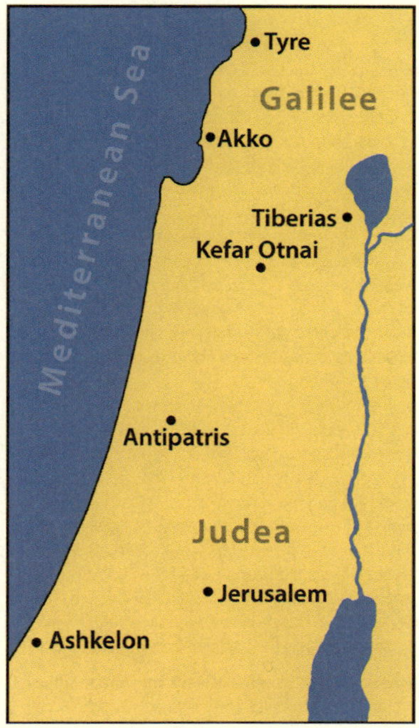

Location of Kefar Otnai

גמ׳ לְמֵימְרָא דְּאַנְטִיפְּרָס בַּגָּלִיל הֲוָה קַיְימָא? וּרְמִינְהִי: אַנְטִיפְּרָס בִּיהוּדָה, וּכְפַר עוֹתְנַאי בַּגָּלִיל, בֵּינְתַיִם – מַטִּילִין אוֹתוֹ לְחוּמְרָא, מְגוֹרֶשֶׁת

GEMARA The Gemara asks: **Is this to say that Antipatris**[N] **was in the Galilee?** It appears from the mishna that Antipatris was on the border of the Galilee, since the condition of the resident of Judea became void by his reaching Antipatris and returning. **And** the Gemara **raises a contradiction** based on what is taught in a *baraita* (*Tosefta* 7:9): **Antipatris is in Judea, and Kefar Otnai is in the Galilee.** And with regard to the area **between them, a stringent** ruling **is placed on it,**[N] and it is treated as though it is located in both Judea and the Galilee. If the husband who made such a condition reached this area and returned home, it is uncertain whether the condition attached to the bill of divorce was fulfilled. Therefore, there is uncertainty whether **she is divorced**

NOTES

Is this to say that Antipatris – לְמֵימְרָא דְּאַנְטִיפְּרָס: According to the explanation of Rashi, the Gemara understands that the husband explicitly stated his intention to travel to the Galilee or Judea, and therefore there are two parts to his condition: That he travel to the Galilee and that he remain there for thirty days. This means that the condition is void only if he travels to the Galilee and returns within this time period. If he did not reach the Galilee, then even if he returns home within this time frame the condition is in effect. Therefore, the Gemara asks: According to the *baraita* the man did not reach the Galilee, so why is his condition void?

A stringent ruling is placed on it – מַטִּילִין אוֹתוֹ לְחוּמְרָא: The meaning is that there is uncertainty whether she is divorced or whether she is not divorced, and all the stringencies of both apply to her.

וְאֵינָהּ מְגוֹרֶשֶׁת!

or whether **she is not divorced.**

אֲמַר אַבַּיֵי, תְּרֵי תְּנָאֵי קָאָמַר לָהּ: אִי מָטֵינָא לַגָּלִיל – לְאַלְתַּר לֶיהֱוֵי גִּיטָּא, וְאִי מִשְׁתַּהֵינָא בְּאוֹרְחָא תְּלָתִין יוֹמִין וְלָא אָתֵינָא – לֶיהֱוֵי גִּיטָּא; הִגִּיעַ לְאַנְטִיפְּרָס וְחָזַר, דְּלָא לַגָּלִיל מְטָא וְלָא אִישְׁתַּהוּיֵי נַמִי אִשְׁתַּהֵי תְּלָתִין יוֹמִין – בָּטֵל תְּנָאוֹ.

Abaye said: It may be that Antipatris is in Judea and Kefar Otnai is in the Galilee. The mishna can be explained as follows: The husband was **saying** a statement including **two conditions to her: If I arrive in the Galilee** then this **will be a bill of divorce immediately, or if I will tarry on the way for thirty days and I do not come** back home, this **will be** a valid **bill of divorce.** If **he reached Antipatris and returned** within thirty days, **as he did not arrive in the Galilee and he also did not tarry for thirty days,** then **his condition is void** and his wife is not divorced.

״הֲרֵי זֶה גִּיטֵּךְ אִם לֹא בָּאתִי מִכָּאן וְעַד שְׁלֹשִׁים יוֹם״ כו׳. לְמֵימְרָא, דְּעַכּוֹ בִּמְדִינַת הַיָּם קַיְימָא? וְהָא אֲמַר רַב סָפְרָא: כִּי הָווּ מִיפַּטְרִי רַבָּנַן מֵהֲדָדֵי – בְּעַכּוֹ הָווּ מִפַּטְרִי, מִשּׁוּם דְּאָסוּר לָצֵאת מֵאֶרֶץ לְחוּצָה לָאָרֶץ!

The continuation of the mishna taught: **This is your bill of divorce if I do not come** back **from now until** the conclusion of **thirty days.** The Gemara asks: **Is this to say that Akko**[N] **is in a country overseas,** and is not considered part of Eretz Yisrael? **But didn't Rav Safra say: When the Sages would take leave from one another**[N] before departing Eretz Yisrael, **they would take** their **leave in Akko, because it is prohibited to leave from Eretz Yisrael**[H] to go **outside of** Eretz Yisrael? This indicates that Akko is within Eretz Yisrael.

אֲמַר אַבַּיֵי, תְּרֵי תְּנָאֵי קָאָמַר לָהּ: אִי מָטֵינָא לִמְדִינַת הַיָּם – לְאַלְתַּר לֶיהֱוֵי גִּיטָּא, אִי מִשְׁתַּהֵינָא בְּאוֹרְחָא תְּלָתִין יוֹמִין וְלָא אָתֵינָא – לֶיהֱוֵי גִּיטָּא; הִגִּיעַ לְעַכּוֹ וְחָזַר, דְּלָא לִמְדִינַת הַיָּם מְטָא וְלָא אִישְׁתַּהוּיֵי נַמִי אִשְׁתַּהֵי תְּלָתִין יוֹמִין – בָּטֵל תְּנָאוֹ.

Abaye said: The husband was **saying** a statement including **two conditions to her: If I arrive in a country overseas,** then this **will be** a valid **bill of divorce immediately,** or **if I tarry thirty days on the way and I do not come** back home, this **will be** a valid **bill of divorce. If he reached Akko and returned, as he did not reach a country overseas and he also did not tarry for thirty days, his condition is void** and his wife is not divorced.

״הֲרֵי זֶה גִּיטֵּךְ כָּל זְמַן שֶׁאֶעֱבוֹר״ וכו׳. וְהָא לָא עֲבַר! אֲמַר רַב הוּנָא: מַאי ״פָּנַיִךְ״? תַּשְׁמִישׁ, וְאַמַּאי קָרֵי לֵיהּ פָּנַיִךְ? לִישָּׁנָא מְעַלְּיָא נְקַט.

§ The continuation of the mishna states: If a husband said to his wife: **This is your bill of divorce** if at **any time I will depart** from your presence for thirty consecutive days, then even if he was continually going and coming, going and coming, since he was not secluded with her during these thirty days this is a valid bill of divorce. The Gemara challenges: **But did he not pass** from her presence during this time, as he was going and coming the entire time? **Rav Huna said: What** is the meaning of the term **your presence** in this context? It means **sexual intercourse.** His actual condition was that if he will not engage in sexual intercourse with her for thirty days then the bill of divorce will be valid. **And why does he call** sexual intercourse **your presence? He employed a euphemistic expression** when he made his condition.

NOTES

Is this to say that Akko, etc. – לְמֵימְרָא דְּעַכּוֹ וכו׳: The question whether Akko is part of Eretz Yisrael was raised in a discussion in the Gemara (6a) on the first mishna of this tractate. An attempt was made in the Jerusalem Talmud to demonstrate from the mishna on 76a that Akko is considered to be part of Eretz Yisrael with regard to stipulations. This is rejected in the Jerusalem Talmud; perhaps it is treated like Eretz Yisrael only with regard to bills of divorce, because the residents of Akko were knowledgeable about writing and signing a bill of divorce for the woman's sake, as discussed on 6a. It may be that if the husband stipulates a condition about a country overseas, perhaps Akko is included in the category of overseas.

The early commentaries discuss another source in the Jerusalem Talmud (1:2), which says that there are two separate portions of Akko, one which is considered to be part of Eretz Yisrael and one which is considered to be outside Eretz Yisrael (see Rabbeinu Tam, *Sefer HaYashar*). The Ramban explains that Abaye could have given this answer, but preferred to explain the mishna in its entirety in accordance with one opinion. The Rashba writes that when the mishna states: If he reached Akko (76a), it means that he reached the city's border, which is considered to be the border of Eretz Yisrael (see Ran).

When the Sages would take leave from one another – כִּי הָווּ מִיפַּטְרִי רַבָּנַן מֵהֲדָדֵי: The early commentaries write that there is a difference between the two groups of Sages with regard to the *halakha*. Those who lived outside of Eretz Yisrael permanently were permitted to return home after their temporary stay in Eretz Yisrael. By contrast, it was prohibited for permanent residents of Eretz Yisrael to travel outside Eretz Yisrael, except in specific circumstances, and even then it was permitted only for a short amount of time.

HALAKHA

Because it is prohibited to leave from Eretz Yisrael, etc. – מִשּׁוּם דְּאָסוּר לָצֵאת מֵאֶרֶץ וכו׳: It is prohibited to leave Eretz Yisrael, even temporarily, unless one is traveling for purposes of studying Torah, finding a wife, saving property from gentiles, or conducting business. In all cases it is prohibited to leave in order to dwell permanently outside of Eretz Yisrael (Rambam *Sefer Shofetim*, *Hilkhot Melakhim UMilḥemoteihem* 5:9).

וְרַבִּי יוֹחָנָן אָמַר: לְעוֹלָם פָּנַיִךְ מַמָּשׁ, מִי קָתָנֵי ״הֲרֵי זוֹ מְגוֹרֶשֶׁת״? ״הֲרֵי זֶה גֵּט״ קָתָנֵי, דְּלָא הָוֵי גֵּט יָשָׁן, וְלִכִי מָלוּ תְּלָתִין יוֹמֵי הָוֵי גִּיטָּא.

And Rabbi Yoḥanan disagreed and **said: Actually,** the husband means **literally: Your presence,**[H] i.e., that he would not be in his wife's presence for thirty consecutive days. **Is the mishna teaching** that **she is divorced** immediately? No, it **is teaching** only that **this** is a valid **bill of divorce.** This means that although the condition was not fulfilled during these thirty days, since he was not secluded with her this **is not considered** to be **an outdated bill of divorce,** which the Sages said may not be used for divorce. **And when,** at some point in the future, **the thirty days** during which he does pass from her presence **are fulfilled, this will be** a valid **bill of divorce.**

תַּנְיָא כְּווֹתֵיהּ דְּרַבִּי יוֹחָנָן: ״הֲרֵי זֶה גִּיטֵּךְ כׇּל זְמַן שֶׁאֶעֱבוֹר מִנֶּגֶד פָּנַיִךְ שְׁלֹשִׁים יוֹם״, וְהָיָה הוֹלֵךְ וּבָא הוֹלֵךְ וּבָא, הוֹאִיל וְלֹא נִתְיַיחֵד עִמָּהּ – הֲרֵי זֶה גֵּט, וּלְגֵט יָשָׁן אֵין חוֹשְׁשִׁין שֶׁהֲרֵי לֹא נִתְיַיחֵד עִמָּהּ.

The Gemara comments that it **is taught** in a *baraita* (*Tosefta* 7:10) **in accordance with** the opinion **of Rabbi Yoḥanan:** If one says to his wife: **This is your bill of divorce** if at **any time I will depart from your presence** for **thirty** consecutive **days, and he was going and coming, going and coming** for the entire thirty days, **since he was not secluded with her** during that time, **this is** a valid **bill of divorce. And one is not concerned** that it is now considered **an outdated bill of divorce, because he was not secluded with her.**

וְלֵיחוּשׁ שֶׁמָּא פִּיֵּיס! אָמַר רַבָּה בַּר רַב הוּנָא, הָכִי אָמַר אַבָּא מָרִי מִשְּׁמֵיהּ דְּרַב: בְּאוֹמֵר: נֶאֱמֶנֶת עָלַי לוֹמַר שֶׁלֹּא בָּאתִי.

The Gemara asks: **But let** there be a **concern** that **perhaps he appeased**[N] his wife during this time that he was going and coming, and he was secluded with her. **Rabba bar Rav Huna said: So said my father, my teacher,** Rav Huna, **in the name of Rav:** The *baraita* is referring to a situation **where** the husband **says: She is deemed credible by me to say that I did not come.** Since the husband states explicitly that he believes her about this, if she said that he was not secluded with her then the bill of divorce remains valid.

אִיכָּא דְּמַתְנֵי לַהּ אַמַּתְנִיתִין: ״מֵעַכְשָׁיו אִם לֹא בָּאתִי מִכָּאן וְעַד שְׁנֵים עָשָׂר חֹדֶשׁ״, וּמֵת בְּתוֹךְ שְׁנֵים עָשָׂר חֹדֶשׁ – הֲרֵי זֶה גֵּט; וְלֵיחוּשׁ שֶׁמָּא פִּיֵּיס! אָמַר רַבָּה בַּר רַב הוּנָא, הָכִי אָמַר אַבָּא מָרִי מִשְּׁמֵיהּ דְּרַב: בְּאוֹמֵר: נֶאֱמֶנֶת עָלַי לוֹמַר שֶׁלֹּא בָּאתִי.

There are those who **teach this** statement of Rav Huna in the name of Rav **with regard to the mishna** mentioned later on, which says that if the husband said to his wife: This is your bill of divorce **from now if I do not come** back **from now until** the conclusion of **twelve months, and he died within twelve months, this is** a valid **bill of divorce.** The Gemara asks: **But let** there be a **concern** that **perhaps he appeased** his wife during this time and was secluded with her. **Rabba bar Rav Huna said: So said my father, my teacher,** Rav Huna, **in the name of Rav:** The mishna is referring to a situation **where** the husband **says: She is deemed credible by me to say that I did not come,** and he did not appease her.

מַאן דְּמַתְנֵי לַהּ אַמַּתְנִיתִין, כׇּל שֶׁכֵּן אַבָּרַיְיתָא;

The Gemara comments: Concerning **the one who taught that** statement of Rav Huna in the name of Rav **with regard to the mishna,**[N] **all the more so** would he teach this statement **with regard to the** ***baraita.*** Since he was constantly going and coming, the bill of divorce would be valid only if the husband stated that he trusts his wife to say that she was not secluded with him.

מַאן דְּמַתְנֵי לַהּ אַבָּרַיְיתָא, אֲבָל אַמַּתְנִיתִין – הָא לָא אֲתָא.

Concerning **the one who taught this** statement **with regard to the** ***baraita,*** it is possible that he taught this only with regard to the *baraita,* **but with regard to the mishna,** this is not the case, **as he did not come**[H] back home within twelve months, but rather died. Therefore, even if he did not specify that he trusts his wife to say whether or not they were secluded, there is no concern that perhaps he was secluded with her without anyone knowing about it.

מתני׳ ״הֲרֵי זֶה גִּיטֵּךְ אִם לֹא בָּאתִי מִכָּאן וְעַד שְׁנֵים עָשָׂר חֹדֶשׁ״, וּמֵת בְּתוֹךְ שְׁנֵים עָשָׂר חֹדֶשׁ – אֵינוֹ גֵּט;

MISHNA If a husband says to his wife: **This is your bill of divorce if I do not come**[H] back **from now until** the conclusion of **twelve months, and he died within twelve months, it is not** a valid **bill of divorce.** This is because the bill of divorce cannot take effect after the husband's death. As a result, she is bound by a levirate bond if her husband has no children.

״הֲרֵי זֶה גִּיטֵּךְ מֵעַכְשָׁיו אִם לֹא בָּאתִי מִכָּאן וְעַד שְׁנֵים עָשָׂר חֹדֶשׁ״, וּמֵת בְּתוֹךְ שְׁנֵים עָשָׂר חֹדֶשׁ – הֲרֵי זֶה גֵּט.

By contrast, if he said to her: **This is your bill of divorce from now if I do not come** back **from now until** the conclusion of **twelve months, and he died within twelve months, this is** a valid **bill of divorce.** This is because the bill of divorce takes effect retroactively. Since he did not return within the year the condition was fulfilled.

HALAKHA

Actually, the husband means literally your presence – לְעוֹלָם פָּנַיִךְ מַמָּשׁ: A husband gave his wife a bill of divorce that was conditional upon his not being seen by her for thirty days, and he was continually coming and going but was not secluded with her, and subsequently she did not see him for thirty days. In such a case it is a valid bill of divorce, in accordance with the opinion of Rabbi Yoḥanan. This applies only when he said to his wife: I trust you to say that I did not appease you. If he did not state that he trusts her there is a concern that perhaps he appeased her and nullified the bill of divorce, in accordance with the opinion of Rabba bar Rav Huna (Rambam *Sefer Nashim, Hilkhot Geirushin* 9:9; *Shulḥan Arukh, Even HaEzer* 144:7).

As he did not come – הָא לָא אֲתָא: If a husband said to his wife: This is your bill of divorce from now if I do not return here within twelve months, and he traveled to another country and it is not known that he returned, she is divorced (Rambam). Some say that even if it is not known that he returned there is concern that he might have come clandestinely (Rabbeinu Ḥananel, Rosh). If he specified that she is trusted to say that he did not come, she is divorced. Even though the *halakha* is in accordance with the first opinion, it is customary to be stringent and stipulate an initial condition that the husband trusts the wife (Rambam *Sefer Nashim, Hilkhot Geirushin* 9:11; *Shulḥan Arukh, Even HaEzer* 144:7).

This is your bill of divorce if I do not come, etc. – הֲרֵי זֶה גִּיטֵּךְ אִם לֹא בָּאתִי וכו׳: If one says to his wife: This is your bill of divorce if I do not come back within twelve months, and he specified neither: From now, nor: On the condition, and died within twelve months, it is uncertain whether the *halakha* is in accordance with the unattributed opinion in the mishna or in accordance with the opinion of Rabbi Yosei, who says that the date written in a document proves when it takes effect (*Shulḥan Arukh, Even HaEzer* 144:2).

NOTES

But let there be a concern that perhaps he appeased – וְלֵיחוּשׁ שֶׁמָּא פִּיֵּיס: The early commentaries disagree about the meaning of the word appeased. According to Rashi the concern is that perhaps he was secluded with her, and afterward he may challenge the bill of divorce by saying that the condition was not fulfilled. According to others there is no concern about seclusion and sexual intercourse, but rather about appeasing her. According to Rabbeinu Ḥananel it is possible that he appeased his wife and canceled the bill of divorce entirely. According to the Rif, cited by the Ramban and the Rashba, the concern is that perhaps he appeased her and convinced her to waive the condition and nullify the bill of divorce even if he does not return within the stated time frame.

The one who taught that with regard to the mishna – מַאן דְּמַתְנֵי לַהּ אַמַּתְנִיתִין: Rashi and Rabbeinu Ḥananel explain this in the following manner: It is much more logical to be concerned about appeasement in the case mentioned in the *baraita*, in which it was said: He was going and coming, as they met several times. By contrast, in the case mentioned in the mishna, where he went and it is not recorded that he came back, there is less of a concern that he appeased her. According to the Rif, the primary concern in the *baraita* is whether he appeased her and in the mishna that perhaps he returned. And if there is concern that perhaps he came back and no one knows about it, then all the more so should there be concern whether he appeased her.

״אם לא בָאתִי מִכָּאן וְעַד שְׁנֵים עָשָׂר חֹדֶשׁ כִּתְבוּ וּתְנוּ גֵּט לְאִשְׁתִּי״, כָּתְבוּ גֵּט בְּתוֹךְ שְׁנֵים עָשָׂר חֹדֶשׁ וְנָתְנוּ לְאַחַר שְׁנֵים עָשָׂר חֹדֶשׁ – אֵינוֹ גֵּט;

If a husband said to others: **If I do not come** back **from now until** the conclusion of **twelve months, write and give**[H] **a bill of divorce to my wife,** and **they wrote a bill of divorce during** the **twelve months and gave** it to her **after twelve months** had elapsed, **it is not** a valid **bill of divorce** because he instructed them to write the bill of divorce only after twelve months had elapsed.

״כִּתְבוּ וּתְנוּ גֵּט לְאִשְׁתִּי אִם לֹא בָאתִי מִכָּאן עַד שְׁנֵים עָשָׂר חֹדֶשׁ״, כָּתְבוּ בְּתוֹךְ שְׁנֵים עָשָׂר חֹדֶשׁ וְנָתְנוּ לְאַחַר שְׁנֵים עָשָׂר חֹדֶשׁ – אֵינוֹ גֵּט, רַבִּי יוֹסֵי אוֹמֵר: כָּזֶה גֵּט.

Similarly, if he said to others: **Write and give a bill of divorce to my wife if I do not come** back **from now until** the conclusion of **twelve months,** and **they wrote** it **during** the **twelve months but gave** it to her **after** the **twelve months, it is not** a valid **bill of divorce** because he instructed them to write the bill of divorce only after twelve months had elapsed, when it was clear that he did not come back. **Rabbi Yosei** disagrees and **says:** In a case **like this,** it is a valid **bill of divorce,** as he did not tell them when to write the bill of divorce. Rather, he stipulated only the time of giving.

כָּתְבוּ לְאַחַר שְׁנֵים עָשָׂר חֹדֶשׁ וְנָתְנוּ לְאַחַר שְׁנֵים עָשָׂר חֹדֶשׁ, וּמֵת, אִם הַגֵּט קוֹדֵם לְמִיתָה – הֲרֵי זֶה גֵּט, וְאִם מִיתָה קָדְמָה לַגֵּט – אֵינוֹ גֵּט, וְאִם אֵין יָדוּעַ – זוֹ הִיא שֶׁאָמְרוּ: מְגוֹרֶשֶׁת וְאֵינָהּ מְגוֹרֶשֶׁת.

If **they wrote** the bill of divorce **after twelve months** had elapsed, **and gave** it **after twelve months** had elapsed, **but** in the interim the husband **died, if** the giving of **the bill of divorce** occurred **before** the husband's **death this is** a valid **bill of divorce. But if** the husband's **death** occurred **before** the giving of **the bill of divorce**[H] it **is not** a valid **bill of divorce. And if it is not known** which occurred first, **this is** a case **where** the Sages **said** there is uncertainty whether **she is divorced or** whether **she is not divorced.**

גמ׳ תָּנָא: רַבּוֹתֵינוּ הִתִּירוּהָ לִינָּשֵׂא.

GEMARA The mishna states that if a husband said to his wife: This is your bill of divorce if I do not come back from now until the conclusion of twelve months, and the husband died within that time, it is not a valid bill of divorce. With regard to this it is **taught** in a *baraita*: **Our Rabbis** disagreed and **permitted her to marry** without requiring *ḥalitza* because they hold that it is a valid bill of divorce.

מַאן רַבּוֹתֵינוּ? אָמַר רַב יְהוּדָה אָמַר שְׁמוּאֵל: בֵּי דִינָא דְּשָׁרוּ מִשְׁחָא, סָבְרִי לַהּ כְּרַבִּי יוֹסֵי, דְּאָמַר: זְמַנּוֹ שֶׁל שְׁטָר מוֹכִיחַ עָלָיו.

The Gemara clarifies: **Who are our Rabbis** mentioned in this *baraita*? **Rav Yehuda said** that **Shmuel said:** They are **the court that permitted** consuming **oil** manufactured by gentiles. Why do they hold that this is a valid bill of divorce? **They hold in accordance with** the opinion of **Rabbi Yosei, who says: The date** written **in a document proves** when **it** takes effect. Whenever a document is dated it is assumed that the intent is for it to take effect from that date even if it does not state explicitly: From now.

HALAKHA

If I do not come…write and give, etc. – אִם לֹא בָאתִי...כִּתְבוּ וּתְנוּ וכו׳: If a husband said: If I do not come back within twelve months, then write and give a bill of divorce to my wife, or if he said: Write and give a bill of divorce to my wife if I do not return within twelve months, then the bill of divorce may not be written until after twelve months have elapsed. If it was written during this time it is not a valid bill of divorce, even if it was given only afterward (Rambam *Sefer Nashim, Hilkhot Geirushin* 9:22; *Shulḥan Arukh, Even HaEzer* 144:5).

If the death occurred before the bill of divorce, etc. – אִם מִיתָה קָדְמָה לַגֵּט וכו׳: If an agent wrote and gave the wife the bill of divorce after the twelve months elapsed, before the husband died, it is a valid bill of divorce. But if he died before the bill of divorce was given she is not divorced. If there is uncertainty with regard to the time of his death then it is uncertain whether or not she is divorced (Rambam *Sefer Nashim, Hilkhot Geirushin* 9:22; *Shulḥan Arukh, Even HaEzer* 144:5).

אָמַר רַבִּי אַבָּא בְּרֵיהּ דְּרַבִּי חִיָּיא בַּר אַבָּא אָמַר רַבִּי יוֹחָנָן: רַבִּי יְהוּדָה נְשִׂיאָה בְּנוֹ שֶׁל רַבָּן גַּמְלִיאֵל בַּר רַבִּי הוֹרָה, וְלֹא הוֹדוּ לוֹ כׇּל סִיעָתוֹ, וְאָמְרִי לַהּ: כׇּל שַׁעְתּוֹ.

Rabbi Abba, son of Rabbi Ḥiyya bar Abba, says that Rabbi Yoḥanan says: Rabbi Yehuda Nesia,[P] **son of Rabban Gamliel** the **son of Rabbi** Yehuda HaNasi, **taught** this matter, **and all of his colleagues** [*siato*] **did not concede to his** opinion. **And some say** that **all of his life** [*she'ato*][N] they did not concede to his opinion.

אָמַר לֵיהּ רַבִּי אֶלְעָזָר לְהַהוּא סָבָא: כִּי שְׁרֵיתוּהָ – לְאַלְתַּר שְׁרֵיתוּהָ, אוֹ לְאַחַר שְׁנֵים עָשָׂר חֹדֶשׁ שְׁרֵיתוּהָ? לְאַלְתַּר שְׁרֵיתוּהָ – דְּהָא לָא אָתֵי, אוֹ דִּלְמָא לְאַחַר שְׁנֵים עָשָׂר חֹדֶשׁ שְׁרֵיתוּהָ – דְּהָא אִיקַּיַּים לֵיהּ תְּנָאוֹ?

Rabbi Elazar[P] **said to a certain elderly man** who was a member of Rabbi Yehuda Nesia's court: **When you permitted** this woman to remarry, did **you permit her** to remarry **immediately** after her husband died **or did you permit her** only **after twelve months?** Did **you permit her** to remarry **immediately** after the husband died, **because he will** certainly **not come** back? **Or perhaps you permitted her** to remarry only **after twelve months, because** only then was the husband's **condition fulfilled?**

וְתִיבְּעֵי לֵיהּ מַתְנִיתִין: "מֵעַכְשָׁיו אִם לֹא בָּאתִי מִכָּאן וְעַד שְׁנֵים עָשָׂר חֹדֶשׁ", וּמֵת בְּתוֹךְ שְׁנֵים עָשָׂר חֹדֶשׁ – הֲרֵי זֶה גֵּט; לְאַלְתַּר הָוֵי – דְּהָא לָא אָתֵי, אוֹ דִּלְמָא לְאַחַר שְׁנֵים עָשָׂר חֹדֶשׁ – דְּהָא אִיקַּיַּים לֵיהּ תְּנָאֵיהּ! אִין הָכִי נָמֵי, וּמִשּׁוּם דַּהֲוָה בְּהַהוּא מַעֲשֶׂה.

The Gemara asks: **And let his dilemma be raised** also with regard to **the mishna,**[H] in the case where the husband said to his wife: This is your bill of divorce **from now if I do not come** back **from now until** the conclusion of **twelve months, and he died within** the **twelve months, this is** a valid **bill of divorce. Is** the bill of divorce valid **immediately** once the husband dies, **because he will** certainly **not come** back? **Or perhaps** the bill of divorce is valid only **after twelve months** have elapsed, **because** only then was **his condition fulfilled?**[N] The Gemara answers: **Yes, indeed so;** this question can be asked with regard to the case in the mishna. **And** Rabbi Elazar asked that particular elder **because** he **was** present **at that incident,** and he could answer based on what actually occurred.

אָמַר אַבָּיֵי: הַכֹּל מוֹדִים, הֵיכָא דְּאָמַר לִכְשֶׁתֵּצֵא חַמָּה מִנַּרְתִּיקָהּ,

§ **Abaye said: Everyone concedes** that in a case **where** the husband **said** to his wife that the bill of divorce will take effect **once the sun emerges from its sheath** [***minnartikah***],[L]

NOTES

All of his colleagues…all of his life – כׇּל סִיעָתוֹ...כׇּל שַׁעְתּוֹ: These two opinions are based on the similarity of the words colleagues [*siato*] and his life [*she'ato*]. Rashi explains that *she'ato* means all of his life. The *Arukh* explains that the term refers to all the other Sages who lived during his lifetime, not only those who were his colleagues.

Because only then was his condition fulfilled – דְּהָא אִיקַּיַּים לֵיהּ תְּנָאֵיהּ: *Tosafot* ask why the court must refrain from giving the bill of divorce until after twelve months have passed, as once the husband is dead it is clear that he will no longer come home, and if so the condition should be fulfilled immediately. They answer that this is technically correct, but the Sages were concerned that people may not know the details of the case, and they will mistakenly think that she may remarry even before the condition was fulfilled.

HALAKHA

And let his dilemma be raised also with regard to the mishna, etc. – וְתִיבְּעֵי לֵיהּ מַתְנִיתִין וכו׳: If a husband says to his wife: This is your bill of divorce from now if I do not return within twelve months, and he died within the twelve months, she is divorced. If the husband died childless and he has a brother [*yavam*], she may not remarry until she performs *ḥalitza* with the brother. As the dilemma of the Gemara is not resolved, then in accordance with the mishna, if she had already remarried she does not need to divorce (*Shulḥan Arukh*, *Even HaEzer* 144:3 and *Beit Shmuel* there).

LANGUAGE

Sheath [*nartik*] **– נַרְתִּיק:** Derived from the Greek ναρθήκιον, *narthēkion*, meaning a container.

PERSONALITIES

Rabbi Yehuda Nesia – רַבִּי יְהוּדָה נְשִׂיאָה: Rabbi Yehuda Nesia was the son of Rabban Gamliel, the latter of whom was the son of Rabbi Yehuda HaNasi. He was called Nesia to differentiate him from his illustrious grandfather, the redactor of the Mishna. One of the earliest *amora'im* in Eretz Yisrael, he was a colleague of Rabbi Yehuda HaNasi's great students. His own students included Rabbi Yoḥanan and Reish Lakish.

Rabbi Yehuda Nesia's court enacted various decrees. It was considered the great Torah center in the Jewish world, to the extent that even the great *amora* Rav deferred to its authority.

Rabbi Yehuda Nesia served as *Nasi* for many years and was probably the last *Nasi* to have outstanding Torah knowledge and to serve as the head of the Sanhedrin. In his honor, he, like his grandfather, is sometimes referred to simply as Rabbi, especially in the Jerusalem Talmud. He was succeeded as *Nasi*, but not as head of the Sanhedrin, by his son, Rabban Gamliel.

Rabbi Elazar – רַבִּי אֶלְעָזָר: In the Gemara, citations of Rabbi Elazar with no patronymic are referring to Rabbi Elazar ben Pedat, a second-generation *amora* in Eretz Yisrael. He was born in Babylonia, where he was a student of both Rav and Shmuel. In his youth he immigrated to Eretz Yisrael, where he married and where he became the primary student of Rabbi Yoḥanan. The connection between Rabbi Elazar and Rabbi Yoḥanan was so close that at times the Gemara raises a contradiction between the statement of one and the statement of the other, under the assumption that it was unlikely that they would hold different opinions in matters of *halakha*.

לְכִי נָפְקָא קָאָמַר לָהּ, וְכִי מָיֵית בְּלֵילְיָא הָוֵי גֵּט לְאַחַר מִיתָה;

he is saying to her that it will be valid **once** the sun **comes out** in the morning. **And** if the husband **dies during the night,** before sunrise, then this **will be** a **bill of divorce after** his **death** and is therefore invalid.

״עַל מְנָת שֶׁתֵּצֵא חַמָּה מִנַּרְתִּיקָהּ״ – מֵעַכְשָׁיו קָאָמַר לָהּ, דְּאָמַר רַב הוּנָא אָמַר רַב: כׇּל הָאוֹמֵר ״עַל מְנָת״ כְּאוֹמֵר ״מֵעַכְשָׁיו״ דָּמֵי;

But if he said to her: **On the condition that the sun will emerge from its sheath,**[H] then **he is saying to** his wife that the bill of divorce will take effect retroactively **from now** once the sun emerges. **As Rav Huna says** that **Rav says: Anyone who states** a condition employing the language: **On the condition, is like** one who **states:** The agreement will take effect retroactively **from now.**

לֹא נֶחְלְקוּ אֶלָּא בְּ״אִם תֵּצֵא״, מָר סָבַר לַהּ כְּרַבִּי יוֹסֵי, דְּאָמַר: זְמַנּוֹ שֶׁל שְׁטָר מוֹכִיחַ עָלָיו, וַהֲוָה לֵיהּ כְּ״מֵהַיּוֹם אִם מַתִּי״, כְּ״מֵעַכְשָׁיו אִם מַתִּי״, מָר לָא סָבַר כְּרַבִּי יוֹסֵי, וַהֲוָה לֵיהּ כְּ״אִם מַתִּי״ גְּרֵידָא.

The *tanna'im* **disagreed only in** the case of one who said to his wife: This will be your bill of divorce **if** the sun **emerges** from its sheath, and the husband died during the night. One **Sage,** referred to as: Our Rabbis, **holds in accordance with** the opinion of **Rabbi Yosei, who** says that **the date** written **in a document proves** when **it** takes effect, **and it is as** if the husband said: **From today if I die,** or **as** if he said: **From now if I die.** And one **Sage,** the unattributed *tanna* of the mishna, **does not hold in accordance with** the opinion of **Rabbi Yosei, and it is as** if the husband said **only: If I die,** in which case the bill of divorce is not valid because it cannot take effect after the husband's death.

״כִּתְבוּ וּתְנוּ גֵּט לְאִשְׁתִּי אִם לֹא בָּאתִי מִכָּאן וְעַד שְׁנֵים עָשָׂר חֹדֶשׁ״, כָּתְבוּ כו׳.

§ The mishna states that if a husband says to others: **Write and give a bill of divorce to my wife if I do not come** back **from now until** the conclusion of **twelve months,** and **they wrote** it within the twelve months but gave it to her after twelve months, it is not a valid bill of divorce. Rabbi Yosei disagrees and says: It is a valid bill of divorce.

אֲמַר לֵיהּ רַב יֵימָר לְרַב אַשִׁי: לֵימָא, קָסָבַר רַבִּי יוֹסֵי: כָּתַב גֵּט עַל תְּנַאי – כָּשֵׁר? לָא, לְעוֹלָם אֵימָא לָךְ: פָּסוּל, וְשָׁאנֵי הָכָא, מִדַּהֲוָה לֵיהּ לְמֵימַר ״אִם לֹא בָּאתִי כִּתְבוּ וּתְנוּ״, וַאֲמַר ״כִּתְבוּ וּתְנוּ אִם לֹא בָּאתִי״, הָכִי קָאָמַר: כִּתְבוּ מֵעַכְשָׁיו וּתְנוּ אִם לֹא בָּאתִי. וְרַבָּנַן? לָא שְׁנָא הָכִי וְלָא שְׁנָא הָכִי.

Rav Yeimar said to Rav Ashi: Shall we say that **Rabbi Yosei holds** that in general, if **he wrote a bill of divorce on condition** then it is **valid,** even if the condition was not fulfilled? Rav Ashi replied: **No, actually I** could **say to you** that according to Rabbi Yosei it is **invalid** if the condition is not fulfilled, **and here it is different. Since he could have said: If I do not come** back within twelve months, **write and give** the bill of divorce to my wife, which would emphasize that they may write the document only if he does not come; **but** instead **he said: Write and give** a bill of divorce **if I do not come** back, **this is what** the husband **is saying: Write** the bill of divorce **from now, and give** it to my wife **if I do not come** back within twelve months. **And** what do **the Rabbis** hold? They hold that **it is no different** whether the husband formulates his instructions like **this and it is no different** if the husband formulates his instructions like **that.** The court cannot differentiate based on the minor differences in the formulation.

HALAKHA

On the condition that the sun will emerge from its sheath – עַל מְנָת שֶׁתֵּצֵא חַמָּה מִנַּרְתִּיקָהּ: If a man gave his wife a bill of divorce at night, and he said to her: This is your bill of divorce on condition that the sun will emerge from its sheath, then even if he died during the night, the bill of divorce is valid once the sun rises. If he said to her: This is your bill of divorce once the sun emerges from its sheath, or he said: If the sun emerges, and he died during the night, she is not divorced. The *halakha* is in accordance with the opinion of the Rabbis, who disagree with Rabbi Yosei (Rambam).

The Ra'avad holds that she is divorced in the case where the husband used the word: If, in accordance with the opinion of Rabbi Yosei. *Tosafot* hold that whether he said: If, or whether he said: Once it emerges, her status is uncertain, as even Rabbi Yosei does not rule definitively. Some hold that even if the husband said: On the condition, the wife's status is uncertain, because it is unclear whether the *halakha* is in accordance with the opinion of Rav Huna with regard to the use of the phrase: On the condition (Rambam *Sefer Nashim, Hilkhot Geirushin* 9:15; *Shulḥan Arukh, Even HaEzer* 144:4).

תָּנוּ רַבָּנַן: ״לְאַחַר שָׁבוּעַ״ – שָׁנָה, ״לְאַחַר שָׁנָה״ – חֹדֶשׁ, ״לְאַחַר חֹדֶשׁ״ – שַׁבָּת.

§ Since the mishna discussed conditions dependent on time, the Gemara cites a *baraita* on a similar topic. **The Sages taught:** If the husband said to his wife: This is your bill of divorce if I do not come back **after a seven**-year Sabbatical cycle,[H] the word after means that the bill of divorce is not valid until a full **year** after the conclusion of the seven-year cycle. If he said: This is your bill of divorce if I do not come back **after** one **year,** it is not valid until one **month** after the end of that year. If he said: This is your bill of divorce if I do not come back **after** one **month,** it is not valid until one **week** after the end of the month.

״לְאַחַר שַׁבָּת״, מַאי? יָתֵיב רַבִּי זֵירָא קַמֵּיהּ דְּרַבִּי אַסִי, וְאָמְרִי לַהּ רַבִּי אַסִי קַמֵּיהּ דְּרַבִּי יוֹחָנָן וְקָאָמַר: חַד בְּשַׁבָּא, וּתְרֵי, וּתְלָתָא – בָּתַר שַׁבְּתָא, אַרְבָּעָה, וַחֲמִשָּׁא וּמַעֲלֵי שַׁבְּתָא – קַמֵּי שַׁבְּתָא.

The Gemara clarifies other similar cases not mentioned in the *baraita*. If the husband said: This is your bill of divorce if I do not come back **after a week,** then **what** is the *halakha*? The Gemara answers: **Rabbi Zeira sat before Rabbi Asi, and some say** that it was **Rabbi Asi** who sat **before Rabbi Yoḥanan, and he said** the following: **Sunday and Monday and Tuesday** are called **after Shabbat. Wednesday and Thursday and Friday** are all called **prior to Shabbat.**

תַּנְיָא, רַבִּי אוֹמֵר: ״לְאַחַר הָרֶגֶל״ – שְׁלֹשִׁים יוֹם. נְפַק רַבִּי חִיָּיא דְּרָשָׁהּ מִשְּׁמֵיהּ דְּרַבִּי וְקִלְּסוּהָ. מִשְּׁמֵיהּ דְּרַבִּים – וְלָא קִלְּסוּהָ; אַלְמָא לֵית הִילְכְתָא כְּוָותֵיהּ

It **is taught** in a *baraita* that **Rabbi** Yehuda HaNasi **says:** If a man says: This is your bill of divorce if I do not come back **after the pilgrimage Festival,**[H] then the document is valid only **thirty days** after the festival. **Rabbi Ḥiyya went out** and **taught** this *halakha* in public **in the name of Rabbi** Yehuda HaNasi, **and they praised it.** He then taught it **in the name of the majority,** as an unattributed opinion, **and they did not praise it. Apparently, the** ***halakha*** **is not in accordance with** this ruling. Consequently, the Sages did not praise Rabbi Ḥiyya when he taught it as if it were a majority ruling, as that would cause it to be accepted as *halakha.*

הדרן עלך מי שאחזו

HALAKHA

After a seven-year cycle, etc. – **לְאַחַר שָׁבוּעַ וכו׳:** If a husband said: This is your bill of divorce if I do not come back after the seven-year Sabbatical cycle, then the bill of divorce takes effect only after the year following the end of the cycle. If he said: After a year, then it takes effect after the month following that year. If he said: After a month, then it takes effect after the first week of the next month. If he said: After Shabbat, it takes effect after Tuesday. This is in accordance with the opinion cited in the *baraita* and Rav Asi's statement (Rambam *Sefer Nashim, Hilkhot Geirushin* 9:23–24; *Shulḥan Arukh, Even HaEzer* 144:6).

After the pilgrimage Festival, etc. – **לְאַחַר הָרֶגֶל וכו׳:** If a husband said: This is your bill of divorce if I do not come back after the pilgrimage Festival, then the bill of divorce does not take effect until fifteen days have passed after the Festival, as the *halakha* is not in accordance with the opinion of Rabbi Yehuda HaNasi (*Tur, Even HaEzer* 144).

Summary of **Perek VII**

While this chapter focused mainly on the giving of bills of divorce and the conditions appended to them, it also included many aggadic discussions, such as the story of King Solomon and the demon Ashmedai. It also described medicinal remedies and charms.

A man who is not mentally competent is unable to give a bill of divorce to his wife. Therefore, even if he instructs others to give a bill of divorce on his behalf, but becomes incompetent before they do so, the document cannot be written or given until the husband recovers his sanity. Once he is restored to sanity, the document may be written and given even without new instructions from the husband.

If a husband is unable to speak, he must demonstrate his sanity. He can then instruct others, through writing or gestures, to write and give a bill of divorce on his behalf.

Any condition placed on a bill of divorce must follow the halakhic principles concerning conditions: It must be a compound condition, the affirmative statement must precede the negative statement, the condition must precede the resultant action, and the condition and the resultant action must concern two separate matters.

Since a bill of divorce can be given only during the lifetime of the husband, any condition indicating that the document takes effect only after the husband's death invalidates the document. In this chapter, there was much discussion with regard to different phrases used verbally to give the instructions, and how they indicate when the bill of divorce takes effect.

Everyone agrees that if the husband says to his wife that the bill of divorce takes effect immediately provided that certain conditions are fulfilled in the future, the document is valid, even if the conditions are fulfilled after the death of the husband. If the husband does not specify that the document is valid immediately, there is no assumption that the date written in a document proves when it takes effect.

If the husband made the bill of divorce conditional on his wife's giving him a certain amount of money, or performing certain actions such as caring for his father or his child, the wife must fulfill his condition for the document to be valid.

During the time between when the bill of divorce is given and when it becomes valid, the woman must separate from her husband to avoid the possibility of the bill of divorce being classified as an outdated bill of divorce, or of the bill of divorce being canceled entirely. Her status during this time is uncertain with regard to whether or not she is divorced. Even though the husband is liable to support her and provide her with sustenance, she is not considered to be his wife.

Introduction to **Perek VIII**

When a man takes a wife, and marries her, and it comes to pass, if she finds no favor in his eyes, because he has found some unseemly matter in her, and he writes her a scroll of severance, and gives it in her hand, and sends her out of his house. And she departs out of his house, and goes and becomes another man's wife. And the latter husband hates her, and he writes her a bill of divorce, and gives it in her hand, and sends her out of his house.

(Deuteronomy 24:1–3)

The Sages received a tradition that the words: "And gives it in her hand" (Deuteronomy 24:1), do not refer only to the woman's actual hand, but include her vicinity and property.

One of the main issues explored in this chapter is the clarification of the exact limitations of this *halakha*. What is considered to be the equivalent of her hand? Is only an area adjacent to her included, or any property that belongs to her? Is a bill of divorce that is deposited near her considered to be in her domain, and how far does that area extend?

Another question pertaining to the giving of a bill of divorce is defining the phrase: "And gives it." Is the divorce effective only if the husband or his agent places the bill of divorce in the woman's hand, or is it effective even if it is thrown to her? Is the divorce effective if she takes the bill from his hand, or is it essential that he give it to her?

This chapter also addresses problems unrelated to the actual giving of the bill of divorce, such as the use of an outdated bill of divorce, meaning that after the writing of the bill of divorce the man and woman were secluded together again; the use of a bill of divorce that was not dated as stipulated by the rabbis; or a specific kind of bill of divorce called a folded and tied bill of divorce, in a case where it is lacking some of the necessary signatures.

With regard to these issues, there are various opinions, ranging from the strictest, which views anything that diverges from the formula coined by the Sages for bills of divorce as totally invalid, to more lenient opinions, which see these *halakhot* as recommendations to be adhered to *ab initio*, but which do not invalidate the bill of divorce after the fact.

An additional issue discussed in the chapter relates specifically to bills of divorce that are technically invalid. The question raised is whether there is sufficient validity to such a divorce to render a woman a divorcée, which disqualifies her from marrying a priest.

מתני׳ הַזּוֹרֵק גֵּט לְאִשְׁתּוֹ, וְהִיא בְּתוֹךְ בֵּיתָהּ אוֹ בְּתוֹךְ חֲצֵרָהּ – הֲרֵי זוֹ מְגוֹרֶשֶׁת; זְרָקוֹ לָהּ בְּתוֹךְ בֵּיתוֹ אוֹ בְּתוֹךְ חֲצֵרוֹ, אֲפִילּוּ הוּא עִמָּהּ בַּמִּטָּה – אֵינָהּ מְגוֹרֶשֶׁת; לְתוֹךְ חֵיקָהּ אוֹ לְתוֹךְ קַלְתָּהּ – הֲרֵי זוֹ מְגוֹרֶשֶׁת.

MISHNA In a case of **one who throws a bill of divorce to his wife, and she is in her house**[H] **or in her courtyard** at the time, then **she is divorced** as though he placed the bill of divorce in her hand. If **he threw it to her in his house**[H] **or in his courtyard, even if** the bill of divorce **is with her in the bed, she is not divorced.** If he threw the bill of divorce **into her lap, or into her basket** [*kaltah*],[L] **she is divorced,** even if she was in her husband's house at the time.

גמ׳ מְנָא הָנֵי מִילֵּי? דְּתָנוּ רַבָּנַן: ״וְנָתַן בְּיָדָהּ״ – אֵין לִי אֶלָּא יָדָהּ; גַּגָּהּ, חֲצֵרָהּ וְקַרְפֵּיפָהּ מִנַּיִן? תַּלְמוּד לוֹמַר: ״וְנָתַן״, מִכׇּל מָקוֹם.

GEMARA **From where are these matters** derived? What is the basis for the *halakha* that when the husband throws the bill of divorce into his wife's house or courtyard, the divorce takes effect? The Gemara answers: It is **as the Sages taught:** The verse states with regard to a bill of divorce: **"And gives it in her hand"** (Deuteronomy 24:1), from which **I have** derived that she is divorced **only** if he actually places it in **her hand.** But **from where** do I derive that she is divorced even if he places it on **her roof,** in **her courtyard, or** in **her enclosure? The verse states: "And gives it,"** indicating that she is divorced **in any case,** regardless of the manner in which he gives her the bill of divorce.

וְתַנְיָא נַמִי הָכִי גַּבֵּי גַּנָּב: ״יָדוֹ״ – אֵין לִי אֶלָּא יָדוֹ; גַּגּוֹ, חֲצֵרוֹ וְקַרְפֵּיפוֹ מִנַּיִן? תַּלְמוּד לוֹמַר: ״הִמָּצֵא תִמָּצֵא״, מִכׇּל מָקוֹם.

And that is also taught in a *baraita* **with regard to a thief.** It is written: "If the theft be found **in his hand"** (Exodus 22:3), from which **I have** derived that one is liable for theft **only** when the stolen item was found in **his hand.** But **from where** do I derive that one is liable for theft even if it was found on **his roof,** in **his courtyard, or** in **his enclosure,**[H] i.e., if the item reached his domain and he secured it with the intent to steal it? **The verse states: "If the theft be found,"** indicating that he is liable **in any case,** whether it was found in his hand or in his domain.

וּצְרִיכָא; דְּאִי אַשְׁמוֹעִינַן גֵּט, מִשּׁוּם דִּבְעַל כׇּרְחָהּ מְגָרְשָׁהּ, אֲבָל גַּנָּב דְּלֵיתֵיהּ בְּעַל כּוֹרְחֵיהּ – אֵימָא לָא;

The Gemara comments: **And** it is **necessary** to teach this *halakha* in both cases. **As if** the Torah **had taught us** only with regard to **a bill of divorce,** one could have said: **Because** a husband **divorces** his wife **against her will,** the divorce is effective regardless of how the husband places the document in her possession. **But a thief, who is not** accountable for theft that he performs **against his will, say no,** he is liable only when he actually steals the item with his hand, and not when it enters his domain by other means.

וְאִי אַשְׁמוֹעִינַן גַּנָּב, מִשּׁוּם דִּקְנָסֵיהּ רַחֲמָנָא, אֲבָל גֵּט – אֵימָא לָא, צְרִיכָא.

And if the Torah **had taught us** only with regard to **a thief,** one could have said: **Because the Merciful One penalized** the thief, obligating him to pay double the value of the item, it is clear that the Torah is strict with a thief. Similarly, the Torah also deemed him responsible for an item that was not actually in his hand. **But** with regard to a **bill of divorce, say no,** the divorce is not effective unless the husband places the document in her hand. Therefore, it is **necessary** to teach this *halakha* in both cases.

״חֲצֵרָהּ״. מַה שֶּׁקָּנְתָה אִשָּׁה קָנָה בַּעְלָהּ!

§ It was taught in the mishna that if the husband threw the bill of divorce into his wife's **courtyard,** she is divorced. The Gemara asks: How can she own a courtyard of her own? There is a principle: **That which a woman acquired** is **acquired** by **her husband,**[H] which indicates that the husband has the rights to all profits generated by his wife's property. Therefore, for all intents and purposes, the courtyard belongs to him for the duration of their marriage.

אָמַר רַבִּי אֶלְעָזָר: בְּכוֹתֵב לָהּ ״דִּין וּדְבָרִים אֵין לִי בִּנְכָסַיִךְ״.

Rabbi Elazar says: The mishna is referring to a case **where** the husband **writes to** his wife: **I have no legal** dealings **or involvement in your property,** thereby relinquishing any ownership rights to her property.

HALAKHA

In her house, etc. – בְּתוֹךְ בֵּיתָהּ וכו׳: The phrase "and gives it in her hand" (Deuteronomy 24:1) is not referring only to her hand. If he placed it in her lap, in her courtyard, or in a place that she rented or borrowed, it is a valid bill of divorce (Rambam *Sefer Nashim, Hilkhot Geirushin* 5:1; *Shulḥan Arukh, Even HaEzer* 139:1).

In his house, etc. – בְּתוֹךְ בֵּיתוֹ וכו׳: If a man threw a bill of divorce to his wife when she was in his house or courtyard, she is not divorced until the bill of divorce reaches her hand or falls into one of her vessels; and if it falls into her vessel, it must be a vessel with regard to which the husband has no concern as to its location, as the Gemara will note (Rambam *Sefer Nashim, Hilkhot Geirushin* 5:8; *Shulḥan Arukh, Even HaEzer* 139:10).

His roof, his courtyard, or his enclosure – גַּגּוֹ חֲצֵרוֹ וְקַרְפֵּיפוֹ: If one stole from another and brought the stolen item into his property, he becomes liable at the time it is secured on his roof, in his courtyard, or in his enclosure, even if he didn't pull it or pick it up (*Shulḥan Arukh, Ḥoshen Mishpat* 348:4).

That which a woman acquired is acquired by her husband – מַה שֶּׁקָּנְתָה אִשָּׁה קָנָה בַּעְלָהּ: Any money found in the possession of a married woman is considered to be in her husband's possession, and he can consume it and its profits, unless she brings proof that it is not his (Rambam *Sefer Nashim, Hilkhot Ishut* 22:30).

LANGUAGE

Basket [*kelet*] – קֶלֶת: From the Greek κάλαθος, *kalathos*, referring to a basket with a narrow base that was used mainly to hold wool and work materials used by women.

Roman statue of a woman with a basket on her head

HALAKHA

Where he writes to her and she is still only betrothed – בְּכוֹתֵב לָהּ וְעוֹדָהּ אֲרוּסָה: If one writes or says to his betrothed: I have no right and no claim to your properties, and his betrothed sold or gave away her properties, even after they were married, her actions stand. This is in accordance with the statement of the Sages from the school of Rabbi Yannai (Rambam *Sefer Nashim, Hilkhot Geirushin* 23:1; *Shulḥan Arukh, Even HaEzer* 92:1).

וְכִי כָּתַב לָהּ הָכִי מַאי הָוֵי? וְהָתַנְיָא: הָאוֹמֵר לַחֲבֵירוֹ ״דִּין וּדְבָרִים אֵין לִי עַל שָׂדֶה זוֹ״, וְ״אֵין לִי עֵסֶק בָּהּ״, וְ״יָדַי מְסוּלֶּקֶת הֵימֶנָּה״ – לֹא אָמַר כְּלוּם!

The Gemara asks: **And when he writes this to her, what** of it? **But isn't it taught** in a *baraita*: **One who says to another** with whom he owns a field in a partnership: **I have no rights and claims to this field, or: I have no involvement with it, or: My hand is removed from it**; it is as though **he said nothing,** since these expressions are not considered to be a withdrawal of his rights to the field.

אָמְרִי דְּבֵי רַבִּי יַנַּאי: בְּכוֹתֵב לָהּ וְעוֹדָהּ אֲרוּסָה; וְכִדְרַב כָּהֲנָא, דְּאָמַר רַב כָּהֲנָא: נַחֲלָה הַבָּאָה לוֹ לְאָדָם מִמָּקוֹם אַחֵר, אָדָם מַתְנֶה עָלֶיהָ שֶׁלֹּא יִרָשֶׁנָּה.

The Gemara answers: **They say in the school of Rabbi Yannai:** The case is one **where he writes to her and she is still** only **betrothed;**[H] he has yet to obtain ownership of her property, being that his rights to his wife's property are only actuated at the time of the marriage. **And** this is **in accordance with** the statement **of Rav Kahana, as Rav Kahana says:** With regard to **an inheritance that comes to a person from another place,** i.e., it is not an inheritance from his father, **a person can stipulate about it** from the outset **that he should not inherit it,** and this condition is effective in annulling his rights to the inheritance. This teaches that as long as the property has not yet entered his possession, he can withdraw his rights to it.

וְכִדְרָבָא, דְּאָמַר רָבָא, הָאוֹמֵר:

And this is **in accordance with** the statement **of Rava, as Rava says: One who says:**

Perek **VIII**
Daf **77** Amud **b**

HALAKHA

I do not want, etc. – אִי אֶפְשִׁי וכו׳: With regard to any ordinance instituted by the Sages concerning monetary matters that benefit a person, that person has the ability to forgo the benefits of that ordinance (see Rambam *Sefer Mishpatim, Hilkhot Malve VeLoveh* 19:6 and *Hilkhot To'en VeNitan* 1:4).

I do not wish to be sustained by you, and I will not do work for you – אֵינִי נִיזּוֹנֶת וְאֵינִי עוֹשָׂה: If a woman says: I will not be sustained by my husband's property, and I will not do work for him, her statement is legally binding. Rema writes that some say (*Beit Yosef*, citing Rambam) she must still take care of the needs of the house even in such a case, but she is not required to perform any other type of work (Rambam *Sefer Nashim, Hilkhot Ishut* 12:4; *Shulḥan Arukh, Even HaEzer* 69:4, 80:15).

Her bill of divorce and her courtyard enter her possession simultaneously – גִּיטָּהּ וַחֲצֵרָהּ בָּאִין כְּאֶחָד: The Ramah rules that since she receives her bill of divorce and acquires ownership of her courtyard simultaneously, she must be standing next to her courtyard when the bill of divorce was placed inside it. If not, she does not acquire them together (*Shulḥan Arukh, Even HaEzer* 139:2).

אִי אֶפְשִׁי בְּתַקָּנַת חֲכָמִים כְּגוֹן זוֹ – שׁוֹמְעִין לוֹ.

I do not want[H] to avail myself of **the ordinance of the Sages** that was instituted on my behalf, **such as** in **this** scenario, **we listen to him.**

מַאי ״כְּגוֹן זוֹ״? כִּדְרַב הוּנָא אָמַר רַב, דְּאָמַר רַב הוּנָא אָמַר רַב: יְכוֹלָה אִשָּׁה שֶׁתֹּאמַר לְבַעְלָהּ ״אֵינִי נִיזּוֹנֶת וְאֵינִי עוֹשָׂה״.

The Gemara asks: **What** is referred to by the words: **Such as** in **this** scenario? What case did Rava refer to that he indicated that in similar situations the *halakha* is the same? The Gemara explains that Rava was referring to **that which Rav Huna says** that **Rav says. As Rav Huna says** that **Rav says: A woman can say to her husband: I do not** wish to **be sustained** by you, **and I will not do** work for you.[H] Although the Sages instituted on her behalf that she would be sustained in exchange for her work, she has the choice of waiving that right if she prefers to retain her earnings. Rava adds that in any similar case where the Sages instituted an ordinance for one's benefit, he can say that he does not wish to accept this rabbinic ordinance if it does not assist him.

רָבָא אָמַר: אַטּוּ יָדָהּ מִי לָא קְנָיָא לֵיהּ לְבַעַל? אֶלָּא גִּיטָּהּ וְיָדָהּ בָּאִין כְּאֶחָד, הָכָא נָמֵי גִּיטָּהּ וַחֲצֵרָהּ בָּאִין כְּאֶחָד.

Rava said that one can resolve the question about the wife's ability to acquire a bill of divorce in a courtyard in a more direct way: **Is that to say** that **her hand is not acquired by her husband?** Yet despite the fact that he owns her hand, she is divorced once she receives a bill of divorce in her hand. **Rather,** one must say that **her bill of divorce and her hand,** i.e., her complete ownership over her hand, **enter** her possession **simultaneously.** Since the bill of divorce releases her from her obligations to her husband, at that moment she acquires full rights to her hand. **Here too,** in the case of her courtyard, one can say that **her bill of divorce and her courtyard enter** her possession **simultaneously,**[H] as her husband's rights to her property are terminated at the time of divorce.

אֲמַר לֵיהּ רָבִינָא לְרַב אָשֵׁי: רָבָא, יַד דְּאִשָּׁה קָא קַשְׁיָא לֵיהּ? נְהִי דְּקָנֵי לֵיהּ לְמַעֲשֵׂה יָדֶיהָ, יָדָהּ גּוּפָהּ מִי קָנֵי לֵיהּ?

Ravina said to Rav Ashi: Was it **difficult for Rava** to understand the *halakha* that one can effect divorce by placing a bill of divorce in **the hand of a woman?** Why is this difficult? **Though** the rights **to her earnings belong to** the husband, **does her hand itself belong to him?** Therefore, since a woman owns her hand, she is divorced once she receives the bill of divorce in her hand; and it is not necessary to apply the principle that the bill of divorce and her hand enter her possession simultaneously. Therefore, there is no proof that the bill of divorce and her courtyard enter her possession simultaneously.

אמר ליה: רבא, יד העבד קא קשיא ליה, למאן דאמר בשטר על ידי עצמו, יד עבד כיד רבו דמיא! אלא גטו וידו באין כאחד, הכי נמי גיטה וחצירה באין כאחד.

Rav Ashi **said to him:** It was **difficult for Rava** to understand the *halakha* that one can effect emancipation by placing a bill of manumission in **the hand of a slave,** as follows: **According to the one who says** that a slave can be emancipated **with a bill** of manumission **by** receiving the bill **himself,**[H] one can ask: How is this effective? Isn't **the hand of a slave like the hand of his master,** as the master owns the slave's body? Therefore, when the master gives the bill of manumission to his slave, it is as though he gave it to himself, and the bill is never considered as having reached the slave's domain. How can the slave be emancipated in this manner? **Rather,** one must say that **his bill** of manumission **and his hand enter** his possession **simultaneously. So too,** with regard to a woman's courtyard, one can explain that **her bill of divorce and her courtyard enter** her possession **simultaneously.**

ההוא שכיב מרע דכתב לה גיטא לדביתהו בהדי פניא דמעלי שבתא ולא הספיק למיתביה לה. למחר תקף ליה עלמא, אתו לקמיה דרבא, אמר להו: זילו אמרו ליה ליקנייה ניהלה להההוא דוכתא דיתיב ביה גיטא, ותיזל איהי ותיחוד ותפתח ותחזיק ביה,

§ The Gemara relates that there was **a certain person on his deathbed who wrote a bill of divorce for his wife toward the evening of the coming of the Shabbat, but he did not manage to give it to her. The next day his condition intensified**[NH] and he was unable to give her the bill of divorce. People **came before Rava** to ask what they should do. **He said to them: Go tell him to transfer to her** ownership **of that place where the bill of divorce is resting, and she should go and close** the door **and open** it **and assert ownership over it,** thereby acquiring the place together with the bill of divorce that is in it.

דתנן: נעל, גדר, פרץ כל שהוא – הרי זו חזקה.

As we learned in a mishna (*Bava Batra* 42a): **If one locked, fenced** in,[H] or **breached any amount, this is** a valid act of **taking possession** through which land is acquired.

אמר ליה רב עיליש לרבא: מה שקנתה אשה קנה בעלה! איכסיף.

Rav Ilish said to Rava: How will it help for her to acquire the place, since **that which a woman acquired is acquired** by **her husband?** Rava **was embarrassed** that he issued an incorrect ruling.

לסוף איגלי מילתא דארוסה הואי, אמר רבא: אם אמרו בנשואה יאמרו בארוסה? הדר אמר רבא: לא שנא ארוסה ולא שנא נשואה, גיטה וחצירה באין כאחד.

Ultimately, it was revealed that she was a betrothed woman. Rava said: I ruled correctly, as even **if they said with regard to a married woman** that everything she acquires belongs to her husband, would **they say** the same **with regard to a betrothed woman?** A betrothed woman's hand is not considered to be like the hand of her husband. **Rava then said:** There **is no difference** if she is **a betrothed woman, and there is no difference** if she is **a married woman,** as **her bill of divorce and her courtyard enter** her possession **simultaneously.**

והא אמרה רבא מעיקרא! כי אמרה רבא – אהאי מעשה אמרה.

The Gemara asks: **But didn't Rava** already **say this** *halakha*, that her bill of divorce and her courtyard enter her possession simultaneously, **at the outset?** The Gemara answers: **When Rava said this** *halakha*, **he said it in connection with this** very **incident.**

"והיא בתוך ביתה". אמר עולא: והוא, שעומדת בצד ביתה ובצד חצרה. רבי אושעיא אמר: אפילו היא בטבריא וחצרה בציפורי, היא בציפורי וחצרה בטבריא – מגורשת.

§ It was taught in the mishna that if a husband throws his wife a bill of divorce **and she is in her house,** then she is divorced. **Ulla says: This is** only **if she is standing next to her house**[H] **and next to her courtyard,** as only then will her house and courtyard acquire it for her. **Rabbi Oshaya says: Even** if **she is in Tiberius and her courtyard** is **in Tzippori,** or if **she is in Tzippori and her courtyard** is in **Tiberius, she is divorced.**

NOTES

His condition intensified – תקף ליה עלמא: The early commentaries note, based on the *Tosefta*, that in principle the Sages prohibited divorcing one's wife on Shabbat. In the case of a person on his deathbed, the Sages permitted the giving of a bill of divorce, lest the dying man become agitated.

HALAKHA

With a bill of manumission by receiving the bill himself – בשטר על ידי עצמו: If one writes a bill of manumission for his Canaanite slave that states: You are a freeman, or any other expression of emancipation, and hands it to him, the slave is emancipated (Rambam *Sefer Kinyan, Hilkhot Avadim* 5:3; *Shulḥan Arukh, Yoreh De'a* 267:41).

The next day his condition intensified – למחר תקף ליה עלמא: A person may not divorce his wife on Shabbat, unless his death is imminent (*Shulḥan Arukh, Oraḥ Ḥayyim* 339:4).

If one locked, fenced in, etc. – נעל, גדר וכו׳: Real estate can be acquired through an act of taking possession. For example, if the purchaser locked, fenced in, or breached any amount effectively, he acquires the property in question (Rambam *Sefer Kinyan, Hilkhot Mekhira* 1:8; *Shulḥan Arukh, Ḥoshen Mishpat* 192:1).

This is only if she is standing next to her house – והוא שעומדת בצד ביתה: If one throws a bill of divorce into his wife's courtyard, the divorce takes effect only if she is standing in her courtyard and the courtyard is consciously secured by her. If she is not standing in her courtyard, even though the bill of divorce is secured in her courtyard, she is not divorced. This is in accordance with Ulla's statement (Rambam *Sefer Nashim, Hilkhot Geirushin* 5:2; *Shulḥan Arukh, Even HaEzer* 139:1).

HALAKHA

Where he lent her the place – דְּאוֹשְׁלָהּ מָקוֹם: If a man lent his wife a place in his courtyard but he did not specify exactly where, and he throws a bill of divorce into the courtyard and it lands on a beam or rocks, the divorce takes effect if the place on which the bill of divorce falls is smaller than four by four cubits, is not ten handbreadths high, and does not have its own name. According to one opinion (see *Maggid Mishne*), she is divorced only when the bill of divorce falls within four cubits of her. If even one of these three conditions is not met, the assumption is that he lent her only one place and not two, and she is not divorced (Rambam *Sefer Nashim, Hilkhot Geirushin* 5:9; *Shulḥan Arukh, Even HaEzer* 139:11).

וְהָא "הִיא בְּתוֹךְ בֵּיתָהּ וּבְתוֹךְ חֲצֵרָהּ" קָתָנֵי! הָכִי קָאָמַר: וְהִיא כְּמִי שֶׁבְּתוֹךְ בֵּיתָהּ וְהִיא כְּמִי שֶׁבְּתוֹךְ חֲצֵרָהּ, דְּכֵיוָן דְּחָצֵר מִשְׁתַּמֶּרֶת לְדַעְתָּהּ הִיא – מִתְגָּרֶשֶׁת.

The Gemara challenges this: **But isn't** it **taught** in the mishna that **she is in her house and in her courtyard?** The Gemara answers: **This is what** the mishna **is saying: And she is** considered to be **like one who is in her house; and she is** considered to be **like one who is in her courtyard.** This means that **since it is a courtyard that is secured with her knowledge,** it is as though she is there, and **she is divorced.**

לֵימָא בְּהָא קָמִיפַּלְגִי, דְּמָר סָבַר: חָצֵר מִשּׁוּם יָדָהּ אִתְרַבַּאי, וּמָר סָבַר: חָצֵר מִשּׁוּם שְׁלִיחוּת אִתְרַבַּאי?

The Gemara suggests: **Let us say that they disagree about this** issue: One **Sage,** Ulla, **holds** that a **courtyard is included** in the areas where she can obtain ownership of a bill of divorce **as** an extension of **her hand.** Consequently, it has the same *halakhot* as her hand, so that just as her hand is close to her, so too, her courtyard must be close to her in order for her to acquire the bill of divorce through it. **And one Sage,** Rabbi Oshaya, **holds** that a **courtyard is included** in the areas where she can obtain ownership of a bill of divorce **as** an extension **of agency,** and therefore, like an agent, her courtyard can acquire the bill of divorce for her when she is far away.

לָא, דְּכוּלֵּי עָלְמָא – חָצֵר מִשּׁוּם יָדָהּ אִיתְרַבַּאי, מָר סָבַר: כְּיָדָהּ, מַה יָּדָהּ בִּסְמוּכָה, אַף חֲצֵרָהּ בִּסְמוּכָה.

The Gemara rejects this: **No, everyone** agrees that a **courtyard is included** in the areas where she can obtain ownership of a bill of divorce **as** an extension of **her hand.** They disagree about how it is compared to her hand. One **Sage,** Ulla, **holds** that it is entirely **like her hand. Just as her** actual **hand is next to** her, **so too, her courtyard,** which is an extension of her hand, acquires the bill of divorce **when** it is **next to** her.

וְאִידָךְ: אִי מַה יָּדָהּ בִּדְבוּקָה, אַף חֲצֵרָהּ בִּדְבוּקָה! אֶלָּא כְּיָדָהּ, מַה יָּדָהּ מִשְׁתַּמֶּרֶת לְדַעְתָּהּ, אַף חֲצֵרָהּ הַמִּשְׁתַּמֶּרֶת לְדַעְתָּהּ, לְאַפּוּקֵי חֲצֵרָהּ הַמִּשְׁתַּמֶּרֶת שֶׁלֹּא לְדַעְתָּהּ.

And the other Sage, Rabbi Oshaya, holds that **if** you derive matters in this way, you should say that **just as her** actual **hand is attached** to her, **so too, her courtyard** can acquire a bill of divorce only **when** it is **attached** to her, which cannot be. **Rather,** the comparison is as follows: Her courtyard is **like her** actual **hand,** and **just as her hand is secured with her knowledge, so too,** only **her courtyard that is consciously secured by her** can acquire a bill of divorce for her. This serves **to exclude her courtyard that is not consciously secured by her,** i.e., that she has no control over, which cannot acquire a bill of divorce for her, since it is not similar to her hand.

הַהוּא גַּבְרָא דִּזְרַק לָהּ גִּיטָּא לִדְבֵיתְהוּ, הֲוָה קַיְימָא בְּחָצֵר, אֲזַל גִּיטָּא נְפַל בְּפִיסְלָא; אֲמַר רַב יוֹסֵף: חָזֵינַן, אִי הָוְיָא אַרְבַּע אַמּוֹת עַל אַרְבַּע אַמּוֹת – פְּלַג לֵיהּ רְשׁוּתָא לְנַפְשֵׁיהּ, וְאִי לָא – חֲדָא רְשׁוּתָא הִיא.

§ The Gemara relates that there was **a certain man who threw a bill of divorce to his wife while she was standing in a courtyard. The bill of divorce went** and **fell onto a board** of wood. **Rav Yosef said: We see** the precise circumstance: **If the** board encompassed an area **of four cubits by four cubits, it** thereby is considered to be **a separate domain of its own** and is not included in the courtyard within which she was standing, and she is consequently not divorced. **And if** the board was **not** that large, **it is** part of the courtyard and it is all **one domain,** and she is therefore divorced.

בְּמַאי עָסְקִינַן? אִילֵימָא בְּחָצֵר דִּידָהּ, כִּי הָוֵי אַרְבַּע אַמּוֹת מַאי הָוֵי? אֶלָּא בְּחָצֵר דִּידֵיהּ, כִּי לָא הָוֵי אַרְבַּע אַמּוֹת מַאי הָוֵי?

The Gemara clarifies: **With what are we dealing** here? **If we say** that the incident occurred **in her courtyard, if** the board **had** an area of **four cubits, what of it?** Since the board belongs to her as well, it should still be an effective divorce. **Rather,** say that the incident occurred **in his courtyard;** but then, even **if** the board did **not have** an area of **four cubits, what of it?** Since none of it belongs to her, why would it be an effective divorce?

לָא צְרִיכָא, דְּאוֹשְׁלָהּ מָקוֹם, דְּחַד מָקוֹם מוֹשְׁלִי אִינָשֵׁי, תְּרֵי מְקוֹמוֹת לָא מוֹשְׁלֵי אִינָשֵׁי.

The Gemara answers: **No,** it is **necessary** in a case **where he lent her the place,**[H] i.e., the courtyard, as a means to acquire the bill of divorce. And **since people lend one place,** but **people do not lend two places,** if the board is considered to be a separate domain then it was not included in the courtyard that was lent to her, and it would therefore not be an effective divorce.

וְלָא אֲמַרַן אֶלָּא דְּלָא גָּבוֹהַּ עֲשָׂרָה, אֲבָל גָּבוֹהַּ עֲשָׂרָה – אַף עַל גַּב דְּלָא הָוֵי אַרְבַּע אַמּוֹת.

The Gemara notes: **And we said** that this is the *halakha* **only** in a case where the place onto which the bill of divorce fell **was not ten** handbreadths **higher** than the courtyard. **But** if the place onto which the bill of divorce fell was **ten** handbreadths **higher, even though** the board did **not have** an area of **four cubits,** it is still considered to be a separate domain.

וְלָא אֲמַרַן אֶלָּא דְּלֵית לֵיהּ

And we said that this is the *halakha* **only** in a case where the place onto which the bill of divorce fell **does not have**

שֵׁם לְוַוי, אֲבָל אִית לֵיהּ שֵׁם לְוַוי – אַף עַל גַּב דְּלָא גָּבוֹהַּ עֲשָׂרָה, וְאַף עַל גַּב דְּלָא הָוֵי אַרְבַּע אַמּוֹת.

a modifier, meaning that this board is not referred to by a unique name. **But if it has a modifier, even though it is not ten** handbreadths **higher** than the courtyard, **and even though** the board did **not have** an area of **four cubits,** it is still considered to be a separate domain, and it would therefore not be an effective divorce.

״אֲפִילּוּ הוּא עִמָּהּ בַּמִּטָּה״ כּוּ׳. אָמַר רָבָא: לֹא שָׁנוּ אֶלָּא בְּמִטָּה שֶׁלּוֹ, אֲבָל בְּמִטָּה שֶׁלָּהּ – מְגוֹרֶשֶׁת.

§ It was taught in the mishna that if he throws a bill of divorce to his wife while she is in his house, she is not divorced, **even if** the bill of divorce **is with her in the bed,** i.e., he throws it onto the bed in which she is sitting or lying. **Rava says: They taught** this **only** in a case where he throws the bill of divorce to her and it is with her **in his bed. But** if he throws the bill of divorce to her and it is with her **in her bed,** then **she is divorced.**

תַּנְיָא נַמִּי הָכִי, רַבִּי אֱלִיעֶזֶר אוֹמֵר: בְּמִטָּה שֶׁלּוֹ – אֵינָהּ מְגוֹרֶשֶׁת, בְּמִטָּה שֶׁלָּהּ – מְגוֹרֶשֶׁת.

This is also taught in a *baraita*: **Rabbi Eliezer says:** If he throws the bill of divorce to her when she is **in his bed, she is not divorced;** if he throws it to her when she is **in her bed,**[H] **she is divorced.**

וּבְמִטָּה שֶׁלָּהּ מְגוֹרֶשֶׁת?! כֵּלָיו שֶׁל לוֹקֵחַ בִּרְשׁוּת מוֹכֵר הוּא! שָׁמְעַתְּ מִינָּהּ: כֵּלָיו שֶׁל לוֹקֵחַ בִּרְשׁוּת מוֹכֵר – קָנָה לוֹקֵחַ?

The Gemara asks: And if he throws the bill of divorce to her **in her bed, is she divorced?** But the bed **is like vessels of a buyer**[H] that are **in the domain of the seller,** since the bed that belongs to her is in the house of the husband. Can **you conclude from** here that even if the **vessels of a buyer** are **in the domain of the seller, the buyer acquires** anything that is deposited into his vessels? This issue is disputed elsewhere. Some hold that when a vessel of the buyer is in the domain of the seller, the vessel cannot serve to acquire an item on behalf of the buyer.

לָא צְרִיכָא, דְּגָבוֹהַּ עֲשָׂרָה. וְהָאִיכָּא מְקוֹם כַּרְעֵי! אַמְּקוֹם כַּרְעֵי לָא קָפְדִי אֱינָשֵׁי.

The Gemara answers: **No,** it is **necessary** to state this *halakha* in a case **where** the bed is **ten** handbreadths **high,** as then the bed is considered to be its own domain. The Gemara challenges this: **But there is the place** on which the **legs** of the bed are standing; the legs are standing in the husband's domain. The Gemara answers: **People are not particular** about **the place of the legs** of the bed since it is so small. Therefore, since the bed is considered to be its own domain, it is not considered to be within the domain of the husband.

״לְתוֹךְ חֵיקָהּ אוֹ לְתוֹךְ קַלְתָּהּ – מְגוֹרֶשֶׁת״. אַמַּאי? כֵּלָיו שֶׁל לוֹקֵחַ בִּרְשׁוּת מוֹכֵר הוּא!

§ It was taught in the mishna that if the husband threw the bill of divorce **into her lap, or into her basket,** then **she is divorced,** even if she is in her husband's house at that time. The Gemara asks: **Why** is she divorced? **Is this** not like a case of **the vessels of a buyer** that are **in the domain of the seller,** with regard to which there is a dispute concerning whether the vessels can serve to acquire an item on the buyer's behalf?

אָמַר רַב יְהוּדָה אָמַר שְׁמוּאֵל: כְּגוֹן שֶׁהָיְתָה קַלְתָּהּ תְּלוּיָה בָּהּ. וְכֵן אָמַר רַבִּי אֶלְעָזָר אָמַר רַבִּי אוֹשַׁעְיָא: כְּגוֹן שֶׁהָיְתָה קַלְתָּהּ תְּלוּיָה בָּהּ. וְרַבִּי שִׁמְעוֹן בֶּן לָקִישׁ אָמַר: קְשׁוּרָה אַף עַל פִּי שֶׁאֵינָהּ תְּלוּיָה.

Rav Yehuda says that **Shmuel says:** The mishna is referring to a case **where her basket was hanging from her** body, and therefore it is not considered to be within the domain of the husband. **And so Rabbi Elazar says** that **Rabbi Oshaya says:** The mishna is referring to a case **where her basket was hanging from her** body. **And Rabbi Shimon ben Lakish says:** If it was **tied** to her then that is enough, **even though it is not hanging** from her body.

HALAKHA

In her bed – בְּמִטָּה שֶׁלָּהּ: If a man threw a bill of divorce to his wife in his domain, and it reached the bed on which the woman was sitting, she is divorced, since the bed is considered to be an independent domain, and the husband is not particular about the place where the legs of the bed stand. If the bed was not ten handbreadths high, it is unclear whether she is divorced, since there is no clear ruling with regard to the *halakha* of vessels of a buyer in the domain of a seller (Rambam *Sefer Nashim, Hilkhot Geirushin* 5:8; *Shulḥan Arukh, Even HaEzer* 139:10, and *Beit Shmuel* there)

Vessels of a buyer, etc. – כֵּלָיו שֶׁל לוֹקֵחַ וכו׳: A person's vessels can serve to acquire items on his behalf if they are placed in a location where he has the right to place them. Therefore, once an item enters a person's vessel, the transaction cannot be retracted. A person's vessels cannot serve to acquire items for him if they are in the public domain or in the domain of the seller, unless the seller said that the vessel should serve to acquire the item for him or he gave permission to the buyer to place the vessel there (Rambam *Sefer Kinyan, Hilkhot Mekhira* 4:1; *Shulḥan Arukh, Ḥoshen Mishpat* 200:3, and *Shakh* there).

רַב אַדָּא בַּר אַהֲבָה אָמַר: כְּגוֹן שֶׁהָיְתָה קַלְתָּהּ מוּנַּחַת לָהּ בֵּין יַרְכוֹתֶיהָ. רַב מְשָׁרְשִׁיָּא בַּר רַב דִּימִי אָמַר: כְּגוֹן שֶׁהָיָה בַּעְלָהּ מוֹכֵר קְלָתוֹת.

Rav Adda bar Ahava says: The mishna is referring to a case **where her basket was placed between her thighs** and is therefore in the place where she is sitting, and since her husband is not particular about the place in which she is sitting, it is considered her domain. **Rav Mesharshiyya bar Rav Dimi says:** The mishna is referring to a case **where her husband was a basket seller,**[H] and therefore is not particular about the place where the basket is since his whole courtyard is full of baskets, and it is therefore considered to be her domain.

רַבִּי יוֹחָנָן אָמַר: מְקוֹם חֵיקָהּ קָנוּי לָהּ, מְקוֹם קַלְתָּהּ קָנוּי לָהּ. אֲמַר רָבָא: מַאי טַעֲמָא דְּרַבִּי יוֹחָנָן? לְפִי שֶׁאֵין אָדָם מַקְפִּיד לֹא עַל מְקוֹם חֵיקָהּ וְלֹא עַל מְקוֹם קַלְתָּהּ.

Rabbi Yoḥanan says: There is no need for these explanations, since **the place of her lap belongs to her,** and **the place of her basket belongs to her. Rava said: What is the reasoning of Rabbi Yoḥanan's** statement? **Because a person is not particular,**[H] **not about the place** of his wife's **lap, nor about the place of her basket,** it is as though he transferred ownership of the place to her for her use.

תַּנְיָא נַמִּי הָכִי: זְרָקוֹ לָהּ לְתוֹךְ חֵיקָהּ אוֹ לְתוֹךְ קַלְתָּהּ, אוֹ לְתוֹךְ כָּל דָּבָר שֶׁהוּא כְּקַלְתָּהּ – הֲרֵי זוֹ מְגוֹרֶשֶׁת.

This is also taught in a *baraita*: If **he threw** the bill of divorce **to her into her lap, or into her basket, or into anything that is like her basket, then she is divorced.**

"כָּל דָּבָר שֶׁהוּא כְּקַלְתָּהּ" לְאִיתוּיֵי מַאי? לְאִיתוּיֵי טַסְקָא דְּאָכְלָה בָּהּ תַּמְרֵי.

The Gemara analyzes the wording of the *baraita*: **What is included** by the expansive term: **Anything that is like her basket?** It serves **to include the basket** [*taska*][L] **from which she eats dates,** as he is not particular about its place as well.

מתני׳ אָמַר לָהּ "כִּנְסִי שְׁטַר חוֹב זֶה", אוֹ שֶׁמְּצָאַתּוּ מֵאֲחוֹרָיו, קוֹרְאָה וַהֲרֵי הוּא גִּיטָּהּ – אֵינוֹ גֵּט, עַד שֶׁיֹּאמַר לָהּ "הֵא גִּיטֵּיךְ".

MISHNA If **he said to** his wife: **Take this promissory note,**[NH] and it was a bill of divorce, **or she found it behind him** and he did not tell her what it was but **she reads** what is written in **it and** discovers that **it is her bill of divorce, it is not** a valid **bill of divorce until he says to her: This is your bill of divorce.**

נָתַן בְּיָדָהּ וְהִיא יְשֵׁנָה, נֵיעוֹרָה, קוֹרְאָה וַהֲרֵי הוּא גִּיטָּהּ – אֵינוֹ גֵּט, עַד שֶׁיֹּאמַר לָהּ "הֵא גִּיטֵּיךְ".

If **he gave** it to her **in her hand and she** was **sleeping,** and he then **woke her, and** when **she reads** what is written in **it,** she finds that **it is her bill of divorce, it is not** a valid **bill of divorce until he says to her: This is your bill of divorce.**

גמ׳ כִּי אָמַר לָהּ "הֵא גִּיטֵּיךְ" מַאי הָוֵי? הָוָה לֵיהּ "טְלִי גִּיטֵּיךְ מֵעַל גַּבֵּי קַרְקַע".

GEMARA Apropos the mishna's statement that if she found the bill of divorce behind him, it is not a valid bill of divorce until he says: This is your bill of divorce, the Gemara asks: And **when he says to her: This is your bill of divorce, what of it?** Why is it considered to be a valid bill of divorce if it was not given to her in the proper manner, being that **it is** as though he told her: **Take your bill of divorce from** where it is placed **on the ground?**

HALAKHA

Basket seller – מוֹכֵר קְלָתוֹת: If a person bought a vessel, placed it in the seller's domain, and placed fruit inside it, he acquires the fruit, since the seller is happy about his sale and therefore is not particular about the placement of the vessel within his domain, as learned from this discussion in the Gemara (Rambam *Sefer Kinyan, Hilkhot Mekhira* 4:1; *Shulḥan Arukh, Ḥoshen Mishpat* 200:4).

Because a person is not particular, etc. – לְפִי שֶׁאֵין אָדָם מַקְפִּיד וכו׳: If a person threw a bill of divorce for his wife into her vessel, and he is not particular about the place where the vessel lies, it is considered to be a valid bill of divorce (Rambam *Sefer Nashim, Hilkhot Geirushin* 5:8; *Shulḥan Arukh, Even HaEzer* 139:10).

Take this promissory note, etc. – כִּנְסִי שְׁטַר חוֹב וכו׳: A man must give a bill of divorce for the sake of divorce. Therefore, if he gave it to her under the assumption that it was a promissory note, she is not divorced unless he said to her afterward: This is your bill of divorce; this is in accordance with the opinion of Rabbi Yehuda HaNasi. Similarly, she is divorced if he informed witnesses of his awareness that it is a bill of divorce from the outset. The Rema writes, citing *Tosafot*, that this is the *halakha* provided that the woman knows that she is being divorced through this bill of divorce, or the witnesses informed her of this afterward (Rambam *Sefer Nashim, Hilkhot Geirushin* 1:9; *Shulḥan Arukh, Even HaEzer* 136:5, 138:4).

LANGUAGE

Basket [*taska*] – טַסְקָא: From the Late Latin tasca, meaning a pocket.

NOTES

Take this promissory note, etc. – כִּנְסִי שְׁטַר חוֹב זֶה וכו׳: The early commentaries ask: Since a woman's consent is not needed for a divorce, as a husband can give his wife a bill of divorce against her will, why is it necessary to tell her that he is giving it to her as a bill of divorce? The Ra'avad explains that it is because there is a concern that perhaps he canceled the bill of divorce by stating it is a promissory note, and he gave it to her in jest. The Rashba writes that the concern is only that he gave it to her in jest, but not that the bill of divorce itself was canceled. Therefore, if he gives it to her again, and says: This is your bill of divorce, it is effective.

By contrast, the Rambam explains that although he can divorce her against her will, a bill of divorce must be given for the sake of severance. Therefore, if he says that it is a promissory note, the divorce does not take effect. The Ramban and the Rashba agree. *Tosafot* and the *Tur* explain that one of the *halakhot* of divorce is that the woman must know that she is divorced so that she does not return to her husband. It is for this reason that a woman who is not halakhically competent cannot be divorced. Therefore, if he does not tell her that it is a bill of divorce, it is not effective.

Some early commentaries write that the disqualification when he tells her it is a promissory note is only when he did not inform witnesses that he is giving it to her for the sake of divorce. If he told this to witnesses, it is a valid bill of divorce even though she does not know about it. The reason for this is that her consent is not required for the divorce; rather, his intentions must be ascertained, something that witnesses can accomplish (see *Halakhot Gedolot* and *Tosefot Rid*).

ואמר רבא: "טלי גיטיך מעל גבי קרקע" – לא אמר כלום! אימא: ששלפתו מאחוריו.

And Rava says that if one says to his wife: **Take your bill of divorce**[H] **from** where it is placed **on the ground,** it is as though **he didn't say anything** and it is not a valid bill of divorce, since a woman is divorced only when the bill of divorce is given to her by her husband. The Gemara answers: **Say that** the bill of divorce was not placed on the ground behind him, but rather **she pulled it out from behind him.** In other words, the bill of divorce was tucked into his belt and she pulled it out. Consequently, she received the bill of divorce from him.

שלפתו נמי, הא בעינא "ונתן בידה" וליכא! לא צריכא, דערק לה חרציה ושלפתיה.

The Gemara challenges this: If **she pulled it out,** it is **also** not a valid bill of divorce, since it is **required** that the directive: **"And gives it in her hand"** (Deuteronomy 24:1), be fulfilled, **and** in this case **it is not** fulfilled, since he did not give it to her; rather, she took it. The Gemara answers: **No,** it is **necessary** in a case **where he bent** [*da'arak*][L] **his waist**[H] over toward her **and she pulled it out,** and by extending his waist to her, it is as though he gave the bill of divorce to her.

תניא נמי הכי: אמר לה "כנסי שטר חוב זה", או ששלפתו מאחוריו, קראתו והרי הוא גיטה – אינו גט, עד שיאמר לה "הא גיטיך", דברי רבי; רבי שמעון בן אלעזר אומר: לעולם אינו גט, עד שיטלנו הימנה ויחזור ויתננו לה ויאמר לה "הא גיטיך".

This is also taught in a *baraita* (*Tosefta* 8:1): If **he said to** his wife: **Take this promissory note, or if she pulled it out from behind him, read it,** and saw that **it is her bill of divorce; it is not** a valid **bill of divorce until he says to her: This is your bill of divorce.** This is **the statement of** Rabbi Yehuda HaNasi. **Rabbi Shimon ben Elazar says: Actually, it is not a valid bill of divorce until he takes it from her and gives it to her again, and says to her: This is your bill of divorce.**

נתנו בידה והיא ישנה, ניעורה וקוראה והרי הוא גיטה – אינו גט, עד שיאמר לה "הא גיטיך", דברי רבי; רבי שמעון בן אלעזר אומר: עד שיטלנו הימנה ויחזור ויתננו לה ויאמר לה "הא גיטיך".

The *baraita* continues: If **he gave it** to her **in her hand, and she** was **sleeping,**[HN] and he then **woke her, and** when **she reads** what is written **in it,** she finds that **it is her bill of divorce; it is not** a valid **bill of divorce until he says to her: This is your bill of divorce.** This is **the statement of Rabbi** Yehuda HaNasi. **Rabbi Shimon ben Elazar says:** It is not a valid bill of divorce **until he takes it from her and gives it to her again, and says to her: This is your bill of divorce.**

וצריכא; דאי איתמר בהך קמייתא, בההיא קאמר רבי, משום דבת איגרושי היא, אבל נתן בידה והיא ישנה, דלאו בת איגרושי היא – אימא מודי ליה לרבי שמעון בן אלעזר.

The Gemara notes: **And** it is **necessary** to mention this dispute in both cases. **As if** this dispute would have **been stated** only **with regard to** the cases in **the first clause,** one could assume that **Rabbi** Yehuda HaNasi **is saying** his opinion specifically **with regard to** the cases in **this** clause, **because she is subject to being divorced,** since she is awake and able to receive a bill of divorce, even though he did not tell her that this is a bill of divorce. **But if he gave it** to her **in her hand and she** was **sleeping, she is not subject to being divorced** since while she is sleeping she is a person who lacks the halakhic competence required to receive a bill of divorce. Therefore, one could **say** that Rabbi Yehuda HaNasi **concedes to Rabbi Shimon ben Elazar** that giving the bill of divorce while she was sleeping is totally not valid. It was therefore necessary to mention that Rabbi Yehuda HaNasi disagrees in this case, as well.

ואי איתמר בהא, בהא קאמר רבי שמעון בן אלעזר, אבל בהך – אימא מודי ליה לרבי, צריכא.

And if this dispute would have **been stated** only **with regard to this** case, where she was sleeping, one could assume that specifically **with regard to this** case **Rabbi Shimon ben Elazar is saying** that he must give her the bill of divorce a second time. **But in the other** case, in which she was awake, one could **say** that **he concedes to Rabbi** Yehuda HaNasi. Therefore, it is **necessary** to mention this dispute in both cases.

אמר רבא: כתב לה גט ונתנו ביד עבדה ישן ומשמרתו – הרי זה גט, ניעור – אינו גט, דהויא ליה חצר המשתמרת שלא לדעתה.

Rava says: If **he wrote a bill of divorce for her, and he placed it in the hand of her slave** when **he is sleeping and she is guarding him, it is** a valid **bill of divorce.** Within the context of the *halakhot* of divorce, a slave has the same status as land, in the sense that both belong to their owner. Therefore, when the husband places the bill of divorce in the slave's hand, it is as though he placed it into her courtyard. If her slave **was awake, it is not** a valid **bill of divorce** because **he is like a courtyard that is not consciously secured by her.** Since he guards himself, he therefore does not acquire it on her behalf.

HALAKHA

Take your bill of divorce, etc. – **טלי גיטיך וכו׳**: A bill of divorce must be given by a man to his wife; she cannot take it on her own. Therefore, if the bill of divorce was resting on the ground and he told his wife to pick it up, it is not a valid bill of divorce. Even if it was resting on the palm of his hand, it is not a valid bill of divorce unless he brought it closer to her or assisted in her taking it, e.g., by opening his clenched hand so that she can take the bill of divorce from him (Rambam *Sefer Nashim, Hilkhot Geirushin* 1:12; *Shulḥan Arukh, Even HaEzer* 138:1).

He bent his waist – **ערק לה חרציה**: If the bill of divorce was stuck into his belt, and he drew in his waist in order to loosen it so that she could take it, and he leaned toward her, it is considered as if he gave it to her. If he did not perform one of these actions, she is not divorced (Rabbeinu Tam). Some say that if he leaned toward her and she removed the bill of divorce, and he said to her: This is your bill of divorce, she is divorced (Rambam *Sefer Nashim, Hilkhot Geirushin* 1:12; *Shulḥan Arukh, Even HaEzer* 138:1).

And she was sleeping – **והיא ישנה**: If a man gave his wife a bill of divorce when she was sleeping, it is not a valid bill of divorce until he says to her, after she wakes up: This is your bill of divorce, provided that the bill of divorce is still in her hand, in accordance with the opinion of Rabbi Yehuda HaNasi. Even if he said to witnesses: See the bill of divorce that I am giving her, it is not valid if he said this when she was sleeping (Rambam *Sefer Nashim, Hilkhot Geirushin* 1:9; *Shulḥan Arukh, Even HaEzer* 138:3).

LANGUAGE

Bent [*arak*] – **ערק**: According to some manuscripts of the Gemara and Mishna, the text should read *de'adak*, apparently related to the word *hadak*, meaning to tighten, though it is not entirely clear what action is referred to by this phrase. The version of the text in the *Arukh* reads *de'avik*, which is related to the Arabic عاق, *'āqa*, meaning to tilt or twist.

NOTES

And she was sleeping – **והיא ישנה**: While she is sleeping, she has less halakhic competence than a deaf-mute, since while asleep she has no mental capabilities at all (*Tosefot HaRosh*). The Ran explains that a bill of divorce must be given in a way such that it is secured; and when he places it in her hand while she is sleeping, it is not secured. The early commentaries disagree with regard to whether she can acquire a bill of divorce by means of her courtyard while she is sleeping (see Rashba and Rabbeinu Crescas Vidal).

יָשֵׁן וּמְשַׁמַּרְתּוֹ – הֲרֵי זֶה גֵּט, אַמַּאי? חָצֵר מְהַלֶּכֶת הִיא, וְחָצֵר מְהַלֶּכֶת לֹא קָנָה!

Rava continues: If **he is sleeping and she is guarding him, it is** a valid **bill of divorce.** The Gemara asks: But **why;** isn't it true that the slave **is like a mobile courtyard, and a mobile courtyard does not acquire** items on behalf of its owner?

וְכִי תֵּימָא יָשֵׁן שָׁאנֵי, וְהָא אָמַר רָבָא: כֹּל שֶׁאִילּוּ מְהַלֵּךְ לֹא קָנָה, עוֹמֵד וְיוֹשֵׁב לֹא קָנָה! וְהִלְכְתָא: בִּכְפוּת.

And if you would say that a case in which he is **sleeping is different** because he is currently not moving, **but didn't Rava say:** In any case in which **if he would be moving** he would **not acquire** items, then even if he is **standing or sitting,** he also does **not acquire** items? The Gemara concludes: **And this** ***halakha*** that Rava said, indicating that it is a valid bill of divorce, applies only **where** the slave is **bound**[H] and sleeping, since in that case placing the bill of divorce in his hand is like placing it in her hand.

מתני׳ הָיְתָה עוֹמֶדֶת בִּרְשׁוּת הָרַבִּים וּזְרָקוֹ לָהּ, קָרוֹב לָהּ – מְגוֹרֶשֶׁת, קָרוֹב לוֹ – אֵינָהּ מְגוֹרֶשֶׁת, מֶחֱצָה עַל מֶחֱצָה – מְגוֹרֶשֶׁת וְאֵינָהּ מְגוֹרֶשֶׁת. וְכֵן לְעִנְיַן קִדּוּשִׁין.

MISHNA If the woman **was standing in the public domain**[H] and her husband took the bill of divorce **and threw it to her,** if it fell **closer to her, she is divorced,** and if it fell **closer to him, she is not divorced.** If it is **equally balanced,** there is uncertainty as to whether **she is divorced or** whether **she is not divorced. And the same** ***halakhot*** apply **with regard to betrothal.**[H]

וְכֵן לְעִנְיַן הַחוֹב: אָמַר לוֹ בַּעַל חוֹבוֹ ״זְרוֹק לִי חוֹבִי״ וּזְרָקוֹ לוֹ, קָרוֹב לַמַּלְוֶה – זָכָה הַמַּלְוֶה, קָרוֹב לַלֹּוֶה – הַלֹּוֶה חַיָּיב, מֶחֱצָה עַל מֶחֱצָה – שְׁנֵיהֶם יַחֲלוֹקוּ.

And the same *halakhot* apply **with regard to a debt.**[H] **If his creditor said to him: Throw** the payment for **my debt to me, and he threw it to him** and the money fell **closer to the creditor,** the **creditor acquired** the payment. The debtor is absolved of his obligation to pay even if the money did not reach the creditor's hand, e.g., it was stolen or lost after it was thrown and before the creditor was able to take it. If it fell **closer to the debtor** and the money was lost, **the debtor** is still **obligated** to pay. If it was **equally balanced** and was lost, **the two of them divide** it, i.e., the debtor owes half of the amount.

גמ׳ הֵיכִי דָּמֵי קָרוֹב לָהּ, וְהֵיכִי דָּמֵי קָרוֹב לוֹ? אָמַר רַב: אַרְבַּע אַמּוֹת שֶׁלָּהּ – זֶהוּ קָרוֹב לָהּ, אַרְבַּע אַמּוֹת שֶׁלּוֹ – זֶהוּ קָרוֹב לוֹ.

GEMARA The Gemara clarifies that which was taught in the mishna: **What is considered closer to her, and what is considered closer to him? Rav says:** If it fell within **four cubits of her, this is** what was meant by the mishna's statement: **Closer to her;** if it fell within **four cubits of him, this is** what was meant by: **Closer to him.**

הֵיכִי דָּמֵי מֶחֱצָה עַל מֶחֱצָה? אָמַר רַבִּי שְׁמוּאֵל בַּר רַב יִצְחָק: כְּגוֹן שֶׁהָיוּ שְׁנֵיהֶן עוֹמְדִין בְּאַרְבַּע אַמּוֹת.

The Gemara asks: **What is considered midway? Rabbi Shmuel bar Rav Yitzḥak says: Such as** when **the two of them were standing within** the same **four cubits.**

וְלֶיחֱזֵי הֵי מִינַּיְיהוּ קָדֵים? וְכִי תֵּימָא דְּאָתוּ תַּרְוַיְיהוּ בַּהֲדֵי הֲדָדֵי, וְהָא אִי אֶפְשָׁר לְצַמְצֵם!

The Gemara asks: **And let us see which of them preceded** the other[H] into these four cubits, and the four cubits would then be considered as belonging to that person. **And if you would say that both of them came simultaneously, but** isn't there a principle that **it is impossible to be** so **precise?**[H] It is not possible that both events occurred at exactly the same time, and it is certain that one of them arrived there before the other.

אֶלָּא אָמַר רַב כָּהֲנָא: הָכָא בִּשְׁמוֹנֶה אַמּוֹת מְצוּמְצָמוֹת עָסְקִינַן,

Rather, Rav Kahana said: Here we are dealing with a case of **precisely eight cubits,** where his four cubits are adjacent to her four cubits,

Perek **VIII**
Daf **78** Amud **b**

וְגֵט יוֹצֵא מֵאַרְבַּע אַמּוֹת שֶׁלּוֹ לְאַרְבַּע אַמּוֹת שֶׁלָּהּ.

and the bill of divorce extends from his four cubits into her four cubits, meaning that part of the bill of divorce is in his four cubits, and part is in hers. Therefore, in this case there is uncertainty whether she is divorced or whether she is not divorced.

HALAKHA

And this *halakha* applies where the slave is bound – וְהִלְכְתָא בִּכְפוּת: If the husband placed the bill of divorce into the hand of the woman's slave, even if the slave was sleeping and the woman was guarding him, it is not a valid bill of divorce unless the slave was bound, in accordance with the statement of Rava. If the slave was awake and bound, and the woman was guarding him, according to the Rambam, it is a valid bill of divorce. The majority of the early commentaries say that both factors are required, i.e., that he is both bound and sleeping (Rambam *Sefer Nashim, Hilkhot Geirushin* 5:17; *Shulḥan Arukh, Even HaEzer* 139:16–17).

If the woman was standing in the public domain – הָיְתָה עוֹמֶדֶת בִּרְשׁוּת הָרַבִּים: If a man threw a bill of divorce to his wife in the public domain or in a domain that does not belong to either of them, if it fell closer to him, she is not divorced, and if it fell midway or closer to her, it is uncertain whether she is divorced, in accordance with the Gemara's explanation of the mishna (Rambam *Sefer Nashim, Hilkhot Geirushin* 5:13; *Shulḥan Arukh, Even HaEzer* 139:13).

And the same *halakhot* apply with regard to betrothal – וְכֵן לְעִנְיַן קִדּוּשִׁין: If a man and a woman were standing in the public domain or in a domain that does not belong to either of them, and the man threw to the woman an item with which he wishes to perform betrothal, if it fell closer to him, she is not betrothed, and if it fell closer to her, she is betrothed. If it fell midway, or if it was unclear whether it was closer to him or to her, it is uncertain whether she is betrothed (Rambam *Sefer Nashim, Hilkhot Ishut* 4:22; *Shulḥan Arukh, Shulḥan Arukh, Even HaEzer* 30:5).

And the same *halakhot* apply with regard to a debt – וְכֵן לְעִנְיַן הַחוֹב: If the creditor said to the debtor: Throw me payment for my debt according to the *halakhot* of bills of divorce, and he threw the payment, if the money fell closer to the debtor, he is still accountable for it. If it fell closer to the creditor, the debtor is absolved of his obligations. If it fell midway and was lost or stolen, the debtor pays half (Rambam *Sefer Mishpatim, Hilkhot Malve VeLoveh* 16:1; *Shulḥan Arukh, Ḥoshen Mishpat* 120:1).

And let us see which of them preceded the other – וְלֶיחֱזֵי הֵי מִינַּיְיהוּ קָדֵים: If the husband came first and stood in the public domain and subsequently the woman came and stood across from him, and he threw her the bill of divorce, if the bill of divorce fell within four cubits of him, it is not a valid bill of divorce, even if she can bend down and pick it up (Rambam *Sefer Nashim, Hilkhot Geirushin* 5:15; *Shulḥan Arukh, Even HaEzer* 139:14).

It is impossible to be so precise – אִי אֶפְשָׁר לְצַמְצֵם: According to the Rambam, it is impossible to place an item with absolute precision, even if it is done by human hands. Therefore, if a murder victim is found and the location of the body is at an equal distance between two cities, the residents of both cities partner together to bring a heifer whose neck is broken and they stipulate that the heifer should be considered as if it was being brought by the closer city. The *Shulḥan Arukh* seems undecided on this issue (Rambam *Sefer Nezikin, Hilkhot Rotze'aḥ UShmirat Nefesh* 9:8; *Shulḥan Arukh, Oraḥ Ḥayyim* 648:11).

וְהָא אֲגִיד גַּבֵּיהּ! אֶלָּא, רַבָּה וְרַב יוֹסֵף דְּאָמְרִי תַּרְוַיְיהוּ: הָכָא בִּשְׁתֵּי כִיתֵּי עֵדִים עָסְקִינַן, אַחַת אוֹמֶרֶת קָרוֹב לוֹ וְאַחַת אוֹמֶרֶת קָרוֹב לָהּ.

The Gemara asks: **But isn't** the bill of divorce still **attached to him,** since part of it is within his four cubits, and therefore it cannot be considered as if he gave her the bill of divorce completely? **Rather,** one should explain as **Rabba and Rav Yosef both say: Here we are dealing with two groups of witnesses; one says** that the bill of divorce fell **closer to him, and one says** that the bill of divorce fell **closer to her.** Therefore, the expression in the mishna, equally balanced, is referring not to distance but to opinions.

רַבִּי יוֹחָנָן אוֹמֵר: ״קָרוֹב לָהּ״ שָׁנִינוּ, אֲפִילּוּ מֵאָה אַמָּה, וְ״קָרוֹב לוֹ״ שָׁנִינוּ, אֲפִילּוּ מֵאָה אַמָּה.

As opposed to Rav, who explained that in the mishna, the word closer meant within four cubits, **Rabbi Yoḥanan says: We learned** that **closer to her** means that the bill of divorce was actually closer to her, **even** if it was **one hundred cubits** away from her. **And we learned** that **closer to him** means that it was actually closer to him, **even** if it was **one hundred cubits** away from him.

הֵיכִי דָּמֵי מֶחֱצָה עַל מֶחֱצָה? אֲמַר רַב שֶׁמֶן בַּר אַבָּא, לְדִידִי מִיפָּרְשָׁא לָהּ מִינֵּיהּ דְּרַבִּי יוֹחָנָן: הוּא יָכוֹל לְשׁוֹמְרוֹ וְהִיא אֵינָהּ יְכוֹלָה לְשׁוֹמְרוֹ – זֶהוּ קָרוֹב לוֹ, הִיא יְכוֹלָה לְשׁוֹמְרוֹ וְהוּא אֵינוֹ יָכוֹל לְשׁוֹמְרוֹ – זֶהוּ קָרוֹב לָהּ, שְׁנֵיהֶם יְכוֹלִין לְשׁוֹמְרוֹ, שְׁנֵיהֶם אֵין יְכוֹלִין – זֶהוּ מֶחֱצָה עַל מֶחֱצָה.

The Gemara asks: According to the explanation offered by Rabbi Yoḥanan, **what are the circumstances** of when it was **equally balanced? Rav Shemen bar Abba said: This was explained to me** personally **by Rabbi Yoḥanan** himself: If it is so positioned that **he can guard it**[H] **and she cannot guard it, this is** considered **closer to him.** If it is so positioned that **she can guard it and he cannot guard it, this is** considered **closer to her.** If it is so positioned that **the two of them can guard it,** or **the two of them cannot** guard it, **this is** considered **equally balanced.**

אֲמַרוּהָ רַבָּנַן קַמֵּיהּ דְּרַבִּי יוֹחָנָן מִשְּׁמֵיהּ דְּרַבִּי יוֹנָתָן הָכִי, אֲמַר: יָדְעִין חַבְרִין בַּבְלָאֵי לְפָרוֹשֵׁי כִּי הַאי טַעְמָא?

The Rabbis said this explanation **before Rabbi Yoḥanan in the name of Rabbi Yonatan,** and Rabbi Yoḥanan **said** in amazement: Do **our Babylonian friends know how to explain in accordance with this explanation?** Rabbi Yoḥanan was astonished that they also understood the issue as he did.

תַּנְיָא נַמִי הָכִי, רַבִּי אֱלִיעֶזֶר אוֹמֵר: כָּל שֶׁהוּא קָרוֹב לָהּ מִלּוֹ, וּבָא כֶּלֶב וּנְטָלוֹ – אֵינָהּ מְגוֹרֶשֶׁת; אֵינָהּ מְגוֹרֶשֶׁת?! כָּל הֵיכִי תִּינַטְרֵיהּ וְתֵיזִיל?

This is also taught in a *baraita* (*Tosefta* 8:1): **Rabbi Eliezer says:** With regard to **any** bill of divorce **that is closer to her than** it is **to him, and a dog came and took it** before the bill of divorce reached her hand, **she is not divorced.** The Gemara asks: Why is it that **she is not divorced?** Once it was closer to her, before the dog took it, the divorce should have taken effect. **Must she continue guarding** her bill of divorce **indefinitely,** even after the bill of divorce took effect?

אֶלָּא לָאו הָכִי קָאָמַר: כָּל שֶׁקָּרוֹב לָהּ מִלּוֹ, וְאִילּוּ בָּא כֶּלֶב וּנְטָלוֹ וְהוּא יָכוֹל לְשׁוֹמְרוֹ וְהִיא אֵינָהּ יְכוֹלָה לְשׁוֹמְרוֹ – אֵינָהּ מְגוֹרֶשֶׁת.

The Gemara answers: **Rather, is it not** that **this is what** Rabbi Eliezer **is saying:** With regard to **any** bill of divorce **that is closer to her than** it is **to him, and if a dog** were to **come and** attempt to **take it, he** would be **able to guard it and she** would **not** be **able to guard it,** in that case **she is not divorced,** as the bill of divorce is considered in his domain.

אֲמַר לֵיהּ שְׁמוּאֵל לְרַב יְהוּדָה: שִׁינָּנָא, כְּדֵי שֶׁתָּשׁוּחַ וְתִטְּלֶנּוּ, וְאַתְּ לָא תַּעֲבֵיד עוּבְדָא עַד דְּמָטֵי גִּיטָּא לְיָדָהּ.

Shmuel said to Rav Yehuda: One with large teeth [*shinnana*],[L] i.e., a nickname for Rabbi Yehuda, when they said: Closer to her, it meant **so that she could bend down and take it.**[H] **And you should not perform**[N] an action to permit a divorcing woman to remarry **until the bill of divorce** actually **reaches her hand.**

HALAKHA

He can guard it, etc. – **הוּא יָכוֹל לְשׁוֹמְרוֹ וכו׳**: What is considered closer to him? When the bill of divorce is so positioned that he can guard it and she cannot. What is considered closer to her? When it is so positioned that she can guard it and he cannot. If it is so positioned that both of them can guard it or both of them cannot guard it, this is considered to be equally balanced, in accordance with Rabbi Yoḥanan's statement (Rambam *Sefer Nashim, Hilkhot Geirushin* 5:14; *Shulḥan Arukh, Even HaEzer* 139:13).

So that she could bend down and take it, etc. – **כְּדֵי שֶׁתָּשׁוּחַ וְתִטְּלֶנּוּ וכו׳**: If a man throws a bill of divorce to his wife and it lands between them, or closer to her, it is uncertain whether she is divorced. Even if it is close enough to her that she can bend down and take it, it is uncertain whether she is divorced. She is not conclusively divorced until the bill of divorce reaches her hand. Once it reaches her hand, she can remarry *ab initio*, in accordance with Shmuel's statement.

It is written in the *Beit Shmuel* that according to most halakhic authorities, if the bill of divorce fell closer to her, by Torah law it is a valid divorce, and Shmuel was only applying a rabbinic stringency. Accordingly, it is questionable if the court would separate a woman from her husband if she remarried on the basis of such a bill of divorce.

The Rema writes that all of these possible cases of divorce are according to the basic *halakha*. *Ab initio*, one should only divorce a woman by placing the bill of divorce in her actual hand and not by placing it in her domain. In addition, even after the fact he recommends stringency, i.e., not permitting her to remarry until she receives the bill of divorce in her actual hand, without any help, and without anything else in her hand at the time (Rambam *Sefer Nashim, Hilkhot Geirushin* 5:13; *Shulḥan Arukh, Even HaEzer* 139:13–14).

LANGUAGE

One with large teeth [*shinnana*] – **שִׁינָּנָא**: This nickname for Rabbi Yehuda, mentioned in numerous places, is interpreted by many as meaning sharp or clever. However, the *ge'onim* write that this term is related to the word for a tooth, *shen*, and is an expression used for someone with large teeth, noting that the expression was also used in their days.

NOTES

And you should not perform, etc. – **וְאַתְּ לָא תַּעֲבֵיד וכו׳**: The reason for this is because a mistake can easily be made about what is considered to be closer to him and what is considered to be closer to her (Ritva). Alternatively, according to the *baraita* that states that the determining factor is whether a dog would come and take it, which is difficult to gauge, the reason is because it is likely that they will err in making that assessment (*Ḥatam Sofer*). Similarly, it is stated in the Jerusalem Talmud: The ideal scenario is when he places it in her hand. Rabbeinu Ḥananel writes that this should be the practice in all cases. He adds that this applies both with regard to the public domain and to her courtyard. Most of the early commentaries (see *Tosafot*, *Tosefot Rid*, and Rashba) write that it seems in the Gemara that this only applies to a bill of divorce thrown in the public domain, not to a bill of divorce given in her courtyard. The early commentaries write that the court should always have the husband give the bill of divorce directly to the wife, as it is difficult to rule leniently contrary to the tradition of Rabbeinu Ḥananel (see *Nimmukei Yosef*).

NOTES

They said this only with regard to bills of divorce, etc. – לְגִיטִּין אָמְרוּ וכו׳: According to the Jerusalem Talmud, the other matter referred to by Rabbi Yoḥanan is with regard to a gift. Rashi explains that the reason for the difference between divorce and other acquisitions is that a bill of divorce can be given against her will and she is divorced through it, immediately, once it reaches her hand or her property. The *Tosefot Rid* explains that the *halakhot* of acquisition are not inherent to the giving of a divorce, since she can be forced to receive the bill of divorce even without her consent, and it is necessary only that the bill of divorce be consciously secured by her. Another explanation is that of the Ramban, Rashba, and their students, that divorce is a unique ordinance instituted to enable the divorce to take effect more easily, and the *halakhot* of divorce cannot be extrapolated to other situations.

אֲמַר לֵיהּ רַב מָרְדְּכַי לְרַב אַשִׁי: הֲוָה עוּבְדָא הָכִי וְאַצְרְכוּהָ חֲלִיצָה.

Rav Mordekhai said to Rav Ashi: There was an incident like this, in which the bill of divorce was closer to the woman than to the man and it was then lost; **and,** after her husband died, **they required** the woman to engage in **the ritual through which the *yavam* frees the *yevama* of her levirate bonds** [***ḥalitza***] in order to permit her to marry, due to uncertainty. They did not rely on the bill of divorce that was given to the woman, since it never actually reached her hand.

״וְכֵן לְעִנְיַן קִדּוּשִׁין״. אָמַר רַבִּי אַסִּי אָמַר רַבִּי יוֹחָנָן: לְגִיטִּין אָמְרוּ וְלֹא לְדָבָר אַחֵר.

§ The mishna stated the *halakha* about a bill of divorce that was closer to him or her, and the mishna added: **And the same** *halakhot* apply **with regard to betrothal. Rabbi Asi says that Rabbi Yoḥanan says: They said** these *halakhot* only **with regard to bills of divorce,**[N] **but not with regard to another matter.**

אֵיתִיבֵיהּ רַבִּי אַבָּא לְרַבִּי אַסִּי: וְכֵן לְעִנְיַן קִדּוּשִׁין! שָׁאנֵי הָתָם דִּכְתִיב: ״וְיָצְאָה... וְהָיְתָה״.

Rabbi Abba raised an objection to the statement of **Rabbi Asi** from what was explicitly taught in the mishna: **And the same** *halakhot* apply **with regard to betrothal.** He responded: **It is different there** with regard to betrothal, **as it is written: "And she departs** out of his house, and goes **and becomes** another man's wife" (Deuteronomy 24:2). The Torah thereby compares betrothal, through the use of the word "becomes," to divorce, through the use of the words "and she departs," so one can learn the *halakhot* of betrothal from the *halakhot* of divorce. One cannot learn *halakhot* concerning other matters from divorce.

אֵיתִיבֵיהּ: וְכֵן לְעִנְיַן הַחוֹב, ״זְרוֹק לִי חוֹבִי״ וּזְרָקוֹ לוֹ, קָרוֹב לַמַּלְוֶה – זָכָה הַלֹּוֶה, קָרוֹב לַלֹּוֶה – הַלֹּוֶה חַיָּיב, מֶחֱצָה עַל מֶחֱצָה – שְׁנֵיהֶם יַחֲלוֹקוּ!

Another objection to his statement was **raised** based on what is taught in a *baraita*: **And the same** *halakhot* apply **with regard to a debt.** If a creditor said to a debtor: **Throw** the payment for **my debt to me, and he threw it to him** and the money fell **closer to the creditor,** the **debtor merits,** i.e., his debt is repaid. If it fell **closer to the debtor** and the money was lost, **the debtor** is still **obligated** to pay. If it was **equally balanced** and was lost, **the two of them divide** it, i.e., the debtor owes half of the amount. Accordingly, the *halakhot* of debts are compared to the *halakhot* of divorce.

הָכָא בְּמַאי עָסְקִינַן – דְּאָמַר לֵיהּ ״זְרוֹק לִי חוֹבִי וְתִיפָּטֵר״. אִי הָכִי, מַאי לְמֵימְרָא? לָא צְרִיכָא, דַּאֲמַר לֵיהּ ״זְרוֹק לִי חוֹבִי בְּתוֹרַת גִּיטִּין״.

The Gemara answers: **Here we are dealing with** a case **where** the creditor **said to** the debtor: **Throw** the payment for **my debt to me, and you will be absolved**[H] of your obligation to pay through this. The Gemara challenges this: **If so, what** is the purpose **of stating** this? Since he made an explicit stipulation, it is obvious that the outcome will be in accordance with his stipulation. The Gemara answers: **No,** it is **necessary** in a case **where** the creditor **said to** the debtor: **Throw** the payment for **my debt to me** according **to the procedure** in effect with **bills of divorce,**[H] meaning that the *halakha* that applies to divorce should apply here too.

וְאַכַּתִּי מַאי לְמֵימְרָא? מַהוּ דְּתֵימָא, מָצֵי אָמַר לֵיהּ: מְשַׁטֶּה אֲנִי בָּךְ, קָא מַשְׁמַע לַן.

The Gemara asks: **And still, what** is the purpose **of stating** this, since the creditor stipulated explicitly: According to the procedure in effect with bills of divorce? The Gemara answers: **Lest you say** that the creditor **can say to** the debtor: **I am teasing you,** and what I stipulated has no validity. Therefore the mishna **teaches us** that if he stipulated that it should be treated as a bill of divorce, then his stipulation takes effect.

HALAKHA

Throw the payment for my debt to me and you will be absolved – זְרוֹק לִי חוֹבִי וְתִיפָּטֵר: If the creditor said to the debtor: Throw the payment for my debt to me and you will be absolved of your obligation to pay, and the debtor threw the payment, the debtor is absolved of his obligation to pay even if it fell far away from the creditor and was lost before it reached him (Rambam *Sefer Mishpatim, Hilkhot Malve VeLoveh* 16:1; *Shulḥan Arukh, Ḥoshen Mishpat* 120:1).

Throw the payment for my debt to me according to the procedure in effect with bills of divorce – זְרוֹק לִי חוֹבִי בְּתוֹרַת גִּיטִּין: If the creditor said to the debtor: Throw payment for my debt to me according to the procedure in effect with bills of divorce, and the debtor threw it and the money fell closer to the debtor, the debtor is still liable for it. If the money fell closer to the creditor, the debtor has fulfilled his obligation to pay. If it was equally balanced and then was lost, the debtor pays half of the sum. The Rema writes that if it fell within four cubits of the creditor, the debtor has fulfilled of his obligation to pay. If it fell more than four cubits from the creditor, but the creditor can guard it and the debtor cannot, the debtor has also fulfilled his obligation to pay. If the debtor can guard it and the creditor cannot, the debtor is liable. If both of them can guard it, it is considered to be equally balanced. If both of them are unable to guard it, the debtor is still liable for the money since it is as though he threw the money away (Rambam *Sefer Mishpatim, Hilkhot Malve VeLoveh* 16:1; *Shulḥan Arukh, Ḥoshen Mishpat* 120:1).

אָמַר רַב חִסְדָּא: גֵּט בְּיָדָהּ וּמְשִׁיחָה בְּיָדוֹ, אִם יָכוֹל לְנַתְּקוֹ וְלַהֲבִיאוֹ אֶצְלוֹ – אֵינָהּ מְגוֹרֶשֶׁת, וְאִם לָאו – מְגוֹרֶשֶׁת;

§ Rav Ḥisda says: If **the bill of divorce was in her hand and a string** tied to the bill of divorce was **in his hand,**[H] as he gave her the bill of divorce in this way, **if** the husband **can** still **pull** the bill of divorce out of her hand **and bring it to him, she is not divorced; and if** he is **not** able to do so, **she is divorced.**

מַאי טַעְמָא? בָּעֵינַן כְּרִיתוּת וְלֵיכָּא.

What is the reason that she is not divorced, despite the fact that he gave her a bill of divorce? The reason is that **we require severance, and it is lacking,** since the husband still has a hold on the bill of divorce.

אָמַר רַב יְהוּדָה: הָיְתָה יָדָהּ עֲשׂוּיָה כְּקַטְפְּרַס וּזְרָקוֹ לָהּ, אַף עַל פִּי שֶׁהִגִּיעַ גֵּט לְיָדָהּ – אֵינָהּ מְגוֹרֶשֶׁת.

Rav Yehuda says: If her hand was positioned like a slope[H] **and he threw it to her, despite** the fact **that the bill of divorce reached her hand, she is not divorced,** since it cannot remain in her hand and will fall out.

אַמַּאי? הָא כִּי נָפֵיל – בְּאַרְבַּע אַמּוֹת דִּידַהּ קָא נָפֵיל! בִּדְלָא נָח.

The Gemara asks: **Why? But when** the bill of divorce **falls** from her hand, **it falls within her four cubits.** The Gemara answers: Rav Yehuda is discussing a case **where** the bill of divorce **did not rest** within her four cubits. Rather, it fell further away.

וְתִיגָּרֵשׁ מֵאֲוִירָא דְּאַרְבַּע אַמּוֹת! תִּפְשׁוֹט דְּבָעֵי רַבִּי אֶלְעָזָר: אַרְבַּע אַמּוֹת שֶׁאָמְרוּ, יֵשׁ לָהֶן אֲוִיר אוֹ אֵין לָהֶן אֲוִיר – תִּפְשׁוֹט דְּאֵין לָהֶן אֲוִיר!

The Gemara asks: **But** why not **let her be divorced** because the bill of divorce was in **the airspace of** her **four cubits?** And if you do not say this, then **resolve** the dilemma **that Rabbi Elazar raised** with regard to **the four cubits that** the Sages **stated** in the *halakhot* of acquisition: **Do they have airspace** with the same legal status **or do they not have airspace? Resolve** that dilemma from here, i.e., **that they do not have airspace.**

הָכָא בְּמַאי עָסְקִינַן – בְּעוֹמֶדֶת עַל גַּב הַנָּהָר, דְּמֵעִיקָּרָא לְאִיבּוּד קָאֵי.

The Gemara rejects this: One cannot resolve the dilemma from here since it is possible to say that **here we are dealing with** a woman who is **standing at the riverbank, as** the bill of divorce **stands to be destroyed from the outset,** since if it does not remain in her hand it will fall into the river. In such a case, everyone agrees that the airspace of the four cubits does not acquire the item.

HALAKHA

If the bill of divorce was in her hand and a string was in his hand – גֵּט בְּיָדָהּ וּמְשִׁיחָה בְּיָדוֹ: If a husband gave a bill of divorce to his wife and a string that remained in the husband's hand was tied to the bill of divorce, if the string was tied tight enough that the husband was able to pull the bill of divorce out of his wife's hand, it is as though he never gave her the bill of divorce, and she is not divorced. In a case where the string was strong enough, but she was clutching the bill of divorce so tightly that he could not pull it out of her hand, the *Tur* cites opposing opinions as to whether it is an effective divorce (Rambam *Sefer Nashim, Hilkhot Geirushin* 5:16; *Shulḥan Arukh, Even HaEzer* 138:2).

If her hand was positioned like a slope – הָיְתָה יָדָהּ עֲשׂוּיָה כְּקַטְפְּרַס: If the woman's hand was on an incline and he threw the bill of divorce into her hand, and it then fell to the ground within four cubits of her, if it was then still, she is divorced. If it continued moving and rolled further than four cubits away from her, it is uncertain whether she is divorced, since Rabbi Elazar's dilemma was not resolved. If she was standing near water or fire and the bill of divorce was destroyed immediately when it fell from her hand, she is not divorced, in accordance with the statement of Rav Yehuda and how it was explained in the Gemara. The Rema writes that all of this applies if she was in the public domain. If she was standing in her own domain, even if it rolled outside of her four cubits, she is divorced. The custom is not to conduct a divorce via placing the bill of divorce in her property. Therefore, if the bill of divorce fell from her hand, even if she was standing within her own property, she is required to go through a second process of divorce (Rambam *Sefer Nashim, Hilkhot Geirushin* 5:12; *Shulḥan Arukh, Even HaEzer* 139:15).

Perek **VIII**
Daf **79** Amud **a**

מתני׳ הָיְתָה עוֹמֶדֶת עַל רֹאשׁ הַגַּג וּזְרָקוֹ לָהּ, כֵּיוָן שֶׁהִגִּיעַ לַאֲוִיר הַגַּג – הֲרֵי זוֹ מְגוֹרֶשֶׁת; הוּא מִלְמַעְלָה וְהִיא מִלְּמַטָּה וּזְרָקוֹ לָהּ, כֵּיוָן שֶׁיָּצָא מֵרְשׁוּת הַגַּג, נִמְחַק אוֹ נִשְׂרַף – הֲרֵי זוֹ מְגוֹרֶשֶׁת.

MISHNA If a woman **was standing on top of the roof**[H] and her husband was standing below, **and he threw** a bill of divorce **to her, once** the bill of divorce **reaches the airspace of the roof, she is divorced.** If **he** was **above**[H] on the roof **and she was below, and he threw it to her, once it leaves the area of the roof,** even if the wording **was erased or** the document **was burned** before it fell to the ground, **she is divorced.**

גמ׳ וְהָא לָא מִינְטַר! אָמַר רַב יְהוּדָה אָמַר שְׁמוּאֵל: בְּגַג שֶׁיֵּשׁ לוֹ מַעֲקָה עָסְקִינַן.

GEMARA The Gemara asks: **But isn't** the airspace of the roof **unsecured?**[N] Since the bill of divorce can be blown away from the roof by the wind, it should be considered an unsecured courtyard, which does not acquire items. If so, why is she divorced once the bill of divorce reaches the airspace of the roof? **Rav Yehuda said that Shmuel said: We are dealing with a roof that has a parapet.** Therefore, it is like a secured courtyard, since the bill of divorce cannot be blown away.

NOTES

But isn't it unsecured – וְהָא לָא מִינְטַר: While the bill of divorce is still in the air, it is liable to be blown away by the wind. Under such circumstances, it cannot be understood to be in the domain of the roof while only in the air above the roof, since an item in the air of a domain is considered to be in that domain only if it will inevitably come to rest there. Therefore, the divorce should not take effect until the bill of divorce actually comes to rest on the roof and not before (Rashi; see Rambam). Others explain that since the bill of divorce can easily be blown away from the roof, the roof is not considered to be a secured courtyard. Therefore, the roof cannot acquire the bill of divorce, and even if the bill of divorce did land on the roof, she would not be divorced (Ritva).

HALAKHA

If she was standing on top of the roof, etc. – הָיְתָה עוֹמֶדֶת עַל רֹאשׁ הַגַּג וכו׳: If the woman was standing on top of a roof that belonged to her, and the husband threw a bill of divorce to the top of the roof, if the roof had a parapet, once the bill of divorce fell within the enclosure of the parapet, she is divorced. If there is no parapet, she is divorced once the bill of divorce comes within three handbreadths of the roof. This is true even if the bill of divorce was burned before it reached her hand, in accordance with the statements of Rav Yehuda and Ulla bar Menashya. According to the *Maggid Mishne* in his explanation of the Rambam, if the bill of divorce was lost or its writing was erased before it landed on the roof, she is not divorced (Rambam *Sefer Nashim, Hilkhot Geirushin* 5:3; *Shulḥan Arukh, Even HaEzer* 139:4–5).

He was above, etc. – הוּא מִלְמַעְלָה וכו׳: If the husband was standing on his roof and he threw a bill of divorce into the woman's courtyard, if the partitions of the courtyard were higher than the roof, so that the bill of divorce entered the confines of the partitions of the courtyard as soon as it was thrown, she is divorced as soon as the bill of divorce enters the confines of the partitions of the courtyard. This is true even if the bill of divorce was burned before it reached the ground, in accordance with the mishna and the explanation of the Gemara (Rambam *Sefer Nashim, Hilkhot Geirushin* 5:4; *Shulḥan Arukh, Even HaEzer* 139:6).

עוּלָּא בַּר מְנַשְּׁיָא מִשְּׁמֵיהּ דַּאֲבִימִי אָמַר: הָכָא בְּפָחוֹת מִשְּׁלֹשָׁה סָמוּךְ לַגַּג עָסְקִינַן, דְּכׇל פָּחוֹת מִשְּׁלֹשָׁה סָמוּךְ לַגַּג – כְּגַג דָּמֵי.

Ulla bar Menashya said in the name of Avimi that there is another answer: **Here we are dealing with** a case in which the bill of divorce is **within three** handbreadths **of the roof, as anything within three** handbreadths **of the roof is** considered to be **like the roof** itself, based on the principle that views two solid surfaces as connected if the gap between them is less than three handbreadths wide.

״הוּא מִלְמַעְלָה״. וְהָא לָא מִינְטַר! אָמַר רַב יְהוּדָה אָמַר שְׁמוּאֵל: כְּגוֹן שֶׁהָיוּ מְחִיצוֹת הַתַּחְתּוֹנוֹת עוֹדְפוֹת עַל הָעֶלְיוֹנוֹת.

§ It was taught in the mishna: If **he** was **above** and she was below, and he threw the bill of divorce to her, once it leaves the area of the roof, she is divorced. The Gemara asks: **But isn't** the airspace of the courtyard **not secured,** since the bill of divorce can be blown out of the courtyard by the wind? **Rav Yehuda says** that **Shmuel says:** We are discussing a case **where the lower partitions** in the courtyard **extend beyond**[B] **the upper** partitions on the roof, so that the bill of divorce will certainly fall in the courtyard.

וְכֵן אָמַר רַבִּי אֶלְעָזָר אָמַר רַבִּי אוֹשַׁעְיָא: כְּגוֹן שֶׁהָיוּ מְחִיצוֹת הַתַּחְתּוֹנוֹת עוֹדְפוֹת עַל הָעֶלְיוֹנוֹת. וְכֵן אָמַר עוּלָּא אָמַר רַבִּי יוֹחָנָן: כְּגוֹן שֶׁהָיוּ מְחִיצוֹת הַתַּחְתּוֹנוֹת עוֹדְפוֹת עַל הָעֶלְיוֹנוֹת.

And so Rabbi Elazar says that **Rabbi Oshaya says:** We are discussing a case **where the lower partitions extend beyond the upper** partitions. **And so Ulla says** that **Rabbi Yoḥanan says:** We are discussing a case **where the lower partitions extend beyond the upper** partitions.

אֲמַר לֵיהּ רַבִּי אַבָּא לְעוּלָּא: כְּמַאן? כְּרַבִּי, דְּאָמַר: קְלוּטָה כְּמִי שֶׁהוּנְחָה דָּמְיָא?

Rabbi Abba said to Ulla: In accordance with whose opinion is this *halakha* that once the bill of divorce enters the woman's domain, it is considered as though it was given to her, even though it was destroyed before it landed on the ground? Is it **in accordance with** the opinion of **Rabbi** Yehuda HaNasi, **who said** that with regard to the prohibition of transferring an item from one domain to another on Shabbat, an object **in airspace is considered at rest?**[H] This means that any item in the airspace of a domain is considered to be placed within that domain.

אֲמַר לֵיהּ: אֲפִילּוּ תֵּימָא רַבָּנַן, עַד כָּאן לָא פְּלִיגִי רַבָּנַן עֲלֵיהּ דְּרַבִּי אֶלָּא לְעִנְיַן שַׁבָּת, אֲבָל הָכָא – מִשּׁוּם אִינְטוּרֵי הוּא, וְהָא קָא מִינְטַר.

Ulla **said to him: You** can **even say** that the mishna is in accordance with the opinion of **the Rabbis,** who disagree with Rabbi Yehuda HaNasi, since **the Rabbis disagree with Rabbi** Yehuda HaNasi **only with regard to Shabbat.** They maintain that with regard to the *halakhot* of Shabbat, the item must actually come to rest in the domain to which it was transferred; while it is in the air, it is not considered as though it has landed on the ground. **But here,** in the case of divorce, **it is because** the bill of divorce **is secured** that she is divorced, **and in this case it is secured** while within the airspace of the partitions.

וְכֵן אָמַר רַבִּי אַסִּי אָמַר רַבִּי יוֹחָנָן: כְּגוֹן שֶׁהָיוּ מְחִיצוֹת הַתַּחְתּוֹנוֹת עוֹדְפוֹת עַל הָעֶלְיוֹנוֹת. אֲמַר לֵיהּ רַבִּי זֵירָא לְרַבִּי אַסִּי: כְּמַאן? כְּרַבִּי, דְּאָמַר: קְלוּטָה כְּמִי שֶׁהוּנְחָה דָּמְיָא?

And so Rabbi Asi says that **Rabbi Yoḥanan says:** We are discussing a case **where the lower partitions** in the courtyard **extend beyond the upper** partitions on the roof. **Rabbi Zeira said to Rabbi Asi: In accordance with whose** opinion is this *halakha*? Is it **in accordance with** the opinion of **Rabbi** Yehuda HaNasi, **who says** that an object **in airspace is considered at rest?**

אֲמַר לֵיהּ: אֲפִילּוּ תֵּימָא רַבָּנַן, עַד כָּאן לָא פְּלִיגִי רַבָּנַן עֲלֵיהּ דְּרַבִּי אֶלָּא לְעִנְיַן שַׁבָּת, אֲבָל הָכָא – מִשּׁוּם אִינְטוּרֵי הוּא, וְהָא קָא מִינְטַר.

Rabbi Asi **said to him: You** can **even say** that the mishna is in accordance with the opinion of **the Rabbis,** since **the Rabbis disagree with Rabbi** Yehuda HaNasi **only with regard to Shabbat. But here, it is because** the bill of divorce **is secured** that she is divorced, **and in this case it is secured** while within the airspace of the partitions.

״נִמְחַק״. אָמַר רַב נַחְמָן אָמַר רַבָּה בַּר אֲבוּהּ: לֹא שָׁנוּ אֶלָּא שֶׁנִּמְחַק דֶּרֶךְ יְרִידָה, אֲבָל נִמְחַק דֶּרֶךְ עֲלִיָּיה – לָא; מַאי טַעְמָא? מֵעִיקָּרָא לָא לְמֵינַח קָאֵי.

§ It was taught in the mishna that once the bill of divorce leaves the domain of the roof, even if the writing **was erased** before it reached her hand, she is divorced with it. **Rav Naḥman says** that **Rabba bar Avuh says: They taught** this *halakha* **only when** the writing **was erased** when it had already left the confines of the roof and was on its **descent,**[H] entering her domain. **But** if the writing **was erased** while it was on its **ascent,** i.e., as it arched upward before falling down, then **no,** she is not divorced. **What is the reason** for this? Because **initially,** before it began its descent, the bill of divorce **is not destined to land** in her domain, since it could be blown elsewhere. Consequently, it cannot be considered as though it is already resting in her courtyard at that time.

BACKGROUND

The lower partitions extend beyond – מְחִיצוֹת הַתַּחְתּוֹנוֹת עוֹדְפוֹת: When the partitions of the courtyard below the house rise higher than the partitions of the roof above, it is clear that an item thrown from the roof, once it leaves the domain of the roof, will immediately enter within the partitions of the courtyard and the airspace of the courtyard.

Courtyard partitions rising higher than the partitions of the roof

HALAKHA

An object in airspace is considered at rest – קְלוּטָה כְּמִי שֶׁהוּנְחָה: One who throws an object from one public domain to another on Shabbat, even if there is a private domain in the middle through which the object passes, is not considered to have transferred an object from one type of domain to another. This is because the *halakha* is not in accordance with Rabbi Yehuda HaNasi, so an object in airspace is not considered at rest with regard to the *halakhot* of Shabbat (Rambam *Sefer Zemanim, Hilkhot Shabbat* 13:16).

Was erased on its descent – שֶׁנִּמְחַק דֶּרֶךְ יְרִידָה: In certain cases, a bill of divorce that enters the confines of partitions is valid even if its writing is erased before it lands. Regardless of whether it is thrown from the courtyard to the roof, or from the roof to the courtyard, it is valid only if its writing is erased after it began its descent. If its writing is erased before it began its descent, it is not a valid bill of divorce, according to the majority of the early commentaries, in accordance with Rav Naḥman's statement. According to the Rambam, if its writing is erased prior to its landing, it is valid only in a case where the bill of divorce is thrown from the roof to the courtyard (Rambam *Sefer Nashim, Hilkhot Geirushin* 5:3–4; *Shulḥan Arukh, Even HaEzer* 139:4–6).

״נִשְׂרַף״. אָמַר רַב נַחְמָן אָמַר רַבָּה בַּר אֲבוּהּ: לֹא שָׁנוּ אֶלָּא שֶׁקָּדַם גֵּט לַדְּלֵיקָה, אֲבָל קָדְמָה דְּלֵיקָה לַגֵּט – לֹא; מַאי טַעְמָא? מֵעִיקָּרָא לִשְׂרֵיפָה קָאָזֵיל.

It was taught in the mishna that once the bill of divorce leaves the domain of the roof, even if the document **was burned** before it reached her hand, she is divorced with it. Here, as well, **Rav Naḥman says** that **Rabba bar Avuh says: They taught** this *halakha* **only when** the throwing of the **bill of divorce preceded the fire.**[H] **But if** the **fire preceded the** throwing of the **bill of divorce,** then the woman is **not** divorced. **What is the reason** for this? Because **initially,** when the bill of divorce was thrown, **it was heading toward being burned,** and therefore it is considered that he never gave her a bill of divorce.

אָמַר רַב חִסְדָּא: רְשׁוּיוֹת חֲלוּקוֹת בְּגִיטִּין.

§ **Rav Ḥisda says: Domains are divided with regard to bills of divorce.** If there are several areas within the same domain, e.g., a house and a courtyard, or a courtyard and a roof, they are not all considered a single domain with regard to bills of divorce. Rather, each one is considered to be a separate domain.

אֲמַר לֵיהּ רָמִי בַּר חָמָא לְרָבָא: מְנָא לֵיהּ לְסָבָא הָא? אֲמַר לֵיהּ, מַתְנִיתִין הִיא: הָיְתָה עוֹמֶדֶת עַל רֹאשׁ הַגַּג וּזְרָקוֹ לָהּ, כֵּיוָן שֶׁהִגִּיעַ גֵּט לַאֲוִיר הַגַּג – הֲרֵי זוֹ מְגוֹרֶשֶׁת.

Rami bar Ḥama said to Rava: From where does the Elder, i.e., Rav Ḥisda, derive **this** *halakha*? Rava **said to him: It is** derived from **the mishna** that taught: If the woman **was standing on the top of the roof and** her husband **threw** a bill of divorce **to her** from below, **once the bill of divorce reaches the airspace of the roof, she is divorced.**

בְּמַאי עָסְקִינַן? אִילֵימָא בְּגַג דִּידָהּ וְחָצֵר דִּידָהּ, לָמָּה לִי אֲוִיר הַגַּג?

Rava explains: **With what are we dealing? If we say** that we are dealing **with** a case of **her roof and her courtyard, why do I** require the bill of divorce to reach **the airspace of the roof** in order for her to be divorced? Even if the bill of divorce remained in the courtyard, she would be divorced, since it is her courtyard.

אֶלָּא בְּגַג דִּידֵיהּ וְחָצֵר דִּידֵיהּ. כִּי הִגִּיעַ לַאֲוִיר הַגַּג מַאי הָוֵי?

Rather, we must be dealing **with** a case of **his roof and his courtyard.** But **when** the bill of divorce **reaches the airspace of the roof, what of it?** Why is she then divorced, if the bill of divorce has not left his domain?

אֶלָּא פְּשִׁיטָא בְּגַג דִּידָהּ וְחָצֵר דִּידֵיהּ. אֵימָא סֵיפָא: הוּא מִלְמַעְלָה וְהִיא מִלְּמַטָּה וּזְרָקוֹ לָהּ, כֵּיוָן שֶׁיָּצָא מֵרְשׁוּת הַגַּג, נִמְחַק אוֹ נִשְׂרַף – הֲרֵי זוֹ מְגוֹרֶשֶׁת; וְאִי בְּגַג דִּידָהּ וְחָצֵר דִּידֵיהּ, אַמַּאי מְגוֹרֶשֶׁת? אֶלָּא בְּגַג דִּידֵיהּ וְחָצֵר דִּידָהּ.

Rather, it **is obvious** that we are dealing **with** a case of **her roof and his courtyard.** Rava questions this conclusion: Say **the latter clause** of the mishna, which taught: If **he** was **above** on the roof **and she** was **below, and he threw it to her, once it leaves the area of the roof,** even if the wording **was erased or** the document **was burned** before it fell to the ground, **she is divorced. And if** we are dealing **with** a case of **her roof and his courtyard, why is she divorced? Rather,** it is necessary to say that we are dealing **with** a case of **his roof and her courtyard.**

רֵישָׁא בְּגַג דִּידָהּ וְחָצֵר דִּידֵיהּ, סֵיפָא בְּגַג דִּידֵיהּ וְחָצֵר דִּידָהּ?

Rava asks: Is it possible that **the first clause** in the mishna is dealing **with** a case of **her roof and his courtyard, and the latter clause** in the mishna is dealing **with** a case of **his roof and her courtyard?** How could the same mishna discuss two *halakhot* where each one is dealing with a different reality, without mentioning this distinction?

אֶלָּא לָאו דְּאוֹשְׁלָהּ מָקוֹם, דְּחַד מָקוֹם מוֹשְׁלֵי אִינָשֵׁי, תְּרֵי מְקוֹמוֹת לָא מוֹשְׁלֵי אִינָשֵׁי.

Rava explains Rav Ḥisda's inference: **Rather, is it not** so **that** the mishna is dealing with a case **where** both the roof and the courtyard belong to him, but **he lent her** a **place** in his domain wherein she could acquire her bill of divorce, and she is standing in that place? In the first clause he lent her the roof, and in the second clause he lent her the courtyard, Consequently, only once it reaches that domain is she divorced. The reason why she does not acquire the bill of divorce until it reaches the specific domain that he lent her is **that people lend** only **one place; people do not lend two places.** Rav Ḥisda understood that one can infer from the mishna that the courtyard and roof remain as separate domains, and concludes that, with regard to bills of divorce, different areas in one domain are considered to be multiple domains.

HALAKHA

When the throwing of the bill of divorce preceded the fire – שֶׁקָּדַם גֵּט לַדְּלֵיקָה: A bill of divorce that entered the confines of partitions, but was burned before it landed, is valid only if first it began to fall and subsequently the fire began burning. If the fire began before the bill of divorce was thrown, it is as though the bill of divorce was thrown away, and it is not a valid bill of divorce, in accordance with Rav Naḥman's statement (Rambam *Sefer Nashim, Hilkhot Geirushin* 5:5; *Shulḥan Arukh, Even HaEzer* 139:4).

אֲמַר לֵיהּ: מִידֵּי אִירְיָא? דִּלְמָא הָא כִּדְאִיתָא וְהָא כִּדְאִיתָא, רֵישָׁא בְּגַג דִּידָהּ וְחָצֵר דִּידֵיהּ, סֵיפָא בְּגַג דִּידֵיהּ וְחָצֵר דִּידָהּ.

Rami bar Ḥama **said to** Rava: **Are the cases comparable? Perhaps this** case is **as it is and that** case is **as it is**, i.e., **the first clause** in the mishna is dealing **with** a case of **her roof and his courtyard,** and **the latter clause** is dealing **with** a case of **his roof and her courtyard.** In some instances, one mishna deals with two different cases. Therefore, the mishna is not an adequate proof for Rav Ḥisda's statement.

אָמַר רָבָא: שָׁלֹשׁ מִדּוֹת בְּגִיטִּין; הָא דְּאָמַר רַבִּי: קְלוּטָה כְּמִי שֶׁהוּנְחָה, וּפְלִיגִי רַבָּנַן עֲלֵיהּ – הָנֵי מִילֵּי לְעִנְיַן שַׁבָּת, אֲבָל הָכָא מִשּׁוּם אִינְטוּרֵי הוּא, וְהָא מִינְּטַר.

Rava says: There are **three** unique **qualities with regard to bills of divorce,** as compared to the *halakhot* of Shabbat. The first is **that which Rabbi** Yehuda HaNasi **says:** An object **in airspace is** considered **at rest; and the Rabbis disagree with him. This matter** about which they disagree **applies** only **with regard to Shabbat. But here,** in the case of divorce, **it is because** the bill of divorce **is secured** that she is divorced; **and** once the bill of divorce is within the airspace of the partitions, **it is secured** and the Rabbis agree that she is divorced.

וְהָא דְּאָמַר רַב חִסְדָּא: נָעַץ קָנֶה בִּרְשׁוּת הַיָּחִיד וּבְרֹאשׁוֹ טְרַסְקַל וְזָרַק וְנָח עַל גַּבָּיו, אֲפִילּוּ גָּבוֹהַּ מֵאָה אַמָּה – חַיָּיב, לְפִי שֶׁרְשׁוּת הַיָּחִיד עוֹלָה עַד לָרָקִיעַ – הָנֵי מִילֵּי לְעִנְיַן שַׁבָּת, אֲבָל הָכָא מִשּׁוּם אִינְטוּרֵי הוּא, וְהָא לָא מִינְּטַר.

And the second matter is **that which Rav Ḥisda says** concerning the *halakhot* of Shabbat: In the case of one who **embedded a reed**[H] in the ground of **a private domain, and on its top was a basket** [***teraskal***],[NL] **and he threw** an object from the public domain and **it rested on top of it, even** if the reed was **a hundred cubits high, he is liable because the private domain extends upward until the sky.** Therefore, the object landed in a private domain. **This matter applies** only **with regard to Shabbat,** as with regard to Shabbat domains are defined based on their partitions and the way in which they are used, which differs from the way domains are defined in other halakhic areas. **But here,** in the case of divorce, **it is because** the bill of divorce **is secured** that she is divorced, **and** when it is on the reed **it is not secured.**[H]

Perek **VIII**
Daf **79** Amud **b**

וְהָא דְּאָמַר רַב יְהוּדָה אָמַר שְׁמוּאֵל: לֹא יַעֲמוֹד אָדָם בְּגַג זֶה וְיִקְלוֹט מֵי גְשָׁמִים מִגַּגּוֹ שֶׁל חֲבֵירוֹ, שֶׁכְּשֵׁם שֶׁדָּיוֹרִין חֲלוּקִין מִלְּמַטָּה כָּךְ דָּיוֹרִין חֲלוּקִין מִלְמַעְלָה,

And the third matter relates to **that which Rav Yehuda says** that **Shmuel says:** On Shabbat **a person should not stand on this roof and collect rainwater from the roof of another** if there is no joining of courtyards. **As just as the residences are separated below, so too, the residences are separated above.** Each residence has a separate domain, and it is forbidden by rabbinic law to transfer an item from a private domain to another private domain if they are not joined. Similarly, despite the fact that the roofs are not totally separated from one another and nobody lives there, each roof is considered to be its own domain.

הָנֵי מִילֵּי לְעִנְיַן שַׁבָּת, אֲבָל לְעִנְיַן גֵּט – מִשּׁוּם קְפֵידָא הוּא, וְכוּלֵּי הַאי לָא קָפְדֵי אֱינָשֵׁי.

Rava explains: **This matter applies** only **with regard to Shabbat. But with regard to a bill of divorce,** if it fell onto another roof that is adjacent to the roof that he lent her for the purpose of acquiring the bill of divorce, she is divorced. The reason that a woman is usually not divorced when a bill of divorce falls into a different place, even though that place also belongs to her husband, is **due to** the fact that a husband **is particular** and does not want to lend her more than one place; **but people are not particular to that extent,**[H] i.e., in this case the husband would not be particular about allowing her to temporarily use an adjacent rooftop that also belongs to him.

HALAKHA

One who embedded a reed, etc. – נָעַץ קָנֶה וכו׳: If, on Shabbat, one embedded a reed in a private domain and then threw an object from a public domain, and the object landed on top of the reed, he is liable. This is true even if the reed is a hundred cubits high, since the private domain extends upward into the sky, in accordance with Rav Ḥisda's statement (Rambam *Sefer Zemanim, Hilkhot Shabbat* 14:17; see *Shulḥan Arukh, Oraḥ Ḥayyim* 345:5).

And it is not secured – וְהָא לָא מִינְּטַר: If a reed was embedded in a woman's courtyard, and it extended higher than the courtyard's partitions, and her husband threw a bill of divorce so that it landed on top of the reed, she is not divorced. This is because the bill of divorce is not secured at the top of the reed, in accordance with Rava's statement and Rashi's version of the text (Rambam *Sefer Nashim, Hilkhot Geirushin* 5:6; *Shulḥan Arukh, Even HaEzer* 139:7).

NOTES

And on its top was a basket – וּבְרֹאשׁוֹ טְרַסְקַל: The Rashba notes that the text of the Gemara before Rashi did not include the words: And on its top was a basket. He explains that with regard to the *halakhot* of Shabbat, the basket is in fact not relevant, as it is the reed which has the status of a separate domain. He suggests, however, that the basket is relevant for the case of the bill of divorce, as the bill of divorce must have a place in which it can land.

LANGUAGE

Basket [*teraskal*] – טְרַסְקַל: Apparently derived from a transposition of the letters of the Greek word **κάρταλλος**, *kartallos*, meaning basket.

HALAKHA

But people are not particular to that extent – וְכוּלֵּי הַאי לָא קָפְדֵי אֱינָשֵׁי: If a husband lent his roof to his wife, and the bill of divorce fell on another roof that was also his, and which was adjacent to the roof that he lent her, she is divorced. Since a roof does not have permanent residents, he is not particular about her using it. This is in accordance with Rav Yehuda's statement as it is understood by Rashi, the Ra'avad, and the Rashba. According to the *Beit Shmuel*, some say that even if he lent her a place in his courtyard and the bill of divorce fell on his roof, it is possible to say that he is not particular about her using the roof and it is still considered a valid bill of divorce. According to the Rambam, even if the bill of divorce fell onto an adjacent roof that belonged to someone else, if she can extend her hand and take it, it is a valid bill of divorce (Rambam *Sefer Nashim, Hilkhot Geirushin* 5:11; *Shulḥan Arukh, Even HaEzer* 139:12).

אמר אביי: שתי חצרות זו לפנים מזו, פנימית שלה וחיצונה שלו, ומחיצות החיצונות עודפות על הפנימיות, וזרקו לה, כיון שהגיע לאויר מחיצות החיצונה – הרי זו מגורשת,

§ **Abaye says:** If there are **two courtyards** that are configured such that **this** courtyard is **within that** courtyard,[H] and the **inner** courtyard **is hers and the outer** courtyard **is his, and the partitions of the outer** courtyard **extend higher than** the partitions of **the inner** courtyard, **and he threw** a bill of divorce **to her** into her courtyard, **once it reaches the airspace of the partitions of the outer** courtyard,[N] i.e., it reaches the area above the inner courtyard at a height lower than the height of the partitions of the outer courtyard, **she is divorced.**

מאי טעמא? פנימית גופה במחיצות החיצונה קא מינטרה.

What is the reason for this? The **inner** courtyard **itself is secured by** the **partitions** of **the outer** courtyard. Therefore, the outer partitions service the inner courtyard as well. If the bill of divorce is secured by being encompassed by the outer partitions, it can be viewed as belonging to the inner courtyard once it reaches its airspace.

מה שאין כן בקופות, שתי קופות זו בתוך זו, פנימית שלה וחיצונה שלו, וזרקו לה, אפילו דגיע לאויר פנימית – אינה מגורשת.

The Gemara comments: **This is not so with regard to baskets.** In a case where there were **two baskets,**[H] **this** one **within that** one, resting in a domain that does not belong to either of them, and **the inner** basket **is hers and the outer** basket **is his, and he threw** a bill if divorce **to her** into her basket, **even** if the bill of divorce **reached the airspace** of **the inner** basket but was burned or taken before it landed therein, **she is not divorced.**

מאי טעמא? דהא לא נח.

What is the reason for this? It is **because** the bill of divorce did **not** yet **rest**[N] within the basket, and in this case, the walls of the outer basket do not service the inner basket.

וכי נח מאי הוי? כליו של לוקח ברשות מוכר הוא!

The Gemara asks: **And when it rests** within the basket, **what of it?** They **are like** the **vessels of a buyer in the domain of the seller,** since her basket is within his basket, which is his domain. She cannot acquire the bill of divorce, despite the fact that it is in her basket, since it is within his domain.

הכא במאי עסקינן – בקופה שאין לה שוליים.

The Gemara answers: **With what are we dealing here? With a basket that has no bottom,**[B] and consequently the inner basket is resting on the ground and not inside the outer basket. Therefore, once the bill of divorce lands inside the inner basket, she is indeed divorced.

מתני׳ בית שמאי אומרים: פוטר אדם אשתו בגט ישן, ובית הלל אוסרין. ואיזהו גט ישן? כל שנתייחד עמה מאחר שכתבו לה

MISHNA **Beit Shammai say: A man may send,** i.e., divorce, **his wife with an outdated bill of divorce,**[H] **and Beit Hillel prohibit** him from doing so. **And what is an outdated bill of divorce? Any case where he was secluded with her after he wrote it for her** and before he gave it to her.

גמ׳ במאי קמיפלגי? בית שמאי סברי, לא אמרינן: גזרה שמא יאמרו גיטה קודם לבנה.

GEMARA The Gemara explains: **With regard to what do they disagree? Beit Shammai hold** that **we do not say** that the bill of divorce is not valid due to a rabbinic **decree, lest they say** that receipt of **her bill of divorce precedes** conception of **her son.** If he gives her the bill of divorce long after it was written, she may give birth to children from him in the interim. There is a concern that people will say that she was actually divorced on the date written on the bill of divorce before the children were born, and the children were conceived through licentious sexual intercourse.

BACKGROUND

A basket that has no bottom – קופה שאין לה שוליים: In this scenario, there are two baskets, one inside the other. The inner basket is not actually in the outer basket, since the outer basket does not have a bottom. Therefore, the inner basket is resting on the ground. According to the conclusion of the Gemara, the inner basket is not considered to be in the outer basket with regard to the *halakhot* of acquisition in monetary law. Nevertheless, it is not considered an independent space, of the kind that would enable the woman to acquire a bill of divorce that is in the airspace of the inner basket.

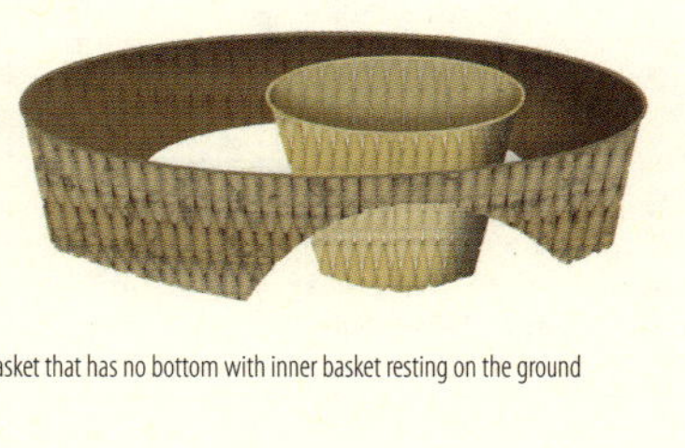

Basket that has no bottom with inner basket resting on the ground

HALAKHA

Two courtyards, such that this courtyard is within that courtyard – שתי חצרות זו לפנים מזו: If there were two courtyards, one situated within than the other, and the inner courtyard belonged to a woman, and the outer courtyard belong to her husband, if the partitions of the outer courtyard are higher than the partitions of the inner courtyard, she is divorced as soon as he throws the bill of divorce into the airspace above the inner courtyard, once it descends lower than the outer partitions (Rambam *Sefer Nashim, Hilkhot Geirushin* 5:6; *Shulḥan Arukh, Even HaEzer* 139:9).

Two baskets – שתי קופות: In this case, there were two baskets, one within the other, and the inner one belonged to the wife and the outer one belonged to the husband. The husband threw a bill of divorce. Even if the bill of divorce reached the airspace of the inner basket, she is not divorced until it actually rests inside the basket, in accordance with Abaye's statement. According to the Rambam, this applies when the basket is in the husband's domain and when the inner basket has no bottom. If both of the baskets had bottoms, she is not divorced, or, according to some, it is uncertain if she is divorced (*Beit Shmuel*, citing *Tur*), since this is like a case of a buyer's vessel in the domain of the seller (Rambam *Sefer Nashim, Hilkhot Geirushin* 5:7; *Shulḥan Arukh, Even HaEzer* 139:9).

An outdated bill of divorce – גט ישן: If a man wrote a bill of divorce for his wife but was secluded with her before he divorced her, if he still wishes to divorce her, he should not do so using that same bill of divorce. Despite this, if he did divorce her with that bill of divorce, she is considered to be divorced, and she can remarry *ab initio*. This is in accordance with the latter formulation of Rabbi Abba's statement. The Ramah and Rosh say that this applies only in a case where the husband handed the bill of divorce to his wife. If he sent her the bill of divorce via an agent and was secluded with her after it was given to the agent, and subsequently the agent gave her the bill of divorce, she should not remarry on the basis of that bill of divorce; if she did remarry, she is not required to leave her second husband (Rambam *Sefer Nashim, Hilkhot Geirushin* 3:5; *Shulḥan Arukh, Even HaEzer* 148:1).

NOTES

The airspace of the partitions of the outer courtyard – אויר מחיצות החיצונה: The commentaries explain that the bill of divorce reached the airspace above the inner courtyard. It is still above the height of the partitions of the inner courtyard, but it has descended within the height of the partitions of the outer courtyard. Since the partitions of the outer courtyard surround the inner courtyard as well, the chance that the wind will blow the bill of divorce away is small. Consequently, it is as though he threw it into her courtyard.

It did not rest – דהא לא נח: The Gemara's language indicates that even if the bill of divorce reaches the airspace of the walls of the inner basket, it still does not take effect. Rashi explains that this is because the function of the walls of a vessel is not to secure, for the long term, items placed inside the vessel, rather to temporarily have items placed inside of it. Consequently, it does not serve to acquire an item for its owner.

Many of the early commentaries disagree with Rashi and state that the airspace of a vessel can also acquire items, and they explain the Gemara differently. According to *Tosafot*, the Gemara is referring to a case in which the bill of divorce did not yet reach the airspace of the walls of the vessel. Therefore, the vessel does not acquire the bill of divorce in this case, since a vessel acquires items only through the airspace within its walls, and not with the airspace above it. This is unlike a courtyard or other domains, where the owner's authority extends upward without limit. Alternatively, Rabbeinu Crescas Vidal explains that since the basket of the woman is within the basket of her husband, meaning that the husband's basket was placed there first, all of the airspace already belongs to the husband. Therefore, even if the bill of divorce were to reach the airspace of the woman's basket, it is ineffective, since all of the airspace belongs to her husband.

וּבֵית הִלֵּל סָבְרִי, אָמְרִינַן: גְּזֵרָה שֶׁמָּא יֹאמְרוּ גִּיטָּהּ קוֹדֵם לִבְנָהּ.

And Beit Hillel hold that **we do say** that this bill of divorce is not valid due to a rabbinic **decree, lest they say** that receipt of **her bill of divorce precedes** conception of **her son.** Consequently, if a woman was secluded with her husband following the writing of the bill of divorce, the bill of divorce is not valid.

אָמַר רַבִּי אַבָּא אָמַר שְׁמוּאֵל: אִם נִישֵּׂאת – לֹא תֵּצֵא.

Rabbi Abba says that **Shmuel says:** Even according to Beit Hillel, **if** the woman **was married** on the basis of an outdated bill of divorce given to her by her previous husband, who did not ask advice from the rabbis, **she** need **not leave** her second husband. In such a case, this decree is not severe enough to invalidate the bill of divorce.

וְאִיכָּא דְּאָמְרִי, אָמַר רַבִּי אַבָּא אָמַר שְׁמוּאֵל: אִם נִתְגָּרְשָׁה – תִּינָּשֵׂא לְכַתְּחִלָּה.

And there are those **who say** that **Rabbi Abba says** that **Shmuel says: If she was divorced** with an outdated bill of divorce, this woman can **marry**[N] even ***ab initio*** on the basis of this bill of divorce. There is no requirement for her to wait for her first husband to write her a new bill of divorce.

מתני׳ כָּתַב לְשׁוּם מַלְכוּת שֶׁאֵינָהּ הוֹגֶנֶת, לְשׁוּם מַלְכוּת מָדַי, לְשׁוּם מַלְכוּת יָוָן, לְבִנְיַן הַבַּיִת, לְחוּרְבַּן הַבַּיִת,

MISHNA If **he wrote** the date on the bill of divorce using a calendrical system that counts years **in the name of a kingdom that is not legitimate,**[N] or he wrote the date **in the name of the kingdom of Medea,** or **in the name of the Greek Empire,** after it ceased to exist, or he wrote the date counting **to the building of the Temple,** or counting **to the destruction of the Temple,** in all these case, the bill of divorce is not valid. In the time of the mishna, the local government was particular that documents be dated with the official government date. Therefore, the Sages instituted that this must be done in bills of divorce as well. If one deviates from this practice, the rabbinic dictates of bills of divorce have been violated, and the bill of divorce is invalid.

הָיָה בַּמִּזְרָח וְכָתַב בַּמַּעֲרָב, בַּמַּעֲרָב וְכָתַב בַּמִּזְרָח – תֵּצֵא מִזֶּה וּמִזֶּה, וּצְרִיכָה גֵּט מִזֶּה וּמִזֶּה.

If **he was in the east and he wrote** the location in the bill of divorce as **in the west,** or if he was **in the west and he wrote** the location in the bill of divorce as **in the east,** the bill of divorce is not valid. If he divorced her with this bill of divorce and she remarried, **she** must **leave** both **this** first husband **and that** second husband, **and she needs a bill of divorce from this** husband **and that** husband.[N]

NOTES

If she was divorced she can marry – אִם נִתְגָּרְשָׁה תִּינָּשֵׂא: Rashi limits this by saying that Shmuel, according to this version, permitted a woman who was divorced with an outdated bill of divorce to marry *ab initio*, only in a case where her husband went overseas and was unable to issue a new bill of divorce, to avoid her becoming a deserted wife. If the husband remained in the same location, he must write a new bill of divorce.

A kingdom that is not legitimate – מַלְכוּת שֶׁאֵינָהּ הוֹגֶנֶת: The Gemara (80a) identifies this unnamed kingdom as the Roman Empire. In his Commentary on the Mishna, the Rambam explains that this term is a general expression for a kingdom that does not have sovereignty in the place in which the bill of divorce was written.

And she needs a bill of divorce from this husband and from that husband – וּצְרִיכָה גֵּט מִזֶּה וּמִזֶּה: Rashi explains that although the first bill of divorce is not valid, and therefore the betrothal to the second man did not take effect at all, she still requires a bill of divorce from the second man so that people will not mistakenly think that a married woman was released without a bill of divorce. Most of the early commentaries explain to the contrary: Since the first bill of divorce is not valid by rabbinic law but valid by Torah law, her betrothal to the second man did take effect, and she requires a bill of divorce from the second husband by Torah law. By the same logic, it is forbidden for her to then return to her first husband since it is as though her first husband is remarrying his divorcée after she married someone else. She must receive a second bill of divorce from her first husband, since the Sages invalidated the first one.

וְאֵין לָהּ לֹא כְּתוּבָּה וְלֹא פֵּירוֹת וְלֹא מְזוֹנוֹת וְלֹא בְּלָאוֹת לֹא עַל זֶה וְלֹא עַל זֶה,

And she does not receive payment of her **marriage contract, and not the profits**[N] from her properties that her husband consumed, **and** she does **not** have a claim to receive **sustenance, and** she does **not** have a claim to **worn clothes**[N] that belonged to her, but which her husband used. She cannot demand these items, **not of this** husband **and not of that** husband.

אִם נָטְלָה מִזֶּה וּמִזֶּה תַּחֲזִיר; וְהַוָּלָד מַמְזֵר מִזֶּה וּמִזֶּה; וְלֹא זֶה וָזֶה מִטַּמְּאִין לָהּ, וְלֹא זֶה וָזֶה זַכָּאִין לֹא בִּמְצִיאָתָהּ וְלֹא בְּמַעֲשֵׂה יָדֶיהָ וְלֹא בַּהֲפָרַת נְדָרֶיהָ.

If she took any of these items **from this husband or from that** husband, **she** must **return** what was taken. **And the child** that was born **from this** husband **or from that** husband that was conceived after she married the second husband is a **son born from an adulterous relationship** [*mamzer*].[NB] **And neither this** husband **nor that** husband, if they are priests, is permitted to **become ritually impure by her**[N] when she dies, which a husband may ordinarily do for his wife. **And neither this** husband **nor that** husband **have the rights**[N] **to objects she finds, or to her earnings, or to the annulment of her vows.**

הָיְתָה בַּת יִשְׂרָאֵל – נִפְסֶלֶת מִן הַכְּהוּנָּה,

If she was an Israelite woman, then through these two marriages **she** becomes **disqualified from** marrying into the **priesthood,**[N] due to the prohibition against a priest marrying a *zona*.

BACKGROUND

Mamzer – מַמְזֵר: A *mamzer* or *mamzeret* is a boy or girl born from an adulterous or incestuous relationship, i.e., a child born from sexual intercourse between a married woman and a man other than her husband, or between relatives who are forbidden to marry by a prohibition punishable by *karet*. The case of a child conceived through intercourse with a menstruating woman is an exception to this principle, as although engaging in sexual intercourse with a menstruating woman is punishable by *karet*, the child is not a *mamzer* or *mamzeret*. Similarly, a child conceived out of wedlock by a man and woman who are permitted to marry is not a *mamzer* or *mamzeret*. A *mamzer* is prohibited from marrying a Jewish woman of unflawed lineage. However, he can marry a convert or a *mamzeret*. Similarly, a *mamzeret* can marry only a convert or a *mamzer*. The offspring of these unions are also *mamzerim*. A *mamzer* inherits from his father and is considered his father's son in all respects.

NOTES

And not profits – וְלֹא פֵּירוֹת: Rashi explains that the term profits in this instance is referring not to the profits from her property, as that is a right a husband enjoys. Rather, it is referring to the right that the Sages instituted for the wife in return for the profits of her property, which the husband takes; namely, his obligation to redeem her from captivity. Many of the early commentaries explain, based on the Jerusalem Talmud, that this is referring to profits from her property. The mishna is ruling that if the second husband, or the first one if she returned to him, profited from her property even though he had no right to do so, she is penalized and cannot demand the return of the profits. She has the right to demand the return of profits that he took after it was known that the bill of divorce was not valid (Rashba).

And not worn clothes – וְלֹא בְּלָאוֹת: Rashi explains that this is referring to clothing that a woman brought into the marriage and that her husband wore. In this case, he is not required to return them to her. Many of the early commentaries (see *Tosafot*) question this statement, since even a married woman who commits adultery does not lose her right to worn cloths. They explain that the mishna is actually referring to payment for worn clothes that no longer exist. However, the Rashba explains Rashi's opinion, stating that the Sages penalized this woman more severely than a woman who committed adultery since a penalty is not an effective deterrent for one who sins intentionally, while a penalty can motivate one acting in good faith to take more care before acting; in this case, to motivate her to ascertain that her bill of divorce was valid.

And the child from this or from that is a *mamzer* – וְהַוָּלָד מַמְזֵר מִזֶּה וּמִזֶּה: Rashi explains that the child from the second husband is a definite *mamzer*, in accordance with his opinion that the bill of divorce provided by the first husband is totally invalid. If the woman returned to her first husband before she was divorced from the second man, the child born to them is a *mamzer* by rabbinic law and is forbidden to marry both an Israelite and a *mamzer*. Others write that the child from the second husband is a *mamzer* only by rabbinic law, in accordance with the opinion that the bill of divorce from her first husband was valid by Torah law. Therefore, if the woman returned to her first husband before she was divorced from her second husband, the child born to them is a *mamzer* by Torah law; and if she returned to her first husband after she was divorced by the second man, the child is unblemished by Torah law (Ramban; Ritva).

And neither this nor that is permitted to become ritually impure by her – וְלֹא זֶה וָזֶה מִטַּמְּאִין לָהּ: If the first and second husbands are priests, they are prohibited to become ritually impure by her when she dies, despite the fact that, normally, a priest may become ritually impure for his wife. If they were not priests or Levites, they are not required to become ritually impure in order to administer her burial, as any other husband would be required to do for his wife (Ritva; see *Tosefot Rabbi Akiva Eiger* on mishnayot).

Neither this nor that have the rights, etc. – וְלֹא זֶה וָזֶה זַכָּאִין וכו׳: Neither husband has the right to objects she finds, since it was instituted that such objects belong to the husband only for the sake of preventing enmity; and here, this issue is not relevant. Neither husband has a right to her earnings, since the Sages instituted that a husband has a right to his wife's earnings in compensation for sustaining her, and in this case she does not receive sustenance. Finally, neither husband has the ability to annul her vows, since this right is connected with the concern of a wife being despised by her husband; and here, this issue is not relevant (Ritva, based on the Gemara in tractate *Yevamot*).

She becomes disqualified from marrying into the priesthood – נִפְסֶלֶת מִן הַכְּהוּנָּה: A woman whose second marriage took place after receiving an invalid bill of divorce from her husband is considered to be a *zona*, a woman who engaged in sexual intercourse with a man forbidden to her by the Torah, as a result of the sexual intercourse with the second man. The early and later commentaries wonder why it is necessary to mention this, since she becomes disqualified from marrying into the priesthood anyway as a result of the first divorce, according to the opinion of some of the early commentaries that the bill of divorce was valid by Torah law. Some explain that it is mentioned due to the continuation of the mishna, which deals with a Levite woman (Ritva; see Maharsha). Alternatively, it is possible to explain that it is mentioned in order to teach that she is considered a *zona* with regard to making a priest liable to be punished with lashes for engaging in sexual intercourse with her (Maharshal).

בַּת לֵוִי – מִן הַמַּעֲשֵׂר, בַּת כֹּהֵן – מִן הַתְּרוּמָה.

If she was the **daughter of a Levite,** through these two marriages she becomes prohibited **from** partaking of **the tithe**[N] that is given to Levites. If she was the **daughter of a priest,** she becomes prohibited **from** partaking of ***teruma*,**[N] even after she returns to the house of her father the priest.

וְאֵין יוֹרְשִׁין שֶׁל זֶה וְיוֹרְשִׁין שֶׁל זֶה יוֹרְשִׁים כְּתוּבָּתָהּ; וְאִם מֵתוּ – אָחִיו שֶׁל זֶה וְאָחִיו שֶׁל זֶה חוֹלְצִין וְלֹא מְיַיבְּמִין.

And the heirs of this husband **and the heirs of that** husband **do not inherit** the rights to collect payment of **her marriage contract**[N] if she dies. **And if** the husbands **die, the brother of this** first husband **and the brother of that** second husband **perform *ḥalitza*,** since she was betrothed to the second one as well, **and they do not consummate the levirate marriage.**

שִׁינָּה שְׁמוֹ וּשְׁמָהּ, שֵׁם עִירוֹ וְשֵׁם עִירָהּ – תֵּצֵא מִזֶּה וּמִזֶּה, וְכׇל הַדְּרָכִים הָאֵלּוּ בָּהּ.

The mishna proceeds to teach an additional *halakha* concerning a bill of divorce written not in accordance with its *halakhot*: **If he changed his name,**[N] i.e., he wrote a different name in the bill of divorce, **or** he changed **her name,**[H] or if he changed **the name of his city or the name of her city,** and she remarried on the basis of this bill of divorce, then **she** must **leave** both **this** first husband **and that**[H] second husband. **And all of those** above-mentioned **ways** of penalizing a woman who remarried based on the bills of divorce detailed in the earlier clause of the mishna apply **to her** in this case as well.

כׇּל עֲרָיוֹת שֶׁאָמְרוּ צָרוֹתֵיהֶן מוּתָּרוֹת,

The mishna teaches another *halakha* associated with the previous *halakhot*: With regard to **all** of those cases in which **they said** that a man who died without children and left behind a widow who is, to the man's brother, one of **those with whom relations are forbidden,** e.g., she is his wife's sister, not only is there no levirate bond for her, but **the rival wives** of the brother who died **are** also **permitted** to marry without either levirate marriage or *ḥalitza*.

NOTES

The daughter of a Levite becomes prohibited from partaking of the tithe – בַּת לֵוִי מִן הַמַּעֲשֵׂר: The tithe given to the Levites becomes the property of the Levites, as if it were any ordinary gift that they receive. It does not have sanctity, and it can be eaten by anyone. Nonetheless, this woman is disqualified from partaking of the tithe, due to a penalty instituted by the Sages (*Yevamot* 91a).

The daughter of a priest becomes disqualified from partaking of *teruma* – בַּת כֹּהֵן מִן הַתְּרוּמָה: According to Rashi, it is derived from a verse in the Torah that a priest's daughter who engages in licentious sexual intercourse is prohibited from partaking of *teruma*. In this case, since the woman illegitimately married a second man, she is considered to be a *zona* and becomes disqualified from eating *teruma*.

Inherit her marriage contract – יוֹרְשִׁים כְּתוּבָּתָהּ: Rashi quotes the Gemara in tractate *Yevamot* that asks: Why is it necessary to mention that the heirs do not inherit the right to collect payment of their mother's marriage contract, after it was stated in the mishna that the mother does not receive payment of her marriage contract? The Gemara there answers that this is referring to the marriage document concerning male children, i.e., a clause within the marriage contract that states that the children born to this woman will inherit the payment of their mother's marriage contract after their father dies, and this is the case even if the woman died during her husband's lifetime. In the case under discussion, if the mother died during her husband's lifetime, although the children are certainly not responsible for their mother's actions, they do not inherit the payment. Since the Sages annulled their mother's marriage contract entirely, it is as though there is no marriage contract.

He changed his name – שִׁינָּה שְׁמוֹ: *Tosafot* note that this is not referring to a real name change, e.g., his name was Abraham and he wrote Isaac, since this is obvious. Rather, it is clarifying that even if he had two names that he used in two different places, and he wrote the name that he does not use in the location where the bill of divorce was written, the bill of divorce is invalid. Likewise, if the city had two names, and he wrote the name that was not used in the location where he wrote the bill of divorce, the bill of divorce is invalid. There are early commentaries who disagree with this explanation (see Rabbeinu Crescas Vidal and *Tosefot Yom Tov*).

HALAKHA

If he changed his name or her name – שִׁינָּה שְׁמוֹ וּשְׁמָהּ: If one gave a bill of divorce to his wife and changed his name, her name, the name of his city, or the name of her city, it is not a valid bill of divorce, even if he wrote in it: Any name that he has, and any name that she has (Rambam *Sefer Nashim, Hilkhot Geirushin* 3:14; *Shulḥan Arukh, Even HaEzer* 129:3).

She must leave this and that – תֵּצֵא מִזֶּה וּמִזֶּה: If a woman is divorced with any bill of divorce that is invalid by Torah law, she remains a married woman. If she marries another man, she must leave him. Any child from this second marriage is a *mamzer*, and she is forbidden to both husbands forever. She must receive a bill of divorce from her first husband to allow her to remarry, and she must receive a bill of divorce from her second husband due to a rabbinic ordinance. She is subject to all of the penalties that were instituted for a woman who was mistakenly told that her husband died, and who remarried.

This includes the following penalties: She does not receive payment of her marriage contract from her first husband or her second husband. They are not required to return profits from her property. They are not required to return the worn clothes of her guaranteed property. In addition, she becomes disqualified from marrying into the priesthood, and from partaking of *teruma* and tithes. Neither of the husbands have rights to the objects she finds, her earnings, or the ability to annul her vows; nor do they become ritually impure for her. If the husbands die, both the brother of the first husband and the brother of the second husband perform *ḥalitza*; and they cannot enter into levirate marriage. All this applies if she had married the second man. If she was only betrothed to him, she returns to her first husband, and she is not required to obtain a bill of divorce from the second man (Rambam *Sefer Nashim, Hilkhot Geirushin* 10:4; *Shulḥan Arukh, Even HaEzer* 150:1, and see 17:56).

הָלְכוּ הַצָּרוֹת הָאֵלּוּ וְנִישְּׂאוּ וְנִמְצְאוּ אֵלּוּ אַיְילוֹנִית – תֵּצֵא מִזֶּה וּמִזֶּה, וְכָל הַדְּרָכִים הָאֵלּוּ בָּהּ.

The mishna discusses another case: **These rival wives went and married** another man without *ḥalitza*, **and these** widows with whom relationships were forbidden **were found** to be **sexually underdeveloped women** incapable of bearing children [***ailonit***].[NBL] Therefore, it became clear, retroactively, that the marriage to the dead brother was never valid, and accordingly, the rival wives were never exempt from the obligation of levirate marriage due to their being the rival wives of a forbidden relationship. Consequently, the rival wives were forbidden to marry anyone else without *ḥalitza*, and the rival wives must **leave** both **this** man whom they remarried, **and that** *yavam*, i.e., they cannot enter into levirate marriage with him. **And all of those** above-mentioned **ways** of penalizing a woman who remarried based on the bills of divorce detailed in the earlier clause of the mishna apply **to her** in this case as well.

הַכּוֹנֵס אֶת יְבִמְתּוֹ, וְהָלְכָה צָרָתָהּ וְנִישֵּׂאת לְאַחֵר, וְנִמְצֵאת זוֹ שֶׁהָיְתָה אַיְילוֹנִית – תֵּצֵא מִזֶּה וּמִזֶּה, וְכָל הַדְּרָכִים הָאֵלּוּ בָּהּ.

Similarly, with regard to **one who marries his** *yevama*, **and her rival wife went and got married to another man, and it was found that this** *yevama* **was a sexually underdeveloped woman,** the rival wife must **leave this** man whom she remarried **and that** *yavam*, i.e., she cannot enter into levirate marriage with him. Because the *yevama* was a sexually underdeveloped woman, the obligation of levirate marriage never applied to her, and her levirate marriage did not exempt her rival wife. **And all of those** aforementioned **ways** of penalizing a woman who remarried based on the bills of divorce detailed in the earlier clause of the mishna apply **to her** in this case as well.

כָּתַב סוֹפֵר גֵּט לָאִישׁ וְשׁוֹבֵר לָאִשָּׁה, וְטָעָה וְנָתַן גֵּט לָאִשָּׁה וְשׁוֹבֵר לָאִישׁ וְנָתְנוּ זֶה לָזֶה,

The mishna now discusses another case: **A scribe wrote a bill of divorce for a man,** so that the man could divorce his wife with it; **and** he wrote **a receipt for the woman,** for her to give to her husband upon receiving payment of her marriage contract, verifying that she received the payment. **And** the scribe **erred and gave** the **bill of divorce to the woman and** the **receipt to the man, and** not knowing what was written in the documents that were in their possession, **they gave** what they received from the scribe **to each other.** The woman gave her husband a bill of divorce and the husband gave his wife a receipt, and consequently, there was no divorce at all.

וּלְאַחַר זְמַן הֲרֵי הַגֵּט יוֹצֵא מִיַּד הָאִישׁ וְשׁוֹבֵר מִיַּד הָאִשָּׁה – תֵּצֵא מִזֶּה וּמִזֶּה, וְכָל הַדְּרָכִים הָאֵלּוּ בָּהּ;

And after some **time, the bill of divorce is in the possession of the man, and the receipt is in the possession of the woman,** and they discover that the divorce never actually transpired. If the woman had remarried another man, **she** must **leave this,** the first husband, **and that,** the second husband. **And all of those** above-mentioned **ways** of penalizing a woman who remarried based on the bills of divorce detailed in the earlier clause of the mishna apply **to her** in this case as well.

רַבִּי אֶלְעָזָר אוֹמֵר: אִם לְאַלְתַּר יָצָא – אֵין זֶה גֵּט, אִם לְאַחַר זְמַן יָצָא – הֲרֵי זֶה גֵּט; לֹא כׇּל הֵימֶנּוּ מִן הָרִאשׁוֹן לְאַבֵּד זְכוּתוֹ שֶׁל שֵׁנִי.

Rabbi Elazar says: If the bill of divorce **is immediately** [***le'altar***][L] in the husband's possession, **this is not** a valid **bill of divorce,** since he clearly never gave it to her. But **if it is in** his possession **after** some **time,** then **this is** a valid **bill of divorce,** since **it is not in the power of the first** husband **to eliminate the right of the second** husband. The assumption is that the husband did in fact give her the bill of divorce in the correct manner, but at some point, he took it back from her.

גמ׳ מַאי מַלְכוּת שֶׁאֵינָהּ הוֹגֶנֶת? מַלְכוּת הָרוֹמִיִּים. וְאַמַּאי קָרֵי לַהּ מַלְכוּת שֶׁאֵינָהּ הוֹגֶנֶת? מִשּׁוּם דְּאֵין לָהֶם לֹא כְּתָב וְלֹא לָשׁוֹן.

GEMARA It was stated in the mishna that if one wrote the date on a bill of divorce according to a kingdom that is not legitimate, it is invalid. The Gemara asks: **What is** the meaning of the description: **A kingdom that is not legitimate?** The Gemara answers: This is referring to **the Roman Empire,** and he wrote the bill of divorce in a different country, such as Babylonia, where the Romans were not in power. **And why is it called: A kingdom that is not legitimate? Because they have neither** their own **script, nor** their own **language,**[B] but rather, they took them from other nations.

NOTES

And these were found to be sexually underdeveloped women – וְנִמְצְאוּ אֵלּוּ אַיְילוֹנִית: Since a sexually underdeveloped woman is unable to give birth, marriage to her is considered to be based on an error and is retroactively void. Additionally, the *halakhot* of levirate marriage and *ḥalitza* do not apply to her, since she cannot give birth to a child who will perpetuate the deceased father's name. There are various indications of a sexually underdeveloped woman, and one of them is that she does not show signs of adulthood by the age of twenty. It was sometimes assumed that a woman who did not show signs of adulthood was merely developmentally delayed, and only later on, once she becomes twenty years old, it is confirmed she is sexually underdeveloped; therefore the use of the expression: These were found to be.

BACKGROUND

Sexually underdeveloped woman [*ailonit*] – אַיְילוֹנִית: From detailed discussions in the Talmud, especially in tractate *Yevamot*, it seems that an *ailonit* is a woman who has some sort of genetic defect preventing her from bearing children. She is different from a barren woman, who also cannot bear children but whose physical and sexual development is normal. An *ailonit* can also be identified by a lack of secondary sexual signs, such as two pubic hairs. It seems that there are different types of defects that give a woman the status of an *ailonit*. While some individuals may have extra male hormones, others may suffer from Turner syndrome.

Neither their own script nor their own language – לֹא כְּתָב וְלֹא לָשׁוֹן: This assertion is based on Roman history. Latin, the language used by the Romans, was originally the language of the Latins, a nation and country that the city of Rome assimilated and incorporated within it. The Roman alphabet is primarily based on the Etruscan alphabet, with the modifications of the Latins. Despite their military and political power, the culture of the Romans was essentially borrowed from other nations.

LANGUAGE

Sexually underdeveloped woman [*ailonit*] – אַיְילוֹנִית: According to the Gemara in tractate *Ketubot* (11a), this word is derived from the word *ayal*, or ram. In Aramaic, the word for ram is *dikhra*, meaning male, and the ram is a symbol of masculinity. The term *ailonit* refers to a woman who, like a man, is incapable of bearing children.

Immediately [*le'altar*] – לְאַלְתַּר: From the Aramaic *al atar*, meaning, on the place, i.e., immediately. In the Jerusalem Talmud, the expression appears in the extended form, as *al atar*, and not as a contraction.

אֲמַר עוּלָּא: מִפְּנֵי מָה תַּקִּינוּ מַלְכוּת בְּגִיטִּין? מִשּׁוּם שְׁלוֹם מַלְכוּת.

Ulla said: For what reason **did** the Sages **institute** that the date should be written according to the years of the local **kingdom, in bills of divorce? Due to** the need to maintain **peaceful** relations with **the kingdom,**[HN] as the government is particular that important documents issued in its domain be written with the date of that government.

וּמִשּׁוּם שְׁלוֹם מַלְכוּת תֵּיצֵא וְהַוָּלָד מַמְזֵר?!

The Gemara asks: **But due to** an ordinance instituted by the Sages solely for the sake of maintaining **peaceful** relations with **the kingdom,** would they be so stringent that the woman would be forced to **leave** her husband, **and** they would declare the status of **the offspring is a *mamzer*?**

אִין, רַבִּי מֵאִיר לְטַעֲמֵיהּ, דְּאָמַר רַב הַמְנוּנָא מִשְּׁמֵיהּ דְּעוּלָּא, אוֹמֵר הָיָה רַבִּי מֵאִיר: כָּל הַמְשַׁנֶּה מִמַּטְבֵּעַ שֶׁטָּבְעוּ חֲכָמִים בְּגִיטִּין – הַוָּלָד מַמְזֵר.

The Gemara answers: **Yes. Rabbi Meir** conforms **to his** line of **reasoning.**[N] **As Rav Hamnuna says in the name of Ulla: Rabbi Meir would say** that **anyone deviating from the formula coined by the Sages for bills of divorce,** even if it is only a minor deviation, the bill of divorce is invalid, and if the woman remarried on the basis of this bill of divorce, then **the offspring** from that marriage **is a *mamzer*.**

"לְשׁוּם מַלְכוּת יָוָן". וּצְרִיכָא; דְּאִי אַשְׁמוּעִינַן מַלְכוּת שֶׁאֵינָהּ הוֹגֶנֶת, מִשּׁוּם דְּמַלִּיכָא, אֲבָל מַלְכוּת מָדַי וּמַלְכוּת יָוָן – מַאי דַּהֲוָה הֲוָה.

It was stated in the mishna: If he wrote the date on a bill of divorce **in the name of the Greek Empire,** then the bill of divorce is invalid. The Gemara comments: **And** it is **necessary** to state this *halakha* and the other *halakhot* as well. **As, if** the mishna **had taught us** this *halakha* only with regard to **a kingdom that is not legitimate,** one could say that the bill of divorce is invalid **because** this kingdom is currently **ruling,** and the local government where he is writing the bill of divorce therefore objects to his writing the date of an another kingdom. **But** with regard to **the kingdom of Medea, and the Greek Empire,** it is not necessary to invalidate the bill of divorce, since **what was, was,** and since these kingdoms are no longer in power, the local government is not particular if they are mentioned in a document.

וְאִי אַשְׁמַעִינַן מַלְכוּת מָדַי וּמַלְכוּת יָוָן, מִשּׁוּם דְּמַלְכוּתָא הָווּ, אֲבָל בִּנְיַן הַבַּיִת – מַאי דַּהֲוָה הֲוָה.

And if the mishna **had taught us** this *halakha* with regard to **the kingdom of Medea and the Greek Empire,** one could understand the concern, **because they were kingdoms,** and the current government objects to another kingdom being mentioned in a document. **But** if he wrote the date counting to **the building of the Temple,** then one could say **what was, was,** and the local government is not particular if this is mentioned in a document. Consequently, it was necessary for the mishna to teach us this *halakha* as well.

HALAKHA

Due to the need to maintain peaceful relations with the kingdom – מִשּׁוּם שְׁלוֹם מַלְכוּת: The Sages instituted that the date should be written in bills of divorce according to the years of the kingdom of that place and era, due to the need of maintaining peaceful relations with the kingdom. However, this is no longer the practice since governments are no longer particular about this (Rambam *Sefer Nashim, Hilkhot Geirushin* 1:27).

NOTES

Due to the need to maintain peaceful relations with the kingdom – מִשּׁוּם שְׁלוֹם מַלְכוּת: Rashi explains that this was done in order to show the authorities that they were respected, as the dates in documents were written according to their kingdom. *Tosafot* and other early commentaries note that it is stated explicitly in the Gemara that it was customary to write the date in other types of legal documents according to the Greek Empire, not the local government. They therefore explain that specifically with regard to bills of divorce, which are documents of great significance as they separate a man from his wife, and especially in lands where women were not customarily divorced, they were particular to write the date according to the local government. The Rid writes that since this was done in order to appease the government, when they saw that the government no longer was particular about this, they began to write other dates in documents, even the date of the Greek Empire (see Ramban). From the Jerusalem Talmud it appears that this was not just meant to pacify the government, but rather the government truly was particular about this, to the extent, that anyone who wrote the date according to a different kingdom was considered to be rebellious. This can be seen from the statement in the Jerusalem Talmud: They deemed the child a *mamzer* due to the danger.

Rabbi Meir conforms to his line of reasoning – רַבִּי מֵאִיר לְטַעֲמֵיהּ: This is an unattributed mishna, and any unattributed mishna is assumed to be in accordance with the opinion of Rabbi Meir. In addition, it is stated explicitly in the Gemara further on: This is the statement of Rabbi Meir.

וְאִי אַשְׁמְעִינַן בְּנִין הַבַּיִת, דְּאָמְרִי: קָמַדְכְּרִי שִׁבְחַיְיהוּ, אֲבָל חוּרְבַּן הַבַּיִת דְּצַעֲרָא הוּא – אֵימָא לָא, צְרִיכָא.

And if the mishna **had taught us** this *halakha* with regard to **the building of the Temple,** then one could say that the reason why this is problematic is because the governments **will say:** The Jews **mention their** own **praise,** instead of honoring the ruling government. **But** with regard to **the destruction of the Temple,**[N] **which is** a cause of **anguish** for us, **say** that **no,** the government is not particular about this. Therefore it is **necessary** to mention all of these *halakhot*.

״הָיָה בַּמִּזְרָח וְכָתַב בַּמַּעֲרָב״. מַאן? אִילֵימָא בַּעַל, הַיְינוּ שִׁינָּה שְׁמוֹ וּשְׁמָהּ, שֵׁם עִירוֹ וְשֵׁם עִירָהּ!

§ It was stated in the mishna, that if **he was in the east and he wrote** the location in the bill of divorce as **in the west,** then the bill of divorce is invalid. The Gemara asks: **Who** is the mishna discussing? **If we say** that the place of the **husband** was changed, then **this is** the same as what is stated later on in the mishna: **He changed his name, or her name; the name of his city or the name of her city.**

אֶלָּא לָאו, סוֹפֵר, כִּדְאָמַר לְהוּ רַב לְסָפְרֵיהּ, וְכֵן אֲמַר לְהוּ רַב הוּנָא לְסָפְרֵיהּ: כִּי יָתְבִיתוּ בְּשִׁילֵי כְּתוֹבוּ בְּשִׁילֵי, וְאַף עַל גַּב דְּמִימְסְרָן לְכוּ מִילֵּי בְּהִינִי, וְכִי יָתְבִיתוּ בְּהִינִי כְּתוֹבוּ בְּהִינִי, וְאַף עַל גַּב דְּמִימְסְרָן לְכוּ מִילֵּי בְּשִׁילֵי.

Rather, is it not referring to **a scribe**[H] who changed the place in which the bill of divorce was written, and did not record the correct location where he was when he wrote the bill of divorce? **As Rav said to his scribes, and similarly, Rav Huna said to his scribes: When you are situated in** the place called **Shili,**[H] **write** the location of the document as: **In Shili, even though the matters were presented to you,** i.e., the transaction recorded in the document took place, **in the place called Hini. And when you are situated in** the place called **Hini, write: In Hini, even though the matters were presented to you in Shili.**[B] One must be careful to write the precise location where the document was written and not somewhere else, as that is considered an illegitimate deviation.

אָמַר רַב יְהוּדָה אָמַר שְׁמוּאֵל:

Rav Yehuda says that Shmuel says:

BACKGROUND

Hini and Shili – **הִינִי וְשִׁילֵי**: These two neighboring towns were separated by approximately a kilometer. They were primarily market towns and centers for the sale of produce. Apparently, Hini and Shili were both adjacent to the Euphrates River and under the judicial jurisdiction of Sura. Some believe that these two towns later joined together to form one small city, called Shilahin, which is located south of the city of Kupa in Iraq.

Location of Hini and Shili

NOTES

But the destruction of the Temple, etc. – **אֲבָל חוּרְבַּן הַבַּיִת וכו׳**: The Ramban explains that there is a problem with deviating from the date of the local government only when the date being written instead is according to another kingdom. For this reason, the date cannot be written according to the building of the Temple, which represents King Solomon's rule, nor according to the destruction of the Temple, which represents the commencement of the rule of Nebuchadnezzar.

By contrast, a date that is not according to another kingdom, such as the years since the creation of the world, is acceptable and is not considered an affront to the local government. The Rashba and Rabbeinu Crescas Vidal write that since counting from the creation of the world shows honor to God, something that all agree to, the local governments are not particular about it, and for this reason it was done *ab initio*, without concern for the mishna. See also the previously mentioned statement of the Rid, who says that since governments are no longer particular about this, the reason for writing the government's date in documents no longer applies.

HALAKHA

Rather is it not referring to a scribe – **אֶלָּא לָאו סוֹפֵר**: It is required to write in a bill of divorce the location of the witnesses at the time of signing, but it is unnecessary to mention the location of the scribe. Therefore, if the bill of divorce was written in one place and signed in another place, only the place in which it was signed should be mentioned (Rosh). Some say that the place of the scribe should be mentioned as well, and therefore the witnesses should sign the bill of divorce in the location where it was written (*Shulḥan Arukh, Even HaEzer* 128:1).

When you are situated in Shili – **כִּי יָתְבִיתוּ בְּשִׁילֵי**: With regard to a case where the husband instructed a scribe to write a bill of divorce, the location where he issued these instructions is not written in the bill of divorce, but rather the date and place where the bill of divorce was written and signed, is recorded, in accordance with Rav Huna's statement (Rambam *Sefer Nashim, Hilkhot Geirushin* 1:25; *Shulḥan Arukh, Even HaEzer* 128:1; see Rambam *Sefer Mishpatim, Hilkhot Malve VeLoveh* 23:6 and *Shulḥan Arukh, Ḥoshen Mishpat* 43:20).

זוֹ דִּבְרֵי רַבִּי מֵאִיר, אֲבָל חֲכָמִים אוֹמְרִים: אֲפִילּוּ לֹא כָּתַב אֶלָּא לְשֵׁם סַנְטָר שֶׁבָּעִיר – הֲרֵי זוֹ מְגוֹרֶשֶׁת.

This is the statement of Rabbi Meir,[H] who is particular about maintaining peaceful relations with the kingdom, with regard to bills of divorce. **But the Rabbis say: Even if he wrote** a date on the bill of divorce **only in the name of** the **guardsman** [*santar*][L] **in the city, she is divorced,** since it is irrelevant which calendrical system was used for the date.

הַהוּא גִּיטָּא דַּהֲוָה כְּתִיב בֵּיהּ לְשֵׁם אִיסְטַנְדְּרָא דְּבַשְׂכָּר, שְׁלַחָה רַב נַחְמָן בַּר רַב חִסְדָּא לְקַמֵּיהּ דְּרַבָּה: כִּי הַאי גַּוְונָא מַאי?

It is related that there was **a certain bill of divorce in which** the date **was written in the name of the governor** [*istandera*] of the city **of Bascar,**[L] i.e., the date was marked according to the years of his government. **Rav Naḥman bar Rav Ḥisda sent this** dilemma **before Rabba: What** is the *halakha* **in a case like this?**

שְׁלַח לֵיהּ: בְּהָא אֲפִילּוּ רַבִּי מֵאִיר מוֹדֵי; מַאי טַעְמָא? מֵאוֹתָהּ מַלְכוּת הוּא.

He sent him in response: **With regard to this, even Rabbi Meir concedes** that the bill of divorce is valid. **What is the reason?** The governor **is** an official **from that kingdom,** so the ruler of the kingdom does not mind.

וּמַאי שְׁנָא מִסַּנְטָר שֶׁבָּעִיר? הָתָם זִילָא לְהוּ מִילְּתָא, הָכָא שְׁבִיחָא לְהוּ מִילְּתָא.

The Gemara asks: **And in what way is this case different from the guardsman in the city?** The Gemara answers: **There, it is demeaning for them** that the date is written in the name of an unimportant official. **Here,** with regard to the governor, **it is complimentary for them** that the date is written in the name of a senior official.

אָמַר רַבִּי אַבָּא אָמַר רַב הוּנָא אָמַר רַב: זוֹ דִּבְרֵי רַבִּי מֵאִיר, אֲבָל חֲכָמִים אוֹמְרִים: הַוָּלָד כָּשֵׁר; וּמוֹדִים חֲכָמִים לְרַבִּי מֵאִיר, שֶׁאִם שִׁינָּה שְׁמוֹ וּשְׁמָהּ, שֵׁם עִירוֹ וְשֵׁם עִירָהּ – שֶׁהַוָּלָד מַמְזֵר.

Rabbi Abba says that **Rav Huna says** that **Rav says: This** mishna is in accordance with **the statement of Rabbi Meir,** who is stringent with regard to this bill of divorce and holds that the child is a *mamzer*. **But the Rabbis say:** The lineage of **the offspring is unflawed.**[N] **And the Rabbis concede to Rabbi Meir, that if he changed his name or her name, the name of his city or the name of her city, the offspring is a *mamzer*.**

אָמַר רַב אַשִׁי, אַף אֲנַן נַמִּי תְּנֵינָא: שִׁינָּה שְׁמוֹ וּשְׁמָהּ, שֵׁם עִירוֹ וְשֵׁם עִירָהּ – תֵּצֵא מִזֶּה וּמִזֶּה, וְכָל הַדְּרָכִים הָאֵלּוּ בָּהּ.

Rav Ashi says: We, too, learn in the mishna: If **he changed his name or her name, the name of his city or the name of her city,** and she remarried on the basis of this bill of divorce, then **she must leave this** husband **and that** husband, **and all of those ways** of penalizing a woman who remarried based on the bills of divorce detailed in the earlier clause of the mishna apply **to her.**

הָא מַאן קָתָנֵי לָהּ? אִילֵימָא רַבִּי מֵאִיר, לִיעָרְבִינְהוּ וְלִיתְנִינְהוּ! אֶלָּא שְׁמַע מִינָּהּ רַבָּנַן, שְׁמַע מִינָּהּ.

It is necessary to clarify **who teaches this *halakha*? If we say** that it is **Rabbi Meir, let him combine** the case of one who writes a different kingdom, and the case of one who changes the names, **and teach them** both as one *halakha*. **Rather, conclude from it** that this *halakha* is the opinion of **the Rabbis.** The Gemara concludes: **Conclude from it** that until this point the mishna was quoting the statement of Rabbi Meir, but subsequently it is the statement of the Rabbis that is quoted, that in a case of such a fundamental change, even in their opinion such a bill of divorce is invalid.

HALAKHA

This is the statement of Rabbi Meir, etc. – זוֹ דִּבְרֵי רַבִּי מֵאִיר וכו׳: The case in question relates to a person who wrote the date on a bill of divorce, and the date was determined using a calendrical system that referred to a government that was not in power in the locale where the bill of divorce was written. A similar question applies to a person who wrote the date on a bill of divorce, and the date was written counting the number of years from the building or the destruction of the Temple. In either of these situations, the bill of divorce is valid if it is customary for people in that locale to count the years in this manner. If they do not ordinarily count in this manner, the bill of divorce is invalid. The *halakha* is in accordance with the opinion of the Rabbis. Nevertheless, even according to the Rabbis, the bill of divorce is invalid *ab initio*; but if the woman remarried, she is not required to leave her husband (*Leḥem Mishne*). It is the accepted practice of all Jewish communities to write the date on the bill of divorce by counting the years from the creation of the world, as is done in the standard Hebrew calendar. In the past, there was a valid practice to record the date by counting from the time of the founding of Alexander the Great's empire. This is known as the count for documents [*minyan hashetarot*]. In recent times, this was practiced only in Yemen. If the date was written according to the local government, it is valid, in accordance with the statement of Rav Yehuda citing Shmuel (Rambam *Sefer Nashim, Hilkhot Geirushin* 1:27; see *Tur, Even HaEzer* 127 and *Shulḥan Arukh, Even HaEzer* 126:5 and 127:10).

If the location written by the scribe is different than the location written by the witnesses who signed the bill of divorce, some say that the *halakha* is in accordance with the opinion of Rabbi Meir, who states that she must leave her second husband, and any child born from him is a *mamzer* (Rabbeinu Ḥananel). Others say that she can remarry on the basis of this bill of divorce *ab initio* (Rif). The *halakha* is that the bill of divorce is invalid, but if she remarried, she is not required to leave her second husband (Rambam *Sefer Nashim, Hilkhot Geirushin* 1:25; *Shulḥan Arukh, Even HaEzer* 128:1).

LANGUAGE

Guardsman [*santar*] – סַנְטָר: According to some commentaries, this word is from the Greek συντηρέω, *suntēreo*, meaning to guard or to uphold rights and commitments. According to other commentaries, it is from a transposition of letters of the Latin saltuarius, meaning guardsman of the fields. There are also commentaries and scholars who believe it originates from the Hebrew root *nun, tet, reish*, meaning to guard, with the addition of the letter *samekh* at the beginning.

The governor [*istandera*] of Bascar – אִסְטַנְדְּרָא דְּבַשְׂכָּר: *Istandera* is from the Persian ostandar, a title for the senior official who rules over a city or province and is the military commander in charge of the troops in that region. He is the one responsible for preserving order and protecting the borders.

Bascar, or as several versions read, Cascar, was the primary city in the province of Mishan in Babylonia. As such, the leader of this city was in command of a very large region and was considered to be like one of the nobles. In non-Jewish sources we also find mention of the Ostan of Cascar and Mishan.

NOTES

But the Rabbis say the lineage of the offspring is unflawed – אֲבָל חֲכָמִים אוֹמְרִים הַוָּלָד כָּשֵׁר: There is a dispute among the early commentaries concerning Rav's statement; namely, to which clause of the mishna does it pertain? Rashi explains that Rav's statement is referring to a case in which the date of the bill of divorce was not written correctly according to the years of the local kingdom. Accordingly, Rav disagrees with Shmuel, who maintains that she is properly divorced, as Rav holds that while the Rabbis disagree with Rabbi Meir in that they hold there is no penalty that renders the offspring a *mamzer*, they do concede that the divorce is flawed and she must leave her second husband. Rabbeinu Tam maintains that Rav's statement is referring to a case where the husband was in the east and the bill of divorce stated that he was in the west, and the other cases in the mishna are grouped with that one. Rav maintains that although even according to the Rabbis she must leave her second husband, the lineage of the offspring is unflawed (see *Tosafot*). Accordingly, Rav agrees with Shmuel's ruling that in a case in which the date of the bill of divorce was not written correctly according to the years of the local kingdom, the woman can remarry *ab initio* (see *Tosafot* and *Sefer HaYashar*).

"כָּל עֲרָיוֹת שֶׁאָמְרוּ" כו׳. נִשְּׂאוּ אִין, זִינּוּ לָא.

§ It was taught in the mishna that in **all** of those cases in **which they said** that a man who died and left behind a widow who is to the *yavam* one of **those with whom relations are forbidden,** and the rival wives were thought to be permitted to remarry, if it later became clear that the forbidden relation was an *ailonit* and therefore they were in fact forbidden from remarrying, then they must leave the man whom they remarried, and they cannot enter into levirate marriage with the *yavam*, and many other penalties apply to them as well. The Gemara comments: It is possible to deduce from the language used by the mishna that only if **they married** other men, then **yes,** these *halakhot* apply to them. But if the rival wives **engaged in licentious sexual intercourse,** then **no,** these *halakhot* do not apply to them.

לֵימָא תֶּיהֱוֵי תְּיוּבְתָּא דְּרַב הַמְנוּנָא, דְּאָמַר רַב הַמְנוּנָא: שׁוֹמֶרֶת יָבָם שֶׁזִּינְּתָה – אֲסוּרָה לִיבָמָהּ?

The Gemara suggests: **Let us say that this is a conclusive refutation of** the opinion **of Rav Hamnuna, as Rav Hamnuna says: A widow awaiting her brother-in-law** to perform levirate marriage **who engaged in licentious sexual intercourse**[H] is likened to a married woman who committed adultery, and **she is prohibited from** entering into levirate marriage with **her *yavam*.**

לָא, נִישְּׂאוּ וְהוּא הַדִּין לְזִינּוּ, וְהַאי דְּקָתָנֵי נִישְּׂאוּ – לִישָּׁנָא מְעַלְּיָא נָקַט.

The Gemara rejects this: **No,** this is not a refutation, since it is possible to explain that the mishna gave the example that **they married, and the same is true in** a case where **they engaged in licentious sexual intercourse. And this that** the mishna **teaches:** If **they married,** is because it **employed a euphemistic expression,** to refrain from discussing a case of licentiousness.

וְאִיכָּא דְּאָמְרִי: נִישְּׂאוּ וְהוּא הַדִּין לְזִינּוּ.

And there are those **who say** that the exchange went as follows: From the mishna's statement about the rival wives that remarried, one can understand, that the *halakha* is so if **they married, and the same is true in** a case where **they engaged in licentious sexual intercourse.**

לֵימָא מְסַיֵּיעַ לֵיהּ לְרַב הַמְנוּנָא, דְּאָמַר רַב הַמְנוּנָא: שׁוֹמֶרֶת יָבָם שֶׁזִּינְּתָה – אֲסוּרָה לִיבָמָהּ?

The Gemara suggests: **Let us say** that it **supports** the opinion **of Rav Hamnuna, as Rav Hamnuna says: A widow awaiting her brother-in-law** to perform levirate marriage **who engaged in licentious sexual intercourse is prohibited from** entering into levirate marriage with **her *yavam*.**

לָא, נִישְּׂאוּ דַּוְקָא, מִשּׁוּם דְּמִיחַלְפָא בְּאִשָּׁה שֶׁהָלַךְ בַּעְלָהּ לִמְדִינַת הַיָּם.

The Gemara rejects this: **No,** it is **specifically** when **they married** that they are forbidden, **because** she **is confused with a woman whose husband traveled to a country overseas** and she went and remarried. In that case she is certainly prohibited from marrying both the first and the second husband. Similarly, they instituted the same decree for a *yevama* who married someone else. By contrast, in the case of a *yevama* who engaged in licentious sexual intercourse, which is completely different, they did not institute this decree.

"הַכּוֹנֵס אֶת יְבִמְתּוֹ" כו׳. וּצְרִיכָא; דְּאִי אַשְׁמְעִינַן בְּהַךְ קַמַּיְיתָא, מִשּׁוּם דְּלָא אִיקַּיַּים מִצְוַת יִבּוּם,

§ It was taught in the mishna that **one who marries his *yevama*,** and her rival wife went and married another man, and ultimately the *yevama* was found to be an *ailonit*, then the rival wife must leave her husband, and she cannot enter into levirate marriage with the *yavam*, and many other penalties apply to her as well. The Gemara comments: **And** it is **necessary** to teach this *halakha* as well, although it seemingly deals with the same issue as the previous *halakha*. **As, if** the mishna **had taught us** this *halakha* only **with regard to the first** case of a rival wife of a woman who is forbidden to the *yavam*, then one could say that the *halakha* is so, **because the mitzva of levirate marriage was not fulfilled** at all, since the rival wife married someone else, and the *yavam* did not perform levirate marriage.

אֲבָל הָכָא דְּאִיקַּיַּים מִצְוַת יִבּוּם – אֵימָא לָא.

But here, in this latter case, **where the mitzva of levirate marriage was fulfilled** in some way when he married the *yevama*, although ultimately it became clear that it was not a legitimate levirate marriage, **say** that the rival wives are **not** penalized, since she is not guilty by not having waited.

HALAKHA

A widow awaiting her brother-in-law to perform levirate marriage who engaged in licentious sexual intercourse – **שׁוֹמֶרֶת יָבָם שֶׁזִּינְּתָה:** A widow awaiting her brother-in-law to perform levirate marriage who engaged in licentious sexual intercourse does not become forbidden to the *yavam*, as long as he is an Israelite and not a priest, unlike the statement of Rav Hamnuna. The *Nimmukei Yosef* says that she is forbidden to the man with whom she engaged in sexual intercourse, as a rabbinic penalty (Rambam *Sefer Nashim*, *Hilkhot Yibbum VaḤalitza* 2:20; *Shulḥan Arukh*, *Even HaEzer* 159:3).

HALAKHA

If she was married, this is considered after some time – **נִישֵּׂאת זֶהוּ לְאַחַר זְמַן**: The case described in the mishna involves a scribe who wrote a receipt and a bill of divorce, and who mistakenly gave the receipt to the man and the bill of divorce to the woman. Consequently, the woman gave the bill of divorce to her husband, and the husband gave the receipt to his wife. In this situation, the *halakha* depends on when the husband claims that he did not divorce his wife, as the bill of divorce is still in his possession. If he claims this after some time, he should divorce her now with the bill of divorce, and she is then permitted to marry anyone. If he does not divorce her, she is considered to be a married woman; and if she remarries, she is considered to be a married woman who married another man. If she remarried before her first husband challenged the divorce, his claim that he did not divorce his wife is not deemed credible, and she is not forbidden to her second husband. She has the presumptive status of a divorcée, and the assumption is that the bill of divorce was first in her possession, was then lost, and was found by her first husband afterward. This is in accordance with the statement of Rabbi Elazar in the mishna and the opinion of Rav Adda (Rambam *Sefer Nashim, Hilkhot Geirushin* 10:11; *Shulḥan Arukh, Even HaEzer* 151:1).

וְאִי אַשְׁמְעִינַן הָכָא, מִשּׁוּם דְּקָא רָמְיָא קַמֵּיהּ, אֲבָל הָתָם דְּלָא רָמְיָא קַמֵּיהּ – אֵימָא לָא, צְרִיכָא.

And if the mishna **had taught us** this *halakha* **here,** with regard to a *yavam* who married a *yevama* who was ultimately found to be an *ailonit*, then one could say that specifically here there is reason to penalize her, **because** this rival wife who remarried **was** also **placed before** the *yavam*, as he could have entered into levirate marriage with any of his brother's wives. Therefore, she could have waited to see if the levirate marriage was effective before remarrying. **But there,** in the first case of a *yevama* who is forbidden to the *yavam*, **that she is not placed before him,** as all of them are entirely exempt from levirate marriage, **say** that the rival wives are **not** penalized. Therefore, it is **necessary** to state both *halakhot*.

״כָּתַב הַסּוֹפֵר וְטָעָה וְנָתַן גֵּט לָאִשָּׁה וְשׁוֹבֵר וכו׳, רַבִּי אֱלִיעֶזֶר אוֹמֵר: אִם לְאַלְתַּר יָצָא״ וכו׳.

§ It was taught in the mishna that if **the scribe wrote** a bill of divorce, **and erred and gave** the **bill of divorce to the woman and the receipt** to the man, and consequently the husband gave his wife a receipt and she gave him a bill of divorce, **Rabbi Eliezer says: If** the bill of divorce **is immediately in** the husband's possession, it is not a valid bill of divorce. But if it is in his possession after some time, the assumption is that she was divorced in a correct manner and the bill of divorce was returned to him later.

הֵיכִי דָּמֵי לְאַלְתַּר, וְהֵיכִי דָּמֵי לְאַחַר זְמַן? אָמַר רַב יְהוּדָה אָמַר שְׁמוּאֵל: כָּל זְמַן שֶׁיּוֹשְׁבִין וַעֲסוּקִין בְּאוֹתוֹ עִנְיָן – זֶהוּ לְאַלְתַּר, עָמְדוּ – זֶהוּ לְאַחַר זְמַן.

The Gemara asks: **What are the circumstances** in which the bill of divorce is **immediately** in the husband's hand **and what are the circumstances** in which it is in his possession **after** some **time? Rav Yehuda says** that **Shmuel says: All** the **while that they are sitting and are engaged in the issue** of the divorce, **this is** considered **immediately.** If **they** already **arose** and concluded the proceedings, **this is** considered **after** some **time.**

וְרַב אַדָּא בַּר אַהֲבָה אָמַר: לֹא נִישֵּׂאת – זֶהוּ לְאַלְתַּר, נִישֵּׂאת – זֶהוּ לְאַחַר זְמַן.

And Rav Adda bar Ahava says: If **she was not married** to someone else, **this is** considered **immediately,** since they can rectify the situation by requiring him to give the bill of divorce properly. If **she was married, this is** considered **after** some **time.**[H]

תְּנַן, לֹא כׇּל הֵימֶנּוּ מִן הָרִאשׁוֹן לְאַבֵּד זְכוּתוֹ שֶׁל שֵׁנִי; בִּשְׁלָמָא לְרַב אַדָּא בַּר אַהֲבָה – הַיְינוּ דְּקָתָנֵי שֵׁנִי, אֶלָּא לִשְׁמוּאֵל מַאי שֵׁנִי?

The Gemara asks: **We learned** in the mishna with regard to Rabbi Elazar's statement: **It is not in the power of the first** husband **to eliminate the right of the second** husband. **Granted, according to** the opinion of **Rav Adda bar Ahava, this** explanation **is** consistent with **that which is taught:** The **second** husband, since the mishna is discussing a case in which she remarried and has a second husband. **But according to** the opinion of **Shmuel, what** is the reference to a **second** husband? Shmuel's opinion is that as soon as they arise and conclude the proceedings, it is considered to be after some time, and in this case there is no second husband. According to Shmuel's opinion, how does Rabbi Elazar's statement apply?

Perek **VIII**
Daf **81** Amud **a**

HALAKHA

He gave it to her conditionally, etc. – **נְתָנוֹ לָהּ עַל תְּנַאי וכו׳**: If one gave a bill of divorce to his wife conditionally and the condition was not fulfilled, the bill of divorce is not valid. The woman who received this bill of divorce does not become disqualified from marrying into the priesthood, in accordance with the opinion of Beit Hillel (*Shulḥan Arukh, Even HaEzer* 6:1, 143:1).

זְכוּת הָרְאוּיָה לַשֵּׁנִי.

The Gemara answers: It is not referring to the right of a second man that she already married, but rather to **the right that is due** to a suitor who wishes to become her **second** husband, meaning that the first husband cannot eliminate the right of a second man who wishes to marry her.

מתני׳ כָּתַב לְגָרֵשׁ אֶת אִשְׁתּוֹ וְנִמְלַךְ, בֵּית שַׁמַּאי אוֹמְרִים: פְּסָלָהּ מִן הַכְּהוּנָּה, וּבֵית הִלֵּל אוֹמְרִים: אַף עַל פִּי שֶׁנְּתָנוֹ לָהּ עַל תְּנַאי וְלֹא נַעֲשָׂה הַתְּנַאי – לֹא פְּסָלָהּ מִן הַכְּהוּנָּה.

MISHNA If **one wrote** a bill of divorce **to divorce his wife, and reconsidered** and did not give it to her, **Beit Shammai say:** Although merely writing the bill of divorce does not dissolve the marriage, by doing so **he disqualified her from marrying into the priesthood. And Beit Hillel say: Even if he gave** the bill of divorce **to her conditionally**[H] **and the condition was not fulfilled,** and therefore the bill of divorce did not take effect, **he did not disqualify her from** marrying into **the priesthood.** A woman is disqualified from marrying into the priesthood only if the divorce takes effect.

גמ׳ שְׁלַח לֵיהּ רַב יוֹסֵף בְּרֵיהּ דְּרַב מְנַשֶּׁה מִדְּוִיל לִשְׁמוּאֵל: יְלַמְּדֵנוּ רַבֵּינוּ, יָצָא עָלָיו קוֹל ״אִישׁ פְּלוֹנִי כֹּהֵן כָּתַב גֵּט לְאִשְׁתּוֹ״, וְיוֹשֶׁבֶת תַּחְתָּיו וּמְשַׁמַּשְׁתּוֹ, מַהוּ?

GEMARA Rav Yosef, son of Rav Menashe from Devil, sent a query to Shmuel: Our teacher, instruct us. In the case of a priest about whom the following rumor circulated:[N] So-and-so the priest wrote a bill of divorce to his wife, but she is still residing under his roof and attending to him; what is the *halakha*? Need one lend credence to this rumor?

שְׁלַח לֵיהּ: תֵּצֵא, וְהַדָּבָר צָרִיךְ בְּדִיקָה. מַאי הִיא? אִילֵימָא דְּאִי מְבַטְּלִינַן קָלָא אוֹ לָא מְבַטְּלִינַן – וְהָא נְהַרְדְּעָא אַתְרֵיהּ דִּשְׁמוּאֵל הִיא, וּבִנְהַרְדְּעָא לָא מְבַטְּלֵי קָלָא! אֶלָּא, דְּאִי קָרוּ לִנְתִינָה ״כְּתִיבָה״.

Shmuel sent the following response to him: She must leave her husband; but the matter requires investigation[N] before he is forced to divorce her. The Gemara asks: What is the investigation that is required? If we say that the investigation is whether we can abolish the rumor that circulated, or we cannot abolish it; that cannot be the question: But isn't Neharde'a the place where Shmuel is the halakhic authority and the rulings there are in accordance with his opinion, and in Neharde'a they do not abolish a rumor? Rather, the required investigation is to determine whether people in that place refer to giving a bill of divorce as writing. If that is the case, the rumor would be that he gave her a bill of divorce.

וְכִי קָרוּ לִנְתִינָה ״כְּתִיבָה״, לִכְתִיבָה גּוּפָהּ מִי לָא קָרוּ לָהּ ״כְּתִיבָה״?

The Gemara asks: And if they refer to giving as writing, it proves nothing, as don't they refer to writing itself as writing? Therefore, the fact that they refer to giving as writing does not mean that he gave the woman the bill of divorce. The same term would be employed even if he only wrote the bill of divorce.

אִין, דְּאִי מִיגַּלְיָא מִילְּתָא דְּקָרוּ לִנְתִינָה ״כְּתִיבָה״, דִּלְמָא נָתַן קָאָמְרִי.

The Gemara answers: Yes, as if it is discovered that they refer to giving as writing,[H] then there is reason to suspect that perhaps they are saying in the rumor that he gave her the bill of divorce, and there is concern that she is actually divorced.

תֵּצֵא?! וְהָאָמַר רַב אַשִׁי: כׇּל קָלָא דְּבָתַר נִישּׂוּאִין לָא חָיְישִׁינַן לֵיהּ!

Apropos Shmuel's statement that she must leave his home, the Gemara asks: She must leave? But doesn't Rav Ashi say: We are not concerned for any rumor that circulates after marriage.[H] According to Rav Ashi, if a rumor circulates that a woman was betrothed to a man, there is concern about the rumor, and she is not allowed to marry someone else until she receives a bill of divorce from her rumored betrothed. But if such a rumor circulates after she has married someone else, there is no concern about such a rumor, and she is not obligated to leave her husband. Here too, in the case of this woman who is suspected of being divorced, she is currently living with her husband. Therefore, perhaps we should not be concerned about such a rumor.

מַאי תֵּצֵא? נַמִי תֵּצֵא מִשֵּׁנִי.

The Gemara answers: What is the meaning of Shmuel's directive: She must leave? This also means that she must leave the second husband. If her first husband dies, and she marries another priest, she must leave him due to the rumor that circulated that her first husband gave her a bill of divorce.

אִם כֵּן, אַתָּה מוֹצִיא לַעַז עַל בָּנָיו שֶׁל רִאשׁוֹן! כֵּיוָן דְּמִשֵּׁנִי הוּא דְּמַפְּקִינַן לַהּ וּמֵרִאשׁוֹן לָא מַפְּקִינַן לַהּ, אָתֵי לְמֵימַר: סָמוּךְ לְמִיתָה גֵּרְשָׁהּ.

The Gemara challenges: If so, you cast aspersions on the children of the first husband. If the reason that she must leave the second husband is because she is assumed to be a divorcée, this means that she remained with her first husband while she was already divorced, and the children they had after the rumor circulated would be disqualified from the priesthood. The Gemara answers: Since we remove her only from the second husband, and we do not remove her from the first husband, they will come to explain the incident by saying as follows: The first husband divorced her proximate to his death, and the children from him are of unflawed lineage. Since he divorced her, she may not marry another priest. Because the assumption here is that the divorce took place proximate to the first husband's death, there is no concern of aspersions being cast on the children from the first husband.

אָמַר רַבָּה בַּר בַּר חָנָה אָמַר רַבִּי יוֹחָנָן מִשּׁוּם רַבִּי יְהוּדָה בַּר אֶילְעַי: בֹּא וּרְאֵה שֶׁלֹּא כַּדּוֹרוֹת הָרִאשׁוֹנִים דּוֹרוֹת הָאַחֲרוֹנִים.

§ Rabba bar bar Ḥana says that Rabbi Yoḥanan says in the name of Rabbi Yehuda bar Elai: Come and see that the later generations are unlike the earlier generations, as the earlier generations were more conscientious about maintaining an unflawed lineage.

NOTES

About whom a rumor circulated – יָצָא עָלָיו קוֹל: The halakhic details of rumors are discussed in the next chapter (88b–89b). Not every rumor carries halakhic weight, and there are several conditions that limit when rumors are cause for concern.

She must leave but the matter requires investigation – תֵּצֵא וְהַדָּבָר צָרִיךְ בְּדִיקָה: Rashi explains that she must leave her husband if the rumor is true. The matter should be investigated before she leaves, to clarify the veracity of the rumor. The Rambam omits mention of an investigation, and it appears that he understood the Gemara in the following manner: She must leave due to the rumor. This is because the matter requires investigation, and since it is impossible to establish the truth, it is necessary to act on the basis of the rumor. The order of the wording appears to support this, for the Gemara initially states that she must leave, and only afterward does it mention: And the matter requires investigation (*Baḥ*).

HALAKHA

That they refer to giving as writing – דְּקָרוּ לִנְתִינָה כְּתִיבָה: If a rumor circulated that a specific priest wrote a bill of divorce for his wife, and in that locale, they refer to the giving of a bill of divorce as writing, even if they also refer to merely writing a bill of divorce as writing, there is concern about the rumor. If in that place they do not refer to the giving of a bill of divorce as writing, then there is no concern about the rumor. The Rambam does not make this distinction (Rambam *Sefer Kedusha, Hilkhot Issurei Bia* 17:19; *Shulḥan Arukh, Even HaEzer* 6:4).

Any rumor that circulates after marriage, etc. – כׇּל קָלָא דְּבָתַר נִישּׂוּאִין וכו׳: If a rumor circulated that a certain woman was betrothed and then divorced, there is concern about the rumor, and she is prohibited from marrying a priest. This is the case only if the rumor circulated before she married the priest. If she married the priest before the rumor circulated, there is no concern about the rumor. If the priest died, she is prohibited from marrying another priest; and if she marries another priest, she must leave him. This is in accordance with the statement of Rav Ashi (Rambam *Sefer Kedusha, Hilkhot Issurei Bia* 17:19; *Shulḥan Arukh, Even HaEzer* 6:3).

דּוֹרוֹת הָרִאשׁוֹנִים – בֵּית שַׁמַּאי, דּוֹרוֹת הָאַחֲרוֹנִים – רַבִּי דּוֹסָא; דְּתַנְיָא: שְׁבוּיָה אוֹכֶלֶת בִּתְרוּמָה, דִּבְרֵי רַבִּי דּוֹסָא.

The Gemara explains: **The earlier generations** is referring to **Beit Shammai.** Beit Shammai were so careful about the sanctity of the priesthood that they said, as stated in the mishna, that the writing of a bill of divorce alone renders a priest's wife forbidden to him. **The later generations** is referring to **Rabbi Dosa, as it is taught** in a mishna (*Eduyyot* 3:6): A priest's wife who was taken **captive** may **partake of *teruma*,**[H] and there is no concern that perhaps she was raped while in captivity and thereby became forbidden to her husband and disqualified from partaking of *teruma*. This is **the statement of Rabbi Dosa.**

אָמַר רַבִּי דּוֹסָא: וְכִי מֶה עָשָׂה לָהּ עַרְבִי זֶה, מִפְּנֵי שֶׁמִּיעֵךְ לָהּ בֵּין דַּדֶּיהָ פְּסָלָהּ מִן הַכְּהוּנָּה?

In explanation of this statement, **Rabbi Dosa says: And what did this Arab do to her** when he took her captive? **Because he fondled her breasts he disqualified her from the priesthood?** As long as it is not determined that her captors actually raped her, she is not prohibited from partaking of *teruma*. It is apparent from here that the later generations are more lenient than the early generations with regard to the sanctity of the priesthood.

וְאָמַר רַבָּה בַּר בַּר חָנָה אָמַר רַבִּי יוֹחָנָן מִשּׁוּם רַבִּי יְהוּדָה בַּר אֶילְעַי: בֹּא וּרְאֵה שֶׁלֹּא כְּדוֹרוֹת הָרִאשׁוֹנִים דּוֹרוֹת הָאַחֲרוֹנִים, דּוֹרוֹת הָרִאשׁוֹנִים מַכְנִיסִין פֵּירוֹתֵיהֶן דֶּרֶךְ טְרַקְסְמוֹן כְּדֵי לְחַיְּיבָן בְּמַעֲשֵׂר, דּוֹרוֹת הָאַחֲרוֹנִים מַכְנִיסִין פֵּירוֹתֵיהֶן דֶּרֶךְ גַּגּוֹת וְדֶרֶךְ קַרְפֵּיפוֹת כְּדֵי לְפוֹטְרָן מִן הַמַּעֲשֵׂר.

And Rabba bar bar Ḥana says that **Rabbi Yoḥanan says in the name of Rabbi Yehuda bar Elai: Come and see that the later generations are unlike the earlier generations. The earlier generations would bring in their produce** from the field by way of the **main entranceway** [***teraksemon***],[L] **in order to obligate** the produce **in tithes.**[N] By contrast, **the later generations** would **bring in their produce by way of roofs and by way of enclosures,**[H] **in order to exempt** the produce[N] **from tithes.**

דְּאָמַר רַבִּי יַנַּאי: אֵין הַטֶּבֶל מִתְחַיֵּיב בְּמַעֲשֵׂר עַד שֶׁיִּרְאֶה פְּנֵי הַבַּיִת, שֶׁנֶּאֱמַר: ״בִּעַרְתִּי הַקֹּדֶשׁ מִן הַבַּיִת״;

The Gemara explains: **As Rabbi Yannai says: Untithed produce does not become obligated in tithes until it sees the entrance of the house,** through which people enter and exit, **as it is stated** in the declaration of the tithes: **"I have put away the hallowed things out of my house"** (Deuteronomy 26:13). As long as untithed produce is not taken into the house through the primary entrance of the house, it is permitted to eat it casually without tithing it. Consequently, they would take the produce in through another entrance in order to exempt it from tithes.

וְרַבִּי יוֹחָנָן אָמַר: אֲפִילּוּ חָצֵר קוֹבַעַת, שֶׁנֶּאֱמַר: ״וְאָכְלוּ בִשְׁעָרֶיךָ וְשָׂבֵעוּ״.

And Rabbi Yoḥanan says with regard to this issue: **Even** entry into the **courtyard establishes**[H] an obligation to tithe, **as it is stated: "That they may eat within your gates, and be satisfied"** (Deuteronomy 26:12). This indicates that once the produce is brought into the courtyard, it is obligated in tithes.

מתני׳ הַמְגָרֵשׁ אֶת אִשְׁתּוֹ וְלָנָה עִמּוֹ בְּפוּנְדְּקִי, בֵּית שַׁמַּאי אוֹמְרִים: אֵינָהּ צְרִיכָה הֵימֶנּוּ גֵּט שֵׁנִי, וּבֵית הִלֵּל אוֹמְרִים: צְרִיכָה הֵימֶנּוּ גֵּט שֵׁנִי.

MISHNA With regard to **one who divorces his wife, and** afterward **she spent the night with him at an inn** [***befundaki***],[L] **Beit Shammai say: She does not require a second bill of divorce from him, and Beit Hillel say: She requires a second bill of divorce from him,** since they may have engaged in sexual intercourse at the inn and thereby betrothed her once again.

NOTES

To obligate it in tithes – לְחַיְּיבָן בְּמַעֲשֵׂר: The obligation to separate *terumot* and tithes from produce depends on several factors, including its stage of readiness for human use. As long as the produce has not reached this proper stage, one can make a casual meal with the produce even before he has separated the tithes. Bringing the produce into the house, in the correct manner, renders it ready to be eaten. According to Rabbi Yoḥanan, bringing it to the house's courtyard, in the correct manner, also renders it ready to be eaten. At that point, one is obligated to separate tithes before eating it, even for a casual meal.

In order to exempt the produce – כְּדֵי לְפוֹטְרָן: Bringing in produce by way of the roofs and enclosures did not engender a complete exemption from tithes. It was still necessary to separate tithes before making a formal meal of the produce. It seems that the later generations attempted to minimize the quantity of the produce that was required to be separated for tithes. By bypassing the main entranceway, they limited the obligation of tithes to produce used for formal meals, and benefited from untithed produce in the form of casual meals.

HALAKHA

A captive can partake of *teruma* – שְׁבוּיָה אוֹכֶלֶת בִּתְרוּמָה: If there are witnesses that a woman was taken captive, she is forbidden to partake of *teruma*, unless there is a witness who testifies that she was not raped. If she herself says: I was taken captive and I was not raped, she is deemed credible. This is unlike the statement of Rabbi Dosa (Rambam *Sefer Kedusha, Hilkhot Issurei Bia* 18:21 and *Sefer Zera'im, Hilkhot Terumot* 6:11; *Shulḥan Arukh, Even HaEzer* 7:4).

By way of roofs and by way of enclosures – דֶּרֶךְ גַּגּוֹת וְדֶרֶךְ קַרְפֵּיפוֹת: Untithed produce does not become obligated in tithes by Torah law until it is taken into the house through the main gate. If one took the produce in through roofs or back entrances, it is exempt from both *teruma* and tithes, and it is permitted to eat a casual meal from it (Rambam *Sefer Zera'im, Hilkhot Ma'aser* 4:1; *Shulḥan Arukh, Yoreh De'a* 331:83).

Entry into the courtyard establishes – חָצֵר קוֹבַעַת: Just as a house determines the obligation for tithes, so too, a courtyard establishes the obligation for tithes. Once the produce is taken into the courtyard through the main gate, it is forbidden to eat from it until it has been tithed (Rambam *Sefer Zera'im, Hilkhot Ma'aser* 4:7; *Shulḥan Arukh, Yoreh De'a* 331:83).

LANGUAGE

Main entranceway [*teraksemon*] – טְרַקְסְמוֹן: According to some of the early commentaries, this is from the late Greek τρέξιμον, *treksimon*, meaning way of the runners, and refers to a wide road.

Inn [*pundaki*] – פּוּנְדְּקִי: From the Greek πανδοκεῖον, *pandokion*, meaning a guest house or inn.

אֵימָתַי? בִּזְמַן שֶׁנִּתְגָּרְשָׁה מִן הַנִּשּׂוּאִין. וּמוֹדִים, בְּנִתְגָּרְשָׁה מִן הָאֵירוּסִין – שֶׁאֵינָהּ צְרִיכָה הֵימֶנּוּ גֵּט שֵׁנִי, מִפְּנֵי שֶׁאֵין לִבּוֹ גַּס בָּהּ.

When did they say this *halakha*? **When she was divorced following the state of marriage.** Beit Hillel **concede that when she was divorced following** the state of **betrothal,**[B] **she does not require a second bill of divorce from him, due to the fact that he is not accustomed to her.** Therefore, there is no concern that they engaged in sexual intercourse, even though they spent the night together at the inn.

גמ׳ אָמַר רַבָּה בַּר בַּר חָנָה אָמַר רַבִּי יוֹחָנָן: מַחֲלוֹקֶת בְּשֶׁרָאוּהָ שֶׁנִּבְעֲלָה,

GEMARA **Rabba bar bar Ḥana says** that **Rabbi Yoḥanan says:** The **dispute** between Beit Shammai and Beit Hillel is specifically **in** a case **where they saw that she engaged in sexual intercourse,**

BACKGROUND

Betrothal and marriage – אֵירוּסִין וְנִישּׂוּאִין: A Jewish wedding is divided into two distinct parts: Betrothal and marriage. Betrothal is the first stage of the process. After betrothal, a woman requires a divorce before she can marry another man. If a betrothed woman engages in sexual intercourse with another man, it is considered adulterous and is punishable by death. A betrothed couple may not engage in sexual intercourse, and most of the couple's mutual obligations do not yet apply.

The second stage of the process, called marriage, follows the betrothal. It takes effect by means of the wedding ceremony, when the bride and groom are together under the bridal canopy symbolizing their union. It immediately confers upon the newlywed couple both the privileges and the responsibilities associated with marriage. After marriage, if one spouse dies, all the *halakhot* of mourning for a close blood relative apply to the surviving spouse. If the wife of a priest dies, he is permitted to make himself ritually impure to bury her. All of the monetary rights and obligations applying to married couples take effect after marriage.

Today, betrothal and marriage are performed in a single ceremony. In talmudic times, there was generally a yearlong gap between the two.

דְּבֵית שַׁמַּאי סָבְרִי: אָדָם עוֹשֶׂה בְּעִילָתוֹ בְּעִילַת זְנוּת,

as Beit Shammai hold: A person does engage in **licentious sexual intercourse.** Although they were seen engaging in sexual intercourse, one cannot assume that he intended to betroth her, since they were recently divorced. The assumption is that they were simply engaging in licentious sexual intercourse. Consequently, he is not required to give her a second bill of divorce.

וּבֵית הִלֵּל סָבְרִי: אֵין אָדָם עוֹשֶׂה בְּעִילָתוֹ בְּעִילַת זְנוּת. אֲבָל לֹא רָאוּהָ שֶׁנִּבְעֲלָה – דִּבְרֵי הַכֹּל אֵינָהּ צְרִיכָה הֵימֶנּוּ גֵּט שֵׁנִי.

And Beit Hillel hold: A person does not engage in **licentious sexual intercourse.**[N] Therefore, he had the intention to betroth her, and he must give her another bill of divorce. **But if they did not see that she engaged in sexual intercourse,** even though they spent the night together at an inn, **everyone agrees** that **she does not require a second bill of divorce from him,** as there is no concern that perhaps they engaged in sexual intercourse.

תְּנַן: וּמוֹדִים בְּנִתְגָּרְשָׁה מִן הָאֵירוּסִין – שֶׁאֵינָהּ צְרִיכָה הֵימֶנּוּ גֵּט שֵׁנִי, שֶׁאֵין לִבּוֹ גַּס בָּהּ; וְאִי בְּשֶׁרָאוּהָ שֶׁנִּבְעֲלָה, מַה לִּי מִן הָאֵירוּסִין וּמַה לִּי מִן הַנִּשּׂוּאִין!

The Gemara challenges this understanding of the mishna: We **learned** in the mishna that Beit Hillel **concede that when she was divorced following** the state of **betrothal, she does not require a second bill of divorce from him because he is not accustomed to her. And if** the mishna is referring to a case in **which they saw that she engaged in sexual intercourse,**[H] **what** is the difference **to me** if it was **following** the state of **betrothal and what** is the difference **to me** if it was **following** the state of **marriage?** In either case, they saw that she engaged in sexual intercourse.

אֶלָּא מַתְנִיתִין בְּשֶׁלֹּא רָאוּהָ שֶׁנִּבְעֲלָה, וְרַבִּי יוֹחָנָן דַּאֲמַר כִּי הַאי תַּנָּא; דְּתַנְיָא, אָמַר רַבִּי שִׁמְעוֹן בֶּן אֶלְעָזָר: לֹא נֶחְלְקוּ בֵּית שַׁמַּאי וּבֵית הִלֵּל עַל שֶׁלֹּא רָאוּהָ שֶׁנִּבְעֲלָה – שֶׁאֵינָהּ צְרִיכָה הֵימֶנּוּ גֵּט שֵׁנִי,

Rather it can be explained that **the mishna** is actually speaking about a case **in which they did not see that she engaged in sexual intercourse. Rabbi Yoḥanan stated** his opinion **in accordance** with the statement of **that *tanna*. As it is taught** in a *baraita* that **Rabbi Shimon ben Elazar said: Beit Hillel and Beit Shammai did not disagree about** a case **where they did not see that she engaged in sexual intercourse.** Everyone agrees **that** in such a scenario, **she does not require a second bill of divorce from him.**

עַל מָה נֶחְלְקוּ? עַל שֶׁרָאוּהָ שֶׁנִּבְעֲלָה, שֶׁבֵּית שַׁמַּאי אוֹמְרִים: אָדָם עוֹשֶׂה בְּעִילָתוֹ בְּעִילַת זְנוּת, וּבֵית הִלֵּל אוֹמְרִים: אֵין אָדָם עוֹשֶׂה בְּעִילָתוֹ בְּעִילַת זְנוּת.

With regard to what case **did they disagree?** They disagreed **about** a case **where they saw that she engaged in sexual intercourse. As Beit Shammai say: A person does engage in licentious sexual intercourse. And Beit Hillel say: A person does not** engage in **licentious sexual intercourse.**[H] Rabbi Shimon ben Elazar disagrees with the mishna.

NOTES

A person does not engage in licentious sexual intercourse – אֵין אָדָם עוֹשֶׂה בְּעִילָתוֹ בְּעִילַת זְנוּת: According to some of the *ge'onim*, this principle is to be accepted literally. If one engaged in sexual intercourse, and, based on the intent of the man and woman, there is a possibility that it was done in a permitted manner, one assumes that it was done permissibly and that the sexual intercourse was not licentious. These *ge'onim* go as far as to say that if one had a son born to him from his non-Jewish maidservant, it can be assumed that he converted her beforehand and that the lineage of the child is unflawed. Similarly, the Ra'avad says that if two people who are not known to be licentious engaged in sexual intercourse, it can be assumed that it was for the sake of betrothal.

The Rambam disagrees and dismisses this presumption that a person does not engage in licentious sexual intercourse. According to the Rambam, this presumption can be assumed only if there is a good reason to do so, such as if he engaged in sexual intercourse with his wife after he divorced her. Similarly, the Rashba writes that if one engaged in sexual intercourse with a woman he first betrothed and then divorced, it can be assumed that they did so for the sake of betrothal.

HALAKHA

And if it is a case in which they saw that she engaged in sexual intercourse – וְאִי בְּשֶׁרָאוּהָ שֶׁנִּבְעֲלָה: If one divorced his wife and subsequently engaged in sexual intercourse with her in the presence of witnesses, it is assumed that they did so for the sake of betrothal, and she is his betrothed. This is the case as long as she was not yet betrothed by another man, regardless of whether she was divorced after marriage or after betrothal (Rambam *Sefer Nashim*, *Hilkhot Geirushin* 10:17; *Shulḥan Arukh*, *Even HaEzer* 149:1).

A person does not engage in licentious sexual intercourse – אֵין אָדָם עוֹשֶׂה בְּעִילָתוֹ בְּעִילַת זְנוּת: The assumption that a person does not engage in licentious sexual intercourse is applied only in a case of one's wife that he divorced, or one who betroths a woman conditionally and later engages in sexual intercourse with her without articulating a condition. In such cases it can be assumed that he intends for the sexual intercourse to serve as betrothal. In all other cases, the assumption is that people engage in licentious sexual intercourse, not for the sake of betrothal (Rambam *Sefer Nashim*, *Hilkhot Geirushin* 10:19; *Shulḥan Arukh*, *Even HaEzer* 149:5).

וּמַתְנִיתִין, דְּאוֹקִימְנָא בְּלֹא רָאוּהָ שֶׁנִּבְעֲלָה, בְּמַאי פְּלִיגִי? דְּאִיכָּא עֵדֵי יִחוּד וְלֵיכָּא עֵדֵי בִיאָה,

The Gemara asks: **And as for the mishna, which we established** as discussing a case in **which they did not see that she engaged in sexual intercourse, with regard to what do they disagree?** The Gemara answers: They disagree about a case in **which there are witnesses** to their **seclusion, but there are no witnesses** to an act of **sexual intercourse.**

בֵּית שַׁמַּאי סָבְרִי: לָא אָמְרִינַן הֵן הֵן עֵדֵי יִחוּד וְהֵן הֵן עֵדֵי בִיאָה, וּבֵית הִלֵּל סָבְרִי: אָמְרִינַן הֵן הֵן עֵדֵי יִחוּד וְהֵן הֵן עֵדֵי בִיאָה,

With regard to such a case, **Beit Shammai hold: We do not** say that **these are the witnesses of seclusion,**[H] **these are the witnesses of sexual intercourse.** According to Beit Shammai, although there are witnesses that they were secluded, this is not considered to be tantamount to testimony that they engaged in sexual intercourse. **And Beit Hillel hold: We do say** that **these are the witnesses of seclusion, these are the witnesses of sexual intercourse.** Since it is assumed that they engaged in sexual intercourse, she is required to obtain a second bill of divorce from him.

וּמוֹדִים בְּנִתְגָּרְשָׁה מִן הָאֵירוּסִין – שֶׁאֵינָהּ צְרִיכָה הֵימֶנּוּ גֵּט שֵׁנִי, דְּכֵיוָן דְּאֵין לִבּוֹ גַּס בָּהּ, לָא אָמְרִינַן הֵן הֵן עֵדֵי בִיאָה.

And Beit Hillel **concede that when she was divorced following** the state of **betrothal, she does not require a second bill of divorce from him,** even if they were alone together. **For since he is not accustomed to her, we do not say** that these are the witnesses of seclusion; **these are the witnesses of intercourse.**

וּמִי אֲמַר רַבִּי יוֹחָנָן הָכִי? וְהָאָמַר רַבִּי יוֹחָנָן: הֲלָכָה כִּסְתַם מִשְׁנָה, וְאוֹקִימְנָא לְמַתְנִיתִין בְּשֶׁלֹּא רָאוּהָ שֶׁנִּבְעֲלָה! אֲמוֹרָאֵי נִינְהוּ וְאַלִּיבָּא דְּרַבִּי יוֹחָנָן.

The Gemara asks: **But did Rabbi Yoḥanan** actually **say this,** that Beit Hillel require a second bill of divorce only when witnesses saw that they engaged in sexual intercourse? **But didn't Rabbi Yoḥanan say:** The ***halakha*** in all cases **is like an unattributed mishna. And we established the mishna** to be discussing a case in which **they did not see that she engaged in sexual intercourse.** How then does Rabbi Yoḥanan rule contrary to the mishna? The Gemara answers: **They are *amora'im*, and** they disagree **with regard to** the opinion of **Rabbi Yoḥanan.** Some of them hold that Rabbi Yoḥanan does not always rule in accordance with an unattributed mishna.

מתני׳ כְּנָסָהּ בְּגֵט קֵרֵחַ – תֵּצֵא מִזֶּה וּמִזֶּה, וְכָל הַדְּרָכִים הָאֵלּוּ בָּהּ.

MISHNA If a woman **was married** by her second husband **on the basis of** receiving **a bare bill of divorce,**[H] i.e., a folded and tied bill of divorce that is missing signatures, **she** must **leave** both **this,** the first husband, **and that,** the second husband. **And all of those** previously mentioned **ways** of penalizing a woman who remarried based on the bills of divorce detailed in the earlier mishna (79b) apply **to her** in this case as well.

גֵּט קֵרֵחַ – הַכֹּל מַשְׁלִימִין עָלָיו, דִּבְרֵי בֶּן נַנָּס. רַבִּי עֲקִיבָא אוֹמֵר: אֵין מַשְׁלִימִין עָלָיו אֶלָּא קְרוֹבִים הָרְאוּיִין לְהָעִיד בְּמָקוֹם אַחֵר.

With regard to **a bare bill of divorce;**[B] **anyone,** even those who are disqualified from bearing witness, **can complete it,**[N] i.e., sign it in addition to the primary witnesses, so that it will not remain bare. This is **the statement of ben Nannas.**[LP] **Rabbi Akiva says: Not** all who are disqualified from bearing witness can **complete it. Rather, only relatives who are fit to testify in another case.** Rabbi Akiva permits only the inclusion of witnesses who would ordinarily be valid witnesses, but who are invalid here because they are relatives of either the husband and wife or the other witnesses.

HALAKHA

These are the witnesses of seclusion, etc. – הֵן הֵן עֵדֵי יִחוּד וכו׳: If a man divorced his wife, and the couple had been married and not merely betrothed, and after the divorce the man was secluded with his wife in the presence of two witnesses, they are suspected of having engaged in sexual intercourse. This applies only if the man and woman were aware that the witnesses could see them, in which case, the witnesses of seclusion count as witnesses to sexual intercourse. If the man had betrothed the woman but had not yet married her, and they were divorced, and subsequently they were secluded together, there is no assumption that the couple engaged in sexual intercourse based on the testimony of witnesses of seclusion. This is because in the case of betrothal, rather than marriage, the man is usually not accustomed to the woman. Nevertheless, if there is a situation where it is clear that the man is accustomed to the woman, even if they are only betrothed, the witnesses of seclusion are considered to be witnesses to sexual intercourse. This is in accordance with the opinion of Beit Hillel (Rambam *Sefer Nashim, Hilkhot Geirushin* 10:18; *Shulḥan Arukh, Even HaEzer* 149:2).

Bare bill of divorce – גֵּט קֵרֵחַ: The *halakhot* of a folded and tied bill of divorce are not mentioned by halakhic authorities following the talmudic era. It is generally understood that this is because the ordinance mandating such bills of divorce was temporary. For many generations, perhaps since the end of the mishnaic period, it was not the practice to write such bills of divorce. Since we are not knowledgeable in this regard, we do not write bills of divorce in this manner (*Smag, Hilkhot Geirushin*).

NOTES

Anyone can complete it – הַכֹּל מַשְׁלִימִין עָלָיו: When the Sages instituted that a folded and tied bill of divorce have more than the two witnesses mandated by Torah law, they did not require that they all be fit to bear testimony. It is sufficient that there be additional signatures on the document.

LANGUAGE

Nannas – נַנָּס: Apparently from the Greek νάννας, *nannas*, meaning uncle. In particular, it refers to a maternal uncle.

PERSONALITIES

Ben Nannas – בֶּן נַנָּס: This Sage, whose full name is Rabbi Shimon ben Nannas, was a *tanna* from the third generation of the *tanna'im*. One of the Sages of Yavne, he was a contemporary of Rabbi Akiva and Rabbi Yishmael, with whom he engaged in halakhic discourse. Rabbi Yishmael once praised ben Nannas by saying: One who wants to acquire wisdom should occupy himself with monetary law…and one who wants to occupy himself with monetary law should serve Shimon ben Nannas. We do not have information about the events of his life, and know only his statements, which are found in the Mishna and in *baraitot*.

BACKGROUND

Bare bill of divorce – גֵּט קֵרֵחַ: In a knotted bill of divorce, the witnesses are supposed to sign behind each fold. When one fold lacks a signature behind it, the bill of divorce is referred to as a bare bill of divorce.

Frontal view of a knotted bill of divorce depicting the text of the bill of divorce

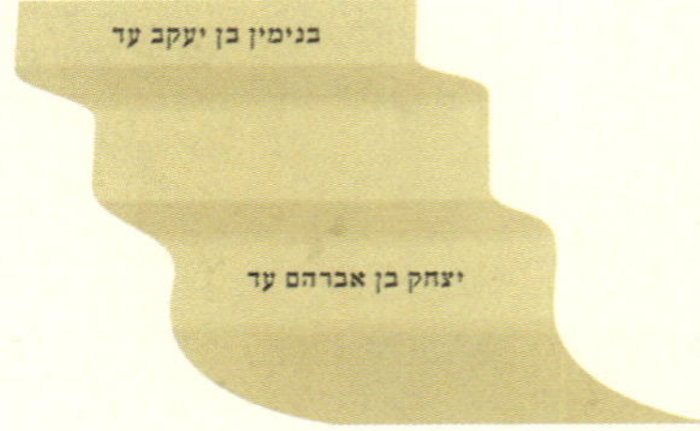

View from behind a knotted bill of divorce with one missing signature

וְאֵיזֶהוּ גֵּט קֵרֵחַ? כָּל שֶׁקְּשָׁרָיו מְרוּבִּין מֵעֵדָיו.

And what is a bare bill of divorce? It is **any** bill of divorce **where** the number of **its folds** is **more than** the number of **its witnesses.**[N] In a folded and tied bill of divorce, the bill of divorce is folded and the folds are then tied. Instead of having two witnesses sign at the bottom of the document, witnesses would sign on each tied fold. A bare bill of divorce has more folds than signatures, i.e., some folds lack signatures.

גמ׳ מַאי טַעֲמָא דְּגֵט קֵרֵחַ? גְּזֵירָה מִשּׁוּם ״כּוּלְּכֶם״.

GEMARA The Gemara asks: **What is the reason that a bare bill of divorce** is not valid, considering that there are more than two witnesses signed on it? The Gemara answers: It is a rabbinic **decree** that was issued **due to** one who says: **All of you** should sign. Since it can be assumed that one who writes a folded and tied bill of divorce wants to have each tied fold signed, there is concern that he may have instructed that all of them sign. If they do not sign, the condition is not fulfilled, and the bill of divorce is not valid.

״גֵּט קֵרֵחַ הַכֹּל מַשְׁלִימִין עָלָיו״.

§ It was stated in the mishna that ben Nannas holds, with regard to **a bare bill of divorce,** that **anyone can complete it.** Rabbi Akiva, however, permits disqualified witnesses to sign only if they are invalid because they are relatives of either the husband and wife or the other witnesses.

וְרַבִּי עֲקִיבָא, עֶבֶד מַאי טַעְמָא לָא? דְּאָתוּ לְמֵימַר כָּשֵׁר לְעֵדוּת. קָרוֹב נַמִּי אָתוּ לְמֵימַר כָּשֵׁר לְעֵדוּת!

The Gemara asks: **And** according to **Rabbi Akiva, what is the reason** that a **slave cannot** sign? The Gemara answers: The Sages were concerned **that** people **will** mistakenly **come to say** that since the slave served as a witness in this case, the slave is **fit to bear witness** in all cases. They will use a slave as a witness in situations that demand testimony accepted only from qualified witnesses. The Gemara challenges this: If so, with regard to **a relative, too, they will come to say** that a relative is **fit to bear witness** in all cases.

אֶלָּא, עֶבֶד הַיְינוּ טַעְמָא – דִּדְלְמָא אָתוּ לְאַסּוֹקֵיהּ לְיוּחֲסִין.

Rather, one could explain that with regard to **a slave, this is the reason** why he is disqualified: There is concern that **perhaps they will come to elevate** his status **with regard to lineage.** If a slave signs the bill of divorce, they might say that if he signed a bill of divorce, he must be an Israelite.

גַּזְלָן דְּבַר יוּחֲסִין הוּא לִיתַּכְשַׁר! אַלְמָה תְּנַן, רַבִּי עֲקִיבָא אוֹמֵר: אֵין מַשְׁלִימִין עָלָיו אֶלָּא קְרוֹבִים הָרְאוּיִין לְהָעִיד בְּמָקוֹם אַחֵר; קָרוֹב אִין, גַּזְלָן לָא!

The Gemara asks: If this is the reason why a slave cannot sign, then **a robber, who is of** unflawed **lineage, should be fit** to complete the signatures of a folded and tied bill of divorce, according to Rabbi Akiva. **Why,** then, did **we learn** in the mishna that **Rabbi Akiva says: Not** all can **complete it. Rather, only relatives who are fit to testify in another case.** The Gemara deduces from this: **A relative, yes; but a robber, no.**

אֶלָּא, עֶבֶד הַיְינוּ טַעְמָא – דְּאָתוּ לְמֵימַר שִׁחְרוּרֵי שַׁחְרְרֵיהּ, גַּזְלָן נַמִּי אָתוּ לְמֵימַר תְּשׁוּבָה עֲבַד; קָרוֹב מַאי אִיכָּא לְמֵימַר? קָרוֹב, כּוּלֵּי עָלְמָא יָדְעִי דְּקָרוֹב הוּא.

The Gemara answers: **Rather, this is the reason** why **a slave** is disqualified: **They will come to say** that his master **emancipated him** and he signed because he is now like any other Israelite. Similarly, with regard to **a robber, they will also come to say** that **he repented** and will allow him to testify in other cases, as well. Therefore, Rabbi Akiva declared him to be unfit as well. With regard to **a relative, what can be said** to disallow him to sign this bill of divorce? With regard to **a relative, everyone knows that he is a relative,** and there is no concern that they will allow him to testify in other cases involving his relatives.

אָמַר רַבִּי זֵירָא אָמַר רַבָּה בַּר שְׁאֵילְתָא אָמַר רַב הַמְנוּנָא סָבָא אָמַר רַב אַדָּא בַּר אַהֲבָה: גֵּט קֵרֵחַ – קְשָׁרָיו שִׁבְעָה וְעֵדָיו שִׁשָּׁה, שִׁשָּׁה וְעֵדָיו חֲמִשָּׁה, חֲמִשָּׁה וְעֵדָיו אַרְבָּעָה, אַרְבָּעָה וְעֵדָיו שְׁלֹשָׁה – עַד כָּאן מַחֲלוֹקֶת בֶּן נַנָּס וְרַבִּי עֲקִיבָא; אֲבָל קְשָׁרָיו שְׁלֹשָׁה וְעֵדָיו שְׁנַיִם – דִּבְרֵי הַכֹּל אֵין מַשְׁלִימִין עָלָיו אֶלָּא קָרוֹב.

§ **Rabbi Zeira**[P] **says** that **Rabba bar She'eilta says** that **Rav Hamnuna the Elder says** that **Rav Adda bar Ahava says:** The **dispute** between **ben Nannas and Rabbi Akiva** with regard to a **bare bill of divorce** that has more tied folds than witnesses is **only** in a case where **its ties** total **seven and its witnesses** total **six,** or its ties total **six and its witnesses** total **five,** or its ties total **five and its witnesses** total **four,** or its ties total **four and its witnesses** total **three.** But if **its ties** total **three and its witnesses** total **two, everyone,** even ben Nannas, **agrees** that **not** all disqualified witnesses can **complete it. Rather, only a relative** can complete it.

NOTES

Where its folds total more than its witnesses – שֶׁקְּשָׁרָיו מְרוּבִּין מֵעֵדָיו: The mishna is referring to a tied and folded bill of divorce. In tractate *Bava Batra* (160b) it is explained that the ordinance of a tied and folded bill of divorce was instituted in a place where there were priests who would get angry at their wives and hastily divorce them. Subsequently, they would regret their actions but would be unable to remarry their divorced wives, since a priest is prohibited from marrying a divorcée. To prevent this situation, the Sages instituted the writing of a folded and tied bill of divorce, which is time-consuming to write and requires additional witnesses, thereby giving the priest time to reconsider his decision to divorce his wife. Once this form of a bill of divorce was instituted, it was applied to other types of documents as well.

With regard to how a folded and tied bill of divorce was written, most commentaries explain that a line of the bill of divorce would be written, and then a line would be left blank. The written line would then be folded over the blank line, and would be sewn down, like a paper fan. This was repeated with the succeeding lines until the whole bill of divorce was written. The witnesses would sign the reverse side of the bill of divorce, between the rows. The Ramah explains that after the document is folded, it is tied with straps that emerge from its sides.

PERSONALITIES

Rabbi Zeira – רַבִּי זֵירָא: Rabbi Zeira, known in the Jerusalem Talmud as Rabbi Ze'eira, was born in Babylonia and became one of the great third-generation *amora'im* of Eretz Yisrael. His father was a tax collector for the Persian government and was praised as one of the few individuals who filled that position properly. When Rabbi Zeira ascended to Eretz Yisrael, he decided to completely identify with the methods of Torah study of Eretz Yisrael, and the Gemara relates that he fasted one hundred fasts in order to forget what he had learned in Babylonia.

אָמַר לֵיהּ רַבִּי זֵירָא לְרַבָּה בַּר שְׁאִילְתָּא: מִכְּדִי כׇּל שְׁלֹשָׁה בִּמְקוּשָּׁר כִּשְׁנַיִם בְּפָשׁוּט דָּמֵי, מָה הָתָם קָרוֹב לָא, אַף הָכָא נַמִּי קָרוֹב לָא!

Rabbi Zeira said to Rabba bar She'eilta: After all, all three witnesses **in** a folded and **tied** bill of divorce are **like** the **two** witnesses **in an ordinary** bill of divorce, since the Sages said that a folded and tied bill of divorce requires at least three witnesses. Therefore, **just as there,** in the case of an ordinary bill of divorce, **a relative cannot** serve as one of the two witnesses, **so too here, a relative** should **not** serve as one of the primary witnesses.

אָמַר לֵיהּ: אַף לְדִידִי קַשְׁיָא לִי וּשְׁאִילְתֵּיהּ לְרַב הַמְנוּנָא, וְרַב הַמְנוּנָא לְרַב אַדָּא בַּר אַהֲבָה, וַאֲמַר לֵיהּ: הַנַּח לִשְׁלֹשָׁה בִּמְקוּשָּׁר, דְּלָאו דְּאוֹרָיְיתָא.

Rabba bar She'eilta **said to him: To me as well** this was **difficult, and I asked that** question **to Rav Hamnuna, and Rav Hamnuna** asked it **to Rav Adda bar Ahava,** who had transmitted this statement, **and he said to him: Leave** the case of **three** witnesses **in a** folded and **tied** bill of divorce, as the requirement **is not by Torah law.** While the requirement to have a minimum of two witnesses in an ordinary bill of divorce is by Torah law, the requirement to have a minimum of three witnesses for a folded and tied bill of divorce is not by rabbinic law. Consequently, it is of no concern if the third witness is not fit to bear witness.

תַּנְיָא נַמִּי הָכִי: גֵּט קֵרֵחַ – קְשָׁרָיו שִׁבְעָה וְעֵדָיו שִׁשָּׁה, שִׁשָּׁה וְעֵדָיו חֲמִשָּׁה, חֲמִשָּׁה וְעֵדָיו אַרְבָּעָה, אַרְבָּעָה וְעֵדָיו שְׁלֹשָׁה – עַד כָּאן מַחְלוֹקֶת בֶּן נַנָּס וְרַבִּי עֲקִיבָא.

The Gemara notes that **this is also taught** in a *baraita* (*Tosefta* 6:9): The **dispute** between **ben Nannas and Rabbi Akiva** with regard to **a bare bill of divorce** that has more tied folds than witnesses is **only** in a case where **its ties** total **seven and its witnesses** total **six,** or its ties total **six and its witnesses** total **five,** or its ties total **five and its witnesses** total **four,** or its ties total **four and its witnesses** total **three.**

הִשְׁלִים עָלָיו עֶבֶד – בֶּן נַנָּס אוֹמֵר: הַוָּלָד כָּשֵׁר, וְרַבִּי עֲקִיבָא אוֹמֵר: הַוָּלָד מַמְזֵר; אֲבָל קְשָׁרָיו שְׁלֹשָׁה וְעֵדָיו שְׁנַיִם – דִּבְרֵי הַכֹּל אֵין מַשְׁלִימִין עָלָיו אֶלָּא קָרוֹב.

The *baraita* continues: If **a slave completed it** with his signature, and the woman remarried on the basis of this bill of divorce, **ben Nannas says: The offspring** of a subsequent marriage **is unflawed. And Rabbi Akiva says: The offspring is a *mamzer*. But** if **its ties** total **three, and its witnesses** total **two, everyone agrees** that **not** all disqualified witnesses can **complete it. Rather,** it can be completed **only** by **a relative** of either the husband and wife or the other witnesses.

רַב יוֹסֵף מַתְנֵי: כָּשֵׁר. וְהָתַנְיָא: קָרוֹב! אָמַר רַב פָּפָּא, תְּנֵי: כָּשֵׁר.

Rav Yosef taught: Only **a valid** witness can complete it. The Gemara challenges: **But isn't it taught** explicitly in a *baraita*: **A relative? Rav Pappa said:** Correct the language of the *baraita,* and **teach: Valid.**

אָמַר רַבִּי יוֹחָנָן: לֹא הוּכְשְׁרוּ בּוֹ אֶלָּא עַד אֶחָד קָרוֹב בִּלְבַד, אֲבָל תְּרֵי לָא, דִּלְמָא אָתֵי לְקַיּוֹמֵי בִּתְרֵי קְרוֹבִים וְחַד כָּשֵׁר.

Rabbi Yoḥanan says: In a folded and tied bill of divorce, the Sages **validated only** the use of **one witness** who is **a relative,** to complete the number of signatures as per the number of knotted folds. **But two** such witnesses, **no,** they did not validate them. The reason for this is that **perhaps they will come to ratify** a bill of divorce **with two** witnesses who are **relatives and one** witness who is **valid.** If the bill of divorce will be challenged, it will be necessary to ratify the document. While this bill of divorce has more than three witnesses signed to it, the court needs to authenticate the signature of only three of the witnesses to ratify the bill of divorce, provided that two of them are not relatives. If there are more than two relatives signed on the bill of divorce, a court may unintentionally authenticate the signatures of two relatives and only one valid witness.

אָמַר רַב אַשִׁי: מַתְנִיתָא נַמִּי דַּיְקָא,

Rav Ashi said: The language of **the *baraita* is also precise,** in accordance with this opinion,

Perek **VIII**
Daf **82** Amud **a**

דְּקָא מְדַלֵּג וְתָנֵי חַד חַד, שְׁמַע מִינַּהּ.

as it teaches by **skipping one** by **one.** The examples given relate to one witness missing, e.g., seven ties and six witnesses, and so on. They do not include a case in which two witnesses are missing, e.g., seven ties and five witnesses. This indicates that the dispute between Rabbi Akiva and Ben Azzai is only with regard to the signature of one witness. The Gemara affirms: **Conclude from it** that this is so.

אָמַר אַבָּיֵי: שְׁמַע מִינַּהּ: הַאי קָרוֹב חָתֵים אִי בָּעֵי בֵּין בַּתְּחִילָּה בֵּין בָּאֶמְצַע בֵּין בַּסּוֹף,

Abaye said: Learn from it that **this relative,** who is allowed to sign a folded and tied bill of divorce, can **sign if he wants** to sign, **either at the beginning,** as the first signature, **in the middle, or at the end.**

מְמַאי? מִדְּלָא קָבַע לֵיהּ מָקוֹם; וּשְׁמַע מִינַּהּ: מִכׇּל תְּלָתָא מְקַיְּימִינַן לָא בָּעֵינַן רְצוּפִין,

From where does Abaye infer this? **From** the fact that **it did not designate a place for him** to sign. **And learn from it,** as well, that **from any three** of the witnesses who signed on a folded and tied bill of divorce, **we** can **ratify** the bill of divorce, i.e., it can be ratified based on their signatures. **And we do not need** to confirm the signatures specifically of three **consecutive** witnesses.

דְּאִי סָלְקָא דַעְתָּךְ בָּעֵינַן רְצוּפִין, לִקְבַּע לֵיהּ מָקוֹם לְהַאי קָרוֹב בַּתְּחִילָּה אוֹ בָּאֶמְצַע אוֹ בַּסּוֹף, וְלַכְשַׁר בֵּיהּ טוּבָא.

As if it enters your mind that **we need consecutive** witnesses, then **they should designate a place for this relative** to sign, **in the beginning, or in the middle, or at the end, and they should** then **validate** the use of **many** disqualified witnesses. It could have been instituted that every third witness may be disqualified. Since in any group of three witnesses, two of them would be valid, more than one disqualified witness could be allowed. Since it is possible to ratify a bill of divorce by confirming signatures that are not consecutive, and therefore there is concern that the court will rely on two disqualified witnesses, the Sages consequently allowed the use of only one disqualified witness.

כִּי אָתוּ לְקַמֵּיהּ דְּרַבִּי אַמִי, אֲמַר לֵיהּ: צֵא וְהַשְׁלֵים עָלָיו עֶבֶד מִן הַשּׁוּק.

With regard to the *halakha* concerning the dispute in the mishna, it is related that **when they came before Rabbi Ami** with a question pertaining to a bare bill of divorce that needed more witnesses, **he said to** the person overseeing: **Go out and complete it** even with **a slave**[H] **from the** general **public,** in accordance with the opinion of ben Nannas.

הדרן עלך הזורק

HALAKHA

Go out and complete it with a slave – צֵא וְהַשְׁלֵים עָלָיו עֶבֶד: The early commentaries disagree with regard to a bare bill of divorce. Some rule that it can be completed with the signature of anyone who is disqualified from bearing witness, in accordance with the opinion of ben Nannas and how Rabbi Ami ruled in practice (Rambam's Commentary on the Mishna; *Tosafot* on *Bava Batra* 162b). Others rule that it can be completed only with the signature of a relative, since the *halakha* is in accordance with the opinion of Rabbi Akiva when he disagrees with his contemporaries. Additionally, the *halakha* is not in accordance with the opinion of Rabbi Ami when he disagrees with Rabbi Yoḥanan, who was his teacher (Rabbeinu Ḥananel; Rid).

Summary of **Perek VIII**

This chapter established that the words: "And gives it in her hand" (Deuteronomy 24:1), do not refer only to a woman's actual hand. If a husband places a bill of divorce in his wife's lap or in a vessel attached to her, it is considered as if he placed the bill of divorce in her hand, and the divorce is effective. Similarly, if a husband threw a bill of divorce into an area that belongs to his wife, such as her house or courtyard, and he threw it in such a way that it entered the airspace over the partitions that delineate the boundaries of her domain, the divorce is effective; or if he threw it and it landed next to her in a public domain, the divorce is effective. Nevertheless, the Sages taught that ideally none of these methods should be employed, and a husband should place a bill of divorce in his wife's hand in order to avoid any uncertainty.

While the Sages explain the meaning of "her hand" in broad terms, they are specific in their explanation of: "He gives it." The bill of divorce must reach the wife through an act of giving performed by the husband. If the bill of divorce reaches her hand without an act of giving by the husband, the bill of divorce is not valid.

After the writing of the bill of divorce, if the man and woman were again secluded, the bill of divorce is considered to be an outdated bill of divorce, which is invalid *ab initio*. The husband must give his wife another bill of divorce. Nevertheless, if a woman received an outdated bill of divorce, she may remarry. An outdated bill of divorce was invalidated by the Sages as a rabbinic decree to prevent aspersions being cast on the children. Though the husband is required to provide a second bill of divorce, if he does not, the wife is still permitted to remarry.

The Sages instituted that the date on a bill of divorce should be written in terms of the years since the establishment of the government of the area in which the bill of divorce is given. If another calendrical system was used, the bill of divorce is valid after the fact, i.e., if she was divorced with it. This *halakha* is no longer relevant because after the days of the Talmud, it became customary to write the date counting the years from the creation of the world or from the founding of Alexander the Great's empire.

In the times of the Talmud, there was a custom to write a folded and tied bill of divorce, on which three or more witnesses would sign. If a signature is lacking, the bill of divorce can be completed by any Jewish man, even by someone who is ordinarily unfit to bear witness. If a woman remarried on the basis of a bill of divorce that was missing a signature, she must leave her second husband, though the lineage of any children who were born is unflawed.

A bill of divorce in which the name of the man or woman was changed is totally invalid. Likewise, if the bill of divorce was accidentally given to the husband and a receipt for the payment of the marriage contract was given to his wife, the bill of divorce is totally invalid. If a woman remarried based on such a divorce, she is like a married woman who cohabited with someone else, and a child resulting from their union is a *mamzer*.

Introduction to **Perek IX**

When a man takes a wife, and marries her, and it comes to pass, if she finds no favor in his eyes, because he has found some unseemly matter in her, and he writes her a scroll of severance, and gives it in her hand, and sends her out of his house.

(Deuteronomy 24:1)

This chapter assembles different *halakhot* of divorce that are not necessarily related to one another, completing the discussion of the *halakhot* of divorce. It continues to examine the topic of conditional divorce, which was discussed in Chapter Seven. The conditions, or qualifications, that are discussed here are those that invalidate the divorce entirely, either because they negate the essence of the bill of divorce as a scroll of severance, i.e., a document that severs the bond between husband and wife, or because they cannot be fulfilled. The chapter discusses cases in which the qualification nullifies the divorce, those in which the qualification is disregarded and the divorce is valid, and those in which the divorce and the qualification are both valid.

A second topic analyzed is the formulation of a bill of divorce. Both the essential, critical formula of the bill of divorce, and the manner in which it should be written *ab initio* are discussed.

The chapter also continues to explore a topic that began in the previous chapter, namely, bills of divorce that were written in a manner that is valid by Torah law but not in accordance with the ordinances of the Sages.

In addition, the chapter details a list of problems that arise when two or more bills of divorce are written on the same paper and it is unclear which bill or bills of divorce the witnesses intended to sign. Cases dealt with are those of bills of divorce that were written one above the other, in opposite directions from one another, one beneath the other, or one next to the other. The latter case can be even more complicated if the witnesses signed in different languages from one another.

Different forms of witnesses' signatures on the bill of divorce are also delineated, e.g., a witness's signature with or without his father's name, with or without adding the word witness, and the use of a nickname for the signature.

Another topic discussed is the manner in which rumors are treated vis-à-vis a woman's marital status. The chapter describes which rumors are treated seriously and which rumors are not, and whether or not a rumor that is found to be baseless should be suppressed by the court.

Finally, the chapter examines the question of when a husband may, should, or must divorce his wife.

מתני׳ הַמְגָרֵשׁ אֶת אִשְׁתּוֹ, וְאָמַר לָהּ ״הֲרֵי אַתְּ מוּתֶּרֶת לְכׇל אָדָם אֶלָּא לִפְלוֹנִי״ – רַבִּי אֱלִיעֶזֶר מַתִּיר, וַחֲכָמִים אוֹסְרִים. כֵּיצַד יַעֲשֶׂה? יִטְּלֶנּוּ הֵימֶנָּה, וְיַחֲזוֹר וְיִתְּנֶנּוּ לָהּ וְיֹאמַר לָהּ ״הֲרֵי אַתְּ מוּתֶּרֶת לְכׇל אָדָם״. כְּתָבוֹ בְּתוֹכוֹ, אַף עַל פִּי שֶׁחָזַר וּמְחָקוֹ – פָּסוּל.

MISHNA With regard to **one who divorces his wife and said to her** while handing her the bill of divorce: **You are hereby permitted to** marry **any man except** [*ella*][H] **for so-and-so, Rabbi Eliezer permits** her to remarry based on this divorce. **And the Rabbis prohibit** her from remarrying, as their bond is not entirely severed by this divorce, and she is therefore still considered his wife. **What should he do** so the divorce may take effect? **He should take it from her**[N] **and hand it to her again, and** he should **say to her: You are hereby permitted to** marry **any man.** If **he wrote** his qualification **inside** the bill of divorce, **even if he then erased it,** the bill **is invalid**[N] since it was not written in a valid manner.

גמ׳ אִיבַּעְיָא לְהוּ: הַאי ״אֶלָּא״, ״חוּץ״ הוּא, אוֹ ״עַל מְנָת״ הוּא?

GEMARA **A dilemma was raised before** the Sages: What is the meaning of **this** word ***ella*** in the husband's statement? Does **it** mean **except,** i.e., the husband intended to divorce his wife in a manner that would render her permitted to marry only a limited group of men? **Or** does **it** mean: **On the condition,** i.e., the husband intended to grant her full divorce on the condition that she would not marry so-and-so?

״חוּץ״ הוּא, וּבְ״חוּץ״ הוּא דִּפְלִיגִי רַבָּנַן עֲלֵיהּ דְּרַבִּי אֱלִיעֶזֶר, דְּהָא שַׁיַּיר לַהּ בְּגֵט, אֲבָל בְּ״עַל מְנָת״ מוֹדוּ לֵיהּ, מִידֵּי דַּהֲוָה אַכׇּל תְּנָאֵי דְּעָלְמָא.

The Gemara elaborates on how this dilemma affects the understanding of the dispute between Rabbi Eliezer and the Rabbis: Does *ella* mean **except, and** therefore **it is** specifically **with** regard to the **exception** of a certain man from the intended divorce **that the Rabbis disagree with Rabbi Eliezer** and hold that the divorce is invalid? This would be **because** in a case where the husband noted an exception, it is as if he **left out** part **of her bill of divorce;** since she is not permitted to remarry anyone she wishes it does not entirely sever the bond between them. **But with** regard to divorce **on the condition** that she will not marry a certain man the Rabbis **agree with** Rabbi Eliezer that it is valid, **just as is** the case **with regard to any typical condition** which the husband attaches to the divorce of his wife.

אוֹ דִּלְמָא ״עַל מְנָת״ הוּא, וּבְ״עַל מְנָת״ הוּא דִּפְלִיג רַבִּי אֱלִיעֶזֶר אַדְּרַבָּנַן, אֲבָל בְּ״חוּץ״ מוֹדֶה, דְּהָא שַׁיַּיר לַהּ בְּגֵט?

Or perhaps this is the meaning of *ella*: **On the condition?** Accordingly, **it is** specifically **with** regard to divorce **on the condition** that the wife will not marry a certain man **that Rabbi Eliezer disagrees with the Rabbis** and allows her to remarry based on this divorce; **but with** regard to **the exception** of a certain man from the woman's right to remarry **he concedes** that the divorce is invalid **as** the husband **left out** part **of her bill of divorce.**

אָמַר רָבִינָא, תָּא שְׁמַע: כׇּל הַבָּתִּים מְטַמְּאִין בִּנְגָעִים אֶלָּא שֶׁל גּוֹיִם; אִי אָמְרַתְּ בִּשְׁלָמָא ״חוּץ״ הוּא – שַׁפִּיר, אֶלָּא אִי אָמְרַתְּ ״עַל מְנָת״ הוּא, עַל מְנָת דְּלָא מִיטַּמּוּ בָּתֵּי גוֹיִם הוּא דְּמִיטַּמּוּ בָּתֵּי יִשְׂרָאֵל, הָא מִיטַּמּוּ בָּתֵּי גוֹיִם לָא מְטַמְּאִי בָּתֵּי יִשְׂרָאֵל?

Ravina said: Come and **hear** a solution to this dilemma from the following mishna (*Nega'im* 12:1): **All houses become ritually impure through leprous sores**[N] of the house **except** [*ella*] **for those belonging to gentiles. Granted, if you say** that the meaning of the word *ella* **is except,** this mishna is **well** understood. **But if you say** that its meaning **is on the condition,** the resulting interpretation of this mishna is that the **houses of Jews become impure only on the condition that** the **houses of gentiles do not become impure; consequently,** if the **houses of gentiles become impure,** the **houses of Jews do not become impure.** Does this interpretation make any sense?

וְעוֹד, בָּתֵּי גוֹיִם מִי מְטַמְּאִי? וְהָתַנְיָא: ״וְנָתַתִּי נֶגַע צָרַעַת בְּבֵית אֶרֶץ אֲחֻזַּתְכֶם״ – אֶרֶץ אֲחוּזַּתְכֶם מִטַּמְּאָה בִּנְגָעִים, וְאֵין בָּתֵּי גוֹיִם מְטַמְּאִין בִּנְגָעִים! אֶלָּא שְׁמַע מִינַּהּ ״חוּץ״ הוּא, שְׁמַע מִינַּהּ.

Moreover, an objection against this interpretation may be raised as follows: **Do** the **houses of gentiles become ritually impure** at all? **But isn't it taught** in a *baraita* that from the verse: **"And I put the plague of leprosy in a house of the land of your possession"** (Leviticus 14:34), it is derived that only **the land of your possession,** i.e., the houses of Jews, **becomes impure through leprous sores** of the house, **but the houses of gentiles do not**[H] **become impure through leprosy? Rather, conclude from** the mishna that the meaning of *ella* **is except.** The Gemara concludes: **Conclude from it** that *ella* means except.

HALAKHA

You are hereby permitted to marry any man except [*ella*], etc. – הֲרֵי אַתְּ מוּתֶּרֶת לְכׇל אָדָם אֶלָּא וכו׳: If a man says to his wife while handing her a bill of divorce: You are hereby permitted to marry any man except for so-and-so, the divorce is invalid. What should he do so that the divorce may take effect? He should take it from her, and hand it to her again, and say to her without qualification: You are hereby permitted to marry any man (Ran), as ruled by the Rabbis. If he says: You are hereby permitted to marry any man on the condition that you will not marry so-and-so, the divorce is valid. The Rema, citing Ramban, rules that even in the case of a condition the divorce is treated as invalid *ab initio* (Rambam *Sefer Nashim, Hilkhot Geirushin* 8:17; *Shulḥan Arukh, Even HaEzer* 137:1).

Houses of gentiles do not, etc. – אֵין בָּתֵּי גוֹיִם וכו׳: Houses of gentiles, even in Eretz Yisrael, do not become ritually impure through leprosy of the house (Rambam *Sefer Tahara, Hilkhot Tumat Tzara'at* 14:11).

NOTES

He should take it from her, etc. – יִטְּלֶנּוּ הֵימֶנָּה וכו׳: It is discussed later on in the Gemara (84b) why it is not sufficient for the husband to retract his qualification by telling her that she is hereby permitted to marry any man, without taking back the bill of divorce and handing in to her again. Ḥizkiyya maintains that the Rabbis are following the opinion of Rabbi Shimon ben Elazar mentioned in the previous chapter (78a), that since the divorce is enacted by a ceremony of the husband handing the bill of divorce to the wife, any statement made by the husband after the bill is already in the wife's possession is legally inconsequential.

Rabbi Yoḥanan, whose explanation is cited by many commentaries on the mishna (see Rabbeinu Crescas Vidal and Ritva), claims that although the Rabbis hold that the divorce in the case of the mishna is invalid, they concede that the woman is considered a divorcée with regard to the prohibition against her marrying a priest (see 82b). Therefore, for the husband to merely retract his qualification would not be sufficient; since the divorce already took effect to some degree, the bill of divorce is already the property of the wife, and the husband can no longer effect the process.

Even if he then erased it the bill is invalid – אַף עַל פִּי שֶׁחָזַר וּמְחָקוֹ פָּסוּל: Since the bill of divorce was written with a disqualifying clause, it is an invalid bill of divorce. Therefore, erasing that clause does not render it valid (*Tosafot* on 84b; Meiri).

All houses become ritually impure through leprous sores – כׇּל הַבָּתִּים מְטַמְּאִין בִּנְגָעִים: Leprosy of the house is a type of leprosy that appears on the walls of a house, in the form of splotches of discoloration on the walls. Its *halakhot* are enumerated in the Torah (Leviticus 14:33–53) and in the Mishna (*Nega'im*). The halakhic definition of this concept is very narrow, and therefore the Sages maintained that there was never a house that was afflicted with actual leprosy and there will never be. The Ramban on Leviticus 13:43 writes that this type of leprosy is the result of spiritual infractions on the part of the residents of the house, and not a natural process.

מַתְנִיתִין דְּלָא כִּי הַאי תַּנָּא; דְּתַנְיָא, אָמַר רַבִּי יוֹסֵי בְּרַבִּי יְהוּדָה: לֹא נֶחְלְקוּ רַבִּי אֱלִיעֶזֶר וַחֲכָמִים עַל הַמְגָרֵשׁ אֶת אִשְׁתּוֹ וְאָמַר לָהּ "הֲרֵי אַתְּ מוּתֶּרֶת לְכָל אָדָם חוּץ מִפְּלוֹנִי" – שֶׁאֵינָהּ מְגוֹרֶשֶׁת. עַל מָה נֶחְלְקוּ? עַל הַמְגָרֵשׁ אִשְׁתּוֹ וְאָמַר לָהּ, "הֲרֵי אַתְּ מוּתֶּרֶת לְכָל אָדָם עַל מְנָת שֶׁלֹּא תִּנָּשְׂאִי לִפְלוֹנִי",

According to this conclusion, **our mishna is not in accordance with** the opinion of **this *tanna*, as it is taught** in a *baraita* that **Rabbi Yosei, son of Rabbi Yehuda, said: Rabbi Eliezer and the Rabbis did not disagree with regard to one who divorces his wife and said to her** while handing her the bill of divorce: **You are hereby permitted to** marry **any man except for so-and-so**; rather, they were in agreement **that** in that case **she is not divorced. With regard to what** case **did they disagree?** It was **with regard to one who divorces his wife and said to her: You are hereby permitted to** marry **any man on the condition that you will not marry so-and-so,**

Perek **IX**
Daf **82** Amud **b**

HALAKHA

She was divorced only from her husband – לֹא נִתְגָּרְשָׁה אֶלָּא מֵאִישָׁהּ: If a man says to his wife while handing her a bill of divorce: You are hereby divorced from me and you are not permitted to marry any man, although she is not permitted to remarry, there is a trace of a bill of divorce, and she is therefore disqualified from marrying a priest (Rambam *Sefer Nashim*, *Hilkhot Geirushin* 10:1; *Shulḥan Arukh*, *Even HaEzer* 6:1).

שֶׁרַבִּי אֱלִיעֶזֶר מַתִּיר לְכָל אָדָם חוּץ מֵאוֹתוֹ הָאִישׁ, וַחֲכָמִים אוֹסְרִים.

as in this case **Rabbi Eliezer permits** her **to** marry **any man except for that man** about whom the condition was made, **and the Rabbis prohibit** her from remarrying, as in their opinion this divorce is not valid.

מַאי טַעְמָא דְּרַבִּי אֱלִיעֶזֶר? מִידֵּי דַּהֲוָה אַכָּל תְּנַאי דְּעָלְמָא. וְרַבָּנַן? כָּל תְּנָאֵי דְעָלְמָא לָא שַׁיֵּיר לֵיהּ בְּגֵט, הָכָא שַׁיֵּיר לָהּ בְּגֵט.

The Gemara asks: **What is the reasoning behind Rabbi Eliezer's** opinion as cited in the *baraita*? The Gemara answers: The ruling here is **just as it is with regard to any typical condition.** The husband has the right to attach conditions to the divorce. **And** how would **the Rabbis** respond to this reasoning? They would reason that by attaching **any typical condition** the husband **did not leave out** part **of the bill of divorce,** as it does not diminish the essential act of severance. By contrast, **here he left out** part **of the bill of divorce,** as she is not permitted to marry any man she wishes. Therefore, the divorce is invalid.

וּמַתְנִיתִין דְּאוֹקִימְנָא בְּ"חוּץ", מַאי טַעְמָא דְּרַבִּי אֱלִיעֶזֶר?

The Gemara asks: **And** according to **the mishna, which we established** as referring to a case of **exception, what is the reason for Rabbi Eliezer's** opinion that the divorce takes effect, despite its lack of complete severance?

אָמַר רַבִּי יַנַּאי מִשּׁוּם זָקֵן אֶחָד: אָמַר קְרָא: "וְיָצְאָה מִבֵּיתוֹ וְהָלְכָה וְהָיְתָה לְאִישׁ אַחֵר", אֲפִילּוּ לֹא הִתִּירָהּ אֶלָּא לְאִישׁ אַחֵר – הֲרֵי זוֹ מְגוֹרֶשֶׁת. וְרַבָּנַן אָמְרִי טַעְמָא דְּרַבִּי אֱלִיעֶזֶר: הַאי "אִישׁ" – לְכָל אִישׁ וְאִישׁ.

Rabbi Yannai said in the name of one elder that **the verse states** with regard to divorce: **"And she departs out of his house, and goes and becomes another man's wife"** (Deuteronomy 24:2), indicating that **even** if he divorced her in a manner that **only permitted her to** marry one **other man, she is divorced,** i.e., this partial severance takes effect. **And the Rabbis would say** in response to **Rabbi Eliezer's explanation** that **this** phrase: Another **man,** which appears in the verse refers not to a specific man but **to any man,** i.e., it must be permitted for her to marry any man for the divorce to take effect.

וְרַבִּי יוֹחָנָן אָמַר, טַעְמָא דְּרַבִּי אֱלִיעֶזֶר מֵהָכָא: "וְאִשָּׁה גְּרוּשָׁה מֵאִישָׁהּ לֹא יִקָּחוּ" – אֲפִילּוּ לֹא נִתְגָּרְשָׁה אֶלָּא מֵאִישָׁהּ – נִפְסְלָה מִן הַכְּהוּנָּה, אַלְמָא הָוֵי גִּיטָּא.

And Rabbi Yoḥanan said that **the reason for Rabbi Eliezer's** opinion **is from** the verse **here,** where it is stated with regard to priests: **"Neither may they take a woman divorced from her husband"** (Leviticus 21:7). This verse indicates that **even** if **she was divorced only from her husband,**[H] and was not permitted to marry others, **she is disqualified from** marrying into **the priesthood** as a divorcée, i.e., she may not marry a priest even after her husband's death. **Apparently,** all the more so, divorce that excludes certain men from the wife's right to remarry **is** considered a valid **bill of divorce.** This is certainly the case when the divorce permits her to marry all men with the exception of one.

וְרַבָּנַן? אִיסּוּר כְּהוּנָּה שָׁאנֵי.

And the Rabbis would respond that **the prohibition** against marrying into the **priesthood is different,** as even a divorce that is otherwise invalid disqualifies a woman from marrying a priest.

בָּעֵי רַבִּי אַבָּא: בְּקִידּוּשִׁין הֵיאַךְ? תִּיבָּעֵי לְרַבִּי אֱלִיעֶזֶר, תִּיבָּעֵי לְרַבָּנַן;

§ **Rabbi Abba raises a dilemma:** If this kind of exception is made **in** a case of **betrothal,** i.e., the man says to the woman that she is hereby forbidden to all men except for so-and-so, **how** is this betrothal treated?[H] The Gemara elaborates: **Let the dilemma be raised according to** the opinion of **Rabbi Eliezer** and **let the dilemma be raised according to** the opinion of **the Rabbis.**

תִּיבָּעֵי לְרַבִּי אֱלִיעֶזֶר: עַד כָּאן לָא קָאָמַר רַבִּי אֱלִיעֶזֶר הָכָא – אֶלָּא מִשּׁוּם דִּכְתִיבִי קְרָאֵי, אֲבָל הָתָם קִנְיָן מַעַלְיָא בָּעֵינַן, אוֹ דִלְמָא ״וְיָצְאָה... וְהָיְתָה״?

Let the dilemma be raised according to Rabbi Eliezer: Is **Rabbi Eliezer saying only here** that the divorce is valid **because verses are written** that support this proposition, as delineated by Rabbi Yannai and Rabbi Yoḥanan; **but there,** in the case of betrothal, **a proper acquisition is necessary,** which is not the case when a certain man is excluded from the prohibition to engage in sexual intercourse with her? **Or** should it **perhaps** be derived from the juxtaposition between the clause: **"And she departs** out of his house," and the clause: **"And becomes** another man's wife" (Deuteronomy 24:2), which serves as a basis for the comparison of the *halakhot* of divorce and betrothal, teaching that just as divorce takes effect in this manner, so does betrothal?

תִּיבָּעֵי לְרַבָּנַן: עַד כָּאן לָא קָאָמְרִי רַבָּנַן הָכָא – אֶלָּא דְּבָעֵינַן כְּרִיתוּת וְלֵיכָּא, אֲבָל הָתָם קִנְיָן כָּל דְּהוּ. אוֹ דִלְמָא ״וְיָצְאָה...וְהָיְתָה״?

Let the dilemma be raised according to the Rabbis: Are **the Rabbis saying here** that the divorce is invalid **only because** the **severance** of the bond between the husband and wife **is necessary** for the divorce to take effect, **and there is no** such severance as long as the woman may not marry any man she wishes; **but there,** in the case of betrothal, **any form of acquisition** is sufficient for it to take effect? **Or** should it **perhaps** be derived from the juxtaposition between the clause beginning: **"And she departs,"** and the clause beginning: **"And becomes,"** that what renders a divorce invalid renders a betrothal invalid as well?

לְבָתַר דְּאִיבַּעְיָא לֵיהּ הֲדַר פְּשָׁטָהּ: בֵּין לְרַבִּי אֱלִיעֶזֶר בֵּין לְרַבָּנַן, בָּעֵינַן ״וְיָצְאָה...וְהָיְתָה״.

After Rabbi Abba **raised the dilemma he then resolved it** in the following manner: **Both according to** the opinion of **Rabbi Eliezer and according to** the opinion of **the Rabbis it is necessary** to compare the *halakha* in the case of betrothal to the ruling with regard to divorce, based on the juxtaposition between **"And she departs"** and: **"And becomes."** Therefore, the dispute remains in this case as well.

אֲמַר אַבַּיֵי: אִם תִּמְצָא לוֹמַר אִיתָא לִדְרַבִּי אַבָּא,

Abaye said: If you say that **Rabbi Abba's** solution **is so,** i.e., if you say that Rabbi Eliezer holds that making an exception in a betrothal is valid, the issue of levirate marriage in such cases must be addressed.

בָּא רְאוּבֵן וְקִידְּשָׁהּ חוּץ מִשִּׁמְעוֹן, וּבָא שִׁמְעוֹן וְקִידְּשָׁהּ חוּץ מֵרְאוּבֵן, וּמֵתוּ שְׁנֵיהֶם – מִתְיַבֶּמֶת לְלֵוִי, וְאֵין אֲנִי קוֹרֵא בָּהּ אֵשֶׁת שְׁנֵי מֵתִים,

If **Reuven came** to a woman **and betrothed her** saying that she is forbidden to all men **except for** his brother **Shimon, and Shimon** then **came and betrothed her** saying that she is forbidden to all men **except for Reuven, and they both died** without children, in this case **she performs levirate marriage with** their brother **Levi, and I do not call her the wife of two dead men.**[H] It is stated in tractate *Yevamot* (31b) that if a woman has a levirate bond with a man due to her two late husbands who were his brothers, she may not perform levirate marriage with him, as it is derived from the verse: "The wife of the dead man shall not be married outside of the family" (Deuteronomy 25:5), that the wife of only one dead man performs levirate marriage, not the wife of two. Abaye stated that in the case under discussion the woman may perform levirate marriage with Levi.

HALAKHA

In a case of betrothal how is it treated – בְּקִידּוּשִׁין הֵיאַךְ: If a man betroths a woman, saying to her: You are hereby betrothed to me and forbidden to all men except for so-and-so, the Rambam rules that the betrothal is of uncertain validity, as Abaye does not accept Rabbi Abba's conclusion (*Maggid Mishne*). The *Shulḥan Arukh* follows the Rambam's ruling. According to *Tosafot* and the Rosh, on the other hand, the betrothal is completely invalid (*Beit Shmuel*). If he said to her: You are hereby betrothed to me on the condition that you will be permitted to marry so-and-so, the betrothal takes effect in full, and the condition is void (Rambam *Sefer Nashim, Hilkhot Ishut* 7:13; *Shulḥan Arukh, Even HaEzer* 38:39).

The wife of two dead men – אֵשֶׁת שְׁנֵי מֵתִים: If three brothers were married to three unrelated women, and one of them died without children, and one of his brothers performed levirate betrothal with his wife but died before he was able to marry her, the third brother performs *ḥalitza* with her and not levirate marriage, as she is rendered the wife of two dead men (Rambam *Sefer Nashim, Hilkhot Yibbum VaḤalitza* 6:27; *Shulḥan Arukh, Even HaEzer* 174:4).

NOTES

Her betrothal to Shimon was not effective – קִידּוּשֵׁי דְּשִׁמְעוֹן לָא אַהֲנוּ: Rashi explains that Shimon's betrothal does not take effect at all (Rabbeinu Crescas Vidal, citing Ra'ah). By contrast, the Rashba claims that it does take effect and the woman is considered his wife as well. The statement that their betrothal is not effective, according to the Rashba, refers to the fact that there is no prohibition against adultery that results from it. Nevertheless, even Reuven is prohibited from engaging in sexual intercourse with her due to the fact that she is his brother's wife.

מַאי טַעְמָא? קִידּוּשֵׁי דִּרְאוּבֵן אַהֲנוּ, קִידּוּשֵׁי דְּשִׁמְעוֹן לָא אַהֲנוּ.

What is the reason that she is not considered to be the wife of two dead men? It is that although her **betrothal to Reuven was effective,** i.e., it took effect, her **betrothal to Shimon was not effective,**[N] as it did not render her forbidden to any man to whom she was not already forbidden due to her betrothal to Reuven. Therefore, she is considered only Reuven's wife.

וְאֶלָּא אֵשֶׁת שְׁנֵי מֵתִים הֵיכִי מַשְׁכַּחַתְּ לַהּ? כְּגוֹן שֶׁבָּא רְאוּבֵן וְקִידְּשָׁהּ חוּץ מִשִּׁמְעוֹן, וּבָא שִׁמְעוֹן וְקִידְּשָׁהּ סְתָם, דְּקִידּוּשֵׁי רְאוּבֵן אַהֲנוּ לְמֵיסְרָא אַעָלְמָא, וְקִידּוּשֵׁי דְּשִׁמְעוֹן אַהֲנוּ לְמֵיסְרָא אַרְאוּבֵן.

Rather, under what circumstances is the case of **a wife of two dead men found** in this context? It is found in a case **where Reuven came and betrothed her,** saying that she is hereby forbidden to all men **except for Shimon, and Shimon** then **came and betrothed her without specifying** any qualifications. **Since Reuven's betrothal was effective in rendering her forbidden to everyone** except for Shimon, **and Shimon's betrothal was effective in rendering her forbidden to Reuven,** the betrothal of both brothers took effect. And if both of them die she may not perform levirate marriage with Levi, as she is the wife of two dead men.

בָּעֵי אַבַּיֵי: אָמַר לַהּ ״הֲרֵי אַתְּ מוּתֶּרֶת לְכָל אָדָם חוּץ מֵרְאוּבֵן וְשִׁמְעוֹן״, וְחָזַר וְאָמַר לַהּ ״לִרְאוּבֵן וְשִׁמְעוֹן״, מַהוּ?

Abaye raises a dilemma: If a man **said to** his wife while handing her a bill of divorce: **You are hereby permitted to** marry **any man except for Reuven and Shimon, and he then said to her:** You are permitted **to** marry **Reuven and Shimon, what is the** *halakha*?

מִי אָמְרִינַן מַאי דַּאֲסַר שְׁרָא, אוֹ דִּלְמָא מַאי דַּאֲסַר שְׁרָא וּמַאי דִּשְׁרָא אֲסַר? אִם תִּמְצָא לוֹמַר

Do we say that **what he forbade** initially **he** then **permitted,** enabling her to marry anyone, including Reuven and Shimon, in which case the severance is complete? **Or perhaps what he forbade** initially **he** then **permitted,** permitting her to marry Reuven and Shimon, **and what he permitted** initially **he** then **forbade,** i.e., he permitted her only to Reuven and Shimon, excluding all other men? **If you say**

Perek **IX**
Daf **83** Amud **a**

HALAKHA

The dilemma shall stand unresolved – תֵּיקוּ: If a man said to his wife while handing her a bill of divorce: You are hereby permitted to marry any man except for Reuven and Shimon, and then said to her: You are hereby permitted to marry Reuven and Shimon, or: You are hereby permitted to marry Reuven, or: You are also permitted to marry Shimon, it is uncertain whether or not she is divorced, as these dilemmas were not resolved by the Gemara (Rosh). The Rambam rules that in the first case she is divorced, in the second case she is not divorced, and in the third case it is uncertain. The Rambam's guiding principle is that the *halakha* is in accordance with any suggestion in the Gemara introduced by the phrase: If you say (Rambam *Sefer Nashim, Hilkhot Geirushin* 8:7–8; *Shulḥan Arukh, Even HaEzer* 137:4).

מַאי דַּאֲסַר שְׁרָא, ״לִרְאוּבֵן״ מַהוּ? לִרְאוּבֵן וְהוּא הַדִּין לְשִׁמְעוֹן, וְהַאי דְּקָאָמַר לִרְאוּבֵן – מִשּׁוּם דִּפְתַח בֵּיהּ, אוֹ דִּלְמָא לִרְאוּבֵן דַּוְקָא?

that **what he** initially **forbade he** then **permitted,** enabling her to marry anyone she wishes, **what is the** *halakha* if he said the second time that she is permitted **to** marry **Reuven?** Did he mean that she is permitted **to** marry **Reuven and the same is true** with regard **to Shimon,** i.e., she is permitted to marry him as well? Is the fact **that he mentioned** only that she is permitted **to** marry **Reuven because he opened** his prior qualification **by** mentioning **him** before he mentioned Shimon, but he intended to permit her to marry Shimon as well? **Or** did he, **perhaps, specifically** intend to permit her **to** marry **Reuven?**

וְאִם תִּמְצָא לוֹמַר לִרְאוּבֵן דַּוְקָא, לְשִׁמְעוֹן מַהוּ? לְשִׁמְעוֹן וְהוּא הַדִּין לִרְאוּבֵן, וְהַאי דְּקָאָמַר שִׁמְעוֹן – מִשּׁוּם דְּסָלֵיק מִינֵּיהּ, אוֹ דִּלְמָא לְשִׁמְעוֹן דַּוְקָא,

And if you say that he intended to permit her **to** marry **specifically Reuven** and not Shimon, **what is** the *halakha* if he said that she is permitted **to** marry **Shimon?** Did he mean that she is permitted **to** marry **Shimon and the same is true** with regard **to Reuven,** and the fact **that he mentioned** only **Shimon is because he ended** his initial previous statement **by** mentioning **him? Or perhaps** he was **specifically** referring only **to Shimon?**

בָּעֵי רַב אַשִׁי: ״אַף לְשִׁמְעוֹן״, מַהוּ? ״אַף״ אַרְאוּבֵן קָאֵי, אוֹ דִּלְמָא ״אַף״ אַעָלְמָא קָאֵי? תֵּיקוּ.

Rav Ashi raises another **dilemma** with regard to the same case: If he said to her the second time: You are **also** permitted **to** marry **Shimon, what is** the *halakha*? Is the word **also referring to Reuven,** i.e., she is permitted to marry Shimon in addition to Reuven, **or perhaps** it is **also referring to everyone,** i.e., she is permitted to marry Shimon in addition to all men, but not Reuven? The dilemma **shall stand** unresolved.[H]

תנו רבנן: לאחר פטירתו של רבי אליעזר, נכנסו ארבעה זקנים להשיב על דבריו, אלו הן: רבי יוסי הגלילי, ורבי טרפון, ורבי אלעזר בן עזריה, ורבי עקיבא.

§ **The Sages taught** (*Tosefta* 9:1): **After the death of Rabbi Eliezer,**[P] **four Sages entered** the discussion **to refute his statement. They were: Rabbi Yosei HaGelili, Rabbi Tarfon, Rabbi Elazar ben Azarya, and Rabbi Akiva.**

נענה רבי טרפון ואמר: הרי שהלכה זו ונישאת לאחיו של זה שנאסרה עליו, ומת בלא בנים, לא נמצא זה עוקר דבר מן התורה? הא למדת, שאין זה כריתות.

Rabbi Tarfon responded to Rabbi Eliezer's opinion, **saying:** If after the husband stipulated that the wife not marry a certain man **she went and married the brother of the one to whom she was prohibited** from marrying, **and** this husband **died without children,** she cannot perform levirate marriage with her husband's brother, because he is forbidden to her due to the stipulation of her first husband. **Is** the first husband **not found** to be **uprooting a matter of Torah law** through his stipulation? **You have therefore derived that this is not** an act of **severance.**[N] The divorce is not valid, as the Torah would not sanction a manner of divorce that can cause a mitzva to be nullified.

נענה רבי יוסי הגלילי ואמר: היכן מצינו אסור לזה ומותר לזה? האסור אסור לכל, והמותר מותר לכל! הא למדת, שאין זה כריתות.

Rabbi Yosei also **responded** to Rabbi Eliezer's opinion, **saying: Where do we find** an example of something that is **forbidden to this** person **and permitted to that** other person? **What is forbidden is forbidden to everyone, and what is permitted is permitted to everyone.** This contradicts Rabbi Eliezer's opinion that a divorcée can be prohibited from marrying a certain man and permitted to marry all other men. **You have therefore derived that this is not** an act of **severance.**

נענה רבי אלעזר בן עזריה ואמר: "כריתות" – דבר הכורת בינו לבינה, הא למדת, שאין זה כריתות.

Rabbi Elazar ben Azarya responded, saying: What is the meaning of the expression: "Scroll of **severance,**" which is used in the Torah for a bill of divorce? It means **something that severs** the bond **between him and her** entirely. This woman, by contrast, is still bound to her husband after their divorce, as his stipulation prevents her from marrying a certain man. **You have therefore derived that this is not** an act of **severance.**

נענה רבי עקיבא ואמר: הרי שהלכה זו ונשאת לאחד מן השוק והיו לה בנים, ונתארמלה או נתגרשה, ועמדה ונישאת לזה שנאסרה עליו, לא נמצא גט בטל ובניה ממזרים? הא למדת, שאין זה כריתות;

Rabbi Akiva responded, saying: If after the husband stipulated that the wife not marry a certain man **she went and married a man from the** general **public, and she had children** with him, **and she was** subsequently **widowed or divorced** from the second husband, **and she** then **arose and married the one to whom she was forbidden** by her first husband's condition, **isn't the bill of divorce** thereby **found** to be **nullified? And** would this not render **her children** from her second marriage as **born from an adulterous relationship** [***mamzerim***],[B] as she is retroactively considered her first husband's wife? **You have therefore derived that this is not** an act of **severance,** as the Torah would not enable a divorce that could lead to such a situation.

דבר אחר: הרי שהיה זה שנאסרה עליו כהן, ומת המגרש, לא נמצאת אלמנה אצלו וגרושה אצל כל אדם?

Rabbi Akiva continued to offer **an alternative** refutation of Rabbi Eliezer's opinion: If **the one to whom she was forbidden was a priest, and** her ex-husband **who divorced** her **died, is she not** thereby **found** to be **a widow with regard to him,** as she was considered a married woman with regard to this priest even after her divorce, **and a divorcée with regard to any** other **man?** Nevertheless, she is forbidden to him too, just as she is forbidden to any other priest.

וקל וחומר: מה גרושה שהיא קלה – אסורה בשביל צד גירושין שבה, אשת איש שהיא חמורה – לא כל שכן! הא למדת, שאין זה כריתות.

And it is therefore **an** ***a fortiori*** inference that **just as** the prohibition for **a divorcée** to marry a priest (see Leviticus 21:14) **is a** relatively **minor** prohibition, yet **she is forbidden** to this priest **due to the element of divorce that applies to her,** even though with regard to him she is not a divorcée but a widow, **all the more so** is it **not** clear that the prohibition against sexual intercourse with **a married woman, which is a major** prohibition, should apply to every man during the lifetime of the ex-husband, due to the fact that she is considered a married woman with regard to this one man? **You have therefore derived that this is not** an act of **severance,** as this divorce does not permit her to marry any man.

PERSONALITIES

Rabbi Eliezer – רבי אליעזר: This is the *tanna* Rabbi Eliezer ben Hyrcanus, also called Rabbi Eliezer the Great, who lived through the destruction of the Second Temple. Rabbi Eliezer was the son of a wealthy family that traced its lineage back to Moses. He began to study Torah only at age twenty, when he went to Jerusalem to learn from Rabban Yoḥanan ben Zakkai. Rabban Yoḥanan ben Zakkai had great esteem for Rabbi Eliezer and considered him the greatest of his disciples, so much so that he claimed he was equal to all the Sages of Israel. Rabban Yoḥanan ben Zakkai described Rabbi Eliezer as a plastered well that does not lose a drop, and his learning was based mostly on the traditions he received from his teacher. Rabbi Eliezer's opinion differed from his teacher in that he tended to agree with the opinions of Beit Shammai. Rabbi Eliezer began to teach Torah before the destruction of the Temple and was among the students of Rabban Yoḥanan ben Zakkai who joined him in founding the great yeshiva in Yavne after the destruction of the Temple.

Rabbi Eliezer married Imma Shalom, the sister of the *Nasi*, Rabban Gamliel of Yavne. Following a fundamental dispute between Rabbi Eliezer and the other Sages with regard to the process of halakhic decision making, Rabban Gamliel had him excommunicated.

Rabbi Eliezer's colleagues were the other disciples of Rabban Yoḥanan ben Zakkai. In particular, there are many recorded discussions between Rabbi Eliezer and Rabbi Yehoshua, who was Rabbi Eliezer's closest colleague. His principal student was Rabbi Akiva, but he taught other scholars in his generation as well. Rabbi Eliezer's son Hyrcanus was one of the talmudic Sages.

NOTES

This is not an act of severance – אין זה כריתות: In contrast to Rabbi Elazar ben Azarya's refutation below, this is not an inference from the literal meaning of the word severance. Rather, the *baraita* is simply referring to the Torah's expression for a bill of divorce, i.e., a scroll of severance (Deuteronomy 24:1).

BACKGROUND

***Mamzer* – ממזר:** A *mamzer* is a child born from an adulterous or incestuous relationship, i.e., a child born from sexual intercourse between a married woman and a man other than her husband, or between relatives who are forbidden to marry by Torah law, where the participants in such relationships are subject to *karet*. An exception to this *halakha* is the offspring conceived with a menstruating woman, with whom sexual intercourse is prohibited to all under penalty of *karet*. The offspring of an unmarried couple is not a *mamzer*.

A *mamzer* inherits from his natural father and is halakhically considered his father's son in all respects. A *mamzer* may marry only a *mamzeret*, i.e., a female *mamzer*, or a convert to Judaism. Likewise, a *mamzeret* may marry only a *mamzer* or a convert. The offspring of that union is a *mamzer* as well.

אָמַר לָהֶן רַבִּי יְהוֹשֻׁעַ: אֵין מְשִׁיבִין אֶת הָאֲרִי לְאַחַר מִיתָה.

Rabbi Yehoshua said to them: Even though your objections are valid, **one does not refute** the opinion of **a lion after** his **death.**[N] After a Sage has passed away one cannot reject his opinion based on a difficulty with it, as he possibly would have provided an answer had it been presented to him while he was still alive.

אָמַר רָבָא: כּוּלְּהוּ אִית לְהוּ פִּירְכָא, לְבַר מִדְּרַבִּי אֶלְעָזָר בֶּן עֲזַרְיָה דְּלֵית לֵיהּ פִּירְכָא. תַּנְיָא נַמִּי הָכִי, אָמַר רַבִּי יוֹסֵי: רוֹאֶה אֲנִי אֶת דִּבְרֵי רַבִּי אֶלְעָזָר בֶּן עֲזַרְיָה מִדִּבְרֵי כּוּלָּן.

Rava said: All of the previously mentioned responses **have refutations** that can be raised against them **except for** the response **of Rabbi Elazar ben Azarya, which does not have a refutation.** The Gemara notes that **this is also taught** in a *baraita*, as **Rabbi Yosei said: I see the statement of Rabbi Elazar ben Azarya** as preferable **to the statements of all** the other Sages.

אָמַר מָר, נַעֲנָה רַבִּי טַרְפוֹן וְאָמַר: הֲרֵי שֶׁהָלְכָה זוֹ וְנִשֵּׂאת לְאָחִיו שֶׁל זֶה שֶׁנֶּאֶסְרָה עָלָיו, וּמֵת בְּלֹא בָנִים, לֹא נִמְצָא זֶה עוֹקֵר דָּבָר מִן הַתּוֹרָה? עוֹקֵר?! אִיהוּ עָקַר?! אֶלָּא, מַתְנֶה לַעֲקוֹר דָּבָר מִן הַתּוֹרָה.

The Gemara commences discussion of the *baraita*: **The Master said** that **Rabbi Tarfon responded, saying:** If **she went and married the brother of the one to whom she was prohibited** from marrying, **and he died without children,** is the first husband **not** thereby **found** to be **uprooting a matter of Torah law?** The Gemara asks: What is the meaning of the question: Is the first husband not **uprooting** a matter of Torah law? Is it **he** who **is uprooting** the mitzva? **Rather,** Rabbi Tarfon means that the husband **is stipulating to uproot a matter of Torah law.**

מַתְנֶה?! מִי קָאָמַר לָהּ: לָא סַגִּי לָהּ דְּלָא מִינַּסְבָא לֵיהּ לַאֲחוּהּ דְּהַהוּא גַּבְרָא? אֶלָּא, גּוֹרֵם לַעֲקוֹר דָּבָר מִן הַתּוֹרָה.

The Gemara questions this assertion as well: Is the husband **stipulating** to uproot a mitzva? **Did he say to her** that **it is not sufficient if she does not marry the brother of that man,** who he rendered forbidden to her? Since he did not stipulate this, he did not uproot the mitzva; it is the woman who uprooted the mitzva by marrying specifically that man's brother. **Rather,** Rabbi Tarfon means that the husband **is causing a matter of Torah law to be uprooted.**

גּוֹרֵם?! אֶלָּא מֵעַתָּה, בַּת אָחִיו לֹא יִשָּׂא, שֶׁמָּא יָמוּת בְּלֹא בָנִים, וְנִמְצָא גּוֹרֵם לַעֲקוֹר דָּבָר מִן הַתּוֹרָה! הַיְינוּ פִּירְכָא.

The Gemara asks: He **is causing** of matter of Torah law to be uprooted? **But if that is so,** one **should not marry his brother's daughter lest he die without children, and he will** thereby **be found** to be **causing a matter of Torah law to be uprooted** in that his brother will not be able to perform levirate marriage with his own daughter, and the Sages laud one who marries his brother's daughter. The Gemara responds: **This is the refutation** against Rabbi Tarfon's response that Rava was referring to.

וּבְמַאי? אִילֵימָא בְּ״חוּץ״, מִשְׁרָא שָׁרֵא רַבִּי אֱלִיעֶזֶר!

The Gemara asks: **And with regard to what** case did Rabbi Tarfon refute Rabbi Eliezer's opinion? **If we say** that it was **with regard to** a case in which the husband said that his wife is permitted to marry any man **except** for so-and-so, the refutation is irrelevant, as **Rabbi Eliezer permits** the woman to marry this man after she married another man.

דְּתַנְיָא: מוֹדֶה רַבִּי אֱלִיעֶזֶר, בִּמְגָרֵשׁ אֶת אִשְׁתּוֹ וְאָמַר לָהּ ״הֲרֵי אַתְּ מוּתֶּרֶת לְכָל אָדָם חוּץ מִפְּלוֹנִי״, וְהָלְכָה וְנִיסֵּת לְאֶחָד מִן הַשּׁוּק וְנִתְאַרְמְלָה אוֹ נִתְגָּרְשָׁה, שֶׁמּוּתֶּרֶת לְזֶה שֶׁנֶּאֶסְרָה עָלָיו!

As it is taught in a *baraita* (*Tosefta* 9:1): **With regard to** a case where a man **divorces his wife and said to her** while handing her the bill of divorce: **You are hereby permitted to** marry **any man except for so-and-so, and she went and married someone from the** general **public and was** subsequently **widowed or divorced** from him, **Rabbi Eliezer concedes that she is** now **permitted to** marry the man **whom she was** initially **prohibited** from marrying[N] by the qualification of her first husband.

NOTES

One does not refute the opinion of a lion after his death – אֵין מְשִׁיבִין אֶת הָאֲרִי לְאַחַר מִיתָה: Later commentaries question this statement, as the Sages of the Talmud would frequently refute the opinions of Sages from earlier generations. Two answers are cited in *Ma'adannei Melekh*. One is that Rabbi Yehoshua made this statement only with regard to Rabbi Eliezer, who was a leading scholar of his generation, and his students were afraid to challenge his opinions. Accordingly, it was not appropriate for these same students to challenge his rulings after his death. The second answer is that these Sages were unsure of what Rabbi Eliezer meant, as the Gemara demonstrates later on. Therefore, they did not have the right to refute his statement. It is also possible that these Sages had the right to disagree with Rabbi Eliezer's ruling; despite this, they could not refute his opinion, since had he still been alive perhaps he would have responded to their objections convincingly.

She is permitted to marry the man whom she was prohibited from marrying, etc. – מוּתֶּרֶת לְזֶה שֶׁנֶּאֶסְרָה עָלָיו: *Tosafot* explain that once a woman remarries, any remaining ties to her ex-husband are nullified, including the qualification he attached to their divorce. Comparing this ruling with Abaye's statement (82b) that partial betrothal can result in a woman being the wife of two men, *Tosafot* explain that the reason remarriage nullifies a woman's remaining bond to her ex-husband is that her remarriage completes the process of the divorce. Therefore, partial marriage is not affected in this manner.

אֶלָּא בְּ״עַל מְנָת״.

Rather, Rabbi Tarfon's refutation was clearly stated **with regard to** a case where the woman was divorced **on the condition** that she would not marry so-and-so. A condition still applies after the woman remarries and its violation nullifies the divorce retroactively.

נַעֲנָה רַבִּי יוֹסֵי הַגְּלִילִי וְאָמַר: הֵיכָן מָצִינוּ אָסוּר לָזֶה וּמוּתָּר לָזֶה? הָאָסוּר אָסוּר לַכֹּל, וְהַמּוּתָּר מוּתָּר לַכֹּל. וְלָא? וַהֲרֵי תְּרוּמָה וְקָדָשִׁים, שֶׁאֲסוּרָה לָזֶה וּמוּתֶּרֶת לָזֶה! בְּאִיסּוּר אִשָּׁה קָא אָמְרִינַן.

The *baraita* states that **Rabbi Yosei HaGelili responded, saying: Where do we find** an example of something that is **forbidden to this** person **and permitted to that** other person? **What is forbidden is forbidden to everyone and what is permitted is permitted to everyone.** The Gemara asks: Is there **not** such an example? **Aren't** ***teruma***, the portion of the produce designated for the priest, **and sacrificial meat forbidden to this** group, i.e., non-priests (see Leviticus 22:10), **and permitted to that** group, i.e., priests? The Gemara answers: **We are referring to a forbidden woman.**

וַהֲרֵי עֲרָיוֹת! בְּאִישׁוּת קָאָמְרִינַן.

The Gemara asks: **Aren't those** women **with whom relations are prohibited** due to familial ties forbidden to some men, i.e., their relatives, and permitted to others? The Gemara answers: **We are referring to** a woman who is forbidden due to **marriage.**

הֲרֵי אֵשֶׁת אִישׁ! הַיְינוּ פִּירְכָא.

The Gemara asks: **Isn't a married woman** forbidden to all men but permitted to her husband? The Gemara responds: **This is the refutation** against Rabbi Yosei HaGelili's response that Rava was referring to.

וּבְמַאי? אִילֵימָא בְּ״עַל מְנָת״, הֲרֵי הוּתְּרָה אֶצְלוֹ בִּזְנוּת! אֶלָּא בְּ״חוּץ״.

The Gemara clarifies: **And with regard to what** case did Rabbi Yosei HaGelili raise this objection? **If we say** that it was **with regard to** a case in which the divorce was granted **on the condition** that she not marry a certain man, she is not entirely forbidden to him, as **she is permitted** to engage **in licentiousness with him;** the condition was with regard to marriage, not licentiousness. **Rather,** he clearly raised the objection **with regard to** a case where the husband told his wife that she is permitted to marry any man **except** for so-and-so, rendering her entirely forbidden to that man.

נַעֲנָה רַבִּי עֲקִיבָא וְאָמַר: הֲרֵי שֶׁהָלְכָה זוֹ וְנִישֵּׂאת לְאֶחָד מִן הַשּׁוּק וְהָיוּ לָהּ בָּנִים, וְנִתְאַרְמְלָה אוֹ נִתְגָּרְשָׁה, וְעָמְדָה וְנִשֵּׂאת לָזֶה שֶׁנֶּאֶסְרָה עָלָיו, לֹא נִמְצָא גֵּט בָּטֵל וּבָנֶיהָ מַמְזֵרִין?

The *baraita* states that **Rabbi Akiva responded, saying:** If **she went and married a man from the** general **public, and she had children** with him, **and she was** subsequently **widowed or divorced** from this second husband, **and she** then **arose and married the one to whom she was forbidden, isn't the bill of divorce** thereby **nullified?** And would this not render **her children** ***mamzerim*****?**

אִי הָכִי, בְּכוּלָּה תְּנָאֵי דְּעָלְמָא נָמֵי לָא תִּנְסִיב, דִּלְמָא לָא מְקַיְּימָא לֵיהּ לִתְנָאֵיהּ, וְנִמְצָא גֵּט בָּטֵל וּבָנֶיהָ מַמְזֵרִין! הַיְינוּ פִּירְכָא.

The Gemara asks: **If that is so,** and there is a concern that she will eventually violate the condition, **in a case of any typical condition** that the husband attaches to the divorce **she should not remarry either,**[N] **lest she not fulfill his condition and the bill of divorce be found** to be **nullified and her children** be rendered ***mamzerim.*** The Gemara responds: **This is the refutation** against Rabbi Akiva's response that Rava was referring to.

וּבְמַאי? אִילֵימָא בְּ״חוּץ״, מִשְׁרָא שָׁרָא רַבִּי אֱלִיעֶזֶר!

The Gemara asks: **And with regard to what** case did Rabbi Akiva raise this objection? **If we say** that it was **with regard to** a case in which the husband said that his wife is permitted to marry any man **except** for so-and-so, the objection is irrelevant, as **Rabbi Eliezer permits** the woman to marry so-and-so after she marries another man.

דְּתַנְיָא: מוֹדֶה הָיָה רַבִּי אֱלִיעֶזֶר, בִּמְגָרֵשׁ אֶת אִשְׁתּוֹ וְאָמַר לָהּ ״הֲרֵי אַתְּ מוּתֶּרֶת לְכָל אָדָם חוּץ מִפְּלוֹנִי״, וְהָלְכָה וְנִשֵּׂאת לְאֶחָד מִן הַשּׁוּק וְנִתְאַרְמְלָה אוֹ נִתְגָּרְשָׁה, שֶׁמּוּתֶּרֶת לָזֶה שֶׁנֶּאֶסְרָה עָלָיו! אֶלָּא בְּ״עַל מְנָת״.

As it is taught in a *baraita*: **With regard to** a case where a man **divorces his wife and said to her: You are hereby permitted** to marry **any man except for so-and-so, and she went and married someone from the** general **public, and was** subsequently **widowed or divorced** from him, **Rabbi Eliezer concedes that she is** now **permitted to** marry the man **whom she was** initially **prohibited** from marrying. **Rather,** Rabbi Akiva's objection was clearly **with regard to** a case of **a condition** that she would not marry so-and-so.

NOTES

In a case of any typical condition she should not remarry either – **בְּכוּלָּה תְּנָאֵי דְּעָלְמָא נָמֵי לָא תִּנְסִיב:** This dispute assumes that a woman who is divorced conditionally may remarry immediately, as there is no concern that the condition will not be fulfilled. The commentaries contrast this statement with the Gemara's ruling in other places that when a condition is attached to a divorce, fulfillment of the condition is a prerequisite for remarriage. *Tosafot* and the Rashba answer that this prerequisite exists only when there is concern that the woman might not be able to fulfill the condition, but here the condition is that she will not marry a certain man, and marriage requires her consent. Therefore, there is no concern that the condition will be violated.

The Rid and the Ramban distinguish between a condition that the wife perform a certain action, the fulfillment of which is a prerequisite for the divorce to take effect, and a condition that she refrain from doing something, which does not prevent her from remarrying immediately. The Ramah claims that according to rabbinic law, fulfillment of the condition is a prerequisite for remarriage, while according to Torah law, the woman may remarry immediately. Therefore, the Gemara rejects Rabbi Akiva's refutation. Rabbeinu Crescas Vidal maintains that the halakhic concern that a person might violate a condition does not exist with regard to divorce, as the consequences of violation after the woman remarries are severe and affect the status of her children and her finances.

דָּבָר אַחֵר: הֲרֵי שֶׁהָיָה זֶה שֶׁנֶּאֶסְרָה עָלָיו כֹּהֵן, וּמֵת הַמְגָרֵשׁ, לֹא נִמְצֵאת אַלְמָנָה אֶצְלוֹ וּגְרוּשָׁה אֵצֶל כׇּל אָדָם, וְקַל וָחוֹמֶר: וּמַה גְּרוּשָׁה שֶׁהִיא קַלָּה – אֲסוּרָה מִשּׁוּם צַד גֵּירוּשִׁין שֶׁבָּהּ, אֵשֶׁת אִישׁ חֲמוּרָה לֹא כׇּל שֶׁכֵּן!

The *baraita* states that Rabbi Akiva added **an alternative** response: If **the one to whom she was forbidden was a priest, and** her ex-husband **who divorced** her **died, is she not found** to be **a widow with regard to him and a divorcée with regard to any** other **man? And** it is therefore **an *a fortiori*** inference that **just as** the prohibition against **a divorcée** marrying a priest **is minor,** and yet **she is forbidden** to this priest **due to the element of divorce that applies to her, all the more so** is it **not** clear that the prohibition against relations with **a married woman, which is major,** should apply to every man during the lifetime of the ex-husband, due to the fact that she is considered a married woman with regard to this one man? Therefore, the divorce does not take effect.

וּבְמַאי? אִילֵימָא בְּ״עַל מְנָת״,

The Gemara asks: **And with regard to what** case was this objection raised? **If we say** that it was **with regard to** a case of **a condition,**

Perek **IX**
Daf **83** Amud **b**

הֲרֵי גְּרוּשָׁה אֶצְלוֹ בִּזְנוּת! אֶלָּא בְּ״חוּץ״.

isn't the woman **a divorcée with regard to** engaging in **licentious** behavior **with him?** The husband stipulated that she not marry that man, but he did not prohibit her from engaging in licentious behavior with him. Therefore, she is considered a divorcée with regard to him as well. This removes the *a fortiori* inference, as with regard to all other men she is not considered married at all. **Rather,** the objection was clearly raised **with regard to** a case of **exception.**

וְרַבִּי עֲקִיבָא, אִי ״חוּץ״ סְבִירָא לֵיהּ – לוֹתִיב ״חוּץ״, וְאִי ״עַל מְנָת״ סְבִירָא לֵיהּ – לוֹתִיב ״עַל מְנָת״!

The Gemara asks: **If Rabbi Akiva holds** that Rabbi Eliezer is referring to a case of **an exception, he should raise an objection** with regard to **an exception, and if he holds** that Rabbi Eliezer is referring to a case of **a stipulation, he should raise an objection** with regard to a case of **a stipulation.** Why does he raise one objection with regard to an exception and then another with regard to a stipulation?

רַבִּי עֲקִיבָא שְׁמִיעַ לֵיהּ דְּאִיכָּא דְּאָמַר ״חוּץ״ וְאִיכָּא דְּאָמַר ״עַל מְנָת״; מַאן דְּאָמַר ״חוּץ״ – הַאי פִּירְכָא, וּמַאן דַּאֲמַר ״עַל מְנָת״ – הַאי פִּירְכָא.

The Gemara answers: **Rabbi Akiva heard that there is** someone **who states** Rabbi Eliezer's ruling with regard to **an exception, and there is** someone else **who states** it with regard to **a stipulation.** He therefore raised objections with regard to both exceptions and stipulations; according to **the one who says** that it is with regard to **an exception, this is the refutation, and** according to **the one who says** that it is with regard to **a stipulation, that is the refutation.**

וּמַאי פִּירְכָא? אִי נֵימָא אִיסּוּר כְּהוּנָּה שָׁאנֵי – הָא רַבִּי אֱלִיעֶזֶר נַמִי מֵאִיסּוּר כְּהוּנָּה קָא מַיְיתֵי לֵיהּ!

The Gemara asks: **What is the refutation** that Rava found for Rabbi Akiva's second objection? **If we say** that it is that **the prohibition** against marrying into the **priesthood is different,** and therefore the *halakhot* of adultery and divorce cannot be inferred from it, **doesn't Rabbi Eliezer also derive** his opinion **from the prohibition** against marrying into **the priesthood?** Rabbi Yoḥanan stated (82b) that Rabbi Eliezer's ruling is derived from the verse that states with regard to priests: "Neither may they take a woman divorced from her husband" (Leviticus 21:7), indicating that even if a woman was divorced only from her husband and was not permitted to marry others, she is disqualified from marrying into the priesthood as a divorcée.

רָבָא, כְּרַבִּי יַנַּאי מִשּׁוּם זָקֵן אֶחָד קָא מַתְנֵי.

The Gemara answers: **Rava taught** his statement **in accordance with** the opinion of **Rabbi Yannai,** who said **in the name of one elder** that Rabbi Eliezer's opinion is derived not from the prohibition against marrying into the priesthood, but from the verse: "And she departs out of his house, and goes and becomes another man's wife" (Deuteronomy 24:2), which indicates that even if he divorced her in a manner that permitted her to marry only one other man, the divorce takes effect. Therefore, Rava refutes Rabbi Akiva's latter objection by claiming that the prohibition against marrying into the priesthood is different from other prohibitions and cannot be compared to them.

אָמַר לָהֶן רַבִּי יְהוֹשֻׁעַ: אֵין מְשִׁיבִין אֶת הָאֲרִי לְאַחַר מִיתָה. לְמֵימְרָא, דְּרַבִּי יְהוֹשֻׁעַ כְּוָותֵיהּ סְבִירָא לֵיהּ? וְהָא אִיהוּ נַמִי מִיפְרַךְ קָפָרֵיךְ!

It is stated in the *baraita* that **Rabbi Yehoshua said to them: One does not refute** the opinion of **a lion after** his **death.** The Gemara asks: **Is this to say that Rabbi Yehoshua holds in accordance with** the opinion of Rabbi Eliezer? **But doesn't he also raise a refutation** against Rabbi Eliezer's opinion?

הָכִי קָאָמַר לְהוּ: לְדִידִי נַמִי אִית לִי פִּירְכָא, מִיהוּ בֵּין לְדִידִי בֵּין לְדִידְכוּ – אֵין מְשִׁיבִין אֶת הָאֲרִי לְאַחַר מִיתָה.

The Gemara answers that **this is what he was saying to them: I also have a refutation** against Rabbi Eliezer's opinion, **but both my** objection **and yours** should not be raised, as **one does not refute** the opinion of **a lion after** his **death.**

וּמַאי פִּירְכָא דְּרַבִּי יְהוֹשֻׁעַ? דְּתַנְיָא, אָמַר רַבִּי יְהוֹשֻׁעַ: מַקִּישׁ קוֹדְמֵי הֲוָיָה שְׁנִיָּה לְקוֹדְמֵי הֲוָיָה רִאשׁוֹנָה, מַה קוֹדְמֵי הֲוָיָה רִאשׁוֹנָה דְּלָא אֲגִידָא בְּאִינִישׁ אַחֲרִינָא, אַף קוֹדְמֵי הֲוָיָה שְׁנִיָּה דְּלָא אֲגִידָא בְּאִינִישׁ אַחֲרִינָא.

The Gemara asks: **And what is Rabbi Yehoshua's refutation?** It is as **it is taught** in a *baraita*: **Rabbi Yehoshua said** that the passage: "When a man takes a wife, and marries her, and it comes to pass, if she finds no favor in his eyes, because he has found some unseemly matter in her, and he writes her a scroll of severance, and gives it in her hand, and sends her out of his house; and she departs out of his house, and goes and becomes another man's wife" (Deuteronomy 24:1–2), **juxtaposes** the woman's status **before the second marriage to** her status **before the first marriage.** It should be derived from here that **just as before the first marriage she is not bound to another man, so too, before the second marriage she is not bound to another man.** Therefore, a woman cannot remarry if she is still bound to her ex-husband due to a qualification that prohibits her from marrying a certain man.

גּוּפָא: מוֹדֶה רַבִּי אֱלִיעֶזֶר, בִּמְגָרֵשׁ אִשְׁתּוֹ וְאָמַר לָהּ "הֲרֵי אַתְּ מוּתֶּרֶת לְכׇל אָדָם חוּץ מִפְּלוֹנִי", וְהָלְכָה וְנִישֵּׂאת לְאֶחָד מִן הַשּׁוּק וְנִתְאַרְמְלָה אוֹ נִתְגָּרְשָׁה, שֶׁמּוּתֶּרֶת לְזֶה שֶׁנֶּאֶסְרָה עָלָיו.

§ The Gemara discusses **the** matter **itself** that was mentioned above in passing: **With regard to** a case where a man **divorces his wife and said to her: You are hereby permitted to** marry **any man except for so-and-so, and she went and married someone from the** general **public and was** subsequently **widowed or divorced** from him, **Rabbi Eliezer concedes that she is** now **permitted to** marry the man **whom she was** initially **prohibited** from marrying.

הֵשִׁיב רַבִּי שִׁמְעוֹן בַּר אֶלְעָזָר תְּשׁוּבָה לְדִבְרֵי רַבִּי אֱלִיעֶזֶר: הֵיכָן מָצִינוּ שֶׁזֶּה אוֹסֵר וְזֶה מַתִּיר!

The *baraita* continues: **Rabbi Shimon bar Elazar raised a refutation to Rabbi Eliezer's statement: Where do we find** a situation **where this** person **prohibits** something **and that** other person **permits** it? How can the first husband render the woman prohibited from marrying a certain man and her second husband render her permitted to do so after his death or their divorce?

וְלָא? וַהֲרֵי יְבָמָה, דְּבַעַל אוֹסֵר וְיָבָם מַתִּיר!

The Gemara questions this refutation: Is there **not** such a situation? **But isn't** there the case of **a *yevama*,** a woman **whose husband** dies childless, and he **deems** her **forbidden** to other men while she waits for his brother, her *yavam*, to perform levirate marriage with her, **and** the ***yavam*,**[B] after performing levirate marriage with her, **deems** her **permitted** in the event of divorce or his death?

הָתָם יָבָם הוּא קָא אָסַר לָהּ, דְּאִי מִבַּעַל הָא שַׁרְיָא וְקַיְימָא.

The Gemara answers: **There, it is the *yavam* who renders her forbidden, since if** not for the *yavam*, i.e., if her deceased husband did not have any brothers, **she would have already been released from** her bond to her **husband** and permitted to marry any man. It is only the existence of the *yavam* that prevents her from marrying other men. Therefore, it is he who renders her permitted.

הֲרֵי נְדָרִים, דְּנוֹדֵר אוֹסֵר וְחָכָם מַתִּיר! הָא אָמַר רַבִּי יוֹחָנָן: אֵין חָכָם מַתִּיר כְּלוּם אֶלָּא בַּחֲרָטָה.

The Gemara asks: **Isn't** there the matter of **vows, where the one who takes the vow prohibits** something **and a halakhic authority renders it permitted**[H] by dissolving the vow? The Gemara answers: **Rabbi Yoḥanan says** that **a halakhic authority dissolves** a vow **only through regret** of the person who took the vow. Since it is necessary for this person to express regret for taking the vow, it is not actually the halakhic authority who causes the dissolution of the vow.

הֲרֵי הֲפָרַת הַבַּעַל, דְּאִשָּׁה נוֹדֶרֶת וּבַעַל מֵיפֵר! הָתָם כִּדְרַב פִּנְחָס מִשְּׁמֵיהּ דְּרָבָא, דְּאָמַר רַב פִּנְחָס מִשְּׁמֵיהּ דְּרָבָא: כׇּל הַנּוֹדֶרֶת – עַל דַּעַת בַּעְלָהּ הִיא נוֹדֶרֶת.

The Gemara asks: **Isn't** there **the nullification of** a wife's vows by **the husband, where the wife vows,** creating a prohibition, **and her husband nullifies** the vow?[BH] The Gemara answers: **There** it can be explained **in accordance with** that which **Rav Pineḥas** reasoned **in the name of Rava, as Rav Pineḥas says in the name of Rava** that with regard to **any woman who takes a vow,** it is from the outset contingent **on her husband's consent** that **she takes the vow.** Therefore, the husband can nullify it.

BACKGROUND

Yavam – יָבָם: A man whose brother died without children is obligated by Torah law to marry his deceased brother's widow or grant her *ḥalitza* (see Deuteronomy 25:5–10). As long as neither levirate marriage nor *ḥalitza* has taken place, it is prohibited for her to marry another man. According to the Torah, levirate marriage is effected by the act of sexual intercourse. The Sages instituted that levirate marriage must be preceded by the practice of *ma'amar*, in which the deceased husband's brother betroths the widow. Sexual intercourse consummates the marriage between the deceased's brother and the widow, and she is thereafter considered his wife in all respects. Nowadays, in most Jewish communities, the brother-in-law is required to free his brother's widow of her obligation through *ḥalitza*, and he is not allowed to marry her through levirate marriage.

Nullification of vows and dissolution of vows – הֲפָרַת נְדָרִים וְהַתָּרַת נְדָרִים: The *halakhot* of vows and their nullification are stated in the Torah (Numbers 30) and are enumerated at length in tractate *Nedarim*. In essence, when either a young woman still under her father's auspices or a married woman takes a vow, her father or her husband respectively can nullify the vow on the day that he hears it if he does not approve of it. The Sages explained, based on the verses, that this is permitted only in certain situations. Only vows taken with regard to matters between the woman and her husband or between the young woman and her father can be nullified. Vows that do not affect the woman's relationship with her husband or father cannot be nullified.

Vows may not only be nullified; one may also request that a Sage dissolve his vow. Although this does not appear explicitly in the Torah, the Sages found allusions to it in the same Torah portion. One who took a vow can request that a single Sage or a court of three dissolve it. Tractate *Nedarim* deals extensively with the problems that arise in this process. The standard scenario involves the person who took the vow declaring that he did not initially anticipate that it would be so difficult to fulfill the vow, and had he known, he would not have taken the vow in the first place. There is no designated time frame for dissolving one's vows and one can request that his vows be dissolved at any time. There are also some vows that a Sage cannot dissolve, e.g., a vow made to another person, which would require that person's agreement to dissolve it. In addition, a vow cannot be dissolved if it was taken before a large group and was contingent on their agreement.

HALAKHA

And a halakhic authority renders it permitted – וְחָכָם מַתִּיר: If one takes an oath or vow and regrets having done so, he can have it dissolved by going to a halakhic authority, who dissolves it for him (Rambam *Sefer Hafla'a*, *Hilkhot Nedarim* 8:5; *Shulḥan Arukh*, *Yoreh De'a* 228:1).

The wife vows and her husband nullifies the vow – אִשָּׁה נוֹדֶרֶת וּבַעַל מֵיפֵר: The husband of a married woman can nullify her vows from the moment they enter the wedding canopy (Rambam *Sefer Hafla'a*, *Hilkhot Nedarim* 11:8; *Shulḥan Arukh*, *Yoreh De'a* 234:2).

NOTES

Something that severs, etc. – **דָּבָר הַכּוֹרֵת וכו׳**: The Rashba writes that this refutation applies both to the case of an exception and to the case of a stipulation, as any qualification that prevents the woman from marrying any man she wishes, even for a limited period of time, precludes severance. By contrast, the Ramah maintains that this refutation refers only to an exception; a divorce that has a condition attached is not lacking severance.

נַעֲנָה רַבִּי אֶלְעָזָר בֶּן עֲזַרְיָה וְאָמַר: ״כְּרִיתוּת״ – דָּבָר הַכּוֹרֵת בֵּינוֹ לְבֵינָהּ, הָא לָמַדְתָּ שֶׁאֵין זֶה כְּרִיתוּת.

§ The Gemara resumes discussion of the previous *baraita*. **Rabbi Elazar ben Azarya responded, saying:** What is the meaning of the expression: "Scroll of **severance** [*keritut*]," that is used in the Torah for a bill of divorce? It means **something that severs**[N] the bond **between him and her** entirely. **You have therefore derived that this** divorce, after which the wife is still bound to her husband due to his qualification, **is not** an act of **severance.**

וְרַבָּנַן הַאי ״כְּרִיתוּת״ מַאי עָבְדִי לֵיהּ? מִיבְּעֵי לְהוּ לְכִדְתַנְיָא: ״הֲרֵי זֶה גִּיטֵּךְ עַל מְנָת שֶׁלֹּא תִּשְׁתִּי יַיִן״, ״עַל מְנָת שֶׁלֹּא תֵּלְכִי לְבֵית אָבִיךְ לְעוֹלָם״ – אֵין זֶה כְּרִיתוּת, שְׁלֹשִׁים יוֹם – הֲרֵי זֶה כְּרִיתוּת.

The Gemara asks: **And what do the** other **Rabbis,** who did not refute Rabbi Eliezer's opinion in this manner, **do with this** term "severance"? How do they interpret it? The Gemara answers: **They need it for that which is taught** in a *baraita*: If a man says to his wife: **This is your bill of divorce on the condition that you will not** ever **drink wine,** or: **On the condition that you will never go to your father's house, that is not** an act of **severance,** as she remains restricted by him indefinitely. If he stipulates that she may not do so for **thirty days, that is** an act of **severance.** The Rabbis derive from the term severance that any indefinite condition prevents the divorce from taking effect.

וְאִידָּךְ? מִ״כָּרֵת כְּרִיתוּת״ נָפְקָא. וְאִידָּךְ? ״כָּרֵת כְּרִיתוּת״ לָא דָּרְשִׁי.

The Gemara asks: **And** from where does **the other** Sage, Rabbi Elazar ben Azarya, derive this principle? The Gemara answers: **It is derived from** the fact that the verse does not utilize the basic form of the word severance, i.e., *karet*, but rather its conjugate, *keritut*. This indicates an additional principle that is derived from the term. The Gemara asks: **And** what do **the other** Sages derive from the seemingly superfluous use of this word? The Gemara answers: **They do not interpret** the distinction between *karet* and *keritut*.

אָמַר רָבָא: ״הֲרֵי זֶה גִּיטֵּךְ עַל מְנָת שֶׁלֹּא תִּשְׁתִּי יַיִן כָּל יְמֵי חַיַּי״ – אֵין זֶה כְּרִיתוּת, ״כָּל יְמֵי חַיֵּי פְלוֹנִי״ – הֲרֵי זֶה כְּרִיתוּת.

§ **Rava says** that if a man says to his wife: **This is your bill of divorce on the condition that you will not drink wine** for **all the days of my life, that is not** an act of **severance,** as she remains bound to his condition for the rest of his life. If he stipulates that she may not drink wine for **all the days of the life of so-and-so, that is** an act of **severance.**

מַאי שְׁנָא ״חַיֵּי פְלוֹנִי״ – דְּדִלְמָא מָאֵית וּמְקַיְּימָא לֵיהּ לִתְנָאֵיהּ? ״חַיַּי״ דִּידֵיהּ נַמִי, דִּלְמָא מָאֵית וּמְקַיְּימָא לֵיהּ לִתְנָאֵיהּ!

The Gemara asks: **What is different** about the case where he mentioned **the life of so-and-so?** Is it **because perhaps** that person **will die and she will** thereby **fulfill the condition,** allowing her to remarry? With regard to **his own life** it is **also** true that **perhaps he will die and she will** thereby **fulfill the condition.** Why is the divorce invalid in that case?

אֶלָּא אֵימָא: ״כָּל יְמֵי חַיַּיִכִי״ – אֵין זֶה כְּרִיתוּת, ״כָּל יְמֵי חַיַּי״ אוֹ ״חַיֵּי פְלוֹנִי״ – הֲרֵי זֶה כְּרִיתוּת.

Rather, say that if the husband tells her: This is your bill of divorce on the condition that you will not drink wine for **all the days of your life,**[H] **that is not** an act of **severance,** as the wife will never be released from this restriction. If he says: For **all the days of my life, or:** For all the days of **so-and-so's life, that is** an act of **severance,** as the condition can potentially be fulfilled during her lifetime.

בְּעָא מִינֵּיהּ רָבָא מֵרַב נַחְמָן: ״הַיּוֹם אִי אַתְּ אִשְׁתִּי וּלְמָחָר אַתְּ אִשְׁתִּי״, מַהוּ? תִּיבָּעֵי לְרַבִּי אֱלִיעֶזֶר, תִּיבָּעֵי לְרַבָּנַן;

§ **Rava raised a dilemma before Rav Naḥman:** If a man hands his wife a bill of divorce and says to her: **Today you are not my wife, and tomorrow you are my wife, what is** the *halakha*? The Gemara elaborates: **Let the dilemma be raised according to** the opinion of **Rabbi Eliezer** and **let the dilemma be raised according to** the opinion of **the Rabbis.**

HALAKHA

All the days of your life, etc. – **כָּל יְמֵי חַיַּיִכִי וכו׳**: If a man hands a bill of divorce to his wife and stipulates that the divorce is on the condition that she will not perform a specific action, e.g., drink wine, for the rest of her life, the divorce is invalid because it does not sever the bond between them. If he stipulates that she may not do so for the rest of his life, or for the rest of a third person's life, or if he specifies a period of time, even if it is an extended period, the divorce is valid. The *Tur* holds that as long as the condition is for a specific period of time, even if it is longer than a person's life span, it is a valid divorce (Rambam *Sefer Nashim, Hilkhot Geirushin* 8:10–11; *Shulḥan Arukh, Even HaEzer* 143:20).

תִּיבְּעֵי לְרַבִּי אֱלִיעֶזֶר: עַד כָּאן לָא קָאָמַר רַבִּי אֱלִיעֶזֶר הָתָם – אֶלָּא דִּלְמַאן דְּקָא שָׁרֵי – קָא שָׁרֵי לְעוֹלָם, אֲבָל הָכָא לָא, אוֹ דִּלְמָא לָא שְׁנָא?

Let the dilemma be raised according to Rabbi Eliezer: Is Rabbi Eliezer saying that **only there,** in the case of the mishna, the divorce is valid **because concerning the one whom** the husband **permits** the wife to marry, **he permits** her **to marry him forever, but here,** the divorce is **not** valid as it is limited in time? **Or perhaps it is no different** from the case in the mishna, and in both cases Rabbi Eliezer holds that the divorce takes effect?

תִּיבְּעֵי לְרַבָּנַן: עַד כָּאן לָא קָאָמְרִי רַבָּנַן הָתָם – אֶלָּא דְּלָא פְּסָקָהּ מִינֵּיהּ לְגַמְרֵי, אֲבָל הָכָא כֵּיוָן דִּפְסָקָהּ – פַּסְקָהּ?

Let the dilemma be raised according to the Rabbis: Perhaps **the Rabbis are saying only there** that the divorce is invalid **because** the husband **did not separate her from himself entirely,** as she is prohibited from marrying a certain man due to his qualification. **But here,** the divorce takes effect, as **once he separates her,** even for a limited period of time, **he has** consequently **separated her**[N] entirely.

בָּתַר דִּבְעָיָא הֲדַר פְּשָׁטָהּ:

After Rava **raised the dilemma he then resolved it** on his own:

Perek **IX**
Daf **84** Amud **a**

מִסְתַּבְּרָא, בֵּין לְרַבִּי אֱלִיעֶזֶר בֵּין לְרַבָּנַן, כֵּיוָן דִּפְסָקָהּ – פַּסְקָהּ.

It stands to reason, both according to Rabbi Eliezer and according to the Rabbis, that **once he separates her,**[H] **he has separated her** entirely. By rendering her entirely permitted for one day he dissolves the bond between them and the divorce takes effect.

תָּנוּ רַבָּנַן: ״הֲרֵי זֶה גִּיטֵּךְ עַל מְנָת שֶׁתִּנָּשְׂאִי לִפְלוֹנִי״ – הֲרֵי זוֹ לֹא תִּנָּשֵׂא, וְאִם נִשֵּׂאת – לֹא תֵּצֵא.

§ **The Sages taught** (*Tosefta* 6:7) that if a man says to his wife: **This is your bill of divorce on the condition that you marry so-and-so,**[H] **she may not marry** that man, **but if she marries** him the marriage is valid and **she** need **not leave** her husband.

מַאי קָאָמַר? אָמַר רַב נַחְמָן, הָכִי קָאָמַר: הֲרֵי זוֹ לֹא תִּנָּשֵׂא לוֹ, שֶׁמָּא יֹאמְרוּ נְשׁוֹתֵיהֶן נוֹתְנִין בְּמַתָּנָה, וְאִם נִשֵּׂאת לְאַחֵר – לֹא תֵּצֵא.

The Gemara asks: **What is the** *baraita* **saying?** She is forbidden from marrying whom? **Rav Naḥman said** that **this is what the** *baraita* **is saying: She may not marry him,** i.e., she may not marry the man mentioned by her husband in the condition, **lest** people **say** that these people **are giving their wives** to each other **as a gift.**[N] **But if she marries another** man[H] **she** need **not leave** him.

וּמִשּׁוּם גְּזֵירָה לָא מַפְּקִינַן מִינֵּיהּ, וְשָׁרֵינַן אֵשֶׁת אִישׁ לְעָלְמָא?!

The Gemara asks: **Do we not remove her from him,** thereby **allowing a married woman to marry anyone, due to a** rabbinic **decree,** lest people say that the husband is giving her as a gift? As long as the condition that she would marry a specific man is not fulfilled, she is a married woman by Torah law.

אֶלָּא אָמַר רַב נַחְמָן, הָכִי קָאָמַר: הֲרֵי זוֹ לֹא תִּנָּשֵׂא לוֹ, שֶׁמָּא יֹאמְרוּ נְשׁוֹתֵיהֶם נוֹתְנִין בְּמַתָּנָה, וְאִם נִשֵּׂאת לוֹ – לֹא תֵּצֵא, דְּמִשּׁוּם גְּזֵירָה לָא מַפְּקִינַן.

Rather, Rav Naḥman said that **this is what the** *baraita* **is saying: She may not marry him,** i.e., the man who was specified in the condition, **lest** people **say** that **they are giving their wives** to each other **as a gift. But if she marries him**[H] **she** need **not leave** him, as **we do not remove** a woman from her husband **due to a decree.**

אֲמַר לֵיהּ רָבָא: לוֹ הוּא דְּלָא תִּנָּשֵׂא, הָא לְאַחֵר תִּנָּשֵׂא? וְהָא בָּעֵי קִיּוּמֵי לִתְנָאָה!

Rava said to Rav Naḥman: It may be inferred from your statement that **it is** specifically **to him that she may not get married, but she may marry another** man *ab initio*. **But isn't she required to fulfill the condition** by marrying the specified man before marrying someone else?

NOTES

These people are giving their wives to each other as a gift – נְשׁוֹתֵיהֶן נוֹתְנִין בְּמַתָּנָה: Such behavior is unquestionably indecent, as a man's wife is not his property and he cannot give her to other people. This behavior is also characteristic of licentiousness. Rav Naḥman's initial interpretation was that the woman is forbidden by rabbinic decree from marrying the man that her husband required her to marry, and the Sages instituted that if she marries another man she is not required to leave him, despite the fact that by Torah law she is still married to her ex-husband as long as she does not fulfill the condition. *Tosafot* explain that due to the seriousness of the matter, Rav Naḥman held that the Sages abrogated the betrothal of the original couple so that the woman would not be restricted by this condition.

NOTES

Once he separates her, he has separated her – כֵּיוָן דִּפְסָקָהּ פַּסְקָהּ: According to one explanation, since the bond is severed entirely, even though it is only for one day, it is a valid divorce (see Ritva). Most commentaries follow Rashi's explanation that once the bond is severed even for one day, they no longer return to being married and the divorce is complete.

HALAKHA

Once he separates her, etc. – כֵּיוָן דִּפְסָקָהּ וכו׳: If a man hands a bill of divorce to his wife and says to her: Today you are not my wife, and tomorrow you are my wife, it is uncertain whether or not the divorce takes effect because the early commentaries disagree concerning this matter. The Rambam holds that the woman is not divorced, based on the Gemara below (86a), while others (Rosh; Rashba), based on the conclusion of Rava and Rav Naḥman here (see 86a), maintain that she is divorced (Rambam *Sefer Nashim, Hilkhot Geirushin* 8:9; *Shulḥan Arukh, Even HaEzer* 137:5).

On the condition that you marry so-and-so – עַל מְנָת שֶׁתִּנָּשְׂאִי לִפְלוֹנִי: If a man hands his wife a bill of divorce and stipulates that she marry so-and-so, and she marries that man, the bill of divorce takes effect, as she has fulfilled the condition. The Sages decreed that she may not marry him, lest people say that they are giving their wives as gifts to each other. The Rema writes that if the husband's behavior indicates that he is divorcing her so that a certain man may marry her, she may not marry him even if it was not stipulated explicitly (Rambam *Sefer Nashim, Hilkhot Geirushin* 8:13; *Shulḥan Arukh, Even HaEzer* 143:15).

If she marries another man, etc. – אִם נִשֵּׂאת לְאַחֵר וכו׳: If a woman marries another man before marrying the man that her ex-husband stipulated that she should marry, the divorce is nullified, her children from her second marriage become *mamzerim*, and she must get divorced from her second husband, in accordance with Rava's statement. The Rema writes, based on the Ra'avad, that if she subsequently marries the man that her ex-husband mentioned, the divorce is retroactively revalidated and her children are no longer considered *mamzerim* (Rambam *Sefer Nashim, Hilkhot Geirushin* 8:13; *Shulḥan Arukh, Even HaEzer* 143:15).

But if she marries him – וְאִם נִשֵּׂאת לוֹ: If a woman was divorced on the condition that she would marry a specific man, although she is prohibited from marrying him by rabbinic law, if she does marry him she does not have to leave him. And if she marries him and is then divorced she is subsequently permitted to marry any man (Rambam *Sefer Nashim, Hilkhot Geirushin* 8:13; *Shulḥan Arukh, Even HaEzer* 143:15).

וְכִי תֵּימָא, אֶפְשָׁר דְּמִינַּסְבָא הַיּוֹם וּמִיגָּרְשָׁה לְמָחָר וּמְקַיְּימָא לִתְנָאָה, וּלְהַךְ דִּפְלִיגַת עֲלֵיהּ דְּרַב יְהוּדָה קָמְדַמֵּית לֵיהּ. דְּאִתְּמַר: ״קוֹנָם עֵינַי בְּשֵׁינָה הַיּוֹם אִם אִישַׁן לְמָחָר״, אָמַר רַב יְהוּדָה: אַל יִישַׁן הַיּוֹם שֶׁמָּא יִישַׁן לְמָחָר,

And if you would say that **it is possible for her to get married today** to someone else **and get divorced** from him **tomorrow and** then **fulfill** her **condition**[N] by marrying the specified man, **and you can compare it to that** *halakha* **over which you disagree with Rav Yehuda. As it was stated** with regard to one who says: **Sleeping** is forbidden to me **as if** it were **an offering** [***konam***][B] **for my eyes today**[H] **if I will sleep tomorrow, Rav Yehuda says** that **he may not sleep today lest he sleep tomorrow,** causing the vow to have been violated today, retroactively.

וְרַב נַחְמָן אָמַר: יִישַׁן הַיּוֹם וְאֵין חוֹשְׁשִׁין שֶׁמָּא יִישַׁן לְמָחָר.

And Rav Naḥman says: He may sleep today, as there is currently no prohibition, **and we are not concerned that perhaps he will sleep tomorrow,** as he will be careful not to sleep. This dispute pertains to the general issue of a prohibition that will take effect retroactively if a condition is not fulfilled. Rav Yehuda holds that the prohibition must be observed until the condition is fulfilled, whereas Rav Naḥman maintains that it is not necessary to observe the prohibition, as he assumes that the condition will be fulfilled. Here too, perhaps Rav Naḥman allows the woman to marry another man because she can fulfill the condition after she is divorced from him.

הָכִי הָשְׁתָּא? הָתָם בִּדִידֵיהּ קַיְימָא, דְּאִי בָּעֵי מַבְרִיז נַפְשֵׁיהּ בְּסִילְוָאתָא וְלָא נָאֵים, הָכָא בְּדִידָהּ קַיְימָא לְאִיגָּרוּשֵׁי?

How can these cases **be compared? There,** in the case of the vow, the fulfillment of the condition **is in his capability, as, if he wants** to prevent himself from falling asleep **he can prick himself with thorns** [*silevata*][L] **and he will not fall asleep. Here, is it in the** woman's power **to get divorced?** Perhaps her husband will not agree to divorce her and the condition will not be fulfilled.

אֶלָּא אָמַר רָבָא: הֲרֵי זוֹ לֹא תִּנָּשֵׂא לֹא לוֹ וְלֹא לְאַחֵר, לוֹ לֹא תִּנָּשֵׂא – שֶׁמָּא יֹאמְרוּ נְשׁוֹתֵיהֶם נוֹתְנִין בְּמַתָּנָה, לְאַחֵר לֹא תִּנָּשֵׂא – דְּבָעֲיָא קִיּוּמֵיהּ לִתְנָאָה;

Rather, Rava said that the *baraita* should be interpreted in the following manner: **This** woman **may marry neither** the man who was specified in the condition **nor another** man. **She may not marry him lest** people **say** that these men **are giving their wives** to each other **as a gift,** and **she may not marry another** man **because she is required to fulfill** the condition.

וְאִם נִשֵּׂאת, לוֹ – לֹא תֵּצֵא, דְּמִשּׁוּם גְּזֵירָה לָא מַפְּקִינַן, לְאַחֵר – תֵּצֵא, דְּבָעֲיָא לְקִיּוּמֵיהּ לִתְנָאָה.

And if she marries the specified man **she** need **not leave** him, **as we do not remove** a woman from her husband **due to a decree.** But if she gets married **to another** man **she must leave** him, **as she is required to fulfill** the **condition** before marrying another man.

תַּנְיָא כְּוָותֵיהּ דְּרָבָא: הֲרֵי זוֹ לֹא תִּנָּשֵׂא, לֹא לוֹ וְלֹא לְאַחֵר, וְאִם נִשֵּׂאת לוֹ – לֹא תֵּצֵא, לְאַחֵר – תֵּצֵא.

It is taught in a *baraita* **in accordance with** the opinion **of Rava: This** woman **may marry neither him nor another** man, **but if she marries him** she need **not leave** him. But if she gets married **to another** man **she must leave** him.

תָּנוּ רַבָּנַן: ״הֲרֵי זֶה גִּיטֵּךְ עַל מְנָת שֶׁתַּעֲלִי לָרָקִיעַ״, ״עַל מְנָת שֶׁתֵּרְדִי לַתְּהוֹם״, ״עַל מְנָת שֶׁתִּבְלְעִי קָנֶה שֶׁל אַרְבַּע אַמּוֹת״, ״עַל מְנָת שֶׁתָּבִיאִי לִי קָנֶה בֶּן מֵאָה אַמָּה״, ״עַל מְנָת שֶׁתַּעַבְרִי אֶת הַיָּם הַגָּדוֹל בְּרַגְלַיִךְ״ – אֵינוֹ גֵּט.

§ **The Sages taught** (*Tosefta* 7:8) that if a man says to his wife: **This is your bill of divorce on the condition that you ascend to the sky,**[H] or **on the condition that you descend to the depths** of the sea, or **on the condition that you swallow a four-cubit reed,** or **on the condition that you bring me a hundred-cubit reed,** or **on the condition that you cross the Great Sea,** i.e., the Mediterranean Sea, **by foot,** or on any other condition that it is impossible to fulfill, **it is not** a valid **bill of divorce.**

רַבִּי יְהוּדָה בֶּן תֵּימָא אוֹמֵר: כָּזֶה גֵּט. כְּלָל אָמַר רַבִּי יְהוּדָה בֶּן תֵּימָא: כָּל תְּנַאי שֶׁאִי אֶפְשָׁר לוֹ לְקַיְּימוֹ בְּסוֹפוֹ וְהִתְנָה עָלָיו מִתְּחִילָּתוֹ, אֵינוֹ אֶלָּא כִּמְפַלִּיגָהּ בִּדְבָרִים, וְכָשֵׁר.

Rabbi Yehuda ben Teima says: A bill of divorce **like this** is a valid **bill of divorce,** as the condition is void. **Rabbi Yehuda ben Teima said** the following **principle:** With regard to **any condition that cannot be fulfilled in the end, yet** even so the husband **stipulated it initially, he is only hyperbolizing.** It is assumed that he did not really intend to attach a condition to the divorce, but rather, to cause her distress, **and** therefore the divorce **is valid** without her fulfilling the condition.

NOTES

And get divorced from him tomorrow and then fulfill her condition – וּמִיגָּרְשָׁה לְמָחָר וּמְקַיְּימָא לִתְנָאָה: *Tosafot* explain that once the woman marries another man and is divorced from him, she is permitted to marry the specified man, as it no longer seems as if her first husband and this man were exchanging wives.

BACKGROUND

Konam – **קוֹנָם:** A *konam* is a type of vow, whose *halakhot* are explained at length in tractate *Nedarim*. The word *konam* refers to a sacrifice, that is to say, one renders an item forbidden to himself as though it were a sacrifice. One of the basic principles of a *konam* is that it cannot apply to an action or an abstract state, but only to an object the likes of which can be consecrated. Therefore, the phrase: Benefiting from so-and-so is *konam* for me, in essence means that I render forbidden deriving benefit from so-and-so, just as an offering is forbidden to me (see *Tosafot*).

HALAKHA

Sleeping is forbidden to me as if it were an offering for my eyes today, etc. – קוֹנָם עֵינַי בְּשֵׁינָה הַיּוֹם וכו׳: If one says: Sleeping is forbidden to me as if it were an offering for my eyes today if I will sleep tomorrow, he may not sleep today lest he forget and sleep tomorrow, in accordance with Rav Yehuda's opinion (Rambam *Sefer Hafla'a, Hilkhot Nedarim* 4:14; *Shulḥan Arukh, Yoreh De'a* 213:3).

On the condition that you ascend to the sky – עַל מְנָת שֶׁתַּעֲלִי לָרָקִיעַ: If he gives her a bill of divorce and attaches a condition that cannot be fulfilled, e.g., that she should ascend to the sky or descend to the depths of the sea, that is not a valid condition, and the divorce takes effect without her having fulfilled the condition. This is in accordance with the statement of Rabbi Yehuda ben Teima (Rambam *Sefer Nashim, Hilkhot Ishut* 6:7; *Shulḥan Arukh, Even HaEzer* 143:12).

LANGUAGE

Thorns [*silevata*] – **סִילְוָאתָא:** This refers to the thorns of a palm tree, like the Arabic سلاء, *sulā'*. They are small leaves that grow on palm fronds and become hard and thorny after a time, and getting pricked by them is very painful. In the language of the mishna thorns are referred to as *sol*, and the word may be connected to the biblical word *sallon* (Ezekiel 2:6, 28:24), which also refers to a prickly thorn.

אָמַר רַב נַחְמָן אָמַר רַב: הֲלָכָה כְּרַבִּי יְהוּדָה בֶּן תֵּימָא. אָמַר רַב נַחְמָן בַּר יִצְחָק: מַתְנִיתִין נַמִּי דַּיְקָא, דְּקָתָנֵי: כָּל שֶׁאֶפְשָׁר לוֹ לְקַיְּימוֹ בְּסוֹפוֹ וְהִתְנָה עָלָיו בִּתְחִילָּתוֹ – תְּנָאוֹ קַיָּים, הָא אִי אֶפְשָׁר – תְּנָאוֹ בָּטֵל, שְׁמַע מִינָּהּ.

Rav Naḥman says that Rav says: **The** *halakha* **is in accordance with** the opinion of **Rabbi Yehuda ben Teima. Rav Naḥman bar Yitzḥak says:** The language of **the mishna is also precisely** formulated in support of this opinion, **as it teaches:** With regard to any condition **that can be fulfilled in the end and** the husband **stipulated** it **initially, his condition stands** (*Bava Metzia* 94a). **Consequently, if his condition cannot** be fulfilled **it is void.** The Gemara concludes: **Learn from it** that the *halakha* is in accordance with the opinion of Rabbi Yehuda ben Teima.

אִיבַּעְיָא לְהוּ: "הֲרֵי זֶה גִּיטֵּיךְ עַל מְנָת שֶׁתֹּאכְלִי בְּשַׂר חֲזִיר", מַהוּ? אָמַר אַבָּיֵי: הִיא הִיא; רָבָא אָמַר: אֶפְשָׁר דְּאָכְלָה וְלָקְיָא.

A dilemma was raised before the Sages: If a husband said to his wife: **This is your bill of divorce on the condition that you eat pig meat, what is** the *halakha*? **Abaye said: It is the same.** This is also a condition that cannot be fulfilled, as it is forbidden by Torah law. Therefore, the condition is void. **Rava said: It is possible for her to eat** it **and be flogged** for it. Consequently, the condition can be fulfilled, although it is forbidden for her to do so.

לְאַבָּיֵי, "כְּלָל" – לְאַתּוֹיֵי בְּשַׂר חֲזִיר; לְרָבָא, "כָּזֶה" – לְמַעוֹטֵי בְּשַׂר חֲזִיר.

The Gemara elaborates: **According to Abaye,** the **principle** stated by Rabbi Yehuda ben Teima serves **to include** a condition to eat **pig meat.** When a *tanna* states a general principle, it expands the *halakha* beyond the specific case mentioned previously. In this case, the stating of the principle serves to apply the *halakha* to a condition subject to a Torah prohibition, in addition to a physical impossibility. **According to Rava,** when Rabbi Yehuda ben Teima stated: A bill of divorce **like this** is a valid bill of divorce, the limiting term of: Like this, serves to emphasize that only when there is a condition that cannot be physically fulfilled is the bill of divorce valid, and serves **to exclude** a condition to eat **pig meat,** which cannot be fulfilled due to a Torah prohibition. Therefore, if she does not fulfill this condition the divorce is invalid.

מֵיתִיבִי: "הֲרֵי זֶה גִּיטֵּךְ עַל מְנָת שֶׁתִּבָּעֲלִי לִפְלוֹנִי", נִתְקַיֵּים הַתְּנַאי – הֲרֵי זֶה גֵּט, וְאִם לָאו – אֵינוֹ גֵּט, "עַל מְנָת שֶׁלֹּא תִּבָּעֲלִי לְאַבָּא וּלְאָבִיךְ" – אֵין חוֹשְׁשִׁין שֶׁמָּא נִבְעֲלָה לָהֶן;

The Gemara **raises an objection** to Rava's opinion from a *baraita*: If a man says to his wife: **This is your bill of divorce on the condition that you engage in sexual intercourse with so-and-so,**[H] and **the condition is fulfilled, this is a** valid **bill of divorce. And if** the condition is **not** fulfilled then **it is not** a valid **bill of divorce.** If he says to her: **On the condition that you do not engage in sexual intercourse with my father**[H] **or your father,** she is permitted to remarry, as **we are not concerned that perhaps she engaged in sexual intercourse with them.**

וְאִילּוּ "עַל מְנָת שֶׁתִּבָּעֲלִי לְאַבָּא וּלְאָבִיךְ" לָא קָתָנֵי; לְאַבָּיֵי נִיחָא, לְרָבָא קַשְׁיָא!

But the *baraita* **does not teach** that the condition is binding when the husband says: **On the condition that you engage in sexual intercourse with my father**[H] **or your father,** which is forbidden by Torah law. **According to Abaye** it **works out well,** as in his opinion a condition that violates Torah law is void. **According to Rava** it is **difficult.**

אָמַר לָךְ רָבָא: בִּשְׁלָמָא בְּשַׂר חֲזִיר – אֶפְשָׁר דְּאָכְלָה וְלָקְיָא, פְּלוֹנִי – נַמִּי אֶפְשָׁר דִּמְשַׁחֲדָא בֵּיהּ בְּמָמוֹנָא, אֶלָּא אַבָּא וְאָבִיךְ בִּדִידָהּ קַיְימָא? נְהִי דְּאִיהִי עָבְדָא אִיסּוּרָא, אַבָּא וְאָבִיךְ מִי עָבְדִי אִיסּוּרָא?

The Gemara answers that **Rava** could have **said to you: Granted,** with regard to **pig meat it is possible for her to eat** it **and be flogged.** Similarly, if the condition is that she engage in sexual intercourse with **so-and-so, it is also possible for her to bribe him**[N] **with money** to engage in sexual intercourse with her. **But** with regard to the case of my **father or your father, is it in her** power to engage in sexual intercourse with them? **Though she** can potentially **perform a forbidden act** in order to fulfill her desire to get married, **would my father or your father perform a forbidden act?** They certainly would not cooperate. Therefore, this is a condition cannot be fulfilled, and it is considered hyperbole.

לְרָבָא, "כְּלָל" – לְאַתּוֹיֵי אַבָּא וְאָבִיךְ, "כָּזֶה" – לְמַעוֹטֵי בְּשַׂר חֲזִיר;

Based on this analysis, **according to Rava,** Rabbi Yehuda ben Teima stated his **principle** in order **to include** the condition of **my father and your father,** as this condition is also considered impossible to fulfill. And the expression: A bill of divorce **like this** is a valid bill of divorce, serves **to exclude** the condition of eating **pig meat,** in which case the divorce is not valid unless she fulfills the condition.

HALAKHA

On the condition that you engage in sexual intercourse with so-and-so – עַל מְנָת שֶׁתִּבָּעֲלִי לִפְלוֹנִי: If the husband stipulated while giving her the bill of divorce that it would be valid on the condition that she engage in sexual intercourse with so-and-so, and she subsequently engages in intercourse with him, whether in the context of marriage or not, the condition is fulfilled and the divorce is valid. It is noted in the Jerusalem Talmud that she may not engage in sexual intercourse with him *ab initio*, as she is not divorced until they engage in sexual intercourse, which renders the beginning of the act of intercourse forbidden (*Shulḥan Arukh, Even HaEzer* 143:18).

On the condition that you do not engage in sexual intercourse with my father – עַל מְנָת שֶׁלֹּא תִּבָּעֲלִי לְאַבָּא: If a man stipulated while giving his wife a bill of divorce that it would be valid on the condition that she may not engage in sexual intercourse with his father, there is no concern that she violated the condition in the past or that she will do so in the future, and she is therefore permitted to remarry *ab initio* (Rema). If there are witnesses who can attest that she engaged in sexual intercourse with him, the divorce is void (*Shulḥan Arukh, Even HaEzer* 143:18).

On the condition that you engage in sexual intercourse with my father – עַל מְנָת שֶׁתִּבָּעֲלִי לְאַבָּא: If the husband stipulated that she perform a forbidden act that requires the participation of others, e.g., engaging in sexual intercourse with his father, the condition is invalid, as his father would not agree to do this (Rambam *Sefer Nashim, Hilkhot Ishut* 6:11; *Shulḥan Arukh, Even HaEzer* 143:12).

NOTES

It is also possible for her to bribe him – נַמִּי אֶפְשָׁר דִּמְשַׁחֲדָא בֵּיהּ: Rashi and the Ramah explain that she can bribe or persuade him to engage in sexual intercourse with her because he can do so in a permitted manner by marrying her. Other commentaries maintain that the condition refers specifically to sexual intercourse outside of marriage, and nevertheless the *baraita* draws a distinction between sexual intercourse with an unrelated man and sexual intercourse with her father or father-in-law (Ritva). The reason for this distinction is that engaging in licentiousness is a relatively minor prohibition and a person can possibly be bribed to transgress it, as opposed to incest, which is an exceptionally grave sin.

HALAKHA

That you eat pig meat, etc. – שֶׁתֹּאכְלִי בְּשַׂר חֲזִיר וכו׳: If a man divorces his wife on the condition that she will perform a forbidden act, such as eating pig meat, the condition is valid. If she does not fulfill the condition then she is not divorced, in accordance with the opinion of Rava (Rambam *Sefer Nashim, Hilkhot Ishut* 6:8; *Shulḥan Arukh, Even HaEzer* 143:12).

Stipulates counter to that which is written in the Torah – הַמַּתְנֶה עַל מַה שֶּׁכָּתוּב בַּתּוֹרָה: If a person stipulates counter to that which is written in the Torah, his condition is void, except with regard to monetary issues, in which case his condition stands. Therefore, if a man betroths a woman on the condition that he is not obligated to provide her with clothing and food, his condition stands, as these are monetary obligations. If he stipulates that he is not obligated to meet her conjugal rights, his condition is void and he is still obligated, as this is not a monetary issue. The Rema cites an opinion that a rabbinic ordinance is treated like Torah law with regard to this issue (Rambam *Sefer Nashim, Hilkhot Ishut* 6:8–10; *Shulḥan Arukh, Even HaEzer* 143:12).

NOTES

As he is definitely uprooting, etc. – דְּוַדַּאי קָא עָקַר וכו׳: This does not mean that he will necessarily violate his obligation to his wife, as he can choose not to fulfill the condition. Rather, the condition itself counters Torah law, as a man cannot betroth a woman without being obligated to provide her with food, clothing, and conjugal rights.

לְאַבַּיֵי, ״כְּלָל״ – לְאַתּוּיֵי בְּשַׂר חֲזִיר, ״כָּזֶה״ – לְמַעוּטֵי פְּלוֹנִי.

And **according to Abaye** this **principle** was stated **to include** the case of a condition that she should eat **pig meat,** and the expression: A bill of divorce **like this** is a valid bill of divorce, serves **to exclude** a condition that she should engage in sexual intercourse with **so-and-so,** in which case the divorce takes effect only once the condition is fulfilled, as it is possible to fulfill this condition in a permitted manner.

מֵיתִיבִי: ״הֲרֵי זֶה גִּיטֵּךְ עַל מְנָת שֶׁתֹּאכְלִי בְּשַׂר חֲזִיר״, וְאִם הָיְתָה זָרָה ״עַל מְנָת שֶׁתֹּאכְלִי בִּתְרוּמָה״, וְאִם הָיְתָה נְזִירָה ״עַל מְנָת שֶׁתִּשְׁתִּי יַיִן״, נִתְקַיֵּים הַתְּנַאי – הֲרֵי זֶה גֵּט, וְאִם לָאו – אֵינוֹ גֵּט; לְרָבָא נִיחָא, לְאַבַּיֵי קַשְׁיָא!

The Gemara **raises an objection** from another *baraita* (*Tosefta* 6:10): If the husband said to his wife: **This is your bill of divorce on the condition that you eat pig meat;**[H] **or** similarly, **if she was a non-priestess,** i.e., the daughter of an Israelite, and he stipulated: **On the condition that you partake of** ***teruma*****; or if she was a nazirite** and he stipulated: **On the condition that you drink wine** (see Numbers 6:3); in all of these cases, if **the condition is fulfilled it is** a valid **bill of divorce, and if not, it is not** a valid **bill of divorce.** This **works out well according to Rava,** who holds that a condition that she should perform a forbidden act is binding; **according to Abaye** it **is difficult.**

אָמַר לָךְ אַבַּיֵי: מִי סָבְרַתְּ דִּבְרֵי הַכֹּל הִיא? הָא מַנִּי – רַבָּנַן הִיא.

The Gemara answers that **Abaye** could have **said to you: Do you hold** that this ruling **is agreed** upon **by everyone?** That is not the case. Rather, in accordance with **whose** opinion **is this** *baraita*? **It is** in accordance with the opinion of **the Rabbis,** who disagree with Rabbi Yehuda ben Teima, maintaining that even a condition that cannot be fulfilled is a valid condition.

וְתֵיפּוֹק לֵיהּ דְּמַתְנֶה עַל מַה שֶּׁכָּתוּב בַּתּוֹרָה הוּא, וְכָל הַמַּתְנֶה עַל מַה שֶּׁכָּתוּב בַּתּוֹרָה – תְּנָאוֹ בָּטֵל!

The Gemara challenges: Regardless of the issue of a condition that cannot be fulfilled, **derive** that this condition is void from the fact **that** the husband **is stipulating counter to that which is written in the Torah, and** there is a principle that with regard to **anyone who stipulates counter to that which is written in the Torah,**[H] **his condition is void.**

אֲמַר רַב אַדָּא בְּרֵיהּ דְּרַב אִיקָא: כִּי אָמְרִינַן מַתְנֶה עַל מַה שֶּׁכָּתוּב בַּתּוֹרָה תְּנָאוֹ בָּטֵל – כְּגוֹן שְׁאֵרָהּ כְּסוּתָהּ וְעוֹנָתָהּ, דְּהוּא קָא עָקַר, אֲבָל הָכָא אִיהִי קָא עָקְרָה.

Rav Adda son of Rav Ika said in response: **When we say** that if one **stipulates counter to that which is written in the Torah his condition is void,** the reference is to a case **such as** a man who betroths a woman on the condition that he will not be obligated to provide her with **her food, her clothing, and her conjugal rights,** as there **he is uprooting** a matter of Torah law by fulfilling the condition. **But here,** it is **she** who **is uprooting** a matter of Torah law by fulfilling the condition and not him.

מַתְקִיף לָהּ רָבִינָא: כְּלוּם קָא עָקְרָה אִיהִי אֶלָּא לְקַיּוּמֵי לִתְנַאי דִּידֵיהּ, אִישְׁתַּכַּח דְּאִיהוּ קָא עָקַר!

Ravina strongly objects to this response: **Isn't she uprooting** it **only** in order **to fulfill his condition?** It is therefore **found that he is uprooting** a matter of Torah law by attaching this condition to the divorce.

אֶלָּא אֲמַר רָבִינָא: כִּי אָמְרִינַן מַתְנֶה עַל מַה שֶּׁכָּתוּב בַּתּוֹרָה תְּנָאוֹ בָּטֵל – כְּגוֹן שְׁאֵרָהּ כְּסוּתָהּ וְעוֹנָתָהּ, דְּוַדַּאי קָא עָקַר, אֲבָל הָכָא מִי קָאָמַר לָהּ לָא סַגְיָא דְּלָא אָכְלָה? לָא תֵּיכוּל וְלָא תִּיגָּרֵשׁ.

Rather, Ravina said: When we say that if one **stipulates counter to that which is written in the Torah,** that **his condition is void,** the reference is to a case **such as** that of a man who stipulates that he will not be obligated to provide his wife with **her food, her clothing, and her conjugal rights, as** by attaching this condition **he is definitely uprooting**[N] a matter of Torah law. **But here, is he saying to her** that it is **not possible for her not to eat? She may not eat and not get divorced.** The condition does not counter Torah law in and of itself, as the wife has the choice of whether or not to fulfill it.

״כֵּיצַד יַעֲשֶׂה? יִטְּלֶנּוּ הֵימֶנָּה״ וכו׳. מַאן תַּנָּא? אָמַר חִזְקִיָּה: רַבִּי שִׁמְעוֹן בֶּן אֶלְעָזָר הִיא;

§ It is stated in the mishna: **What should he do** after giving her the bill of divorce and stipulating that she is not permitted to so-and-so? **He should take it from her,** and hand it to her again, and say to her: You are hereby permitted to marry any man. The Gemara asks: **Who** is the *tanna* who **taught** that? **Ḥizkiyya said** that **it is Rabbi Shimon ben Elazar.**

דְּתַנְיָא, רַבִּי שִׁמְעוֹן בֶּן אֶלְעָזָר אוֹמֵר: עַד שֶׁיִּטְּלֶנּוּ הֵימֶנָּה, וְיַחֲזוֹר וְיִתְּנֶנּוּ לָהּ וְיֹאמַר לָהּ ״הֵי גִּיטֵּיךְ״.

As it is taught in a *baraita*: If a husband gives his wife a bill of divorce without her knowledge, **Rabbi Shimon ben Elazar says** that it does not take effect **until he takes it from her, and hands it to her again, and says to her: This is your bill of divorce.** Rabbi Yehuda HaNasi holds that it is not necessary for him to hand it to her a second time; rather, it is sufficient for him to tell her that he is giving her a bill of divorce. The mishna is therefore in accordance with the opinion of Rabbi Shimon ben Elazar, who holds that the husband must hand it to her again.

רַבִּי יוֹחָנָן אָמַר: אֲפִילּוּ תֵּימָא רַבִּי, דִּילְכוֹן אָמַר: שָׁאנֵי הָכָא, הוֹאִיל וּקְנָאַתּוּ לִיפָּסֵל בּוֹ לִכְהוּנָּה.

Rabbi Yoḥanan said: You can **even say** that it is in accordance with the opinion of **Rabbi** Yehuda HaNasi.[H] **Your** Sage, referring to Rav Kahana, who came from Babylonia to study in Eretz Yisrael, **said**[N] that **it is different here, since**[N] the wife has already **acquired** the bill of divorce with regard **to** her **becoming disqualified** from marrying **into the priesthood due to it,** and Rabbi Yehuda HaNasi holds that he need not take it back and give it to her again. Since the bill of divorce was already partially effective, it is in the wife's possession and cannot be used by the husband to divorce her in full unless she gives it back to him and he gives it to her again. Therefore, even Rabbi Yehuda HaNasi agrees that he must give it to her a second time.

״כְּתָבוֹ בְּתוֹכוֹ״. אָמַר רַב סָפְרָא: כְּתָבוֹ בְּתוֹכוֹ תְּנַן.

§ It is stated in the mishna that if the husband **wrote** his qualification **inside** the bill of divorce, it is invalid even if he subsequently erased it. **Rav Safra said: We learned** in the mishna that the bill is invalid only if **he wrote** the qualification **inside** the bill of divorce, not if he stated it orally.

פְּשִׁיטָא, ״כְּתָבוֹ בְּתוֹכוֹ״ תְּנַן! מַהוּ דְּתֵימָא הָנֵי מִילֵּי לְאַחַר הַתּוֹרֶף, אֲבָל לִפְנֵי הַתּוֹרֶף – אֲפִילּוּ עַל פֶּה נַמִּי פָּסוּל, קָא מַשְׁמַע לָן.

The Gemara asks: It **is obvious** that this is the case, as **we learned** in the mishna explicitly that **he wrote it inside.** The Gemara answers: Rav Safra stated this **lest you say** that **this matter applies** only when the qualification was written **after the essential** part of the bill of divorce, which contains the names of the husband and wife and the date, **but before the essential** part[H] was written; **even** if the qualification was stated **orally,** the bill of divorce is **invalid,** as it was written with the intention that the wife would not be permitted to marry any man. Rav Safra therefore **teaches us** that only a written qualification in the bill of divorce renders it invalid, and an oral statement does not render it invalid. Consequently, the husband can hand this bill of divorce to his wife without stating the qualification and it will be valid.

וְרָבָא אָמַר: לֹא שָׁנוּ אֶלָּא לְאַחַר הַתּוֹרֶף, אֲבָל לִפְנֵי הַתּוֹרֶף – אֲפִילּוּ עַל פֶּה נַמִּי פָּסוּל.

And Rava said: They taught that it is specifically writing the qualification that invalidates the bill of divorce **only** when the qualification is stated **after** the writing of **the essential part.**[N] **But** if the qualification is stated **before the essential** part of the bill of divorce is written, **even** if it is stated **orally,** the bill of divorce **is invalid.**

וְאָזְדָא רָבָא לְטַעְמֵיהּ, דַּאֲמַר לְהוּ רָבָא לְהָנְהוּ דְּכָתְבִי גִּיטֵּי: שַׁתְּקוּ שְׁתוּקֵי לְבַעַל עַד דְּכָתְבִיתוּ לֵיהּ לַתּוֹרֶף דְּגִיטָּא.

And Rava followed his line of **reasoning, as Rava said to those who write bills of divorce: Silence** the **husband until you write the essential** part **of the bill of divorce,** lest he state a condition, thereby rendering the bill of divorce invalid.

NOTES

Your Sage said – דִּילְכוֹן אָמַר: In the Jerusalem Talmud it is explicit that Rabbi Yoḥanan is referring to Rav Kahana. This can be inferred in the Babylonian Talmud as well from tractate *Bava Kamma* (117b). Rashi explains that Rabbi Yoḥanan said this to Ḥizkiyya, who was originally from Babylonia. *Tosafot* question this explanation, as Rav Kahana apparently went to Eretz Yisrael only after Ḥizkiyya's death. They explain, therefore, that Rabbi Yoḥanan said this to his Babylonian students, as many of his greatest students were from Babylonia. The Rashba answers that the Ḥizkiyya mentioned here is not Ḥizkiyya, son of Rabbi Ḥiyya the Great, who was Rabbi Yoḥanan's teacher; rather, it refers to another Ḥizkiyya, who was the grandson of the *amora* Rav.

It is different here since, etc. – שָׁאנֵי הָכָא, הוֹאִיל וכו׳: Rashi and most early commentaries explain that although the husband did not render his wife permitted to marry any man, which invalidates the divorce according to the Rabbis, there is still the trace of a bill of divorce, which disqualifies her from marrying a priest, as mentioned earlier (82b). Since the divorce took effect to some degree, the bill can be used to complete the divorce only if the husband takes it back and hands it to her again.

The Rashba questions this explanation, asking how a bill of divorce can be used a second time after it already took effect. Based on the opinion of the Rambam that this woman is disqualified from marrying a priest only by rabbinic law, the Rashba suggests that the first use of the document was not significant enough to prevent it from being used again. Nevertheless, he questions the validity of the Rambam's opinion.

Rabbeinu Ḥananel has a version of the text that replaces: It is different here, with: It is different there. According to this version, in the case of a husband who handed a bill of divorce to his wife without her knowledge, it is unnecessary for him to hand it to her a second time because the divorce is essentially valid, as by Torah law the wife's consent is not a requirement. Here, the initial act of handing her the bill of divorce was worthless, since he did not render her permitted to marry any man. The Rashba rejects this version of the text.

Only after the writing of the essential part, etc. – אֶלָּא לְאַחַר הַתּוֹרֶף וכו׳: There are two approaches to understanding Rava's opinion. One approach is that stating an exception before the essential part of the bill of divorce is written renders the bill of divorce fundamentally invalid, as the bill was written with the intention that it would enact a partial divorce. In *Tosefot HaRosh* it is noted that this reasoning accords with the opinion of the *tanna* Rabbi Elazar, who maintains that a bill of divorce must be written with appropriate intention (see 23a). Consequently, the Sages issued a decree that stating an exception even after the essential part is written, but before the standard part is written, renders the bill invalid, so that people do not confuse the two cases. Likewise, they issued a decree that before the essential part is written, any stipulation that the husband states invalidates the bill, so that people do not assume that it is valid in a case of exception as well. Nevertheless, a mere stipulation that is stated, or even written, after the writing of the essential part does not invalidate the bill of divorce, as that would constitute a decree that is enacted in order to prevent the violation of a decree (Rashi; *Tosafot*).

Another approach is that stating an exception orally before the essential part is written does not render the bill of divorce fundamentally invalid, as by handing it to his wife without qualification the husband is considered as having retracted his qualification. Rather, this is a rabbinic decree, issued due to the case of an exception written in the bill. Consequently, this decree pertains only to a case of exception, as ruling that a condition to invalidate the bill of divorce, even if it is stated before the essential part, would constitute a decree that is enacted in order to prevent the violation of a decree (*Sefer HaIttur*; Ramban; Rabbeinu Crescas Vidal).

HALAKHA

You can even say that it is in accordance with the opinion of Rabbi Yehuda HaNasi, etc. – אֲפִילּוּ תֵּימָא רַבִּי וכו׳: If a man hands his wife a bill of divorce and says to her: You are hereby permitted to marry any man except for so-and-so, he can rectify the matter by taking it back, handing it to her a second time, and saying to her: You are hereby permitted to marry any man. This is in accordance with the opinion of Rabbi Yoḥanan that all *tanna'im* agree with the ruling of the mishna (Rambam *Sefer Nashim, Hilkhot Geirushin* 8:17; *Shulḥan Arukh, Even HaEzer* 137:1).

Before the essential part – לִפְנֵי הַתּוֹרֶף: If the husband stated a condition orally before the essential part of the bill of divorce was written, the Rambam rules that by Torah law this is considered an uncertain divorce, even if it is an ordinary condition. It is cited in the *Beit Shmuel* that many authorities hold that the divorce is invalid only in a case of exception, and only by rabbinic law. With regard to a condition, they hold that even by rabbinic law the divorce is valid. The conclusion reached in the *Beit Shmuel*, as well as in the *Beit Yosef*, is that where the husband attaches a condition in this manner and it is fulfilled, the divorce should be relied upon so as to avoid a situation where the woman is left as a deserted wife.

In a case of exception all authorities agree that the bill of divorce is invalid, in accordance with the opinion of Rava, but they disagree with regard to the degree to which the document is invalid. Rashi and *Tosafot* claim that it is completely invalid by Torah law, while the Rambam holds that it is considered an uncertain divorce, and others (Ra'avad; Ramban) maintain that it is invalid by rabbinic law (Rambam *Sefer Nashim, Hilkhot Geirushin* 8:4; *Shulḥan Arukh, Even HaEzer* 147:2).

תָּנוּ רַבָּנַן: כׇּל הַתְּנָאִין פּוֹסְלִין בְּגֵט, דִּבְרֵי רַבִּי; וַחֲכָמִים אוֹמְרִים: כׇּל שֶׁפּוֹסֵל עַל פֶּה פּוֹסֵל בִּכְתָב, וְכׇל שֶׁאֵינוֹ פּוֹסֵל עַל פֶּה אֵינוֹ פּוֹסֵל בִּכְתָב, "חוּץ" שֶׁפּוֹסֵל עַל פֶּה – פּוֹסֵל בִּכְתָב, "עַל מְנָת" שֶׁאֵינוֹ פּוֹסֵל עַל פֶּה – אֵינוֹ פּוֹסֵל בִּכְתָב.

The Sages taught: All conditions that are written **in a bill of divorce invalidate** it, this is **the statement of Rabbi** Yehuda HaNasi. **And the Rabbis say: Any** qualification **that invalidates** the divorce when stated **orally** by the husband while he hands the bill of divorce to his wife **invalidates** it **when written,**[N] **and any** qualification **that does not invalidate** it when stated **orally does not invalidate** it **when written.** Therefore, issuing a qualification that she is permitted to marry any man **except** for so-and-so, **which invalidates** the divorce when stated **orally, invalidates** it as well **when written,** whereas attaching a standard **condition, which does not invalidate** it when stated **orally, does not invalidate** it **when written.**

אֲמַר רַבִּי זֵירָא: מַחֲלוֹקֶת – לִפְנֵי הַתּוֹרֶף, דְּרַבִּי סָבַר: גָּזְרִינַן "עַל מְנָת" אַטּוּ "חוּץ", וְרַבָּנַן סָבְרִי: לָא גָּזְרִינַן "עַל מְנָת" אַטּוּ "חוּץ". אֲבָל לְאַחַר הַתּוֹרֶף

Rabbi Zeira said: This **dispute** applies to a case where the condition was written in the bill of divorce **before the essential** part was written, as **Rabbi** Yehuda HaNasi **holds** that **we issue a decree** that a **stipulation** invalidates the bill of divorce **due to** a case of an **exception, and the Rabbis hold** that **we do not issue a decree** that a **stipulation** invalidates it **due to** a case of **an exception. But** if it was written **after the essential** part,

NOTES

Any qualification that invalidates the divorce when stated orally invalidates it when written – כָּל שֶׁפּוֹסֵל עַל פֶּה פּוֹסֵל בִּכְתָב: The Meiri points out that the term orally in this *baraita* refers here not to the manner in which the qualification was made, but rather, to the stage at which it was made, i.e., the handing of the bill of divorce to the woman, as opposed to the writing of the bill.

While the commentaries agree with regard to the understanding of the term orally, they disagree with regard to the reference of the term written. Some explain that this too refers to the stage at which the bill of divorce is being written. According to Rabbi Yehuda HaNasi, any qualification that is stated while the bill of divorce is being written renders it invalid. The Rabbis, on the other hand, hold that only adding an exception of a certain man from the wife's permission to remarry, which invalidates the divorce if stated while the bill of divorce is being handed to her, invalidates the bill of divorce if it is stated while it is being written.

The Ramban and the Rashba reject this explanation and claim that the term written refers to the qualification being actually written into the bill of divorce. They explain that according to Rabbi Yehuda HaNasi, any condition written anywhere in the bill of divorce renders it invalid by rabbinic decree, even if the condition is erased or fulfilled, due to the fundamental invalidity of the bill of divorce in a case of exception. According to the Rabbis, a bill of divorce is rendered invalid only when it is written with an exception.

A third opinion is that of the *Ba'al HaMaor* and Rabbeinu Yitzḥak, cited by *Tosafot*. They explain that Rabbi Yehuda HaNasi renders a bill of divorce in which a condition was written invalid, even if it was erased before the bill was handed to the wife, unless the condition is fulfilled; if it is fulfilled, the divorce is valid. The Rabbis' opinion, according to this explanation, is that if the condition is erased before the bill is handed to the wife, it is valid, and the condition does not need to be fulfilled. Only a condition that is present at the time that the bill is delivered must be fulfilled.

HALAKHA

We do not issue a decree due to a case where it is written before the essential part – לָא גָּזְרִינַן אַטּוּ לִפְנֵי הַתּוֹרֶף: If a qualification was written in the bill of divorce after the essential part, whether it was written before or after the witnesses' signatures, the bill is valid, in accordance with the opinion of the Rabbis. If it is a qualification that invalidates the divorce, such as an exception or a condition that applies to the wife's entire lifetime, the bill of divorce is rendered invalid, even if the qualification is erased (*Beit Shmuel*). No condition should be written in a bill of divorce *ab initio*, even after the essential part, because not everyone is knowledgeable about the different parts of a bill of divorce and the different types of conditions (Rambam *Sefer Nashim*, *Hilkhot Geirushin* 8:3–4; *Shulḥan Arukh*, *Even HaEzer* 147:1–2).

דִּבְרֵי הַכֹּל כָּשֵׁר; וּמַתְנִיתִין דְּקָתָנֵי "כְּתָבוֹ" וְאוֹקִימְנָא בְּ"חוּץ", אֲבָל "עַל מְנָת" לָא פָּסֵיל, אִיבָּעֵית אֵימָא: לִפְנֵי הַתּוֹרֶף וְרַבָּנַן, וְאִיבָּעֵית אֵימָא: לְאַחַר הַתּוֹרֶף וְדִבְרֵי הַכֹּל.

everyone agrees that it **is valid. And the mishna, which teaches** that if **he wrote** his qualification in the bill of divorce it is invalid, **and we established** that it is referring only **to** a case of **an exception, but a condition does not render** the bill of divorce **invalid,** does not contradict this *baraita*. As **if you wish, say** that the mishna is referring to a case where the qualification is written **before the essential** part of the bill of divorce, **and** it is in accordance with the opinion of **the Rabbis. And if you wish, say** that it is referring to a case where the qualification is written **after the essential** part, **and everyone,** even Rabbi Yehuda HaNasi, **agrees** with regard to its ruling.

וְרָבָא אֲמַר: מַחֲלוֹקֶת – לְאַחַר הַתּוֹרֶף, דְּרַבִּי סָבַר: גָּזְרִינַן אַטּוּ לִפְנֵי הַתּוֹרֶף, וְרַבָּנַן סָבְרִי: לָא גָּזְרִינַן אַטּוּ לִפְנֵי הַתּוֹרֶף, אֲבָל לִפְנֵי הַתּוֹרֶף – דִּבְרֵי הַכֹּל פָּסוּל;

And Rava said: The **dispute** between Rabbi Yehuda HaNasi and the Rabbis **is** with regard to a case where the condition is written **after the essential** part, **as Rabbi** Yehuda HaNasi **holds** that **we issue a decree** rendering the bill of divorce invalid **due to** a case where the condition is written **before the essential** part, **and the Rabbis hold** that **we do not issue a decree due to** a case where it is written **before the essential** part.[H] **But** if it is written **before the essential** part, **everyone agrees** that it **is invalid.**

וּמַתְנִיתִין דְּקָתָנֵי ״כְּתָבוֹ״ וְאוֹקִימְנָא בְּ״חוּץ״, אֲבָל ״עַל מְנָת״ לָא פָּסֵיל – אַחַר הַתּוֹרֶף וְרַבָּנַן הִיא.

And accordingly, **the mishna, which teaches** that if **he wrote** his qualification in the bill of divorce it is invalid, **and we established** that it is referring only **to** a case of **an exception, but a condition does not render** the bill of divorce **invalid,** does not contradict this *baraita*. It is referring to a case where he wrote the condition **after the essential** part, **and it is** in accordance with the opinion of **the Rabbis,** who hold that a condition written after the essential part does not render the bill of divorce invalid.

תָּנֵי אֲבוּהּ דְּרַבִּי אָבִין קַמֵּיהּ דְּרַבִּי זֵירָא: כָּתַב גֵּט עַל תְּנַאי – דִּבְרֵי הַכֹּל פָּסוּל. דִּבְרֵי הַכֹּל פָּסוּל? וְהָא מִיפְלַג פְּלִיגִי!

The father of Rabbi Avin taught a *baraita* **before Rabbi Zeira:** If one **wrote a conditional bill of divorce, everyone agrees** that it **is invalid.** Rabbi Zeira asked him: **Everyone agrees** that it **is invalid? But don't they disagree** about this?

אֶלָּא, אֵימָא: לְדִבְרֵי הַכֹּל כָּשֵׁר, וְהֵיכִי דָּמֵי? לְאַחַר הַתּוֹרֶף.

Rabbi Zeira therefore modified the *baraita* in accordance with his opinion: **Rather, say** that **everyone agrees** that it **is valid. And what are the circumstances** in which both sides agree that it is valid? It is referring to a case where the condition is written **after the essential** part of the bill of divorce.

וְלֵימָא: הֲרֵי זֶה פָּסוּל, וְרַבִּי! תַּנָּא דִּבְרֵי הַכֹּל אַתְנְיֵיהּ, כָּשֵׁר בְּפָסוּל מִיחַלַּף לֵיהּ, ״הֲרֵי זֶה״ בְּ״דִבְרֵי הַכֹּל״ לָא מִיחַלַּף לֵיהּ.

The Gemara counters: **Let** Rabbi Zeira **say** an alternative modification of the *baraita*: **It is invalid,** omitting the words: Everyone agrees, **and** this *baraita* is in accordance with the opinion of **Rabbi** Yehuda HaNasi. The Gemara answers: **The *tanna* taught him** that **everyone agrees,** which is a conspicuous statement. Although **he may** conceivably **confuse** the word **valid with invalid,** he certainly **does not confuse** the phrase: **It is, with** the phrase: **Everyone agrees.** Therefore, Rabbi Zeira modified the *baraita* the way he did.

מתני׳ הֲרֵי אַתְּ מוּתֶּרֶת לְכָל אָדָם אֶלָּא לְאַבָּא וּלְאָבִיךְ, לְאָחִי וּלְאָחִיךְ, לְעֶבֶד וּלְגוֹי, וּלְכָל מִי שֶׁאֵין לָהּ עָלָיו קִדּוּשִׁין – כָּשֵׁר.

MISHNA If a man says to his wife while handing her a bill of divorce: **You are hereby permitted to** marry **any man, except to** marry **my father or to** marry **your father,** to marry **my brother or to** marry **your brother, to** marry **a slave or to** marry **a gentile, or to** marry **anyone** to whom **she cannot** legally become **betrothed,**[H] the divorce **is valid.** Since these men cannot betroth her anyway, his qualification is meaningless.

הֲרֵי אַתְּ מוּתֶּרֶת לְכָל אָדָם אֶלָּא אַלְמָנָה לְכֹהֵן גָּדוֹל, גְּרוּשָׁה וַחֲלוּצָה לְכֹהֵן הֶדְיוֹט, מַמְזֶרֶת וּנְתִינָה לְיִשְׂרָאֵל, בַּת יִשְׂרָאֵל לְמַמְזֵר וּלְנָתִין, וְכָל מִי שֶׁיֵּשׁ לָהּ עָלָיו קִדּוּשִׁין אֲפִילּוּ בַּעֲבֵירָה – פָּסוּל.

If he says to her: **You are hereby permitted to** marry **any man, except** for when doing so violates the following: The prohibition against **a widow** being married **to a High Priest;** the prohibition against **a divorcée or a *yevama* who performed *ḥalitza* [*ḥalutza*]** being married **to a common priest; a *mamzeret* or a Gibeonite woman**[B] being married **to an Israelite** man; **an Israelite woman** being married **to a *mamzer* or to a Gibeonite** man; or marrying **anyone** to whom **she can** legally become **betrothed,**[H] **even** if this betrothal would be **a transgression,** such as in the aforementioned cases; in all of these cases the divorce **is invalid.** His statement renders it a partial divorce, as the woman is still not permitted to marry any man who is eligible to betroth her.

גמ׳ כְּלָלָא דְּרֵישָׁא – לְאֲתוּיֵי שְׁאָר חַיָּיבֵי כָרֵיתוֹת, כְּלָלָא דְּסֵיפָא – לְאֲתוּיֵי שְׁאָר חַיָּיבֵי לָאוִין, כְּגוֹן עַמּוֹנִי וּמוֹאָבִי, נְתִינֵי, מִצְרִי וַאֲדוֹמִי.

GEMARA The stating of **the generalization in the first clause** of the mishna: Anyone to whom she cannot legally become betrothed, serves **to include the rest of those liable** to receive *karet* for engaging in sexual intercourse with her, who are not listed explicitly in the mishna. The stating of **the generalization in the last clause** of the mishna: Anyone to whom she can legally become betrothed, serves **to include the rest of those liable by a prohibition** for engaging in sexual intercourse with her, **such as an Ammonite and a Moabite, a Gibeonite, an Egyptian, and an Edomite** (Deuteronomy 23:4, 8–9). Although they are all prohibited from engaging in sexual intercourse with her due to a prohibition or a positive mitzva, she can legally become betrothed to them.

HALAKHA

To anyone to whom she cannot legally become betrothed – לְכָל מִי שֶׁאֵין לָהּ עָלָיו קִדּוּשִׁין: If a man divorces his wife and stipulates that she is permitted to marry any man except for so-and-so, and that man is a gentile, or a slave, or a forbidden relation, to whom she cannot legally become betrothed, it is a valid divorce (Rambam *Sefer Nashim, Hilkhot Geirushin* 8:5; *Shulḥan Arukh, Even HaEzer* 137:2).

Anyone to whom she can legally become betrothed – כָּל מִי שֶׁיֵּשׁ לָהּ עָלָיו קִדּוּשִׁין: If the husband stipulates, while handing her the bill of divorce, that she is not permitted to marry so-and-so, if so-and-so is otherwise eligible to marry her, the divorce is not valid, even if their marriage is prohibited by Torah law. Despite this, she is disqualified from marrying a priest due to the trace of a bill of divorce (Rambam *Sefer Nashim, Hilkhot Geirushin* 8:5; *Shulḥan Arukh, Even HaEzer* 137:2, and *Beit Shmuel* there).

BACKGROUND

A Gibeonite woman – נְתִינָה: This term refers to a descendant of the Gibeonites, one of the ten categories of lineage within the Jewish people who returned from Babylonia. According to most authorities, by Torah law the Gibeonites could have been treated as ordinary converts. Nevertheless, first Joshua (see Joshua, chapter 9) and then King David issued decrees that accorded them the status of *mamzerim*, thereby prohibiting Jews from marrying them. There were hardly any Gibeonites during the talmudic period, and eventually they completely disappeared.

HALAKHA

Will reach the age of eligibility for betrothal – אָתְיָא לִכְלַל הֲוָיָה: If he stipulated while handing her the bill of divorce that she is permitted to marry any man except for so-and-so, who is a minor boy, it is not a valid divorce. The *Tur*, citing Rabbeinu Ḥananel, holds that it is uncertain whether she is divorced (Rambam *Sefer Nashim*, *Hilkhot Geirushin* 8:5; *Shulḥan Arukh*, *Even HaEzer* 137:2).

NOTES

Death is common – מִיתָה שְׁכִיחָא: In other words, death is a more common occurrence than conversion (Rashba).

בְּעָא מִינֵּיהּ רָבָא מֵרַב נַחְמָן: חוּץ מִקִּידּוּשֵׁי קָטָן, מַהוּ? מִי אָמְרִינַן הָשְׁתָּא מִיהָא לָאו בַּר הֲוָיָה הוּא, אוֹ דִּלְמָא אָתֵי לִכְלַל הֲוָיָה?

§ **Rava raised a dilemma before Rav Naḥman:** If the husband says that she is permitted to marry any man **except for a betrothal to** so-and-so, who is **a minor boy** at that time, **what is** the *halakha*? **Do we say** that **now,** since **he is in any event not eligible for betrothal,** as a minor boy cannot betroth a woman, the husband's qualification does not prohibit his wife to anyone, and it is a complete act of severance? **Or perhaps,** since **he will reach** eligibility for **betrothal,** is the husband's qualification considered as prohibiting her to someone to whom betrothal could apply?

אֲמַר לֵיהּ, תְּנֵיתוּהָ: קְטַנָּה מִתְגָּרֶשֶׁת בְּקִידּוּשֵׁי אָבִיהָ;

Rav Naḥman **said to him: You learned** the solution to this dilemma in a *baraita*: **A minor girl can get divorced** from her husband even if she was betrothed to him **through her father's betrothal,** i.e., her father betrothed her to her husband (see Deuteronomy 22:16).

אַמַּאי? וְהָא בָּעֵינַן ״וְיָצְאָה...וְהָיְתָה״! אֶלָּא אָתְיָא לִכְלַל הֲוָיָה, הָכָא נַמִּי אָתְיָא לִכְלַל הֲוָיָה.

Why can she? **But don't we need** there to be a broad similarity between the *halakhot* of divorce and betrothal, as derived from the juxtaposition between the clause: **"And she departs,"** and the clause: **"And becomes"** (Deuteronomy 24:2), which serves as the basis for the comparison of the *halakhot* of divorce and betrothal? Accordingly, since she will not be eligible to receive her own betrothal until she reaches majority, she should not be able to receive her bill of divorce. **Rather,** evidently, since **she will** eventually **reach** the age of eligibility to receive her own **betrothal** she is considered essentially eligible for betrothal now as well. **Here also,** since the minor boy, whom the husband prohibited the wife from marrying, **will reach** the age of eligibility for **betrothal,**[H] the divorce is invalid.

״חוּץ מִן הַנּוֹלָדִים״, מַהוּ? הָשְׁתָּא מִיהָא לָא אִיתְיְלִיד, אוֹ דִּלְמָא עֲתִידֵי דְּמִתְיַילְדֵי?

Rava raised another dilemma: If the husband says that she is permitted to marry any man **except for those who will be born** in the future, **what is** the *halakha*? Should it be reasoned that **now,** since **in any event they are not yet born,** the qualification is void, as it pertains to people who do not exist? **Or perhaps** they are considered forbidden to her as **they will be born in the future.**

אֲמַר לֵיהּ, תְּנֵיתוּהָ: ״לְעֶבֶד וּלְגוֹי״, אִם אִיתָא, עֶבֶד וְגוֹי נַמִּי עֲבִידִי דְּמִיגַּיְירִי!

Rav Naḥman **said to him: You learned** the solution to your dilemma in the mishna, which states that if the husband says that she is forbidden **to** marry **a slave or to** marry **a gentile** the divorce is valid; **if it is so** that future situations are taken into account, **a slave and a gentile are also likely to convert.** Therefore, the husband is prohibiting her from marrying a man whom she might be able to marry in the future, which should render the divorce invalid. Evidently, only the present situation is taken into consideration.

הָנָךְ לָאו לְאִיגַּיּוּרֵי קָיְימִי, הָנֵי לְאִיתְיְלוּדֵי קָיְימִי.

The Gemara rejects this solution: **Those** people **do not stand** before the court ready **to convert.** It is only a possibility that they will convert, as there is no reason to assume that they will do so. By contrast, **these** people who will be born **stand** ready **to be born.** Therefore, this solution cannot be inferred from the mishna.

״חוּץ מִבַּעַל אֲחוֹתָהּ״, מַהוּ? הָשְׁתָּא מִיהָא לָא חַזְיָא לֵיהּ, אוֹ דִּלְמָא זִמְנִין דְּמֵתָה אֲחוֹתָהּ וְחַזְיָא לֵיהּ?

Rava raised another dilemma: If he permits her to marry any man **except for her sister's husband, what is** the *halakha*? Should it be reasoned that **now,** since **in any event she is not yet fit for him,** as sexual intercourse between them is punishable by *karet*, the divorce is valid? **Or perhaps** should it be reasoned that **sometimes** a woman's **sister dies and she is** thereby **fit to** marry her husband?

אֲמַר לֵיהּ, תְּנֵיתוּהָ: ״לְעֶבֶד וּלְגוֹי״, עֶבֶד וְגוֹי נַמִּי עֲבִידִי דְּמִיגַּיְירִי! גֵּירוּת לָא שְׁכִיחָא, מִיתָה שְׁכִיחָא.

Rav Naḥman **said to him: You learned** the solution to your dilemma in the mishna, which states that if the husband says that she is forbidden **to** marry **a slave or to** marry **a gentile** the divorce is valid. And **a slave and a gentile are also** potentially fit to marry her as they are **likely to convert.** Evidently, only the current situation is taken into account. The Gemara rejects this; whereas **conversion is uncommon, death is common.**[N]

"חוּץ מִזְּנוּתַיִךְ", מַהוּ? בְּנִשּׂוּאִין הָא לָא שַׁיֵּיר, אוֹ דִּלְמָא שַׁיֵּיר בְּבִיאָה?

Rava raised another dilemma: If he says to her: You are hereby permitted to any man **except for your licentiousness,** meaning she may get married to any man but she may not engage in sexual intercourse outside of a second marriage, as she is still rendered a married woman in that regard, **what is the** *halakha* in this case? Is the divorce valid? Should it be reasoned that **with regard to marriage he did not leave** anything **out** of the divorce, as she is permitted to marry any man, **or perhaps he left out** part of the divorce **with regard to sexual intercourse?**

אֲמַר לֵיהּ, תְּנֵיתוּהָ: לְאַבָּא וּלְאָבִיךְ, וּבְמַאי? אִילֵימָא בְּנִשּׂוּאִין, אַבָּא וְאָבִיךְ בְּנֵי נִשּׂוּאִין נִינְהוּ? אֶלָּא לָאו בִּזְנוּת, וּלְאַבָּא וּלְאָבִיךְ הוּא דְּלָא שַׁיֵּיר, הָא לְאַחֵר שַׁיֵּיר.

Rav Naḥman **said to him: You learned** the solution in the mishna: If the husband says while handing her the bill of divorce: You are hereby forbidden **to my father or to your father,** the divorce is valid. **And with regard to what** action is this stated? **If we say** that it is **with regard to marriage, are my father and your father eligible for marriage?** Her betrothal to them would not take effect. **Rather, is it not with regard to** them engaging in **licentiousness** with her? **And** it may be inferred from the mishna that only if he renders her forbidden **to my father or to your father is it not** considered as if **he left out** part of the divorce, rendering the divorce valid; but if he renders her forbidden **to** engage in licentiousness with **another** man, it is considered as if **he left out** part of the divorce, and it will not take effect.

דִּלְמָא בְּנִשּׂוּאִין, דְּעָבַר וְאִינְסֵיב.

The Gemara rejects this: **Perhaps** the mishna is referring **to marriage, where** the father **transgresses** the prohibition **and marries** her anyway. Therefore, the *halakha* with regard to licentiousness cannot be inferred from here.

"חוּץ מִשֶּׁלֹּא כְּדַרְכָּהּ", מַהוּ? בִּכְדַרְכָּהּ הָא לָא שַׁיֵּיר, אוֹ דִּלְמָא "מִשְׁכְּבֵי אִשָּׁה" כְּתִיב?

Rava raised another dilemma: If he says to her that she is permitted to any man **except for** engaging in **intercourse in an atypical manner,** i.e., anal intercourse, **what is the** *halakha*? Should it be reasoned that **with regard to typical** sexual intercourse **he did not leave out** part of the divorce, rendering the divorce valid? **Or perhaps** from the fact that the expression: **"Cohabitations of a woman"** (Leviticus 20:13), **is written** in the plural, it is derived that typical and atypical sexual intercourse have the same status, and accordingly this is considered a partial divorce, and it will not take effect.

"חוּץ מֵהֲפָרַת נְדָרַיִךְ", מַהוּ? בְּנִשּׂוּאִין הָא לָא שַׁיֵּיר, אוֹ דִּלְמָא "אִישָׁהּ יְקִימֶנּוּ וְאִישָׁהּ יְפֵרֶנּוּ" כְּתִיב?

The Gemara raises a similar dilemma: If he says to her that she is permitted to marry any man: **Except** for the *halakhot* of **the nullification of your vows,**[N] i.e., no man who marries her can nullify her vows other than her ex-husband, who retains his power to do so, **what is** the *halakha*? Should it be reasoned that **with regard to** her ability to enter into **marriage, he did not leave out** anything from his act of severance? **Or perhaps** is it derived from that which **is written: "Her husband may sustain it, or her husband may nullify it"** (Numbers 30:14), that a husband's power to nullify his wife's vows is an intrinsic component of being married, and therefore this divorce is not a complete severance?

NOTES

Except for the nullification of your vows – חוּץ מֵהֲפָרַת נְדָרַיִךְ: Rashi and the Meiri explain that this means that even though he is divorcing her he will still have the power to nullify her vows. Accordingly, the citation of the verse "Or her husband may make it void" comes to indicate that as long as the husband can still nullify her vows he is still considered her husband to some degree. Others explain that this means that her future husband will not be able to nullify her vows. According to this explanation, the question is whether a husband's power to nullify his wife's vows is considered a fundamental component of marriage, without which the marriage is incomplete (Ritva).

"חוץ מִתְּרוּמָתֵיךְ", מַהוּ? בְּנִשּׂוּאִין הָא לָא שַׁיֵּיר, אוֹ דִּלְמָא "קִנְיַן כַּסְפּוֹ" כְּתִיב?

The Gemara raises another dilemma: If he says to her: You are hereby permitted to marry any man **except for your** partaking of *teruma*,[N] i.e., if she marries a priest she will not be able to partake of *teruma*, **what is** the *halakha*? Should it be reasoned that **with regard to** her ability to enter into **marriage, he did not leave out** anything from his act of severance? **Or perhaps** is it derived from that which **is written: "The purchase of his money,** he may eat of it" (Leviticus 22:11), indicating that a priest's wife partakes of *teruma* because she is his acquisition, and that if she is prohibited from partaking of *teruma*, then his acquisition of her is not complete?

"חוץ מִירוּשָּׁתֵיךְ", מַהוּ? בְּנִשּׂוּאִין הָא לָא שַׁיֵּיר, אוֹ דִּלְמָא "לִשְׁאֵרוֹ...וְיָרַשׁ אוֹתָהּ" כְּתִיב?

The Gemara raises another dilemma: If he says to her: You are hereby permitted to marry any man **except for your inheritance,**[N] i.e., her future husband will not be considered her husband with regard to the *halakhot* of inheritance, **what is** the *halakha*? Should it be reasoned that **with regard to** her ability to enter into **marriage, he did not leave out** anything from his act of severance? **Or perhaps** since it is derived that a husband inherits from his wife, who is considered his next of kin, from that which **is written: "To his kinsman**[N] that is next to him of his family **and he shall possess it"** (Numbers 27:11), then if a husband does not become his wife's beneficiary, is their marriage not complete?

"חוץ מִקִּידּוּשַׁיִךְ בִּשְׁטָר", מַהוּ? מִי אָמְרִינַן: אֶפְשָׁר דִּמְקַדֵּשׁ לָהּ בְּכֶסֶף וּבְבִיאָה, אוֹ דִּלְמָא "וְיָצְאָה...וְהָיְתָה", אִיתְּקוּשׁ הֲוָויוֹת לַהֲדָדֵי?

The Gemara raises another dilemma: If he says to her: You are hereby permitted to marry any man **except for your** ability to enter **betrothal by** receiving **a document,** i.e., if another man betroths her by giving her a document of betrothal, the betrothal will not take effect, **what is** the *halakha*? **Do we say** that since one **can** still **betroth her with money or with sexual intercourse,** the act of severance is complete? **Or perhaps** is it derived from the juxtaposition between the clause: **"And she departs"** and the clause: **"And becomes"** (Deuteronomy 24:2), that the different ways of **becoming** a wife **are compared to each other,** so that the inability to perform one of them renders the severance incomplete?

תֵּיקוּ.

The Gemara comments: These dilemmas shall all **stand**[B] unresolved.[H]

מתני׳ גּוּפוֹ שֶׁל גֵּט: "הֲרֵי אַתְּ מוּתֶּרֶת לְכׇל אָדָם";

MISHNA **The basic,** essential, element **of a bill of divorce**[HN] **is: You are hereby permitted to marry any man.**

BACKGROUND

Shall stand – תֵּיקוּ: Various explanations have been offered with regard to the etymology of this term. One explanation is that the word is an abbreviated version of *tikom*, let it stand. Another is that its source is the word *tik*, a case or pouch, whose contents are unknown. Similarly, the resolution is unknown to us as if it were hidden inside a case (*Arukh*). Although not the literal meaning of the word, some raise the suggestion that the term alludes to an acrostic: The Tishbite, i.e., Elijah the Prophet, will resolve questions and dilemmas (*Tosafot Yom Tov*).

HALAKHA

These dilemmas shall all stand unresolved – תֵּיקוּ: If he handed her a bill of divorce and said that she is permitted to any man except for her sister's husband or someone who will be born in the future, or if he said to her: Except for your engaging in licentiousness or atypical intercourse, or if he prohibited her from marrying through one of the methods of betrothal, or if he prevented her future husband from receiving one of his marital rights, it is uncertain whether she is divorced. This is because these dilemmas are left unresolved in the Gemara and are therefore treated stringently, as they pertain to Torah law (Rambam *Sefer Nashim, Hilkhot Geirushin* 8:6; *Shulḥan Arukh, Even HaEzer* 137:3).

The basic element of a bill of divorce – גּוּפוֹ שֶׁל גֵּט: The essential part of the bill of divorce is the statement: You are hereby permitted to marry any man. Even if other expressions of divorce are also mentioned, this statement is still considered the essential part. If it is not written, the bill of divorce is invalid (Rambam *Sefer Nashim, Hilkhot Geirushin* 1:4; *Shulḥan Arukh, Even HaEzer* 126:41, and *Beit Shmuel* and *Taz* there).

NOTES

Except for your partaking of *teruma* – חוּץ מִתְּרוּמָתֵיךְ: According to Rashi, this means that if she marries a priest it will be prohibited for her to partake of *teruma*. *Tosafot* question this explanation, as a divorcée cannot marry a priest in any case, and if she does she is disqualified from partaking of *teruma* due to their engaging in sexual intercourse. One possible answer is that a divorcée who marries a priest may partake of *teruma* before they engage in sexual intercourse (see Ritva). *Tosafot* explain that this is referring to a case where the first husband is a priest, and he stipulates when giving her the bill of divorce that she will still be considered his wife with regard to her permission to partake of *teruma*. The Meiri establishes the case in a different manner: The husband is an Israelite and the wife is the daughter of a priest, and they got divorced without having children. Although the wife normally goes back to partaking of *teruma* in such a case, here the husband stipulates that she may not do so (see *Ḥatam Sofer*).

Except for your inheritance – חוּץ מִירוּשָּׁתֵךְ: Rashi and the Meiri explain that he stipulated that he should inherit her, while others explain that he stipulated that her future husband will not inherit her (Ritva).

To his kinsman – לִשְׁאֵרוֹ: The premise of this derivation is that a husband and wife are considered one flesh (see Genesis 2:24). Therefore, if the second husband is prevented from becoming his wife's beneficiary by the ex-husband's qualification, the marriage is considered incomplete.

The basic element of a bill of divorce – גּוּפוֹ שֶׁל גֵּט: Ritva writes that this does not mean that if he writes this sentence alone it is a valid bill of divorce, as he certainly must write the names of the husband and wife. Rather, it means that if he does not write this sentence it is not a valid bill of divorce. The Rid, on the other hand, writes that even if he does not write their names it is valid if there are witnesses who can testify that the husband gave it to her.

רַבִּי יְהוּדָה אוֹמֵר: ״וְדֵין דִּיהֱוֵי לִיכִי מִינַּאי סֵפֶר תֵּירוּכִין וְאִגֶּרֶת שְׁבוּקִין וְגֵט פִּטּוּרִין לִמְהַךְ לְהִתְנַסְּבָא לְכָל גְּבַר דִּיתִצְבְּיִין״. גּוּפוֹ שֶׁל גֵּט שִׁחְרוּר: ״הֲרֵי אַתְּ בַּת חוֹרִין״, ״הֲרֵי אַתְּ לְעַצְמֵךְ״.

Rabbi Yehuda says that there is also another essential sentence: **And this**[N] **that you shall have**[H] **from me is a scroll of divorce, and a letter of leave, and a bill of dismissal to go to marry any man that you wish. And the basic** element **of a bill of manumission**[H] for a maidservant is: **You are hereby a free woman,** or: **You are hereby your own.**

גמ׳ פְּשִׁיטָא, אָמַר לָהּ לְאִשְׁתּוֹ ״הֲרֵי אַתְּ בַּת חוֹרִין״ – לֹא אָמַר וְלֹא כְלוּם, אָמַר לָהּ לְשִׁפְחָתוֹ ״הֲרֵי אַתְּ מוּתֶּרֶת לְכָל אָדָם״ – לֹא אָמַר וְלֹא כְלוּם,

GEMARA It is obvious that if one **stated** in a bill of divorce **for his wife: You are hereby a free woman,**[H] **he has stated nothing,**[N] as that is not a statement of divorce. Similarly, if one **stated** in a bill of manumission **for his maidservant: You are hereby permitted to** marry **any man,**[H] **he has stated nothing,** as that is not a statement of manumission.

אָמַר לָהּ לְאִשָּׁה ״הֲרֵי אַתְּ לְעַצְמֵךְ״, מַהוּ? לְגַמְרֵי קָאָמַר לָהּ, אוֹ לִמְלָאכָה קָאָמַר לָהּ?

The Gemara asks: If **he stated** in a bill of divorce **for** his **wife: You are hereby your own, what is the** *halakha*? **Is he saying to her:** You are **entirely** your own, meaning that she has full control over her status and may marry another man? **Or is he saying to her:** You are your own with regard **to work,** meaning that she may keep the revenue from her work? If so, this is not a statement of divorce.

אֲמַר לֵיהּ רָבִינָא לְרַב אַשִׁי: תָּא שְׁמַע, דִּתְנַן: גּוּפוֹ שֶׁל גֵּט שִׁחְרוּר ״הֲרֵי אַתְּ בַּת חוֹרִין״, ״הֲרֵי אַתְּ לְעַצְמֵךְ״; וּמָה עַבְדָּא דְּקָנֵי לֵיהּ גּוּפֵיהּ, כִּי אָמַר לֵיהּ ״הֲרֵי אַתְּ לְעַצְמֵךְ״ – קָנֵי גּוּפֵיהּ, אִשָּׁה דְּלָא קָנֵי גּוּפָהּ – לֹא כָּל שֶׁכֵּן?

Ravina said to Rav Ashi: Come and **hear** a solution **that we learned** in the mishna: **The basic** element **of a bill of manumission is: You are hereby a free woman,** or: **You are hereby your own. And just as** with regard to **a slave, whose body is acquired** by the master, if the master **states** in a bill of manumission **for the** slave: **You are hereby your own,** the slave **acquires his body, all the more so** with regard to **a wife, whose body is not acquired**[H] by her husband, is it **not** clear that by his writing in a bill of divorce: You are hereby your own, she is completely released from their marriage?

אֲמַר לֵיהּ רָבִינָא לְרַב אַשִׁי: אָמַר לוֹ לְעַבְדּוֹ ״אֵין לִי עֵסֶק בְּךָ״, מַהוּ?

Ravina said to Rav Ashi: If **he stated** in a bill of manumission **for his slave: I have no business with you,**[H] **what is the** *halakha*? Is this a valid statement of manumission?

אֲמַר לֵיהּ רַב חָנִין לְרַב אַשִׁי, וְאָמְרִי לָהּ רַב חָנִין מְחוֹזְנָאָה לְרַב אַשִׁי: תָּא שְׁמַע, דְּתַנְיָא: הַמּוֹכֵר עַבְדּוֹ לְגוֹי – יָצָא לְחֵירוּת, וְצָרִיךְ גֵּט שִׁחְרוּר מֵרַבּוֹ רִאשׁוֹן; אָמַר רַבָּן שִׁמְעוֹן בֶּן גַּמְלִיאֵל: בַּמֶּה דְּבָרִים אֲמוּרִים שֶׁלֹּא כָּתַב עָלָיו אוֹנוֹ, אֲבָל כָּתַב עָלָיו אוֹנוֹ – זֶהוּ שִׁחְרוּרוֹ.

Rav Ḥanin said to Rav Ashi, and some say that it was **Rav Ḥanin from Meḥoza** who said this **to Rav Ashi: Come** and **hear** a solution **that we learned** in a *baraita*: With regard to **one who sells his slave**[N] **to a gentile,** the slave **is emancipated but** nevertheless **requires a bill of manumission**[H] **from his first master. Rabban Shimon ben Gamliel said: In what case is this statement said?** It is **when** the master **did not write his document for** the slave when he sold him; **but if he wrote his document for him, that is** the slave's bill of **manumission.**

HALAKHA

And this that you shall have, etc. – וְדֵין דִּיהֱוֵי וכו׳: A bill of divorce must include the formulation stated by Rabbi Yehuda, and other additions are included to complete and clarify the wording. While the statement: You are hereby permitted to marry any man, is included as well, the Rema rules that it is not critical, as its content is already included in Rabbi Yehuda's version. Others disagree, maintaining that this statement is critical (Rambam *Sefer Nashim, Hilkhot Geirushin* 4:12; *Shulḥan Arukh, Even HaEzer* 126:1 and *Beit Shmuel* there).

The basic element of a bill of manumission – גּוּפוֹ שֶׁל גֵּט שִׁחְרוּר: How does one write a bill of manumission for his slave? He writes on paper or on any other surface suitable for writing: You are hereby a freeman, or: You are hereby your own, and he hands it to him (Rambam *Sefer Kinyan, Hilkhot Avadim* 5:3; *Shulḥan Arukh, Yoreh De'a* 267:41).

If one stated in a bill of divorce for his wife, you are hereby a free woman – אָמַר לָהּ לְאִשְׁתּוֹ הֲרֵי אַתְּ בַּת חוֹרִין: If a man writes in a bill of divorce for his wife: You are hereby a free woman, it is not a valid bill of divorce (Rambam *Sefer Nashim, Hilkhot Geirushin* 1:4; *Shulḥan Arukh, Even HaEzer* 136:4).

If one stated in a bill of manumission for his maidservant, you are hereby permitted to marry any man – אָמַר לָהּ לְשִׁפְחָתוֹ הֲרֵי אַתְּ מוּתֶּרֶת לְכָל אָדָם: If one writes in a bill of manumission for his maidservant: You are hereby permitted to marry any man, she is not emancipated, as that is not a statement of manumission (Rambam *Sefer Kinyan, Hilkhot Avadim* 5:3; *Shulḥan Arukh, Yoreh De'a* 267:43).

A wife whose body is not acquired, etc. – אִשָּׁה דְּלָא קָנֵי גּוּפָהּ וכו׳: If one writes in a bill of divorce: You are sent away, or: You are your own, she is divorced, in accordance with the conclusion of the Gemara (Rambam *Sefer Nashim, Hilkhot Geirushin* 1:4; *Shulḥan Arukh, Even HaEzer* 136:4).

I have no business with you – אֵין לִי עֵסֶק בְּךָ: If one wrote in a bill of manumission for his slave: I have no business with you, this sentence constitutes the basic part of the bill of manumission, and it is valid (Rambam *Sefer Kinyan, Hilkhot Avadim* 5:3; *Shulḥan Arukh, Yoreh De'a* 267:41).

Requires a bill of manumission, etc. – צָרִיךְ גֵּט שִׁחְרוּר וכו׳: If one sells his slave to the gentiles, the slave is emancipated. Furthermore, the master must repurchase the slave from the gentile for up to ten times his value, as a penalty, and the master must then write him a bill of manumission, in accordance with the opinion of the first *tanna* in the *baraita* (Rambam *Sefer Kinyan, Hilkhot Avadim* 8:1; *Shulḥan Arukh, Yoreh De'a* 267:80).

NOTES

Rabbi Yehuda says: And this, etc. – רַבִּי יְהוּדָה אוֹמֵר וְדֵין וכו׳: The early commentaries discuss whether the version suggested by Rabbi Yehuda, which is written nowadays in all bills of divorce, replaces the sentence: You are hereby permitted to marry any man, as Rabbi Yehuda's version explicitly renders the wife permitted to marry any man she wishes, or whether Rabbi Yehuda's formulation is in addition to: You are hereby permitted to marry any man. Some commentaries hold that if Rabbi Yehuda's version is written, the sentence: You are hereby permitted to marry any man, is not critical, and it is written nowadays only so that the bill of divorce is as explicit as possible (Rashba). Many commentaries maintain that Rabbi Yehuda is merely adding to the previously mentioned sentence, which is a critical component of the divorce in his opinion as well (Rambam; Ramah; Ramban). In fact, some even rule that if that sentence is not written, and the wife remarries based on the bill of divorce, she must leave her second husband.

Some commentaries explain that Rabbi Yehuda's version is deficient, as it mentions only that the wife may marry any man she wishes, without mentioning her right to engage in sexual intercourse without committing adultery. Therefore, only the inclusion of the sentence: You are hereby permitted to any man, renders it a full divorce, following which the woman is completely unmarried. Others reject this explanation, claiming that her right to engage in sexual intercourse without committing adultery does not need to be mentioned specifically; this becomes an issue only if the husband states explicitly that she is prohibited from engaging in sexual intercourse (*Sefer HaIttur*; Rid).

You are hereby a free woman, he has stated nothing – הֲרֵי אַתְּ בַּת חוֹרִין לֹא אָמַר וְלֹא כְלוּם: The woman's marital status remains the same, as a married woman is also considered a free woman. Although she cannot marry another man, and has several obligations toward her husband, the marriage is merely an agreement and does not negate her freedom.

One who sells his slave, etc. – הַמּוֹכֵר עַבְדּוֹ וכו׳: Rashi adds that although the Sages instituted that one who sells his slave to a gentile is required to redeem him for up to ten times his value, after redeeming him the master does not have the right to take him back as a slave. This requirement is due to the master's responsibility for putting the slave in this unacceptable situation.

מַאי אוֹנוֹ? אָמַר רַב שֵׁשֶׁת: דְּכָתַב לֵיהּ: לִכְשֶׁתִּבְרַח מִמֶּנּוּ אֵין לִי עֵסֶק בְּךָ.

The Gemara asks: **What is** the phrase: **His document,** referring to? **Rav Sheshet says that he writes for him** as follows: **When you will escape from** the gentile to whom I sold you, **I have no business with you.** Consequently, as soon as he escapes his gentile master in any manner, he is entirely emancipated. It may be derived from here that the statement: I have no business with you, is valid with regard to manumission.

״רַבִּי יְהוּדָה אוֹמֵר: וְדֵן דִּיהֱוֵי לִיכִי מִינַּאי סֵפֶר תֵּירוּכִין וְאִיגֶּרֶת שְׁבוּקִין״. בְּמַאי קָמִיפַּלְגִי? רַבָּנַן סָבְרִי: יָדַיִם שֶׁאֵין מוֹכִיחוֹת הָוְיָין יָדַיִם, וְאַף עַל גַּב דְּלָא כָּתַב לַהּ ״וְדֵן״ מוֹכְחָא מִילְּתָא דִּבְהַאי גִּיטָּא קָא מְגָרֵשׁ לַהּ;

§ It is stated in the mishna that **Rabbi Yehuda says** that in addition to the statement: You are hereby permitted to marry any man, there is another essential sentence in the bill of divorce: **And this** [*veden*] **that you shall have from me is a scroll of divorce and a letter** [*ve'iggeret*] **of leave.** The Gemara asks: **With regard to what** principle **do** Rabbi Yehuda and the Rabbis **disagree?** The Gemara answers: **The Rabbis hold** that **ambiguous intimations are valid intimations.** An incomplete statement is sufficient as long as the intention is clear from the context. **And** therefore, **even if he does not write for her** explicitly: **And this** that you shall have from me is a scroll of divorce and a letter of leave, the bill of divorce is valid as **it is evident that he is divorcing her with this bill of divorce.**

וְרַבִּי יְהוּדָה סָבַר: יָדַיִם שֶׁאֵין מוֹכִיחוֹת לָא הָוְיָין יָדַיִם, וְטַעְמָא דְּכָתַב לַהּ ״וְדֵן״ דְּמוֹכְחָא מִילְּתָא דִּבְהַאי גִּיטָּא קָא מְגָרֵשׁ לַהּ, אֲבָל לָא כָּתַב לַהּ ״וְדֵן״, אָמְרִי: בְּדִיבּוּרָא גָּרְשַׁהּ, וּשְׁטָרָא רְאָיָה בְּעָלְמָא הוּא.

And Rabbi Yehuda holds that **ambiguous intimations are not valid intimations, and** therefore **the reason** that the bill of divorce is valid is **that he writes for her: And this** that you shall have from me is a scroll of divorce and a letter of leave, **so it is evident that he is divorcing her with this bill of divorce. But if he does not write for her: And this** that you shall have from me is a scroll of divorce and a letter of leave, people **will say** that **he is divorcing her orally,** and will mistakenly assume that the husband's statement to her when he hands her the bill of divorce is what causes the divorce to take effect, **and** that **the document is merely evidence** of the divorce, rather than the divorce itself.

אָמַר אַבַּיֵי: הַאי מַאן דְּכָתַב גִּיטָּא, לָא לִכְתּוֹב ״וְדֵין״ דְּמַשְׁמַע וְדִין, אֶלָּא וְדֵן;

§ The Gemara relates several rulings concerning the precise terminology to be used in writing a bill of divorce. **Abaye said: This person who writes a bill of divorce**[N] **should not write** the word meaning: **And this,**[H] by spelling it *vav, dalet, yod, nun,* **as** that can be misread as having the vowel of a *ḥirik* under the letter *dalet*, not a *tzeire*. Read with a *ḥirik*, it **indicates: And** there is a **law** that we should get divorced. **Rather,** he should make sure to write the word meaning: **And this,** without a *yod*, so that it is clear that it should be read with a *tzeire*.

וְלָא לִכְתּוֹב ״אִיגֶּרֶת״ דְּמַשְׁמַע אִיגֶּרֶת, אֶלָּא אִגֶּרֶת; וְלָא לִכְתּוֹב ״לִימְהַךְ״ דְּמַשְׁמַע לִי מֵהָךְ; וְלָא לִכְתּוֹב ״לְמִחַךְ״ דְּמַשְׁמַע כִּי חוּכָא;

And he should not write the word meaning: **A letter,**[H] by spelling it *alef, yod, gimmel, reish, tav,* **as** that can be confused with another identically spelled word that **indicates a roof.**[N] **Rather,** he should write the word meaning: **A letter,** without a *yod*. **And he should not write: To go,**[NH] by spelling it *lamed, yod, mem, heh, khaf,* as that could be read as a conjunction which **indicates: For me from this. And he should** be sure **not to write** ***limḥakh,***[H] i.e., he must be careful that the letter *heh* not look like a *ḥet*, **as that indicates** that it is **like a joke.**

NOTES

This person who writes a bill of divorce, etc. – הַאי מַאן דְּכָתַב גִּיטָּא וכו׳: The Rambam holds that a bill of divorce that was not written according to the instructions outlined in the Gemara is invalid. By contrast, several early commentaries cite a geonic tradition that a bill of divorce spelled not in accordance with the instructions in the Gemara is invalid only if it was written by the husband himself, who later claims that he deliberately wrote it in an incorrect manner because he did not really intend to divorce his wife. If the error was made by a scribe, although he should correct it *ab initio*, if he does not correct it and the woman remarries based on this bill of divorce, it is deemed a scribal error and the bill of divorce is valid.

As that also indicates a roof – דְּמַשְׁמַע אִיגֶּרֶת: Rashi explains that when the word *iggeret* is written with a *yod* it can also mean roof, *igra*. *Tosafot* add that although the word carries both meanings whether with or without a *yod*, when this word was used to have the meaning of: A letter, it was commonly written without a *yod*, as that is the Hebrew meaning of the word, and it appears in that form in the Bible. When referring to a roof it is generally written with a *yod*, as that is the Aramaic meaning of the word.

The *ge'onim*, followed by the Rambam, have a different explanation: If the word is written with a *yod*, perhaps a space will be left after the *yod* and it will read *ve'i gart*, which means: If you committed adultery, indicating that the husband is divorcing the wife only if she committed adultery.

According to a different version of the text, Abaye stresses that one should make sure to write *ve'iggeret* with the prefix *vav*, since if it is omitted the word might be understood as referring to some other letter, not a bill of divorce (see *Tosafot*).

And he should not write to go [*limhakh*], etc. – וְלָא לִכְתּוֹב לִימְהַךְ וכו׳: According to Rashi's version of the text there are two instructions with regard to the word *limhakh*. The first is not to write it with a *yod* so that it does not look like two words and come out *li mehakh*, meaning for me from this, indicating that she will be his by the serving of this bill, i.e., it is a bill of betrothal, not divorce. The second instruction is to make sure the *heh* does not look like a *ḥet*, as the word formed with a *ḥet* would indicate that he is joking.

The Rambam apparently had a version of the text that combines both instructions. Making both errors causes it to be read as: It is a joke to me, *li meḥakh*. While in the *Beit Yosef* this version is deemed a mistake, Rabbi Eliyahu Mizraḥi (responsum 87) considers it preferable.

HALAKHA

Should not write, and this, etc. – לָא לִכְתּוֹב וְדֵין וכו׳: When writing a bill of divorce one should not write *vedein* with a *yod*, lest it be read *vedin*, meaning law (Rambam *Sefer Nashim, Hilkhot Geirushin* 4:13; *Shulḥan Arukh, Even HaEzer* 126:9).

And he should not write, a letter, etc. – וְלָא לִכְתּוֹב אִיגֶּרֶת וכו׳: One should not write *iggeret* with a *yod*, lest it be read as two separate words, meaning: And if you committed adultery (Rambam *Sefer Nashim, Hilkhot Geirushin* 1:4; *Shulḥan Arukh, Even HaEzer* 126:9).

And he should not write, to go, etc. – וְלָא לִכְתּוֹב לִימְהַךְ וכו׳: One should not write the word *limhakh* in a bill of divorce with a *yod*, lest it be read *li meḥakh*, meaning: It is a joke for me (Rambam *Sefer Nashim, Hilkhot Geirushin* 1:4; *Shulḥan Arukh, Even HaEzer* 136:13).

And he should be sure not to write *limḥakh* – וְלָא לִכְתּוֹב לְמִחַךְ: When writing the word *limhakh* he must make sure that the *heh* does not look like a *ḥet*, as the word would then mean to joke (Rambam *Sefer Nashim, Hilkhot Geirushin* 1:4; *Shulḥan Arukh, Even HaEzer* 126:14).

״דִּיתִיהֱוְיִין״ ״דִּיתִיצְבְּיִין״ תְּלָתָא תְּלָתָא יוּדִי״ן דְּמַשְׁמַע תֶּהֶוְיָן וְתִצְבְּיָן. וְלוֹרְכֵיהּ לוי״ו דְּ״תֵירוּכִין״ ולוי״ו דְּ״שְׁבוּקִין״ דְּמַשְׁמַע תְּרִיכִין וּשְׁבִיקִין;

Abaye continues: In the clause: That you shall be permitted to go marry any man that you wish, the words *ditihevyin* and *ditiztviyin* must include **three** instances of the letter ***yod***[HL] in a row in each word, **as** with only two instances of the letter *yod* these words **indicate:** That **they shall be** [*tehevyan*], **and:** That **they wish** [*titzviyan*], referring to other women. **And he should extend the** ***vav***[N] **of** ***teirukhin***[H] **and the** ***vav*** **of** ***shevukin*****,** as otherwise, the *vav* may be mistaken for a *yod*, and those words spelled with a *yod* **indicate divorced** [*terikhin*] **and left** [*shevikin*] women. In other words, it will change the meaning from describing the document as one that divorces or sends away to describing the women as divorced and sent away.

וְלוֹרְכֵיהּ לוי״ו דְּ״כְדוּ״ דְּמַשְׁמַע וּכְדִי; וְלָא לִיכְתּוֹב ״לְאִיתְנַסְּבָא״ דְּמַשְׁמַע לָא יִתְנַסְּבָא, אֶלָּא ״לְהִתְנַסְּבָא״.

And in the clause: And now [*ukhedu*] I have dismissed and ousted and divorced you, **he should extend the** ***vav*** **of** ***khedu*****,**[H] as otherwise, the *vav* may be mistaken for a *yod*, and spelled with a *yod* it **indicates: And with nothing** [*ukhedi*].[N] **And** in the expression: To go marry [*lehitnasseva*] **he should not write** ***le'itnasseva***[H] with an *alef* and a *yod*, **as,** if he leaves space between the letters it will **indicate: Will not get married** [*la yitnasseva*]. **Rather,** he should write ***lehitnasseva*****,**[L] with a *heh* and without a *yod*, so there will be no room for this error.

אִיבַּעְיָא לְהוּ: בָּעֵינַן ״וְדֵין״, אוֹ לָא בָּעֵינַן ״וְדֵין״?

§ **A dilemma was raised before them: Do we need** to write: **And this** that you shall have from me is a scroll of divorce, and a letter of leave, and a bill of dismissal to go to marry any man that you wish, **or do we not need** to write the clause beginning with the words: **And this?** Is the *halakha* in accordance with the opinion of Rabbi Yehuda or the Rabbis?

תָּא שְׁמַע, דְּאַתְקֵין רָבָא בְּגִיטֵּי: ״אֵיךְ פְּלָנְיָא בַּר פְּלָנְיָא פְּטַר וְתָרֵיךְ יַת פְּלוֹנִיתָא אִינְתְּתֵיהּ דַּהֲוַת אִינְתְּתֵיהּ מִן קֳדַם דְּנָא מִיּוֹמָא דְּנַן וּלְעָלַם״, וְאִילּוּ ״וְדֵין״ לָא קָאָמַר.

Come and hear a solution, **as Rava instituted** the following wording **in bills of divorce:** We saw **how so-and-so,**[N] **son of so-and-so,**[H] **dismissed and divorced so-and-so, his wife, who was his wife from beforehand, from this day and forever.**[H] **But he did not state** the clause beginning with the words: **And this.**

וּלְטַעֲמִיךְ, כּוּלְּהוּ מִי קָאָמַר? אֶלָּא בָּעֵינַן, הָכָא נַמִי בָּעֵינַן.

The Gemara challenges this solution: **And according to your reasoning, did** Rava **state all** of the other necessary clauses[N] of a bill of divorce? **Rather, we need** to write them even though they were not mentioned explicitly in Rava's formulation. **Here too, we need** to write the clause beginning with the words: And this, even though it was not mentioned specifically by Rava.

״מִיּוֹמָא דְּנַן״ – לְאַפּוּקֵי מִדְּרַבִּי יוֹסֵי, דְּאָמַר: זְמַנּוֹ שֶׁל שְׁטָר מוֹכִיחַ עָלָיו;

§ The Gemara analyzes the wording instituted by Rava: The expression: **From this day,** is written **to the exclusion of** the statement **of Rabbi Yosei, who said:**[N] **The date** written **in a document proves** when **it** takes effect, and therefore it is not necessary to write the expression: From this day. Rava added this expression to take the opposite opinion into account.

״וּלְעָלַם״

The expression: **And forever,**

NOTES

And he should extend the *vav*, etc. – וְלוֹרְכֵיהּ לוי״ו וכו׳: *Tosafot* explain that the *vav* does not need to be longer than a normal *vav*; rather, one should make sure the *vav* is of the right length, since if it is too short it looks like a *yod* and causes the word to be read differently. The commentaries cite the custom to write a longer *vav* in these words, which is advantageous because one who makes sure to write a longer *vav* will certainly not write one that is too short (Rashba).

And with nothing [*ukhedi*] – וּכְדִי: Rashi explains this word according to its Aramaic meaning, with nothing, while the Rambam interprets it as *ukedei*, which is Hebrew for: And in order to, i.e., I will divorce you under a certain condition.

How so-and-so, etc. – אֵיךְ פְּלָנְיָא וכו׳: This cannot be the exact wording of the bill of divorce, as this statement relates to the divorce in third person and not in first person as the bill should be written. A bill of divorce written in this manner, as is the practice of the Karaites, would be invalid. The wording here is clearly inaccurate in this regard (Ran).

Did Rava state all of the other clauses – כּוּלְּהוּ מִי קָאָמַר: Rashi explains that this refers to the sentence: That you shall be permitted to go marry any man that you wish. The Rashba explains that it refers to the statement: You are hereby permitted to marry any man.

To the exclusion of the statement of Rabbi Yosei who said – לְאַפּוּקֵי מִדְּרַבִּי יוֹסֵי דְּאָמַר: Since several sources imply that the *halakha* is in accordance with Rabbi Yosei's opinion, the commentaries maintain that this does not indicate that Rabbi Yosei's opinion was rejected by Rava. Rather, he added this phrase to prevent a court that does not rule according to Rabbi Yosei from rendering this bill of divorce invalid.

HALAKHA

Three instances of the letter *yod* – תְּלָתָא יודי״ן: The words *ditihevyin*, that you shall be, and *ditiztviyin*, that you wish, should each include three instances of the letter *yod* in a row, as with two instances of the letter *yod* the words are in plural form and indicate that the reference is to two wives. *Tosafot* and Rosh, citing Rabbi Yosef Tuv-Elem, note that the custom is to write these words with five instances of the letter *yod*, including the other two instances of the letter *yod* that are included in the spelling (Rambam *Sefer Nashim, Hilkhot Geirushin* 1:4; *Shulḥan Arukh, Even HaEzer* 136:10).

And he should extend the *vav* of *teirukhin* – וְלוֹרְכֵיהּ לוי״ו דְּתֵירוּכִין: When writing the words *teirukhin*, divorce, and *shevukin*, leave, one should make sure to extend the *vav* so that it is longer than an ordinary *vav*. This is so that the *vav* does not appear like a *yod*, causing the word to be read as *terikhin* or *shevikin*, meaning that he is divorced by her (Rambam *Sefer Nashim, Hilkhot Geirushin* 1:4; *Shulḥan Arukh, Even HaEzer* 136:11).

He should extend the *vav* of *khedu* – לוֹרְכֵיהּ לוי״ו דִּכְדוּ: One should be careful to extend the *vav* of the word *khedu* so that it does not look like a *yod*, causing the word to be read *kedei*, meaning that he is divorcing her under a condition (Rambam *Sefer Nashim, Hilkhot Geirushin* 1:4; *Shulḥan Arukh, Even HaEzer* 136:11).

And he should not write *le'itnasseva* – וְלָא לִיכְתּוֹב לְאִיתְנַסְּבָא: He should not write *le'itnasseva*, with an *alef* and a *yod*, as that might be mistakenly read *la yitnasseva*, will not get married; rather, he should write *lehitnasseva*, with a *heh* and without a *yod*. If he wrote *litnasseva*, with neither an *alef* nor a *heh*, the Rema rules, based on the Rashba, that the bill of divorce is valid (*Shulḥan Arukh, Even HaEzer* 136:15).

How so-and-so, son of so-and-so, etc. – אֵיךְ פְּלָנְיָא בַּר פְּלָנְיָא וכו׳: The Rambam's formulation of the bill of divorce reads: How I, so-and-so, son of so-and-so. The *Tur*, citing the Rosh, comments that this is not correct, as the word how belongs in a document written by witnesses, not in a bill of divorce, which a husband writes for his wife (Rambam *Sefer Nashim, Hilkhot Geirushin* 1:12; *Shulḥan Arukh, Even HaEzer* 126:8).

From this day and forever – מִיּוֹמָא דְּנַן וּלְעָלַם: A bill of divorce must include the expression: From this day and forever (Rambam *Sefer Nashim, Hilkhot Geirushin* 1:12; *Shulḥan Arukh, Even HaEzer* 154:101).

LANGUAGE

Three instances of the letter *yod* – תְּלָתָא יודי״ן: Three instances of the letter *yod* in a row do not exist in the normal spelling of any word. Despite this, these words are written in this manner in a bill of divorce in order to prevent any other possible reading. If the words are written with a single *yod* it might be read as a vowel, e.g., the word *tihevyin* would read *tihevin*. And with two instances of the letter *yod* it could be read as a consonant alone, e.g., *tihevyan*. Therefore, it is written unconventionally with three instances of the letter *yod*, in order to emphasize that it is to be read *tihevyin*.

To go marry [*lehitnasseva*] – לְהִתְנַסְּבָא: This is the form of the word in Old Aramaic, as in the earlier form of Aramaic the passive form was written with the letter *heh*, as is found in the Aramaic of the Bible. This letter was dropped later on due to the general fading of the guttural consonants.

לְאַפּוֹקֵי מִדִּבְעָא מִינֵּיהּ רָבָא מֵרַב נַחְמָן, דְּאָמַר ״הַיּוֹם אִי אַתְּ אִשְׁתִּי וּלְמָחָר אַתְּ אִשְׁתִּי״.

was instituted **to the exclusion of that which Rava asked Rav Naḥman,** with regard to a case **where** the husband **said** to his wife while handing her the bill of divorce: **Today you are not my wife and tomorrow you are my wife.** Does this limitation take effect? Although the conclusion of that inquiry was that once the wife is divorced she is divorced forever, Rava instituted the addition of this expression in the text of the bill of divorce to remove any uncertainty with regard to such a case.

״גּוּפוֹ שֶׁל גֵּט שִׁחְרוּר הֲרֵי אַתְּ בַּת חוֹרִין, הֲרֵי אַתְּ לְעַצְמֵךְ״. אַתְקֵין רַב יְהוּדָה בִּשְׁטַר זְבִינֵי דְעַבְדֵי: ״עַבְדָּא דְּנַן מוּצְדָּק לְעַבְדּוּ, וּפְטִיר וַעֲטִיר מִן חֵרוּרֵי וּמִן עֲלוּלֵי וּמִן עֲרוּרֵי מַלְכָּא וּמַלְכְּתָא, וְרֹשׁוּם דְּאִינִישׁ לָא אִית עֲלוֹהִי, וּמְנוּקֶּה מִכׇּל מוּם וּמִן שְׁחִין דְּנָפֵיק עַד טַצְהַר חֲדַת וְעַתִּיק״.

§ It is stated in the mishna: **The basic** element **of a bill of manumission** for a maidservant is: **You are hereby a free woman,** or: **You are hereby your own. Rav Yehuda instituted** the following formulation **in a document of sale for slaves: This slave is justified,** i.e., fit for slavery, **and he is dismissed and removed from manumission and from accusations and from contests of the king and queen,** meaning that he was not sentenced to death by the governmental court. **And there is not a sign** [*reshum*] **of** ownership of another **person on him.**[N] **And he is clean of any blemish and of boils that emerge on him for four** [*tatzhar*][L] years, whether **new or old.**

מַאי אַסּוּתֵיהּ? אָמַר אַבָּיֵי: גִּינְבָּרָא וּמָרְתְּכָא וְכַבְרִיתָא, וְחַלָּא דְחַמְרָא, וּמִשְׁחָא דְזֵיתָא וְנֵטְפִיק חִיוָּרָא, וְשָׁיֵיף לֵיהּ בְּגַדְפָּא דְאַוְּוזָא.

The Gemara asks tangentially: **What is the cure for** boils?[B] **Abaye said:** One takes **ginger** [*ginebara*],[L] **and slag from silver, and sulfur** [*kavrita*],[L] **and wine vinegar, and olive oil, and white naphtha** [*natpik*],[L] **and spreads it with a goose feather.**

מתני׳ שְׁלֹשָׁה גִּיטִּין פְּסוּלִין, וְאִם נִשֵּׂאת – הַוָּלָד כָּשֵׁר:

MISHNA **Three bills of divorce are invalid** *ab initio*, **but if** the woman **marries** another man on the basis of one of these bills of divorce the lineage of **the offspring** from this marriage **is unflawed.** In other words, she is not considered to be a married woman who engaged in sexual intercourse with another man, which would impair the lineage of their child.

כָּתַב בִּכְתַב יָדוֹ וְאֵין עָלָיו עֵדִים, יֵשׁ עָלָיו עֵדִים וְאֵין בּוֹ זְמַן, יֵשׁ בּוֹ זְמַן וְאֵין בּוֹ אֶלָּא עֵד אֶחָד, הֲרֵי אֵלּוּ שְׁלֹשָׁה גִּיטִּין פְּסוּלִין, וְאִם נִשֵּׂאת – הַוָּלָד כָּשֵׁר.

These three bills are: A bill of divorce that the husband **wrote in his handwriting**[NH] **but has no** signatures of **witnesses on** the document at all, a case where **there are** signatures of **witnesses on** the document **but there is no date** written **on it,**[H] and a case where **there is a date** written **on it, but it contains only one witness. These are** the **three invalid bills of divorce** with regard to which the Sages said: **And if she marries,** the lineage of **the offspring is unflawed.**

NOTES

And there is not a sign [*reshum*] of ownership of another person on him – וְרֹשׁוּם דְּאִינִישׁ לָא אִית עֲלוֹהִי: Rashi explains that slaves would wear tags that would identify their owners. The version held by many commentaries replaces *reshum*, ownership, with *reshu*, possession, meaning that he is not liened to anyone (*Tosafot*), or that no one else has authority over him (*Arukh*).

Wrote in his handwriting – כָּתַב בִּכְתַב יָדוֹ: *Tosafot* (3b) explain that although the husband's signature is considered equivalent to the signatures of two witnesses, he is not deemed credible with regard to the date. Therefore, this bill of divorce is treated the same as a bill of divorce in which no date is written.

BACKGROUND

Boils – שְׁחִין: The treatment process for boils serves two purposes. Some of the substances mentioned, such as olive oil, are used to alleviate the itchiness of the skin. Other substances, such as sulfur and mercury, serve to disinfect and remove the illness.

HALAKHA

Wrote in his handwriting – כָּתַב בִּכְתַב יָדוֹ: If the husband wrote a bill of divorce in his handwriting and one witness signed it, it is invalid; despite this, the wife is disqualified from marrying a priest as a divorcée (Rambam *Sefer Nashim, Hilkhot Geirushin* 1:14; *Shulḥan Arukh, Even HaEzer* 130:20).

But there is no date written on it – וְאֵין בּוֹ זְמַן: If a bill of divorce does not include the date it is invalid (Rambam *Sefer Nashim, Hilkhot Geirushin* 1:25; *Shulḥan Arukh, Even HaEzer* 127:1).

LANGUAGE

Four [*tatzhar*] – טַצְהַר: The *ge'onim* correctly note that this is the Persian word čahār, meaning four.

Ginger [*ginebara*] – גִּינְבָּרָא: There are different opinions as to the meaning of this word. Some assert that it refers to the ginger plant, called *gingembre* in French. Others maintain that it is the sap of a juniper, of the genus *Juniperus*, which is its scientific name today. The juniper is a coniferous tree bearing juicy fruits whose sap is extracted from the bark of several of its species. Still others claim that it refers to mercury sulfide, HgS, called κιννάβαρι, *kinnabari*, in Greek, which was used as a base for paints and as a major source for mercury.

Sulfur [*kavrita*] – כַּבְרִיתָא: According to Rashi this is sulfur, and this is how sulfur is translated in several Aramaic translations of the Bible. In the version of the text according to the *Arukh*, the word is *kakrita*, meaning honeycomb.

Naphtha [*natpik*] – נֵטְפִיק: This word means crude oil, and probably derives from the Akkadian *naptu*.

רבי אליעזר אומר: אף על פי שאין עליו עדים אלא שנתנו לה בפני עדים – כשר, וגובה מנכסים משועבדים, שאין העדים חותמים על הגט אלא מפני תיקון העולם.

Rabbi Eliezer says: Even though there are no signatures of **witnesses on** the document, **but he handed it to her in the presence of** two **witnesses,**[H] it **is a valid** bill of divorce.[N] And on the basis of this bill of divorce the woman **can collect** the amount written for her in her marriage contract even **from liened property, as** Rabbi Eliezer maintains that **the witnesses sign the bill of divorce only for the betterment of the world.**[B] If no witnesses sign a bill of divorce the husband can contest its validity at any time by denying that he wrote it. Nevertheless, the witnesses' signatures are not an essential part of a bill of divorce.

גמ׳ ותו ליכא? והא איכא: גט ישן! התם לא תצא, הכא תצא.

GEMARA The Gemara asks: **But are there no other** invalid bills of divorce? **But isn't there an outdated bill of divorce,** where the husband and wife were secluded after it was written and before it was handed to her? The Gemara answers that there is a difference between the cases: **There,** in the case of an outdated bill of divorce, if the woman remarries on the basis of that bill of divorce **she** need **not leave** her husband; **here, she must leave** him.

הניחא למאן דאמר הכא תצא, אלא למאן דאמר הכא לא תצא, מאי איכא למימר?

The Gemara asks: **This works out well according to the one who says** that **here she must leave** her husband, even though the lineage of their children is unflawed. **But according to the one who says** that **here she** need **not leave, what is there to say?** Why is an outdated bill of divorce not mentioned in the mishna?

התם תינשא לכתחלה, הכא דיעבד.

The Gemara answers: There is still a difference between the cases, as **there,** in the case of an outdated bill of divorce, **she may remarry *ab initio*;** while **here,** it is only **after the fact,** if she remarried, that she need not leave her second husband.

והא איכא גט קרח! התם הולד ממזר, הכא הולד כשר.

The Gemara asks: **But isn't there a bare bill of divorce,** i.e., one that is missing a signature, which is also invalid? The Gemara answers: **There,** if the woman remarries based on this bill of divorce **the offspring** of her second marriage **is a *mamzer*; here,** the lineage of **the offspring is unflawed.**

הניחא לרבי מאיר, דאמר: כל המשנה ממטבע שטבעו חכמים בגיטין הולד ממזר, אלא לרבנן מאי איכא למימר?

The Gemara asks: **This works out well according to Rabbi Meir, who said** that **anyone who deviates from the formula coined by the Sages with regard to bills of divorce** renders **the offspring a *mamzer*.** Therefore, a bare bill of divorce is completely invalid, and if the woman remarries the offspring is a *mamzer*. **But according to the Rabbis,** who hold that the offspring is not a *mamzer*, **what is there to say?** Why is a bare bill of divorce not listed in the mishna?

התם תצא, הכא לא תצא

The Gemara answers that there is still a distinction between the cases: **There,** if the woman remarries **she must leave** her husband, even according to the Rabbis who hold that the offspring is not a *mamzer*; **here, she** need **not leave** her husband.

הניחא למאן דאמר הכא לא תצא, אלא למאן דאמר הכא תצא מאי איכא למימר? במקושר לא קא מיירי.

The Gemara asks: **This works out well according to the one who says** that **here she** need **not leave** her husband; **but according to the one who says** that **here she must leave** her husband, **what is there to say?** The Gemara answers: Apparently the mishna **is not speaking about** a folded and **tied** bill of divorce, which requires a signature on every fold, but rather, an open bill of divorce. There are only three cases in which this type of a bill of divorce is invalid in a manner that obligates the woman, if she remarries, to leave her second husband, although the lineage of their children would be unflawed.

HALAKHA

He handed it to her in the presence of two witnesses – שנתנו לה בפני עדים: If a bill of divorce that is not signed by witnesses is transmitted to a woman in the presence of witnesses, the bill of divorce is valid after the fact, in accordance with the opinion of Rabbi Eliezer (Rambam *Sefer Nashim, Hilkhot Geirushin* 1:18; *Shulḥan Arukh, Even HaEzer* 133:1).

NOTES

Even though there are no signatures of witnesses on it… it is a valid bill of divorce – אף על פי שאין עליו עדים...כשר: The dispute in the mishna with regard to a bill of divorce that was not signed by witnesses but was handed to the wife in the presence of two witnesses pertains directly to the fundamental dispute between Rabbi Meir and Rabbi Elazar, mentioned several times throughout the tractate (see 3b), over which witnesses effect the divorce. Rabbi Meir holds that it is the signatory witnesses who effect the divorce, whereas Rabbi Elazar maintains that it is the witnesses of the transmission of the bill of divorce from the husband to the wife that effect the divorce.

In this mishna, Rabbi Eliezer's statement clearly accords with the opinion of Rabbi Elazar. Furthermore, according to the version of the mishna cited below (86b), it is actually Rabbi Elazar, not Rabbi Eliezer, who makes this statement. However, identifying Rabbi Meir as the first *tanna* in the mishna is difficult, as in his opinion a bill of divorce that is not signed by witnesses is entirely invalid, not only *ab initio*. Therefore, Rashi claims that this is a third opinion, according to which the handwriting of the husband suffices.

Nevertheless, in the Jerusalem Talmud it is asserted that this is the opinion of Rabbi Meir, and that is how most commentaries interpret it as well. They explain that Rabbi Meir concedes that the husband's handwriting can supplant the signatures of witnesses, based on the principle that the admission of a litigant is equivalent to testimony of one hundred witnesses. Rashi also mentions this alternative interpretation, and one later commentary suggests that it was added by Rashi himself in a later edition of his commentary (see *Migdal David*).

BACKGROUND

The betterment of the world – תיקון העולם: This term refers to various *halakhot* enacted by the Sages in order to improve Jewish society. The Mishna records a series of these *halakhot* in the fourth chapter, many of which were intended to protect women from becoming chained to their husbands or to prevent the birth of *mamzerim*. Perhaps the most well-known of these enactments is the document, known as a *prosbol*, which prevents the Sabbatical Year from abrogating an outstanding debt, an institution introduced by Hillel. Although by Torah law all loans are canceled at the end of the Sabbatical Year, by signing this document a lender would be permitted to collect his loan even after that time. In this way, Hillel ensured that people would continue to provide loans even as the Sabbatical Year was approaching. Although it bears the same name, this term is not related to *tikkun olam*, the improvement of the world, which is central to Jewish mysticism.

וְהָא אִיכָּא: שְׁלוֹם מַלְכוּת! הָתָם תֵּיצֵא, הָכָא לֹא תֵּיצֵא.

The Gemara asks: **But isn't there** a bill of divorce that is invalid **due to** the need to maintain **peaceful** relations with **the kingdom,** as it mentions the year of the divorce according to the age of another kingdom? Why is this not mentioned in the mishna? The Gemara answers: **There, she must leave** her husband; **here, she** need **not leave** her husband.

הָנִיחָא לְמַאן דְּאָמַר הָכָא לֹא תֵּיצֵא, אֶלָּא לְמַאן דְּאָמַר תֵּיצֵא, מַאי אִיכָּא לְמֵימַר? (הָתָם הַוָּלָד מַמְזֵר, הָכָא הַוָּלָד כָּשֵׁר.)

The Gemara asks: **This works out well according to the one who says that here she** need **not leave** her husband. **But according to the one who says that she must leave** her husband, **what is there to say?** The Gemara answers: **There, the offspring is a** *namzer*; **here,** the lineage of **the offspring is unflawed.**

(הָנִיחָא לְרַבִּי מֵאִיר, אֶלָּא לְרַבָּנַן מַאי אִיכָּא לְמֵימַר?) מוֹקִים לַהּ כְּדְרַבִּי מֵאִיר, וְהָתָם הַוָּלָד מַמְזֵר, הָכָא הַוָּלָד כָּשֵׁר.

The Gemara asks: **This works out well according to Rabbi Meir; but according to the Rabbis,** who hold that in the case of a bill of divorce in which the date is written according to the age of another kingdom, the offspring is not a *mamzer*, **what is there to say?** The Gemara answers: The one who holds that in the cases in the mishna the woman must leave her husband **establishes it in accordance with** the opinion of **Rabbi Meir,** according to whom **there, the offspring is a** *mamzer*. **Here,** the lineage of **the offspring is unflawed.**

מִנְיָנָא דְּרֵישָׁא לְמַעוּטֵי מַאי, וּמִנְיָנָא דְּסֵיפָא לְמַעוּטֵי מַאי?

The mishna emphasizes twice that there are three bills of divorce that are invalid. The Gemara asks: **What** does **the quantity in the first clause** serve **to exclude? And what** does **the quantity in the latter clause** serve **to exclude?**

מִנְיָנָא דְּרֵישָׁא – לְמַעוּטֵי הָנֵי דַּאֲמַרַן,

The Gemara answers: **The quantity** mentioned **in the first clause** serves **to exclude those** invalid bills of divorce **that we** previously **mentioned,** which are treated either more or less stringently than the cases in the mishna.

מִנְיָנָא דְּסֵיפָא – לְמַעוּטֵי הָא דְּתַנְיָא: הַמֵּבִיא גֵּט מִמְּדִינַת הַיָּם, נְתָנוֹ לָהּ וְלֹא אָמַר לָהּ ״בְּפָנַי נִכְתַּב וּבְפָנַי נֶחְתַּם״ – יוֹצִיא וְהַוָּלָד מַמְזֵר, דִּבְרֵי רַבִּי מֵאִיר,

The quantity mentioned **in the latter clause** serves **to exclude that which is taught** in a *baraita*: With regard to an agent **who brings a bill of divorce** for a certain woman **from a country overseas,** and **gives it to her but does not say to her: It was written in my presence and it was signed in my presence,** and she remarries, her second husband **must divorce** her, **and the offspring** of their marriage **is a** *mamzer*. This is **the statement of Rabbi Meir.**

וַחֲכָמִים אוֹמְרִים: אֵין הַוָּלָד מַמְזֵר, כֵּיצַד יַעֲשֶׂה? יִטְּלֶנּוּ הֵימֶנָּה, וְיַחֲזוֹר וְיִתְּנֶנּוּ לָהּ בִּפְנֵי שְׁנַיִם וְיֹאמַר ״בְּפָנַי נִכְתַּב וּבְפָנַי נֶחְתַּם״.

And the Rabbis say: The offspring of the second marriage **is not a** *mamzer*; rather, **how should** the agent **act** to rectify the situation? **He should take** the bill of divorce **from her, and give it to her again in the presence of two** witnesses **and say: It was written in my presence and it was signed in my presence.** Since this problem can be corrected, it is not listed in the mishna as one of the invalid bills of divorce.

״כָּתַב בִּכְתַב יָדוֹ וְאֵין עָלָיו עֵדִים״. אָמַר רַב: כְּתַב יָדוֹ שָׁנִינוּ.

§ It is stated in the mishna: A bill of divorce that the husband **wrote in his handwriting, but has no** signatures of **witnesses on it** at all, is invalid; nevertheless, if the woman remarries, the lineage of the child born from her second husband is unflawed. **Rav says: We learned** that this is referring to **his handwriting.**

אַהֵיָיא? אִילֵימָא אַרֵישָׁא – פְּשִׁיטָא, כְּתַב יָדוֹ קָתָנֵי!

The Gemara asks: **With regard to which** clause of the mishna is this referring? **If we say** that it is referring **to the first clause,** what Rav said **is obvious,** as the case of **his handwriting is** explicitly **taught** in that clause.

וְאֶלָּא אַמְּצִיעֲתָא, הֲרֵי יֵשׁ עָלָיו עֵדִים! אֶלָּא אַסֵּיפָא: יֵשׁ בּוֹ זְמַן וְאֵין בּוֹ אֶלָּא עֵד אֶחָד,

And if it is **rather** referring **to the middle clause,** i.e., an undated bill of divorce, why does it matter whether it was written in the husband's handwriting? **Aren't there** signatures of **witnesses on it? Rather,** it must be referring **to the latter clause** in the mishna, i.e., a bill of divorce that **has a date** written **on it but has only** the signature of **one witness.**

וְדַוְקָא כְּתַב יָדוֹ וְעֵד, אֲבָל כְּתַב סוֹפֵר וְעֵד – לָא.

And Rav is saying that **specifically** when the bill of divorce is written in **his handwriting and** has the signature of one **witness,**[H] the woman's child from her second husband is of unflawed lineage. **But** if it is written in **a scribe's handwriting,** even if it includes the signature of one **witness,** the child's lineage is **not** unflawed, but rather he is a *mamzer*, as the bill of divorce is completely invalid.

וּשְׁמוּאֵל אָמַר: אֲפִילּוּ כְּתַב סוֹפֵר וְעֵד, שֶׁהֲרֵי שָׁנִינוּ: כְּתַב סוֹפֵר וְעֵד – כָּשֵׁר.

And Shmuel says: Even where it is written in **a scribe's handwriting and** it has the signature of **a witness,** the lineage of the child is unflawed, **as we learned** in a mishna (87b): In the case of a bill of divorce in which **the scribe's handwriting** is recognizable **and** there is one **witness** signed, it is **valid.**

וְרַב: מִי דָּמֵי? הָתָם תִּינָּשֵׂא לְכַתְּחִילָּה, הָכָא דִּיעֲבַד.

And Rav would respond: **Is** that case **comparable? There,** in that case, the mishna indicates that the woman **may marry *ab initio*.** Therefore, it must be a case where the scribe also signed as a second witness. But **here,** in the case of this mishna, the bill of divorce is invalid and the woman may not remarry; it is only if she remarried and had a child that his lineage is rendered unflawed **after the fact.** Therefore, it must be referring to a case where the husband wrote it.

וּשְׁמוּאֵל: לָא קַשְׁיָא, הָא בְּסַפְרָא דִּמוּבְהָק, וְהָא בְּסַפְרָא דְּלָא מוּבְהָק.

And Shmuel, who holds that both cases are referring to a bill of divorce that was written by a scribe but not signed by the scribe as one of the witnesses, would respond that the contradiction is **not difficult. That** mishna, where the bill of divorce is rendered valid *ab initio*, is referring **to** the handwriting of **an expert scribe,**[N] who can presumably be relied upon to have written the bill of divorce properly and only according to the husband's instructions, **and this** mishna is referring **to** the handwriting of **a scribe who is not expert.** Since the bill of divorce was not signed by two witnesses, there is concern that the scribe did not write it properly.

וְכֵן אָמַר רַבִּי יוֹחָנָן: כְּתַב יָדוֹ שָׁנִינוּ. אֲמַר לֵיהּ רַבִּי אֶלְעָזָר: הֲרֵי יֵשׁ עָלָיו עֵדִים! אֲמַר לֵיהּ: אַסֵּיפָא.

And similarly, Rabbi Yoḥanan says in accordance with the opinion of Rav: **We learned** that the mishna is referring to **his handwriting. Rabbi Elazar,** assuming that Rabbi Yoḥanan was explaining the middle clause, **said to him: Aren't there** signatures of **witnesses in** the bill of divorce? Why is the husband's handwriting necessary? Rabbi Yoḥanan **said to him:** I was referring **to the latter clause,** in which there is only one witness.

זִימְנִין אֲמַר רַב: תֵּצֵא, זִימְנִין אֲמַר רַב: לֹא תֵּצֵא,

§ With regard to the three invalid bills of divorce mentioned in the mishna, **sometimes Rav said** that if the woman remarries based on one of these bills of divorce **she must leave** her second husband, and **sometimes Rav said** that **she** need **not leave.**

הָא כֵּיצַד? יֵשׁ לָהּ בָּנִים – לֹא תֵּצֵא, אֵין לָהּ בָּנִים – תֵּצֵא.

How so? How can the contradiction between Rav's statements be explained? If **she** already **has children** from her second husband then **she** need **not leave** him, as, if she is required to leave him there will be slander that their children are *mamzerim*. But if **she does not have children** from him, **she must leave** him.

מְתִיב מָר זוּטְרָא בַּר טוֹבִיָּה: וְכוּלָּן שֶׁהָיוּ בָּהֶן סְפֵק קִידּוּשִׁין אוֹ סְפֵק גֵּירוּשִׁין – הֲרֵי אֵלּוּ חוֹלְצוֹת וְלֹא מִתְיַבְּמוֹת,

Mar Zutra bar Toviya raises an objection to Rav's opinion from a mishna (*Yevamot* 30b). With regard to a woman whose husband died childless [*yevama*] but who is prohibited from marrying her late husband's brother [*yavam*] because he is a forbidden relative to her, not only is she herself exempt from levirate marriage, but she causes any rival wives of hers to be exempt as well, even if they are not forbidden relatives to the brother. The mishna lists fifteen examples of such forbidden relatives (*Yevamot* 2a). **And** if **any of these** fifteen women **had undergone a betrothal or divorce** whose status is **uncertain**[H] with the deceased brother, **those** rival wives **must perform the ritual through which the *yavam* frees the *yevama* of her levirate bonds [*ḥalitza*] and** may **not enter into levirate marriage,** since they are possibly the rival wives of a forbidden relative.

HALAKHA

His handwriting and one witness – כְּתַב יָדוֹ וְעֵד: If the husband wrote a bill of divorce in his handwriting and handed it to his wife without two witnesses, it is an invalid bill of divorce by rabbinic law. Despite this, she is disqualified from marrying a priest. If it was written by a scribe, it is not considered a bill of divorce at all, even if there was one witness. This is in accordance with the opinion of Rav and Rabbi Yoḥanan, in opposition to the opinion of Shmuel (Rambam *Sefer Nashim, Hilkhot Geirushin* 1:13–14; *Shulḥan Arukh, Even HaEzer* 130:20).

And if any of these women had undergone a betrothal or divorce whose status is uncertain, etc. – וְכוּלָּן שֶׁהָיוּ בָּהֶן סְפֵק קִידּוּשִׁין אוֹ סְפֵק גֵּירוּשִׁין וכו׳: If a *yevama* is forbidden to her *yavam* but her betrothal to her late husband was uncertain, or if he granted her a divorce whose status is uncertain, her rival wife must perform *ḥalitza* and not enter into levirate marriage (Rambam *Sefer Nashim, Hilkhot Yibbum VaḤalitza* 6:22; *Shulḥan Arukh, Even HaEzer* 173:6).

NOTES

That mishna is referring to the handwriting of an expert scribe – הָא בְּסַפְרָא דִּמוּבְהָק: Several commentaries explain that an expert scribe presumably writes the bill of divorce only after the husband instructs him to. Therefore, his handwriting is equivalent to the signature of a witness, and in total there are two witnesses. A scribe who is not an expert may have written it without the instruction of the husband, and therefore the signatures of two witnesses are necessary (Rashi; Rashba). The Rid explains that if the scribe is an expert his handwriting is accepted as testimony, since everyone knows that he is qualified to give testimony. If he is not well known people might think that he is not qualified to give testimony, and that is why he did not sign the bill of divorce. They might conclude that any bill of divorce that has only one qualified witness is valid.

HALAKHA

She is never required to leave him – **לְעוֹלָם לֹא תֵּצֵא**: If a woman was divorced with an undated bill of divorce, she may not remarry. If she does remarry she need not leave her second husband, even if they do not have children, in accordance with the ruling of Rabbi Levi and Rabbi Yoḥanan (Rambam *Sefer Nashim*, *Hilkhot Geirushin* 1:25; *Shulḥan Arukh*, *Even HaEzer* 127:1).

All birds disqualify, etc. – **כָּל הָעוֹפוֹת פּוֹסְלִין וכו׳**: If an animal or bird drinks from water of purification, it is disqualified. However a pigeon does not disqualify the waters, since it sucks in such a way that its saliva does not mix with the water (Rambam *Sefer Tahara*, *Hilkhot Para Aduma* 9:12).

BACKGROUND

Kartzit – **קַרְצִית**: Although in modern Hebrew this refers to a tick, that is clearly not the reference here, as ticks feed on blood and, in addition, are not insects but arachnids. Rather, it apparently refers to a kind of winged insect with oral suckers. Although the Gemara interprets it as a fly [*didveta*], it is not necessarily referring to what is called a fly nowadays, especially since flies are not generally found in crops. It may be referring to a grain-eating species of beetle.

Pigeon – **יוֹנָה**: Most birds drink water by dipping the ends of their beaks in water and then raising their heads so the water descends into their throats. In this manner some of the bird's saliva becomes mixed with the water, part of which spills back from the bird's beak into the basin. By contrast, pigeons drink by sucking the water, so they swallow all of it and none of it spills back.

כֵּיצַד סְפֵק קִידּוּשִׁין? זָרַק לָהּ קִידּוּשִׁין סָפֵק קָרוֹב לָהּ סָפֵק קָרוֹב לוֹ – זֶהוּ סְפֵק קִידּוּשִׁין.

How could there be a betrothal whose status is **uncertain? If he threw her** money or a document as **betrothal** in the public domain, and the item was **possibly closer to her,** whereby she could acquire the object and become betrothed, and **possibly closer to him,** preventing her from acquiring it, **this is** a case of **a betrothal** whose status is **uncertain.**

סְפֵק גֵּירוּשִׁין? כָּתַב בִּכְתַב יָדוֹ וְאֵין עָלָיו עֵדִים, יֵשׁ עָלָיו עֵדִים וְאֵין בּוֹ זְמַן, יֵשׁ בּוֹ זְמַן וְאֵין בּוֹ אֶלָּא עֵד אֶחָד – הֲרֵי זֶה סְפֵק גֵּירוּשִׁין;

How can there be **a divorce** whose status is **uncertain?**[N] It is in the cases of invalid bills of divorce mentioned in the mishna here: A bill of divorce that the husband **wrote in his handwriting but has no** signatures of **witnesses on** the document at all, a case where **there are** signatures of **witnesses on** the document **but there is no date** written **on it,** and a case where **there is a date** written **on it but it contains only one witness.** In each of the three cases, **this is** considered **a divorce** whose status is **uncertain.**

וְאִי אָמְרַתְּ לֹא תֵּצֵא, צָרָתָהּ אָתְיָא לְיַבּוּמֵי!

And if you say that despite this woman's problematic divorce **she** need **not leave** her second husband, **her rival wife** from her first marriage might **come to enter into levirate marriage** after the first husband's death, assuming that she was already divorced. This would violate the ruling of the mishna in tractate *Yevamot* that she may not do so, as the status of the divorce is uncertain and therefore it is uncertain whether she is the rival wife of a forbidden relative.

תִּתְיַבֵּם וְאֵין בְּכָךְ כְּלוּם, חֲשָׁשָׁא דְּרַבָּנַן הִיא.

The Gemara answers: **She may enter into levirate marriage, and** there is **no** problem **with that,** as the difficulty with the bill of divorce **is** merely **a concern by rabbinic law.** By Torah law it is a complete bill of divorce, and the rival wife is fit for levirate marriage.

לֵוִי אָמַר: לְעוֹלָם לֹא תֵּצֵא. וְכֵן אָמַר רַבִּי יוֹחָנָן: לְעוֹלָם לֹא תֵּצֵא.

Contrary to Rav's opinion that a woman who remarries based on one of these bills of divorce must leave her second husband unless they have children, **Levi says** that **she** is **never** required to **leave** him,[H] whether or not they have children. **And similarly, Rabbi Yoḥanan says** that **she** is **never** required to **leave** him.

וְכֵן אָמַר לְהוּ רַבִּי יוֹחָנָן לִבְנֵי רַבִּי חֲלַפְתָּא דְּמִן הוּנָא הָכִי אָמַר אֲבוּכוֹן: לְעוֹלָם לֹא תֵּצֵא; וְקַרְצִית שֶׁבָּעֳמִיר אֵינָהּ פּוֹסֶלֶת בְּמֵי חַטָּאת.

And similarly, Rabbi Yoḥanan said to the sons of Rabbi Ḥalafta of Huna: Your father said the following two statements that I heard from him: That **she** is **never** required to **leave** him, **and** that **a** ***kartzit***[B] **in the sheaf does not disqualify water of purification** (see Numbers 19:17–19). Even if a *kartzit* drinks from this water, it may still be sprinkled on a person in order to purify him from ritual impurity imparted by a corpse.

מַאי קַרְצִית? אָמַר אַבָּיֵי: דִּידְבְתָּא דְּבֵינֵי כֵּיפֵי.

The Gemara asks: **What is a** ***kartzit*****? Abaye said** that it is a species of **fly** [***didveta***] **that is found between the sheaves.**

מְתִיב רַב דָּנִיאֵל בַּר רַב קְטִינָא: כָּל הָעוֹפוֹת פּוֹסְלִין בְּמֵי חַטָּאת חוּץ מִן הַיּוֹנָה, מִפְּנֵי שֶׁמּוֹצֶצֶת; וְאִם אִיתָא, נִיתְנֵי: חוּץ מִיּוֹנָה וְקַרְצִית!

Rav Daniel bar Rav Ketina raises an objection to this ruling from the Mishna (*Para* 9:3): **All birds disqualify**[H] **water of purification**[N] by drinking from it, because some of the water spills from the bird's beak back into the basin after being disqualified by having been in the bird's mouth. This is the *halakha* with regard to all birds **except for the pigeon,**[B] **because it sucks** the water, which prevents it from spilling back. **And if it is so** that a *kartzit* does not disqualify water of purification, **let** the mishna **teach** that all birds disqualify **except for the pigeon and the** ***kartzit.***

NOTES

How can there be a divorce whose status is uncertain – **סְפֵק גֵּירוּשִׁין**: If a husband throws the bill of divorce to his wife and it is uncertain whether it fell closer to him or to her, that is also a divorce whose status is uncertain, just as with regard to betrothal. The Gemara in tractate *Yevamot* (30b) discusses why this case is not mentioned in the mishna. It is not discussed here because the mishna is cited in a different context (Rashba; *Tosafot*; Ritva, citing Ramah).

All birds disqualify water of purification – **כָּל הָעוֹפוֹת פּוֹסְלִין בְּמֵי חַטָּאת**: This *halakha* is explained in numerous ways. Rashi explains that while in the bird's beak the water loses its status as water of purification. It then disqualifies the rest of the water when it spills back into it. *Tosafot* elaborate that the Gemara (*Sota* 16b) derives from the fact that purification waters are referred to in the verse as: "Running water in a vessel" (Numbers 19:17), that they must be sprinkled from the same vessel from which they were drawn, and they must not be moved from vessel to vessel. Therefore, when the bird drinks the water from the basin, it loses its status as running water in a vessel.

Rashi suggests in tractate *Ḥullin* (9b) that the water is disqualified because it was used; *Tosafot* reject this suggestion. Another suggestion is that it is disqualified because attention was diverted from it, and diversion of attention disqualifies water of purification. The Rambam and Rabbi Shimshon of Saens both explain in their commentaries on this mishna that the water spills back into the basin mixed with the bird's saliva, which disqualifies it as water of purification. Rabbeinu Crescas Vidal adopts this explanation here.

לָא פְּסִיקָא לֵיהּ, דִּגְדוֹלָה לָא פָּסְלָה, וּקְטַנָּה פָּסְלָה. וְעַד כַּמָּה? אָמַר רַבִּי יִרְמְיָה, וְאִיתֵּימָא רַבִּי אַמִי: עַד כַּזַּיִת.

The Gemara answers: The matter **is not clear-cut, as, while a large** *kartzit* **does not disqualify** the water, **a small one does disqualify** it. This ruling is not mentioned in the mishna, as it is not common to all species of *kartzit*. The Gemara asks: **And how** small must a *kartzit* be to disqualify water of purification? **Rabbi Yirmeya said, and some say** that it was **Rabbi Ami** who said: The size is **up to an olive-bulk.**

״רַבִּי אֶלְעָזָר אוֹמֵר: אַף עַל פִּי״ וכו׳. אָמַר רַב יְהוּדָה אָמַר רַב: הֲלָכָה כְּרַבִּי אֶלְעָזָר בְּגִיטִּין. כִּי אָמְרִיתַהּ קַמֵּיהּ דִּשְׁמוּאֵל, אָמַר: אַף בִּשְׁטָרוֹת.

§ It is stated in the mishna that **Rabbi Elazar says: Even if** there are no signatures of witnesses on the document, but rather he handed it to her in the presence of two witnesses, it is a valid bill of divorce. **Rav Yehuda said** that **Rav said** that **the** ***halakha*** **is in accordance with** the opinion of **Rabbi Elazar with regard to bills of divorce.**[H] But **when I said this** ***halakha*** **before Shmuel, he said** that the *halakha* is in accordance with Rabbi Elazar **with regard to** monetary **documents as well.**[H]

וְרַב סָבַר בִּשְׁטָרוֹת לָא? הָא קָתָנֵי: וְגוֹבָה מִנְּכָסִים מְשׁוּעְבָּדִים!

The Gemara asks: **But does Rav hold** that **with regard to** monetary **documents** the *halakha* is **not** in accordance with Rabbi Elazar? **Doesn't** Rabbi Elazar **teach** in the mishna that on the basis of this bill of divorce a woman **can collect** the amount written in her marriage contract even **from liened property?** Apparently, Rabbi Elazar's ruling has monetary ramifications as well.

רַבִּי אֶלְעָזָר תַּרְתֵּי אָמַר, וְרַב סָבַר כְּוָותֵיהּ בַּחֲדָא וּפְלִיג עֲלֵיהּ בַּחֲדָא.

The Gemara answers: **Rabbi Elazar made two statements,**[N] i.e., his ruling was both with regard to divorce and with regard to monetary documents. **And Rav holds in accordance with his** opinion **with regard to one** issue, i.e., divorce, **and disagrees with his** opinion **with regard to one** issue, monetary documents.

וְכֵן אָמַר רַבִּי יַעֲקֹב בַּר אִידִי אָמַר רַבִּי יְהוֹשֻׁעַ בֶּן לֵוִי: הֲלָכָה כְּרַבִּי אֶלְעָזָר בְּגִיטִּין; וְרַבִּי יַנַּאי אָמַר: אֲפִילּוּ רֵיחַ הַגֵּט אֵין בּוֹ.

And similarly, Rabbi Ya'akov bar Idi says that **Rabbi Yehoshua ben Levi says:** The ***halakha*** **is in accordance with** the opinion **of Rabbi Elazar with regard to bills of divorce. And Rabbi Yannai says:** This **does not have even the trace of a bill of divorce.**

וְרַבִּי יַנַּאי לֵית לֵיהּ דְּרַבִּי אֶלְעָזָר? הָכִי קָאָמַר: לְרַבָּנַן, אֲפִילּוּ רֵיחַ הַגֵּט אֵין בּוֹ.

The Gemara asks: **But does Rabbi Yannai not hold** in accordance with the opinion **of Rabbi Elazar** at all, as opposed to the other *amora'im*? The Gemara answers: Rather, **this is what** Rabbi Yannai **is saying: According to the Rabbis,** who disagree with Rabbi Elazar, this bill of divorce **does not have even the trace of a bill of divorce.**

וְכֵן אָמַר רַבִּי יוֹסֵי בְּרַבִּי חֲנִינָא אָמַר רֵישׁ לָקִישׁ: הֲלָכָה כְּרַבִּי אֶלְעָזָר בְּגִטִּין; וְרַבִּי יוֹחָנָן אָמַר: אֲפִילּוּ רֵיחַ הַגֵּט אֵין בּוֹ.

And similarly, Rabbi Yosei, son of Rabbi Ḥanina, says that **Reish Lakish says:** The ***halakha*** **is in accordance with** the opinion of **Rabbi Elazar with regard to bills of divorce. And Rabbi Yoḥanan says:** This **does not have even the trace of a bill of divorce.**

לֵימָא רַבִּי יוֹחָנָן לֵית לֵיהּ דְּרַבִּי אֶלְעָזָר? הָכִי קָאָמַר: לְרַבָּנַן, אֲפִילּוּ רֵיחַ הַגֵּט אֵין בּוֹ.

The Gemara asks: **Let us say** that **Rabbi Yoḥanan does not hold** in accordance with the opinion **of Rabbi Elazar** at all. The Gemara answers: Rather, **this is what** Rabbi Yoḥanan **is saying: According to the Rabbis,** who disagree with Rabbi Elazar, this **does not have even the trace of a bill of divorce.**

שְׁלַח לֵיהּ רַבִּי אַבָּא בַּר זַבְדָּא לְמָרֵי בַּר מָר: בְּעִי מִינֵּיהּ מֵרַב הוּנָא: הֲלָכָה כְּרַבִּי אֶלְעָזָר בְּגִיטִּין, אוֹ אֵין הֲלָכָה?

Rabbi Abba bar Zavda sent the following request **to Marei bar Mar: Ask Rav Huna** whether the ***halakha*** **is in accordance with** the opinion of **Rabbi Elazar with regard to bills of divorce or** whether the ***halakha*** **is not** in accordance with his opinion.

אַדְּהָכִי נָח נַפְשֵׁיהּ דְּרַב הוּנָא. אֲמַר לֵיהּ רַבָּה בְּרֵיהּ, הָכִי אָמַר אַבָּא מִשְּׁמֵיהּ דְּרָבָא: הֲלָכָה כְּרַבִּי אֶלְעָזָר בְּגִיטִּין, וְרַבּוֹתֵינוּ הַבְּקִיאִין בְּדִבְרֵי הֲלָכָה, מִשּׁוּם רַבֵּינוּ אָמְרוּ: הֲלָכָה כְּרַבִּי אֶלְעָזָר בְּגִיטִּין, דְּאָמַר רַב חָמָא בַּר גּוּרְיָא אָמַר רַב: הֲלָכָה כְּרַבִּי אֶלְעָזָר בְּגִיטִּין.

Meanwhile, before this request reached him, **Rav Huna died. Rabba, son of** Rav Huna, **said** to Marei bar Mar: **My father said in the name of Rava like this:** The ***halakha*** **is in accordance with** the opinion of **Rabbi Elazar with regard to bills of divorce. And our teachers who are well-versed in matters of** ***halakha*** also said **in the name of our teacher** that the ***halakha*** **is in accordance with** the opinion of **Rabbi Elazar with regard to bills of divorce, as Rav Ḥama bar Gurya,** referred to as our teachers, **says** that our teacher **Rav says:** The ***halakha*** **is in accordance with** the opinion **of Rabbi Elazar with regard to bills of divorce.**

HALAKHA

The ***halakha*** **is in accordance with the opinion of Rabbi Elazar with regard to bills of divorce – הֲלָכָה כְּרַבִּי אֶלְעָזָר בְּגִיטִּין:** If a bill of divorce was handed to a wife by her husband in the presence of witnesses, the divorce is valid even if it was not signed by witnesses (Rambam *Sefer Nashim, Hilkhot Geirushin* 1:18; *Shulḥan Arukh, Even HaEzer* 133:1).

With regard to monetary documents as well – אַף בִּשְׁטָרוֹת: If a document was transmitted before witnesses, it is valid even if it was not signed by witnesses. It can be used even to collect from property on which there is a lien, in accordance with the opinion of Shmuel, following the principle that Shmuel's opinion is accepted with regard to monetary law. The *Shakh* cites many authorities who disagree with this ruling, maintaining that signatory witnesses are necessary for monetary documents, as they are meant to serve as proof. He therefore suggests that a litigant can reject a document that does not contain the signatures of witnesses, claiming that he follows the authorities who render it invalid. The *Shakh* concludes that the matter requires further investigation (Rambam *Sefer Mishpatim, Hilkhot Malve VeLoveh* 11:2; *Shulḥan Arukh, Ḥoshen Mishpat* 51:7).

NOTES

Made two statements, etc. – תַּרְתֵּי אָמַר וכו׳: Why does Rav distinguish between bills of divorce and monetary documents with regard to the requirement of signatory witnesses? Rashi explains that the source for this requirement is a verse in Jeremiah (32:44) that refers to sale documents. Therefore, it is unique to monetary documents. The logic behind this distinction is as follows. The main purpose of a bill of divorce is to effect the divorce. The witnesses of the divorce do not need to sign it because their job is not to publicize its existence but to testify that it was given to the wife properly. On the other hand, monetary documents are usually documents of proof, and as such they must be signed by witnesses. Furthermore, these documents obligate other parties as well, as they can be used to collect liened property. Therefore, this type of document must be written in a manner that publicizes it, i.e., in the presence of witnesses.

איכָּא דְּאָמְרִי: וַחֲבֵרֵינוּ הַבְּקִיאִין בִּדְבַר הֲלָכָה, וְתַלְמִידֵי רַבֵּינוּ, מִשּׁוּם רַבֵּינוּ אָמְרוּ: הֲלָכָה כְּרַבִּי אֶלְעָזָר בְּגִיטִּין, דְּאָמַר רַב חִסְדָּא אָמַר רַב חָמָא בַּר גּוּרְיָא אָמַר רַב: הֲלָכָה כְּרַבִּי אֶלְעָזָר בְּגִיטִּין.

There are those who say a different version of this statement: **And our colleagues who are well versed in matters of *halakha* and the disciples of our teacher said in the name of our teacher** that **the *halakha* is in accordance with** the opinion of **Rabbi Elazar with regard to bills of divorce, as Rav Ḥisda**, Rabba bar Rav Huna's colleague, **said that Rav Ḥama bar Gurya**, his teacher, **said** that **Rav said:** The ***halakha* is in accordance with** the opinion of **Rabbi Elazar with regard to bills of divorce.**

וְכֵן כִּי אֲתָא רָבִין, אָמַר רַבִּי אֶלְעָזָר אָמַר רַב: הֲלָכָה כְּרַבִּי אֶלְעָזָר בְּגִיטִּין.

And similarly, when Ravin came from Eretz Yisrael he said that **Rabbi Elazar**, the *amora*, **says** that **Rav says:** The ***halakha* is in accordance with** the opinion of **Rabbi Elazar with regard to bills of divorce.**

מתני׳ שְׁנַיִם שֶׁשָּׁלְחוּ שְׁנֵי גִיטִּין שָׁוִין וְנִתְעָרְבוּ – נוֹתֵן שְׁנֵיהֶם לָזוֹ וּשְׁנֵיהֶם לָזוֹ; לְפִיכָךְ אָבַד אֶחָד מֵהֶן – הֲרֵי הַשֵּׁנִי בָּטֵל.

MISHNA With regard to a case of **two men who sent**[H] their wives **two identical bills of divorce** with an agent, as both their names and their wives' names are identical, **and** the two bills of divorce **were mixed up**, the agent **should hand both** bills of divorce **to this** wife **and both** of them **to that** wife, so that each wife definitely receives her bill of divorce, although it is unclear which one is hers. **Therefore, if one of** the bills of divorce **was lost**[H] before it was given to both women, **the other is void,**[N] because it is unknown which bill of divorce was meant for which woman.

חֲמִשָּׁה שֶׁכָּתְבוּ כְּלָל בְּתוֹךְ הַגֵּט: אִישׁ פְּלוֹנִי מְגָרֵשׁ פְּלוֹנִית, וּפְלוֹנִי פְּלוֹנִית, וְהָעֵדִים מִלְּמַטָּה – כּוּלָּן כְּשֵׁרִין, וְיִנָּתֵן לְכָל אַחַת וְאַחַת;

With regard to **five** husbands **who wrote a general wording in the bill of divorce**, i.e., who wrote one common bill of divorce for their wives with a single formula, writing that **so-and-so divorces** his wife **so-and-so, and so-and-so** divorces **so-and-so, and the witnesses** signed **below**, in this case **all** of these bills of divorce that were combined into one bill **are valid; and** the bill **must be handed to each and every** wife individually, so they will all be divorced by it.

הָיָה כּוֹתֵב טוֹפֶס לְכָל אֶחָד וְאֶחָד וְהָעֵדִים מִלְּמַטָּה, אֶת שֶׁהָעֵדִים נִיקְרִין עִמּוֹ – כָּשֵׁר.

If the scribe **was writing** a separate **formula** in the bill of divorce **for each and every** couple, **and the witnesses** signed **below**, the formula **with which the witnesses'** signatures **are read is valid.** In other words, the formula directly underneath which they signed is valid, and the others are not valid.

גמ׳ מַאן תַּנָּא? אָמַר רַבִּי יִרְמְיָה: דְּלָא כְּרַבִּי אֶלְעָזָר, דְּאִי רַבִּי אֶלְעָזָר, כֵּיוָן דְּאָמַר עֵדֵי מְסִירָה כָּרְתִי, הָא לָא יָדְעִי בְּהֵי מִינַּיְיהוּ קָא מִגָּרְשָׁה.

GEMARA Who is the *tanna* who **taught** that the two bills of divorce that were mixed up should be handed to both wives? **Rabbi Yirmeya said:** It **is not in accordance with** the opinion of **Rabbi Elazar, as had** it been in accordance with the opinion of **Rabbi Elazar, since he says** that **witnesses of the transmission** of the bill of divorce **effect** the divorce,[B] handing both bills of divorce to both wives would not enable the divorce of each woman to take effect. This is because the witnesses **do not know** at the time of the transmission **with which one of** the bills of divorce **she is being divorced.**

אַבַּיֵי אָמַר: אֲפִילּוּ תֵּימָא רַבִּי אֶלְעָזָר, אֵימָא דְּבָעֵי רַבִּי אֶלְעָזָר – כְּתִיבָה לִשְׁמָהּ, נְתִינָה לִשְׁמָהּ מִי בָּעֵי?

Abaye said: You can **even say** that it is in accordance with the opinion of **Rabbi Elazar. Say that** although **Rabbi Elazar requires the writing** of the bill of divorce to be **for her sake**, i.e., with the specific woman and man for whom it is designated in mind, **does he require giving** it to her **for her sake?** Although the transmission of the bill of divorce is what causes it to take effect, it need not be done with the designated woman in mind. Therefore, the divorce here is valid, as the bill of divorce was definitely given to the wife for whom it was intended.

HALAKHA

Two men who sent, etc. – שְׁנַיִם שֶׁשָּׁלְחוּ וכו׳: If two men who shared the same name were married to women with the same name and they both sent bills of divorce to their wives, and the bills of divorce were mixed up so that it is unclear for whom each bill was written, both bills of divorce must be given to each of the two wives, and the witnesses of the transmission render them valid (Rambam *Sefer Nashim, Hilkhot Geirushin* 3:12; *Shulḥan Arukh, Even HaEzer* 132:3).

Therefore, if one of the bills of divorce was lost – לְפִיכָךְ אָבַד אֶחָד מֵהֶן: If one of two identical bills of divorce was lost, the remaining one should not be given to either wife. If the agent gives it to one or both of them, it is uncertain whether the woman is divorced (Rambam *Sefer Nashim, Hilkhot Geirushin* 3:12; *Shulḥan Arukh, Even HaEzer* 132:3).

NOTES

The other is void – הֲרֵי הַשֵּׁנִי בָּטֵל: This does not mean that the bill of divorce is actually invalidated; it is a valid bill of divorce. Rather, since it is unknown for which wife it was intended, it cannot be used to divorce either of them, because if one or both of them receives it, it is uncertain whether or not she is divorced, and therefore she is not permitted to remarry (Ran).

BACKGROUND

Witnesses of the transmission of the bill of divorce effect the divorce – עֵדֵי מְסִירָה כָּרְתִי: There is a disagreement throughout the Talmud with regard to what renders a document effective. It may be having the witnesses sign the document. Alternatively, the signatures might simply prevent forgeries, while the main strength of a document stems from the transmission of the document under the watch of witnesses. Rabbi Elazar believes the latter is true; therefore, it is unclear whether or not he would agree with the mishna's ruling that the wife is divorced even in a case where the witnesses of the transmission of the bill of divorce cannot identify the precise moment that she receives it.

"חֲמִשָּׁה שֶׁכָּתְבוּ כְּלָל" כו׳. הֵיכִי דָּמֵי כְּלָל, הֵיכִי דָּמֵי טוֹפֶס?

§ It is stated in the mishna: With regard to **five** husbands **who wrote a general wording** in a bill of divorce, all of them can divorce their wives with it. But if a separate formula was written for each, only the last one is valid. The Gemara asks: **What are the circumstances of** the case of the **general wording, and what are the circumstances of** the case of the separate **formula** that was written for each couple?

אָמַר רַבִּי יוֹחָנָן: זְמַן אֶחָד לְכוּלָּן – זֶהוּ כְּלָל, זְמַן לְכָל אֶחָד וְאֶחָד – זֶהוּ טוֹפֶס;

Rabbi Yoḥanan says: If there is **one date** and one formula written **for all of them,** such as: On such-and-such a date so-and-so divorced so-and-so, and so-and-so divorced so-and-so, **that is a general wording.**[H] If a separate **date** and formula was written **for each and every one** of them, **that is** considered a separate **formula.**

וְרֵישׁ לָקִישׁ אָמַר:

And Reish Lakish says:

HALAKHA

If there is one date for all of them, that is a general wording – זְמַן אֶחָד לְכוּלָּן זֶהוּ כְּלָל: If five men wrote bills of divorce for their wives with a general wording, e.g., they wrote the date and then wrote that so-and-so divorces his wife so-and-so, and so-and-so divorces his wife so-and-so, and continued to write the entire formula of a bill of divorce, and the witnesses signed it, it is a valid bill of divorce, and it should be handed to each of the wives before witnesses. If there are no witnesses of the transmission, any one of these women who produces the bill of divorce is divorced (Rambam *Sefer Nashim, Hilkhot Geirushin* 4:18; *Shulḥan Arukh, Even HaEzer* 130:9).

אֲפִילּוּ זְמַן אֶחָד לְכוּלָּן נַמִי הָוֵי טוֹפֶס. אֶלָּא הֵיכִי דָּמֵי כְּלָל? דִּכְתַב "אָנוּ פְּלוֹנִי וּפְלוֹנִי גֵּירַשְׁנוּ נְשׁוֹתֵינוּ פְּלוֹנִית וּפְלוֹנִית".

Even if one date was written **for all of them it is still** considered a separate **formula** if the divorce of each couple is mentioned separately. **Rather, what are the circumstances of** the case of a **general wording?** It is a case **where one wrote: We, so-and-so and so-and-so,** have hereby **divorced our wives**[N] **so-and-so and so-and-so.**

מַתְקִיף לַהּ רַבִּי אַבָּא: לְרַבִּי יוֹחָנָן, דְּאָמַר זְמַן אֶחָד לְכוּלָּן זֶהוּ כְּלָל, לֵיחוּשׁ דִּלְמָא כִּי חָתְמוּ סָהֲדֵי – אַבַּתְרָא הוּא דַּחֲתִימִי! מִי לָא תַּנְיָא: עֵדִים חֲתוּמִין עַל שְׁאֵילַת שָׁלוֹם בְּגֵט – פָּסוּל, חָיְישִׁינַן שֶׁמָּא עַל שְׁאֵילַת שָׁלוֹם חָתְמוּ?

Rabbi Abba objects to this: According to Rabbi Yoḥanan, who says that when there is **one date** written **for all of them that is a general wording, we should be concerned** that **perhaps when the witnesses signed**[N] the bill of divorce **they** intended to **sign** for only **the last** couple. **Isn't it taught** in a *baraita* (*Tosefta* 9:9) that if **witnesses are signed on a greeting** that was written **in a bill of divorce,** i.e., after the formulation of the bill of divorce the scribe extended greetings to someone and the witnesses signed underneath, it is **invalid, as we are concerned** that **perhaps they signed** the **greeting** and not the bill of divorce?

לָאו אִיתְּמַר עֲלַהּ: אָמַר רַבִּי אֲבָהוּ, לְדִידִי מְפָרְשָׁא לִי מִינֵּיהּ דְּרַבִּי יוֹחָנָן: "שַׁאֲלוּ" – פָּסוּל, "וְשַׁאֲלוּ" – כָּשֵׁר, הָכָא נַמִי – דִּכְתִיב בֵּיהּ "פְּלוֹנִי וּפְלוֹנִי וּפְלוֹנִי".

The Gemara answers: **Wasn't it stated with regard to** this *baraita* that **Rabbi Abbahu says: It was explained to me by Rabbi Yoḥanan** that if the wording of the greeting is: **Ask** about the well-being of so-and-so, it is **invalid,**[H] as perhaps the witnesses intended to witness only the greeting. But if the wording is: **And ask** about the well-being of so-and-so, with the conjunctive prefix *vav*, thereby making it appear as a continuation of the previous matter, it is **valid,** as the witnesses presumably signed the bill of divorce as well. **Here too,** it should be explained that this is a bill of divorce **in which it is written: So-and-so** has divorced his wife so-and-so, **and so-and-so**[H] has divorced so-and-so, **and so-and-so** has divorced so-and-so, as the conjunctive prefix indicates continuation.

NOTES

We...have hereby divorced our wives, etc. – אָנוּ גֵּירַשְׁנוּ נְשׁוֹתֵינוּ וכו׳: The Rambam apparently holds that according to both Rabbi Yoḥanan and Reish Lakish, the standard formula of the divorce must be written just once; only the names of the couples are written separately. According to Reish Lakish, for example, the formulation would be: We, so-and-so and so-and-so, have hereby divorced our wives so-and-so and so-and-so; so-and-so has divorced so-and-so, and so-and-so has divorced so-and-so, and each one of them said to his wife: I hereby divorce, and so forth. In Rabbi Yoḥanan's opinion, the statement: We, so-and-so and so-and-so, have hereby divorced our wives, etc., is unnecessary. Otherwise, the formulation is the same. Most commentaries on the Rambam interpret his ruling in this manner, although there are those who disagree. By contrast, the Ramah claims that according to both opinions, a separate formula must be written for each couple, and otherwise the bill of divorce is invalid, since a separate bill of divorce is necessary for each of the women, as explained later in the Gemara. The general wording that enables the witnesses to sign once for all the divorces is merely the date according to Rabbi Yoḥanan and the statement: We...have hereby divorced our wives, etc., according to Reish Lakish. The rest of the bill of divorce reads: I, so-and-so, hereby divorce so-and-so, so that she shall be permitted, etc., for each and every couple.

We should be concerned that perhaps when the witnesses signed, etc. – לֵיחוּשׁ דִּלְמָא כִּי חָתְמוּ סָהֲדֵי וכו׳: This wording indicates that it is only a concern; perhaps the witnesses intended to sign all of the bills of divorce and perhaps they intended to sign only the last one. Therefore, the Rambam rules that if such a bill of divorce is given, it is considered a divorce whose status is uncertain. By contrast, the Ran maintains that the bills of divorce before the last are invalid by Torah law; since the signatures do not clearly indicate testimony as to these bills of divorce, they are meaningless with regard to them.

HALAKHA

Ask, it is invalid, etc. – שַׁאֲלוּ פָּסוּל וכו׳: One should not write anything between the text of the bill of divorce and the witnesses' signatures that does not relate to the divorce *ab initio*. If such a statement is written, e.g., if it says: Send her greetings, the bill of divorce is invalid, as it is possible that the witnesses signed only the greeting. If it is written with a conjunctive prefix, i.e., it says: And send her greetings, thereby making it appear as a continuation of the previous matter, it is valid. This is in accordance with the opinion of Rabbi Yoḥanan as explained by Rabbi Abbahu (Rambam *Sefer Nashim, Hilkhot Geirushin* 4:25; *Shulḥan Arukh, Even HaEzer* 130:3).

In which it is written, so-and-so and so-and-so, etc. – דִּכְתִיב בֵּיהּ פְּלוֹנִי וּפְלוֹנִי וכו׳: If a bill of divorce that was written for several couples says: So-and-so has divorced so-and-so, and afterward it says: And so-and-so has divorced so-and-so, with the conjunctive prefix *vav*, the entire bill of divorce is valid provided that certain conditions are fulfilled. If with regard to each couple it is written: So-and-so has divorced so-and-so, without a conjunctive prefix, only the final bill of divorce is valid. The *Beit Shmuel* disagrees (*Shulḥan Arukh, Even HaEzer* 130:9, and in the comment of Rema).

וְתוּ, לְרַבִּי יוֹחָנָן, דְּאָמַר זְמַן לְכָל אֶחָד זֶהוּ טוֹפֶס, מַאי אִירְיָא מִשּׁוּם טוֹפֶס? וְתֵיפוֹק לֵיהּ דַּהֲוָה לֵיהּ נִכְתַּב בַּיּוֹם וְנֶחְתַּם בַּלַּיְלָה!

The Gemara raises another challenge: **And furthermore, according to Rabbi Yoḥanan, who says** that when there is a separate **date** written **for each** couple, **that is** considered a separate **formula, why** is it rendered invalid **specifically due to** it being considered a separate **formula? Derive** that it is invalid **because it is** like a bill of divorce that **was written during the day and signed at night,** which is invalid because it was signed on a different calendar date than it was written. Here too, since a different date was written for each couple, and the witnesses signed only after the last formula, they clearly signed only on that date, and with regard to the previous couples it is therefore an invalid bill of divorce.

אֲמַר לֵיהּ מָר קַשִׁישָׁא בְּרֵיהּ דְּרַב חִסְדָּא לְרַב אַשִׁי, הָכִי אָמְרִינַן מִשְּׁמֵיהּ דְּרַבִּי יוֹחָנָן: דִּכְתִיב בְּהוּ ״בְּחַד בְּשַׁבָּא״, ״בְּחַד בְּשַׁבָּא״.

Mar Kashisha, son of Rav Ḥisda, said to Rav Ashi: We say the following explanation of the case **in the name of Rabbi Yoḥanan:** It is a case **where it is written in** the respective formulations: **On Sunday, on Sunday.**[H] In other words, the date written in each bill of divorce is the same, as they were all written on the same date.

אֲמַר לֵיהּ רָבִינָא לְרַב אַשִׁי: לְרֵישׁ לָקִישׁ, דְּאָמַר זְמַן אֶחָד לְכוּלָּן נַמִי טוֹפֶס הָוֵי, וְהֵיכִי דָמֵי כְּלָל – דִּכְתִיב בֵּיהּ הָכִי: ״אָנוּ פְּלוֹנִי וּפְלוֹנִי גֵּירַשְׁנוּ נְשׁוֹתֵינוּ פְּלוֹנִית וּפְלוֹנִית״, נִמְצְאוּ שְׁתֵּי נָשִׁים מִתְגָּרְשׁוֹת בְּגֵט אֶחָד, וְהַתּוֹרָה אָמְרָה: ״וְכָתַב לָהּ״ – וְלֹא לָהּ וְלַחֲבֶרְתָּהּ!

Ravina said to Rav Ashi: According **to Reish Lakish, who says** that if the divorce of each couple is mentioned separately, then even if **one date** was written **for all of them it is still** considered a separate **formula, and** he explains that **what are the circumstances of** the case of **a general wording;** a case **where the following** wording **is written in** the bill of divorce: **We, so-and-so and so-and-so, have** hereby **divorced our wives so-and-so and so-and-so.** Accordingly, **two women are found being divorced with one bill of divorce.** All of these women are divorced with the same bill of divorce that contains a list of several couples. **And the Torah said: "And he writes her"** (Deuteronomy 24:1), **and** it is derived from this phrase that he **cannot** write it both **for her and for another** woman.[H] Rather, each woman requires a separate bill of divorce.

דַּהֲדַר כְּתַב ״פְּלוֹנִי גֵּירֵשׁ פְּלוֹנִית וּפְלוֹנִי גֵּירֵשׁ פְּלוֹנִית״.

The Gemara answers: It is valid **because he then wrote** after the general formulation: **So-and-so**[H] **has divorced so-and-so, and so-and-so has divorced so-and-so.**

אֲמַר לֵיהּ רָבִינָא לְרַב אַשִׁי, וּמַאי שְׁנָא מֵהָא, דְּתַנְיָא: הַכּוֹתֵב כָּל נְכָסָיו לִשְׁנֵי עֲבָדָיו – קָנוּ וּמְשַׁחְרְרִין זֶה אֶת זֶה!

Ravina said to Rav Ashi: And in **what** way **is** this case **different from that which is taught** in a *baraita*: With regard to **one who writes** a document granting **all of his property to his two slaves, they** both **acquire** the property **and** must **emancipate each other?** Since the slaves are included in the property, by acquiring the property together they each have ownership over half of the other slave. Consequently, they must emancipate each other. Since the *halakhot* of emancipation of slaves are compared to the *halakhot* of divorce, it can be proven from here that one bill of divorce can be written for two wives.

וְלָאו אוֹקִימְנָא בִּשְׁנֵי שְׁטָרוֹת?

The Gemara answers: **But didn't we establish** that that *baraita* is referring **to** a case where the master wrote **two documents,** one for each slave, stating that he is giving him all of his property, and he gave them to them simultaneously? Certainly each slave needs his own bill of emancipation.

תַּנְיָא כְּוָותֵיהּ דְּרַבִּי יוֹחָנָן, תַּנְיָא כְּוָותֵיהּ דְּרֵישׁ לָקִישׁ.

It **is taught** in a *baraita* **in accordance with** the opinion **of Rabbi Yoḥanan,** and similarly it **is taught** in a *baraita* **in accordance with** the opinion **of Reish Lakish.**

תַּנְיָא כְּוָותֵיהּ דְּרַבִּי יוֹחָנָן: חֲמִשָּׁה שֶׁכָּתְבוּ בְּתוֹךְ הַגֵּט ״אִישׁ פְּלוֹנִי מְגָרֵשׁ פְּלוֹנִית, וּפְלוֹנִי פְּלוֹנִית, וּפְלוֹנִי פְּלוֹנִית״, וּזְמַן אֶחָד לְכוּלָּן, וְהָעֵדִים מִלְּמַטָּה – כּוּלָּן כְּשֵׁרִים וְתִנָּתֵן לְכָל אַחַת וְאַחַת.

It **is taught** in a *baraita* **in accordance with** the opinion **of Rabbi Yoḥanan** as follows: With regard to **five** men **who wrote in the bill of divorce: So-and-so** hereby **divorces so-and-so, and so-and-so** divorces **so-and-so, and so-and-so** divorces **so-and-so,** and wrote **one date for all of them, and the witnesses** signed **below,** in this case **all of them are valid; and** this document **must be handed to each and every one** of the women mentioned in it.

HALAKHA

On Sunday, on Sunday – בְּחַד בְּשַׁבָּא, בְּחַד בְּשַׁבָּא: If one document was written for several couples, and it was formulated as follows: On such-and-such a date so-and-so has hereby divorced so-and-so, until the completion of the formula of the bill of divorce, and then it says: On this date so-and-so has hereby divorced so-and-so, etc., with several bills of divorce written in this manner, and the witnesses are signed below, in this case all of the women are divorced with this bill of divorce, as long as it is handed to each of the women before witnesses. If there are no witnesses of the transmission, and the document is produced by one of the women, if she is the last woman mentioned in the bill of divorce she is considered divorced, and with regard to the other women it is considered a divorce whose status is uncertain (Rambam *Sefer Nashim, Hilkhot Geirushin* 4:19; *Shulḥan Arukh, Even HaEzer* 130:9).

He cannot write it both for her and for another woman – לֹא לָהּ וְלַחֲבֶרְתָּהּ: If it is written in the bill of divorce: We, so-and-so and so-and-so, have hereby divorced our wives so-and-so and so-and-so, and it continues until the completion of the formula of a bill of divorce, it is not valid, because two women cannot be divorced with one bill of divorce (Rambam *Sefer Nashim, Hilkhot Geirushin* 4:19; *Shulḥan Arukh, Even HaEzer* 130:10).

Because he then wrote: So-and-so, etc. – דַּהֲדַר כְּתַב פְּלוֹנִי וכו׳: If the bill of divorce is initially written in the plural: We have hereby divorced, etc., and it then states in detail that so-and-so has hereby divorced so-and-so, and so-and-so has hereby divorced so-and-so, it is a valid bill of divorce (Rambam *Sefer Nashim, Hilkhot Geirushin* 4:19; *Shulḥan Arukh, Even HaEzer* 130:10).

זְמַן לְכָל אֶחָד וְאֶחָד וְהָעֵדִים מִלְּמַטָּה, אֶת שֶׁהָעֵדִים נִקְרָאִים עִמּוֹ – כָּשֵׁר; רַבִּי יְהוּדָה בֶּן בְּתֵירָא אוֹמֵר: אִם יֵשׁ רֶיוַח בֵּינֵיהֶן – פָּסוּל, וְאִם לָאו – כָּשֵׁר, שֶׁאֵין זְמַן מַפְסִיקָן.

Nevertheless, if a separate **date** is written **for each and every one and the witnesses** signed **below,** the bill of divorce **with which the witnesses'** signatures **are read is valid. Rabbi Yehuda ben Beteira says: If there is space**[N] **between them** it is **invalid,** as the witnesses' signatures appear to be referring only to the last couple. **But if** there is **not** a space it is **valid,** as the **date** written for each couple **does not separate** between **them.** Rather, they are still considered the same bill of divorce with regard to the witnesses' signatures.

תַּנְיָא כְּוָותֵיהּ דְּרֵישׁ לָקִישׁ: חֲמִשָּׁה שֶׁכָּתְבוּ כְּלָל בְּתוֹךְ הַגֵּט ״אָנוּ פְּלוֹנִי וּפְלוֹנִי גֵּירַשְׁנוּ נְשׁוֹתֵינוּ פְּלוֹנִית וּפְלוֹנִית, פְּלוֹנִי גֵּירֵשׁ פְּלוֹנִית וּפְלוֹנִי גֵּירֵשׁ פְּלוֹנִית״, וּזְמַן אֶחָד לְכוּלָּן וְהָעֵדִים מִלְּמַטָּה – כּוּלָּן כְּשֵׁרִין וְתִנָּתֵן לְכָל אַחַת וְאַחַת.

It **is taught** in a *baraita* **in accordance with** the opinion **of Reish Lakish:** With regard to **five** men **who wrote a general wording in the bill of divorce: We, so-and-so and so-and-so,** have hereby **divorced our wives so-and-so and so-and-so; so-and-so has divorced so-and-so, and so-and-so has divorced so-and-so, and** they wrote **one date for all of them, and the witnesses** signed **below,** in this case **all of them are valid; and it must be handed to each and every** woman.

זְמַן לְכָל אֶחָד וְאֶחָד, וְרֶיוַח לְכָל אֶחָד וְאֶחָד, וְהָעֵדִים מִלְּמַטָּה, אֶת שֶׁהָעֵדִים נִקְרָאִין עִמּוֹ – כָּשֵׁר; רַבִּי מֵאִיר אוֹמֵר: אַף עַל פִּי שֶׁאֵין רֶיוַח בֵּינֵיהֶם – פָּסוּל שֶׁהַזְּמַן מַפְסִיקָן.

If a separate **date** was written **for each and every one, and** there is a **space for each and every one, and the witnesses** signed **below,** only **the one with which the witnesses'** signatures **are read is valid;** the others are not. **Rabbi Meir says: Even if there is no space between them,** the upper ones are **invalid,** as the **date separates them.**

וְרֵישׁ לָקִישׁ, מַאי אִירְיָא זְמַן לְכָל אֶחָד וְאֶחָד? הָא אָמַר: זְמַן אֶחָד לְכוּלָּן נַמִּי טוֹפֶס הָוֵי!

The Gemara asks: **And** according to **Reish Lakish, why** is the *baraita* referring **specifically** to a case in which a separate **date** was written **for each and every one? Didn't he say** that if **one date** was written **for all of them it is still** considered a separate **formula?**

הָנֵי מִילֵּי הֵיכָא דְּלָא עַרְבִינְהוּ מֵעִיקָּרָא, אֲבָל הָכָא דְּעַרְבִינְהוּ מֵעִיקָּרָא, אִי פָּלֵיג לְהוּ זְמַן – אִין, אִי לָא – לָא.

The Gemara answers: **This matter** applies **where he did not merge them at the outset** but instead wrote the divorce of each couple separately. **But here, he merged them at the outset,** writing: So-and-so and so-and-so have hereby divorced their wives so-and-so and so-and-so. Therefore, **if the date separates them** they **are** considered to be separate bills of divorce, and **if not,** then they are **not** considered separate bills of divorce.

מתני׳ שְׁנֵי גִיטִּין שֶׁכְּתָבָן זֶה בְּצַד זֶה, וּשְׁנַיִם עֵדִים עִבְרִים בָּאִים מִתַּחַת זֶה לְתַחַת זֶה וּשְׁנַיִם עֵדִים יְוָנִים בָּאִים מִתַּחַת זֶה לְתַחַת זֶה, אֶת שֶׁהָעֵדִים הָרִאשׁוֹנִים נִקְרָאִין עִמּוֹ – כָּשֵׁר.

MISHNA With regard to **two bills of divorce that** a scribe **wrote** on the same paper **one next to the other,**[H] **and** the signatures of **two Hebrew witnesses,** i.e., witnesses who signed in Hebrew from right to left, **extend from underneath this** bill of divorce on the right **to underneath that** bill of divorce on the left, **and** the signatures of **two Greek witnesses,** i.e., who signed in Greek from left to right, **extend from underneath that** bill of divorce on the left **to underneath this** bill of divorce on the right, the bill of divorce **with which the** names of the **first** two **witnesses are read** [*nikra'in*] **is valid.** The other bill of divorce is invalid, as it is not considered signed by these witnesses.

עֵד אֶחָד עִבְרִי וְעֵד אֶחָד יְוָנִי, וְעֵד אֶחָד עִבְרִי וְעֵד אֶחָד יְוָנִי בָּאִין מִתַּחַת זֶה לְתַחַת זֶה – שְׁנֵיהֶם פְּסוּלִין.

If **one witness** signed in **Hebrew** from right to left, **and one witness** signed beneath him in **Greek**[B] from left to right, **and** underneath that signature **one witness** signed in **Hebrew, and** beneath him **one witness** signed in **Greek,** with the signatures **extending from underneath this** bill of divorce **to underneath that** bill of divorce, **both** bills of divorce **are invalid.**

HALAKHA

Bills of divorce that a scribe wrote one next to the other – גִּיטִּין שֶׁכְּתָבָן זֶה בְּצַד זֶה: If one writes two bills of divorce in two separate columns in a single scroll, and the signatures of the witnesses extend from beneath one column to beneath the other so that the name of each witness is below the first bill of divorce and the name of his father is under the second bill of divorce, the bill of divorce under which the witnesses' names appear is valid (Rambam *Sefer Nashim*, *Hilkhot Geirushin* 4:21; *Shulḥan Arukh*, *Even HaEzer* 130:8).

NOTES

If there is space – אִם יֵשׁ רֶיוַח: According to *Tosefot HaRosh*, this refers to a gap wide enough for witnesses to sign between one bill of divorce and another. Rabbeinu Crescas Vidal claims that the word space should not necessarily be understood literally. Whenever the basic statements of divorce, i.e., so-and-so has hereby divorced so-and-so, are not conjoined by the prefix *vav*, that is called space.

BACKGROUND

One witness signed in Hebrew and one witness signed in Greek – עֵד אֶחָד עִבְרִי וְעֵד אֶחָד יְוָנִי: According to Rashi, all the witnesses, even the witnesses whose names are Greek, signed their names in Hebrew letters. In addition, Rashi holds that the two middle signatures were not signed on one line; rather, they continued on the following line. It is important to note that in Greek the patronym precedes the name of the individual and therefore, Josephus *filius* Simon means the son of Josephus, Simon.

Had the witnesses signed the two bills of divorce in the configuration that appears in the diagram, there would be two first names, Reuven and Simon, appearing beneath the bill of divorce on the right, and two first names, Yitzhak and Aristobolus, appearing beneath the bill of divorce on the left side. The concern, as explained later in the Gemara (87b), is that perhaps when signing his name, one of the witnesses with a Greek name imitated a witness who signed with a Hebrew name and reversed the order, placing his name before his patronym. The result is that the name of the second signatory that was actually son of Josephus, Simon, will be written: Son of Simon, Josephus. In that case, there would be only one first name, Reuven, beneath the bill of divorce on the right side and three first names, Simon, Yitzḥak, and Aristobolus beneath the bill of divorce on the left side.

According to the Rambam, the signatures of the witnesses with the Greek names were signed in Greek and each of the signatures appeared on one line. The witnesses who signed their names in Hebrew intended to sign the bill of divorce beneath which their signature began, i.e., the bill of divorce on the right, and the witnesses who signed their names in Greek intended to sign the bill of divorce beneath which their signature began, i.e., the bill of divorce on the left, the result being that each bill of divorce was signed by two witnesses. The concern is that perhaps one of the witnesses signing in Greek imitated the witnesses signing in Hebrew and his intent was to sign the bill of divorce on the right, resulting in three signatures on the bill of divorce on the right and one signature on the bill of divorce on the left. Or, perhaps the second witness signing in Hebrew imitated the witnesses signing in Greek and his intent was to sign the bill of divorce on the left, resulting in three signatures on the bill of divorce on the left and one signature on the bill of divorce on the right.

Hebrew and transliterated Greek signatures according to Rashi

Hebrew and Greek signatures according to the Rambam

GEMARA It is stated in the first case of the mishna that the bill of divorce under which the names of the first two witnesses appear is valid and the other is not, even though the signatures extend to that bill of divorce as well. The Gemara says: **But let this** bill of divorce **be validated by** the name **Reuven** alone,[H] **and** let **that** bill of divorce be validated **by** the continuation: **Son of Ya'akov, witness,** which can be considered a separate signature. **Didn't we learn** in a subsequent mishna (87b) that a signature that reads: **Son of so-and-so, witness,**[H] **is valid?**

גמ׳ וְלִיתַּכְשַׁר הַאי בִּ״רְאוּבֵן״ וְהַאי בְּ״בֶן יַעֲקֹב עֵד״, דְּהָא תְּנַן: ״בֶּן אִישׁ פְּלוֹנִי עֵד״ – כָּשֵׁר!

The Gemara answers: It is a case **where** the words: **Reuven, son of, are written on the** side of the **first** bill of divorce, **and** the words: **Ya'akov, witness,** are written **on the** side of the **latter** bill of divorce, indicating that it is one signature.

דִּכְתַב ״רְאוּבֵן בֶּן״ אַקַּמָּא וְ״יַעֲקֹב עֵד״ אַבַּתְרָא.

The Gemara says: **But let this** bill of divorce, on the first, left-hand, side, **be validated by** the words: **Reuven, son of,**[N] **and let that** bill of divorce on the other, right-hand, side **be validated by** the words: **Ya'akov, witness. Didn't we learn** in the same mishna that a signature that reads: **So-and-so, witness,** without the father's name, **is valid?**

וְלִיתַּכְשַׁר הַאי בִּ״רְאוּבֵן בֶּן״, וְלִיתַּכְשַׁר הַאי בְּ״יַעֲקֹב עֵד״, דְּהָא תְּנַן: ״אִישׁ פְּלוֹנִי עֵד״ – כָּשֵׁר!

The Gemara answers: It is a case **where** the word **witness is not written.** The latter side includes only a name, which is not sufficient. **And if you wish, say: Actually,** it is a case **where** the expression: Ya'akov, **witness, is written** underneath the second bill of divorce; **but** it is a case **where we know that this signature is not Ya'akov's.** Evidently it is part of the signature of Reuven, son of Ya'akov, and cannot serve as a separate signature for the second bill of divorce.

דְּלָא כְּתַב ״עֵד״. וְאִיבָּעֵית אֵימָא: לְעוֹלָם דִּכְתַב ״עֵד״, וּדְיָדְעִינַן בְּהָא חֲתִימָה דְּלָאו דְּיַעֲקֹב הוּא.

HALAKHA

But let this bill of divorce be validated by the name Reuven alone, etc. – **וְלִיתַּכְשַׁר הַאי בִּרְאוּבֵן וכו׳**: If the witnesses' signatures are written so that the names of the witnesses are under the first bill of divorce and the expression: Son of so-and-so, is under the second bill of divorce, both bills of divorce are valid (*Shulḥan Arukh, Even HaEzer* 130:8).

Son of so-and-so, witness – **בֶּן אִישׁ פְּלוֹנִי עֵד**: If a witness signs his name and writes: Witness, or if he writes: Son of so-and-so, witness, or if he signs both his name and his father's name but does not write the word witness, the signature is valid. If he writes only his name and does not write the word witness, the signature is invalid (*Shulḥan Arukh, Even HaEzer* 130:11–12).

NOTES

Let this bill of divorce be validated by the words Reuven, son of – **וְלִיתַּכְשַׁר הַאי בִּרְאוּבֵן בֶּן**: How can the expression: Reuven, son of, serve as a signature? Rashi explains that the expression is interpreted as: Son of Reuven, as Greek Jews would reverse the word order when signing.

Perek **IX**
Daf **87** Amud **b**

The Gemara asks: **But perhaps** Reuven signed both bills of divorce, and **he signed** the second one **with his father's name?**[N] The Gemara answers: **One does not leave out** his own **name and** instead **sign in the name of his father.**

וְדִלְמָא בִּשְׁמָא דַּאֲבוּהּ חָתֵים! לָא שָׁבֵיק אִינִישׁ שְׁמֵיהּ וְחָתֵים שְׁמָא דַּאֲבוּהּ.

The Gemara asks: **But perhaps he made** his father's name **a symbol** for his own signature? **As Rav would draw a fish** instead of signing his name, **Rabbi Ḥanina** would draw **a date palm, Rav Ḥisda** would write **a *samekh*, Rav Hoshaya** would write **an *ayin*,** and **Rabba bar Rav Huna would draw a sail.**

וְדִילְמָא סִימָנָא שַׁוְיֵיהּ! דְּהָא רַב צַיֵּיר כַּוָּורָא, רַבִּי חֲנִינָא – חָרוּתָא, רַב חִסְדָּא – סמ״ך, רַב הוֹשַׁעְיָא – עי״ן, רַבָּה בַּר רַב הוּנָא צַיֵּיר מְכוֹתָא!

The Gemara answers: **A person would not be so brazen**[N] as **to make his father's name a symbol.** Therefore, it is assumed that the word Ya'akov is a continuation of Reuven's signature on the first bill of divorce, not a separate signature on the second bill of divorce.

לָא חָצֵיף אִינִישׁ לְשַׁוּוֹיֵי לִשְׁמָא דַּאֲבוּהּ סִימָנָא.

The Gemara raises a different question: **But let this** bill of divorce **be validated by the two Hebrew witnesses, and let that** bill of divorce **be validated by the two Greek witnesses, as we learned** in the subsequent mishna that **a bill of divorce that was written in Hebrew and its witnesses** signed **in Greek,** or that was written **in Greek and its witnesses** signed **in Hebrew, is valid.**

וְלִיתַּכְשַׁר הַאי בִּשְׁנֵי עֵדִים עִבְרִים, וְלִיתַּכְשַׁר הַאי בִּשְׁנֵי עֵדִים יְוָנִים, דִּתְנַן: גֵּט שֶׁכְּתָבוֹ עִבְרִית וְעֵדָיו יְוָנִית, יְוָנִית וְעֵדָיו עִבְרִית – כָּשֵׁר!

And if you would say that since the signatures of the witnesses of the second bill of divorce **are two lines away**[H] from the bill of divorce itself, it is **not** valid, as that is the *halakha* with regard to a document that has a gap between the text and the signatures, **but didn't Ḥizkiyya say** that if the gap was **filled,** even **with** the signatures **of relatives**[H] who are disqualified from serving as witnesses, it is **valid?**

וְכִי תֵּימָא, כֵּיוָן דְּמוּפְלָג בִּשְׁנֵי שִׁיטִין לָא, וְהָאָמַר חִזְקִיָּה: מִלְאָהוּ בִּקְרוֹבִים – כָּשֵׁר!

NOTES

He signed with his father's name – **בִּשְׁמָא דַּאֲבוּהּ חָתֵים**: It was customary in several places for people to refer to themselves by their father's name, similar to the custom of writing one's surname and not his first name. *Tosafot* add that in this case there is a logical reason to assume that the son signed using his father's name, since he signed the adjacent bill of divorce using his own name, and together both signatures form his name in full.

A person would not be so brazen – **לָא חָצֵיף אִינִישׁ**: As these alternative forms of identification were considered to be somewhat informal, it would be disrespectful for one to employ his father's name in this manner.

HALAKHA

Since the signatures are two lines away, etc. – **כֵּיוָן דְּמוּפְלָג בִּשְׁנֵי שִׁיטִין וכו׳**: When witnesses sign a bill of divorce they should not leave a space of two lines between the bill of divorce and their signatures. It is ruled in the *Mordekhai* and the *Tur* that if there is such a space, the bill of divorce is invalid. According to the Rambam and the Ramban it is possible to validate such a bill of divorce by handing it to the wife in the presence of witnesses (Rambam *Sefer Nashim, Hilkhot Geirushin* 1:18; *Shulḥan Arukh, Even HaEzer* 130:1).

Filled with the signatures of relatives – **מִלְאָהוּ קְרוֹבִים**: If the witnesses' signatures are two lines apart from the text of a document, it is invalid. If the space is filled with the signatures of relatives or other people who are disqualified from giving testimony, it is valid, as that prevents an additional clause from being forged (Rambam *Sefer Mishpatim, Hilkhot Malve VeLoveh* 27:4; *Shulḥan Arukh, Ḥoshen Mishpat* 45:6, 14).

הָא תָּנֵי זְעֵירִי: שְׁנֵיהֶן כְּשֵׁרִין. וְתַנָּא דִּידַן? דִּלְמָא גּוּנְדְּלִית חֲתִימִי, וְכוּלְּהוּ אַחַד הוּא דַּחֲתִימִי.

The Gemara comments: **Ze'eiri** in fact **teaches** that **both of** the two bills of divorce **are valid,** not only the one beneath which the names of the first two witnesses appear. The Gemara asks: **And** what is the reasoning of **the *tanna* of our** mishna, who does not agree with this ruling? The Gemara answers: He is concerned that **perhaps** the bottom two witnesses **signed in reverse** [*gundalit*].[LN] For example, if the top two signatures are in Hebrew, perhaps the witnesses who signed in Greek reversed the word order of their signatures, imitating the Hebrew style, **and** in actuality **all of the** witnesses **signed one** bill of divorce.

"עֵד אֶחָד עִבְרִי וְעֵד אֶחָד יְוָנִי". וְלִיתַּכְשַׁר הַאי בְּעֵד אֶחָד עִבְרִי וְעֵד אֶחָד יְוָנִי, וְהַאי בְּעֵד אֶחָד עִבְרִי וְעֵד אֶחָד יְוָנִי, דְּהָא תְּנַן: עֵד אֶחָד עִבְרִי וְעֵד אֶחָד יְוָנִי – כָּשֵׁר!

§ It is stated in the mishna that if **one witness** signed in **Hebrew and** then **one witness** signed in **Greek,** and then one more witness signed in Hebrew and one in Greek, both bills of divorce are invalid. The Gemara asks: **But let this** bill of divorce **be validated by one Hebrew witness**[N] **and one Greek witness, and that** bill of divorce be validated **by** the other pair composed of **one Hebrew witness and one Greek witness. Didn't we learn** in the subsequent mishna that a bill of divorce that was signed by **one witness** in **Hebrew and one witness** in **Greek is valid?**

הָא תָּנֵי זְעֵירִי: שְׁנֵיהֶם כְּשֵׁרִים. וְתַנָּא דִּידַן? דִּלְמָא גּוּנְדְּלִית חֲתִים, וּתְלָתָא אַחַד, וְחַד אַחַד.

The Gemara answers: **Ze'eiri** in fact **teaches** that **both of them are valid.** The Gemara asks: **And** what is the reasoning of **the *tanna* of our** mishna? The Gemara answers: He is concerned that **perhaps they signed in reverse,** i.e., perhaps one of the witnesses who signed in Greek reversed the word order of his signature, **and** in actuality he signed the other bill of divorce. Consequently, **three** witnesses signed **one** bill of divorce **and** only **one** witness signed the other **one.** Therefore, they are both rendered invalid.

מתני׳ שִׁיֵּיר מִקְצָת הַגֵּט וּכְתָבוֹ בַּדַּף הַשֵּׁנִי, וְהָעֵדִים מִלְּמַטָּה – כָּשֵׁר. חָתְמוּ עֵדִים בְּרֹאשׁ הַדַּף, מִן הַצַּד, אוֹ מֵאַחֲרָיו, בְּגֵט פָּשׁוּט – פָּסוּל.

MISHNA If a scribe **left out part of the bill of divorce**[H] **and wrote it in the second column,** i.e., the bill of divorce is written in two columns on one paper, **and the** signatures of the **witnesses are beneath** the second column, it is a **valid** bill of divorce. If the **witnesses signed at the top of the column,**[H] **on the side, or on the back**[N] **of an ordinary,** non-folded **bill of divorce,** it is **invalid.**

NOTES

Signed in reverse [*gundalit*] – גּוּנְדְּלִית חֲתִים: The *ge'onim* write that the word *gundalit* refers to the left hand and is also used to describe writing from left to right. In the context of this discussion the term refers to the case of a Hebrew signature written from right to left, where the Hebrew signatures are under the Greek signatures (Responsa of the *Ge'onim*). Early commentaries add that the term came to mean any backward behavior, e.g., a Greek witness signing from right to left or a Hebrew witness signing from left to right (Rashi; Rid). The Meiri cites another definition of the word *gundalit*: A mimic. Here it refers to the latter witnesses imitating the style of the signatures of the former witnesses.

But let this bill of divorce be validated by one Hebrew witness, etc. – וְלִיתַּכְשַׁר הַאי בְּעֵד אֶחָד עִבְרִי וכו׳: Rashi explains that the two middle signatures start on one line and end on the next line. Therefore each Greek signature is on a different bill of divorce, and if one of them reversed the order of his signature there are three signatures on one bill of divorce and three on the other. *Tosafot* and most other early commentaries maintain that each witness signed on one line. According to their version of the text, the Gemara's question is why the bill of divorce on the right is not rendered valid, since even if the Greek witnesses reversed the order of their signatures, they are all signed on the right-hand side bill of divorce. The answer is that the second Hebrew witness, who signed third, also may have reversed his signature, so perhaps three of the signatures are on the left-hand side bill of divorce and only one on the right (see Ramban and Rashba).

Or on the back – אוֹ מֵאַחֲרָיו: The mishna specifies that this ruling relates to a simple bill of divorce, because a folded and sewn bill of divorce requires that the witnesses sign on the back. The reverse is not true; a folded and sewn bill of divorce that was signed inside can be opened and turned into a simple bill of divorce and is thereby valid. According to some commentaries this distinction is true with regard to signatures that appear on the side of the bill of divorce as well (see Ritva).

LANGUAGE

In reverse [*gundalit*] – גּוּנְדְּלִית: The *ge'onim* write that this was the term for a left-handed person. The source of the word is unknown.

HALAKHA

Left out part of the bill of divorce, etc. – שִׁיֵּיר מִקְצָת הַגֵּט וכו׳: If a scribe wrote part of a bill of divorce in one column and continued writing it in the next column, and the witnesses signed below the end of the bill of divorce, it is valid (Rambam *Sefer Nashim, Hilkhot Geirushin* 4:24; *Shulḥan Arukh, Even HaEzer* 130:7).

The witnesses signed at the top of the column, etc. – עֵדִים בְּרֹאשׁ הַדַּף וכו׳: If witnesses signed at the top of a bill of divorce, on its side, or on the back of it, it is invalid. If it is given to the wife in the presence of witnesses it is valid (Rambam *Sefer Nashim, Hilkhot Geirushin* 4:22; *Shulḥan Arukh, Even HaEzer* 130:4, 6).

הִקִּיף רֹאשׁוֹ שֶׁל זֶה בְּצַד רֹאשׁוֹ שֶׁל זֶה וְהָעֵדִים בָּאֶמְצַע – שְׁנֵיהֶם פְּסוּלִין; סוֹפוֹ שֶׁל זֶה בְּצַד סוֹפוֹ שֶׁל זֶה וְהָעֵדִים בָּאֶמְצַע, אֶת שֶׁהָעֵדִים נִקְרִין עִמּוֹ – כָּשֵׁר; רֹאשׁוֹ שֶׁל זֶה בְּצַד סוֹפוֹ שֶׁל זֶה וְהָעֵדִים בָּאֶמְצַע, אֶת שֶׁהָעֵדִים נִקְרִין בְּסוֹפוֹ – כָּשֵׁר.

If the scribe **placed the top of this** bill of divorce[H] **next to the top of that**[B] bill of divorce so that both are written in the same column but with the text in opposite directions, **and the witnesses** signed **in the middle,** between the bills of divorce, **both** bills of divorce **are invalid.** If he placed **the end of this** bill of divorce **next to the end of that**[H] bill of divorce, **and the witnesses** signed **in the middle** between them, the bill of divorce **with which the witnesses'** signatures **are read,** i.e., the bill that is written in the same direction as the signatures, **is valid.** If he placed **the top of this** bill of divorce **next to the end of that**[HB] bill of divorce, **and the witnesses** signed **in the middle,** the bill of divorce **at the end of which the witnesses are read,** i.e., the upper bill of divorce, **is valid.**

גֵּט שֶׁכְּתָבוֹ עִבְרִית וְעֵדָיו יְוָנִית, יְוָנִית וְעֵדָיו עִבְרִית, עֵד אֶחָד עִבְרִי וְעֵד אֶחָד יְוָנִי, כְּתַב סוֹפֵר וְעֵד – כָּשֵׁר.

With regard to **a bill of divorce that was written in Hebrew and its witnesses** signed **in Greek,**[H] or that was written **in Greek and its witnesses** signed **in Hebrew,** or in which **one witness** signed **in Hebrew and one witness** signed **in Greek,** or if a bill of divorce has **the writing of a scribe,** and the scribe identifies his handwriting, **and** one **witness** verifies his signature, it is **valid** as though two witnesses testified to ratify their signatures.

HALAKHA

Placed the top of this bill of divorce, etc. – **הִקִּיף רֹאשׁוֹ שֶׁל זֶה וכו׳**: If there are two bills of divorce, the tops of which are adjacent to each other, and the witnesses signed in between, both of them are invalid because the witnesses' signatures are not read with either of them. If they are given to the wife in the presence of witnesses, both are valid (Rambam *Sefer Nashim, Hilkhot Geirushin* 4:23).

The end of this bill of divorce next to the end of that, etc. – **סוֹפוֹ שֶׁל זֶה בְּצַד סוֹפוֹ שֶׁל זֶה וכו׳**: If two bills of divorce are written so that their ends face each other, and the witnesses' signatures are in between, the bill of divorce with which the witnesses' signatures are read is valid. The other one is invalid, as any bill of divorce in which the signatures are written in the opposite direction of the text is invalid. If the bill of divorce is given to the wife in the presence of witnesses it is valid (*Tur, Even HaEzer* 130; *Shulḥan Arukh, Even HaEzer* 130:5–6).

The top of this bill of divorce next to the end of that, etc. – **רֹאשׁוֹ שֶׁל זֶה בְּצַד סוֹפוֹ שֶׁל זֶה וכו׳**: If the top of one bill of divorce is next to the end of another bill of divorce and the witnesses signed in between, the uppermost bill of divorce is valid. The bottom bill of divorce is invalid, and if the document is produced by the woman stated in the bottom bill of divorce she is not divorced (Rambam *Sefer Nashim, Hilkhot Geirushin* 4:22; *Shulḥan Arukh, Even HaEzer* 130:5–6).

That was written in Hebrew and its witnesses signed in Greek – **שֶׁכְּתָבוֹ עִבְרִית וְעֵדָיו יְוָנִית**: If a bill of divorce was written in one language and the witnesses signed it in another language, it is valid as long as the witnesses understand what is written and what they signed (Rambam *Sefer Nashim, Hilkhot Geirushin* 4:7; *Shulḥan Arukh, Even HaEzer* 130:14).

BACKGROUND

The top of this bill of divorce next to the top of that – **רֹאשׁוֹ שֶׁל זֶה בְּצַד רֹאשׁוֹ שֶׁל זֶה**: These two bills of divorce are positioned so that the beginning of one is inverted and placed directly above the beginning of the other. Therefore, the signatures in between are not associated with either bill of divorce (see 88a).

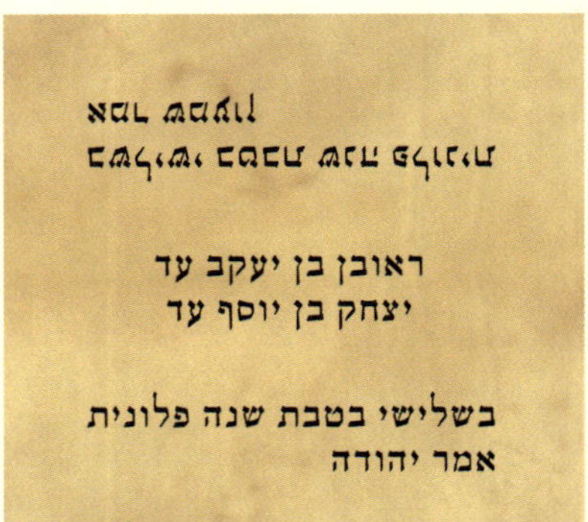

Top of one bill of divorce inverted and directly above the top of another bill of divorce

The top of this bill of divorce next to the end of that – **רֹאשׁוֹ שֶׁל זֶה בְּצַד סוֹפוֹ שֶׁל זֶה**: Here the two bills of divorce are written so that one is directly above the other. Therefore the signatures of the witnesses are directly below the upper bill of divorce and not at all associated with the lower bill of divorce.

Top of one bill of divorce next to the end of another bill of divorce

״אִישׁ פְּלוֹנִי עֵד״ – כָּשֵׁר; ״בֶּן אִישׁ פְּלוֹנִי עֵד״ – כָּשֵׁר; ״אִישׁ פְּלוֹנִי בֶּן אִישׁ פְּלוֹנִי״ וְלֹא כָּתַב ״עֵד״ – כָּשֵׁר; וְכָךְ הָיוּ נְקִיֵּי הַדַּעַת שֶׁבִּירוּשָׁלַיִם עוֹשִׂין. כָּתַב חֲנִיכָתוֹ וַחֲנִיכָתָהּ – כָּשֵׁר.

As for the wording of the signature, if a witness signed: **So-and-so, witness,**[H] without mentioning his father's name, it is **valid.** Similarly, if he did not write his name and instead wrote: **Son of so-and-so, witness,** it is **valid.** If he wrote: **So-and-so, son of so-and-so, but did not write** the word **witness, it is valid. And this is what the scrupulous people of Jerusalem**[B] **would do,**[N] i.e., they would sign without the word witness. As for the names of the husband and wife, if the scribe **wrote his surname** [*ḥanikhato*][NL] or nickname **and her surname**[H] or nickname, it is **valid.**

גמ׳ וְלֵיחוּשׁ דִּלְמָא הָנֵי תְּרֵי גִּיטֵּי הֲווֹ, וְאִיתְרַמִּי לֵיהּ זְמַן דְּקַמָּא וְעֵדִים דְּבַתְרָא, וְגַזְיֵיהּ לִזְמַן דְּבַתְרָא וְעֵדִים דְּקַמָּא!

GEMARA With regard to a bill of divorce that is written in two columns, **let us be concerned** that **perhaps these were two** adjacent **bills of divorce,** the second one higher up on the page than the first, **and the date** written at the top **of the first** bill of divorce **and the** signatures of the **witnesses** written at the bottom **of the latter** bill of divorce **happened** to be written next to each other, **and** someone **cut out the date of the latter** bill of divorce **and** the signatures of **the witnesses of the first**[N] so that it appears to be a single bill of divorce written in two columns.

אָמַר רַבִּי אַבָּא אָמַר רַב: כְּשֶׁיֵּשׁ רֶיוַח מִלְּמַטָּה. וְדִלְמָא זְמַן דְּבַתְרָא מֵיגַז גַּזְיֵיהּ! כִּדְאָמַר רַבִּי אַבָּא אָמַר רַב: כְּשֶׁיֵּשׁ רֶיוַח מִלְּמַטָּה,

Rav Abba says that **Rav says:** It is a case **where there is space** on the paper **below** the first bill of divorce, so it is clear that nothing was cut out. The Gemara asks: **And perhaps he cut out the date of the latter** bill of divorce, making it look like a continuation of the first one, which was actually never finished? The Gemara answers: **Just as Rabbi Abba says** that **Rav says** that it is a case **where there is space below** the first bill of divorce,

NOTES

And this is what the scrupulous people of Jerusalem would do – וְכָךְ הָיוּ נְקִיֵּי הַדַּעַת שֶׁבִּירוּשָׁלַיִם עוֹשִׂין: Rashi explains that these men of virtue would express themselves as concisely as possible, and therefore they would not write the word witness, as that could be inferred from the context of their signatures. According to a different version of the text, this sentence relates to the following ruling in the mishna, with regard to the use of surnames, stating that the scrupulous people of Jerusalem would sign their surnames (see *Tosefot Yom Tov*).

Surname [*ḥanikha*], etc. – חֲנִיכָתוֹ וכו׳: Rashi explains that this term is referring to a name by which his family is known. Other commentaries write that this is referring to a nickname by which the husband or wife is known, although it is not his or her given name (*Ge'onim*; Rabbeinu Ḥananel; Rabbeinu Tam).

Cut out the date of the latter bill of divorce and the witnesses of the first – גַּזְיֵיהּ לִזְמַן דְּבַתְרָא וְעֵדִים דְּקַמָּא:

Two adjacent bills of divorce before being cut

Two adjacent bills of divorce after being cut, resembling one bill of divorce written in two columns

HALAKHA

So-and-so, witness – אִישׁ פְּלוֹנִי עֵד: A witness should sign *ab initio*: So-and-so, son of so-and-so, witness. If he wrote only: So-and-so, witness, or: Son of so-and-so, witness, or if he wrote both his name and his father's name but did not write the word witness, it is valid (Rambam *Sefer Nashim, Hilkhot Geirushin* 4:12; *Shulḥan Arukh, Even HaEzer* 130:11).

Wrote his surname and her surname – כָּתַב חֲנִיכָתוֹ וַחֲנִיכָתָהּ: If the scribe wrote only the husband's surname and the wife's surname in the bill of divorce, it is valid. According to the *Beit Shmuel* it is valid only after the fact. The Rosh distinguishes between a nickname that is the way the person is referred to by everyone, which the Rosh holds to be valid *ab initio*, and one that is not always used when referring to him, which in the opinion of the Rosh is valid only after the fact (Rambam *Sefer Nashim, Hilkhot Geirushin* 3:13; *Shulḥan Arukh, Even HaEzer* 129:1).

BACKGROUND

The scrupulous people of Jerusalem – נְקִיֵּי הַדַּעַת שֶׁבִּירוּשָׁלַיִם: These people are mentioned several times by the Sages. The expression apparently refers to people who were scrupulous in their actions. They were very careful about their manners and made sure not to cause embarrassment or perplexity to themselves or others. The Sages taught several *halakhot* based on the customs of this circle.

LANGUAGE

Surname [*ḥanikha*] – חֲנִיכָה: This word means nickname, whether a personal nickname, a surname, or any other kind of moniker. The source of the term is unknown. Some claim that it comes from the root *ḥet, nun, kaf*, which means education, since this is not the person's given name but rather a name that people have become accustomed, or educated, to using.

הָכָא נַמִי – כְּשֶׁיֵּשׁ רֶיוַח מִלְמַעְלָה.

so too, it is a case **where there is space above** the latter one, so it is clearly not a separate bill of divorce that was cut.

וְדִלְמָא אִימְּלוּכֵי אִימְּלִיךְ וְכָתַב!

The Gemara asks: **But** although it is clearly one bill of divorce, **perhaps** the scribe wrote the first part of the bill of divorce and then the husband **changed his mind**[N] about divorcing his wife, thereby canceling the bill of divorce, and afterward he changed his mind again **and** the scribe then **wrote** the rest of the bill of divorce in the second column, after the first part was already canceled.

דְּכָתַב "הֲרֵי אַתְּ" מִלְּמַטָּה וּ"מוּתֶּרֶת" מִלְּמַעְלָה. וְדִלְמָא אִיתְרְמִי לֵיהּ! כּוּלֵּי הַאי לָא חָיְישִׁינַן.

The Gemara answers: It is a case **where he wrote: You are hereby, on the bottom** of the first column, **and** continued: **Permitted** to marry any man, **at the top** of the second column. In this case there is obvious continuity between the columns, and he certainly did not change his mind in the meantime. The Gemara asks: **But perhaps it happened** that he stopped in the middle of the sentence? The Gemara answers: **We are not concerned to such a degree;** it is highly unlikely that he changed his mind in the middle of a sentence.

רַב אָשֵׁי אָמַר: דִּידִיעָה בֵּיהּ מִתְחִתָּא דִּמְגִילְּתָא.

Rav Ashi said: The mishna is referring to a case **where the stretch of the scroll is clear,**[HN] so it is obvious that it is a complete piece of parchment and that nothing was cut out of it.

"חָתְמוּ עֵדִים בְּרֹאשׁ הַדַּף" וכו׳. אִינִי? וְהָא רַב חָתֵים מִן הַצַּד! הָתָם בְּשֶׁגַּגּוֹ כְּלַפֵּי כְּתָב.

§ It is stated in the mishna: If **the witnesses signed at the top of the column** or on the side, the bill of divorce is invalid. The Gemara raises an objection: **Is that so? Wouldn't Rav sign on the side?** The Gemara answers: **There,** in the case of Rav, he would sign **with the roof,** i.e., the top, **of** his signature **facing the text**[B] of the document, so it was clear that he was signing the document.

אֶלָּא הָא דְּקָתָנֵי: הִקִּיף רֹאשׁוֹ שֶׁל זֶה בְּצַד רֹאשׁוֹ שֶׁל זֶה וְהָעֵדִים בָּאֶמְצַע – שְׁנֵיהֶם פְּסוּלִין, וְלֵיחְזֵי הֵי מִינַּיְיהוּ כְּלַפֵּי כְּתָב וְלִיתַּכְשַׁר!

The Gemara asks: **But** this contradicts **that which is taught** in the mishna: If the scribe **placed the top of this** bill of divorce **next to the top of that** bill of divorce, writing both bills of divorce in the same column in opposite directions, **and the witnesses** signed **in the middle** between them, **both** bills of divorce **are invalid.** According to the above answer, **let us see** with regard to **which one of them** the top of the witnesses' signatures **faces the text, and let it be rendered valid.**

הָתָם דִּרְמֵי לֵיהּ כְּעִיבְּרָא.

The Gemara answers: **There,** in the mishna, it is a case **where** the signatures are not parallel to the text. Rather, **they are placed like** a door **bolt,**[B] perpendicular to the text, so they are not written in the same direction as either of the bills of divorce.

NOTES

Changed his mind – אִימְּלוּכֵי אִימְּלִיךְ: Why is the husband's reconsidering tantamount to his canceling of the bill of divorce? Rashi cites two possible explanations for this *halakha*. The first explanation is that the husband canceled the first part of the bill of divorce by changing his mind, and a bill of divorce that was canceled can no longer be rendered valid again. According to Rashi's second explanation, it is invalid due to concern that the scribe resumed writing the bill of divorce on a later date, rendering it a bill of divorce that was written and signed on different dates. *Tosafot* reject these explanations. They suggest that the concern is that perhaps the scribe began writing the bill of divorce for a different husband, who subsequently changed his mind about divorcing his wife. Consequently, the bill of divorce was not written for the sake of this woman. The Ramban interprets this ruling in a manner similar to Rashi's first explanation: The scribe's writing of the bill of divorce must stem from one appointment, and since the husband's change of mind discontinues the scribe's appointment, he cannot continue writing the bill of divorce without a second appointment (Rashba; Rabbeinu Crescas Vidal; Ran).

Where the stretch of the scroll is clear – דִּידִיעָה בֵּיהּ מִתְחִתָּא דִּמְגִילְּתָא: Rashi points out that this answers all of the Gemara's questions. Since it is clearly a complete piece of parchment and no space was left at the end of the first column, there is no reason for concern that anything was cut out or that the husband changed his mind in the middle of the writing, as the bill of divorce was presumably written in two columns in the first place.

HALAKHA

Where the stretch of the scroll is clear – דִּידִיעָה בֵּיהּ מִתְחִתָּא דִּמְגִילְּתָא: When is a bill of divorce valid even though it is written in two columns? It is valid when it is evident from the appearance of the scroll that nothing was cut out from it, and that the scribe intended to continue writing it in the second column. If it is not clear, then even if the bill of divorce is handed to the wife in the presence of witnesses it is uncertain whether she is divorced, as it is possible that there were two bills of divorce and the husband cut out the end of one and the beginning of the other, in accordance with Rav Ashi's assertion. The Rema writes, citing the *Maggid Mishne*, that if there are witnesses that it was one bill of divorce from the beginning, and it is handed to the wife before witnesses, it is valid (Rambam *Sefer Nashim*, *Hilkhot Geirushin* 4:24; *Shulḥan Arukh*, *Even HaEzer* 130:7).

BACKGROUND

With the roof of his signature facing the text – בְּשֶׁגַּגּוֹ כְּלַפֵּי כְּתָב: In the example pictured here, both signatures are on the sides of the bill of divorce. The text faces the bottom of Yosef ben Shimon's signature and the top of Ya'akov ben Yitzḥak's signature.

Signatures on both sides of a bill of divorce

Where they are placed like a door bolt – דִּרְמֵי לֵיהּ כְּעִיבְּרָא: A door bolt is inserted into the doorpost perpendicular to it. Here too, the signatures are perpendicular to the two bills of divorce, so they are not associated with either of them.

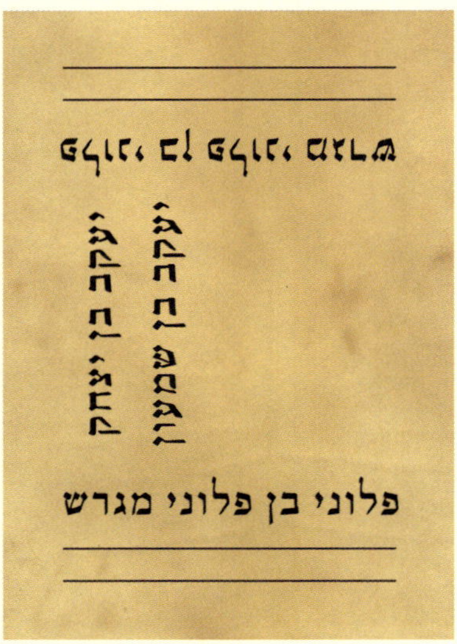

Signatures placed like a door bolt

אִי הָכִי, סֵיפָא דְּקָתָנֵי: רֹאשׁוֹ שֶׁל זֶה בְּצַד סוֹפוֹ שֶׁל זֶה וְהָעֵדִים בָּאֶמְצַע, אֶת שֶׁהָעֵדִים נִיקְרִין בְּסוֹפוֹ – כָּשֵׁר; וְאִי דִּרְמִי בְּעִיבְרָא, לָאו בַּהֲדֵי הַאי מִיקְּרֵי וְלָאו בַּהֲדֵי הַאי מִיקְּרֵי!

The Gemara challenges: **If so,** consider **the latter clause** of the mishna, **which teaches** that if the scribe placed **the top of this** bill of divorce **next to the end of that** bill of divorce, **and the witnesses** signed **in the middle,** the bill of divorce **at the end of which the witnesses are read is valid. And if** the mishna is referring to a case **where** the signatures **are placed like a bolt,** perpendicular to the text, **they are neither read with this** bill of divorce, **nor are they read with that** one.

אֶלָּא, רַב בְּדִיסְקֵי הֲוָה חָתֵים.

Rather, a different answer must be offered: **Rav would sign** only **letters**[H] and rulings on the side, where the location of his signature is inconsequential. By contrast, bills of divorce and monetary documents must be signed beneath the text.

״גֵּט שֶׁכְּתָבוֹ עִבְרִית וכו׳ כְּתַב סוֹפֵר וְעֵד – כָּשֵׁר״. אָמַר רַבִּי יִרְמְיָה: חָתַם סוֹפֵר שָׁנִינוּ.

§ It is stated in the mishna: With regard to **a bill of divorce that was written in Hebrew** and its witnesses signed in Greek, or that was written in Greek and its witnesses signed in Hebrew, or in which one witness signed in Hebrew and one witness signed in Greek, or if a bill of divorce has **the writing of a scribe,** and the scribe identifies his handwriting, **and** one **witness** verifies his signature, it is **valid** as though two witnesses testified to ratify their signatures. **Rabbi Yirmeya says: We learned** that the mishna means that **the scribe signed**[H] the bill of divorce as a witness; his handwriting in the text is not sufficient.

אָמַר רַב חִסְדָּא: הָא מַנִּי? רַבִּי יוֹסֵי הִיא.

Rav Ḥisda says: In accordance with **whose** opinion **is this? It is** in accordance with the opinion of **Rabbi Yosei** that there is no concern that the scribe signed unlawfully.

הַהִיא כְּתוּבַּת חֲתָנִים דְּאָתְיָא לְקַמֵּיהּ דְּרַבִּי אַבָּהוּ, דַּהֲווּ יָדְעִי לֵיהּ לְטוֹפְסָא וְלַחֲתִימַת יָדָא דְּחַד סָהֲדָא, סָבַר לְאַכְשׁוּרָהּ, אֲמַר לֵיהּ רַבִּי יִרְמְיָה: חָתַם סוֹפֵר שָׁנִינוּ.

The Gemara relates: There was **a certain marriage contract that was brought before Rabbi Abbahu, which** people **recognized** and verified **its formula,** i.e., the scribe's handwriting, **and the signature of one witness.** Rabbi Abbahu **thought to deem it valid** based on the scribe's handwriting and the witness. **Rabbi Yirmeya said to him: We learned** that the mishna means that **the scribe signed** the bill of divorce; his handwriting alone is not sufficient.

״כָּתַב חֲנִיכָתוֹ וַחֲנִיכָתָהּ – כָּשֵׁר״. תָּנוּ רַבָּנַן: חֲנִיכַת אָבוֹת בְּגִיטִּין – עַד עֲשָׂרָה דּוֹרוֹת; רַבִּי שִׁמְעוֹן בֶּן אֶלְעָזָר אוֹמֵר: שְׁלֹשָׁה דּוֹרוֹת – כָּשֵׁר, מִכָּאן וְאֵילָךְ – פָּסוּל.

§ It is stated in the mishna: With regard to the names of the husband and wife, if the scribe **wrote his surname** or nickname **and her surname** or nickname, it is **valid. The Sages taught** (*Tosefta* 8:6): **A surname** from one's **forefathers**[HN] is valid **with regard to bills of divorce until ten generations** after the forefather. **Rabbi Shimon ben Elazar says:** It is **valid** for only **three generations; from this** point **forward** it is **invalid.**

כְּמַאן אָזְלָא הָא דְּאָמַר רַבִּי חֲנִינָא: כְּתַב חֲנִיכַת אָבוֹת בְּגִיטִּין עַד שְׁלֹשָׁה דּוֹרוֹת, כְּמַאן? כְּרַבִּי שִׁמְעוֹן בֶּן אֶלְעָזָר.

The Gemara asks: **In accordance with whose** opinion **is that which Rabbi Ḥanina said,** that **the writing of a surname** from one's **forefathers** is valid **with regard to bills of divorce until three generations** after the forefather? It is **in accordance with** the opinion of **Rabbi Shimon ben Elazar.**

אֲמַר רַב הוּנָא: מַאי קְרָאָה? ״כִּי תוֹלִיד בָּנִים וּבְנֵי בָנִים וְנוֹשַׁנְתֶּם״.

Rav Huna said: What is the verse from which this opinion is derived? It is the verse: **"When you will beget children, and children's children, and you will have been long [*venoshantem*]** in the land" (Deuteronomy 4:25). Since the word *venoshantem* stems from the word *yashan,* meaning old, it is derived that after one's grandchildren, or three generations, a matter is considered old and forgotten.

אָמַר רַבִּי יְהוֹשֻׁעַ בֶּן לֵוִי: לֹא חָרְבָה אֶרֶץ יִשְׂרָאֵל עַד שֶׁעָבְדוּ בָּהּ שִׁבְעָה בָּתֵּי דִינִים עֲבוֹדָה זָרָה, וְאֵלּוּ הֵן: יָרָבְעָם בֶּן נְבָט, וּבַעְשָׁא בֶּן אֲחִיָּה, וְאַחְאָב בֶּן עָמְרִי, וְיֵהוּא בֶּן נִמְשִׁי, וּפֶקַח בֶּן רְמַלְיָהוּ, וּמְנַחֵם בֶּן גָּדִי, וְהוֹשֵׁעַ בֶּן אֵלָה, שֶׁנֶּאֱמַר: ״אוּמְלְלָה יוֹלֶדֶת הַשִּׁבְעָה נָפְחָה נַפְשָׁהּ בָּאָה שִׁמְשָׁהּ בְּעוֹד יוֹמָם בּוֹשָׁה וְחָפֵרָה״.

§ The Gemara cites another derivation from this verse. **Rabbi Yehoshua ben Levi says:** The first **destruction of Eretz Yisrael did not** occur **until seven** dynasties and their **courts**[N] **committed idol worship in it, and they are these: Jeroboam, son of Nevat; and Baasa, son of Ahijah; and Ahab, son of Omri; and Jehu, son of Nimshi; and Pekah, son of Remaliah; and Menahem, son of Gadi; and Hoshea, son of Elah, as it is stated: "She who has given birth to seven languishes; her spirit droops; her sun is gone down while it was yet day, she is ashamed and confounded"** (Jeremiah 15:9).

HALAKHA

Rav would sign only letters – רַב בְּדִיסְקֵי הֲוָה חָתֵים: A judge may sign a court summons on the side of the document (*Shulḥan Arukh, Ḥoshen Mishpat* 11:6).

We learned that the mishna means that the scribe signed – חָתַם סוֹפֵר שָׁנִינוּ: Though the Rambam permits the scribe to sign the bill of divorce as one of the witnesses, he should not do so, as other authorities hold that this renders the bill of divorce invalid. If a woman remarries based on a bill of divorce that was signed by the scribe, she need not leave her husband (*Beit Shmuel*, based on Rivash). In a case where two witnesses signed and the scribe signed as well there is a dispute among the authorities. The *Beit Shmuel* notes that most of them validate the bill of divorce after the fact (Rambam *Sefer Nashim, Hilkhot Geirushin* 9:27; *Shulḥan Arukh, Even HaEzer* 130:18).

A surname from one's forefathers – חֲנִיכַת אָבוֹת: If the name of the head of the witness's family is written in the bill of divorce instead of his own name, that is sufficient if the gap between them is three generations or less. This is in accordance with the opinion of Rabbi Shimon ben Elazar, according to whom Rabbi Ḥanina ruled (*Tur, Even HaEzer* 130, citing Rif and Rosh).

NOTES

A surname from one's forefathers – חֲנִיכַת אָבוֹת: Some commentaries explain that this refers to a case where the name or nickname of the person's forefather was written instead of his father's name. Others claim that it refers to a case where this is the only name written for him. They note the custom in certain generations of referring to a person by the name of the head of the family generations ago. Accordingly, this name is rendered invalid either three or ten generations after the forefather. The Meiri writes that if the name becomes a surname shared by the family, independent of reference to the forefather it comes from, it is considered their own surname and is valid even after this period. Another interpretation is that if a surname has been obsolete in the family for three or ten generations, it becomes invalid (Meiri).

Seven dynasties and their courts – שִׁבְעָה בָּתֵּי דִינִים: Even though there were kings of Israel who did not belong to any of these dynasties, e.g., Zimri, they are not counted because they each ruled for less than one year (Rashi).

LANGUAGE

Guards [*pardesei'ot*] – פַּרְדֵּסִיאוֹת: This word has variant versions in manuscripts of the Talmud, i.e., *parsaddeot* and *perozdaot*. The source of the word is the Latin praesidia, meaning guards.

NOTES

By advancing their exile by two years – שֶׁהִקְדִּים שְׁתֵּי שָׁנִים: The 850 years are calculated as follows: It is mentioned in I Kings 6:1 that the Temple was built 480 years after the exodus from Egypt. The forty years that the Jewish people were in the desert are subtracted. To the remaining 440 years, the 410 years that the Temple stood are added. Therefore, 850 years passed from the entrance of the Jewish people into Eretz Yisrael until their exile with the destruction of the First Temple.

אֲמַר רַב אַמִי: מַאי קְרָאָה? ״כִּי תוֹלִיד בָּנִים וּבְנֵי בָנִים״.

Rabbi Ammi said: What is the verse from which it is derived that it was seven dynasties? **"When you will beget children, and children's children,** and you will have been long in the land, and will deal corruptly, and make a graven image, even the form of anything…you will soon utterly perish from off the land" (Deuteronomy 4:25–26). The phrase "when you will beget children and children's children" is interpreted homiletically as indicating seven generations. This is because the term "you will beget [*tolid*]," written in the singular form, indicates one generation, and the word "children," written in the plural form, indicates two generations. Since the word "children" is mentioned three times, seven generations are indicated in total.

אֲמַרוּ לֵיהּ רַב כָּהֲנָא וְרַב אַסִי לְרַב: כְּתִיב בֵּיהּ בְּהוֹשֵׁעַ בֶּן אֵלָה: ״וַיַּעַשׂ הָרַע בְּעֵינֵי ה׳ רַק לֹא כְּמַלְכֵי יִשְׂרָאֵל״, וּכְתִיב: ״עָלָיו עָלָה שַׁלְמַנְאֶסֶר״ וגו׳!

Rav Kahana and Rav Asi said to Rav: It is written with regard to **Hoshea ben Elah: "And he did that which was evil in the eyes of the Lord, yet not as the kings of Israel** that were before him" (II Kings 17:2). **But it is written** subsequently: **"Against him came up Shalmaneser,** king of Assyria" (II Kings 17:3) and exiled the people of Israel. If Hoshea performed less evil than the previous kings of Israel, why was his generation the one that was punished?

אֲמַר לְהוּ: אוֹתָן פַּרְדֵּסִיאוֹת שֶׁהוֹשִׁיב יָרָבְעָם עַל הַדְּרָכִים כְּדֵי שֶׁלֹּא יַעֲלוּ יִשְׂרָאֵל לָרֶגֶל – בָּא הוֹשֵׁעַ וּבִיטְּלָן, וְאַף עַל פִּי כֵן לֹא עָלוּ יִשְׂרָאֵל לָרֶגֶל, אָמַר הַקָּדוֹשׁ בָּרוּךְ הוּא: אוֹתָן שָׁנִים שֶׁלֹּא עָלוּ יִשְׂרָאֵל לָרֶגֶל יֵלְכוּ בַּשְּׁבִי.

Rav **said to them: Hoshea came and canceled those guards** [*pardesei'ot*][L] **that Jeroboam placed on the roads in order to prevent** the subjects of the kingdom of **Israel from ascending** to Jerusalem **on the pilgrimage Festival, and even so** the subjects of the kingdom of **Israel did not ascend** to Jerusalem **on the pilgrimage Festival. The Holy One, Blessed be He,** therefore **said** that for **those years that** the subjects of the kingdom of **Israel did not ascend** to Jerusalem **on the pilgrimage Festival they will go into captivity.**

אֲמַר רַב חִסְדָּא אֲמַר מָר עוּקְבָא, וְאָמְרִי לָהּ אֲמַר רַב חִסְדָּא אֲמַר רַבִּי יִרְמְיָה: דָּרַשׁ מָרֵימָר, מַאי דִּכְתִיב: ״וַיִּשְׁקוֹד ה׳ עַל הָרָעָה וַיְבִיאֶהָ עָלֵינוּ כִּי צַדִּיק ה׳ אֱלֹהֵינוּ״? מִשּׁוּם דְּצַדִּיק ה׳ אֱלֹהֵינוּ וַיִּשְׁקוֹד ה׳ עַל הָרָעָה וַיְבִיאֶהָ עָלֵינוּ?!

Rav Ḥisda said that **Mar Ukva said, and some say** that it was **Rav Ḥisda** who **said** that **Rabbi Yirmeya said,** that **Mareimar interpreted** a verse **homiletically** as follows: **What** is the meaning of **that which is written: "And so the Lord has watched over the evil, and brought it upon us; for the Lord our God is righteous** [*tzaddik*]" (Daniel 9:14)? How can it be that **because the Lord, our God, is righteous, the Lord watched over the evil and brought it upon us?**

אֶלָּא, צְדָקָה עָשָׂה הַקָּדוֹשׁ בָּרוּךְ הוּא עִם יִשְׂרָאֵל שֶׁהֶגְלָה גָּלוּת צִדְקִיָּהוּ וַעֲדַיִין גָּלוּת יְכָנְיָה קַיֶּימֶת, דִּכְתִיב בֵּיהּ בְּגָלוּת יְכָנְיָה: ״הֶחָרָשׁ וְהַמַּסְגֵּר אֶלֶף״,

Rather, it must be interpreted as follows: **The Holy One, Blessed be He, performed charity** [*tzedaka*] **with** the people of **Israel by exiling** them in **the exile of Zedekiah while the exile of Jeconiah still existed** in Babylonia, **as it is written with regard to the exile of Jeconiah: "And the craftsmen** [*ḥarash*] **and the smiths** [*masger*] **a thousand"** (II Kings 24:16). The great scholars, referred to in this verse as craftsmen and smiths, of the generation were exiled with Jeconiah, and they were therefore able to give guidance to those who were exiled in the time of Zedekiah when they came to Babylonia.

חָרָשׁ – שֶׁבְּשָׁעָה שֶׁפּוֹתְחִין נַעֲשׂוּ הַכֹּל כְּחֵרְשִׁין, מַסְגֵּר – כֵּיוָן שֶׁסּוֹגְרִין שׁוּב אֵינָן פּוֹתְחִין, וְכַמָּה? אֶלֶף.

Why are the great scholars referred to as craftsmen [*ḥarash*] and smiths [*masger*]? ***Ḥarash***, containing the same letters as *ḥeresh*, meaning deaf, is an allusion to the fact **that when they would introduce** a statement of Torah **everyone would become like deaf persons,** as they would not understand. ***Masger***, which stems from the root *samekh, gimmel, reish*, meaning to close, alludes to the fact that **once they would close** a certain matter that they did not comprehend, **no** one **would introduce** it **again,** as no one was capable of solving such a problem. **And how many** scholars were there? There were **one thousand.**

עוּלָּא אָמַר: שֶׁהִקְדִּים שְׁתֵּי שָׁנִים לְ״וְנוֹשַׁנְתֶּם״.

Ulla says that God performed charity with the people of Israel **by advancing** their exile **by two years**[N] relative to the numerical value of the word ***venoshantem*** that appears in the verse. Although the numerical value of the word is 852, God exiled the Jewish people from the land after only 850 years, so that the punishment mentioned subsequently, i.e., utter annihilation, would not be fulfilled either.

אָמַר רַב אַחָא בַּר יַעֲקֹב: שְׁמַע מִינָּהּ, ״מְהֵרָה״ דְּמָרֵי עָלְמָא – תְּמָנֵי מְאָה וְחַמְשִׁין וְתַרְתֵּי הוּא.

Rav Aḥa bar Ya'akov said: Learn from this numerical value that **soon** [*mehera*] **for the Master of the World is eight hundred and fifty-two** years, as it is stated in the verse in Deuteronomy: "You will soon [*maher*] utterly perish." Since the Jewish people dwelled in Eretz Yisrael for almost this amount of time, it is apparently considered soon.

מתני׳ גֵּט מְעוּשֶּׂה, בְּיִשְׂרָאֵל – כָּשֵׁר, וּבְגוֹיִם – פָּסוּל; וּבְגוֹיִם, חוֹבְטִין אוֹתוֹ וְאוֹמְרִים לוֹ: עֲשֵׂה מַה שֶּׁיִּשְׂרָאֵל אוֹמְרִים לְךָ (וְכָשֵׁר).

MISHNA With regard to **a bill of divorce** that the husband **was compelled** by the court to write and give his wife,[N] if he was compelled **by a Jewish** court[H] it is **valid, but** if he was compelled **by gentiles**[H] it is **invalid. But with regard to gentiles they may beat him**[N] at the request of the Jewish court **and say to him: Do what the Jews are telling you,**[H] **and it is a valid** divorce.

גמ׳ אָמַר רַב נַחְמָן אָמַר שְׁמוּאֵל: גֵּט הַמְעוּשֶּׂה בְּיִשְׂרָאֵל, כַּדִּין – כָּשֵׁר, שֶׁלֹּא כַּדִּין – פָּסוּל וּפוֹסֵל;

GEMARA Rav Naḥman says that **Shmuel says:** With regard to **a bill of divorce** that the husband **was compelled by a Jewish** court to give his wife, if they did so **lawfully,** as the *halakha* obligated the husband to divorce his wife, it is **valid.** This is referring to cases where sexual intercourse is forbidden or specific cases where the Sages instituted that the husband is obligated to divorce his wife. If they did so **unlawfully,** the bill of divorce is **invalid, but** it is not considered entirely invalid, as it **disqualifies** the wife from marrying a priest after her husband's death.

וּבְגוֹיִם, כַּדִּין – פָּסוּל וּפוֹסֵל, שֶׁלֹּא כַּדִּין – אֲפִילּוּ רֵיחַ הַגֵּט אֵין בּוֹ.

And in a case where the husband was compelled **by gentiles,** if he was compelled **lawfully,** the bill of divorce is **invalid, but** it also **disqualifies** the wife from marrying a priest. But if he was compelled **unlawfully it does not have even the trace of a bill of divorce,** and the wife is not even disqualified from marrying a priest.

מַה נַּפְשָׁךְ? אִי גּוֹיִם בְּנֵי עִשּׂוּיֵי נִינְהוּ, אִיתַּכְשׁוּרֵי נָמֵי לִיתַּכְשַׁר! אִי לָאו בְּנֵי עִשּׂוּיֵי נִינְהוּ, מִיפְסַל לָא לִיפְסֵל!

The Gemara raises an objection: With regard to the statement that if the husband was compelled by gentiles the divorce is invalid but it also disqualifies the wife from marrying a priest, **whichever way you look at it,** the statement is difficult. **If gentiles are** legally **capable of compulsion, it should be rendered valid** with regard to the woman's permission to remarry **as well. If they are not** legally **capable of compulsion, it should not disqualify** her either.

אָמַר רַב מְשַׁרְשִׁיָּא: דְּבַר תּוֹרָה גֵּט מְעוּשֶּׂה בְּגוֹיִם כָּשֵׁר, וּמָה טַעַם אָמְרוּ פָּסוּל? שֶׁלֹּא תְּהֵא כׇּל אַחַת וְאַחַת הוֹלֶכֶת וְתוֹלָה עַצְמָהּ בְּגוֹי, וּמַפְקַעַת עַצְמָהּ מִיַּד בַּעְלָהּ.

Rav Mesharshiyya says: By **Torah** law **a bill of divorce** that the husband **was compelled by gentiles** to write and give his wife **is valid, and what is the reason** the Sages **said** that it is **invalid?** It is **so that each and every woman will not go and depend on a gentile** to compel her husband to divorce her through temptation or bribery, **and** thereby she will **release herself from her husband** unlawfully.

NOTES

A bill of divorce that the husband was compelled to write and give his wife – גֵּט מְעוּשֶּׂה: The Gemara in tractate *Bava Batra* (48a) discusses how a divorce can take effect against the will of the husband. It cites the mishna in tractate *Arakhin* (21a) that states that the husband is compelled to say that he wants this divorce. The Gemara explains that although an expression of willingness that was extracted under duress is generally considered meaningless, here it is accepted due to the mitzva to obey the rulings of the Sages. The Rambam explains this reasoning as follows: It is assumed that everyone wants to observe the mitzvot, and if a person expresses objection it is due to his evil inclination. Therefore, by using force the court neutralizes this man's evil inclination and allows him to express his genuine will.

But with regard to gentiles they may beat him, etc. – וּבְגוֹיִם חוֹבְטִין אוֹתוֹ וכו׳: The Rosh maintains that as long as the compulsion is performed at the instruction of a Jewish court, it is not necessary for the gentiles to say to the husband explicitly: Do what the Jews are telling you to do. By contrast, the Ramah holds that the gentiles must make this statement; otherwise the divorce is invalid.

HALAKHA

A bill of divorce that the husband was compelled…by a Jewish court – גֵּט מְעוּשֶּׂה בְּיִשְׂרָאֵל: If a man is obligated to divorce his wife and he is not willing to do so, the court can compel him to divorce her, and it is a valid bill of divorce. If they compel him to divorce her unlawfully, then even if he says under duress that he wants to divorce her, and even if he cancels a preemptive declaration of his invalidating the divorce, the divorce is invalid. In the *Beit Shmuel* it is added that the divorce is invalid by Torah law. The wife is nevertheless disqualified from marrying a priest, in accordance with Shmuel's statement (Rambam *Sefer Nashim, Hilkhot Geirushin* 2:20; *Shulḥan Arukh, Even HaEzer* 134:5–7).

A bill of divorce that the husband was compelled…by gentiles – גֵּט מְעוּשֶּׂה...בְּגוֹיִם: If gentiles compel the husband to divorce his wife, the divorce is invalid whether or not he is legally obligated to divorce her. If he is obligated to divorce her she is disqualified by this divorce from marrying a priest. If he is not obligated to divorce her, she is not disqualified. This is in accordance with Shmuel's statement (Rambam *Sefer Nashim, Hilkhot Geirushin* 2:20; *Shulḥan Arukh, Even HaEzer* 134:8).

Do what the Jews are telling you – עֲשֵׂה מַה שֶּׁיִּשְׂרָאֵל אוֹמְרִים לְךָ: If a court compels a husband to divorce his wife using gentiles who beat him, saying: Do what the Jews are telling you, he is considered as having been compelled by a Jewish court (Rambam *Sefer Nashim, Hilkhot Geirushin* 2:20; *Shulḥan Arukh, Even HaEzer* 134:9).

אִי הָכִי, שֶׁלֹּא כַּדִּין אֲפִילּוּ רֵיחַ הַגֵּט אֵין בּוֹ?! וְנֶהֱוֵי שֶׁלֹּא כַּדִּין כְּיִשְׂרָאֵל, וּמִפְסִיל נַמִי לִפְסוֹל!

The Gemara asks: **If that is so,** that where the husband was compelled by gentiles the bill of divorce is valid by Torah law, why did Shmuel rule that if he was compelled **unlawfully it does not have even the trace of a bill of divorce? Let** a bill of divorce that the husband was compelled **unlawfully** by gentiles to give his wife **be compared to** a case where he was compelled unlawfully by **Jews, and disqualify** the wife from marrying a priest **as well.**

אֶלָּא, הָא דְּרַב מְשָׁרְשִׁיָּא בְּדוּתָא הִיא.

Rather, that statement **of Rav Mesharshiyya,** that by Torah law a bill of divorce is valid even if the husband was compelled by gentiles to write it and give it to his wife, **is a mistake.** In principle it does not have even the trace of a bill of divorce, even if the husband is required by law to divorce his wife.

וְטַעֲמָא מַאי? כַּדִּין בְּכַדִּין דְּיִשְׂרָאֵל מִיחַלַּף, שֶׁלֹּא כַּדִּין בְּכַדִּין יִשְׂרָאֵל לָא מִיחַלַּף.

And what is the reason that the wife is disqualified from marrying a priest in this case? It is because the case where the husband was compelled **lawfully** by gentiles **can be confused with** a case where he was compelled **lawfully by Jews.** If a bill of divorce that gentiles compelled the husband to write and give to his wife carries no weight, people might think that this is likewise the *halakha* with regard to a case where Jews compelled the husband to do so. Therefore, the Sages issued a decree that even if the husband was compelled by gentiles the wife is disqualified from marrying a priest. By contrast, the case where the husband was compelled **unlawfully** by gentiles **cannot be confused with** a case where he was compelled **lawfully by Jews,** as they are too dissimilar. Therefore, a bill of divorce that gentiles unlawfully compelled the husband to write and give his wife is entirely invalid.

אַבָּיֵי אַשְׁכְּחֵיהּ לְרַב יוֹסֵף דְּיָתֵיב וְקָא מְעַשֶּׂה אַגִּיטֵּי, אֲמַר לֵיהּ: וְהָא אֲנַן הֶדְיוֹטוֹת אֲנַן, וְתַנְיָא, הָיָה רַבִּי טַרְפוֹן אוֹמֵר: כׇּל מָקוֹם שֶׁאַתָּה מוֹצֵא אָגוֹרִיאוֹת שֶׁל גּוֹיִם, אַף עַל פִּי שֶׁדִּינֵיהֶם כְּדִינֵי יִשְׂרָאֵל, אִי אַתָּה רַשַּׁאי לְהִיזָּקֵק לָהֶם, שֶׁנֶּאֱמַר: ״וְאֵלֶּה הַמִּשְׁפָּטִים אֲשֶׁר תָּשִׂים לִפְנֵיהֶם״, ״לִפְנֵיהֶם״ וְלֹא לִפְנֵי גּוֹיִם, דָּבָר אַחֵר: ״לִפְנֵיהֶם״ – וְלֹא לִפְנֵי הֶדְיוֹטוֹת!

§ **Abaye**[P] **found Rav Yosef**[P] **sitting** in court as the judge **and compelling** husbands to give their wives **bills of divorce. He said to him: But aren't we ordinary people,** not ordained judges? **And it is taught** in a *baraita* that **Rabbi Tarfon would say:** With regard to **any place where you find gentile courts [*agoriot*],**[HBL] **even if their laws are like Jewish laws, you may not attend them, as it is stated: "Now these are the ordinances which you shall set before them"** (Exodus 21:1). It is derived from here that one may go to court only **before them,** i.e., Jewish judges, **and not before gentiles. Alternatively,** it is derived that one may go to court **before them,** i.e., ordained judges, **and not before ordinary people.** Since we are not ordained judges, how can you perform a distinctly judicial act?

HALAKHA

Gentile courts – אֲגוֹרִיאוֹת שֶׁל גּוֹיִם: It is prohibited to go for judgment before a gentile court or gentile judges, even if they judge according to Jewish law, and even if both parties agree to do so. One who does so is considered wicked, as it is a disgrace to the Torah. If the Jewish court is incapable of enforcing its decision, it can grant permission to go to a gentile court (Rambam *Sefer Mishpatim, Hilkhot Sanhedrin* 26:7; *Shulḥan Arukh, Ḥoshen Mishpat* 26:1).

BACKGROUND

Gentile courts [*agoriot*] – אֲגוֹרִיאוֹת: The Sages rendered it prohibited for Jews to use gentile courts to settle disputes, even in cases where gentile law is the same as *halakha* (see *Gittin* 88b). They based this prohibition on the verse: "Now these are the ordinances which you shall set before them" (Exodus 21:1), indicating that the *halakhot* must be adjudicated before them, i.e., Jewish courts, and not before gentile ones. Extremely harsh terms were used to refer to violators. Various sources accuse them of heresy, betraying the Torah, and profaning God's name. This attitude seemed to stem from the need to maintain the last bastion of Jewish autonomy during the exile, when the Jews were no longer sovereign in their own state. Nevertheless, there were certain unusual circumstances under which the later authorities did permit using gentile courts, primarily when the issue was one over which the secular government had authority, e.g., land ownership and physical assaults. Although there were communities in which this *halakha* was neglected, in general the religious leadership managed to preserve the integrity of Jewish courts, both through the institution of communal ordinances as well as by taking special measures against violators.

LANGUAGE

Courts [*agoriot*] – אֲגוֹרִיאוֹת: From the Greek ἀγορά, *agora*, meaning assembly and place of assembly, where the leaders of a community gather and pronounce judgment.

PERSONALITIES

Abaye – אַבָּיֵי: One of the outstanding Sages of the Talmud, Abaye was a fourth-generation Babylonian *amora*. Abaye was orphaned at the time of his birth and raised by his paternal uncle, Rabba. Some say that his real name was Naḥmani or Kilil and that Abaye was merely a nickname. The woman who assisted his uncle in raising him impressed upon him many life lessons that he quotes in her name. There are several incidents related in the Gemara that illustrate his intelligence even as a child, including some where his adoptive father, Rabba, tests his knowledge. Although Rabba was a priest and the head of his yeshiva, he lived in poverty, as did Abaye.

Abaye was the primary student of Rabba and of Rav Yosef. After Rav Yosef's death, Abaye succeeded him as the head of the yeshiva in Pumbedita. He honored the study of Torah and would announce a celebration for the scholars whenever one of them completed a tractate.

Growing up in his uncle's home, he was aware of the difficulties of scholars who were without financial means. The Gemara in tractate *Berakhot* (35b) relates that he testified that many were successful in following the path of Rabbi Yishmael, who instructed his students to plow, plant, and harvest in the appropriate time; only very few were successful in following the path of Rabbi Shimon bar Yoḥai, who taught that one should devote himself entirely to Torah and ignore worldly concerns.

Abaye's exchanges and halakhic disputes with his uncle, and even more so with Rav Yosef, can be found throughout the Talmud. His disputes with his colleague Rava are especially significant. Their disagreements are examples of profound and edifying disputes and constitute in part the foundations of the Babylonian Talmud. In these disputes, with six exceptions, the *halakha* is ruled in accordance with the opinion of Rava.

In addition to Abaye's prominence as a Torah scholar, he was known for his righteousness and his acts of kindness.

Rav Yosef – רַב יוֹסֵף: Rav Yosef bar Ḥiyya was one of the greatest third-generation Babylonian *amora'im*. Rav Yosef was given the nickname Sinai, in contrast to his colleague, Rabba, who was called: The one who uproots mountains. Sinai denotes one who received the Torah itself, i.e., one who is exceedingly knowledgeable with regard to *halakha* and whose opinions are based on the most authoritative sources. Due to this knowledge, he was recommended as the replacement for Rav Yehuda as the head of the yeshiva in Pumbedita. However, he deferred to Rabba and took the position only after Rabba's death. He served in that position for only two years until his own passing in the year 323.

In his later years Rav Yosef was blind. He explained that he preferred the opinion that a blind person is exempt from the performance of mitzvot. Since he performed the mitzvot anyway, he believed that he would receive a greater reward as one who performed the mitzvot voluntarily. When he learned that the reward for one who is commanded in mitzvot is greater than that for one who performs them voluntarily, he declared that he prefers the opinion that a blind person is obligated in the performance of mitzvot (*Kiddushin* 31a).

He was respected greatly by other Sages, most notably by his prominent students Abaye and Rava.

אֲמַר לֵיהּ: אֲנַן שְׁלִיחוּתַיְיהוּ קָא עָבְדִינַן, מִידֵּי דַּהֲוָה אַהוֹדָאוֹת וְהַלְוָאוֹת.

Rav Yosef **said to him:** We see ourselves as agents of the ordained judges in Eretz Yisrael, and **we are performing** our task as judges on the basis of **their agency,**[NH] **just as is** the case **with regard to** cases of **admissions and loans,**[H] which we attend to on the same basis.

אִי הָכִי, גְּזֵילוֹת וַחֲבָלוֹת נַמִי! כִּי עָבְדִינַן שְׁלִיחוּתַיְיהוּ – בְּמִילְּתָא דִּשְׁכִיחָא, בְּמִילְּתָא דְּלָא שְׁכִיחָא – לָא עָבְדִינַן שְׁלִיחוּתַיְיהוּ.

The Gemara asks: **If so,** why is the *halakha* that judges living outside Eretz Yisrael do not judge in cases of **robbery and** personal **injury?** They should judge in these cases **as well.** The Gemara answers: **When we perform** our tasks as judges on the basis of **their agency,** it is **with regard to common matters,** e.g., cases that pertain to the *halakhot* of admissions and loans, which arise frequently between people. But **with regard to uncommon matters,** e.g., cases of robbery or personal injury, **we do not perform** our tasks as judges on the basis of **their agency.**

מתני׳ יָצָא שְׁמָהּ בָּעִיר מְקוּדֶּשֶׁת – הֲרֵי זוֹ מְקוּדֶּשֶׁת, מְגוֹרֶשֶׁת – הֲרֵי זוֹ מְגוֹרֶשֶׁת, וּבִלְבַד שֶׁלֹּא יְהֵא שָׁם אֲמַתְלָא.

MISHNA If **a rumor circulated in the city** that an unmarried woman is **betrothed,**[H] **she is** considered to be **betrothed.**[N] Similarly, if a rumor circulated that a married woman is **divorced, she is divorced, provided there is no** valid alternative **explanation** [*amatla*][HL] for the rumor.

אֵיזוֹ הִיא אֲמַתְלָא? גֵּירֵשׁ אִישׁ פְּלוֹנִי אֶת אִשְׁתּוֹ עַל תְּנַאי, זָרַק לָהּ קִידּוּשֶׁיהָ סָפֵק קָרוֹב לָהּ סָפֵק קָרוֹב לוֹ – זוֹ הִיא אֲמַתְלָא.

What is considered a valid **explanation?** For example, it is a case where there is a rumor that **so-and-so divorced his wife** but that the bill of divorce was given to her **conditionally.** It is therefore possible that the condition was not fulfilled and she is not actually divorced. Similarly, if there is a rumor that a woman was betrothed but that the man **threw her betrothal,** i.e., the money or document of betrothal, **to her,** and it is **uncertain** whether it was **closer to her** and **uncertain** whether it was **closer to him,** and therefore the status of their betrothal is likewise uncertain, **this is** considered a valid **explanation.**

גמ׳ וְאָסְרִינַן לָהּ אַגַּבְרָא? וְהָא אֲמַר רַב אַשִׁי: כׇּל קָלָא דְּבָתַר נִישּׂוּאִין – לָא חָיְישִׁינַן לֵיהּ!

GEMARA With regard to the statement that a woman who is rumored to be divorced is divorced, **do we render her forbidden to her husband**[H] if she is married to a priest? **But didn't Rav Ashi say** that **we are not concerned about any rumor that** circulates **after marriage?** Accordingly, a woman should not be compelled to leave her husband merely on the basis of a rumor.

הָכִי קָאָמַר: יָצָא שְׁמָהּ בָּעִיר מְקוּדֶּשֶׁת – הֲרֵי זוֹ מְקוּדֶּשֶׁת, מְקוּדֶּשֶׁת וּמְגוֹרֶשֶׁת

The Gemara answers that **this is what** the mishna **is saying:** If **a rumor circulated in the city** that a woman is **betrothed, she is betrothed,** and she may not marry another man until she receives a bill of divorce from the man to whom she is rumored to be betrothed. If she is rumored to have been **betrothed** to a certain man **and** subsequently **divorced**[H] from him,

HALAKHA

We are performing our task as judges on the basis of their agency – אֲנַן שְׁלִיחוּתַיְיהוּ קָא עָבְדִינַן: Since ordination of judges is no longer performed, courts do not have the full status of judges. Rather, they act as agents of the ordained courts of previous generations and do not have the authority to implement the *halakhot* of fines and penalties in Torah law (Rambam *Sefer Mishpatim, Hilkhot Sanhedrin* 5:8).

Admissions and loans – הוֹדָאוֹת וְהַלְוָאוֹת: The *halakhot* of fines may be implemented in court only by three ordained judges. In cases of monetary law, i.e., loans and admissions, as well as other cases that are common and involve monetary loss, an expert judge is not necessary, and they may instead be judged by three ordinary judges. Therefore, such cases can be judged outside of Eretz Yisrael, and nowadays as well (Rambam *Sefer Mishpatim, Hilkhot Sanhedrin* 5:8; *Shulḥan Arukh, Ḥoshen Mishpat* 1:1).

If a rumor circulated in the city that an unmarried woman is betrothed – יָצָא שְׁמָהּ בָּעִיר מְקוּדֶּשֶׁת: A woman who is rumored to be betrothed to a certain man is assumed to be betrothed, even if there is no clear evidence of this (Rambam *Sefer Nashim, Hilkhot Ishut* 9:22; *Shulḥan Arukh, Even HaEzer* 46:1).

Provided there is no explanation – וּבִלְבַד שֶׁלֹּא יְהֵא שָׁם אֲמַתְלָא: A rumor is treated seriously when it is not weakened by an explanation. An example of an explanation is when a woman is rumored to have been betrothed to a certain man conditionally, or in an uncertain manner. Since there is no testimony of the betrothal and the rumor is not substantial, the explanation offered by the woman is relied upon (Rambam *Sefer Nashim, Hilkhot Ishut* 9:23; *Shulḥan Arukh, Even HaEzer* 46:3).

Do we render her forbidden to her husband – וְאָסְרִינַן לָהּ אַגַּבְרָא: If a rumor circulated that a certain priest divorced his wife, and she is living with him, she is not obligated to leave him, as a rumor that circulates after marriage is of no concern (*Shulḥan Arukh, Even HaEzer* 6:3).

Betrothed and subsequently divorced – מְקוּדֶּשֶׁת וּמְגוֹרֶשֶׁת: If a rumor circulated that a woman was betrothed to a certain man and subsequently was divorced from him, it is assumed that she is not married to him, and it is prohibited for her to marry a priest due to the rumor that she is a divorcée. Different opinions are cited in the *Beit Shmuel* with regard to a case where she is rumored to have been betrothed to a certain man and then divorced from him conditionally (Rambam *Sefer Nashim, Hilkhot Geirushin* 10:20; *Shulḥan Arukh, Even HaEzer* 46:7).

NOTES

We are performing our task as judges on the basis of their agency – שְׁלִיחוּתַיְיהוּ קָא עָבְדִינַן: *Tosafot* write that although today there are no ordained judges even in Eretz Yisrael, all Jewish judges today are considered agents of the ordained judges from previous generations, as those judges granted permission and authority to the Sages of all generations to judge the people.

She is considered betrothed – הֲרֵי זוֹ מְקוּדֶּשֶׁת: In other words, she may not remarry without receiving a bill of divorce from the man to whom it is rumored that she is betrothed.

LANGUAGE

Explanation [*amatla*] – אֲמַתְלָא: Apparently from the Aramaic *matla*, which means parable and which also refers to a story or occurrence. An *amatla* is a story that serves as a justification for or explanation of something that happened.

הֲרֵי זוֹ מְגוֹרֶשֶׁת; מַאי טַעְמָא? קוֹל וְשׁוֹבְרוֹ עִמּוֹ.

she is considered to be **divorced** and may remarry. **What is the reason** for this? The **rumor** came **with its receipt.** The rumor that she is betrothed is canceled by the rumor that she is divorced.

אֲמַר רָבָא: יָצָא לָהּ שֵׁם מְזַנָּה בָּעִיר – אֵין חוֹשְׁשִׁין לָהּ; מַאי טַעְמָא? פְּרִיצוּתָא בְּעָלְמָא הוּא דַּחֲזוֹ לַהּ.

§ **Rava said:** If **a rumor circulated in the city** that a woman **engaged in licentious sexual intercourse,**[H] **we are not concerned** that the rumor is true with regard to her eligibility to marry a priest. **What is the reason** for this? It is assumed that people **saw her** engage in **merely licentious behavior,** in a manner that does not disqualify her from marrying a priest.

כְּתַנָּאֵי: אָכְלָה בַּשּׁוּק, גִּירְגְּרָה בַּשּׁוּק, הֵנִיקָה בַּשּׁוּק – בְּכוּלָּן רַבִּי מֵאִיר אוֹמֵר: תֵּצֵא, רַבִּי עֲקִיבָא אוֹמֵר: מִשֶּׁיִּשָּׂאוּ וְיִתְּנוּ בָּהּ מוֹזְרוֹת בַּלְּבָנָה;

This statement is **parallel to** one side of a dispute among the *tanna'im*: If a woman **ate in the marketplace, walked with her neck stretched forward**[N] in an arrogant manner **in the marketplace,** or **nursed in the marketplace, with regard to all** of these cases **Rabbi Meir says** that **she must leave** her husband, since all of these behaviors are considered licentious behavior. **Rabbi Akiva says** that she must leave him only **once the women who spin** [*mozerot*][L] **by the moonlight converse about her** having engaged in promiscuous sexual intercourse, as this indicates that the matter is well known and accepted as fact.

אָמַר לוֹ רַבִּי יוֹחָנָן בֶּן נוּרִי: אִם כֵּן, לֹא הִנַּחְתָּ בַּת לְאַבְרָהָם אָבִינוּ שֶׁיּוֹשֶׁבֶת תַּחַת בַּעְלָהּ, וְהַתּוֹרָה אָמְרָה: ״כִּי מָצָא בָהּ עֶרְוַת דָּבָר״, וּלְהַלָּן הוּא אוֹמֵר: ״עַל פִּי שְׁנַיִם עֵדִים אוֹ עַל פִּי שְׁלֹשָׁה עֵדִים יָקוּם דָּבָר״, מָה לְהַלָּן דָּבָר בָּרוּר, אַף כָּאן דָּבָר בָּרוּר!

Rabbi Yoḥanan ben Nuri said to him: If so, you have not allowed any **daughter of Abraham our forefather to remain with her husband,** i.e., all wives will be forced to leave their husbands, as it is common for women to slander their peers. **And the Torah said: "Because he has found some unseemly matter in her,** and he writes her a scroll of severance" (Deuteronomy 24:1), **and it says over there: "At the mouth of two witnesses, or at the mouth of three witnesses, a matter shall be established"** (Deuteronomy 19:15). **Just as there,** the word "matter" is referring to **a clear matter,** as it is established through witnesses, **so too here,** the unseemly matter that is considered a cause for divorce is also referring to **a clear matter** that was not established merely through a rumor. Rava's statement is in accordance with this opinion.

תָּנוּ רַבָּנַן: בְּעוּלָה – אֵין חוֹשְׁשִׁין לָהּ, נְשׂוּאָה – אֵין חוֹשְׁשִׁין לָהּ, אֲרוּסָה – אֵין חוֹשְׁשִׁין לָהּ, שֶׁלֹּא לִפְלוֹנִי – אֵין חוֹשְׁשִׁין לָהּ, בְּעִיר אַחֶרֶת – אֵין חוֹשְׁשִׁין לָהּ,

The Sages taught: If a rumor circulated that a certain unmarried woman is **a non-virgin, one is not concerned**[N] **about it,**[H] and she may marry a High Priest. If a rumor circulated that she is **a married woman, one is not concerned about it.** If a rumor circulated that she is **a betrothed woman, one is not concerned about it.** If a rumor circulated that she is betrothed, but **not to so-and-so,**[H] i.e., the man who betrothed her is not specified, **one is not concerned about it.** If a rumor circulated that she was betrothed **in another city, one is not concerned about it.**

מַמְזֶרֶת – אֵין חוֹשְׁשִׁין לָהּ, שִׁפְחָה – אֵין חוֹשְׁשִׁין לָהּ;

If a rumor circulated that she is **a daughter born from an incestuous or adulterous relationship** [*mamzeret*], **one is not concerned about it.** If a rumor circulated that she is **a maidservant, one is not concerned**[H] **about it.**

הִקְדִּישׁ פְּלוֹנִי נְכָסָיו, הִפְקִיר פְּלוֹנִי נְכָסָיו – אֵין חוֹשְׁשִׁין לָהֶן.

Similarly, if a rumor circulated that **so-and-so consecrated his property,**[H] or that **so-and-so renounced ownership of his property, we are not concerned about these** rumors, and his property cannot be taken away by the Temple treasury or another person.

HALAKHA

If a rumor circulated…that a woman engaged in licentious sexual intercourse – יָצָא לָהּ שֵׁם מְזַנָּה: One should not pay heed to a rumor that a woman engaged in licentious sexual intercourse, even if her husband left her due to her transgression of the Jewish customs of modesty, or if testimony was given about her licentious behavior. Therefore, if her husband died before managing to give her a bill of divorce, it is permitted for her to marry a priest. This is in accordance with Rava's statement (Rambam *Sefer Kedusha, Hilkhot Issurei Bia* 17:21; *Shulḥan Arukh, Even HaEzer* 6:16).

If a rumor circulated that a woman is a non-virgin, one is not concerned about it – בְּעוּלָה אֵין חוֹשְׁשִׁין: If a woman who has the presumptive status of a virgin is rumored to be a non-virgin, the rumor is disregarded, and it is permitted for her to marry even a High Priest. If a rumor circulated that a woman is a *ḥalutza*, some authorities rule that the rumor is disregarded and it is permitted for her to marry a priest, in accordance with the version of the Rif and the Rosh, and others hold that the rumor is treated seriously, like a rumor that a woman is a divorcée (Ra'avad), in accordance with the printed version of the Gemara (Rambam *Sefer Kedusha, Hilkhot Issurei Bia* 17:20; *Shulḥan Arukh, Even HaEzer* 6:5).

If a rumor circulated that she is betrothed, but not to so-and-so, etc. – שֶׁלֹּא לִפְלוֹנִי וכו׳: If a rumor circulated that a woman is betrothed but the man to whom she is purportedly betrothed is not specified, or if it is rumored that she was betrothed in another city, the rumor is not considered credible and is disregarded (*Shulḥan Arukh, Even HaEzer* 46:1, in the comment of Rema).

If a rumor circulated that she is a maidservant one is not concerned – שִׁפְחָה אֵין חוֹשְׁשִׁין: If a rumor circulated about a woman that she is a maidservant, the rumor is disregarded, and she may marry even a priest (Rambam *Sefer Kedusha, Hilkhot Issurei Bia* 17:21).

So-and-so consecrated his property, etc. – הִקְדִּישׁ פְּלוֹנִי נְכָסָיו וכו׳: If a rumor circulated that so-and-so consecrated all of his property or renounced his ownership of it, the rumor is disregarded unless there is clear evidence indicating it is true (Rambam *Sefer Hafla'a, Hilkhot Arakhin VaḤaramim* 7:20).

NOTES

Walked with her neck stretched forward [*girgera*] – גִּירְגְּרָה: Rashi interprets this word as walking with an extended neck, which is a licentious manner of behavior. Others suggest that it is related to the word *gargeran*, meaning glutton, and means that she grabbed food from a man in the marketplace and ate it, which is also considered licentious behavior (Ritva; see *Arukh*).

If a rumor circulated that a woman is a non-virgin, one is not concerned – בְּעוּלָה אֵין חוֹשְׁשִׁין: What would be the ramifications if this rumor were considered true? Rashi explains that it would be prohibited for the woman to marry a High Priest, who may not marry a non-virgin. *Tosafot* explain that an unmarried woman who engaged in sexual intercourse is suspected as having engaged in sexual intercourse with a man who is prohibited from marrying her, and she would thereby be disqualified from marrying any priest. Rabbeinu Crescas Vidal adds an additional practical ramification: A non-virgin receives one hundred dinars in her marriage contract, whereas a virgin receives two hundred.

In the version of the Rif and the Rosh, the Gemara states here: If a rumor circulated that a woman is a *yevama* who performed *ḥalitza* [*ḥalutza*], one is not concerned about it.

LANGUAGE

The women who spin [*mozerot*] – מוֹזְרוֹת: *Mozerot* means to spin yarn or thread. The *baraita* refers to women who sit and spin together by moonlight, conversing about local gossip and news while they spin. This *baraita* is discussed in the Jerusalem Talmud as well (*Sota* 6:1), where another version is mentioned that reads *motzerot*. It is explained that *motzerot* refers to combing wool, whereas *mozerot* refers to spinning flax.

אָמַר עוּלָּא: לֹא שֶׁשָּׁמְעוּ קוֹל הֲבָרָה, אֶלָּא כְּדֵי שֶׁיְּהוּ נֵרוֹת דּוֹלְקוֹת וּמִטּוֹת מוּצָּעוֹת, וּבְנֵי אָדָם נִכְנָסִין וְיוֹצְאִין וְאוֹמְרִים ״פְּלוֹנִית מִתְקַדֶּשֶׁת הַיּוֹם״.

§ **Ulla says:** The rumor mentioned in the mishna with regard to betrothal is **not** referring to a case **where** people only **heard an echo. Rather,** it is referring to a case **where** there is circumstantial evidence, as **there are candles lit and beds made** in the woman's house, as was the custom for brides, **and people entering and leaving and saying** that **so-and-so is becoming betrothed today.**

מִתְקַדֶּשֶׁת?! וְדִלְמָא לָא אִקַּדְּשָׁה! אֵימָא: ״פְּלוֹנִית נִתְקַדְּשָׁה הַיּוֹם״.

The Gemara asks: If people merely are saying that she is **becoming betrothed,** what is the reason for concern? **Perhaps she was not betrothed** in the end. Rather, **say** that people are saying that **so-and-so was betrothed today.**

וְכֵן תָּנֵי לֵוִי: לֹא שֶׁיִּשְׁמְעוּ קוֹל הֲבָרָה, אֶלָּא כְּדֵי שֶׁיְּהוּ נֵרוֹת דּוֹלְקוֹת וּמִטּוֹת מוּצָּעוֹת, וְנָשִׁים טוֹוֹת לְאוֹר הַנֵּר וּשְׂמֵחוֹת לָהּ, וְאוֹמְרוֹת ״פְּלוֹנִית מִתְקַדֶּשֶׁת הַיּוֹם״. מִתְקַדֶּשֶׁת?! וְדִלְמָא לָא אִקַּדְּשָׁה! אָמַר רַב פַּפָּא, אֵימָא: ״פְּלוֹנִית נִתְקַדְּשָׁה הַיּוֹם״.

And similarly, Levi taught a *baraita*: The mishna is **not** referring to a case **where** people only **hear an echo. Rather,** it is referring to a case **where candles are lit and beds are made, and women are spinning by candlelight and rejoicing for her and saying** that **so-and-so is becoming betrothed today.** The Gemara asks: If they are merely saying that she is **becoming betrothed,** what is the reason for concern? **Perhaps she was not betrothed** in the end. **Rav Pappa said: Say** that they are saying that **so-and-so was betrothed today.**

אָמַר רַבָּה בַּר בַּר חָנָה אָמַר רַבִּי יוֹחָנָן: לֹא שֶׁשָּׁמְעוּ קוֹל הֲבָרָה, אֶלָּא כְּדֵי שֶׁיְּהוּ נֵרוֹת דּוֹלְקוֹת וּמִטּוֹת מוּצָּעוֹת וּבְנֵי אָדָם נִכְנָסִין וְיוֹצְאִין, אָמְרוּ דָּבָר – זֶה הוּא קוֹל, לֹא אָמְרוּ דָּבָר – זֶהוּ אֲמַתְלָא.

Rabba bar bar Ḥana says that **Rabbi Yoḥanan says:** The mishna is **not** referring to a case **where** people only **heard an echo.**[H] **Rather,** it is referring to a case **where there are candles lit and beds made and people entering and leaving. If they made** an explicit **statement** that the woman was betrothed, **this is a rumor** that renders her betrothed. If **they did not make** such a **statement, this is** the **explanation** mentioned in the mishna.

לֹא אָמְרוּ?! וְהָא לֹא אָמְרוּ לֹא כְּלוּם! לְאַפּוּקֵי מִדְּרַבָּה בַּר רַב הוּנָא, דְּאָמַר: אֲמַתְלָא שֶׁאָמְרוּ – אֲפִילוּ מִכָּאן וְעַד עֲשָׂרָה יָמִים, קָא מַשְׁמַע לָן: לֹא אָמְרוּ הוּא דְּהָוְיָא אֲמַתְלָא, הָא אָמְרוּ – לָא הָוְיָא אֲמַתְלָא.

The Gemara asks: If **they did not make** such **a statement,** why is it considered an explanation? **But they did not say anything** that requires an explanation. The Gemara answers that Rabbi Yoḥanan did not mean that the people did not say anything, but rather that they did not state unequivocally that the woman is betrothed, **to the exclusion of that which Rabba bar Rav Huna said: The explanation mentioned** in the mishna negates the rumor **even** if it circulates at some point **from now until ten days** after the rumor begins to circulate. Rabbi Yoḥanan therefore **teaches us** that only if the people **did not say** unequivocally that she is betrothed **is it considered an explanation** that negates the rumor. But if **they said** so unequivocally, any later explanation **is not considered an explanation** that negates the rumor.

אָמַר רַבִּי אַבָּא אָמַר רַב הוּנָא אָמַר רַב: לֹא שֶׁשָּׁמְעוּ קוֹל הֲבָרָה, אֶלָּא כְּדֵי שֶׁיֹּאמְרוּ: פְּלוֹנִי מֵהֵיכָן שָׁמַע? מִפְּלוֹנִי, וּפְלוֹנִי מִפְּלוֹנִי, וּבוֹדְקִין וְהוֹלְכִין עַד שֶׁמַּגִּיעִין לְדָבָר הַבָּרוּר.

Rabbi Abba said that **Rav Huna said** that **Rav said:** The mishna is **not** referring to a case **where** people only **heard an echo. Rather,** it is referring to a case **where** people **say: From where did so-and-so hear** that this woman is betrothed? **From so-and-so, and so-and-so** heard it **from so-and-so. And** as a result, the judges **investigate** the rumor **continuously,** tracing the hearsay **until they reach a clear matter,** i.e., eyewitnesses.

HALAKHA

Is not referring to a case where people only heard an echo, etc. – לֹא שֶׁשָּׁמְעוּ קוֹל הֲבָרָה וכו׳: What type of rumor gives a woman the presumptive status of being betrothed? It is one where, for example, two witnesses who are fit to give testimony come to court and testify that they saw candles lit and beds made in the woman's house, and people entering and leaving, and women rejoicing for her and saying that so-and-so was betrothed today. If they merely heard them say that so-and-so will be betrothed today, the rumor is disregarded, in accordance with the statements of Ulla, Levi, and Rav Pappa (Rambam *Sefer Kedusha, Hilkhot Ishut* 9:22; *Shulḥan Arukh, Even HaEzer* 46:1).

דָּבָר הַבָּרוּר, עֵדוּת מַעַלְיְיתָא הוּא! אֶלָּא, כִּי אֲתָא רַב שְׁמוּאֵל בַּר יְהוּדָה, אָמַר רַבִּי אַבָּא אָמַר רַב הוּנָא אָמַר רַב: לֹא שֶׁשָּׁמְעוּ קוֹל הֲבָרָה, אֶלָּא כְּדֵי שֶׁיֹּאמְרוּ: פְּלוֹנִי מֵהֵיכָן שָׁמַע? מִפְּלוֹנִי, וּפְלוֹנִי מִפְּלוֹנִי, וְהָלְכוּ לָהֶם לִמְדִינַת הַיָּם.

The Gemara raises an objection: If the court reaches **a clear matter it is proper testimony,** not a rumor. **Rather, when Rav Shmuel bar Yehuda came** from Eretz Yisrael he taught that **Rabbi Abba said** that **Rav Huna said** that **Rav said:** The mishna is **not** referring to a case **where** people only **heard an echo. Rather,** it is referring to a case **where** people **say: From where did so-and-so hear** this? **From so-and-so, and so-and-so** heard it **from so-and-so, and they went overseas,**[H] so that the court cannot investigate further.

אֲמַר לֵיהּ אַבַּיֵּי לְרַב יוֹסֵף: מְבַטְּלִינַן קָלָא אוֹ לָא מְבַטְּלִינַן? אֲמַר לֵיהּ: מִדְּאָמַר רַב חִסְדָּא: עַד שֶׁיִּשְׁמְעוּ מִפִּי הַכְּשֵׁרִים, שְׁמַע מִינָּהּ: מְבַטְּלִינַן קָלָא.

§ **Abaye said to Rav Yosef: Do we suppress a rumor**[HN] that was not substantiated by the court, **or do we not suppress** it? **He said to him: Since Rav Ḥisda says** that a rumor is not treated stringently **until** the court **hears** it **from valid** witnesses, which indicates that rumors are generally treated leniently, **learn from it** that **we suppress a rumor.**

אֲמַר לֵיהּ: אַדְּרַבָּה, מִדַּאֲמַר רַב שֵׁשֶׁת: אֲפִילּוּ מִפִּי נָשִׁים הָוֵי קוֹל, שְׁמַע מִינָּהּ: לָא מְבַטְּלִינַן קָלָא!

Abaye **said to him: On the contrary, since Rav Sheshet said** that **even** if the court hears it **from women it is** considered a serious **rumor,** indicating that rumors are treated stringently, **learn from it** that **we do not suppress a rumor.**

אֲמַר לֵיהּ: אַתְרָוָותָא נִינְהוּ, בְּסוּרָא מְבַטְּלֵי קָלָא, בִּנְהַרְדְּעָא לָא מְבַטְּלֵי קָלָא.

Rav Yosef **said to him: These** opinions correspond to the local custom in two different **places. In Sura they suppress a rumor,** whereas **in Neharde'a they do not suppress a rumor.**

הַהִיא דִּנְפַק עֲלָהּ קָלָא דְּאִיקַּדְשָׁה לְבַר בֵּי רַב, אַתְיֵיהּ רַב חָמָא לַאֲבוּהּ, אֲמַר לֵיהּ: אֵימָא לִי הֵיכִי הֲוָה עוּבְדָא? אֲמַר לֵיהּ: עַל תְּנַאי קַדֵּישׁ, אַדַּעְתָּא דְּלָא אָזֵיל לְבֵי חוֹזַאי, וַאֲזַל. אֲמַר לֵיהּ: כֵּיוָן דִּבְעִידָּנָא דַּהֲוַאי קָלָא לָא הֲוַאי אֲמַתְלָא, לָאו כׇּל כְּמִינָּךְ דִּמְחַזְּקַתְּ אֲמַתְלָא.

The Gemara relates several incidents: **A rumor circulated that a certain woman**[H] **was betrothed to a student** of Torah. **Rav Ḥama summoned her father and said to him: Tell me** exactly **how the incident** transpired. The father **said to him:** The student **betrothed** her **conditionally, with the intention that he would not go to** the city of **Bei Ḥozai, and he** subsequently **went** there, thereby nullifying the betrothal. Rav Ḥama **said to him: Since at the time that the rumor existed** this **explanation did not exist, it is not in your power to create the presumption of an explanation.** Therefore, the rumor must be treated stringently.

הַהִיא דִּנְפַק עֲלָהּ קָלָא דְּאִיקַּדְשָׁה בַּאֲצִיפָּא דְּתוֹחְלָא בְּעֵינָא דְּבֵי שִׁיפֵי, שְׁלַחָהּ רַב אִידִי בַּר אָבִין לְקַמֵּיהּ דְּאַבַּיֵּי: כִּי הַאי גַּוְונָא מַאי? אֲמַר לֵיהּ: אֲפִילּוּ לְמַאן דְּאָמַר לָא מְבַטְּלִינַן קָלָא, בְּהָא מְבַטְּלִינַן קָלָא, מֵימַר אָמְרִי: עַיִּינוּ בְּהוּ רַבָּנַן בְּקִידּוּשֶׁיהָ וְלָא הֲוָה בְּהוּ שָׁוֶה פְּרוּטָה.

A rumor circulated that a certain woman **was betrothed with a mat of dates** [*atzifa detoḥela*][N] **from the spring of Bei Shifei. Rav Idi bar Avin sent** the case to be presented **before Abaye,** asking him: **What is the** *halakha* **in a case like this?** Should this rumor be suppressed? Abaye **said to him: Even according to the one who said** that **we do not suppress a rumor, in this** case **we suppress the rumor.** This is because if she marries someone else people will not slander her. Rather, **they will say** that **the Sages investigated her betrothal,** i.e., the value of the mat of dates with which she was betrothed, **and** concluded that **it was not worth one** ***peruta*** and therefore the betrothal was invalid.

הַהִיא דִּנְפַק עֲלָהּ קָלָא דְּאִיקַּדְשָׁה

A rumor circulated that a certain woman **was betrothed**

HALAKHA

And they went overseas – וְהָלְכוּ לָהֶם לִמְדִינַת הַיָּם: If two men testify that they saw a celebration that appeared to be a betrothal celebration, and they heard from so-and-so who heard from so-and-so that so-and-so was betrothed to so-and-so in the presence of two witnesses, but the witnesses went overseas or died, the woman is considered betrothed based on this rumor. The Rema adds that according to some opinions (*Tur*, citing Rosh), if only one person testifies that he heard the rumor from two people the rumor is disregarded, in accordance with Rav Huna's statement in the name of Rav (Rambam *Sefer Kedusha, Hilkhot Ishut* 9:22; *Shulḥan Arukh, Even HaEzer* 46:2).

Do we suppress a rumor – מְבַטְּלִינַן קָלָא: If a rumor is proven baseless, the court must suppress the rumor and should not be concerned about it, even if it has no explanation. The Rema cites the opinion of the Ran, based on the Rif, that nowadays courts should not suppress rumors, since the *halakha* depends on the local custom, which is not clear nowadays and is rendered an uncertainty. However, it is pointed out in the *Beit Shmuel* that the Rema writes in his book *Darkhei Moshe* that since rumors are given weight only by rabbinic law, in a case of uncertainty such as this one, the court should rule leniently and suppress the rumor. The Rema, citing Rashba, notes that a rumor must be disregarded wherever it is not necessary to treat it seriously, so that wicked people will not be empowered to spread slander about Jewish women (*Shulḥan Arukh, Even HaEzer* 6:5, 46:4).

A rumor circulated that a certain woman, etc. – הַהִיא דִּנְפַק עֲלָהּ קָלָא וכו׳: If a rumor circulated that a certain woman was betrothed to so-and-so, and afterward her father was asked about it, and he said that the betrothal was conditional and the condition was not fulfilled, his statement is not deemed credible and it is considered uncertain whether or not the woman is betrothed (Rambam *Sefer Kedusha, Hilkhot Ishut* 9:25).

NOTES

Do we suppress a rumor – מְבַטְּלִינַן קָלָא: To what case is this dilemma referring? Rashi raises two suggestions. One is a case where the rumor circulates among people who are disqualified from giving testimony, and the source of the rumor cannot be ascertained. The other suggestion is that those to whom the initial rumor was attributed are found, and they deny having seen the behavior in question. *Tosafot* and several other commentaries prefer the latter explanation. However, the Ramah rejects it, claiming that if they deny having seen the behavior in question, it is obvious that the rumor must be suppressed. The Ritva defends the opinion that the rumor should not be suppressed, explaining that if the woman marries based on the court's ruling, there is concern that people will slander the court, claiming that it unlawfully permitted her to marry.

Mat of dates [*atzifa detoḥela*] – אֲצִיפָא דְּתוֹחְלָא: Rashi explains that this refers to a species of date that does not ripen on the tree. Rather, it becomes edible only after it is placed in palm baskets for some time. Other explanations are suggested in the *Arukh*. According to one explanation, it refers to a vessel or bundle of cress, called *taḥlei* in Aramaic. Another suggestion is that it refers to date pits.

לְחַד מִבְּנֵי פְּלָנְיָא, אָמַר רָבָא: אֲפִילּוּ לְמַאן דְּאָמַר לָא מְבַטְּלִינַן קָלָא, בְּהָא מְבַטְּלִינַן קָלָא, מֵימַר אָמְרִי: עַיְּינוּ בְּהוּ רַבָּנַן בְּקִידּוּשֵׁי, וְקִידּוּשֵׁי קָטָן הֲווּ.

to one of the sons of so-and-so, who had both adult and minor sons. The son to whom she was betrothed was not specified. **Rava said: Even according to the one who says** that **we do not suppress a rumor, in this** case **we suppress the rumor.** People will not slander her. Rather, **they will say** that **the Sages investigated the betrothal and** concluded that **it was the betrothal of a minor.**

הַהִיא דִּנְפַק עֲלַהּ קָלָא דְּאִיקַּדְּשָׁה לְקָטָן הַנִּרְאֶה כְּגָדוֹל, אֲמַר לֵיהּ רַב מָרְדֳּכַי לְרַב אָשֵׁי: הֲוָה עוּבְדָא, וְאָמְרוּ: עֲדַיִין לֹא הִגִּיעַ לִפְלַגּוֹת רְאוּבֵן, שֶׁנֶּאֱמַר: ״לִפְלַגּוֹת רְאוּבֵן גְּדוֹלִים חִקְרֵי לֵב״.

A rumor circulated that a certain woman was betrothed to a minor boy who looked like an adult, as his body was developed like an adult. **Rav Mordekhai said to Rav Ashi: There was a precedent in which** the Sages **said** that there is no concern that people will think that the woman is betrothed, since the boy **did not yet reach the divisions of Reuben,**[N] i.e., the competence of adulthood, **as it is stated: "Among the divisions of Reuben there were major resolves of heart"** (Judges 5:16). Therefore, the betrothal is rendered entirely invalid, and there is no concern of slander.

״וּבִלְבַד שֶׁלֹּא תְּהֵא שָׁם אֲמַתְלָא״. אָמַר רַבָּה בַּר רַב הוּנָא: אֲמַתְלָא שֶׁאָמְרוּ – אֲפִילּוּ מִכָּאן וְעַד עֲשָׂרָה יָמִים. רַב זְבִיד אָמַר: בִּמְקוֹם אֲמַתְלָא חוֹשְׁשִׁין לַאֲמַתְלָא.

§ It is stated in the mishna that a rumor is treated seriously only **provided there is no explanation. Rabba bar Rav Huna said: The explanation mentioned** in the mishna negates the rumor **even** if it circulates at some point **from now,** i.e., from the time the rumor circulated, **until ten days**[N] afterward. **Rav Zevid says: Where** there is the reasonable possibility of **an explanation,**[H] **we are concerned about** the possibility of **an explanation** even if it is not mentioned explicitly, and the rumor is therefore disregarded.

אֵיתִיבֵיהּ רַב פָּפָּא לְרַב זְבִיד: וּבִלְבַד שֶׁלֹּא תְּהֵא שָׁם אֲמַתְלָא! אֲמַר לֵיהּ: בִּמְקוֹם אֲמַתְלָא קָאָמַר.

Rav Pappa raised an objection to the opinion **of Rav Zevid** from the expression in the mishna: **Provided there is no explanation,** which indicates that the explanation must be mentioned for it to be regarded. Rav Zevid **said to him:** The mishna **is saying** that **where** there is the reasonable possibility of **an explanation** the rumor is disregarded, even if it was not mentioned.

אֲמַר לֵיהּ רַב כָּהֲנָא לְרַב פָּפָּא: וְאַתְּ לָא תִּסְבְּרָא? וְהָתְנַן: נִתְקַדְּשָׁה וְאַחַר כָּךְ בָּא בַּעְלָהּ – מוּתֶּרֶת לַחֲזוֹר; לָאו מִשּׁוּם דְּאָמְרִינַן עַל תְּנַאי קַדֵּישׁ?

Rav Kahana said to Rav Pappa: And you, do you not hold Rav Zevid's statement to be true? **But didn't we learn** in a mishna that if a woman **was betrothed** after her husband was taken for dead, **and then her husband came** back,[H] **she is permitted to return** to him (*Yevamot* 92a), which would not have been the case if she had been married and not merely betrothed? **Isn't this because we say** that the second man **betrothed her conditionally,**[N] stipulating that if her husband is found to be alive the betrothal is null, even though this explanation did not circulate explicitly?

שָׁאנֵי הָתָם, דְּאָתֵי בַּעַל וְקָא מְעַרְעֵר.

The Gemara answers: **It is different there because the husband comes and contests** the betrothal, which shows clearly that he never divorced her and that her betrothal was mistaken. Therefore, there is no need for an additional explanation.

HALAKHA

Where there is the reasonable possibility of an explanation, etc. – **בִּמְקוֹם אֲמַתְלָא וכו׳**: If a rumor circulated that a woman is betrothed to so-and-so, and afterward an explanation circulated, then, if the explanation appears to the court to be true, it is deemed credible and the woman is not considered betrothed. Otherwise, in accordance with the opinion of Rav Zevid and Rabbi Yoḥanan (89a), the explanation is disregarded (Rambam *Sefer Nashim, Hilkhot Ishut* 9:24; *Shulḥan Arukh, Even HaEzer* 46:4).

If a woman was betrothed and then her husband came back – **נִתְקַדְּשָׁה וְאַחַר כָּךְ בָּא בַּעְלָהּ**: If a woman heard that her husband died, or she received from him a bill of divorce, and she then became betrothed to another man, only to discover later that her husband was still alive or that the bill of divorce was invalid, her betrothal is of no consequence, as betrothal does not take effect with a married woman. She may return to her husband, as there is no concern that people will think that she was married to the second husband and left him without receiving a bill of divorce. It is also permitted for her to marry the other man if her husband dies or divorces her (Rambam *Sefer Nashim, Hilkhot Geirushin* 10:6; *Shulḥan Arukh, Even HaEzer* 17:58).

NOTES

Did not yet reach the divisions of Reuben – **עֲדַיִין לֹא הִגִּיעַ לִפְלַגּוֹת רְאוּבֵן**: In other words, his actions indicate that he is a minor who has not reached the competence of adulthood. Therefore, the woman may marry and does not need a divorce from him (Meiri). Rashi adds that the rumor should be suppressed, as there is no concern of slander.

The Ritva infers from here that majority is determined not only based on physical development but based on competence and behavior as well. Therefore, this boy was deemed a minor.

Rabbeinu Ḥananel has a version of the text that reads: We have not reached the divisions of Reuben. In other words, we do not have the acuteness of the Sages of Reuben, who were able to discern whether a certain boy who looks and acts like an adult could be determined as having reached majority. Rather, we follow the halakhic principle that defines majority based on puberty and age (Rosh; *Arukh*).

Until ten days – **וְעַד עֲשָׂרָה יָמִים**: Some commentaries explain that if the explanation circulates more than ten days after the rumor, its veracity is doubted. Others claim that Rabba bar Rav Huna is not referring specifically to ten days; if the explanation circulates afterward, it is still valid (Rabbeinu Crescas Vidal).

Betrothed her conditionally – **עַל תְּנַאי קַדֵּישׁ**: This explanation is accepted even though there are witnesses, not only a rumor, of her betrothal. If so, certainly in a case where a woman is rumored to be only betrothed, an implicit explanation should be accepted.

אִי הָכִי, נִישֵּׂאת נַמִי! נִישֵּׂאת דְּעָבְדָה אִיסּוּרָא – קַנְסוּהָ רַבָּנַן, נִתְקַדְּשָׁה דְּלָא עָבְדָה אִיסּוּרָא – לָא קַנְסוּהָ רַבָּנַן.

The Gemara asks: **If so,** in a case where **she married** the second man, it should **also** be permitted for her to return to her first husband. Why do the Sages render it prohibited for her to do so? The Gemara answers: In a case where **she married** him, **since she performed a prohibited** action,[H] albeit unintentionally, by engaging in sexual intercourse with a man who is not her husband while she was married, **the Sages penalized her.** By contrast, in a case where **she was** merely **betrothed, since she did not perform a prohibited** action, **the Sages did not penalize her.**

אֲמַר רַב אַשִׁי: כָּל קָלָא דְּלָא אִיתַּחְזַק בְּבֵי דִּינָא לָאו קָלָא הוּא. וְאָמַר רַב אַשִׁי: כָּל קָלָא דְּבָתַר נִישּׂוּאִין לָא חָיְישִׁינַן לֵיהּ; הָא דְּבָתַר אֵירוּסִין חָיְישִׁינַן לֵיהּ. רַב חֲבִיבָא אֲמַר: אֲפִילּוּ דְּבָתַר אֵירוּסִין נַמִי לָא חָיְישִׁינַן לֵיהּ. וְהִלְכְתָא: לָא חָיְישִׁינַן לֵיהּ.

§ **Rav Ashi said: Any rumor that was not confirmed**[N] **in court**[H] **is not** regarded as a significant **rumor. And Rav Ashi said:** With regard to **any rumor that** was spread about a woman **after** her **marriage, we are not concerned about it.** She need not leave her husband, and he need not divorce her. The Gemara infers that if the rumor circulated **after** her **betrothal we are concerned about it,** and she must be divorced from her betrothed. **Rav Ḥaviva said: Even** if it circulated **after** her **betrothal,**[H] **we are still not concerned about it.** The Gemara concludes: **And the** ***halakha*** **is that we are not concerned about it.**

אֲמַר רַב יִרְמְיָה בַּר אַבָּא, שָׁלְחוּ לֵיהּ מִבֵּי רַב לִשְׁמוּאֵל: יְלַמְּדֵנוּ רַבֵּינוּ, יָצָא עָלֶיהָ קוֹל מֵרִאשׁוֹן, וּבָא אַחֵר וְקִדְּשָׁהּ קִידּוּשֵׁי תוֹרָה, מַהוּ? שְׁלַח לְהוּ: תֵּצֵא, וְהַעֲמִידוּ הַדָּבָר עַל בּוּרְיוֹ וְהוֹדִיעוּנִי.

Rav Yirmeya bar Abba said that a group of students **from the study hall of Rav sent** the following question **to Shmuel** after Rav's death: **Teach us, our master:** If **a rumor circulated about** a woman that she is betrothed **to a first** man, **and another** man **came and betrothed her** in a manner of **betrothal** that is recognized **by Torah law,** as there is clear testimony of it, **what is the** ***halakha*****? He sent them** an answer: **She must leave** the second man, **and you clarify the matter**[H] to figure out exactly what happened **and inform me.**

מַאי "וְהַעֲמִידוּ הַדָּבָר עַל בּוּרְיוֹ"? אִילֵימָא דְּאִי מִגַּלְיָא מִילְּתָא דְּקִידּוּשֵׁי דְּקַמָּא לָאו קִידּוּשֵׁי מַעַלְיָא נִינְהוּ מְבַטְּלִינַן קָלָא – וְהָא נְהַרְדְּעָא אַתְרֵיהּ דִּשְׁמוּאֵל הוּא וְלָא מְבַטְּלֵי קָלָא! אֶלָּא, דְּאִי מִיגַּלְיָא מִילְּתָא דְּקִידּוּשֵׁי קַמָּא קִידּוּשֵׁי מַעַלְיָא נִינְהוּ, לָא צְרִיכָה גֵּט מִשֵּׁנִי.

The Gemara asks: **What** is meant by: **And you clarify the matter? If we say that** he said this so that **if it is discovered that the betrothal of the first** man **was not a proper betrothal we** should **suppress the rumor,** thereby permitting her to marry the second man, **isn't Neharde'a Shmuel's locale? And** as mentioned above, in Neharde'a **they would not suppress a rumor. Rather,** he must have instructed them in this manner **because if it is discovered that the betrothal of the first man was a proper betrothal, she does not need a bill of divorce from the second** man.

וּפְלִיגָא דְּרַב הוּנָא, דְּאָמַר רַב הוּנָא: אֵשֶׁת אִישׁ שֶׁפָּשְׁטָה יָדָהּ וְקִיבְּלָה קִידּוּשִׁין מֵאַחֵר – מְקוּדֶּשֶׁת,

And in ruling that she does not need a bill of divorce from the second man, Shmuel **is in disagreement with Rav Huna, as Rav Huna says:** In the case of **a married woman who extended her hand**[HN] **and received** money or a document of **betrothal from another** man, it is considered uncertain whether or not the woman **is betrothed** to him, and she needs a bill of divorce from him.

מִדְּרַב הַמְנוּנָא; דְּאָמַר רַב הַמְנוּנָא: הָאִשָּׁה שֶׁאָמְרָה לְבַעְלָהּ "גֵּירַשְׁתַּנִי" – נֶאֱמֶנֶת, חֲזָקָה אֵין אִשָּׁה מֵעִיזָּה פָּנֶיהָ בִּפְנֵי בַעְלָהּ.

Rav Huna's opinion is based on a principle stated **by Rav Hamnuna, as Rav Hamnuna says** that **a woman who said to her husband: You divorced me, is deemed credible,** due to the **presumption** that **a wife is not so brazen** to lie in this manner **before her husband.** Therefore, in the case brought before Shmuel, the fact that the woman received money or a document of betrothal from the second man should be considered sufficient basis for the rumor to be suppressed, since if she were already betrothed she certainly would not have accepted the betrothal from him.

HALAKHA

In a case where she married…she performed a prohibited action – נִישֵּׂאת דְּעָבְדָה אִיסּוּרָא וכו׳: If a woman's husband goes overseas and she is subsequently told that he died, and she remarries, after which her husband returns, she must leave both men, whether she relied on the testimony of one or two witnesses. She requires a bill of divorce from both men and does not collect her marriage contract from either of them (Rambam *Sefer Nashim, Hilkhot Geirushin* 10:5; *Shulḥan Arukh, Even HaEzer* 17:56).

Any rumor that was not confirmed in court – כָּל קָלָא דְּלָא אִיתַּחְזַק בְּבֵי דִּינָא: A rumor is taken seriously only if it was confirmed by the court, following an investigation that led the court to the conclusion that it has a substantial basis. Otherwise it is disregarded. The Rema comments that if there is a strong reason to assume that a rumor is true, the court is required to investigate it (Rambam *Sefer Nashim, Hilkhot Ishut* 9:22; *Shulḥan Arukh, Even HaEzer* 46:1–2).

Any rumor that was spread about a woman after her marriage…after her betrothal – כָּל קָלָא דְּבָתַר נִישּׂוּאִין...דְּבָתַר אֵירוּסִין: If a rumor was spread about a married or betrothed woman that she was previously betrothed to another man, it is disregarded, in accordance with the statement of Rav Ḥaviva (Rambam *Sefer Nashim, Hilkhot Geirushin* 10:20; *Shulḥan Arukh, Even HaEzer* 46:8).

And you clarify the matter – וְהַעֲמִידוּ הַדָּבָר עַל בּוּרְיוֹ: If a rumor was spread that a certain woman was betrothed, and afterward another man betrothed her in the presence of the court, the court must investigate the first betrothal. If witnesses come to court with clear evidence that she was betrothed to the first man, then the second man's betrothal is disregarded, in accordance with Shmuel's opinion (Rambam *Sefer Nashim, Hilkhot Ishut* 9:26; *Shulḥan Arukh, Even HaEzer* 46:5).

A married woman who extended her hand, etc. – אֵשֶׁת אִישׁ שֶׁפָּשְׁטָה וכו׳: If a married woman extended her hand and received money for betrothal in the presence of her husband, she is betrothed to the second man. Similarly, if a woman said to her husband, or in his presence, that he divorced her, her statement is deemed credible and accepted, as a woman would presumably not be so brazen as to lie in this manner in the presence of her husband. This is in accordance with Shmuel's understanding of Rav Hamnuna's principle. The Rema notes that according to the Ra'avad, her statement is accepted only with regard to her needing a bill of divorce from her second husband. She is otherwise still considered married to her first husband, and she may not marry her second husband nor collect her marriage contract from him without evidence of her divorce. The Rema adds that according to the Ramah, nowadays the woman is certainly not rendered divorced with regard to the lenient ramifications of this status. This is because brazenness is more common today, and it cannot be presumed that a woman would not be so brazen (Rambam *Sefer Nashim, Hilkhot Ishut* 4:13; *Shulḥan Arukh, Even HaEzer* 17:2).

NOTES

That was not confirmed – דְּלָא אִיתַּחְזַק: Rashi and the Ramban explain that if a rumor is not investigated by the court due to the court's assessment that it is not serious enough to deserve an investigation, it should be disregarded. By contrast, the Ramah explains that this refers to a rumor with regard to which the court did not find a reliable source. Similarly, it is stated in the Jerusalem Talmud that if the court investigated the rumor and found it to be based on the testimony of women or minors, the rumor should be suppressed.

Who extended her hand – שֶׁפָּשְׁטָה יָדָהּ: The Rashba explains that Rav Huna does not mean to say that she is considered fully betrothed to the second man and it is permitted for her to marry him, as this action of hers is not sufficient evidence that the presumption that she is a married woman is incorrect. Rather, it is considered uncertain whether or not the woman is betrothed to the second man, insofar as she needs a bill of divorce from him, without which she is forbidden even to her first husband.

וְאִידָךְ? כִּי אִתְּמַר דְּרַב הַמְנוּנָא – בְּפָנָיו, שֶׁלֹּא בְּפָנָיו מְעִיזָּה וּבְעִיזָּה.

The Gemara asks: **And** how does **the other** Sage, Shmuel, who disagrees with Rav Huna, relate to this principle? The Gemara answers: He holds that **Rav Hamnuna's** principle **was stated** in reference to a case **when** the wife says **in** her husband's **presence** that he divorced her, but when she is **not in his presence she is certainly brazen** enough to lie in this manner. Therefore, in the case brought before Shmuel, the woman may have accepted the betrothal of the other man because it was not in her husband's presence.

לֹא מָצְאוּ דָּבָר עַל בּוּרְיוֹ, מַהוּ?

The Gemara asks: **What is** the *halakha* if **they did not find a clear matter,**[H] i.e., they could not establish with certainty whether she was betrothed to the first man?

אָמַר רַב הוּנָא: מְגָרֵשׁ רִאשׁוֹן וְנוֹשֵׂא שֵׁנִי, אֲבָל מְגָרֵשׁ שֵׁנִי וְנוֹשֵׂא רִאשׁוֹן – לֹא; מַאי טַעְמָא? אָתֵי לְמֵימַר מַחֲזִיר גְּרוּשָׁתוֹ מִן הָאֵירוּסִין.

Rav Huna says: The **first** man **divorces** her **and** the **second** man **marries** her. **But** for the **second** man to **divorce her and** the **first** man to **marry** her is **not** permitted. The Gemara explains: **What is the reason** that it is not permitted? It is prohibited lest people **come to say** that the first man is **remarrying his divorcée after** her **betrothal** to another man, as they will mistakenly assume that the first man betrothed her and then divorced her, thereby enabling her to be betrothed to the second man. Therefore, if he marries her after she is divorced from the second man, people will conclude that he is in violation of the Torah prohibition of remarrying one's divorcée after she was married to another man.

רַב שִׁינָּנָא בְּרֵיהּ דְּרַב אִידִי אָמַר: אַף מְגָרֵשׁ שֵׁנִי וְנוֹשֵׂא רִאשׁוֹן, מֵימַר אָמְרִי: עַיְּינִי רַבָּנַן בְּקִידּוּשֵׁי, וְקִידּוּשֵׁי טָעוּת הֲוָה.

Rav Shinnana, son of Rav Idi, says: For the **second** man to **divorce** her **and** the **first** man to **marry** her **is also** permitted. There is no concern that people will assume that the first man is remarrying his divorcée, as **they will say** that **the Sages investigated the** second man's **betrothal**[N] **and** found that **it was a mistaken betrothal.**[B]

יָצָא עָלֶיהָ קוֹל מִזֶּה וּמִזֶּה, מַהוּ? אָמַר רַב פָּפָּא: אַף זוֹ, מְגָרֵשׁ רִאשׁוֹן וְנוֹשֵׂא שֵׁנִי. אַמֵּימָר אָמַר: מוּתֶּרֶת לִשְׁנֵיהֶם.

The Gemara asks: **What is** the *halakha* if **a rumor circulated about her** having been betrothed **to this** man **and** then another rumor was spread that she became betrothed **to that** man? **Rav Pappa says:** In **this** case **too,** the **first** man **divorces** her **and** the **second** man **marries** her, due to the previously mentioned concern that people will think that he is remarrying his divorcée after she was betrothed to another man. **Ameimar says: She is permitted to both** the first and the second man. One of them must divorce her while the other may marry her.

HALAKHA

They did not find a clear matter – **לֹא מָצְאוּ דָּבָר עַל בּוּרְיוֹ**: If it was rumored that a certain woman was betrothed, and she was subsequently betrothed to another man in the presence of the court, but it was never clarified whether the rumor was true or false, the first man to whom she was purportedly betrothed must give her a bill of divorce. The second man may marry her, as his betrothal of her is deemed valid. Nevertheless, if the second man divorces her, the first one may not marry her, lest people think that he is remarrying his divorcée after she was betrothed to another man, in accordance with Rav Huna's opinion (Rambam *Sefer Nashim, Hilkhot Ishut* 9:26; *Shulḥan Arukh, Even HaEzer* 46:5).

NOTES

The Sages investigated the second man's betrothal – **עַיְּינִי רַבָּנַן בְּקִידּוּשֵׁי**: Rashi explains that the Sages investigated her betrothal to the second man and concluded that it was mistaken. Rabbeinu Crescas Vidal concurs. The Ra'avad, in his comments on the Rif, the Ramah, and the Rid, interpret this to mean that the Sages investigated the first man's betrothal and found that it was mistaken. Therefore, once the woman is divorced from the second man, the first is permitted to marry her, like any other man, as he is not remarrying his divorcée (see Maharsha and Maharam Schiff).

BACKGROUND

A mistaken betrothal – **קִידּוּשֵׁי טָעוּת**: This is a betrothal in which one of the participants was under a false impression with regard to its terms. Any transaction conducted under false pretenses is considered in error and the injured party can nullify it. For example, if one buys an animal and discovers it to be diseased, he can nullify the sale. A related concept is the nullification of a transaction. If an object is overpriced or underpriced by more than one-sixth, the sale is invalid and either party may reconsider. Similarly, if a man marries a woman and subsequently discovers that she has serious physical defects of which he was unaware at the time of the marriage, he can divorce her without paying her marriage contract.

Perek **IX**
Daf **90** Amud **a**

וְהִלְכְתָא: מוּתֶּרֶת לִשְׁנֵיהֶם.

And the *halakha* is that **she is permitted to both of them.**[H]

מתני׳ בֵּית שַׁמַּאי אוֹמְרִים: לֹא יְגָרֵשׁ אָדָם אֶת אִשְׁתּוֹ אֶלָּא אִם כֵּן מָצָא בָהּ דְּבַר עֶרְוָה, שֶׁנֶּאֱמַר: ״כִּי מָצָא בָהּ עֶרְוַת דָּבָר״;

MISHNA **Beit Shammai say: A man may not divorce his wife unless he finds out about her** having engaged in **a matter of forbidden sexual intercourse** [*devar erva*], i.e., she committed adultery or is suspected of doing so, **as it is stated: "Because he has found some unseemly matter** [*ervat davar*] **in her,** and he writes her a scroll of severance" (Deuteronomy 24:1).

וּבֵית הִלֵּל אוֹמְרִים: אֲפִילּוּ הִקְדִּיחָה תַּבְשִׁילוֹ, שֶׁנֶּאֱמַר: ״כִּי מָצָא בָהּ עֶרְוַת דָּבָר״;

And Beit Hillel say: He may divorce her **even** due to a minor issue, e.g., because **she burned** or over-salted **his dish,**[N] **as it is stated: "Because he has found some unseemly matter in her,"** meaning that he found any type of shortcoming in her.

רַבִּי עֲקִיבָא אוֹמֵר: אֲפִילּוּ מָצָא אַחֶרֶת נָאָה הֵימֶנָּה, שֶׁנֶּאֱמַר: ״וְהָיָה אִם לֹא תִמְצָא חֵן בְּעֵינָיו״.

Rabbi Akiva says: He may divorce her **even** if **he found another woman** who is **better looking than her** and wishes to marry her, **as it is stated** in that verse: **"And it comes to pass, if she finds no favor in his eyes"** (Deuteronomy 24:1).

HALAKHA

She is permitted to both of them – **מוּתֶּרֶת לִשְׁנֵיהֶם**: If a rumor was spread that a certain woman was betrothed to so-and-so, and afterward another rumor circulated that she became betrothed to a different man, one of them must give her a bill of divorce and the other may marry her, in accordance with Ameimar's opinion (Rambam *Sefer Nashim, Hilkhot Ishut* 9:27; *Shulḥan Arukh, Even HaEzer* 46:6).

NOTES

She burned or over-salted his dish – **הִקְדִּיחָה תַּבְשִׁילוֹ**: The Rambam apparently understands that he may also divorce her if he decides that she is not a good match for him due to her attributes or her behavior. In the *Ḥatam Sofer* it is explained that according to the Rambam, Beit Hillel's statement is a figurative expression, meaning that what she presents to him is not to his liking.

גמ׳ תַּנְיָא, אָמְרוּ בֵּית הִלֵּל לְבֵית שַׁמַּאי: וַהֲלֹא כְּבָר נֶאֱמַר "דָּבָר"! אָמְרוּ לָהֶם בֵּית שַׁמַּאי: וַהֲלֹא כְּבָר נֶאֱמַר "עֶרְוַת"!

GEMARA It **is taught** in a *baraita* that **Beit Hillel said to Beit Shammai: But isn't** the word **"matter" already stated** in the verse, indicating that any disadvantageous matter is a legitimate reason for divorce? **Beit Shammai said to them: But isn't** the word **"unseemly** [*ervat*]**" already stated?**

אָמְרוּ לָהֶם בֵּית הִלֵּל: אִם נֶאֱמַר "עֶרְוַת" וְלֹא נֶאֱמַר "דָּבָר", הָיִיתִי אוֹמֵר: מִשּׁוּם עֶרְוָה תֵּצֵא, מִשּׁוּם דָּבָר לֹא תֵּצֵא, לְכָךְ נֶאֱמַר "דָּבָר"; וְאִילּוּ נֶאֱמַר "דָּבָר" וְלֹא נֶאֱמַר "עֶרְוַת", הָיִיתִי אוֹמֵר: מִשּׁוּם דָּבָר תִּנָּשֵׂא לְאַחֵר, וּמִשּׁוּם עֶרְוָה לֹא תִּנָּשֵׂא לְאַחֵר, לְכָךְ נֶאֱמַר "עֶרְוַת".

Beit Hillel said to them: If the word **"unseemly" had been stated and** the word **"matter" had not been stated, I would have said** that a wife **should leave** her husband **due to forbidden sexual intercourse,** but **she should not** have to **leave** him **due to** any other **matter. Therefore,** the word **"matter" is stated. And if** the word **"matter" had been stated and** the word **"unseemly" had not been stated, I would have said** that if he divorced her merely **due to** a disadvantageous **matter she may marry another** man, as the Torah continues: "And she departs out of his house, and goes and becomes another man's wife" (Deuteronomy 24:2). **But** if she was divorced **due to** her engaging in **forbidden sexual intercourse, she may not marry another** man, as she is prohibited from remarrying. **Therefore,** the word **"unseemly" is stated,** indicating that even a wife who is divorced due to adultery is permitted to remarry.

וּבֵית שַׁמַּאי הַאי "דָּבָר" מַאי עָבְדִי לֵיהּ? נֶאֱמַר כָּאן "דָּבָר" וְנֶאֱמַר לְהַלָּן "דָּבָר" – "עַל פִּי שְׁנֵי עֵדִים אוֹ עַל פִּי שְׁלֹשָׁה עֵדִים יָקוּם דָּבָר", מָה לְהַלָּן בִּשְׁנֵי עֵדִים, אַף כָּאן בִּשְׁנֵי עֵדִים.

The Gemara asks: **And what do Beit Shammai do with this** word **"matter"?** How do they interpret it? It seems superfluous, as in their opinion the verse refers specifically to a wife who engaged in forbidden sexual intercourse. The Gemara answers: The word **"matter" is stated here,** with regard to divorce, **and** the word **"matter" is stated there,** with regard to testimony: **"At the mouth of two witnesses, or at the mouth of three witnesses, a matter shall be established"** (Deuteronomy 19:15). **Just as there,** it is stated that a matter is established only **through two witnesses, so too here,** a matter of forbidden sexual intercourse justifies divorce only if it is established **through two witnesses.**[H]

וּבֵית הִלֵּל: מִי כְּתִיב "עֶרְוָה בְּדָבָר"? וּבֵית שַׁמַּאי: מִי כְּתִיב "אוֹ עֶרְוָה אוֹ דָּבָר"?

And Beit Hillel would respond to this analogy in the following manner: **Is it written:** Because he has found something **unseemly in a matter** [*erva bedavar*], indicating that it was established through the testimony of two witnesses that she engaged in adultery? **And Beit Shammai** would respond to Beit Hillel's interpretation as follows: **Is it written:** Because he has found **either** something **unseemly or** another **matter** [*o erva o davar*], in accordance with Beit Hillel's understanding?

וּבֵית הִלֵּל: לְהָכִי כְּתִיב "עֶרְוַת דָּבָר", דְּמַשְׁמַע הָכִי וּמַשְׁמַע הָכִי.

And Beit Hillel would respond that **for this** reason the expression **"some unseemly matter** [*ervat davar*]**" is written, as it indicates that** interpretation, i.e., that a husband is not obligated to divorce his wife unless there are two witnesses to her having engaged in forbidden sexual intercourse, **and it** also **indicates this** interpretation, i.e., that he may divorce her due to any deficiency, be it adultery or any other shortcoming.

"רַבִּי עֲקִיבָא אוֹמֵר: אֲפִילּוּ מָצָא אַחֶרֶת". בְּמַאי קָא מִיפַּלְגִי? בִּדְרֵישׁ לָקִישׁ, דְּאָמַר רֵישׁ לָקִישׁ: "כִּי" מְשַׁמֵּשׁ בְּאַרְבָּעָה לְשׁוֹנוֹת: אִי, דִּלְמָא, אֶלָּא, דְּהָא;

§ It is stated in the mishna that **Rabbi Akiva says:** He may divorce her **even if he found another woman** who is better looking than her. **With regard to what do they disagree?** They disagree **with regard to** the application of **Reish Lakish's** statement, **as Reish Lakish said** that the term ***ki*** actually **has** at least **four** distinct **meanings:**[L] **If, perhaps, rather,** and **because.**

בֵּית שַׁמַּאי סָבְרִי: "וְהָיָה אִם לֹא תִמְצָא חֵן בְּעֵינָיו כִּי מָצָא בָהּ עֶרְוַת דָּבָר" – דְּהָא מָצָא בָהּ עֶרְוַת דָּבָר, וְרַבִּי עֲקִיבָא סָבַר: "כִּי מָצָא בָהּ עֶרְוַת דָּבָר" – אִי נַמִי מָצָא בָהּ עֶרְוַת דָּבָר.

Beit Shammai hold[N] that the verse **"And it comes to pass, if she finds no favor in his eyes, because** [*ki*] **he has found some unseemly matter in her"** means that she did not find favor in his eyes **due to** the fact that **he has found some unseemly matter in her. And Rabbi Akiva holds** that the phrase **"because** [*ki*] **he has found some unseemly matter in her"** means: **Or if he has found some unseemly matter in her.**

אֲמַר לֵיהּ רַב פַּפָּא לְרָבָא: לֹא מָצָא בָהּ לֹא עֶרְוָה וְלֹא דָּבָר, מַהוּ?

§ **Rav Pappa said to Rava:** According to Beit Hillel, if the husband **found about her neither**[N] **forbidden sexual intercourse nor** any other **matter,** but divorced her anyway, **what is** the *halakha*? Is the divorce valid?

HALAKHA

So too here it is established through two witnesses – **אַף כָּאן בִּשְׁנֵי עֵדִים:** If two witnesses testify in court that a married woman committed adultery, it is prohibited for her to remain with her husband. If one witness testifies and the husband does not believe him, she is permitted to remain with him. Similarly, if two witnesses see her perform an action that suggests adultery, but they did not see her actually commit adultery, the husband may divorce her without paying her marriage contract if he wishes (Rambam *Sefer Nashim, Hilkhot Ishut* 24:15; *Shulḥan Arukh, Even HaEzer* 178:9).

LANGUAGE

The term *ki* has four distinct meanings – **כִּי מְשַׁמֵּשׁ בְּאַרְבַּע לְשׁוֹנוֹת:** This word is a conjunction and has several meanings. Sometimes it introduces a reason and means because. Other times it introduces a contrast and means rather. It can also mean perhaps or if. The differences between these variant meanings are often subtle and sometimes converge (see Rashi and *Tosafot*).

NOTES

Beit Shammai hold, etc. – **בֵּית שַׁמַּאי סָבְרִי וכו׳:** Why is Rabbi Akiva's opinion compared to that of Beit Shammai and not that of Beit Hillel? *Tosafot* suggest that Rabbi Akiva agrees with Beit Shammai that the expression "some unseemly matter" refers to forbidden sexual intercourse. Therefore, the only difference between them is whether or not the verse mentions an additional justification for divorce, i.e., that the wife does not find favor in the husband's eyes. *Tosafot* also mention another version of the text that reads: Beit Hillel and Beit Shammai hold, etc. Similarly, the Ritva's version of the text reads: The Rabbis hold, etc. Another version simply reads: Beit Hillel hold (see Maharshal).

If the husband found about her neither, etc. – **לֹא מָצָא בָהּ וכו׳:** Rashi explains that the question is whether or not the husband is obligated to remarry her. In the *Ḥatam Sofer* it is explained that perhaps if he divorced her without justification the divorce is ineffective.

אֲמַר לֵיהּ, מִדְּגַלֵּי רַחֲמָנָא גַּבֵּי אוֹנֵס: ״לֹא יוּכַל לְשַׁלְּחָהּ כׇּל יָמָיו״ – כׇּל יָמָיו בַּעֲמוֹד וְהַחֲזֵיר קָאֵי, הָתָם הוּא דְּגַלֵּי רַחֲמָנָא, אֲבָל הָכָא מַאי דַּעֲבַד עֲבַד.

Rava **said to him** that the answer can be derived **from what the Merciful One reveals** in the Torah **with regard to a rapist: "He may not send her away all his days"** (Deuteronomy 22:29), indicating that even if he divorces the woman whom he raped and was subsequently commanded to marry, **all his days he stands** commanded **to arise and remarry** her as his wife. Evidently, **specifically there** the husband is obligated to remarry his divorcée, **as the Merciful One reveals** as much. **But here, what he did, he did.**

אֲמַר לֵיהּ רַב מְשַׁרְשִׁיָּא לְרָבָא: אִם לִבּוֹ לְגָרְשָׁהּ וְהִיא יוֹשֶׁבֶת תַּחְתָּיו וּמְשַׁמַּשְׁתּוֹ, מַהוּ? קָרֵי עֲלֵיהּ: ״אַל תַּחֲרֹשׁ עַל רֵעֲךָ רָעָה וְהוּא יוֹשֵׁב לָבֶטַח אִתָּךְ״.

Rav Mesharshiyya said to Rava: If he intends to divorce her and she is living with him and serving him, what is the *halakha*? Rava **read** the following verse **about** such a person: **"Devise not evil against your neighbor,**[H] **seeing he dwells securely by you"** (Proverbs 3:29).

תַּנְיָא, הָיָה רַבִּי מֵאִיר אוֹמֵר: כְּשֵׁם שֶׁהַדֵּעוֹת בְּמַאֲכָל, כָּךְ דֵּעוֹת בְּנָשִׁים; יֵשׁ לְךָ אָדָם שֶׁזְּבוּב נוֹפֵל לְתוֹךְ כּוֹסוֹ וְזוֹרְקוֹ וְאֵינוֹ שׁוֹתֵהוּ, וְזוֹ הִיא מִדַּת פַּפּוֹס בֶּן יְהוּדָה, שֶׁהָיָה נוֹעֵל בִּפְנֵי אִשְׁתּוֹ וְיוֹצֵא;

§ **It is taught in a** *baraita* (*Tosefta, Sota* 5:9) that **Rabbi Meir would say: Just as there are** different **attitudes with regard to food, so too, there are** different **attitudes with regard to women.** With regard to food, **you have a person who,** when **a fly falls into his cup, he throws out** the wine with the fly **and does not drink it. And this is** comparable to **the demeanor of Pappos**[L] **ben Yehuda**[NP] with regard to his wife, **as he would lock** the door **before his wife and leave** so that she would not see any other man.

וְיֵשׁ לְךָ אָדָם שֶׁזְּבוּב נוֹפֵל לְתוֹךְ כּוֹסוֹ וְזוֹרְקוֹ וְשׁוֹתֵהוּ, וְזוֹ הִיא מִדַּת כׇּל אָדָם, שֶׁמְּדַבֶּרֶת עִם אַחֶיהָ וּקְרוֹבֶיהָ וּמַנִּיחָהּ;

And you have a person who, when **a fly falls into his cup, he throws out** the fly **and drinks** the wine. **And this is** comparable to **the demeanor of any** common **man, whose wife speaks with her siblings and relatives, and he lets her** do so.

וְיֵשׁ לְךָ אָדָם שֶׁזְּבוּב נוֹפֵל לְתוֹךְ תַּמְחוּי, מוֹצְצוֹ וְאוֹכְלוֹ, זוֹ הִיא מִדַּת אָדָם רַע, שֶׁרוֹאֶה אֶת אִשְׁתּוֹ יוֹצְאָה וְרֹאשָׁהּ פָּרוּעַ, וְטוֹוָה בַּשּׁוּק,

And you have a man who, when **a fly falls into** his **serving bowl, he sucks** the fly **and eats** the food. **This is the demeanor of a bad man, who sees his wife going out** into the street **with her head uncovered, and spinning in the marketplace** immodestly,

HALAKHA

Devise not evil against your neighbor, etc. – אַל תַּחֲרֹשׁ עַל רֵעֲךָ רָעָה וכו׳: A husband who intends to divorce his wife may not continue to live with her and have her serve him (Rambam *Sefer Nashim, Hilkhot Ishut* 10:21; *Shulḥan Arukh, Even HaEzer* 119:2).

LANGUAGE

Pappos – פַּפּוֹס: From the Greek πάππος, *pappos*, meaning grandfather.

NOTES

Pappos ben Yehuda – פַּפּוֹס בֶּן יְהוּדָה: Rashi and other commentaries mention, based on *Shabbat* 104b, that his wife eventually committed adultery. In other words, for one to protect his wife excessively is not praiseworthy and is likely to backfire, as it may cause her to hate him and eventually commit adultery. Rather, it is preferable for one to be neither overly strict nor overly permissive.

PERSONALITIES

Pappos ben Yehuda – פַּפּוֹס בֶּן יְהוּדָה: Pappos ben Yehuda was a contemporary of Rabbi Akiva. Apparently he was a Torah scholar, as he is mentioned in several sources as having suggested to Rabbi Akiva various homiletic interpretations of verses and as having engaged with him in the study of different topics as a colleague. Some sources refer to him as Rabbi Pappos or Rabbi Papayyes.

He is described as an esteemed figure whose wealth and determination rendered him a benefactor and leader of the Jewish community. He was apparently imprisoned and may have been executed during the period of religious persecution that took place during Hadrian's rule.

Perek **IX**
Daf **90** Amud **b**

וּפְרוּמָה מִשְּׁנֵי צְדָדֶיהָ, וְרוֹחֶצֶת עִם בְּנֵי אָדָם.

and with her garment open from both sides, and bathing with men, and ignores it.

עִם בְּנֵי אָדָם סָלְקָא דַּעְתָּךְ? אֶלָּא בְּמָקוֹם שֶׁבְּנֵי אָדָם רוֹחֲצִין.

The Gemara asks: **Can it enter your mind** that the *baraita* is referring to a wife who bathes **with men?** Even a man of the lowest moral character would not allow his wife to act in this manner. **Rather,** the *baraita* means that she bathes **in a place where men** often **bathe.**[N]

זוֹ – מִצְוָה מִן הַתּוֹרָה לְגָרְשָׁהּ, שֶׁנֶּאֱמַר: ״כִּי מָצָא בָהּ עֶרְוַת וגו׳ וְשִׁלְּחָהּ מִבֵּיתוֹ... וְהָלְכָה וְהָיְתָה לְאִישׁ אַחֵר״, הַכָּתוּב קְרָאוֹ ״אַחֵר״, לוֹמַר, שֶׁאֵין זֶה בֶּן זוּגוֹ לָרִאשׁוֹן, זֶה הוֹצִיא רְשָׁעָה מִבֵּיתוֹ וְזֶה הִכְנִיס רְשָׁעָה לְתוֹךְ בֵּיתוֹ.

The *baraita* continues: With regard to **this** kind of wife, **it is a mitzva by Torah law to divorce her,**[H] **as it is stated: "Because he has found some unseemly** matter in her, and he writes her a scroll of severance, and gives it in her hand, **and he sends her out of his house… And she goes and becomes another** [*aḥer*] **man's wife"** (Deuteronomy 24:1–2). **The verse called** the second husband *aḥer*, other, **to state that this man is not a peer of the first** husband. They are morally distinct, as **that** first husband **evicted a wicked woman from his house and this** second man **introduced a wicked woman into his house.**[H]

זָכָה שֵׁנִי – שִׁלְּחָהּ, שֶׁנֶּאֱמַר: ״וּשְׂנֵאָהּ הָאִישׁ הָאַחֲרוֹן״, וְאִם לָאו – קוֹבַרְתּוֹ, שֶׁנֶּאֱמַר: ״אוֹ כִי יָמוּת הָאִישׁ הָאַחֲרוֹן״, כְּדַאי הוּא בְּמִיתָה, שֶׁזֶּה הוֹצִיא רְשָׁעָה מִבֵּיתוֹ וְזֶה הִכְנִיס רְשָׁעָה לְתוֹךְ בֵּיתוֹ.

If **the second** man **merits, he will send her out, as it is stated** in the following verse: **"And the latter husband hates** her… and he sends her out of his house" (Deuteronomy 24:3). **And if not, she will bury him, as it is stated** in the same verse: **"Or if the latter husband dies."** It is **appropriate for him** to receive the punishment **of death, as that** first man **evicted a wicked woman from his house and this** second husband **introduced a wicked woman into his house.**

NOTES

In a place where men often bathe – בְּמָקוֹם שֶׁבְּנֵי אָדָם רוֹחֲצִין: Rashi explains that she enters the water in the presence of men after they have already emerged from the water and dressed. The Ritva explains that she does not bathe in the presence of men at all. Nevertheless, since men often bathe there, it is possible that a man would enter to bathe. By disregarding this possibility, the wife displays her licentiousness.

HALAKHA

It is a mitzva by Torah law to divorce her – מִצְוָה מִן הַתּוֹרָה לְגָרְשָׁהּ: If a woman is not modest like upright Jewish women, it is a mitzva to divorce her (Rambam *Sefer Nashim, Hilkhot Geirushin* 10:22; *Shulḥan Arukh, Even HaEzer* 119:4).

And this second man introduced a wicked woman into his house – וְזֶה הִכְנִיס רְשָׁעָה לְתוֹךְ בֵּיתוֹ: If a woman was divorced from her husband due to licentious behavior, it is inappropriate for an upright man to marry her (Rambam *Sefer Nashim, Hilkhot Geirushin* 10:22; *Shulḥan Arukh, Even HaEzer* 119:5).

"כִּי שָׂנֵא שַׁלַּח" – רַבִּי יְהוּדָה אוֹמֵר: אִם שְׂנֵאתָהּ שַׁלַּח, רַבִּי יוֹחָנָן אוֹמֵר: שָׂנְאוּי הַמְשַׁלֵּחַ.

§ The prophet Malachi states in rebuke of those who divorce their wives: **"For I hate sending away,** says the Lord, the God of Israel" (Malachi 2:16). **Rabbi Yehuda says:** The verse means that **if you hate** your wife, **send** her away. Do not continue living with a woman whom you hate. **Rabbi Yoḥanan says:** The verse means that **one who sends** his wife away **is hated** by God.

וְלָא פְּלִיגִי: הָא בְּזוּג רִאשׁוֹן, הָא בְּזוּג שֵׁנִי;

And the Gemara explains that **they do not disagree. This** statement **is with regard to a first marriage,**[NH] i.e., one should tolerate his first wife and not divorce her, and **that** statement **is with regard to a second marriage,** in which case the husband should divorce his wife if he hates her.

דְּאָמַר רַבִּי אֶלְעָזָר: כׇּל הַמְגָרֵשׁ אִשְׁתּוֹ רִאשׁוֹנָה – אֲפִילּוּ מִזְבֵּחַ מוֹרִיד עָלָיו דְּמָעוֹת, שֶׁנֶּאֱמַר: "וְזֹאת שֵׁנִית תַּעֲשׂוּ כַּסּוֹת דִּמְעָה אֶת מִזְבַּח ה׳ בְּכִי וַאֲנָקָה מֵאֵין עוֹד פְּנוֹת אֶל הַמִּנְחָה וְלָקַחַת רָצוֹן מִיֶּדְכֶם, וַאֲמַרְתֶּם עַל מָה עַל כִּי ה׳ הֵעִיד בֵּינְךָ וּבֵין אֵשֶׁת נְעוּרֶיךָ אֲשֶׁר אַתָּה בָּגַדְתָּה בָּהּ וְהִיא חֲבֶרְתְּךָ וְאֵשֶׁת בְּרִיתֶךָ".

As Rabbi Elazar says: With regard to **anyone who divorces his first wife, even the altar sheds tears over him, as it is stated: "And this further you do: You cover the altar of the Lord with tears, with weeping, and with sighing, insomuch that He does not regard the offering anymore, nor does He receive it with goodwill from your hand. Yet you say: What for? Because the Lord has been witness between you and the wife of your youth, against whom you have dealt treacherously, though she is your companion, and the wife of your covenant"** (Malachi 2:13–14). Clearly one should not divorce the wife of his youth, i.e., his first wife, as one who does so is hated by God for divorcing the woman to whom he was bound in companionship and covenant.

הדרן עלך המגרש
וסליקא לה מסכת גיטין

NOTES

This statement is with regard to a first marriage, etc. – **הָא בְּזוּג רִאשׁוֹן וכו׳**: There are different opinions among the commentaries and halakhic authorities with regard to the relationship between this distinction and the opinions stated in the mishna. Some explain that the dispute in the mishna is with regard to a first wife, whom one should not divorce lightly. One does not need any special justification to be permitted to divorce his second wife. Others maintain that the dispute in the mishna is with regard to a second wife as well; nevertheless, with regard to divorcing a first wife one should be especially hesitant, even if he discovers a shortcoming of hers. In this context, the Meiri mentions the ordinance of Rabbeinu Gershom Meor HaGola that it is prohibited for a husband to divorce his wife against her will.

HALAKHA

This statement is with regard to a first marriage, etc. – **הָא בְּזוּג רִאשׁוֹן וכו׳**: A man should not divorce his first wife unless he finds that she engaged in licentiousness, and it is inappropriate to divorce her hastily. With regard to his second wife, if he hates her he may divorce her. The later authorities interpret this ruling in accordance with the opinion of Beit Hillel (see Gra; Rambam *Sefer Nashim, Hilkhot Geirushin* 10:21; *Shulḥan Arukh, Even HaEzer* 119:3).

Summary of **Perek IX**

The main principle formulated in this chapter with regard to the *halakhot* of conditions or qualifications is that a divorce must sever the relationship between the husband and wife, leaving no bond between them and no limitation to the woman's freedom. Any qualification that limits the wife's right to remarry, e.g., a condition that she will not marry a certain man, negates the essence of the divorce and therefore invalidates it. By contrast, a condition that restricts the wife for only a limited period of time, or one that predicates the divorce on a specific action, even a prohibited action, which the woman is capable of performing, is a valid condition, and the divorce is therefore valid as well. If the condition cannot be fulfilled by the wife, the divorce is valid and the condition is null. Any condition written in the essential part of the bill of divorce invalidates it.

The essential formula of a bill of divorce is the statement permitting her to marry any man she wishes. The wording of the bill of divorce should be clear and unequivocal *ab initio*. It should be written and worded with great care to prevent it from being contested in any fashion.

Although it is important to write a bill of divorce accurately, not every deviation from its proper form invalidates it after the fact. Three cases are listed in which, although the bill of divorce is invalid *ab initio*, if the wife remarries after receiving it she need not leave her second husband. These are a case in which the bill of divorce was written by the husband but was not signed by witnesses, a case in which it was signed by one witness, and a case in which the date was not written on it. According to the accepted *halakha*, if the bill of divorce was given to the wife in the presence of two witnesses, it is valid *ab initio* even if it was not signed by any witnesses, as the witnesses of the transmission of the bill of divorce effect the divorce.

If two identical bills of divorce were written for two different couples with the same names and they were mixed up, both bills of divorce should be given to both women, and they are both consequently divorced, even though it is unknown which bill of divorce was written for whom.

In a case where several bills of divorce are written on the same paper one below the other, and the signatures are at the bottom, if a common date is written for all the bills of divorce and the names of each couple are specified separately, the signatures count for all the bills of divorce and they are all valid. If they do not have a common date, only the bottommost bill of divorce is valid.

If two bills of divorce are written on the same paper in any other form, and the witnesses signed only once, it is presumed that they intended to sign the one that is above their signatures and adjacent to them. If the bills of divorce are written parallel to one another and the signatures extend from one bill of divorce to the other, the one that they appear to be associated with is validated by them.

A witness may sign in any language and in several different forms. He may sign his nickname or surname. What matters is that it is clear that he is the one signing the bill of divorce.

Although generally a divorce is valid only if it is performed willingly by the husband, a Jewish court can compel a husband to divorce his wife in a case where he is obligated to do so. If the husband is compelled by a gentile court, the divorce is invalid.

If a rumor circulates that a certain woman is betrothed or divorced, the court must seek out the source of the rumor. If a substantial basis is found, e.g., specific eyewitnesses are mentioned, the rumor is treated seriously, with stringent ramifications. If the rumor has a reasonable explanation, it is often disregarded.

If a husband divorces his wife, the divorce takes effect regardless of the reason that led him to do so. However one should refrain from divorcing his wife against her will, especially if she is the wife of his youth. Rabbeinu Gershom Meor HaGola decreed excommunication against any husband who divorces his wife against her will. If she commits adultery or behaves with licentiousness, it is a mitzva for the husband to divorce her.

Image Credits

All images are copyright © Koren Publishers Jerusalem Ltd., except:

p400 ©Antony Grossy; **p404** top right © H. Zell; **p404** bottom left © Firooo2, www.Flagstaffotos.com.au; **p405** top right image © Hectonichus; **p405** bottom left image © Kousvet.

My Notes

My Notes

My Notes

My Notes

My Notes

My Notes

My Notes

My Notes

תלמוד בבלי

— מהדורת נאה —

גיטין חלק ד

Steinsaltz Center

KOREN

Please note that the number ranges that appear at the bottom of each daf of the Vilna pages indicate the corresponding pages of the Koren Talmud Bavli translation and commentary.

תלמוד בבלי

הוצאת קֹורֵן ירושלים

— מהדורת נאה —

מסכת גיטין
דף סז: עד דף צ:

COMMENTARY BY

Rabbi Adin Even-Israel
Steinsaltz

EDITOR-IN-CHIEF

Rabbi Dr Tzvi Hersh Weinreb

EXECUTIVE EDITOR

Rabbi Joshua Schreier

•

STEINSALTZ CENTER
KOREN PUBLISHERS JERUSALEM

עין משפט
נר מצוה

סו א מיי' פ"ט מהל' גירושין הל' כו סמג עשין נ טוש"ע אה"ע סי' קכ סעי' ז וסי' קמא סעי' כא כג:
סז ב מיי' שם הלכ"ז סמג שם טוש"ע אה"ע סי' קכ סעי' ט:
סח ג מיי' שם הלכ"ח טוש"ע שם סעי' יא:
א ד מיי' שם פ"ב הלי"ד סמג שם טוש"ע אה"ע סי' קכא סעי' א:
ב ה מיי' שם הלט"ז טוש"ע שם סעיף ה:
ג ו מיי' פ"ד מהל' דעות הל"ב והל' יד טו:

וְאִיכָּא דְּאַפֵּיךְ לְהוּ.§ "אָמַר לַעֲשָׂרָה כִּתְבוּ גֵּט".§ ת"ר: אאָמַר לַעֲשָׂרָה "כִּתְבוּ גֵּט וּתְנוּ לְאִשְׁתִּי" – אֶחָד כּוֹתֵב עַל יְדֵי כּוּלָּם, "כּוּלְּכֶם כְּתוֹבוּ" – אֶחָד כּוֹתֵב בְּמַעֲמַד כּוּלָּם; *"הוֹלִיכוּ גֵּט לְאִשְׁתִּי" – אֶחָד מוֹלִיךְ ע"י כּוּלָּם, "כּוּלְּכֶם הוֹלִיכוּ" – אֶחָד מוֹלִיךְ בְּמַעֲמַד כּוּלָּם. אִיבַּעְיָא לְהוּ: מָנָה אוֹתָן, מַהוּ? רַב הוּנָא אָמַר: מָנָה – אֵינוֹ כְּ"כוּלְּכֶם", ר' יוֹחָנָן מִשּׁוּם ר' אֶלְעָזָר דְּמִן רוֹמָה אָמַר: במָנָה – הֲרֵי הוּא כְּ"כוּלְּכֶם". אָמַר רַב פַּפָּא, וְלָא פְּלִיגֵי: הָא דְּמָנָה כּוּלְּהוּ, וְהָא דְּמָנָה מִקְצָתַיְיהוּ. גאָמְרִי לָהּ לְהַאי גִּיסָא, וְאָמְרִי לָהּ לְהַאי גִּיסָא. אַתְקֵין רַב יְהוּדָה בְּגִיטָּא דְ"כוּלְּכֶם": "כְּתוֹבוּ אוֹ כּוּלְּכוֹן אוֹ כָּל חַד וְחַד מִינַּכוֹן, חֲתוֹמוּ אוֹ כּוּלְּכוֹן אוֹ כָּל תְּרֵי מִינַּכוֹן, אוֹבִילוּ אוֹ כּוּלְּכוֹן אוֹ כָּל חַד וְחַד מִינַּכוֹן". אָמַר רָבָא: זִימְנִין דְּגָאֵיז לֵיהּ לְדִיבּוּרֵיהּ, וְאָמַר "כּוּלְּכוֹן" וְלָא אָמַר "כָּל חַד מִינַּכוֹן", וְאָתֵי לְאִיפְּסוּלֵי! אֶלָּא אָמַר רָבָא: ג"כְּתוֹבוּ כָּל חַד מִינַּכוֹן, חֲתוֹמוּ כָּל תְּרֵי מִינַּכוֹן, אוֹבִילוּ כָּל חַד מִינַּכוֹן".§

ואיכא דאפיך להו. לרבה ורב יוסף. ע"י כולן. בשביל כולן. מוליך במעמד כולן. כולן ילכו עמו. מנה מהו. אם לא אמר "כולכם", אבל מנאן: א' ב' ג' ד', ואמר: "כתבו גט לאשתי" מהו? *מדמנינהו לכולהו – הנך מנויין איכוין, או דלמא כיון דלא אמר להו: כולכם המנויין כתבו – לא בעינן כולם? אמרי לה להאי גיסא. מנה כולהו – אכולהו קפיד, מנה מקצתייהו – לא קפיד אלא אמנויין; השנים מהני מנויין חתמו, למעוטי השאר שלא נמנו אתה, ולא לכל הני מנויין איכוין שיחתמו כולם. כיון דלא מנה לכולהו – הוברר שטורח הדבר עליו וחדל לו מדעתו הראשונה, ואפי' המנויין אינם צריכין לחתום, אלא מקצתן. ואמרי לה להאי גיסא. מנה מקצתן – גלי דעתיה דאהני קפיד, וצריכין כולן המנויין לחתום. מנה כולן, כיון דלא אמר "כולכם" – לא הקפיד, אלא לומר בפני מנין זה, ולא שיחתמו כולם. אתקין רב יהודה בגיטא דכולכם. בגט שאדם אומר במעמד רבים, ויש לחוש שמא יאמר: לכולכם איכוין, ולא יחתמו כולם, ונמצא גט בטל. התקין שיהו כותבין בו: כך אמר לנו פלוני: כתבו או כולכון או כל חד מנכון. "כולכון" – אחד כותב במעמד כולם, "או כל חד מנכון" – אפי' אין חביריו עמו. אובילו. הוליכו. ואתי לאיפסולי. שמא לא יהא אחד מהן במעמד כתיבתו, או לא יחתמו כולן. חתומו כל תרין מנכון. ולא לימא (אינש) כולכם.

מי שאחזו קורדייקוס ואמר כתבו גט לאשתי לא אמר כלום. ואפי' אמר "כתבו ותנו".

כרכה בסודריה. משום דאסכת דיה טעמא דחיורא הוא דעבד הכי. והגמרא לא פירשו עד לבסוף.

דאמר

הדרן עלך האומר

מִי דשֶׁאֲחָזוֹ קוֹרְדְּיָיקוֹס, וְאָמַר "כִּתְבוּ גֵּט לְאִשְׁתִּי" – לֹא אָמַר כְּלוּם. אָמַר "כִּתְבוּ גֵּט לְאִשְׁתִּי" וַאֲחָזוֹ קוֹרְדְּיָיקוֹס, וְחָזַר וְאָמַר "לֹא תִּכְתְּבוּהוּ" – אֵין דְּבָרָיו הָאַחֲרוֹנִים כְּלוּם. הנִשְׁתַּתֵּק, וְאָמְרוּ לוֹ "נִכְתּוֹב גֵּט לְאִשְׁתְּךָ" וְהִרְכִּין בְּרֹאשׁוֹ, *בּוֹדְקִין אוֹתוֹ שְׁלֹשָׁה פְּעָמִים, אִם אָמַר עַל לָאו לָאו וְעַל הֵן הֵן – הֲרֵי אֵלּוּ יִכְתְּבוּ וְיִתְּנוּ.§

גמ' מַאי קוֹרְדְּיָיקוֹס? אָמַר שְׁמוּאֵל: דְּנַכְתֵיהּ חַמְרָא חֲדַתָּא דְּמַעֲצַרְתָּא. וְלִיתְנֵי: מִי שֶׁנְּשָׁכוֹ יַיִן חָדָשׁ! הָא קמ"ל, דְּהָא רוּחָא קוֹרְדְּיָיקוֹס שְׁמָהּ. לְמַאי נָפְקָא מִינָּהּ? לְקָמֵיעָא. מַאי אָסוּתֵיהּ? *בִּישְׂרָא סוּמָּקָא אַגּוּמְרֵי, וְחַמְרָא מַרְקָא. אָמַר אַבָּיֵי, *אָמְרָה לִי אֵם: לְשִׁימְשָׁא בַּת יוֹמָא – כּוּזָא דְּמַיָּא; בַּת תְּרֵי יוֹמֵי – סִיכּוּרֵי; בַּת תְּלָתָא יוֹמֵי – בִּשְׂרָא סוּמָּקָא אַגּוּמְרֵי, וְחַמְרָא מַרְקָא. לְשִׁימְשָׁא עַתִּיקָתָא – לֵיתֵי תַּרְנְגוֹלְתָּא אוּכַּמְתִּי וְלִיקְרְעָהּ שְׁתִי וָעֵרֶב, וְלִיגַלְּחֵיהּ לִמְצִיעָתָא דְּרֵישֵׁיהּ וְלוֹתְבֵיהּ עִילָּוֵיהּ, וְנִנְחֵיהּ עִילָּוֵיהּ עַד דְּמִיסְרַךְ, וְלֵינְחוֹת וְלֵיקוּם בְּמַיָּא עַד צַוָּארֵיהּ עַד דְּחָלֵישׁ עָלְמָא עִילָּוֵיהּ, וְלֵימוּד וְלִסְלֵיק וְלֵיתֵיב. וְאִי לָא, לֵיכוּל כַּרְתֵי, וְלֵינְחוֹת וְלֵיקוּם בְּמַיָּא עַד צַוָּארֵיהּ עַד דְּחָלֵישׁ עָלְמָא עִילָּוֵיהּ, וְלֵימוּד וְלִסְלֵיק וְלֵיתֵיב. לְשִׁימְשָׁא – בִּישְׂרָא סוּמָּקָא אַגּוּמְרֵי, וְחַמְרָא מַרְקָא. לְתַלְגָּא – בִּישְׂרָא שְׁמִינָא אַגּוּמְרֵי, וְחַמְרָא חַיָּיא. רַב עַמְרָם חֲסִידָא כִּי הֲוָה מְצַעֲרִין לֵיהּ בֵּי רֵישׁ גָּלוּתָא, הָווּ מַגְנוּ לֵיהּ *אַתַּלְגָּא, לְמָחָר אֲמַרוּ לֵיהּ: מַאי נִיחָא לֵיהּ לְמָר דְּלַיְיתוּ לֵיהּ? אֲמַר: הָנֵי כָּל דְּאָמִינָא לְהוּ מֵיפַּךְ אַפְּכִי, אֲמַר לְהוּ: בִּישְׂרָא סוּמָּקָא אַגּוּמְרֵי וְחַמְרָא מַרְקָא, אַיְיתוּ לֵיהּ אִינְהוּ בִּישְׂרָא שְׁמִינָא אַגּוּמְרֵי וְחַמְרָא חַיָּיא; שָׁמְעָה יַלְתָּא וּמְעַיְּילָה לֵיהּ לְבֵי מַסּוּתָא, וּמוֹקְמֵי לֵיהּ בְּמַיָּא דְּבֵי מַסּוּתָא עַד דְּמִהַפְּכִי מַיָּא דְּבֵי מַסּוּתָא וְהָווּ דָּמָא, וְקָאֵי בִּישְׂרֵיהּ פְּשִׁיטֵי פְּשִׁיטֵי. רַב יוֹסֵף אִיעֲסַק בְּרֵיחַיָּא. רַב שֵׁשֶׁת אִיעֲסַק בְּכַשּׁוּרֵי, אָמַר: וגְּדוֹלָה מְלָאכָה שֶׁמְּחַמֶּמֶת אֶת בְּעָלֶיהָ. א"ל רֵישׁ גָּלוּתָא לְרַב שֵׁשֶׁת: מ"ט לָא סָעֵיד מָר גַּבָּן? א"ל: דְּלָא מַעֲלוּ עַבְדֵי, דַּחֲשִׁידֵי אַאֵבֶר מִן הַחַי. א"ל: מִי יֵימַר? אֲמַר לֵיהּ: הָשְׁתָּא מַחֲוֵינָא לָךְ. א"ל לְשַׁמָּעֵיהּ: זִיל גְּנוֹב, אַיְיתִי לִי חֲדָא כַּרְעָא מֵחֵיוָתָא, אַיְיתֵי לֵיהּ. אֲמַר לְהוּ: אַהֲדָמוּ לִי הַדְמֵי דְּחֵיוָתָא, אַיְיתוּ תְּלָת כַּרְעֵי אוֹתִיבוּ קַמֵּיהּ. אֲמַר לְהוּ: הָא בַּעֲלַת שָׁלֹשׁ רַגְלַיִם הֲוַאי? פְּסוּק אַיְיתוּ חֲדָא מֵעָלְמָא, אוֹתִיבוּ קַמֵּיהּ. אֲמַר לֵיהּ לְשַׁמָּעֵיהּ: אוֹתְבֵיהּ נַמִי לְהָךְ דִּידָךְ, אוֹתְבָהּ. אֲמַר לְהוּ: הַאי בַּת חָמֵשׁ רַגְלַיִם הֲוַאי? אֲמַר לֵיהּ: אִי הָכִי, לִיעַבְדוּ קַמֵּיהּ (שַׁמָּעֵיהּ) דְּמָר וְלֵיכוּל, א"ל: לֶחֱיֵי. קְרִיבוּ תַּכָּא קַמַּיְיהוּ, וְאַיְיתוּ קַמֵּיהּ בִּישְׂרָא וְאוֹתִיבוּ קַמֵּיהּ *רִיסְתְּנָא דְּחַנְקָא חַמְתָא, גַּשְּׁשֵׁיהּ וּשְׁקַלָה כְּרָכָהּ בְּסוּדָרֵיהּ. לְבָתַר דְּאָכֵיל, אָמְרִי לֵיהּ: איגניב

מי שאחזו קורדייקוס. שם שידה השולטת כששותה יין הרבה מגיתו. לא אמר כלום. שאין דעתו מיושבת. נשתתק. לאו אשאחזו קורדייקוס קאי, אלא אדם שנעשה אלם מחמת חולי. הרכין. הטה, "ויט שמים" מתרגמינן: וארכין שמיא (תהלים יח). בודקין אותו. בדברים אחרים, שואלין לו דברים שהוא ראוי להשיב עליהן, (א) אם ראו דעתו מיושבת, שמרמז על תשובת לאו הרכנה שדרך בני אדם להרכין על לאו, ועל הין הרכנת הין, שלשה פעמים לכל אחד – כותבין ונותנין, אם מרכין על הגט הרכנת הין. **גמ'** נכתיה. נשכו, כלומר ששתה הימנו, והרגיש בו. רוחא. שד האוחז על ידי כך. לקמיעא. שמשביעין בה את הרוח בשמו. סומקא. כחוש. מרקא. מזוג במים הרבה. לשמשא בת יומא. חולי שאחזו מחמת חום בו ביום. כוזא דמיא. ישתה. סיכורי. הקזת דם בקרן. סומקא. כחוש. עתיקתא. מימים רבים. למציעתא דרישיה. דחולה. דחליש ליה עלמא. פג לבו. ולימוד. ישוט, כמו נחית בר *אמוראי (ב"ב דף עד.). לשמשא בשרא סומקא כו'. כדאמר. לתלגא. חולי שאחזו מחמת ליגה. חייא. בלא מזיגת מים. הוו מצערי ליה. העבדים, מפני שהיה חסיד ופרוש, ומחמיר עליהן באיסורין. ילתא. אשת רב נחמן, והיא בת הנשיא ואשת אב בית דין, וחשובה, כדאמרי' ב"העור והרוטב" (חולין דף קכד.) דרב נחמן חתנא דבי נשיאה הוה. מסותא. מרחץ. דמתהפכי. מחמת זיעה אדומה היוצאה ממנו ע"י בשרא שמינא וחמרא חייא. פשיטי פשיטי. בקרות עגולות. רב יוסף איעסק. לתלגא בריחיא, כדי שיתחמם ויזיע. בכשורי. לשאת קורות ומשאות. אהדמו לי הדמי דחיותא. סדרו לפני נתחי הבהמה לנתחיה. אהדמו. הנתיחו, כלומר ערכו הנתחים. א"ל. ריש גלותא. אי הכי. דמשום דחשידי הוא. ליעבדו קמיה שמעיה דמר. כלומר, קמיה שמעיה דמר יסדרו המאכל בהיתר. תכא. שולחן. ריסתנא דחנקא חמתא. אמנסטרייסו"ן, עצם קטן שעל כף הירך, שאדם בולעו ונחנק. משום דרב ששת סגי נהור הוה, ולא יראנו, ויאכל ויחנק. גששה. משמשה, והרגיש באותו עצם. שקל. כל החתיכה וכרכה בסודריה. איגניב

מסורת הש"ס

מדלי' מנהגה. גי' רש"ל

[תוספתא פ"ד]

[ע' מ"ש תוס' על זה לקמן עו: ד"ה בודקין]

[לקמן עו:]

[קדושין לח: וש"נ]

ס"א כולי ליליא

[נ"ל אמודאי וכ"ה בערוך עי' ערך מד ב]

ס"א ל"ג

[דסתנא גירסת ערוך]

הגהות הב"ח

(א) רש"י ד"ה בודקין וכו' להשיב עליהם לאו או הן ואם ראו דעתו:

גליון הש"ס

גמ' אמרי לה להאי גיסא. כעין זה כ"ב דף מב ע"ב וש"נ:

תוספות רי"ד

אמר לעשרה כתבו [ותנו] גט לאשתי א' כותב ושני' חותמין דכך אמר להם כל שנים מכם כתבו ותנו גט לאשתי. אבל אם אמר כולכם כתובו קפידא הוי שרצה לבזותה בפני כולן וא' כותב וכולן חותמין ואם מת אחד מהן הרי הגט בטל שלא נתקיים תנאו: ת"ר אמר לעשרה כתבו גט לאשתי אחד כותב על ידי כולם. פי' לא צוה להם לחותמו אלא לכותבו בלבד כולכם כתבו א' כותב במעמד כולם פי' בהסכמת כולן שכולם ידעו כשכתוב: הוליכו גט לאשתי אחד מוליך ע"י כולם כולכם הוליכו אחד מוליך במעמד כולם. פי' לא דמיא ברייתא למתני' דבמתני' צוה אותם בין על הכתיבה בין על החתימה משום הכי תנן אחד מהן כותב ושנים חותמין ואם אמר כולכם א' כותב (ושנים) [וכולם] חותמין אבל הברייתא מיירי כגון שלא צוה אותם אלא בכתיבת הגט והוא רוצה אח"כ להחתימו: איבעיא להו מנה אותן מהו רב הונא אמר מנה אותם אינו ככולכם ור' יוחנן משום ר' אלעזר אמר מנה אותם הרי הוא ככולכם אמר רב פפא ולא פליגי הא דמנה כולהו הא דמנה מקצתייהו אמרי לה להאי גיסא ואמרי לה להאי גיסא והילכך עבדינן לחומרא בין מנה כולם בין מנה מקצתם אותם שמנה ככולכם דמי: אתקין רב בגיטא כתובו כל חד מנכון א) פי' כתובו חתומו כל תרי מנכון אובילו כל חד מנכון פי' כשמצוה הבעל במעמד אנשים כתבו גט לאשתי התקין שיאמר כך כתובו כל חד מנכון חתומו כל תרי מנכון אובילו כל חד מנכון גזירה שמא יאמר כולכם ויתבטל הגט משום הכי מלמדין אותו שיאמר כן:

סליק פירקא

מי שאחזו קורדייקוס ואמר כתבו גט לאשתי לא אמר כלום אמר כתבו גט לאשתי ואחזו קורדייקוס וחזר ואמר אל תכתבוהו אין בדבריו האחרונים כלום: נשתתק ואמרו לו נכתוב גט לאשתך והרכין בראשו בודקין אותו ג' פעמים אם אמר על לאו לאו ועל הן הן הרי אלו יכתבו ויתנו. פי' קורדייקוס הוא רוח רעה השורה על האדם ששותה יין מגיתו ומפני זה לא אמר כלום שמשועמם הוא ואינו עומד על דעתו ואם מתחילה צוה ואמר כתבו גט לאשתי ואח"כ אחזו קורדייקוס וחזר ואמר אל תכתבוהו אין בדבריו האחרונים כלום ולא בטלה שליחותו: נשתתק לאו אמי שאחזו קורדייקוס קאי אלא אדם שנאלם מחמת חולי ועומד על דעתו ואם אמר לו נכתוב גט לאשתך והוא הרכין והטה להם בראשו סימן [הוא] שמתרצה בדבר בודקין אותו ג' פעמים בדברים אחרים אם משיב על לאו לאו ועל הן הן על דעתו הוא עומד וסומכין בהרכנת ראשו וכותבין גט לאשתו:

א) נראה דל"ל כתובו כל חד מנכון חתומו כל תרי מנכון וכו'.

אמר

איגניב לן כסא דכספא! בהדי דקא מעייני ואתי, אשכחוה דכרוכה בסודריה, אמרי ליה: חזי מר, דלא מיכל קא בעי אלא לצעורן! אמר להו: אנא מיכל אכלי, וטעמי ביה טעמא דחיורא. אמרי ליה: חיורא לא עביד לן האידנא. אמר להו: בדקו בדוכתיה; *דאמר רב חסדא: אוכמא בחיורא וחיורא באוכמתא — לקותא היא; בדוק אשכחוה. כי קא נפיק, כרו ליה בירא ושדו ליה ציפתא עילויה, ואמרי ליה: ליתי מר לינח, נחר ליה רב חסדא מאחוריה. אמר ליה לינוקא: פסוק לי פסוקיך, אמר ליה: ש"ב ב °"נטה לך על ימינך או על שמאלך". אמר ליה לשמעיה: מאי קא חזית? אמר ליה: ציפיתא דשדיא, אמר ליה: הדר מינה. לבתר דנפק, אמר ליה רב חסדא: מנא הוה ידע מר? אמר ליה: חדא, דנחר לי מר; ועוד, דפסק לי ינוקא פסוקא; ועוד, דחשידי עבדי דלא מעלו. קהלת ב °"עשיתי לי שרים ושרות ותענוגות בני האדם שדה ושדות", "שרים ושרות" — אלו מיני זמר, "ותענוגות בני האדם" — אלו בריכות ומרחצאות, "שדה ושדות" — הכא תרגימו: שידה ושידתין, במערבא אמרי: שידתא. אמר רבי יוחנן: שלש מאות מיני שדים היו בשיחין, ושידה עצמה איני יודע מה היא. אמר מר, הכא תרגימו: שידא ושידתין. שידה ושידתין למאי איבעי ליה? מ"א ו דכתיב: °"והבית בהבנותו אבן שלמה מסע נבנה" וגו', אמר להו לרבנן: היכי אעביד? אמרו ליה: איכא שמירא דאייתי משה לאבני אפוד. אמר להו: היכא אישתכח? אמרו ליה: אייתי שידה ושידתין כבשינהו אהדדי, אפשר דידעי ומגלו לך. אייתי שידה ושידתין כבשינהו אהדדי, אמרי: אנן לא ידעינן, דילמא אשמדאי מלכא דשידי ידע. אמר להו: היכא איתיה? אמרי ליה: איתיה בטורא פלן; כריא ליה בירא ומליא ליה מיא ומיכסיא בטינרא וחתמיה בגושפנקיה, וכל יומא סליק לרקיע וגמר מתיבתא דרקיעא, ונחית לארעא וגמר מתיבתא דארעא, ואתי סייר ליה לגושפנקיה ומגלי ליה ושתי, ומכסי ליה וחתים ליה ואזיל. שדריה לבניהו בן יהוידע, יהב ליה שושילתא דחקיק עלה שם ועזקתא דחקיק עלה שם, וגבבי דעמרא וזיקי דחמרא. אזל כרא בירא מתתאי, ושפינהו למיא וסתמינהו בגבבי דעמרא, וכרא בירא מעילאי ושפכינהו לחמרא וטמינהו, סליק יתיב באילנא. כי אתא סיירי' לגושפנקא, גלייה, אשכחיה חמרא, משלי כ אמר, כתיב: °"לץ היין הומה שכר וכל שוגה בו לא יחכם", הושע ד וכתיב: °"זנות ויין ותירוש יקח לב", לא אישתי. כי צחי, לא סגיא ליה, *אישתי רוה וגנא. נחית, אתא, שדא ביה שושילתא, סתמיה כי אתער הוה קא מיפרזל, א"ל: שמא דמרך עלך! שמא דמרך עלך! כי נקיט ליה ואתי, מטא דיקלא חף ביה שדייה, מטא לביתא שדייה, מטא גבי כובא דההיא ארמלתא, נפקא איתחננא

איגניב לן כסא דכספא. שהיו רואים אותו כרך בסודריא, ורוצין לבדוק מהו. אמרי ליה. לריש גלותא. דחיורא. בשר בעלת שחין. מיכל אכלי וטעמי. טעמתי. חיורא לא עביד לן האידנא. לא שחטנו היום בהמה בעלת שחין. בדוכתא. בעור היו בודקין במקום ריסתנא זו בכף הירך, תורה אור ותמצאהו בעור שהוא לבן. דאמר רב חסדא חיורא באוכמתא לקותא היא. טלאי לבן בעור שחור — לקותא היה שם בבשר, ונהפך העור ללבן. כרו ליה בירא. חפרו גומץ שיפול בו. ושדו ליה ציפתא. השליכו מחצלת על פי הבור כדי שלא יבין נזיר לח: *מושבו. ליתי מר לינח. לשכב במשכבו. נחר ליה רב חסדא. עשה לו סימן, כמו "נחרת סוסיו" (ירמיה ח). א"ל. רב ששת לינוקא: פסוק לי פסוקיך. נטה לך. פסוק הוא בעשהאל. הדר מינה. חזור מעליה, לימין או לשמאל. בריכות. לרחוץ בהן כלונ. הכא תרגימו. בבבל. שידה ושידתין. שד זכר ושד נקבה. שידתא. שידה, עגלה למרכבת נשים ושרים. בי שיחין. באותו מקום. מה היא. מה דמותה ומה טיבה. ויש אומרים שידה עצמה — ראש כולן, ואמן איני יודע מאי היא. היכי איעביד. בלי כלי ברזל. שמיר. בריה מששת ימי בראשית, ואין כל דבר קשה יכול לעמוד מפניו. לאבני אפוד. דאמרינן במסכת סוטה (דף מח.): אבנים הללו אין כותבין עליהם בדיו, שנאמר: "פתוחי חותם", ואין מסרטין עליהם באיזמל, שנאמר: "במלואותם" שלא יהו חסרות כלום, אלא כותב עליהם בדיו, ומראה להן שמיר מבחוץ, והן נבקעות מאליהן. כבשינהו. כפאם ביסורין לומר לו היכן הוא. כבשינהו. לחצן, לשון "מכבש של בגדים" (שבת דף קמא.). היכא איתיה. אשמדאי, שאוכל לכבשו. בטורא פלן. בהר פלוני. כריא ליה בירא. כרה לו שם בור. טינרא. אבן. וחתמיה בגושפנקיה. בחותמו. סייר לגושפנקיה. בודקו, שלא נגע אדם בו לגלות בורו. בגבבי דעמרא. גיזות צמר. וזיקי דחמרא. נודות יין. בירא מתתאי. במורד ההר, למטה מבורו של אשמדאי. ושפינהו למיא. כגון "השופה יין *לחמריה" (ב"מ דף ס.), הריק מי בור העליון לתוך התחתון דרך נקב שנקב בשפה שבין שתי הבורות, ומתוך שהראשון קרקעיתו גבוהה מקרקעית התחתון — נרוקו המים לתוכו מאליהן. וסתמינהו. לנקבים שבין זה לזה, כדי שכששפשים יין בעליון — לא יזוב ממנו לתחתון. וכרא בירא. אחרינא מעילאי לבורו של אשמדאי. וטמינהו. מילא אותן שתי בורות עפר, כדי שלא יבין אשמדאי. טמינהו. סתמן, כדמתרגמינן: "סתמום פלשתים" (בראשית כו) — טמנון פלשתאי. כי אתא. אשמדאי. סיירי' לגושפנקיה. ומצאו שלם. לא סגי ליה. לא יכול להתאפק. רוה וגנא. נשתכר ונרדם. נחית אתא. בניהו מן האילן. סתמיה. סגר השלשלת סביב צוארו, שלא יוכל ראשו לצאת. הוה קא מפרזל. משתגע ומתעסק לנתקה הימנו. דמרך. הקב"ה. חף ביה. נתחכך בו. *כובא. צריף קטן, כמו כוכא דציידי. דארמלתא. אלמנה היתה דרה בו. איתחננא

דאמר רב חסדא אוכמא בחיורא וחיורא באוכמא לקותא היא. פירוש: טלאי שחור בעור לבן, או טלאי לבן בעור שחור — אין זה אלא מחמת נגע שהיה שם. הקשה רבינו תם: דבנזיר בריש פרק "בית שמאי" (דף לח:) משמע דלא איירי רב חסדא אלא בשור שחור בין שוורים לבנים, שהשחור מגרע כולם ומתקלקל מקחם על ידו. ופריך התם ממתני' דהתם, דמשמע שהלבן גרוע, ומסיק דרב חסדא איירי בתורא דקרמנאי, דהתם שחור גרוע טפי. ואור"ת: דתרי מילי נינהו, ומילתיה דהכא איירי בטלאי שחור בעור לבן ולבן בעור שחור, והתם מיירי בשור שחור בין שוורים לבנים. ותדע, דבכל הספרים ישנים לא גרסינן התם במילתיה דרב חסדא אלא: אוכמא בחיורא לקותא, ותו לא. וכן נראה, דאי גרסינן תרווייהו כמו הכא, ונפרש חד לטלאי וחד לשור בין השוורים — אם כן מאי פריך התם? דמנא ליה דאוכמא בחיורא קאי אשור בין השוורים? נימא איפכא, ולא יקשה כלום! רבינו תם. **איכא** שמיר דאייתי משה לאבני אפוד. הכא משמע דלאבני אפוד בעי שמיר, ובפ"ק דקידושין (דף לא.) גבי עובדא דדמא בן נתינה בקשו ממנו אבנים לאפוד, וזה היה בבית שני, מדקאמר: לשנה נולדה לו פרה אדומה כו'. דבבית ראשון לא עשו פרה, כדאמר*: שניה עשה עזרא. ואם כן היה שמיר בבית שני! ואין להקשות, דבפרק בתרא דסוטה (דף מח.) תנן: משמתו נביאים הראשונים — בטלו אורים ותומים, ומשחרב בית המקדש — בטל שמיר. דהיינו בית המקדש שני, מדנקט בית המקדש סתם, והתם בגמרא נקט בית המקדש ראשון על מילי אחריני. ועוד: מדלא ערבינהו בהדי אורים ותומים, והוי ליה למיתני: משמתו נביאים הראשונים בטלו אורים ותומים והשמיר, דמשמתו נביאים הראשונים — היינו משחרב בית המקדש ראשון, בטלו אורים ותומים! וצריך לומר ששמרוהו מימי שלמה עד חורבן בית שני. הקשה ה"ר אלחנן: במסכת ע"ז בפ' "ר' ישמעאל" (דף נב:) גבי אבני מזבח ששקצום אנשי יון: ליתברינהו — "אבנים שלמות" אמר רחמנא, לינסרינהו — "לא תניף עליהם ברזל" אמר רחמנא. ולינסרינהו ע"י שמיר? ואומר ר"י: דע"י שמיר אין נעשין חלקות, דהגירת לפורן פוסלת במזבח*. והך סוגיא אתיא כמ"ד בסוטה (דף מח:) דאיצטריך שמיר לאבני בית המקדש, והא דכתיב מגוררות במגירה — מוקי לה באבני ביתו*. **זיל** אייתי שידה כו'. כי לא רצו לשאול באורים ותומים כשיכולין לשאול על ידי דבר אחר.

וכתיב זנות ויין ותירוש. אף על פי שזה הפסוק לא נכתב עדיין — היו יודעין, כמו "ארור עושה מלאכת ה' רמיה" בפ' "לא יחפור" (ב"ב דף כא:) °גבי יואב. לברוקתי

[פרה פ"ג מ"ה]

[חולין יח.]

[ועי"ע תוס' זבחים נד: ד"ה אבנים ותוס' חולין יח. ד"ה וכמה]

נ"ל מושכו

נ"א לחבריה

ס"א דלא אישתא אמר כריב ויין ישמח לבב אנוש

[בי' הערוך ערך ככא ג' כוכא ובזה עולה יפה פרש"י כוכא צריף קטן כמו כוכא דציידי תענית דף כב.]

גליון הש"ס

תום' ד"ה וכתיב וכו' גבי יואב. ע' לעיל דף נה ע"ב וכמ"ש שם על הגליון:

איחַנְנָא לֵיהּ, כְּפָא לְקוֹמָתֵיהּ מִינֵּיהּ אִיתְּבַר בֵּיהּ גַּרְמָא, אֲמַר, הַיְינוּ דִּכְתִיב: °"וְלָשׁוֹן רַכָּה תִּשְׁבָּר גָּרֶם". חֲזָא סַמְיָא דַּהֲוָה קָא טָעֵי בְּאוֹרְחָא, אַסְקֵיהּ לְאוֹרְחֵיהּ. חֲזָא רַוְיָא דַּהֲוָה קָא טָעֵי בְּאוֹרְחָא, אַסְקֵיהּ לְאוֹרְחֵיהּ. חֲזָא חֶדְוָותָא דְּהָווּ קָמְחַדֵּי לָהּ, בָּכָה. שְׁמַעֵיהּ לְהַהוּא גַּבְרָא דַּהֲוָה קָאָמַר לְאוּשְׁכָּפָא: עֲבֵיד לִי מְסָאנֵי לְשַׁב שְׁנֵי, אָחֵיךְ. חֲזָא הַהוּא קָסְמָא דַּהֲוָה קָסֵים, אָחֵיךְ. כִּי מְטָא לְהָתָם, לָא עַיְילוּהּ לְגַבֵּיהּ דִּשְׁלֹמֹה עַד תְּלָתָא יוֹמֵי. יוֹמָא קַמָּא אֲמַר לְהוּ: אַמַּאי לָא קָא בָּעֵי לִי מַלְכָּא לְגַבֵּיהּ? א"ל: אָנְסֵיהּ מִשְׁתְּיָא; שְׁקַל לְבֵינְתָא אוֹתֵיב אַחֲבֶרְתָּהּ. אָתוּ אֲמַרוּ לֵיהּ לִשְׁלֹמֹה, אֲמַר לְהוּ, הָכִי אֲמַר לְכוּ: הֲדוּר אַשְׁקְיוּהּ. לְמָחָר אֲמַר לְהוּ: וְאַמַּאי לָא קָא בָּעֵי לִי מַלְכָּא לְגַבֵּיהּ? אֲמַרוּ לֵיהּ: אָנְסֵיהּ מֵיכְלָא; שְׁקַל לְבֵינְתָא מֵחֲבֶרְתָּהּ אוֹתְבָהּ אַאַרְעָא. אָתוּ אֲמַרוּ לֵיהּ לִשְׁלֹמֹה, אֲמַר לְהוּ, הָכִי אֲמַר לְכוּ: נִגְדּוּ מִינֵּיהּ מֵיכְלֵיהּ. [לְסוֹף] תְּלָתָא יוֹמֵי עַיֵּיל לְקַמֵּיהּ; שְׁקַל קַנְיָא וּמְשַׁח אַרְבָּעָה גַּרְמִידֵי וּשְׁדָא קַמֵּיהּ, א"ל: מִכְּדֵי כִּי מָיֵית הַהוּא גַּבְרָא לֵית לֵיהּ בְּהָדֵין עָלְמָא אֶלָּא ד' גַּרְמִידֵי, הַשְׁתָּא כַּבְשַׁתֵּיהּ לְכוּלֵּי עָלְמָא וְלָא שָׂבַעְתְּ עַד דְּכָבְשַׁתְּ נַמִּי לְדִידִי? א"ל: לָא קָא בָּעֵינָא מִינָּךְ מִידֵּי, בָּעֵינָא דְּאִיבְנְיֵיהּ לְבֵית הַמִּקְדָּשׁ וְקָא מִיבָּעֵי לִי שָׁמִירָא. א"ל: לְדִידִי לָא מְסִיר לִי, לְשָׂרָא דְּיַמָּא מְסִיר לֵיהּ, וְלָא יָהֵיב לֵיהּ אֶלָּא לְתַרְנְגוֹלָא בָּרָא דִּמְהֵימַן לֵיהּ אַשְׁבּוּעָתֵיהּ. וּמַאי עָבֵד בֵּיהּ? מַמְטֵי לֵיהּ לְטוּרֵי דְּלֵית בְּהוּ יִשּׁוּב, וּמַנַּח לָהּ אַשִּׁינָּא דְּטוּרָא וּפָקַע טוּרָא, וּמְנַקֵּיט מַיְיתֵי בִּיזְרָנֵי מֵאִילָנֵי וְשָׁדֵי הָתָם וְהָוֵי יִשּׁוּב. וְהַיְינוּ דְּמְתַרְגְּמִינַן: נַגַּר טוּרָא. בָּדְקוּ קִינָּא דְּתַרְנְגוֹלָא בָּרָא דְּאִית לֵיהּ בְּנֵי, וַחֲפוּיָהּ לְקִינֵּיהּ זוּגִיתָא חִיוַּרְתֵּי. כִּי אֲתָא בָּעֵי לְמֵיעַל וְלָא מָצֵי, אֲזַל אַיְיתֵי שָׁמִירָא וְאוֹתְבֵיהּ עִלָּוֵיהּ; רְמָא בֵּיהּ קָלָא, שָׁדְיֵיהּ, שְׁקַלֵיהּ, אֲזַל חָנֵק נַפְשֵׁיהּ אַשְׁבּוּעָתֵיהּ. אֲמַר לֵיהּ בְּנָיָהוּ: מַאי טַעְמָא כִּי חֲזִיתֵיהּ לְהַהוּא סַמְיָא דַּהֲוָה קָא טָעֵי בְּאוֹרְחָא, אַסִּיקְתֵּיהּ לְאוֹרְחֵיהּ? אֲמַר לֵיהּ: מַכְרְזֵי עֲלֵיהּ בִּרְקִיעָא דְּצַדִּיק גָּמוּר הוּא, וּמַאן דְּעָבֵד לֵיהּ נַיְחָא נַפְשֵׁיהּ זָכֵי לְעָלְמָא דְּאָתֵי. וּמַאי טַעְמָא כִּי חֲזִיתֵיהּ לְהַהוּא רַוְיָא דְּקָטָעֵי בְּאוֹרְחָא, אַסִּיקְתֵּיהּ לְאוֹרְחֵיהּ? א"ל: מַכְרְזֵי עֲלֵיהּ בִּרְקִיעָא דְּרָשָׁע גָּמוּר הוּא, וַעֲבַדִי לֵיהּ נַיְחָא נַפְשֵׁיהּ כִּי הֵיכִי דְּלֵיכְלֵיהּ לְעָלְמָא. מַאי טַעְמָא כִּי חֲזִיתֵיהּ לְהַהוּא חֶדְוָותָא, בָּכֵית? אֲמַר לֵיהּ: בָּעֵי מֵימַת גַּבְרָא בְּגוֹ תְּלָתִין יוֹמִין, וּבָעְיָא מִינְטַר לְיָבָם קָטָן תְּלֵיסַרִי שְׁנִין. מַאי טַעְמָא כִּי שְׁמַעְתֵּיהּ לְהַהוּא גַּבְרָא דַּאֲמַר לֵיהּ לְאוּשְׁכָּפָא: עֲבֵיד לִי מְסָאנֵי לְשַׁב שְׁנִין, אַחֵיכְתְּ? אֲמַר לֵיהּ: הַהוּא שִׁבְעָה יוֹמֵי לֵית לֵיהּ, מְסָאנֵי לְשַׁב שְׁנִין בָּעֵי?! מ"ט כִּי חֲזִיתֵיהּ לְהַהוּא קָסְמָא דַּהֲוָה קָסֵים, אַחֵיכְתְּ? אֲמַר לֵיהּ: דַּהֲוָה יָתֵיב אַבֵּי גַּזָּא דְּמַלְכָּא, לִקְסוֹם מַאי דְּאִיכָּא תּוּתֵיהּ. *תַּרְחֵיהּ גַּבֵּיהּ עַד דִּבְנְיֵיהּ לְבֵית הַמִּקְדָּשׁ. יוֹמָא חַד הֲוָה קָאֵי לְחוּדֵיהּ, אֲמַר לֵיהּ, כְּתִיב: °"כְּתוֹעֲפוֹת רְאֵם לוֹ", וְאָמְרִינַן: "כְּתוֹעֲפוֹת" – אֵלּוּ מַלְאֲכֵי הַשָּׁרֵת, "רְאֵם" – אֵלּוּ הַשֵּׁדִים, מַאי רְבוּתַיְיכוּ מִינַּן? א"ל: שְׁקוֹל שׁוֹשִׁילְתָּא מִינַּאי וְהַב לִי עִיזְקְתָךְ, וְאַחְוֵי לָךְ רְבוּתַאי. שְׁקַלֵיהּ לְשׁוֹשִׁילְתָּא מִינֵּיהּ וִיהֵיב לֵיהּ עִיזְקְתֵיהּ, *בְּלָעֵיהּ, אוֹתְבֵיהּ לְחַד גַּפֵּיהּ בִּרְקִיעָא וּלְחַד גַּפֵּיהּ בְּאַרְעָא, פַּתְקֵיהּ אַרְבַּע מְאָה פַּרְסֵי. עַל הַהִיא שַׁעְתָּא אֲמַר שְׁלֹמֹה: °"מַה יִּתְרוֹן לָאָדָם בְּכָל עֲמָלוֹ שֶׁיַּעֲמֹל תַּחַת הַשָּׁמֶשׁ". *°"וְזֶה הָיָה חֶלְקִי מִכָּל עֲמָלִי" *מַאי "וְזֶה"? רַב וּשְׁמוּאֵל, חַד אָמַר: מַקְלוֹ, וְחַד אָמַר: גּוּנְדוֹ. הָיָה מְחַזֵּר עַל הַפְּתָחִים, כָּל הֵיכָא דִּמְטָא אֲמַר: °"אֲנִי קֹהֶלֶת הָיִיתִי מֶלֶךְ עַל יִשְׂרָאֵל בִּירוּשָׁלָיִם". כִּי מְטָא גַּבֵּי סַנְהֶדְרִין, אֲמַרוּ רַבָּנַן: מִכְּדֵי שׁוֹטֶה בַּחֲדָא מִילְּתָא לָא סְרִיךְ, מַאי הַאי? אֲמַרוּ לֵיהּ לִבְנָיָהוּ: קָא בָּעֵי לָךְ מַלְכָּא לְגַבֵּיהּ? אֲמַר לְהוּ: לָא. שְׁלַחוּ לְהוּ לְמַלְכְּוָותָא: קָאָתֵי מַלְכָּא לְגַבַּיְיכוּ? שְׁלַחוּ לְהוּ: אִין, קָאָתֵי. שְׁלַחוּ לְהוּ: בִּידְקוּ בְּכַרְעֵיהּ, שְׁלַחוּ לְהוּ: בְּמוֹקֵי קָאָתֵי, וְקָא תָּבַע לְהוּ בְּנִדּוּתַיְיהוּ, וְקָא תָּבַע לָהּ נַמִּי לְבַת שֶׁבַע אִימֵּיהּ. אַתְיוּהּ לִשְׁלֹמֹה וַהֲבוּ לֵיהּ עִיזְקְתָא וְשׁוֹשִׁילְתָּא דַּחֲקוּק עֲלֵיהּ שֵׁם, כִּי עַיֵּיל חַזְיֵיהּ, פָּרַח. וַאֲפִילּוּ הָכִי הֲוָה לֵיהּ בִּיעֲתוּתָא מִינֵּיהּ, וְהַיְינוּ דִּכְתִיב: °"הִנֵּה מִטָּתוֹ שֶׁלִּשְׁלֹמֹה שִׁשִּׁים גִּבֹּרִים סָבִיב לָהּ מִגִּבֹּרֵי יִשְׂרָאֵל כֻּלָּם אֲחֻזֵי חֶרֶב מְלֻמְּדֵי מִלְחָמָה אִישׁ חַרְבּוֹ עַל יְרֵכוֹ מִפַּחַד בַּלֵּילוֹת"! *רַב וּשְׁמוּאֵל, חַד אָמַר: מֶלֶךְ וְהֶדְיוֹט, וְחַד אָמַר: מֶלֶךְ וְהֶדְיוֹט וּמֶלֶךְ. לְדָמָא דְּרֵישָׁא – לֵיתֵי שׁוּרְבִינָא וּבִינָא וְאָסָא דָּרָא, וְזֵיתָא וְחִילְפָא, *וְחִילְפֵי דְּיַמָּא וְיַבְלָא, וְלִישְׁלוֹקִינְהוּ בַּהֲדֵי הֲדָדֵי, וְלִנְטוֹל תְּלָת מְאָה כָּסֵי אַהַאי גִּיסָּא דְּרֵישָׁא, וּתְלָת מְאָה כָּסֵי אַהַאי גִּיסָּא דְּרֵישָׁא. וְאִי לָא, לֵיתֵי וַרְדָּא חִיוָּרָא דְּקָאֵי בְּחַד דָּרָא, וְלִישְׁלְקֵיהּ, וְלִינְטוֹל שִׁיתִּין כָּסֵי אַהַאי גִּיסָּא דְּרֵישָׁא, וְשִׁיתִּין כָּסֵי אַהַאי גִּיסָּא דְּרֵישָׁא. לְצִלִּיחְתָּא – לֵיתֵי תַּרְנְגוֹלָא בָּרָא, וְלִישְׁחֲטֵיהּ בְּזוּזָא חִיוָּרָא אַהַהוּא גִּיסָּא דְּכָיֵיב לֵיהּ, וְנִזְדַּהַר מִדְּמֵיהּ דְּלָא לְסַמְיִנְהוּ לְעֵינֵיהּ, וְלִיתְלְיֵיהּ בְּסִיפָא דְּבָבָא, דְּכִי עַיֵּיל חָיֵיף בֵּיהּ, וְכִי נָפֵיק חָיֵיף בֵּיהּ. לִבְרוֹקְתִּי

תורה אור: מִשְׁלֵי כה — במדבר כד — קהלת א — ס"א וכתיב וזה שם ב — שם א — שיר ג

איחַנְנָא לֵיהּ. לִימָּשֵׁךְ מֵעָלָיו שֶׁלֹּא יָחוּף בּוֹ. כְּפָא לְקוֹמָתֵיהּ. לְצַד אַחֵר, וְאִיסְתַּלַּק עוֹבִי כְּתֵיפָיו מִן הַבַּיִת. וְלָשׁוֹן רַכָּה תִּשְׁבָּר גָּרֶם. עַל יְדֵי לָשׁוֹן רַכָּה, שֶׁתְּחִנָּה מַעֲנֶה רַךְ – נִשְׁבְּרָה עַצְמִי. אַסְקֵיהּ. הֶעֱלָהוּ, לְהַטּוֹתוֹ אֶל הַדֶּרֶךְ. רַוְיָא. שִׁיכּוֹר. אַסְקֵיהּ. אֶל הַדֶּרֶךְ. חֲזָא חֶדְוָותָא דְּהָווּ מְחַדֵּי לָהּ. רָאָה הַכְנָסַת כַּלָּה, שֶׁהָיוּ מַרְבִּין בְּשִׂמְחָה מְאֹד. אָנְסֵיהּ מִשְׁתְּיָא. שָׁתָה הַרְבֵּה. נִגְדּוּ מֵיכְלָא מִינֵּיהּ. מָשְׁכוּ יְדֵיכֶם מִלְּהַאֲכִילוֹ, כִּי אִם מְעַט. קַנְיָא. קָנֶה. דִּמְהֵימַן לֵיהּ אַשְׁבּוּעָתֵיהּ. מַאֲמִינוֹ בִּשְׁבוּעָתוֹ, כְּשֶׁנִּשְׁבַּע לוֹ לְהַחֲזִירוֹ לוֹ. דְּלֵית בְּהוּ יִישּׁוּב. שֶׁל זְרָעִים וְאִילָנוֹת, לְהִתְפַּרְנֵס שָׁם. וּפָקַע טוּרָא. מִתְבַּקֵּעַ מְעַט כְּמִין חָרִיץ, עַד שֶׁמַּשְׁלִיךְ שָׁם זֶרַע הָאִילָנוֹת, וּגְדֵלִים אִילָנוֹת שָׁם וּמִתְפַּרְנֵס מֵהֶם. בָּדְקוּ קִינָּא. בָּדְקוּ עַד שֶׁהָיוּ בְּקִיאִין הֵיכָן יֵשׁ קֵן שֶׁל דּוּכִיפַת, דְּהוּא תַּרְנְגוֹלָא בָּרָא. זוּגִיתָא. זְכוּכִית, כְּדֵי שֶׁיִּרְאֶה אֶת בָּנָיו וְלֹא יוּכַל לִיכָּנֵס אֶצְלָם, וִיהֵא צָרִיךְ לַשָּׁמִיר לְבַקֵּעַ הַזְּכוּכִית. רְמָא בֵּיהּ. שְׁלוּחוֹ שֶׁל שְׁלֹמֹה, קָלָא. חָנֵק נַפְשֵׁיהּ. הַתַּרְנְגוֹל. אַסִּיקְתֵּיהּ. מָה חָשַׁשְׁתָּ לוֹ? וּבָעְיָא מִינְטַר לְיָבָם קָטָן. עַד שֶׁיָּבִיא שְׁתֵּי שְׂעָרוֹת וִיהֵא רָאוּי לַחֲלִיצָה, וְיוֹדֵעַ הָיָה זֶה שֶׁעֲתִידָה לְהַמְתִּין שְׁלֹשׁ עֶשְׂרֵה שָׁנָה. שִׁבְעָה יוֹמֵי לֵית לֵיהּ. אֵינוֹ בָּטוּחַ לִחְיוֹת שִׁבְעָה יָמִים, שֶׁמָּא לְמָחָר יָמוּת. אַבֵּי גַּזָּא. תַּחְתָּיו הָיָה אוֹצָר גָּדוֹל זָהָב וָכֶסֶף טָמוּן. תַּרְחֵיהּ גַּבֵּיהּ. אִיחֵר אֶצְלוֹ שְׁלֹמֹה לְאַשְׁמְדַאי, "תָּרַח" בִּלְשׁוֹן אֲרַמִּי אִיחוּר, כִּדְאָמְרִינַן בְּבָבָא קַמָּא (דף פ.): מַאן תָּרַח – נִיתְרַח שְׁמוּאֵל. הֲוָה קָאֵי לְחוּדֵיהּ. שְׁלֹמֹה אֵצֶל אַשְׁמְדַאי. כְּתוֹעֲפוֹת רְאֵם לוֹ. לְהַקָּדוֹשׁ בָּרוּךְ הוּא, יֵשׁ לוֹ תּוֹעֲפוֹת רְאֵמִים לְמִשְׁלַחְתּוֹ, וְלִיפָּרַע פּוּרְעָנוּת בִּשְׁלִיחוּתוֹ. מַאי רְבוּתַיְיכוּ. שֶׁנִּשְׁתַּבֵּחַ הקב"ה בָּכֶם. עִיזְקְתָךְ. טַבַּעְתּוֹ הָיָה שֵׁם חָקוּק עָלֶיהָ. פַּתְקֵיהּ. דְּחָהוּ. גּוּנְדוֹ. לְבוּשׁוֹ. וּבְאִיסּוּרֵי טְהָרוֹת דְּרַב הַאי רָאִיתִי: קוּדוּ מְקֵידָה שֶׁל חֶרֶס לִשְׁתּוֹת מַיִם (סוטה דף לג.). לָא סְרִיךְ. אֵינוֹ נִדְבָּק לוֹמַר דָּבָר אֶחָד שֶׁל שְׁטוּת כָּל הַיָּמִים, שֶׁזֶּה אוֹמֵר: הָיִיתִי מֶלֶךְ, וְאֵינוֹ אוֹמֵר דְּבַר שְׁטוּת אַחֶרֶת. בָּדְקוּ בְּכַרְעֵיהּ. שֶׁרַגְלָיו שֶׁל שֵׁד דּוֹמוֹת לְשֶׁל תַּרְנְגוֹלִים. בְּמוֹקֵי קָאָתֵי. אֵינוֹ בָּא לִשְׁכַּב יָחֵף אֶלָּא בְּאַנְפִּילָאוֹת, קאלצו"ש בְּלַעַ"ז. מֶלֶךְ וְהֶדְיוֹט. הָיָה שְׁלֹמֹה, לֹא חָזַר שׁוּב לְמַלְכוּתוֹ*. לְדָמָא דְּרֵישָׁא. חוֹלִי כְּאֵב הָרֹאשׁ הַבָּא מֵחֲמַת דָּם. שׁוּרְבִינָא. מִין אֶרֶז, כִּדְאָמְרִינַן בְּרֹאשׁ הַשָּׁנָה (דף כג.) תְּאַשּׁוּר – שׁוּרְבִינָא. וּבִינָא. עֲרָבָה. וְאָסָא דָּרָא. הֲדַס לַח. חִילְפָא. לַפְלָפָה, עֵץ שֶׁשְּׁמוֹ פופליי"ר. וְחִילְפֵי יַמָּא. גירופל"א*. °יַבְלָא. מִין עֵשֶׂב. וַרְדָּא. רוס"א. דְּקָאֵי בְּחַד דָּרָא. כָּל עָלִין שֶׁלּוֹ מִצַּד אֶחָד, זֶה לְמַעְלָה מִזֶּה. לְצִלִּיחְתָּא. כְּאֵב חֲצִי הָרֹאשׁ. בְּזוּזָא חִיוָּרָא. בְּדִינָר שֶׁל כֶּסֶף צָרוּף יִשְׁחָטֶנּוּ. לְהַאי גִּיסָּא דְּכָאֵיב לֵיהּ. שֶׁיָּזוּב הַדָּם עַל חֲצִי הָרֹאשׁ שֶׁשָּׁם הַכְּאֵב. וְלִיתְלְיֵיהּ. לְתַרְנְגוֹלָא שָׁחוּט. בְּסִיפֵי דְּבָבָא. בִּמְזוּזוֹת הַפֶּתַח.

גליון הש"ס

רש"י ד"ה יבלא מין עשב. וכן בחולין דף קה ע"ב כך ריפתא איבלא:

ר"ל כעין מלכות ראשונה שמלך על העליונים. רש"ל

נעגליך בל"ר

[גי' הערוך ערך תרה תרהייה]

פי' בלע לשלמה ס"א בלעה ופי' בלע לטיחקה. מ"ד

סנהדרין כ:

מגילה יא:

[בערוך ערך תלף פי' רוזמרינ"ן]

לְבְרוֹקְתִי – לֵיתֵי עַקְרַבָּא דְּשַׁב חוּמְרֵי וְנֵיבְּשֵׁיהּ בְּטוּלָּא, וְנִישְׁחוֹק תַּרְתֵּי מְנָתָא כּוּחְלָא וַחֲדָא מְנָתָא מִינֵּיהּ, וְלִימְלֵי תְּלָתָא מַכְחֲלֵי בְּהַאי עֵינָא וּתְלָתָא מַכְחֲלֵי בְּהַאי עֵינָא, טְפֵי לָא לִימְלֵי, דְּאִי לָא – פָּקַע עֵינֵיהּ. לְשַׁבְרִירֵי דְּלֵילְיָא – נֵיתֵי שׁוּדְרָא בִּרְקָא וְנֵיסַר חֲדָא כַּרְעָא מִינֵּיהּ וַחֲדָא כַּרְעָא מִכַּלְבָּא, וְנִיטְרְפוּ יָנוּקֵי חַסְפָּא אַבַּתְרֵיהּ, וְלֵימְרוּ לֵיהּ: *"אָסָא כַּלְבָּא אַכְסָא תַּרְנְגוֹלָא", וְלִיגְבֵּי שַׁב אוּמְצֵי מִשִּׁבְעָה בָּתֵּי וְלֵיתְבִינְהוּ נִיהֲלֵיהּ בְּצִינּוֹרָא דְּדַשָּׁא, וְנֵיכְלִינְהוּ *בְּקִלְקוּלֵי דְּמָתָא. בָּתַר הָכִי לִפְשׁוֹט שׁוּדְרָא בִּרְקָא וְנֵימְרוּ הָכִי: "שַׁבְרִירֵי דִּפְלוֹנִי בַּר פְּלוֹנִיתָא שְׁבַקִינְהוּ לִפְלוֹנִי בַּר פְּלוֹנִיתָא וְלִיחֲרוּ לְכַלְבָּא בְּבָבִיתָא דְּעֵינֵיהּ". לְשַׁבְרִירֵי דִּימָמָא – לֵיתֵי שִׁבְעָה סוּמָּקֵי מִגַּוּוֹא דְּחֵיוָתָא וְנִיטְוִינְהוּ אַחַסְפָּא דְּאוּמָּנָא, וְלֵיתִיב אִיהוּ מִגַּוַּאי וְאִינִישׁ אַחֲרִינָא מֵאַבְּרַאי, וְנֵימָא לֵיהּ: "עֲוִירָא, הַב לִי דְּאֵיכוֹל", וְנֵימָא לֵיהּ הָאֵיךְ: "פְּתִיחָא, סַב אֵיכוֹל", וּבָתַר דְּאָכֵיל לִיתַבְרֵיהּ לְחַסְפָּא, דְּאִי לָא – הָדְרִי עִילָּוֵיהּ. לְדָמָא דְּאָתֵי מִנְּחִירָא – לֵיתֵי גַּבְרָא כֹּהֵן דִּשְׁמֵיהּ לֵוִי, וְלִיכְתּוֹב לֵיהּ לֵוִי לְמַפְרֵעַ. וְאִי לָא, לֵיתֵי אִינִישׁ מֵעָלְמָא, וְנִיכְתּוֹב לֵיהּ: "אֲנָא פַּפִּי שֵׁילָא בַּר סוּמָּקֵי" לְמַפְרֵעַ. וְאִי לָא, נִיכְתּוֹב לֵיהּ הָכִי: "טַעַם דְּלִי בְּמֵי כֶסֶף טַעַם דְּלִי בְּמֵי פְּגַם". וְאִי לָא, לֵיתֵי עִיקָּרָא דְּאַסְפַּסְתָּא, וְאַשְׁלָא דְּפוּרְיָיא עַתִּיקָא, וְקוּרְטָסָא, וּמוֹרִיקֵי וְסוּמָּקָא דְּלוּלִיבָא, וְנִקְלִינְהוּ בַּהֲדֵי הֲדָדֵי, וְלֵיתֵי גְּבָבָא דְּעַמְרָא וְנִיגְדּוֹל תַּרְתֵּי פְּתִילָתָא, וְלִטְמִישׁ בְּחַלָּא וְנִיגְדַּבַּל בְּקִיטְמָא הָדֵין, וְנֵיתִיב בִּנְחִירֵיהּ. וְאִי לָא, לֵיחֲזֵי אַמַּת הַמַּיִם דְּאָזְלַת מִמִּזְרָח כְּלַפֵּי מַעֲרָב, וְנִפְסַע וְנֵיקוּם חַד כַּרְעָא לְהַאי גִּיסָא וְחַד כַּרְעָא לְהַאי גִּיסָא, וְנִישְׁקוֹל טִינָא בִּידֵיהּ דִּימִינָא מִתּוּתֵי כַּרְעָא דִּשְׂמָאלֵיהּ, וּבִידֵיהּ דִּשְׂמָאלָא מִתּוּתֵי כַּרְעָא דִּימִינֵיהּ, וְנִיגְדּוֹל תַּרְתֵּי פְּתִילָתָא דְּעַמְרָא וְנִיטְמִישׁ בְּטִינָא, וְנֵיתִיב בִּנְחִירֵיהּ. וְאִי לָא, לֵיתִיב תּוּתֵי מַרְזְבָא וְנַיְיתוּ מַיָּא וְלִישְׁדוּ עֲלֵיהּ, וְלֵימְרוּ: "כִּי הֵיכִי דְּפָסְקִי הָנֵי מַיָּא, לִיפְסוֹק דָּמֵיהּ דִּפְלָנְיָא בַּר פְּלָנִיתָא". לְדָמָא דְּאָתֵי מִפּוּמָּא – בָּדְקִינַן לֵיהּ בְּגִילָא דְּחִיטְתָא, אִי סָרֵיךְ – מֵרֵיאָה קָאָתֵי וְאִית לֵיהּ תַּקַּנְתָּא, וְאִי לָא – מִכַּבְדָּא קָאָתֵי וְלֵית לֵיהּ תַּקַּנְתָּא. אֲמַר לֵיהּ רַב אַמִּי לְרַב אַשִׁי, וְהָאֲנַן אִיפְּכָא תְּנַן: *"נִיטַּל הַכָּבֵד וְלֹא נִשְׁתַּיֵּיר הֵימֶנָּה כְּלוּם, הָרֵיאָה שֶׁנִּיקְּבָה אוֹ שֶׁחָסְרָה! אֲמַר לֵיהּ: כֵּיוָן דְּמִפּוּמֵיהּ קָאָתֵי, אֵימַר אִיתְמוּחֵי אִיתְמַח. אָמַר מָר: אִי מֵרֵיאָה קָאָתֵי אִית לֵיהּ תַּקַּנְתָּא. מַאי תַּקַּנְתֵּיהּ? לֵיתֵי שִׁבְעָה *כּוּנֵי מִפִּירְמָא דְּסִילְקָא, וְשִׁבְעָה כּוּנֵי פִּירְמָא דְּכָרְתֵי, וַחֲמִשָּׁה כּוּנֵי פְּרִידָא, וּתְלָתָא כּוּנֵי דְּטַלְפְּחֵי, וְכוּנָא דְּכַמּוֹנָא וְכוּנָא דְּחַבְלֵי, וּכְנֶגְדָּן כַּנְתָּא פְּטִירְתָא, וְלִיבְשִׁיל וְלֵיכוֹל, וְלִישְׁתֵּי אַבַּתְרֵיהּ שִׁיכְרָא חֲרִיפָא דְּטֵבֵת. לְכָבָא – אָמַר רַבָּה בַּר רַב הוּנָא: לֵיתֵי תּוּמָא יְחִידָאָה וְנִימְרְסֵיהּ בְּמִשְׁחָא וּמִילְחָא, וְנֶתְבֵּיהּ אַטּוּפְרַאי דְּאַלְיוֹנָא דְּהַהוּא גִּיסָא דְּכָיֵיב לֵיהּ, וְנֶהְדַּר לֵיהּ גַּדַּנְפָּא דְּלִישָׁא, וְנִיזְדַּהַר לְבִישְׂרֵיהּ דְּקָשֵׁי לְחִיוָּרָא. לְחִינְכֵי – אָמַר רַבִּי יוֹחָנָן: *חוּמְתִּי כִּי מַמְרוּ, וְעִיקָּרָא דְּחוּמְתִּי עָדִיף מִמַּמְרוּ, וְנִינְקוֹט בְּפוּמֵּיהּ; הָנֵי לְאוּקוּמֵי. לְבַשּׁוּלֵי – לַיְיתֵי פָּאֲרֵי דְּרֵישׁ נַפְיָא, וְטַלְפְּחֵי בְּעַפְרַיְיהוּ, וְשׁוּבְלִילְתָא וְחוּמְרְתָא דִּכְשׁוּתָא, וְנִינְקוֹט כְּאַמְגּוּזָא בְּפוּמֵּיהּ. לְאִיפְתּוּחֵי – לִינְפַּח לֵיהּ חַבְרֵיהּ תַּחְלֵי חִיוָּרְתָא בְּגִילָא דְּחִיטְתָא. לְאַסּוּקֵי – לֵיתֵי עַפְרָא מְטוּלָּא דְּבֵית הַכִּסֵּא, וְנִיגְבּוֹל בְּדוּבְשָׁא וְנֵיכוֹל, דְּמַעֲלֵי לֵיהּ. לְבִרְסָם – לֵיתֵי כִּי פִּיסְתְּקָא דְּנִישְׁדּוֹר, וְכִי אַמְגּוּזָא דְּחֶלְבְּנִיתָא דּוּבְשָׁנִיתָא, וּמְלֵי תַּרְוָודָא דּוּבְשָׁא חִיוָּרָא, וּמְלֵי נַטְלָא בַּת מְחוֹזָא חַמְרָא נְקִידָא, וְנִישְׁלוֹקִינְהוּ בַּהֲדֵי הֲדָדֵי, וְכִי בַּשֵּׁיל נִשְׁדּוֹר בַּשֵּׁיל לֵיהּ כּוּלֵּיהּ. וְאִי לָא, לֵיתֵי רְבִיעֲתָא דַּחֲלָבָא דְּעִיזָּא חִיוַּרְתִּי וְנִיטַּיְיפֵיהּ

רש"י

לִבְרוֹקְתִי. חוֹלִי שֶׁבָּעַיִן, שֶׁקּוֹרִין טייל"א. דְּשַׁב חוּמְרֵי. מְנוּמָּר בְּשֶׁבַע גְּוָונִין מֵחֲמַת זִקְנָה. וְנֵיבְּשֵׁיהּ בְּטוּלָּא. כְּלוֹמַר, שֶׁלֹּא מֵחֲמַת שֶׁמֶשׁ. תַּרְתֵּי מְנָתָא כּוּחְלָא וַחֲדָא מְנָתָא מִינֵּיהּ. שְׁנֵי חֲלָקִים כְּחוֹל וְחֵלֶק אֶחָד מִמֶּנּוּ. תְּלָתָא מַכְחֲלֵי. מִכְחוֹל הוּא כְּנַף עוֹף אוֹ כַּף רָחָב דַּק שֶׁל עֵץ שֶׁנּוֹטֵל בּוֹ הַכְּחוֹל וְנוֹתֵן בָּעַיִן. תְּלָתָא מַכְחֲלֵי. שְׁלֹשָׁה פְּעָמִים. לִימְלֵי. יָשׂוּם בְּעֵינוֹ. דְּאִי לָא. מִיזְדַּהַר, דְּלָא לִימְלֵי טְפֵי – פָּקַע עֵינֵיהּ. לְשַׁבְרִירֵי דְּלֵילְיָא. סַנְוֵרִים הַבָּאוֹת עַל הָאָדָם בַּלַּיְלָה. שׁוּדְרָא בִּרְקָא. חֶבֶל שֶׁל שֵׂיעָר בְּהֵמָה, וְשֶׁל זְנַב סוּס וּפָרָה. וְנֵיסַר חֲדָא כַּרְעָא מִינֵּיהּ וַחֲדָא כַּרְעָא מִכַּלְבָּא. יִקְשׁוֹר אֶחָד מֵרַגְלָיו וְרֶגֶל הַכֶּלֶב בִּשְׁנֵי רָאשֵׁי הַחֶבֶל. וְנִטְרְפוּ יָנוּקָא חַסְפָּא אַבַּתְרֵיהּ. יַקִּשְׁקְשׁוּ תִּינוֹקוֹת שִׁבְרֵי חֲרָסִים אַחֲרָיו. וְיֹאמְרוּ. לַחַשׁ זֶה. אָסָא כַּלְבָּא אַכְסָא תַּרְנְגוֹל. זָקֵן כֶּלֶב, שׁוֹטֶה תַּרְנְגוֹל. אוּמְצֵי. חֲתִיכוֹת בָּשָׂר. וְנִתְבִינְהוּ נִיהֲלֵיהּ. בְּנֵי הַבָּתִּים לְהָנָךְ אוּמְצֵי בְּצִינּוֹרָא דְּדַשָּׁא. קִלְקוּלֵי. אַשְׁפּוֹת. לִיפְשׁוֹט. יַתִּיר הַקֶּשֶׁר מֵרַגְלוֹ. בְּבָבִיתָא דְּעֵינֵיהּ. בְּבָבַת עֵינוֹ. סוּמָּקֵי. טְחוֹלִים. אַחַסְפָּא דְּאוּמָּנָא. כְּלִי חֶרֶס מְנוּוָּל, שֶׁמַּקִּיזִין לְתוֹכוֹ דָּם. וְנֵימָא לֵיהּ עֲוִירָא. לִפְתִיחָא: הַב לִי וְאֵיכוֹל. פַּפִּי שֵׁילָא כו'. לַחַשׁ הוּא. טַעַם דְּלִי בְּמֵי כֶסֶף. לַחַשׁ הוּא. אַשְׁלָא דְּפוּרְיָא. חֶבֶל שֶׁל מִטָּה. וְקוּרְטָסָא. נְיָיר שֶׁל מוֹכִין. וּמוֹרִיקָא. קרו"ג. וְסוּמָּקָא דְּלוּלָבָא. דָּבָר אָדוֹם הַגָּדֵל בַּלּוּלָב. וְנִגְדִּיל פְּתִילָתָא. לְשׁוֹן גְּדִילִים, יַעֲשֶׂה פְּתִילָה מִן הַצֶּמֶר. וְלִטְמִישׁ בְּחַלָּא. יַשְׁרֶה בְּחוֹמֶץ. וְנִיגְדַּבֵּיל. יְגַלְגְּלוּ בָּאֵפֶר, וְיִדָּבֵק הָאֵפֶר בּוֹ. וְנִשְׁדוּ עֲלֵיהּ. דֶּרֶךְ מַרְזֵב. סָרֵיךְ. נִדְבָּק הַקַּשׁ בַּדָּם. גִּילָא. אישטריי"ש. כֵּיוָן. דְּדָמָא דְּכַבְדָּא שֶׁהִיא תְּלוּיָה לְמַטָּה מִן הָרֵיאָה, עוֹלֶה לְמַעְלָה וְנָפֵיק דֶּרֶךְ הַפֶּה. אֵימַר אִתְמוּחֵי אִתְמַח. כּוּלָּהּ כַּבְדָּא, וְלֹא נִשְׁתַּיֵּיר הֵימֶנָּה כְּלוּם, וְנָפַל לָרֵיאָה דֶּרֶךְ קְנֵה הַכָּבֵד, שֶׁמְּחוּבָּר לַקָּנֶה שֶׁל רֵיאָה. כּוּנֵי. מְלֹא אֶגְרוֹף. פִּירְמָא דְּסִילְקָא. קְנִיבַת תְּרָדִים, מלינדור"א. פְּרִידָא. מִין עֵשֶׂב, וי"א: מדיירישר"ש. וּכְנֶגְדָּן. כְּשִׁיעוּר כָּל אֵלּוּ. כַּנְתָּא פְּטִירְתָּא. אנטריי"ל שֶׁל בְּהֵמָה שֶׁהָיְתָה פֶּטֶר רֶחֶם לְאִמָּהּ. לְכָבָא. חוֹלִי הַשִּׁינַּיִם הַפְּנִימִים. תּוּמָא יְחִידָאָה. רֹאשׁ שׁוּם שֶׁלֹּא הָיָה בּוֹ אֶלָּא צֶלַע אֶחָד. וְנִמְרְסֵיהּ. יִשְׁחָקֶנּוּ. אַטּוּפְרָא דְּאַלְיוֹנָא. עַל צִפּוֹרֶן שֶׁל בּוֹהֶן יָד. וְנִזְדַּהַר לְבִשְׂרֵיהּ. שֶׁלֹּא יִגַּע אוֹתוֹ שׁוּם בִּבְשָׂרוֹ. דְּקָשֵׁי לְחִיוָּרָא. צָרַעַת. לְחִינְכֵי. הָאֲבַעְבּוּעוֹת הַגְּדֵלִים בַּגָּרוֹן כְּמִין גלנ"ט, וּבִלְשׁוֹן רוֹמִי אשטרנגיילו"ן. חוּמְתִּי כִּי מַמְרוּ. עָלֵי שֶׁל חוֹמֶס = פילטר"ו, טוֹב לִרְפוּאָה זוֹ, כְּמִין עֵשֶׂב שֶׁקּוֹרִין "מַמְרוּ" בִּלְשׁוֹן אֲרַמִּי. וְעִיקָּרָא דְּחוּמְתִּי. שׁוֹרֶשׁ הַחִימּוּס, פילטר"ו. עָדִיף. לִרְפוּאָה מִמַּמְרוּ, מַמְרוּ – שבדמוני', לְשׁוֹן מוֹרִי. הָנֵי. חוּמְתִּי וּמַמְרוּ. לְאוּקוּמֵי. הַחוֹלִי שֶׁלֹּא יִנְפַּח יוֹתֵר מִדַּאי. לְבַשּׁוּלֵי. הָאֲבַעְבּוּעוֹת, שֶׁתִּתְבַּקֵּעַ לֵחָה שֶׁלָּהֶן לְתוֹכָן, שֶׁתְּהֵא יוֹצְאָה כְּשֶׁיִּבָּקְעוּ אוֹתוֹ. פָּאֲרֵי דְּרֵישׁ נַפְיָא. סוּבִּים גְּדוֹלִים שֶׁצָּפִין לְמַעְלָה בַּנָּפָה כְּשֶׁמְּרַקְּדִין. וְטַלְפְּחֵי בְּעַפְרַיְיהוּ. עֲדָשִׁים עִם עָפָר שֶׁנִּתְלַשׁוּ בָּהֶן. וְשׁוּבְלִילְתָא. תִּלְתָּן פינוגר"י. וְחוּמְרְתָא דִּכְשׁוּתָא. פֶּרַח שֶׁבַּכְּשׁוּת, הומלו"ן. כְּאַמְגּוּזָא. כְּשִׁיעוּר אֱגוֹז. לְפַתּוּחֵי. הָאֲבַעְבּוּעוֹת שֶׁל אשטרנגיילו"ן, שֶׁיִּבָּקְעוּ וְתֵצֵא הַלֵּיחָה. לִינְפַּח לֵיהּ. בִּגְרוֹנוֹ. בְּגִילָא דְּחִיטְתָא. שֶׁהוּא חָלוּל, וְיַכְנִיס זֶרַע הַשַּׁחֲלַיִם לְתוֹכוֹ בְּרֹאשׁוֹ אֶחָד וְיַכְנִיסֶנּוּ בְּתוֹךְ פִּיו שֶׁל חוֹלֶה עַד הַבְּלִיעָה, וְיִנְפַּח חֲבֵירוֹ בָּרֹאשׁ הָאַחֵר וְיֵלְכוּ הַשַּׁחֲלַיִם וְיִפְּלוּ, וְיֵחָנוּ עַל הַחוֹלִי. לְאַסּוּקֵי. לְהַעֲלוֹת בָּשָׂר לִרְפוּאוֹת הַבִּיקּוּעַ. מְטוּלָּא דְּבֵית הַכִּסֵּא. מִתַּחַת צֵל אֲבָנִים הַמְסוּדָּרוֹת לְבֵית הַכִּסֵּא בַּשָּׂדוֹת, וּמְתוּקָּנוֹת כְּעֵין מוֹשָׁב. לְבִרְסָם. חוֹלִי שֶׁקּוֹרִין לוריי"ר, וְהוּא בָּא מִן הָרֹאשׁ דֶּרֶךְ הַחוֹטֶם. כִּי פִּיסְתְּקָא דְּנִשְׁדּוֹר. כְּשִׁיעוּר גלנט שֶׁל אֶרֶז, מִסֵּס נִשְׁדּוֹר שֶׁקּוֹרִין אמוניק"א. חֶלְבְּנִיתָא דּוּבְשָׁנִיתָא. חֶלְבְּנָה מְתוּקָה, שֶׁקּוֹרִין גלמ"א. תַּרְוָודָא. כַּף. נַטְלָא. כְּלִי מַחֲזִיק רְבִיעִית. חַמְרָא נְקִידָא. יַיִן צָלוּל יָפֶה, שֶׁאֵינוֹ אָדוֹם. וְכִי בַּשֵּׁיל נִשְׁדּוֹר בַּשֵּׁיל כּוּלֵּיהּ. זֶה סִימָן יִהְיֶה לְךָ: לִכְשֶׁיִּתְבַּשֵּׁל הַנִּשְׁדּוֹר – בְּיָדוּעַ שֶׁשְּׁאָר סַמָּנִין מְבוּשָּׁלִין, לְפִי שֶׁהוּא קָשֶׁה. וְנִטַּיְיפֵיהּ

תוספות

לברוקתי • הכא משמע דיש לה רפואה, וכן בפ' "המוציא יין" (שבת דף עח.) נמי קאמר: שכן כוחלין לברוקתי. וקשה: דבבכורות (דף לח:) חשיב ליה גבי מומין הקבועין! ואומר רבינו יצחק: דכל מה שאינו עובר מאיליו, או ע"י רפואה קלה – חשיב מום קבוע. אי נמי, רפואה דהכא וד"המוציא" – היינו בתחילת החולי, אבל בסוף החולי – אין לו רפואה.

לכבא • שינים, כדפי' בקונטרס כאן, ולא כמו שפירש בעלמא (ע"ז דף כח.*) דהיינו חניכיים. מדאמרינן ב"ערבי פסחים" (דף קיג.): לא תעקר ככא, וכן בחולין (דף נט:): נתור ככי ושיני דגברי – וזה לא שייך לומר בחניכיים.

רב

[גירסת הערוך אשא]

[עי' תוס' שם ד"ה ככי]

[ב"ק כא. ובע"ז כח. כתב רש"י תרגום מאשפות יריס אביון מקלקלתא מריס תשוכא]

חולין מב.

[נ"א בוני אבל בגירסת ערוך ערך כן ג איתא כוני ופירושו חופן ועי' בשבת קי: הגירסא שלפנינו בוני ופרש"י שם בוני מלא אגרוף ובעירובין כט: פרש"י בוני מדות ולקמן ע"ב ודף ע. בוני פרש"י מלא אגרוף וע"ע שבת סב. ד"ה ושבעה]

[בערוך ערך חמת איתא חומתי וממרו פי' בלע"ז פילטרו"ן]

וְנִיטַיְיפֵיהּ אַתְּלָת קִלְחֵי כְּרָבָא, וְנִיבְחֲשֵׁיהּ בְּגַוְוזָא דְּמַרְמְהִין, וְכִי בַּשֵּׁיל גַּוְוזָא בְּמַרְמְהִין בַּשֵּׁיל לֵיהּ כּוּלֵּיהּ. וְאִי לָא, לֵיתֵי נִפְקֵי דְּכַלְבָּא חִיוָּרָא וְנִיגְבּוֹל בְּנַטְפָּא, וְכַמָּה דְּאֶפְשָׁר נִפְקָא לָא נֵיכוֹל, דִּמְפָרֵיק. לְגִירָא — לֵיתֵי גִּירָא דְּלֵילִיתָא וְנֵיפְכֵיהּ, וְנִשְׁדֵּי מַיָּא עִלָּוֵיהּ וְנִשְׁתֵּי. וְאִי לָא, לֵיתֵי מִמַּיָּא דְּאִישְׁתֵּי מִינַּיְיהוּ כַּלְבָּא בְּלֵילְיָא, וְנִיזְדַּהַר מִגִּילּוּיָא. לְגִילּוּיָא — *אַנְפָּקָא דְּחַמְרָא חַיָּיא. לְמוּרְסָא — אַנְפָּקָא דְּחַמְרָא בְּאָהֳלָא *תּוֹלָאנָא. לְפִירְחָא דְּלִיבָּא — לֵיתֵי תְּלָת בְּרוֹשְׁיָיאתָא דְּשַׂעֲרֵי וְנִשְׁטְרִינְהוּ בְּכַמְכָּא דְּלָא עֲבַר עִלָּוֵיהּ אַרְבְּעִין יוֹמִין, וְנֵיכוֹל, וְנִשְׁתֵּי אַבַּתְרַיְיהוּ חַמְרָא מַרְקָא. א"ל רַב אַחָא מִדִּיפְתִּי לְרָבִינָא: וְכָל שֶׁכֵּן דְּפָרַח לִיבֵּיהּ! אֲמַר לֵיהּ: אֲנָא — לְיוּקְרָא דְּלִיבָּא אֲמַרִי. לְפִירְחָא דְּלִיבָּא — לֵיתֵי תְּלָת בְּרוֹשְׁיָיאתָא דְּחִיטֵּי וְנִישְׁטְרִינְהוּ בְּדוּבְשָׁא וְנֵיכוֹל, וְנִישְׁתֵּי אַבַּתְרַיְיהוּ חַמְרָא חַיָּיא. לְצַרְחָא דְּלִיבָּא — *לֵיתֵי תְּלָת *בֵּיעֵי נִינְיָיא וּבֵיעֲתָא דְּכַמּוֹנָא וּבֵיעֲתָא דְּשׁוּמְשְׁמֵי וְלֵיכוֹל. לְכָאֵב מֵעַי — לֵיתֵי תְּלָת מְאָה פִּלְפְּלֵי אֲרִיכָתָא, וְכָל יוֹמֵי נִשְׁתֵּי מְאָה מִינַּיְיהוּ בְּחַמְרָא. רָבִין דְּמִן נֶרֶשׁ עֲבַד לָהּ לִבְרַתֵּיהּ דְּרַב אַשִׁי מְאָה וְחַמְשִׁין מֵהָנֵי דִּידָן, וְאִתַּסְיָא. לְכִירְצָא — אַנְפָּקָא דְּחַמְרָא בְּאַטְרְפָא דַּעֲרָאָה. לְכִירְצָא חִיוָּרָא — לֵיתֵי בִּיזְרָא גַּלְגִּילָא וְנִיצַיְירָה בְּשִׁיסְתַּג, וְנִיתַיְירֵיהּ בְּמַיָּא וְנִשְׁתֵּיהּ, וְנִזְדַּהַר מִבִּינְתָא, דְּאִי לָא — מְנַקְּבָא לָהּ לְמַעְיָינֵיהּ. לְמֵיסַר — סִיסִין רְטִיבָא בְּמַיָּא; לְמִישְׁרָא — יְבִישְׁתָּא בְּמַיָּא, וְסִימָנָךְ: אִיצָא רְטִיבָא דְּסָכַר נַהֲרָא. לִטְחָלָא — לֵיתֵי שַׁב בִּינֵּי דְּמַיָּא וְנֵייבְּשִׁינְהוּ בְּטוּלָּא, וְכָל יוֹמָא נִישְׁתֵּי תַּרְתֵּי וּתְלָתָא בְּחַמְרָא. וְאִי לָא, לֵיתֵי טְחָלָא דְּצִיפַּרְתָּא דְּלָא אִיפַּתַּח וְנַטְּחְיָא בְּתַנּוּרָא, וְנוֹקֵי לַהֲדֵיהּ וְנֵימָא: "כִּי הֵיכִי דְּיָבֵישׁ הַאי טְחָלָא, נֵייבַשׁ טְחָלְיָא דִּפְלוֹנִי בַּר פְּלוֹנִיתָא". וְאִי לָא, נִיטַחְיֵיהּ בֵּינֵי אוּרְבֵּי דְּבֵיתָא חֲדַתָּא, וְנֵימָא הָכִי. וְאִי לָא, *לִיבָּקֵי שַׁכְבָא דְּשָׁכֵיב בְּשַׁבְּתָא, וְנִישְׁקְלֵיהּ לְיָדֵיהּ וְנוֹתְבָה אַטְּחָלֵיהּ, וְנֵימָא: כִּי הֵיכִי דְּיָבֵישׁ הָא יָדָא, נֵייבַשׁ טְחָלְיָא דִּפְלוֹנִי בַּר פְּלוֹנִיתָא. וְאִי לָא, נֵיתֵי בִּינִיתָא וְנִיטְוְויֵיהּ בֵּי נַפָּחָא, וְנֵיכְלֵיהּ בְּמַיָּא דְּבֵי נַפָּחָא וְנִישְׁתֵּי מִמַּיָּא דְּבֵי נַפָּחָא. הַהִיא עִיזָּא דַּהֲוַת שָׁתְיָא מַיָּא דְּבֵי נַפָּחָא, אִישְׁתְּחִיט וְלָא אִישְׁתַּכַּח לָהּ טְחָלָא. וְאִי לָא, לִיפְתַּח חָבִיתָא דְּחַמְרָא לִשְׁמֵיהּ. א"ל רַב אַחָא בְּרֵיהּ דְּרָבָא לְרַב אַשִׁי: אִי אִית לֵיהּ חָבִיתָא דְּחַמְרָא, לָא אָתֵי לְקַמֵּיהּ דְּמָר! אֶלָּא, מַרְגַּל בְּפַת שַׁחֲרִית, דִּמְעַלְּיָא לְכוּלֵּי גּוּפֵיהּ. לְרוֹשְׁחַתָּא — לֵיתֵי אַקִיקָא וְאִילָוָא, וְאַסְפִּירְכָא וּמַרְתְּכָא, וְחוּמְרְתָא דְּפִילוֹן וְשִׁיאֲפָא דַּחֲמִימְתָּא, וְנִינְקַט בְּשַׁחֲקֵי דְּכִיתָנָא בְּקַיְיטָא וְדַעֲמַר גּוּפְנָא בְּסִיתְוָא. וְאִי לָא, לִישְׁתֵּי שִׁיכְרָא מַרְקָא. לְשִׁיגְרוֹנָא — לֵיתֵי פַּתְיָא דְּמוֹנִינֵי, וְנִיגַנְדְּרֵיהּ שִׁיתִּין זִימְנֵי אַהָא מְטַחְתֵּיהּ, וְשִׁיתִּין זִימְנֵי אַהָא מְטַחְתֵּיהּ. לְצַמִירְתָּא — נֵיתֵי תְּלָת נִיטוֹפַיְיתָא מִישְׁחָא דְּכוּפְרָא, וּתְלָת נִיטוֹפַיְיתָא אִיצְרָא דְּכַרְתֵּי, וּתְלָת נִיטוֹפַיְיתָא דְּחַמְרָא נְקִידָא, וְלִישְׁדֵּי לֵיהּ לְאִישׁ בְּאַמָּה וּלְאִשָּׁה בְּאוֹתוֹ מָקוֹם. וְאִי לָא, לֵיתֵי אוּנָא דְּזִיקָא, וְלִתְלֵי לֵיהּ לְאִישׁ בְּאַמָּה וּלְאִשָּׁה בַּדַּדִּין. וְאִי לָא, לֵיתֵי חוּטָא דְּזְהוֹרִיתָא דְּשַׁדְתֵּיהּ דּוֹמָה בַּת דּוֹמָה, וְלִיתְלֵי לֵיהּ לְאִישׁ בְּאַמָּה וּלְאִשָּׁה בַּדַּדִּין. וְאִי לָא, לֵיתֵי כִּינָּה *דְּזָכָר וּנְקֵבָה, *וְלִיתְלֵי לֵיהּ לְאִישׁ בְּאַמָּה וּלְאִשָּׁה בְּאוֹתוֹ מָקוֹם, וְכִי מַשְׁתִּין — נַשְׁתִּין אַסִּיסְנָא יְבֵישְׁתָּא בְּצִינּוֹרָא דְּדַשָּׁא; וְנֶעֱיַין בְּחוּמְרְתָא דְּנָפְקָ' מִינֵּיהּ, דִּמְעַלְּיָא לְכוּלְּהוּ צִימְרָא. לְצִימְרָא בָּרָא — לֵיתֵי תְּלָתָא גְּרִיבֵי סוּפְלֵי וּתְלָתָא גְּרִיבֵי אַטְרַף אַדְרָא, וְנִישְׁלוֹקִינְהוּ כָּל חַד לְחוּדֵיהּ וְלֵיתִיב בֵּינַיְיהוּ, וְלִתְבִינְהוּ בְּתַרְתֵּי מְשִׁיכְלֵי וְנֵיתֵי פְּתוּרָא וּנְנַח עִילָּוֵיהּ, וְנִיקוּם מֵעִילָּוֵי הַאי וְלוֹתִיב עִילָּוֵי הַאי, וּמֵעִילָּוֵי הַאי וְלוֹתִיב עִילָּוֵי הַאי, עַד דְּנֵיסַק בֵּיהּ הַבְלָא, וְלִסְחֵי מִינַּיְיהוּ. וְכִי שָׁתֵי, מִמַּיָּא דְּאַדְרָא לִישְׁתֵּי, מִמַּיָּא דְּסוּפְלֵי לָא לִישְׁתֵּי, מִשּׁוּם דִּמְעַקְּרֵי. לְצִימְרָא גַּוְּונָא — לֵיתֵי שִׁבְעָה בּוּנֵי דְּסִילְקָא מִשַּׁב מִשָּׁארֵי, וְנִישְׁלוֹקִינְהוּ בְּעַפְרַיְיהוּ וְנֵיכוֹל, וְנִישְׁתֵּי אַטְרַף אַדְרָא בְּשִׁיכְרָא אוֹ
עִנְבֵי

ונטייפיה אתלת קלחי דכרבא. יטיפנו על שלשה קלחי כרוב בכלי. ונבחשיה בגוזא דמרמהין. יגיס את הקדירה בקיסם של עץ ששמו מרמהי"ן. נפקא דכלבא חיורא. צואה של כלב לבן. ונגבול בנטפא. נרי. וכמה דאפשר. לו ברפואה אחרת, או להתאפק בחוליו. ניפקא לא ניכול. לא יאכל צואת הכלבים. דמפרק. מנתק אבריו. לגירא. חולי שקורין אשפונט"א. גירא דליליתא. חץ של לילית, אבן שעשויה כחץ ונופלת עם הברד. וניפכיה. העוקץ למטה ובית יד למעלה. וניזדהר מגילויא. שיהו במקום שאין נחש מצוי. אנפקא. זהו רביעית, וכן שם הכלי. למורסא. קלו"ג. אהלא תלאנא. *אהלות אדום, כמין תולעת שני. לפירחא דליבא. שלבו פורח, פשמיי"ר בלע"ז. ברושייתא. חלות. ונשטרינהו בכמכא. ישרה אותם בכותח, טרכנריי"ד בלע"ז. דלא עבר עליה ארבעין יומין. שנעשה הכותח. מרקא. מזוג במים הרבה. דפרח ליביה. שדברים חלשים הן כל אלו, ומתישין כחו של אדם. ליוקרא דליבא. שלבו כבד עליו. לצרחא דליבא. כאב הלב. ניניא. מינט"ה. מהני דידן. פילפלין שלנו. לכירצא. תולעים שבמעים. אטרפא דעראה. עלה של עץ ארע שקורין לורי"ר ופריו קורין ביי"ש. ביזרא דגלגילא. זרע אורוג"א. וניצירה בשיסתג. יקשרנו במטלית בגד של צמר גפן. ונזדהר מבינתא. יזהר שלא יבלע את גרגיר הזרע. למעייניה. למעיו. למיסר. לעצור את השלשול. סיסין. פוליאו"ל. למישרי. לשלשל אדם עצור. וסימניך. שלא תחליף לשתות לח לשלשל ויבש לעצור. איצא. שם עשב, וכשהוא לח סוכרין בו נהרות – כך הלח סותם. לטחלא. שטחול שלו נפוח וגדול, מחמת חולי. שב ביני דמיא. שבע עלוקות של מים, בלע"ז שנשוא"ש. ציפרתא דלא איפתח. עז שלא ילדה. וניקו להדיה. יעמוד כנגדו. ואי לא. אי ליכא תנורא. ניטחייה. לההוא טחלא. ביני אורבי. יטיח אותו בכותל, וידבק בין שורות הכותל, וייבש שם. ולימא הכי. כי היכי דיביש האי טחלא כו'. ליבקי שכבא. יטרח עד שידע היכן יש מת שמת בשבת. ליבקי. לשון בקיאות. ונשקליה לידיה. דשכבא. וניתיב להדיה טחלא. דחולה.

ביניתא. דג. ונטווייה בנורא דבי נפחא. יצלנו בגחלים שלפני הנפח. מיא דבי נפחא. אותם שמכבה בהן את הברזל. ליפתח חביתא דחמרא לשמיה. יקנה חבית של יין לשתייתו. כלומר, ישתה יין טוב תמיד הרבה. לא אתי קמי דמר. לשאול רפואה, שהיין רפואה לו. לרושחתא. תחתוניות. אקיקא. עשב ששמו קקול"י. אילוא. אלואיי"ן. אספרכא. כסף חי. מרתכא. קוגילו"ן, והוא מפסולת הכסף, מקום שחופרין כסף מן הקרקע ויוצקים אותו ומעלה ריתחא, והוא מרתכא. חומרתא דפילון. בוטו"ן שהנשים תולות בצואריהן, של זהב או של כסף, ונותן בו שמן שמעורב בו מין בושם ששמו פילון, ודומה לעלי גפנים, כדתניא בת"כ: שלא יערב קימום במר, מי גלובקיא בשמן, עלי גפנים בפילון. ושיאפא דחמימתא. צואת יונים, ולשון מורי: צואת תרנגולין. ונינקיט. כל אלו. בשחקי דכיתנא. שהם קרים בקייטא. ובדעמר גופנא. שהן חמים בסתוא, ויניח באותו מקום. לשגרונא. חולי הירכים והקלבוסת, שקורין הנק"א. פתיא דמוניני. כלי מלא ציר דגים קטנים. ולגנדריה שתין זמני אהא מטחתא. יגלגלו ששים פעמים על ירך זה למעלה, בקילבוסת שקורין הנק"א. לצמרתא. אבן הגדילה בגיד, ועוצרת השתן. ניטופייתא. טיפות. משחא דכופרא. פסולת של זפת, והוא עיטרן. איצרא דכרתי. סחיטת כרישין. חמרא נקידא. יין נקי. אונא דזיקא. אוזן של נוד. חוטא דזהוריתא דשדתי' דומה בת דומה. חוט של זהורית שטוותו אשה חשודה בת חשודה. אסיסנא יבישתא. על סנה יבש. ונעיין בחומרתא דנפקא מיניה. יהא זהיר באבן היוצאת ממנו לשומרה. דמעלי לכולה צמרי. חולי שקורין *פיוור"י. גריבי. סאין. סופלי. גרעיני תמרים. אטרף אדרא. עלין של עץ ששמו אדר. משיכלי. עריבות. וכי שתי. דקיימא לן: הרוחץ בחמין שותה מהם, והם רפואה לו, במסכת שבת (דף מא.). ממיא דאדרא. לישתי, אבל ממיא דסופלי – לא לישתי. דמעקרי. עושין אותו עקר מלהוליד. בוני. מלא יד. משב משארי. משבעת ערוגות. בעפרייהו. עפר העולה בשרשיהם.
ענבי

מלשון הבורית והאהל. רש"ל

[גי' הערוך ערך אהל א תולענא]

ס"א ליכול תלת ביעי ביעתא בניניא וביעתא וכו'

[פי' ענין חיפוש. ערוך ערך בק ב]

פי' מאוס ומאסה

[ב"ב מח: ב"מ פו.]

פי' כשיעור ביעי

פי' קדחת

ס"א ולישדי

ענבי תאלא במים. לחזזיתא — ליתי שב חיטי ארזנייתא וניקלינהו אמרא חדתא, ונפיק משחא מינייהו ונישוף. רב שימי בר אשי עבד ליה להההוא גוי לדבר אחר, ואיתסי. אמר שמואל: האי מאן דמחו ליה *באלונכי דפרסאי מיחייא לא חיי, אדהכי והכי ניספו ליה בשרא שמינא אגומרי וחמרא חייא, אפשר דחיי פורתא ומפקיד אביתיה. *אמר רב אידי בר אבין: האי מאן דבלע זיבורא מיחייא לא חיי, אדהכי והכי נשקיה רביעתא דחלא *שמזג, אפשר דחיי פורתא ומפקיד לביתיה. א"ר יהושע בן לוי: אכל בשר שור בלפת, ולן בלבנה בלילי י"ד או ט"ו בתקופת תמוז — אחזתו אחילו. תנא: והממלא כריסו מכל דבר — אחזתו אחילו. אמר רב פפא: אפי' מתמרי. פשיטא! סד"א, הואיל *ואמר מר: תמרי — משבען ומשחנן ומשלשלן ומאשרן ולא מפנקן, אימא לא, קמ"ל. *מאי אחילו? א"ר אלעזר: אש של עצמות. מאי אש של עצמות? אמר אביי: אש גרמי. מאי אסותיה? אמר אביי, *אמרה לי אם: כולהו שקייני — תלתא ושבעא ותריסר, והאי — עד דמתסי; כולהו שקייני — אליבא ריקנא, והאי — בתר דאכל ושתי ועייל לבית הכסא ונפיק ומשי ידיה, ומייתו ליה בונא דשתיתא דטלפחי ובונא דחמרא עתיקא, וניגבלינהו בהדי הדדי וניכול, וניכרוך בסדיניה וניגניה, וליכא דנוקמיה עד דקאי מנפשיה, וכי קאי לישקליה לסדיניה מיניה, ואי לא — הדר עילויה. אמר ליה אליהו לר' נתן: °אכול שליש ושתה שליש והנח שליש, לכשתכעוס תעמוד על מילואך. תני ר' חייא: הרוצה שלא יבא לידי חולי מעיים, יהא רגיל בטיבול קיץ וחורף, אסעודתך שהנאתך ממנה משוך ידך הימנה, בואל תשהה עצמך בשעה שאתה צריך לנקביך. אמר מר עוקבא: האי מאן דשתי טיליא חיורא — אחזתו ויתק. אמר רב חסדא: שיתין מיני חמרא הוו, מעליא דכולהו — סומקא ריחתנא, גריעא דכולהו — טיליא חיורא. אמר רב יהודה: האי מאן דיתיב בצפרני ניסן גבי נורא, ושייף משחא ונפיק ויתיב בשמשא — אחזתו ויתק. תנו רבנן: *גהקיז דם ושימש מטתו — הוויין לו בנים ויתקין, הקיזו שניהם ושימשו — הוויין להן בנים בעלי ראתן. אמר רב פפא: לא אמרן אלא דלא טעים מידי, אבל טעים מידי — לית לן בה. אמר רבה בר רב הונא: דבא מן הדרך* ושימש מטתו — הוויין לו בנים ויתקין. תנו רבנן: *הבא מבית הכסא, אל ישמש מטתו עד שישהה שיעור חצי מיל, מפני ששד בית הכסא מלוה עמו, ואם שימש — הוויין לו בנים נכפים. תנו רבנן: ההמשמש מטתו מעומד — אוחזתו עוית, מיושב — אוחזתו *דלריא, היא מלמעלה והוא מלמטה — אוחזתו דלריא. מאי דלריא? אמר רבי יהושע בן לוי: סם דלריא — דרדרא. מאי דרדרא? אמר אביי: מוריקא דחוחי. רב פפא אלים ובלע ליה; רב פפי אלים ושדי ליה. אמר אביי: מי שאינו בקי בדרך ארץ, ליתי ג' קפיזי קורטמי דחוחי, ונידוקינהו ונישליקינהו בחמרא ונישתי. *אמר רבי יוחנן: הן הן החזירוני לנערותי. § שלשה דברים מכחישים כחו של אדם, ואלו הן: פחד, דרך, ועון. פחד, דכתיב: °"לבי סחרחר עזבני כחי"; דרך, דכתיב: °"ענה בדרך כחי"; עון, דכתיב: °"כשל בעוני כחי". § שלשה דברים *מתישין גופו של אדם, ואלו הן: יאכל מעומד, ושתה מעומד, ושימש מטתו מעומד. *חמשה קרובין למיתה יותר מן החיים. ואלו הן: אכל ועמד, שתה ועמד, הקיז דם ועמד, ישן ועמד, שימש מטתו ועמד. § ששה העושה אותן — מיד מת, ואלו הן: הבא בדרך ונתייגע, יהקיז דם, ונכנס לבית המרחץ, ושתה ונשתכר, וישן על גבי קרקע, ושימש מטתו. אמר רבי יוחנן: והוא שעשאן כסידרן. אמר אביי: כסידרן — מת, שלא כסידרן — חליש. איני? והא מעוררת עבדה ליה לעבדה תלת מינייהו ומית! ההוא כחוש הוה. § *שמונה רובן קשה ומיעוטן יפה, ואלו הן: דרך, חודרך ארץ, עושר, ומלאכה, יין, ושינה, חמין, טוהקזת דם. שמונה ממעטים את הזרע, ואלו הן: המלח, והרעב, והנתק, בכייה, ושינה על גבי קרקע, וגדגדניות, וכשות שלא בזמנה, והקזת דם למטה — כפלים. תנא: כשם שקשה למטה כפלים, כך יפה למעלה כפלים. אמר רב פפא:

למטה

תהלים לח | שם קב | שם לא

רש"י:

ענבי תאלא. ענבי גפן המודלת בדקל. לחזזיתא. ילפת. חיטי ארזנייתא. חטין גסים. אמרא חדתא. על ברזל של פוסוי"ר חדש. ונישוף. ימשח. לדבר אחר. לרעת. באלונכי פרסאי. *בנוכליות של פרסיים, שמצרפין אותן בדמי סם המות. דמפקיד אביתיה. לצוואה על נכסיו. חלא *שמזג. חומץ חזק. מכל דבר. שהוא טוב לו ומתוק לחיכו ואוכל ממנו כל תאוותו — מביאו לידי חולי ששמו אחילו. הואיל ואמר מר. שהתמרים יפין לגוף כל כך. משחנן. מחממות. משלשלן. משלשלות. מאשרן. נותנות כח. ולא מפנקן. אינן מתענגות את הלב להיות איסטניס, ואע"פ שהן מתוקות. כל שקייני. כל משקין שאדם שותה לרפואה — יש להן מנין ימים לשתותם; יש מהן ג', יש מהן ז', יש מהן י"ב. בונא דשתיתא דטלפחי. מלא אגרוף מן שתיתא — שם מאכל העשוי מקמח עדשים ומלח. וניכרוך גופיה בסדינים. כדי שיתחמם גופו ויזיע. וליכא דנוקמיה. ולא יהיה אדם שיקימנו, לפי שהזיעה יפה לו. אכול שליש. מלא מעיך שליש, ושתה שליש, והנח שליש בטנך ריקם. ולכשתכעוס. וימלא בטנך כעס — תעמוד על מילואך, אבל אם תמלא מעיך אכילה ושתיה, לכשתכעוס — תבקע. בטיבול. לטבול *בחומץ או פת ביין. שהנאתך. שערבה לך. משוך ידך הימנה. שלא תמלא את כריסך. טיליא. יין רע. ויתק. חלשות. ריחתנא. שיש לו ריח טוב מאד. בצפרני. לבקרים. הוויין לו. אם נתעברה באותו תשמיש. בעלי ראתן. חלשים הרבה, מחמת שיש להן שרץ במוח, כדאמרינן בכתובות (דף עז.). דלא טעים מידי. בין הקזה לתשמיש. נכפים. נופלין מאותו חולי. עוית. קרנפ"א. סם דלריא. סם רפואתה של דלריא דרדרא שמה. קורטמי דחוחי. קרו"ג הגדל בקרקע מזובל בזבל הצאן. מוריקא דחוחי. קרו"ג הגדל בגדר של היזמי, שקורין שבי"ל. אלים. לועס בשיניו. בדרך ארץ. שאין לו כח לשמש. קפיזא. כלי מחזיק ג' רביעיות. ונדוקינהו. יכתשם הדק. לנערותי. בתשמיש. פחד. דאגה, שדואג על דבר העתיד, כגון טירוד מזונות או פחד אויב, וקורין סיינש"א. סחרחר. מוקף דאגה. אכל ועמד. מיד, קודם ששהה מעט. העושה אותן. כולן כאחת. מעוררת. שם אשה. ומיעוטן יפה. כשיש לאדם מעט מהם — יפה לגופו לרפואה, וטוב שיהא לו קלת משלא יהא לו כלום. אבל רובן קשה. כשיש לו הרבה. דרך. להלך בדרכים. ודרך ארץ. תשמיש. עושר. מיעוטו יפה ורובו קשה, שמבטלו מת"ת ומגביה לבו. חמין. לרחוץ ולשתות. נתק. לרעת. גדגדניות. איילנדר"א. שלא בזמנה. לקמיה מפרש. והקזת דם למטה. היא ממעטת כפלים בכולן.

תורה אור

תוספות:

רב שימי בר אשי עבד ליה להההוא גוי כו'. הקשה ה"ר אלחנן: אמאי לא אסור לרפאות הגוי, כדאמרינן בפ' "אין מעמידין" (ע"ז דף כו.) גבי מילדת ומניקה אפילו בשכר לפי שמגדלו לעבודה זרה! ואור"י: דשמא כדי להתחכם ברפואה שרי, כדי שידע לרפאות ישראל ע"י כן. א"נ: הגוי היה יודע שהיה בקי ברפואה זאת, ושרי משום איבה. או שמא לא שייך כאן מגדל בן לעבודה זרה כמו במילדת ומניקה*. **דרך** ועון. דאגת העון. א"נ: עונש העון. **חמשה** קרובין למיתה אכל ועמד כו'. משמע אפילו עושה אחד מהן בלבד, מדלא קאמרינן עלה דבעינן כסדרן.

דקתני

מסורת הש"ס:

פ' רומח
כ"ל שמגז
[גי' הערוך כך לנך בלונכי פי' המוסף שכן בלשון יוני קורין לרומח לונכי]
[ע"ז יב:]
כ"ל שמגז
כתובות י:
ברכות לב.
[קדושין לח. וש"נ]
[נ"ל פת בחומץ]
כתובות עז: נדה יז.
ס"א בנהריס
[נ"ל אליא פי' מפסק ערוך ערך פסק]
שבת קיח.
[בתוספ' אליהו רבה איתא מתשי"ש וכ"ה בערוך ובע"י]
[מס' ד"א רבה פ"ג ברכות לז. ע"ש]
[מסכת כלה]
שם לא
שבת קכט:

עין משפט נר מצוה:

ד א מיי' פ"ד מהלכות דעות הלכה טו:
ה ב מיי' שם הלכה א:
ו ג ד ה מיי' שם הלכ' יט טוש"ע א"ח סי' רמ סעיף טו:
ז ו מיי' שם הלכה ג:
ח ז מיי' שם הלכה יח:
[וע"ע תוס' ע"ז כו: ד"ה לאפוקי]
ט ח מיי' שם הלכה יט טוש"ע א"ח סי' רמ סעיף יד:
י ט מיי' שם הלכה יח:

גליון הש"ס

גמ' אכול שליש ושתה שליש וכו'. עי' נדה דף כד ע"ב תד"ה אכילתו:

לְמַטָּה — לְמַטָּה מִן הַבֵּיצִים, לְמַעְלָה — לְמַעְלָה מִן הַבֵּיצִים. וּכְשׁוּת שֶׁלֹּא בִּזְמַנָּהּ. תָּנָא: כְּשֵׁם שֶׁקָּשָׁה שֶׁלֹּא בִּזְמַנָּהּ, כָּךְ יָפָה בִּזְמַנָּהּ. אָמַר רַב פַּפָּא: זְמַנָּהּ — תַּמּוּז, שֶׁלֹּא בִּזְמַנָּהּ — טֵבֵת, יוֹמֵי נִיסָן וְיוֹמֵי תִשְׁרֵי — לָא מַעֲלוּ וְלָא קָשׁוּ.§ "אָמַר "כִּתְבוּ גֵּט לְאִשְׁתִּי" וַאֲחָזוֹ קוֹרְדְיָיקוֹס וְחָזַר וְאָמַר "אַל תִּכְתְּבוּ" — אֵין דְּבָרָיו הָאַחֲרוֹנִים כְּלוּם".§ אר"ש בֶּן לָקִישׁ: כּוֹתְבִין וְנוֹתְנִין גֵּט לְאַלְתַּר, וְר' יוֹחָנָן אָמַר: אאֵין כּוֹתְבִין אֶלָּא לִכְשֶׁיִּשְׁתַּפֶּה. מ"ט דר"ל? דְּקָתָנֵי: אֵין בִּדְבָרָיו הָאַחֲרוֹנִים כְּלוּם. וְר' יוֹחָנָן אָמַר לָךְ: אֵין בִּדְבָרָיו הָאַחֲרוֹנִים כְּלוּם — דִּלְכִי מִתְצִיל לָא צָרִיךְ לְמִיהֲדַר אִימְּלוֹכֵי בֵּיהּ, וּלְעוֹלָם אֵין כּוֹתְבִין אֶלָּא לִכְשֶׁיִּשְׁתַּפֶּה. בְּמַאי קָמִיפַּלְגִי? ר"ל מְדַמֵּי לֵיהּ לְיָשֵׁן, וְר' יוֹחָנָן מְדַמֵּי לֵיהּ לְשׁוֹטֶה. וְר' יוֹחָנָן נַמִי לִידַמְיֵיהּ לְיָשֵׁן! יָשֵׁן לָא מְחוּסַּר מַעֲשֶׂה, הַאי מְחוּסַּר מַעֲשֶׂה. וְר"ל נַמִי נִידַמְיֵיהּ לְשׁוֹטֶה! שׁוֹטֶה לָא סַמֵּיהּ בְּיָדָן, הַאי סַמֵּיהּ בְּיָדָן, *בִּשְׂרָא סוּמָּקָא אַגּוּמְרֵי וְחַמְרָא מַרְקָא. וּמִי אָמַר ר' יוֹחָנָן הָכִי? *וְהָאָמַר רַב יְהוּדָה אָמַר שְׁמוּאֵל: בשָׁחַט בּוֹ שְׁנַיִם אוֹ רוֹב שְׁנַיִם, וְרָמַז וְאָמַר "כִּתְבוּ גֵּט לְאִשְׁתִּי" — הֲרֵי אֵלּוּ יִכְתְּבוּ וְיִתְּנוּ, וְתַנְיָא: *גרָאוּהוּ מְגוּיָּד אוֹ צָלוּב עַל הַצְּלִיבָה, וְרָמַז וְאָמַר "כִּתְבוּ גֵּט לְאִשְׁתִּי" — הֲרֵי אֵלּוּ יִכְתְּבוּ וְיִתְּנוּ! הָכִי הַשְׁתָּא?! הָתָם דַּעְתָּא צִילּוּתָא הִיא, וּכְחִישׁוּתָא הוּא דְּאַתְחִילָה בֵּיהּ, הָכָא דַּעְתָּא שְׁגִישְׁתָּא הִיא. וּמִי אָמַר שְׁמוּאֵל הָכִי? וְהָאָמַר רַב יְהוּדָה אָמַר שְׁמוּאֵל: דשָׁחַט בּוֹ שְׁנַיִם אוֹ רוֹב שְׁנַיִם וּבָרַח — מְעִידִין עָלָיו; וְאִי ס"ד חַי הוּא, אַמַּאי מְעִידִין עָלָיו? האָמְרִי: חַי הוּא וְסוֹפוֹ לָמוּת. אֶלָּא מֵעַתָּה, יְהֵא גּוֹלֶה עַל יָדוֹ! אַלְמָה תַּנְיָא: ושָׁחַט בּוֹ שְׁנַיִם אוֹ רוֹב שְׁנַיִם — ה"ז אֵינוֹ גּוֹלֶה? הָא אִיתְּמַר עֲלָהּ, א"ר הוֹשַׁעְיָא: זחָיְישִׁינַן שֶׁמָּא הָרוּחַ בִּלְבַּלְתּוֹ; אִי נַמִי, הוּא קֵירֵב אֶת מִיתָתוֹ. מַאי בֵּינַיְיהוּ? חאִיכָּא בֵּינַיְיהוּ, דְּשַׁחֲטֵיהּ בְּבֵיתָא דְּשַׁיְשָׁא וּפִירְכֵּס; אִי נַמִי, דְּשַׁחֲטֵיהּ בְּבָרָא וְלָא פִּירְכֵּס.§ "נִשְׁתַּתֵּק, וְאָמְרוּ לוֹ נִכְתּוֹב גֵּט לְאִשְׁתְּךָ" כו'.§ וְלֵיחוּשׁ דִּלְמָא שִׁיחַיָּא דְּ"לָאו לָאו" נַקְטֵיהּ, אִי נַמִי שִׁיחַיָּא דְּ"הֵן הֵן" נַקְטֵיהּ! א"ר יוֹסֵף בַּר מַנְיוֹמֵי אָמַר רַב נַחְמָן: דְּאָמְרִינַן לֵיהּ בְּסֵירוּגִין. וְלֵיחוּשׁ דִּלְמָא שִׁיחַיָּא דְּסֵירוּגִין נַקְטֵיהּ! טדְּאָמְרִינַן לֵיהּ חַד לָאו וּתְרֵין הֵן, וּתְרֵין לָאו וְחַד הֵן. דְּבֵי רַבִּי יִשְׁמָעֵאל תָּנָא: יאוֹמְרִים לוֹ דְּבָרִים שֶׁל יְמוֹת הַחַמָּה בִּימוֹת הַגְּשָׁמִים, וְשֶׁל יְמוֹת הַגְּשָׁמִים בִּימוֹת הַחַמָּה. מַאי נִיהוּ? אִילֵימָא *גְּלוּפְקְרֵי וּסְדִינֵי — לֵיחוּשׁ דִּלְמָא קוּרָא אַחֲדֵיהּ, א"נ חַמָּה אַחֲדֵיהּ!

אֶלָּא

לְמַטָּה מִן הַבֵּיצִים. כְּמוֹ בְּרַגְלָיו וּבְשׁוֹקָיו. לְמַעְלָה מִן הַבֵּצִים. בַּכְּתֵפַיִם וּבַגּוּף וּבַקִּילְבּוֹסֶת. כּוֹתְבִין וְנוֹתְנִין גֵּט לְאַלְתַּר. וַאֲפִילּוּ בְּתוֹךְ חוֹלְיוֹ, הוֹאִיל וְאָמַר קוֹדֶם לָכֵן. וְלָא אָמְרִינַן שׁוֹטֶה הוּא, וְאֵינוֹ יָכוֹל לְגָרֵשׁ. אִימְּלוֹכֵי בֵּיהּ. לִיטּוֹל רְשׁוּת. הַאי מְחוּסַּר מַעֲשֶׂה. שֶׁצָּרִיךְ רְפוּאָה, בִּשְׂרָא סוּמָּקָא אַגּוּמְרֵי. לָאו סַמֵּיהּ בְּיָדָן. אֵין סַם רְפוּאָתוֹ בְּיָדֵינוּ. מְגוּיָּד. מְחוּתָּךְ בַּחֲתִיכוֹת, לְשׁוֹן "גּוֹדּוּ אִילָנָא" (דניאל ד). צִילּוּתָא הִיא. צְלוּלָה הָיָה דַּעְתּוֹ, אֶלָּא שֶׁכָּחַשׁ כֹּחוֹ מִלְּהוֹצִיא דָּבָר בְּפִיו. שְׁגִישְׁתָּא. תַּרְגּוּם שֶׁל מְהוּמָה, כְּלוֹמַר: דַּעַת מְבוּלְבָּל. וּמִי אָמַר שְׁמוּאֵל. שָׁחַט בּוֹ שְׁנַיִם כּוֹתְבִין גֵּט לְאִשְׁתּוֹ, אַלְמָא: גֵּט מְחַיֵּים הוּא. מְעִידִין עָלָיו. שֶׁמֵּת, לְהַשִּׂיא אֶת אִשְׁתּוֹ. חַי הוּא. וְגִיטּוֹ מְחַיֵּים, אֲבָל סוֹפוֹ לָמוּת, לְכָךְ מְעִידִין עָלָיו לְאַחַר זְמַן לְהַשִּׂיא אֶת אִשְׁתּוֹ, הֵיכָא דְּלֹא גֵּירְשָׁהּ. אֶלָּא מֵעַתָּה. הוֹאִיל וְסוֹפוֹ לָמוּת. יְהֵא גּוֹלֶה עַל יָדוֹ. הַשּׁוֹחֲטוֹ בְּשׁוֹגֵג. הָרוּחַ בִּלְבַּלְתּוֹ. וְאִלְמָלֵא הָרוּחַ לֹא מֵת. הוּא קֵירֵב אֶת מִיתָתוֹ. עַל יְדֵי שֶׁפִּירְכֵּס, וְנִמְצָא שֶׁלֹּא הֲרָגוֹ זֶה. אֲבָל מִכָּל מָקוֹם סוֹפוֹ לָמוּת. שִׁיחַיָּא דְּלָאו לָאו נַקְטֵיהּ. חוֹלִי שֶׁל שִׁגָּעוֹן, הַמְלַמְּדוֹ תָּמִיד לְהַרְכִּין רֹאשׁוֹ בְּהַרְכָּנַת לָאו אוֹ הֵין, וְאֵינוֹ מֵשִׁיב עַל דִּבְרֵי שְׁאֵלָתָם. שִׁיחַיָּא. הִשְׁתַּחֲוָיָה. בְּסֵירוּגִין. מַמְתִּינִין בֵּין הַרְכָּנָה לִשְׁאֵלָה שָׁעָה, וְחוֹזְרִין וְשׁוֹאֲלִין לוֹ אוֹתָהּ שְׁאֵלָה עַצְמָהּ. שִׁיחַיָּא דְּסֵירוּגִין. לִשְׁחוֹת וּלְהַרְכִּין בְּעִנְיָן זֶה לְשָׁעוֹת. הָכִי גָּרְסִינַן: חַד לָאו וּתְרֵין הֵין וּתְרֵין לָאו וְחַד הֵין. דְּכִי הַךְ שִׁיחַיָּא לָא נַקְטֵיהּ. אוֹמְרִים לוֹ. כְּשֶׁבּוֹדְקִין אוֹתוֹ עַל לָאו שׁוֹאֲלִין לוֹ אִם מְבַקֵּשׁ דְּבָרִים הָרְאוּיִן לוֹ בִּימוֹת הַחַמָּה, וְעַכְשָׁיו יְמוֹת הַגְּשָׁמִים. גְּלוּפְקְרִין. קוט"א בְּלַעַ"ז. וּסְדִינֵי. אִם יְכַסּוּהוּ בִּסְדִינֵי פִּשְׁתָּן בִּימוֹת הַגְּשָׁמִים. דִּלְמָא קוּרָא אַחֲדֵיהּ. בִּימוֹת הַחַמָּה, וְאַף עַל פִּי שֶׁמֵּשִׁיב הֵין עַל הַגְּלוּפְקְרִין — לָאו שׁוֹטֶה הוּא.

בְּפֵירֵי

דקתני אין בדבריו האחרונים כלום. מייתור הלשון דייק דהוה ליה למימר: הרי אלו יכתבו ויתנו. אי נמי דייק מדלא תנא: אין צריך לבודקו פעם שניה, דהוה משמע שממתינים מיהא עד שישתפה. ומי אמר רבי יוחנן הכי והא אמר שמואל שחט בו שנים כו'. וא"ת: השתא דמדמי ליה לאחזו קורדייקוס – תקשי ליה מתני', דקתני: מי שאחזו קורדייקוס ואמר "כתבו גט לאשתי" – לא אמר כלום, והכא בשחט בו שנים ואמר "כתבו" הרי אלו יכתבו ויתנו! י"ל: דהא פשיטא דבשעה שאמר "כתבו" – אכתי דעתא צילותא היא ולא דמי לאחזו קורדייקוס. אבל קודם שיכתוב ויתן יתחלש ויתקלקל, ועל שעת נתינה נראה לו לדמות לאחזו קורדייקוס, וקשה לרבי יוחנן דאמר אין כותבין ונותנין עד שישתפה. הקשה הרב רבי אלחנן: דאמאי פריך לרבי יוחנן? לריש לקיש נמי תיקשי, דהא טעמא דריש לקיש באחזו קורדייקוס משום דסמיה(א) בידיה. והכא דאין סמיה בידיה – מודה ר"ל דאין כותבין ונותנין, דמדמי ליה לשוטה! ולספרים דלא גרסי "ומי אמר רבי יוחנן הכי" א"ש, דפריך לתרוייהו. אי נמי, נקט רבי יוחנן – משום דקאמר בהדיא: אין כותבין. ורמז ואמר כתבו גט לאשתי. כגון שאמרו לו: "נכתוב גט לאשתך", והרכין בראשו. ושמא אין צריך לבודקו כמו במתניתין, משום דאית ביה דעתא צילותא, כדאמרינן בסמוך. התם דעתא צילותא היא. לא ידע רבינו יצחק עד מתי יחשב דעתא צילותא, דליכא למימר דבדקוהו בשעת נתינת הגט – דאם כן לא הוה פריך מידי לרבי יוחנן. ושמא עד שיודע שנטרפה דעתו יחשב דעתא צילותא. ובגט שכיב מרע אומר ר"י דצריך ליזהר שלא יתקלקל בין כתיבה לנתינה, דאם נתקלקל בינתיים, אפילו נתפקח לבסוף – אין מועיל, אפי' לריש לקיש, דהא לא סמיה בידיה. ופעמים ששכיב מרע אינו בדעתו, ומספקא אי חשבינן ליה כשוטה או שמא תונבא בעלמא הוא דנקטיה, וכישן דמי. ואי סלקא דעתך חי הוא אמאי מעידין כו'. דסלקא דעתך דמעידין עליו שכבר מת קאמר. ומשני: חי וסופו למות לאלתר, קודם שיתירוה ב"ד לינשא. אלא מעתה יהא גולה על ידו. לשמואל פריך, דכיון דקאמר דמת לאלתר – היה לו לגלות! ולאו אשינויא דחי הוא וסופו למות פריך, דכ"ש אי חשבת ליה כבר מת דקשה טפי, דקס"ד דגלות תלי במת לאלתר, ואם לא מת לאלתר – אינו גולה. דס"ד דבהכי תלי, דלישנא דכתיב גבי גלות "ויפל עליו וימות" (במדבר לה) משמע ליה לאלתר. אע"פ שבמזיד חייב אפילו לא מת לאלתר – יש חילוק בין מיתה לגלות, כדמפלגי בגלות בין דרך ירידה לדרך עליה, ובמזיד אין שום חלוק. ולית ליה השתא הא דפריך ב"אלו נערות" (כתובות דף לג:): ממאי דבמזיד "ונקה המכה" – מקטלא? ודלמא בשוגג, ומאי "ונקה" – מגלות! דמשמע דחייב גלות אפילו לא מת לאלתר*. *°חיישינן שמא הרוח בלבלתו. דווקא בגלות חיישינן להני טעמי, אבל במזיד לעולם חייב. ושמא יש שום דרשא גבי גלות כמו שיש חילוק בין גלות למיתה לענין דרך ירידה ועליה. והא דמשמע ב"אלו נערות" (גם זה שם) כי מוקי "ונקה המכה" אשוגג דחייב גלות אפי' לא מת לאלתר – מיירי בביתא דשישא וכגון דלא פירכס. בביתא דשישא או דלא פירכס. מר חשיב בלבול הרוח קירוב מיתה יותר מפרכוס, ומר חשיב פרכוס קירוב מיתה יותר מבלבול הרוח. ותרוייהו בעו שימות מחמת הרולא, ולא מחמת דבר אחר. אי נמי: מר חשיב פירכוס מחמת רולא, משום דכל אדם דרכו לפרכס מחמת שחיטה. ומר חשיב בלבול רוח מחמת רולא, משום דאתי ממילא. אי נמי: לא פליגי הני לישני, ואינו חייב אלא בביתא דשישא ולא פרכס. והש"ס מפרש נפקותא בין הנך טעמי. בודקין אותו שלש פעמים. (שייך לעיל דף סז:) פי': שלש פעמים על לאו, ושלש פעמים על הן, דהיינו ששה פעמים בין הכל. ובגמרא דקאמר וניחוש דלמא שיחיא דלאו לאו נקטיה, אי נמי שיחיא דהן הן – לאו משום דלא ניבעי תרוייהו, דתרוייהו בעינן כדפירשנו. אלא כלומר: ובחד מהן, או בלאו או בהן, אינו בדעתו. וי"ס דל"ג "אי נמי". ובדיקה זו מפרש בירושלמי כילד בודקין לאו והן; אומרים לו: נכתוב גט לאשתך – אומר הן, לאמך – אומר לאו(ב), *לאחותך – אומר לאו, לבתך – אומר לאו כו'. דבי רבי ישמעאל תנא. אין נראה לומר דפליגי, דבדיקה דמתני' למה לא תועיל? אלא דקתני בדיקה עדיפא טפי הכי, דליכא למימר ביה דשיחיא דלאו או דהן הן נקטיה, שהיא חכמה גדולה, כיון שאינו טועה בין ימות החמה לימות הגשמים – אפילו בעינן. שלשה לאו ושלשה הן סירוגין – לא בעי. וניחוש שמא קרירות אחדיה. ולמה לנו לחושבו כשוטה, ונאמר שאינו גט, ונעגן אשתו חנם!

אלא

יא א מיי' פ"ב מהלכות גירושין הלכה טו סמג עשין נ טוש"ע אה"ע סימן קמא סעיף ב בהג"ה:
יב ב ג טוש"ע שם סעיף ח:
יג ד ה מיי' שם פי"ג הלכה יז סמג שם טוש"ע אה"ע סימן יז סעיף לו:
יד ו ז ח מיי' פ"ה מהלכות רוצח ושמירת נפש הלכה ב:
טו ט י מיי' פ"ב מהל' גירושין הלכה טז סמג עשין נ טוש"ע אה"ע סימן קמא סעי' ה:

תוספות רי"ד

אמר כתבו גט לאשתי ואחזו וכו'. ר"ל אמר כותבין ונותנין לאלתר ור' יוחנן אמר אין כותבין אלא לכשישתפה מ"ט דר"ל דקתני אין דבריו האחרונים כלום ור' יוחנן אמר לך אין דבריו האחרונים כלום דלכי מיתציל לא צריך מיהדר ולאמלוכי ביה ולעולם אין כותבין אלא לכשישתפה במאי קמיפלגי ר"ל מדמה ליה לישן ור' יוחנן מדמה ליה לשוטה וקי"ל כר' יוחנן הלכה כרבי יוחנן. איני והאמר רב יהודה אמר שמואל שחט בו שנים או רוב שנים מעידים עליו [ומשני] חי הוא וסופו למות: נשתתק בודקין אותו ג' פעמים וניחוש דלמא שיחיא דלאו לאו או דהין הין נקטיה אמר רב יוסף בר מנויומי אמר רב נחמן דאמרינן ליה בסירוגין חד לאו ותרי הין תרי לאו וחד הין דבי ר' ישמעאל תנא אומרים לו דברים של ימות החמה בימות הגשמים ושל ימות הגשמים בימות החמה מאי [ניהו אילימא] גושפקי וסדיני וניחוש דלמא קררה אחדיה או חמה אחדיה אלא בפירי.

לעיל סז:
יבמות קכ:
[תוספתא רפ"ה]
ס"א גושפקר [בכתוב ערך גשפק גורס גושפקי פי' כן גלופקרין]
[וע"ע תוס' כתובות לג: ד"ה דלמא ותוס' יבמות קכ: ד"ה אלא מעתה ול"ה חיישינן ותוס' שבועות לג. ד"ה על פי]
פי' בין כל פעם אומרים לו לאשתך ואומר הן

הגהות הב"ח

(א) תוס' ד"ה ומי אמר וכו' משום דסמיה בידן והיכי דלאין סמיה בידן מודה: (ב) ד"ה בודקין וכו' לאמך אומר לאו לאשתך אומר הן לאחותך אומר לאו לאשתך אומר הן לבתך

גליון הש"ס

תוס' ד"ה חיישינן. עי' שבועות ד' לב ע"ב תוס' ד"ה על פי עדים:

אֶלָּא בְּפֵירֵי.§ *אָמַר רַב כָּהֲנָא אָמַר רַב: אחֵרֵשׁ שֶׁיָּכוֹל לְדַבֵּר מִתּוֹךְ הַכְּתָב, כּוֹתְבִין וְנוֹתְנִין גֵּט לְאִשְׁתּוֹ. אָמַר רַב יוֹסֵף: מַאי קָא מַשְׁמַע לָן? תָּנֵינָא: נִשְׁתַּתֵּק, וְאָמְרוּ לוֹ "נִכְתּוֹב גֵּט לְאִשְׁתְּךָ" וְהִרְכִּין בְּרֹאשׁוֹ, בּוֹדְקִין אוֹתוֹ שְׁלֹשָׁה פְּעָמִים, אִם אָמַר עַל לָאו לָאו וְעַל הֵן הֵן — הֲרֵי אֵלּוּ יִכְתְּבוּ וְיִתְּנוּ! אֲמַר לֵיהּ רַבִּי זֵירָא: אִלֵּם קָאָמְרַתְּ? שָׁאנֵי אִלֵּם, *דְּתַנְיָא: במְדַבֵּר וְאֵינוֹ שׁוֹמֵעַ — זֶהוּ חֵרֵשׁ, שׁוֹמֵעַ וְאֵינוֹ מְדַבֵּר — זֶהוּ אִלֵּם, וְזֶה וָזֶה הֲרֵי הֵן כְּפִקְחִין לְכָל דִּבְרֵיהֶם. וּמִמַּאי דִּמְדַבֵּר וְאֵינוֹ שׁוֹמֵעַ זֶהוּ חֵרֵשׁ, שׁוֹמֵעַ וְאֵינוֹ מְדַבֵּר זֶהוּ אִלֵּם? דִּכְתִיב: °"וַאֲנִי כְחֵרֵשׁ לֹא אֶשְׁמָע וּכְאִלֵּם לֹא יִפְתַּח פִּיו". וְאִי בָּעֵית אֵימָא, כִּדְאָמְרִי אֱינָשֵׁי: אִישְׁתַּקִּיל מִילּוּלֵיהּ. אֲמַר ר' זֵירָא: אִי קַשְׁיָא לִי הָא קַשְׁיָא לִי, דְּתַנְיָא: °"אִם לֹא יַגִּיד" — גפְּרָט לְאִלֵּם שֶׁאֵינוֹ יָכוֹל לְהַגִּיד; אַמַּאי? הָא יָכוֹל לְהַגִּיד מִתּוֹךְ הַכְּתָב! אֲמַר לֵיהּ אַבַּיֵי: דעֵדוּת קָאָמְרַתְּ? שָׁאנֵי עֵדוּת, *דְּרַחֲמָנָא אָמַר: מִפִּיהֶם — וְלֹא מִפִּי כְתָבָם. מֵיתִיבִי: *הכְּשֵׁם שֶׁבּוֹדְקִין אוֹתוֹ לְגִיטִּין, כָּךְ בּוֹדְקִין אוֹתוֹ לְמַשָּׂאוֹת וּלְמַתָּנוֹת, וּלְעֵדִיּוֹת וְלִירוּשׁוֹת; קָתָנֵי מִיהַת עֵדִיּוֹת! אָמַר רַב יוֹסֵף בַּר מַנְיוּמֵי אָמַר רַב שֵׁשֶׁת: ובְּעֵדוּת אִשָּׁה, דְּאַקִּילוּ בָּהּ רַבָּנַן. וְהָא קָתָנֵי יְרוּשׁוֹת! אָמַר רַבִּי אַבָּהוּ: זיְרוּשַּׁת בְּנוֹ הַבְּכוֹר. קָתָנֵי מִיהַת לְמַשָּׂאוֹת וּלְמַתָּנוֹת, מַאי לָאו לְעָלְמָא? לָא, לְדִידֵיהּ. מֵיתִיבִי: חחֵרֵשׁ, לֹא הָלְכוּ בּוֹ אַחַר רְמִיזוֹתָיו וְאַחַר קְפִיצוֹתָיו וְאַחַר כְּתַב יָדוֹ אֶלָּא בְּמִטַּלְטְלִין, טאֲבָל לֹא לְגִיטִּין! תַּנָּאֵי הִיא; דְּתַנְיָא, אָמַר רַבָּן שִׁמְעוֹן בֶּן גַּמְלִיאֵל: בַּמֶּה דְּבָרִים אֲמוּרִים — בְּחֵרֵשׁ מֵעִיקָּרוֹ, אֲבָל פִּקֵּחַ וְנִתְחָרֵשׁ — הוּא כּוֹתֵב וְהֵן חוֹתְמִין. וְחֵרֵשׁ מֵעִיקָּרוֹ לָא? *כְּשֵׁם ישֶׁכּוֹנְסָהּ בִּרְמִיזָה כָּךְ מוֹצִיאָהּ בִּרְמִיזָה! אִי בְּאִשְׁתּוֹ — ה"נ, הָכָא בְּמַאי עָסְקִינַן — בִּיבִמְתּוֹ. יְבִמְתּוֹ מִמַּאן? אִילֵימָא דְּנָפְלָה לֵיהּ מֵאָחִיו חֵרֵשׁ? ככְּשֵׁם שֶׁכְּנִיסָתָהּ בִּרְמִיזָה כָּךְ יְצִיאָתָהּ בִּרְמִיזָה! אֶלָּא לדְּנָפְלָה לֵיהּ מֵאָחִיו פִּקֵּחַ. וְאִיבָּעֵית אֵימָא: לְעוֹלָם דְּנָפְלָה לֵיהּ מֵאָחִיו חֵרֵשׁ, וּגְזֵירָה אָחִיו חֵרֵשׁ אַטּוּ אָחִיו פִּקֵּחַ. אִי הָכִי, אִשְׁתּוֹ נַמִי! יְבִמְתּוֹ בִּיבִמְתּוֹ מִיחַלְּפָא, אִשְׁתּוֹ בִּיבִמְתּוֹ לָא מִיחַלְּפָא. וּמִי גָּזְרִינַן חֵרֵשׁ אַטּוּ פִּקֵּחַ? וְהָתְנַן

[תהלים לח] [ויקרא ה] [תוספתא רפ"ה]

רש"י

בְּפֵירֵי. שֶׁאֵינָם מְצוּיִם בְּאוֹתָהּ שָׁעָה, כְּגוֹן לריש"ש בִּימוֹת הַגְּשָׁמִים, וּבִימוֹת הַחַמָּה ניספל"ה. חֵרֵשׁ. שֶׁהָיָה פִּיקֵּחַ כְּשֶׁכְּנָסָהּ, וְקִדּוּשָׁיו קִידּוּשִׁין גְּמוּרִין, וּתְנַן בִּיבָמוֹת (דף קיג.): נִתְחָרֵשׁ הוּא אוֹ נִשְׁתַּטָּה — לֹא יוֹצִיא עוֹלָמִית, לְפִי שֶׁאֵין כֹּחַ בְּגֵירוּשֵׁי חֵרְשׁוּת לְהַפְקִיעַ קִידּוּשֵׁי חָכְמָה. וְקָאָמַר רַב דְּאִם יָכוֹל לְדַבֵּר מִתּוֹךְ הַכְּתָב, דְּיוֹדֵעַ לִכְתּוֹב עַל הַקְּלָף "כִּתְבוּ וּתְנוּ גֵּט לְאִשְׁתִּי אַתֶּם פְּלוֹנִי וּפְלוֹנִי" וּמָסַר לָהֶם — פִּיקֵּחַ גָּמוּר הוּא, וְכוֹתְבִין וְנוֹתְנִין. אִלֵּם קָאָמְרַתְּ שָׁאנֵי אִלֵּם. דְּכֵיוָן דְּשׁוֹמֵעַ הוּא — הֲרֵי הוּא כְּפִיקֵּחַ לְכָל דְּבָרָיו. אֲבָל חֵרֵשׁ שֶׁאֵינוֹ שׁוֹמֵעַ וְאֵינוֹ מְדַבֵּר, אִי לָאו דְּיָכוֹל לְדַבֵּר מִתּוֹךְ הַכְּתָב — בִּרְמִיזָה לָא מַפֵּיק. וְאִי לָאו דְּאַשְׁמְעִינַן רַב — לָא הֲוָה יָדַעְנָא. חֵרֵשׁ הַמְדַבֵּר וְאֵינוֹ שׁוֹמֵעַ זֶהוּ חֵרֵשׁ. וְלֹא זֶהוּ חֵרֵשׁ שֶׁדִּבְּרוּ בּוֹ חֲכָמִים בְּכָל מָקוֹם וְהִשְׁווּהוּ לְשׁוֹטֶה. דְּזֶהוּ כְּפִיקֵּחַ לְכָל דְּבָרָיו, כִּדְקָתָנֵי בְּהֶדְיָא. אֲבָל חֵרֵשׁ דְּרַב כָּהֲנָא — (אֵינוֹ) לֹא שׁוֹמֵעַ וְלֹא מְדַבֵּר. אִישְׁתַּקִּיל מִילּוּלֵיהּ. נוֹטָרִיקוֹן דְּאִלֵּם. אִי קַשְׁיָא לִי. בְּהָא דְּרַב כָּהֲנָא. פְּרָט לְאִלֵּם. שֶׁאֵינוֹ חַיָּיב קׇרְבַּן שְׁבוּעָה עַל שְׁבוּעַת הָעֵדוּת, אִם הִשְׁבִּיעוֹ וְהִרְכִּין בְּרֹאשׁוֹ שֶׁאֵינוֹ יוֹדֵעַ. הֲרֵי יָכוֹל לְהַגִּיד מִתּוֹךְ הַכְּתָב. וְאִם אִיתָא לִדְרַב כָּהֲנָא — לִיחַיַּיב! מִפִּיהֶם. "עַל פִּי שְׁנַיִם עֵדִים"*. וְלֹא מִפִּי כְּתָבָם. יָעִידוּ בְּבֵ"ד, דְּלָא דָּמֵי לִשְׁטָר שֶׁחֲתָמוּהוּ בְּיוֹמוֹ — דְּהַהוּא אוֹרְחֵיהּ לְהָכִי. כְּשֵׁם שֶׁבּוֹדְקִים. אַנִּשְׁתַּתֵּק וְהִרְכִּין בְּרֹאשׁוֹ קָאֵי. לְמַשָּׂאוֹת וּמַתָּנוֹת. לִמְכּוֹר בִּנְכָסָיו. לְעֵדִיּוֹת וְלִירוּשׁוֹת. כּוּלְּהוּ מְפָרֵשׁ וְאָזֵיל. קָתָנֵי מִיהָא לְעֵדִיּוֹת. שֶׁיָּעִיד עֵדוּתוֹ מִפִּי הַכְּתָב. וְהָאָמְרַתְּ: מִפִּיהֶם, וְזֶה נֶאֱלָם! בְּעֵדוּת אִשָּׁה. לְהַשִּׂיאָהּ. דְּאַקִּילוּ בָּהּ. בְּעֵד אֶחָד, קָרוֹב וְשִׁפְחָה. וּפָרְכִינַן. קָתָנֵי יְרוּשׁוֹת. וְקָא סָלְקָא דַּעְתָּךְ לְהָעִיד עַל יְרוּשָּׁה שֶׁהוֹרִישׁ אָדָם מֵעָלְמָא. אָמַר רַבִּי אַבָּהוּ. מַאי יְרוּשׁוֹת — בְּנוֹ דִּידֵיהּ, אִם רָצָה לְהַשְׁווֹת אֶת הַבְּכוֹר כְּאֶחָד מִבָּנָיו. וּלְהָכִי נָקַט יְרוּשַּׁת בְּנוֹ הַבְּכוֹר, דְּאִם לֹא לְשַׁנּוֹת עַל מִשְׁפַּט הַיְרוּשָּׁה שֶׁל תּוֹרָה הוּא בָּא — לָמָּה לָנוּ לִדְבָרָיו? הַיְרוּשָּׁה מֵאֵילֶיהָ תִּפּוֹל! מַאי לָאו דְּעָלְמָא. דְּהַיְינוּ עֵדוּת. לֹא הָלְכוּ אַחַר רְמִיזָתוֹ. לְחָשְׁבוֹ כְּפִיקֵּחַ. אֲבָל לֹא לְגִיטִּין. הֵיכָא דְּקִידּוּשָׁיו הָיוּ קִידּוּשִׁין גְּמוּרִין. וּתְיוּבְתָּא דְּרַב כָּהֲנָא. בַּמֶּה דְּבָרִים אֲמוּרִים. דְּלֹא הָלְכוּ בּוֹ בְּגִיטִּין. בְּחֵרֵשׁ מֵעִיקָּרוֹ. שֶׁאֵין לוֹ כְּתַב יָד שֶׁל דַּעַת, שֶׁלֹּא הָיְתָה לוֹ דַּעַת צְלוּלָה מִיָּמָיו. וּלְקַמֵּיהּ פָּרֵיךְ: וְכֵיוָן דְּחֵרֵשׁ מֵעִיקָּרוֹ הוּא — הֲרֵי כָּנַס בִּרְמִיזָה, וְלֹא הָיוּ קִידּוּשִׁין גְּמוּרִין! וּמוֹקֵי לָהּ בְּיָבָם. אֲבָל פִּיקֵּחַ. שֶׁלָּמַד לִכְתּוֹב מִדַּעַת צְלוּלָה. הוּא כּוֹתֵב. גֵּט, וַאֲחֵרִים חוֹתְמִין, וְהַיְינוּ כְּרַב כָּהֲנָא. כְּשֵׁם שֶׁכּוֹנֵס בִּרְמִיזָה כו'. מִשְׁנָה הִיא בִּיבָמוֹת, דְּחֵרֵשׁ שֶׁנָּשָׂא אִשָּׁה, אִם רָצָה — יוֹצִיא. בִּיבִמְתּוֹ. שֶׁקִּידּוּשֶׁיהָ גְּמוּרִין, וְזִיקָתָהּ גְּמוּרָה, וְהוּא אֵין יָכוֹל לַחֲלוֹץ — לְפִי שֶׁאֵינוֹ בְּ"וְעָמַד וְאָמַר לֹא חָפַצְתִּי לְקַחְתָּהּ" (דברים כה), וְכוֹנֵס וְאֵינוֹ מוֹצִיא לְעוֹלָם, דְּגֵט דִּידֵיהּ לָא מַפְקַע זִיקָה דְּאוֹרַיְיתָא. אִשְׁתּוֹ נַמִי. נִיגְזוֹר אַטּוּ יְבִמְתּוֹ, שֶׁקִּידּוּשֶׁיהָ גְּמוּרִין. יְבִמְתּוֹ בִּיבִמְתּוֹ. אֵשֶׁת אָחִיו פִּיקֵּחַ בְּאֵשֶׁת אָחִיו חֵרֵשׁ. וּמִי גָּזְרִינַן. אָחִיו חֵרֵשׁ אַטּוּ פִּיקֵּחַ? שְׁנֵי

[לקמן עב.] [חגיגה ג: [תוס' תרומות פ"א]] [יבמות לח:] [דברים יז] [יבמות קיב:]

תוספות

אלא בפירי · אין לפרש שעואלין לו אם רוצה פירי של ימות הגשמים בימות החמה או איפכא, ואומר "הן" – כי זה אפשר למצוא בכבושים בדבש, או בענין אחר. אלא שעואלין לו אם רוצה שילקטו לו מן האילן. **אמר** רב יוסף מאי קמ"ל תנינא נשתתק כו'. תימה לר"י: אדרבה, דתיקשי ליה מתני' כיון דאינו מחלק בין אלם לחרש – דלמה לי יכול לדבר מתוך הכתב? בהרכנה סגי! ואומר ר"י: דהא ודאי דבחרש לא סגי בהרכנה, אע"פ שכותבין לו "נכתוב גט לאשתך" ומרכין בראשו, ובודקין אותו ג"פ לאו והן. אלא דמדמי רב יוסף הרכנה דאלם לכתיבה דחרש, כמו שאלם ע"י הרכנה ניכר שמבין ומתרצה, ועל ידי זה כותבים גט – הוא הדין חרש ששאלוהו בכתב והשיב בכתב – יש הוכחה שהוא מבין בטוב, אע"פ שאם שאלוהו בכתב והרכין בראשו – אינו מועיל כלום. **אמר** רבי זירא אי קשיא כו'. תימה לר"י: דמשמע דפריך לרב כהנא, מדקאמר: והא יכול לדבר מתוך הכתב, ואמאי לא פריך אמתניתי' דהרי יכול להגיד ע"י הרכנה? ואור"י: דמתניתין לא קשיא ליה, דפשיטא ליה דגבי גט אין צריך הגדה בפה, רק שמתרצה, כמו שצריך גבי עדות דבור. אבל לרב כהנא, דחשיב יכול לדבר מתוך הכתב אפי' בחרש – א"כ דבור מעליא הוא, ויש לחושבה הגדה. וי"מ: דאמתניתין לא קשיא ליה, דאיכא למימר דהא דאמר "פרט לאלם שאינו יכול להגיד" – היינו אלם שאינו שומע, דהיינו חרש. אבל אלם לא משמע הכי. **והא** יכול לדבר מתוך הכתב. דהגדה חשיבה ע"י הכתב, כדפרישית. אע"ג דממעט *חרש וחרשת מחליצה לפי שאינם ב"אמר" ו"אמרה" – אמירה ודאי לא הוי אלא בפה. ועוד דהתם* יליף "וענתה" מ"וענו הלוים" שצריך בלשון הקדש, ומינה נמי שמעינן דהויא בפה כמו בלוים. **מפיהם** ולא מפי כתבם. בפ' שני דכתובות (דף כ:*) הארכתי בה. **קתני** מיהת עדיות. אמאי דקתני: פרט לאלם שאינו יכול להגיד, פריך. ומיהו, לר"י נראה דהאי פירכא נמי הויא לרב, דהא תיובתא דבתר הכי הויא לדידיה. והכי פירושו: בשלמא אי לאו דרב, אע"פ שלענין עדות חשיבה הגדה מה שמרכין בראשו, כדקתני הכא דבודקין אותו לעדות – מ"מ פטר קרא אלם שאינו יכול להגיד, דלענין קרבן שבועה לא חשיבה הגדה, אלא הגדה מעליא. אלא לרב, דחשיב דיכול לדבר מתוך הכתב עדות מעליא, כיון דאפילו בחרש מהני, אע"ג דהרכנה לא מהניא ביה כלל – וא"כ צריך לומר הא דממעט קרא אלם שאינו יכול להגיד, אע"פ שיכול לדבר מתוך הכתב – משום דרחמנא אמר "מפיהם" ולא מפי כתבם, וא"כ איך בודקין אותו לעדות? הא בעינן מפיהם ולא מפי כתבם! ולמאי דפירשנו פרט לאלם שאינו יכול להגיד, דהיינו חרש – א"ש, דאי לאו דרב באלם סגי בהרכנה בכל דבר, אבל חרש לא סגי, אפי' יכול לדבר מתוך הכתב – לא לענין גט, ולא לענין עדות. אבל לרב, אע"ג דפסול לענין עדות – כשר גבי גט, תקשי ליה, דהא הכא מכשרינן עדות כמו גט. **והא** קתני ירושות. השתא דקסבר ירושות דעלמא, ומשאות ומתנות דעלמא, ולענין עדות קאמר – צ"ל דסלקא דעתיה דפרושי קא מפרש: למשאות ומתנות וירושות – היינו עדות. אי נמי הוי מצי למימר: ולטעמיך היינו עדות! **ירושת** בנו הבכור. פרש"י: שהשוה בכור לפשוט. ואין נראה לר"י, אם כן הוה ליה למימר: שריבה לזה ומיעט לזה! אלא אומר רבינו יצחק: דהיינו שאומר על בן בין הבנים שהוא בכור, וקא משמע לן דנאמן לכך על ידי הרכנה. **תנאי** היא דתניא אמר רשב"ג כו'. לא בעי לשנויי דרב מיירי בפיקח מעיקרו, וברייתא בחרש מעיקרו, כמו שמחלק רשב"ג. משום דקים לן דרשב"ג פליג על הך ברייתא, כדאמר רבי יוחנן בסמוך. אי

[יבמות קד:] [סוטה לב.] [ד"ה ור"י]

עין משפט נר מצוה

טז א מיי' פ"ב מהלכות גירושין הלכה טז סמג עשין נ [עיין כ"מ]:

יז ב מיי' פ"ב מהלכות אישות הלכ' כו ופכ"ט מהל' מכירה הל' ג סמג עשין פב טוש"ע ח"מ סי' רלה סעיף יח:

יח ג מיי' פ"ט מהלכות עדות הלכה יא סמג לאוין ריד טוש"ע ח"מ סי' לה סעיף (יח) [יא]:

יט ד מיי' שם ופ"ג שם הלכה ד סמג שם טוש"ע שם וסי' כח סעיף יא:

כ ה מיי' פכ"ט מהל' מכירה הלכה ג סמג עשין פב טוש"ע ח"מ סי' רלה סעיף יח:

כא ו מיי' פ"ט מהל' עדות הלכה יא סמג לאוין ריד טוש"ע ח"מ סי' לה סעיף יא:

כב ז מיי' פ"ד מהל' נחלות הלכה א סמג עשין צו טור ש"ע ח"מ סי' רעט סעיף א:

כג ח מיי' פכ"ט מהל' מכירה הלכה ב ג סמג עשין פב טור ש"ע ח"מ סי' רלה סעיף יז:

כד ט י מיי' פ"ב מהל' גירושין הלכה יז סמג עשין נ טור ש"ע אה"ע סימן קכ סעיף ה:

כה כ ל מיי' פ"ז מהל' יבום הלכ' טז יז סמג עשין נג טוש"ע אה"ע סי' קעב סעיף יב וסי' קכא סעי' ו:

גליון הש"ס

תום' ד"ה א"ר זירא כו' דהיינו חרש. קשה לי דה"ל למאי לריך לשמעתא דאינו יכול להגיד הא בלאו הכי לאו בר שבועה הוא ועל כל חייבי כריתות אינו חייב והוא כשוטה לכל דבר:

תוספות רי"ד

אמר רב כהנא אמר רב חרש שיכול לדבר מתוך הכתב כותבים ונותנין גט לאשתו. פי' אין לפרש דבחרש מעיקרא הוא דאמר רב דא"כ מאי אריא בכתיבה בכל רמזיו יכול להוציא כדאמרינן בפ' חרש כשם שכנס ברמיזה כך מוציא ברמיזה אלא בפקח ונתחרש קאמר שהיה פקח כשכנסה וקדושיו קדושין גמורין ותנן ביבמות נתחרש הוא או נשתטה אינו מוציא עולמית לפי שאין כח בגירושי חרשת להפקיע קדושי חכמה וקאמר רב שאם יכול לדבר מתוך הכתב ויודע לכתוב על הקלף כתבו גט ותנו לאשתי אתם פלוני ופלוני ומסר להם סומכין על כתיבתו וכותבין ונותנין אמר רב נחמן מאי קמ"ל תנינא נשתתק ואמרו לו נכתוב גט לאשתך וכו' כיון דקא מחוי כתבי' פי' סומכין ברמזיו וכותבין גט לאשתו ואין לך רמז גדול מכתיבת ידו א"ל רב זירא אלם קאמרת שאני אלם דתניא חרש המדבר ואינו שומע זהו חרש שומע ואינו מדבר זהו אלם וזה וזה הרי הם כפקחים לכל דבריהם. פי' ונשתתק במתני' פקח גמור הוא אלא שמתוך חליו נאלם ואינו מדבר אבל שפוי הוא בדעתו ולפיכך בודקים אותו אם לא נטרפה דעתו סומכין על רמזיו וכ"ש על כתב ידו אבל חרש גמור שאינו שומע ואינו מדבר שאין סומכין על רמזיו להפקיע קדושיו שנתן בעודו פקח כדתנן נתחרש הוא או נשתטה לא יוציא עולמית הוה אמינא שגם על כתבו לא נסמוך דכשאר רמזיו דמיא קמ"ל רב דסומכין על כתיבתו שהכתיבה אינה נעשית אלא בדעת ובכוונה: א"ר זירא אי ק' לי הא ק' לי דתניא אם לא יגיד פרט לאלם שאינו יכול להגיד. ואמאי והא יכול להגיד מתוך הכתב. פי' ממתני' דנשתתק לא ק' ליה מפני שהוא פקח ומחמת חליו נשתתק ואלם דממעט מלא יגיד י"ל דהוא חרש גמור שאינו בר דעת מ"ה ממעט ליה אלא דרב ק' דאמר סומכין על כתיבתו להפקיע קדושי פקחות שנעשו מדעת וא"כ אמאי ממעט ליה מאם לא יגיד הרי יכול להגיד מתוך הכתב ואע"פ שאין לסמוך על רמזיו על כתיבתו יש לסמוך: א"ל אביי עדות קאמרת שאני עדות דרחמנא אמר מפיהם ולא מפי כתבם. פי' האי אלם דקא ממעט מלא יגיד לא בחרש מיירי ומשום שאין בו דעת [אלא] באלם שהוא שומע ואינו מדבר שהוא כפקח לכל דבריו וטעמא דמלתא משום דלגבי עדות בעי' מפיהם ולא מפי כתבם אבל לענין ליתן גט לאשתו לא מיבעיא שהוא פקח אלא אפילו חרש גמור ע"י כתיבתו כותבין ונותנין גט לאשתו להפקיע קדושי פקחותו שכתיבתו מדעת היא נעשית כדקאמר רב ואי ק' אלם שהוא פקח אמאי אינו יכול להעיד מפי הכתב ומ"ש מכל שטרי דעלמא שהן כשרים בדיני ממונות ואמרי' בהו עדים החתומים על השטר נעשה כמי שנחקרה עדותן בב"ד וגם הוא מקרא מלא שדות בכסף יקנו וכתוב בספר וחתום. תשובה כל שיכול להגיד על פה כשר בכתיבה ועשו חתימתו כמו שנחקרה בב"ד עדותו וכל שאינו יכול להגיד על פה אינו כשר בכתיבה ומשום הכי אלם פסול בכתיבה דליתיה על פה ומיהו אינו יכול העד כשיבא לב"ד לכתוב עדותו ולהגיד על ידי כתב אלא בפיו דבעי' מפיהם ולא מפי כתבם. ולא דמיא לחתימת השטר דהתם כיון דמסר החתימה להוא דמסהיד נעשה כמי שנחקרה עדותו בב"ד אבל אי בעי איהו לאסהודי גבי דינא לא מצי לאסהודי בכתב דאכתי לא מסר סהדותיה להוא דמסהיד ליה הלכך צריך להעיד על פה שלא נתקנה החתימה אלא למסור למי שהוא מעיד לו ומפני תיקון העולם שמא ימותו העדים או ילכו למדינת הים אבל לא למוסרה לב"ד כיון דאיהו קאי קמייהו ואלם אין חתימתו מועלת אפילו למוסרה למי שמעיד לו אחרי שאינו בר הגדה משום הכי פטור משבועת העדות שאינו בר דעת לא בפה ולא בחתימה: מיתיבי כשם שבודקין אותו לגיטין כך בודקין אותו למתנות ולמשאות ולירושות ולעדיות קתני מיהת לעדיות מאי לאו לעדיות דעלמא. פי' אלמא שבודקין משנשתתק ומקבל עדותו בהרכנת ראשו וכ"ש בכתיבתו והיכי אמרת דאלם אינו יכול להעיד מתוך הכתב אמר ר' יוסף בר חמא אמר רב ששת בעדות אשה דאקילו בה רבנן להכשיר עד א' ואפילו עד מפי עד הכשירו נמי להעיד בכתיבה ובבדיקה ואפי' אינו מעיד בפה אבל בשאר עדיות לא [והא] ירושות קתני מיהת למאי לאו ירושות דעלמא אמר רב דימי ירושת בנו הבכור דנכסי דידיה נינהו ולכל מאן דבעי מזכה קתני מיהת למשאות ומתנות מאי לאו משאות ומתנות דידיה. מיתיבי חרש לא הלכו אחר רמיזותיו ואחר קפיצותיו ואחר כתב ידו אלא במטלטלין אבל לא בגיטין. פי' בפקח ולבסוף נתחרש מיירי שהיו קדושיו קדושי

כו א מיי' פ"ז מהל' יבום הלכה כב סמג עשין נא טוש"ע אה"ע סי' קעב סעיף יג:

כז ב ג מיי' פ"ו מהל' גירושין הלכה כב סמג עשין נ טוש"ע אה"ע סימן קיט סעי' ו:

כח ד מיי' שם פ"ב הלכה ה סמג שם טוש"ע אה"ע סי' קכ סעיף ז:

*וְהָתְנַן: אשְׁנֵי אַחִין חֵרְשִׁין נְשׂוּאִין שְׁתֵּי אֲחָיוֹת פִּיקְחוֹת, אוֹ שְׁתֵּי אֲחָיוֹת חֵרְשׁוֹת, אוֹ שְׁתֵּי אֲחָיוֹת אַחַת פִּיקַחַת וְאַחַת חֵרֶשֶׁת, וְכֵן שְׁתֵּי אֲחָיוֹת חֵרְשׁוֹת נְשׂוּאוֹת לִשְׁנֵי אַחִין פִּיקְחִין, אוֹ לִשְׁנֵי אַחִין חֵרְשִׁין, אוֹ לִשְׁנֵי אַחִין אֶחָד פִּיקֵּחַ וְאֶחָד חֵרֵשׁ — הֲרֵי אֵלּוּ פְּטוּרוֹת מִן הַחֲלִיצָה וּמִן הַיִּבּוּם, וְאִם הָיוּ נָכְרִיּוֹת — יִכְנְסוּ, וְאִם רָצוּ לְהוֹצִיאָן — יוֹצִיאוּ! *אֶלָּא, מְחַוַּורְתָּא כִּדְשַׁנִּין מֵעִיקָּרָא. אָמַר רַבִּי יוֹחָנָן: חֲלוּקִין עָלָיו חֲבֵירָיו עַל רשב"ג. אָמַר אַבַּיֵי, אַף אֲנַן נַמִּי תָּנֵינָא: *בנִשְׁתַּטֵּית — לֹא יוֹצִיא, נִתְחָרֵשׁ הוּא אוֹ נִשְׁתַּטָּה — לֹא יוֹצִיא עוֹלָמִית; מַאי "עוֹלָמִית"? לָאו אע"ג דְּיָכוֹל לְדַבֵּר מִתּוֹךְ הַכְּתָב? אָמַר רַב פַּפָּא: אִי לָאו דְּאַשְׁמוּעִינַן ר' יוֹחָנָן, הֲוָה אָמִינָא, רשב"ג לְפָרוּשֵׁי טַעְמָא דְּת"ק הוּא דְּאָתָא, וּמַאי "עוֹלָמִית"? אע"ג דְּחָזֵינָא לֵיהּ דְּחָרִיף; אִי נַמִּי, לְכִדְרַבִּי יִצְחָק, *דְּא"ר יִצְחָק: דְּבַר תּוֹרָה שׁוֹטָה מִתְגָּרֶשֶׁת, מִידֵּי דַּהֲוָה אַפִּיקַּחַת בְּעַל כָּרְחָהּ, וּמַה טַּעַם אָמְרוּ אֵינָהּ מִתְגָּרֶשֶׁת? גשֶׁלֹּא יִנְהֲגוּ בָּהּ מִנְהַג הֶפְקֵר.§ **מתני'** דאָמְרוּ לוֹ "נִכְתּוֹב גֵּט לְאִשְׁתְּךָ"? וְאָמַר לָהֶן "כְּתוֹבוּ", אָמְרוּ לַסּוֹפֵר וְכָתַב וְלָעֵדִים וְחָתְמוּ, אע"פ שֶׁכְּתָבוּהוּ וַחֲתָמוּהוּ וּנְתָנוּהוּ לוֹ וְחָזַר וּנְתָנוֹ לָהּ — הֲרֵי הַגֵּט בָּטֵל, עַד שֶׁיֹּאמַר לַסּוֹפֵר "כְּתוֹב" וְלָעֵדִים "חֲתוֹמוּ".§ **גמ'** טַעְמָא דְּלָא אֲמַר "תְּנוּ", הָא אֲמַר "תְּנוּ" — נוֹתְנִין, מַנִּי? ר"מ הִיא, דְּאָמַר: מִילֵּי מִימְסְרָן לְשָׁלִיחַ; אֵימָא סֵיפָא: עַד שֶׁיֹּאמַר לַסּוֹפֵר "כְּתוֹב" וְלָעֵדִים "חֲתוֹמוּ", אֲתָאן לְר' יוֹסֵי, דְּאָמַר: *מִילֵּי לָא מִימְסְרָן לְשָׁלִיחַ; רֵישָׁא ר"מ וְסֵיפָא רַבִּי יוֹסֵי? *אִין, רֵישָׁא ר"מ וְסֵיפָא רַבִּי יוֹסֵי. אַבַּיֵי אָמַר: כּוּלָּהּ רַבִּי מֵאִיר הִיא, וְהָכָא בְּמַאי עָסְקִינַן — דְּלָא אֲמַר "תְּנוּ". אִי הָכִי, "עַד שֶׁיֹּאמַר תְּנוּ" מִיבָּעֵי לֵיהּ! אֶלָּא הָכָא בְּמַאי עָסְקִינַן — דְּלָא אֲמַר לְבֵי תְּלָתָא. א"ה, "עַד שֶׁיֹּאמַר לִשְׁלֹשָׁה" מִיבָּעֵי לֵיהּ! אֶלָּא כּוּלָּהּ רַבִּי יוֹסֵי הִיא, וְהָכָא בְּמַאי עָסְקִינַן — דְּלָא אֲמַר "אִמְרוּ". אִי הָכִי, "עַד שֶׁיֹּאמַר אִמְרוּ" מִיבָּעֵי לֵיהּ! וְעוֹד, *מִי מוֹדֶה רַבִּי יוֹסֵי בְּאוֹמֵר "אִמְרוּ"? *וְהָתְנַן: כָּתַב סוֹפֵר וְעֵד — כָּשֵׁר, *וְאָמַר רַבִּי יִרְמְיָה: חָתַם סוֹפֵר שָׁנִינוּ, וַאֲמַר רַב חִסְדָּא: מַתְנִיתִין מַנִּי? ר'

שְׁנֵי אַחִין חֵרְשִׁים. כֵּיוָן דְּהֵם חֵרְשִׁים לָא אִיכְפַּת לָן בִּנְשׂוּאֵיהֶן אִם הֵן (א) *אַחַת פִּקְּחוֹת, דְּמ"מ הֵם לֹא כָּנְסוּ אֶלָּא בִּרְמִיזָה. וְכֵן שְׁתֵּי אֲחָיוֹת חֵרְשׁוֹת. לָא אִיכְפַּת לָן בַּפִּקְּחוּת שֶׁל בְּעָלִים, דְּהֵן לֹא נִכְנְסוּ אֶלָּא בִּרְמִיזָה, לְפִיכָךְ פְּטוּרוֹת מִן הַחֲלִיצָה, דְּיוֹצְאָה מִשּׁוּם אֲחוֹת אִשָּׁה, דְּכָל עֲרָיוֹת פְּטוּרוֹת מִן הַחֲלִיצָה. וְאִם הָיוּ נָכְרִיּוֹת. וּמֵת אֶחָד מֵהֶן – הַשֵּׁנִי אֵינוֹ יָכוֹל לַחֲלוֹץ, מִפְּנֵי שֶׁהוּא חֵרֵשׁ אוֹ שֶׁהִיא חֵרֶשֶׁת וְאֵינָהּ יְכוֹלָה לוֹמַר "מֵאֵן יְבָמִי", אֶלָּא יִכָּנְסוּ. וְאִם רָצוּ לְהוֹצִיאָן. אַחֲרֵי כֵן – יוֹצִיאוּ, דְּאָתֵי גֵּט חֵרֵשׁ וּמַפְקַע זִיקַּת קִידּוּשֵׁי חֵרֵשׁ. אַלְמָא, הֵיכָא דְּנָפְלָה לֵיהּ מֵאָחִיו חֵרֵשׁ – מַפִּיק, וְלָא גָּזְרִינַן אַטּוּ אָחִיו פִּקֵּחַ! כִּדְשַׁנִּין מֵעִיקָּרָא. דְּנָפְלָה לֵיהּ מֵאָחִיו פִּקֵּחַ. חֲלוּקִין עָלָיו חֲבֵירָיו. דַּאֲפִי' פִּקֵּחַ וְנִתְחָרֵשׁ אֵינוֹ יָכוֹל לְגָרֵשׁ, וַאֲפִי' יוֹדֵעַ לִכְתּוֹב. וְלָא תֵּימָא רשב"ג מְפָרֵשׁ מִילְּתֵיהּ דְּתַנָּא קַמָּא, דְּהָכִי שְׁמִיעַ לֵיהּ לְרַבִּי יוֹחָנָן דְּמִיפְלַג פָּלֵיג. נִשְׁתַּטֵּית. הִיא, מִשֶּׁנִּיסֵּאת. לֹא יוֹצִיא. אָסוּר לְהוֹצִיאָהּ. וְאע"פ שֶׁפִּקַּחַת וְנִתְחָרְשָׁה יוֹצִיאָהּ, דְּאִשָּׁה לָא בָּעֵינַן דַּעְתָּהּ, שֶׁהֲרֵי יוֹצְאָה לִרְצוֹנָהּ וְשֶׁלֹּא לִרְצוֹנָהּ – הֵיכָא דְּנִשְׁטֵית אָמוּר רַבָּנַן לֹא יוֹצִיא, דְּכֵיוָן שֶׁאֵינָהּ יוֹדַעַת לִשְׁמוֹר עַצְמָהּ – יִנְהֲגוּ בָּהּ הֶפְקֵר בִּזְנוּת, וְכֵן מְפָרֵשׁ לְקַמָּן. וְאע"ג דְּחָרִיף. אֲבָל מְדַבֵּר מִתּוֹךְ הַכְּתָב – לֹא מְמַעֵט. אִי נַמִּי. הַאי "עוֹלָמִית" לְכִדְרַבִּי יִצְחָק אַתָּא לְמֵידַק מִינֵּיהּ, מִדְּקָתָנֵי סֵיפָא עוֹלָמִית, וְרֵישָׁא לָא תְּנָא עוֹלָמִית – מִשּׁוּם דְּרֵישָׁא דְּרַבָּנַן כִּדְרַבִּי יִצְחָק, וְסֵיפָא דְּאוֹרַיְיתָא. דְּגַבֵּי מְגָרֵשׁ בָּעֵינַן דַּעְתּוֹ, שֶׁהָאִישׁ אֵינוֹ מוֹצִיא אֶלָּא לִרְצוֹנוֹ. אַפִּיקַּחַת בְּעַל כָּרְחָהּ. מִתְגָּרֶשֶׁת, וְאע"פ שֶׁלֹּא מִדַּעְתָּהּ. **מתני'** אָמְרוּ לוֹ. לְבָרִיא, אוֹ לִשְׁכִיב מְרַע חָכָם. נִכְתּוֹב גֵּט לְאִשְׁתְּךָ. שֶׁלֹּא תִּזָּקֵק לְיָבָם. וְאָמַר לָהֶם כְּתוֹבוּ. וְהֵם אָמְרוּ לוֹ לַסּוֹפֵר כו'. **גמ'** טַעְמָא דְּלָא אָמַר לָהֶם תְּנוּ. בְּלֹא "כִּתְבוּ", דְּכֵיוָן דְּאָמַר לָהֶם "כִּתְבוּ" מַקְפִּיד הָיָה בַּדָּבָר שֶׁלֹּא יֹאמְרוּ לְאַחֵר וְיִכְתּוֹב, שֶׁבּוּשָׁת הוּא לוֹ לְגַלּוֹת שֶׁאֵינוֹ יוֹדֵעַ לִכְתּוֹב גֵּט. וּדְהָא אֲפִי' ר"מ מוֹדֶה, *לְקַמָּן בְּפֶרֶק "הִתְקַבֵּל" שֶׁאִם אָמַר "כִּתְבוּ גֵּט לְאִשְׁתִּי", אֲפִילּוּ אָמַר לְב"ד – לֹא עֲשָׂאָם ב"ד לְהַרְשׁוֹת אֶת אֲחֵרִים עַל כָּךְ. הָא אָמַר תְּנוּ. גֵּט לְאִשְׁתִּי, וְלֹא אָמַר "כִּתְבוּ" – אוֹמְרִים לַאֲחֵרִים וְיִכְתְּבוּ וְיִתְּנוּ, דַּעֲשָׂאָן ב"ד. וְעַל כָּרְחִין כְּגוֹן שֶׁהָיוּ שְׁלֹשָׁה, דְּאִילּוּ לִשְׁנַיִם – אֲפִי' ר"מ מוֹדֶה שֶׁאֲפִי' לֹא אָמַר "כִּתְבוּ" אֶלָּא "תְּנוּ" צְרִיכִים הֵם עַצְמָם לִכְתּוֹב. דְּהָכִי תְּנַן לְקַמָּן: *אָמַר לִשְׁנַיִם "תְּנוּ גֵּט לְאִשְׁתִּי" אוֹ לִשְׁלֹשָׁה "כִּתְבוּ וּתְנוּ גֵּט לְאִשְׁתִּי" – יִכְתְּבוּ הֵם עַצְמָם וְיִתְּנוּ. אֲבָל אָמַר לִשְׁלֹשָׁה "תְּנוּ" – יֹאמְרוּ לַאֲחֵרִים וְיִכְתְּבוּ וְיִתְּנוּ, מִפְּנֵי שֶׁעֲשָׂאָם ב"ד, דִּבְרֵי ר"מ, וּפְלֵיג רַבִּי יוֹסֵי עֲלֵיהּ, דַּאֲפִילּוּ לִשְׁלֹשָׁה נַמִּי, אע"ג דְּלֹא אָמַר "כִּתְבוּ" – צְרִיכִין הֵם עַצְמָם לִכְתּוֹב. וּמַתְנִיתִין דְּנָקַט "כִּתְבוּ" – מַשְׁמַע דְּאִי לֹא אָמַר "כִּתְבוּ" לָא הָוֵי פָּסֵיל הַאי גִּיטָּא, וּכְגוֹן שֶׁהָיוּ שְׁלֹשָׁה, וְרַבִּי מֵאִיר הִיא. דְּאָמַר מִילֵּי מִימְסְרָן לְשָׁלִיחַ. דֶּרֶךְ אֶרֶץ הוּא לַעֲשׂוֹת שָׁלִיחַ דְּבָרִים, וַהֲוֵי נַמִּי בִּדְבָרִים שְׁלוּחוֹ שֶׁל אָדָם כְּמוֹתוֹ. הִלְכָּךְ הֵיכָא דַּהֲווּ ג', דְּאִיכָּא לְמֵימַר עֲשָׂאָן ב"ד, לוֹמַר לַאֲחֵרִים: אִמְרוּ לַסּוֹפֵר וְיִכְתּוֹב, וְלָעֵדִים וְיַחְתְּמוּ. עַד שֶׁיֹּאמַר לַסּוֹפֵר כְּתוֹב. מַשְׁמַע דְּאֵין לְךָ כַּל הֵיתֵּר לוֹמַר לַאֲחֵרִים לִכְתּוֹב, אֶלָּא הַשּׁוֹמֵעַ מִפִּיו הוּא יִכְתּוֹב, וַאֲפִילּוּ שְׁלֹשָׁה, וַאֲפִי' לֹא אָמַר "כִּתְבוּ". הָכָא בְּמַאי עָסְקִינַן. הַךְ סֵיפָא דְּקָתָנֵי: עַד שֶׁיֹּאמַר לַסּוֹפֵר עַצְמוֹ. דְּלָא אָמַר תְּנוּ. בְּלֹא "כִּתְבוּ". וְהָכִי קָאָמַר: הָאוֹמֵר "כִּתְבוּ" – אֵינוֹ כָּשֵׁר, אֶלָּא א"כ אָמַר לַסּוֹפֵר עַצְמוֹ. אִי הָכִי. כֵּיוָן דְּאִיכָּא לַד הֵיתֵּר לוֹמַר לַאֲחֵרִים, הָכִי אִיבָּעֵי לֵיהּ לְמִיתְנֵי: אֵינוֹ גֵּט עַד שֶׁיֹּאמַר "תְּנוּ", בְּלֹא "כִּתְבוּ", וְכָל שֶׁכֵּן פְּשִׁיטָא דְּכִי אָמַר לַסּוֹפֵר עַצְמוֹ! אֶלָּא וַדַּאי דַּוְקָא קָאָמַר סֵיפָא בְּאוֹמֵר "תְּנוּ". וְהָכָא בְּמַאי עָסְקִינַן דְּלָא אָמַר לִשְׁלֹשָׁה. וּבִשְׁנַיִם מוֹדֶה ר"מ דַּאֲפִילּוּ אָמַר "תְּנוּ" – כּוֹתְבִין הֵן עַצְמָן, דְּלָא עֲשָׂאָם ב"ד. אֶלָּא כּוּלָּהּ רַבִּי יוֹסֵי הִיא. וְהָא דְּנָקַט בְּרֵישָׁא "כְּתוֹבוּ" – לָאו לְמֵידַק דְּאִילּוּ אָמַר "תְּנוּ" בְּלֹא "כִּתְבוּ" אוֹמְרִים לַאֲחֵרִים וְיִכְתְּבוּ, אֶלָּא הַיְינוּ טַעְמָא דְּפָסוּל – דְּלָא אָמַר "אִמְרוּ". וְהָכִי דָּיְיקַת מִינַּהּ: טַעְמָא דְּלֹא אָמַר "אִמְרוּ", הָא אָמַר לִשְׁנַיִם "אִמְרוּ לִפְלוֹנִי וְיִכְתּוֹב, וְלִפְלוֹנִי וּפְלוֹנִי וְיַחְתְּמוּ", וְאָמְרוּ לְאוֹתוֹ סוֹפֵר וְכָתַב, וּלְאוֹתָן עֵדִים וְחָתְמוּ – שַׁפִּיר דָּמֵי, דְּמוֹדֵי רַבִּי יוֹסֵי בְּהָא, שֶׁהֲרֵי עֲשָׂאָן שְׁלוּחִין לְכָךְ. וְא"ר יִרְמְיָה חָתַם סוֹפֵר שָׁנִינוּ. לָא תֵּימָא דְּמִתְכַּשַּׁר גֵּט בַּחֲתִימַת עֵד אֶחָד וּכְתַב יַד סוֹפֵר שֵׁנִי, אֶלָּא הָכִי קָאָמַר: חָתַם הַסּוֹפֵר בְּגֵט עֵד, וְעֵד שֵׁנִי עִמּוֹ – כָּשֵׁר. וְאָמַר רַב חִסְדָּא. מַתְנִי' דְּמַכְשַׁר לְהַחְתִּים סוֹפֵר בְּגֵט. ר'

אי נמי לכדרבי יצחק. אביי נמי דייק "עולמית" לכדרבי יצחק בפרק "חרש" (יבמות קיג:), דקאמר התם: אף אנן נמי תנינא(ב) כדרבי יצחק, ודייק מדקתני "עולמית" גבי נשתטה, ולא תנא גבי נישטת היא. אלא דהכא דייק מדקתני "עולמית" אתרוייהו, אנתחרש ונשתטה; הא דקתני ליה אחרש – אשמועינן אפי' יכול לדבר ע"י כתב, ואנשתטה – לכדרבי יצחק. ורב פפא דחי, דמ"מ איכא למימר דלא אתא "עולמית" אלא לכדרבי יצחק גרידא. **הכא** במאי עסקינן דלא אמר תנו. וא"ת: וכי לא ידע שיקשה לו "עד שיאמר תנו מיבעי ליה"? דמכח זה דקדק תחלה דסיפא כרבי יוסי, מדקתני "עד שיאמר לסופר כתוב" ולא קתני: עד שיאמר "תנו"! וי"ל: דהמתרץ סבר דלהכי לא תנא: עד שיאמר "תנו" – משום דככר שמעינן ליה מדיוקא דרישא דקתני "כתבו", משמע: הא אמר "תנו" – נותנין. ולהכי אשמועינן בסיפא דב"כתבו" לא מהני עד שיאמר לסופר "כתוב". וטעמא דרישא קמפרש, דלהכי לא מהני מה שעשו אחרים בלשון "כתובו" – משום דמילי לא מימסרן לשליח, ולא מהני עד שיאמר לסופר "כתוב" ולעדים "חתומו". ופריך: עד שיאמר "תנו" מיבעי ליה, דכיון דלא שמעינן ליה אלא מדיוקא דרישא – הוה ליה למיתני בסיפא בהדיא: עד שיאמר "תנו". **הכא** במאי עסקינן דלא אמר לתלתא. ה"נ תימה: וכי לא ידע שיקשה לו, עד שיאמר "לג' מיבעי ליה"? ועוד: דאי בדלא אמר לתלתא – מאי איריא "כתבו"? "תנו" נמי לא מהני! וי"ל: דהשתא מוקי רישא בכל ענין, בין אמר לב' בין אמר לשלשה, ומשום שלשה נקט "כתבו", דהא אם אמר "תנו" – נותנין. ולהכי לא מצי למיתני בסיפא "עד שיאמר לשלשה", דהא בשלשה נמי מיירי, ד"כתבו" לא מהני אפי' בשלשה. ומ"מ פריך: דה"ל למיתני בסיפא, ולפרש בהדיא: עד שיאמר לשלשה "תנו". **הכא** במאי עסקינן דלא אמר אמרו. סלקא דעתא דלא שייך לאקשויי "עד שיאמר "אמרו" מיבעי ליה", דניחא ליה למינקט דומיא דרישא, שהבעל מלוה לעדים עצמם לעשות. אבל אומר "אמרו" – אומר לאחרים שיאמרו לעדים לעשות. וא"ת: השתא דמוקי לה כרבי יוסי – אמאי נקט "כתבו"? הוה ליה למינקט "תנו", וכ"ש "כתבו"! ועוד: כיון ד"כתבו" לאו דוקא, והוא הדין "תנו" – נימא דהוא הדין נמי "אמרו", ותיתי שפיר סיפא: עד שיאמר לסופר כתוב כו'! ויש לומר: דלא חש למיתני "תנו", דמסיפא שמעינן דהוא הדין "תנו", מדלא תנא: עד שיאמר "תנו". ומשום

תוספות רי"ד

קדושי תורה ואין לו כח להפקיעם לא ברמיזה ולא בכתבו וק' לרב כהנא אמר רב ומהדר תנאי הוא דתניא ארשב"ג בד"א בחרש מעיקרו אבל פקח ונתחרש הוא כותב ואחרים חותמין על כתב ידו. פי' בד"א שאין סומכין על כתב ידו אלא בחרש מעיקרא שלא למד לכתוב מדעת אבל פקח ונתחרש שלמד הכתיבה בעודו פקח סומכין על כתבו והוא כותב הגט ואחרים חותמין עליו ונותנו לאשתו ומפקיע קדושי פקחותו כרב כהנא אמר רב: ומקשה חרש מעיקרו לא אדרבה (מיקלקל) כשם שכנס ברמיזה כך מוציא ברמיזה ובכל רמזיו סומכין וכ"ש על כתיבתו ומהדר אי באשתו הכי נמי הכא במאי עסקינן ביבמתו יבמתו דנפלה ליה ממאן אילימא דנפלה ליה מאחיו חרש סוף סוף כשם שכנס ברמיזה כך מוציא ברמיזה אלא דנפלה ליה מאחיו פקח נמצא עכשיו דפליגי רבנן ורשב"ג בכתיבת החרש דרבנן סברי חרש לא יועילו רמזיו ולא כתיבתו לגבי גט וכגון שכנס בעודו פקח שקדושיו קדושי תורה דאי בחרש מעיקרו ליכא מאן דפליג דכשם שכנס ברמיזה כך מוציא ברמיזה ואתא רשב"ג למימר איזו כתיבת חרש אין סומכין עליה מחרש מעיקרו שלא למדה מדעת אותה כתיבה ודאי לא מהניא גבי יבמתו שנפלה לפניו מאחיו פקח שאין ביאתו וגיטו חשובים להפקיע זיקה דאורייתא ואפילו ע"י כתב אבל בכתיבת פקח ונתחרש שלמדה בעודו פקח מהניא כתיבתו לאחר שנתחרש להפקיע קדושי פקחותו ואע"פ שרמזיו אין מועילין כתיבתו מועלת ורב כהנא אמר רב דאמרי כרשב"ג: א"ר יוחנן חלוקים עליו חביריו על רשב"ג. פי' היא הברייתא שהבאנו למעלה ואתא ר' יוחנן למימר דרשב"ג דאמר בד"א בחרש מעיקרו לאו לפרושי דת"ק קאמר ולא אתי לאיפלוגי עליה אלא קים ליה לר' יוחנן דמיפליג פליגי: אמר אביי אף אנן נמי תנינא נשתטת לא תצא. פי' מפני שאין לה יד ואין לה דעת לשמור גיטה. נתחרש הוא או נשתטה לא יוציא עולמית מאי עולמית לאו אע"ג שיכול לדבר מתוך הכתב שאין לחלק בין כתיבתו לשאר רמזיו וכיון דרבנן פליגי עליה דרשב"ג וסתם מתני' דיבמות נמי פליגא עליה הלכה כסתם מתני' ולקמן בפרקין נמי אמרינן לאפוקי מדרב כהנא אלמא לית הלכתא כותיה שאין סומכין על כתיבתו כמו שאין סומכין על רמיזותיו שהפקיע קדושי פקחותו: מתני' אמרו לו נכתוב גט לאשתך אמר להם כתובו אמרו לסופר וכתב ולעדים וחתמו אף על פי שכתבוהו וחתמוהו ונתנוהו לו וחזר ונתנו לה הרי הגט בטל עד שיאמר לסופר כתוב ולעדים חתומו: ודייקינן טעמא דלא אמר תנו הא אמר תנו [נותנין] ומתני' מני ר' מאיר היא דאמר מילי ממסרן לשליח אימא סיפא עד שיאמר לסופר כתוב ולעדים חתומו אתאן לר' יוסי דאמר מילי לא מימסרן לשליח ואבקה

[נ"ל אחיות]

יבמות קיג: קיב:

ס"א אלמא לא גזרינן חרש אטו פקח

שם

שם קיג:

[לעיל כט. וש"נ]

אמר אביי אין רישא ר"מ וסיפא ר' יוסי רבא אמר כולה ר"מ ס"ל מ"ד

[ולפנינו הוא לעיל סו:] עי' תוס' לעיל ד"ה התקבל

[לעיל סו: לקמן עב.]

לעיל סו: לקמן פו:

[לעיל סו: לקמן פח.]

[ולפנינו הוא לעיל סו:]

הגהות הב"ח

(א) רש"י ד"ה שני אחין וכו' אם הן פקחות כצ"ל ותיבת אחת נמחק: (ב) תוס' ד"ה אי נמי וכו' נמי תנינא לכדרבי יצחק:

ר' יוֹסֵי הִיא, דְּאָמַר: *מִילֵּי לָא מִימְסְרָן לְשָׁלִיחַ; וְאִי ס"ד מוֹדֶה ר' יוֹסֵי בְּאוֹמֵר "אִמְרוּ", נָפֵיק מִינָּהּ חוּרְבָא, דְּזִימְנִין דְּאָמַר לְהוּ לִשְׁנַיִם "אִמְרוּ לַסּוֹפֵר וְיִכְתּוֹב וְלִפְלוֹנִי וּפְלוֹנִי וְיַחְתְּמוּ", וּמִשּׁוּם כִּיסּוּפָא דְּסוֹפֵר חָיְישִׁי וּמַחְתְּמִי לֵיהּ, וּבַעַל לָא אָמַר הָכִי! אֶלָּא מְחַוַּורְתָּא, רֵישָׁא ר"מ וְסֵיפָא ר' יוֹסֵי. רַב אַשִׁי אָמַר: כּוּלָּהּ ר' יוֹסֵי הִיא, וְלָא מִיבָּעֲיָא קָאָמַר; לָא מִבָּעֲיָא הֵיכָא דְּלֹא אָמַר "תְּנוּ", אֶלָּא אֲפִי' אָמַר "תְּנוּ" — לָא; וְלָא מִיבָּעֲיָא הֵיכָא דְּלֹא אָמַר לְבֵי תְּלָתָא, אֶלָּא אֲפִי' אָמַר לְבֵי תְּלָתָא — לָא; וְלָא מִיבָּעֲיָא הֵיכָא דְּלֹא אָמַר "אִמְרוּ", אֶלָּא א אֲפִילּוּ אָמַר "אִמְרוּ" — נַמִי לָא. תַּנְיָא כְּוָותֵיהּ דְּרַב אַשִׁי: כָּתַב סוֹפֵר לִשְׁמָהּ וְחָתְמוּ עֵדִים לִשְׁמָהּ, אע"פ שֶׁכְּתָבוּהוּ וַחֲתָמוּהוּ וּנְתָנוּהוּ לוֹ וּנְתָנוֹ לָהּ — הֲרֵי הַגֵּט בָּטֵל, עַד שֶׁיִּשְׁמְעוּ קוֹלוֹ שֶׁיֹּאמַר לַסּוֹפֵר "כְּתוֹב" וְלָעֵדִים "חֲתוֹמוּ"; יִשְׁמְעוּ — לְאַפּוּקֵי מִמ"ד: *מוֹדֶה רַבִּי יוֹסֵי בְּאוֹמֵר "אִמְרוּ"; קוֹלוֹ — לְאַפּוּקֵי *מִדְּרַב כָּהֲנָא אָמַר רַב.§ **מתני'** *ב "זֶה גִּיטֵּיךְ אִם מַתִּי", "זֶה גִּיטֵּיךְ מֵחוֹלִי זֶה", "זֶה גִּיטֵּיךְ לְאַחַר מִיתָה" — *לֹא אָמַר כְּלוּם; ג "מֵהַיּוֹם אִם מַתִּי", "מֵעַכְשָׁיו אִם מַתִּי" — ד ה"ז גֵּט; "מֵהַיּוֹם וּלְאַחַר מִיתָה" — גֵּט וְאֵינוֹ גֵּט, וְאִם מֵת — חוֹלֶצֶת וְלֹא מִתְיַיבֶּמֶת. ה "זֶה גִּיטֵּיךְ מֵהַיּוֹם אִם מַתִּי מֵחוֹלִי זֶה", וְעָמַד וְהָלַךְ בַּשּׁוּק וְחָלָה וּמֵת, אוֹמְדִין אוֹתוֹ, אִם מֵחֲמַת חוֹלִי הָרִאשׁוֹן מֵת — ה"ז גֵּט, וְאִם לָאו — אֵינוֹ גֵּט.§ **גמ'** אַלְמָא "אִם מַתִּי" כִּ"לְאַחַר מִיתָה" דָּמֵי; וַהֲדַר תָּנֵי "מֵהַיּוֹם אִם מַתִּי" "מֵעַכְשָׁיו אִם מַתִּי", אַלְמָא "אִם מַתִּי" לָאו כִּ"לְאַחַר מִיתָה" דָּמֵי! אָמַר אַבַּיֵי: "אִם מַתִּי" — שְׁתֵּי לְשׁוֹנוֹת מַשְׁמַע, מַשְׁמַע כְּ"מֵעַכְשָׁיו" וּמַשְׁמַע כִּ"לְאַחַר מִיתָה"; אָמַר לָהּ "מֵהַיּוֹם" — כְּמַאן דְּאָמַר לָהּ "מֵעַכְשָׁיו" דָּמֵי, לֹא אָמַר לָהּ "מֵהַיּוֹם" — כְּמַאן דְּאָמַר לָהּ "לְאַחַר מִיתָה" דָּמֵי.§ "זֶה גִּיטֵּךְ אִם מַתִּי" — לֹא אָמַר כְּלוּם".§ אָמַר רַב הוּנָא: וְחוֹלֶצֶת. וְהָא "לֹא אָמַר כְּלוּם" קָתָנֵי! לֹא אָמַר כְּלוּם, דַּאֲסִירָא לְעָלְמָא, וּלְיָבָם נַמִי אֲסִירָא. וְהָא מִדְּסֵיפָא חוֹלֶצֶת, מִכְּלָל דְּרֵישָׁא יַבּוּמֵי נַמִי מְיַבְּמָהּ! מַתְנִי' כְּרַבָּנַן, וְרַב הוּנָא (א) דְּאָמַר — כְּר' יוֹסֵי, *דְּאָמַר: זְמַנּוֹ שֶׁל שְׁטָר מוֹכִיחַ עָלָיו. אִי רַבִּי יוֹסֵי, חֲלִיצָה נַמִי לָא תִּיבָּעֵי! וְכ"ת, מְסַפְּקָא לֵיהּ לְרַב הוּנָא אִי הִלְכְתָא כְּר' יוֹסֵי אוֹ אֵין הֲלָכָה כְּר' יוֹסֵי — וּמִי מְסַפְּקָא לֵיהּ? ו *וְהָא רַבָּה בַּר אֲבוּהּ חֲלַשׁ, עוּל לְגַבֵּיהּ רַב הוּנָא וְרַב נַחְמָן; א"ל רַב הוּנָא לְר"נ: בְּעֵי מִינֵּיהּ מֵרַבָּה בַּר אֲבוּהּ, הֲלָכָה כְּרַבִּי יוֹסֵי אוֹ אֵין הֲלָכָה? א"ל: טַעְמָא דְּרַבִּי יוֹסֵי לָא יָדַעְנָא, הֲלָכָה אִיבָּעֵי מִינֵּיהּ? א"ל: אַתְּ בְּעֵי מִינֵּיהּ הֲלָכָה, וְטַעֲמֵיהּ דְּרַבִּי יוֹסֵי אֲנָא אָמֵינָא לָךְ; בָּעֵי מִינֵּיהּ. א"ל, הָכִי אֲמַר רַב: ו הֲלָכָה כְּרַבִּי יוֹסֵי; לְבָתַר דִּנְפַק א"ל: הַיְינוּ טַעְמָא דְּרַבִּי יוֹסֵי, דְּקָסָבַר: ז זְמַנּוֹ שֶׁל שְׁטָר מוֹכִיחַ עָלָיו! אֶלָּא מְסַפְּקָא לֵיהּ אִי

ר' יוֹסֵי הִיא. הִלְכָּךְ לֵיכָּא לְמֵיחַשׁ לְחוּרְבָּא. דְּאִילּוּ לְר' מֵאִיר — אִיכָּא לְמֵיחַשׁ, דִּלְמָא זִימְנִין דְּאָמַר לִשְׁנַיִם "אִמְרוּ לִפְלוֹנִי וְיִכְתּוֹב וְלִפְלוֹנִי וּפְלוֹנִי וְיַחְתְּמוּ" וְאָזְלִי הָנֵי שְׁלוּחֵי וְחָיְישִׁי לְכִיסּוּפָא דְּסוֹפֵר, וּמַחְתְּמִי לֵיהּ בְּלֹא דַּעַת הַבַּעַל. אֲבָל לְר' יוֹסֵי — לֵיכָּא לְמֵיחַשׁ לְהָכִי, שֶׁהֲרֵי לֹא יִכְתּוֹב סוֹפֵר גֵּט אֶלָּא אִם כֵּן יִשְׁמַע מִפִּי הַבַּעַל עַצְמוֹ. וְאִי ס"ד מוֹדֶה ר' יוֹסֵי בְּאוֹמֵר אִמְרוּ. הַךְ חוּרְבָּא גּוּפָהּ לְר' יוֹסֵי אִיתָא. כּוּלָּהּ ר' יוֹסֵי הִיא. וְרֵישָׁא דְּאָמַר "כִּתְבוּ" — לָאו דַּוְוקָא, דַּאֲפִילּוּ "תְּנוּ" נַמִי פָּסוּל, כִּדְקָתָנֵי סֵיפָא: עַד שֶׁיֹּאמַר לַסּוֹפֵר וְיִכְתּוֹב. וְאוֹרְחָא דְּתַנָּא לְמִיתְנֵי וּלְאוֹסוֹפֵי, וְנָקַט לְמִילְּתֵיהּ בְּלָשׁוֹן: לָא מִיבָּעֲיָא הַךְ, אֶלָּא אֲפִילּוּ הָא נַמִי פָּסֵיל עַד שֶׁיֹּאמַר כו'. תַּנְיָא כְּוָותֵיהּ דְּרַב אַשִׁי. דְּבְאוֹמֵר "אִמְרוּ" נַמִי פָּסֵיל רַבִּי יוֹסֵי. לְאַפּוּקֵי מִדְּרַב כָּהֲנָא. דְּאָמַר לְעֵיל (דף עא.): חֵרֵשׁ שֶׁיָּכוֹל לְדַבֵּר מִתּוֹךְ הַכְּתָב — כּוֹתְבִין וְנוֹתְנִין גֵּט לְאִשְׁתּוֹ. **מתני'** אִם מַתִּי לֹא אָמַר כְּלוּם. דְּמַשְׁמַע לִכְשֶׁאָמוּת, וְאֵין גֵּט לְאַחַר מִיתָה. זֶה גִּיטֵּךְ מֵחוֹלִי זֶה. מַשְׁמַע מֵחוֹלִי זֶה וְאֵילָךְ, וְכֵיוָן שֶׁמֵּת מִתּוֹךְ הַחוֹלִי — נִמְצָא שֶׁאֵין הַגֵּט חָל אֶלָּא לְאַחַר מִיתָה. מֵהַיּוֹם וּלְאַחַר מִיתָה גֵּט וְאֵינוֹ גֵּט. מְסַפְּקָא לָן אִי תְּנָאָה הָוֵי: מֵהַיּוֹם אִם אָמוּת, וְכֵיוָן שֶׁמֵּת — נִתְקַיֵּים הַתְּנַאי, וְנִמְצָא שֶׁהוּא גֵּט מִשְּׁעַת נְתִינָתוֹ. אוֹ חֲזָרָה הָוֵי, שֶׁחָזַר בּוֹ מִמַּאי דְּאָמַר "מֵהַיּוֹם", וְאָמַר "לְאַחַר מִיתָה יְהֵא גֵּט" וְאֵינוֹ כְּלוּם. דִּבְשְׁלָמָא גַּבֵּי מַתָּנָה — אִיכָּא לְמֵימַר גּוּפָא מֵהַיּוֹם וּפֵירָא לְאַחַר מִיתָה, אֲבָל הָכָא — לֵיכָּא לְמֵימַר הָכִי. וְאִי מִשּׁוּם תְּנָאָה — ה"ל לְמֵימַר "מֵהַיּוֹם אִם מַתִּי". וּבַגְּמָרָא פָּרֵיךְ: מ"ש מֵרֵישָׁא. חוֹלֶצֶת. שֶׁמָּא אֵינוֹ גֵּט. וְלֹא מִתְיַיבֶּמֶת. שֶׁמָּא גֵּט הֲוֵה, וַהֲוְיָא לָהּ גְּרוּשַׁת אָחִיו, וְקַיְימָא עֲלֵיהּ בְּכָרֵת הוֹאִיל וְלֹא הֶחֱזִירָהּ. **גמ'** וַהֲדַר תָּנֵי כו' אַלְמָא לָאו כִּלְאַחַר מִיתָה דָּמֵי. דְּאִילּוּ כְּ"מֵהַיּוֹם וּלְאַחַר מִיתָה" תָּנֵי סֵיפָא: גֵּט וְאֵינוֹ גֵּט. מַשְׁמַע כְּמֵעַכְשָׁיו. אִם יִתְקַיֵּים תְּנַאי זֶה שֶׁאָמוּת, וּכְשֶׁמֵּת הֲוֵה גֵּט לְמַפְרֵעַ. אֲבָל לְאַחַר מִיתָה — לָא מַשְׁמַע תְּנָאָה, וְסַפּוּקֵי מְסַפְּקָא לָן. וְחוֹלֶצֶת. כְּלוֹמַר: אֲסוּרָה לְהִתְיַיבֵּם, דִּמְסַפְּקָא לֵיהּ אִי הֲוֵה גֵּט אִי לָא. וּלְקַמֵּיהּ מְפָרֵשׁ וְאָזֵיל. וְהָא מִדְּסֵיפָא. גַּבֵּי "מֵהַיּוֹם וּלְאַחַר מִיתָה" תָּנָא: חוֹלֶצֶת, וּבְרֵישָׁא לָא תָּנָא, מִכְּלָל דְּדַוְוקָא קָתָנֵי! מַתְנִי'. דְּבָעֵי "מֵהַיּוֹם". כְּרַבָּנַן. דִּפְלִיגִי עֲלֵיהּ דְּרַבִּי יוֹסֵי בְּ"יֵשׁ נוֹחֲלִין" (ב"ב קלו.) דְּקָא תָּנֵי: הַכּוֹתֵב כָּל נְכָסָיו לִבְנוֹ צָרִיךְ שֶׁיִּכְתּוֹב "מֵהַיּוֹם וּלְאַחַר מִיתָה", וְאִי לָא — ה"ל מַתָּנָה לְאַחַר מִיתָה, וְה"נ גֵּט לְאַחַר מִיתָה הוּא. וְרַב הוּנָא כְּר' יוֹסֵי דְּאָמַר. הָתָם: אֵינוֹ צָרִיךְ, דְּקָא סָבַר: זְמַנּוֹ שֶׁל שְׁטָר מוֹכִיחַ עָלָיו דְּמֵהַיּוֹם נָתַן לוֹ אֶת גּוּף הַקַּרְקַע, וְהַפֵּירוֹת יֹאכַל הוּא בְּחַיָּיו. דְּאִם לֹא נָתַן לוֹ הַגּוּף מֵעַכְשָׁיו — לָמָּה נִכְתַּב זְמַן בִּשְׁטַר הַמַּתָּנָה? חֲלִיצָה נַמִי לָא לִיבָּעֵי. דְּהָא אָמַר: אע"ג דְּלֹא כָּתַב "מֵהַיּוֹם" — כְּמַאן דְּכָתַב מֵהַיּוֹם דָּמֵי, וּ"מֵהַיּוֹם אִם מַתִּי" תְּנַן בְּמַתְנִי' דְּכָשֵׁר! טַעְמָא דְּר' יוֹסֵי לָא יָדַעְנָא. אַמַּאי קָאָמַר א"ל. בְּעַל

ומשום כיסופא דסופר חיישי ומחתמי ליה. הוה מצי לשנויי: כיון דאמר מר כשר ולא תעשה כו', ולאסוקי כדמסיק ב"התקבל" (לעיל סו.). אלא לפי שכבר דקדק, *ולא חש לחזור ולהאריך. ומכאן יש להוכיח דפרק "מי שאחזו" סדרו אחר "התקבל"*.

לא מיבעיא היכא דלא אמר לבי תלתא כו'. "לא מיבעיא" קמא אתי אפי' לר"מ, דקאמר: לא מיבעיא "כתבו" אלא אפי' "תנו", כיון דמיירי בב', כדקאמר בתר הכי: לא מיבעיא היכא דלא אמר לבי תלתא. אע"ג דקאי לרבי יוסי – אין לחוש, דמדקדק כל "לא מיבעיא" שיכול לומר. ויש ספרים דגרסי: לא מיבעיא היכא דלא אמר לבי תלתא "תנו", אלא אפילו אמר לבי תלתא "תנו".

תניא כוותיה דרב אשי. לכאורה משמע דלא מייתי מינה ראיה אלא דלא מודה ר' יוסי באומר "אמרו". אבל הרב רבי אלחנן פירש בשם ר' יצחק דמוכח מינה ד"לא מיבעיא" קאמר, כדמשני רב אשי. דודאי אי הוי תני: "נכתוב גט לאשתך" כו' – הוה דייקינן: הא אמר "תנו" – נותנין, כדדייק אמתני', והוי רישא ר"מ. אבל השתא דנקט כתב הסופר לשמה, דמשמע: הא אם אמר לשום אדם – מהני, והא ליתא, דאפילו לר"מ לא מהני. אלא ודאי לא מיבעיא קאמר; לא מיבעיא לא אמר "כתבו" אלא אפי' אמר "כתבו", ולא מיבעיא דלא אמר "תנו" כו', כדדייק אמתני'. **קולו** לאפוקי מדרב כהנא כו'. וא"ת: ואמאי נקט מדרב כהנא? ממתני' נמי אתיא לאפוקי, דמכשרה בהרכנת הראש בלא קול! וי"ל: דמסתברא דהרכנה דמתני' מהני כמו קול, כיון דקים לן שמתרצה – לא בעינן שמיעת הקול. כמו "תן גט זה לאשתי" אם היה זכות לה – לא היה יכול לחזור בו, ואע"פ שהיא אינה אומרת כלום, כיון שהיא מתרצה בלא שמיעת קולה – הוי שלוחה. ובברייתא דנקט "עד שישמעו קולו" – לא שנה אלא למעוטי חרש דרב כהנא, דמסתבר למעוטי.

מהיום אם מתי מעכשיו אם מתי הרי זה גט. כתב ר"ת: "מהיום אם מתי" אם מת בו ביום – לא ידענא מה אדון בה. ולרבינו אלחנן נראה ד"מהיום" הוי כמו "מעכשיו", ודעתו שיהא גט לאלתר, דמסתמא דלכך נותן גט, שירא למות, וכי אין לו לירא שמא ימות בו ביום? אלא ודאי לאלתר קאמר שיהא גט. ומכל מקום נכון להחמיר. **הכי** אמר רב הלכה כרבי יוסי. והא דאמרינן בפרק בתרא (לקמן פה:): התקין רב בגיטא "מן יומא דנן ולעלם" ולאפוקי מדרבי יוסי – אין זה אלא לשופרא בעלמא, דהא כרבי יוסי ס"ל, כדאמר הכא. ואית דגרים לקמן "רבא", לפי זה צריך לומר נמי דלשופרא דשטרא תקן, דהא אמר בסמוך דלרבא פשיטא ליה דהלכה כרבי יוסי אפילו בעל פה. וכן פירש בקונטרס לקמן*). אי

*) [ועי' תוס' לעיל לט: ד"ה מקום]

[נ"ל לא]

[וע"ע תוס' ריש נדרים בשם ר"י וב"ב יב. ד"ה אטו ועי' תוס' ביצה לז. ד"ה ורמינהי וקל"ע]

כט א מיי' פ"ב מהל' גירושין הלכה ה סמג עשין נ טוש"ע אה"ע סי' קכ סעיף ד:
ל ב מיי' פ"ט מהלכ' גירושין הלכה יב סמג שם טוש"ע אה"ע סימן קמה סעיף א:
לא ג מיי' שם הלכ' יג טוש"ע שם סעיף ב:
לב ד מיי' שם הלכה יד טוש"ע שם סעיף ג:
לג ה מיי' שם הלכה יח טוש"ע שם סעיף ז:
לד ו ז מיי' פי"ב מהל' זכייה הלכה טו סמג עשין פב טוש"ע ח"מ סימן רנח סעיף א:

[עי' מה שפי' תוספות כתובות ב: ד"ה הרי זה]

[לעיל כט. וש"נ]

[לעיל סו:]

[לעיל עח.]

כתובות ב: ב"ב קלז.

קדושין ס. ב"ב קלו.

[לקמן עו: עז. פה: ב"ב קלו. ע"ש לז. תוספתא דכתובות פ"ח]

ב"ב קלו.

הגהות הב"ח

(א) גמ' ורב הונא דאמר כר' יוסי כצ"ל ותיבת דאמר נמחק:

תוספות רי"ד

ואסקה רב אסי כולה ר' יוסי היא לא מבעיא קאמר לא מבעיא היכא דלא אמר תנו אלא אפי' אמר תנו נמי לא. ולא מיבעיא היכא דלא אמר אמרו אלא אפילו אמר אמרו נמי לא: תניא כותיה דרב אסי כתב הסופר לשמה וחתמו עדים לשמה אף על פי שכתבוהו וחתמוהו ונתנוהו לו וחזר ונתנו לה הרי הגט בטל עד שישמעו קולו שיאמר לסופר כתוב ולעדים חתומו ישמעו לאפוקי ממ"ד מודה ר' יוסי באומר אמרו קולו לאפוקי מדרב כהנא אמר רב [דאמר] חרש שיכול לדבר מתוך הכתב כותבים ונותנין גט לאשתו: **מתני'** זה גיטיך אם מתי זה גיטיך מחולי זה [זה] גיטיך לאחר מיתתי לא אמר כלום: מהיום אם מתי מעכשיו אם מתי הרי זה גט מהיום ולאחר מיתה גט ואינו גט ואם מת חולצת ולא מתיבמת. פי' זה גיטיך אם מתי משמע שיהא גט לאחר שאמות ומשום הכי לא אמר כלום שאין גט לאחר מיתה דבעי' שיהא המגרש חי בשעת קנין הגט והגט הזה אינו קונה כ"א לאחר מיתה. זה גיטיך מחולי זה פי' (האי) [על] אם מתי קאי בין אם אומר לה זה גיטיך אם מתי בין אם אמר לה זה גיטיך אם מתי מחולי [זה] ומת לא אמר כלום ומתיבמת (ולא אמרינן שמא נשתנה חליו ולא מת מאותו החולי) הכי משמע אם מתי מחולי או אם לא אעמוד מחולי והרי מת ולא עמד וכיון דאינו קונה אלא לאחר מיתה לא אמר כלום. אבל אם אמר מהיום אם מתי או מעכשיו אם מתי הרי זה גט דכיון דאמר מהיום או מעכשיו למפרע הוא קונה משעה שמסרו בידה ואין זה גט לאחר מיתה וכשאמר מהיום ולאחר מיתה מספקא לן אי תנאה הוי וכאילו אמר מהיום אם מתי דמי וקונה למפרע אי חזרה הוי שתחילה אמר מהיום ואח"כ חזר ואמר שלא יהא גט אלא לאחר מיתה ואינו כלום הלכך מספיקא חולצת דלמא חזרה הוי ולא הוי גיטא ואינה מתיבמת דלמא תנאה הוי והוי גיטא ולא דמי למתנה דכתב ביה מהיום ולאחר מיתה והיא קיימת דהתם אמרינן גופא מהיום ופירא לאחר מיתה אבל הכא ליכא למימר הכי: רבה בר אבוה חלש עייל לגביה רב הונא ורב נחמן ורבא א"ל רב הונא לרב נחמן בעי מיניה מרבה הלכה כר' יוסי דאמר זמנו של שטר מוכיח עליו ולא בעינן מהיום אי לא בעא מיניה א"ל הכי אמר רב הלכה כר' יוסי ולית הלכתא כר' יוסי מדאמרי' לקמן בפרקין ורבותינו התירוה לינשא וסברי לה כר' יוסי דאמר זמנו של שטר מוכיח עליו ולא הודו לו כל סייעתו אלמא אין הלכה כמותו ובפרקין לקמן אמרינן מן יומא דין

עין משפט נר מצוה

לה א מיי' פ"ח מהל' זכייה הלכה יד סמג עשין פב טוש"ע ח"מ סי' רנ סעיף ב:

לו ב מיי' פ"ב מהל' גירושין הלכה יב סמג עשין נ טוש"ע אה"ע סי' קמה סעי' טז:

לז ג מיי' פ"ח מהל' זכייה הלכה יז סמג עשין פב טוש"ע ח"מ סי' רנ סעי' א:

אִי א"ר יוֹסֵי בְּעַל פֶּה אִי לֹא אָמַר. וּמִי מִסַּפְּקָא לֵיהּ? וְהָתְנַן: "ה"ז גִּיטֵּיךְ אִם לֹא בָּאתִי מִכָּאן וְעַד י"ב חֹדֶשׁ", וּמֵת בְּתוֹךְ י"ב חֹדֶשׁ – אֵינוֹ גֵּט; וְתָנֵי עֲלָהּ: *רַבּוֹתֵינוּ הִתִּירוּהָ לְהִינָּשֵׂא; וְאָמְרִי': מַאן רַבּוֹתֵינוּ? אָמַר רַב יְהוּדָה אָמַר שְׁמוּאֵל: בֵּי דִינָא דְּשָׁרוּ מִשְׁחָא, וְסָבְרִי לָהּ כְּר' יוֹסֵי, דְּאָמַר: זְמַנּוֹ שֶׁל שְׁטָר מוֹכִיחַ עָלָיו! אֶלָּא מִסַּפְּקָא לֵיהּ אִי הֲלָכָה כְּר' יוֹסֵי בְּעַל פֶּה אוֹ אֵין הֲלָכָה. וּמִי מִסַּפְּקָא לֵיהּ? וְהָאָמַר רָבָא: "ה"ז גִּיטֵּיךְ אִם מַתִּי" וְ"שֶׁאֲנִי מֵת" – ה"ז גֵּט, "כְּשֶׁאָמוּת" וּ"לְאַחַר מִיתָה" – אֵין זֶה גֵּט; הֵיכִי דָּמֵי? אִילֵימָא דְּאָמַר לָהּ "מֵהַיּוֹם" וְרַבָּנַן, צְרִיכָא לְמֵימַר? וְהָתְנַן: "מֵהַיּוֹם אִם מַתִּי" – ה"ז גֵּט! וְאֶלָּא לָאו דְּלֹא אָמַר לָהּ "מֵהַיּוֹם" וְר' יוֹסֵי, ש"מ הֲלָכָה כְּר' יוֹסֵי! לְרָבָא פְּשִׁיטָא לֵיהּ, לְרַב הוּנָא מִסַּפְּקָא לֵיהּ. וְאב"א: לְעוֹלָם דְּאָמַר לָהּ "מֵהַיּוֹם" וְרַבָּנַן, וְהָנֵי לִישָּׁנֵי אִיצְטְרִיכִי לֵיהּ, "שֶׁאֲנִי מֵת" כְּ"אִם מַתִּי" דָּמֵי, "כְּשֶׁאָמוּת" כִּ"לְאַחַר מִיתָה" דָּמֵי. וְאִיכָּא דְּמַתְנֵי לָהּ אַסֵּיפָא: "זֶה גִּיטֵּיךְ לְאַחַר מִיתָה" – לֹא אָמַר כְּלוּם; אָמַר רַב הוּנָא: וּלְדִבְרֵי ר' יוֹסֵי חוֹלֶצֶת. פְּשִׁיטָא, מִדְּסֵיפָא לְרַבָּנַן חוֹלֶצֶת, רֵישָׁא נַמִי לְר' יוֹסֵי חוֹלֶצֶת! מַהוּ דְּתֵימָא, רַבִּי יוֹסֵי בְּהָא כְּרַבִּי ס"ל, דְּאָמַר: גִּיטָּא מַעַלְיָא הָוֵי, וַחֲלִיצָה נַמִי לָא תִּיבָּעֵי, קמ"ל, דְּלָא רַבִּי סָבַר לָהּ כְּר' יוֹסֵי וְלָא ר' יוֹסֵי סָבַר לָהּ כְּרַבִּי; רַבִּי לָא סָבַר לָהּ כְּרַבִּי יוֹסֵי, דְּקָתָנֵי "כָּזֶה גֵּט" לְמַעוּטֵי דְּרַבִּי יוֹסֵי; וְר' יוֹסֵי לָא סָבַר לָהּ כְּרַבִּי, דְּקָתָנֵי "כָּזֶה גֵּט" לְמַעוּטֵי דְּרַבִּי. רַבִּי מַאי הִיא? *דְּתַנְיָא: "מֵהַיּוֹם וּלְאַחַר מִיתָה" – גֵּט וְאֵינוֹ גֵּט, דִּבְרֵי חֲכָמִים, רַבִּי אוֹמֵר: כָּזֶה גֵּט. רַבִּי יוֹסֵי מַאי הִיא? דִּתְנַן: *"כִּתְבוּ וּתְנוּ גֵּט לְאִשְׁתִּי אִם לֹא בָּאתִי מִיכָּן וְעַד י"ב חֹדֶשׁ", כְּתָבוּהוּ בְּתוֹךְ י"ב חֹדֶשׁ וְנָתְנוּ לְאַחַר י"ב חֹדֶשׁ – אֵינוֹ גֵּט, ר' יוֹסֵי אוֹמֵר: כָּזֶה גֵּט.§ "זֶה גִּיטֵּיךְ מֵהַיּוֹם אִם מַתִּי מֵחוֹלִי זֶה, וְעָמַד וְהָלַךְ בַּשּׁוּק" כו'.§ *אָמַר רַב הוּנָא: גִּיטּוֹ כְּמַתְּנָתוֹ, מַה מַּתְּנָתוֹ [א]אִם עָמַד חוֹזֵר, אַף גִּיטּוֹ אִם עָמַד חוֹזֵר; וּמָה גִּיטּוֹ אע"ג דְּלָא פָּרֵישׁ, [ב]כֵּיוָן דְּאָמַר "כְּתוֹבוּ" – אע"ג דְּלֹא אָמַר "תְּנוּ", [ג]אַף מַתְּנָתוֹ כֵּיוָן דְּאָמַר "תְּנוּ" – אע"ג דְּלֹא קָנוּ מִינֵּיהּ. תְּנַן: "זֶה גִּיטֵּיךְ מֵהַיּוֹם אִם מַתִּי מֵחוֹלִי זֶה", וְעָמַד וְהָלַךְ בַּשּׁוּק וְחָלָה וּמֵת, אוֹמְדִים אוֹתוֹ, אִם מֵחֲמַת חוֹלִי הָרִאשׁוֹן מֵת – ה"ז גֵּט, אִם לָאו – אֵינוֹ גֵּט; וְא"א: אִם עָמַד חוֹזֵר, לָמָּה לִי אוּמְדָּנָא? הֲרֵי עָמַד! אָמַר מָר בְּרֵיהּ דְּרַב יוֹסֵף מִשְּׁמֵיהּ דְּרָבָא: שֶׁנִּיתַּק מֵחוֹלִי לְחוֹלִי. וְהָא "עָמַד" קָתָנֵי! עָמַד מֵחוֹלִי זֶה וְנָפַל לְחוֹלִי אַחֵר. וְהָא "הָלַךְ בַּשּׁוּק" קָתָנֵי! הָלַךְ עַל מִשְׁעַנְתּוֹ. וְהָא

בְּעַל פֶּה. כְּגוֹן גַּבֵּי גֵּט שֶׁכָּתַב כְּהִלְכָתוֹ, וּכְשֶׁמְּסָרוֹ לָהּ אוֹמֵר "זֶה גִּיטֵּיךְ אִם מַתִּי". הִלְכָּךְ לָא דָּמֵי לִשְׁטָר, שֶׁכֵּיוָן שֶׁכָּתַב הַתְּנַאי אֵצֶל הַזְּמַן בִּשְׁטָר – אִיכָּא לְמֵימַר דִּזְמַן מוֹכִיחַ דְּמֵהַיּוֹם קָאָמַר, אֲבָל עַל פֶּה – דִּלְמָא כִּי מְסָרֵיהּ נִיהֲלָהּ הֲדַר בֵּיהּ מִזְּמַן דִּשְׁטָרָא, וּמְסָרֵיהּ נִיהֲלָהּ ע"מ לְאַחַר מִיתָה, הוֹאִיל וְלָא אָמַר "מֵהַיּוֹם". אֵינוֹ גֵּט. דְּהָא לָא הַוְיָא גֵּט עַד י"ב חֹדֶשׁ, וַהֲוָה לֵיהּ גֵּט לְאַחַר מִיתָה. בֵּי דִינָא דְּשָׁרוּ מִשְׁחָא. ר' יְהוּדָה נְשִׂיאָה שֶׁהִתִּיר שֶׁמֶן שֶׁל גּוֹיִם, בְּמַסֶּכֶת ע"ז (דף לז.). אִם מַתִּי וְשֶׁאֲנִי מֵת. אֵיזֶה מִשְּׁתֵּי לְשׁוֹנוֹת הַלָּלוּ, דִּלְשׁוֹן תְּנַאי הֵם. שֶׁאָמוּת. מַשְׁמַע: לִכְשֶׁאָמוּת יְהֵא גֵּט. צְרִיכָא לְמֵימַר. הָא בְּהֶדְיָא תְּנַן לָהּ בְּמַתְנִי': מֵהַיּוֹם אִם מַתִּי – ה"ז גֵּט. וְר' יוֹסֵי. וְאַשְׁמְעִינַן רָבָא דִּבְעַל פֶּה נַמִי אֲמָרָהּ ר' יוֹסֵי, וְהִלְכְתָא כְּוָתֵיהּ. דְּמַתְנֵי לָהּ. לִדְרַב הוּנָא לְעֵיל. וּלְדִבְרֵי ר' יוֹסֵי. דְּאָמַר: כִּי לָא אָמַר "מֵהַיּוֹם", כְּמַאן דְּאָמַר "מֵהַיּוֹם" דָּמֵי. חוֹלֶצֶת. דִּזְמַן הַשְּׁטָר הוי"ל כְּ"מֵהַיּוֹם", וְכִי מְסָרֵיהּ נִיהֲלַהּ וְאָמַר: "זֶה גִּיטֵּיךְ לְאַחַר מִיתָה" – מְסַפְּקָא לָן אִי תְּנָאָה הוּא, אִי חֲזָרָה הוּא. מִדְּסֵיפָא. כִּי אָמַר "מֵהַיּוֹם וּלְאַחַר מִיתָה" תְּנָא מַתְנִי' חוֹלֶצֶת לְרַבָּנַן, מִכְּלָל דִּ"לְאַחַר מִיתָה" לְר' יוֹסֵי – נַמִי חוֹלֶצֶת, דְּהָא לְרַבִּי יוֹסֵי כְּ"מֵהַיּוֹם וּלְאַחַר מִיתָה" דָּמֵי. וְר' יוֹסֵי וְרַבָּנַן לָא אִיפְלוּג אֶלָּא בְּהָא לְחוּדָהּ, דִּלְר' יוֹסֵי בְּלָאו "מֵהַיּוֹם" כְּ"מֵהַיּוֹם", וּלְרַבָּנַן יֵשׁ חִילּוּק. כְּרַבִּי ס"ל. דְּאָמַר לְקַמָּן: גֵּט הוּא, וּפָלֵיג אַדְּרַבָּנַן, וְקָסָבַר תְּנָאָה הוּא. וְהוֹאִיל וְאַשְׁכַּחַן לְרַבִּי דְּפָלֵיג – אֵימָא ר' יוֹסֵי נַמִי פָּלֵיג, דְּהָא שָׁמְעִינַן לֵיהּ דְּמֵיקֵל בִּתְנַאי. דְּקָתָנֵי כָּזֶה גֵּט. בְּמִילְּתֵיהּ דְּרַבִּי. לְמַעוּטֵי דְּר' יוֹסֵי. הֵיכָא דְּלָא אָמַר "מֵהַיּוֹם", דְּכֵיוָן דְּקָתָנֵי "כָּזֶה" – מַשְׁמַע דְּכִי הַאי גַּוְונָא הוּא דְּמַכְשַׁר, אֲבָל בְּלָאו "מֵהַיּוֹם" – פָּסוּל. דְּקָתָנֵי כָּזֶה גֵּט. ר' יוֹסֵי גַּבֵּי תְּנַאי, לְקַמָּן (עו.). וְעַל כָּרְחָיךְ לְמַעוּטֵי אֲתָא, וְלָא אַשְׁכַּחַן דִּלְמַעֲטֵיהּ אִי לָאו הָא דְּ"מֵהַיּוֹם וּלְאַחַר מִיתָה", וּלְאַשְׁמוּעִינַן דְּאַע"ג דְּגַבֵּי מַתָּנָה כָּשֵׁר – הָתָם הוּא דְּהָכִי קָאָמַר לֵיהּ: גּוּפָא מֵהַיּוֹם, וּפֵירֵי לְאַחַר מִיתָה. אֲבָל בְּגֵט, כֵּיוָן דְּלָאו לְשׁוֹן תְּנַאי הוּא – הָוְיָא לֵיהּ סְפֵק תְּנָאָה סְפֵק חֲזָרָה. *רַבִּי יוֹסֵי מַאי הִיא. הֵיכָא קָתָנֵי "כָּזֶה גֵּט"? ר' יוֹסֵי אוֹמֵר כָּזֶה גֵּט. מִדַּהֲוָה לֵיהּ לְמֵימַר "אִם לֹא בָּאתִי כִּתְבוּ וּתְנוּ", וְאָמַר "כִּתְבוּ וּתְנוּ אִם לֹא בָּאתִי" – ה"ק: כִּתְבוּ עַכְשָׁיו, וּתְנוּ אִם לֹא בָּאתִי. *וְהָלַךְ גָּרְסִינַן. גִּיטּוֹ. דְּשכ"מ, כְּמַתְּנָתוֹ. מַה מַּתְּנָתוֹ. אָמְרִינַן בְּב"ב (דף קנא.): אִם עָמַד – חוֹזֵר. אַף גִּיטּוֹ אִם עָמַד חוֹזֵר. וְלָא מִיבַּעְיָא הֵיכָא דְּאָמַר "אִם מַתִּי" – דְּהָא לָא מֵת. אֶלָּא אֲפִילּוּ לָא אָמַר "אִם מַתִּי", אֶלָּא יְהַב לָהּ גֵּט סְתָמָא, אִם עָמַד – חוֹזֵר, דְּמִסְתָמָא אַדַּעְתָּא דְּמִיתָה יְהַב לָהּ, וְהָא לָא מֵת. אע"ג דְּלֹא אָמַר תְּנוּ. כִּדְתְנַן בְּ"הָאוֹמֵר הִתְקַבֵּל" (לְעֵיל סה.) רַבִּי שִׁמְעוֹן שְׁזוּרִי אוֹמֵר: אַף הַמְסוּכָּן, כֵּיוָן דְּאָמַר "כִּתְבוּ" אַף עַל גַּב דְּלָא אָמַר "תְּנוּ" – אַדַּעְתָּא לְמֵיתַב קָאָמַר. הֲרֵי עָמַד. וּבָטֵל הַגֵּט מֵאֵלָיו. שֶׁנִּיתַּק מֵחוֹלִי לְחוֹלִי. וְאֵין זוֹ עֲמִידָה, אֶלָּא אִם כֵּן בָּא לִכְלַל רְפוּאָה שָׁעָה אַחַת. עַל מִשְׁעַנְתּוֹ. נִשְׁעָן עַל מַקְלוֹ, וּלְעוֹלָם חוֹלֶה הוּא. וְהָא דְּנָקַט הָלַךְ – לָאו מִשּׁוּם דַּעֲמִידָה הִיא, דְּתֵילַף מִינַּהּ: אִם עָמַד אֵינוֹ חוֹזֵר, אֶלָּא הָא קַמַּשְׁמַע לָן: טַעְמָא דְּהָלַךְ הוּא דְּבָעֵי אוּמְדָּנָא אִם מֵחֲמַת חוֹלִי הָרִאשׁוֹן מֵת, דְּאִיכָּא לְמֵיחַשׁ: הוֹאִיל וְהָלַךְ – נִיצַּל מֵאוֹתוֹ הַחוֹלִי, וּמֵת מֵחוֹלִי אַחֵר, וְהוּא אָמַר(א) מֵחוֹלִי זֶה. *אִידָךְ. מִי שֶׁלֹּא הָלַךְ בַּשּׁוּק, מִסְתָמָא אע"פ שֶׁנִּיתַּק לְחוֹלִי אַחֵר – יֵשׁ בּוֹ מֵחוֹלִי הָרִאשׁוֹן, וְלָא בָּעֵי אוּמְדָּנָא. מַתְּנָתוֹ

אי א"ר יוסי בעל פה. אם מבטל בדבורו הוכחת זמן השטר, כיון שאין כתוב בו "מהיום". **לרבא** פשיטא ליה. מכאן קשה על רשב"ם, דפי' ב"יש נוחלין" (ב"ב קלו.) גבי: בעי מיניה רבא מרב נחמן: בהקנאה מהו, פי': אם מועיל הקנאה כמו "מהיום", א"ל: בהקנאה אינו צריך, ופי' רשב"ם: היינו דלא כר' יוסי, והכא משמע דסבר רבא כר' יוסי! ואור"י: דהתם איירי באין כתוב זמן בשטר, ומתוקם כר' יוסי.

אמר רב הונא גיטו כמתנתו מה מתנתו כו'. פרש"י ור"ת: מה מתנת שכיב מרע בלא שום תנאי – חוזר, אף גיטו נמי, אם עמד, חוזר ממילא – בלא שום תנאי. ומסיק דרבה ורבא לא ס"ל הא דרב הונא, דכיון דאם עמד חוזר, וכי מיית הוי גיטא – אמרי יש גט לאחר מיתה, כמו מתנה שאינה חלה עד לאחר מיתה, כמו כן גט. ואין להקשות לפירושו: דכיון דבסתם אם עמד חוזר – מה צריך במתני' למיתני "מהיום אם מת" "מעכשיו אם מת"? בסתם נמי הוי כמהיום וכמעכשיו! דאיצטריך לאשמועינן איזה לשון משמע מחיים ואיזה לאחר מיתה. אבל קשה: דאמאי הוצרך שמואל לתקן בגט דשכיב מרע לקמן בפרקין (דף עה:): אם ימות – יהא גט, ואם לאו – לא יהא גט, כיון דבסתם נמי חוזר אם עמד! ומיהו, י"ל: דשמואל לא סבר כרב הונא אלא כרבה ורבא. ומיהו, קשה: דהא אמרי' ב"איזהו נשך" (ב"מ דף סו.): ההוא שכיב מרע דכתב גט לדביתהו, איתנח, אמרה ליה דביתהו: אמאי קא מיתנחת? אי קיימת – דידך אנא. וקאמר דפטומי מילי נינהו. ופריך: פשיטא! ואמאי פשיטא? והא רב הונא אית ליה הכא אם עמד חוזר! ע"כ נראה לר"ת: שכ"מ שנתן גט ולא התנה, דאם עמד – אינו חוזר. ולא דמי למתנת שכ"מ דאם עמד חוזר, דמתנה אינה חלה כלל אלא לאחר מיתה, אבל גט – חל מחיים, דדעתו שיחול מיד – הלכך אינו חוזר אם לא פירש. וגיטו כמתנתו דקאמר רב הונא – אומר ר"ת: מדקאמר "גיטו", ולא קאמר "גט שכ"מ" – משמע דקאי אמתני' ד"מהיום אם מת מחולי זה". וקאמר: מה מתנתו, אפילו בלא תנאי, אם עמד – חוזר, אף גיטו בתנאי, אם עמד – חוזר ממילא, שאין כאן עוד תנאי, כיון דעמד, אע"פ שחזר ונפל באותו חולי הראשון ומת. רבה ורבא לא סבירא להו הא דרב הונא, דאפי' עמד והלך בלא משענת, כיון דשוב מת מאותו חולי – אינו חוזר, והוה גט, דאי לא הוי גט אע"פ שמת מאותו חולי – יאמרו שאין תנאי החולי הזה גורם אע"פ שהתנה, שהרי מת זה מאותו חולי, אלא מיתה גורמת, ולכך לא הוי גט כשעמד, ויש גט לאחר מיתה. אבל השתא דעמד אינו חוזר, כיון דמת מאותו החולי יאמרו שתנאי החולי גורם, ולא מיתה. ופריך: אם אמרת אם עמד חוזר – למה לי אומדנא? לפי' רש"י פריך מכ"ש, דכיון דאמרת דאם עמד חוזר, אף כשנתן גט סתם – כ"ש דהיכי דפירש מהיום אם מת. ולפי' ר"ת פריך בפשיטות. והא

תוספות רי"ד

דין לאפוקי מדר' יוסי דאמר זמנו של שטר מוכיח עליו: **מתני'** הרי זה גיטך מהיום אם מתי מחולי זה ועמד והלך בשוק וחלה ומת אומדין אותו אם מחמת חולי הראשון מת הרי זה גט ואם לאו אינו גט: אמר רב הונא גיטו כמתנתו מה מתנתו אם עמד חוזר אף גיטו אם עמד חוזר. פי' מתנתו דש"מ אע"ג דסתמא קא יהיב ולא פירש אם מתי אם עמד מחליו מתנתו בטלה דאנן סהדי דלא נתן אלא מחמת מיתה לא אם יבריא אף גיטו נמי אע"ג דיהיב לה בסתמא ולא פי' אם מתי אם עמד חוזר שלא נתן לה אלא ע"ד מיתה לא ע"ד שיבריא

הגהות הב"ח

(א) רש"י ד"ה על משענתו וכו' והוא אמר אם מתי מחולי זה:

מסורת הש"ס

כתובות ב: [לקמן עו: ע"ז לז.]

כתובות ב: לקמן עו: [ע"ז לז. תוספתא פ"ה]

תוספתא פ"ה ע"ש קדושין

נט: [לקמן עד:] לקמן עו:

לעיל סו.

נ"א רבי מהי

שייך למתני'

שייך לדף עג.

והא קמ"ל, דהלך על משענתו הוא דבעינן אומדנא, [א]אידך – אומדנא נמי לא בעינן. [ב]שמעת מינה: שכיב מרע שניתק מחולי לחולי – מתנתו מתנה? אין, דאמר רבי אלעזר משמיה דרב: שכיב מרע שניתק מחולי לחולי – מתנתו מתנה. רבה ורבא [ג]לא סבירא להו הא דרב הונא, גזירה שמא יאמרו יש גט לאחר מיתה. ומי איכא מידי, דמדאורייתא לא הוי גיטא, ומשום גזירה שרינן אשת איש לעלמא? אין, *כל דמקדש אדעתא דרבנן מקדש, ואפקעינהו רבנן לקדושין מיניה. א"ל רבינא לרב אשי: תינח דקדיש בכספא, קדיש בביאה מאי איכא למימר? א"ל: שויוה רבנן לבעילתו בעילת זנות. ת"ר: *[ד]הרי זה גיטך מהיום אם מתי מחולי זה", ונפל הבית עליו או הכישו נחש – אינו גט; "אם לא אעמוד מחולי זה", ונפל עליו בית או הכישו נחש – ה"ז גט; מאי שנא רישא ומאי שנא סיפא? *[ה]שלחו מתם: אכלו ארי, אין לנו. ההוא גברא דזבין ארעא לחבריה, קביל עליה כל אונסא דמתיליד, לסוף אפיקו בה נהרא; אתא לקמיה דרבינא, א"ל: זיל שפי ליה, דהא קבילת עלך כל אונסא דמתיליד. א"ל רב אחא בר תחליפא לרבינא: אונסא דלא שכיח הוא! איגלגל מילתא ומטא לקמיה דרבא, אמר להו: אונסא דלא שכיח הוא. איתיביה רבינא לרבא: "אם לא אעמוד מחולי זה", ונפל עליו בית או הכישו נחש – ה"ז גט! אמר ליה רבא: ואימא מרישא: אינו גט. א"ל רב אחא מדפתי לרבינא: ומשום דקשיא רישא אסיפא, לא מותבינן תיובתא מינה? אמר ליה: אין, כיון דקשיא רישא אסיפא – לא איתמר בי מדרשא, ומשבשתא היא, זיל בתר סברא. רב פפא ורב הונא בריה דרב יהושע זבן שומשמי *אגידא דנהר מלכא, אגור מלחי לעבורינהו, קבילו עלייהו כל אונסא דמתיליד, לסוף איסתכר נהר מלכא, אמרו להו: אגורו חמרי אפקעינהו ניהלן, דהא קבילתו עלייכו כל אונסא דמיתליד; אתו לקמיה דרבא, *אמר להו: קאקי חיורי משלחי גלימי דאינשי, [ו]אונסא דלא שכיח הוא.§

מתני' *[ז]לא תתייחד עמו אלא בפני עדים, אפי' על פי עבד אפי' ע"פ שפחה, חוץ משפחתה, מפני שלבה גס בה בשפחתה. *מה היא באותן הימים? רבי יהודה אומר: כאשת

כאשת

רש"י

מתנתו מתנה. אם מת מחולי האחר, דהא אמרה: לאו עמידה היא. וגבי גט דמתני' הוא דבעינן אומדנא – משום ד"מחולי זה" קאמר לה. **לא סבירא להו הא** דרב הונא. דהיכא דלא אמר לה "אם מתי" סבירא להו דאם עמד – אינו חוזר. גזירה **שמא יאמרו** יש גט לאחר מיתה. דאי עמד חוזר, אתו למימר לא הוי גט עד דמיית, וקא חזינן דלכי מיית הוי גיטא, ש"מ: יש גט לאחר מיתה, ואתי לאכשורי "זה גיטך לאחר מיתה". ולא ידעו דכיון דלא פריש מידי – להכי יהבינא ניהלה, שיהא גט מעכשיו, וע"מ שימות. **לא הוי גיטא.** דהא אדעתא דמיית יהב לה, והא לא מת. **אינו גט.** דאונסא דלא שכיח הוא ולא מסיק אדעתיה, ולא אמר אלא דימות ע"י החולי. **מאי שנא רישא כו'.** אי אונסא דלא שכיח אסיק אדעתיה – רישא נמי ליהוי גיטא, דהא מתוך אותו חולי מת, ד"מחולי זה" לא משמע אלא מתוך חולי זה. **שלחו מתם.** על ידי מעשה שאירע באחד שאמר "אם לא אעמוד מחולי זה" ואכלו ארי, ושלחו הדבר לארץ ישראל, והשיבו: אין לנו שיהא גט, דאונסא דלא שכיח לא אסיק אדעתיה. **קביל עליה.** המוכר. **כל אונסא** דמתיליד בה. שיפסיד את הלוקח. **אפיקו בה נהרא.** צוה המלך שיעבירו את הנהר דרך אותה שדה. **שפי ליה.** העמידה לפניו בשופי. **ואימא מרישא.** אדמותבת לי מסיפא, תסייעי לי מרישא. **לא איתמר בי מדרשא.** במקום ישיבת תלמידי חכמים שיתקבלוה. **זיל בתר סברא.** ומסתבר דאונסא דלא שכיח לא אסיק אדעתיה. **זבון שומשמין.** לקחו שומשמין. **אגור מלחי.** שכרו להם ספנים להוליכם לביתם. **קבילו עלייהו.** המוכרים. **כל אונסא דמתיליד.** עלייהו בדרך. **אסתכר נהר מלכא.** ולא יכלו ספינות לעבור, שעשו בו סכר שקורין איסקלוס"א. **אמרו להו.** רב פפא ורב הונא למוכרים: אגורו חמרי כו'. **קאקי חיורי.** אווזים לבנים, לפי שהיו זקנים. **משלחי גלימי.** מפשיטין בגדי אנשים. כלומר, פוסקים עליהם דין להנאתן. **מתני' לא תתייחד** עמו. זה שנתן גט ואמר לה "מהיום אם מתי" – לא תתייחד עמו, שמא יבא עליה. דאיכא למ"ד חיישינן שמא בעל לשם קידושין, וצריכה גט שני. ולמאן דלא חייש נמי, מ"מ פנויה היא, ואסור להתייחד עם הפנויה*.

כאשת

תוספות

והא קא משמע לן דהלך על משענתו. פי': בשלמא כדקס"ד דהלך ממש, ואם עמד אינו חוזר – ניחא, דנקט הלך לרבותא, אע"ג דהלך ממש – צריך אומדנא, כיון דעמד אינו חוזר. אבל למאי דקאמר דהלך לאו ממש, אלא על משענתו – אם כן פשיטא דצריך אומדנא, ולהכי קאמר: קמ"ל דהלך על משענתו כו'. **מאי שנא רישא ומ"ש סיפא.** בירושלמי מפרש: טעמא רבה איכא, דברישא הרי לא מת מחולי זה, אבל בסיפא "אם לא יעמוד" קאמר – והרי לא עמד, ד"לא עמד" משמע בין ע"י החולי בין ע"י דבר אחר. אבל גמרא שלנו אינו סובר חילוק זה, אלא בכולם משמע ליה שימות מתוך חולי זה.

איתיביה רבינא לרבא אם לא אעמוד מחולי זה ונפל עליו הבית. תימה: מאי פריך ליה רבינא לרבא מגט? הא אית ליה לרבא בפרק קמא דכתובות (דף ג:) ללישנא קמא, שהוא עיקר, כדמוכח ב"השולח" (לעיל דף לד.), דאין טענת אונס בגיטין, כדמפרש התם: משום צנועות ומשום פרוצות! ומאי מהדר ליה רבא נמי: ואימא מרישא דאינו גט? והא סבר רבא התם דאין טענת אונס בגיטין! ואפי' באונסא דלא שכיחא איירי התם, דשכיח אמרינן התם דלכ"ע אין אונס, דמייתי מהא דפסקיה מברא, ודחי: אונס דשכיח שאני, דהוה ליה לאסוקי אדעתיה. ואור"י: דאיכא שלשה גווני אונס; דאונס דשכיח לגמרי – לכ"ע אין אונס, ואונס דלא שכיח כלל, כגון דשמעתין – אפילו לרבא יש אונס, אפילו בגיטין, דליכא למיגזר משום צנועות דסברא דאנים – כיון דלא שכיח כלל, ומשום פרוצות נמי לא גזור רבנן, כיון דלא שכיח כלל. ופלוגתא דאין טענת אונס – היינו בשכיח ולא שכיח. ועוד אור"י: דאפילו הוי הכא אונס שכיח כי ההוא דכתובות – פריך שפיר רבינא, דדוקא גבי "אם לא באתי מכאן עד י"ב חדש" אמרינן אין טענת אונס בגיטין – משום צנועות ומשום פרוצות, אע"ג דלא אסיק אדעתיה אונס דלא שכיח – מ"מ הוי בכלל משמעות לשונו ד"אם לא באתי" – משמע בכל ענין שלא יבא. אבל "אם מת מחולי זה" או "לא יעמוד מחולי זה" – משמע שרוצה לומר שאם ימות ע"י החולי – יהא גט, אבל אם ימות מחמת דבר אחר – לא יהא גט. ולהכי פריך רבינא: דאם איתא דלא אסיק אדעתיה אונס דלא שכיח, משום צנועות ופרוצות אין לנו לומר שיהא גט, דדמי לחוכא ואיטלולא, דכיון דבכלל משמעות לשונו נמי לא הוי נפילת בית או נשיכת נחש. אלא ודאי כל אונס מסיק אדעתיה, וכיון דאסיק אדעתיה דעתו לפוטרה בכל ענין שימות, ומתוך חולי זה הוא קאמר, ולא מחמת חולי זה. ורבא מהדר ליה דמשובשת היא, דהא קשיא רישא לסיפא, ולא משום סייעתא דנפשיה קאמר. **לא** תתייחד עמו **אלא בפני עדים.** לפי' הקונט' ניחא, דפירש: מה היא באותן הימים – מילתא באפי נפשה היא, אבל ב"זה גיטך מהיום אם מתי" דרישא – לכ"ע הוי גט משעת נתינה. לפיכך אתי שפיר דתלי בגמרא טעמא דמתניתין דלא תתייחד – משום חשש קדושין, ולא משום גט ישן, שהרי כבר היה גט משעת נתינה. אבל לפי' ר"ת ור"ח, דמפ' ד"מה היא באותן הימים" קאי ארישא – א"מהיום אם מתי", ואפילו הכי לרבי יהודה הרי היא כאשת איש לכל דבריה, ואינה מגורשת עד שעה אחת סמוך למיתה, וקשה לר"י: דא"כ אמאי תלי טעמא בגמרא משום חששא דקידושין, כיון דעדיין אינה מגורשת? ואור"י: דודאי לרבי יהודה הוי טעמא משום גט ישן, אבל לרבי יוסי דאמר מגורשת ואינה מגורשת, ולרבי מאיר דאמר בגמרא דבעילתה תלויה – איכא למיחש לקדושין*.

ראוה

לח א מיי' פ"ט מהל' גירושין הלכה יח סמג עשין נ טוש"ע אה"ע סימן קמה סעי' ז:
לט ב מיי' פ"ח מהל' זכייה ומתנה הלכה כה סמג עשין פב טוש"ע ח"מ סי' רנ סעיף ב:
מ ג מיי' פ"ט מהלכות גירושין הלכה יח סמג עשין נ טוש"ע אה"ע סי' קמה סעיף ד:
מא ד ה מיי' שם הלכ' יז טוש"ע שם סעיף ו:
מב ו מיי' פי"ט מהל' מכירה הלכה ה סמג לאוין קע טוש"ע ח"מ סי' רכה סעי' ג וסעי' ד:
מג ז מיי' פ"ח מהל' גירושין הלכה ב סמג עשין נ טוש"ע אה"ע סי' קמח סעי' ב:

כתובות ג. ב"ב מח. יבמות
ג) קי. לעיל לג. תוספתא רפ"ה ע"ש
[סנהדרין יז: וש"נ]
[נ"ל אגודא פי' כמו על כל גדותיו והן גפי הנהרות. ערוך]
כתובות פב.
[ע"ז לו:]
כתובות כז:
לעיל כה:
[וע"ע תוס' כתובות כז: ד"ה לא]

תוספות רי"ד

רבה ורבא לא ס"ל להא דרב הונא גזירה שמא יאמרו יש גט לאחר מיתה. פי' היכא דיהיב לה גט סתם הוי גט ואע"פ שעמד שאם אתה אומר שלא יהא גט אלא אם ימות יאמרו יש גט לאחר מיתה ויכשירו אע"ג דאמר לה זה גיטך אם מתי ולא ידעו דכיון דלא פירש מידי להכי יהביה ניהלה שיהא גט מעכשיו אם ימות: ומי איכא מידי דמדאורייתא לא הוי גיטא ומשום גזירה שמא יאמרו יש גט לאחר מיתה שרינן אשת איש לעלמא אין מאן דמקדש אדעתא דרבנן מקדש ואפקעינהו רבנן לקדושין מיניה והלכתא כרבה ורבא והכי אמרינן לקמן בפרקין אתקין שמואל בגיטא דש"מ אם לא מתי לא יהא גט ואם מתי יהא גט ואם לא מתי [לא] יהא גט למימרא שאם יתנו בסתם מיד הוי גט: א"ר אלעזר משמיה דרב ש"מ שניתק מחולי לחולי מתנתו מתנה: ת"ר הרי זה גיטך מהיום אם מתי מחולי זה ונפל עליו בית או נשכו נחש או אכלו ארי אינו גט פי' דאונסא דלא שכיח א) אדעתיה לאקנויי עליה דלא להוי גיטא אם יאנס ואדעתא דהכי לא גמר ומקניה. ההוא גברא דזבין ארעא לחבריה קביל עליה כל אונסא דמתיליד לסוף אפיקו בה נהרא. פי' צוה המלך שיביאו הנהר דרך עליה. אתו לקמיה דרבינא א"ל זיל שפי ליה דהא קבילת עלך כל אונסא דמתיליד בה א"ל רב תחליפא לרבינא אונסא דלא שכיח הוא איגלגל מילתא ומטא לקמיה דרבא אמר להו אונסא דלא שכיח הוא: רב פפא ורב הונא בריה דרב יהושע זבין שומשמי אגודא דנהר מלכא אגירו מלחי למעברינה וקבילו עלייהו כל אונסא דמתיליד ביה לסוף מסתכר נהר מלכא. פי' נסתם ולא היו הספינות יכולות לעבור אמרו להו אגירו חמרי ואסקינהו ניהלן דקא קבליתו עלייכו כל אונסא דמתיליד אתו לקמיה דרבא [א"ל] קאקי חיורי משלחי גלימא דאינשי אונסא דלא שכיח הוא והלכתא כרבא: **מתני'** לא תתיחד עמו אלא בפני עדים אפילו עבד אפילו שפחה חוץ משפחתה מפני שלבה גס בשפחתה ומה היא באותן הימים

רבי

א) נראה דצ"ל דלא שכיח הוא ולאו אדעתיה לאקנויי עליה וכו'.

מד א מיי׳ פ״י מהל׳ גירושין הלכה יז סמג עשין נ טור ש״ע אה״ע סימן קמט סעיף א:

כְּאֵשֶׁת אִישׁ לְכָל דְּבָרֶיהָ, רַבִּי יוֹסֵי אוֹמֵר: מְגוֹרֶשֶׁת וְאֵינָהּ מְגוֹרֶשֶׁת.§ **גמ׳** ת״ר: *רְאוּהָ שֶׁנִּתְיַחֲדָה עִמּוֹ בַּאֲפֵלָה, אוֹ שֶׁיְּשֵׁנָה עִמּוֹ תַּחַת מַרְגְּלוֹת הַמִּטָּה — אֵין חוֹשְׁשִׁין שֶׁמָּא נִתְעַסְּקוּ בְּדָבָר אַחֵר; *וְחוֹשְׁשִׁין מִשּׁוּם זְנוּת וְאֵין חוֹשְׁשִׁין מִשּׁוּם קִדּוּשִׁין, רַבִּי יוֹסֵי בְּרַבִּי יְהוּדָה אוֹמֵר: אַף (א) חוֹשְׁשִׁין מִשּׁוּם קִדּוּשִׁין. מַאי קָאָמַר? אָמַר רַב נַחְמָן אָמַר רַבָּה בַּר אֲבוּהּ, ה״ק: רְאוּהָ שֶׁנִּבְעֲלָה — חוֹשְׁשִׁין מִשּׁוּם קִדּוּשִׁין, נָתַן לָהּ כְּסָפִים — חוֹשְׁשִׁין מִשּׁוּם זְנוּת, דְּאָמְרִי׳: בְּאֶתְנַנָּה נָתַן לָהּ, וְאֵין חוֹשְׁשִׁין מִשּׁוּם קִדּוּשִׁין, רַבִּי יוֹסֵי בְּר׳ יְהוּדָה אוֹמֵר: אאַף בְּזוֹ חוֹשְׁשִׁין מִשּׁוּם קִדּוּשִׁין. כְּמַאן אָזְלָא הָא דְּאָמַר* רַבָּה בַּר בַּר חָנָה אָמַר רַבִּי יוֹחָנָן: מַחֲלוֹקֶת — כְּשֶׁרְאוּהָ שֶׁנִּבְעֲלָה, אֲבָל לֹא רְאוּהָ שֶׁנִּבְעֲלָה — דִּבְרֵי הַכֹּל אֵין צְרִיכָה הֵימֶנּוּ גֵּט שֵׁנִי, כְּמַאן? כְּדִבְרֵי הַכֹּל. מַתְקִיף לָהּ אַבָּיֵי: מִידֵּי כְּסָפִים קָתָנֵי? אֶלָּא אָמַר אַבָּיֵי, ה״ק: רְאוּהָ שֶׁנִּבְעֲלָה — חוֹשְׁשִׁין מִשּׁוּם זְנוּת וְאֵין חוֹשְׁשִׁין מִשּׁוּם קִדּוּשִׁין, ר׳ יוֹסֵי בְּרַבִּי יְהוּדָה אוֹמֵר: אַף חוֹשְׁשִׁין מִשּׁוּם קִדּוּשִׁין. כְּמַאן אָזְלָא הָא דְּאָמַר רַבָּה בַּר בַּר חָנָה א״ר יוֹחָנָן: מַחֲלוֹקֶת — כְּשֶׁרְאוּהָ שֶׁנִּבְעֲלָה, אֲבָל לֹא רְאוּהָ שֶׁנִּבְעֲלָה — דִּבְרֵי הַכֹּל אֵין צְרִיכָה הֵימֶנּוּ גֵּט שֵׁנִי, כְּמַאן? כְּר׳ יוֹסֵי בְּר׳ יְהוּדָה. מַתְקִיף לָהּ רָבָא: א״כ, מַאי ״אַף״? אֶלָּא אָמַר רָבָא, ה״ק: *רַבִּי יוֹסֵי בַּר רַבִּי יְהוּדָה אוֹמֵר: אַף לֹא רְאוּהָ שֶׁנִּבְעֲלָה — חוֹשְׁשִׁין מִשּׁוּם קִדּוּשִׁין. כְּמַאן אָזְלָא הָא דְּאָמַר רַבָּה בַּר בַּר חָנָה א״ר יוֹחָנָן: מַחֲלוֹקֶת — כְּשֶׁרְאוּהָ שֶׁנִּבְעֲלָה, אֲבָל לֹא רְאוּהָ שֶׁנִּבְעֲלָה — דִּבְרֵי הַכֹּל אֵינָהּ צְרִיכָה הֵימֶנּוּ גֵּט, כְּמַאן? דְּלָא כְּחַד.§ ״מַה הִיא בְּאוֹתָן הַיָּמִים? רַבִּי יְהוּדָה אוֹמֵר: כְּאֵשֶׁת אִישׁ לְכָל דְּבָרֶיהָ, ר׳ יוֹסֵי אוֹמֵר: מְגוֹרֶשֶׁת וְאֵינָהּ מְגוֹרֶשֶׁת״.§ תָּנָא: וּבִלְבַד שֶׁיָּמוּת. וְלִכִי מָיֵית הָוֵי גִּיטָּא? וְהָא קַיְימָא לָן דְּאֵין גֵּט לְאַחַר מִיתָה! אָמַר רַבָּה: בְּאוֹמֵר ״מֵעֵת שֶׁאֲנִי בָּעוֹלָם״.§ תָּנוּ רַבָּנַן: *יָמִים שֶׁבֵּינְתַיִם — בַּעְלָהּ זַכַּאי בִּמְצִיאָתָהּ וּבְמַעֲשֵׂה יָדֶיהָ וּבַהֲפָרַת נְדָרֶיהָ, וְיוֹרְשָׁהּ, וּמִטַּמֵּא

רש״י

כְּאֵשֶׁת אִישׁ. וְהַבָּא עָלֶיהָ בְּמֵזִיד בְּחֶנֶק וּבְשׁוֹגֵג בְּחַטָּאת, וְאַע״ג דְּמֵת מֵאוֹתוֹ חוֹלִי, לְפִי שֶׁלֹּא גֵּירְשָׁהּ אֶלָּא סָמוּךְ לְמִיתָה. וּבַגְּמָ׳ מוֹקֵי לָהּ בְּאוֹמֵר לָהּ בִּמְסִירַת הַגֵּט ״הֲרֵי זֶה גִּיטֵּךְ וְהִתְגָּרְשִׁי בּוֹ מֵעֵת שֶׁאֲנִי בָּעוֹלָם אִם מַתִּי״. הִלְכָּךְ רַבִּי יְהוּדָה סָבַר: סָמוּךְ לְמִיתָה הוּא דְּהָוֵי גֵּט וּמִקַּמֵּי הָכִי אֵשֶׁת אִישׁ הִיא, וְרַבִּי יוֹסֵי סָבַר: מִכִּי יָהֵב לָהּ גִּיטָּא כָּל שַׁעְתָּא מְסַפְּקָא לָן בְּ״מֵעֵת שֶׁאֲנִי בָּעוֹלָם״, הִלְכָּךְ סְפֵיקָא הִיא וְהַבָּא עָלֶיהָ בְּאָשָׁם תָּלוּי. **גמ׳** בְּדָבָר אַחֵר. בְּתַשְׁמִישׁ. וְחוֹשְׁשִׁין מִשּׁוּם זְנוּת. שֶׁמָּא בָּא עָלֶיהָ. וּלְקַמָּן פָּרֵיךְ: מַאי קָאָמַר? וְאֵין חוֹשְׁשִׁין. שֶׁמָּא בָּעַל לְשֵׁם קִידּוּשִׁין, לְהַצְרִיכָהּ גֵּט שֵׁנִי. מַאי קָאָמַר. קָתָנֵי: אֵין חוֹשְׁשִׁין שֶׁמָּא נִתְעַסְּקוּ בְּדָבָר אַחֵר, וַהֲדַר תָּנֵי: וְחוֹשְׁשִׁין מִשּׁוּם זְנוּת! חוֹשְׁשִׁין מִשּׁוּם קִידּוּשִׁין. וּצְרִיכָה גֵּט שֵׁנִי מִשּׁוּם קִדּוּשִׁין, וְאֵין כָּאן טַעַם גֵּט יָשָׁן (ב) שֶׁכְּבָר מְסָרוֹ לָהּ קוֹדֶם לָכֵן, אֶלָּא טַעַם קִידּוּשִׁין הַלָּלוּ מַצְרִיכִין אוֹתָהּ גֵּט. נָתַן לָהּ כְּסָפִים. אַחַר בְּעִילָה. חוֹשְׁשִׁין מִשּׁוּם זְנוּת. כְּלוֹמַר, תּוֹלִין בִּיאָה זוֹ בִּזְנוּת. וְאֵין חוֹשְׁשִׁין לְקִדּוּשִׁין. לְהַצְרִיכָהּ גֵּט. דְּאִי לְשֵׁם קִדּוּשִׁין בָּעַל — לָא הֲוָה יָהֵיב לָהּ אֶתְנָן. וְהַאי חוֹשְׁשִׁין דִּזְנוּת — לָאו דַּוְוקָא, דְּמַאי חֲשָׁשָׁא אִיכָּא? אִי מִשּׁוּם כְּהוּנָּה — הָא גְּרוּשָׁה הִיא, וְנִפְסְלָה, וְאִי לִתְרוּמָה — בַּת כֹּהֵן לָא מִיפַּסְלָא אֶלָּא בְּבִיאַת עֲבֵירָה, כְּגוֹן גּוֹי חָלָל נָתִין וּמַמְזֵר וְהָנָךְ דִּמְפָרְשֵׁי בִּיבָמוֹת וּבְקִדּוּשִׁין. אֶלָּא אַיְּידֵי דְּנָקַט ״אֵין חוֹשְׁשִׁין״ בְּסֵיפָא, נָקַט לְשׁוֹן חוֹשְׁשִׁין בְּרֵישָׁא. אַף בְּזוֹ. שֶׁנָּתַן לָהּ כְּסָפִים — חוֹשְׁשִׁין מִשּׁוּם קִידּוּשִׁין, דִּלְמָא הָנֵי כְּסָפִים לָאו אֶתְנָן נִינְהוּ אֶלָּא מַתָּנָה. כְּמַאן אָזְלָא הָא. דְּאוֹקֵי רַבִּי יוֹחָנָן בְּ״הַזּוֹרֵק״ (ג) מַחֲלוֹקֶת ב״ש וּב״ה בִּמְגָרֵשׁ אֶת אִשְׁתּוֹ וְלָנָה עִמּוֹ בְּפוּנְדְּקִי, דְּמַצְרְכִי לָהּ ב״ה גֵּט שֵׁנִי — בְּשֶׁרָאוּהָ שֶׁנִּבְעֲלָה, אֲבָל לֹא רָאוּהָ — לָא חָיְישִׁינַן. כְּמַאן כְּדִבְרֵי הַכֹּל. דְּבֵין לְת״ק בֵּין לְר׳ יוֹסֵי אָמְרִינַן: הֵיכָא דְּלָא רָאוּהָ — לָא חָיְישִׁינַן, וְהֵיכָא דְּרָאוּהָ — חָיְישִׁינַן, אִי לָאו מִשּׁוּם כְּסָפִים. מִידֵּי כְּסָפִים קָתָנֵי. אִי אִתְנַיֵּיהּ לְתַנָּא כְּסָפִים — לָא הֲוָה טָעֵי בְּגִירְסָא לְמִינְקְטֵיהּ לְגַמְרֵי. אַף חוֹשְׁשִׁין. לְקַמֵּיהּ פָּרֵיךְ: מַאי ״אַף״? כְּמַאן אָזְלָא הָא. דְּאוֹקֵי ר׳ יוֹחָנָן אַלִּיבָּא דְּב״ה, דְּהֵיכָא דְּרָאוּהָ צְרִיכָה גֵּט. כְּרַבִּי יוֹסֵי בְּר׳ יְהוּדָה. דְּאִילּוּ לְת״ק לָא נֶחְלְקוּ בֵּית שַׁמַּאי וּבֵית הִלֵּל בְּדָבָר זֶה, דְּלָא שָׁבֵיק ב״ה וְסָתֵים כְּב״ש. אֲבָל רַבִּי יוֹסֵי סָבַר לָהּ כְּרַבִּי יוֹחָנָן, וְלָא כְּמַאן דְּמוֹקֵי פְּלוּגְתַּיְיהוּ אַף בְּשֶׁלֹּא רָאוּהָ שֶׁנִּבְעֲלָה, דְּהָא הָכָא כִּי לֹא רָאוּהָ — כּוּלְּהוּ מוֹדוּ דְּלָא חָיְישִׁינַן. מַאי אַף. דְּהָא חֲשָׁשָׁא דִּזְנוּת לָאו דַּוְוקָא חֲשָׁשָׁא, אֶלָּא קוּלָּא הִיא, לוֹמַר: תּוֹלִין אוֹתָהּ בִּזְנוּת וְאֵין חוֹשְׁשִׁין לְקִידּוּשִׁין. וְר׳ יוֹסֵי הֲוָה לֵיהּ לְמֵימַר: חוֹשְׁשִׁין לְקִידּוּשִׁין וְאֵין תּוֹלִין לְהָקֵל בִּזְנוּת. אַף לֹא רְאוּהָ כו׳. דְּכֵיוָן שֶׁרָאוּהָ שֶׁנִּתְיַחֲדָה — עֵדֵי הַיִּחוּד הֵן הֵן עֵדֵי בִיאָה, דְּכֵיוָן דְּגַיְיסֵי אַהֲדָדֵי — חוֹשְׁשִׁין לְבִיאָה. דְּלָא כְּחַד. דְּאִי לְת״ק — אֲפִי׳ רָאוּהָ נַמִי, הָאָמַר: תּוֹלִין בִּזְנוּת, וְאֵינָהּ צְרִיכָה גֵּט. וְאִי לְרַבִּי יוֹסֵי — כִּי לֹא רָאוּהָ נַמִי קָאָמַר חוֹשְׁשִׁין. וּסְבִירָא לֵיהּ כְּמַאן דְּמוֹקֵי הָתָם פְּלוּגְתַּיְיהוּ בְּשֶׁלֹּא רָאוּהָ, וְקָמַצְרְכִי לָהּ ב״ה גֵּט. תָּנָא וּבִלְבַד שֶׁיָּמוּת. אֲבָל אִי לֹא מֵת — אִיגְּלַאי מִלְּתָא דְּלָאו גִּיטָּא הוּא, וְחַיָּיב חַטָּאת. וּפָרְכִינַן: בֵּין לְר׳ יוֹסֵי דִּמְשַׁוֵּי לָהּ אֵשֶׁת אִישׁ סָפֵק, בֵּין לְרַבִּי יְהוּדָה דִּמְשַׁוֵּי לָהּ אֵשֶׁת אִישׁ וַדַּאי, וְלִכִי מָיֵית הֵיכִי הָוֵי גִּיטָּא? הָא לְדִידְהוּ לָא הָוֵי גֵּט לְמַפְרֵעַ מִשְּׁעַת מְסִירָה, אִם כֵּן לָא הָוֵי גֵּט עַד לְאַחַר מִיתָה! וּמְשַׁנֵּי. אָמַר רַבָּה. מַתְנִי׳ לָאו בְּאוֹמֵר ״מֵהַיּוֹם אִם מַתִּי״ — דְּהַהִיא וַדַּאי לִכִי מָיֵית אִיגְּלַאי מִילְּתָא דְּהָוֵי גֵּט מִשְּׁעַת נְתִינָה, וְהַבָּא עָלֶיהָ פָּטוּר. אֶלָּא בְּאוֹמֵר ״מֵעֵת שֶׁאֲנִי בָּעוֹלָם לֶהֱוֵי גֵּט״. הִלְכָּךְ, לְרַבִּי יְהוּדָה סָמוּךְ לְמִיתָה חָיֵיל גִּיטָּא, וּמֵעִיקָּרָא אֵשֶׁת אִישׁ הִיא. וְרַבִּי יוֹסֵי סָבַר: מִשְּׁעַת נְתִינָה מְסַפְּקָא לָן דִּלְמָא זוֹ הִיא שָׁעָה הַסְּמוּכָה לְמִיתָה, וְהָוֵי גֵּט סָפֵק, וְאַע״ג דְּחָיֵי טְפֵי — אֵין בְּרֵירָה. שֶׁבֵּינְתַיִם. בֵּין נְתִינָה לְמִיתָה. וּמִטַּמֵּא

תוספות

ראוה שנתייחדה עמו באפילה. ב״הזורק״ (לקמן דף פא.) תנן: המגרש את אשתו ולנה עמו בפונדקי, ובסמוך מייתי לה. ה״ה נתייחדה עמו באפילה כדמשמע הכא. **נתן** לה כספים חוששין משום זנות א]. פי׳: אפילו ראוה שנבעלה, כיון שנתן לה כספים. פרש״י: דבזנות אין שייך לשון ״חוששין״, דלכהונה כבר נפסלה — שהרי היא גרושה, ולתרומה לא מיפסלא בת כהן אלא בביאת עבירה, שנבעלה לכותי חלל, נתין, ממזר. ואגב קידושין נקט חוששין. ומיהו, לרבי אלעזר דאמר*: פנוי הבא על הפנויה שלא לשם אישות ◉עשאה זונה — נקט נמי שפיר ״חוששין״ בזנות. ומיהו, סתמא דתלמודא ביבמות (דף סא:) לא אשכח משנה או ברייתא כרבי אלעזר. **אם** כן מאי אף. דהני תרי מילי סתרן אהדדי, דאי חוששין לזנות — אין חוששין לקדושין. **תנא** ובלבד שימות. פי׳ בקונטרס: הא דקאמר רבי יוסי מגורשת ואינה מגורשת — היינו אם מת לבסוף, ובשעת מיתה הויא מגורשת גמורה, כדאמרינן: ולכי מיית — הוי גיטא. אבל אם לא מת — איגלאי מילתא דלאו גיטא הוא, וחייב חטאת. וטעמא דרבי יוסי מפרש הקונטרס בסמוך — משום דאין ברירה, ולא אמרינן לכשמת הוברר הדבר שמתחלה היו אותן שעות רחוקות מן המיתה, והיתה אשת איש בודאי. אלא, אין ברירה, ונחשבה משעת נתינה ועד שעת מיתה ספק גרושה. ואין נראה לרבינו יצחק, דאי סבר אין ברירה א״כ כי היכי דעד שעת מיתה הויא ספק מגורשת, אע״ג שהוברר הדבר לבסוף שאותן שעות היו רחוקות מן המיתה, משעת מיתה ואילך נמי לא תהא מגורשת ודאי, אע״פ שהוברר הדבר לבסוף שאותה שעה היתה סמוכה למיתה, כיון דבשעה שהיה לגט לחול לא היה מבורר. ולעיל בריש פרק ״כל הגט״ (דף כה:) דייקינן בהדיא דיש ברירה, כיון דכי מיית הוי גט, ואפילו לא מת מאותו חולי — יהיה לנו לומר שתהא מגורשת מספק כל אותם הימים, ולא נאמר הוברר הדבר שלא חלו כלל הגירושין. ועוד: דבפרק ״בכל מערבין״ (עירובין לז:) אמר דלמ״ד אין ברירה — לא חייל עירוב כלל, ואם כן — הכא נמי לא היה להם לגירושין לחול כלל, אע״ג דהוברר הדבר לבסוף. על כן נראה לרבינו יצחק, דטעמא דרבי יוסי דאמר: מגורשת ואינה מגורשת — משום דמספקא לן אם חלין הגירושין משעת נתינה כר׳ מאיר, או חלין שעה אחת קודם מיתה כר׳ יהודה. וכן פירש ריב״ס. **אמר** רבה באומר מעת שאני בעולם. פי׳ בקונטרס: שאמר בפירוש ״הרי זה גיטך מעת שאני בעולם״. ומילתא באפי נפשיה היא, ולא קאי ארישא א״הרי זה גיטך מהיום אם מתי״, דהתם לכולי עלמא מגורשת משעת נתינה. ואין נראה לר״ת, דלישנא ד״מה היא באותן הימים״ משמע דקאי אמאי דאיירי לעיל. ועוד אומר רבינו יצחק: דבתוספתא בהדיא משמע דקאי א״מהיום אם מתי״, דקתני: ״הרי זה גיטך מהיום אם מתי מחולי זה״ — הימים שבינתים בעלה זכאי במציאתה כו׳, ומייתי פלוגתא דהנך תנאי דבסמוך. ונראה לר״ת כמו שכתב בפי׳ רבינו חננאל: נעשה ״כאומר״ בכ״ף ״מעת שאני בעולם״ א). כלומר, ״מהיום״ דקאמר — היינו מחיים, שדעתו לאחר הגט כל מה שיוכל, רק שיחול מחיים שעה אחת סמוך למיתתו. ואע״ג דקאי ארישא, א״מהיום אם מתי״, פריך שפיר: והא אין גט לאחר מיתה, כיון דקתני: הרי היא כאשת איש לכל דבריה — א״כ אין גט חל משעת נתינה אלא לאחר מיתה, אע״ג דאמר ״מהיום״. וכן ר׳ יוסי דאמר מגורשת ואינה מגורשת — אינה מגורשת ודאי אלא משעת מיתה ואילך, והא אין גט לאחר מיתה! וא״ת: והא דאמר ב): כל היוצא למלחמת בית דוד גט כריתות כותב לאשתו, ופירש בקונטרס שהיה כותב גט על תנאי אם

א) [עי׳ תוס׳ יבמות כה: ד״ה כאומר] ב) [שבת נו: וש״נ]

תוספות רי״ד

ר׳ יהודה אומר הרי היא כאשת איש לכל דבר ר׳ יוסי אומר מגורשת ואינה מגורשת. פי׳ לא תתייחד עמו אלא בעדים שמא יבא עליה ויתבטל הגט ותהא צריכה גט שני לבעילה זו ולקמן בפ׳ הזורק פליגי ב״ש וב״ה במגרש את אשתו ולנה עמו בפונדקי ומצרכי לה ב״ה גט שני ואע״פ שהגט זה אינו גומר אלא לאחר מיתה כיון דאמר מהיום אם מתי למפרע הוא קונה ואינו פוטר הביאה שעשה בה לאחר מיכן הלכך אם יבא עליה צריכה ממנו גט שני: ומה היא באותן הימים. פי׳ בעל כרחיה פשטא דמתני׳ הכי משמע דקאי אמתני׳ דלעיל דתנן מהיום אם מתי מעכשיו אם מתי ועלה קאי מה היא באותן הימים שאם נתן ראובן גט לאשתו באחד בניסן ואמר לה מהיום אם מתי ולא מת אלא בא׳ באייר מה היא כל ימי ניסן ר׳ יהודה אומר כאשת איש לכל דבריה. פי׳ דקסבר ר׳ יהודה לא קנה הגט אלא בשעת המיתה אבל כל ימי ניסן היא אשתו גמורה והבא עליה בשגגה מביא חטאת קבועה. ר׳ יוסי אומר מגורשת וכו׳. פי׳ גם ר״י סובר שאין הגט גט אלא בשעת מיתה מיהו כל ימי ניסן לא דיינינן לה כאשת איש גמורה לחייב הבא עליה בחטאת קבועה אלא ספק אשת איש והבא עליה מביא אשם תלוי: תאנא ובלבד שימות פי׳ התם פליג ר׳ יוסי על ר׳ יהודה אבל אם הבריא ולא מת אגלאי מילתא דכל אותן הימים אשת איש גמורה היא שהרי בטל הגט מעיקרו ומקשה ולכי מיית הוי גיטא והא קי״ל אין גט לאחר מיתה פי׳ היכי עבדי לה ר׳ יוסי ור׳ יהודה אשת איש כל ימי ניסן אטו כי מיית הוי גיטא והא אין גט לאחר מיתה אלא ודאי למפרע קונה הגט וכיון דלמפרע קונה הגט והוא אמר לה מהיום איגלאי מלתא שכל ימי ניסן היתה מגורשת ולמה מחזיקה ר׳ יהודה אשת איש גמורה ור׳ יוסי מחזיקה בספק א) אמר רבא נעשה כאומר לה מעת שאני בעולם. פי׳ אע״פ שאמר לה מהיום קסבר ר׳ יהודה ור׳ יוסי אנן סהדי שלא רצה לגרשה אלא לאחר מיתה כדי שלא תהיה זקוקה ליבם ומפני שאין גט לאחר מיתה אמר לה מהיום ודי לנו בשעה א׳ סמוך למיתה שיקנה הגט באותה שעה ולא יהא גט לאחר מיתה הלכך אע״ג דאמר לה מהיום לא נתכוון להקנותו לה אלא שעה א׳ סמוך למיתה ומפני שכל שעה ושעה היא בספק שמא עכשיו ימות ונמצא שזאת היא שעת קנין הגט נחלקו בדבר זה ר׳ יהודה ור׳ יוסי דר׳ יהודה סבר אע״פ שבעת הבעילה היא בספק כיון שלא מת מיד אלא חיה עד א׳ באייר הוברר הדבר שכל חודש ניסן היתה אשת איש גמורה ולא קנה הגט אלא באותה שעה שהיתה סמוכה למיתה וקסבר ר׳ יהודה יש ברירה ור׳ יוסי ב) בדאין ברירה אלא כיון שבשעת הבעילה היה הדבר בספק הבא עליה מביא אשם תלוי שכפי המעשה שבאותה שעה אנו דנין אותו ואע״פ שמתברר לאחר מיכן שאין זו שעת קנין הגט לא סמכינן אברירה אלא כשעת הבעילה אנו דנין אותו ואין זה דומה לספק חלב המתחייב אשם תלוי ואם מתברר לאחר מיכן מביא חטאת דהתם אם אצלו היה ספק היה יכול להתברר מאחרים אבל זה הספק אין אדם בעולם שיכול לבררו שמי יודע אם ימות מיד ותהיה זו השעה של קנין הגט או לא ימות מיד הלכך אע״פ שהוברר לאחר מיכן שלא מת מיד לא סמכינן אברירה אלא כעת הבעילה אנו דנין אותו והכי אמרי׳ לעיל בפ׳ כל גט בגמ׳ דבברירה פליגי רבי יוסי ורבי יהודה דלרבי יהודה יש ברירה ולרבי יוסי אין ברירה: ת״ר ימים שבינתיים בעלה זכאי במציאתה ובמעשה ידיה ובהפרת נדריה ויורשה ומיטמא

א) גירסת רבינו כגי׳ הר״ת שהובא בתוס׳ כאן ד״ה אמר. ב) נ״ל ור׳ יוסי סבר דאין ברירה אלא כיון שבשעת הבעילה וכו׳.

מסורת הש״ס

[לקמן דף פא.] [יבמות סא:] [תוספתא פ״ה] [מלינו חוששין לקולא ועמ״ש רש״י שבת קנג. ד״ה ושמואל] לקמן פא. [תוספתא פ״ה ע״ש]

ראוה שנבעלה חוששין משום זנות ואין חוששין משום קידושין ר״י ס״א מ״ד

הגהות הב״ח

(א) גמ׳ ר׳ יוסי ברבי יהודה אומר אף בזו חוששין: (ב) רש״י ד״ה חוששין וכו׳ גט ישן כו׳ לקמן דף עט ע״ב: (ג) ד״ה כמאן וכו׳ בהזורק כ״ג דף פא:

גליון הש״ס

תום׳ ד״ה נתן לה כספי׳ וכו׳ עשאה זונה נקט. ע׳ יבמות ד׳ סט ע״א תד״ה לא פוסלין:

הגהות מהר״ב רנשבורג

א] תום׳ ד״ה נתן לה כספים חוששין משום זנות פי׳ אפילו ראוה וכו׳ עד סופו. עיין סנהדרין ד׳ נ ע״ב תום׳ ד״ה ת״ל ובת כהן וכו׳ ושוב ראיתי בספר מחנה ראובן ביבמות ד׳ סא ע״א עמד בזה:

מה א מיי' פ"ט מהל' גירושין הל' יט וע"ש:
מו ב מיי' פרק יח מהל' איסורי ביאה הלכה כה טוש"ע אה"ע סימן לג סעיף ב:
מז ג מיי' פ"ח מהלכות גירושין הל' א סמג עשין נ טוש"ע אה"ע סי' קמג סעיף א:
מח ד מיי' שם הל' כב טוש"ע שם סעיף ב:
מט ה ו ז מיי' פ"ז מהל' אישות הלכה י יא סמג עשין מח טוש"ע אה"ע סי' לח סעיף ו:
נ ח ט מיי' פ"ח מהל' גירושין הל' א סמג עשין נ טוש"ע אה"ע סימן קמג סעיף ב:
נא י מיי' שם הל' כב טוש"ע שם סעיף ג:
נב כ מיי' פ"ו מהל' אישות הלכה יז ופ"ג מהל' זכייה הלכה ח סמג עשין מח טוש"ע אה"ע סי' לח סעיף ג:

ומטמא לה. כללו של דבר: הרי היא כאשתו לכל דבר – אלא שאינה צריכה הימנו גט שני, דברי ר' יהודה; ר"מ אומר: בעילתה תלויה; ר' יוסי אומר: בעילתה ספק; וחכ"א: [א]מגורשת ואינה מגורשת, ובלבד שימות. מאי איכא בין ר"מ לרבי יוסי? אמר רבי יוחנן: אשם תלוי איכא בינייהו, לר"מ לא מייתי אשם תלוי, ולר' יוסי מייתי אשם תלוי. "וחכ"א: מגורשת ואינה מגורשת". חכמים היינו רבי יוסי – איכא בינייהו דרבי זירא, *דאמר רבי זירא אמר רבה בר ירמיה אמר שמואל: [ב]כל מקום שאמרו חכמים "מגורשת ואינה מגורשת" – בעלה חייב במזונותיה.§ **מתני'** [ג]"הרי זה גיטך ע"מ שתתני לי מאתים זוז" – הרי זו מגורשת, ותתן. "ע"מ שתתני לי מיכן ועד שלשים יום", אם נתנה לו בתוך שלשים יום – מגורשת, ואם לאו – אינה מגורשת. אמר רבן שמעון בן גמליאל: מעשה בצידן, באחד שאמר לאשתו "ה"ז גיטך ע"מ שתתני לי איצטליתי" ואבדה איצטליתו, ואמרו חכמים: תתן לו את דמיה.§ **גמ'** מאי "ותתן"? *רב הונא אמר: והיא תתן, רב יהודה אמר: לכשתתן. מאי בינייהו? איכא בינייהו, שנתקרע הגט או שאבד; רב הונא אמר והיא תתן – [ד]אינה צריכה הימנו גט שני, רב יהודה אמר לכשתתן – צריכה הימנו גט שני. ותנן נמי גבי קידושין כי האי גוונא, דתנן: *[ה]האומר לאשה "הרי את מקודשת לי על מנת שאתן לך מאתים זוז" – הרי היא מקודשת, ויתן; ואיתמר: מאי "ויתן"? רב הונא אמר: והוא יתן, רב יהודה אמר: לכשיתן. מאי בינייהו? איכא בינייהו, [ו]שפשטה ידה וקיבלה קידושין מאחר, רב הונא אמר והוא יתן, [ז]תנאה בעלמא הוא, מקיים תנאיה ואזיל; רב יהודה אמר לכשיתן, לכי יהיב לה הוא דהוו קידושין, השתא לא הוו קידושין. וצריכא; דאי אשמעינן גבי קידושין, בהא קאמר רב הונא והוא יתן, משום דלקרובה קאתי, אבל גבי גירושין דלרחוקה קאתי – אימא מודה ליה לרב יהודה; ואי אשמעינן גבי גירושין, בהא קאמר רב הונא והיא תתן, משום דלא כסיף למיתבעה, אבל גבי קידושין דכסיפא למיתבעיה – אימא מודי ליה לרב יהודה; ואי אשמעינן גבי קידושין, בהא קאמר רב יהודה לכשיתן, משום דכסיפא למיתבעיה, אבל גבי גירושין דלא כסיף למיתבעה – אימא מודה ליה לרב הונא; ואי אשמעינן גבי גירושין, בהא קאמר רב יהודה לכשתתן, משום דלרחוקה קאתי, אבל גבי קידושין דלקרובה קאתי – אימא מודה ליה לרב הונא, צריכא. מיתיבי: *[ח]"ה"ז גיטך על מנת שתתני לי מאתים זוז", אע"פ שנקרע הגט או שנאבד – מגורשת, [ט]ולאחר לא תנשא עד שתתן; ועוד תניא: *[י]"ה"ז גיטך על מנת שתתני לי מאתים זוז" ומת, נתנה – אינה זקוקה ליבם, לא נתנה – זקוקה ליבם. רבן שמעון בן גמליאל אומר: נותנת לאביו או לאחיו או לאחד מן הקרובים; עד כאן לא פליגי, אלא דמר סבר: לי – ולא ליורשי, ומר סבר: לי – ואפילו ליורשי, וכ"ע מיהא תנאה הוי, תיובתא דרב יהודה! אמר לך רב יהודה: הא מני? רבי היא, *דאמר רב הונא אמר רבי: [כ]כל האומר "על מנת" כאומר "מעכשיו" דמי, ופליגי רבנן עליה, ואנא דאמרי – כרבנן. *וא"ר זירא: כי הוינן בבבל, אמרינן, הא דאמר רב הונא אמר רבי: כל האומר "על מנת" כאומר "מעכשיו" דמי – פליגי רבנן עליה. כי סליקי, אשכחתיה לרבי אסי דיתיב וקאמר משמיה דרבי יוחנן: הכל מודים באומר "על מנת" כאומר "מעכשיו" דמי, לא נחלקו אלא ב"מהיום ולאחר מיתה". והתניא

ומטמא לה. אי כהן הוא. שאינה צריכה הימנו גט שני. אם מת, דסמוך למיתה הוי גט. בעילתה תלויה. הדבר תלוי עד שימות או עד שיעמוד מחולי זה, אם מת מן החולי הבא עליה פטור. דלר' מאיר משמע ליה "מעת שאני בעולם" – היינו משעת נתינה, והכי קאמר לה: ה"ז גיטך מעת שאני בעולם אם מתי. הלכך כשמת איגלאי מילתא דגרושה הואי בשעת ביאה, ואם לא מת – הבא עליה בחטאת. רבי יוסי אומר בעילתה ספק. לכשימות. דמשמע ליה: מעת שאני בעולם. ומיהו מספקא לן על שעת ביאה אי גרושה הואי אי לא, שמא זו היא שעה הראויה ליסמך למיתה שמא אינה זו, ואינה גרושה. הילכך, אם ימות – מביא הבא עליה אשם תלוי, ואם לא ימות – בחטאת ודאי. מגורשת ואינה מגורשת ובלבד שימות. והיינו נמי כרבי יוסי, דמייתי אשם תלוי, דספיקא משוו לה. ולקמן מפרש: מזוני איכא בינייהו. לא מייתי אשם תלוי. אם ימות, אלא פטור לגמרי, כדפרישית לעיל. ולר' יוסי. אם ימות – מביא זה אשם תלוי. איכא בינייהו דר' זירא. כלומר, איכא בינייהו מזוני, וכדר' זירא. ולא דפליגי בדר' זירא, דתרוייהו אית להו דרבי זירא, ומשום הכי לא קרי לה רבי יוסי "מגורשת ואינה מגורשת" – דקסבר לית לה מזוני. ואע"ג דר' יוסי דמתני' תנא "מגורשת ואינה מגורשת" – תרי תנאי ואליבא דרבי יוסי, והיינו חכמים דברייתא. **מתני'** מעשה בצידן. בגמ' פריך: מאי תנא דתנא מעשה. **גמ'** שנתקרע הגט. קודם מתן מעות. והיא תתן. תנאי בעלמא הוא, וכי מקיימא ליה – איגלאי מילתא דמשעת נתינה גיטא הוי, דכל "ע"מ" מעכשיו הוא, וע"מ כן דליקיים. צריכה גט שני. דלכשתתן כבר אזל ליה גיטא. שפשטה ידה כו'. קודם מתן מעות. מקיים תנאיה ואזיל. והוו קידושיו קידושין למפרע, ושל שני אינו כלום. דלקרובה קאתי. הילכך, מעכשיו קאמר לה, משעה שחפץ בה. אבל גט דלרחוקה קאתי. ומסתמא בקושי הוא מגרשה, הילכך לכשתתן קאמר, וקסבר: אדהכי והכי מפייסנא לה. לא כסיף למתבעה. מעותיו, הילכך לא צריך ליה למתלי גיטא במתן מעות, ומעכשיו קאמר לה. ולאחר לא תנשא עד שתתן. דדילמא לא יהבה, ונמצא גט בטל. נתנה. לפני מותו, אינה זקוקה ליבם. לא נתנה זקוקה ליבם. ולא סגי לה ליתן ליורשים. ומ"ס. ר"ש. לי. משמע אפילו ליורשים, כשאיני. אבל דכו"ע תנאה הוי. ולא תלה הגט בשעת מתן מעות, דאי לכשתתן קאמר, נהי נמי ד"לי" ואפילו ליורשי משמע – מיהו הוה ליה גט לאחר מיתה. כאומר מעכשיו דמי. דה"ק: מעכשיו יהא גט ע"מ שתקיימי התנאי. לא נחלקו. אלא ב"מהיום ולאחר מיתה" דרבנן מספקא להו אי תנאה הוי אי חזרה הוי, ולרבי ודאי תנאה הוי. והתניא

אם ימות במלחמה. והא אמרי' הכא: הרי היא כאשת איש לכל דבריה, לפי' ר"ת, דקאי א"מהיום אם מתי"! ומיהו, [לפי' הקונטרס] י"ל: שהיו מפרשין בהדיא [שמהיום] תהיה מגורשת. אבל קשה: דאפילו לפירוש הקונט' דהכא, ד"מהיום אם מתי" הויא מגורשת לאלתר משעת נתינה – מ"מ קשה, דהא אילו לא נהרג אוריה – היתה בת שבע אשת איש! ועוד קשה: דאם לא היה נותן גט אלא על תנאי אם ימות – א"כ מאי "כל היוצא"? הלא לא היה צריך תנאי זה אלא למי שאין לו בנים ויש לו אח! ומיהו, זה י"ל דלאו דווקא נקט "אם ימות", אלא כלומר: אם לא יבא בסוף המלחמה, ומשום עיגונא. ונראה לר"ת: שהיו כותבין גט גמור בלא שום תנאי, בלינעא, וכשהיה חוזר מן המלחמה – היה כונסה. והיתה בת שבע פנויה. והא דאמרי' ב"הזהב" (ב"מ דף נט.): מוטב שיבעול אדם ספק אשת איש ולא ילבין פני חבירו ברבים, מנא לן – מדוד. קרי לה ספק אשת איש, אע"ג שהיתה פנויה גמורה – לפי שגרשה בלינעא, ולא היה ידוע לעולם אם היא מגורשת אם לאו. **אשם** תלוי איכא בינייהו. דלר"מ דאמר בעילתה תלויה – לא מייתי אשם תלוי, אלא הדבר תלוי ועומד, אם מת מאותו חולי – מגורשת משעת כתיבה, ואם לא מת – חייב חטאת [א]. ושמא אי הוה מספקא לן אם מת מאותו חולי אם לאו – היה לר"מ מייתי נמי אשם תלוי.

רבי יוסי אומר בעילתה ספק. ומביא אשם תלוי. ולא בעי ר' יוסי חתיכה משתי חתיכות. וה"נ סבר בס"פ "דם שחיטה" (כריתות דף כג.).

רב הונא אמר והיא תתן. וכן הלכה, דקיי"ל כרבי, דכל האומר "ע"מ" כאומר "מעכשיו" דמי. דבפ' קמא דקידושין (דף ח.) פסקינן הלכתא כר"א דאמר: "התקדשי לי במנה" *ונתן לה מנה חסר דינר – הרי זו מקודשת, וישלים, דכמאן דאמר "ע"מ" דמי, כדרב הונא אמר *רב: דכל האומר "ע"מ" כאומר "מעכשיו" דמי.

[נ"ל ונתן לה דינר עי' קדושין מז.]

[נ"ל רבי]

איכא בינייהו שפשטה ידה וקבלה כו'. ולעיל גבי גט הוה מצי למימר נמי שפשטה ידה כו', וה"נ הוה מצי למימר שנקרע שטר קידושין. אבל לא מצי למימר שנתאכלו מעות של קדושין, דאע"ג דנתאכלו – מקודשת, דברשות' דידה קא מתאכלי, כדאמרינן בריש "האומר" (קדושין דף נט.). אדמיפלגי

ב"ב מז: ע"ש ב"מ יב: ע"ש
כתובות נז: ע"ש

קדושין ס.

שם ע"ש

[שם כל הסוגיא תוספתא פ"ה]

[תוספתא פ"ה]

קדושין ח. ע"ש ודף ס: ע"ז לז. ע"ש לקמן עה: עז. ע"ש

נ"א א"ר זירא

הגהות מהר"ב רנשבורג

א] תוס' ד"ה אשם תלוי איכא בינייהו דלר"מ וכו' ושמא אי הוה מספקא לן וכו'. עי' כוונתם במהרש"א דמספקא להו אי בעי ר"מ חתיכה אחת מב' חתיכות ונ"ע דתלמוד ערוך הוא במסכת כריתות דף י"ח ע"א דר"מ לא בעי חתיכה אחת מב' חתיכות וצ"ע:

תוספות רי"ד

ומטמא לה כללו של דבר הרי היא כאשתו לכל דבר אלא שאינה צריכה ממנו גט שני דברי רבי יהודה ר"מ אומר בעילתה תלויה ר' יוסי אומר בעילתה ספק וחכ"א מגורשת ואינה מגורשת מאי איכא בין ר' מאיר לר' יוסי א"ר יוחנן אשם תלוי איכא בינייהו. פי' דקס"ד כך משמע בעילתה תלויה כמו בעילתה ספק ואמר ר' יוחנן אשם תלוי איכא בינייהו לר' מאיר דאמר בעילתה תלויה לא מייתי אשם תלוי לרבי יוסי דאמר בעילתה ספק מייתי אשם תלוי דר"מ סבר האי דקאמר מהיום דוקא קאמר מהיום ולכי מיית בא' באייר איגלי מילתא למפרע שמאחד בניסן קנה הגט וכל חודש ניסן היתה מגורשת הלכך בעילתה בכל חודש ניסן תלויה היא אם לא ימות ויבריא איגלי מילתא דאשת איש הוה ומייתי חטאת ואם ימות איגלי מילתא דמחד מניסן הות מיגרשא ופטורה לגמרי ור' יוסי [סבר] לא מיגרשא מחד בניסן אלא שעה א' קודם למיתתו וכיון שכל ימי ניסן היו ספק בעת הבעילה מביא אשם תלוי ור' יהודה סבר אע"פ שבעת הבעילה היה ספק כיון שראינו שהיה כל חודש ניסן הוברר הדבר שכל חודש ניסן היתה אשת איש גמורה ומביא חטאת קבועה דסמכינן אברירה נמצא שג' חלוקות בדבר ר' יהודה סבר אם מת בא' באייר כל חודש ניסן היא אשת איש גמורה והבא עליה מביא חטאת קבועה ור' יוסי סבר כל חודש ניסן הוא ספק והבא עליה מביא אשם תלוי ור' מאיר סבר כל חודש ניסן היא בחזקת מגורשת כיון שמת דאיגלי מילתא דמחד בניסן איגרשא אבל אם הבריא ולא מת כולן שוין בדבר שכל אותן הימים אשת איש היא שהרי הגט בטל: וחכ"א מגורשת ואינה מגורשת חכמים היינו ר' יוסי דר' זירא איכא בינייהו דא"ר זירא אמר רבה בר ירמיה אמר שמואל מגורשת ואינה מגורשת בעלה חייב במזונותיה לרבנן חייב לר' יוסי דאמר ספק המע"ה: **מתני'** הרי זה גיטך ע"מ שתתני לי מאתים זוז הרי זו מגורשת ותתן ע"מ שתתני לי מכאן ועד ל' יום נתנה בתוך ל' יום מגורשת ואם לאו אינה מגורשת ארשב"ג מעשה בצידן באחד שאמר לאשתו הרי זה גיטך ע"מ שתתנו לי אצטליתי ואבדה אצטליתו ואמרו חכמים תתן לו את דמיה. איתמר רב הונא אמר והיא תתן. פי' הגט קונה למפרע משעת נתינת הגט והיא תתן לו הזוזים ורב יהודה אמר לכשתתן פי' אין הגט קונה אלא לכשתתן לו הזוזים ולא למפרע משעת הגט מאי איכא בינייהו שנקרע הגט או שאבד קודם שתתן לו הזוזים. רב הונא אמר והיא תתן אינה צריכה ממנו גט שני תנאה הוי מקיימה תנאיה ואזיל שכל האומר ע"מ כאומר מעכשיו דמי אם תתני לי מאתים זוז והילכך כל זמן שהיא נותנת לו מתקיים הגט למפרע ואם נקרע או אבד קודם נתינת הזוזים אין בכך כלום ורב יהודה אמר לכשתתן צריכה ממנו גט שני דלכי תתן הוא דהוי גיטא אבל השתא לא הוי גיטא דלית ליה כל האומר על מנת כאומר מעכשיו דמי והלכך אין הגט קונה אלא בשעת נתינת הזוזים ובעי' שיהא הגט קיים באותה שעה. וה"ה נמי אם בטל הגט קודם שתתן לו מאתים זוז לרב הונא אינו מבוטל דלמפרע מקיים גיטא כי יהבה ליה זוזים והלכך משהגיע גט לידה אינו מבטלו והכי אמרינן גבי אשה לענין קדושין דאם פשטה ידה וקבלה קדושין מאחר אינה מקודשת וכך חורה דאשה לגבי קדושין כחורה דבעל לגבי גט וכן ש"מ שאמר מעכשיו אם מתי משהגיע גט לידה אינו יכול לבטלו דלכי מיית למפרע קונה הגט והלכתא כרב הונא דקי"ל כל האומר ע"מ כאומר מעכשיו דמי ותניא כותיה הרי זה גיטך ע"מ שתתני לי מאתים זוז אע"פ שנקרע הגט או אבד הרי זו מגורשת ולאחר לא תנשא עד שתתן. פי' דבעיא לקיומיה תנאה ולכי מיקיימא ליה הוי גיטא למפרע ועוד תניא הרי זה גיטך ע"מ שתתני לי מאתים זוז ומת נתנה לו אינה זקוקה ליבם [לא] נתנה לו זקוקה ליבם רשב"ג אומר נותנת לאביו או לאחיו או לא' מן היורשין ע"כ לא פליגי אלא דמר סבר לי ולא ליורשי ומר סבר לי ואפילו ליורשי אבל לכו"ע תנאה הוי ומיקיים תנאיה ואזיל והוי גיטא למפרע דאי לא הוי גיטא לאחר מיתה ואין הלכה כרשב"ג דאע"ג דאיפסקא הלכתא כותיה דוקא במשנתינו אבל בברייתא יחיד ורבים הלכה כרבים:

מעשה

וְהָתַנְיָא: *"מֵהַיּוֹם וּלְאַחַר מִיתָה" — גֵּט וְאֵינוֹ גֵּט, דִּבְרֵי חֲכָמִים, רַבִּי אוֹמֵר: כָּזֶה גֵּט. וּלְרַב יְהוּדָה דְּאָמַר: בְּ"עַל מְנָת" *פְּלִיגִי, אַדְמִיפַּלְגִי בְּ"מֵהַיּוֹם וּלְאַחַר מִיתָה", לִיפְלְגִי בְּ"עַל מְנָת"! לְהוֹדִיעֲךָ כֹּחוֹ דְּרַבִּי. וְלִיפְלְגוּ בְּ"עַל מְנָת" וּלְהוֹדִיעֲךָ כֹּחָן דְּרַבָּנַן! *כֹּחַ דְּהֶיתֵּירָא עָדִיף לֵיהּ.§ א"עַל מְנָת שֶׁתִּתְּנִי לִי מִכָּאן וְעַד שְׁלֹשִׁים יוֹם" וכו'.§ פְּשִׁיטָא! מַהוּ דְּתֵימָא: קְפֵידֵיהּ לָאו קְפֵידָא וּלְזָרְזָהּ קָאָתֵי, קָא מַשְׁמַע לָן.§ "אָמַר רַבָּן שִׁמְעוֹן בֶּן גַּמְלִיאֵל: מַעֲשֶׂה בְּצַיְדָּן" כו'.§ מַאי תְּנָא דְּקָתָנֵי מַעֲשֶׂה? חַסּוּרֵי מִיחַסְּרָא וְהָכִי קָתָנֵי: אִם אָמַר לָהּ "ע"מ שֶׁתִּתְּנִי לִי אִיצְטְלִיתִי" וְאָבְדָה אִיצְטְלִיתוֹ, אִיצְטְלִיתִי בדַּוְקָא קָאָמַר לָהּ. רַבָּן שִׁמְעוֹן בֶּן גַּמְלִיאֵל אוֹמֵר: תִּתֵּן לוֹ אֶת דָּמֶיהָ; וְאָמַר רַבָּן שִׁמְעוֹן בֶּן גַּמְלִיאֵל: מַעֲשֶׂה נַמִי בְּצַיְדָּן, בְּאֶחָד שֶׁאָמַר לְאִשְׁתּוֹ "הֲרֵי זֶה גִּיטֵּךְ עַל מְנָת שֶׁתִּתְּנִי לִי אִצְטְלִיתִי" וְאָבְדָה אִצְטְלִיתוֹ, וְאָמְרוּ חֲכָמִים: תִּתֵּן לוֹ אֶת דָּמֶיהָ. בְּעָא מִינֵּיהּ רַבִּי אַסִּי מֵרַבִּי יוֹחָנָן: "הֲרֵי זֶה גִּיטֵּךְ עַל מְנָת שֶׁתִּתְּנִי לִי מָאתַיִם זוּז", וְחָזַר וְאָמַר לָהּ "מְחוּלִים לָךְ", מַהוּ? תִּיבָּעֵי לְרַבָּנַן, תִּיבָּעֵי לְרשב"ג; תִּיבָּעֵי לְרַבָּנַן: עַד כָּאן לָא קָאָמְרִי רַבָּנַן הָתָם — אֶלָּא דְּלָא אַחֲלַהּ גַּבָּהּ, אֲבָל הָכָא — הָא קָאָמַר לָהּ "מְחוּלִי' לָךְ". אוֹ דִּלְמָא אֲפִילּוּ רשב"ג לָא קָאָמַר אֶלָּא דְּקָא מְפַיְּיסָהּ לֵיהּ בְּדָמֵי, אֲבָל לְגַמְרֵי — לָא? אֲמַר לֵיהּ: גאֵינָהּ מְגוֹרֶשֶׁת. אֵיתִיבֵיהּ: *הָאוֹמֵר לַחֲבֵירוֹ "קוֹנָם שֶׁאַתָּה נֶהֱנֶה לִי אִם אִי אַתָּה נוֹתֵן לִבְנִי כּוֹר אֶחָד שֶׁל חִטִּין וּשְׁתֵּי חָבִיּוֹת שֶׁל יַיִן", ר"מ אוֹמֵר: אָסוּר עַד שֶׁיִּתֵּן, וַחֲכָמִים אוֹמְרִים: דאַף זֶה יָכוֹל לְהַתִּיר אֶת נִדְרוֹ שֶׁלֹּא ע"פ חָכָם, וְאוֹמֵר: הֲרֵינִי כְּאִילּוּ הִתְקַבַּלְתִּי! הָכִי הַשְׁתָּא?! *הָתָם לְצַעוּרָהּ קָא מִכַּוֵּין וְלָא צִיעֲרָהּ, *הָכָא מִשּׁוּם הַרְוָוחָה הוּא, וְהָא לָא אִיצְטְרִיךְ! הַהוּא גַּבְרָא דַּאֲמַר לֵיהּ לַאֲרִיסֵיהּ: כּוּלֵּי עָלְמָא דָּלוּ תְּלָת דַּלְוָותָא וְאָכְלִי רִיבְעָא, אַתְּ דְּלֵי אַרְבְּעָה וֶאֱכוֹל תִּילְתָּא. לְסוֹף אֲתָא מִיטְרָא. אֲמַר רַב יוֹסֵף: הָא לָא דְּלָה, רַבָּה אֲמַר: ההָא לָא אִיצְטְרִיכָא. לֵימָא, רַב יוֹסֵף דְּאָמַר כְּרַבָּנַן, וְרַבָּה דְּאָמַר כְּרַבָּן שִׁמְעוֹן בֶּן גַּמְלִיאֵל? וְתִיסְבְּרָא? וְהָא קַיְימָא לָן הִילְכְתָא כְּוָותֵיהּ דְּרַבָּה, וּבְהָא אֵין הֲלָכָה כְּרַבָּן שִׁמְעוֹן בֶּן גַּמְלִיאֵל! אֶלָּא לְעוֹלָם כְּרַבָּנַן, רַב יוֹסֵף כְּרַבָּנַן, וְרַבָּה אָמַר לָךְ: אֲנָא דַּאֲמָרִי אֲפִילּוּ לְרַבָּנַן, עַד כָּאן לָא קָאָמְרִי רַבָּנַן הָתָם — אֶלָּא דִּלְצַעוּרָהּ קָא מִיכַּוֵּין, אֲבָל הָכָא מִשּׁוּם הַרְוָוחָה הוּא, וְהָא לָא אִיצְטְרִיךְ. *תְּנַן הָתָם: בָּרִאשׁוֹנָה הָיָה נִטְמָן יוֹם שְׁנֵים עָשָׂר חֹדֶשׁ, כְּדֵי שֶׁיְּהֵא חָלוּט לוֹ, והִתְקִין הִלֵּל הַזָּקֵן שֶׁיְּהֵא חוֹלֵשׁ אֶת מְעוֹתָיו לַלִּשְׁכָּה, וִיהֵא שׁוֹבֵר אֶת הַדֶּלֶת וְנִכְנָס, וְאֵימָתַי שֶׁיִּרְצֶה הַלָּה יָבוֹא וְיִטּוֹל אֶת מְעוֹתָיו. וְאָמַר רָבָא: מִתַּקַּנְתּוֹ שֶׁל הִלֵּל נִשְׁמַע: ז"הֲרֵי זֶה גִּיטֵּךְ עַל מְנָת שֶׁתִּתְּנִי לִי מָאתַיִם זוּז", וְנָתְנָה לוֹ מִדַּעְתּוֹ — מְגוֹרֶשֶׁת, עַל כּוֹרְחוֹ — אֵינָהּ מְגוֹרֶשֶׁת; מִדְּאִיצְטְרִיךְ לֵיהּ לְהִלֵּל לְתַקּוּנֵי נְתִינָה בְּעַל כּוּרְחֵיהּ דְּהָוְיָא לָהּ נְתִינָה, מִכְּלָל

ס"א ל"ג

וְהָתַנְיָא. בְּנִיחוּתָא. דְּשָׁמְעִינַן מִינָּהּ, מִדְּאִצְטְרִיכוּ לְאִיפְלוּגֵי בְּהָא — מִכְּלָל דְּבְ"עַל מְנָת" מוֹדוּ. וּלְרַב יְהוּדָה. אַדְּמִיפַּלְגִי בְּהַךְ מַתְנִיתָא בְּ"מֵהַיּוֹם וּלְאַחַר מִיתָה" — לְאַשְׁמוּעִינַן דִּבְ"עַל מְנָת" פָּסְלִי רַבָּנַן, וְכ"ש הָא! וּמְשַׁנֵּי: לְהָכִי אִיפְלִיגוּ בְּהָכִי — לְהוֹדִיעֲךָ כֹּחוֹ דְּרַבִּי. מִיהוּ, רַבָּנַן בְּ"עַל מְנָת" נַמִי פָּסְלִי. מַאי תְּנָא. לְעֵיל מִינָּהּ בְּדָמִים, דְּקָתָנֵי: מַעֲשֶׂה בְּצַיְדָן כו', מַאי רְאָיָה? אֵין שׁוֹנִין מַעֲשֶׂה בַּמִּשְׁנָה אֶלָּא לִרְאָיָה. תִּתֵּן אֶת דָּמֶיהָ. דְּלָא אִיכַּוֵּין אֶלָּא לְהַרְוָוחָה דִּידֵיהּ. מַהוּ. מִי הָוְיָא הַךְ מְחִילָה קִיּוּם תְּנַאי, כְּאִילּוּ נְתַנְתָּן לוֹ אוֹ לָא? תִּיבָּעֵי לְרַבָּנַן. דְּאָמְרֵי: דָּמִים לָאו בִּמְקוֹם אִיצְטְלִית קָיְימִי, וְדָמִים לָאו אִיצְטְלִית הֵן. אֲבָל הָכָא — הָא אַחֲלִינְהוּ, וַהֲוֵי כְּאִילּוּ קִבֵּל מָעוֹת מַמָּשׁ, דִּמְחִילָה כְּקַבָּלָה. קוֹנָם שֶׁאַתָּה נֶהֱנֶה לִי. קוֹנָם תְּהֵא עָלֶיךָ כָּל הֲנָאָה שֶׁתֵּהָנֶה מִמֶּנִּי. אַף זֶה. אִם רָצָה הַנּוֹדֵר — יָכוֹל לְהַתִּירוֹ מֵאֵלָיו, בְּלֹא שְׁאֵלַת הַתָּרַת חָכָם, וְאוֹמֵר לוֹ: הֲרֵינִי כְּאִילּוּ הִתְקַבַּלְתִּי. אַלְמָא מְחִילָה כְּקַבָּלָה. מִשּׁוּם הַרְוָוחָה. שֶׁהָיָה צָרִיךְ לְצוֹרֶךְ בְּנוֹ. תְּלָתָא דַּלְוָותָא. כָּל שְׁאָר הָאֲרִיסִים שֶׁבְּמָקוֹם זֶה מַשְׁקִין הַתְּבוּאָה שָׁלֹשׁ פְּעָמִים בַּשָּׁנָה. וְשָׁקְלִי רִיבְעָא. וּמִנְהַג הָאֲרִיסִין לִיטּוֹל רְבִיעַ הַתְּבוּאָה, בִּשְׁבִיל טוֹרַח חֲרִישָׁה וּזְרִיעָה וְנִיכּוּשׁ וְהַשְׁקָאָה וְכָל צָרְכֵי הַשָּׂדֶה. אַתְּ דְּלֵי אַרְבַּע. הַשְׁקֵה אֶת הַשָּׂדֶה אַרְבָּעָה פְּעָמִים. אֲתָא מִטְרָא. בִּזְמַן הַשְׁקָאָה רְבִיעִית. הָא לָא דָּלָה. וְלָא שָׁקֵיל אֶלָּא רִיבְעָא, כְּמִנְהַג הַמָּקוֹם. הָא לָא אִיצְטְרִיךְ. וּמַזָּלוֹ גָּרַם. כְּרַבָּן שִׁמְעוֹן. דְּדָמִים בִּמְקוֹם אִצְטְלִית, הָכָא נַמִי — מָטָר בִּמְקוֹם הַשְׁקָאָה. הִלְכְתָא כְּרַבָּה. בְּכָל מָקוֹם שֶׁנֶּחֱלַק עִם רַב יוֹסֵף, חוּץ מִשָּׂדֶה עִנְיָן וּמֶחֱצָה*. אֵין הֲלָכָה כְּרַבָּן שִׁמְעוֹן. דְּאָמַר לְקַמָּן: חוּץ מֵעָרֵב וְצַיְדָן וּרְאָיָה אַחֲרוֹנָה. הָכִי גָּרְסִי': אֶלָּא לְעוֹלָם כְּרַבָּנַן. כְּלוֹמַר, תַּרְוַיְיהוּ אַלִּיבָּא דְּרַבָּנַן אָמְרִי לָהּ. דִּלְצַעוּרָהּ אִיכַּוֵּין. דְּסְתָם מְגָרֵשׁ אֶת אִשְׁתּוֹ מִתּוֹךְ אֵיבָה הוּא מְגָרְשָׁהּ, הִלְכָּךְ מִסְפֵּיקָא אָמְרִי' לְצַעוּרָהּ אִיכַּוֵּין, וְלָא תָּלִינַן לְמֵימַר לְהַרְוָוחָה אִיכַּוֵּין, לְקוּלָּא. תְּנַן הָתָם. בְּמַסֶּ' עֲרָכִין (דף לא.). הָיָה נִטְמָן. הַקּוֹנֶה בַּיִת בְּעִיר חוֹמָה הָיָה נִטְמָן יוֹם שְׁנֵים עָשָׂר חוֹדֶשׁ, שֶׁלֹּא יִמְצָאֶנּוּ הַמּוֹכֵר לָתֵת מְעוֹתָיו, כְּדֵי שֶׁיְּהֵא חָלוּט לוֹ, כִּדְכְתִיב (ויקרא כה): "וְאִם לֹא יִגָּאֵל עַד מְלֹאת לוֹ" וגו'. חוֹלֵשׁ. זוֹרֵק, כְּמוֹ "חוֹלֵשׁ עַל גּוֹיִם" (ישעיה יד) — מַטִּיל גּוֹרָל. לַלִּשְׁכָּה. מְתוּקֶּנֶת לְכָךְ. וִיהֵא שׁוֹבֵר הַדֶּלֶת. שֶׁל בֵּיתוֹ וְנִכְנָס. מִתַּקַּנְתּוֹ שֶׁל הִלֵּל. דְּאִיצְטְרִיךְ לְתַקּוּנֵי נְתִינָה עַל כָּרְחוֹ תְּהֵא נְתִינָה. מִכְּלָל

אדמיפלגי במהיום ולאחר מיתה ליפלגי בעל מנת. תימה: דודאי, אי הוה שמעינן מילתא דרבנן ב"מהיום", אי הוו פליגי ב"ע"מ" הוה פריך שפיר. אבל אין ענין זה לזה כלום, דאפילו הוו אמרי רבנן ב"על מנת" גט ואינו גט, דלמא ב"מהיום" הוו מודו דהוי גט גמור, דתנאה הוי, או שמא לא הוי גט כלל, דחזרה הוי! ועוד: דמשמע "ליפלגו בעל מנת" – דב"על מנת" יאמרו חכמים גט ואינו גט, הא סבר רב יהודה דב"על מנת" לא הוי גט כלל, אלא לכשיתן! ונראה לר"י: דלרב יהודה לכשיתן הוי גט ודאי, אבל עד שיתן – הוי ספק, והוי גט ואינו גט, דמספקא ליה באומר "על מנת" אי כ"מעכשיו" דמי. ואין סברא לומר כלל דלרב יהודה עד שיתן ודאי לא הוי גט, דפשיטא ליה דלרבנן דרבי "ע"מ" לאו כאומר "מעכשיו" דמי אע"ג דב"מהיום ולאחר מיתה" מספקא להו, דא"כ הוה איפכא מר' יוחנן, דלרבי יוחנן ב"ע"מ" מודו רבנן לרבי דהוי כאומר "מעכשיו" דמי, וב"מהיום ולאחר מיתה" – אין מעשה נגמר מיד לרבנן, א"כ "ע"מ" הוי טפי כאומר "מעכשיו" מ"מהיום ולאחר מיתה". ולהכי פריך: וליפלגו ב"על מנת" וישמיענו דאפי' ב"על מנת" לרבנן גט ואינו גט, כ"ש ב"מהיום ולאחר מיתה". וליכא למימר דאי הוו פליגי ב"ע"מ" הוה אמינא "מהיום ולאחר מיתה" לא הוי גט כלל לרבנן – דא"כ מתני' דקתני "מהיום ולאחר מיתה" גט ואינו גט, אמאן תרמייה? ועוד יש לומר: דהכי קאמר: אדמיפלגי ב"מהיום ולאחר מיתה" ולא השמיענו בהך ברייתא אלא מילתא דרבי, דמילתייהו דרבנן דאמרי גט ואינו גט תנא לה במתני' – לפלוג ב"ע"מ", ולאשמועינן מילתא דתרוייהו, דאינה שנויה בשום דוכתא. ועוד הארכתי בפרק "האומר" בקידושין (דף ס.). חסורי מיחסרא וכו'. וא"ת: למה הוצרך להגיה דפליגי רבנן אדרבן שמעון בן גמליאל? מנא ליה דפליגי עליה? ואומר ר"י: דקבלה היתה בידו דפליגי רבנן. (ושהלכה כמותו ולא כרשב"ג, כדמיירי בסמוך). רבה אמר הא לא איצטריך. וא"ת: דבפרק "האומנין" (ב"מ דף עז. ושם) אמרי': שכר את הפועלים ואתא מטרא – הפסד דפועלים! וי"ל: דשאני התם, שאינו אלא שכיר יום, שלא שכרו בעל הבית אלא לדלות, וכיון שלא הולרך – אינו שכירו. אבל הכא, שהוא אריס ועושה כל מלאכות שבשדה, ויש לו חלק בקרקע כמו בעל השדה, ומיד כשהתנה עמו לדלות ארבעה – זכה בשליש שדה, ואפי' אתא מטרא ולא איצטריך, כמו שאר אריסים דמשמע דנטלי רבעא ואפילו לא יצטרכו לדלות. ורב יוסף סבר: כיון דמשנה עצמו משאר אריסות – אמרינן הא לא דלה. הא קיי"ל הלכתא כרבה. ®מכאן משמע דכולי התלמוד הלכתא כרבה לגבי רב יוסף, מדלא קאמר: והא בהא קיי"ל כרבה, כדקאמר "ובהא לא קיי"ל כרשב"ג". ודלא כאומר: הא דקאמר *) הילכתא כרבה לגבי רב יוסף בר משדה ענין ומחצה – היינו דוקא במילי דאיפלגו בבבא בתרא. והא דאיצטריך התלמוד לפסוק הלכה בקידושין בפרק קמא (דף ט.) כרבה גבי שיראי לא צריכי שומא – פירשנו שם [ד"ה והילכתא]**).

תוספות רי"ד

מעשה בצידן וכו' מאן תנא דקתני מעשה חסורי מחסרא והכי קתני אם אמר לה ע"מ שתתני לי אצטליתי ואבדה אצטליתו [אצטלתי] דוקא קא"ל רשב"ג אומר תתן את דמיה ומעשה בצידן וכו' אמר רבה בר בר חנה אמר ר' יוחנן כל מקום ששנה ר"ג במשנתינו הלכה כמותו חוץ מערב וצידן וראיה אחרונה (ערב בפ' גט פשוט צידן בפ' מי שאחזו וראיה אחרונה בפ' דיני ממונות) והלכך אי לא יהבה ליה אצטליתו דוקא לא הויא מגורשת: בעא מיניה ר' אמי מר' יוחנן הרי זה גיטיך ע"מ שתתני לי מאתים זוז וחזר ואמר מחולין הן לך מהו א"ל אינה מגורשת דלצעורה איכוין והא לא ציערה: ההוא גברא דא"ל לאריסיה כ"ע דלו תלת דלוותא ואכלי רבעא את דלי ד' ואכיל תילתא לסוף אתא מיטרא ולא איצטריך אמר רב יוסף הא לא דלה רבה אמר הא לא איצטריך וקי"ל הלכה כרבה תנן התם בראשונ' היה נטמן יום י"ב חודש כדי שיהא חלוט לו התקין הלל שיהא חולש את מעותיו ללשכה [ויהא] שובר את הדלת ונכנס ואימתי שירצה יבא הלה ויטול את מעותיו:

נג א מיי' פ"ח מהל' גירושין הלכה כא:
נד ב מיי' שם הל' כג סמג עשין נ טוש"ע אה"ע סי' קמג סעיף ו:
נה ג מיי' שם הל' כא טוש"ע שם סעיף ה:
נו ד מיי' פ"ח מהל' נדרים הלכה יד סמג לאוין רמב טוש"ע י"ד סימן רלב סעיף כ:
[ברכות ס. וש"נ]
נז ה מיי' פ"ע מהל' שכירות הלכה ו סמג עשין פט טוש"ע ח"מ סימן שלד סעיף ג:
נח ו מיי' פי"ב מהל' שמיטה ויובל הל' ו:
נט ז מיי' פ"ח מהלכות גירושין הלכה כא סמג עשין נ טוש"ע אה"ע סי' קמג סעיף ז:

לעיל עב: וש"נ

[נ"ל נמי פליגי]

גליון הש"ס

תוס' ד"ה הא קיי"ל כו' מכאן משמע. עיין במלחמות סוף פי"ט דשבת:

נדרים כד. סג.

[ב"ב ק"ד: קמג:]

[נ"ל הכא]

[נ"ל ההם]

ערכין לא.

---

*) [ב"ב קיד: וקמג:] **) [ועי' תוס' ב"ב קיד: ותוס' מגילה כט: ותוס' מנחות לב. ד"ה מנעל ותוס' ב"מ כט. סד"ה והוי ותוס' שבועות מז. ד"ה שומר]

מכלל

מִכְּלָל דִּבְעָלְמָא נְתִינָה בְּעַל כָּרְחֵיהּ לָא הָוְיָא נְתִינָה. מַתְקִיף לָהּ רַב פַּפָּא, וְאִיתֵימָא רַב שִׁימִי בַּר אַשִׁי: וְדִלְמָא כִּי אִצְטְרִיךְ לֵיהּ לְתַקּוּנֵי — שֶׁלֹּא בְּפָנָיו, אֲבָל בְּפָנָיו — בֵּין מִדַּעְתּוֹ בֵּין בְּעַל כָּרְחוֹ הָוְיָא נְתִינָה! וְאִיכָּא דְּאָמְרִי, אָמַר רָבָא: מִתַּקָּנָתוֹ שֶׁל הִלֵּל, "ה"ז גִּיטֵּךְ עַל מְנָת שֶׁתִּתְּנִי לִי מָאתַיִם זוּז", וְנָתְנָה לוֹ — בֵּין מִדַּעְתּוֹ וּבֵין בְּעַל כָּרְחוֹ הָוְיָא נְתִינָה; וְכִי אִיצְטְרִיךְ לֵיהּ לְהִלֵּל לְתַקּוּנֵי — שֶׁלֹּא בְּפָנָיו, אֲבָל בְּפָנָיו — בֵּין מִדַּעְתּוֹ בֵּין בְּעַל כָּרְחוֹ הָוְיָא נְתִינָה. מַתְקִיף לָהּ רַב פַּפָּא, וְאִיתֵימָא רַב שִׁימִי בַּר אַשִׁי: וְדִלְמָא אֲפִילּוּ בְּפָנָיו נַמִי — מִדַּעְתּוֹ אִין, עַל כָּרְחוֹ לָא, וְהִלֵּל מַאי דְּאִיצְטְרִיךְ לֵיהּ תַּקֵּין! *אָמַר רַבָּה בַּר בַּר חָנָה א"ר יוֹחָנָן: כׇּל מָקוֹם שֶׁשָּׁנָה רשב"ג בְּמִשְׁנָתֵינוּ — הֲלָכָה כְּמוֹתוֹ, חוּץ מֵעָרֵב, וְצַיְדָּן, וּרְאָיָה אַחֲרוֹנָה. *ת"ר: "הֲרֵי זֶה גִּיטֵּךְ וְהַנְּיָיר שֶׁלִּי" — אֵינָהּ מְגוֹרֶשֶׁת, "עַל מְנָת שֶׁתַּחֲזִירִי לִי אֶת הַנְּיָיר" — מְגוֹרֶשֶׁת. מַאי שְׁנָא רֵישָׁא וּמַאי שְׁנָא סֵיפָא? אָמַר רַב חִסְדָּא: הָא מַנִּי? רשב"ג הִיא, דְּאָמַר: תִּתֵּן לוֹ אֶת דָּמֶיהָ, ה"נ אֶפְשָׁר דִּמְפַיְּיסָה לֵיהּ בְּדָמֵי. מַתְקִיף לָהּ אַבָּיֵי: אֵימוּר דְּאָמַר רשב"ג — הֵיכָא דְּלֵיתֵיהּ בְּעֵינֵיהּ, הֵיכָא דְּאִיתֵיהּ בְּעֵינֵיהּ מִי אָמַר? אֶלָּא אָמַר אַבָּיֵי: הָא מַנִּי? *ר"מ הִיא, דְּאָמַר: אבָּעֵינַן תְּנַאי כָּפוּל, וְהָכָא הָא לָא כַּפְלֵיהּ לִתְנָאֵיהּ. מַתְקִיף לָהּ רָבָא: טַעְמָא דְּלָא כַּפְלֵיהּ לִתְנָאֵיהּ, הָא כַּפְלֵיהּ לִתְנָאֵיהּ לָא הָוֵי גִּיטָּא? מִכְּדֵי כׇּל תְּנָאֵי מֵהֵיכָא גָּמְרִינַן לְהוּ — מִתְּנַאי בְּנֵי גָד וּבְנֵי רְאוּבֵן; מַה הָתָם תְּנַאי קוֹדֵם לְמַעֲשֶׂה, באַף כׇּל תְּנַאי קוֹדֵם לְמַעֲשֶׂה, לְאַפּוּקֵי הָכָא דְּמַעֲשֶׂה קוֹדֵם לִתְנַאי! אֶלָּא אָמַר רָבָא: מִשּׁוּם דְּמַעֲשֶׂה קוֹדֵם לִתְנַאי. מַתְקִיף לָהּ רַב אַדָּא בַּר אַהֲבָה: טַעְמָא דְּמַעֲשֶׂה קוֹדֵם לִתְנַאי, הָא תְּנַאי קוֹדֵם לְמַעֲשֶׂה לָא הָוֵי גִּיטָּא? מִכְּדֵי כׇּל תְּנָאֵי מֵהֵיכָא גָּמְרִינַן לְהוּ — מִתְּנַאי בְּנֵי גָד וּבְנֵי רְאוּבֵן; מַה הָתָם תְּנַאי בְּדָבָר אֶחָד וּמַעֲשֶׂה בְּדָבָר אַחֵר, גאַף כֹּל, לְאַפּוּקֵי הָכָא

דִּתְנַאי

רש"י

מִכְּלָל דִּבְעָלְמָא [נְתִינָה בְּע"כ] לָאו נְתִינָה הִיא. וְגַבֵּי גֵּט דְּאִיסּוּרָא הוּא לָא תַּקֵּין הִלֵּל. שֶׁלֹּא בְּפָנָיו. כִּי הָכָא, שֶׁאֵינוֹ בַּלִּשְׁכָּה. מַאי דְּאִיצְטְרִיךְ לֵיהּ תַּקֵּין. רָאָה שֶׁהָיָה נִטְמָן, וְהִתְקִין דִּבְעַל כָּרְחוֹ וְשֶׁלֹּא בְּפָנָיו תְּהֵא נְתִינָה. וְאִי הֲוָה נַמִי קָאֵי קַמָּן, וְאָמַר "לָא מְקַבֵּילְנָא" — הֲוָה אִיצְטְרִיךְ לְהִלֵּל נַמִי לְתַקּוּנֵי דְּתֶיהֱוֵי נְתִינָה. אֶלָּא מַה שֶּׁלֹּא הוּצְרַךְ — לֹא הוּצְרַךְ, וְגַבֵּי גֵּט דְּאִיסּוּרָא הוּא — לָא קַיְימָא תַּקַּנְתָּא דְּהִלֵּל. עָרֵב. בִּשְׁלְהֵי גֵּט פָּשׁוּט. צַיְדָּן. דְּמַתְנִי'. רְאָיָה אַחֲרוֹנָה. בְּ"אֶחָד דִּינֵי מָמוֹנוֹת" (סנהדרין דף לא.), דְּאִפְלִיגִי בְּאָמְרוּ לוֹ: כׇּל רְאָיוֹת שֶׁיֵּשׁ לְךָ הָבִיא — הָבֵא עַד שְׁלֹשִׁים, וְלֹא הֵבִיא עַד לְאַחַר שְׁלֹשִׁים. וְאָמְרוּ לוֹ: הָבֵא רְאָיָה, וְאָמַר: אֵין לִי רְאָיָה. בְּקַמַּיְיתָא — הִלְכְתָא כְּוָותֵיהּ, וּבְבַתְרַיְיתָא — לֵית הִלְכְתָא כְּוָותֵיהּ. וְהַנְּיָיר שֶׁלִּי. לָא יָהֵיב לָהּ וְלָא מִידֵּי, וְרַחֲמָנָא אָמַר: "וְנָתַן בְּיָדָהּ"*. מַאי שְׁנָא רֵישָׁא כו'. קָא סָלְקָא דַּעְתֵּיהּ: "עַל מְנָת" לָאו "מֵעַכְשָׁיו" הוּא, כְּרַבָּנַן דִּפְלִיגִי עֲלֵיהּ דְּרַבִּי, וַהֲוֵי כְּמוֹ: לִכְשֶׁתַּחֲזִירִי לִי הַנְּיָיר — לֶיהֱוֵי גֵּט. וְא"כ אַמַּאי מְגוֹרֶשֶׁת? הָא בִּשְׁעַת גֵּירוּשִׁין לָאו מִידֵּי נְקִיטָא! הֵיכָא דְּלֵיתֵיהּ. לְאִצְטְלִית. לָא כַּפְלֵיהּ. ר"מ בְּמַסֶּכֶת קִידּוּשִׁין (דף סא.): כׇּל תְּנַאי שֶׁאֵינוֹ כִּתְנַאי בְּנֵי גָד וּבְנֵי רְאוּבֵן וכו'. דְּנֵימָא: אִם לֹא תַּחֲזִירִי — לֹא יְהֵא גֵּט, הִלְכָּךְ בָּטֵל תְּנָאֵיהּ. הָא כַּפְלֵיהּ לָא הָוֵי גִּיטָּא. לְר"מ. מִכְּדֵי. לְר"מ, כׇּל תְּנַאי מֵהֵיכָא גָּמְרִינַן לְכוֹפְלוֹ. מִתְּנַאי בְּנֵי גָד. שֶׁהָיָה כָּפוּל: "אִם יַעַבְרוּ" "וְאִם לֹא יַעַבְרוּ" (במדבר לב), וְכֵיוָן דְּמִינַּיְ' גָּמְרִי' — בָּעֵינַן כִּי הָתָם: תְּנַאי שֶׁתָּלוּ בּוֹ הַמַּעֲשֶׂה הוּזְכַּר קוֹדֶם לַמַּעֲשֶׂה, "אִם יַעַבְרוּ" — זֶה הַתְּנַאי, "וּנְתַתֶּם לָהֶם" — זֶה הַמַּעֲשֶׂה. ה"נ בָּעֵינַן דְּנֵימָא: אִם תַּחֲזִירִי — יְהֵא גֵּט. לְאַפּוּקֵי הָכָא. דְּאָמַר לָהּ "זֶה גִּיטֵּךְ" בְּרֵישָׁא, וַהֲדַר "ע"מ שֶׁתַּחֲזִירִי". מִשּׁוּם דַּהֲוֵי לֵיהּ כו'. וּבֵין לְר"מ וּבֵין לְרַבָּנַן, דְּלָא אִפְלִיג אֶלָּא בִּכְפִילָה, כִּדְמְפָרֵשׁ טַעְמָא הָתָם: (א) הוּצְרַךְ הַדָּבָר לְאוֹמְרוֹ, שֶׁאִלְמָלֵא כֵּן — יֵשׁ בְּמַשְׁמַע שֶׁאַף בְּאֶרֶץ כְּנַעַן לֹא יִנְחָלוּ. בְּדָבָר אֶחָד. לַעֲבוֹר הַיַּרְדֵּן. וּמַעֲשֶׂה בְּדָבָר אַחֵר. נַחֲלַת עֵבֶר הַיַּרְדֵּן מִזְרָחָה.

בְּדָבָר

תוספות

מכלל דבעלמא נתינה בעל ברחו לא הויא נתינה. וא"ת: דהשתא לא מפליג בין בפניו בין שלא בפניו, דבכל ענין בעל כרחו לא הויא נתינה, א"כ למה היה נטמן בראשונה? וי"ל: דבפניו לא היה יכול להעיז מלוה מלקבלם כדי שיהיה הבית שלו, וגם אם היה בפניו — יעשוהו ב"ד לקבלם בעל כרחו. וא"ת: בבתי ערי חומה, דהוי כפרעון החוב, דעליו לקבלם — פשיטא דהוי פרעון, כדקאמרינן: *הלוהו בישוב — לא יחזיר לו במדבר, משמע דבישוב — יחזיר לו אפילו בעל כרחו. וכן ב"הזהב" (ב"מ דף מט.) כי אמר ליה "שקול זוזך" — לא הוי אפילו כשומר חנם. ומה אילטריך הלל הזקן לתקן? וי"ל: דוקא בעלמא פשיטא דהוי נתינה, שאין המלוה מפסיד בקבלת הפרעון. אבל הכא, דע"י הפרעון צריך להחזיר הבית, וכן ע"י קבלתו הוי הגט גט — לא הויא נתינה. וא"ת: גבי גט פשיטא דלא הויא נתינה, ומה צריך ללמוד מתקנתו של הלל? וכי אם יתן מתנה לחבירו יקבלנה בעל כרחו?! ואור"י: די"ל, דכיון דאמר לה "ה"ז גיטך ע"מ שתתני לי מאתים זוז" — תלה הדבר בדעתה, ועליו לקבלם, והוי כמו בבתי ערי חומה, וקמ"ל דאפ"ה בע"כ לא הויא נתינה.

לאפוקי הכא דמעשה קודם לתנאי. פי' בקונטרס: דר' מאיר ור' חנינא לא פליגי אלא בכפלות, כדקאמרינן התם טעמא דהוצרך לאומרו, שאלמלא כן יש במשמע שאף בארץ כנען לא ינחלו. וקשה: דבפרק "השוכר את הפועלים" (ב"מ דף צד.) משמע בהדיא דפליגי רבנן נמי אר"מ במעשה קודם לתנאי, גבי מתנה שומר חנם להיות כשואל! וא"ת: בשלמא תנאי כפול, ותנאי קודם למעשה, והן קודם ללאו — ילפינן שפיר מתנאי בני גד ובני ראובן, מדנכתבו בזה הענין — שמע מינה בעינן כי האי גוונא. אבל שלא יהא מתנה על מה שכתוב בתורה, ואפשר לקיימו ע"י שליח, היכי ילפינן מהתם כדאמרינן בכתובות (דף עד.)? דלמא בלאו הכי נמי מועיל תנאי, אלא דהכי הוה מעשה! וי"ל: *משום דכל התנאים הכתובים דמייתי בקידושין בפרק "האומר" (דף סא.) הוו בענין זה — שמע מינה דבעינן ממש כי האי גוונא. ו"אם בחקותי תלכו" ו"אם תאבו ושמעתם" נמי — רוב מלות ע"י שליח. ונראה דהלכה כר"מ, דבעי' תנאי כפול כו', דשמואל ורבא בסמוך סברי כוותיה. וכל הני דמתניתין איירי בתנאי כפול אע"ג דלא פירש, דה"נ מוקי לה לקמן ברייתא בדכפליה לתנאיה, אע"פ שלא פירש. ובכל "ע"מ" שבש"ס, כגון (סוכה מא:) "ע"מ שתחזירהו לי" דאתרוג, וכיוצא בו — בעי כפילות. ובכל מקום בעינן תנאי כפול, אלא דוקא בשתויי יין ופרועי ראש — דהוי איסורי, בפ' "שבועת העדות" (שבועות דף לו:). והא דבעינן כפילות בסוטה — משום דהוי איסורא דאית ביה ממונא, דאיכא שאר וכסות ועונה וכתובה. והא דאמרינן בירושלמי בפרק "האומר": א"ר יוסי א"ר בון: בכל אתר אית ליה לר"מ מכלל לאו אתה שומע הן, והכא לית ליה. ונראה להרב ר' אלחנן דגרסינן: בכל אתר לית ליה לר"מ וכו' והכא אית ליה. ומשני ר' חנינא: חומר הוא בערוה. כלומר, אע"ג דלא כפל תנאו, ומן הדין התנאי בטל ומעשה קיים, ומשום חומר אין הגט גט ולא הקידושין קידושין, שאם קבלה קידושין מאחר — צריכה גט משניהם, ובהכי איירי התם לעיל. הקשה הרב ר' אלחנן: כיון דבעינן תנאי כפול ב"איזהו נשך" (ב"מ דף סו.) גבי "אי קיימת דידך אנא", דקאמר: פטומי מילי בעלמא הוא, משמע שאם התנה הוא כמו שהיא אמרה — היה מועיל, ואמאי? הא לא כפליה לתנאיה! ואומר רבינו יצחק: הא דנקט פטומי מילי — משום דלא מהני אפי' לרבנן דר"מ. וג' ענייניס יש: דיש מקומות דבעינן תנאי גמור, ולר"מ תנאי כפול. ויש מקומות דלא בעינן אלא גלוי דעת. ויש מקומות דאפי' גלוי דעת לא בעינן, ובפ' "האיש מקדש" (קדושין דף מט: ד"ה דברים) מפורש. **אלא אמר רבא משום דמעשה קודם לתנאי.** לאו משום דלית ליה לרבא "כל האומר על מנת כאומר מעכשיו דמי" דהא הכי הילכתא, כדפרישית לעיל. ועוד: דבהדיא קאמר רבא *ב"הילך אתרוג זה על מנת שתחזירהו לי", החזירו — יצא, ואם לאו כאומר "מעכשיו" דמי — היכי יצא? והא לא חלה המתנה אלא כשהחזירו, ואז אינו בידו! ואין נראה לומר דהתם מיירי כגון שאמר "מעכשיו" — דא"כ היה לו לפרש בדבריו. ואע"ג דלא פירש נמי כפילות — היינו משום דלא מפרש ליה במשנתינו, אבל אי מיירי באומר "מעכשיו" — היה לו לפרש. אלא שרוצה רבא ליישב ברייתא זו אפילו כרבנן ורבי, אבל לרבי אתיא שפיר, כדמסיק רב אשי. ואביי נמי משמע לקמן בסוף פירקין דסבר כרבי, דקאמר: הכל מודין ב"על מנת שתאכלי חמה מגרתיקה" — ד"מעכשיו" קאמר, וכדרבי כו'. ומיהו, אין משם ראיה, דלא מצי למימר איפכא: הכל מודין ד"על מנת" לאו כאומר "מעכשיו" דמי, דהא ב"אם תאכלי" פליגי, כ"ש ב"על מנת" דעדיף.

דתנאי

עין משפט נר מצוה

ס א ב מיי' פ"ו מהל' אישות הל' ב סמג עשין מח טוש"ע אה"ע סימן לח סעיף ב:
סא ג טוש"ע שם סעיף ד בהג"ה:

מסורת הש"ס

[ב"ק קיח.]

[בכורות כד. ב"מ לח:] ב"ק סט. ב"ב קעד. כתובות עז. סנהדרין לא. לעיל לח.

דברים כד

לעיל כ: [תוספתא פ"ב]

[קדושין סא.]

[כתובות עד. ד"ה תנאי תירצו באופן אחר]

[סוכה מא:]

תוספות רי"ד

אמר רבא מתקנתו של הלל הרי זה גיטך ע"מ שתתני לי מאתים זוז ונתנה לו בין מדעתו בין בעל כרחו מגורשת דמתנה בעל כרחה שמה מתנה וכי איצטריך ליה להלל לתקוני שלא בפניו אבל בפניו בין מדעתו בין שלא מדעתו הויא נתינה: ת"ר הרי זה גיטך והנייר שלי אינה מגורשת ע"מ שתחזירי את הנייר הרי זו מגורשת מ"ש רישא ומ"ש סיפא פי' דקס"ד דלא קניא גיטא עד שתחזיר לו את הנייר ונמצא דבעת קניית הגט לא יהיב לה מידי ורחמנא אמר ונתן בידה

הגהות הב"ח

(א) רש"י ד"ה משום וכו' התם דהולך:

דתנאי ומעשה בדבר אחד! אלא אמר רב אדא בר אהבה: משום דתנאי ומעשה בדבר אחד. רב אשי אמר: הא מני? רבי היא, דאמר* רב הונא אמר *רב: כל האומר "על מנת" כאומר "מעכשיו" דמי. אתקין שמואל בגיטא דשכיב מרע: "אם לא מתי לא יהא גט, ואם מתי יהא גט". ולימא: אם מתי יהא גט, ואם לא מתי לא יהא גט! *לא מקדים איניש פורענותא לנפשיה. ולימא: לא *יהא גט אם לא מתי! בעינן תנאי קודם למעשה. מתקיף לה רבא: מכדי כל תנאי מהיכא גמרינן? מתנאי בני גד ובני ראובן, מה התם "הן" קודם ל"לאו", אף כל, לאפוקי הכא ד"לאו" קודם ל"הן"! אלא אמר רבא: [א]"אם לא מתי לא יהא גט, אם מתי יהא גט אם לא מתי לא יהא גט"; "אם לא מתי לא יהא גט" — לא מקדים איניש פורענותא לנפשיה, "אם מתי יהא גט אם לא מתי לא יהא גט" — בעינן "הן" קודם ל"לאו".§ **מתני'** [ב]"הרי זה גיטך ע"מ שתשמשי את אבא", "על מנת שתניקי את בני", כמה היא מניקתו? [ג]שתי שנים, *רבי יהודה אומר: שמונה עשר חדש; מת הבן או שמת האב — הרי זה גט. "הרי זה גיטך ע"מ שתשמשי את אבא שתי שנים" — ע"מ שתניקי את בני שתי שנים", מת הבן, או *שאמר האב "אי אפשי שתשמשני", שלא בהקפדה — אינו גט, רבן שמעון בן גמליאל אומר: כזה גט. כלל אמר רבן שמעון בן גמליאל: כל עכבה שאינה הימנה — הרי זה גט.§ **גמ'** ומי בעינן כולי האי? ורמינהי: *שמשתו יום אחד, הניקתו יום אחד — ה"ז גט! אמר רב חסדא, לא קשיא: הא רבנן והא רבן שמעון בן גמליאל, מתניתין רשב"ג וברייתא רבנן. הא מדסיפא רבן שמעון בן גמליאל הוי, מכלל דרישא לאו רשב"ג! אלא, ברייתא רשב"ג היא דמיקל בתנאי, מתני' רבנן. רבא אמר, לא קשיא: כאן בסתם, כאן במפרש. רב אשי אמר: [ד]כל סתם נמי כמפרש יום אחד דמי. תנן: כמה היא מניקתו? שתי שנים, רבי יהודה אומר: שמונה עשר חדש; בשלמא לרבא ניחא, אלא לרב אשי, למה לי שתי שנים? למה לי שמונה עשר חדש? ביום אחד סגי! [ה]הכי קאמר: יום אחד משתי שנים — לאפוקי לאחר שתי שנים, דלא; יום אחד משמונה עשר חדש — לאפוקי לאחר שמונה עשר חדש, דלא. מיתיבי: "הרי זה גיטך על מנת שתשמשי את אבא שתי שנים", "על מנת שתניקי את בני שתי שנים", מת הבן, או שאמר האב "אי אפשי שתשמשני", שלא בהקפדה — אינו גט; בשלמא

בדבר אחד. בגט עצמו, הוא התנאי להחזירו, והוא המעשה להיות גט. רב אשי אמר הא מני. דקתני "על מנת שתחזירי" – מגורשת. רבי היא דאמר וכו' כאומר מעכשיו דמי. ואשתכח דבשעת גירושין נקיטא לגט, ולאחר זמן היא מחזרת ומתנה על מנת להחזיר – שמה מתנה. אתקין שמואל כו'. כשמוסרו לה יאמר: "אם לא מתי לא יהא גט אם מתי יהא גט" דבעי' תנאי כפול, דאי לא כפליה – הוי גיטא מיד, ואי כהן הוא – מפסלא עליה. ה"ג ונימא אם מתי. ברישא. לא מקדים כו'. הן קודם. "אם יעברו ונתתם" (במדבר לב). ה"ג אלא אמר רבא אם לא מתי לא יהא גט. לימא ברישא, משום דלא מקדים כו'. והדר נימא הן ולאו, דבעינן הן קודם ללאו. **מתני'** כמה היא מניקתו ב' שנים. שיהא לולד שתי שנים, שכך הוא זמן הנקתו. ולענין לשמש את אביו – כל ימי חייו. רבי יהודה אומר שמונה עשר חדש. לר' יהודה זמן הנקת תינוק עד שיהו לו י"ח חדשים, בכתובות בפרק "אע"פ" (דף ס.). מת הבן. קודם הזמן, או מת האב. ה"ז גט. דכיון דלא פריש מידי – לא איכוון אלא להרווחה, כל ימים שהוא צריך, ומכאן ואילך אינו צריך. שלא בהקפדה. היא לא הכעיסתו ואפי' הכי, שאין העכבה הימנה – אינו גט. וכ"ש אם בהקפדה. רשב"ג אומר כזה גט. הואיל ולא הקפידתו, ואין העכבה הימנה. **גמ'** מתני' רשב"ג. דאמר לעיל (דף עד.): תתן דמיה. אלמא להרווחה מיכוין, ולאו דוקא קאמר. הא נמי להרווחה איכוין, וכל זמן שהוא צריך לינק קאמר. וברייתא רבנן. דאמרי (שם.) אצטלית דוקא, הכא נמי – שימוש והנקה דוקא, וביום אחד סגי. דמיקל בתנאי. דאמר: תתן דמיה, וקאמר נמי: כל עכבה שאינה הימנה ה"ז גט. כאן בסתם. מתני' דאמר שתי שנים תניקי – בסתם, וברייתא – במפרש יום אחד. רב אשי אמר. ברייתא בסתם, דכל סתם כמפרש יום אחד דמי. ומתני' – רב אשי משני לה לקמיה. ורב אשי לאו לשנויי מתניתין וברייתא אתא, אלא לאפלוגי עליה דרבא דאמר: סתם – שתי שנים. יום אחד משתי שנים. של תינוק. לאפוקי. שאם הניקתו לאחר שעברו לו שתי שנים. דלא. שאין זה הנקה. בשלמא

דתנאי ומעשה בדבר אחד. פירוש: שהתנאי סותר המעשה, דאין הגט חל אלא אחר שנתקיים התנאי – ואז אין הגט בידה. אבל "הילך אתרוג זה במתנה *על מנת שתחזירהו" – לא הוי תנאי ומעשה בדבר אחד, דס"ל "על מנת" כאומר "מעכשיו", והמתנה חלה מיד, ויצא בו מיד כשיצא לידו*.

מת הבן או מת האב ה"ז גט. פי' בקונטרס: מת הבן בתוך ב' שנים. משמע שרוצה לומר דאם לא הניקה ושמשה כלל – דלא הוי גט. וכן משמע בפירושו בגמרא גבי "בשלמא לרבא כו' אלא לרב אשי" כו'. ואין נראה, דאם מת האב כששימשתו יום אחד – פשיטא דהוי גט, כיון ששימשתו עד שמת, דמה יש לה לשמש יותר? וליכא למימר דאשמועינן אע"פ שמת קודם הוי גט, דלא בעינן שתשמשנו כל ימי חייה – דהא ודאי לא בעינן, דאי הוה בעינן – לא הוה גט, דאין זה כריתות, כדאמרינן בפרק בתרא (לקמן דף פג:): "כל ימי חייכי" – אין זה כריתות. אלא נראה לרבינו יצחק לפרש: דמת קודם שהניקה ושימשה כלל, דלא איכוין אלא להרווחה ולא לצעורה, והא לא איצטריך. ואפי' לרב יוסף דאמר לעיל:* והא לא דלה – יש לחלק, דהכא מסתמא אם היה יודע שימות אביו או בנו – לא היה מקפיד בתנאו. אבל התם – אדרבה, אם היה יודע דאתי מטרא – לא היה משכירו כלל.

כלל אמר רשב"ג כל עכבה שאינה הימנה ה"ז גט. הקשה ה"ר אלחנן: א"כ אמאי קאמר רבא לעיל* דנתינה בעל כרחו לא הויא נתינה, ולא הוי גט! והא עכבה אינה ממנה, והלכה כרשב"ג במשנתנו! ועוד: מאי שנא מת האב או הבן מ"מחולין לך", דבעי למימר *דאפילו לרשב"ג אינה מגורשת? וי"ל: דהכא ודאי להרווחה בעלמא עשה כן, וכיון שמת ולא אצטריך – הוי כאילו נתקיים התנאי. אבל התם, "שתתני לי מאתים זוז" – בדעתו שיקבלם, ולבסוף כשאינו רוצה לקבלם – לא נתקיים התנאי. והא דמספקא ליה לעיל ב"מחולין לך" – דלמא אפי' לרבנן הוי גט. ואע"ג דהכא לא הוי גט – היינו משום דהתם בעצמו מחל לה, אבל הכא לא מחל לה כלום.

ורמינהו שימשתו יום אחד ה"ז גט. אין להקשות: לפי' הקונטרס, דמפרש דמת הבן או מת האב דמתני' אחר שהניקתו, אמאי לא מוקי להך ברייתא דהכא שמת לאחר ששימשתו והניקתו יום אחד? דא"כ הוה ליה למיתני בהדיא: ומת. אבל אין לתרץ דא"כ מאי איריא יום א' – אפי' שעה אחת נמי, דהא לרש"י שפירש בסמוך גבי "אלא לרב אשי מאי שנא רישא ומאי שנא סיפא" – ה"נ יום אחד לאו דוקא, אלא אפילו שעה אחת, דאי דוקא – לא הוי פריך מידי. **מתניתין** רשב"ג. דאמר גבי אצטלית: תתן לו את דמיה, דלהרווחה קא מיכוין. ומתניתין נמי להרווחה קא מכוין, והנקה ושימוש כל הצורך קאמר. וברייתא רבנן, דאמרי: לצעורה קא מיכוין, וכיון דליערה יום אחד – סגי בהכי, כיון דלא להרווחה קא מכוין. ולפירוש זה, אם מת קודם שהניקה ושימשה כלל – אינו גט, דהא לא ליערה. אי נמי: הכא לא נתכוון לצעורה בחנם, אלא לצורך בנו ואביו, וכי מת – הא לא אצטריך. אבל גבי אצטלית – לעולם הוא צריך לאצטלית ולא לדמי', ולכך כשאבדה – יכול לומר: איני חפץ בדמי אצטלית. וכן צריך לפרש בסמוך דמוקי מתני' כרבנן. **ברייתא** רשב"ג היא דמיקל בתנאי. ובהרווחה פורתא סגי, אבל רבנן דמחמרי – אית לן למימר דכל הצורך קאמר. **כאן** במפרש. ברייתא במפרש יום אחד, וקא משמע לן: דוקא הניקתו ושימשתו יום אחד, אבל מת ולא הניקתו ושמשתו כלל – אינו גט. דסלקא דעתין, כיון שהיקל עליה כל כך, שלא הצריכה אלא יום אחד, אף על פי דפירש, כי מת ולא הניקתו ושמשתו כלל – ליהוי גט, קא משמע לן דלא אמרינן הכי.

בשלמא

[סוכה מא: קדושין ו: בבא בתרא קלז:]

[ועי' תוס' קדושין ו: ד"ה לא החזירו ותוס' סוכה מא: ד"ה הילך ותוס' ב"ב קלז: ד"ה לא]

[דף עד:]

[דף עד:]

[לעיל עד:]

סב א מיי' פ"ט מהל' גירושין הל' כ סמג עשין נ טוש"ע אה"ע סימן קמה סעיף ה:

סג ב ג ד ה מיי' פ"ח שם הלכה יט סמג שם טוש"ע אה"ע סימן קמג סעיף ח:

[לעיל עד. וש"נ]

[נ"ל רבי]

[לעיל יח.]

[בכתובות פ' מכות סי' קלה איתא ולימא לא יהא גט אם לא מתי יהא גט אם מתי בעינן תנאי וכו']

[כתובות ס:]

[גי' סדר המשנה וכן ברי"ף ורא"ש או שמת האב או שאמר כו']

[תוספתא פ"ה]

תוספות רי"ד

ואסיק רב אשי הא מני ר' היא דאמר רב הונא אמר רבי כל האומר ע"מ כאומר מעכשיו דמי. פי' והגט קונה למפרע משעה שמסרו בידה קודם שתחזיר לו הנייר והחזרת הנייר הוי תנאה ומקיימה ליה לתנאה והוי גיטא למפרע ובההיא שעתא הנייר שלה היה ומתנה ע"מ להחזיר שמה [מתנה] אתקין שמואל בגיטא דש"מ אם לא מתי לא יהא גט ואם מתי יהא גט פי' הכי צריך למימר אם מתי יהא גט מהיום או מעכשיו דאי לא אמר הכי הוה ליה גט לאחר מיתה ומשום דתנינן ליה בפירוש במתני' לא איצטריך שמואל למימרי': ולימא אם מתי יהא גט ואם לא מתי לא יהא גט לא מקדים איניש פורענותא לנפשיה הלכך מתחיל באם לא מתי ומשום דבעי' תנאי כפול אומר שניהם שאם לא יכפול תנאו אין זה תנאי והוי גט מיד ואם הוא כהן מיפסלא עילויה מתקיף לה רבא מכדי כל תנאי מהיכא גמרי' ליה מבני גד ובני ראובן מה התם הן קודם ללאו אף וכו' לאפוקי הכא דלאו קודם להן אלא אמר רבא הכי לימא אם לא מתי לא יהא גט ואם מתי יהא גט ואם לא מתי לא יהא גט מ"ש לא מתי לא יהא גט דלא מקדים איניש פורענותא לנפשיה ואם מתי יהא גט ואם לא מתי לא יהא גט דבעי' תנאי כפול והן קודם ללאו. תניא אבא חלפתא איש כפר חנניה אומר משום ר' מאיר תנאי קודם למעשה הרי זה תנאי. מעשה קודם לתנאי אין זה תנאי. פי' כגון אם מתי יהא גט זהו תנאי קודם למעשה כמו אם יעברו ונתתם. יהא גט אם מתי זה מעשה קודם לתנאי שאין זה תנאי אלא מיד הוי גט. והלכתא כר' מאיר משום דתנן סתמא כותיה בפ' השוכר את הפועלים כל המתנה על מה שכתוב בתורה תנאו בטל וכל תנאי שמעשה קודם מתחילתו תנאו בטל וכל תנאי שאפשר לו לקיימו בסופו והתנה עליו מתחילתו תנאו קיים. ואי קשה והיכי תנן בפרקין זה גיטך אם מתי זה גיטך מחולי זה לא אמר כלום מהיום אם מתי מעכשיו אם מתי הרי זה גט. והא הרי זה גיטך הוי מעשה אם מתי הוי תנאה ואנן בעי' תנאי קודם למעשה י"ל התנא קיצר את לשונו. וה"ק זה גיטך אם מתי יהא גט דהוי תנאי קודם למעשה עיין בשלהי פרקין שהוכחתי כרבנן ועי' בפ' האומר בקידושין. מתני' הרי זה גיטך ע"מ שתשמשי את אבא ע"מ שתניקי את בני כמה היא מניקתו שתי שנים ר' יהודה אומר י"ח חודש מת הבן או שמת האב הרי זה גט ע"מ שתשמשי את אבא שתי שנים וע"מ שתניקי את בני שתי שנים מת הבן או שמת האב או שאמר האב אי אפשי שתשמשני שלא בהקפדה אינו גט רשב"ג אומר הרי זה גט אמר רשב"ג כל עכבה שאינה ממנה הרי זה גט. פי' הרי היא מניקתו שתי שנים שיהו לולד כ"ד חודש מניקתו ולענין לשמש את אביו כל ימי חייו מת הבן או וכו' פי' דוקא אם התחילה להניקה ואח"כ מת אבל אם לא הניקה כלל ומת הבן אינו גט שהרי לא נתקיים התנאי של יניקה כלל ודמי לסיפא כשאמר הבן בתוך שתי שנים שלא נתקיים התנאי של שתי שנים. או שאמר האב וכו'. פי' אע"פ שלא הקפידתו האשה שאין העכבה ממנה אפ"ה אינו גט כיון שלא נתקיים התנאי. רשב"ג אומר כל עכבה וכו' ומי בעי' כולי האי. ורמינהו שמשתו יום א' הניקתו יום א' הרי זה גט. אמר רבא לא קשה כאן בסתם כאן במפרש פי' מתני' בסתם דאמר לה ע"מ שתניקי את בני ולא פירש לה כמה צריכה להניקו שתי שנים שהוא זמן יניקת הולד. וברייתא במפרש דאמר לה ע"מ שתניקי את בני יום אחד והוא גופיה קא משמע לן שאם שמשתו יום אחד והניקתו יום אחד שיתקיים התנאי הוי גט ואם לאו כגון שמת הבן או האב אינו גט הוא ולאפוקי מדרבי שמעון בן גמליאל רב אשי אמר כל בסתם נמי כמפרש יום אחד דמי. פי' ברייתא דתני יום אחד אף על פי שאמר לה על מנת שתניקי את בני סתם די לה ביום אחד כיון שלא פירש לה זמן. תנן כמה היא מניקתו שתי שנים בשלמא לרבא ניחא אלא לרב אשי למה לי שתי שנים יום אחד סגי ה"ק יום אחד משתי שנים. לאפוקי לאחר שתי שנים דלא יום אחד מי"ח חודש לאפוקי אחר י"ח חודש דלא. פי' שכבר עבר זמן היניקה. מיתיבי הרי זה גיטך ע"מ שתשמשי את אבא שתי שנים על מנת שתניקי את בני שתי שנים מת הבן או שאמר האב אי אפשי שתשמשני שלא בהקפדה אינו גט

בשלמא

סד א ב מיי' פ"ח מהל' גירושין הלכה יח סמג עשין נ טוש"ע אה"ע סי' קמג סעיף י:

סה ג מיי' שם פרק ט הלכה ט סמג שם טוש"ע אה"ע סי' קמד סעיף ז:

בשלמא לרבא, רישא בדלא פריש סיפא דפריש, אלא לרב אשי, מאי שנא רישא ומאי שנא סיפא? קשיא. ת"ר: *"הרי זה גיטך על מנת שתשמשי את אבא שתי שנים", ו"על מנת שתניקי את בני שתי שנים", אע"פ שלא נתקיים התנאי — הרי זה גט, לפי שלא אמר לה "אם תשמשי" "אם לא תשמשי", "אם תניקי" ו"אם לא תניקי", דברי רבי מאיר; וחכ"א: נתקיים התנאי — ה"ז גט, ואם לאו — אינו גט; רשב"ג אומר: אין לך תנאי בכתובים שאינו כפול. איכא דאמרי: לר' מאיר קאמר ליה, ואיכא דאמרי: לרבנן קאמר להו; איכא דאמרי לר' מאיר קאמר ליה, והכי קאמר ליה: אין לך תנאי בכתובים שאינו כפול, והוו להו שני כתובים הבאין כאחד, *וכל שני כתובים הבאין כאחד אין מלמדין. איכא דאמרי לרבנן קאמר להו, והכי קאמר להו: אין לך תנאי בכתובים שאינו כפול, וגמרינן מינייהו. ורמינהו: "הרי זה גיטך ע"מ שתשמשי את אבא שתי שנים", "על מנת שתניקי את בני שתי שנים", מת האב או מת הבן — אינו גט, דברי ר' מאיר; וחכמים אומרים: אע"פ שלא נתקיים התנאי — הרי זה גט, יכולה היא שתאמר לו: תן לי אביך ואשמשנו, תן לי בנך ואניקנו; קשיא דרבי מאיר אדרבי מאיר, קשיא דרבנן אדרבנן! דרבי מאיר אדרבי מאיר לא קשיא, התם בדלא כפליה לתנאיה, הכא בדכפליה לתנאיה; ורבנן אדרבנן לא קשיא, *מאן חכמים דהכא? רבן שמעון בן גמליאל היא, דאמר: כל עכבה שאינה הימנה — הרי זה גט. תנו רבנן: *[א]אמר לה בפני שנים — "הרי זה גיטך על מנת שתשמשי את אבא ב' שנים", וחזר ואמר לה בפני שנים "הרי זה גיטך על מנת שתתני לי מאתים זוז" — לא ביטל דברי האחרון את הראשון, רצתה — משמשתו, רצתה — נותנת לו מאתים זוז; אבל אמר לה בפני שנים "הרי זה גיטך ע"מ שתתני לי מאתים זוז", וחזר ואמר לה בפני שנים "הרי זה גיטך על מנת שתתני לי ג' מאות זוז" — ביטל דברי האחרון את הראשון. ואין אחד מן הראשונים ואחד מן האחרונים מצטרפין. אהייא? אילימא אסיפא — הרי בטל! [ב]אלא ארישא — פשיטא! מהו דתימא: כל לקיומא תנאי מצטרפין, קמ"ל.

§ **מתני'** "הרי זה גיטך אם לא באתי מכאן עד שלשים יום", והיה הולך מיהודה לגליל, הגיע לאנטיפרס וחזר — בטל תנאו. "הרי זה גיטך אם לא באתי מכאן עד שלשים יום", והיה הולך מגליל ליהודה, והגיע לכפר עותנאי וחזר — בטל תנאו. "הרי זה גיטך אם לא באתי מכאן עד שלשים יום", והיה הולך למדינת הים, והגיע לעכו וחזר — בטל תנאו. [ג]"הרי זה גיטך כל זמן שאעבור מכנגד פניך שלשים יום", היה הולך ובא הולך ובא, הואיל ולא נתיחד עמה — הרי זה גט.

§ **גמ'** למימרא דאנטיפרס בגליל הוה קיימא? ורמינהי: *אנטיפרס ביהודה, וכפר עותנאי בגליל, בינתים — מטילין אותו לחומרא, מגורשת ואינה

רש"י

בשלמא לרבא. דאוקי רישא דמתני' ב' שנים ממש, ואע"ג דסתם. **רישא.** דקאמר: מת הבן בתוך שתי שנים ה"ז גט. **בדלא פריש.** ב' שנים, והרי הניקתו כל צרכו. **סיפא דפריש.** על כרחיך דווקא קאמר, דהא לא איצטריך לפרושי, ופריש. **אלא לרב אשי.** דאמר: רישא דמתני' יום אחד קאמר – על כרחך מת הבן או האב דקתני – כגון שמת ולא הניקתו כלל, ואמאי ה"ז גט? הרי לא נתקיים כלום מן התנאי! **לפי שלא אמר לה.** אם תניקי – יהא גט, אם לא תניקי – לא יהא גט. דבעינן תנאי כפול כתנאי בני גד ובני ראובן. **ר"ש כו'.** מיפרשא בהדיא ואזלא. **איכא דאמרי** לר"מ קאמר ליה. אין לנו ללמוד מתנאי בני גד, שאין לך תנאי בכל המקרא שאינו כפול, כגון: "אז תנקה מאלתי" (בראשית כד), וכגון: "אם שכב אם לא שכב" (במדבר ה), "אם תאבו ושמעתם אם תמאנו ומריתם" (ישעיה א) – הלכך הוי להו שני כתובין הבאים כאחד, ואין מלמדין. **ואיכא דאמרי** לרבנן קאמר להו אין לך תנאי בכתובין שאינו כפול. ויש לנו ללמוד מהן, דכולהו צריכי, כדמתרצינן להו בקדושין ב"האומר לחבירו" (ד' סא.). **מאן חכמים.** בהך מתניתא בתרייתא – ר"ש [ב"ג] היא. **אמר לה בפני שנים ה"ז גיטך כו'.** ולא מסרו לה בפניהם, דאי מסרו לה – איגרשה לה בהאי תנאי, ותו לא מצי לאתנויי תנאה אחרינא. אלא כך אמר בפניהם: כשאמסרנו לה – לא אמסרנו אלא על מנת כן. וחזר ואמר לה בפני שנים כו'. ומסרו לה. **לא ביטל כו'.** שלא בא זה להוסיף, מדלא אמר לה: שתתני מאתים זוז תוספת על תנאי הראשון, ולעקור נמי לא בא – מדלא ביטל דברו הראשון בפני אלו, אלא הכי קאמר לה: או תנאי ראשון או מאתים זוז. **ג' מאות זוז.** ודאי עקר ליה לתנאיה קמא. **ואין אחד מן העדים הראשונים ואחד מן האחרונים מצטרפים.** להעיד שהיה תנאי בגט זה. כל זמן שלא יבואו שנים כאחד [ויעידו כאחד] מן התנאים – כשר ע"י עדי חתימה, ולא כל כמינייהו דהנך לשוויי תנאה בגיטא. **אילימא אסיפא.** פשיטא דאין אחד מן הראשונים כלום, שהרי אפילו באו שניהם אינן כלום, דהא בטיל ליה ההוא תנאה. **אלא ארישא.** דקאמר: או האי או האי. **מהו דתימא.** הואיל ומקיים גיטא בחד מהני תנאי – הוו להו כחד תנאה, וכל סהדי דמסהדי לקיומי תנאה דהאי גיטא – ליצטרפו, קא משמע לן. **מתני' והגיע לאנטיפרס וחזר. מיד. תנאו בטל.** כלומר, ושוב אינו כשר לגרש בו. ואפילו חזר והלך לגליל ונשתהה שלשים יום – אינו גט. דקא סלקא דעתך אנטיפרס בתחילת גליל היא, והרי מתנאי הראשון הלך לגליל ולא שהה שלשים יום, וביטל הגט – שהרי בא. אבל אם לא הגיע לאנטיפרס, וחזר, ולאחר ימים הלך לגליל ונשתהה שלשים יום – הרי זו מגורשת, שזמן השלשים לא נקבע אלא משילך לגליל, והרי לא הלך עד עתה, ונשתהה. **לכפר עותנאי.** קס"ד כפר עותנאי בריש יהודה, כבואו מגליל ליהודה, והרי הלך ליהודה ובא בתוך שלשים, ואין כאן עוד לא תנאי ולא גט להתקיים עוד. **לעכו.** קא סלקא דעתיה עכו במדינת הים קיימא. **כל זמן שאעבור מכנגד פניך.** כשאשתהה שלשים יום עובר מכנגד פניך – מיד יהא גט. **והיה הולך ובא כו'.** בגמרא פריך: והא לא עבר, שהיה הולך ובא בתוך שלשים! **גמ' אנטיפרס ביהודה וכפר עותנאי בגליל.** סמוכים זה לזה בספר, זה בראש יהודה וזה בראש גליל. הלכך, היה הולך מיהודה לגליל, והגיע לאנטיפרס וחזר – לא בטל תנאו, דאכתי לא אזיל לגליל. וכי אזיל ומשתהי – הוי גיטא, לכך הזכיר לה בתנאי: "שאני הולך מיהודה לגליל", דלא לימני תלתין יומין אלא מיום שיגיע לגליל. היה הולך מגליל ליהודה והגיע לכפר עותנאי וחזר – לא ביטל תנאו, דאכתי לא מטא ליהודה. **בינתים.** היה הולך מיהודה לגליל, ועבר את אנטיפרס, ולכפר עותנאי לא בא, וחזר בתוך שלשים, ולאחר זמן חזר והלך לגליל ממש ושהה. **מטילין אותו לחומרא.** ואמרינן מגורשת ליפסל לכהונה. ואינה

[תוספתא פ"ה] [קדושין כז. וש"נ] [עירובין פג. וש"נ] [תוספתא פ"ד] [תוספתא פ"ה]

תוספות

בשלמא לרבא רישא בדלא פריש וסיפא בדפריש. פי' בקונט': כיון דלא אצטריך לפרושי, ופירש – אמרי' דאתיא למימר דאפילו מת לא הוי גט. ואין נראה לר"י: דהא גבי אביו אצטריך לפרושי, וגבי בן אצטריך לפרושי, לר' יהודה דאמר י"ח חודש. ומה שפירש נמי: אלא לרב אשי מאי שנא רישא ומאי שנא סיפא, כיון דרישא כמפרש יום אחד דמי – על כרחין מת האב או הבן דקתני – כגון שמת ולא הניקתו כלל. ואמאי ה"ז גט? הא לא נתקיים כלום מן התנאי. ואין נראה, דלכ"ע מת הבן היינו שלא הניקתו כלל, כדפירש במתני'. ונראה לר"י לפרש: בשלמא לרבא כו' וסיפא בדפריש, דהואיל ופירש שתי שנים – ודאי לצעורה קא מכוין, ואפילו מת אינו גט. אלא לרב אשי, כיון דרישא נמי הוי במפרש יום א' – הרי נמי נתכוין לצעורה, כיון דפירש, ואפילו מת – לא ליהוי גט, כמו בסיפא. **והוו** להו שני כתובין הבאין כאחד. הקשה ה"ר אלחנן: בפרק "האומר" (קדושין דף סא:) דפריך מקראי טובא לר' חנינא בן גמליאל דלא בעי תנאי כפול – לימא דהויא ב' כתובין הבאים כאחד! וי"ל: דהתם כ"איכא דאמרי" דהכא, דלרבנן קאמר להו. אי נמי: אי הוה פריך ליה התם מכולהו בהדי הדדי – הוי משני להו דהוו שני כתובין הבאין כאחד. ועוד: דשפיר מצריך להו רבי חנינא בן גמליאל התם. **וגמרינן** מינייהו. פי' בקונטרס: ולא הוו שני כתובים הבאין כאחד, דכולהו מצריך להו ר' חנינא בן גמליאל בקדושין (ג"ז שם). ואין נראה להרב רבי אלחנן, דהתם לא מצריך להו, אלא דמשני להו, דאין משום אחד מהן ללמוד דניבעי תנאי כפול. אבל לרבי מאיר, דיליף מינייהו – לא עביד שם צריכותא. ויש לומר: דיש בהן שום צריכותא.

תוספות רי"ד

בשלמא לרבא רישא בדלא פריש סיפא בדפריש אלא לרב אשי מ"ש רישא ומ"ש סיפא. פי' בשלמא לרבא דאוקי רישא דמתני' שתי שנים ממש ואף על גב דסתם. רישא דקאמר מת הבן בתוך שתי שנים ה"ז [גט] בדלא פריש שתי שנים והרי הניקתו כל צרכו. סיפא בדפריש על כרחיך דוקא קאמר דהא לא איצטריך לפרושי ופירש. אלא לרב אשי דאמר רישא דמתני' יום א' קאמר על כרחיך מת הבן או מת האב דקתני כגון שמת ולא הניקתו כלל ואמאי הרי זה גט הרי לא נתקיים כלום מן התנאי: קשיא. וכיון דאיתוקם רב אשי בקושיא ש"מ כרבא הלכתא דאמר סתמא כל זמן היניקה א) משמע שתי שנים לולד: ת"ר הרי זה גיטך ע"מ שתשמשי את אבא שתי שנים וע"מ שתניקי את בני שתי שנים אע"פ שלא נתקיים התנאי הרי זה גט לפי שלא אמר לה אם תשמשי ואם לא תשמשי אם תניקי ואם לא תניקי דברי ר' מאיר וחכמים אומרים נתקיים התנאי הרי זה גט ואם לאו אינו גט וקי"ל יחיד ורבים הלכה כרבים. וכתב ר"י ז"ל והלכתא כרבנן. ואע"ג דקי"ל דבעי' תנאי כפול הני מילי באם תשמשי ואם לא תשמשי כענין שנאמר אם יעברו ואם לא יעברו וכדאתקין שמואל בגיטא דש"מ אבל בע"מ לא דקי"ל כל האומר ע"מ כאומר מעכשיו דמי. ואינו נ"ל לחלק (ס"א דיש חילוק) בין ע"מ ובין אם דאדרבה כיון דע"מ כאומר מעכשיו דמי. כ"ש דלא מהני ביה תנאה לאורועי האי גיטא דהשתא באם לא מהני בע"מ לא כ"ש אבל נ"ל דמדאתקין שמואל לא מצינו למפסק כר' מאיר דכיון דלא איפסיקא בהדיא הלכה כר' מאיר לא מצינו למסמך אתקנתא דשמואל דנ"ל שמואל לחומרא הוא דאתקין הכי בגיטא דש"מ שלא תפסל עליו מעכשיו אליבא דרבי מאיר אם הוא כהן אבל לעולם להתירה לעולם בגט זה אע"ג דלא איקיים תנאיה משום דלא כפליה לתנאיה לא מצינו בהדיא שפסק כר' מאיר דאילו כן אמאי לא פסק בהדיא הלכה כר' מאיר ב) לא בגיטין ולא בקדושין דפליג נמי התם ר"מ עם רבנן והלכך יש להחמיר בדבר כרבנן שהם רבים שלא תנשא לעלמא עד שתקיים תנאו והכי נמי אמרינן לקמן בפרק המגרש אתקין רב בגיטין וכו' מן יומא דין לאפוקי מדר' יוסי דאמר זמנו של שטר מוכיח עליו והא איהו הוא דאמר בפרק יש נוחלין הלכה כרבי יוסי. אלא ודאי חומרא בעלמא הוא דאתקין בגיטא לאפוקי נפשיה מפלוגתא וה"ה הכי אית למימר הכא דחומרא בעלמא הוא דאתקין שמואל שלא תפסל עליו מעכשיו אליבא דר' מאיר ולעולם הלכה כרבנן וכי היכי דפליגי רבנן עליה דר' מאיר בתנאי כפול הכי נמי פליגי עליה בהין קודם ללאו דהא לא בעי רבנן הין ולאו כלל והכי נמי פליגי עליה בתנאי קודם למעשה דהכי אמרי' בשלהי השוכר את הפועלים מאן שמעת ליה דאית ליה האי סברא דבעי' תנאי קודם למעשה ר' מאיר דתניא אבא חלפתא אומר משום ר' מאיר וכו' ובשלהי פירקין מוכח בפירוש דרבנן פליגי עליה ולא בעי תנאי קודם למעשה: ת"ר אמר לה בפני שנים הרי זה גיטך ע"מ שתשמשי את אבא שתי שנים וע"מ שתניקי את בני שתי שנים וחזר ואמר בפני שנים הרי זה גיטך ע"מ שתתני לי מאתים זוז לא בטלו דבריו הראשונים את האחרונים רצתה משמשתו רצתה נותנת לו ר' זוז. פי' אמר בפני שנים וכו' ולא מסרו לה בפניהם שאם מסרו לה איגרשא לה בהאי תנאה ותו לא מצי לאתנויי תנאה אחרינא אלא כך אמר בפניהם כשאמסרנו לך לא אמסרנו אלא ע"מ כן וחזר ואמר לה בפני שנים וכו' ומסרו לה לא בטלו וכו' שלא בא זה להוסיף מדלא אמר לה שתתני לי מאתים זוז תוספת על תנאי הראשון ולעקור נמי לא בא מדלא בטל תנאו הראשון בפני אלו אלא הכי קא"ל או תנאי ראשון או מאתים זוז אבל אם אמר לה בפני שנים הרי זה גיטך על מנת שתתני לי מאתים זוז וחזר ואמר לה בפני שנים אחרים ג' מאות זוז בטלו דבריו האחרונים את הראשונים ואין אחד מן הראשונים וא' מן האחרונים מצטרפים. אהייא אילימא אסיפא הרי ביטל אלא ארישא פשיטא שמה שמעיד זה אינו מעיד זה ולאו כל כמינייהו לשווי תנאה בגיטא עד דמספרי חדא מילתא מהו דתימא כל קומי תנאה מצטרפי קמ"ל. פי' מהו דתימא הואיל ושניהם מעידים שהיה תנאי בגט זה יהיו נאמנים שלא תנשא עד שלא תקיימנו קמ"ל כיון שאין עדותן מכוונת אינן נאמנים לשווי תנאה בגיטא והואיל והגט יוצא מתחת ידי האשה נאמנת לומר בעלי נתנו לי בלי תנאי ותנשא בו: **מתני'** הרי זה גיטך אם לא באתי מכאן ועד שלשים יום והיה הולך מיהודה לגליל והגיע לאנטיפרס וחזר בטל התנאי. הרי זה גיטך אם לא באתי מכאן ועד שלשים יום והיה הולך מגליל ליהודה והגיע לכפר עותנאי וחזר בטל התנאי. הרי זה גיטך אם לא באתי מכאן ועד שלשים יום והיה הולך למדינת הים והגיע לעכו וחזר בטל התנאי. הרי זה גיטך כל שאעבור מכנגד פניך שלשים יום היה הולך ובא הולך ובא הואיל ולא נתיחד עמה הרי זה גט. אוקימנא בגמרא דאנטיפרס היא בסוף ארץ יהודה ששתי העיירות הללו הן עומדין בין גבול יהודה וגליל. ועותנאי היא ראש גליל ואנטיפרס ראש יהודה והדרך שיש בין אנטיפרס

א) נראה דל"ל דזה קאמר דהיינו שתי שנים. ב) נראה דל"ל דלא מצינו שפסק כר"מ לא בגיטין ולא בקדושין וכו'.

ואינה מגורשת! אמר אביי, תרי תנאי קאמר לה: אי מטינא לגליל — לאלתר ליהוי גיטא, ואי משתהינא באורחא תלתין יומין ולא אתינא — ליהוי גיטא; הגיע לאנטיפרס וחזר, דלא לגליל מטא ולא אישתהויי נמי אשתהי תלתין יומין — בטל תנאו.§ "הרי זה גיטך אם לא באתי מכאן ועד שלשים יום" כו'.§ למימרא, דעכו במדינת הים קיימא? והא אמר רב ספרא: כי הוו מיפטרי רבנן מהדדי — *בעכו הוו מפטרי, משום דאסור לצאת *מארץ לחוצה לארץ! אמר אביי, תרי תנאי קאמר לה: אי מטינא למדינת הים — לאלתר ליהוי גיטא, אי משתהינא באורחא תלתין יומין ולא אתינא — ליהוי גיטא; הגיע לעכו וחזר, דלא למדינת הים מטא ולא אישתהויי נמי אשתהי תלתין יומין — בטל תנאו.§ "ה"ז גיטך כל זמן שאעבור" וכו'.§ והא לא עבר! אמר רב הונא: מאי "פניך"? תשמיש, ואמאי קרי ליה פניך? *לישנא מעליא נקט. ורבי יוחנן אמר: לעולם פניך ממש, מי קתני "הרי זו מגורשת"? "ה"ז גט" קתני, דלא הוי גט ישן, אולכי מלו תלתין יומי הוי גיטא. תניא כוותיה דרבי יוחנן: *"ה"ז גיטך כל זמן שאעבור מנגד פניך שלשים יום", והיה הולך ובא, הואיל ולא נתייחד עמה — ה"ז גט, *ולגט ישן אין חוששין שהרי לא נתייחד עמה. וליחוש שמא פייס! אמר רבה בר רב הונא, הכי אמר אבא מרי משמי' דרב: *בבאומר: נאמנת עלי לומר שלא באתי. איכא דמתני לה אמתניתין: "מעכשיו אם לא באתי מכאן ועד י"ב חדש", ומת בתוך י"ב חדש — ה"ז גט; וליחוש שמא פייס! אמר רבה בר רב הונא, הכי אמר אבא מרי משמיה דרב: באומר: נאמנת עלי לומר שלא באתי. מאן דמתני לה אמתני', כל שכן אברייתא; מאן דמתני לה אברייתא, אבל אמתני' — גהא לא אתא.§

מתני' *ד"ה"ז גיטך אם לא באתי מכאן ועד י"ב חדש", ומת בתוך י"ב חדש — אינו גט; *ה"ה"ז גיטך מעכשיו אם לא באתי מכאן ועד י"ב חדש", ומת בתוך י"ב חדש — הרי זה גט. ו"אם לא באתי מכאן ועד י"ב חדש כתבו ותנו גט לאשתי", כתבו גט בתוך י"ב חדש ונתנו לאחר י"ב חדש — אינו גט; *"כתבו ותנו גט לאשתי אם לא באתי מכאן עד י"ב חדש", כתבו בתוך י"ב חדש ונתנו לאחר י"ב חדש — אינו גט, רבי יוסי אומר: כזה גט. זכתבו לאחר י"ב חדש ונתנו לאחר י"ב חדש, ומת, אם הגט קודם למיתה — ה"ז גט, ואם מיתה קדמה לגט — אינו גט, ואם אין ידוע — זו היא שאמרו: מגורשת ואינה מגורשת.§ **גמ'** *תנא: רבותינו התירוה לינשא. מאן רבותינו? אמר רב יהודה אמר שמואל: בי דינא דשרו מישחא, סברי לה כרבי יוסי, *דאמר: זמנו של שטר מוכיח עליו. א"ר אבא בריה דרבי חייא בר אבא א"ר יוחנן: *ר' יהודה נשיאה בנו של ר"ג בר רבי הורה, ולא הודו לו כל *סיעתו, ואמרי לה: כל *שעתו. א"ל ר' אלעזר לההוא סבא: כי שריתוה — לאלתר שריתוה, או לאחר שנים עשר חדש שריתוה? לאלתר שריתוה — דהא לא אתי, או דלמא לאחר י"ב חדש שריתוה — דהא איקיים ליה תנאו? *ותיבעי ליה מתניתין: "מעכשיו אם לא באתי מכאן ועד י"ב חדש", ומת בתוך י"ב חדש — הרי זה גט; לאלתר הוי — דהא לא אתי, או דלמא לאחר י"ב חדש — דהא איקיים ליה תנאיה! חאין הכי נמי, ומשום דהוה בההוא מעשה. *אמר אביי: הכל מודים, היכא דאמר לכשתצא חמה מנרתיקה — לכי

תניא כוותיה דרבי יוחנן. מייתי ראיה מדקאמר: ולגט ישן אין חוששין – משמע דאם נתיחד עמה לא הוי אלא גט ישן. אבל לרב הונא אם נתיחד עמה בטל הגט לגמרי. **וניחוש** שמא פיים. מפורש לעיל (דף יח: ד"ה שמא). **ולא** הודו לו כל סיעתו כו'. אין להוכיח מכאן דאין הלכה כרבי יוסי אע"ג דרב פסק כוותיה, משום דרבי יוחנן קאמר הכא: לא הודו לו כל סיעתו, ורב ור' יוחנן הלכה כרבי יוחנן. דהא ר' יוחנן גופיה יכול לסבור כרבי יוסי, או שמא דוקא הכא דבעל פה לא סבר כרבי יוסי. **דהא** אקיים ליה תנאיה. וא"ת: לאלתר מה יש לחוש? דהא ודאי יתקיים התנאי, דכיון דמת לא ישוב עוד לביתו! וי"ל: דאיכא למיגזר אטו לא מת, כי אין העולם יודעין שמת, ויתמהו על שמתירין לינשא. אבל לאחר שנים עשר חדש הכל יודעין שנתקיים התנאי. **הכל** מודים לכשתצא לכי נפקא קאמר. ולרבי יוסי גט ואינו גט, כדאמר לעיל ב"אחר מיתה". לאחר

ואינה מגורשת. ליפשא בגט זה. ספק בטל במהלך הראשון, הואיל ועבר אנטיפרס הוה ליה ספק יהודה ספק גליל ובטל שהרי חזר בתוך שלשים, או שמא ספק יהודה הוא ולא בטל תנאו ונתקיים במהלך השני והוי גט. **אמר אביי.** מתני' נמי אית לה דאנטיפרס ביהודה, וכגון דאמר לה תרי תנאי. **אי מטינא** לגליל לאלתר ליהוי גיטא. ואפי' לא משתהינא. **ואי משתהינא באורחא** תלתין יומין ולא **אתינא** ליהוי גיטא. ואפי' לא מטינא לגליל. הלכך הגיע לאנטיפרס וחזר לאלתר – תנאו בטל, ואין כאן עוד לקיימו, שהרי לא לגליל בא ולא נשתהה. ואפי' קיימו לאחר זמן – הרי לא התנה אלא על מהלך הראשון, וכשהזכיר גליל לא הזכיר למנות השלשים משם והלאה אלא שיהא מיד גט כשיגיע שם, והרי לא הגיע וגם לא נשתהה. והכי משמע מתני': הרי זה גיטך אם לא באתי מכאן ועד שלשים יום מיום שאלא מכאן, והיה הולך מיהודה לגליל, ותלה הגט גם בביאתו לגליל. **למימרא** דעכו במדינת הים קיימא. אמאי דהוה סלקא דעתין מעיקרא קאי, ולאו אמירולא דאביי. **כי הוו מיפטרי** רבנן מהדדי. בני מדינת הים שהיו הולכין ללמוד תורה בארץ ישראל, כשחוזרים לבתיהם היו חבריהם בני ארץ ישראל מלוים אותן עד עכו, ומשם נפטרים מהם. **שאסור.** לבני ארץ ישראל לצאת לחוצה לארץ. **והא לא עבר.** שלשים יום רצופין. **תשמיש.** והרי שלשים יום רצופים בלא תשמיש, כדקתני: הואיל ולא נתיחד עמה. **לישנא מעליא.** פנים של מטה. **הרי זה גט קתני.** דאין הגט נפסל משום גט ישן, הואיל ולא נתיחד עמה, ולכי מקיים תנאיה – ליהוי גיטא. **גט ישן.** כל שנתיחד עמה בין כתיבה לנתינה. ופסלוהו רבנן משום שמא יאמרו גיטה קודם לבנה, לקמן ב"הזורק" (דף עט.). **שמא פיים.** כשהיה בא אצלה פיים קטטה שביניהם, ונתיחד עמה. ולאחר זמן אתי בעל מערער, ואמר: פייסתי. **באומר.** בשעת התנאי: על מנת כן אני מוסר לה, שתהא נאמנת עלי כמאה עדים כל זמן שתאמר שלא באתי ונתיחדתי ופייסתי. **כל שכן אברייתא.** דכיון דהיכא דלא בא חיישי' שמא פיים, אי לאו דאתני ברישא "נאמנת עלי" – כ"ש אברייתא שהיה הולך ובא. **אבל אמתני'.** דמת בתוך י"ב חדש, ולא ראינו שבא בעיר משילה – לא חיישינן שמא פיים, ואפי' לא הימנה עליה מעיקרא – הוי גט, דהא לא אתא. **מתני'** אינו גט. דכיון דלא אמר "מעכשיו" – משמע: לאחר י"ב חדש יהא גט, והרי מת בתוך הזמן, וזקוקה ליבם. **גמ'** התירוה לינשא. דאף על גב דלא אמר "מעכשיו" כמאן דאמר "מעכשיו" דמיא, דמסתמא מעכשיו קאמר לה. **בי דינא** דשרי מישחא. שמנן של גוים. והיינו ר' יהודה נשיאה שהיה בימי האמוראים, בן בנו של רבינו הקדוש, כדאמרינן במסכת ע"ז (דף לז.): מסתמיך ואזיל ר' יהודה נשיאה אכתפיה דר' שמלאי כו'. **כרבי יוסי.** בב"ב (דף קלו.): הכותב נכסיו לבנו לאחר מותו – צריך שיכתוב: "מהיום ולאחר מיתה", רבי יוסי אומר: אינו צריך, שזמנו של שטר מוכיח עליו. דלהכי איכתיב זמן בשטרא – לידע שמהיום נתן לו גוף הקרקע, שלא יירשו אחיו עמו, והפירות לאחר מותו. **בנו של ר"ג בר רבי.** בנו של רבינו הקדוש. **הורה.** שתהא מותרת. **ולא** הודו לו כל שעתו. כל ימי חייו. **לאלתר שריתוה.** כששמעו בו שמת, ואפילו קודם י"ב חדש. **הא לא אתי.** שהרי ודאי לא יבא עוד, ויש כאן קיום תנאי. **ותבעי ליה.** נמי אמתני', היכא דאמר "מעכשיו" ודברי הכל, אמאי בעי לה אפלוגתא? **אין ה"נ.** דאיכא למבעי אמתני'. ולהכי בעייה מההוא סבא ואליבא דרבותינו – משום דהוה בההוא מעשה דשריותא, ויש לו להשיבו מפי השמועה ששמע וידע היאך התירו. אבל אי הוה בעי מסתמא או מגברא אחרינא – הוי בעי לה אמתני'. **הכל מודים.** באומר לאשתו בלילה: "זה גיטך כשתצא חמה מנרתיקה". לכי

סו א ב ג מיי' פ"ט מהל' גירושין הל' ט ויא סמג עשין נ טוש"ע אה"ע סי' קמד סעיף ז:
סז ד (מיי' שם הל' יא) טוש"ע שם סעיף ב:
סח ה מיי' שם טוש"ע שם סעיף ג:
סט ו ז מיי' שם הלכה כב טוש"ע שם סעיף ה:
ע ח מיי' שם הל' יא טוש"ע שם סעיף ג:

תוספות רי"ד

אנטיפרס לעותנאי היא מסופקת ספק שהיא נחשבת מארץ יהודה ספק אם היא נחשבת מארץ הגליל ותרי תנאי קאמר לה כשהיה הולך מיהודה לגליל התנה עמה אי מטינא לגליל לאלתר ליהוי גיטא אי משתהינא הכא ביהודה תלתין יומין ולא אתינא (לאלתר) נמי ליהוי גיטא ואע"ג דלא מטינא לגליל וזה האיש הלך כל ארץ יהודה והגיע לאנטיפרס שהיא עומדת בסוף יהודה סמוך לגליל וחזר לביתו קודם ל' בטל הגט דהא לא לגליל אזיל ולא אשתהויי אישתהי תלתין יומין ביהודה ובטל תנאו שעשה בנתינה זו כשנתן גט לאשתו על תנאי זה ואע"פ שאח"כ הולך בגליל או שוהה ביהודה ל' יום אינו גט שכבר בטלה נתינה הראשונה אבל אם נוטלו ממנה וחוזר ונותנו לה פעם שניה יכול לגרש בו להתנות מה שרוצה דקי"ל גט שבטלו חוזר ומגרש בו. ואם היה הולך מגליל ליהודה והתנה עמה אלו שני התנאים דאי מטינא ליהודה לאלתר ליהוי גיטא ואי משתהינא הכא בגליל תלתין יומין ולא אתינא (לאלתר) ליהוי גיטא ואע"ג דלא מטינא ליהודה והיה מהלך כל ארץ הגליל והגיע לכפר עותנאי שעומדת בראש הגליל וחזר לביתו קודם ל' יום בטל התנאי דהא לא ליהודה אזל ולא אשתהויי אשתהי תלתין יומין בגליל ואם יצא חוץ מכפר עותנאי והגיע לדרך שבין עותנאי לאנטיפרס שהיא מסופקת מאיזו נחשבת היא מגורשת ואינה מגורשת ואם מת חולצת ולא מתיבמת וכן אם היה הולך מא"י למדינת הים והתנה לה אלו שני התנאים והגיע לעכו שהיא בקצה א"י עומדת ולא שהה שם ל' יום וחזר בטל התנאי דלאו למדינת הים אזל ולא אשתהויי אשתהי. ה"ז גיטך כל זמן וכו' והא לא עבר. פי' דהא הולך ובא קתני וכיון שלא עבר מכנגד עיניה ל' יום רצופים למה יהיה הגט גט: אמר רב הונא מאי פניך תשמיש ואמאי קרי ליה פניך (לימא מילתא) [לישנא מעליא] נקיט והלכך אע"פ שהיה הולך ובא הואיל ולא נתיחד עמה הוי גט: ור' יוחנן אמר לעולם פניך ממש והאי דקתני הרי זו' מגורשת ה"ז גט דלא הוי גט ישן ולכי מלו תלתין יומין הוי גיטא. פי' לעולם פניך קאמר ממש שכל זמן שלא נעלם מעיניה ל' יום אינו גט ומאי דקשה לך והא לא עבר והיכי תני הרי זה גט לא קתני הרי זה גט כשר דלכי מלו תלתין יומין ונעלם ממנה ל' יום מגורשת היא ולא אמרי' כיון שהיה הולך ובא ניחוש לגט ישן אלא כיון שלא נתיחד עמה אין לחוש לגט ישן. תניא כותיה דר' יוחנן הרי זה גיטך כל זמן שאעבור מכנגד פניך ל' יום והיה הולך ובא הואיל ולא נתיחד עמה הרי זה גט ולאחר לא תנשא עד ל' יום ולגט ישן אין חוששין שהרי לא נתיחד עמה פי' הרי זה גט כשר שאם ישלים ל' יום ולא יבא היא מגורשת ונשאת לאחר ולא חיישינן לגט ישן שהרי לא נתיחד עמה. ופי' המורה גט ישן כל שנתיחד עמה בין כתיבה לנתינה ופסלוהו רבנן שמא יאמרו גיטה קודם לבנה לקמן בפרק הזורק וקשה לי בהאי פירושא חדא בגט ישן דלקמן אמרי' אם נתגרשה בו תנשא לכתחלה דאין בו שום איסור שבעולם וגרושה גמורה היא ולא אמרי' אלא שלא תתגרש בו לכתחלה (אלא) מפני לעז הולד וא"כ אמאי מקשי' וניחוש שמא פיים ואפילו אם פיים ובא עליה כיון שמותרת להנשא בו לכתחלה מאי איכפת לן ותו בגט ישן דהתם היחוד הוא קודם הנתינה והלכך הוא כשר שהגט בא ועוקר כל הקדושין שהיו לפניו אבל הכא היחוד הוא לאחר נתינת הגט וי"ל קדשה בביאה וצריכה גט אחר הלכך נ"ל לפרש בגט ישן דהכא חמור מגט ישן דהתם דהתם אמרי' אם נתגרשה בו תנשא לכתחלה אבל הכא אם נתיחד עמה לאחר שנתנו לה הגט בטל שאם אמר לה הרי זה גיטך מעכשיו כל זמן שאעבור מכנגד פניך ל' יום שאינו יכול לבטלו בנתיים אלא כל זמן שיעבור הגט קונה למפרע אבל היחוד שנתיחד עמה מבטל הגט דחיישינן שמא בא עליה וקדשה בביאה והגט לא עקר אלא קדושים הראשונים וצריכה גט אחר לביאה זו ואם לא אמר לה מעכשיו אלא כל זמן שאעבור שאין הגט מתקיים אלא לכשיעבור ולא למפרע ועד אז היא אשת איש גמורה שאין לומר קדשה בההוא יחוד מ"מ י"ל שבטל הגט באותה ביאה שעשה שהרי כיון שלא אמר מעכשיו יכול הוא לבטלו כל זמן שרוצה וכיון שבא עליה בתורת אישות ולא בתורת בעילת זנות אין לך בטול גדול מזה ואפילו עבר מכנגד פניה ל' יום לאחר מיכן אינה מגורשת בנתינה הראשונה שעשה כיון שיש יחוד אחריה וצריך ליטול הגט מידה ולחזור וליתנו לה ולהתנות עמה פעם אחרת שאע"פ שבטלו אם רוצה לחזור ולגרש בו יכול לגרש בו. וניחוש שמא פיים. פי' אמאי תני ולגט ישן אין חוששין ניחוש שמא כשהיה בא אצלה פיים קטטה שביניהם ונתיחד עמה ולאחר זמן אתי בעל ומערער ואומר פייסתי. אמר רבה בר רב הונא הכי אמר אבא מרי משמיה דרב באומר נאמנת עלי לומר שלא באתי. פי' בשעת התנאי אמר ע"מ כן אני מוסר לה שתהא נאמנת עלי כמאה עדים כל זמן שתאמר שלא באתי ונתיחדתי עמה: ואיכא דמתני להא אמתני' מעכשיו אם לא באתי מכאן ועד י"ב חדש ומת בתוך י"ב חדש הרי זה גט וניחוש שמא פיים אמר רבה בר רב הונא הכי אמר אבא מרי משמיה דרב באומר נאמנת עלי לומר שלא באתי. מאן דמתני לה אמתני' כ"ש אברייתא ומאן דמתני לה

אִלְכִי נָפְקָא קָאָמַר לָהּ, וְכִי מָיְית בְּלֵילְיָא הָוֵי גֵּט לְאַחַר מִיתָה; בּ"עַל מְנָת שֶׁתֵּצֵא חַמָּה מִנַּרְתִּיקָהּ" – מֵעַכְשָׁיו קָאָמַר לָהּ, *דְּאָמַר רַב הוּנָא אָמַר *רַב: [נ"ל רב] כָּל הָאוֹמֵר "עַל מְנָת" כְּאוֹמֵר "מֵעַכְשָׁיו" דָּמֵי; גלֹא נֶחְלְקוּ אֶלָּא בְּ"אִם תֵּצֵא", מָר סָבַר לָהּ כְּרַבִּי יוֹסֵי, דְּאָמַר: *זְמַנּוֹ שֶׁל שְׁטָר מוֹכִיחַ עָלָיו, וַהֲוָה לֵיהּ כְּ"מֵהַיּוֹם אִם מַתִּי", כְּ"מֵעַכְשָׁיו אִם מַתִּי", מָר לָא סָבַר כְּרַבִּי יוֹסֵי, וַהֲוָה לֵיהּ כְּ"אִם מַתִּי" גְּרֵידָא.§ "כִּתְבוּ וּתְנוּ גֵּט לְאִשְׁתִּי אִם לֹא בָּאתִי מִכָּאן וְעַד י"ב חֹדֶשׁ", כִּתְבוּ כו'.§ אֲמַר לֵיהּ רַב יֵימָר לְרַב אַשִׁי: לֵימָא, קָסָבַר ר' יוֹסֵי: כָּתַב גֵּט עַל תְּנַאי – כָּשֵׁר? לָא, לְעוֹלָם אֵימָא לָךְ: פָּסוּל, וְשָׁאנֵי הָכָא, מִדַּהֲוָה לֵיהּ לְמֵימַר "אִם לֹא בָּאתִי כִּתְבוּ וּתְנוּ", וְאָמַר "כִּתְבוּ וּתְנוּ אִם לֹא בָּאתִי", הָכִי קָאָמַר: כִּתְבוּ מֵעַכְשָׁיו וּתְנוּ אִם לֹא בָּאתִי. וְרַבָּנַן? לָא שְׁנָא הָכִי וְלָא שְׁנָא הָכִי. ת"ר: ד"לְאַחַר שָׁבוּעַ" – שָׁנָה, "לְאַחַר שָׁנָה" – חֹדֶשׁ, "לְאַחַר חֹדֶשׁ" – שַׁבָּת. "לְאַחַר שַׁבָּת", מַאי? *יָתֵיב ר' זֵירָא קַמֵּיהּ דְּרַבִּי אַסִי, וְאָמְרִי לָהּ רַבִּי אַסִי קַמֵּיהּ דְּרַבִּי יוֹחָנָן וְקָאָמַר: החַד בְּשַׁבָּא, וּתְרֵי, וּתְלָתָא – בָּתַר שַׁבְּתָא, אַרְבְּעָה, וְחַמְשָׁא וּמַעֲלֵי שַׁבְּתָא – קַמֵּי שַׁבְּתָא. תַּנְיָא, רַבִּי אוֹמֵר: "לְאַחַר הָרֶגֶל" – שְׁלֹשִׁים יוֹם. נְפַק ר' חִיָּיא *דְּרָשָׁהּ מִשְּׁמֵיהּ דְּרַבִּי וְקִלְּסוּהָ. מִשְּׁמֵיהּ דְּרַבִּים – וְלָא קִלְּסוּהָ; (א) אַלְמָא לֵית הִילְכְתָא כְּוָותֵיהּ.§

הדרן עלך מי שאחזו

הַזּוֹרֵק יגֵּט לְאִשְׁתּוֹ, וְהִיא בְּתוֹךְ בֵּיתָהּ אוֹ בְּתוֹךְ חֲצֵרָהּ – הֲרֵי זוֹ מְגוֹרֶשֶׁת; יזְרָקוֹ לָהּ בְּתוֹךְ בֵּיתוֹ אוֹ בְּתוֹךְ חֲצֵרוֹ, אֲפִילּוּ הוּא עִמָּהּ בַּמִּטָּה – אֵינָהּ מְגוֹרֶשֶׁת; *לְתוֹךְ חֵיקָהּ אוֹ לְתוֹךְ קַלְתָּהּ – הֲרֵי זוֹ מְגוֹרֶשֶׁת.§ **גמ'** מְנָא הָנֵי מִילֵּי? *דְּתָנוּ רַבָּנַן: °"וְנָתַן בְּיָדָהּ" – אֵין לִי אֶלָּא יָדָהּ; גַּגָּהּ, חֲצֵרָהּ וְקַרְפֵּיפָהּ מִנַּיִן? ת"ל: "וְנָתַן", מִכָּל מָקוֹם. *וְתַנְיָא נַמִי הָכִי גַּבֵּי גַּנָּב: "יָדוֹ" – אֵין לִי אֶלָּא יָדוֹ; גַּגּוֹ, חֲצֵרוֹ וְקַרְפֵּיפוֹ מִנַּיִן? ת"ל: °"הִמָּצֵא תִמָּצֵא", מִכָּל מָקוֹם. וּצְרִיכָא; דְּאִי אַשְׁמוּעִי' גֵּט, מִשּׁוּם דִּבְעַל כָּרְחָהּ מְגָרְשָׁהּ, אֲבָל גַּנָּב דְּלֵיתֵיהּ בְּעַל כּוֹרְחֵיהּ – אֵימָא לָא; וְאִי אַשְׁמוּעִינַן גַּנָּב, מִשּׁוּם דִּקְנָסֵיהּ רַחֲמָנָא, אֲבָל גֵּט – אֵימָא לָא, צְרִיכָא. "חֲצֵרָהּ". *מַה שֶּׁקָּנְתָה אִשָּׁה חקָנָה בַּעְלָהּ! א"ר אֶלְעָזָר: בְּכוֹתֵב לָהּ "דִּין וּדְבָרִים אֵין לִי בִּנְכָסַיִךְ". וְכִי כָּתַב לָהּ הָכִי מַאי הָוֵי? וְהָתַנְיָא: *הָאוֹמֵר לַחֲבֵירוֹ "דִּין וּדְבָרִים אֵין לִי עַל שָׂדֶה זוֹ", וְ"אֵין לִי עֵסֶק בָּהּ", וְ"יָדַי מְסוּלֶּקֶת הֵימֶנָּה" – לֹא אָמַר כְּלוּם! אָמְרִי דְּבֵי ר' יַנַּאי: טבְּכוֹתֵב לָהּ וְעוֹדָהּ אֲרוּסָה; וְכִדְרַב כָּהֲנָא, דְּאָמַר רַב כָּהֲנָא: נַחֲלָה הַבָּאָה לוֹ לָאָדָם מִמָּקוֹם אַחֵר, אָדָם מַתְנֶה עָלֶיהָ שֶׁלֹּא יִרָשֶׁנָּה; וְכִדְרָבָא, *דְּאָמַר רָבָא, הָאוֹמֵר: אִי

[דברים כד] [שמות כב] [תורה אור]

רש"י

לְכִי נָפְקָא קָאָמַר לָהּ. וְאִי מָיֵית בַּלַּיְלָה לָא הָוֵי גִּיטָּא, וְגַבֵּי מַתְנִי' נַמִי, "הֲרֵי זֶה גִּיטֵּךְ לִכְשֶׁלֹּא אָבֹא לְאַחַר שְׁנֵים עָשָׂר חֹדֶשׁ" – לָאו גֵּט הוּא, וְלֵיכָּא לְמִיסְמַךְ אַזְּמַנּוֹ שֶׁל שְׁטָר מוֹכִיחַ עָלָיו, דְּהָא בְּהֶדְיָא אָמַר: לִכְשֶׁלֹּא אָבֹא – יְהֵא גֵּט, אֲבָל לֹא מֵעַכְשָׁיו. בְּאִם תֵּצֵא. וְדִכְוָותֵהּ "אִם לֹא בָּאתִי". וְאָמְרִי' לְעֵיל בְּפִירְקִין (דף עג.) גַּבֵּי "אִם מַתִּי", "אִם" – שְׁתֵּי לְשׁוֹנוֹת מַשְׁמַע, מַשְׁמַע מֵעַכְשָׁיו וּמַשְׁמַע לִכְשֶׁיַּגִּיעַ, אָמַר "מֵהַיּוֹם" – הָוֵי מֵעַכְשָׁיו, לֹא אָמַר "מֵהַיּוֹם" – הָוֵי לִכְשֶׁיַּגִּיעַ. הִלְכָּךְ רַבּוֹתֵינוּ סָבְרִי לָהּ כְּרַבִּי יוֹסֵי כו'. כְּאִם מַתִּי גְּרֵידָא. וַאֲמָרַן לְעֵיל ד"לְאַחַר מִיתָה" הוּא, לִכְשֶׁאָמוּת. וְהָכָא נַמִי מַשְׁמַע: לִכְשֶׁלֹּא אָבֹא לְאַחַר שְׁנֵים עָשָׂר חוֹדֶשׁ. כָּתַב גֵּט עַל תְּנַאי כָּשֵׁר. וַאֲפִילּוּ לֹא נִתְקַיֵּים הַתְּנַאי. דְּהָא הָכָא הוּא נָוֶה לִכְתּוֹב לְאַחַר י"ב חֹדֶשׁ. וְהֵם קָדְמוּ וּכְתָבוּהוּ, וּמַכְשַׁר רַבִּי יוֹסֵי, וְנֵימָא נַמִי דְּאַרֵישָׁא פָּלֵיג. מִדַּהֲוָה לֵיהּ לְמֵימַר כו'. אֲבָל בְּרֵישָׁא מוֹדֶה. וְרַבָּנַן. דִּפְלִיגִי עֲלֵיהּ, סָבְרִי: ל"ש אָמַר "כִּתְבוּ אִם לֹא בָּאתִי", ל"ש "אִם לֹא בָּאתִי כִּתְבוּ" – לֹא נָוֶה לִכְתּוֹבוֹ אֶלָּא לְאַחַר י"ב חֹדֶשׁ. לְאַחַר שָׁבוּעַ שָׁנָה. "זֶה גִּיטֵּךְ אִם לֹא אָבֹא לְאַחַר שָׁבוּעַ זוֹ", "שְׁמִטָּה זוֹ" – מַמְתִּינִים לוֹ שָׁנָה שְׁמִינִית, דְּכָל שָׁנָה שְׁמִינִית קְרוּיָה אַחַר שָׁבוּעַ. חַד בְּשַׁבָּא תְּרֵי בְּשַׁבָּא וּתְלָת בְּשַׁבָּא. קָרֵי בָּתַר שַׁבָּת שֶׁעָבְרָה. אֲבָל רְבִיעִי חֲמִישִׁי וְשִׁשִּׁי נִקְרָאִין עַל שֵׁם שַׁבָּת הַבָּאָה. קַמֵּי שַׁבְּתָא. הַאי שַׁבָּת דְּקָאָמַר – יוֹם שַׁבָּת מַמָּשׁ קָאָמַר. לְאַחַר הָרֶגֶל. "אִם לֹא אָבֹא לְאַחַר הָרֶגֶל" – צָרִיךְ לְהַמְתִּין ל' יוֹם. וְקִלְּסוּהָ. יָפֶה אָמַרְתָּ, דְּוַדַּאי יְחִידָאָה אֲמָרָהּ. וְלָא קִלְּסוּהָ. לֹא הוֹדוּ לוֹ שֶׁנֶּאֶמְרָה מִפִּי רַבִּים, מִשּׁוּם דְּלֵית הִלְכְתָא כְּוָותֵיהּ.

הדרן עלך מי שאחזו

הַזּוֹרֵק גֵּט וְהִיא בְּתוֹךְ בֵּיתָהּ. שֶׁל נִכְסֵי מְלוֹג, וּזְרָקוֹ לָהּ ע"ג קַרְקַע. הֲרֵי זוֹ מְגוֹרֶשֶׁת. דְּקָנְתָה לָהּ חֲצֵרָהּ כְּאִילּוּ נְתָנוֹ בְּיָדָהּ, כִּדְמְפָרֵשׁ בַּגְּמָ'. לְתוֹךְ חֵיקָהּ אוֹ לְתוֹךְ קַלְתָּהּ הֲרֵי זוֹ מְגוֹרֶשֶׁת. וַאֲפִילּוּ הִיא בְּתוֹךְ בֵּיתוֹ, וְטַעְמָא מְפָרֵשׁ בַּגְּמָ'. קַלְתָּהּ. סַל שֶׁהַנָּשִׁים נוֹתְנוֹת לְתוֹכוֹ מַחֲטִין וְצִנּוֹרִיּוֹת. **גמ'** ת"ל וְנָתַן מ"מ. וְדָרְשִׁי' לֵיהּ בְּכַנְפֵי נַפְשֵׁיהּ, מִדְּלָא כְּתִיב "וּבְיָדָהּ יִתְּנֶנּוּ" – מַשְׁמַע לָן נְתִינָה כָּל דְּהוּא, וְיָדָהּ דִּכְתַב רַחֲמָנָא – דְּבָעֵינַן דּוּמְיָא דְּיָדָהּ דְּמִשְׁתַּמֶּרֶת לְדַעְתָּהּ, כִּדְמְפָרֵשׁ לְקַמֵּיהּ. מִשּׁוּם דִּבְעַל כָּרְחָהּ. כְּלוֹמַר, דְּכִי יָהֵיב לֵיהּ נַמִי בְּיָדָהּ – עַל כָּרְחָהּ הִיא, וַאֲפִילּוּ הָכִי אָמַר רַחֲמָנָא דְּתִתְגָּרֵשׁ. הִלְכָּךְ חֲצֵרָהּ נַמִי קָנֵי לָהּ. אֲבָל גַּנָּב. דְּלָא מִיחַיַּיב אִי שַׁדְיֵיהּ אִינִישׁ עַל כָּרְחֵיהּ. אֵימָא. מִדַּעְתֵּיהּ נַמִי לָא תִּיקְנֵי לֵיהּ חֲצֵרוֹ, אִם לֹא מָשַׁךְ, כְּגוֹן נִכְנְסָה לַחֲצֵרוֹ וְנָעַל בְּפָנֶיהָ. קָנָה בַּעְלָהּ. לַפֵּירוֹת, לְהִשְׁתַּמֵּשׁ בָּהּ, וְהִלְכָּךְ לָא נָפֵיק גֵּט מִידֵיהּ דְּבַעַל. דְּכָתַב לָהּ כו'. הַשְׁתָּא מַשְׁמַע דְּכָתַב לָהּ כֵּן לְאַחַר שֶׁכְּנָסָהּ. עַל שָׂדֶה זוֹ. שֶׁהָיְתָה לוֹ עִמּוֹ שׁוּתָּפוּת בָּהּ. וְאֵין לִי עֵסֶק בָּהּ. אַחַת מִכָּל לְשׁוֹנוֹת הַלָּלוּ. לֹא אָמַר כְּלוּם. דְּמֵאַחַר שֶׁהִיא שֶׁלּוֹ – צָרִיךְ לִכְתּוֹב לְשׁוֹן מַתָּנָה. בְּכוֹתֵב לָהּ. דִּין וּדְבָרִים כו' בְּעוֹדָהּ אֲרוּסָה, קוֹדֶם שֶׁזָּכָה בַּנְּכָסִים. וְא"צ לִכְתּוֹב לְשׁוֹן מַתָּנָה – דְּיָכוֹל לְהַתְנוֹת, כִּדְרַב כָּהֲנָא. מִמָּקוֹם אַחֵר. שֶׁאֵינָהּ יְרוּשַּׁת אֲבוֹתָיו מִן הַתּוֹרָה. מַתְנֶה עָלֶיהָ. קוֹדֶם שֶׁזָּכָה. אִי

[לעיל עג. עה: [ע"ש] ע"ז לז. קדושין ח. ס: [ע"ש]] [לעיל עב. וש"נ] [פסחים קו.] [לעיל כ.] [ב"ב פה: [ב"מ ט:]] [ב"ק סה: ב"מ י: נו:] [נזיר כד: סנהדרין עח.] [כריתות כד: ב"ב מג. מט. כתובות פג. לה.] [ג"ז שם וב"ק ח:]

תוספות

לאחר שבוע שנה. נראה דאפילו עומד בסוף שבוע הוי שנה, כיון שהזכיר לשון שבוע.

הדרן עלך מי שאחזו

הזורק · ת"ל ונתן. וא"ת: ונימא: "ונתן" – כלל, "בידה" – פרט, ואין בכלל אלא מה שבפרט! וי"ל: "ושלחה" חזר וכלל, ודיינינן כעין הפרט. וכן י"ל בסמוך גבי "המצא תמצא" דהוי כלל ופרט וכלל, דשדי "ידו" בין "המצא תמצא". וא"ת: א"כ היכי פריך בריש "מרובה" (ב"ק סד:) גבי שדי חמור בין המצא תמצא: והא מיבעי ליה לכדתניא אין לי אלא ידו כו'? ומאי פריך? כיון דהכא נמי שדינן "ידו" בין "המצא תמצא", הכי נמי נישדי חמור! וי"ל: כיון דשדינן "ידו", דאיירי ברשות, ודמי ל"המצא תמצא" – תו לא נישדי חמור, דהוי דבר הנגנב.

בכותב לה דין ודברים כו'. וא"ת: והא אכתי אית ליה לבעל פירי, כדאמרינן ב"הכותב" (כתובות פג.) שהבעל אוכל פירות בחייה! וי"ל: דכתב לה "דין ודברים אין לי בנכסייך ובפירותיהן", דאז לית ליה, כדאמרי' התם. ולר"ת דמפרש בסמוך דלא תלי באכילת פירות – אתי שפיר, כמו שאפרש בסמוך.

והתניא האומר לחבירו כו'. הוה מצי לשנויי בשכותב לה בלשון טוב המועיל, או שנתן לה הבעל במתנה, דאמרינן ב"חזקת הבתים" (ב"ב דף נא:) דקנתה, ואין הבעל אוכל פירות. אלא משום דבפרק "הכותב" (כתובות פג.) אצטריך לשנויי הכי, משני נמי הכא. וכדרב כהנא דאמר רב כהנא נחלה כו'. ואע"ג דלא מייתי ראיה כיון דעדיין לא זכה בנכסים שיכול לסלק עצמו אפילו בלשון גרוע, דהא בהנהו דמייתי לא איירי בלשון "דין ודברים", ועוד: ד"אי אפשי" דמייתי הוי לשון טוב טפי מ"דין ודברים", כדמשמע בכריתות (דף כד:). אלא מייתי דלא תיקשי: היכי יכול להתנות שלא יירשנה הואיל שלא בא לעולם עדיין, כמו שאינו יכול להתנות על נחלת אביו? ואפילו לר"מ דאמר ב"על מנת שאין לך עלי שאר כסות ועונה" – תנאו בטל, משום דמתנה על מה שכתוב בתורה – הא בדרבנן תנאו קיים – שאני התם שהוא עושה תנאי גמור, אבל הכא אין עושה כל כך תנאי. ועוד, דאמרינן ב"איזהו נשך" (ב"מ דף סו.) דבעינן שיעשה התנאי אותו שצריך לתנאי, והכא עושהו הבעל שאינו צריך לתנאי. ומביא שפיר מדרב כהנא דאדם מתנה עליה שלא יירשנה. וכי תימא: מאי שנא מנחלת אביו שאינו יכול להתנות? לא דמי, שהרי הכא תקנת חכמים היא, וכדרבא, דאמר: האומר "אי אפשי בתקנת חכמים כגון זו" – שומעין לו. דכלום עשו אלא להנאתו – אי אפשי לו באותה הנאה. ואע"ג דלרב אית ליה ב"הכותב" (כתובות פג.) דאפילו בדאורייתא יכול להתנות – התלמוד דהכא לא סבר הכי, ועוד: דמסקנא דהתם לא קאי הכי.

דין ודברים אין לי על שדה זו לא אמר כלום. כל הני לישני לא מהני כלום, משום דמדין ודברים ומעסק ידיו ורגליו סליק נפשיה, ולא מגופה דשדה, כדאמרינן בפ"ב דכריתות (דף כד:). והא דמהני גבי עבד "אין לי עסק בך" – לא כמו שמפרש ר"ת דזכו ביה שמיא, דא"כ היכי מייתי ראיה לקמן בפ"ב (דף פה.) דבאשה מהני "הרי את לעצמך" מק"ו מעבד? אלא היינו טעמא: ד"אין לי עסק בך" – משמע: אלא תהא לעצמך, וזה לא שייך בשדה.

עין משפט נר מצוה

עא א ב ג מיי' פ"ט מהל' גירושין הלכה טו סמג עשין נ טוש"ע אה"ע סי' קמג סעיף ז:

עב ד ה מיי' שם הלכה כג טוש"ע שם סעיף ו:

א ו מיי' פ"ה שם הלכה א סמג שם טוש"ע אה"ע סי' קלט סעיף א:

ב ז מיי' שם הלכה ח טוש"ע שם סעיף ו:

ג ח מיי' פכ"ה מהל' אישות הל' ו סמג עשין מח טוש"ע אה"ע סימן פה סעיף ז:

ד ט מיי' פכ"ג מהל' אישות הל' א ה סמג שם טוש"ע אה"ע סי' צב סעיף א וסעיף ג וסעיף ז וסי' סט סעיף ז:

תוספות רי"ד

לה אברייתא אבל למתני' אם לא באתי קתני והרי לא בא פי' בברייתא דתני היה הולך ובא יש לחוש שמא פיים אבל מתני' דלא תני ובא לא חיישינן שמא בא: **מתני'** הרי זה גיטך אם לא באתי מכאן ועד שנים עשר חודש ומת בתוך שנים עשר חודש אינו גט. מעכשיו אם לא באתי מכאן ועד י"ב חדש ומת בתוך י"ב חדש הרי זה גט. תנא רבותינו התירוה לינשא פי' אע"ג דלא אמר לה מעכשיו. מאן רבותינו אמר רב יהודה אמר שמואל בי דינא דשרו משחא פי' הוא ר' יהודה נשיאה בן בנו של רבינו הקדוש דתנן בפ' אין מעמידין רבי יהודה הנשיא ובית דינו התירו השמן. וסבר לה כר' יוסי דאמר זמנו של שטר מוכיח עליו פי' דתנן בבבא בתרא הכותב נכסיו לבנו לאחר מותו צריך שיכתוב מהיום ולאחר מיתה רבי יוסי אומר אינו צריך: אמר ר' אבא בריה דר' חייא בר אבא א"ר יוחנן ר' יהודה הנשיא בנו של ר"ג בר רבי התירה לינשא ולא הודו לו כל שעתו ואמרי לה כל סייעתו למימרא דלית הלכתא כותיה. א"ל רבי אלעזר להוא סבא כי שריתוה לאלתר שריתוה או לאחר י"ב חדש שריתוה לאלת' שריתוה דהא לא אתי או דלמא לאחר י"ב חדש שריתוה דאיקיים לה תנאיה א"ל ותבעי לך מתני' מעכשיו אם לא באתי מכאן ועד י"ב חדש ומת בתוך י"ב חדש הרי זה גט לאלתר הוי גט דהא לא אתי או דלמא לאחר י"ב חדש דאיקיים תנאה. א"ל אין הכי נמי דמתני' קא מיבעיא לי ודקא שאילנא לך בה משום דהוית בההוא מנינא ולא איפשטא ולחומרא עבדי' עד שישלימו י"ב חדש: אמר אביי הכל מודים היכא דאמר לה לכשתצא חמה מנרתקה לכי נפק קא"ל וכי מיית בליליא הוי גט לאחר מיתה פי' ודכוותא גבי מתני' נמי אם אמר לה על מנת שתצא חמה מנרתקה מעכשיו קא"ל דאמר רב הונא כל האומר ע"מ כאומר מעכשיו דמי. לא נחלקו אלא באם תצא חמה מנרתקה מר סבר לה כר' יוסי דאמר זמנו של שטר מוכיח עליו והוה ליה כמהיום אם מתי כמעכשיו אם מתי ומר לא סבר לה כר' יוסי והוה ליה כאם מתי גרידה: **מתני'** אם לא באתי מכאן ועד י"ב חדש כתבו גט ותנו לאשתי כתבו בתוך י"ב חדש ונתנו לאחר י"ב חדש אינו גט פי' שהוא לא הרשה אותם לכתוב אלא אם לא יבא לאחר י"ב חדש ולא בתוך י"ב חדש כתבו גט ותנו לאשתי אם לא באתי [מכאן] ועד י"ב חדש כתבו בתוך י"ב חדש ונתנו לאחר י"ב חדש אינו גם ר' יוסי אומר כזה גט פי' ת"ק סבר אע"פ שאמר תחילה כתבו ותנו גט לאשתי ה"ק כתבו ותנו אם לא באתי וכו' אבל קודם לכן לא הרשה אותם ואלה שכתבו בתוך י"ב חדש שלא ברשות עשו ואינו גט ור' יוסי סבר כזה גט דמדהוה ליה למימר אם לא באתי כתבו ותנו ואמר כתבו ותנו אם לא באתי ה"ק כתבו מעכשיו ותנו אם לא באתי ורבנן סברי לא שנא הכי ול"ש הכי וקי"ל כרבנן ובעל כרחין דוקא קתני מדפליג ר' יוסי בסיפא ולא פליג ברישא וקשה לי ואמאי הוי תנאה כלל והא הוי מעשה קודם לתנאי שאמר כתבו ותנו שהוא מעשה קודם ואח"כ אמר אם לא באתי שהוא תנאי אלא ודאי מכאן מוכיח דלא בעי תנאי קודם למעשה אלא ר' מאיר מדיליף מבני גד ובני ראובן אבל רבנן כי היכי דלא בעו תנאי כפול הכי נמי לא בעו תנאי קודם למעשה אלא אפילו מעשה קודם לתנאי נמי תנאו קיים. וסתמא זו דלא כר' מאיר וא"כ הלכה כרבנן ואע"ג דתנן סתמא כר' מאיר בשלהי פרק השוכר את הפועלים. כתבו לאחר י"ב חדש ונתנו לאחר י"ב חדש ומת אם גט קודם למיתה הרי זה גט ואם מיתה קדמה לגט אינו גט אין ידוע זהו שאמרו מגורשת ואינה מגורשת: ת"ר לאחר שבוע שנה לאחר שנה חדש לאחר חדש שבת. פי' זה גיטך אם לא אבא לאחר שבוע של שמיטה זו ממתינים לו שנה שמינית דכל שנה שמינית קרויה אחר שבוע. אבל אם אמר לה לאחר שבע שנים כיון שהזכיר המנין מיד משמע וכיון שהשלימו ז' שנים מיד הוי גט וכן אם אמר לה לאחר י"ב חדש וכן לאחר ז' ימים אבל כשאמר לאחר שבוע אנו דנין דבריו כאילו אמר מוצאי השבוע וכל שנה שמינית קרי מוצאי שביעית וכן לאחר השנה כל החדש יקרא לאחר שנה וכל לאחר חדש כל שבוע הבא יקרא לאחר חדש וכן לאחר השבת יקרא עד חצי השבוע אבל כשהזכיר המנין בין בשנים בין בחדשים בין בימים מיד הוא גט לאחר שבת מאי יתיב ר' זירא קמיה דרבי אסי ואמרי לה ר' אסי קמיה דר' יוחנן ויתיב וקאמר חד בשבא תרי ותלתא בתר שבתא ארבעה חמשה ומעלי שבתא קמי שבתא תניא רבי אומר לאחר הרגל ל' יום נפק ר' חייא דרשה משמי' דרבי' ולא קלסוה אלמא דלית הלכתא כותיה:

פ"ח הזורק גט לאשתו והיא בתוך ביתה או בתוך חצירה הרי זו מגורשת זרקו לה בתוך ביתו או בתוך חצרו אפילו עמו במטה אינה מגורשת לתוך חיקה או לתוך קלתה הרי זו מגורשת. פי' הזורק גט לאשתו והיא בתוך ביתה או בתוך חצרה של נכסי מלוג וזרקו לה ע"ג קרקע הרי זו מגורשת אבל בתוך ביתו או בתוך חצרו אפילו הוא עמה במטה וזרקו שם אינה מגורשת ואם זרקו לה בתוך חיקה או בתוך קלתה שהוא סל שהנשים נותנות בתוכו מחטים וצנורות אפילו בתוך ביתו הרי זו מגורשת מנא ה"מ דת"ר ידה אין לי אלא ידה גגה חצרה וקרפיפה מניין ת"ל ונתן בידה מ"מ. פי' תרי ונתן בידה כתיב. ומקשה חצרה מה שקנתה אשה

הגהות הב"ח

(א) גמ' אלמא לית. נ"ב עי' לעיל פ"ב בדף כ ע"א:

עין משפט
נר מצוה

ה א מיי' פי"ט מהלכות מלוה ולוה הלכה ו:
ו ב מיי' פי"ב מהלכות אישות הלכה ד סמג עשין מח טוש"ע אה"ע סימן סט סעיף ד וסימן פ סעיף טו בהג"ה וסי' פא סעיף א בהג"ה:
ז ג מיי' פ"ה מהלכות גירושין הלכה א סמג עשין נ טוש"ע אה"ע סי' קלט סעיף א:

[וע"ע תוס' עירובין עח. ד"ה ומקני ותוס' ב"ב קנו: ד"ה קונין ותוס' ביצה יז. ד"ה מאי טעמא]

ח ד מיי' פ"ה מהלכות עבדים הלכה ג סמג עשין פז טוש"ע י"ד סי' רסז סעיף מח:
ט ה מיי' פ"א מהלכות מכירה הלכה ח סמג עשין פב טוש"ע ח"מ סי' קלב סעיף א:
י ו מיי' פכ"ג מהל' אישות הלכה א סמג עשין מח טוש"ע אה"ע סימן נב סעיף א וסעיף ג וסעיף ז וסימן סט סעיף ז:
יא ז מיי' פ"ה מהלכות גירושין הל' ב סמג עשין נ טוש"ע אה"ע סימן קלט סעיף א ב:
יב ח מיי' פי"ז מהל' אבידה הלכה י:
יג ט מיי' פ"ה מהלכות גירושין הלכה ב ו סמג עשין נ טוש"ע אה"ע סי' קלט סעיף א:
יד י כ ל מ מיי' שם הלכה ט טוש"ע שם סעיף יא:

אי אפשי בתקנת חכמים כגון זו — שומעין לו. מאי "כגון זו"? כדרב הונא אמר רב, *דאמר רב הונא אמר רב: ביכולה אשה שתאמר לבעלה "איני ניזונית ואיני עושה". רבא אמר: אטו ידה מי לא קניא ליה לבעל? אלא גיטה וידה באין כאחד, גהכא נמי גיטה וחצרה באין כאחד. אמר ליה רבינא לרב אשי: רבא, יד דאשה קא קשיא ליה? נהי דקני ליה למעשה ידיה, ידה גופה מי קני ליה? אמר לי': רבא, יד העבד קא קשיא לי', למ"ד *דבשטר על ידי עצמו, יד עבד כיד רבו דמיא! אלא גטו וידו באין כאחד, ה"נ גיטה וחצירה באין כאחד. ההוא שכיב מרע דכתב לה גיטא לדביתהו בהדי פניא דמעלי שבתא ולא הספיק למיתביה לה. למחר תקף ליה עלמא, אתו לקמיה דרבא, אמר להו: זילו אמרו ליה ליקנייה ניהלה להההוא דוכתא דיתיב ביה גיטא, ותיזל איהי ותיחוד ותפתח ותחזיק ביה, *דתנן: הנעל, גדר, פרץ כל שהוא — הרי זו חזקה. אמר ליה רב עיליש לרבא: מה שקנתה אשה קנה בעלה! ◦איכסיף. לסוף איגלי מילתא דארוסה הואי, *אמר רבא: ואם אמרו בנשואה יאמרו בארוסה? הדר אמר רבא: לא שנא ארוסה ולא שנא נשואה, גיטה וחצירה באין כאחד. והא אמרה רבא מעיקרא! כי אמרה רבא — אהאי מעשה אמרה.§ "והיא בתוך ביתה".§ *אמר עולא: ◦זוהוא, שעומדת בצד ביתה *ובצד חצרה. ר' אושעיא אמר: אפילו היא בטבריא וחצרה בציפורי, היא בציפורי וחצרה בטבריא — מגורשת. והא "היא בתוך ביתה ובתוך חצרה" קתני! ה"ק: והיא כמי שבתוך ביתה והיא כמי שבתוך חצרה, דכיון דחצר משתמרת לדעתה היא — מתגרשת. לימא בהא קמיפלגי, דמר סבר: *חצר משום ידה אתרבאי, ומר סבר: חצר משום שליחות אתרבאי? לא, דכולי עלמא — החצר משום ידה איתרבאי, מר סבר: כידה, מה ידה בסמוכה, אף חצרה בסמוכה; ואידך: אי מה ידה בדבוקה, אף חצרה בדבוקה! אלא כידה, מה ידה משתמרת לדעתה, טאף חצרה המשתמרת לדעתה, לאפוקי חצרה המשתמרת שלא לדעתה. ההוא גברא דזרק לה גיטא לדביתהו, הוה קיימא בחצר, *אזל גיטא נפל בפיסלא; אמר רב יוסף: יחזינן, אי הויא ארבע אמות על ארבע אמות — פלג ליה רשותא לנפשיה, ואי לא — חדא רשותא היא. במאי עסקינן? אילימא בחצר דידה, כי הוי ד' אמות מאי הוי? אלא בחצר דידיה, כי לא הוי ארבע אמות מאי הוי? כלא צריכא, *דאושלה מקום, דחד מקום מושלי אינשי, תרי מקומות לא מושלי אינשי. לולא אמרן אלא דלא גבוה עשרה, אבל גבוה עשרה — אע"ג דלא הוי ארבע אמות. מולא אמרן אלא דלית ליה
שם

[לפנינו ליתא] [לעיל כד. ולקמן פח.] [ולקמן עט.]

תוספות

ידה גופיה מי קניא ליה. וא"ת: חצרה נמי לא קניא ליה גופיה אלא פירי! ◦וי"ל: כיון דקנוי לו לפירא — הוי כאילו קנוי לו גוף החצר. אבל מעשה ידיה — מעלמא קאתו. ועוד: דחצר קנוי לו בעל כרחה של אשה, אבל ידיה — אינס קנויים לו על כרחה, דיכולה היא לומר "איני ניזונית ואיני עושה".

ותיזיל איהי ותיחוד ותפתח. פירש רש"י: לפי שהגט אסור לטלטל למוסרו לה. אף על גב דבתוספתא* בפרק "משילין" תניא: אין מגרשין בשבת — בשכיב מרע הקילו, דלא תפול קמי יבם. להכי בפ' "משילין" (ביצה דף לז.) קתני: אין מקדשין, ולא קתני אין מגרשין כמו בתוספתא, משום דשכיב מרע שרי לגרש. *ולא הוי כמו "טלי גיטיך מעל גבי קרקע"* דכיון שהגט בא מרשות הבעל לרשותה — הוי כאילו נתנו לה. מה שקנתה אשה קנה בעלה. וא"ת: והא אמרינן ב"חזקת הבתים" (ב"ב דף נא:): במתנה קנתה ואין הבעל אוכל פירות! ואור"י, דהכא איירי בשאלה, דלא אלימא כמו מתנה, ובמתנה דוקא אמרי' קנתה ואין הבעל אוכל פירות. ור"ת מפרש: דאע"ג דבמתנה אין הבעל אוכל פירות, כיון דאם מכרה ונתנה אינו קיים, כדאמרי' ב"חזקת הבתים" (שם) — חשיב כאילו הוי דבעל, ואינה יכולה לקנות על ידו מה שבתוכו. ואין תלוי באכילת פירות. ותדע, דהא שני לעיל: בכותב לה "דין ודברים אין לי בנכסייך" ואע"ג דאכתי הבעל אוכל פירות, כדאמרי' ב"הכותב" (כתובות דף פג.), אלא הואיל ואם מכרה ונתנה קיים, כדתנן ב"הכותב" — חשיב ליה חצרה. ואור"י: דאין ראיה, דאיכא לאוקומי בכותב לה "דין ודברים אין לי בנכסייך ובפירותיהן" כדפי' לעיל. וכן צריך לומר ב"חזקת הבתים" (ב"ב מט.) גבי אין לאיש חזקה בנכסי אשתו — כגון שכתב לה "ובפירותיהם", ואע"ג דלא קאמר ליה גמרא הכי, הכא נמי לעיל. ועוד: דבירושלמי משמע בהדיא דבפירות תליא מילתא, דפריך התם: גגה וחצרה אינן משועבדים לאיש לאכילת פירות? ומשני רבי יוחנן בשם רבי ינאי: עד שיכתוב לה "דין ודברים אין לי בנכסייך ובפירותיהן".

והוא שעומדת בצד ביתה. בפ"ק דבבא מציעא (דף יא:) אמרי': דוקא בגט, דחוב הוא לה — בעינן שתהא עומדת בצד ביתה, ולא במציאה.

פליג רשותא לנפשיה. וקשה לר"י: דבפ' "המוציא יין" (שבת דף פ.) וב"חזקת הבתים" (ב"ב נו.) גבי המוציא מרשות לרשות, אמר רבה: והוא שיש חיוב חטאת ביניהם, אבל כרמלית — לא, אביי אמר: אפילו כרמלית, אבל פיסלא — לא, רבא אמר: אפי' פיסלא. ואזדא רבא לטעמיה, דאמר רבא: רשות שבת כרשו' גיטין. פירוש: ובגיטין חשיב פיסלא רשות בפני עצמו, כדאמרינן הכא. והשתא דהא פיסלא הוי ממש כרמלית, דלא גבוה עשרה, ובגבוה שלשה איירי, דאי לאו הכי הוי כלבוד, וגם מסתמא הוי רחב ארבעה — דאם לא כן לא היה דבר חשוב בפני עצמו, אם כן אמאי קאמר אביי: אבל פיסלא לא? ויש לומר: דיש לחלק בין כרמלית גמור לכרמלית המיטלטל.
אמקום

רש"י

אי אפשי בתקנת חכמים כגון זו. אמילתא אחריתי אמרה רבא. שומעין לו. הואיל והתקנה לצורכו נעשית — יכול לומר: כלום עשו אלא להנאתי, אני אי אפשי בהנאה זו. מאי כגון זו. אהייא אמרה רבא. איני ניזונית. משל בעלי. ואיני עושה. לו מלאכה. דכי תקון רבנן מזוני — להנאתה תקון, זמנין דלא ספקה במעשה ידיה, ואחר כך תקנו מעשה ידיה לבעלה משום איבה, הלכך יכולה לומר "אי אפשי". רבא אמר. לעולם בדלא כתב לה "דין ודברים", ודקשיא לך: מה שקנתה אשה קנה בעלה. אטו ידה מי לא קניא ליה לבעל כו'. ולקמיה פריך: מאי היא? גיטה וידה באין כאחד. על ידי הגט באה ידה לה, עם נתינתו. אמר ליה רבינא לרב אשי רבא. דקשיא ליה לעיל: אטו ידה מי לא קניא ליה לבעל. יד אשה קשיא ליה. בתמיה. נהי דקניא ליה למעשה ידיה. אבל גופא מי קני ליה? וכיון דגופא לא קני ליה — מכי יהב גיטא לידה נפק לה גט מרשותיה, ולא משום דגיטה וידה באין כאחד. הלכך גבי חצר דקניא ליה — היכי מיגרשא? יד דעבד קשיא ליה. שגופו קנוי, ומקבל שחרורו בעצמו. למאן דאמר. ב"האשה נקנית" (קדושין דף כג.) שהעבד קונה עצמו בשטר שיחרור. על ידי עצמו. כלומר, בקבלת עצמו. תקף ליה עלמא. והיה ירא פן ימות, ותזקק ליבם, ואסור לטלטל גט בשבת ולמוסרו לה. ליקנייה. הבעל לדוכתא דמונח ביה גיטא לאשה, בחזקה, דקרקע נקנה בחזקה. ותיחוד ותפתח. תסגור דלת החדר שיקנה לה לשום חזקה. דתנן נעל. דלת, או גדר פרצה, או פרץ גדר כל שהוא. הרי זו חזקה. לקנות, שאין המוכר יכול לחזור בו. דהשתא קא יהיב לה חצר וגיטה בתוכו, ותנן: נכסים שאין להם אחריות נקנין עם נכסים שיש להן אחריות, בכסף בשטר ובחזקה. אם אמרו בנשואה. שהבעל יזכה בנכסים, יאמרו בארוסה? והך מילתא דרבא אתמר מקמי ההיא דאמר רבא לעיל: גיטה וחצרה באין כאחד, דבתר הכי הדר ביה רבא, ואמר: לא שנא ארוסה ולא שנא נשואה כו' כדמפרש ואזיל. והא אמרה רבא. לעיל, ואמאי איכסיף כי פרכה רב עיליש להא מילתא? ומשנינן: מעיקרא נמי כי אמרה רבא. להאי תירוצא דלעיל — אהאי מעשה אמרה, בתר דהדר סברה, ואמר דגיטה וידה באין כאחד. הכי גרסינן: מעיקרא כי אמרה רבא אהאי מעשה אמרה. כמי שבתוך ביתה. כאילו היא בתוך ביתה, ומאי היא — דבעי' דתיהוי חצרה משתמרת לדעתה, כלומר על פיה ועל צוויה. לאפוקי הא דאמרי' בפרקין לקמן (דף עח.): נתן גט ביד עבדה ניעור — אינו גט, דהויא לה חצר המשתמרת שלא לדעתה, שהוא משמר עצמו מדעתו. משום ידה אתרבאי. הלכך סמוכה לה בעינן, דומיא דידה. נפל בפיסלא. על גבי חתיכת עץ. פליג רשותא לנפשיה. ואינו בטל לגבי חצר, ואינה מגורשת. ולקמיה פריך: היכי דמי. אי נימא בחצר דידה. דאשה. כי הוי ארבע אמות מאי הוי. הרי שניהם שלה! דאושלה מקום. בחצרו לקנות בו גט. דאושלה. השאילה.
שם

תוספות רי"ד

אשה קנה בעלה פי' שכל נכסי האשה קנויין לו לבעל הפירות וכיון שפירות החצר הוא של בעל מה כח יש לאשה באותו חצר שיקנה לה הגט: אמר רב' אטו ידה מי לא קנייה ליה לבעל אלא גיטא וידה באין כאחד הכי נמי גיטא וחצרה באין כאחד א"ל רבינא לרב אשי רב' יד האשה קא קשה ליה נהי דקני ליה למעשה ידיה גופא מי קנייא ליה פי' דוקא מעשה ידיה הן שלו אבל גוף היד אינה שלו שיעשה הבעל בה כל תשמיש שהוא רוצה כ"א מעשה ידיה שהן קצובים כדתנן בכתובות ומה היא עושה לו משקל ה' סלעים וכו' אבל אינו יכול להכריחה לעשות לו יותר מן השיעור או אם רוצה שתעשה לו שמוש קשה בידה כגון לחפור בשדהו וכיוצא בו אינו רשאי שאין כל שמוש היד קנוי לו לפיכך הוי גט אבל חצרה כל השמוש שלה הוא של בעל כל זמן שהיא תחתיו ואין האשה רשאית להשתמש בה כלל בלא רשותו והילכך לא יהא גט א"ל רבא יד דעבד קא קשה ליה למ"ד בשטר ע"י עצמו יד עבד כיד רבו דמיא אלא גיטו וידו באין כא' הכא נמי גיטה וחצרה באין כאחד: (ההוא גברא דזרק גיטא לדביתהו הוה קיימא בחצר אינגדר ואזל גיטא נפל בפסלא פי' בפסל שלו א"ר יוסף חזינן אי הוי ד' אמות על ד' אמות לא) אלא בחצר דידיה כי לא הוי ד' אמות מאי הוה לא צריכא דאושלא מקום דחד מקום מושלי אינשי שני מקומות לא מושלי אינשי ולא אמרן דלא גבוה י' אבל גבוה י' אע"ג דלא הוי ד' אמות): ההוא ש"מ דכתב גיטא לדביתהו אפניא דמעלי שבתא ולא אספיק למיתביה ניהלה למחר תקף ליה עלמא. פי' והיה ירא פן ימות ותזקק ליבם ואסור לטלטל הגט בשבת ולמוסרו לה: אתי לקמיה דרבא אמר להו ליקנייה לה להאי דוכתא דיתיב בה גיטא ותיתי ותיחוד ותפתח באפיה כי היכי דתתחזיק ביה דתנן נעל גדר פרץ כל שהוא הרי זו חזקה פי' אמר רבא שיקנה הבעל לאשה אותו המקום שהגט מונח שם ע"י חזקה שבקנין אסור להקנות בשבת אלא יאמר לה מקום פלוני יהא שלך במתנה והחזיק בו ותקנה אותו והיא תחזיק *תקנה אותו המקום וכיון שהגט מונח שם הוה ליה כמקנה לה הגט והחצר ביחד ורבא לטעמיה דאמרי' לעיל בהמביא אמר רבא כתב לה גט ונתנו בחצרו וכתב לה שטר מתנה עליה קנאתו ומתגרשת בו דגיטו וחצירו באין לה כאחד. והוא בתוך ביתה אמר עולא והיא שעומדת בתוך ביתה או בתוך חצרה ור' הושעיא אמר אפילו היא בטבריה וחצרה בציפורי היא בציפורי וחצרה בטבריה והא היא בתוך חצרה קתני ה"ק והיא כמו שבתוך חצרה דהוא לה חצר המשתמרת לדעתה והלכתא כעולא דהכי אמר רב אשי בפ' שנים אוחזין האי חצר איתרבי משום יד ולא גריעא משליחות גבי גט דחוב הוא לה אין חבין לאדם אלא בפניו גבי מתנה דזכות הוא לה זכין לאדם שלא בפניו ב):

א) חסר כאן איזה תיבות. ב) כאן צ"ל ד"ה ההוא גברא דזרק גיטא כו' עד אע"ג דלא הוי ד' אמות.
ברוך

מסורת הש"ס

כתובות נח: ע: פג. קז: ב"ק ח: ע"ש [ב"ב מט:]
[קדושין כג:]
ב"ב מב.
לעיל כט:
ב"מ יא.
נ"ל או בצד
[לעיל כא. ב"מ י:]
[גירסת הערוך בערך גנדר אינגדר גיטא וכן העתיק רש"י בשבת פ. ד"ה כרשות גיטין וכו' אינגדר גיטא]

גליון הש"ס

גמ' איכסיף לסוף איגלאי. עי' לעיל דף כט ע"ב ב"מ דף נז ע"א ע"ז דף כב ע"א: שם והוא שעומדת בצד ביתה. עי' עירובין דף לב ע"ב תד"ה אשה: תוד"ה דה כו' וי"ל כיון דקנוי לו לפירי. עיין כתובות דף מז ע"ב תוד"ה זמנין בסה"ד:

שם לווי, אבל אית ליה שם לווי – אע"ג דלא גבוהה עשרה, ואע"ג דלא הוי ארבע אמות.§ "אפילו הוא עמה במטה" כו'.§ אמר רבא: אלא שנו אלא במטה שלו, אבל במטה שלה – מגורשת. תניא נמי הכי, רבי אליעזר אומר: במטה שלו – אינה מגורשת, במטה שלה – מגורשת. ובמטה שלה מגורשת?! כליו של לוקח ברשות מוכר הוא! שמעת מינה: *כליו של לוקח ברשות מוכר – קנה לוקח? לא צריכא, בדגבוהה עשרה. והאיכא מקום כרעי! אמקום כרעי לא קפדי אינשי.§ "לתוך חיקה או לתוך קלתה – מגורשת".§ אמאי? *כליו של לוקח ברשות מוכר הוא! *אמר רב יהודה אמר שמואל: כגון שהיתה קלתה תלויה בה. וכן אמר ר' אלעזר אמר רבי אושעיא: כגון שהיתה קלתה תלויה בה. ור' שמעון בן לקיש אמר: קשורה אע"פ שאינה תלויה. רב אדא בר אהבה אמר: כגון שהיתה קלתה מונחת לה בין ירכותיה. רב משרשיא בר רב דימי אמר: כגון שהיה בעלה מוכר קלתות. ר' יוחנן אמר: מקום חיקה קנוי לה, מקום קלתה קנוי לה. אמר רבא: מ"ט דר' יוחנן? גלפי שאין אדם מקפיד לא על מקום חיקה ולא על מקום קלתה. תניא נמי הכי: זרקו לה לתוך חיקה או לתוך קלתה, או לתוך כל דבר שהוא כקלתה – הרי זו מגורשת. "כל דבר שהוא כקלתה" לאיתויי מאי? לאיתויי טסקא דאכלה בה תמרי.§ **מתני'** דאמר לה "כנסי שטר חוב זה", או שמצאתו מאחוריו, קוראה והרי הוא גיטה – אינו גט, עד שיאמר לה "הא גיטיך". הנתן בידה והיא ישנה, ניעורה, קוראה והרי הוא גיטה – אינו גט, עד שיאמר לה "הא גיטיך".§ **גמ'** כי אמר לה "הא גיטיך" מאי הוי? הוה ליה "טלי גיטיך מעל גבי קרקע", ואמר רבא: *ו"טלי גיטיך מעל גבי קרקע" – לא אמר כלום! אימא: ששלפתו מאחוריו. שלפתו נמי, הא בעינא "ונתן בידה" וליכא! לא צריכא, *חדעריק לה חרציה ושלפתיה. תניא נמי הכי: אמר לה "כנסי שטר חוב זה", או ששלפתו מאחוריו, קראתו והרי הוא גיטה – אינו גט, עד שיאמר לה "הא גיטיך", דברי רבי; *רבי שמעון בן אלעזר אומר: לעולם אינו גט, "עד שיטלנו הימנה ויחזור ויתננו לה ויאמר לה "הא גיטיך". נתנו בידה והיא ישנה, ניעורה וקוראה והרי הוא גיטה – אינו גט, עד שיאמר לה "הא גיטיך", דברי רבי; רבי שמעון בן אלעזר אומר: עד שיטלנו הימנה ויחזור ויתננו לה ויאמר לה "הא גיטיך". וצריכא; דאי איתמר בהך קמייתא, בההיא קאמר רבי, משום דבת איגרושי היא, אבל נתן בידה והיא ישנה, דלאו בת איגרושי היא – אימא מודי ליה לרבי שמעון בן אלעזר; ואי איתמר בהא, בהא קאמר ר' שמעון בן אלעזר, אבל בהך – אימא מודי ליה לרבי, צריכא. *אמר רבא: כתב לה גט ונתנו ביד עבדה ישן ומשמרתו – ה"ז גט, ניעור – אינו גט, דהויא ליה חצר המשתמרת שלא לדעתה. ישן ומשמרתו – הרי זה גט, אמאי? *חצר מהלכת היא, וחצר מהלכת לא קנה! וכי תימא ישן שאני, *והא*) אמר רבא: כל שאילו מהלך לא קנה, עומד ויושב לא קנה!

*(א) טוהלכתא: בכפות.§ **מתני'** **)יהיתה עומדת ברשות הרבים וזרקו לה, קרוב לה – מגורשת, קרוב לו – אינה מגורשת, מחצה על מחצה – מגורשת ואינה מגורשת. כוכן לענין קדושין. לוכן לענין החוב: אמר לו בעל חובו "זרוק לי חובי" וזרקו לו, קרוב למלוה – זכה *המלוה, קרוב ללוה – הלוה חייב, מחצה על מחצה – שניהם יחלוקו.§ **גמ'** היכי דמי קרוב לה, והיכי דמי קרוב לו? אמר רב: ארבע אמות שלה – זהו קרוב לה, ארבע אמות שלו – זהו קרוב לו. היכי דמי מחצה על מחצה? אמר ר' שמואל בר רב יצחק: כגון שהיו שניהן עומדין בארבע אמות. מוליחזי הי מינייהו קדים? וכי תימא דאתו תרוייהו בהדי הדדי, *והא אי אפשר לצמצם! אלא אמר רב כהנא: הכא בח' אמות מצומצמות עסקינן, וגט

*) לעיל כא. ב"ק יב. ב"מ ט: **) יבמות לא.

רש"י

שם לווי. כולהו פיסלא מיקרו, ואי הוי להאי שם לעצמו – הוה ליה חשוב, ולא בטיל. אבל במטה שלה. אע"פ שבתוך ביתו – מגורשת. וקא סלקא דעתין טעמא משום דקסבר: כליו של לוקח ברשות מוכר – קונה חפץ הנתון לתוכו לבעליו, ופלוגתא היא בב"ב (פה.). דגבוהה י'. דהוי רשותא לנפשיה, ולא חשיב ההוא אוירא רשות מוכר, לבטל את רשות הכלי. והא איכא מקום כרעי. שמונחים לארץ. ה"ג: אמקום כרעי לא קפדי אינשי. הואיל וגבוה מן הארץ עשרה, שנוחה להשתמש תחתיה. קשורה אע"פ שאינה תלויה. אלא נגררת בקרקע וקשור בה. ולא גרסי': תלויה אע"פ שאינה קשורה. בין ירכותיה. ואע"פ שמונחת בקרקע – אין אדם מקפיד על כל מקום מושב אשתו, ועד עכשיו היה אותו מקום קנוי לה. מוכר קלתות. לכך אינו מקפיד על מקומה, שיש לו בית לכך. תניא נמי הכי. דמשום דאינו מקפיד הוא, מדקתני: או בכל דבר שהוא כקלתה, שמיוחד לתשמישה תמיד, שהמכניס אשתו לתוך ביתו – על מנת להיות כלי תשמישיה קטנים עמה הוא מכניסה. טסקא. טסק"א בלע"ז. **מתני'** עד שיאמר לה הא גיטיך. ואפי' לאחר שבא לידה אומר לה כן, ודיו. קוראה והרי הוא גיטה. כשהיא קוראה בו רואה שהוא גיטה. **גמ'** טלי גיטיך מעל גבי קרקע לא אמר כלום. דבעינן "ונתן". שלפתו. שהיה תחוב בין חגורו למתניו, ושלפתו משם. דעריק לה חרציה. עקם לה מתניו, להקריב לה הגט. שלפתו. גרס בברייתא. לעולם אינו גט. הואיל ובא לידה שלא בהכשר, עד שיטלנו כו'. דבת איגרושי היא. שהרי ניעורה ולא מיחסרא אלא אמירת "הי גיטך", הלכך כי אמר לה בתר הכי – שפיר דמי, שקבלתה הוגנת. הרי זה גט. דהוי חצרה המשתמרת לדעתה, הואיל והוא ישן – אינו משתמר אלא על ידה. ניעור אינו גט. שהעבד משמר את עצמו ואת מה שבידו, והויא לה חצרה המשתמרת שלא לדעתה. חצר מהלכת לא קנה. רבא גופיה אמרה ב"שנים אוחזין בטלית"*. כל שאילו מהלך כו'. רבא נמי אמרה התם: היה מהלך בספינה וקפצו דגים לתוך הספינה כו'. בכפות. שאינו ראוי להלך, בההוא קאמר רבא דהוי גט. **מתני'** קרוב לה. מפרש בגמ'. אמר לו. מלוה ללוה. זרוק לי חובי. ברה"ר. וזרקו לו. ואבד. **גמ'** ד' אמות שלו. שאין בינו לגט ד' אמות, דאמרינן ב"שנים אוחזין" (ב"מ דף י.) דד' אמות של אדם קונות לו. כגון שהיו שניהם עומדים בד' אמות. לגט, זו מכאן וזה מכאן, שכל הגט מונח בתוך ארבע אמות שלו ובתוך ארבע אמות שלה. ולא גרסינן: מצומצמות. וליחזי הי מינייהו קדים. לבא במעמדו, אם קדם הוא לבא – זכה בכל ארבע אמות, ואם קדמה היא לבא – זכתה בכל ד' אמות הסמוכות לה, ושוב לא נכנסה זכותו לתוכו. א"א לצמצם. שלא יקדים האחר. מצומצמות. שהיו שניהם עומדים בח' אמות מצומצמות, לא פחות ולא יותר יש בין שניהם.

תוספות

אמקום כרעי לא קפדי אינשי. לכל הפחות באשתו, וכן באויר המטה. כגון שקלתה תלויה בה. וא"ת: ותיפשוט איפכא מדמתרצי כל הני אמוראי, וב"המוכר את הספינה" (ב"ב דף פה:) רוצה לפשוט מדברי אמוראי ואינו יכול! ויש לומר: דהכא לכולהו מספקא להו, אלא דדחו למתני' דלא נפשוט מינה. א"נ: אפי' בעלמא כליו של לוקח ברשות מוכר קנה – הכא לענין גט, דלרחוקה קאתי, לא קנה. מקום חיקה קנוי לה. וא"ת: פשיטא, דהא חיקה הוי ממש כידה! ואומר ר"י: דר' יוחנן קשורה ותלויה בעי, ומיירי כשבגדיה נגררין בארץ. והשתא, אי לאו טעמא דמקום חיקה קנוי לה – לא הוי מהני מידי, כיון דאינה קשורה ותלויה. אינו גט עד שיאמר לה הא גיטיך. ר"י היה מצריך לנותן גט לאשתו לומר "הי גיטיך" וגם "הרי את מותרת לכל אדם" כדמשמע ב"המגרש" (לקמן דף פה:) שהיו רגילים לומר ג"כ "ודן". ומיהו, קשה דב"הניזקין" (לעיל דף נה.) משמע דאפילו לא אמר כשר, גבי: מעדותו של רבי יוחנן בן גודגדא נשמע: אמר לעדים ראו גט זה וכו'! וי"ל: דהתם נמי אחר כך יגידו לה העדים שהיא מגורשת. אף על פי דהאשה מתגרשת בעל כרחה – מכל מקום צריך לומר לה "הי גיטיך" ו"הרי את מותרת לכל אדם" – שתדע שהיא מגורשת, ולא תהא חוזרת, דבעינן שיהא משלחה ואינה חוזרת*.

תוספות רי"ד

בתוך ביתו או בתוך חצרו אפילו עמה במטה וכו' אמר רבא ל"ש אלא במטה שלו אבל במטה שלה מגורשת תניא נמי הכי ר' אליעזר אומר במטה שלה מגורשת ש"מ כלי של לוקח ברשות מוכר קני פי' ופלוגתא היא בפ' המוכר את הספינה וא"כ תקשה מהכא למ"ד לא קנה לא צריכא במטה דגבוהה עשרה פי' דהוי רשותא לנפשיה ולא חשיב ההוא אוירא רשות מוכר לבטל את הכלי: והא איכא מקום כרעים פי' כרעי המטה שהן מונחים בבית הבעל אמקום כרעים לא קפדי אינשי שהואיל והיא גבוהה י' נוח להשתמש תחתיה: לתוך חיקה או לתוך קלתה הרי זו מגורשת קלתה כליו של לוקח ברשות מוכר הוא א"ר יוחנן מקום חיקה קנוי לה מקום קלתה קנוי לה אמר רבא מ"ט דר' יוחנן לפי שאין אדם מקפיד לא על מקום חיקה ולא על מקום קלתה: **מתני'** אמר לה כנסי שט"ח זה או שמצאתו מאחוריו קוראה והרי הוא גיטה אינו גט עד שיאמר לה הרי זה גיטך נתן בידה והיא ישנה ונתעוררה קוראה והרי היא גיטה אינו גט עד שיאמר לה הרי זה גיטך: או שמצאתו מאחוריו וכי אמר לה הרי הוא גיטך מאי הוי טלי גיטך מעל גבי קרקע הוא ואמר רבא טלי גיטך מע"ג קרקע לא אמר כלום דבעינן ונתן בידה וליכא והכא נמי לא איהו יהיב לה אימא שלפתו מאחוריו ואכתי הא בעינן ונתן בידה וליכא לא צריכא דעייק לה חרציה ושלפתיה ועקימת מתניו שעיקם לה חשיבה נתינה תניא נמי הכי אמר לה כנסי ש"ח או ששלפתו מאחוריו קוראה והרי היא גיטה אינו גט עד שיאמר לה הרי הוא גיטך דברי ר' ר"ש בן אלעזר אומר אינו גט עד שיטלנו ממנה ויחזיר ויתננו לה ויאמר לה הרי זה גיטך וקי"ל הלכה כרבי מחברו וכ"ש דהיא סתם מתני' ומחלוקת דברייתא דהלכה כסתם ודוקא בכנסי שט"ח זה ונתן בידה א) והיא ישנה שהבעל נותנו לה לשם גירושין והיא לא הרגישה בדבר ואילו היה מודיע לעדים קודם לכך שלשם גירושין הוא נותנו לה אע"פ שאמר לאשה כנסי שט"ח זה היתה מגורשת כדילפינן מעדותו של ר' יוחנן בן גודגודא דלא בעינן דעת אשה בגט אלא כיון שלא הודיע לעדים ב) אלא אמר לה עכשיו הרי זה גיטך וכן כשנתן בידה והיא ישנה יש כאן נתינה אלא מפני שאינה יכולה לשומרו אומר לה כשניעורה הרי זה גיטך ודי לו אבל אילו נתנו לה מתחלה לשם פקדון נתינה זו אינה כלום ולא די שיחזור ויאמר לה הרי זה גיטך ומפני זה (עשה) [תנא] התנא זה (הסבוב) אמר לה כנסי שט"ח זה (ול"ש) [ולא תנא] הנותן גט לאשתו לשומרו ואח"כ אמר לה הרי זה גיטך מגורשת שאילו היה כן היה צריך ליטלו ממנה ולחזור וליתנו לשם גירושין: אמר רבא כתב לה גט ונתנו ביד עבדה ישן ומשמרתו ה"ז גט נעור ומשמרתו אינו גט דהוה לה חצר המשתמרת שלא לדעתה ישן ומשמרתו הרי זה גט אמאי חצר מהלכת היא וחצר מהלכת לא קנה וכ"ת ישן שאני האמר רבא כל שאילו מהלך לא קנה עומד ויושב לא קנה והלכתא בכפות: **מתני'** היתה עומדת ברה"ר וזרקו לה קרוב לה מגורשת קרוב לו אינה מגורשת מחצה על מחצה מגורשת ואינה מגורשת וכן לענין קדושין ולענין החוב אמר לו זרוק לי חובי וזרקו לו קרוב למלוה זכה הלוה קרוב ללוה הלוה חייב מחצה על מחצה שניהם יחלוקו היתה עומדת על ראש הגג וזרקו לה כיון שהגיע לאויר הגג הרי זו מגורשת הוא מלמעלה והיא מלמטה וזרקו לה כיון שיצא מרשות הגג נשרף או נמחק הרי זו מגורשת היכי

א) נראה דצ"ל או כשהיא ישנה. ב) נראה דצ"ל אלא כיון שלא הודיע לעדים לכן צריך שיאמר לה עכשיו הרי זה גיטך וכו'.

עין משפט נר מצוה

טו א ב ג מיי' פ"ה מהלכות גירושין הל' ח סמג עשין נ טוש"ע אה"ע סימן קלט סעי' י:
טז ד מיי' פ"א שם הלכה ט סמג שם טוש"ע אה"ע סימן קלו סעיף א וסימן קלח סעיף ד:
יז ה מיי' שם סמג שם טוש"ע שם סימן קלח סעיף ג:
יח ו ז ח מיי' שם הל' יב טוש"ע שם סעיף א:
יט ט מיי' פ"ה שם הל' יז סמג שם טוש"ע אה"ע סימן קלט סעיף טז וסעיף יז:
כ י טוש"ע שם סעיף יג:
כא כ מיי' פ"ד מהל' אישות הלכה כב סמג עשין מח טוש"ע אה"ע סימן ל סעיף ה:
כב ל מיי' פט"ז מהל' מלוה ולוה הלכה א סמג עשין צד טוש"ע ח"מ סימן קכ סעיף א:
כג מ מיי' פ"ה מהל' גירושין הלכה יג סמג עשין נ טוש"ע אה"ע סימן קלט סעיף יד ועיין במ"מ ובכ"מ:

מסורת הש"ס

[ב"ב פה:]
[לקמן עט:]
ב"ב פה:
[לעיל כז.]
[נ"ל דעייק ערוך ערך עקף ב ובערך עיק כתב בפי' ר"ח כתב לאדיק וכו' וכתב המוסיף דעדיק כתוב בנוסחא דיכן עכ"ל ובהרא"ש איתא דעויק]
[ב"מ ט:]
לקמן פד:
קדושין מד:
[לעיל כא. וש"נ]
ס"א הא כל כו'
ס"א אלא בכפות
[במשנה שבמשניות איתא הלוה וכ"א ברב אלפס אכן בהרא"ש איתא המלוה]
[בכורות יז. ועי' תוספות עירובין ה: ד"ה וספק ותוס' סוכה טו: ד"ה פרוץ ותוספות בכורות יז: ד"ה אפשר ותוספות חולין כח: ד"ה לפי]
[יבמות קיג:]

הגהות הב"ח

(א) גמ' והלכתא בכפות. נ"ב עי' לעיל בפ' שני בדף כא.:

כד א מיי' פ"ה מהל' גירושין הלכה יד ופ"ד מהלכות אישות הל' כב סמג עשין מט נ טור ש"ע אה"ע סימן ל סעיף ה וסימן קלט סעיף יג:
כה ב מיי' פ"ה מהל' גירושין הלכה יג סמג עשין נ טור ש"ע אה"ע סי' קלט סעי' יג:
כו ג ד ה מיי' פט"ז מהלכות מלוה ולוה הלכה א סמג עשין צד טוש"ע ח"מ סימן קכ סעיף א:
כז ו מיי' פ"ה מהלכות גירושין הלכה טז סמג עשין נ טוש"ע אה"ע סי' קלח סעיף ב:
כח ז ח מיי' שם הלכה יב סמג שם טוש"ע שם סימן קלט סעיף טו:

וְגֵט יוֹצֵא מֵאַרְבַּע אַמּוֹת שֶׁלּוֹ לְד' אַמּוֹת שֶׁלָּהּ. וְהָא אֲגִיד גַּבֵּיהּ! אֶלָּא, *רַבָּה וְרַב יוֹסֵף דְּאָמְרִי תַּרְוַיְיהוּ: הָכָא בִּשְׁתֵּי כִּיתֵּי עֵדִים עָסְקִינַן, אַחַת אוֹמֶרֶת קָרוֹב לוֹ וְאַחַת אוֹמֶרֶת קָרוֹב לָהּ. רַבִּי יוֹחָנָן אוֹמֵר: "קָרוֹב לָהּ" שָׁנִינוּ, אֲפִילּוּ מֵאָה אַמָּה, וְ"קָרוֹב לוֹ" שָׁנִינוּ, אֲפִילּוּ מֵאָה אַמָּה. הֵיכִי דָּמֵי מֶחֱצָה עַל מֶחֱצָה? אָמַר רַב שֶׁמֶן בַּר אַבָּא, לְדִידִי מִיפָּרְשָׁא לָהּ מִינֵּיהּ דְּרַבִּי יוֹחָנָן: אהוּא יָכוֹל לְשׁוֹמְרוֹ וְהִיא אֵינָהּ יְכוֹלָה לְשׁוֹמְרוֹ — זֶהוּ קָרוֹב לוֹ, הִיא יְכוֹלָה לְשׁוֹמְרוֹ וְהוּא אֵינוֹ יָכוֹל לְשׁוֹמְרוֹ — זֶהוּ קָרוֹב לָהּ, שְׁנֵיהֶם יְכוֹלִין לְשׁוֹמְרוֹ, שְׁנֵיהֶם אֵין יְכוֹלִין — זֶהוּ מֶחֱצָה עַל מֶחֱצָה. אֲמַרוּהָ רַבָּנַן קַמֵּיהּ דְּרַבִּי יוֹחָנָן מִשְּׁמֵיהּ דְּרַבִּי יוֹנָתָן הָכִי, אֲמַר: *יָדְעִין חַבְרִין בַּבְלָאֵי לְפָרוּשֵׁי כִּי הַאי טַעְמָא? תַּנְיָא נַמִּי הָכִי, רַבִּי אֱלִיעֶזֶר אוֹמֵר: *כָּל שֶׁהוּא קָרוֹב לָהּ מִלּוֹ, וּבָא כֶּלֶב וּנְטָלוֹ — אֵינָהּ מְגוֹרֶשֶׁת; אֵינָהּ מְגוֹרֶשֶׁת?! כָּל הֵיכִי תִּינַטְרֵיהּ וְתֵיזִיל? אֶלָּא לָאו ה"ק: כָּל שֶׁקָּרוֹב לָהּ מִלּוֹ, וְאִילּוּ בָּא כֶּלֶב וּנְטָלוֹ וְהוּא יָכוֹל לְשׁוֹמְרוֹ וְהִיא אֵינָהּ יְכוֹלָה לְשׁוֹמְרוֹ — אֵינָהּ מְגוֹרֶשֶׁת. אֲמַר לֵיהּ שְׁמוּאֵל לְרַב יְהוּדָה: *בשִׁינָּנָא, כְּדֵי שֶׁתָּשׁוּחַ וְתִטְּלֶנּוּ, וְאַתְּ לָא תַּעֲבֵיד עוּבְדָא עַד דְּמָטֵי גִּיטָּא לְיָדָהּ. אֲמַר לֵיהּ רַב מָרְדֳּכַי לְרַב אַשִׁי: הֲוָה עוּבְדָא הָכִי וְאַצְרְכוּהָ חֲלִיצָה.§ "וְכֵן לְעִנְיַן קִדּוּשִׁין".§ אָמַר ר' אַסִּי אָמַר ר' יוֹחָנָן: לְגִיטִּין אָמְרוּ גוְלֹא לְדָבָר אַחֵר. אֵיתִיבֵיהּ רַבִּי אַבָּא לְר' אַסִּי: וְכֵן לְעִנְיַן קִדּוּשִׁין! שָׁאנֵי הָתָם *דִּכְתִי': °"וְיָצְאָה וְהָיְתָה". [דברים כד] אֵיתִיבֵיהּ: וְכֵן לְעִנְיַן הַחוֹב, "זְרוֹק לִי חוֹבִי" וּזְרָקוֹ לוֹ, קָרוֹב לַמַּלְוֶה — זָכָה *הַלֹּוֶה, קָרוֹב לַלֹּוֶה — הַלֹּוֶה חַיָּיב, מֶחֱצָה עַל מֶחֱצָה — שְׁנֵיהֶם יַחֲלוֹקוּ! הָכָא בְּמַאי עָסְקִינַן — דדְּאָמַר לֵיהּ "זְרוֹק לִי חוֹבִי וְתִיפָּטֵר". אִי הָכִי, מַאי לְמֵימְרָא? לָא צְרִיכָא, הדְּאָמַר לֵיהּ "זְרוֹק לִי חוֹבִי בְּתוֹרַת גִּיטִּין". וְאַכַּתִּי מַאי לְמֵימְרָא? מַהוּ דְּתֵימָא, מָצֵי אָמַר לֵיהּ: מְשַׁטֶּה אֲנִי בָּךְ, קמ"ל. *אָמַר רַב חִסְדָּא: גֵּט בְּיָדָהּ וּמְשִׁיחָה בְּיָדוֹ, ואִם יָכוֹל לְנַתְּקוֹ וּלְהָבִיאוֹ אֶצְלוֹ — אֵינָהּ מְגוֹרֶשֶׁת, וְאִם לָאו — מְגוֹרֶשֶׁת; מַאי טַעְמָא? בָּעֵינַן כְּרִיתוּת וְלֵיכָּא. [ב"מ ז.] אָמַר רַב יְהוּדָה: זהָיְתָה יָדָהּ עֲשׂוּיָה כְּקַטַפְרֵס וּזְרָקוֹ לָהּ, אַף עַל פִּי שֶׁהִגִּיעַ גֵּט לְיָדָהּ — אֵינָהּ מְגוֹרֶשֶׁת. אַמַּאי? הָא כִּי נָפֵיל — בְּאַרְבַּע אַמּוֹת דִּידַהּ קָא נָפֵיל! בִּדְלָא נָח. וְתִיגָּרֵשׁ מֵאֲוִירָא דְּאַרְבַּע אַמּוֹת! תִּפְשׁוֹט דְּבָעֵי רַבִּי אֶלְעָזָר: אַרְבַּע אַמּוֹת שֶׁאָמְרוּ, יֵשׁ לָהֶן אֲוִיר אוֹ אֵין לָהֶן אֲוִיר — תִּפְשׁוֹט דְּאֵין לָהֶן אֲוִיר! חהָכָא בְּמַאי עָסְקִינַן — בְּעוֹמֶדֶת עַל גַּב הַנָּהָר, דְּמֵעִיקָּרָא לְאִיבּוּד קָאֵי.§

מתני'

וגט יוצא. מאלו לאלו, מקלתו בד' אמות שלה ומקלתו בד' אמות שלו. **והא אגיד גביה.** עדיין הגט ברשותו קלת, ותנן "ונתן בידה" בעינן, עד שיהא כולו ברשותה. **אמרוה קמיה דר' יוחנן.** להאי פירושא דמתני'. **משמיה דר' יונתן הכי.** כדפרשה ר' יוחנן ביכולין לשומרו. **רבי יונתן** מבבל הוה ועלה לארץ ישראל. **תניא נמי הכי.** דקורבה דמתני' שמירה היא. **כל שקרוב לה מלו.** השתא משמע: אע"פ שקרוב לה יותר ממנו, ובא כלב ונטלו – אינה מגורשת. וקשיא לן בה: אמאי אינה מגורשת? מכי אתא לקורבה דידה איגרשה לה, ומאי איכפת לן אם נטלו כלב? כל היכי תנטריה ותיזיל. וכי כל הימים צריכה לשומרו? אלא לאו הכי קאמר. אע"פ שקרוב לה מלו, אם יש הפסק נהר או גבשושית בינה לגט, שאילו היה בא כלב ונטלו אינה יכולה לשומרו הימנו, אבל הוא יכול לשומרו – אינה מגורשת. **כדי שתשוח ותטלנו.** הוא דהויא קורבה דמתני', ואפ"ה את לא תעביד עובדא להתירה ליגשא. **עד דמטי גט לידה.** גזירה שמא יאמרו על רחוק שהוא קרוב. **הוה עובדא.** שזרקו קרוב לה, ומת, ואצרכוה חליצה. **לגיטין אמרו.** דמשום קורבה מגורשת. **ולא לדבר אחר.** כגון אם זרק לו חוב קרוב לו ואבד דגט הוא דבעל כרחה קנויה לה הלכך לאלתר הוי גיטא אבל בעלמא – לא. **ותיפטר.** דהא פטריה. אבל "זרוק לי חובי" סתמא – זרוק ושומרו קאמר. **ומשיחה.** חוט שהגט קשור בו, ליי"ל בלע"ז. **גט בידה.** שנתנו לה, וראש המשיחה עדיין בידו. **בקטפרס.** מדרון, ראשי אצבעותיה מטין לקרקע, שלא פשטה ידה וקופה כדרך פושטי יד. ופרכינן. **והא כי נפיל לד' אמות דידה נפיל.** ומה לי אי אין ידה ראויה לקבל בפשיטתה. **בדלא נח.** לארץ, אלא כשנפל מתוך ידה נשרף, וקבלה שבא לידה – לאו קבלה היא. ופריך: וכי לא נח מאי הוי? מכי מטא לתוך ארבע אמות שלה תיגרש מאויריהן, ומדקאמר אינה מגורשת – פשוט דאין להן אויר, והיא בעיא דרבי אלעזר. **על גב הנהר.** דאויר שאינו ראוי לנוח לא קני.

גמ'

רבי יוחנן אמר קרוב לה שנינו אפילו מאה אמה. וקשה: דבפ"ק דב"מ (דף י:) קא"ר יוחנן דקטנה יש לה חלר, ויש לה ד' אמות, וקאמר התם דיליף מליאה מגט, משמע דבגט לרבי יוחנן אינה מגורשת אלא תוך ד' אמות, והכא קאמר אפילו מאה אמה! וי"ל: דבד' אמות שלה אפילו יכול לשמור כמוה – מגורשת, וחוץ לארבע אמות – לריך שתהא היא יכולה לשומרו, ולא הוא. ועוד קשה: דרב אשי אית ליה התם דברה"ר לא תקנו ארבע אמות, והכא תנן: היתה עומדת ברה"ר קרוב לה מגורשת! וי"ל: דהתם באין יכול לשומרו, והכא – ביכולה לשומרו. א"נ י"ל: דהכא לאו דוקא נקט רה"ר, אלא בסמטא או בלדי רה"ר.

***והא** א"א לצמצם. וא"ת: ולישני: כגון דלא ידעינן הי מינייהו קדים, ולכך הוי ספיקא! וי"ל: דלישנא דמחלה על מחלה לא משמע הכי, ולכך מוקי לה בשתי כיתי עדים כו'. וא"ת: ונימא: אוקי תרי בהדי תרי, ואוקי איתתא בחזקת אשת איש, ולא תהא מגורשת כלל! וי"ל: כיון דספיקא דרבנן היא, כדאמרינן בפ' "ארבעה אחין" (יבמות דף לא.) – נתנו לה דין מגורשת ואינה מגורשת.

***שניהם** אין יכולים זה הוא מחצה על מחצה. פי': אין יכולין לשומרו כל אחד לבדו, אלא שניהם יחד. אבל אם אין יכולין לשומרו כלל – פשיטא דאינה מגורשת כלל כל עיקר.

ואת לא תעביד עובדא עד דמטי גט לידה. והיינו דוקא ברה"ר, אבל בחלרה – אין לריך שיגיע לידה, כדאמר לעיל: תיזיל איהי ותחוד ותפתח. ומיהו, בערוך בערך גט כתב: קבלנו מרבותינו, אפי' זרקו לה בתוך חלרה – לא משתריא לעלמא עד דמטא גיטא לידה. ומייתי מהא דאמר בירושלמי: המחמיר שבכולן עד שיתננו לידה. ואינה ראיה, דאיכא למימר דמיירי ברה"ר, דבהדיא מסיק לה *אקרוב לו וקרוב לה, ומסתמא לא אתא לאפוקי חלרה.

לגיטין אמרו ולא לדבר אחר. פי' בקונטר': משום דבגט נתינה בעל כרחה הויא נתינה. והקשה ר"י לר' יהודה, דלדבר אחר נמי אמרו לעיל ב"מי שאחזו" (דף עה.) דנתינה בעל כרחו הויא נתינה! ומשיב: דבדבר אחר אשכחן דוכתא דלא הויא נתינה, כגון *הלוהו בישוב – לא יחזיר לו במדבר, אבל בגט – בכל מקום הויא נתינה. **אי** הכי מאי למימרא. וא"ת: אדרבה, תקשי ליה אמאי קרוב ללוה חייב לוה? כיון דאמר "זרוק חובי ותפטר" – קרוב ללוה נמי ליפטר! וי"ל: דמיירי מסתמא דמפרש לו שיזרוק לו למקום שיוכל לשומרו הוא.

***מחצה** על מחצה שניהם יחלוקו. הכא לא שייך לומר המוליא מחבירו עליו הראיה, דאין כאן ספק. **אם** יכול לנתקו ולהביאו כו'. נראה דלא מיירי כשהיתה ידה פתוחה, ולאחר שנתן הגט בידה קפלה ידה – דא"כ אפילו אין יכול להביאו אללו אינה מגורשת, כיון דבשעת נתינה היה יכול להביאו אללו, ומה שקופלת ידה אח"כ – זה אינו עושה הבעל אלא היא, והוה ליה כמו "טלי גיטיך מעל גבי קרקע" ואינו גט. אלא נראה לר"י דמיירי שכבר היתה ידה קפולה, והוא תחב הגט לתוך ידה, ואם תחב כל כך בחוזק עד שאינו יכול להביאו אללו – הויא מגורשת. ור"ת מפרש: דבידה פתוחה איירי שפיר, ו"אם אינו יכול להביאו אללו" – היינו כשהגט כבד, ואם ימשוך אללו – תינתק המשיחה. ולריך ליזהר שתהא יד האשה פתוחה עד שיניח כל הגט בידה, דאם תקפוץ ידה בעוד שהבעל אוחז בראש הגט בידו – לא הוי גט, דהוי כמו גט בידה ומשיחה בידו. ונראה דכשר, דלא גרע מערק לה חרליה ושלפתו, דהוי גט אע"ג דביד הבעל להדק מתניו שלא תטול. והמחמיר תבא עליו ברכה. **והא** בארבע אמות דידה קא נפיל. הוה מלי לשנויי דמיירי שהאשה עומדת בחלר דידיה, דלית לה ארבע אמות, או ברה"ר *לרב אשי דפ"ק דב"מ (דף י:).

ותתגרש מאוירא דארבע אמות. וא"ת: והא לא מינטר, כדאמרינן בסמוך באויר גג! וי"ל: דאויר ארבע אמות חשיב ליה מינטר, ועומדת על ראש הגג – מיירי אפילו חוץ לארבע אמות. ולהכי פריך: והא לא מינטר. ור"י אומר: דרבי אלעזר גופיה מספקא ליה אם מה שתיקנו חכמים ארבע אמות תיקנו גם באויר, ואע"ג דלא מינטר עשאוהו כמינטר, כמו שעשו ארבע אמות רשותו ואע"פ שאינה רשותו.

היתה

תוספות רי"ד

היכי דמי קרוב לו והיכי דמי קרוב לה אמר רבא ד' אמות שלה הוא קרוב לה ד' אמות שלו הוא קרוב לו. היכי דמי מחצה על מחצה ואסיק הכא בשתי כתי עדים עסקינן אחת אומר' קרוב לה ואחת אומרת קרוב לו ור' יוחנן אמר קרוב לה שנינו אפילו ק' אמה קרוב לו שנינו אפי' ק' אמה ה"ד מחצה על מחצה הוא יכול לשמרו והיא אינה יכולה לשמרו זה הוא קרוב לו היא יכולה לשמרו והוא אינו יכול לשמרו זהו קרוב לה שניהם יכולין לשמרו שניהם אינן יכולין לשמרו זהו מחצה על מחצה א"ל רב שמואל לרב יהודה שיננא איזהו קרוב לה כדי שתשוח ותטלנו ואת לא תעביד עובדא עד דמטי גיטא לידה א"ל רב מרדכי לרב אשי הוה עובדא ואצרכוה חליצה פי' הוה עובדא שזרק הגט קרוב לה ולא מטיא גיטא לידה ומת ואצריכוה חליצה. כתב ר"ח ז"ל ואנו קבלנו מרבותינו אפילו זרקו לה בחצרה לא משתריא לעלמא עד דמטי גיטא לידה דגרסי' בתלמוד א"י המחוור מכלן עד שיתנו לה. ואינו נראה לי דהאי דאמר שמואל ואת לא תעביד עובדא עד דמטי גיטא לידה דוקא כשזרקו לה ברה"ר שאין לאשה זכות בו אבל כשזרקו לה בתוך חצרה יש לגמגם בדבר שלא יהיה גט והלכך אע"ג דלא מטי גיטא לידה הויא מגורשת וחצרה קני לה: א"ר אסי א"ר יוחנן לגיטין אמרו ולא לדבר אחר פי' שאין ד' אמות קונות אלא לענין גיטין ולא לדבר אחר עד שיגיע לידו איתיביה ר' אבא לר' אסי וכן לענין קדושין שאני התם דכתיב ויצאה והיתה איתיביה וכן לענין החוב אמר לו (צריך) זרק וכו' הכא במאי עסקינן דאמר לו זרוק לי חובי בתורת גיטין והפטר אי הכי מאי למימרא מהו דתימא מצי אמר משטה אני בך קמ"ל פי' קנין הגט אינו דומה לשאר הקנין דקנין דעלמא אין אדם יכול להקנות לחבירו בעל כרחו והגט מקנהו לאשתו בעל כרחה א"כ טעם החצר דרבי ליה רחמנא לא בעבור קנין הוא א) אלא שהרי היא עצובה בו ואינה חפצה לקנותו וחצרה קונה לה ומתגרשת אלא טעם הדבר הוא מפני שהוא כשתמר לדעתה א"כ בכל מקום שהוא משתמר לדעתה היא מגורשת משא"כ בשאר קנינים דעלמא משום הכי א"ר יוחנן לגיטין אמרו ולא לדבר אחר ובשנים אוחזין אמרינן דדוקא בסימטא שהוא רה"י ד' אמות של אדם קונות לו לענין מציאה בכי האי גוונא דלא ליתי לאינצויי אבל ברה"ר לא ודוקא מציאה אבל לענין מקח וממכר לא ודוקא משיכה קונה בסימטא ולא ד' אמות ולענין זריקת החוב נמי לא קנה שיפטר הלוה עד דמטי ליה לידיה דמלוה ולא לד' אמותיו. גרס' התם אמר ר"ל משום אבא כהן ברדלי ד' אמות של אדם קונות לו בכל מקום מ"ט תקינו ליה רבנן דלא ליתו לאינצויי וקפריש גאון בכל מקום דאמרינן לאו כל מקום ממש אלא בשדה בעלמא אי נמי בסימטא אי נמי בצידי רה"ר דלא דחיקו בהו רבים אבל ברה"ר דדחיקו רבים אי נמי בשדה חבירו לא קני ליה ד' אמות דידיה: אמר רב חסדא גט בידה ומשיחה בידו אם יכול לנתקו ולהביאו אצלו אינה מגורשת ואם לאו מגורשת מאי טעמא בעינן כריתות וליכא: אמר רב יהודה היתה ידה עשויה כקטפרס וזרקו לה אף על פי שהגיע גט לידה אינה מגורשת פי' היתה ידה משופעת שאינה יכולה לקבל גיטה: דלא נח כגון ששרפתו (כלתה) קודם

א) נראה דצ"ל לא בעבור קנין הוא אלא שהרי היא עזובה וכו' [illegible]

עננה

[יבמות לה.] [פסחים פט: חולין מה. זבחים לג:] [תוספתא פ"ח] [ברכות לו. וש"נ ועיין פירושו של ... בחגיגה טו:] [קדושין ה. וש"נ] [ואולי צ"ל המלה כלאי במשנה עמוד ...] שייך לעיל ע"א במתני' | שייך לע"א | עיין ברש"ל | אאין קרוב כצ"ל | ב"ק קיח. | צ"ל לרב אשי

מתני' [א]הָיְתָה עוֹמֶדֶת עַל רֹאשׁ הַגַּג וּזְרָקוֹ לָהּ, כֵּיוָן שֶׁהִגִּיעַ לַאֲוִיר הַגַּג — הֲרֵי זוֹ מְגוֹרֶשֶׁת; [ב]הוּא מִלְמַעְלָה וְהִיא מִלְּמַטָּה וּזְרָקוֹ לָהּ, כֵּיוָן שֶׁיָּצָא מֵרְשׁוּת הַגַּג, נִמְחַק אוֹ נִשְׂרַף — הֲרֵי זוֹ מְגוֹרֶשֶׁת.§ **גמ'** וְהָא לָא מִינְטַר! אָמַר רַב יְהוּדָה אָמַר שְׁמוּאֵל: [ג]בְּגַג שֶׁיֵּשׁ לוֹ מַעֲקֶה עָסְקִינַן. עוּלָּא בַּר מְנַשְּׁיָא מִשְּׁמֵיהּ דַּאֲבִימִי אָמַר: [ד]הָכָא בִּפְחוֹת מִשְּׁלֹשָׁה סָמוּךְ לַגַּג עָסְקִינַן, דְּכָל פָּחוֹת מִשְּׁלֹשָׁה סָמוּךְ לַגַּג — כְּגַג דָּמֵי.§ "הוּא מִלְמַעְלָה".§ וְהָא לָא מִינְטַר! א"ר יְהוּדָה אָמַר שְׁמוּאֵל: [ה]כְּגוֹן שֶׁהָיוּ מְחִיצוֹת הַתַּחְתּוֹנוֹת עוֹדְפוֹת עַל הָעֶלְיוֹנוֹת. וְכֵן אָמַר רַבִּי אֶלְעָזָר א"ר אוֹשַׁעְיָא: כְּגוֹן שֶׁהָיוּ מְחִיצוֹת הַתַּחְתּוֹנוֹת עוֹדְפוֹת עַל הָעֶלְיוֹנוֹת. וְכֵן אָמַר עוּלָּא א"ר יוֹחָנָן: כְּגוֹן שֶׁהָיוּ מְחִיצוֹת הַתַּחְתּוֹנוֹת עוֹדְפוֹת עַל הָעֶלְיוֹנוֹת. א"ל ר' אַבָּא לְעוּלָּא: כְּמַאן? כְּרַבִּי, דְּאָמַר: *קְלוּטָה כְּמִי שֶׁהוּנְחָה דָּמְיָא? א"ל: אֲפִילּוּ תֵּימָא רַבָּנַן, עַד כָּאן לָא פְּלִיגִי רַבָּנַן עֲלֵיהּ דְּרַבִּי אֶלָּא לְעִנְיַן שַׁבָּת, אֲבָל הָכָא — מִשּׁוּם אִינְטוּרֵי הוּא, וְהָא קָא מִינְטַר. וְכֵן אָמַר ר' אַסִּי א"ר יוֹחָנָן: כְּגוֹן שֶׁהָיוּ מְחִיצוֹת הַתַּחְתּוֹנוֹת עוֹדְפוֹת עַל הָעֶלְיוֹנוֹת. א"ל רַבִּי זֵירָא לְר' אַסִּי: כְּמַאן? כְּרַבִּי, דְּאָמַר: קְלוּטָה כְּמִי שֶׁהוּנְחָה דָּמְיָא? א"ל: אֲפִילּוּ תֵּימָא רַבָּנַן, עַד כָּאן לָא פְּלִיגִי רַבָּנַן עֲלֵיהּ דְּרַבִּי אֶלָּא לְעִנְיַן שַׁבָּת, אֲבָל הָכָא — מִשּׁוּם אִינְטוּרֵי הוּא, וְהָא קָא מִינְטַר.§ "נִמְחַק".§ א"ר נַחְמָן אָמַר רַבָּה בַּר אֲבוּהּ: לֹא שָׁנוּ [ו]אֶלָּא שֶׁנִּמְחַק דֶּרֶךְ יְרִידָה, אֲבָל נִמְחַק דֶּרֶךְ עֲלִיָּיה — לָא; מַאי טַעְמָא? מֵעִיקָּרָא לָא לְמֵינָח קָאֵי.§ "נִשְׂרַף".§ אָמַר ר"נ אָמַר רַבָּה בַּר אֲבוּהּ: לֹא שָׁנוּ [ז]אֶלָּא שֶׁקָּדַם גֵּט לַדְּלֵיקָה, אֲבָל קָדְמָה דְּלֵיקָה לַגֵּט — לֹא; מ"ט? מֵעִיקָּרָא לִשְׂרֵיפָה קָאָזֵיל. אָמַר רַב חִסְדָּא: רְשׁוּיוֹת חֲלוּקוֹת בְּגִיטִּין. א"ל רָמִי בַּר חָמָא לְרָבָא: מְנָא לֵיהּ לְסָבָא הָא? א"ל, מַתְנִי' הִיא: הָיְתָה עוֹמֶדֶת עַל רֹאשׁ הַגַּג וּזְרָקוֹ לָהּ, כֵּיוָן שֶׁהִגִּיעַ גֵּט לַאֲוִיר הַגַּג — הֲרֵי זוֹ מְגוֹרֶשֶׁת; בְּמַאי עָסְקִינַן? אִילֵימָא בְּגַג דִּידָהּ וְחָצֵר דִּידָהּ, לָמָּה לִי אֲוִיר הַגַּג? אֶלָּא בְּגַג דִּידֵיהּ וְחָצֵר דִּידֵיהּ, כִּי הִגִּיעַ לַאֲוִיר הַגַּג מַאי הָוֵי? אֶלָּא פְּשִׁיטָא [ח]בְּגַג דִּידָהּ וְחָצֵר דִּידֵיהּ. אֵימָא סֵיפָא: הוּא מִלְמַעְלָה וְהִיא מִלְּמַטָּה וּזְרָקוֹ לָהּ, כֵּיוָן שֶׁיָּצָא מֵרְשׁוּת הַגַּג, נִמְחַק אוֹ נִשְׂרַף — הֲרֵי זוֹ מְגוֹרֶשֶׁת; וְאִי בְּגַג דִּידָהּ וְחָצֵר דִּידָהּ, וְחָצֵר דִּידֵיהּ, אַמַּאי מְגוֹרֶשֶׁת? [ט]אֶלָּא בְּגַג דִּידֵיהּ וְחָצֵר דִּידָהּ; רֵישָׁא בְּגַג דִּידָהּ וְחָצֵר דִּידֵיהּ, סֵיפָא בְּגַג דִּידֵיהּ וְחָצֵר דִּידָהּ? אֶלָּא לָאו *דְּאוֹשְׁלָהּ מָקוֹם, דְּחַד מָקוֹם מוֹשְׁלֵי אֱינָשֵׁי, תְּרֵי מְקוֹמוֹת לָא מוֹשְׁלֵי אֱינָשֵׁי. א"ל: מִידֵּי אִירְיָא? דִּלְמָא הָא כִּדְאִיתָא וְהָא כִּדְאִיתָא, רֵישָׁא בְּגַג דִּידָהּ וְחָצֵר דִּידֵיהּ, סֵיפָא בְּגַג דִּידֵיהּ וְחָצֵר דִּידָהּ. אָמַר רָבָא: שָׁלֹשׁ מִדּוֹת בְּגִיטִּין; הָא דְּאָמַר רַבִּי: קְלוּטָה כְּמִי שֶׁהוּנְחָה, וּפְלִיגִי רַבָּנַן עֲלֵיהּ — הָנֵי מִילֵּי לְעִנְיַן שַׁבָּת, אֲבָל הָכָא מִשּׁוּם אִינְטוּרֵי הוּא, וְהָא מִינְטַר; וְהָא *דְּאָמַר רַב חִסְדָּא: [י]נָעַץ קָנֶה בִּרְשׁוּת הַיָּחִיד וּבְרֹאשׁוֹ טְרַסְקָל וְזָרַק וְנָח עַל גַּבָּיו, אֲפִילּוּ גָּבוֹהַּ מֵאָה אַמָּה — חַיָּיב, לְפִי שֶׁרְשׁוּת הַיָּחִיד עוֹלָה עַד לָרָקִיעַ — הָנֵי מִילֵּי לְעִנְיַן שַׁבָּת, אֲבָל הָכָא מִשּׁוּם אִינְטוּרֵי הוּא, [כ]וְהָא לָא מִינְטַר; וְהָא

[שבת ד. לז. ב"ק ע:]
[לעיל עז:]
שבת ז. ע"ש

גמ' והא לא מינטר. אויר הגג, דאתי זיקא ושדי ליה מקמי דלינח. וכי לא שדיה זיקא, ואירע לו דבר אחר, שבא כלב וקלטו או גשמים מחקוהו – אמאי קתני מגורשת מן האויר? הא בעינן אויר שסופו לנוח! **בפחות מג' כו'.** אויר דמתני' בהכי עסקינן, דהוי כמאן דנח. והלכך קנאתו בהנחתו, דכיון דהגג גבוה י' הוא – הויא לה חצר המשתמרת לכל דניח בגויה. **והא לא מינטר.** דקס"ד שהגג גבוה מחומת החצר, והיכי קתני: כיון שיצא מרשות הגג מגורשת? הא אין סופו לנוח, אפילו לא באת דליקה, דאתי זיקא ודחי ליה חוץ למחיצות! **שהיו מחיצות התחתונות.** של חצר. **עודפות.** על מעקה של גג, דכי נפיק מגג – מטא לאויר מחיצות חצר. ומשום הכי בעינן עודפות, דהאי דקאי בתוך מחיצות מעקת הגג וזרקו כלפי מעלה כדי שיעבור את המעקה – יפול לחצר. **קלוטה.** בתוך האויר. **כמי שהונחה.** לארץ. דתניא: הזורק בשבת מרה"ר לרה"ר ורה"י באמצע – רבי מחייב וחכמים פוטרים. **וא"ל רבי זירא לרבי אסי כו'.** גרסי' בה כדשני עולא: אפילו תימא רבנן כו'. **דרך ירידה.** כשזרקו כלפי מעלה, כדי להעבירו את המעקה, לא נמחק עד שהגיע לחזור ולירד. **אבל נמחק דרך עלייה.** אע"פ שיצא מאויר הגג לאויר חצר, ומחיצות התחתונות עודפות. **אינה מגורשת.** דדרך סילוקו לא מיקרי נתינה, אלא דרך הנחתו לבא לרשותה. **שקדם גט לדליקה.** שקדמה זריקת הגט בחצר קודם שתהא הדליקה באויר החצר. **רשויות חלוקות לגיטין.** אם השאילה הבעל מקום בחצירו לקבלת גיטה – לא השאילה גגו או ביתו, ולא אמרינן לא קפיד, דתרי מקומות לא מושלי. משום דמייתי עלה ראיה ממתני' נקט לה הכא. **הא כדאיתא והא כדאיתא.** רישא בגג דידה וחצר דידיה, ובעינן אויר הגג. **סיפא** בגג דידיה וחצר דידה. מיגרשא באויר חצר. אבל אי תרווייהו דידיה, ואושלה מקום – אימא לך דלא קפיד. **שלש מדות בגיטין.** חלוקות מדין שאר איסורין. **הני מילי.** דפליגי רבנן. **והא דאמר רב חסדא נעץ קנה.** בחצר, גבוה ממחיצת החצר. **וזרק.** מרה"ר. **ונח על גביו חייב.** דהויא לה הנחה ברה"י, שאויר רה"י עולה עד לרקיע. אע"ג דאויר רשות הרבים אינו למעלה מעשרה, כדאמרי' במס' שבת (דף ז. ח.). **הני מילי.** דהוי כמונח לארץ – לענין שבת. **אבל.** אם היה חצר של אשה, וקנה נעוץ גבוה מן המחיצות – אינה מגורשת, שאין סופו לנוח לארץ, דרמי ליה זיקא חוץ למחיצות. **וטעמא דגיטא** – משום חצר המשתמרת הוא, דומיא דידה, והא לא מינטר. והא

היתה עומדת בראש הגג. לרבי הושעיא דאמר לעיל: אפילו היא בטבריא וחצרה בציפורי – האי עומדת היינו: כמי שעומדת, כלומר כגון שמשתמרת, כדמשני לעיל אעומדת בתוך ביתה או בתוך חצרה. אי נמי: נקט עומדת לאשמועינן דבגג דידה מיירי, שעומדת ברשותה, כדמוקי לה בגמרא.

כגון שהיו מחיצות התחתונות עודפו' על העליונות. דמיד שיצא מרשות גג נכנס לרשות חצר. וא"ת: ומה מועיל דעודפות? מ"מ כשזרקו מעל המעקה לא מנטר כנגד הגג! וי"ל: דכיון דשלש מחיצות עודפות – חשיב משתמר, ואין לחוש למחיצה רביעית. אי נמי: כשהגג קצר, וחצר רחב הרבה ועודפות המחיצות גם רביעית, מצד זה ומצד זה, וכנגד המעקה אינו כי אם פתח בעלמא. אי נמי: כשהגג עומד באמצע החצר ולא מן הצד, ומחיצות החצר מוקפות לו מכל צד. וא"ת: דאמרינן ב"מרובה" (ב"ק דף ע:) באומר "זרוק גניבתך לחצרי ותיקני לי חצרי גניבתך", דאיסור שבת ואיסור גניבה באין כאחד, והיכי באין כאחד? והא לענין שבת מיחייב אפילו למעלה מן המחיצות, עד שלא נכנס עדיין תוך המחיצות, דרה"י עולה עד לרקיע, ולענין קנין – עד דמטי לתוך המחיצות! וי"ל: דמיירי כשזורק דרך פתח, ולא מעל המחיצות. **כמאן** כרבי דאמר קלוטה כמי שהונחה דמיא. תימה: דנקט רבי, דלא איירי אלא ברשות היחיד מקורה, משום דבית כמאן דמליא דמיא, כדאמרינן בריש שבת (דף ה.). ודר"ע הוה ליה למינקט, דאית ליה קלוטה כמי שהונחה דמיא אפילו ברה"ר! ונראה: דהשתא סלקא דעתין דטעמא דרבי לאו משום קירוי, אלא משום מחיצה אית ליה, דכמאן דמליא דמיא. ולהכי קאמר: כמאן – כרבי, דכר"ע לא מיתוקמא, מדמצרכת מחיצות החיצונות עודפות, ולר"ע אית ליה דכמי שהונחה דמיא אפילו ברה"ר. אלא ודאי כרבי מוקמת לה. ומשני: אפילו תימא רבנן כו'. ולפי זה יכול להיות טעמא דרבי משום קירוי, כדאמרינן בשבת*).

דרך עלייה אינה מגורשת מ"ט מעיקרא לא למינח קאי. ולא דמי להא דבעי רבא בפ"ק דב"מ (דף יב.): זרק ארנקי בפתח זה ויצא בפתח אחרת מהו? אויר שאין סופו לנוח כמונח דמי, או לא. הכא, דבדרך עלייה – אין דומה כל כך שיהא עומד לנוח. אי נמי: התם בבית מקורה – דומה יותר עומד לנוח. והא

כט א מיי' פ"ה מהל' גירושין הל' ג סמג עשין נ טוש"ע אה"ע סימן קלט סעיף ד:
ל ב מיי' שם הלכה ד טוש"ע שם סעיף ו:
לא ג ד מיי' שם הלכה ג טוש"ע שם סעי' ד:
לב ה ו מיי' שם טוש"ע שם סעיף ו:
לג ז ח מיי' שם טוש"ע שם סעיף ד:
לד ט מיי' שם הלכה ד טוש"ע שם סעיף ו:
לה י מיי' פי"ד מהל' שבת הלכה יז סמג לאוין סה טוש"ע א"ח סימן שמה סעיף ה:
לו כ מיי' פ"ה מהלכות גירושין הלכה ו סמג עשין נ טוש"ע אה"ע סימן קלט סעיף ז:

תוספות רי"ד

שנה בקרקע: היתה עומדת על ראש הגג וכו' והא לא מינטר פי' א) דאפילו דיקא ואמרת ליה לבראי ואמאי קתני כיון שהגיע לאויר הגג ואע"ג דלא נח אם נשרף או נמחק היא מגורשת אמר רב יהודה אמר שמואל בגג שיש לו מעקה עסקינן עולא בר מנשה משמיה דאבימי אמר הכא בפחות מג' סמוך לגג עסקינן וכל פחות מג' סמוך לגג כגג דמי: הוא מלמעלה וכו' פי' רישא בגג דידה וחצר דידיה סיפא בגג דידיה וחצר דידה: והא לא מינטר פירוש דקס"ד שהגג גבוה מחומות החצר דאתי זיקא ושדי ליה לבראי והיכי תני כיון שיצא מרשות הגג ונמחק או נשרף קודם שינוח באויר החצר הרי זו מגורשת אמר רב יהודה אמר שמואל כגון שהיו מחיצות התחתונות עודפות על העליונות וכי נפיק מאויר הגג מיד מגיע לתוך מחיצות החצר:

א) נ"ל פי' דאתי זיקא ושדי ליה לבראי וכו'.

*) [ועי' תוספות שבת ה. ד"ה לא וב"ק ע: ד"ה כמאן]

לז א מיי' פ"ה מהל' גירושין הלכה יא סמג עשין נ טוש"ע אה"ע סי' קלט סעי' יב:

לח ב ג מיי' שם הלכה ו ז טוש"ע שם סעיף ט:

לט ד ה ו מיי' שם פ"ג הלכה ה סמג שם טוש"ע אה"ע סימן קמח סעיף א:

וְהָא דְּאָמַר רַב יְהוּדָה אָמַר שְׁמוּאֵל: לֹא יַעֲמוֹד אָדָם בְּגַג זֶה וְיִקְלוֹט מֵי גְשָׁמִים מִגַּגּוֹ שֶׁל חֲבֵירוֹ, שֶׁכְּשֵׁם שֶׁדָּיוֹרִין חֲלוּקִין מִלְּמַטָּה כָּךְ דָּיוֹרִין חֲלוּקִין מִלְמַעְלָה, הָנֵי מִילֵּי לְעִנְיַן שַׁבָּת, [א]אֲבָל לְעִנְיַן גֵּט — מִשּׁוּם קְפֵידָא הוּא, וְכוּלֵּי הַאי לָא קָפְדִי אֱינָשֵׁי. *אָמַר אַבָּיֵי: [ב]שְׁתֵּי חֲצֵרוֹת זוֹ לִפְנִים מִזּוֹ, פְּנִימִית שֶׁלָּהּ וְחִיצוֹנָה שֶׁלּוֹ, וּמְחִיצוֹת הַחִיצוֹנוֹת עוֹדְפוֹת עַל הַפְּנִימִיּוֹת, וּזְרָקוֹ לָהּ, כֵּיוָן שֶׁהִגִּיעַ לַאֲוִיר מְחִיצוֹת הַחִיצוֹנָה — הֲרֵי זוֹ מְגוֹרֶשֶׁת, מַאי טַעְמָא? פְּנִימִית גּוּפָהּ בִּמְחִיצוֹת הַחִיצוֹנָה קָא מִינַּטְרָה; מַה שֶּׁאֵין כֵּן בְּקוּפּוֹת, שְׁתֵּי קוּפּוֹת זוֹ בְּתוֹךְ זוֹ, פְּנִימִית שֶׁלָּהּ וְחִיצוֹנָה שֶׁלּוֹ, וּזְרָקוֹ לָהּ, אֲפִילּוּ הִגִּיעַ לַאֲוִיר פְּנִימִית — אֵינָהּ מְגוֹרֶשֶׁת; מַאי טַעְמָא? דְּהָא לָא נָח. [ג]וְכִי נָח מַאי הָוֵי? *כֵּלָיו שֶׁל לוֹקֵחַ בִּרְשׁוּת מוֹכֵר הוּא! הָכָא בְּמַאי עָסְקִינַן — בְּקוּפָּה שֶׁאֵין לָהּ שׁוּלַיִים.§ **מתני'** *ב"ש אוֹמְרִים: פּוֹטֵר אָדָם אִשְׁתּוֹ בְּגֵט יָשָׁן, וּבֵית הִלֵּל [ד]אוֹסְרִין. וְאֵיזֶהוּ גֵּט יָשָׁן? כָּל שֶׁנִּתְיַיחֵד עִמָּהּ מֵאַחַר שֶׁכְּתָבוֹ לָהּ.§ **גמ'** בְּמַאי קָמִיפַּלְגִי? ב"ש סָבְרִי, לָא אָמְרִינַן: גְּזֵירָה שֶׁמָּא יֹאמְרוּ גִּיטָּהּ קוֹדֵם לִבְנָהּ; וּב"ה סָבְרִי, אָמְרִי': [ה]גְּזֵירָה *שֶׁמָּא יֹאמְרוּ גִּיטָּהּ קוֹדֵם לִבְנָהּ. א"ר אַבָּא אָמַר שְׁמוּאֵל: אִם נִישֵּׂאת — לֹא תֵּצֵא. וְא"ד, אָמַר רַבִּי אַבָּא אָמַר שְׁמוּאֵל: [ו]*אִם נִתְגָּרְשָׁה — תִּינָּשֵׂא לְכַתְּחִלָּה.§ **מתני'** *כָּתַב לְשׁוּם מַלְכוּת שֶׁאֵינָהּ הוֹגֶנֶת, לְשׁוּם מַלְכוּת מָדַי, לְשׁוּם מַלְכוּת יָוָן, לְבִנְיַן הַבַּיִת, לְחוּרְבַּן הַבַּיִת, *הָיָה בַּמִּזְרָח וְכָתַב בַּמַּעֲרָב, בַּמַּעֲרָב וְכָתַב בַּמִּזְרָח — תֵּצֵא מִזֶּה וּמִזֶּה, וּצְרִיכָה גֵּט מִזֶּה וּמִזֶּה; וְאֵין לָהּ לֹא כְּתוּבָּה וְלֹא פֵּירוֹת וְלֹא מְזוֹנוֹת וְלֹא בְּלָאוֹת לֹא עַל זֶה וְלֹא עַל זֶה, אִם נָטְלָה מִזֶּה וּמִזֶּה — תַּחֲזִיר; וְהַוָּלָד מַמְזֵר מִזֶּה וּמִזֶּה; וְלֹא זֶה וְזֶה מִטַּמְּאִין לָהּ, וְלֹא זֶה וְזֶה זַכָּאִין לֹא בִּמְצִיאָתָהּ וְלֹא בְּמַעֲשֵׂה יָדֶיהָ וְלֹא בַּהֲפָרַת נְדָרֶיהָ; הָיְתָה בַּת יִשְׂרָאֵל — נִפְסֶלֶת מִן הַכְּהוּנָּה,

וְהָא דְּאָמַר רַב יְהוּדָה לֹא יַעֲמוֹד אָדָם עַל גַּגּוֹ וְיִקְלוֹט מֵי גְשָׁמִים. הַנּוֹפְלִין עַל גַּגּוֹ שֶׁל חֲבֵירוֹ, דְּהָוֵי מוֹצִיא מֵרְשׁוּת לִרְשׁוּת אִם לֹא עֵירְבוּ. שֶׁאַע"פ שֶׁאֵינָם דָּרִים עַל הַגַּגּוֹת — שַׁיָּיךְ נַמִי בְּהוּ אִיסּוּר חִילּוּק רְשׁוּת. הָנֵי מִילֵּי. דַּחֲלוּקַת רְשׁוּיוֹת גַּגִּין כִּרְשׁוּיוֹת בָּתִּים לְעִנְיַן שַׁבָּת. אֲבָל בְּגִיטִּין. הָיוּ לוֹ שְׁנֵי גַגִּין סְמוּכִין זֶה לָזֶה, וְהִשְׁאִילָהּ מָקוֹם בָּזֶה לְקַבֵּל אֶת גִּיטָּהּ, וְקִיבְּלַתּוּ בָּזֶה — לָא אָמְרִינַן הָכָא רְשׁוּיוֹת חֲלוּקוֹת. דְּהָא דַּאֲמַרַן לְעֵיל: תְּרֵי מְקוֹמוֹת לָא מוֹשְׁלֵי אֱינָשֵׁי — מִשּׁוּם קְפֵידָא הוּא, יֵשׁ מַשְׁאִיל חֲצֵרוֹ וּמַקְפִּיד עַל בֵּיתוֹ. אֲבָל כּוּלֵּי הַאי גַּגִּין סְמוּכִין, וְאֵין תַּשְׁמִישׁ רָגִיל בָּהֶן — לָא קָפְדִי אֱינָשֵׁי. בִּמְחִיצוֹת הַחִיצוֹנָה קָא מִינַּטְרָה. רְגִילָה לְהִשְׁתַּמֵּר. הִלְכָּךְ מְשׁוּעְבָּדוֹת הֵן לָהּ, וְקָנוּ לָהּ. דְּהָא לָא נָח. וְאֵין מְחִיצּוֹת כְּלֵי עֲשׂוּיִין לְאַוֵּירָן לִשְׁמוֹר, דְּאֵין כְּלֵי עָשׂוּי אֶלָּא לְהַנִּיחַ בְּתוֹכוֹ. ה"ג: וְכִי נָח מַאי הָוֵי כו'. שֶׁאֵין לָהּ שׁוּלַיִים. פוּנ"ץ, דִּפְנִימִית מוּנַּחַת ע"ג קַרְקַע. גִּיטָּהּ קוֹדֵם לִבְנָהּ. שֶׁמָּא יַשְׁהֶה אֶת הַגֵּט שְׁנָתַיִם וְשָׁלֹשׁ בֵּין כְּתִיבָה לִנְתִינָה, וְיִהְיוּ לָהּ בָּנִים מִמֶּנּוּ בְּתוֹךְ הַזְּמַן, וְאַחַר כָּךְ יְגָרְשֶׁנָּה בּוֹ. וּלְיָמִים כְּשֶׁיִּשְׁתַּכַּח הַדָּבָר, יִרְאוּ זְמַן הַגֵּט קוֹדֵם לְלֵידַת הַבֵּן, וִיהוּ סְבוּרִין שֶׁנִּיתַּן לָהּ מִשְּׁעַת כְּתִיבָה, וְיֹאמְרוּ: מִן הַפְּנוּיָה נוֹלַד, מִשֶּׁגֵּירְשָׁהּ, וְהָוֵי פְּגָם. אִם נִתְגָּרְשָׁה. בְּגֵט יָשָׁן, וְהָלַךְ בַּעְלָהּ לְמדה"י — תִּינָּשֵׂא לְכַתְּחִלָּה. **מתני'** כָּתַב לְשֵׁם מַלְכוּת שֶׁאֵינָהּ הוֹגֶנֶת. מִי שֶׁהָיָה בְּבָבֶל וְכָתַב: בִּשְׁנַת כָּךְ וְכָךְ לְמַלְכוּת אַחֶרֶת. וּבַגְּמָרָא מְפָרֵשׁ אַמַּאי קָרֵי לָהּ שֶׁאֵינָהּ הוֹגֶנֶת. אוֹ שֶׁכָּתַב לְשֵׁם מָדַי כו' — לְפִי שֶׁצָּרִיךְ לִכְתּוֹב לְשֵׁם מַלְכוּת שֶׁנִּכְתַּב בָּהּ, כִּדְמְפָרֵשׁ בַּגְּמָ'. אוֹ שֶׁכְּתָבָהּ לְבִנְיַן הַבַּיִת אוֹ לְחוּרְבָּנוֹ פָּסוּל. מִפְּנֵי שֶׁלֹּא כָּתַב לְשֵׁם הַמַּלְכוּת. תֵּצֵא מִזֶּה וּמִזֶּה. אִם נִיסֵּת בְּגֵט זֶה — תֵּצֵא מִן הָרִאשׁוֹן וּמִן הַשֵּׁנִי, וּצְרִיכָה גֵּט שֵׁנִי מִן הָרִאשׁוֹן וְגֵט מִן הַשֵּׁנִי. וְאַע"פ שֶׁקִּדּוּשֵׁי שֵׁנִי לָא הָווּ קִדּוּשִׁין. וּבִיבָמוֹת (פח.) מְפָ' טַעְמָא: גְּזֵירָה שֶׁמָּא יֹאמְרוּ גֵּירֵשׁ רִאשׁוֹן גֵּט גָּמוּר, וְנָשָׂא שֵׁנִי, וְנִמְצֵאת אֵשֶׁת אִישׁ יוֹצְאָה בְּלֹא גֵּט. וְלֹא פֵּירוֹת. דִּין פֵּירוֹת שֶׁתִּקְּנוּ לָהּ לָאִשָּׁה, פִּירְקוֹנָהּ מִשִּׁבְיָהּ תַּחַת פֵּירוֹת, וְעַל אֵלּוּ אֵין לָהּ כְּלוּם. וְלֹא בְּלָאוֹת. הַקַּיָּימִים מִבְּגָדִים שֶׁהִכְנִיסָהּ לוֹ. וּקְנָסָא הוּא דְּקָנְסוּהָ, כִּדְמְפָ' בִּיבָמוֹת (צא.) דְּאִיבָּעֵי לָהּ אַקְרוּיֵיהּ לְגִיטָּא. וְהַוָּלָד מַמְזֵר מִזֶּה וּמִזֶּה. אִם הֶחֱזִירָהּ הָרִאשׁוֹן וְיָלְדָה לוֹ בֵּן — הָוֵי מַמְזֵר מִדְּרַבָּנַן. וּבִיבָמוֹת (פט.) אָמְרִינַן דְּאָסוּר בְּמַמְזֶרֶת, הוֹאִיל וְכָשֵׁר מִן הַתּוֹרָה. מִטַּמְּאִין לָהּ. אִם כֹּהֲנִים הֵם. נִפְסֶלֶת מִן הַכְּהוּנָּה. דְּזוֹנָה הִיא, דִּסְתָם זוֹנָה הַיְינוּ אֵשֶׁת אִישׁ שֶׁמְּזַנָּה תַּחַת בַּעְלָהּ לַאֲחֵרִים, דְּהַיְינוּ נָפְקָא בָּרָא.

בַּת

והא דאמר רב יהודה אמר שמואל לא יעמוד אדם בגג זה כו'. וא"ת: והא שמואל פסיק כר"ש, דאמר גגין רשות אחד הן, בפ' "כל גגות" (עירובין דף צא.)! וי"ל: דהכא להוליך מגג לבית קאמר. וא"ת: א"כ אמאי נקט מגגו של חבירו? אפי' מגג של עצמו לא יקלוט להוליך לביתו, לפי שגגו נפרץ לגג של חבירו שהוא אסור לו! וי"ל: דשמואל סבר התם דאפי' במחיצות שאינן ניכרות אמרינן גוד אסיק מחיצות הבית למעלה, ומותר לטלטל מגג לבית. ומיהו, אנן כרב קי"ל, דמצריך מחיצות ניכרות. ומיהו, לישנא ד"כשם שדיורין חלוקין למטה" כו' — משמע דמגג לגג קאמר. ושמא שמואל נמי נקט מילתיה ככולי עלמא, לרבנן מגג לגג, לר"ש מגג לבית. וא"ת: מאי קמ"ל שמואל? מתני' היא ברים פ' "כל גגות" (שם דף פט:)! וי"ל: קמ"ל אפילו קליטת גשמים שלא נחו בגגו של חבירו, ואפ"ה דיורין חלוקין, למר כדאית ליה ולמר כדאית ליה. והכי הוה מצי לאיתויי מתני', אלא דניחא ליה לאיתויי מילתא דשמואל*. **פנימית** גופה במחיצות החיצונות מינטרה. מה שפירש בקונט': שמחיצות החיצונות משועבדות לפנימיות — לאו דוקא משועבדות, דא"כ אדמפליג בין חצרות לקופות — ליפלוג בחצרות גופייהו בין משועבדות לשאינם משועבדות. אלא טעמא: כיון שהמחיצות החיצונות קבועות, ועתידות לישאר שם — חשיבא פנימית מינטרא בהו. ומיירי כשמחיצות החיצונות מפסיקות בין חיצונה לפנימית. דאי אין מפסיקות, כשהגיע הגט לאויר פנימית ולא נכנס תוך מחיצות — אמאי מגורשת? הא אינו משתמר מפני בני חיצונה, וא"כ לא חשיב חצר המשתמרת, כדפריך גבי עובדא דר"ג וזקנים בב"מ (דף יא:): וכי בצד שדהו היו עומדין? אע"פ שהתבואה היתה בביתו של ר"ג שהיה משתמר, כדמוכח בירושלמי, שכבר היה בבית — מ"מ לא הויא משתמרת, לגבי זקנים, מפני בני ביתו של ר"ג. ועוד י"ל: דמיירי שפיר באין מחיצות החיצונות מפסיקות, ומיירי שהאשה עומדת בצד חצרה, הלכך הוי חצר המשתמרת ע"י מחיצות החיצונות, דלא לישדיא זיקא לרה"ר. אבל גבי זקנים — לא היו מועילין מחיצות בית של ר"ג כיון שהזקנים לא היו עומדין בצד הבית. והא דאמרינן בשלהי "השואל" (שם דף קב.) דהזבל של בעל הבית, פי': של משכיר, בתורי דאתו ליה מעלמא, דקנתה לו חצרו אע"פ שאינה משתמרת מן *השוכר — י"ל: דמיירי שיש גם למשכיר בית באותו חצר, דהוי עומד בצד חצרו. אי נמי: שוכר הוי כמו שומר, ושלוחו של משכיר*. **דהא** לא נח. פי' בקונטרס: ואין מחיצות של כלי עשויות אלא להניח בתוכן. משמע מפירושו דאויר כלי אינו קונה. ואין נראה דבפרק בתרא דע"ז (דף עב:) אמר גבי יין נסך: מכי מטא לאוירא דמנא — קנייה, יין נסך לא הוי עד דמטא לארעיה דמנא. משמע דאויר כלי קונה! אלא נראה דהכי פירושו: דהא לא נח באויר כלי. אבל גבי חצרות, אע"ג דלא נח תוך מחיצות הפנימיות, כיון שהוא תוך מחיצות החיצונה — מגורשת, כיון דמחיצות החיצונות הם קבועות, כדפירשנו לעיל. וגרסי' גבי חצרות: כיון שהגיע לאויר מחיצות הפנימית, פירוש: כנגד הפנימי, למעלה ממחיצותיה, ותוך מחיצות חיצונה. וגבי קופות גרסי': אפילו הגיע לאויר פנימית, פירוש: ולמעלה ממחיצותיה, דאי הוה בתוך חלל קופה הפנימית — הויא מגורשת, כדפרישית. ואית ספרים דגרסי גבי חצרות: כיון שהגיע לאויר מחיצה חיצונה. ולפי גירסא זו, כיון דגבי קופות נקט פנימית — הוי משמע אפילו מונח בחלל פנימית אינה מגורשת עד שינוח בשוליו, כדפי' בקונט'. ולא יתכן, דאויר כלי קונה, כדפרישית. **ב"ש** סברי לא אמרינן גזרה שמא יאמרו גיטה קודם לבנה. בירושל' מפרש דאזלי לטעמייהו, דב"ש אית להו בפ' "המגרש" (לקמן דף צ.): לא יגרש אדם את אשתו אא"כ מצא בה דבר ערוה, הלכך מזוהמת היא בעיניו, ואינו בא עליה. וב"ה אית להו אפילו הקדיחתו תבשילו יכול לגרשה, ואינה מזוהמת בעיניו, ויאמרו כי בא עליה. וכי האי גוונא פליגי לקמן (דף פא.) במגרש ולנה עמו בפונדקי, למאן דמוקי לה בלא ראוה שנבעלה. **כתב** לשם מלכות שאינה הוגנת. אומר רבינו אלחנן: דלהכי קרי לה "שאינה הוגנת" — לאשמועינן דאע"פ שאין לה לא כתב ולא לשון, אף על פי כן מתקנאין בה.

ולא בלאות. פירש בקונטרס: בלאותיה קיימים. ואין נראה, דבהדיא אמרינן בסוף פרק "אלמנה ניזונית" (כתובות דף קא.): זינתה — לא הפסידה בלאותיה קיימין. אלא בשאין קיימין איירי הכא. **וצריכה** גט מזה ומזה. פי' בקונטרס: אע"פ שקדושי השני לא היו קדושין, כדמפרש ביבמות (דף פח:): גזרה שמא יאמרו גירש ראשון גט גמור, ונשא שני, ונמצאת אשת איש יוצאה בלא גט. ואינו נראה לה"ר יוסף: דהתם ודאי היא אשת ראשון אינה מקודשת לשני, אבל הכא מה"ת צריכה גט משני, שהרי גט גמור היה אותו שגירש בו ראשון, ואינו פסול אלא מדרבנן.

שינה

תוספות רי"ד

מתני' בש"א פוטר אדם את אשתו בגט ישן וב"ה אוסרים איזהו גט ישן כל שנתיחד עמה מאחר שכתבו לה. במאי קמיפלגי ב"ש סברי לא אמרינן גזירה שמא יאמרו גיטה קודם לבנה וב"ה סוברים אמרינן גזירה שמא יאמרו גיטה קודם לבנה. פי' שנתיחד עמה לאחר שכתבו לה גזרינן שמא תתעבר ואם יגרשנה בגט זה שזמנו קודם לעיבורה יאמרו העולם בראותן זמן גיטה קודם כי מאז נתגרשה וכשבא עליה גרושתו היתה ובעילתו היתה בעילת זנות ומזונות נולד הבן הזה: אמר ר' אבא אמר שמואל ואם נשאת לא תצא איכא דאמרי אמר ר' אבא אמר שמואל אם נתגרשה בו תינשא לכתחלה פי' דגט כשר הוא שאפילו נתיחד עמה עכשיו כשמוסר לה הגט עוקר כל קדושין הראשונים ואינה צריכה גט אחר ומפני חששא זו אין מצריכין אותה גט אחר (דאפילו איתמר כדבריהם הולד כשר): **מתני'** כתב לשם מלכות שאינה הוגנת לשם מלכות מדי לשם מלכות יון לבנין הבית לחרבן הבית היה במזרח וכתב במערב במערב וכתב במזרח תצא מזה ומזה וצריכה גט מזה ומזה [א]אין לה כתובה ולא פירות ולא מזונות ולא בלאות על זה ועל זה ואם נטלה מזה ומזה תחזיר והולד ממזר מזה ומזה לא זה וזה מטמאין לה ולא זה וזה זכאין במציאתה ולא במעשה ידיה ולא בהפרת נדריה היתה בת ישראל פסלה מן הכהונה בת לוי מן המעשר בת כהן מן התרומה אין יורשיו של זה ויורשיו של זה יורשין כתובתה מתו אחיו של זה ואחיו של זה חולצין ולא מיבמין שינה שמו ושמה שם עירו ושם עירה תצא מזה ומזה וכל הדרכים האלו בה [א] אם היה בדרך וכתב הגט בשנת כך וכך למלכות פרס ולא שם המלך המולך: ואמאי קרי לה מלכות שאינה הוגנת שאין לה לא כתב ולא לשון אלא מאומה אחרת לקחו והיינו דכתיב בזוי אתה מאד

[א] נראה דל"ל כתב לשם מלכות כו' פי' אם היה בדרך.

שאין

(עירובין כ.)

[לעיל עח.]

עדיות פ"ד מ"ז [לקמן פו.]

[לעיל כו:]

[לקמן פו.] יבמות לא:

גליון הש"ס

גמ' אם נתגרשה תינשא לכתחלה. עיין יבמות דף יד ע"ב תוספות ד"ה בגט ישן.

[ועיין היטב תוס' עירובין ...]

[פי' תוספות יבמות לא: ד"ה היה במזרח וכו' ועוד בתוספות לקמן פ. ד"ה כין]

לא. ד"ה ושמואל [נ"ל המשכיר]

[ועיין תוספות ב"מ יא: ד"ה וכי בצד]

בַּת לֵוִי — מִן הַמַּעֲשֵׂר, בַּת כֹּהֵן — מִן הַתְּרוּמָה; וְאֵין יוֹרְשִׁין שֶׁל זֶה וְיוֹרְשִׁין שֶׁל זֶה יוֹרְשִׁים כְּתוּבָּתָהּ; וְאִם מֵתוּ — אָחִיו שֶׁל זֶה וְאָחִיו שֶׁל זֶה חוֹלְצִין וְלֹא מְיַיבְּמִין. *אשִׁינָּה שְׁמוֹ וּשְׁמָהּ, שֵׁם עִירוֹ וְשֵׁם עִירָהּ — תֵּצֵא מִזֶּה וּמִזֶּה, וְכָל הַדְּרָכִים הָאֵלּוּ בָּהּ. *כָּל עֲרָיוֹת שֶׁאָמְרוּ צָרוֹתֵיהֶן מוּתָּרוֹת, הָלְכוּ הַצָּרוֹת הָאֵלּוּ וְנִישְּׂאוּ וְנִמְצְאוּ אֵלּוּ אַיְילוֹנִית — תֵּצֵא מִזֶּה וּמִזֶּה, וְכָל הַדְּרָכִים הָאֵלּוּ בָּהּ. *הַכּוֹנֵס אֶת יְבִמְתּוֹ, וְהָלְכָה צָרָתָהּ וְנִישֵּׂאת לְאַחֵר, וְנִמְצֵאת זוֹ שֶׁהָיְתָה אַיְילוֹנִית — תֵּצֵא מִזֶּה וּמִזֶּה, וְכָל הַדְּרָכִים הָאֵלּוּ בָּהּ. *כָּתַב *סוֹפֵר גֵּט לָאִישׁ וְשׁוֹבֵר לָאִשָּׁה, וְטָעָה וְנָתַן גֵּט לָאִשָּׁה וְשׁוֹבֵר לָאִישׁ וְנָתְנוּ זֶה לָזֶה, וּלְאַחַר זְמַן הֲרֵי הַגֵּט יוֹצֵא מִיַּד הָאִישׁ וְשׁוֹבֵר מִיַּד הָאִשָּׁה — תֵּצֵא מִזֶּה וּמִזֶּה, וְכָל הַדְּרָכִים הָאֵלּוּ בָּהּ; רַבִּי *אֱלִיעֶזֶר אוֹמֵר: באִם לְאַלְתַּר יָצָא — אֵין זֶה גֵּט, אִם לְאַחַר זְמַן יָצָא — הֲרֵי זֶה גֵּט; לֹא כָּל הֵימֶנּוּ מִן הָרִאשׁוֹן לְאַבֵּד זְכוּתוֹ שֶׁל שֵׁנִי.§

גמ' מַאי מַלְכוּת שֶׁאֵינָהּ הוֹגֶנֶת? מַלְכוּת הָרוֹמִיִּים. וְאַמַּאי קָרֵי לָהּ מַלְכוּת שֶׁאֵינָהּ הוֹגֶנֶת? מִשּׁוּם דְּאֵין לָהֶם לֹא כְּתָב וְלֹא לָשׁוֹן. אָמַר עוּלָּא: מִפְּנֵי מָה תִּקְּנוּ מַלְכוּת בְּגִיטִּין? גמִשּׁוּם שְׁלוֹם מַלְכוּת. וּמִשּׁוּם שְׁלוֹם מַלְכוּת תֵּצֵא וְהַוָּלָד מַמְזֵר?! אִין, ר"מ לְטַעֲמֵיהּ, *דְּא"ר הַמְנוּנָא מִשְּׁמֵיהּ דְּעוּלָּא, אוֹמֵר הָיָה ר"מ: כָּל הַמְשַׁנֶּה מִמַּטְבֵּעַ שֶׁטָּבְעוּ חֲכָמִים בְּגִיטִּין — *הַוָּלָד מַמְזֵר.§ "לְשׁוּם מַלְכוּת יָוָן".§ וּצְרִיכָא; דְּאִי אַשְׁמוּעִינַן מַלְכוּת שֶׁאֵינָהּ הוֹגֶנֶת, מִשּׁוּם דְּמַלִּיכָא, אֲבָל מַלְכוּת מָדַי וּמַלְכוּת יָוָן — מַאי דַּהֲוָה הֲוָה; וְאִי אַשְׁמַעִי' מַלְכוּת מָדַי וּמַלְכוּת יָוָן, מִשּׁוּם דְּמַלְכוּתָא הָווּ, אֲבָל בִּנְיַן הַבַּיִת — מַאי דַּהֲוָה הֲוָה; וְאִי אַשְׁמוּעִינַן בִּנְיַן הַבַּיִת, דְּאָמְרִי: קָמַדְכְּרִי שִׁבְחַיְיהוּ, אֲבָל חוּרְבַּן הַבַּיִת דְּצַעֲרָא הוּא — אֵימָא לָא, צְרִיכָא.§ ד"הָיָה בַּמִּזְרָח וְכָתַב בַּמַּעֲרָב".§ מַאן? אִילֵימָא בַּעַל, הַיְינוּ שִׁינָּה שְׁמוֹ וּשְׁמָהּ, שֵׁם עִירוֹ וְשֵׁם עִירָהּ! האֶלָּא *לָאו, סוֹפֵר, *כִּדְאָמַר לְהוּ רַב לְסָפְרֵיהּ, וְכֵן אֲמַר לְהוּ רַב הוּנָא לְסָפְרֵיהּ: וכִּי יָתְבִיתוּ בְּשִׁילֵי כְּתוּבוּ בְּשִׁילֵי, וְאע"ג דְּמִימְסְרָן לְכוּ מִילֵּי בְּהִינֵי, וְכִי יָתְבִיתוּ בְּהִינֵי כְּתוּבוּ בְּהִינֵי, וְאע"ג דְּמִימְסְרָן לְכוּ מִילֵּי בְּשִׁילֵי. אָמַר רַב יְהוּדָה אָמַר שְׁמוּאֵל:
זו

[ב"ב קעב. יבמות קטז.]

רש"י

בת לוי מן המעשר. קנסא הוא, כדמפרש התם (יבמות צא.). מן התרומה. כדאמרי' בסוטה (דף כח.) מ"ונטמאה" "ונטמאה" ג"פ, אחד – לבעל, ואחד – לבועל, ואחד – לתרומה. ואין יורשין של זה. בנים שהיו לה ממנו. יורשין כתובתה. ביבמות (דף צא.) פרכינן: כתובה מאי עבידתה? הא קתני: אין לה כתובה! ומשני: כתובת בנין דיכרין, שתקנו חכמים שירשו בניה יתר על חולקיהון דעם אחוהון כשמתה בחיי בעלה, ואע"פ שבעלה יורשה – הכא לא שקלי, דקנסא קנסו. אחיו. של שני חולץ מדרבנן, כדפירשנו גבי גט, שמא יאמרו גירש זה ונשא זה. ואחיו של ראשון צריך לחלוץ מן התורה. ולא מייבמין. משום קנסא. שינה שמו ושמה. בגט. וכל הדרכים. המפורשים למעלה במשנתינו. כל עריות שאמרו צרותיהן מותרות. חמש עשרה עריות שאמרו חכמים שצרותיהן מותרות ליבא לשוק בלא חליצה, כשמתו בעליהן בלא בנים. הלכו הצרות. של עריות. ונישאו. לשוק. ונמצאו. העריות איילונית, ואיגלאי מילתא שהיו קדושי המת בטעות, ונמצאו שלא היו אלו צרותיהן, ולא פטרום העריות האלו מן החליצה. תצא מזה. מבעל שנישאת לו. ומזה. מן היבם. וכל הדרכים האלו בה. וביבמות (דף נב.) מוקמינן לה כר"ע, דאמר: יש ממזר מחייבי לאוין. והלכה צרתה ונישאת לאחר. וקיי"ל: ביאת האחת פוטרת צרתה. ונמצאת. זו שנתייבמה. איילונית. ואין לה יבומים, שהרי לא אשת המת היתה, ונמצא שלא נפטרה צרתה, ונישאת לשוק בלא חליצה. תצא מזה ומזה. מבעל זה ומיבמה הראשון. כתב סופר. אחד גט לאיש לגרש בו אשתו. ושובר. לאשתו, שתמסור לבעל כשיפרע לה כתובתה. וטעה הסופר כשמסר להן השטרות, ונתן גט לאשה ושובר לאיש, והם מסרו זה לזה. והלכה זו ונישאת, כסבורה שזה גט שמסר לה בעלה, וזה סבור שמסרה לו אשתו שובר. יוצא מתחת ידי האיש. שמוציאו לפנינו להראות שוברו – והרי הוא גט. אם לאלתר. בגמ' מפרש. לא כל הימנו. אין הכל כדבריו להאמינו. לאבד זכותו של שני. שנשאה, דאמרי': קנוניא היא ביניהם והחליפו השטרות לאחר שניסת.

גמ' שאין להם לא כתב ולא לשון. אלא משל אומה אחרת. משום שלום מלכות. שיהא לנו שלום עמהם, שיאמרו: חשובים אנו בעיניהם שכותבים שטרותיהם בשמינו. יוציא והולד ממזר. בתמיה. ר"מ לטעמיה. סתם משנה. ולקמן נמי אמרינן: זו דברי ר"מ. משום דמליכא. עכשיו היא מולכת, לפיכך יתקנא בה המלך של מלכות זו, ויקפיד עמנו. מאי דהוה הוה. כבר עברו, ואבדה קנאתם, שאין מתקנא בהן. דהא דקתני מתני': "לשום מלכות מדי ויון" – שמונה למנין שהתחילה מדי למלוך בימי דריוש, או למנין שהתחילה יון למלוך. דאיכא שם מלכות. הלכך חיישינן דלמא קפיד המלך הזה. כי יתביתו בהיני. לכתוב שטר. כתבו. בתוכו שבהיני נכתב, ואף על גב דמימסרן כו'.
זו

[יבמות נא:]
שם
שם
שם
[עי' תוס' ע"ב ד"ה כתב]
[בסדר המשנה וברי"ף ורמב"ם איתא אליעזר]
לעיל ה: [ב"מ נה:]
[לעיל ה: ובב"מ נה: איתא יוצא והולד ממזר]
[תיבת לאו משולל הבנה ויוקן הגירסא לאו כרש"ש אלא אסופר כדאמר להו רב וכו' ובתוס' יבמות לה: ד"ה הוה וכו' העתיקו אלא סופר]

תוספות

שינה שמו ושמה כו'. לא שינה ממש, כדאמר *בפ"ב (דף כ) וכן שם עירו ושם עירה – לא ששינה ממש, אלא שיש לאותה העיר שני שמות בשני מקומות. **ושם** עירו ושם עירה. אומר ר' יצחק: דהיינו דווקא עיר שדרין בה, אבל עיר שנולד בה – אפי' שינה כשר, כיון שא"צ לכותבו כלל. שהקדמונים שהרגילו לכותבו – משום שאם יארע שיש שם יוסף בן שמעון אחר יהיה בו סימן ע"י מקום לידה. ותדע, כי כמה פעמים כותבים מקום הלידה על פי הבעל או האשה, ואם שינה פסול – לא היה נכון לכותבו אלא ע"פ עדים. ולא דמי לאשתמודעינהו, דאפי' מפי קרוב או אשה נאמן, ב"החולץ" (יבמות דף לט:) – דשם קל הדבר לברר, ועביד לאיגלויי טובא. ועוד, דאשתמודעינהו צריכין להעיד כדי שלא תתעגן, אבל כאן מה לנו לתקן לכתוב מקום הלידה בחנם, כיון שע"י כך יכול לבא לידי פסול אם ישנה? אלא ודאי, אפי' שינה – כשר. ור"ת הביא ראיה שאין שטר נפסל כשנשתנה בו דבר שאין צריך, מדאמר בפ"ב דכתובות (דף כד:) דאין מעלין משטרות ליוחסין – דלאו אכולה מילתא קא מסהדי, אלא אמנה שבשטר, ולא על מה שכתוב שהוא כהן. אלמא, אפילו אינו כהן – השטר כשר. וסברא הוא דעדים לא קיימי אלא על עיקר מעשה. ומעשה באחד ששינה בגט מקום לידתו, והכשירו ר"י. והרבה פעמים כשלא היה להם ברור מקום הלידה הי' אומר: אל תכתבוהו כלל. ומקום עמידה נמי א"צ לכתוב, דהא כל גיטין הבאים ממדינת הים אין כותבין מקום עמידת האשה. ולהכי לא מוקי ליה בבעל ובשינה מקום עמידתו, כדמוקי אסופר, משום דפשיטא דאין צריך לכתוב מקום עמידתו. **מפני** מה תקנו מלכות בגיטין. וא"ת: והא אמרינן בפ"ק דמסכת ע"ז (דף י.): ובגולה אין מונין אלא למלכות יון בלבד, אלמא לא חיישינן לשלום מלכות! ואור"י: דדוקא בגיטין יש לחוש לשלום מלכות, שמקפידין, לפי שהוא דבר גדול שמפרידין איש מאשתו*). **כי** יתביתו בהיני כו'. ואור"י: דאלו שתי מקומות סמוכין הן זה לזה, כדאמרינן בפ"ג דביצה (דף כה:): רב הונא הוו מכתפי לי' משילי להיני ומהיני לשילי – משמע דקרובות הן זו לזו. ולרבותא נקטינהו הני, דאע"פ שאין דומה כל כך לשיקרא, כיון שיכול לבא מזה לזה ביום אחד – יש להחמיר. ואור"י: דאע"ג דבגט פסלינן היה במזרח וכתב במערב, *וה"ה עדים שלא יחתמו – מ"מ בשאר שטרות אם כתב שילי בהיני – כשר, כדאמרי' ב"אחד דיני ממונות" (סנהדרין לב.): שטר שכתבו באחד בניסן בשמיטה, ובאו עדים ואמרו: בא' בניסן עמנו הייתם – כשר, דחיישינן שמא איחרוהו וכתבוהו. אלמא, אע"פ שלא היה בעיר ביום הכתוב בשטר – כשר. מ"מ אור"י: שאין עושין יפה אותם שרגילים לכתוב כתובה בעיר אחרת שאין מקום החופה, אע"פ שלא יהיה הסופר שם ביום החופה, דלכתחילה צריך ליזהר אף בשאר שטרות, כדאמר ליה רב לספריה: כי יתביתו בהיני וכו'. אך קשה לר"י: דבפ' "גט פשוט" (ב"ב דף קס.) משמע דגיטין מאוחרין כשרים, דאמר: גט מקושר שעדיו מתוכו – כשר, לפי שיכול לעשותו פשוט. דאז הוה מאוחר, דבמקושר מלך שנה מונין לו שנים (שם קסד:). וביבמות נמי בפרק "ר"ג" (דף נב.) אמר: לכשאכנסנה אגרשנה – ה"ז גט, אע"פ שכתב מן האירוסין זמן של אחר נישואין. א"כ אמאי פסלינן הכא היה במזרח וכתב במערב? והלא אם ירצו שלא היה סופר בעיר ביום כתיבת הגט – יאמרו שאחרוהו וכתבוהו! ודוחק הוא לומר דגט מאוחר לעולם פסול, והיא דמקושר שכתב עדיו מתוכו – לא איירי בגט אשה אלא מיירי בשטר, והיא ד"כשאכנסנה אגרשנה" – שכתבו בו ביום של נישואין, קודם הנישואין. דלא משתמיט בשום מקום שיהא גט מאוחר פסול! וי"ל: שמא גט מאוחר אינו כשר אם לא יהיו לבסוף באותה העיר ביום שכתוב בגט הסופר והעדים. ועוד י"ל: דגט מאוחר ודאי כשר טפי שכתוב מקום שעומד בשעת כתיבה, אע"פ שכשיגיע הזמן הכתוב בו לא יעמדו שם הסופר והעדים – יתלו שאיחרוהו וכתבוהו. אבל היה במזרח וכתב במערב, שאינו כותב מקום שעומד באותה שעה – פסול, משום מיחזי כשיקרא. ועוד: כי פעמים נודע שלא איחרוהו, ויסברו העולם שהקדימוהו.

*) [עי' תוס' יבמות לה: ד"ה מלכות וכו' כתבו דבר זה בשם ר"ת]

עין משפט נר מצוה

[נ"ל בפרק רביעי לד:]

מ א מיי' פ"ג מהלכות גירושין הלכה יד ופ"י הלכה ד סמג עשין נ טוש"ע אה"ע סימן קכט סעיף יג וסי' קנ סעי' א:

מא ב מיי' שם פ"י הל' יא סמג שם טוש"ע אה"ע סימן קנח:

מב ג מיי' שם פ"א הלכה כז סמג שם טור אה"ע סימן קכ:

מג ד ה מיי' שם פ"א הלכה כד סמג שם טוש"ע אה"ע סימן קכח סעיף א:

מד ו מיי' שם ופכ"ג מהלכות מלוה הל' ו סמג שם (וסימן לד) טוש"ע אה"ע סימן קכז סעיף ו וטוש"ע ח"מ סימן מג סעיף כ:

תוספות רי"ד

שאין להם לא כתב ולא לשון. או שכתבו לשם מלכות מדי או יון או שמנה לחרבן הבית או לבנינו ולא הזכירו בו שנת המלך המולך בבבל הוא פסול: אמר עולא מפני מה תקנו מלכות בגיטין משום שלום מלכות פי' שיאמרו כל כך חשובין אנו בעיניהם שכותבין זמן שטרותיהן על שמינו: ומשום שלום מלכות תצא והולד ממזר אין ר"מ לטעמיה דאמר רב המנונא משמיה דעולא אומר היה ר"מ כל המשנה ממטבע שטבעו חכמים בגיטין הולד ממזר. גרסי' בפ"ק דע"ז אמר ליה רב נחמן בגולה אין מונין אלא למלכי יון הוא סבר דחויי קא מדחי ליה נפק דק ואשכח דתניא בגולה לא מונין אלא למלכי יון ומהכא מוכח דלא קפדינן [בשטרות] בשלום מלכות ואף בגיטין נמי הוו מונין למלכי יון ואע"ג דתנן כתב לשם מלכות שאינה הוגנת וכו' עד תצא מזה ומזה וכל הדרכים האלו בה ואפי' רבנן דפליגי עליה דר' מאיר ואמרי הולד כשר מודו דתצא כדאמרינן לקמן בפ' המגרש אפ"ה נהגו לכתוב למלכות יון ולא חיישינן לשלום מלכות משום דחזו דלא הוו קפדי עלייהו ואין לומר דוקא לשטרות קאמר ולא לגיטין דכל טעמא דמילתא אינו אלא משום שלום מלכות ואם לא חשו בשטרות לא יחושו בגיטין אלא ודאי כל גט נהגו לכתוב למלכי יון וכיון דבמנהגא תליא מילתא ולא חיישינן למתני' וגם מה שאנו נוהגין למנות לבריאת העולם בין לגיטין בין לשטרות כשר הוא ואין לחוש לשלום מלכות: היה במזרח וכתב במערב וכו'. מאן אילימא בעל היינו שינה שמו ושמה שם עירו ושם עירה אלא לאו סופר וכדאמר להו רב לספריה כי יתביתו בשילה כתביתו בשילה ואע"ג דמסירי לכי מילי בהינו וכי יתביתו בהינו כתביתו בהינו ואע"ג דמסירי לכו מילי בשילה פי' אם נמסר להם לכתוב גט לאשה בהינו באחד בניסן ואחרו לכתבו עד שבאו לשילה בעשרה בניסן שהן צריכין לכתוב הזמן בעשרה בניסן שאם יכתבו בא' בניסן הוה ליה נכתב ביום ונחתם בלילה דפסול וצריך להשוות זמן כתיבתו עם חתימתו והלכך כותבין בעשרה בניסן בזמן שכותבין אותו והלכך הן צריכין לכתוב שבשילה נכתב הגט שהרי בעשרה בניסן בשילה הן עומדין ואע"פ שהדברים נמסרו להן בהינו אין כותבין אלא בשילה מפני שבזמן הכתוב בגט בשילה היו עומדים ואם שינו וכתבו שבהינו נכתב הוא פסול שלמה כותבין המקום בגטין או בשטרות כדי שתראה עדות שאתה יכול להזימה שההזמה היא תלויה בזמן ובמקום כדתנן בסנהדרין באיזה יום ובאיזה שעה באיזה מקום ואם יבא להזימן יאמרו להם והלא ביום פלוני עמנו הייתם במקום פלוני נמצא שעיקר ההזמה היא תלויה במקום ובזמן והלכך אם שינו המקום פסול הוא דהויא לה עדות שאי אתה יכול להזימה וכל עדות שאי אתה יכול להזימה ק"ל דלא שמה עדות: [מתני'] תצא מזה ומזה. פי' אם נשאת בגט זה תצא מן השני מפני שנשאת בגט פסול ואע"פ שחזור הראשון ונותן לה גט כשר אסורה היא לו מפני שנבעלה לו באיסור וכאשת איש המזנה תחת בעלה דיינינן לה שאסורה לבעל ואסורה לבועל ולראשון נמי אסורה לחזור מפני שזנתה תחתיו וצריכה גט מזה ומזה מן הראשון צריכה גט שהרי הראשון היה פסול ומן השני צריכה גט לא מיבעיא בשלום מלכות או היה במזרח וכתב במערב שפסולין מדרבנן וכשרין הן מדאורייתא ותפסו בה קדושי שני שהיא צריכה גט ממנו אלא אפילו בשינה שמו ושמה שהוא פסול מדאורייתא והיא אשת איש ולא תפסי בה קדושי [שני] צריכה גט ממנו שמא יאמרו העולם גירשה הראשון בגט כשר ומש"ה נשאה השני ועכשיו אשת איש יוצאה בלא גט הלכך גט מן השני כדאמרן בהאשה רבה: אין לה כתובה וכו' דמאי טעמא תקינו רבנן כתובה כדי שלא תהא קלה בעיניו להוציאה הא תהא קלה וקלה: ולא פירות ולא מזונות ולא בלאות. מ"ט תנאי כתובה ככתובה: ולא פירות. פי' דין פירות שתקנו לאשה פדייה מן השביה תחת נכסי מלוג לא אית לה כלום: ולא מזונות אפילו לוותה ואכלה אינו משלם לה: ולא בלאות אפילו בלאותיה שהם בעין מנכסי נדונייתה קנסוה חכמים להפסידם מפני שנשאת בגט זה ולא הראתו לחכמים ואם נטלה מזה ומזה תחזיר ולא אמרינן מאי דתפס תפס והולד ממזר מזה ומזה מן השני הוי ממזר מדאורייתא היכא דהגט הוא פסול מדאורייתא כגון שינה שמו ושמה שהוא ממזר מדבנן ואסור בממזרת ואינו לוקח לו כשרה ובשלום מלכות והיה במזרח וכתב במערב שהוא פסול מדרבנן הוי ממזר מדרבנן ולא ממזרת דמדאורייתא הוי כשר אלא לוקח גיורת דקהל גרים לא אקרי קהל וכן אם החזיר לה הראשון הוי ממזר מדרבנן לא זה וזה מטמאין לה דאמר מר מטמא הוא לאשתו כשרה ואינו מטמא לאשתו פסולה ואפילו בגט פסול מדרבנן דמדאורייתא חזיא ליה ואמרינן לה יטמא מצוה ב"ד עוקרין דברי תורה בשב ואל תעשה: ולא זה וזה זכאין במציאתה מ"ט אמרו חכמים מציאת אשה לבעלה משום איבה הא תהוי לה איבה. ולא במעשה ידיה דמאי טעמא אמור רבנן מעשה ידיה לבעלה משום דקאכלה מזוני הכא כיון דמזוני לית לה מעשה ידיה לאו דידיה הוי: ולא בהפרת נדריה. טעמא מאי אמור רבנן בעל מיפר כדי שלא תתגנה על בעלה הכא תתגנה ותתגנה היתה

מה א מיי' פ"ו מהל' יבום הלכה כג סמג עשין נא טוש"ע אה"ע סימן קעג סעיף י:
מו ב מיי' שם פ"ב הל' כ סמג לאוין פג טוש"ע אה"ע סימן קנט סעיף ג:
מז ג מיי' פ"י מהלכות גירושין הלכה יא סמג עשין נ טוש"ע אה"ע סימן קנא:

זוֹ דִּבְרֵי ר"מ, אֲבָל חֲכָמִים אוֹמְרִים: אֲפִילּוּ לֹא כָּתַב אֶלָּא לְשֵׁם סַנְטָר שֶׁבָּעִיר – הֲרֵי זוֹ מְגוֹרֶשֶׁת. הַהוּא גִּיטָּא דַּהֲוָה כְּתִיב בֵּיהּ לְשֵׁם אִיסְטַנְדְּרָא דְּבַשְׂכָּר, שְׁלָחָהּ רַב נַחְמָן בַּר רַב חִסְדָּא לְקַמֵּיהּ דְּרָבָא: כִּי הַאי גַּוְונָא מַאי? שְׁלַח לֵיהּ: בְּהָא אֲפִילּוּ ר"מ מוֹדֵי; מַאי טַעְמָא? מֵאוּתָהּ מַלְכוּת הוּא. וּמַאי שְׁנָא מִסַּנְטָר שֶׁבָּעִיר? הָתָם זִילָא לְהוּ מִילְּתָא, הָכָא שְׁבִיחָא לְהוּ מִילְּתָא. אָמַר ר' אַבָּא אָמַר רַב הוּנָא אָמַר רַב: זוֹ דִּבְרֵי ר"מ, אֲבָל חֲכָמִים אוֹמְרִים: הַוָּלָד כָּשֵׁר; וּמוֹדִים חֲכָמִים לְר"מ, שֶׁאִם שִׁינָּה שְׁמוֹ וּשְׁמָהּ, שֵׁם עִירוֹ וְשֵׁם עִירָהּ – שֶׁהַוָּלָד מַמְזֵר. אָמַר רַב אַשִׁי, אַף אֲנַן נַמִי תָּנֵינָא: שִׁינָּה שְׁמוֹ וּשְׁמָהּ, שֵׁם עִירוֹ וְשֵׁם עִירָהּ – תֵּצֵא מִזֶּה וּמִזֶּה, וְכָל הַדְּרָכִים הָאֵלּוּ בָּהּ; הָא מַאן קָתָנֵי לָהּ? אִילֵימָא ר"מ, לִיעָרְבִינְהוּ וְלִיתְנִינְהוּ! אֶלָּא ש"מ רַבָּנַן, ש"מ.§ א"כָּל עֲרָיוֹת שֶׁאָמְרוּ" כו'.§ ב"נִישְּׂאוּ אִין, זִינּוּ לָא; לֵימָא תֶּיהֱוֵי תְּיוּבְתָּא דְּרַב הַמְנוּנָא, *דְּאָמַר רַב הַמְנוּנָא: שׁוֹמֶרֶת יָבָם שֶׁזִּינְּתָה – אֲסוּרָה לִיבָמָהּ? לָא, נִישְּׂאוּ וְה"ה לְזִינּוּ, וְהַאי דְּקָתָנֵי נִישְּׂאוּ – *לִישָּׁנָא מְעַלְּיָא נָקַט. וְאִיכָּא דְּאָמְרִי: נִישְּׂאוּ וְה"ה לְזִינּוּ; לֵימָא מְסַיַּיע לֵיהּ לְרַב הַמְנוּנָא, דְּא"ר הַמְנוּנָא: שׁוֹמֶרֶת יָבָם שֶׁזִּינְּתָה – אֲסוּרָה לִיבָמָהּ? לָא, נִישְּׂאוּ דַּוְקָא, מִשּׁוּם דְּמִיחַלְפָא בְּאִשָּׁה שֶׁהָלַךְ בַּעְלָהּ לִמְדִינַת הַיָּם.§ "הַכּוֹנֵס אֶת יְבִמְתּוֹ" כו'.§ וּצְרִיכָא; דְּאִי אַשְׁמְעִינַן בְּהָךְ קַמַּיְיתָא, מִשּׁוּם דְּלָא אִיקַּיֵּים מִצְוַת יִבּוּם, אֲבָל הָכָא דְּאִיקַּיֵּים מִצְוַת יִבּוּם – אֵימָא לָא; וְאִי אַשְׁמְעִי' הָכָא, מִשּׁוּם דְּקָא רַמְיָא קַמֵּיהּ, אֲבָל הָתָם דְּלָא רַמְיָא קַמֵּיהּ – אֵימָא לָא, צְרִיכָא.§ "כָּתַב הַסּוֹפֵר וְטָעָה וְנָתַן גֵּט לָאִשָּׁה וְשׁוֹבֵר וכו', ר"א אוֹמֵר: אִם לְאַלְתַּר יָצָא" וכו'.§ הֵיכִי דָּמֵי לְאַלְתַּר, וְהֵיכִי דָּמֵי לְאַחַר זְמַן? אָמַר רַב יְהוּדָה אָמַר שְׁמוּאֵל: כָּל זְמַן שֶׁיּוֹשְׁבִין וַעֲסוּקִין בְּאוֹתוֹ עִנְיָן – זֶהוּ לְאַלְתַּר, עָמְדוּ – זֶהוּ לְאַחַר זְמַן; וְרַב אַדָּא בַּר אַהֲבָה אָמַר: גלֹא נִישֵּׂאת – זֶהוּ לְאַלְתַּר, *נִישֵּׂאת – זֶהוּ לְאַחַר זְמַן. תְּנַן, לֹא כָּל הֵימֶנּוּ מִן הָרִאשׁוֹן לְאַבֵּד זְכוּתוֹ שֶׁל שֵׁנִי; בִּשְׁלָמָא לְרַב אַדָּא בַּר אַהֲבָה – הַיְינוּ דְּקָתָנֵי שֵׁנִי, אֶלָּא לִשְׁמוּאֵל מַאי שֵׁנִי?
זְכוּת

זוֹ דִּבְרֵי ר"מ. דְּגֵט נִפְסָל מִשּׁוּם שְׁלוֹם מַלְכוּת. סַנְטָר. מְפָרֵשׁ בְּבָבָא בַּתְרָא (דף סח.): בַּר מַתְוָונְיָא, זָקֵן הַמְּמוּנֶּה לִהְיוֹת בָּקִי בְּנַחֲלַת גְּבוּל שְׂדֵה כָּל אִישׁ וְאִישׁ. אִיסְטַנְדְּרָא דְּבַשְׂכָּר. שִׁלְטוֹן שֶׁל בַּשְׂכָּר, עַבְדּוֹ שֶׁל מֶלֶךְ. וּמַאי שְׁנָא מִסַּנְטָר דְּעִיר. דְּשָׁמְעִינַן לְר"מ דְּפָלֵיג. זִילָא לְהוּ מִילְּתָא. שֶׁאֵין שׁוּלְטָנוּת גְּרוּעָה מִזּוֹ, וּבוּשֶׁת הוּא לַמֶּלֶךְ שֶׁנִּזְכַּר זֶה וְהִנִּיחוּ כָּל שְׁאָר מְשָׁרְתָיו. שְׁבִיחָא. לְפִי שֶׁשּׁוּלְטָנוּתוֹ חֲשׁוּבָה. הַוָּלָד כָּשֵׁר. אַשְּׁלוֹם מַלְכוּת קָאֵי. לִיעָרְבִינְהוּ וְלִיתְנִינְהוּ. בַּהֲדֵי מְשַׁנֶּה שֵׁם מַלְכוּת, דְּחַד פְּסוּלָא הוּא. זִינּוּ לָא. אֵינָהּ אֲסוּרָה לְהִתְיַיבֵּם, דְּנִישְּׂאוּ חָמוּר, שֶׁמָּא יֹאמְרוּ חָלַץ לָהּ וְנִיסֵּת, וְחָזַר לְכוֹנְסָהּ מִשֶּׁנִּתְגָּרְשָׁה, וַהֲוָה לֵיהּ נוֹשֵׂא אֶת חֲלוּצָתוֹ, דְּקָם לֵיהּ *בְּ"לֹא יִבְנֶה". דְּמִיחַלְפָא בְּאִשָּׁה שֶׁהָלַךְ בַּעְלָהּ לִמְדִינַת הַיָּם. וּבָאוּ וְאָמְרוּ לָהּ: מֵת בַּעְלֵיךְ, וְנִיסֵּת, דְּאָסְרִינַן לָהּ לְמֶיהְדַּר, וְאע"פ שֶׁבְּאוֹנֶס, מִשּׁוּם שֶׁמָּא יֹאמְרוּ: גֵּירֵשׁ רִאשׁוֹן, וְנָשָׂא זֶה, וְחָזַר הָרִאשׁוֹן וְהֶחֱזִירָהּ לְאַחַר גֵּירוּשֵׁי שֵׁנִי, וְנִמְצָא מַחֲזִיר גְּרוּשָׁתוֹ מִשֶּׁנִּיסֵּת. הָכִי נַמִי אָמְרִי' הָכָא: שֶׁמָּא יֹאמְרוּ חָלַץ זֶה וְנָשָׂא זֶה כו'. אֲבָל זְנוּת לֵית לֵיהּ קָלָא כּוּלֵּי הַאי, וּמֵידַע יָדְעִי דִּפְרִיצוּתָא הֲוַאי, וְלָא חָשְׁדִי לָהּ בַּחֲלוּצָה. דְּלָא אִקַּיֵּים מִצְוַת יִבּוּם. שֶׁע"י הָעֶרְוָה נִישֵּׂאת הַצָּרָה לַשּׁוּק. הִילְכָּךְ, כִּי אִגַּלַּאי דְּלָאו צָרַת עֶרְוָה הֲוַאי – קָנְסִינַן לָהּ מִשּׁוּם דְּלֹא הִמְתִּינָה, וְאָסְרִינַן לָהּ אַיַּבָּם. אֲבָל. סֵיפָא, דְּאִיקַּיֵּים מִצְוַת יִבּוּם, כְּשֶׁנִּיסֵּת זוֹ לַשּׁוּק ע"י שֶׁנִּתְיַיבְּמָה צָרָתָהּ, אֵימָא תּוּ לָא הֲוָה לָהּ לְאַמְתּוּנֵי, וְלֹא נִקְנְסָהּ. וְאִי. תָּנָא סֵיפָא – מִשּׁוּם דְּרַמְיָא קַמֵּיהּ, שְׁתֵּיהֶן נָפְלוּ תְּחִילָּה לְהִתְיַיבֵּם כְּאַחַת, וּכְשֶׁנִּתְיַיבְּמָה הָאַחַת קוֹדֶם שֶׁתָּבִיא שְׁתֵּי שְׂעָרוֹת – הָיָה לָהּ לְצָרָתָהּ לְהַמְתִּין עַד שֶׁתִּרְאֶה שֶׁיְּהוּ יִבּוּמֵי חֲבֶרְתָּהּ כְּשֵׁרִין, דְּכֵיוָן דְּאִתְרַמַּאי קַמֵּיהּ – צְרִיכָה לָצֵאת מִידֵי זִיקָּתוֹ בְּיִבּוּמִין וַדָּאִין. אֲבָל. צָרַת עֶרְוָה, מִתְּחִילַּת נְפִילָתָן הָיְתָה הַצָּרָה הַזּוֹ סְבוּרָה דְּלָא רַמְיָא קַמֵּיהּ לְיִבּוּם, שֶׁהֲרֵי הָעֶרְוָה מוֹצִיאַתָּהּ מִידֵי זִיקָּתוֹ. הִלְכָּךְ, לָא הֲוָה לָהּ לְאַסּוּקֵי אַדַּעְתָּא וּלְאַמְתּוּיֵי שֶׁמָּא תִּמָּצֵא הָעֶרְוָה אַיְילוֹנִית, הוֹאִיל וּמְסוּלֶּקֶת הִיא מִמֶּנּוּ – לָא מַסְּקָא אַדַּעְתָּא, וְלָא לִיקַנְסָהּ מִלְּהִתְיַיבֵּם וּמִלִּיטּוֹל כְּתוּבָּה, דְּהָא אֲנוּסָה הִיא – קָא מַשְׁמַע לָן. בְּאוֹתוֹ עִנְיָן. בְּדִבְרֵי גֵּירוּשֶׁיהָ.
זכות

זו דברי ר"מ אבל חכמים אומרים הולד כשר. פי' בקונט': דאשלום מלכות קאי. וקשה לר"ת: דא"כ פליגי אדרב יהודה אמר שמואל דלעיל, דאמר: אבל חכמים אומרים אפי' לא כתב אלא לשם סנטר שבעיר – הרי זו מגורשת. דמשמע מגורשת, ותינשא לכתחילה, אע"פ שלא נכתב לשם מלכות. א"כ היאך אנו כותבין בגיטין לבריאת עולם? הא קיי"ל כרב באיסורי, ולדידיה אסור לגרש בו לכתחילה! ולספרים דגרסי לעיל: אמר רב יהודה אמר רב – קשה דרב אדרב! ונצטרך לומר דאמוראי נינהו אליבא דרב. ואומר הרב רבי אלחנן: דלא קשה מידי, דבסנטר העיר כשר טפי, לפי שהוא ממלכות העיר, אבל לשם מלכות אחרת – אסור לגרש בו, ובדיעבד הולד כשר. ומשום דר"מ בעי מלכות חשובה קאמר: אבל חכמים אומרים אפילו סנטר, דגרע – הויא מגורשת כיון דהוא מאותה מלכות, ועדיף ממלכות אחרת. ומה שאנו כותבין לבריאת עולם – משום דהשתא ליכא שלום מלכות בכך, שאפי' גוים אינם מונין לשנות מלכים. אבל בימי חכמים היו רגילין למנות לשנות מלכים, כדאמרינן ב"גט פשוט" (ב"ב דף קסד:): מנהגה של אומה זו מלך שנה מונין לו שתים. פי': שהיו כותבין כן בשטרותיהן לכבוד המלך, לומר: מלך הרבה. והרב ר' יוסף פי': דעכשיו אין המלכות מקפדת, ולהכי לא כתבינן לשנות מלכים. תדע, דהא ר"מ מודה דכתבו לשם איסטנדרא כשר – משום דאין מלכות מקפדת. ור"ת מפרש: דלאו אשלום מלכות קאי "זו דברי ר"מ", אלא א"היה במזרח וכתב במערב". אבל לשום מלכות אחרת – מותר לגרש בו לכתחילה לרבנן, ולא פליג אדרב יהודה דלעיל. ו"מגורשת" – היינו שתתגרש בו לכתחילה קאמר, אפי' נכתב לשם סנטר, דזילא בהו מילתא, וכל שכן השתא שמותר לכתוב לבריאת עולם, דלא זילא בהו מילתא כלל, דלא מתקנאים בזה. וקיי"ל כחכמים, ואע"ג דסתם לן תנא כר' מאיר – מ"מ מדקאמר לעיל: ומשום שלום מלכות הולד ממזר? אין, ר"מ לטעמיה כו', וכן בפ"ק (לעיל ה:): משום דלא אמר "בפני נכתב ובפני נחתם" יוציא והולד ממזר? ומשני: אין, ר"מ לטעמיה כו'. משמע דלית הלכתא כוותיה. והשתא אתי שפיר דקאמר: דיקא נמי דמודים חכמים לר"מ בשינה שמו ושמה, מדלא ערבינהו בהדי "היה במזרח" כו' דדמיא ליה. ומיהו, קשה לפירוש רבינו תם: דלקמן בפרק בתרא (דף פו.) פריך אההיא דשלשה גיטין פסולין: ותו ליכא? והא איכא שלום מלכות! התם הולד ממזר, הכא – הולד כשר. הניחא לר"מ, אלא לרבנן דאמרי הולד כשר מאי איכא למימר? אלמא משמע דשלום מלכות דווקא בדיעבד הולד כשר לרבנן, אבל לכתחילה – אסור לגרש בו! *ורבינו תם גריס לקמן, וכן נמצא בפי' רבינו חננאל: והא איכא שלום מלכות וכו', ולא פריך משלום מלכות אלא מבבא שאחריה, דהיה במזרח וכתב במערב. **נישאו** אין זינו לא לימא תיהוי תיובתא דרב המנונא. פירש בקונטרס: דנישאו גזרינן שמא יאמרו חלץ זה ונשא זה וגירש, ונמצא זה מחזיר חלוצתו. אבל זינו, דפריצותא בעלמא הוא – לא חשדי לה בחלוצה. וקשה לר"י: דמאי קאמר בסמוך דמיחלפא באשה שהלך בעלה למדינת הים, כיון דהך גזירה גופה שייכא בה. דלשון מיחלפא משמע דהכא לא שייכא ההיא גזירה! ועוד: לאיכא דאמרי נישאו וה"ה לזינו, מאי ס"ד? כיון דההיא גזירה דמיחלפא באשה שהלך בעלה כו' לא שייכא אלא בנישאו! ועוד: אמאי לא דייק נמי הש"ס ב"האשה רבה" (יבמות דף לב.) גבי: אמרו לה "מת בעליך" וניסת, ניסת – אין, זינתה – לא, כדדייק הכא! ואור"י: דאי שומרת יבם שזינתה מותרת לייבם, דלא כרב המנונא – בנישאת נמי לא גזרי' בה שמא יאמרו חלץ זה ונשא זה ונמצא מחזיר חלוצתו, כיון דזינתה במזיד לא מיתסרא. דהכי אמרינן ב"האשה רבה" (שם דף לד.) גבי מי שהלך אשתו למדינת הים, דאשה שהלך בעלה למדינת הים – אסור להחזירה, משום דבמזיד מיתסרא – בשוגג נמי גזרו בה רבנן, שמא יאמרו גירש זה ונשאה זה. והכי פירושו: נישאו אין – מדלא נקט זינו, דהוה משמע תרוייהו, ונקט נישאו – שמע מינה נישאו דוקא, אבל זינו – לא, משום דמיחלפא באשה שהלך וכו'. אבל בגופה לא שייכא הך גזירה, כיון דבמזיד לא מיתסרא. ומשני: נישאו, והוא הדין לזינו. וכיון דזינתה אסורה ליבם, כדרב המנונא, בנישאת נמי גזרינן בה, שמא יאמרו חלץ זה ונשאת. איכא דאמרי נישאת והוא הדין לזינו – השתא לא מסתבר טעמא דמיחלפא כו', ולהכי קאמר: לימא מסייע ליה לרב המנונא, דאי בזינו שריא – בנישאת נמי ליכא למיגזר בה בגופה. ודחי: אף ע"ג דליכא למיגזר בה, מכל מקום מיחלפא באשה שהלך כו'. וה"ה דהוי מצי למידחי: הא מני – ר"ע היא, דמשוי חייבי לאוין כערוה, ורב המנונא אליבא דרבנן קאמר, כדדחי ליה בסוטה בפ"ב (דף יח:). אלא עדיפא מיניה קא דחי, שאין צריך להעמידה כר"ע, ואפי' הכי ליכא סייעתא לרב המנונא. מיהו, מצא רבינו יהודה בתוספתא דקתני על מתניתין: דברי ר"מ שאמר משום ר' עקיבא, דמשמע דכרבנן לא מתוקמא מתניתין. לפי זה חולקת על הש"ס שלנו. *כתב גט לאיש ושובר לאשה. ליכא למידק מהכא דכותבין שובר, דהיכא דלא אפשר – ודאי כותבין, כדאמר ב"הכותב" (כתובות פט:).
לא

תוספות רי"ד

היתה בת ישראל נפסלה מן הכהונה פי' דחשבינן לה זונה וכן בת כהן מן התרומה ובת לוי מן המעשרות משום קנסא: מתו אחיו של זה וכו' פי' חולצין דהא אשת אחיו היא ולא מייבמת משום קנסא או משום גזירה דהויא לה גרושת אחיו ושמא יאמרו גירש זה ונשא זה והויא לה גרושת אחיו. ואין יורשיו של זה וכו' זו היא כתובת בנין דכרין הכי מפרש לה ביבמות: אמר רב הונא אמר רב זו דברי ר"מ אבל חכמים אומרים הולד כשר. פי' בולד ממזר פליגי רבנן דלא משוו ליה ממזר ומותר בישראלית אבל בתצא מזה ומזה לא פליגי רבנן דהכי אמרי' בפירקין דלקמן דבשלום מלכות לרבנן תצא ולא פליגי רבנן אלא שהולד כשר: ומודים חכמים לר"מ בשינה שמו ושמה שם עירו ושם עירה שתצא מזה ומזה וכל הדרכים האלו בה מפני שהוא פסול תורה: אמר רב אשי אף אנן תנינא שינה שמו ושמה שם עירו ושם עירה תצא מזה ומזה וכל הדרכים האלו בה הא מאן קתני לה אילימא ר' מאיר ניערבינהו וניתנגהו אלא לאו ש"מ רבנן היא ש"מ: **מתני'** כל העריות שאמרו צרותיהן מותרות הלכו הצרות ונשאו ונמצאו אלו איילונית תצא מזה ומזה וכל הדרכים האלו בה: הכונס את יבמתו והלכה צרתה ונשאת לאחר ונמצאת זו איילונית תצא מזה ומזה וכל הדרכים האלו בה. פי' כל העריות שאמרו צרותיהן מותרות אלו ט"ו עריות שאמרו חכמים שצרותיהן מותרות לינשא לשוק בלא חליצה כשמתו בעליהן בלא בנים אם הלכו הצרות האלו ונשאו לשוק ונמצאו העריות איילונית ואיגלי מילתא שהיו קדושי המת בהן בטעות ונמצאו שלא היו אלו צרותיהן ולא פטרום העריות האלו מן החליצה תצא מזה ומזה פי' מהבעל שנישאת לו ומיבם וכל הדרכים האלו בה: וכן הכונס את יבמתו ונפטרה צרתה בביאתה כדאמרן בית א' הוא בונה ולא שתים ונמצאת זו שנתיבמה אילונית ואין יבומיה יבומין שהרי לא היתה אשת המת ונמצאת שלא נפטרה צרתה ונשאת לשוק בלא חליצה תצא מזה ומזה וכל הדרכים האלו בה: גרסי' בהאשה רבה ת"ר זו דברי ר' עקיבא דאמר יש ממזר מחייבי לאוין אבל חכ"א אין ממזר מיבמה: אמר רב המנונא שומרת יבם שזנתה אסורה ליבמה ואמרינן בשלהי פ"ב דסוטה אמרי במערבא אין הלכה כרב המנונא: **מתני'** כתב הסופר וטעה ונתן גט לאשה ושובר לאיש ונתנו זה לזה ולאחר זמן הרי גט יוצא מיד האיש ושובר מיד האשה תצא מזה ומזה וכל הדרכים האלו בה ר' אלעזר אומר אם לאלתר יצא אינו גט ואם לאחר זמן יצא הרי זה גט שלא כל הימנו מן הראשון לאבד זכותו של שני פי' אלה הם דברי הבעל המערער שאומר כי הסופר טעה ונתן הגט שהיה צריך ליתן לו נתנו לאשה והשובר שהיה צריך לתת לאשה נתן לו וכשנתנו זה לזה נמצא שאני נתתי לאשתי השובר והיא נתנה לי הגט וסברתי לגרש את אשתי בגט וגרשתיה בשובר והרי רגלים לדבר שהשובר יוצא מתחת יד האשה והגט מתחת יד האיש ת"ק סבר חיישינן לדברי הבעל ואם נשאת תצא מזה ומזה וכל הדרכים האלו בה: ור' אלעזר סבר אם לאלתר יצא זה הספק לפנינו חיישינן ואינו גט אבל אם לאחר זמן יצא הרי זה גט שלא כל הימנו מן בעל הראשון וכו' אלא אמרינן קנוניא עשה עם האשה נותן לה השובר והיא נתנה לו הגט כדי לאוסרה על השני הלכך לא מהמנינן ליה: היכי דמי לאלתר והיכי דמי לאחר זמן אמר רב יהודה אמר שמואל כל זמן שיושבין זהו לאלתר עמדו זהו לאחר זמן ורב אדא בר אהבה אומר אם לא נשאת זהו לאלתר

עי' רש"ל וגש"א

סוטה יח: יבמות פח. לב: לה. נו.

[לעיל טו: וש"נ]

רש"ל וה"ה נתאחשה

גליון הש"ס

גמ' לישנא מעליא נקט. עי' כתובות דף יז ע"א וש"נ: תוס' ד"ה דברי ר"מ וכו' וה"ה ר"מ גריס לקמן וכו'. כעין זה כתב בשבועות דף מח ע"א תד"ה מאן דמתני וכן דף ט ע"ב תד"ה כדאמר ורש"י כתבו תוס' נזיר דף כב ע"ב ד"ה ומשני וכן כתבו תוספות שבת דף קכ ע"ב ד"ה אמטו וברכות דף מה ע"א תד"ה ג' שאכלו ובמעילה דף יב ע"ב תוספות ד"ה חלב מוקדשין:

[שייך לעיל ע"א במשנה]

תורה אור

זְכוּת הָרְאוּיָה לַשֵּׁנִי.§ **מתני'** כָּתַב לְגָרֵשׁ אֶת אִשְׁתּוֹ וְנִמְלַךְ, ב"ש אוֹמְרִים: פְּסָלָהּ מִן הַכְּהוּנָּה, וּב"ה אוֹמְרִים: אאע"פ שֶׁנְּתָנוֹ לָהּ עַל תְּנַאי וְלֹא נַעֲשָׂה הַתְּנַאי — לֹא פְּסָלָהּ מִן הַכְּהוּנָּה.§ **גמ'** שְׁלַח לֵיהּ רַב יוֹסֵף בְּרֵיהּ דְּרַב מְנַשֶּׁה מִדְּוִיל לִשְׁמוּאֵל: יְלַמְּדֵנוּ רַבֵּינוּ, יָצָא עָלָיו קוֹל "אִישׁ פְּלוֹנִי כֹּהֵן כָּתַב גֵּט לְאִשְׁתּוֹ", וְיוֹשֶׁבֶת תַּחְתָּיו וּמְשַׁמַּשְׁתּוֹ, מַהוּ? שְׁלַח לֵיהּ: תֵּצֵא, וְהַדָּבָר צָרִיךְ בְּדִיקָה. מַאי הִיא? אִילֵימָא דְּאִי מְבַטְּלִינַן קָלָא אוֹ לָא מְבַטְּלִינַן — *וְהָא נְהַרְדְּעָא אַתְרֵיהּ דִּשְׁמוּאֵל הִיא, *וּבִנְהַרְדְּעָא לָא מְבַטְּלִי קָלָא! אֶלָּא, דְּאִי קָרוּ לִנְתִינָה "כְּתִיבָה". וְכִי קָרוּ לִנְתִינָה "כְּתִיבָה", לִכְתִיבָה גּוּפַהּ מִי לָא קָרוּ לַהּ "כְּתִיבָה"? באִין, דְּאִי מִיגַּלְיָא מִילְּתָא דְּקָרוּ לִנְתִינָה "כְּתִיבָה", דִּלְמָא נָתַן קָאָמְרִי. תֵּצֵא?! *וְהָא"ר אַשִׁי: גכָּל קָלָא דְּבָתַר נִישּׂוּאִין לָא חָיְישִׁינַן לֵיהּ! מַאי תֵּצֵא? נַמִי תֵּצֵא דמִשֵּׁנִי. א"כ, אַתָּה מוֹצִיא לַעַז עַל בָּנָיו שֶׁל רִאשׁוֹן! כֵּיוָן דְּמִשֵּׁנִי הוּא דְּמַפְּקִינַן לָהּ וּמֵרִאשׁוֹן לָא מַפְּקִינַן לָהּ, אָתֵי לְמֵימַר: סָמוּךְ לְמִיתָה גֵּרְשָׁהּ. אָמַר רבב"ח א"ר יוֹחָנָן מִשּׁוּם רַבִּי יְהוּדָה בַּר אֶלְעַי: בֹּא וּרְאֵה שֶׁלֹּא כַּדּוֹרוֹת הָרִאשׁוֹנִים דּוֹרוֹת הָאַחֲרוֹנִים; דּוֹרוֹת הָרִאשׁוֹנִ' — ב"ש, דּוֹרוֹת הָאַחֲרוֹנִים — רַבִּי דּוֹסָא; *דְּתַנְיָא: *שְׁבוּיָה אוֹכֶלֶת בִּתְרוּמָה, דִּבְרֵי ר' דּוֹסָא. א"ר דּוֹסָא: וְכִי מֶה עָשָׂה לָהּ עַרְבִי זֶה, מִפְּנֵי שֶׁמִּיעֵךְ לָהּ בֵּין דַּדֶּיהָ פְּסָלָהּ מִן הַכְּהוּנָּה? *וְאָמַר רבב"ח א"ר יוֹחָנָן מִשּׁוּם ר' יְהוּדָה בַּר אֶלְעַי: בֹּא וּרְאֵה שֶׁלֹּא כַּדּוֹרוֹת הָרִאשׁוֹנִים דּוֹרוֹת הָאַחֲרוֹנִים, דּוֹרוֹת הָרִאשׁוֹנִים — מַכְנִיסִין פֵּירוֹתֵיהֶן דֶּרֶךְ טְרַקְסְמוֹן כְּדֵי לְחַיְּיבָן בְּמַעֲשֵׂר, דּוֹרוֹת הָאַחֲרוֹנִים — מַכְנִיסִין פֵּירוֹתֵיהֶן דֶּרֶךְ גַּגּוֹת וְדֶרֶךְ קַרְפֵּיפוֹת כְּדֵי לְפוֹטְרָן מִן הַמַּעֲשֵׂר; *דְּאָמַר רַבִּי יַנַּאי: אֵין הַטֶּבֶל מִתְחַיֵּיב בְּמַעֲשֵׂר עַד שֶׁיִּרְאֶה פְּנֵי הַבַּיִת, שֶׁנֶּאֱמַר: °"בִּעַרְתִּי הַקֹּדֶשׁ מִן הַבַּיִת"; וְרַבִּי יוֹחָנָן אָמַר: האֲפִילּוּ חָצֵר קוֹבַעַת, שֶׁנֶּאֱמַר: °"וְאָכְלוּ בִשְׁעָרֶיךָ וְשָׂבֵעוּ".§ **מתני'** *הַמְגָרֵשׁ אֶת אִשְׁתּוֹ וְלָנָה עִמּוֹ בְּפוּנְדְּקִי, ב"ש אוֹמְרִים: אֵינָהּ צְרִיכָה הֵימֶנּוּ גֵּט שֵׁנִי, וּבה"א: וצְרִיכָה הֵימֶנּוּ גֵּט שֵׁנִי. אֵימָתַי? בִּזְמַן שֶׁנִּתְגָּרְשָׁה מִן הַנִּשּׂוּאִין. וּמוֹדִים, בְּנִתְגָּרְשָׁה מִן הָאֵירוּסִין — שֶׁאֵינָהּ צְרִיכָה הֵימֶנּוּ גֵּט שֵׁנִי, מִפְּנֵי שֶׁאֵין לִבּוֹ גַּס בָּהּ.§ **גמ'** *אָמַר רַבָּה בַּר בַּר חָנָה א"ר יוֹחָנָן: מַחֲלוֹקֶת בְּשֶׁרָאוּהָ שֶׁנִּבְעֲלָה, דב"ש

כתובות לו: [עדיות פ"ג מ"ו] · דברים כו · שם

רש"י

זְכוּת הָרְאוּיָה. מִשֶּׁיָּצְאָתָה מִלִּפְנֵי הָעֵדִים בְּחֶזְקַת מְגוֹרֶשֶׁת — זָכְתָה לִינָּשֵׂא לַשֵּׁנִי. **אִישׁ פְּלוֹנִי כֹּהֵן.** מַעֲשֶׂה בָּא לְפָנָיו שֶׁכָּתַב כֹּהֵן לְגָרֵשׁ אֶת אִשְׁתּוֹ, וְיָצָא קוֹל בָּעִיר עַל כָּךְ שֶׁכָּתַב לָהּ גֵּט. **מַהוּ.** מִי מַפְּקִינַן לָהּ מִינֵּיהּ מִשּׁוּם קָלָא, שֶׁלֹּא יֹאמְרוּ: גֵּירְשָׁהּ וְהֶחֱזִירָהּ, וְנִמְצָא כֹּהֵן מַחֲזִיר גְּרוּשָׁתוֹ. **תֵּצֵא.** מִפְּנֵי הַקּוֹל. אֲבָל הַדָּבָר צָרִיךְ בְּדִיקָה קוֹדֶם שֶׁנּוֹצִיאֶנָּה מִמֶּנּוּ. **דְּאִי מְבַטְּלִינַן קָלָא.** אִם נוּכַל לְשַׁתֵּק בְּנֵי הָעִיר, וּלְהוֹצִיאָהּ מִן הַקּוֹל הַזֶּה — לֹא תֵּצֵא מִבַּעְלָהּ. **וּבִנְהַרְדְּעָא לָא מְבַטְּלִי קָלָא.** לֹא הָיוּ נוֹהֲגִין דַּיָּינֵי הָעִיר לְשַׁתְּקָם, מִפְּנֵי הַחֲשָׁד שֶׁלֹּא יוֹצִיאוּ קוֹל שֶׁמַּחֲזִיקִים יְדֵי עוֹבְרֵי עֲבֵירָה. דְּהָכִי אָמְרִינַן בְּ"הַמְגָרֵשׁ":* בְּסוּרָא מְבַטְּלֵי קָלָא, בִּנְהַרְדְּעָא לָא מְבַטְּלֵי קָלָא. **דְּאִי קָרוּ לִנְתִינָה כְּתִיבָה.** אִם רְגִילִין בָּעִיר לִקְרוֹת לִנְתִינָה "כְּתִיבָה" — הָוֵי קוֹל, שֶׁהֲרֵי אוֹמְרִי' שֶׁכָּתַב לָהּ, וְהַאי "כָּתַב" נָתַן הוּא, דְּהָא קָרוּ לִנְתִינָה "כְּתִיבָה". וְאִי לָא קָרוּ לִנְתִינָה "כְּתִיבָה" — אֵין זֶה קוֹל, וְלֹא יַחְשְׁדוּהוּ בְּמַחֲזִיר גְּרוּשָׁתוֹ, שֶׁהֲרֵי לֹא יָצָא קוֹל שֶׁנָּתַן אֶלָּא שֶׁכָּתַב. וּפָרְכִינַן: נְהִי נַמִי דְּקָרוּ לִנְתִינָה "כְּתִיבָה", אַמַּאי מַפְּקִינַן לָהּ בְּהָכִי? וְכִי לִכְתִיבָה גּוּפָהּ מִי לָא קָרוּ לָהּ "כְּתִיבָה"? וּמַאן לֵימָא לָן דְּהַאי "כָּתַב" דְּקָא אָמְרִי "נָתַן" הוּא? דִּלְמָא כְּתִיבָה בְּעָלְמָא הוּא! וּמְשַׁנֵּינַן. **אִי מִיגַּלְיָא מִילְּתָא.** שֶׁרְגִילִין בְּנֵי הָעִיר לִקְרוֹת לִנְתִינָה "כְּתִיבָה", אַע"ג דְּלִכְתִיבָה לְחוּדָא נַמִי קָרוּ "כְּתִיבָה" מַחְמְרִינַן לְמֵיחַשׁ לְקָלָא, וְאָמְרִינַן: כָּתַב וְנָתַן קָאָמְרִי, וְתֵצֵא מִפְּנֵי חֲשַׁד הַקּוֹל. **כָּל קָלָא דְּבָתַר נִשּׂוּאִין כו'.** אַע"פ שֶׁשָּׁנִינוּ בְּ"הַמְגָרֵשׁ" *דְּחָיְישִׁינַן לְקָלָא, דִּתְנַן: יָצָא שְׁמָהּ בָּעִיר מְקוּדֶּשֶׁת לִפְלוֹנִי — מְקוּדֶּשֶׁת, וַאֲסוּרָה לִינָּשֵׂא לְאַחֵר, עַד שֶׁיִּתֵּן לָהּ אוֹתוֹ פְּלוֹנִי גֵּט. ה"מ כְּשֶׁיָּצָא הַקּוֹל קוֹדֶם שֶׁתִּנָּשֵׂא לְאַחֵר, אֲבָל יָצָא לְאַחַר נִשּׂוּאִין — לָא חָיְישִׁי' לֵיהּ. וְזוֹ נְשׂוּאָה וְעוֹמֶדֶת לְכֹהֵן זֶה הֲרֵי יָמִים וְשָׁנִים, וּמִפְּנֵי שֶׁיָּצָא עָלֶיהָ קוֹל גֵּירוּשִׁין נוֹצִיאֶנָּה מִתַּחְתָּיו? הָא קָלָא דְּבָתַר נִשּׂוּאִין הוּא. **מַאי תֵּצֵא נַמִי תֵּצֵא מִשֵּׁנִי.** אִם מֵת כֹּהֵן זֶה וּנְשָׂאָהּ כֹּהֵן אַחֵר — תֵּצֵא, שֶׁהֲרֵי יָצָא עָלֶיהָ קוֹל גְּרוּשָׁה זֶה כַּמָּה שָׁנִים. וּפָרְכִינַן: וַהֲרֵי אַתָּה מוֹצִיא לַעַז עַל בָּנָיו שֶׁל רִאשׁוֹן לוֹמַר חֲלָלִים הֵם, שֶׁהֲרֵי הוֹצֵאתָהּ מִן הַשֵּׁנִי, שֶׁבָּדְקוּ אַחַר הַדְּבָרִים וְנִמְצְאוּ אֱמֶת. **אָתֵי לְמֵימַר סָמוּךְ לְמִיתָה גֵּרְשָׁהּ.** הָרִאשׁוֹן, לְפִיכָךְ חֲכָמִים מוֹצִיאִים אוֹתָהּ מִן הַשֵּׁנִי. וְלָא אָתֵי לְאַחֲזוּקֵי קָלָא קַמָּא בְּהָכִי, הוֹאִיל וּמֵרִאשׁוֹן לֹא אַפְּקוּהָ, וְאֵין לַעַז. **ב"ש.** שֶׁהָיוּ מַחֲמִירִים בִּקְדוּשַּׁת יוֹחֲסִין, שֶׁאוֹסְרִין אוֹתָהּ לַכְּהוּנָּה מִפְּנֵי כְּתִיבַת הַגֵּט. **שֶׁמִּיעֵךְ לָהּ.** שֶׁשִּׂחֵק עִמָּהּ, לָא חָיְישִׁינַן שֶׁמָּא בָּא עָלֶיהָ. **דֶּרֶךְ טְרַקְסְמוֹן.** דֶּרֶךְ הַכְּבוּשָׁה מִחוּץ לִיכָּנֵס לִפְנִים. וְדוֹמֶה לִי שֶׁהוּא לְשׁוֹן יְוָנִי, כְּמוֹ "טְרַקְסִין" (יומא דף נא.). **כְּדֵי לְחַיְּיבוֹ בְּמַעֲשֵׂר.** דְּקַיְימָא לָן: אֵין הַטֶּבֶל מִתְחַיֵּיב בְּמַעֲשֵׂר עַד שֶׁיִּרְאֶה פְּנֵי הַבַּיִת, וּדְעָיֵיל לֵיהּ דֶּרֶךְ שַׁעַר — לְאַפּוֹקֵי דֶּרֶךְ חֲצֵרוֹת וְדֶרֶךְ גַּגּוֹת דְּלָא. וְיָלֵיף מִ"וְאָכְלוּ בִשְׁעָרֶיךָ" בְּב"מ בְּ"הַשּׂוֹכֵר" (פח.). **מתני' צְרִיכָה גֵּט שֵׁנִי.** מְפָ' בַּגְּמָ'. **לִבּוֹ גַּס בָּהּ.** פריוו"ך בְּלַעַ"ז. **גמ' בְּשֶׁרָאוּהָ שֶׁנִּבְעֲלָה.** ב"ש סָבְרִי: אָדָם עוֹשֶׂה בְּעִילָתוֹ בְּעִילַת זְנוּת, וְכָל כַּמָּה דְּלָא אָמַר: הֲרֵינִי בּוֹעֵל לְשֵׁם קִדּוּשִׁין — לָא אָמְרִינַן לְשֵׁם קִדּוּשִׁין בָּעַל.

מַה

[לקמן פט.] · [לקמן פט:] · שם. · יבמות נב. לקמן פח: [פט:] · לקמן פח: · [ריטב"א דמילתא איתא במשנה עדיות פ"ג מ"ו אבל הך דקאמר ר' דוסא וכי מה עשה לה ליתא שם ולכך שפיר גרסי' דתניא] · ברכות לה: · ג"ז שם וב"מ פח: · קדושין שם. עדיות פ"ד מ"ז [תוספתא דעדיות פ"ב ע"ש ודמכילתין פ"ו ע"ש] · לעיל עג:

תוספות

***לא** כל הימנו לאבד זכותו של שני. ואם תאמר: לרב אדא בר אהבה, דמוקי לה בשניסת, מה שפירש בקונטרס משום חששא דקוניא — מה קוניא שייך? דכיון דניסאת לשני — לא מצי להחזירה, דתלא מזה ומזה! וי"ל: דפעמים דאין הבעל שם על לבו שאסור להחזירה, ועושה קוניא.

ובנהרדעא לא מבטלי קלא. אפילו ע"י עדים. והא דאמרינן ב"חזקת הבתים" (ב"ב דף לב.) ובפ' שני דכתובות (דף כו: ושם) גבי מעלין לכהונה על פי עד אחד דמבטלין קלא — התם משום דנפסל מתרומה לעולם, אבל משום דנאסרה לבעלה משום גרושה — אין לבטלו. א"נ: שאני התם, דלתרומה דרבנן אין לחוש אי מבטלי קלא. **דורות** אחרונים ר' דוסא. אע"ג דב"אלו נערות" (כתובות דף לו:) קאמר ר' יוחנן: רבי יהודה ור' דוסא אמרו דבר אחד, והכא קאמר ר"י גופיה: בא וראה שלא כדורות כו' — גם על עצמו היה קורא תגר. אי נמי: לאו דבר אחד ממש קאמר, שלא היה מיקל כמו ר' דוסא. ובכמה מקומות אמרינן "אמרו דבר אחד", אע"פ שאינן שוין.

וכי מה עשה לה ערבי זה. לרבותא נקט, דאפילו ערביים שטופין בזימה, כדאמרינן בפ"ב דקדושין (דף מט:): י' קבין זנות ירדו לעולם, ט' נטלו ערביים ואחת לכל העולם — אפ"ה ליכא למיחש. **טרקסמון** · לשון שער, כמו "טרוקו גלי" (ברכות דף כח.). ובערוך פי': טרקסמון — מין ירק, דבמשניו' חשיב ירק ששמו טרקסמון. רוצה לומר: דרך שמכניסין ירק שפטור ממעשר. ואין נראה, דא"כ הל"ל "ירק" סתם, ועוד ל"ע במשניות אם דרך טרקסמון פטור אפילו מדרבנן. **דרך** גגות כדי לפוטרן מן המעשר. היינו דווקא אכילת עראי, אבל אכילת קבע — אסורה, כדאמר רבי אושעיא (פסחים דף ט.): מערים אדם על תבואתו ומכניסה במוץ שלה, כדי שתהא בהמתו אוכלת ופטורה מן המעשר. ואכילת בהמה אכילת עראי הוא, כדתנן (פאה פ"א מ"ו): מאכילין לבהמה ולחיה ולעוף עד שיתמרח בכרי. **ורבי** יוחנן אמר אפילו חצר קובעת. וא"ת: ור' ינאי היכי פליג עליה? והא כמה תנאי אית להו דחצר קובעת, כההוא דמייתי בפ' "יוצא דופן" (נדה מז:): אי זו היא חצר שקובעת למעשר? רבי ישמעאל אומר: שהכלים נשמרים לתוכה כו', וכן (ביצה לה.): היה אוכל באשכול ונכנס מגינה לחצר, ר"א אומר: יגמור, ור' יהושע אומר: לא יגמור! וי"ל: דרבי ינאי מוקי להו מדרבנן, אבל מה"ת — צריך שיראה פני הבית. אבל אין לתרץ דהא דחצר קובעת — היינו דבעינן שיבא דרך חצר לבית, אבל חצר לבד אינה קובעת אפי' מדרבנן. דההוא דהיה אוכל באשכול משמע דחצר קובעת בלא בית, וכן בכמה משניו'. ועוד הקשה ה"ר אלחנן: דההוא בסוף פ' "יוצא דופן" (נדה דף מז:) מסיים בה הכי: ר' יהודה אומר: שתי חצרות זו לפני' מזו, הפנימי' — חייבת, והחיצונה — פטורה. ואי צריך להביא לבית — פשיטא דלעולם לא יתחייב עד שיכנים דרך פנימית, כי דרך חיצונה לבדה לא יוכל לבא.

בית

עין משפט נר מצוה

שייך לעיל פ:

מח א מיי' פ"ח מהל' גירושין הלכה א סמג עשין נ טוש"ע אה"ע סימן קמג סעיף א וסימן ו סעיף א:

מט ב טוש"ע אה"ע סי' ו סעיף ד:

נ ג מיי' פ"י שם הלכה כ סמג שם טוש"ע אה"ע סימן מו סעיף ח וסימן ו סעיף ג:

נא ד מיי' פי"ז מהל' איסורי ביאה הלכה יט טוש"ע אה"ע סימן ו סעיף ג:

נב ה מיי' פ"ג מהל' מעשר הלכה ג ופ"ד הלכה ז סמג עשין קלה טוש"ע י"ד סימן שלא סעיף פג:

נג ו מיי' פ"י מהלכות גירושין הלכה יח סמג עשין נ טוש"ע אה"ע סימן קמט סע"א:

תוספות רי"ד

לאלתר ואם נשאת זהו לאחר זמן תנן לא כל הימנו מן הראשון לאבד זכותו של שני בשלמא לרב אדא בר אהבה היינו דקתני שני אלא לשמואל מאי שני זכות הראויה לשני שמשיצאת מלפני העדים בחזקת מגורשת זכתה להנשא לשני ומדקמפרשי אמוראי למילתא דרבי אלעזר ש"מ דהלכתא כותיה ומסתמא [הלכתא] כותיה דרב אדא בר אהבה דדיקא מתניתין כותיה ופירוקא דשמואל שינויא היא ואשינויא לא סמכינן: **מתני'** כתב לגרש את אשתו ונמלך בש"א פסלה מן הכהונה ובה"א אע"פ שנתנו לה על תנאי ולא נעשה התנאי לא פסלה מן הכהונה: שלח ליה רב יוסף בריה דרב מנשיא לשמואל ילמדנו רבינו יצא עליו קול איש פלוני כהן כתב גט לאשתו והרי היא יושבת תחתיו ומשמשתו מהו שלח ליה תצא והדבר צריך בדיקה מאי צריך בדיקה אילימא דאי מיגליא מילתא דקרי אינשי מתא לנתינה כתיבה דלמא כתב ונתן קאמרי והאמר רב (שמואל) [אשי] כל קלא דבתר נישואין לא חיישינן ליה. פי' ואע"ג דאמרינן בפירקין דלקמן דחיישי' לקלא ה"מ קלא דקמי נישואין כדתנן יצא שמה בעיר מקודשת הרי זו מקודשת ואסורה לינשא עד שיתן לה אותו פלוני גט אבל לאחר נשואין לא חיישינן וזו נשואה ועומדת היא והיכי אמר תצא ומהדר מאי תצא דאמר שמואל משני שאם מת כהן זה ונשאה כהן אחר תצא שהרי יצא עליה קול גרושה זה כמה שנים ופרכינן והרי אתה מוציא לעז על בניו של ראשון שיאמרו חללים הם שהרי הוציאוה מן השני מפני שבדקו אחר הדברים ונמצאו אמת ומהדר כיון דמפקת לה משני ולא מפקת לה מראשון אתו למימר סמוך למיתה גירשה הראשון ולפיכך הוציאוה מן השני ולא אתי לאחזוקי קלא קמא הואיל ולא אפיקנה מראשון: **מתני'** המגרש את אשתו ולנה עמו בפונדקי בש"א אינה צריכה ממנו גט שני ובה"א צריכה ממנו גט שני אימתי בזמן שנתגרשה מן הנשואין ומודים בנתגרשה מן האירוסין שאינה צריכה ממנו גט שני מפני שאין לבו גס בה: כנסה בגט קרח תצא מזה ומזה וכל הדרכים האלו בה: גט קרח הכל משלימים עליו דברי בן ננס ר' עקיבא אומר אין משלימים עליו אלא קרובי' הראוין להעיד במקום אחר: איזהו גט קרח

כל

נד א מיי' פ"י מהלכות גירושין הלכה יז סמג עשין נ טוש"ע אה"ע סימן קמט סעיף א:
נה ב מיי' שם הלכה יח טור ש"ע שם סעיף ב:

דב"ש סברי: אדם עושה בעילתו בעילת זנות, וב"ה סברי: *אין אדם עושה בעילתו בעילת זנות. אבל לא ראוה שנבעלה – דברי הכל אינה צריכה הימנו גט שני. תנן: ומודים בנתגרשה מן האירוסין – שאינה צריכה הימנו גט שני, שאין לבו גס בה; ואי בשראוה שנבעלה, אמה לי מן האירוסין ומה לי מן הנשואין! אלא מתני' בשלא ראוה שנבעלה, ור' יוחנן דאמר כי האי תנא; דתניא, *א"ר שמעון בן אלעזר: לא נחלקו ב"ש וב"ה על שלא ראוה שנבעלה – שאינה צריכה הימנו גט שני, על מה נחלקו? על שראוה שנבעלה, שבש"א: אדם עושה בעילתו בעילת זנות, ובה"א: אין אדם עושה בעילתו בעילת זנות. ומתני', דאוקימנא בלא ראוה שנבעלה, במאי פליגי? *דאיכא עדי יחוד וליכא עדי ביאה, ב"ש סברי: לא אמרי' הן הן עדי יחוד והן הן עדי ביאה, וב"ה סברי: באמרינן הן הן עדי יחוד והן הן עדי ביאה, ומודים בנתגרשה מן האירוסין – שאינה צריכה הימנו גט שני, דכיון דאין לבו גס בה, לא אמרינן הן הן עדי ביאה. ומי אמר ר' יוחנן הכי? והאמר רבי יוחנן: *הלכה כסתם משנה, ואוקימנא למתניתין בשלא ראוה שנבעלה! *)אמוראי נינהו ואליבא דרבי יוחנן.§ **מתני'** *כנסה בגט קרח – תצא מזה ומזה, וכל הדרכים האלו בה. גט קרח – הכל משלימין עליו, דברי בן ננס. ר"ע אומר: אין משלימין עליו אלא קרובים הראויין להעיד במקום אחר. ואיזהו גט קרח? כל שקשריו מרובין מעדיו.§ **גמ'** מ"ט דגט קרח? *גזירה משום "כולכם".§ "גט קרח הכל משלימין עליו".§ ור"ע, עבד מאי טעמא לא? דאתו למימר כשר לעדות. קרוב נמי אתו למימר כשר לעדות! אלא, עבד היינו טעמא – דדלמא אתו לאסוקיה ליוחסין. גזלן דבר יוחסין הוא ליתכשר! אלמה תנן, ר"ע אומר: אין משלימין עליו אלא קרובים הראויין להעיד במקום אחר; קרוב אין, גזלן לא! אלא, עבד היינו טעמא – דאתו למימר שחרורי שחרריה, גזלן נמי אתו למימר תשובה עבד; קרוב מאי איכא למימר? קרוב, כולי עלמא ידעי דקרוב הוא.§ א"ר זירא, אמר רבה בר שאילתא, א"ר המנונא סבא, א"ר אדא בר אהבה: גט קרח – קשריו שבעה ועדיו ששה, ששה ועדיו חמשה, חמשה ועדיו ארבעה, ארבעה ועדיו שלשה – עד כאן מחלוקת בן ננס ור"ע; אבל קשריו שלשה ועדיו שנים – דברי הכל אין משלימין עליו אלא קרוב. א"ל רבי זירא לרבה בר שאילתא: מכדי כל שלשה במקושר כשנים בפשוט דמי, מה התם קרוב לא, אף הכא נמי קרוב לא! אמר ליה: אף לדידי קשיא לי ושאילתיה לרב המנונא, ורב המנונא לרב אדא בר אהבה, וא"ל: הנח לשלשה במקושר, דלאו דאורייתא. תניא נמי הכי: *גט קרח – קשריו שבעה ועדיו ששה, ששה ועדיו חמשה, חמשה ועדיו ארבעה, ארבעה ועדיו שלשה – עד כאן מחלוקת בן ננס ורבי עקיבא; השלים עליו עבד – בן ננס אומר: הולד כשר, ורבי עקיבא אומר: הולד ממזר; אבל קשריו שלשה ועדיו שנים – דברי הכל אין משלימין עליו אלא קרוב. רב יוסף מתני: כשר. והתניא: קרוב! אמר רב פפא, תני: כשר. אמר רבי יוחנן: לא הוכשרו בו אלא עד אחד קרוב בלבד, אבל תרי לא, דלמא אתי לקיומי בתרי קרובים וחד כשר. אמר רב אשי: מתניתא נמי דיקא,

דקא

*) [יבמות עז: מנחות נב: חולין מג. ועמ"ש על הגליון נדה נו:]

מה לי מן האירוסין. הא חזינן דבעל, ואין אדם בועל את אשתו בזנות לב"ה. בשלא ראוה שנבעלה. והא (א) דמצרכינן גט שני – משום דאמרי': כיון דלבו גס בה – ודאי בעל, ואין אדם בועל בעילת זנות, ואיכא קדושין. ומודים. במן האירוסין, דכל כמה דלא חזינן – לא אמרינן בעל, דהא לא גייסי אהדדי. הן הן כו'. כלומר, כיון דראו שנתייחדו – אין צריך עדות של ביאה גדול מזה, ודאי אנן סהדי כיון דגייסי אהדדי – לא פרשו זה מזה. מי אמר ר' יוחנן הכי. כדלעיל, דהיכא דלא ראוה שנבעלה לא בעי גט. מתני' גט קרח. מפרש בסיפא במתני': שקשריו מרובין מעדיו, בב"ב (דף קס.) אמרי' דתקון רבנן גט מקושר משום כהנים קפדנים, שהיו כותבין גט פתאום לנשותיהן, ומתחרטין לאחר זמן, ואין יכולים להחזירן. ותקנו להם גט מקושר, שאינו נוח ליכתב מהרה, שמא בתוך כך יתפייס. וחותמין עדיו מבחוץ. וכותב שיטה או שתים וכורכן על החלק ותופר, ועד א' חותם על הכרך מבחוץ. וחוזר וכותב שני שיטין או יותר מבפנים, וכורכן על החלק, וחותם עד שני על הכרך מבחוץ, וכן עד שלישי. ואם יש קשר כרוך ואין עד חתום מאחוריו – זה קרח, ופסול. כדמפרש בגמרא משום "כולכם", דמסתמא למנין קשריו היו עדיו מתחלה, וחיישי' דלמא אמר להו "כולכם חתומו" והרי אחד שלא חתם. הכל משלימין עליו. ואפי' פסולין, דליתא להא השלמה אלא משום חששא בעלמא, שמא כשיצא לאחר זמן בבית דין יפסלוהו, שיהו סבורים שהזמין הבעל עדיו למנין קשריו, ולא חתמו בו כולם. אלא קרוב שהוא ראוי להעיד. בעדות אחרת, שאין עליו פסול עדות אלא קורבה. אבל גנב וגזלן – לא. וטעמא מפרש בגמ'. גמ' קרוב נמי אתו למימר כשר לעדות. אלא מדמכשר בקרוב – ש"מ בקיאי אינשי בהלכות עדות, ולא אתו לאכשורי פסולים וקרובים. לאסוקי ליוחסין. דאמרי: מדאחתמוהו בגיטא – לאו עבד הוא, ויהבי ליה בת ישראל. אלא. לעולם טעמא משום דאתי לאכשורי לעדות, ודקשיא לך קרוב נמי – לא דמי, דעבד איכא למימר שחרורי שחרריה. אפילו המכירים אותו שהוא עבד ובקיאין בהלכות עדות – אתו לאכשוריה לעדות, דאמרי: מדאחתמוהו – ש"מ שחרריה מריה. וכן גזלן, אתו למימר: מדאחתמוהו – ש"מ תשובה עבד. אין משלימין עליו. שלישי פסול. אלא כשר או קרוב. דגט מקושר צריך שלשה עדים, כדאמרינן בפרק "גט פשוט" דרבנן תקון שמא בתוך כך שלא ימלא ג' עדים ינוח כעסו. כל שלשה במקושר. כיון דעיקרו בג'. כשנים בפשוט דמי. ואמאי מכשרת קרוב? גט קרח קשריו שבעה. כלומר, שקשריו שבעה כו'. עד כאן מחלוקת בן ננס ור"ע. שאם השלים עבד כו'. הולד כשר גרסי' בבן ננס. רב יוסף מתני. במילתיה דר' זירא אמר רבה בר שאילתא: אבל קשריו ג' ועדיו שנים – אין משלימין עליו אלא כשר. לא הוכשרו בו. אם היה קרח. דבשני קשרים אין משלימין בו שני קרובים, אלא אחד קרוב ואחד כשר, ואפילו היו חתומים בו כבר ג' כשרים. דלמא אתי לקיומיה. היום, ולמחר אם יקרא עליו ערעור לפוסלו, ויביאוהו לב"ד ואין העדים בפנינו, ויבאו עדים מן השוק שיכירו שלש מן החתימות הללו ויקיימוהו בכך, ושמא לא יכירו אלא חתימת שני הקרובים ואחד מן הכשרים, ובית דין אינן יודעין שהן קרובים – ויקיימוהו בעדות פסולה. מתניתא נמי דיקא. הך ברייתא דקתני קשריו שבעה ועדיו ששה, או קשריו ששה ועדיו חמשה כו' – לא אישתמיט ותנא בחד מינייהו שני קרחות, כגון קשריו חמשה ועדיו שלשה – שמע מינה לא פליגי בה, דאפילו קרוב לא מיתכשר.

דקא

בית שמאי סברי אדם בועל בעילת זנות. ואע"ג דביבמות פ' "ב"ש" (דף קז.) אמרי ב"ש דאין ממאנין אלא ארוסות, ולא נשואות, ומפרש רב יוסף ורבה טעמא דב"ש – משום דאין אדם בועל בעילתו בעילת זנות, ולהכי נשואות אין יכולות למאן, דלאו אדעתא דהכי נסבה. איכא למימר: דהתם, כיון שראינו שקידשה – ודאי אינו רוצה לבעול בעילתו בעילת זנות. אבל הכא, שלא ראינו הקדושין – סברי דבועל בעילת זנות. וב"ה סברי דלעולם אין אדם בועל בעילת זנות. ואע"ג דאית להו התם אפילו נשואות ממאנות – היינו משום דכיון שע"י קדושין *ונשואין בא עליה – לא חשיב ליה בעילת זנות, כדאמרי' התם. בגט קרח תצא מזה ומזה. הא דלא תני לה בהדי הנהו דלעיל, אומר ה"ר יוסף: דאיידי דתנא לעיל: כתב סופר גט כו' – תנא: כתב לגרש את אשתו, והדר תנא: המגרש את אשתו ולנה עמו בפונדקי, דהוי נמי פלוגתא דב"ש וב"ה כמו כתב לגרש כו', והדר תנא גט קרח. וכל הדרכים האלו בה. לקמן בפ' בתרא (דף פו.) מוקי לה כר"מ, אבל לרבנן – תלא, והולד כשר.

תוספות רי"ד

כל שקשריו מרובים מעדיו. אוקימנא למתני' בשלא ראוה שנבעלה ובמאי פליגי כגון דאיכא עדי יחוד וליכא עדי ביאה ב"ה סברי אמרי' הן הן עדי יחוד הן הן עדי ביאה ואין אדם עושה בעילתו בעילת זנות ולשם קדושין בעל הלכך צריכה ממנו גט שני וב"ש סברי לא אמרי' הן הן עדי יחוד הן הן עדי ביאה ומודים בנתגרשה מן האירוסין שאינה צריכה ממנו גט שני דכיון דאין לבו גס בה לא אמרי' הן הן עדי יחוד הן הן עדי ביאה: כנסה בגט קרח וכו'. פי' דגט קרח מפרש בסיפא דמתני' אי זה גט קרח וכו' ובגט פשוט אמרי' דרבנן תקנו גט מקושר משום כהנים קפדנים שהיו קופדים עם נשותיהן וכותבין להן גט פתאום ומתחרטין לאחר זמן ואין יכולין להחזירן ותקינו להו גט מקושר שאינו נוח ליכתב ושמא בתוך כך מתפיים עם אשתו וחותמין עדיו מבחוץ כותב שיטה א' מכפנים וכורכה על שיטה חלקה ותופר ועד אחד חותם על הכרך מבחוץ וחוזר וכותב שיטה אחרת וכורכה על שיטה חלקה וחותם על הכרך מבחוץ (וכן עד שני) וכן עד ג' ואם הרבה בו קשרים יותר מג' ויש שם קשר כרוך ואין עד חתום מאחריו זהו גט קרח ופסול: ואמרי' מ"ט דגט קרח גזירה משום כולכם. פי' דאמרינן מסתמא למנין קשריו היו עדיו מתחלה וחיישינן דלמא אמר להו כולכם חתומו והרי אחד לא חתום ותנן לעיל כולכם חתומו א' כותב וכולן חותמין ולפיכך אם מת אחד מהן הרי הגט בטל וק' לי אמאי לא תניא לעיל גבי הנך דתנא בהו תצא מזה ומזה ואפסקה בכתב לגרש את אשתו ונמלך ובמגרש את אשתו ולנה עמו וכו': גט קרח הכל משלימין עליו פי' אפי' פסולין כגון עבד וגזלן דליתיה להשלמה זו אלא משום חששא בעלמא שמא כשיצא לאחר זמן בב"ד יפסלהו שיהו סבורים שהזמין הבעל עדיו למנין קשריו ולא חתמו בו כולן הלכך אפילו בפסולין משלימין אותו והשלמה זו אינה אלא מדעת הבעל שיצוה לו שיחתום בו דאי שלא מדעתו היאך רשאי זה לחתום ולהעיד עדות שקר תדע דהכי הוא מדאמרינן לקמן לא הכשירו בו אלא עד אחד קרוב בלבד אבל תרי לא דלמא אתו לקיומיה בשני קרובים וחד כשר ואי שלא מדעת הבעל משלימין אותו ניחוש דלמא איהו מקיים אפומיה דההוא כשר וקרוב שחתמו שלא מדעת הבעל ששניהם פסולין כיון שלא צוה להן הבעל וכן הם פסולין הכשרין כמו הקרובים כיון שעשו שלא מדעת הבעל אלא ודאי אין משלימין אלא מדעת הבעל: ר' עקיבא אומר אין משלימין וכו' פי' דוקא בקרוב משלימין אותו שאין עליו פסול אחר אלא קורבה אבל עבד וגזלן לא אמרינן: ור"ע עבד מ"ט לא לאו דלמא אתו למימר עבד כשר לעדות קרוב נמי אתו למימר כשר לעדות אלא [עבד] היינו טעמא דלא דלמא אתו לאסוקיה ליוחסין גזלן דבר יוחסין הוא ליתכשר אלמה תאני קרוב אין גזלן לא אלא עבד היינו טעמא דלא דלמא אתו למימר שחרורי שחרריה גזלן נמי אתו למימר תשובה עבד אלא קרוב מאי איכא למימר כולי עלמא ידעי דקרוב הוא ואי ק' והרי כל טעמא בגט קרח לא הוי אלא משום גזירת כולכם ולעיל בהמביא תנין אמרי' איתמר אמר לעשרה כתבו גט לאשתי אמר ר' יוחנן שנים משום עדים וכולן משום תנאי ור"ל אמר כולם משום עדים ומוקמינן פלוגתייהו דאמר להו כולכם ואיכא בינייהו כגון שנמצא א' מהן קרוב או פסול למ"ד משום תנאי כשר ואמרי' נמי התם מיחתם בתחלה קרוב או פסול אמרי לה כשר ואמרי לה פסול אלמא ע"כ לא פליגי אלא להחתימו (ולכתחלה) [בתחילה] אבל באמצע או בסוף לר' יוחנן הוא כשר וקי"ל ר"ל ור' יוחנן הלכה כר' יוחנן בר מתלת ור' עקיבא לא מכשר אלא קרוב אבל פסול לא ואי חתם בו פסול א"ר עקיבא הולד ממזר כדאמרינן לקמן בהלכתין ור' יוחנן מתיר להחתים הפסול לכתחלה וקי"ל הלכה כר"ע מחביריו כ"ש דבן ננס תלמיד חבר הוה לר"ע כדאמרי' בשלהי פ' מי שמת יש לתרץ דהתם בעל הוא דקפיד ואמר חתמו בו כלכם הלכך אי מחתמי' ביה פסול לא נפיק מיניה חורביה לאכשורי בשאר עדיות דאנן לא הוה מחתימ' ליה אי לאו משום דבעל קפיד אבל בגט קרח שב"ד מורים לו להחתימו אם יורו לו ב"ד להחתים בו פסול אתו לאכשוריה בשאר עדיות ומשום הך גזירה אמרינן שאם חתם בו הולד ממזר: אמר רב אדא בר אהבה גט קרח קשריו שבעה ועדיו ששה ששה ועדיו ה' ה' ועדיו ד' ד' ועדיו ג' עד כאן מחלוקת בן ננס ור' עקיבא אבל קשריו ג' ועדיו ב' דברי הכל אין משלימין עליו אלא קרוב א"ל ר' זירא לרבה בר שילא מיכדי כל ג' במקושר כשנים בפשוט דמי מה התם קרוב לא אף הכא נמי קרוב לא א"ל אף לדידי קשיא ושאילתיה לרב המנונא ורב המנונא לרב אדא בר אהבה וא"ל הנח לג' במקושר דלאו דאורייתא: א"ר יוחנן לא הכשירו בו אלא עד אחד קרוב בלבד אבל תרי לא דלמא אתו לקיומיה בשני קרובים וחד כשר. פי' אם היה קרח בשני קשרים אין משלימין בו שני קרובים אלא א' קרוב וא' כשר ואפילו היו חתומים בו כבר ג' כשרים דלמא אתו לקיומיה היום ומחר אם יקרא עליו ערעור לפוסלו ויביאוהו לב"ד ואין העדים בפנינו ויבואו עדים מן השוק שיכירו שלשה מהחתימות האלו ויקיימוהו בכך ושמא לא יכירו אלא חתימת שני הקרובים וא' מן הכשרים וב"ד אינם יודעין שהן קרוביו ויקיימוהו. ואי ק' ובפשוט היכי מכשרי' שום קרוב כדאמרינן בגט פשוט תניא היו חתומים בו ד' וה' עדים ונמצא א' קרוב או פסול תתקיים העדות בשאר ואמר חזקיה מילאהו בקרובים כשר וניחוש שמא יתקיים השטר ע"פ א' קרוב וא' כשר ובשלהי תוספ' דמסכתין תניא גט שחתמו עליו ה' עדים ונמצאו שלשה הראשונים קרובים או פסולים תתקיים העדות בשאר נ"ל דלכתחלה אסור להחתים עד קרוב בגט פשוט דומיא כב' במקושר אבל אי איקרי וחתם לא פסלינן ליה אלא תתקיים העדות בשאר ומתניתא שחתמו בו תניא דיעבד וחזקיה נמי מילאהו קאמר דיעבד אבל הכא הכל משלימין עליו תנן לכתחלה ומשום הכי אמר רבי יוחנן לא הכשירו בו אלא עד אחד קרוב והוא הדין דאי איקרו וחתמו בו תרי לא פסלינן ליה.

אמר

[שם ביבמות קז. בגמ' איתא וכתובה]

[יבמות קז. כתובות עג.]

[תוספתא פ"ד ותוספתא לעדיות פ"ב ע"ש]

[קדושין סה:]

[שבת מו. וש"נ]

[יבמות לא:]

לעיל ד: [וע' תוס' לקמן פב. ד"ה גזירה משום]

תוספתא ספ"ו כ"ש

הגהות הב"ח

(א) רש"י ד"ה בשלא וכו' והא דמצרכינן גט:

דקא מדלג ותני חד חד, שמע מינה. אמר אביי: שמע מינה: האי קרוב חתים אי בעי בין בתחילה בין באמצע בין בסוף, ממאי? מדלא קבע ליה מקום; ושמע מינה: מכל תלתא מקיימינן ולא בעינן רצופין, דאי סלקא דעתך בעינן רצופין, לקבע ליה מקום להאי קרוב בתחילה או באמצע או בסוף, ולכשר ביה טובא. כי אתו לקמיה *דרבי אמי, אמר ליה: צא והשלם עליו עבד מן השוק.§

הדרן עלך הזורק

המגרש את אשתו, ואמר לה "הרי את מותרת לכל אדם אלא לפלוני" — ר' אליעזר מתיר, וחכמים אאוסרים. כיצד יעשה? ביטלנו הימנה, ויחזור ויתננו לה ויאמר לה "הרי את מותרת לכל אדם". *כתבו בתוכו, אע"פ שחזר ומחקו — פסול.§ **גמ'** איבעיא להו: האי "אלא", "חוץ" הוא, או "על מנת" הוא? "חוץ" הוא, וב"חוץ" הוא דפליגי רבנן עליה דר' אליעזר, דהא שייר לה בגט, גאבל ב"על מנת" מודו ליה, מידי דהוה אכל תנאי דעלמא. או דלמא "על מנת" הוא, וב"ע"מ" הוא דפליג ר' אליעזר אדרבנן, *אבל ב"חוץ" מודה, דהא שייר לה בגט? אמר רבינא, ת"ש: *דכל הבתים מטמאין בנגעים אלא של גוים; אי אמרת בשלמא "חוץ" הוא — שפיר, אלא אי אמרת "על מנת" הוא, על מנת דלא מיטמו בתי גוים הוא דמיטמו בתי ישראל, הא מיטמו בתי גוים לא מטמאי בתי ישראל?! ועוד, בתי גוים מי מטמאי? והתניא: °"ונתתי נגע צרעת בבית ארץ אחוזתכם" — ארץ אחוזתכם מטמאה בנגעים, ואין בתי גוים מטמאין בנגעים! אלא השמע מינה "חוץ" הוא, ש"מ. מתני' דלא כי האי תנא; דתניא, אמר ר' יוסי בר' יהודה: לא נחלקו רבי אליעזר וחכמים על המגרש את אשתו ואמר לה "הרי את מותרת לכל אדם חוץ מפלוני" — שאינה מגורשת, על מה נחלקו? על המגרש אשתו ואמר לה, "הרי את מותרת לכל אדם על מנת שלא תנשאי לפלוני", שר"א

ויקרא יד

רש"י

דקא מדלג ותני חד חד. שהולך ומחסר העדים מן הקשרים אחד אחד. בכל דילוג ודילוג שמנה במשנתנו לא דילג אלא אחד במנין הקשרים. שמע מינה האי קרוב חתים. בין בתחילה קודם – לכשרים, בין באמצעו, בין בסופו. מדלא קבע ליה מקום. לקרוב במתני'. ושמע מינה. מדלא קבע מקום – שמע מינה דכל גיטין ושטרות מקושרים היוצאין בבית דין להעיד על חתימת העדים לקיימו. מכל תלתא. סהדי דחתימי ביה, שיכירו עדי השוק את חתימתן – מקיימינן ליה לגיטא, ואפילו הן מפוזרין. כגון אם יש בו י' עדים, ועדי השוק מכירין את כתב הראשון והשלישי והחמישי. ולא בעינן שיכירו אותן שלשה רצופין. דאי ס"ד בעינן רצופין. אמאי לא הוכשרו בו אלא השלמת קרוב אחד? ומשום דלמא אתי לקיומיה בשני קרובים וחד כשר, כדאמרינן לעיל. ליקבע ליה מקום. להשלמת קרובים. או בתחילה. קודם לשנים הכשרים, דכל שלשה ושלשה החתומין בו. או באמצע. כל ג' וג' חתומין יכשיר קרוב אחד, כגון: כשר וקרוב וכשר, וחוזר וחותם כשר וקרוב וכשר, וכן לעולם. או בסוף. כל ג' וג' יקבע מקומו. ולכשר ביה. קרובים טובא, וליכא למיחש דלמא אתי לקיומיה בשני קרובים וחד כשר – דהא לא משכחת שני קרובין בכל ג' רצופין שבו, שאין לך בו שנים קרובים שלא יהא הפסק ב' כשרים ביניהם. אלא מדלא אשכח תקנתא להשלמת שני קרובים בקביעות מקום – שמע מינה לא בעינן רצופין, הלכך חיישינן דלמא מקיים ליה בקרובין מפוזרין. כי אתו לקמיה דר' אמי. גט מקושר שלא הזמין לו עדים למנין קשריו, והסופר והעדים בפנינו, ועדיין לא נמסר לה. א"ל כו'. כאן נגס. כן הוא עיקרה של סוגיא זו. ולא שמעתיה כן, אלא כביאורה בקונטרס מורי הזקן.

הדרן עלך הזורק גט

המגרש · ואמר לה. בשעת מסירה. **גמ'** על מנת הוא. על מנת שלא תנשאי לפלוני. אבל בעל מנת מודו. רבנן, דבגט לא שייר, שהתירה במסירת הגט לכל אדם, אלא שהתנה עמה: על מנת שלא תנשאי לזה, ואין זה אלא כתנאי בעלמא. אלא של גוים. דכתיב: "אחוזתכם".

הכא

תוספות

צא והשלם עליו עבד מן השוק. אומר ר"י: דהך דהכא פליג אדחזקיה דאמר בפרק "גט פשוט" (ב"ב דף קסב:): מילאהו בקרובים – כשר. דמשמע: דוקא קרובים כשרים למילוי. ומעשה בא לפני רבינו משולם באחד שכתב גט לאשתו, והחתים עליו ב' עדים, ואחר זמן החתים עליו עד שלישי, והכשירו מסברא, דהא דאמרינן דאין עדי הגט חותמין זה בלא זה – היינו בשנים, או שזימן שלשה יחד, שאין הגט יכול להיות בפחות – אז יחתמו כולם זה בפני זה. אבל כשהגט נגמר בשנים, ולא היה אז דעתו להחתים יותר, כשחזר והחתים שלישי – אין נפסל בכך, כיון שנגמר ע"י הראשונים. ור"ת הביא ראיה מכאן דכשר: דלישנא ד"צא והשלם עליו עבד מן השוק" – משמע שכבר חתמו הראשונים, ולא היה צריך כי אם להשלים. אלמא, כיון שכבר הוכשר הגט ע"י הראשונים – תו לא מיפסיל בהשלמת אחרים זה שלא בפני זה. ומיהו בקונטרס פירש: והסופר והעדים בפנינו, ועדיין לא נמסר. משמע שסובר דבעינן זה בפני זה. ומה שפירש: ועדיין לא נמסר לה – ר"ל שהעדים לא חתמו עדיין, ולהכי לא נמסר לה, וחותמין כולן זה בפני זה. אך מה שפי': שהסופר בפנינו – בחנם פירש, דמה לנו אם הלך לו הסופר? וכן פירש הר' אלחנן דנראה לפוסלו, דכיון שבא להחתים שלישי – גילה בדעתו שלא יהא גט עד שהחתים שלישי, וחתימתו אין כלום, כיון שלא חתמו זה בפני זה. לעיל פא. **גזירה** משום כולכם. פירש בקונטרס: דמסתמא למנין קשריו היו עדיו מתחלה, וחיישינן דלמא אמר להו "כולכם חתומו" והרי אחד מהם שלא חתם. ותימה: מאחר דפסלינן גט קרח משום "כולכם" – מאותו טעם נפסל קרוב להחתים בתוכו, כדאמרינן לעיל בפ' ב' (דף יח:) דאם אמר הבעל "כולכם", למ"ד משום עדים – נמצא אחד מהן קרוב או פסול – פסול הגט! ויש לחלק: דהכא במקושר, דעדיו ג' – הכשירו בו אחד קרוב. ולעיל בפ"ב (שם ד"ה אמרי) הארכתי.

הדרן עלך הזורק גט

המגרש · אבל בעל מנת מודו ליה. לכאורה היה נראה דדוקא ב"על מנת שלא תינשאי" מודו דלא הוי שיור, משום דהותרה אצלו בזנות, אבל ב"על מנת שלא תיבעלי ולא תינשאי" – הוי שיור כמו "חוץ". ולהכי נקט בברייתא בסמוך "על מנת שלא תינשאי" גרידא, דב"שלא תינשאי ולא תיבעלי" – מודה ר' אליעזר דהוי שיור כמו "חוץ". וכן משמע קצת, דהא לקמן פריך ארבי יוסי הגלילי דאמר: היכן מצינו אסור לזה ומותר לזה. במאי? אי ב"על מנת" – הרי הותרה אצלו בזנות, אלא ב"חוץ". ואי ב"על מנת שלא תינשאי ולא תיבעלי" קאמר רבי אליעזר נמי לא הוי שיורא – מאי קאמר "הרי הותרה אצלו בזנות"? ועוד, למאי דמוקי לה ב"חוץ", אדמקשה ר' יוסי הגלילי לרבי אליעזר מ"חוץ", ליפרוך להו לרבנן דמודו ב"על מנת שלא תינשאי ושלא תיבעלי" דלא הותרה אצלו בזנות. ומיהו, נראה לר"י: דאפילו ב"על מנת שלא תינשאי ושלא תיבעלי" מודו רבנן דלא הוי שיורא, דכיון דאין אוסרה אלא בלשון תנאי – הוי כאילו הותרה לכל, ולהכי לא מצי פריך מידי רבי יוסי הגלילי אדרבנן. וכי קאמר "אילימא בעל מנת – הרי הותרה אצלו בזנות", הוה מצי למיפרך, שאפילו לא הותרה אצלו בזנות, כגון "על מנת שלא תינשאי ולא תיבעלי" דהרי הותרה לכל, כיון דלא אסרה אלא דרך תנאי. אלא נקט קושיא פשוטה "ע"מ שלא תינשאי" גרידא הנזכר בברייתא. דא"כ, אדמפליג בסמוך בין "ע"מ" ל"חוץ" – לפלוג ב"ע"מ" גופיה. ועוד, דקאמר "או דלמא האי אלא ע"מ הוא כו'" – אף על גב דב"אלא" אסיר נשואין ובעילה, אפ"ה לא הוי שיור, אף על גב דב"חוץ" מודו להו. ובסמוך דקאמר "ומתניתין דאוקימנא בחוץ מאי טעמא דרבי אליעזר", אבל לרבנן אפילו ב"על מנת שלא תינשאי ולא תיבעלי" – אתי שפיר, מידי דהוי אכל תנאים דעלמא.

אמר רבינא תא שמע כל הבתים כו'. ומדתנן בריש זבחים (דף ב.): כל הזבחים שנזבחו שלא לשמן כשירין, אלא שלא עלו לבעלים לשם חובה – לא הוה מצי לאיתויי ראיה, דהתם לא שייך לא "על מנת", ולא "חוץ", ואותו "אלא" לא הוי אלא לשון "רק" או "אבל".

שרבי

עין משפט נר מצוה

א א מיי' פ"ח מהל' גירושין הלכה יז סמג עשין נ טוש"ע אה"ע סימן קלז סעיף א:

ב ב מיי' וסמג שם טוש"ע שם וסימן קמז סעיף ג:

ג ג מיי' שם הלכה טז סמג שם טוש"ע אה"ע סימן קלז סעיף א:

ד ד מיי' פי"ד מהל' טומאת צרעת הל' יא:

ה ה מיי' פ"ח מהל' גירושין הלכה טז סמג עשין נ טוש"ע אה"ע סימן קלז סעיף א:

מסורת הש"ס

[גי' הרא"ש דר' ינאי]

[עי' תוס' לקמן פד: ד"ה אם כתבו]

ס"א מודי דהוי אבל תנאי דעלמא

נגעים פי"ב מ"א

תוספות רי"ד

אמר אביי האי קרוב חתים בין בתחלה בין באמצע בין בסוף ממאי מדלא קא קבע ליה מקום. פי' וה"ה נמי בפשוט אם היו חתומים בו ד' וה' עדים ונמצא א' מהן קרוב או פסול תתקיים העדות בשאר ולא חיישינן לקרוב בכל היכא דאיתא חתום ואי ק' הא אמרן לעיל בהמביא תנין מיחתם בתחלה קרוב או פסול אמרי זה כשר ואמרי לה פסול דאתי לאיחלופי בקיום שטרות דעלמא יש לתרץ התם חתום קרוב תחילה ואין שם עדים אחרים והרואה סובר שעל הקרוב סומך אבל הכא כבר חתום הוא בכשרים ואינו חותם בקרוב אלא על הקשר קרח ויודעים שעל שאר העדים סומכי כדתרצינן התם גבי מילאהו בקרובים כשר: ושמעת מינה מכל תלתא מקיימינן ולא בעינן רצופים דאי ס"ד בעינן רצופים ליקבע ליה להאי קרוב מקום או בתחלה או באמצע או בסוף וליתכשרו ביה טובא פי' וה"ה לפשוט שהיו חתומים בו עדים הרבה מכל תרי מניהו מקיימי ולא בעי' רצופים פי' שכך הם שנים בפשוט כמו ג' במקושר: **סליק פירקא**

המגרש את אשתו וא"ל הרי את מותרת לכל אדם אלא לפלוני ר' אליעזר מתיר וחכמים אוסרין כיצד יעשה יטלנו ממנה ויחזור ויתננו לה ויאמר לה הרי את מותרת לכל אדם ואם כתבו בתוכו אע"פ שחזר ומחקו פסול. פי' בעת שמסר לה הגט לא אמר הרי זה גיטיך סתם אלא אמר לה הרי את מותרת לכל אדם אלא לפלוני: כיצד יעשה וכו'. פירוש שהגט לא נתבטל בכך ובכשרותו עומד אלא שהנתינה הראשונה לא היתה יפה ויטלנו ממנה ויחזור ויתננו לה ויאמר לה הרי את מותרת לכל אדם ודוקא יטלנו ממנה ויחזור ויתננו לה בכשרות אז היא מגורשת אבל אם לא נטלו ממנה וחזר ואמר לה הרי את מותרת לכל אדם אינו כלום דבעינן ונתן בידה ונתינה ראשונה כיון שהיתה בפסול כמאן דליתא דמיא הילכך בעינן נתינה בכשרות והאי דתני שיאמר לה בנתינה שניה הרי את מותרת לכל אדם לאו דוקא אלא אם אמר לה הרי זה גיטך סתם די לנו דכשאומר לה הרי זה גיטיך סתם הכי משמע שתהא מותרת לכל אדם אלא מפני ששנה תחילה אלא לפלוני חזר ושנה הרי את מותרת לכל אדם ולאו דוקא אלא שאמר לה הרי זה גיטיך סתם דיו דהאי דתנן לקמן גופו של גט הרי את מותרת לכל אדם דוקא בכתיבת הגט מיירי לא שיהא צ"ל לה בעת המסירה דומיא דסיפא דקתני ר' יהודה אומר ודין דיהבי ליך מנאי שאין זה (מכבר) [מדבר] אלא שיכתבנו בגט לא שיאמר לה בפה כך וכך הרי את מותרת לכל אדם דוקא בכתיבת הגט מיירי אבל במסירתו לה אינו צ"ל אלא הרי זה גיטיך סתם שבכתיבה מתגרשת האשה לא באמירה וכיון שהגט כתוב כהלכתו אומר לה הרי זה גיטיך והיא מגורשת: איבעיא להו האי אלא חוץ הוא או ע"מ הוא חוץ הוא ובחוץ הוא דפליגי רבנן עליה דר' אליעזר דהא שייר ליה בגט אבל בע"מ מודו ליה מידי דהוה אכל תנאי דעלמא או דלמא ע"מ הוא ובע"כ הוא דפליג רבי אליעזר עלייהו דרבנן אבל בחוץ מודה להו דהא שייר ליה בגט אמר רבינא ת"ש כל הבתים מיטמאין בנגעים אלא של גוים אי אמרת בשלמא חוץ הוא שפיר אלא אי אמרת ע"מ הוא ע"מ

דלא

תוספות רי"ד

דלא מיטמאו בתי גוים הוא דמיטמאו בתי ישראל הא כשמטמאו בתי גוים לא מיטמאו בתי ישראל ותו בתי גוים מי מיטמאי בנגעים והכתיב אמר רחמנא אחוזתכם מיטמא בנגעים ולא אחוזת הגוים אלא לאו ש"מ חוץ הוא ש"מ ודוקא בחוץ פליגי רבנן אבל בע"מ מודו והכי נמי אמרינן לקמן ת"ר כל התנאים פוסלים בגט דברי רבי וחכ"א כל שפוסל בפה פוסל בכתב וכל שאינו פוסל בפה אינו פוסל בכתב חוץ שפוסל בפה פוסל בכתב ע"מ שאינו פוסל בפה אינו פוסל בכתב וכתב ר"ח ז"ל ואפשר בחוץ פליגי והלכה כחכמים אבל בע"מ תנאה הוי ולכשימשות זה שנאסרה עליו הרי היא מותרת לכל אדם שהרי נתקיים התנאי ואינו נ"ל שאינה זקוקה להמתין עד שימות אותו פלוני שנאסרה עליו אלא מיד היא מותרת לינשא לכל אדם חוץ מאותו פלוני דהכי אמרינן לקמן בהלכתי' ת"ר לאחר פטירתו של רבי אלעזר נכנסו ד' זקנים להשיב על דבריו ר' טרפון ורבי יוסי הגלילי ור' אלעזר בן עזריה ור' עקיבא נענה ר' טרפון ואמר הרי שהלכה זו ונשאת לאחיו של זה שנאסרה עליו ומת בלא בנים לא נמצא זה שהוא גורם לעקור דבר מן התורה ואי אמרת דאסורה להנשא לאחר כל זמן שזה שנאסרה עליו קיים היאך גורם לעקור דברי התורה והרי אסורה היא להנשא לכל אדם כ"ש לאחיו ואם עברה ונישאת לאחיו בעבירה נישאת לו שהרי עדיין לא נתקיים התנאי והיאך תהיה בת ייבום שלא היו נישואיו נישואין אלא ודאי מכאן מוכיח שמיד היא מותרת לינשא לכל אדם ולא חיישינן שמא תתאלמן או תתגרש ותנשא לזה ויתבטל הגט. תו אמרינן נענה ר' עקיבא הרי שהלכה זו ונשאת לא' מן השוק והיו לה בנים ונתאלמנה או נתגרשה ועברה ונשאת לזה שנאסרה עליו לא נמצא גט בטל ובניה ממזרים. ומוקמינן לה דרבי עקיבא סבר דבע"מ פליגי אלמא תפשוט מהכא דמאן דשרי בע"מ לא מזקקינן לה לאמתוני עד שימות אותו פלוני שנאסרה עליו ותו דפריך עליה רבא ואמר אי הכי בכולהו תנאי דלמא לא תינסיב דדלמא לא מקיימא תנאה ונמצא גט בטל ובניה ממזרים מכאן מוכיח דקים ליה לרבא דבכל תנאים דעלמא מתירין אותה לינשא מיד ולקמן נמי בהרי זה גיטיך על מנת שלא תשתי יין כל ימי חיי פלוני הרי זה כריתות. פי' המורה הרי זה כריתות מיד והיא תתקיים התנאי וכ"כ גם בעל ה"ג כל ימי חיי וחיי פלוני הרי זה כריתות ומיקיים תנאיה וכ"ת לכי מיית איהו למה לה גיטא [אלא ודאי ש"מ] דכל תנאה דבידה לקיימו אנן לאלתר שרינן לה ואמרינן לה קיים תנאך. ואי ק' היכי אמרינן דבכל תנאין דעלמא שרינן לה לאלתר והא אמרן לעיל בפ' מי שאחזו תניא הרי זה גיטיך ע"מ שתתני לי מאתים זוז ונקרע הגט או אבד הרי זו מגורשת ולאחר לא תנשא עד שתתן אלמא כל זמן דלא מיקיימה תנאה אסורה להנשא והכא היכי שרינן לה מיד. תשובה כל זמן שמתנה ואומר לה ע"מ שתעשי דבר פלוני תלה קיום הגט בעשיית המעשה שאם תעשה האשה אותו המעשה הגט קיים ואם לאו אינו קיים כגון שתתני מאתים זוז או שתניקי את בני או שתשמשי את אבא וכיוצא בהן בכל אלה עשיית מעשה האשה היא באה כדי לקיים הגט ומ"ה אין הגט קיים אלא בעשיית אותו המעשה שהרי הבעל תלה קיום הגט בעשיית אותו המעשה אבל כשאמר לה הרי זה גיטיך על מנת שלא תנשאי לפלוני ע"מ שלא תשתי יין כל ימי חיי פלוני וכיוצא בהן שעשיית המעשה אינה באה לקיום הגט אלא לבטל הגט שאם תנשאי לו או תשתי יין נמצא גט בטל לא תלה הבעל קיום הגט בעשיית המעשה אלא הגט גט מיד ובלבד שתזהר האשה שלא תעשה אותו המעשה שיתבטל הגט בשבילו והילכך אע"פ שעשיית המעשה מבטלת הגט למפרע אפ"ה מתירין אותה להנשא מיד ולא חיישינן שמא

תעשה

שר"א מתיר לכל אדם חוץ מאותו האיש, וחכמים אוסרים. מאי טעמא דר"א? מידי דהוה אכל תנאי דעלמא. ורבנן? כל תנאי דעלמא לא שייר ליה בגט, הכא שייר לה בגט. ומתני' דאוקימנא ב"חוץ", מאי טעמא דר"א? א"ר ינאי *משום זקן אחד: אמר קרא: °"ויצאה מביתו והלכה והיתה לאיש אחר", אפילו לא התירה אלא לאיש אחר – הרי זו מגורשת. (א) ורבנן *(אמרי טעמא דר"א:) האי "איש" – לכל איש ואיש. *ורבי יוחנן אמר, טעמא דר"א מהכא: °"ואשה גרושה מאישה לא יקחו" – *אאפילו לא נתגרשה אלא מאישה – נפסלה מן הכהונה, אלמא הוי גיטא. ורבנן? איסור כהונה שאני. בבעי רבי אבא: בקידושין היאך? תיבעי לר"א, תיבעי לרבנן; תיבעי לר"א: עד כאן לא קאמר רבי אליעזר הכא – אלא משום דכתיבי קראי, אבל התם קנין מעליא בעינן, או דלמא *"ויצאה והיתה"? תיבעי לרבנן: עד כאן לא קאמרי רבנן הכא – אלא דבעינן כריתות וליכא, אבל התם קנין כל דהו, או דלמא "ויצאה והיתה"? לבתר דאיבעיא ליה הדר פשטה: בין לרבי אליעזר בין לרבנן, בעינן "ויצאה והיתה". אמר אביי: אם תמצא לומר איתא לדרבי אבא, בא ראובן וקידשה חוץ משמעון, ובא שמעון וקידשה חוץ מראובן, ומתו שניהם – מתיבמת ללוי, *ואין אני קורא בה אשת שני מתים, מאי טעמא? קידושי דראובן אהנו, קידושי דשמעון לא אהנו. ואלא אשת שני מתים היכי משכחת לה? כגון שבא ראובן וקידשה חוץ משמעון, ובא שמעון וקידשה סתם, דקידושי ראובן אהנו למיסרא אעלמא, וקידושי דשמעון אהנו למיסרא אראובן. בעי אביי: אמר לה "הרי את מותרת לכל אדם חוץ מראובן ושמעון", וחזר ואמר לה "לראובן ושמעון", מהו? מי אמרינן מאי דאסר שרא, או דלמא מאי דאסר שרא ומאי דשרא אסר? גאם תמצא לומר מאי

רש"י

הכא שייר בגיטא. כיון דקתני בהדה שלא לינשא לזה – נמצא שלא התירה גט זה לכל אדם. אלא מאישה. דאמר לה: הרי את מגורשת ממני, ואי את מותרת לכל אדם. וזהו ריח הגט שפוסל בכהונה. ומדפוסל לכהונה – אלמא גט הוא, והכא דשרייה לכל אדם חוץ מזה – מותרת לאחרים. איסור כהונה שאני. שריבה בהן הכתוב מצות יתירות. בקידושין היאך. "התקדשי לי ליאסר לכל אדם חוץ מפלוני" מהו? דכתיבי קראי. כדאמרן: "לאיש אחר" "גרושה מאישה". ויצאה והיתה. אקיש הויה ליציאה, וכיון דבגירושין הוי גט – הכא נמי הוו קידושין, ונאסרה לכל חוץ מאותו האיש. בעינן כריתות וליכא. דהא אגידא ביה לגביה דההוא גברא. הדר פשטה בין לר"א כו'. לר"א הוו קידושין, לרבנן לא הוו קידושין. אם תמצי לומר איתא לדרבי אבא. אליבא דר"א, דהוו קידושין – אפילו הכי בא ראובן וקדשה לגבי כולי עלמא חוץ משמעון אחיו, ובא שמעון וקדשה חוץ מראובן, ומתו שניהם – מתייבמת ללוי אחיהם. ואין אני קורא בה אשת שני מתים. לאוסרה ללוי מפני זיקת שני יבמין, דתנן ביבמות (דף לא.): שלשה אחין ומת אחד מהם ועשה השני מאמר ביבמתו ומת – חולצת ולא מתייבמת, שנאמר: "ומת אחד מהם יבמה יבא עליה" מי שעליה זיקת יבם אחד, ולא שעליה זיקת שני יבמין. כגון זו, שעדיין לא יצתה מזיקת יבומי המת הראשון, דאין יבמה יוצאה מזיקתה אלא בביאה, ונתוספה עליה זיקה מחמת מאמרו של שני. והכא אשמועינן אביי: אפילו איתא לדרבי אבא, שקידושין כאלו הוו קידושין לגבי עלמא, ונמצאו שניהם קידושין – אין אני קורא בה אשת שני מתים. מאי טעמא? קדושי דראובן אהנו, אבל קדושי שמעון לא מהני מידי. דכיון דאמר: "חוץ מראובן" – לא אסרה על שום אדם המותר, שהרי אסורה ועומדת היא על הכל חוץ מראובן. ואלא אשת שני מתים היכי משכחת לה. בהאי ענינא דרבי אבא? כגון בא ראובן כו'. מאי

תוספות

שרבי אליעזר מתיר לכל אדם חוץ מאותו האיש. משמע דאפילו בחיי אותו האיש מתירה לינשא. והקשה רבינו שמואל: אמאי לא חיישינן דלמא לא תקיים תנאה, כדאמר לעיל ב"מי שאחזו" (דף עד.) גבי "הרי זה גיטיך על מנת שתתני לי מאתים זוז" (*ולאחר) לא תנשא עד שתתן! ועוד מביא ראיה רבינו יצחק מברייתא דלקמן (דף פד.): "על מנת שלא תיבעלי לאבא ולאביך" – אין חוששין שמא תיבעל להם, הא לאחר – חוששין שתיבעל לו! °ותירץ הרב רבי אלחנן: דשאני גבי מאתים זוז, דיש לחוש פן תפסיד את אשר לה ולא תוכל לקיים תנאה. וכן גבי "שלא תיבעלי לאחר" – חיישינן שמא יבא עליה באונס. אבל הכא, "על מנת שלא תינשאי" – ליכא למיחש שישאנה בעל כרחה, דנישואין אי אפשר בעל כרחה. אפילו לא נתגרשה אלא מאישה פסולה לכהונה. וא"ת: והא ודאי דאיסור כהונה שאני, דהא אם לא נתגרשה אלא מאישה ולא הותרה לשום אדם – פשיטא דאפילו לר"א לא הוי גט כלל בעלמא, ואם מת – מותרת להתייבם, ואע"פ שפסולה לכהונה! וי"ל דהכי מייתי: דכיון דאפילו לא נתגרשה אלא מאישה פסולה לכהונה, א"כ כי אמר "חוץ מפלוני" – הוי גט גמור. דאם לא הוי גט – סברא הוא דבלא נתגרשה אלא מאישה, אפילו ריח הגט לא הוי, ולא היה אוסרה הכתוב לכהנים. וא"ת: לר"א דלא חשיב ב"על מנת" שיור, ולתנא דמתני' דרבנן נמי מודו דלא הוי שיורא, אמאי לא תנא ביבמות ברישא (דף ב.) ט"ז נשים פוטרות צרותיהן, ולחשוב בהדייהו אשת איש דפוטרת צרתה – כגון שגירשה זה ב"על מנת שלא תינשא לפלוני" ונשאה אחיו של פלוני, ומת בלא בניס? ומ"על מנת שלא תנשא" גרידא, דמותרת בזנות, או "לא תיבעלי" גרידא, שיכולה להתקדש – אין קשה, דלא דמי לאחות אשה שאסורה גם בזנות, ואינה יכולה להתקדש. אבל מ"על מנת שלא תינשא ושלא תיבעלי" – קשיא! וי"ל: דלא תני לה משום דלא דמי לאחות אשה, דהתם בשעת נפילה הויא לה אחות אשה, אבל הכא – בשעת נפילה אכתי לא הויא אשת איש עד שתיבעל ליבם, ותעבור על תנאו. ואפילו תתחבנה כאילו היא אשת איש, כיון שמטעם אשת איש אסורה ליבעל לו – מ"מ לא מצי למיתני', דהא אם תיבעל לו – נמצא שלא היתה אשת אחיו מעולם, ולא דמי לאחות אשה, הלכך לא פטרה. ומיהו, לא יתיישב אלא למאן דנפקא ליה מאחות אשה. ועוד קשה לרבינו יצחק: דאכתי משכחת לה אף בצרת צרה, כגון דקידשה אחד חוץ מראובן ושמעון אחיו, ובא ראובן וקידשה חוץ משמעון אחיו, דאהני קידושי דידיה למיסרא אקמא, ומת ראובן בלא בנים ולו אשה אחרת, ויבם שמעון צרתה ולו אשה אחרת, ומת בלא בנים, ונפלו לפני לוי, דצרת צרה פטורה מן החליצה ומן הייבום! וי"ל: כיון שנאסרה על יבם זה לפני קידושי אחיו משום אשת איש – לא חשיבא לגבי יבם אשת אח. אבל אי אשת שני מתים דאורייתא, כדמשמע בסמוך, משכחת לה שש עשרה צרות וצרת צרה, כגון שקידש ראובן חוץ משמעון ולוי אחיו, ובא שמעון וקידשה חוץ מלוי, דאהני קידושי שמעון למיסרא אראובן. ומתו ראובן ושמעון, ויבם לוי צרת אשת שני מתים, שאשת שני מתים לא נאסרה ללוי, שלא אסרוה עליו. ומת לוי ולו אשה אחרת, ונפלו לפני יהודה, דצרת [צרה] אשת שני מתים פטורה מן החליצה ויבום. ומיהו, איכא למימר בפלוגתא לא קמיירי, דרבנן פליגי אדר"א בקידושין כמו בגירושין, כדמסיק "ויצאה והיתה", ולדידהו לא משכחת אשת שני מתים. ואפילו ללוי דמיירי בפלוגתא פ"ק דיבמות (דף ט.) לא מיירי אלא בפלוגתא דסבירא ליה לתנא כוותיה. תדע, דלא תנא לוי חייבי לאוין, ואע"ג דלר"ע לאו בני חליצה ויבום נינהו, כחייבי כריתות. אבל למאי דסלקא דעתיה דר' אבא דרבנן מודו בקידושין – הוי מצי למיתני ט"ז. ובירושלמי דמכילתין פריך לה: וליתני ט"ז נשים לר"א! ומשני: התם התורה אסרה עליו, ברם הכא – הוא אסרה עליו. פירוש: כל ט"ו נשים אסרה תורה ליבם, והאיסור בא ממילא על ידי קידושין בלא שום תנאי. אבל כאן – אסרה על ידי תנאי שלו. א"נ י"ל: תמן התורה אסרתה ואין לה היתר להתייבם, דאין איסור שלה תלוי בשום אדם אלא בתורה, שאסרתה עליו. אבל באשת איש – האיסור תלוי במגרש, שאם ירצה – יתירנה ליבם קודם שימות אחיו המת שנשאה*. אלא אשת שני מתים היכי משכחת לה. הכא משמע דאשת שני מתים דאורייתא. וקשה מפ"ג דיבמות (דף לא:) ומפ"ק (דף י:), ושם מפורש*. כגון שבא ראובן וקידשה חוץ משמעון ובא שמעון וקידשה סתם. תימה לרבינו יצחק: כשבא שמעון וקידשה סתם, אמאי לא פקע איסות דראובן? מ"ש מ"הרי את מותרת לכל אדם חוץ מפלוני" וניסאת לאחר ומת, דפקע איסות ראשון, ומותרת לזה שנאסרה עליו? ואין סברא לחלק משום דהתם הוי שיור מועט ופקע. ויש לומר: דהתם בגירושין, כיון שהתחיל לנתקה – ע"י שניסאת לאחר מנתקה לגמרי. אבל הכא שבא לקדשה – ע"י שנתקדשה לאחר לא נתקה. וחזר ואמר לה לראובן ושמעון. כל הך בעיא מיתוקמא שפיר אף כרבנן. אף

עין משפט נר מצוה

ו א מיי' פ"י מהל' גירושין הל' א סמג עשין נ טוש"ע אה"ע סימן ו סעיף א וסימן קנ סעיף ג:

[טעות הדפוס]

ז ב מיי' פ"ז מהל' אישות הלכה יג סמג עשין מח טוש"ע אה"ע סי' לח סעיף לט וע"ש:

ח ג מיי' פ"ח מהל' גירושין הלכה ז סמג עשין נ טוש"ע אה"ע סי' קלז סעיף ד:

[גי' רש"ל ורבנן אמרי וכו' פי' הרבנן שהיו בימי רבי ינאי אבל המהרש"א בתוס' דלקמן פג ע"ב ד"ה רבא וכו' כתב לקיים הגירסא שלפנינו ורבי יוחנן אמר וכו' ע"ש ועי' בגירסת הילקוט בפ' אמור ובפ' תצא איתא אביי אמר טעמא דר"א מהכא ואשה גרושה וכו']

תוספות רי"ד

תעשה אותו מעשה ויבטל הגט למפרע: מ"ט דר' אליעזר דכתיב ואשה גרושה מאישה לא יקחו אפילו לא נתגרשה אלא מאישה נפסלה מן הכהונה אלמא הוי גיטא פי' והכא דשרייה לכל אדם חוץ מפלוני מותרת לאחרים ורבנן איסור כהונה שאני שהתורה רבתה בהן מצות יתירות: בעי ר' אבא בקידושין היאך. פי' אם אמר לה התקדשי לי להיאסר לכל אדם חוץ מפלוני: תיבעי לר' אליעזר תיבעי לרבנן תיבעי לר' אליעזר דע"כ לא קאמר ר' אליעזר הכא אלא משום דכתיב קרא אבל התם כי יקח כתיב קנין מעליא בעיא או דלמא ויצאה והיתה. תיבעי לרבנן ע"כ לא אמרי רבנן הכא אלא דבעינן כריתות וליכא אבל התם קנין כל דהו או דלמא ויצאה והיתה בתר דבעיא הדר פשטה בין לר' אליעזר בין לרבנן ויצאה והיתה. נ"ל דע"כ לא מהני שיור בקידושין בין בחוץ לר' אליעזר בין בע"מ לרבנן אלא כי שייר לעלמא ולדידיה לא שייר כגון דאמר לה הרי את מקודשת לי חוץ משמעון או ע"מ שתהי מותרת לשמעון אבל אם שייר לעצמו כגון דא"ל הרי את מקודשת לי ויאסרו עלי כל קרובותיך חוץ מפלונית גם רבי אליעזר מודה דלא הוו קידושין כיון ששייר בקידושין דהא לא יליף לה רבי אליעזר אלא מלאיש אחר וההוא שיורא באחריני הוא אבל ממנו גירשה לגמרי וה"ה הכי נמי גבי קידושין אם לא שייר לעצמו שנאסר בכל קרובותיה אע"פ ששייר לאחרים הוו קידושין אבל אם שייר לעצמו לא הוו קידושין

תניא

מסורת הש"ס

[לקמן פג:]

[טעות הדפוס וכן בילקוט פרשת אמור ופ' תצא ליתא]

יבמות נב. לד

[קדושין ה. וש"נ]

[לעיל מג:]

[ועי' תוספות יבמות י: ד"ה לעולם]

[ד"ה מדרבנן וד"ה לעולם]

תורה אור: דברים כד; ויקרא כא

הגהות הב"ח

(א) גמ' ורבנן האי איש לכל איש ואיש ורבנן אמר טעמא דר"א מהכא אשר כנ"ל וכ"כ ע"ל בדף פג בתוס' בד"ה רבא:

גליון הש"ס

תוס' ד"ה שר"א מתיר וכו' ותירץ הר"ר אלחנן עי' קידושין דף ס ע"ב תד"ה אבל:

מַאי דַּאֲסַר שְׁרָא, "לִרְאוּבֵן" מַהוּ? לִרְאוּבֵן וְהוּא הַדִּין לְשִׁמְעוֹן, וְהַאי דְּקָאָמַר לִרְאוּבֵן — מִשּׁוּם דִּפְתַח בֵּיהּ, אוֹ דִּלְמָא לִרְאוּבֵן דַּוְקָא? [א]וְאִם תִּמְצָא לוֹמַר לִרְאוּבֵן דַּוְקָא, לְשִׁמְעוֹן [ב]מַהוּ? לְשִׁמְעוֹן וְה"ה לִרְאוּבֵן, וְהַאי דְּקָאָמַר שִׁמְעוֹן — מִשּׁוּם דְּסָלֵיק מִינֵּיהּ, אוֹ דִּלְמָא לְשִׁמְעוֹן דַּוְקָא? בָּעֵי רַב אַשִׁי: "אַף לְשִׁמְעוֹן", מַהוּ? "אַף" אַרְאוּבֵן קָאֵי, אוֹ דִּלְמָא "אַף" אַעָלְמָא קָאֵי? [ג]תֵּיקוּ.§ ת"ר: *לְאַחַר פְּטִירָתוֹ שֶׁל ר"א, נִכְנְסוּ אַרְבָּעָה זְקֵנִים לְהָשִׁיב עַל דְּבָרָיו, אֵלּוּ הֵן: *רַבִּי יוֹסֵי הַגְּלִילִי, ור"ט, וְרַבִּי אֶלְעָזָר בֶּן עֲזַרְיָה, וְר"ע. נַעֲנָה ר"ט וְאָמַר: הֲרֵי שֶׁהָלְכָה זוֹ וְנִישֵּׂאת לְאָחִיו שֶׁל זֶה שֶׁנֶּאֶסְרָה עָלָיו, וּמֵת בְּלֹא בָּנִים, לֹא נִמְצָא זֶה עוֹקֵר דָּבָר מִן הַתּוֹרָה? הָא לָמַדְתָּ, שֶׁאֵין זֶה כְּרִיתוּת. נַעֲנָה רַבִּי יוֹסֵי הַגְּלִילִי וְאָמַר: הֵיכָן מָצִינוּ אָסוּר לָזֶה וּמוּתָּר לָזֶה? הָאָסוּר אָסוּר לַכֹּל, וְהַמּוּתָּר מוּתָּר לַכֹּל! הָא לָמַדְתָּ, שֶׁאֵין זֶה כְּרִיתוּת. נַעֲנָה רַבִּי אֶלְעָזָר בֶּן עֲזַרְיָה וְאָמַר: "כְּרִיתוּת" — דָּבָר הַכּוֹרֵת בֵּינוֹ לְבֵינָהּ, הָא לָמַדְתָּ, שֶׁאֵין זֶה כְּרִיתוּת. נַעֲנָה ר"ע וְאָמַר: הֲרֵי שֶׁהָלְכָה זוֹ וְנִשֵּׂאת לְאֶחָד מִן הַשּׁוּק וְהָיוּ לָהּ בָּנִים, וְנִתְאַרְמְלָה אוֹ נִתְגָּרְשָׁה, וְעָמְדָה וְנִישֵּׂאת לָזֶה שֶׁנֶּאֶסְרָה עָלָיו, לֹא נִמְצָא גֵּט בָּטֵל וּבָנֶיהָ מַמְזֵרִים? הָא לָמַדְתָּ, שֶׁאֵין זֶה כְּרִיתוּת; דָּבָר אַחֵר: הֲרֵי שֶׁהָיָה זֶה שֶׁנֶּאֶסְרָה עָלָיו כֹּהֵן, וּמֵת הַמְגָרֵשׁ, לֹא נִמְצֵאת אַלְמָנָה אֶצְלוֹ וּגְרוּשָׁה אֵצֶל כָּל אָדָם? וְק"ו: מַה גְּרוּשָׁה שֶׁהִיא קַלָּה — אֲסוּרָה בִּשְׁבִיל צַד גֵּירוּשִׁין שֶׁבָּהּ, אֵשֶׁת אִישׁ שֶׁהִיא חֲמוּרָה — לֹא כ"ש! הָא לָמַדְתָּ, שֶׁאֵין זֶה כְּרִיתוּת. אָמַר לָהֶן רַבִּי יְהוֹשֻׁעַ: אֵין מְשִׁיבִין אֶת הָאֲרִי לְאַחַר מִיתָה. אָמַר רָבָא: כּוּלְּהוּ אִית לְהוּ פִּירְכָא, לְבַר מִדְּר' אֶלְעָזָר בֶּן עֲזַרְיָה דְּלֵית לֵיהּ פִּירְכָא. תַּנְיָא נַמִי הָכִי, *א"ר יוֹסֵי: רוֹאֶה אֲנִי אֶת דִּבְרֵי ר' אֶלְעָזָר בֶּן עֲזַרְיָה מִדִּבְרֵי כּוּלָּן.§ אָמַר מָר, נַעֲנָה ר"ט וְאָמַר: הֲרֵי שֶׁהָלְכָה זוֹ וְנִשֵּׂאת לְאָחִיו שֶׁל זֶה שֶׁנֶּאֶסְרָה עָלָיו, וּמֵת בְּלֹא בָּנִים, לֹא נִמְצָא זֶה עוֹקֵר דָּבָר מִן הַתּוֹרָה? עוֹקֵר?! אִיהוּ עָקַר?! אֶלָּא, מַתְנֶה לַעֲקוֹר דָּבָר מִן הַתּוֹרָה. מַתְנֶה?! מִי קָאָמַר לָהּ: לָא סַגֵּי לָהּ דְּלָא מִינַּסְבָא לֵיהּ לַאֲחוּהּ דְּהַהוּא גַּבְרָא? אֶלָּא, גּוֹרֵם לַעֲקוֹר דָּבָר מִן הַתּוֹרָה. גּוֹרֵם?! [ד]אֶלָּא מֵעַתָּה, בַּת אָחִיו לֹא יִשָּׂא, שֶׁמָּא יָמוּת בְּלֹא בָּנִים, וְנִמְצָא גּוֹרֵם לַעֲקוֹר דָּבָר מִן הַתּוֹרָה! [ה]הַיְינוּ פִּירְכָא. וּבְמַאי? אִילֵימָא בְּ"חוּץ", מִשְׁרָא שָׁרָא ר"א! דְּתַנְיָא: [ו]*מוֹדֶה ר"א, בִּמְגָרֵשׁ אֶת אִשְׁתּוֹ וְאָמַר לָהּ "הֲרֵי אַתְּ מוּתֶּרֶת לְכָל אָדָם חוּץ מִפְּלוֹנִי", וְהָלְכָה וְנִיסֵּת לְאֶחָד מִן הַשּׁוּק וְנִתְאַרְמְלָה אוֹ נִתְגָּרְשָׁה, שֶׁמּוּתֶּרֶת לָזֶה שֶׁנֶּאֶסְרָה עָלָיו! אֶלָּא בְּ"עַל מְנָת". נַעֲנָה ר' יוֹסֵי הַגְּלִילִי וְאָמַר: הֵיכָן מָצִינוּ אָסוּר לָזֶה וּמוּתָּר לָזֶה? הָאָסוּר אָסוּר לַכֹּל, וְהַמּוּתָּר מוּתָּר לַכֹּל. וְלָא? וַהֲרֵי תְּרוּמָה וְקָדָשִׁים, שֶׁאֲסוּרָה לָזֶה וּמוּתֶּרֶת לָזֶה! בְּאִיסּוּר אִשָּׁה קָא אָמְרִינַן. וַהֲרֵי עֲרָיוֹת! בְּאִישׁוּת קָאָמְרִינַן. הֲרֵי אֵשֶׁת אִישׁ! הַיְינוּ פִּירְכָא. וּבְמַאי? אִילֵימָא בְּ"עַל מְנָת", הֲרֵי הוּתְּרָה אֶצְלוֹ בִּזְנוּת! אֶלָּא בְּ"חוּץ". נַעֲנָה ר"ע וְאָמַר: הֲרֵי שֶׁהָלְכָה זוֹ וְנִישֵּׂאת לְאֶחָד מִן הַשּׁוּק וְהָיוּ לָהּ בָּנִים, וְנִתְאַרְמְלָה אוֹ נִתְגָּרְשָׁה, וְעָמְדָה וְנִשֵּׂאת לָזֶה שֶׁנֶּאֶסְרָה עָלָיו, לֹא נִמְצָא גֵּט בָּטֵל וּבָנֶיהָ מַמְזֵרִין? אִי הָכִי, בְּכוּלָּה תְּנָאֵי דְּעָלְמָא נַמִי לָא תִּנְסִיב, דִּלְמָא לָא מְקַיְּימָא לֵיהּ לִתְנָאֵיהּ, וְנִמְצָא גֵּט בָּטֵל וּבָנֶיהָ מַמְזֵרִין! הַיְינוּ פִּירְכָא. וּבְמַאי? אִילֵימָא בְּ"חוּץ", מִשְׁרָא שָׁרָא ר"א! דְּתַנְיָא: מוֹדֶה הָיָה ר"א, בִּמְגָרֵשׁ אֶת אִשְׁתּוֹ וְאָמַר לָהּ "הֲרֵי אַתְּ מוּתֶּרֶת לְכָל אָדָם חוּץ מִפְּלוֹנִי", וְהָלְכָה וְנִשֵּׂאת לְאֶחָד מִן הַשּׁוּק וְנִתְאַרְמְלָה אוֹ נִתְגָּרְשָׁה, שֶׁמּוּתֶּרֶת לָזֶה שֶׁנֶּאֶסְרָה עָלָיו! אֶלָּא בְּ"עַל מְנָת". דָּבָר אַחֵר: הֲרֵי שֶׁהָיָה זֶה שֶׁנֶּאֶסְרָה עָלָיו כֹּהֵן, וּמֵת הַמְגָרֵשׁ, לֹא נִמְצֵאת אַלְמָנָה אֶצְלוֹ וּגְרוּשָׁה אֵצֶל כָּל אָדָם, וְקַל וָחוֹמֶר: וּמַה גְּרוּשָׁה שֶׁהִיא קַלָּה — אֲסוּרָה מִשּׁוּם צַד גֵּירוּשִׁין שֶׁבָּהּ, אֵשֶׁת אִישׁ חֲמוּרָה לֹא כָּל שֶׁכֵּן! וּבְמַאי? אִילֵימָא בְּ"עַל מְנָת",

הֲרֵי

רש"י

*מַאי דַּאֲסַר שְׁרָא. דְּהַאי "לִרְאוּבֵן וְשִׁמְעוֹן" — דְּהַדַר אָמַר לָהּ קוֹדֶם מְסִירָה — אַף לִרְאוּבֵן וְשִׁמְעוֹן קָאָמַר, וְאֵינוֹ שִׁיּוּר. אוֹ דִּלְמָא. הַאי לִרְאוּבֵן וְשִׁמְעוֹן דְּהֲדַר קָאָמַר — חֲזָרָה הִיא, שֶׁחָזַר וְהָפַךְ תְּנָאוֹ, לוֹמַר: לִרְאוּבֵן וְשִׁמְעוֹן אֲנִי מַתִּירָהּ לְבַדָּהּ וְתֵאָסְרִי עַל הַכֹּל. בָּעֵי רַב אַשִׁי אַף לְשִׁמְעוֹן מַהוּ. אָמַר לָהּ "חוּץ מֵרְאוּבֵן וְשִׁמְעוֹן" וְחָזַר וְאָמַר "אַף לְשִׁמְעוֹן" מַהוּ? אִם תִּימְצֵי לוֹמַר הֵיכָא דְּחָזַר וְאָמַר "לְשִׁמְעוֹן", וְלֹא אָמַר "אַף" — דַּוְקָא לְשִׁמְעוֹן קָאָמַר, הָכָא מַאי? כֵּיוָן דְּאָמַר "אַף" — וַדַּאי הִתִּירָהּ לִשְׁנֵיהֶם, דְּהַאי "אַף" אַרְאוּבֵן קָאֵי, וְאַע"ג דְּלֹא הִזְכִּיר שְׁמוֹ. אוֹ דִּלְמָא. לְשִׁמְעוֹן וְלֹא לִרְאוּבֵן, וְהַאי "אַף" — אַכּוּלֵּי עָלְמָא קָאֵי. נַעֲנָה. הֵרִים קוֹלוֹ. כָּל עֲנִיָּה הַכְּתוּבָה בַּתּוֹרָה הֲרָמַת קוֹל הִיא. הֲרֵי שֶׁהָלְכָה זוֹ. אַחַר גֵּירוּשֶׁיהָ. וְנִיסֵּת לְאָחִיו. שֶׁל אוֹתוֹ הָאִישׁ שֶׁנֶּאֶסְרָה עָלָיו בַּגֵּירוּשִׁין. עוֹקֵר דָּבָר. מִצְוַת יִבּוּם, שֶׁאֲסוּרָה לְהִתְיַבֵּם לוֹ. שֶׁאֵין זֶה כְּרִיתוּת. הָאֲמוּרָה בַּתּוֹרָה, שֶׁלֹּא אָמְרָה תּוֹרָה כְּרִיתוּת הָעוֹקֵר דָּבָר מִן הַתּוֹרָה. הַכּוֹרֶתֶת בֵּינוֹ לְבֵינָהּ. וַהֲרֵי אַכַּתִּי אֲגִידָא בֵּיהּ, לֵיאָסֵר עַל אוֹתוֹ הָאִישׁ. לֹא נִמְצָא גֵּט בָּטֵל לְמַפְרֵעַ. שֶׁהֲרֵי אָמַר לָהּ: עַל מְנָת שֶׁלֹּא תִּנָּשְׂאִי לִפְלוֹנִי. וּבָנֶיהָ. מִן הָאֶמְצָעִי, מַמְזֵרִין. שֶׁאֵין זֶה כְּרִיתוּת. לֹא אָמְרָה תּוֹרָה כְּרִיתוּת הַמֵּבִיא אֶת יִשְׂרָאֵל לִידֵי פְּסוּל. לֹא נִמְצֵאת אַלְמָנָה. אֵצֶל כֹּהֵן זֶה, דְּהָא לְגַבֵּיהּ לָא אִיגָּרְשָׁה. גְּרוּשָׁה אֵצֶל כָּל אָדָם. וְעַל יְדֵי צַד גֵּירוּשִׁין שֶׁבָּהּ אֲסָרָהּ הַכָּתוּב עָלָיו, כְּדַאֲמַרַן לְעֵיל: גְּרוּשָׁה מֵאִישָׁהּ לְבַדּוֹ אֲסוּרָה לִכְהוּנָּה. וְק"ו. וַהֲרֵי דְּבָרִים ק"ו, שֶׁאַתָּה לָמֵד הֵימֶנּוּ שֶׁלִּפְנֵי מִיתַת הַמְגָרֵשׁ תְּהֵא אֲסוּרָה לַכֹּל מִפְּנֵי צַד אִישׁוּת שֶׁבָּהּ. וּמַה. אִיסּוּר גְּרוּשָׁה שֶׁהוּא קַל, דְּלֵיתָא אֶלָּא בְּלָאו בְּעָלְמָא, מָצִינוּ שֶׁאֲסוּרָה עַל כֹּהֵן זֶה שֶׁהִיא אַלְמָנָה אֶצְלוֹ, מִפְּנֵי צַד גֵּירוּשִׁין שֶׁבָּהּ. אֵשֶׁת אִישׁ שֶׁהִיא חֲמוּרָה. אֵינוֹ דִּין שֶׁתֵּאָסֵר אֵצֶל מִי שֶׁהִתִּירוֹ אֶצְלוֹ, מִפְּנֵי צַד אִישׁוּת שֶׁבָּהּ. אֵין מְשִׁיבִין אֶת הָאֲרִי לְאַחַר מִיתָה. אִם הָיָה קַיָּים — שֶׁמָּא יַחֲזִיר לָכֶם תְּשׁוּבָה. אִית לְהוּ פִּירְכָא. כִּדְמְפָרֵשׁ וְאָזֵל לְקַמֵּיהּ, בָּתַר סַיְּיעְתָּא דְּבָרַיְיתָא. אִיהוּ עָקַר. כְּלוֹמַר, וְכִי הוּא עוֹקְרוֹ מַמָּשׁ? הֲרֵי נֶעֱקַר מֵאֵלָיו בְּגַרְמָתוֹ שֶׁל זֶה. עוֹקֵר — מַשְׁמַע הָעוֹשֶׂה אִיסּוּר בְּיָדַיִם, וְיִבּוּמִין הַלָּלוּ אֵינָן מוּטָּלִין עָלָיו לְיַבְּמָהּ, שֶׁיְּהֵא הוּא עוֹקְרָן. בַּת אָחִיו לֹא יִשָּׂא. שֶׁלֹּא יוּכַל הָאָב לְיַבֵּם אֶת בִּתּוֹ. הַיְינוּ פִּירְכָא. דְּאָמַר רָבָא: לְכוּלְּהוּ אִית לְהוּ פִּירְכָא. וּבְמַאי. מוֹקֵי ר"ט פְּלוּגְתָּא דְּר"א וְרַבָּנַן. אִי בְּחוּץ מִישְׁרָא שָׁרֵי לָהּ רַבִּי אֱלִיעֶזֶר. לְהִתְיַבֵּם לוֹ, מֵאַחַר שֶׁנִּיסֵּת לְאַחֵר וְנִתְּקָהּ מֵאִישׁוּת הָרִאשׁוֹן לְגַמְרֵי. אֶלָּא בְּעַל מְנָת. מוֹקֵי לָהּ, דְּכֵיוָן דִּתְנָאָה הוּא וְלָא אִיתְקַיַּים — נִמְצָא גֵּט בָּטֵל לְמַפְרֵעַ, וְקַיְימָא בְּאִיסּוּר אֵשֶׁת אִישׁ. תְּרוּמָה וְקָדָשִׁים. אֲסוּרִין לְיִשְׂרָאֵל וּמוּתָּרִין לְכֹהֲנִים. עֲרָיוֹת. בִּתּוֹ וַאֲחוֹתוֹ. בְּאִישׁוּת קָאָמְרִינַן. נֶאֶסְרָה ע"י קִידּוּשִׁין. אֵשֶׁת אִישׁ. מוּתֶּרֶת לְבַעְלָהּ וַאֲסוּרָה לְכָל אָדָם. הַיְינוּ פִּירְכָא. דְּקָאָמַר רָבָא לְעֵיל. הֲרֵי הוּתְּרָה אֶצְלוֹ בִּזְנוּת. דְּהָא "עַל מְנָת שֶׁלֹּא תִּנָּשְׂאִי" הוּא דְּקָאָמַר לָהּ, וְקָרֵינָא בָּהּ מוּתֶּרֶת לַכֹּל. אֶלָּא בְּחוּץ. מוֹקֵי רַבִּי יוֹסֵי הַגְּלִילִי לִפְלוּגְתָּא דְּר"א, הִילְכָּךְ פָּרֵיךְ לֵיהּ: הָא שֶׁאֲסָרָהּ עָלָיו לְגַמְרֵי דִּלְגַבֵּיהּ לָא אִיגָּרְשָׁה.

הֲרֵי

תוספות

אף לשמעון מהו. נראה ד"אף לראובן" נמי מספקא ליה.

ועמדה ונישאת לזה שנאסרה עליו לא נמצא גט בטל. וא"ת: והלא אין נישואין חלין, שהרי אסורה עליו משום איסור אשת איש, ומאי שנא מדתניא בתוספתא: "על מנת שלא תינשאי לאבא ולאביך" — ה"ז גט, "על מנת שלא תבעלי לאבא ולאביך" — אינו גט, חוששין שמא תבעל להם. משמע דבע"מ שלא תנשא להם — אפילו נישאת ה"ז גט, והכא אמאי הגט בטל? וי"ל: דהכא עמדה ונישאת לאחר מיתת המגרש קאמר, וכה"ג צ"ל לקמן גבי "שלא תבעלי לאבא ולאביך" — אין חוששין שמא תבעל להם, משום דאסורה להם, הא לאחר — חוששין שמא תבעל. אע"ג דאסורה לו נמי משום אשת איש, מ"מ חוששין שמא תבעל לו לאחר מיתת המגרש. והיא דתוספתא יש ליישב שלא תחלוק על הש"ס שלנו, דהא דקתני התם "על מנת שלא תבעלי לאבא ולאביך" — אינו גט, חוששין שמא תבעל להם, היינו כלומר שאם נראה שתבעל להם — שלא יהא גט, ובא להשמיענו דב"על מנת שלא תינשא" כו' — אפילו נישאת להם הוי גט. א"נ: קא משמע לן ד"על מנת שלא תבעלי לאבא ולאביך" לא בעי למימר דרך נשואין, אלא דרך זנות בעלמא.

אילימא בחוץ לר' אליעזר מישרא שרי. וטעמא: כיון דנשאת זה שהותרה לו — נתרוקן לו כל האישות, ופקע אישות של ראשון לגמרי.

רבא

מסורת הש"ס

עייך לדף פב: | [תוספתא פ"ז] | [תוספתא שם] | [כתוס' איתא ר' טרפון ורבי יוסי הגלילי ור"א בן עזריה ור"ע וטי' תוספת ע"ז מה. ד"ה אמר ר"ע ומה שרשמתי שם] | [עי' תוספות ע"ב ד"ה מודה]

עין משפט נר מצוה

ט א ב ג מיי' פ"ה מהל' גירושין הלכה ח סמג עשין נ טוש"ע אה"ע סימן קלז סעיף ז:

גליון הש"ס

גמ' אלא מעתה בת אחיו לא ישא. עי' יבמות דף לט ע"א תוס' ד"ה ספק א"א: **שם** אלא מעתה בת אחיו כו' היינו פירכא. לא זכיתי להבין דאינו מהדמה דהתם לא נופלת לפניו ליבום ולא הוי עקירה משא"כ בתנאי דנופלת לפניו לייבום דהא הגט התירה גם ליבם אלא דא"א לו לייבם דאז יעקר התנאי ויתבטל הגט וכמ"ש תוס' לעיל דמה"ט אינה פוטרת צרתה דלא דמי לאחות אשה דהכתי לא הוי ערוה עד שתבעל. וגם כיון דזקוקה לו ואעפ"כ אינו יכול לייבם מחמת תנאו זהו הוי גרם עקירת המצוה ולע"ג: **שם** מודה ר"א וכו'. תמיה לי על הסכמת הפוסקים ראשונים ואחרונים את זאת הא כ"מ לדידן באומר חוץ מעובד כוכבים פלוני דהגט כשר ובזה קיימא הסברא דבנשאת לאחר דמותרת אח"כ גם לזה העובד כוכבים לכשיתגייר דהוטיל ופסקה פסקה.

הֲרֵי גְּרוּשָׁה אֶצְלוֹ בִּזְנוּת! אֶלָּא בְּ"חוּץ". וְר"ע, אִי "חוּץ" סְבִירָא לֵיהּ – לוֹתִיב "חוּץ", וְאִי "עַל מְנָת" ס"ל – לוֹתִיב "עַל מְנָת"! ר"ע שְׁמִיעַ לֵיהּ דְּאִיכָּא דְּאָמַר "חוּץ" וְאִיכָּא דְּאָמַר "עַל מְנָת"; מ"ד "חוּץ" – הַאי פִּירְכָא, וּמ"ד "עַל מְנָת" – הַאי פִּירְכָא. וּמַאי פִּירְכָא? אִי נֵימָא אִיסּוּר כְּהוּנָּה שָׁאנֵי – הָא ר"א נַמִי מֵאִיסּוּר כְּהוּנָּה קָא מָיְיתֵי לֵיהּ! רָבָא, *כְּרַבִּי יַנַּאי מִשּׁוּם זָקֵן אֶחָד קָא מַתְנֵי.§ אָמַר לָהֶן ר' יְהוֹשֻׁעַ: אֵין מְשִׁיבִין אֶת הָאֲרִי לְאַחַר מִיתָה. לְמֵימְרָא, דְּר' יְהוֹשֻׁעַ כְּוָותֵיהּ סְבִירָא לֵיהּ? וְהָא אִיהוּ נַמִי מִיפְרַךְ קָפָרֵיךְ! ה"ק לְהוּ: לְדִידִי נַמִי אִית לִי פִּירְכָא, מִיהוּ בֵּין לְדִידִי בֵּין לְדִידְכוּ – אֵין מְשִׁיבִין אֶת הָאֲרִי לְאַחַר מִיתָה. וּמַאי פִּירְכָא דְּר' יְהוֹשֻׁעַ? דְּתַנְיָא, א"ר יְהוֹשֻׁעַ: מַקִּישׁ קוֹדְמֵי הֲוָיָה שְׁנִיָּה לְקוֹדְמֵי הֲוָיָה רִאשׁוֹנָה, מַה קּוֹדְמֵי הֲוָיָה רִאשׁוֹנָה דְּלָא אֲגִידָא בְּאִינִישׁ אַחֲרִינָא, אַף קוֹדְמֵי הֲוָיָה שְׁנִיָּה דְּלָא אֲגִידָא בְּאִינִישׁ אַחֲרִינָא. גּוּפָא: מוֹדֶה ר"א, בִּמְגָרֵשׁ אִשְׁתּוֹ וְאָמַר לָהּ "הֲרֵי אַתְּ מוּתֶּרֶת לְכָל אָדָם חוּץ מִפְּלוֹנִי", וְהָלְכָה וְנִישֵּׂאת לְאֶחָד מִן הַשּׁוּק וְנִתְאַרְמְלָה אוֹ נִתְגָּרְשָׁה, שֶׁמּוּתֶּרֶת לָזֶה שֶׁנֶּאֶסְרָה עָלָיו. *הֵשִׁיב ר"ש בַּר אֶלְעָזָר תְּשׁוּבָה לְדִבְרֵי ר"א: הֵיכָן מָצִינוּ שֶׁזֶּה אוֹסֵר וְזֶה מַתִּיר! וְלָא? וַהֲרֵי יְבָמָה, דְּבַעַל אוֹסֵר וְיָבָם מַתִּיר! הָתָם יָבָם הוּא קָא אָסַר לָהּ, דְּאִי מִבַּעַל – הָא שַׁרְיָא וְקַיְּימָא. הֲרֵי נְדָרִים, דְּנוֹדֵר אוֹסֵר [א]וְחָכָם מַתִּיר! הָא א"ר יוֹחָנָן: [ב]אֵין חָכָם מַתִּיר כְּלוּם אֶלָּא בַּחֲרָטָה. הֲרֵי הֲפָרַת הַבַּעַל, דְּאִשָּׁה נוֹדֶרֶת [ג]וּבַעַל מֵיפֵר! הָתָם כִּדְרַב פִּנְחָס מִשְּׁמֵיהּ דְּרָבָא, *דְּאָמַר רַב פִּנְחָס מִשְּׁמֵיהּ דְּרָבָא: כָּל הַנּוֹדֶרֶת – עַל דַּעַת בַּעְלָהּ הִיא נוֹדֶרֶת. נַעֲנָה רַבִּי אֶלְעָזָר בֶּן עֲזַרְיָה וְאָמַר: "כְּרִיתוּת" – דָּבָר הַכּוֹרֵת בֵּינוֹ לְבֵינָהּ, הָא לָמַדְתָּ שֶׁאֵין זֶה כְּרִיתוּת. וְרַבָּנַן הַאי "כְּרִיתוּת" מַאי עָבְדִי לֵיהּ? מִיבָּעֵי לְהוּ *לִכְדְתַנְיָא: [ד]ה"ז גִּיטֵּךְ ע"מ שֶׁלֹּא תִּשְׁתִּי יַיִן", "ע"מ שֶׁלֹּא תֵּלְכִי לְבֵית אָבִיךְ לְעוֹלָם" – אֵין זֶה כְּרִיתוּת, שְׁלֹשִׁים יוֹם – ה"ז כְּרִיתוּת. וְאִידַּךְ? מִ"כְּרֵת כְּרִיתוּת" נָפְקָא. וְאִידַּךְ? "כְּרֵת כְּרִיתוּת" לָא דָּרְשִׁי. *אָמַר רָבָא: "ה"ז גִּיטֵּךְ ע"מ שֶׁלֹּא תִּשְׁתִּי יַיִן כָּל יְמֵי חַיַּי" – אֵין זֶה כְּרִיתוּת, "כָּל יְמֵי חַיֵּי פְלוֹנִי" – ה"ז כְּרִיתוּת. מַאי שְׁנָא "חַיֵּי פְלוֹנִי" – דְּדִלְמָא מָאֵית וּמְקַיְּימָא לֵיהּ לִתְנָאֵיהּ? "חַיַּי" דִּידֵיהּ נַמִי, דִּלְמָא מָאֵית וּמְקַיְּימָא לֵיהּ לִתְנָאֵיהּ! אֶלָּא אֵימָא: ה"כָּל יְמֵי חַיַּיִךְ" – אֵין זֶה כְּרִיתוּת, "כָּל יְמֵי חַיַּי" אוֹ "חַיֵּי פְלוֹנִי" – ה"ז כְּרִיתוּת.§ בְּעָא מִינֵּיהּ רָבָא מֵרַב נַחְמָן: *"הַיּוֹם אִי אַתְּ אִשְׁתִּי וּלְמָחָר אַתְּ אִשְׁתִּי", מַהוּ? תִּיבָּעֵי לְר' אֱלִיעֶזֶר, תִּיבָּעֵי לְרַבָּנַן; תִּיבָּעֵי לְרַבִּי אֱלִיעֶזֶר: עַד כָּאן לָא קָאָמַר רַבִּי אֱלִיעֶזֶר הָתָם – אֶלָּא דִּלְמַאן דְּקָא שָׁרֵי – קָא שָׁרֵי לְעוֹלָם, אֲבָל הָכָא לָא, אוֹ דִּלְמָא לָא שְׁנָא? תִּיבָּעֵי לְרַבָּנַן: עַד כָּאן לָא קָאָמְרִי רַבָּנַן הָתָם – אֶלָּא דְּלָא פְּסָקָהּ מִינֵּיהּ לְגַמְרֵי, אֲבָל הָכָא כֵּיוָן דִּפְסָקָהּ – פְּסָקָהּ? בָּתַר דְּבַעְיָא הֲדַר פְּשָׁטָהּ:

מִסְתַּבְּרָא

הֲרֵי גְּרוּשָׁה אֶצְלוֹ בִּזְנוּת. גָּרְסִינַן. הֲרֵי לֹא אֲסָרָהּ עָלָיו אֶלָּא לִינָּשֵׂא, אֲבָל לִזְנוּת – גְּרוּשָׁה הִיא אֶצְלוֹ מִיָּד. הִלְכָּךְ אִם יָמוּת בַּעְלָהּ הָרִאשׁוֹן נַמִי שֵׁם גֵּירוּשִׁין עָלֶיהָ אֶצֶל זֶה עוֹלָמִית. וּמֵעַתָּה אֵין כָּאן ק"ו, דְּאִיכָּא לְמִפְרַךְ דְּמָה אִם נֶאֶסְרָה עָלָיו מִשּׁוּם צַד גֵּירוּשִׁין שֶׁבָּהּ – שֶׁהֲרֵי אַף אֶצְלוֹ הָיָה עָלֶיהָ צַד גֵּירוּשִׁין – תֹּאמַר שֶׁתֵּאָסֵר עַל כָּל אָדָם בִּשְׁבִיל צַד אִישׁוּת שֶׁיֵּשׁ בָּהּ אֶצֶל זֶה לְבַדּוֹ? שֶׁאֵין עָלֶיהָ שׁוּם צַד אִישׁוּת אֶצֶל שְׁאָר כָּל אָדָם. אֶלָּא בַּחוּץ. סְבִירָא לֵיהּ לְרַבִּי עֲקִיבָא מִילְּתֵיהּ דְּר' אֱלִיעֶזֶר. וּפָרְכִינַן. לְר"ע, דְּפָרֵיךְ הָנֵי תְּרֵי פִּרְכֵי, חֲדָא אַ"חוּץ" וַחֲדָא אַ"עַל מְנָת", אִי סְבִירָא לֵיהּ פְּלוּגְתָּא דְּרַבִּי אֱלִיעֶזֶר וְרַבָּנַן בַּ"חוּץ" – נוֹתִיב הַךְ פִּירְכָא בַּתְרַיְיתָא דְּ"חוּץ". וְאִי בְּעַל מְנָת מוֹקֵי לָהּ, נוֹתְבֵיהּ פִּירְכָא קַמַּיְיתָא, וְתוּ לָא! אִיכָּא דְּאִית לֵיהּ בַּחוּץ. פְּלִיגִי, וְאִיכָּא דְּאִית לֵיהּ בְּ"עַל מְנָת" פְּלִיגִי. הַאי פִּירְכָא. "הֲרֵי שֶׁהָיָה זֶה כֹּהֵן" כו'. וּלְמַאן דְּאִית לֵיהּ ע"מ הַאי פִּירְכָא. "הֲרֵי שֶׁהָלְכָה" כו'. וּמַאי פִּירְכָא. אִיכָּא לְמִיפְרַךְ אַפִּירְכֵיהּ דְּרַבִּי עֲקִיבָא בַּתְרַיְיתָא, דְּקָאָמַר רָבָא לְעֵיל: וּלְכוּלְּהוּ אִית לְהוּ פִּירְכָא. אִי נֵימָא אִיסּוּר כְּהוּנָּה שָׁאנֵי. הוֹאִיל וְרִיבָּה בָּהֶן הַכָּתוּב מִצְוֹת יְתֵירוֹת. הָא ר' אֱלִיעֶזֶר. דְּקָאָמַר: מוּתֶּרֶת לְכָל אָדָם חוּץ מִמֶּנּוּ. מֵאִיסּוּר כְּהוּנָּה יָלֵיף לָהּ. מִגְּרוּשָׁה מֵאִישָׁהּ לְבַדָּהּ, שֶׁפָּסוּל לִכְהוּנָּה – מֵהָתָם יָלְפָא לְעֵיל, דְּמִדְּפָסִיל לִכְהוּנָּה הָוֵי גִּיטָּא, וְאַע"ג דְּשַׁיֵּיר. וְיָלֵיף מִינָּהּ קוּלָּא, וְלָא אָמְרִינַן אִיסּוּר כְּהוּנָּה שָׁאנֵי. כ"ש דְּמָצֵי לְמִיפְרַךְ אַלִּיבֵּיהּ: נֵילַף מֵאִיסּוּר כְּהוּנָּה לְחוּמְרָא, וְנֵימָא: כִּי הֵיכִי דְּצַד גֵּירוּשֶׁיהָ פּוֹסְלָהּ לִכְהוּנָּה אִם יָמוּת – יְהֵא צַד אִישׁוּתָהּ פּוֹסְלָהּ לְכָל אָדָם! רָבָא. דְּאָמַר לְעֵיל: כּוּלְּהוּ אִית לְהוּ פִּירְכָא. כְּר' יַנַּאי מִשּׁוּם זָקֵן אֶחָד מַתְנֵי לָהּ. דְּאָמַר לְעֵיל טַעַם דְּר' אֱלִיעֶזֶר מִ"וְהָיְתָה לְאִישׁ אַחֵר", וְלָא יָלֵיף מֵאִיסּוּרֵי כְהוּנָּה. הִילְכָּךְ פָּרְכִינַן לְר"ע: אִיסּוּר כְּהוּנָּה שָׁאנֵי, וְלָא תִּיקְשֵׁי לְרַבִּי אֱלִיעֶזֶר. וְהָא אִיהוּ נַמִי מִיפְרַךְ פָּרְכֵיהּ. לְר' אֱלִיעֶזֶר לְקַמָּן בַּבָּרַיְיתָא. מַקִּישׁ קוֹדְמֵי הֲוָיָה שְׁנִיָּה. צַד פָּנוּי שֶׁבָּהּ, בֵּין גֵּירוּשִׁין לְנִשּׂוּאִין. לְקוֹדְמֵי הֲוָיָה רִאשׁוֹנָה. צַד פָּנוּי שֶׁהָיָה בָּהּ קוֹדֶם קִידּוּשִׁין שֶׁל רִאשׁוֹן. דְּהָא אִיתְקוּשׁ, דִּכְתִיב לְעֵיל מִינֵּיהּ: "כִּי יִקַּח אִישׁ" וגו' – הַיְינוּ קִידּוּשֵׁי רִאשׁוֹן, "וְהָיְתָה לְאִישׁ אַחֵר" – הַיְינוּ קִידּוּשֵׁי שֵׁנִי. שֶׁזֶּה אוֹסֵר וְזֶה מַתִּיר. נִישּׂוּאֵי בַּעְלָהּ הָרִאשׁוֹן אֲסָרוּהָ עַל זֶה, וְנִישּׂוּאֵי שֵׁנִי יַתִּירוּהָ לוֹ. בַּחֲרָטָה. שֶׁפּוֹתֵחַ פֶּתַח לַנּוֹדֵר, בַּדְּבָרִים הַבָּאִים לוֹ ע"י נֶדֶר זֶה, שֶׁאִילּוּ יָדַע מִתְּחִילָּה שֶׁכֵּן עָתִיד לִהְיוֹת – לֹא הָיָה נוֹדֵר. נִמְצָא שֶׁמִּתְּחִילָּתוֹ אֵינוֹ נֶדֶר. וַהֲרֵי הֲפָרַת הַבַּעַל. שֶׁהוּא בְּלֹא חֲרָטָה. עַל דַּעַת בַּעְלָהּ. עַל מְנָת שֶׁאִם יִרְצֶה, וְאִם לָאו – לֹא יְהֵא נֶדֶר. וְרַבָּנַן. כָּל הָנָךְ רַבָּנַן דִּלְעֵיל, דְּלָא יָלְפֵי מֵהָכָא פִּירְכַיְיהוּ. אֵין זֶה כְּרִיתוּת. שֶׁאֵין מַפְרִידָן אֶלָּא הַמָּוֶת, דְּעַד יוֹם מוֹתָהּ קְשׁוּרָה בּוֹ. ה"ז כְּרִיתוּת. מִיָּד, וְהִיא תְּקַיֵּים הַתְּנַאי. הַיּוֹם אִי אַתְּ אִשְׁתִּי. נָתַן לָהּ גֵּט וְאָמַר לָהּ: הַיּוֹם לְבַדּוֹ יְהוּ גֵּירוּשִׁין, וּלְמָחָר לֹא יְהוּ גֵּירוּשִׁין, דְּשַׁיֵּיר בְּגִיטָּהּ, מַהוּ? תִּיבָּעֵי לְר' אֱלִיעֶזֶר. דְּמַכְשִׁיר בְּשִׁיּוּר. תִּיבָּעֵי לְרַבָּנַן. דְּפָסְלִי בְּשִׁיּוּר. כֵּיוָן דִּפְסָקָהּ. מִינֵּיהּ הַיּוֹם לְגַמְרֵי אֵצֶל כָּל אָדָם. פְּסָקָהּ. לְכָל אָדָם לְעוֹלָם, וְשׁוּב אֵינָהּ אִשְׁתּוֹ עַד שֶׁיַּחֲזוֹר וִיקַדְּשֶׁנָּה. הִלְכָּךְ, אֵין תְּנַאי זֶה כְּלוּם.

מַאי

רבא כרבי ינאי משום זקן אחד סבירא ליה. וא"ת: א"כ ר' יוסי דקאמר: רואה אני את דברי רבי אלעזר בן עזריה מדברי כולן, ואית ליה הני פירכי – סבר נמי כר' ינאי משום זקן אחד, א"כ תיקשי (א)לר' יוחנן דפליג לעיל אר' ינאי! וי"ל: דאיכא למימר ד"רואה אני את דברי רבי אלעזר" – לא משום הני פירכי קאמר. וא"ת: כיון דר"א מקרא יליף, הנהו זקנים מה משיבין על דבריו? דגזירת הכתוב הוא! וי"ל: דמשום דיש להשיב על דבריו – מסתבר לאוקמי קרא טפי כדדרשי רבנן. **מה** קודמי הויה ראשונה דלא אגידא ביה כו'. אע"ג דלגמרי על כרחיך לא דמו, דהא בקודמי הויה ראשונה שרי לכ"ע, ובקודמי הויה שניה אסורה לקרובי בעלה הראשון, מ"מ הוקשו לענין: כי היכי דלא הוי אשת איש מעיקרא – ה"נ בעיא בקודמי הויה שניה שתהא מופקעת לגמרי ממנו מדין אשת איש, ולא תהא אגידא ביה כלל.

*__מודה__ ר"א במגרש כו'. תימה: למאן מודה? דלרבנן דפליגי עליה – לא הויא גט, ואינה מותרת לשום אדם!. **ואידך** כרת כריתות לא דרשי. והא דרבי יוסי הגלילי דהוי בכלל רבנן דריש בפ"ב (לעיל דף כא:) "כרת כריתות", והכא קאמר דלא דרשי – היינו דלא דרשי ליה להנהו דרשא, אלא לדרשא אחרינא. **כל** ימי חייכי אין זה כריתות כל ימי חיי וחיי פלוני ה"ז כריתות. תימה לרבינו יצחק: דבפ"ק דיומא (דף יג.) גבי "אף אשה אחרת מתקינין לו" מייתי מילתא דרבא דהכא בענין אחר, דקאמר: אלא דאמר לה "ע"מ שתמות אחת מכס" כו', וקאמר: כי האי גוונא מי הוי גיטא? והאמר רבא: "ה"ז גיטך ע"מ שלא תשתי יין כל ימי חיי וחייכי" – אין זה כריתות, "כל ימי חיי פלוני" – ה"ז כריתות. ואין זה כדמסיק הכא, ולא כדבעי למימר הכא מעיקרא, דלא מידכר "כל ימי חייכי"! ושמא התלמוד אינו חושש, ומייתי בכל ענין "כל ימי חיי" כדבעי למימר מעיקרא, ו"חייכי" דאין זה כריתות, כדמסיק. ומיהו, קשה לר"י: התם אמאי לא הוי כריתות ב"על מנת שתמות אחת מכס"? דמאי שנא מ"חיי פלוני" דהוי כריתות, דבשביל דתלה אף במיתתה – לא גרע. **כיון** דפסקה פסקה. הכא לא קאמר "או דלמא לא שנא", כדאמרינן לעיל. דמיד כשאמר כיון דפסקה פסקה – הדין שכן הוא.

מסתברא

תוספות רי"ד

תניא הרי זה גיטך ע"מ שלא תשתי יין על מנת שלא תלכי לבית אביך לעולם אין זה כריתות עד ל' יום הרי זה כריתות. אמר רבא הרי זה גיטך ע"מ שלא תשתי יין כל ימי חיי וחייכי אין זה כריתות כל ימי חיי פלוני הרי זה כריתות מ"ט חיי פלוני דאפשר דמיית ומקיימית ליה לתנאיה חיי דידיה נמי אפשר דמיית ומקיימית ליה לתנאיה אלא אימא כל ימי חייכי אין זה כריתות כל ימי חיי וחיי פלוני הרי זה כריתות ומכאן מוכיח שמיד מותרת לינשא ואינה צריכה להמתין עד שימות אותו פלוני דאי איתא שצריכה להמתין א"כ הרבה יש בידיהן שאילו אמר כל ימי חיי אסורה להנשא כל ימי חייו ולאחר מיתתו היא מותרת בלא גט שהיא אלמנה וא"כ אין זה כריתות ואמאי הדר ואמר הרי זה כריתות אלא ודאי לאלתר שריא לה לאינסובי ולא חיישינן שמא תעבר על תנאה ונמצא גט בטל ומיבעיא לי א"ל ע"מ שלא תשתי יין עד ק' שנה או עד זמן גדול שהיא תזקין ולא ישלים הזמן מהו מי אמרינן כיון דרובא דעלמא חיין עד ע' דכתיב ימי שנותינו בהם שבעים שנה ככל ימי חייכי דמי ואין זה כריתות או דלמא כיון דאיכא דחיין טפי א' מני אלף הרי זה כריתות וכן כתב בעל ה"ג א) א"ל כל ימי חיי פלוני ואנסיבא לה לאלתר והוו לה בנין מן בעל שני ומית ליה בעלה ראשון והדר הוו לה בנין לאחר מיתתו ועדיין ההוא פלוני דאתני לתנאה בגויה מיקיים ואי שתי בחיי' לאחר מיתת הבעל הראשון בטיל ליה גט למפרע וביניה קמאי ממזרים בתראי לאו ממזרים ואסורה לשני דכיון דבטל גט למפרע כי דר גבה אשת איש הואי ותנן כשם שאסורה לבעל כך אסורה לבועל והוי פליגי רבנן דהוו קאמרינן דכיון דבחיי בעלה לא עברה עילויה תנאיה ולאחר מיתה היא דעברה כיון דמית ליה בטיל ליה לתנאיה ולא בטיל ליה גט למפרע [עכ"ל בבה"ג] ואינו נ"ל סברת הני רבנן דאם איתא דכיון דמית בעל בטל תנאיה ואם עברה ובטיל תנאיה לא בטיל גיטא למפרע אי הכי אפילו כי אמר לה כל ימי חייכי אמאי אמרינן דאין זה כריתות הא אפשר דמית איהו ברישא ומשתריא למישתי חמרא אלא לאו ש"מ אע"ג דמית בעל ברישא תנאיה לא ובטיל והלכך אין זה כריתות דאכתי אסורה לשתות אחר מותו ואי שתיא בטיל ליה גיטא למפרע וה"ה הכי נמי בחיי פלוני אי מיית בעל ברישא ושתיא בחיי אותו פלוני בטיל גיטא למפרע והכי אמרן לעיל בפ' מי שאחזו תניא הרי זה גיטך ע"מ שתתני לי מאתים זוז ומת נתנה לו אינה זקוקה ליבם לא נתנה לו זקוקה ליבם רשבג"א נותנת לאביו או לאחיו או לאחד מן היורשין אלמא קיום תנאה דגיטא מהני לאחר מותו וה"ה נמי דמהני בטולי גיטא לאחר

א) כ"ה בה"ג שלפנינו בהלכות גיטין סי' לט.

י א ב מיי' פ"ו מהל' שבועות הל' א ופ"ח מהל' נדרים הלכה ה סמג לאוין רלח טוש"ע י"ד סי' רכח סעיף א:

יא ג מיי' פי"א מהל' נדרים הל' ח סמג לאוין רמב טוש"ע י"ד סי' רלד סעיף ב:

יב ד ה מיי' פ"ח מהל' גירושין הל' י יא סמג עשין נ טוש"ע אה"ע סימן קמג סעיף כ:

[שייך לע"א]

[לעיל פב:]

הגהות הב"ח

(א) תום' ד"ה רבא וכו' תיקשי לרבנן דפליגי לעיל אר' ינאי:

תוספתא פ"ז ע"ש

שבת מו: נדה מו: נדרים עג עד. יבמות כט:

[תוספתא ספ"ה] עירובין טו סוכה כד: לעיל כח: יומא יג. [קדושין ה.]

[יומא יג.]

[לקמן פו.] (נדרים כט.)

גמרא

אמסתברא, בין לרבי אליעזר בין לרבנן, כיון דפסקה – פסקה.§ ת"ר: "הרי זה גיטך ע"מ שתנשאי לפלוני" – הרי זו לא תנשא, ואם נשאת – לא תצא. מאי קאמר? אמר רב נחמן, ה"ק: הרי זו לא תנשא לו, שמא יאמרו נשיהן נותנין במתנה, ואם נשאת לאחר – לא תצא. ומשום גזרה לא מפקינן מיניה, ושרינן אשת איש לעלמא?! אלא אמר רב נחמן, הכי קאמר: הרי זו לא תנשא לו, שמא יאמרו נשיהם נותנין במתנה, ואם נשאת לו – לא תצא, דמשום גזרה לא מפקינן. א"ל רבא: לו הוא דלא תנשא, הא לאחר תנשא? והא בעי קיומי לתנאה! וכי תימא, אפשר דמינסבא היום ומיגרשה למחר ומקיימא לתנאה, ולהך דפליגת עליה דרב יהודה קמדמית ליה. *דאתמר: "קונם עיני בשינה היום אם אישן למחר", אמר רב יהודה: באל יישן היום שמא יישן למחר, ורב נחמן אמר: יישן היום ואין חוששין שמא יישן למחר. הכי השתא? התם בדידיה קיימא, דאי בעי מבריז נפשיה בסילוואתא ולא נאים, הכא בדידה קיימא לאיגרושי? אלא אמר רבא: גהרי זו לא תנשא לא לו ולא לאחר, לו לא תנשא – שמא יאמרו נשותיהם נותנין במתנה, לאחר לא תנשא – דבעיא קיומיה לתנאה; ואם נשאת, לו – לא תצא, דמשום גזרה לא מפקינן, לאחר – תצא, דבעיא לקיומיה לתנאה. תניא כוותיה דרבא: הרי זו לא תנשא, לא לו ולא לאחר, ואם נשאת לו – לא תצא, לאחר – תצא.§ *ת"ר: "ה"ז גיטך ע"מ שתעלי לרקיע", "ע"מ שתרדי לתהום", "ע"מ שתבלעי קנה של ד' אמות", "ע"מ שתביאי לי קנה בן ק' אמה", "ע"מ שתעברי את הים הגדול ברגליך" – אינו גט. רבי יהודה בן תימא אומר: כזה גט. כלל אמר ר' יהודה בן תימא: כל תנאי שאי אפשר לו לקיימו בסופו והתנה עליו מתחילתו, אינו אלא כמפליגה בדברים, וכשר. אמר רב נחמן אמר רב: דהלכה כר' יהודה בן תימא. א"ר נחמן בר יצחק: מתני' נמי דיקא, דקתני: *כל שאפשר לו לקיימו בסופו והתנה עליו בתחילתו – תנאו קיים, הא אי אפשר – תנאו בטל, ש"מ. איבעיא להו: "הרי זה גיטך ע"מ שתאכלי בשר חזיר", מהו? אמר אביי: היא היא; רבא אמר: אפשר דאכלה ולקיא. לאביי, "כלל" – לאתויי בשר חזיר; לרבא, "כזה" – למעוטי בשר חזיר. מיתיבי: *ה"הרי זה גיטך ע"מ שתבעלי לפלוני", נתקיים התנאי – הרי זה גט, ואם לאו – אינו גט, ו"על מנת שלא תבעלי לאבא ולאביך" – אין חוששין שמא נבעלה להן; ואילו "על מנת שתבעלי לאבא ולאביך" לא קתני; לאביי ניחא, לרבא קשיא! אמר לך רבא: בשלמא בשר חזיר – אפשר דאכלה ולקיא, פלוני – נמי אפשר דמשחדא ביה בממונא, זאלא אבא ואביך בדידה קיימא? נהי דאיהי עבדא איסורא, אבא ואביך מי עבדי איסורא? לרבא, "כלל" – לאתויי אבא ואביך, "כזה" – למעוטי בשר חזיר; לאביי

רש"י

מאי קאמר. האי "לא תינשא" דקאמר – למאן קאמר? לאותו פלוני או לכל אדם? לא תינשא לו. כדמפרש, שמא יאמרו נשיהם נותנין במתנה, ואין לך לעז גדול מזה. ואם ניסת לאחר לא תצא. שלא להחזיק תנאי זה. ומשום הך גזירה לא מפקינן לה. בתמיה: והא לא איתקיים התנאי ובטל הגט. ה"ג: אלא אמר רב נחמן הכי קאמר הרי זה גיטך ע"מ שתנשאי לפלוני הרי זו לא תינשא לו משום גזירה שמא יאמרו נשיהן נותנין במתנה ואם ניסת לו לא תצא. שאין כאן איסור אלא חשש לעז בעלמא. הא לאחר תינשא. והוי גיטא, הואיל ולא אמר "ע"מ שלא תנשאי אלא לפלוני", אלא "ע"מ שתנשאי לפלוני" – סוף סוף הא בעיא לקיומי תנאה. וכי תימא אפשר דמיגרשה. מן השני היום, ולמחר תינשא לאותו פלוני, לקיים תנאה. ולהא דפליגת עליה דרב יהודה קמדמית לה. דלא חיישת דלמא לא מיקיים. שמא יישן למחר. ונמצא שעבר על נדרו. ורב נחמן אמר יישן היום. ולמחר יתקיים תנאו ולא יישן. דאי בעי מבריז נפשיה בסילוותא. ינקוז בשרו תמיד בקוץ. בדידה קיימא לאגרושי. בתמיה. מפליגה. דוחה אותה, לצערה בדברי הבאי. מתני' נמי דיקא. בב"מ ב"השוכר את הפועלים" (דף לד.). אפשר דאכלה ולקיא. ולכן תימא גופיה תנאו קיים. כלל לאתויי בשר חזיר. קתני: כלל אמר ר' יהודה בן תימא. כזה גט. דקאמר ר' יהודה בן תימא. למעוטי בשר חזיר. דה"ק: כזה גט, דאי אפשר לקיימו כלל – הלכך תנאו בטל. אבל לעבור על דברי תורה – אפשר לקיימו באיסור, ותלקה על שעברה. שתבעלי. גרסינן גבי פלוני, וגבי אביו ואביך גרסינן: "שלא תבעלי". שתבעלי. בין בזנות בין בנשואין. אין חוששין שמא נבעלה להם. כלומר, מותרת לינשא מיד, ואין חוששין שמא תבעל להן ויבטל הגט. אבל אמר לה: "ע"מ שלא תבעלי לפלוני" – אינו גט, שמא תבעל לו, דומיא ד"ע"מ שלא תלכי לבית אביך לעולם". ואילו גבי אבא ואביך שתבעלי לא קתני. דניהוי תנאה, אלמא לא הוי תנאה. לאביי ניחא כו'. [משום דלדידיה לר' יהודה בן תימא אפילו לא יתקיים הרי זה גט, אלא לרבא קשיא, דהא אמר] אפילו רבי יהודה בן תימא מודה בה. אמר לך רבא. לא דמיא לבשר חזיר. דאילו בשר חזיר בידה לקיימו באיסור, ושתבעלי לפלוני נמי אפשר – דמשחדא ליה בממונא, ואם אינו רוצה לבועלה באיסור – ישאנה ויבעול בהיתר. אלא אבא ואביך – בדידה קיימא? לרבא כלל. דקתני רבי יהודה בן תימא. לאתויי אבא ואביך. דהוי נמי א"א לקיימו. כזה למעוטי בשר חזיר. דאפשר לקיימו הוא. ולאביי

תוספות

מסתברא בין לר' אליעזר בין לרבנן כיון דפסקה פסקה. פי': ומגורשת לעולם. ואע"ג דלמאי דבעי למימר לרבי אליעזר או דלמא לא שנא, משמע דבעי למימר דאין הגט חל אלא אותו היום, כמו חוץ מפלוני דלא חל אלא מעלמא – מ"מ לישנא ד"פסקה" משמע לגמרי. והא דקאמר לקמן (דף פו.): לעולם לאפוקי *(מדרבא אמר רב נחמן) – לאו לאפוקי ממש, אלא שופרא דשטרא אתקין: מיומא דנן ולעלם, שלא תטעה לומר שאינה מגורשת אלא אותו יום. אלא א"ר נחמן ה"ק. וא"ת: דמעיקרא לא אמר כן! וי"ל: דמעיקרא סבר דאפקעי רבנן קידושין מינה, ולבסוף חזר בו, שאין נראה לו סברא דבשביל חשש מועטת כזו יפקיעו רבנן קידושין. ומיגרשה למחר ומקיים לתנאיה. דהשתא לא שייך שמא יאמרו נשותיהן נותנין במתנה, כיון דניסאת לאחר בינתים. הכא בדידה קיימא לאגרושי. אע"ג דכיון שאינה יכולה לקיים תנאה (א) *הויא אשת איש לזה שנשאת לו עכשיו – מ"מ אינה יכולה לקיים תנאה ולינשא בלא גירושין, דלעולם צריכה גט מספיקא, שמא יתקיים תנאה ותנשא גם לשני ע"י מיתת הראשון, או יגרשה. וקשה *לרבי יהודה: והא ודאי בדידה קיימא לאיגרושי, שיכולה לומר "מאיס עלי" וכייפינן ליה! ולפי פי' רש"י ורבינו תם דלא כייפינן ליה – ניחא. ועוד קשיא: דכייפינן ליה לגרשה, שהרי היא עליו באיסור אשת איש, וא"כ מאי קאמר "אטו בדידה קיימא לאיגרושי"? ואי הוה מפרש: בדידה קיימא לאיגרושי ולאינסובי, דודאי אין בידה שישאנה זה – הוי אתי שפיר, אך אין הלשון משמע כן! וי"ל: כיון דמכל מקום יכול הבעל לדחותה – לא בדידה קיימא לאיגרושי. על מנת שתעלי לרקיע אינו גט. ב"השוכר את הפועלים" בסופו (ב"מ דף לד.) גרסינן: אם נתקיים התנאי – הרי זה גט. ואם לאו – אינו גט. ותימה: היאך יכול לקיימו? וי"ל: ע"י שם. קשה להרב ר' אלחנן: דהוה לן למילף מתנאי בני גד ובני ראובן שיכול לקיימו, אבל היכא שלא יוכל לקיימו כי הכא, הוה לן למימר דאף על גב דתנאי בטל – מעשה קיים, כי היכי דילפינן בפרק *"מצות חליצה" (יבמות דף קו) דבעינן שיוכל לעשות ע"י שליח! וי"ל: דהתם לא ילפינן אלא שהמעשה יכול לעשות ע"י שליח, אבל תנאי – אין לחוש אם לא יוכל לעשות ע"י שליח, או אינו יכול לעשות כלל. על מנת שתבעלי לפלוני ואילו לאבא ולאביך לא קתני. יש ספרים שהוגהו בברייתא: ע"מ שלא תבעלי לאבא ולאביך – אין חוששין שמא תבעל להם. משום דקשיא להו מאי דייק "ואילו לאבא ולאביך לא קתני"? אבא ואביך מאן דכר שמייהו? מיהו, משום כן אין צריך להגיה. דשפיר דייק, מדקתני "ע"מ שתבעלי לפלוני" – משמע דוקא לפלוני, דלא חשיב הפלגה בדברים במה שיש שם איסור פנויה, אבל אבא ואביך – לא. ותיפוק

עין משפט נר מצוה

יג א מיי' פ"ח מהל' גירושין הל' ט סמג עשין נ טוש"ע אה"ע סי' קלז סעיף ה וע"ש במ"מ:

[נ"ל מדבעא מיניה רבא מרב נחמן]

יד ב מיי' פ"ד מהל' נדרים הל' יד סמג לאוין רמב טוש"ע י"ד סימן ריג סעיף ג:

טו ג מיי' פ"ח מהל' גירושין הל' יג סמג עשין נ טוש"ע אה"ע סי' קמג סעיף טו:

טז ד מיי' פ"ו מהל' אישות הל' ז סמג עשין נ טוש"ע אה"ע סי' קמג סעיף יב וסי' לח סעיף ב:

יז ה טוש"ע שם סימן קמג סעיף יח:

יח ו טוש"ע שם סעי' יג:

גי' רש"ל לא הויא ועי' במהרש"א

יט ז מיי' שם הל' יא טוש"ע שם סעיף יב:

[נ"ל לרבינו]

מסורת הש"ס

נדרים יד: ע"ש

ב"מ לד. [תוספתא פ"ה]

רש"ל [ב"מ שם]

[תוספתא פ"ד]

הגהות הב"ח

(א) תוס' ד"ה הכא וכו' לקיים תנאה לא הויא אשת איש. נ"ב פי' האשה [אינה מקודשת לזה] להיות אשת איש ותלא ותינשא לפלוני בלא גירושין

גליון הש"ס

תוס' ד"ה הכא בדידה וכו' ולפי פרש"י ור"ת. בכתובות דף סג ע"ב: ד"ה על מנת וכו' וי"ל ע"י שם. ע' חגיגה דף יד ע"ב תד"ה נכנסו:

תוספות רי"ד

לאחר מותו: ת"ר הרי זה גיטך ע"מ שתנשאי לפלוני הרי זו לא תנשא לא לו ולא לאחר לא לו שמא יאמרו נשותיהן נותנין במתנה זה לזה ולאחר [לא תנשא] דבעיא לקיומה לתנאה ואם נשאת לו לא תצא דמשום גזירה לא מפקינן לה ואם נשאת לאחר תצא דבעיא לקיומיה לתנאה שעדיין לא נתקיים התנאי ולא הוי גט: איתמר קונם עיני בשינה היום אם אישן למחר אמר רב יהודה אל ישן היום שמא ישן למחר נמצא עובר על נדרו למפרע ורב נחמן אמר ישן היום ואין חוששין שמא ישן למחר. עלה בדעתו לומר דפלוגתא דרב יהודה ורב נחמן דפליגי בהא שייכי נמי בהרי זה גיטך ע"מ שלא תשתי יין כל ל' יום או כל ימי חיי פלוני דהיא היא דכי היכי דהתם אמר רב נחמן ישן היום ואין חוששין שמא ישן למחר ה"ה הכי נמי נימא הכא תנשא מיד ולא חיישינן שמא תשתה יין ויבטל הגט למפרע וכי היכי דאמר רב יהודה התם אל יישן היום שמא ישן למחר ה"ה הכי נמי הכא לא תנשא עד שישלימו ל' יום או עד שימות אותו פלוני שמא תשתה יין ויבטל הגט למפרע ולא היא דלא דמי דהתם כי אמר קונם עיני בשינה היום אם אישן למחר אם ישן למחר לא חייל עליה שום איסורא שהאיסור לא יחול אלא על מה שישן אתמול ומאי דהוה הוה והילכך לא זהיר ביה וחיישינן שמא יישן למחר אבל הכא דאי שתיא חמרא חייל עלה איסורא דמיבטיל גיטא והויא אשת איש והיא אסורא מיזהר זהירא בה ולא שתיא והכי אמרינן בנדרים בפ' ואלו מותרין ומודה רב יהודה באומר קונם עיני בשינה למחר אם אישן היום שישן היום דאי לא זהיר בתנאיה באיסוריה מזהיר זהיר פי' אם יישן היום חל עליו איסורא שלא יישן למחר ולא חיישינן שמא יישן גם למחר שכיון שאסור לו לישן מיזהר זהיר שלא יישן ויעשה אסור אבל בפלוגתא דרב יהודה אם יישן למחר שום איסורא לא חייל עליה השתא אלא תנאה הוי על איסורא דעבר עליה אתמול ומאי דהוה הוה והכי נמי אם תשתה יין חייל עליה איסור אשת איש בין למפרע בין להבא והילכך מיזהר זהירה בה שלא תשתה ומודה בה רב יהודה: ת"ר הרי זה גיטך ע"מ שתעלי לרקיע ע"מ שתרדי לתהום ע"מ שתבלעי קנה בן ק' אמה ע"מ שתפרחי באויר ע"מ שתעברי הים הגדול ברגליך אינו גט ר' יהודה בן בתירא אומר כזה גט כלל א"ר יהודה בן תימא כל שא"א לקיימו בסופו והתנה עליו מתחילתו אינו אלא כמפליגה בדברים וכשר אמר רב נחמן הלכה כר' יהודה בן תימא אמר רב נחמן בר יצחק מתני' נמי דייקא דקתני כל שאפשר לקיימו בסופו והתנה עליו מתחילתו תנאו קיים הא שא"א לו לקיימו בסופו תנאו בטל ש"מ: איבעיא להו הרי זה גיטך ע"מ שתאכלי בשר

לאביי, "כלל" — לאתויי בשר חזיר, "כזה" — למעוטי פלוני. *אמיתיבי: "הרי זה גיטך ע"מ שתאכלי בשר חזיר", ואם היתה זרה "על מנת שתאכלי בתרומה", ואם היתה נזירה "ע"מ שתשתי יין", נתקיים התנאי — הרי זה גט, ואם לאו — אינו גט; לרבא ניחא, לאביי קשיא! אמר לך אביי: מי סברת ד"ה היא? הא מני — רבנן היא. ותיפוק ליה דמתנה על מה שכתוב בתורה הוא, *וכל המתנה על מה שכתוב בתורה — תנאו בטל! אמר רב אדא בריה דרב איקא: כי אמרינן מתנה על מה שכתוב בתורה תנאו בטל — כגון שארה כסותה ועונתה, דהוא קא עקר, אבל הכא איהי קא עקרה. מתקיף לה רבינא: כלום קא עקרה איהי אלא לקיומי לתנאי דידיה, אישתכח דאיהו קא עקר! אלא אמר רבינא: בכי אמרינן מתנה על מה שכתוב בתורה תנאו בטל — כגון שארה כסותה ועונתה, דודאי קא עקר, אבל הכא מי קאמר לה? לא סגיא דלא אכלה? גלא תיכול ולא תיגרש.§ "כיצד יעשה? יטלנו הימנה" וכו'.§ מאן תנא? אמר חזקיה: ר"ש בן אלעזר היא; *דתניא, ר"ש בן אלעזר אומר: עד שיטלנו הימנה, ויחזור ויתננו לה ויאמר לה "הי גיטך". ר' יוחנן אמר: אפילו תימא רבי, דילכון אמר: שאני הכא, הואיל וקנאתו ליפסל בו לכהונה.§ "כתבו בתוכו".§ אמר רב ספרא: כתבו בתוכו תנן. פשיטא, "כתבו בתוכו" תנן! מהו דתימא: ה"מ לאחר התורף, אבל לפני התורף — אפילו על פה נמי פסול, קמ"ל. דורבא אמר: לא שנו אלא לאחר התורף, אבל לפני התורף — אפילו על פה נמי פסול. ואזדא רבא לטעמיה, דאמר להו רבא להנהו דכתבי גיטי: שתקו שתוקי לבעל עד דכתביתו ליה לתורף דגיטא. ת"ר: כל התנאין פוסלין בגט, דברי רבי; וחכמים אומרים: כל שפוסל על פה פוסל בכתב, וכל שאינו פוסל על פה אינו פוסל בכתב, "חוץ" שפוסל על פה — פוסל בכתב, "ע"מ" שאינו פוסל על פה — אינו פוסל בכתב. אמר רבי זירא: מחלוקת — לפני התורף, דרבי סבר: גזרינן "ע"מ" אטו "חוץ", ורבנן סברי: לא גזרינן "ע"מ" אטו "חוץ". אבל לאחר התורף —
דברי

ולאביי כזה למעוטי פלוני. דאינו גט עד שתיבעל לו, דבידה להשחידו בממון, וישאנה בהיתר. ותיפוק ליה כו'. נהי נמי דאפשר לה לקיימו באיסור — מיהו תנאי היכי הוי? הא הוה ליה מתנה על מה שכתוב בתורה, וקיימא לן: תנאו בטל! דודאי קא עקר. שהרי מסר לה קידושין והרי היא אשתו להתחייב בכולן, וכי אתני ע"מ שלא יתחייב — הוה ליה עוקר. מאן תנא. דצריך ליטלו הימנה ולא סגי באמירה בעלמא, שיחזור ויאמר לה: הרי את מותרת לכל אדם. ר"ש בן אלעזר היא. בפרק "הזורק",* אמר לה כנסי שטר חוב זה כו'. אפילו תימא רבי. דפליג התם עליה דר"ש בן אלעזר. דילכון אמר. רב כהנא שהיה משלכם, מבבל, שעלה לא"י ללמוד תורה מרבי יוחנן, כדאמרינן ב"הגוזל בתרא" (ב"ק דף קיז.), ושאל ממנו הרבה דברים, ועליו קא"ר יוחנן בכל דוכתי "דילכון אמר". שאני הכא. משום הכי צריך לחזור וליטלו, דקנאתו בנתינה קמייתא ליפסל בו לכהונה, הילכך, אי לאו דהדר שקיל לה מינה — לא מהניא אמירה, שהרי כבר זכתה בו על מנת תנאי ראשון. אבל ההוא ד"הזורק" — לא זכתה בו לכלום. כתבו בתוכו תנן. דוקא כתבו בתוכו הוא דלית ליה תקנתא, אבל לא כתבו בתוכו, אפילו אמר לעדים ע"מ כן — אינו נפסל בכך, ובלבד שיאמר לה בשעת מסירה: הרי את מותרת לכל אדם. הני מילי. דבעינן כתבו בתוכו, ולא מיפסל במאי דאמר לסהדי לכותבו ע"מ כן — היכא דאמר לאחר כתיבת התורף "ע"מ שלא תנשאי לפלוני", דכיון דנכתב עיקר הגט קודם הזכרת תנאי — לא מיפסל במאי דאמר לסהדי לכותבו ע"מ כן, אי לא כתבי ליה בתוכו בהדיא. אפילו על פה. שהרי עיקר הגט ע"מ כן נכתב. קמ"ל. רב ספרא: בתוכו דוקא קאמר. שתוקי שתקיה. נזפו בו, שלא יזכיר שום תנאי. פוסלין בגט. אם כתבו בתוכו, ואפילו נתקיים התנאי. חוץ שפוסל בעל פה. דהוי שיור בגט. מחלוקת. ד"ע"מ" דרבי ורבנן — בשכתבו לפני התורף.
ואוקימנא

ותיפוק ליה דהוה מתנה על מה שכתוב בתורה. אומר ה"ר אלחנן: ד"קרע את כסותי *ע"מ לפטור", אע"ג דנזקין חשיב להו גמרא בערכין (דף ו:), מלוה כתובה בתורה — מ"מ לא חשיב מתנה על מה שכתוב בתורה, כיון שמוחל בהדיא. אבל ודאי, אם היה אומר "קרע את כסותי ע"מ שאין לך עלי דין נזק" — חשיב מתנה על מה שכתוב בתורה, כמו ב"על מנת שאין לך עלי אונאה"*.

אמר חזקיה ר"ש בן אלעזר היא. הא דתניא בפ"ק (לעיל דף ה:), ולקמן (דף פו.) נמי מייתי: המביא גט ולא אמר "בפני נכתב" וכו' כיצד יעשה — יטלנו הימנה ויחזור ויתננו לה, אתיא אפילו כרבי. דכיון שניתן הגט כהילכתו מן התורה, מה שהוא אומר אחר הנתינה "בפני נכתב ובפני נחתם" לא היה מועיל כלום. ועוד: דשליח דוקא כשיאמר בשעת נתינה — מידק דייק.

רבי יוחנן אומר אפילו תימא רבי דילכון אמר. מתוך פירוש הקונטרס משמע דלחזקיה רבו היה אומר כן, דעלה קאי. לפי שרב כהנא היה מבבל, וחזקיה גם הוא היה מבבל, כדאמר בסוכה (דף כ. ודף מד.): עלו ר' חייא ובניו ויסדוה. ואין נראה לר"י, דהא מסתמא כשפשט רב כהנא לר' יוחנן כמה ספיקות ששאל, כדאמר ב"הגוזל בתרא" (ב"ק דף קיז:) — כבר נפטר חזקיה, דאילו היה קיים — לא היה שואל ספיקותיו ר' יוחנן מרב כהנא אלא מחזקיה, שהיה רבו, כדאמר ב"אלו קשרים" (שבת דף קיב:) דקא"ר יוחנן: כבר שנית לנו סנדל. וגם רב כהנא לא היה מניח חזקיה ויושב לפני רבי יוחנן, ור' יוחנן בעצמו לא היה בעל ישיבה בעוד שחזקיה קיים. אלא נראה שלתלמידיו מבבל שהיו לפניו היה אומר ר' יוחנן: דילכון אמר כך, כמו שפירש ר"ת בקידושין בפ"ק (דף כט:): הא לן והא להו. ואע"ג דבזבחים בפרק "קדשי קדשים" (דף נט.) אמר: כי סליק רב כהנא אשכחיה לר"ש ברבי — משמע שר"ש ברבי היה עדיין קיים, והוא היה גדול ואפילו מר' חייא אביו של חזקיה, דהא אגמריה ספר תהלים כדאמרינן בפ"ק דקידושין (דף לג.), ואין נראה כלל שהיה מניח ר"ש ולומד לפני ר' יוחנן, שר' יוחנן היה צריך לרב כהנא דאגמריה כל ספיקי דהוו ליה! אלא י"ל: דשני פעמים עלה רב כהנא לארץ ישראל*). *אם כתבו בתוכו אע"פ שחזר ומחקו פסול. פירוש: לפי שלא נכתב הגט אלא על תנאי זה, ואין כאן כריתות. משמע דוקא "חוץ" דלא הוה כריתות — חזר ומחקו פסול, אבל שאר מחקין כשרין בגט, רק שיעשה קיום המחק לפני "שריר וקיים". ומ"מ נהגו העולם להחמיר. מהו דתימא הני מילי לאחר התורף. פי': כשאמר הבעל לפני התורף, אפילו בעל פה, שלא כתבו הסופר — פסול, שעל תנאי זה כתבו, ואין זה כריתות — קמ"ל דאפ"ה כשר, דסופר לא כתב אלא ע"מ כמו שיאמר הבעל בסוף, וכיון שחזר בו — כשר. ומ"מ, אע"ג דמתני' איירי לפני התורף, כתבו לאחר התורף — נמי פסול, כדאמרינן בסמוך: ואיבעית אימא לאחר התורף ודברי הכל, ור' זירא סבר כרב ספרא דהכא. שתוקי שתקיה לבעל כו'. בכל שאר תנאים איירי, כדפי' בקונטרס. ורבא לטעמיה, דלפני התורף גזר "ע"מ" אטו "חוץ" לרבנן דרבי. כל התנאים פוסלין בגט. פירש בקונטרס: שנכתב בגט, ואפילו נתקיימו התנאים. ואין נראה לרבינו יצחק, דמה שייך לגזור ב"ע"מ שתתני לי מאתים זוז" וכיוצא בו אטו "חוץ", כיון שאין שם שיור כמו ב"חוץ"? ולא היה שייך כלל בשאר תנאים לגזור אטו "חוץ" אם לא "ע"מ שלא תינשאי לפלוני" גרידא, דהוי שיור! ועוד קשה לרבינו יצחק: דא"כ אפילו בעל פה נמי נגזור אטו "חוץ", ויפסל כל גט שיש בו תנאי אפילו על פה, אפילו נתקיים התנאי. ובסמוך מכשיר ר' זירא "ע"מ" אחר התורף אפילו לרבי, אפילו כתבו בתוכו! ועוד: מדקא מהדרי ליה רבנן: כל שאינו פוסל על פה אינו פוסל בכתב — מכלל דבעל פה מודה להו רבי דאינו פוסל! ונראה לר"י: דכל תנאים, אם נתקיימו, אפילו נכתבו בגט — כשר, כמו בעל פה, דלא שייך למגזר אטו "חוץ" כדפירשנו. והכא בלא נתקיים התנאי קאמר רבי דפוסלים בגט כשנכתבו ומחקם, דאין מועלת מחיקה בהם כי היכי דאינה מועלת ב"חוץ", דגזרינן מחיקה ד"ע"מ" אטו מחיקת "חוץ". ותכ"א: "חוץ" שפוסל בעל פה, פירוש בשעת נתינה — פוסל בכתב אפילו נמחק, משום דלא נכתב לשם כריתות, "ע"מ" שאין פוסל על פה, משום דהוי כריתות — אינו פוסל בכתב, אע"פ שלדעת התנאי נכתב — אין נפסל בכך כיון שחזר ומחקו, אע"פ שלא קיימה. ולא דמי ל"על מנת שתתני לי מאתים זוז" וחזר ואמר "מחולין לך", דאמרינן ב"מי שאחזו" (לעיל דף עד:) דאינה מגורשת — דהיינו דוקא בשעת נתינה, אבל בכתב תנאי בגט קודם הנתינה, וחזר בו מן התנאי ומחקו — כשר, ואינה צריכה לקיים אלא רק מה שמתנה עמה בשעת נתינה, שאז חלים הגירושין. אבל לאחר התורף דברי הכל כשר. נראה לרבינו יהודה: דכשר אפילו אמר הבעל קודם כתיבת התורף, דב"חוץ" נמי ליכא פסולא דאורייתא אלא כשנכתב קודם התורף, אבל נכתב אחר התורף, אפילו אמר בעל קודם לכן — לא חשיב נכתב שלא לשם כריתות, דאין דעת הסופר לשם תנאי ד"חוץ לפלוני" בשעת כתיבת התורף, כיון שלא כתבו בגט עדיין. וכיון דב"חוץ" ליכא פסול דאורייתא — ב"ע"מ" הוי כשר, דלא גזרינן גזירה לגזירה. ותדע, דרב ספרא דלעיל דקאי כר' זירא דהכא, סבר לעיל דבעל פה אינו פוסל אפילו אמר הבעל לפני התורף, כשלא נכתב כלל — וה"ה כשנכתב אחר התורף, שלא נפסל מן התורה מפני שאמר תחילה על פה. ומיהו, לרבא ודאי אמר הבעל לפני התורף ד"ה פסול, אפילו נכתב אחר כך, דלרבא פסול אפילו "על מנת", אפילו בעל פה, שלא נכתב כלל לא בתחילה ולא בסוף, כשלא נתקיים התנאי.
דברי

*) [ועי' תוס' מנחות כג: ד"ה כי סליק]

תוספות רי"ד

בשר חזיר מהו אמר אביי היא היא רבא אמר אפשר דאכלה ולקיא: תניא הרי זה גיטך ע"מ שתאכלי בשר חזיר ואם היתה זרה על מנת שתאכל בתרומה ואם היתה נזירה ע"מ שתשתי יין נתקיים התנאי הרי זה גט ואם לאו אינו גט: תניא הרי זה גיטך ע"מ שתבעלי לפלוני נתקיים התנאי הרי זה גט ואם לאו אינו גט: ואי ק' כיון שקיום הגט תלוי בבעילתו וכל זמן שלא בעל אשת איש היא א"כ היאך מתירין אנו לבעול אשת איש. תשובה הוי ליה גיטא ובעילה באין כאחד כ"ש שהגט קונה למפרע שכל האומר ע"מ כאומר מעכשיו דמי ואף אם נבעלה לאחרים ביני וביני פטורים הן: אם כתבו בתוכו אע"פ שחזר ומחקו פסול פי' כיון שנכתב הגט לשם שיור אע"פ שחזר ומחקו פסול הוא ואין לו תקנה עד שיכתוב א' וסתם מתני' ר' אלעזר היא דלא בעי עדי חתימה והאי דכתיב וכתב לה על כתב הגט קאי דאי ר' מאיר כיון דאמר עדי חתימה כרתי לא איכפת לן בכתיבת הגט כלל כדאמרן בפ' כל הגט אמר רב נחמן אומר היה ר' מאיר אפילו מצאו באשפה חתמו ונתנו לה כשר אי נמי י"ל דאפילו תימא ר' מאיר וע"כ לא מכשיר ר' מאיר אלא התם דאיכתיב לשם גירושין אבל האי דלא איכתיב שהרי יש בו שיור אפילו ר' מאיר מודה דפסול: אמר רב ספרא כתבו בתוכו תנן פי' דוקא אם כתבו בתוכו אין לו תקנה אבל אם התנה ע"פ יש לו תקנה שיחזור ויתננו לה בלי שיור פשיטא כתבו בתוכו תנן פי' דמשמע דוקא בכתיבה מיפסיל לגמרי אבל במימרא לא ומאי איצטריכא רב ספרא לאשמועינן מהו דתימא הני מילי לאחר תורף אבל לפני התורף אפילו ע"פ נמי פסול קמ"ל רב ספרא דאפילו לפני התורף נמי דוקא אם כתבו אין לו תקנה אבל באמירה יש לו תקנה שיחזור מתנאו ואע"פ שנכתב התורף ע"ד שיור אין בכך כלום כיון שחוזר בו ונותנו לה בלי שיור ורבא אמר ל"ש אלא לאחר התורף אבל לפני התורף אפילו ע"פ נמי פסול פי' לא שנו מאי דתני כתבו דמשמע ודאי כתבו אבל בפה לא זהו לאחר התורף אבל לפני התורף אפילו בפה נמי פסול פי' דכיון דאיכתיב תורפו של גט על זה התנאי כאילו נתנו לה על זה התנאי (מאי) דמי ודוקא בחוץ הוא דפסיל רבא ע"פ לפני התורף משום דקסבר דכמאן דאיכתיב תורפו של גט על זה התנאי דמי אבל בע"מ ושאר תנאים לא פסל ע"פ אפילו לפני התורף דהא (אז) [אפילו] יהביה לה על תנאי זה לא מיפסיל ואזדא רבא לטעמיה דאמר להו רבא להני דכתיבי גיטי שתקו שתוקי לבעל עד דכתביתו לתורפיה דגיטא פי' דאי אתני שום תנאי בעת כתיבת תורפו של גט צריכה האשה לקיים אותו התנאי ואם רוצה הבעל לחזור מתנאו אינו יכול לגרשה באותו הגט עד שיכתוב לה גט אחר והלכתא כרבא ומאי דאמר רבא לקמן מחלוקת לאחר [התורף] אבל לפני התורף דברי הכל פסול דמשמע דכל תנאים דעלמא פוסלין לפני התורף דוקא בכתיבה קאמר ולא בפה: אישתכח השתא דחוץ פוסל לפני התורף אפילו ע"פ וכל תנאים פוסלין לפני התורף בכתיבה אבל ע"פ לא אלא שצריך שיתקיים אותו התנאי שנכתב הגט עליו: ת"ר כל התנאים פוסלין בגט דברי רבי וחכ"א כל שפוסל בפה פוסל בכתב וכל שאינו פוסל בפה אינו פוסל בכתב חוץ שפוסל בכתב ע"פ

[כלאי' בבא קמא דף לב.]

כ א מיי' פ"ז מהל' אישות הלכה ח סמג עשין מח טוש"ע אה"ע סי' קמג סעיף יב:

[וע"ע תוס' כתובות נו. ד"ה הרי זו]

כא ב מיי' שם סמג עשין מח טוש"ע אה"ע סי' לח סעיף ה:

כב ג מיי' שם סמג שם טוש"ע שם סי' קמג סעיף יב:

כג ד מיי' פ"ח מהל' גירושין הל' ד סמג עשין נ טוש"ע אה"ע סי' קמז סעיף ג וע"ש במ"מ ובכ"מ:

[תוספתא פ"ד]

[לקמן עח.]

[כתובות נו. פד: קדושין יט: נזיר יא. ב"ב נא. נב. ב"ב קטו: מכות ג.]

לעיל עח.

[שייך לעיל במתני' פב.]

דברי הכל כשר; ומתני' דקתני "כתבו" ואוקימנא ב"חוץ", אבל "ע"מ" לא פסיל, איבעית אימא: לפני התורף ורבנן, ואיבע"א: לאחר התורף ודברי הכל. ורבא אמר: מחלוקת — לאחר התורף, דרבי סבר: גזרינן אטו לפני התורף, אורבנן סברי: לא גזרינן אטו לפני התורף, אבל לפני התורף — דברי הכל פסול; ומתני' דקתני "כתבו" ואוקימנא ב"חוץ", אבל "על מנת" לא פסיל — אחר התורף ורבנן היא. תני אבוה דרבי אבין קמיה דרבי זירא: כתב גט על תנאי — דברי הכל פסול. דברי הכל פסול? והא מיפלג פליגי! אלא, אימא: לדברי הכל כשר, והיכי דמי? בלאחר התורף. ולימא: הרי זה פסול, ורבי! תנא דברי הכל אתנייה, כשר בפסול מיחלף ליה, "הרי זה" ב"דברי הכל" לא מיחלף ליה.§ **מתני'** גהרי את מותרת לכל אדם אלא לאבא ולאביך, לאחי ולאחיך, לעבד ולגוי, ולכל מי שאין לה עליו קידושין — כשר. הרי את מותרת לכל אדם אלא אלמנה לכהן גדול, גרושה וחלוצה לכהן הדיוט, ממזרת ונתינה לישראל, בת ישראל לממזר ולנתין, וכל מי שיש לה עליו קידושין אפילו בעבירה — פסול.§ **גמ'** דכללא דרישא — לאתויי שאר חייבי כריתות, כללא דסיפא — לאתויי שאר חייבי לאוין, (כגון עמוני ומואבי, נתיני, מצרי ואדומי.) [ס"א ל"ג] בעא מיניה רבא מרב נחמן: חוץ מקידושי קטן, מהו? מי אמרינן השתא מיהא לאו בר הויה הוא, או דלמא אתי לכלל הויה? א"ל, תניתוה: קטנה מתגרשת בקידושי אביה; אמאי? והא בעינן "ויצאה והיתה"! אלא אתיא לכלל הויה, ההכא נמי אתיא לכלל הויה. ו"חוץ מן הנולדים", מהו? השתא מיהא לא איתיליד, או דלמא עתידי דמתיילדי? א"ל, תניתוה: "לעבד ולגוי", אם איתא, עבד וגוי נמי עבידי דמיגיירי! הנך לאו לאיגיורי קיימי, הני לאיתילודי קיימי. ז"חוץ מבעל אחותה", מהו? השתא מיהא לא חזיא ליה, או דלמא זמנין דמתה אחותה וחזיא ליה? אמר ליה, תניתוה: "לעבד ולגוי", עבד וגוי נמי עבידי דמיגיירי! גירות לא שכיחא, *מיתה שכיחא. ח"חוץ מזנותיך", מהו? בנשואין הא לא שייר, או דלמא שייר בביאה? א"ל, תניתוה: "לאבא ולאביך", ובמאי? אילימא בנשואין, אבא ואביך בני נשואין נינהו? אלא לאו בזנות, ולאבא ולאביך הוא דלא שייר, הא לאחר שייר. דלמא בנשואין, דעבר ואינסיב. ט"חוץ משלא כדרכה", מהו? בכדרכה הא לא שייר, או דלמא °"משכבי אשה" [ויקרא כ] כתיב? י"חוץ מהפרת נדריך", מהו? בנשואין הא לא שייר, או דלמא °"אישה יקימנו ואישה יפירנו" [במדבר ל] כתיב? כ"חוץ מתרומתיך", מהו? בנשואין הא לא שייר, או דלמא °"קנין כספו" [ויקרא כב] כתיב? "חוץ מירושתיך", מהו? בנשואין הא לא שייר, או דלמא °"לשארו וירש אותה" [במדבר כז] כתיב? "חוץ מקידושיך בשטר", מהו? מי אמרינן: אפשר דמקדש לה בכסף ובביאה, או דלמא "ויצאה והיתה", *איתקוש הוויות להדדי? לתיקו.§ **מתני'** *)מגופו של גט: "הרי את מותרת לכל אדם"; רבי

*) נדרים ה.

רש"י

ואוקימנא בחוץ. ברים פירקין, ושמעינן מינה דאילו ב"על מנת", אפילו כתבו בתוכו – כשר. אימא דברי הכל כשר כו'. ר' זירא לטעמיה, דאוקי פלוגתא בלפני התורף, הלכך ד"ה פסול לא משכחת לה. ולימא. ליה רבי זירא לתנא: תני "ה"ז פסול", ולא תיתני "דברי הכל", ונימא רבי היא. תנא ד"ה אתנייה. ע"כ "דברי הכל" [תורה אור] אתנייה רביה לתנא, דאי אתנייה "הרי זה" – לא הוה מיחלף ליה ב"דברי הכל", אפילו שכח גירסא שלו. אבל כשר בפסול – מיחלף ליה, אם שכח שמועתו. להכי אמר ליה: תני "דברי הכל כשר", דמסתברא דהכי אגמריה רביה. **מתני'** אלא לאבא ולאביך כו'. לאו שיורא הוא, דבלאו איסור אישות נמי לא תפסי להו בה קידושין. אלמנה לכהן גדול. כיון דקידושין תופסין בחייבי לאוין, כדאמרינן בפ"ק דקידושין (דף יח.), ולהאי לא תפסי משום איסור אישות שבה – אשתכח דשייר בגיטא. ולכל מי שיש לה עליו קידושין. אם היתה פנויה, ואפילו בעבירה דאיסור לאו. פסול. דהוי שיור. **גמ'** כללא דרישא. "ולכל מי שאין לה עליו קידושין". נתיני. מן הגבעונים, שהיו משבעה אומות, ואיכא לאו ד"לא תתחתן בם". מצרי ואדומי. בתוך שלשה דורות, שהם באיסור עשה. חוץ מקידושי קטן. חוץ מפלוני, וקטן הוא. קטנה מתגרשת. אם קיבלה גיטה לאחר מיתת אביה. בקידושי אביה. כלומר, ואפילו קידשה אביה לאיש הזה, דהוו להו קידושין גמורין. והא בעינן ויצאה והיתה. דלא מיגרשה אא"כ ראויה לקדש את עצמה לאיש אחר. אלא אתיא לכלל הויה. לאחר זמן, וקא חשיב ליה מעכשיו. דלא דק קרא למימר דתיהוי השתא בת הויה. לענין שיורא נמי הוי שיור. הנולדים. עתידין להולד. או דלמא עתידין דמתילדי. ומיתסרא עליהן מפני *(אשתו) [צ"ל אישותו] של זה, הלכך הוי שיור. עבד וגוי נמי. הא מצית למימר בהו עתידי דמיגיירי, ואפ"ה לא הוי שיור. השתא מיהת לא חזיא ליה. כל זמן שאחותה קיימת, ולא הוי שיור. חוץ מזנותיך. שלא תבעלי בזנות. או דלמא שייר בביאה. בעלמא, וגם אישות קרינן בה. אבא ואביך בני נישואין נינהו. דתיסק אדעתיה דבעי לאתנויי בהדה? הא לא תפסי בה קידושין! [לעיל ל: כתובות פג:] אלא לאו בזנות. ואבא ואביך הוא דלא הוי שיור, דבלאו הכי נמי אסירא להו. ודלמא בנישואין. קתני מתני', ואף על גב דלאו אורחא הוא. הלכך, לאחר הוי שיור – אבל בזנות אימא לא הוי שיור! משכבי אשה כתיב. הקיש שני משכבי' לכל דבר. ואישה יפרנו. וכיון דשייר הפרת נדרים לגביה – אישה קרינא ביה. מתרומתיך. שאם תנשאי לכהן לא יאכילך בתרומה. קנין כספו. "הוא יאכל בו" כתיב, והאי כיון דלאו בר הכי הוא – [כתובות מו: וש"נ] לא הויא קנין כספו, ואשתכח דשייר בקדושין אצל כהנים. חוץ מירושתך. שאם תמותי אני יורשך. ממשפחתו וירש אותה. מכאן שהבעל יורש את אשתו, וכיון דאיהו ירית לה – אשתו היא. חוץ מקידושיך בשטר. שאם יקדשוך בשטר – לא יהו קידושין. כלומר, ששייר אחד מדרכי קידושין ולא שייר את כולם. ואיתקש הוויות להדדי. והיכא דשייר חדא מינייהו לא קרינא ביה "ויצאה". **מתני'** גופו של גט. עיקר כתב הגט כך יכתבו בו.

ודן

תוספות

דברי הכל כשר. אע"ג דב"חוץ" פסול אפילו אחר התורף, כדאמרינן בסמוך: ואי בעית אימא לאחר התורף ודברי הכל – מ"מ לא גזרינן ביה "ע"מ" אטו "חוץ", ד"חוץ" אחר התורף אינו פסול אלא מדרבנן, גזירה אטו לפני תורף, ולא גזרינן גזירה לגזירה. **רבא** אמר מחלוקת לאחר התורף. דרבי גזר "ע"מ" דלאחר התורף אטו "ע"מ" דלפני התורף. אע"ג דלפני התורף נמי אינו אלא גזירה אטו "חוץ" – כולה חדא גזירה היא. **אבל** לפני התורף דברי הכל פסול. דגזרינן אטו "חוץ", וב"חוץ" הוא פסול גמור אפילו על פה, דסבר רבא דלא נכתב לשם כריתות.

ומתני' דקתני כתבו ואוקימנא בחוץ אבל על מנת לא פסול לאחר התורף ורבנן. והוא הדין דבלאו האי טעמא צריך לאוקומי מתני' אחר התורף, מדקתני "כתבו", דמשמע: אבל על פה – כשר.

תניתוה קטנה מתגרשת בקידושי אביה. וא"ת: ודלמא מן האירוסין איירי, ויש לה אב, דבת הויה היא! ועוד: אמאי לא קא מייתי מתניתין דפרק "התקבל" (לעיל דף סה.): קטנה שאמרה "התקבל לי גיטי" – אינו גט עד שיגיע גט לידה, ומוקמינן לה בפ"ב דקדושין (דף מד:) באין לה אב! ואור"י: דהך ברייתא משמע ליה בכל ענין, אפילו אין לה אב, או מן הנשואין דאין לאביה רשות בה. אבל מתניתין ד"התקבל" מצי למדחיה בדיש לה אב, כדמשמע פשט דמתניתין, דקתני בתר הכי: ואם אמר אביה כו'. והכי הוה בעי למידק בפרק שני דקדושין (דף מד:) דיש לה אב עסקינן.

חוץ מתרומתיך מהו. פי' בקונטרס: שאם תנשאי לכהן – לא תאכל בתרומה. ואין נראה לר"י, דבלאו הכי לא אכלה בתרומה, דגרושה מתחללת בביאת כהן. ואפילו קידשה ונשאה ולא בא עליה, דמשתמרת לביאה פסולה היא. אע"ג דאהני מה שמשייר שתהא אסורה לאכול מן התורה – מכל מקום נראה דוחק לפרש כן. ונראה לפרש: חוץ מתרומה – שהוא כהן, ומגרשה לכל דבר חוץ שלא תיאסר באכילתה. אי הוי שיור, ד"קנין כספו" אמר רחמנא דע"י קידושין אוכלת בתרומה – אם כן עדיין קידושין עליה, ואין זה כריתות. או דילמא בקידושין הא לא שייר, שתוכל להתקדש למי שתרצה. וכי האי גוונא פי' בקונטרס עצמו גבי "חוץ מירושתך ומהפרת נדריך".

עין משפט נר מצוה

כד א ב מיי' פ"ח מהל' גירושין הל' ז סמג עשין נ טוש"ע אה"ע סי' קמז סעיף ב:
כה ג ד ה מיי' שם הל' ה סמג שם טוש"ע אה"ע סימן קלז סעיף ב:
כו ו ז ח ט י מיי' שם הלכה ו טוש"ע שם סעיף ג:
כז כ מיי' שם הלכה ו:
כח ל מיי' שם סמג שם טוש"ע שם סעיף ג:
כט מ מיי' שם פ"א הלכה ז סמג שם טוש"ע אה"ע סימן קנ סעיף מא:

תוספות רי"ד

ע"מ שאינו פוסל בפה אינו פוסל בכתב: א"ר זירא מחלוקת לפני התורף דר' סבר גזרינן ע"מ אטו חוץ ורבנן סברי לא גזרינן אבל לאחר התורף דברי הכל כשר: ורבא אמר מחלוקת לאחר התורף דר' סבר גזרינן לאחר התורף אטו לפני התורף ורבנן סברי לא גזרינן אבל לפני התורף דברי הכל פסול. פי' ס"ל לרבא כל תנאים דמיכתבי בגיטא מקמי התורף פסול מן התורה שאין זה ספר כריתות כיון שתנאי כתוב בתוכו ואע"פ שהוא תנאי כשר והאשה רוצה לקיימו אלא צריך לכתוב הגט בלי תנאי ואפילו שרוצה להתנות יתנה בעת שמוסרו לה. ור' זירא סבר אם תנאי כשר הוא אינו פוסל ומקרי ספר כריתות כיון שיכולה לקיימו והלכתא כרבא. נמצא מעכשיו לפי פסק ההלכה דלפני התורף פוסל חוץ בין בכתב כגון שכתבו בתוכו בין בעל פה כגון שהודיעו לסופר והסופר כתבו ע"ד כן שאין לו תקנה עולמית לגט זה וע"מ שהוא תנאי כשר הוא פוסל דוקא בכתב שאין לו תקנה עולמית אבל בעל פה לא פסיל אבל מיהו צריך ליתנו לה באותו התנאי כיון שנכתב התורף ע"ד כן ואם רוצה הבעל לחזור מן התנאי ולגרשה בלא תנאי צריך לכתוב לה גט אחר בלא תנאי ולאחר התורף חוץ פוסל דוקא בכתב אבל בעל פה לא פסיל ליה אלא יכול ליתנו לה בלא חוץ והוא כשר וע"מ אינו פוסל אפילו בכתב שכל מה שרוצה להתנות אחר התורף בין בכתב בין בעל פה יכול להתנות ואם רוצה לחזור מתנאו ולגרשה בו בלא תנאי הרשות בידו כיון שהתורף נכתב בלא תנאי: **מתני'** הרי את מותרת לכל אדם אלא לאבא ולאביך לאחי ולאחיך לעבד ולגוי ולכל מי שאין לה עליו קידושין כשר. פי' דכיון דאסירי עלה מדאורייתא לאו שיור הוא וכשר הרי את מותרת לכל אדם אלא אלמנה לכה"ג גרושה וחלוצה לכ"ה ממזרת ונתינה לישראל בת ישראל לנתין ולממזר ולכל מי שיש לה עליו קידושין אפילו בעבירה פסול: בעא מיניה רבא מרב נחמן חוץ מקדושי קטן מהו השתא מיהו לאו בר הויה הוא או דלמא אתי לכלל הויה ופשט ליה דכיון דאתי לכלל הויה שיורא הוא: חוץ מן הנולדים מהו השתא מיהו לא איתילידו או דלמא עתידי דמתילדי. חוץ מבעל אחותה מהו השתא מיהא לא חזיא ליה או דלמא זמנין דמיתה אחותה וחזיא ליה חוץ מזנותיך מהו בנישואין הא לא שייר או דלמא הא שייר בביאה חוץ משלא כדרכה מהו בכדרכה הא לא שייר או דלמא משכבי אשה כתיב: חוץ מהפרת נדריך מהו בנישואין הא לא שייר או דלמא אישה יקימנו ואישה יפרנו כתיב חוץ מתרומתיך מהו בנישואין הא לא שייר או דלמא קנין כספו כתיב חוץ מירושתיך מהו בנישואין הא לא שייר או דלמא לשארו וירש אותה כתיב חוץ מקידושיך בשטר מהו אפשר דמקדש לה בכסף ובביאה או דלמא והיתה כתיב איתקש הויות להדדי ואיתוקמו בתיקו וכל תיקו דאיסורא לחומרא: **מתני'** גופו של

גליון הש"ס

תוס' ד"ה תניתוה קטנה וכו' בכפ"ב דקדושין דיש לה אב עסקינן. עי' לעיל דף סד ע"ב תד"ה נערה.

רַבִּי יְהוּדָה אוֹמֵר: "וְדֵן דִּיהֱוֵי לִיכִי מִינַּאי סֵפֶר תֵּירוּכִין וְאִגֶּרֶת שְׁבוּקִין וְגֵט פִּטּוּרִין לִמְהַךְ לְהִתְנַסְּבָא לְכָל גְּבַר דִּיתִצְבְּיִין". *אגּוּפוֹ שֶׁל גֵּט שִׁחְרוּר: "הֲרֵי *אַתְּ בַּת חוֹרִין", "הֲרֵי אַתְּ לְעַצְמֵךְ".§

גמ' בפְּשִׁיטָא, *אָמַר לָהּ לְאִשְׁתּוֹ "הֲרֵי אַתְּ בַּת חוֹרִין" — לֹא אָמַר וְלֹא כְלוּם, גאָמַר לָהּ לְשִׁפְחָתוֹ "הֲרֵי אַתְּ מוּתֶּרֶת לְכָל אָדָם" — לֹא אָמַר וְלֹא כְלוּם, אָמַר לָהּ לְאִשָּׁה "הֲרֵי אַתְּ לְעַצְמֵךְ", מַהוּ? לְגַמְרֵי קָאָמַר לָהּ, אוֹ לִמְלָאכָה קָאָמַר לָהּ? א"ל רָבִינָא לְרַב אַשִׁי: ת"ש, דִּתְנַן: *גּוּפוֹ שֶׁל גֵּט שִׁחְרוּר "הֲרֵי אַתְּ בַּת חוֹרִין", "הֲרֵי אַתְּ לְעַצְמֵךְ"; וּמָה עַבְדָּא דְּקָנֵי לֵיהּ גּוּפֵיהּ, כִּי א"ל "הֲרֵי אַתְּ לְעַצְמֵךְ" — קָנֵי גּוּפֵיהּ, אִשָּׁה דְּלָא קָנֵי גּוּפָהּ — דלֹא כ"ש? א"ל רָבִינָא לְרַב אַשִׁי: א"ל לְעַבְדּוֹ "אֵין לִי עֵסֶק בְּךָ", מַהוּ? א"ל רַב חָנִין לְרַב אַשִׁי, וְאָמְרִי לָהּ רַב חָנִין מֵחוֹזְנָאָה לְרַב אַשִׁי: הת"ש, *דְּתַנְיָא: והַמּוֹכֵר עַבְדּוֹ לְגוֹי — יָצָא לְחֵירוּת, וְצָרִיךְ גֵּט שִׁחְרוּר מֵרַבּוֹ רִאשׁוֹן; אָמַר רַבָּן שִׁמְעוֹן בֶּן גַּמְלִיאֵל: בד"א — שֶׁלֹּא כָּתַב עָלָיו אוֹנוֹ, אֲבָל כָּתַב עָלָיו אוֹנוֹ — זֶהוּ שִׁחְרוּרוֹ. מַאי אוֹנוֹ? אָמַר רַב שֵׁשֶׁת: דְּכָתַב לֵיהּ: לִכְשֶׁתִּבְרַח מִמֶּנּוּ אֵין לִי עֵסֶק בְּךָ.§ "ר' יְהוּדָה אוֹמֵר: וְדֵן דִּיהֱוֵי לִיכִי מִינַּאי סֵפֶר תֵּירוּכִין וְאִגֶּרֶת שְׁבוּקִין".§ בְּמַאי קָמִיפַּלְגִי? רַבָּנַן סָבְרִי: *יָדַיִם שֶׁאֵין מוֹכִיחוֹת הָוְיָין יָדַיִם, וְאַף עַל גַּב דְּלָא כָּתַב לָהּ "וְדֵן" מוֹכְחָא מִילְּתָא דִּבְהַאי גִּיטָּא קָא מְגָרֵשׁ לָהּ; וְר' יְהוּדָה סָבַר: יָדַיִם שֶׁאֵין מוֹכִיחוֹת לָא הָוְיָין יָדַיִם, וְטַעְמָא דְּכָתַב לָהּ "וְדֵן" דְּמוֹכְחָא מִילְּתָא דִּבְהַאי גִּיטָּא קָא מְגָרֵשׁ לָהּ, אֲבָל לָא כָּתַב לָהּ "וְדֵן", אָמְרִי: בְּדִיבּוּרָא גֵּרְשָׁהּ, וּשְׁטָרָא רְאָיָה בְּעָלְמָא הוּא. אָמַר אַבַּיֵי: הַאי מַאן דְּכָתַב גִּיטָּא, זלָא לִכְתּוֹב "וְדִין" דְּמַשְׁמַע וְדִין, אֶלָּא וְדֵן; חוְלָא לִכְתּוֹב "אִיגֶּרֶת" דְּמַשְׁמַע אִיגֶּרֶת, אֶלָּא אִגֶּרֶת; טוְלָא לִכְתּוֹב "לִימְהַךְ" דְּמַשְׁמַע לִי מַהֵךְ; יוְלָא לִכְתּוֹב "לְמַחַךְ" דְּמַשְׁמַע כִּי חוּכָא; כ"דִיתִיהֱוְיִין" "דִיתִיצְבְּיִין" תְּלָתָא תְּלָתָא יוּדִי"ן דְּמַשְׁמַע תֶּהֶוְיָין וְתִצְבְּיָין; לוּלְאוֹרְכֵיהּ לְוָי"ו דְ"תֵירוּכִין" וּלְוָי"ו דִ"שְׁבוּקִין" דְּמַשְׁמַע תְּרִיכִין וּשְׁבִיקִין; מוּלְאוֹרְכֵיהּ לְוָי"ו דְ"כְדוּ" דְּמַשְׁמַע וּכְדִי; נוְלָא לִיכְתּוֹב "לְאִיתְנַסְּבָא" דְּמַשְׁמַע לָא יִתְנַסְּבָא, אֶלָּא "לְהִתְנַסְּבָא". אִיבַּעְיָא לְהוּ: בָּעֵינַן "וְדֵן", אוֹ לָא בָּעֵינַן "וְדֵן"? תָּא שְׁמַע, סדְּאַתְקֵין *רָבָא בְּגִיטֵּי: "אִיךְ פְּלָנְיָא בַּר פְּלָנְיָא פָּטַר וְתָרֵיךְ יַת פְּלוֹנִיתָא אִינְתְּתֵיהּ דַּהֲוַת אִינְתְּתֵיהּ מִן קֳדָם דְּנָא מִיּוֹמָא דְּנַן וּלְעָלַם", וְאִילּוּ "וְדֵן" לָא קָאָמַר. וּלְטַעְמֵיךְ, כּוּלְּהוּ מִי קָאָמַר? אֶלָּא בָּעֵינַן, עהָכָא נַמִי בָּעֵינַן.§ "מִיּוֹמָא דְּנַן" — לְאַפּוֹקֵי מִדְּרַבִּי יוֹסֵי, דְּאָמַר: *זְמַנּוֹ שֶׁל שְׁטָר מוֹכִיחַ עָלָיו; "וּלְעָלַם" — לְאַפּוֹקֵי

רש"י

וְדֵן דִּי יֶהֱוֵי לִיכִי מִינַּאי כו'. וְזֶה הַסֵּפֶר אֲשֶׁר יִהְיֶה לִיךְ מֵאִתִּי. סֵפֶר תֵּירוּכִין וְאִגֶּרֶת שְׁבוּקִין. שֶׁצָּרִיךְ לְהוֹכִיחַ בְּתוֹכוֹ שֶׁעַל יְדֵי סֵפֶר זֶה הוּא מְגָרְשָׁהּ. **גמ'** אָמַר לָהּ לְאִשְׁתּוֹ. לִכְתּוֹב בְּגִיטָּהּ: "הֲרֵי אַתְּ בַּת חוֹרִין" וְלֹא כָּתַב בּוֹ "הֲרֵי אַתְּ מוּתֶּרֶת לְכָל אָדָם". לֹא אָמַר כְּלוּם. דְּלֹא שַׁיָּיךְ בְּגֵירוּשִׁין לְשׁוֹן חֵירוּת, דְּבַת חוֹרִין הָיְתָה קוֹדֶם לָכֵן. אָמַר לְשִׁפְחָתוֹ הֲרֵי אַתְּ מוּתֶּרֶת לְכָל אָדָם לֹא אָמַר כְּלוּם. דִּלְגַבֵּי מְלָאכָה לֹא אַפְקָהּ מִינֵּיהּ, וְכֵיוָן דְּשִׁפְחָה הִיא, וְשֵׁם שִׁפְחָה עָלֶיהָ — לֹא מִשְׁתַּרְיָא נַמִי לְבֶן חוֹרִין. יָצָא לְחֵירוּת. אע"פ שֶׁקְּנָסוּהוּ לִפְדוֹתוֹ עַד עֲשָׂרָה בְּדָמָיו — לֹא יִשְׁתַּעְבֵּד לוֹ עוֹד. וְצָרִיךְ גֵּט שִׁחְרוּר. לְהַתִּירוֹ בְּבַת יִשְׂרָאֵל. שֶׁלֹּא כָּתַב עָלָיו אוֹנוֹ. שְׁטָר כְּשֶׁמְּכָרוֹ לַגּוֹי. לִכְשֶׁתִּבְרַח מִמֶּנּוּ. מִן הַגּוֹי, אִם תּוּכַל לְהִמָּלֵט מִן הַגּוֹי. אַלְמָא "אֵין לִי עֵסֶק בְּךָ" — לְשׁוֹן חֵירוּת הוּא. יָדַיִם שֶׁאֵין מוֹכִיחוֹת. בֵּית (א) אֲחִיזָה לַדָּבָר, לֶאֱחוֹז בּוֹ, וְלוֹמַר: הוֹכִיחַ שֶׁעַל יְדֵי סֵפֶר זֶה גֵּירְשָׁהּ. אפ"ה — הָוֵי בֵּית יָד, וְאָמְרִינַן: מִדְּכָתַב גֵּט וְיָהֵיב — גַּלֵּי דַּעְתֵּיהּ דִּבְהַאי גִּיטָּא גֵּירְשָׁהּ. בְּדִיבּוּרָא. דְּאָמַר לָהּ בִּשְׁעַת מְסִירָה: הֲרֵי אַתְּ מוּתֶּרֶת לְכָל אָדָם. רְאָיָה בְּעָלְמָא הוּא. לִהְיוֹת בְּיָדָהּ לְעֵדוּת בְּכָל אֲשֶׁר תֵּלֵךְ, לְהַרְאוֹת שֶׁהִיא פְּנוּיָה. לָא לִכְתּוֹב וְדִין. דְּמַשְׁמַע: דִּין הוּא שֶׁאֲגָרְשֵׁךְ, אֲבָל אִם אֵינוֹ דִּין עָלַי שֶׁאֲגָרְשֵׁךְ — לֹא תִּתְגָּרְשִׁי. וְלָא לִכְתּוֹב אִיגֶּרֶת. שֶׁיִּבּוּקִין בְּיו"ד, דְּמַשְׁמַע אִיגָּרָא, לְשׁוֹן גַּג. וְלָא לִכְתּוֹב לִימְהַךְ לְהִתְנַסְּבָא לְכָל מַאן דִּיתִיצְבְּיִין. דְּמַשְׁמַע: לִי מֵהֵךְ, לִי תְּהִי מִסֵּפֶר הַזֶּה וְאֵילָךְ. אֶלָּא לִמְהַךְ. בְּלֹא יו"ד. וְלָא לִכְתּוֹב לְמַחַךְ. צָרִיךְ שֶׁיַּבְדִּיל רַגְלוֹ שֶׁל הֵ"א, שֶׁיִּהְיֶה אֲוִיר בֵּין רַגְלוֹ לְגַגּוֹ, דְּלָא לִיתְחֲזֵי כְּחֵי"ת. דְּמַשְׁמַע לְמַחַךְ. לִצְחֵק, כְּלוֹמַר: מְצַחֵק אֲנִי בָּךְ, כִּי חוּכָא. זֶהוּ טוֹפֶס הַגֵּט: פְּטָרִית יָתִיכִי לִיכִי אַנְתְּ פְּלוֹנִית בַּת פְּלוֹנִי דַּהֲוֵית אִינְתְּתִי מִקַּדְמַת דְּנָא וּכְדוּ פְּטָרִית וּשְׁבָקִית וְתָרוֹכִית יָתִיכִי דִּי תֶּהֶוְיָין רַשָּׁאָה וְשַׁלְטָאָה בְּנַפְשַׁיְכִי לִמְהַךְ לְהִתְנַסָּבָא לְכָל מַאן דִּיתִיצְבְּיִין וֶאֱנָשׁ לָא יִמְחֵי בִּידַיְכִי מִן יוֹמָא דְּנַן וּלְעָלַם וְדֵן דִּי יֶהֱוֵי לִיכִי מִינַּאי גֵּט פְּטוּרִין וְסֵפֶר תֵּירוּכִין וְאִגֶּרֶת שְׁבוּקִין כְּדַת מֹשֶׁה וְיִשְׂרָאֵל. "דִּי תֶּהֶוְיָין רַשָּׁאָה" לִיתֵּן בֵּיהּ תְּלָתָא יוּדִי"ן רְצוּפִין, דְּנִיקְרֵי דִּי תִּיהֶוְיָין. דְּאִי לָא שַׁדְיָא בֵּיהּ אֶלָּא תְּרֵין יוּדִי"ן מִיתְקְרֵי: דִּי *דְּהָוְיָין, לָשׁוֹן דְּעָלְמָא. וְכֵן "דִּי תִיצְבְּיִין", דְּכִי כָּתַב תְּלָתָא יוּדִי"ן — מַשְׁמַע שֶׁתְּהֵא רַשָּׁאָה לְהִנָּשֵׂא לְכָל מִי שֶׁתִּרְצֶה. וּלְאוֹרְכֵיהּ לְוָי"ו דְּתֵירוּכִין. יַאֲרִיךְ וָי"ו שֶׁבְּסֵפֶר תֵּירוּכִין, וָוי"ו שֶׁבְּאִגֶּרֶת שְׁבוּקִין, דְּאִי לָא מַאֲרִיךְ לֵיהּ — מִיחְזֵי כְּיו"ד, מַשְׁמַע: סֵפֶר תְּרִיכִין — גְּרוּשׁוֹת דְּעָלְמָא, וּשְׁבִיקִין — אִגֶּרֶת נָשִׁים עֲזוּבוֹת דְּעָלְמָא, וְלֹא שֶׁלָּהּ הוּא. וּלְאוֹרְכֵיהּ לְוָי"ו דְּוּכְדוּ. פְּטָרִית יָתִיכִין וָי"ו הָאַחֲרוֹנָה מַאֲרִיךְ שֶׁלֹּא יֵרָאֶה כְּיו"ד, דְּאִי לָא מַאֲרִיךְ לֵיהּ — מַשְׁמַע: (ב) וּכְדִי, כְּלוֹמַר: בְּוְלֹא כְלוּם, בְּאֵין סֵפֶר. כְּמוֹ "כְּדֵי נַסְבַהּ" (ר"ה דף ה.), *וּכְמוֹ: וְאָמְרִי לָהּ כְּדִי, שֵׁם חָכָם (ב"מ דף ב). וְלָא לִכְתּוֹב לְאִיתְנַסְּבָא. בְּאָלֶף, אֶלָּא לְהִתְנַסְּבָא בְּהֵ"א. שֶׁמָּא יַרְחִיק "לֹא" מִן "יִתְנַסְּבָא", וּמַשְׁמַע: לֹא יִתְנַסְּבָא — לֹא תִּנָּשֵׂא. מִי בָּעֵינַן. כְּלוֹמַר, הֲלָכָה כְּר"י אוֹ כְּרַבָּנַן? כּוּלְּהוּ מִי קָאָמַר. כָּל שְׁאָר דְּבָרִים הַנִּכְתָּבִים בַּגֵּט, כְּגוֹן "דִּי תִיהֶוְיָין" וכו' מִי הִזְכִּירָם רָבָא בְּתַקָּנָה זוֹ? אֶלָּא. אע"ג דְּלָא אַזְכְּרִינְהוּ רָבָא בָּעֵינַן דְּלִכְתְּבִינְהוּ. הָכָא נַמִי. "וְדֵן" בָּעֵינַן, וּמִיהוּ רָבָא לֹא הוּצְרַךְ לְתַקֵּן אֶלָּא אֵלּוּ, כִּדְמְפָרֵשׁ וְאָזֵיל. מִן יוֹמָא דְּנַן וּלְעָלַם לְאַפּוֹקֵי מִדְּר' יוֹסֵי דְּאָמַר. אֵין צָרִיךְ לִכְתּוֹב "מֵהַיּוֹם" בְּגֵט דִּשְׁכִיב מְרַע, דִּזְמַנּוֹ שֶׁל שְׁטָר מוֹכִיחַ עָלָיו, וְלָא הָוֵי כְּגֵט לְאַחַר מִיתָה. לְכָךְ תִּקֵּן רָבָא בְּכָל הַגִּיטִּין לִהְיוֹת הַסּוֹפְרִים רְגִילִין בּוֹ. וְאע"ג דְּקַיְימָא לָן כְּר' יוֹסֵי — בָּעֵינַן לְאַפּוֹקֵי נַפְשִׁין מִפְּלוּגְתָּא, שֶׁיְּהֵא הַדָּבָר בְּהֶיתֵּר וְלֹא יֵצֵא שֵׁם פְּסוּל מִמִּשְׁפְּחוֹת יִשְׂרָאֵל. לְאַפּוֹקֵי

תוספות

רבי יהודה אומר ספר תירוכין ואגרת שבוקין. בספרים לא היה כתוב "גט פטורין", ובגמרא נמי כי קאמר: ולורכיה לוי"ו דתירוכין ולוי"ו דשיבוקין – לא קאמר לוי"ו דפטורין. ומיהו בפ"ק דנדרים (דף ה:) כתיב בספרים נמי "גט פיטורין", ונראה דהכא נמי גרסינן ליה, דהא "ספר כריתות" מתרגמינן: פיטורין, וגם בגיטין רגילין לכותבו. **אע"ג** דלא כתב ודן מוכחא מילתא דבהאי גיטא מיגרשה לה. הכא משמע דפליגי ב"ודן", ובריש נדרים משמע דפליגי ב"מינאי", דלרבנן הויין ידים, ואע"ג דלא כתיב "מינאי" – מגורשת, דאין אדם מגרש אשת חברו. ואומר ר"י: דבתרוייהו פליגי, ושם מפורש. ולא תיקשי לאביי דאמר התם: ידים שאינם מוכיחות הויין ידים, ובסמוך אמר אביי: לא ליכתוב "ודין". ושמא לשופרא דשטרא קאמר הכי. **ולא** ליכתוב איגרת ביו"ד דמשמע איגרא. אע"ג דב"אגרת" מן הדין אין יו"ד, מ"מ "איגרא" שהוא לשון גג – רגילות לכותבו ביו"ד, לפי שאינו כתוב בעברי. אבל ב"אגרת" שהוא לשון אגרת – כתוב בעברי בלא יו"ד, כדכתיב (אסתר ט) "על כל דברי אגרת הזאת", וכן כולם כתובין כן. ובסדר תיקון שטרות שכתב הרב ר"י ט"ע כתב: ולא ליכתוב "אגרת" בלא וי"ו דמשמע אגרתא בעלמא, שאדם שולח לחברו, אלא "ואגרת" בוי"ו, דמשמע דקאי אגיטא, וא"ודן" דלעיל. **דתהויין** דתצביין בתלתא יודי"ן. ואומר ר"י: שראה בתיקון גיטין קדמונים דחמשה יודי"ן צריכי, תלתא יודי"ן ביחד בסוף התיבה, ואחר הדל"ת ואחר התי"ו דיתיהויין דיתילביין. וכן כתוב בתיקון שטרות של ה"ר יוסף ט"ע: "ודי תיהויין" הם שתי תיבות, "ודי" במקום אשר. אבל "דיתבא על נהר פלוני" – הכל תיבה אחת כלומר: היושבת, ואין לכתוב "די יתבא" – אשר יושבת. **ולורכיה** לוי"ו כו'. ושמא אין צריך להאריך, אלא כלומר שלא יעשה קצרה, שתהא נראית יו"ד. וכן רגל ה"א ד"למהך" להרחיק מן הגג – שמא אין צריך להרחיק, אלא שלא יחבר בגגה. ושמא צריך להאריך הווי"ן ולהרחיק רגל הה"א, שלא יטעו העולם בזה. ונהגו להאריך ולהרחיק. ומיהו, ודאי דאין הגט פסול אם לא האריכן, וכן הה"א של "מהך", אם לא הרחיקה יותר מדאי. ומעשה בגט שלא היה ניכר היטב בין וי"ו ליו"ד, שבא לפני רבינו אליהו, והביא תינוק דלא חכים ולא טיפש לקרות אותה התיבה, כדאמר במנחות גבי תפילין (דף כט:): זיל אייתי תינוק דלא חכים ולא טיפש, אי קרי "ויהרג" – כשר, אי לא – "ייהרג" הוא ופסול. מן

מג א מיי' פ"ח מהל' גירושין הל' ע סמג עשין נ טוש"ע אה"ע סי' קלו סעיף ה:
מד ב מיי' שם הל' יד סמג שם טוש"ע אה"ע סי' קל סעי' ב:
מה ג מיי' שם פ"א הל' כח סמג שם טוש"ע אה"ע סימן קכז סעי' א:
מו ד מיי' שם פ"א הל' עו סמג שם טוש"ע אה"ע סי' קלו סעיף א:
מז ה מיי' שם הל' כד ופ"ג שם הל' ג סמג שם טוש"ע שם:
מח ו מיי' שם פ"א הל' יד סמג שם טוש"ע אה"ע שם סימן קל סעיף ג:

גמרא

אלְאַפּוּקֵי מִדְּבָעָא מִינֵּיהּ *רָבָא מֵרַב נַחְמָן, דְּאָמַר "הַיּוֹם אִי אַתְּ אִשְׁתִּי וּלְמָחָר אַתְּ אִשְׁתִּי".§ "גּוּפוֹ שֶׁל גֵּט שִׁחְרוּר הֲרֵי אַתְּ בַּת חוֹרִין, הֲרֵי אַתְּ לְעַצְמֵךְ".§ אַתְקֵין רַב יְהוּדָה בִּשְׁטַר זְבִינֵי דְּעַבְדֵי: "עַבְדָּא דְּנַן מוּצְדָּק לְעַבְדוּ, וּפְטִיר וַעֲטִיר מִן חֲרוּרֵי וּמִן עֲלוּלֵי וּמִן עֲרוּרֵי מַלְכָּא וּמַלְכְּתָא, וְרֹשׁוּם דְּאִינִישׁ לָא אִית עֲלוֹהִי, וּמְנוּקֶּ' מִכָּל מוּם וּמִן שְׁחִין דְּנָפֵיק עַד טַצְהַר חֲדַת וְעַתִּיק". מַאי אָסוּתֵיהּ? אָמַר אַבַּיֵי: גִּינְבָּרָא וּמַרְתְּכָא וְכַבְרִיתָא, וְחָלָא דְּחַמְרָא, וּמִשְׁחָא דְּזֵיתָא וְנַטְפִּיק חִיוָּרָא, וְשָׁיְיפִי לֵיהּ בְּגַדְפָּא דְּאַוְזָא.§ **מתני'** *שְׁלֹשָׁה גִּיטִּין פְּסוּלִין, וְאִם נִשֵּׂאת – הַוָּלָד כָּשֵׁר: בכָּתַב בִּכְתַב יָדוֹ וְאֵין עָלָיו עֵדִים, גיֵשׁ עָלָיו עֵדִים וְאֵין בּוֹ זְמַן, יֵשׁ בּוֹ זְמַן וְאֵין בּוֹ אֶלָּא עֵד אֶחָד, הֲרֵי אֵלּוּ שְׁלֹשָׁה גִּיטִּין פְּסוּלִין, וְאִם נִשֵּׂאת – הַוָּלָד כָּשֵׁר. רַבִּי *אֱלִיעֶזֶר אוֹמֵר: האע"פ שֶׁאֵין עָלָיו עֵדִים אֶלָּא שֶׁנְּתָנוֹ לָהּ בִּפְנֵי עֵדִים – כָּשֵׁר, וְגוֹבָה מִנְּכָסִים מְשׁוּעְבָּדִים, השֶׁאֵין הָעֵדִים חוֹתְמִים עַל הַגֵּט אֶלָּא מִפְּנֵי תִּיקּוּן הָעוֹלָם.§ **גמ'** וְתוּ לֵיכָּא? וְהָא אִיכָּא: *גֵּט יָשָׁן! הָתָם לֹא תֵּצֵא, הָכָא תֵּצֵא. הָנִיחָא לְמ"ד הָכָא תֵּצֵא, אֶלָּא לְמ"ד הָכָא לֹא תֵּצֵא, מַאי אִיכָּא לְמֵימַר? הָתָם תִּינָּשֵׂא לְכַתְּחִלָּ', הָכָא דִּיעֲבַד. וְהָא אִיכָּא *גֵּט קֵרֵחַ! הָתָם הַוָּלָד מַמְזֵר, הָכָא הַוָּלָד כָּשֵׁר. הָנִיחָא לְרַבִּי מֵאִיר, דְּאָמַר: כָּל הַמְשַׁנֶּה מִמַּטְבֵּעַ שֶׁטָּבְעוּ חֲכָמִים בְּגִיטִּין הַוָּלָד מַמְזֵר, אֶלָּא לְרַבָּנַן מַאי אִיכָּא לְמֵימַר? הָתָם תֵּצֵא, הָכָא לֹא תֵּצֵא. הָנִיחָא לְמ"ד הָכָא לֹא תֵּצֵא, אֶלָּא לְמ"ד הָכָא תֵּצֵא מַאי אִיכָּא לְמֵימַר? בִּמְקוּשָּׁר לָא קָא מַיְירֵי. וְהָא *אִיכָּא: שְׁלוֹם מַלְכוּת! הָתָם תֵּצֵא, הָכָא לֹא תֵּצֵא. הָנִיחָא לְמ"ד הָכָא לֹא תֵּצֵא, אֶלָּא לְמ"ד תֵּצֵא, מַאי אִיכָּא לְמֵימַר? (הָתָם הַוָּלָד מַמְזֵר, הָכָא הַוָּלָד כָּשֵׁר. הָנִיחָא לְר' מֵאִיר, אֶלָּא לְרַבָּנַן מַאי אִיכָּא לְמֵימַר?) מוֹקִים לָהּ כְּדְרַבִּי מֵאִיר, וְהָתָם הַוָּלָד מַמְזֵר, הָכָא הַוָּלָד כָּשֵׁר. מִנְיָנָא דְּרֵישָׁא לְמַעוּטֵי מַאי, וּמִנְיָנָא דְּסֵיפָא לְמַעוּטֵי מַאי? מִנְיָנָא דְּרֵישָׁא – לְמַעוּטֵי הָנֵי דַּאֲמַרַן, מִנְיָנָא דְּסֵיפָא – לְמַעוּטֵי הָא *דְּתַנְיָא: הַמֵּבִיא גֵּט מִמְּדִינַת הַיָּם, נְתָנוֹ לָהּ וְלֹא אָמַר (לָהּ) "בְּפָנַי נִכְתַּב וּבְפָנַי נֶחְתַּם" – יוֹצִיא וְהַוָּלָד מַמְזֵר, דִּבְרֵי רַבִּי מֵאִיר, וַחכ"א: אֵין הַוָּלָד מַמְזֵר, כֵּיצַד יַעֲשֶׂה? יִטְּלֶנּוּ הֵימֶנָּה, וְיַחֲזוֹר וְיִתְּנֶנּוּ לָהּ בִּפְנֵי שְׁנַיִם וְיֹאמַר "בְּפָנַי נִכְתַּב וּבְפָנַי נֶחְתַּם".§ "כָּתַב בִּכְתַב יָדוֹ וְאֵין עָלָיו עֵדִים".§ אָמַר רַב: כְּתַב יָדוֹ שָׁנִינוּ. אַהַיָּיא? אִילֵימָא אַרֵישָׁא – פְּשִׁיטָא, כְּתַב יָדוֹ קָתָנֵי! וְאֶלָּא אַמְּצִיעֲתָא, הֲרֵי יֵשׁ עָלָיו עֵדִים! ואֶלָּא אַסֵּיפָא: יֵשׁ בּוֹ זְמַן וְאֵין בּוֹ אֶלָּא עֵד אֶחָד, וְדַוְקָא

רש"י

לְאַפּוּקֵי מִדְּבָעָא מִינֵּיהּ רָבָא מֵרַב נַחְמָן הַיּוֹם אִי אַתְּ אִשְׁתִּי וּלְמָחָר הֲרֵי אַתְּ אִשְׁתִּי. מַהוּ, וּפָשַׁט לֵיהּ כֵּיוָן דְּפָסְקָהּ פָּסְקָהּ. אַפְּ"ה תִּקֵּן דְּלָא לַעֲבֵיד הָכִי, שֶׁלֹּא לְהוֹצִיא לַעַז עַל הַגֵּט. מוּצְדָּק לְעַבְדוּ. דִּינוֹ פָּסוּק לְעַבְדוּת, שֶׁאֵין שׁוּם עִרְעוּר בַּמְּכִירָה. וּפְטִיר וַעֲטִיר מִן חֲרוּרֵי. וּפָרוּשׁ וּמוּפְלָג מִכָּל חֵירוּת, כְּמוֹ "הַנִּפְטָר מֵרַבּוֹ" (יומא דף נג.). [לעיל פג:] וַעֲטִיר. כְּמוֹ "עִיטְרָא", שְׁטַר חֲלוּקָה, "רַק הַבָּמוֹת לֹא סָרוּ" (מלכים ב יב) מְתַרְגְּמִינַן: לָא עטרא. וּמִן עֲרוּרֵי מַלְכָּא וּמַלְכְּתָא. וּמֵעִרְעוּר הַמֶּלֶךְ וְהַמַּלְכָּה, שֶׁלֹּא חָטָא לִהְיוֹת מוּכְתָּב לַמַּלְכוּת לֵיהָרֵג. שֶׁאִם הָיָה מוּכְתָּב לַמַּלְכוּת – מִקָּחוֹ בָּטֵל, כִּדְאָמַר [דף פ.] בְּב"מ בְּ"הַשּׂוֹכֵר"*. וְרֹשׁוּם דְּאִינִישׁ. רוֹשֶׁם – סִימָן שֶׁעוֹשִׂין עַל הָעֲבָדִים, כִּדְאָמְרִי' בְּמַסֶּכֶת שַׁבָּת (דף נח.). לָא אִית עִילָּוֵי'. מֵאָדָם אַחֵר חוּץ מִן הַמּוֹכֵר הַזֶּה. וּמְנוּקֶּה מִכָּל מוּם. כְּמוֹ לִסְטִים מְזוּיָּין, דְּמִקָּחוֹ בָּטֵל. [לעיל ג: יז: ב"ב קטו.] וּמִן שְׁחִין דְּנָפֵיק עַד טַצְהַר. וּמִכָּל שְׁחִין שֶׁיֵּצֵא בְּפָנָיו עַד שְׁתֵּי שָׁנִים, דְּמָאִיס לְמֵיקַם קַמֵּיהּ. עַד טַצְהַר. בִּל' פַּרְסִי שְׁתֵּי שָׁנִים. וְהַאי [כתובות נז:] דְּקָא אָמְרִי': *סִמְפּוֹן בַּעֲבָדִים לֵיכָּא – הַיְינוּ הֵיכָא דְּזַבֵּין סְתָמָא, אֲבָל הָכָא כֵּיוָן דְּאַתְנֵי – מִקָּחוֹ בָּטֵל. וְזֶה עַכְשָׁיו אֵין לוֹ שְׁחִין, וְדֶרֶךְ שְׁחִין יָשָׁן שֶׁהוֹלֵךְ לוֹ – חוֹזֵר עַד שְׁתֵּי שָׁנִים, לְפִיכָךְ עַד ב' שָׁנִים מַתְנֶה עִמּוֹ שֶׁאִם יֵצֵא בּוֹ אוֹתוֹ שְׁחִין עַד שְׁתֵּי שָׁנִים שֶׁיְּהֵא מִקָּחוֹ בָּטֵל, לְפִי שֶׁכְּבָר הָיָה בּוֹ הַמּוּם הַזֶּה וְלֹא רָאָהוּ. [לעיל עט:] גִּינְבָּרָא. כְּמַשְׁמָעוֹ, זנגבי"ל. וּמַרְתְּכָא. פְּסוֹלֶת סִיגֵי כֶּסֶף, שֶׁיּוֹצֵא מִמֶּנּוּ בַּמָּקוֹם שֶׁמַּתִּיכִין אוֹתוֹ בִּשְׁעַת הֲסִירָתוֹ מִן הֶהָרִים, [לעיל פח:] וְקוֹרִין לוֹ קוגילו"ן. וְכַבְרִיתָא. גָּפְרִית. [ס"א ל"ג] וְשָׁיְיפִי לֵיהּ בְּגַדְפָּא דְּאַוְזָא. וְסָךְ אוֹתוֹ בְּנוֹצָה שֶׁל אַוָּז. **מתני'** וְאִם נִיסֵּת הַוָּלָד כָּשֵׁר. הַאי תַּנָּא לָאו כְּרַבִּי מֵאִיר סְבִירָא לֵיהּ, דְּאָמַר: עֵדֵי חֲתִימָה כָּרְתִי, דִּלְרַבִּי מֵאִיר הַוָּלָד מַמְזֵר, (א) וּלְמַאן דְּמוֹקֵי לָהּ בַּגְּמָ' כְּרַבִּי מֵאִיר – אִיכָּא [לעיל עט:] לְמֵימַר דִּכְתַב יָדוֹ כְּמֵאָה עֵדִים דָּמֵי. וְלָאו כְּרַבִּי אֶלְעָזָר סְבִירָא לֵיהּ, דְּאָמַר עֵדֵי מְסִירָה כָּרְתִי – דְּהָא פָּלֵיג רַבִּי אֶלְעָזָר בְּסֵיפָא, אֶלָּא כֵּיוָן דִּכְתַב יָדוֹ הוּא – "וְכָתַב וְנָתַן" קָרֵינָא בֵּיהּ, וְאַע"ג דְּלֵיכָּא עֵדֵי מְסִירָה – כָּשֵׁר מִדְּאוֹרַיְיתָא. וּמִיהוּ, רַבָּנַן פַּסְלִינְהוּ דִּלְמָא אָתֵי לְאַכְשׁוּרֵי בִּכְתַב סוֹפֵר, הִלְכָּךְ, לֹא תִּינָּשֵׂא, וְאִם נִיסֵּת – הַוָּלָד כָּשֵׁר. וְדַוְקָא כְּתַב יָדוֹ, אֲבָל כְּתַב סוֹפֵר וְאֵין שָׁם עֵד – הַוָּלָד מַמְזֵר. וּזְמַן תַּקַּנְתָּא דְּרַבָּנַן, מִשּׁוּם בַּת אֲחוֹתוֹ, כִּדְאָמְרִינַן בְּפ"ק (לעיל דף יז.), הִלְכָּךְ הַוָּלָד כָּשֵׁר. אֶלָּא עֵד אֶחָד. פְּלִיגֵי בָּהּ בַּגְּמָרָא; אִיכָּא לְמ"ד: אַכְּתַב יָדוֹ קָאֵי, אֲפִילּוּ הָכִי אַשְׁמוּעִינַן דִּלְכַתְּחִלָּה לָא. וְרֵישָׁא אַשְׁמוּעִינַן דַּאֲפִי' אֵין בּוֹ עֵד, אִם נִיסֵּת – הַוָּלָד כָּשֵׁר. וְאִיכָּא לְמַאן דְּאָמַר: אַכְּתַב סוֹפֵר קָאֵי, וַאֲפִי' הָכִי הַוָּלָד כָּשֵׁר, דְּסוֹפֵר הֲוָה לֵיהּ בִּמְקוֹם עֵד שֵׁנִי. ר' אֶלְעָזָר אוֹמֵר אַף עַל פִּי שֶׁאֵין עָלָיו עֵדִים. וְאֵינוֹ כְּתַב יָדוֹ. אֶלָּא שֶׁנְּתָנוֹ לָהּ בִּפְנֵי עֵדִים כָּשֵׁר. לִינָּשֵׂא לְכַתְּחִילָּה. תִּיקּוּן הָעוֹלָם. שֶׁמָּא יָמוּתוּ עֵדֵי מְסִירָה, וְיָבֹא הַבַּעַל וִיעַרְעֵר לוֹמַר: לֹא גֵירַשְׁתִּיהָ. **גמ'** וְתוּ לֵיכָּא. גִּיטִּין פְּסוּלִין לְכַתְּחִילָּה וְהַוָּלָד כָּשֵׁר? וְהָאִיכָּא גֵּט יָשָׁן. דְּאָמְרִינַן לְעֵיל(ב) בַּגְּמָ': אִם נִיסֵּת לֹא תֵּצֵא. הָכָא תֵּצֵא. רַב וְלֵוִי פְּלִיגֵי בָּהּ לְקַמָּן בִּשְׁמַעְתִּין. הָתָם. אָמְרִינַן בַּגְּמָ': אִם נִתְגָּרְשָׁה תִּנָּשֵׂא לְכַתְּחִלָּה, בְּפֶרֶק "הַזּוֹרֵק" (לעיל עט.). הָנִיחָא לְרַבִּי מֵאִיר. דְּאָמַר: כָּל הַמְשַׁנֶּה מִמַּטְבֵּעַ שֶׁטָּבְעוּ חֲכָמִים בְּגִיטִּין – הַוָּלָד מַמְזֵר. אֶלָּא לְרַבָּנַן. אִי מַתְנִי' דְּהָכָא דְּרַבָּנַן הִיא, נִיתְנֵי נַמִי הָכָא גֵּט קֵרֵחַ! הָתָם תֵּצֵא. אֲפִילּוּ לְרַבָּנַן. שְׁלוֹם מַלְכוּת. דְּאָמְרִינַן בְּ"הַזּוֹרֵק" (שם עט.): כָּתַב לְשֵׁם מַלְכוּת כו'. מִנְיָינָא דְּרֵישָׁא. שְׁלֹשָׁה גִּיטִּין פְּסוּלִין. מִנְיָינָא דְּסֵיפָא. "הֲרֵי אֵלּוּ ג' גִּיטִּין פְּסוּלִין" – מַשְׁמַע מִיעוּטָא, הָנֵי וְתוּ לָא. הָנֵי דַּאֲמַרַן. וְאַשְׁמְעִינַן דְּמַתְנִי' ר"מ הִיא, דְּאָמַר הָתָם הַוָּלָד מַמְזֵר. לְמַעוּטֵי הָא דְּתַנְיָא. דְּהָכָא הַוָּלָד מַמְזֵר כְּר' מֵאִיר, וְאַשְׁמְעִינַן מַתְנִי' דְּבָרַיְיתָא מְתַרְלְתָּא הִיא, דַּאֲפִילּוּ כה"ג מְשַׁוֵּי לֵיהּ ר"מ מַמְזֵר. אִי נֵימָא אַרֵישָׁא. דְּלֵיכָּא שׁוּם עֵד. אֶלָּא אַמְּצִיעֲתָא. שֶׁפָּסוּל מִשּׁוּם זְמַן, מַה לִּי כְּתַב יָדוֹ מַה לִּי כְּתַב סוֹפֵר? הֲרֵי יֵשׁ עָלָיו עֵדִים! וְדַוְקָא

תוספות

מן עלולי ומן ערורי מלכא ומלכתא. נראה לר"י דגרסי' איפכא: "מן ערורי ומן עלולי מלכא", ומלכתא דלשון עלילה שייך במלך וערעורי גבי שאר כל אדם. **רושם**. פי' בקונטרס: רושם וסימן שעושין לעבדים. ואית ספרים דגרסי "ורשו דאינשי", פי': שאין עליו מלוה.

מן עלולי מלכא. כן הוא כמו שפי' בקונטרס כאן, דמוכתב למלכות הוי מקח טעות, כדאמרי' ב"האומנין" (ב"מ פ.) וב"המוכר פירות" (ב"ב צג:) אמרינן בהדיא דאומר לו: הרי שלך לפניך. ובפ"ק דקידושין (דף יא.) ובפ' "אע"פ" (כתובות נח.) גבי סימפון בעבדים ליכא, דאמר: מאי אמרת ליסטים מזויין או מוכתב למלכות – הנהו קלא אית להו, צריך לפרש כמו שפי' ר"ת: קלא אית להו – ולא שכיחא, ולא כמו שפי' בקונטר' התם: קלא אית להו, וסבר וקביל. ומאי דאתקין לכתוב בשטרא – לא הוי אלא לשופרא, שלא יטעו העולם. כמו חרורי, דפשיטא שאם משוחרר הוא שהמקח בטל*. **עד** טצהר. והא דאמרינן סימפון בעבדים ליכא, אי בבראי – הא קא חזי ליה, אי בגואי – לא איכפת ליה, היינו במומין שהן עליו עתה. אבל באותן שיבאו עליו אחר כך, ולא יהיה אז ראוי למיקם קמיה – ודאי הוה מקח טעות. אף על גב דכי האי גוונא משכחת סימפון בעבדים, איכא למימר דהא לא שכיחא.

שלשה גיטין פסולין. לעיל (דף ג:) פירשתי. ומה שפי' בקונטרס דהך משנה לא כרבי אלעזר ולא כר"מ – אין נראה, דאיכא בגמ' דמוקי לה כר' מאיר.

מוקי להדיא כר' מאיר. נראה דלא גרסי' "הדיא", דאמתני' קאי. **מניינא** דסיפא למעוטי הא דתניא כו'. כל משניות מפיק מחד מיעוטא – ממניינא דרישא, והך ברייתא – ממניינא דסיפא. ואשמעינן דמתרלתא היא. ורבינו יצחק אומר: דהך ברייתא איצטריכא מיעוטא לחוד, לפי שיש תקנה אפי' לר"מ, אפילו לכתחלה לינשא, שיוכל ליטלו הימנה וליתנו לה קודם נישואין. **אמר** רב כתב ידו שנינו כו'. דוקא כתב ידו ועד, אבל כתב סופר ועד – לא, אפי' בספרא מובהק, דסבירא ליה לרב: חתם סופר שנינו, כדפירש בקונט'. ורבינו חננאל גרים: דוקא כתב ידו ועד הוא דפסול, ואם ניסאת – הוולד כשר. אבל כתב סופר ועד – תינשא לכתחילה. ושמואל אמר: אפילו כתב סופר ועד דוקא בדיעבד כשר. והתנן כתב סופר ועד כשר! ומשני: התם בסופר מובהק. וגירסא זו אינה בשום ספר. ועוד יש לומר: דלרב כתב סופר מובהק ועד כשר לכתחילה, אבל בסופר שאינו מובהק ועד – פסול אפילו בדיעבד.

יש

[וע"ע תוס' כתובות נח. ותוס' קדושין יא. ד"ה הנהו]

תוספות רי"ד

מתי הנה כל כונתו היא להקנותו לה לאחר מיתה ומה יודע הוא שבגט כתוב בו מהיום בודאי עיקר הגט אין צריך הבעל לדעת אותו כראוי והבעל יאמר לה הרי זה גיטך והיא מגורשת שספר כריתות נתן לה ואינו צריך שיבין הוא דברי הספר שאם היה צ"ל לה דברי הספר בפה היו זקוקין להבינו אלא כיון שאין האשה מתגרשת אלא בספר ולא בדברים אע"פ שאינו יודע מה כתוב בו היא מגורשת באומרו לה הרי זה גיטך אבל התנאי שתלוי באמירת הבעל מה יועיל לכתבו בגט והבעל לא יבין בו הלכך הטעם שנתן המורה שמא חזר בו אין ראוי לתתו אלא לחבר לא להדיוטות ולפיכך תיקן רב שיכתבו בו מיומא דין שיעידו העדים כי כך אמר הבעל כשהיה ש"מ כדי שיהיו זריזין ללמד ש"מ לומר כך שאם לא יאמר כך נמצא שמעידין עדות שקר (ויגיד עליו דינו) ולעלם לאפוקי מדבעא מיניה רבא מרב נחמן אילו אמר הבעל היום אי את אשתי ולמחר את אשתי א) ואנו כותבין גט ולעלם מועיל כלום אלא תקן שיכתבו כך כדי להרגילם בכך שאם הבעל רוצה לומר היום אי את אשתי ולמחר את אשתי שישתקוהו ליתן גט לצמיתות כמו שכותבים בגט ולעלם ותהא עדותן קיימת וה"ה הכי נמי מיומא דין ולעלם תקן לכותבו בגיטין בעבור ש"מ שיתן גט לאשתו בתנאי אם מתי שיהו מרגילים אותו לומר מהיום ולא יסמכו על זמן שכתבו בגט כר' יוסי ותהא עדותן קיימת שכותבין בגט מהיום ודומה זה למאי דאמרי' בפ' הזהב אמר רב ששת בריה דרב אידי כמאן כתבי' האידנא במנא דכשר למקנייא ביה במנא לאפוקי מדרב ששת דאמר קונין בפירות. דכשר לאפוקי מדשמואל דאמר קונין במורינגא. למקניא לאפוקי מר' לוי דאמר קונין בבליו של מקנה ביה למעוטי מטבע שכל זה שאנו כותבין בשטרות הוא כדי להרגילם שלא יעשום בענין אחר שאם יעשום בענין אחר מה מועלת כתיבתם הלא הן מעידים שקר אלא ודאי העיקר הוא שהם יעשו כך ועל מה שעשו הם אנו מעידים. גם הנה בש"מ צריך לומר מהיום ואנו מעידים שכך אמר. והכי הוא משמעות דברי רב מדקאמר איך פלוני פטר ותריך וזהו לשון עדות שמעידים העדים כי כך היה המעשה: גופו של גט שחרור הרי את בן חורין הרי את לעצמך אתקין רב יהודה בשטר זביני דעבדי עבדא מוצדק לעבדו ופטור ועטור מן חרורי ומן עלולי מלכא ומלכתא ורשם דאינש לית עילוהי מנוקה מכל מום ומכל שחין דנפיק ביה עד שצהר וחדת ועתיק פי' מוצדק לעבדו דינו פסוק לעבדות שאין שום ערעור במכירה זו ופטיר ועטיר מן חרורי פרוש ומופלג מכל חירות כמו הנפטר מרבו ועטור כמו עטרא שטר חלוקה רק הבמות לא סרו תרגומי' לא עטרא ומן ערורי מלכא ומלכתא פי' מערעור (ועלילות) המלך והמלכה שלא חטא שיהא מוכתב למלכות שאם היה מוכתב למלכות מקחו בטל כדאמרינן בהשוכר בבבא מציעא רושם סימן שעושין על העבדים כדאמרן במס' שבת לא איתא עילויה מאדם אחר חוץ מן המוכר הזה ומנוקה מכל מום ומכל שחין דנפיק ביה עד שצהר מכל שחין שיצא בפניו עד ב' שנים דמאיס למיקם קמיה שצהר בלשון פרסי ב' שנים דהאי דאמרי' סמפון בעבדים ליכא היינו היכא דזבין סתמא אבל הכא דאתני מקחו בטל ואלה מוכי שחין קודם שיתגלו עליהם השחינים יש חולי בגופן שמחמת אותו

[לעיל פג:] [דף פ.] [לעיל ג: יז: ב"ב קטו.] [כתובות נז:] [צ"ל אלעזר ועי' תוי"ט דגרסי' אלעזר בלא יו"ד וכן בפיסקא לקמן ובכל הסוגיא וכן ברש"י דהכא ושאר מקומות איתא רבי אלעזר] [לעיל עט:] [לעיל פח:] ס"א ל"ג [לעיל עט:]

הגהות הב"ח

(א) רש"י ד"ה ואם ניסת וכו' דלר' מאיר הוולד ממזר (ולמאן דמוקי לה וכו' כמאה עדים דמי) תא"מ ונ"ב נ"ל הגה"ה היא ומתוס' דרפ"ק לקחו לפרש כך: (ב) ד"ה והאיכא וכו' לעיל כ"ב דף עט ע"ב:

ב"מ נה: לעיל ה:

תוספות רי"ד

של שטר מוכיח: ולעלם לאפוקי מדבעא מיניה רבא מרב נחמן היום אי את אשתי ולמחר (אין) את אשתי מהו פי' המורה אע"ג דרב גופיה פסק הלכה כר' יוסי בפ' יש נוחלין הכא אמר לאפוקי מדר' יוסי משום דבעא לאפוקי נפשיה מפלוגתא ויש מי שאומר דהדר ביה מההוא ועקרה לדר' יוסי דלית הלכתא כותיה אף בשטרות ויש מי שאומר דלכתחלה לא עבדינן כר' יוסי ואי עבד כר' יוסי עבד ויש מי שאומר הלכה כר' יוסי בשטרות אבל לא בגיטין. והנכון בעיני שזהו העיקר שחילוק יש בין שטרות לגיטין כדאמרן לעיל בפ' מי שאחזו במאי דתנן זה גיטך אם מתי לא אמר כלום אמר רב הונא וחולצת ולא מתיבמת ושקלינן וטרינן בה טובא ומסקינן דר' יוסי אמר זמנו של שטר מוכיח עליו בין בשטר שלאחר מיתה הוא בתוכו וכן בגט שהוא ע"פ אבל רב הונא פשיט ליה דבשטר הלכה כר' יוסי מפני שהתנאי שלאחר מיתה כתוב בתוכו וגם הזמן כתוב בתוכו אבל בגט שהזמן כתוב בתוכו והתנאי שלאחר מיתה אמר לה על פה מספקא ליה אי הלכה כר' יוסי בהא שיועיל זמנו של גט שהוא כתוב לתנאי דלאחר מיתה שהוא בפה ומ"ה אמר חולצת ולא מתיבמת ורב הונא דפסיק הלכה כר' יוסי מרב פשטו ליה כדאמרי' התם א"ל הכי אמר רב הלכה כר' יוסי וכמו שרב הונא חולק בין גט לשטר דבשטר פסק הלכה כר' יוסי ובגט לא ה"ה הכי נמי חולק רב אע"ג דפסק הלכה כר' יוסי בשטרות בגטין לא נראו לו דבריו ומ"ה אמרינן לאפוקי מדר' יוסי ולא ק' דידיה אדידיה. והתקין שיכתבו בגיטין כך כדי שיהו רגילין להרגיל את ש"מ לומר כך בשעה שנותנו לה מהיום אם מתי אבל אם השכיב מרע לא אמר בפיו מהיום הכתיבה שאנו כותבין בתוך הגט מיומא דין אינה מועלת כלום דהא לר' יוסי כך מועיל זמן הגט כמו מהיום לרבנן ורב הונא ס"ל כר' יוסי ואפ"ה קאמר דלא מהני זמן שהוא ככתיבה לתנאי דלאחר מיתה שהוא בפה (והם) [וה"ה] הכי לרבנן אע"ג דכתיב מהיום לא מהני לתנאי דהוא ע"פ כדפריש המורה די"ל חזר בו ממה שכתב מהיום ולא נתנו לה אלא שיקנה לאחר מיתה ואין גט לאחר מיתה. וזה הטעם צריך לתת לחבר שהוא יודע מה כתוב בגט אבל ההדיוטות שאין יודעים מה כתוב בו בלתי זה הטעם אינו כלום שהרי אנו מלמדין אותו שיאמר לה הרי זה גיטך אם

א) נראה דצ"ל אי הוי גיטא או לא ולכן אנו כותבין בגט ולעלם ואף דאינו מועיל כלום כו'.

וְדַוְקָא כְּתַב יָדוֹ וְעֵד, אאֲבָל כְּתַב סוֹפֵר וְעֵד – לָא. וּשְׁמוּאֵל אָמַר: אֲפִי' כְּתַב סוֹפֵר וְעֵד, שֶׁהֲרֵי שָׁנִינוּ: *כְּתַב סוֹפֵר וְעֵד – כָּשֵׁר. וְרַב: מִי דָּמֵי? הָתָם תִּינָּשֵׂא לְכַתְּחִילָּה, הָכָא דִּיעֲבַד. וּשְׁמוּאֵל: לָא קַשְׁיָא, הָא בְּסַפְרָא דְּמוּבְהָק, וְהָא בְּסַפְרָא דְּלָא מוּבְהָק. וְכֵן אָמַר ר' יוֹחָנָן: (כְּתַב יָדוֹ שָׁנִינוּ.) אָמַר לֵיהּ רַבִּי אֶלְעָזָר: הֲרֵי יֵשׁ עָלָיו עֵדִים! אָמַר לֵיהּ: אַסֵּיפָא. זִימְנִין אָמַר רַב: תֵּצֵא, זִימְנִין אָמַר רַב: לֹא תֵּצֵא, הָא כֵּיצַד? יֵשׁ לָהּ בָּנִים – לֹא תֵּצֵא, אֵין לָהּ בָּנִים – תֵּצֵא. מְתִיב מָר זוּטְרָא בַּר טוֹבִיָּה: *בוְכוּלָּן שֶׁהָיוּ בָּהֶן סְפֵק קִידּוּשִׁין אוֹ סְפֵק גֵּירוּשִׁין – הֲרֵי אֵלּוּ חוֹלְצוֹת וְלֹא מִתְיַבְּמוֹת, כֵּיצַד סְפֵק קִידּוּשִׁין? זָרַק לָהּ קִידּוּשִׁין סָפֵק קָרוֹב לָהּ סָפֵק קָרוֹב לוֹ – זֶהוּ סְפֵק קִידּוּשִׁין. סְפֵק גֵּירוּשִׁין? כָּתַב בִּכְתַב יָדוֹ וְאֵין עָלָיו עֵדִים, יֵשׁ עָלָיו עֵדִים וְאֵין בּוֹ זְמַן, יֵשׁ בּוֹ זְמַן וְאֵין בּוֹ אֶלָּא עֵד אֶחָד – הֲרֵי זֶה סְפֵק גֵּירוּשִׁין; וְאִי אָמְרַתְּ לֹא תֵּצֵא, צָרָתָהּ אַתְיָא לְיַבּוּמֵי! תִּתְיַבֵּם וְאֵין בְּכָךְ כְּלוּם, חֲשָׁשָׁא דְּרַבָּנַן הִיא. לֵוִי אָמַר: לְעוֹלָם לֹא תֵּצֵא. וְכֵן אָמַר ר' יוֹחָנָן: גלְעוֹלָם לֹא תֵּצֵא. וְכֵן אֲמַר לְהוּ ר' יוֹחָנָן לִבְנֵי ר' חֲלַפְתָּא דְּמִן *הוּנָא, הָכִי אָמַר אֲבוּכוֹן: *לְעוֹלָם לֹא תֵּצֵא; וְקַרְצִית שֶׁבָּעֳמִיר אֵינָהּ פּוֹסֶלֶת בְּמֵי חַטָּאת. מַאי קַרְצִית? אָמַר אַבַּיֵי: דִּידְבְתָּא דְּבֵינֵי כֵּיפֵי. מְתִיב רַב דָּנִיאֵל בַּר רַב קְטִינָא: *דכָּל הָעוֹפוֹת פּוֹסְלִין בְּמֵי חַטָּאת חוּץ מִן הַיּוֹנָה, מִפְּנֵי שֶׁמּוֹצֶצֶת; וְאִם אִיתָא, נִיתְנֵי: חוּץ מִיּוֹנָה וְקַרְצִית! לָא פְּסִיקָא לֵיהּ, דִּגְדוֹלָה לָא פָּסְלָה, וּקְטַנָּה פָּסְלָה. וְעַד כַּמָּה? אָמַר ר' יִרְמְיָה, וְאִיתֵימָא ר' אַמִּי: עַד כַּזַּיִת.§ "ר' אֶלְעָזָר אוֹמֵר: אַף עַל פִּי" וכו'.§ *אָמַר רַב יְהוּדָה אָמַר רַב: הֲלָכָה כְּר' אֶלְעָזָר בְּגִיטִּין. כִּי אָמְרִיתַהּ קַמֵּיהּ דִּשְׁמוּאֵל, *אָמַר: הַאַף בִּשְׁטָרוֹת. וְרַב סָבַר בִּשְׁטָרוֹת לָא? הָא קָתָנֵי: וְגוֹבָה מִנְּכָסִים מְשׁוּעְבָּדִים! רַבִּי אֶלְעָזָר תַּרְתֵּי אָמַר, וְרַב סָבַר כְּוָותֵיהּ בַּחֲדָא וּפְלִיג עֲלֵיהּ בַּחֲדָא. וְכֵן אָמַר ר' יַעֲקֹב בַּר אִידִי אָמַר ר' יְהוֹשֻׁעַ בֶּן לֵוִי: הֲלָכָה כְּר' אֶלְעָזָר בְּגִיטִּין; וְרַבִּי יַנַּאי אָמַר: אֲפִילּוּ רֵיחַ הַגֵּט אֵין בּוֹ. וְרַבִּי יַנַּאי לֵית לֵיהּ דְּר' אֶלְעָזָר? הָכִי קָאָמַר: לְרַבָּנַן, אֲפִילּוּ רֵיחַ הַגֵּט אֵין בּוֹ. וְכֵן אָמַר ר' יוֹסֵי בְּר' חֲנִינָא אָמַר רֵישׁ לָקִישׁ: הֲלָכָה כְּרַבִּי אֶלְעָזָר בְּגִיטִּין; וְר' יוֹחָנָן אָמַר: אֲפִילּוּ רֵיחַ הַגֵּט אֵין בּוֹ. לֵימָא ר' יוֹחָנָן לֵית לֵיהּ דְּר' אֶלְעָזָר? הָכִי קָאָמַר: לְרַבָּנַן, אֲפִילּוּ רֵיחַ הַגֵּט אֵין בּוֹ. שְׁלַח לֵיהּ ר' אַבָּא בַּר זַבְדָּא לְמָרֵי בַּר מָר: בָּעֵי מִינֵּיהּ מֵרַב הוּנָא: הֲלָכָה כְּר' אֶלְעָזָר בְּגִיטִּין, אוֹ אֵין הֲלָכָה? אַדְּהָכִי נָח נַפְשֵׁיהּ דְּרַב הוּנָא, אֲמַר לֵיהּ רַבָּה בְּרֵיהּ, הָכִי אָמַר אַבָּא מִשְּׁמֵיהּ *דְּרָבָא: הֲלָכָה כְּר' אֶלְעָזָר בְּגִיטִּין, וְרַבּוֹתֵינוּ הַבְּקִיאִין בִּדְבַר הֲלָכָה, מִשּׁוּם רַבֵּינוּ אָמְרוּ: הֲלָכָה כְּר' אֶלְעָזָר בְּגִיטִּין, דְּאָמַר רַב חָמָא בַּר גּוּרְיָא אָמַר רַב: הֲלָכָה כְּר' אֶלְעָזָר בְּגִיטִּין. אִיכָּא דְּאָמְרִי: וַחֲבֵרֵינוּ הַבְּקִיאִין בִּדְבַר הֲלָכָה, וְתַלְמִידֵי רַבֵּינוּ, מִשּׁוּם רַבֵּינוּ אָמְרוּ: הֲלָכָה כְּרַבִּי אֶלְעָזָר בְּגִיטִּין, דְּאָמַר רַב חִסְדָּא אָמַר רַב חָמָא בַּר גּוּרְיָא אָמַר רַב: הֲלָכָה כְּרַבִּי אֶלְעָזָר בְּגִיטִּין. וְכֵן כִּי אֲתָא רָבִין, אָמַר ר' אֶלְעָזָר אָמַר רַב: הֲלָכָה כְּרַבִּי אֶלְעָזָר בְּגִיטִּין.§

מתני' ושְׁנַיִם שֶׁשָּׁלְחוּ שְׁנֵי גִיטִּין שָׁוִין •וְנִתְעָרְבוּ – נוֹתֵן שְׁנֵיהֶם לָזוֹ וּשְׁנֵיהֶם לָזוֹ; לְפִיכָךְ אָבַד אֶחָד מֵהֶן – הֲרֵי הַשֵּׁנִי בָּטֵל. זחֲמִשָּׁה שֶׁכָּתְבוּ כְּלָל בְּתוֹךְ הַגֵּט: אִישׁ פְּלוֹנִי מְגָרֵשׁ פְּלוֹנִית, וּפְלוֹנִי פְּלוֹנִית, וְהָעֵדִים מִלְּמַטָּה – כּוּלָּן כְּשֵׁרִין, וְיִנָּתֵן לְכָל אַחַת וְאַחַת; הָיָה כּוֹתֵב טוֹפֶס לְכָל אֶחָד וְאֶחָד וְהָעֵדִים מִלְּמַטָּה, אֵת שֶׁהָעֵדִים נִקְרָאִין עִמּוֹ – כָּשֵׁר.§ **גמ'** מַאן תַּנָּא? אָמַר ר' יִרְמְיָה: דְּלָא כְּר' אֶלְעָזָר, דְּאִי ר' אֶלְעָזָר, *כֵּיוָן דְּאָמַר חעֵדֵי מְסִירָה כָּרְתִי, הָא לָא יָדְעִי בְּהֵי מִינַּיְיהוּ קָא מְגָרְשָׁה. אַבַּיֵי אָמַר: אֲפִי' תֵּימָא ר' אֶלְעָזָר, אֵימָא דְּבָעֵי ר' אֶלְעָזָר – כְּתִיבָה לִשְׁמָהּ, נְתִינָה לִשְׁמָהּ מִי בָּעֵי?§ "חֲמִשָּׁה שֶׁכָּתְבוּ כְּלָל" כו'.§ הֵיכִי דָּמֵי כְּלָל, הֵיכִי דָּמֵי טוֹפֶס? אָמַר רַבִּי יוֹחָנָן: טזְמַן אֶחָד לְכוּלָּן – זֶהוּ כְּלָל, זְמַן לְכָל אֶחָד וְאֶחָד – זֶהוּ טוֹפֶס; וְרֵישׁ לָקִישׁ אָמַר: אֲפִילּוּ

תוספות

יש לה בנים לא תצא כו'. וא"ת: מאי פריך לעיל: הניחא למ"ד לא תצא, אלא למ"ד תצא – מאי איכא למימר. ומאי קושיא? נימא דבשלש מלכות אפילו יש לה בנים תצא! וי"ל: דבשלש מלכות נמי, כיון דלרבנן הולד כשר – יש לה בנים לא תצא.

זרק לה קדושין ספק קרוב כו'. בפ' "ד' אחין" (יבמות ל:) דייק: ואילו בגירושין ספק קרוב לו כו' לא קתני, ומפרש לה.

כל העופות פוסלין במי חטאת. טעמא – משום שתהא חיותו בכלי. אבל משום מלאכה אין נפסל אחר קידוש, כדאמרינן בספרי ובמס' פרה (פ"ד מ"ד). ומיהו, משום היסח הדעת נראה דנפסלין לאחר קידוש. ובמקום אחר הארכתי*.

וליתכשר

רש"י

וְדַוְקָא כְּתַב יָדוֹ וְעֵד. הוּא דְּאָמְרִינַן הַוָּלָד כָּשֵׁר. וְכִי תֵּימָא: הָא מֵרֵישָׁא שָׁמְעִינַן לָהּ, דַּאֲפִילּוּ בְּלֹא שׁוּם עֵד הַוָּלָד כָּשֵׁר! אִי לָאו סֵיפָא הֲוָה אָמִינָא: הֵיכָא דְּאִיכָּא עֵד אֶחָד עִם כְּתַב יָדוֹ – תִּינָּשֵׂא לְכַתְּחִלָּה. דְּהָא תְּנַן. לְקַמָּן בְּפִירְקִין. כְּתַב סוֹפֵר וְעֵד כָּשֵׁר. כְּלוֹמַר, כָּתַב סוֹפֵר וְחָתַם עֵד אֶחָד – כָּשֵׁר. וְרַב. אָמַר לָךְ: מִי דָּמֵי? הָתָם כָּשֵׁר לְכַתְּחִילָּה מַשְׁמַע, דְּהָתָם חָתַם סוֹפֵר עִם הָעֵד שָׁנִינוּ, כִּדְמִתָּרֵץ לָהּ רַבִּי יִרְמְיָה לְקַמָּן. וּשְׁמוּאֵל. לֵית לֵיהּ דְּרַבִּי יִרְמְיָה, אֶלָּא כָּתַב סוֹפֵר וְלֹא חָתַם וְהַיְינוּ טַעַם דְּכָשֵׁר לְכַתְּחִילָּה – בְּסַפְרָא דְּמוּבְהָק וּבָקִי בְּתוֹרַת גִּיטִּין, וְלֹא יִכְתְּבֶנּוּ אֶלָּא אִם שָׁמַע מִפִּי הַבַּעַל. וְכֵן א"ר יוֹחָנָן. כְּרַב, דְּאָמַר: כְּתַב יָדוֹ שָׁנִינוּ. אֲבָל כְּתַב סוֹפֵר – הַוָּלָד מַמְזֵר. הֲרֵי יֵשׁ עָלָיו עֵדִים. ר' אֶלְעָזָר סָבַר דְּאַמַּתְנִיתָא קָאֵי. זִימְנִין אָמַר רַב. בְּהָנֵי שְׁלֹשָׁה גִּיטִּין דְּמַתְנִי': אִם נִשֵּׂאת תֵּצֵא. יֵשׁ לָהּ בָּנִים. קוֹדֶם שֶׁנּוֹדַע לָנוּ שֶׁבַּגֵּט הַזֶּה נִשֵּׂאת. לֹא תֵּצֵא. שֶׁלֹּא לְהוֹצִיא לַעַז מַמְזֵרוּת עַל בָּנֶיהָ. וְכוּלָּן. חֲמֵשׁ עֶשְׂרֵה עֲרָיוֹת שֶׁאָמְרוּ שֶׁפּוֹטְרוֹת צָרוֹתֵיהֶן מִן הַחֲלִיצָה, אִם הָיוּ בָּהֶן לְבַעֲלֵיהֶן הַמֵּת קִידּוּשֵׁי סָפֵק, אוֹ שֶׁגֵּרְשָׁן לִפְנֵי מוֹתוֹ גֵּירוּשֵׁי סָפֵק – נִמְצֵאת צָרָתָהּ סָפֵק שֶׁהִיא צָרַת עֶרְוָה וּפְטוּרָה, סָפֵק שֶׁאֵינָהּ צָרַת עֶרְוָה וּזְקוּקָה לְיַבֵּם. הֲרֵי אֵלּוּ. הַצָּרוֹת. חוֹלְצוֹת. שֶׁמָּא זְקוּקָה הִיא. וְלֹא מִתְיַבְּמוֹת. שֶׁמָּא אֵינָהּ זְקוּקָה וְנִמְצָא נוֹשֵׂא אֵשֶׁת אָח שֶׁלֹּא בִּמְקוֹם מִצְוָה. זֶהוּ סְפֵק גֵּירוּשִׁין. דְּכֵיוָן דְּמִדְּאוֹרַיְיתָא כָּשֵׁר – זְקוּקָה צָרָתָהּ לְיַבֵּם. וְאִי אָמְרַתְּ לֹא תֵּצֵא. אִם נִשֵּׂאת בְּגֵט זֶה. אָתֵי לְמֵימַר. גֵּט זֶה מְעַלְּיָא, וְצָרָתָהּ לָאו צָרַת עֶרְוָה הִיא, וְאָתֵי לְיַבּוּמָהּ. וּמְשַׁנֵּינַן: תִּתְיַבֵּם וְאֵין בְּכָךְ כְּלוּם. כְּלוֹמַר, אִי אָתֵי לְיַבּוּמָהּ – לָא אִיכְפַּת לָן כּוּלֵּי הַאי, דְּנִגְזוֹר הָא אַטּוּ הָא, דְּכֵיוָן דְּכָשֵׁר מִדְּאוֹרַיְיתָא – חֲשָׁשָׁא דְּרַבָּנַן בְּעָלְמָא הִיא, וְלָאו צָרַת עֶרְוָה הִיא. לְעוֹלָם לֹא תֵּצֵא. וַאֲפִי' אֵין לָהּ בָּנִים. וְקַרְצִית שֶׁבָּעֳמִיר כו'. וְעוֹד שְׁמוּעָה זוֹ אָמַר אֲבִיכֶם: דְּקַרְצִית הַנִּמְצֵאת בָּעֳמָרִים אֵינָהּ פּוֹסֶלֶת בְּמֵי חַטָּאת, אִם שָׁתָת מֵהֶן. מִפְּנֵי שֶׁמּוֹצֶצֶת. וְאֵינָהּ מַחֲזֶרֶת מִמַּיִם שֶׁבְּפִיהָ לַחֲזוֹר וּלְטַפְטֵף בְּתוֹךְ הַכְּלִי. דִּתְנַן הָתָם:* שָׁתְתָה מֵהֶן בְּהֵמָה חַיָּה וְעוֹף – פְּסוּלִין, מִפְּנֵי שֶׁמְּקִיאִים מִפִּיהֶם לְתוֹכָן, וּכְבָר בָּטְלוּ בְּפִיהֶן מִתּוֹרַת מֵי חַטָּאת. דִּידְבְתָּא. זְבוּב גָּדוֹל, כְּמִין חָגָב. דְּבֵינֵי כֵּיפֵי. הַנִּמְצָא בֵּין הָעֳמָרִים. עַד כַּמָּה. הָוְיָא קְטַנָּה וּפָסְלָה. עַד כַּזַּיִת. וּמִכַּזַּיִת וָמַעְלָה הָוְיָא גְּדוֹלָה וְלָא פָּסְלָה. וַהֲלָכָה כְּר' אֶלְעָזָר בְּגִיטִּין. דְּעֵדֵי מְסִירָה כָּרְתִי, וַאֲפִילּוּ פְּסוּלָא דְּרַבָּנַן לֵיכָּא. אֲבָל לֹא בִּשְׁטָרוֹת, דִּכְתִיב בְּהֶן: "וְכָתוֹב בַּסֵּפֶר וְחָתוֹם" בְּיִרְמְיָה (לב) בְּסֵפֶר הַמִּקְנָה. אֲפִי' בִּשְׁטָרוֹת. דְּהָתָם עָלָה טוֹבָה קמ"ל, מִפְּנֵי תִּיקּוּן הָעוֹלָם. וְהָא קָתָנֵי. מַתְנִיתִין. גּוֹבָה מִנְּכָסִים מְשׁוּעְבָּדִים. אִם שְׁטָר הוּא, אוֹ גֵּט זֶה – גּוֹבָה כְּתוּבָּה מִנְּכָסִים מְשׁוּעְבָּדִים, דִּתְנַן בִּכְתוּבּוֹת (דף פט.): הוֹצִיאָה גֵּט וְאֵין עִמּוֹ כְּתוּבָּה – גּוֹבָה כְּתוּבָּתָהּ. תַּרְתֵּי אָמַר. בְּגִיטִּין וּשְׁטָרוֹת. רֵיחַ הַגֵּט. לִיפָּסֵל בִּכְהוּנָּה לְהַחְמִיר, וְכָל שֶׁכֵּן לְהָתִּיר. וְרַבּוֹתֵינוּ הַבְּקִיאִין בִּדְבַר הֲלָכָה. הָנָךְ דְּמִפַּלְגִי וְאָזִיל, רַב חָמָא בַּר גּוֹרְיָא. רַב חִסְדָּא. מִשּׁוּם רַבֵּינוּ. רַב. חֲבֵרֵינוּ. רַב. **מתני'** שְׁנֵי גִיטִּין שָׁוִין. בִּשְׁמוֹתֵיהֶן. הֲרֵי הַשֵּׁנִי בָּטֵל. דְּלָא יָדְעִינַן דְּמַאן נִיהוּ. טוֹפֶס לְכָל אֶחָד וְאֶחָד. בַּגְּמָ' מְפָרֵשׁ לָהּ. אֶת שֶׁהָעֵדִים נִקְרָאִים עִמּוֹ. הַיְינוּ תַּחְתּוֹן, אֲבָל עֶלְיוֹנִים פְּסוּלִים – שֶׁמָּא לֹא הֵעִידוּ אֶלָּא עַל הָאַחֲרוֹן. **גמ'** מַאן תַּנָּא. דְּקָתָנֵי דְּאִיכָּא תַּקַּנְתָּא בְּנוֹתֵן שְׁנֵיהֶם לָזוֹ וּשְׁנֵיהֶם לָזוֹ. דְּלָא כְּר' אֶלְעָזָר. אֶלָּא כְּר' מֵאִיר, הִלְכָּךְ כָּל אַחַת מֵהֶן מִתְגָּרֶשֶׁת בְּשֶׁלָּהּ, שֶׁהֲרֵי בָּא לְיָדָהּ וְעֵדָיו חֲתוּמִים בּוֹ. וְר' מֵאִיר, כֵּיוָן דְּלָא בָּעֵי עֵדֵי מְסִירָה – שַׁפִּיר דָּמֵי, דְּהָא כָּל גִּיטִּין נַמֵּי, מִשֶּׁחֲתָמוּהוּ הָעֵדִים אֵינָן יוֹדְעִין לְמִי יִנָּתֵן. הָא לָא יָדְעִי. עֵדֵי מְסִירָה בְּהֵי מִינַּיְיהוּ מִיגָּרְשָׁה, וְאֵין זוֹ נְתִינָה לִשְׁמָהּ מְבוֹרֶרֶת. וְרַבִּי אֶלְעָזָר, כֵּיוָן דַּחֲתִימָה לִשְׁמָהּ לָא בָּעֵי – עַל כָּרְחֵיךְ לִשְׁמָהּ דִּכְתִיב בִּקְרָא אַ"כָּתַב וְנָתַן" קָאֵי.

אֲפִילּוּ

עין משפט נר מצוה

מט א מיי' פ"א מהל' גירושין הלכה יד סמג עשין נ טוש"ע אה"ע סימן קל סעיף כ:

נ ב מיי' פ"ו מהל' יבום הל' ז סמג עשין נא טוש"ע אה"ע סי' קעג סעיף ו:

נא ג מיי' פ"א מהל' גירושין הל' יד ופ"י הלכה ב סמג עשין נ טוש"ע אה"ע סי' קכז ס"א וסי' קנ ס"א:

נב ד מיי' פ"ט מהל' פרה אדומה הל' יב סמג עשין רלג:

נג ה מיי' פי"א מהל' מלוה ולוה הל' ב סמג עשין צד טוש"ע ח"מ סי' מ סעי' ב וסי' נא סעי' ז:

[וע' תוספות פסחים יח. ד"ה בטלו]

נד ו מיי' פ"ג מהל' גירושין הל' יב סמג עשין נ טוש"ע אה"ע סי' קלב סעיף ג:

נה ז מיי' פ"ד מהלכות גירושין הל' יח סמג עשין נ טוש"ע אה"ע סי' קל סעי' ט:

נו ח מיי' פ"א מהלכות גירושין הל' יח סמג

מסורת הש"ס

[לעיל סו: עי"ש: לקמן פז:]

ס"א ל"ג

יבמות ל:

חיפא ס"א

משמיה דרב ס"א

פרה פ"ט מ"ג חולין סב.

[לעיל ז.] כתובות לג:

[עי' תוס' לעיל ז. ד"ה דקי"ל]

[נ"ל דרב]

[פרה פ"ט מ"ג]

גליון הש"ס

מתני' ונתערבו נותן שניהם. עיין טורי אבן ר"ה כז ע"א ד"ה בהם קול:

תוספות רי"ד

אֲפִילּוּ זְמַן אֶחָד לְכוּלָּן נַמִי הָוֵי טוֹפֶס. אֶלָּא הֵיכִי דָּמֵי כְּלָל? דְּכָתַב "אָנוּ פְּלוֹנִי וּפְלוֹנִי גֵּירַשְׁנוּ נְשׁוֹתֵינוּ פְּלוֹנִית וּפְלוֹנִית". מַתְקִיף לָהּ רַבִּי אַבָּא: לְר' יוֹחָנָן, דְּאָמַר זְמַן אֶחָד לְכוּלָּן זֶהוּ כְּלָל, לֵיחוּשׁ דִּלְמָא כִּי חָתְמוּ סָהֲדֵי — אַבַּתְרָא הוּא דַּחֲתִימִי! מִי לָא *תַּנְיָא: אעֵדִים חֲתוּמִין עַל שְׁאֵילַת שָׁלוֹם בְּגֵט — פָּסוּל, חָיְישִׁינַן שֶׁמָּא עַל שְׁאֵילַת שָׁלוֹם חָתְמוּ? לָאו אִיתְּמַר עֲלַהּ: א"ר אַבָּהוּ, בלְדִידִי מְפָרְשָׁא לִי מִינֵּיהּ דְּרַבִּי יוֹחָנָן: "שַׁאֲלוּ" — פָּסוּל, "וְשַׁאֲלוּ" — כָּשֵׁר, ה"נ — גדִּכְתִיב בֵּיהּ "פְּלוֹנִי וּפְלוֹנִי". וְתוּ, לְרַבִּי יוֹחָנָן, דְּאָמַר זְמַן לְכָל אֶחָד זֶהוּ טוֹפֶס, מַאי אִירְיָא מִשּׁוּם טוֹפֶס? וְתֵיפוֹק לֵיהּ דַּהֲוָה לֵיהּ נִכְתָּב בַּיּוֹם וְנֶחְתַּם בַּלַּיְלָה! א"ל מָר קַשִּׁישָׁא בְּרֵיהּ דְּרַב חִסְדָּא לְרַב אַשִׁי, הָכִי אָמְרִינַן מִשְּׁמֵיהּ דְּרַבִּי יוֹחָנָן: דדִּכְתִיב בְּהוּ "בְּחַד בְּשַׁבָּא", "בְּחַד בְּשַׁבָּא". א"ל רָבִינָא לְרַב אַשִׁי: לְרֵישׁ לָקִישׁ, דְּאָמַר זְמַן אֶחָד לְכוּלָּן נַמִי טוֹפֶס הָוֵי, (א) וְהֵיכִי דָּמֵי כְּלָל — דִּכְתִיב בֵּיהּ הָכִי: "אָנוּ פְּלוֹנִי וּפְלוֹנִי גֵּירַשְׁנוּ נְשׁוֹתֵינוּ פְּלוֹנִית וּפְלוֹנִית", נִמְצְאוּ שְׁתֵּי נָשִׁים מִתְגָּרְשׁוֹת בְּגֵט אֶחָד, וְהַתּוֹרָה אָמְרָה: "וְכָתַב לָהּ" — *הוְלֹא *לָהּ וְלַחֲבֶרְתָּהּ! ודַּהֲדַר כָּתַב "פְּלוֹנִי גֵּירֵשׁ פְּלוֹנִית וּפְלוֹנִי גֵּירֵשׁ פְּלוֹנִית". א"ל רָבִינָא לְרַב אַשִׁי, וּמַאי שְׁנָא מֵהָא, *דְּתַנְיָא: הַכּוֹתֵב כָּל נְכָסָיו לִשְׁנֵי עֲבָדָיו — קָנוּ וּמְשַׁחְרְרִין זֶה אֶת זֶה! וְלָאו אוֹקִימְנָא בִּשְׁנֵי שְׁטָרוֹת? תַּנְיָא כְּוָותֵיהּ דְּר' יוֹחָנָן, תַּנְיָא כְּוָותֵיהּ דְּרֵישׁ לָקִישׁ. תַּנְיָא כְּוָותֵיהּ דְּר' יוֹחָנָן: חֲמִשָּׁה שֶׁכָּתְבוּ בְּתוֹךְ הַגֵּט "אִישׁ פְּלוֹנִי מְגָרֵשׁ פְּלוֹנִית, וּפְלוֹנִי פְּלוֹנִית, וּפְלוֹנִי פְּלוֹנִית", וּזְמַן אֶחָד לְכוּלָּן, וְהָעֵדִים מִלְּמַטָּה — כּוּלָּן כְּשֵׁרִים וְתִנָּתֵן לְכָל אַחַת וְאַחַת. זְמַן לְכָל אֶחָד וְאֶחָד וְהָעֵדִים מִלְּמַטָּה, יֵאת שֶׁהָעֵדִים נִקְרָאִים עִמּוֹ — כָּשֵׁר; ר' יְהוּדָה בֶּן בְּתֵירָא אוֹמֵר: אִם יֵשׁ רֶיוַח בֵּינֵיהֶן — פָּסוּל, וְאִם לָאו — כָּשֵׁר, שֶׁאֵין זְמַן מַפְסִיקָן. תַּנְיָא כְּוָותֵיהּ דְּרֵישׁ לָקִישׁ: חֲמִשָּׁה שֶׁכָּתְבוּ כְּלָל בְּתוֹךְ הַגֵּט "אָנוּ פְּלוֹנִי וּפְלוֹנִי גֵּירַשְׁנוּ נְשׁוֹתֵינוּ פְּלוֹנִית וּפְלוֹנִית, פְּלוֹנִי גֵּירֵשׁ פְּלוֹנִית וּפְלוֹנִי גֵּירֵשׁ פְּלוֹנִית", וּזְמַן אֶחָד לְכוּלָּן וְהָעֵדִים מִלְּמַטָּה — כּוּלָּן כְּשֵׁרִין וְתִנָּתֵן לְכָל אַחַת וְאַחַת. זְמַן לְכָל אֶחָד וְאֶחָד, וְרֶיוַח לְכָל אֶחָד וְאֶחָד, וְהָעֵדִים מִלְּמַטָּה, אֶת שֶׁהָעֵדִים נִקְרָאִין עִמּוֹ — כָּשֵׁר; ר"מ אוֹמֵר: אע"פ שֶׁאֵין רֶיוַח בֵּינֵיהֶם — פָּסוּל שֶׁהַזְּמַן מַפְסִיקָן. וְרֵישׁ לָקִישׁ, מַאי אִירְיָא זְמַן לְכָל אֶחָד וְאֶחָד? הָא אָמַר: זְמַן אֶחָד לְכוּלָּן נַמִי טוֹפֶס הָוֵי! הָנֵי מִילֵּי הֵיכָא דְּלָא עָרְבִינְהוּ מֵעִיקָּרָא, אֲבָל הָכָא דְּעָרְבִינְהוּ מֵעִיקָּרָא, אִי פָּלֵיג לְהוּ זְמַן — אִין, אִי לָא — לָא.§ **מתני'** חשְׁנֵי גִיטִּין שֶׁכְּתָבָן זֶה בְּצַד זֶה, וּשְׁנַיִם עֵדִים עִבְרִים בָּאִים מִתַּחַת זֶה לְתַחַת זֶה וּשְׁנַיִם עֵדִים יְוָנִים בָּאִים מִתַּחַת זֶה לְתַחַת זֶה, אֵת שֶׁהָעֵדִים הָרִאשׁוֹנִים נִקְרָאִין עִמּוֹ — כָּשֵׁר. *עֵד אֶחָד עִבְרִי וְעֵד אֶחָד יְוָנִי, וְעֵד אֶחָד עִבְרִי וְעֵד אֶחָד יְוָנִי בָּאִין מִתַּחַת זֶה לְתַחַת זֶה — שְׁנֵיהֶם פְּסוּלִין.§ **גמ'** טוְלִיתַּכְשַׁר הַאי בִּ"רְאוּבֵן" וְהַאי בְּ"בֶן יַעֲקֹב עֵד", דְּהָא תְּנַן: "בֶּן אִישׁ פְּלוֹנִי עֵד" — כָּשֵׁר! דְּכָתַב "רְאוּבֵן בֶּן" אַקַּמָּא וְ"יַעֲקֹב עֵד" אַבַּתְרָא. וְלִיתַּכְשַׁר הַאי "בִּרְאוּבֵן בֶּן", וְלִיתַּכְשַׁר הַאי בְּ"יַעֲקֹב עֵד", דְּהָא תְּנַן: "אִישׁ פְּלוֹנִי עֵד" — כָּשֵׁר! ידְּלָא כָּתַב "עֵד". וְאִיבָּעֵית אֵימָא: כלְעוֹלָם דְּכָתַב "עֵד", וּדְיָדְעִינַן בְּהָא חֲתִימָה דְּלָאו דְּיַעֲקֹב הוּא.

וְדִלְמָא

רש"י

אֲפִילּוּ זְמַן אֶחָד לְכוּלָּן נַמִי הָוֵי טוֹפֶס. לְכָל אֶחָד וְאֶחָד, לִפְסוֹל הָעֶלְיוֹנִים. (*א"כ כִּי כָּתְבוּ: אִישׁ פְּלוֹנִי מְגָרֵשׁ פְּלוֹנִית וּפְלוֹנִי פְּלוֹנִית), הוֹאִיל וְהִזְכִּיר שֵׁם אִישׁ וְאִשָּׁה יַחַד לְכָל אֶחָד וְאֶחָד — הָוֵי כָּל חַד גֵּט לְעַצְמוֹ, וְנִמְצָא אַחֲרוֹן מַפְסִיק בְּעֵדוּת, וְאֵין עֵדִים מְעִידִים אֶלָּא עָלָיו. לְר' יוֹחָנָן דְּאָמַר כו'. הוֹאִיל וְכָל אִישׁ וְאִשָּׁה נִכְתָּבִים לְבַד לְבַד, אַמַּאי כּוּלָּן כְּשֵׁרִים? עַל שְׁאֵילַת שָׁלוֹם חָתְמוּ. וְלֹא עַל הַגֵּט. שַׁאֲלוּ. בִּשְׁלוֹמוֹ. פָּסוּל. דַּהֲוֵי מִלְּתָא בְּאַפֵּי נַפְשֵׁיהּ, וּמַפְסֶקֶת. זְמַן לְכָל אֶחָד וְאֶחָד. קָא סָלְקָא דַּעְתִּין: בַּיּוֹם שֶׁנִּכְתַּב זֶה לֹא נִכְתַּב זֶה. מַאי אִירְיָא. דְּמִפַּסְלֵי עֶלְיוֹנִים מִשּׁוּם דְּאֵין הָעֵדִים נִקְרָאִים עִמָּם? וְתֵיפוֹק לֵיהּ. דַּהֲווּ כּוּלְּהוּ, בַּר מִבַּתְרָא, נִכְתְּבוּ הַיּוֹם וְנֶחְתְּמוּ לְאַחַר זְמַן, שֶׁהֲרֵי לֹא חָתְמוּ הָעֵדִים עַד שֶׁנִּכְתַּב הָאַחֲרוֹן! נֶחְתַּם בַּלַּיְלָה לָאו דַּוְקָא, אֶלָּא מִשּׁוּם לִישָּׁנָא דְּמַתְנִי' נְקַט לֵיהּ, דִּתְנַן בְּפֶרֶק שֵׁנִי (לעיל יז.): נִכְתַּב בַּיּוֹם וְנֶחְתַּם בַּלַּיְלָה — פָּסוּל, וְכ"ש לְמָחָר אוֹ לְיוֹמָא אוֹחֲרָא. בְּחַד בְּשַׁבָּא. גֵּירֵשׁ פְּלוֹנִי פְּלוֹנִית, וַהֲדַר כָּתַב: בְּחַד בְּשַׁבָּא גּוּפֵיהּ גֵּירֵשׁ פְּלוֹנִי פְּלוֹנִית, דְּהַשְׁתָּא לָא מִיפַּסְלֵי קַמָּאֵי אֶלָּא מִשּׁוּם הַפְסָקָה. דַּהֲדַר כְּתַב הָכִי כו'. דַּהֲווּ לְהוּ כָּל חַד בְּאַפֵּי נַפְשֵׁיהּ. וּמִיהוּ, אַהֲנֵי לִישָּׁנֵי קַמָּאֵי לְאַשְׁמוּעִינַן שֶׁהָעֵדִים יָדְעוּ בְּכָל הַגִּיטִּין הַלָּלוּ. וּמַאי שְׁנָא הָא מֵהָא דְּתַנְיָא כו'. וְעֶבֶד גָּמַר "לָהּ" "לָהּ" מֵאִשָּׁה, וְלָא פָּסְלִינַן לְהוּ מִשּׁוּם "וְלֹא לָהּ וְלַחֲבֶרְתָּהּ" (ב) שֶׁשִּׁחְרֵר שְׁנֵיהֶם בְּבַת אַחַת, וְדָמֵי לְקַמַּיְיתָא דְּרֵישׁ לָקִישׁ: "אָנוּ פְּלוֹנִי וּפְלוֹנִי גֵּירַשְׁנוּ נָשֵׁינוּ פְּלוֹנִית וּפְלוֹנִית", וְאַמַּאי בָּעֵי לְמֵיהְדַּר וּמִכְתַּב "פְּלוֹנִי גֵּירֵשׁ פְּלוֹנִית וּפְלוֹנִי פְּלוֹנִית"? הָא הָכָא כָּתַב: "כָּל נְכָסַי לִפְלוֹנִי וּפְלוֹנִי עֲבָדַי", וְקָתָנֵי: קָנוּ כָּל הַנְּכָסִים, וְנִמְצָא כָּל אֶחָד חֶצְיוֹ בֶּן חוֹרִין וְחֶצְיוֹ עֶבֶד לַחֲבֵרוֹ, וּמְשַׁחְרְרִים זֶה אֶת זֶה חֲלָקֵיהֶן! וְלָאו אוֹקִימְנָא. בְּפֶרֶק "הַשּׁוֹלֵחַ גֵּט". בִּשְׁנֵי שְׁטָרוֹת. שֶׁכָּתַב בִּשְׁטָר: "כָּל נְכָסַי לִפְלוֹנִי עַבְדִּי", וּבִשְׁטָר הַשֵּׁנִי: "כָּל נְכָסַי נְתוּנִים לִפְלוֹנִי עַבְדִּי" וּמְסָרָן לָהֶן בְּבַת אַחַת, שֶׁלֹּא קָדַם זֶה לָזֶה. הִלְכָּךְ קָנוּ שְׁנֵיהֶם, דְּהַאי אָמַר: כּוּלְּהוּ דִּידִי, וְהַאי אָמַר: כּוּלְּהוּ דִּידִי. אִישׁ פְּלוֹנִי כו'. הַיְינוּ כְּרַבִּי יוֹחָנָן, דְּלָא קָתָנֵי "אָנוּ פְּלוֹנִי וּפְלוֹנִי גֵּירַשְׁנוּ" כו'. וּלְרֵישׁ לָקִישׁ. אַמַּאי קָתָנֵי בְּהַךְ דִּמְסַיְּיעָא לֵיהּ: זְמַן לְכָל אֶחָד וְאֶחָד כו' אֶת שֶׁהָעֵדִים נִקְרָאִין עִמּוֹ — כָּשֵׁר? בְּלָאו זְמַן לְכָל אֶחָד וְאֶחָד נַמִי פְּסִילֵי עֶלְיוֹנִים! אֲבָל הָכָא דְּעָרְבִינְהוּ מֵעִיקָּרָא. דְּהָא דְּקָתָנֵי זְמַן לְכָל אֶחָד וְאֶחָד — כְּגוֹן דְּכָתַב הָכִי כִּדְקָתָנֵי רֵישָׁא: אָנוּ פְּלוֹנִי וּפְלוֹנִי גֵּירַשְׁנוּ נָשֵׁינוּ פְּלוֹנִית וּפְלוֹנִית, פְּלוֹנִי גֵּירֵשׁ פְּלוֹנִית בְּאֶחָד בְּשַׁבָּת, וּפְלוֹנִי גֵּירֵשׁ פְּלוֹנִית בְּאֶחָד בְּשַׁבָּת. דְּכֵיוָן דְּעָרְבִינְהוּ מֵעִיקָּרָא, אִי לָא הֲדַר אַפְסְקִינְהוּ בִּזְמַן — לָא מִיפְסְקִי. **מתני'** שְׁנֵי גִיטִּין שֶׁכְּתָבָן זֶה בְּצַד זֶה. בְּרוֹחַב הַמְּגִילָּה. שְׁנַיִם עִבְרִים בָּאִים מִתַּחַת. הָרִאשׁוֹן לְתַחַת הַשֵּׁנִי, שֵׁם הָעֵד תַּחַת הָרִאשׁוֹן וְשֵׁם אָבִיו תַּחַת הַשֵּׁנִי, וְכֵן עֵד שֵׁנִי תַּחְתָּיו. וְחָזְרוּ וְחָתְמוּ תַּחְתֵּיהֶן שְׁנֵי יִשְׂרְאֵלִים יְוָנִים, הַדָּרִים בְּאֶרֶץ יָוָן, וּבִלְשׁוֹן יְוָנִית, כְּדֶרֶךְ הַזּוּ. אֲבָל חֲתִימַת הַיְּוָנִים אֵינָהּ נִקְרֵאת כַּחֲתִימַת הָעִבְרִים, שֶׁכְּשֶׁהַיְּוָנִי חוֹתֵם יוֹסֵף בֶּן שִׁמְעוֹן — בְּיָדוּעַ שֶׁשְּׁמוֹ שִׁמְעוֹן בֶּן יוֹסֵף, שֶׁכָּךְ מִתְפָּרֶשֶׁת חֲתִימָתָן: יוֹסֵף בֶּן שִׁמְעוֹן, כְּלוֹמַר: בְּנוֹ שֶׁל יוֹסֵף שִׁמְעוֹן, וְנִמְצָא שֵׁם הָעֵד חָתוּם עַל גֵּט שֵׁנִי, וְשֵׁם אָבִיו חָתוּם עַל הָרִאשׁוֹן. הִלְכָּךְ, עַל כָּרְחִיךְ הַיְּוָנִים תַּחַת הַשֵּׁנִי חָתְמוּ כָּזֶה*. אֶת שֶׁהָעֵדִים הָרִאשׁוֹנִים נִקְרָאִים עִמּוֹ כָּשֵׁר. אִם הָעִבְרִיִּים חֲתוּמִים לְמַעְלָה — הַיְּמִינִי כָּשֵׁר, וְאִם הַיְּוָנִים חֲתוּמִים לְמַעְלָה — הַשְּׂמָאלִי כָּשֵׁר. וּבַגְּמָרָא פָּרֵיךְ: אִידָךְ אַמַּאי מִיפְּסַל? עֵד אֶחָד עִבְרִי וְעֵד אֶחָד יְוָנִי וְעֵד עִבְרִי וְעֵד א' יְוָנִי בָּאִים מִתַּחַת זֶה לְתַחַת זֶה. עֵד עִבְרִי וְעֵד יְוָנִי בָּאִים מִתַּחַת גֵּט הַיָּמִין לְתַחַת גֵּט הַשְּׂמֹאל, וְעֵד עִבְרִי וְעֵד יְוָנִי עוֹד תַּחְתֵּיהֶן בָּאִין מִתַּחַת הַשְּׂמֹאל לְתַחַת גֵּט הַיָּמִין. כְּגוֹן שֶׁהַיְּוָנִי הָרִאשׁוֹן חָתַם תַּחַת הַשְּׂמָאלִי יוֹסֵף (ג) *בְּסוֹף שִׁיטָּה, וְחָזַר וְחָתַם בֶּן שִׁמְעוֹן בְּרֹאשׁ שִׁיטָּה שְׁנִיָּה תַּחַת הַיְּמִינִי, נִמְצָא שְׁמוֹ תַּחַת הַיְּמִינִי. דְּהָכִי מִיפָּרְשָׁה חֲתִימָה דִּידְהוּ: בְּנוֹ שֶׁל יוֹסֵף שִׁמְעוֹן, נִמְצָא שֶׁמִּתַּחַת גֵּט הַיָּמִין בָּא לְתַחַת גֵּט הַשְּׂמֹאל, שֵׁם אָבִיו עַל הַשְּׂמֹאל, וּשְׁמוֹ עַל הַיָּמִין. וְהָעִבְרִי הַשֵּׁנִי חָתַם שְׁמוֹ תַּחַת גֵּט הַשְּׂמָאלִי בְּסוֹף שִׁיטָּה, וְשֵׁם אָבִיו תַּחַת הַיְּמִינִי בְּרֹאשׁ שִׁיטָּה שֶׁתַּחְתֶּיהָ, [שֶׁלֹּא כְּדַרְכּוֹ]. נִמְצָא בָּא מִתַּחַת גֵּט שֵׁנִי לְתַחַת גֵּט רִאשׁוֹן. וְהַיְּוָנִי הַשֵּׁנִי חָתַם תַּחְתָּיו כְּדַרְכּוֹ בְּשִׁיטָּה אַחַת יִשְׁמָעֵאל בֶּן תַּחַת הָרִאשׁוֹן, וְנַפְתָּלִי תַּחַת הַשֵּׁנִי, נִמְצָא שְׁמוֹ חָתוּם עַל הַשֵּׁנִי. שְׁנֵיהֶם פְּסוּלִים. וּבַגְּמָרָא מְפָרֵשׁ טַעְמָא. **גמ'** וְלִיתַּכְשַׁר קַמָּא בִּרְאוּבֵן וּבַתְרָא בְּבֶן יַעֲקֹב עֵד. וְיוּכְשְׁרוּ שְׁנֵיהֶם עַל יְדֵי שְׁנֵי עֵדִים רִאשׁוֹנִים. דְּהָא תְּנַן. בְּמַתְנִיתִין בְּפִירְקִין. וְלִיתַּכְשַׁר הַאי בִּרְאוּבֵן בֶּן. דְּמַשְׁמַע: אֲנִי בְּנוֹ שֶׁל רְאוּבֵן, כְּדֶרֶךְ פֵּירוּשׁ חֲתִימַת הַיְּוָנִים, וְזֶה שֶׁחָתַם תַּחַת הַשֵּׁנִי — אִישׁ אַחֵר הָיָה, וּשְׁמוֹ יַעֲקֹב. דְּלָא כְּתִיב עֵד. וּמַתְנִיתִין דַּוְקָא נְקַט "אִישׁ פְּלוֹנִי עֵד", דְּהֵיכָא דְּלָא חָתַם "פְּלוֹנִי בֶּן פְּלוֹנִי" — בָּעֵינַן עֵד. דְּלָאו יַעֲקֹב הוּא. אֶלָּא (ד) שֶׁל זֶה בְּנוֹ הָיָה.

וְדִלְמָא

בכך לירח	בכך לירח
ראובן בן	יעקב עברי
. . . . .	יוסף יווני
בן שמעון	קהת עברי
בן לוי	. . . . .
ישמאל בן	נפתלי יווני

תוספות

וליתכשר האי בראובן והאי בבן יעקב עד. תימה לר"י: היכי ליתכשר בראובן? הא לא תנא אלא "איש פלוני עד" כשר, אבל "איש פלוני" בלא "עד" – לא! ואור"י: דפשיטא ליה דראובן קאי א"בן יעקב עד" דבתריה, והוי כאילו כתב בהדיה דראובן "עד".

וליתכשר האי בראובן בן והאי ביעקב עד. פירש בקונטרס: ד"ראובן בן" משמע: אני בנו של ראובן, כדרך פירוש חתימת יונים. וזה שחתם תחת השני – איש אחר היה, ושמו יעקב. ולפירושו שפי' שחתם כחתימת יונית – בחנם פירש שיעקב הוא איש אחר, שיוכל לפרש הוא יעקב הוא עצמו בן ראובן. ופירוש דחוק לומר שהעברי חתם כדרך חתימת יונים. ונראה לפרש: ד"ראובן בן" דקאמר – הוא בן יעקב, ולא חש ראובן לכתוב שם יעקב אביו לפי שהוא כתוב וחתום על גט שני, ונקרא יפה ראובן בן יעקב.

דידעינן ביה בהאי חתימת ידא דלאו דיעקב. משמע דבסתמא היה לנו לתלות ביעקב, אע"ג דבעי קיום חותמין – מסתמא השליח שאומר "בפני נכתב" וכו' מכיר חתימת ידו. אי נמי, איכא למימר דמיירי בא"י, דאין צריך קיום חותמין, כיון שאין עליו עוררים.

ודלמא

תוספות רי"ד

אפילו זמן אחד לכולן זהו תופס. ה"ד כלל דכתיב ביה הרי אנו פלוני ופלוני גרשנו נשותינו פלונית ופלונית. מתקיף לה ר' אבא לר' יוחנן דאמר זמן אחד לכולן זהו כלל ליחוש כי חתימי שהדי אבתרא הוא דחתימי פי' הואיל וכל שם איש ואשה נכתבים לבד דילמא דעדים אבתרא חתימי ולא אכולהו מי לא תניא עדים החתומים על שאלת שלום בגט חיישינן שמא על שאלת שלום חתמו ולאו מי איתמר עלה א"ר אבהו לדידי מיפרשא לי מיניה דר' יוחנן שאלו פסול ושאלו כשר הכא נמי דכתיב ביה איש פלוני גירש פלונית ופלוני פלונית ופלוני פלונית פי' שהוא"ו מוסיף על ענין ראשון ומחבר את כולן ואכולהו משהדי: ותו לר' יוחנן דאמר זמן לכל אחד זהו תופס מאי איריא משום תופס תיפוק לי דהוה ליה נכתב ביום ונחתם בלילה פי' דקס"ד שביום שנכתב זה לא נכתב זה וכולהו הוו נכתבו ביום ונחתמו לאחר זמן א"ל מר קשישא בריה דרב אידי לרב אשי הכי אמרינן משמיה דר' יוחנן דכתיב ביה הכי בחד בשבא בחד בשבא בחד בשבא א"ל רבינא לרב אשי לר"ל דאמר ה"ד כלל דכתב ביה הכי אנו פלוני ופלוני ופלוני גירשנו את נשותינו פלונית ופלונית ופלונית נמצאו ב' נשים מתגרשות בגט אחד והתורה אמרה וכתב לה ולא לה ולחברתה דהדר נכתבים פלוני גירש פלונית ופלוני פלונית ופלוני פלונית וקי"ל ר"ל ור'

רבנו חננאל

יוחנן הלכה כר' יוחנן: **מתני'** ב' גיטין שכתבן זה בצד זה ושני עדים עברים באין מתחת זה לזה ושני עדים יונים באין מתחת זה לזה את שהעדים הראשונים נקראין עמו כשר. עד א' עברי ועד א' יוני באין מתחת זה לתחת זה שניהם פסולין. פי' ב' גיטין שכתבן זה בצד זה לרוחב המגילה א' מימין וא' משמאל. ושני עדים עברים באין מתחת זה לתחת זה וכו' וב' עדים עברים חתומים בלשון קודש והיו חתומים מתחת זה לתחת זה שלא היו חתומים שמם ושם אבותם תחת גט אחד כמו שעושין כל העדים החותמים תחת כל גט וכל שטר אלא כתבו שם תחת גט הימיני ושם אבותם תחת השמאלי וכן השני כתב יוסף תחת הימיני בן שמואל תחת השמאלי נמצאת משוכות מגט זה לגט זה שמותם כתבו תחת הימיני ושמות אבותיהם תחת השמאלי ועוד חזרו וחתמו תחתיהן שני ישראל יונים הדרים בארץ יון ולא חתמו בלשון קודש אלא בלשון יונית והיתה חתימתן נמי משוכה מתחת הימיני לתחת השמאלי ומנהג היונים הוא בשמותם ראובן בן יעקב [יעקב] הוא שם העד וראובן הוא שם האב שכך מתפרש ראובן מי הוא בנו יעקב וחתמו שני היונים כך תחת העברים דן בן נפתלי גד בן אשר כתוב תחת הימיני ונפתלי בן דן וכן השני גד בן היה כתוב תחת הימיני ואשר תחת השמאלי נמצא עכשיו שני עברים חתומים תחת הימיני ושני עדים יוונים חתומים תחת השמאלי אך שהעדים הראשונים נקראים עמו כשר. דהיינו הימיני שהעברים נקראים עמו וקורא אותן ראשונים לפי סדר המשנה דתני שני עדים עברים ושני עדים יונים וגט השמאלי שהעדים נקראים עמו פסול.

ומקשה

עין משפט נר מצוה

נח א ב מיי' פ"ד מהל' גירושין הל' כה סמג עשין נ טוש"ע אה"ע סימן קל סעיף ג:

נט ג מיי' שם טוש"ע שם סעיף ט ובהג"ה:

ס ד ה ו מיי' שם הל' יט טוש"ע שם וסע"י:

סא ז טוש"ע שם סעיף ט:

סב ח ט מיי' שם הל' כא טוש"ע שם סעיף ח:

סג י מיי' שם טוש"ע שם סעיף יב:

סד כ מיי' שם טוש"ע שם סעיף ח:

[ע' תוס' עירובין טו: ד"ה ורבנן ותוס' לעיל כח: ד"ה בכתיבה]

מסורת הש"ס

ברש"י בדפוסי ליתא לכל זה

ב"ב כטו. [תוספ' פ"ז]

[קדושין יז.]

לעיל מב.

[תוספות על זה לקמן ע"ב]

ס"א ברא"ש

הגהות הב"ח

(א) גמ' כדפס הוי אלא היכי דמי: (ב) רש"י ד"ה ומאי שנא וכו' כששחרר: (ג) ד"ה עד אחד עברי וכו' תחת השמאלי יוסף בן בסוף שיטה וחזר וחתם שמעון כל"ל: (ד) ד"ה דלאו יעקב הוא אלא בנו של זה היה:

וְדִלְמָא בִּשְׁמָא דַּאֲבוּהּ חָתִים! לָא שָׁבֵיק אִינִישׁ שְׁמֵיהּ וְחָתֵים שְׁמָא דַּאֲבוּהּ. וְדִילְמָא סִימָנָא שַׁוְיֵיהּ! דְּהָא *רַב צָיֵיר כַּוְורָא, רַבִּי חֲנִינָא — חָרוּתָא, רַב חִסְדָּא — סָמֶךְ, רַב הוֹשַׁעְיָא — עַ"ןְ, רַבָּה בַּר רַב הוּנָא צָיֵיר מַכּוֹתָא! לָא חָצֵיף אִינִישׁ לְשַׁוּוֹיֵי לִשְׁמָא דַּאֲבוּהּ סִימָנָא. וְלִיתַּכְשַׁר הַאי בִּשְׁנֵי עֵדִים עִבְרִים, וְלִיתַּכְשַׁר הַאי בִּשְׁנֵי עֵדִים יְוָנִים, דִּתְנַן: גֵּט שֶׁכְּתָבוֹ עִבְרִית וְעֵדָיו יְוָנִית, יְוָנִית וְעֵדָיו עִבְרִית — כָּשֵׁר! וְכ"ת, כֵּיוָן [א]דְּמוּפְלָג בִּשְׁנֵי שִׁיטִּין לָא, *וְהָאָמַר חִזְקִיָּה: [ב]מִלְאָהוּ בִּקְרוֹבִים — כָּשֵׁר! הָא תָּנֵי זְעֵירִי: שְׁנֵיהֶן כְּשֵׁרִין. וְתַנָּא דִּידָן? דִּלְמָא *גּוּנְדָּלִית חָתִים, וְכוּלְּהוּ אַחַד הוּא דַּחֲתִימִי.§ "עֵד אֶחָד עִבְרִי וְעֵד אֶחָד יְוָנִי".§ וְלִיתַּכְשַׁר הַאי בְּעֵד אֶחָד עִבְרִי וְעֵד אֶחָד יְוָנִי, וְהַאי בְּעֵד אֶחָד עִבְרִי וְעֵד אֶחָד יְוָנִי, דְּהָא תְּנַן: עֵד אֶחָד עִבְרִי וְעֵד אֶחָד יְוָנִי — כָּשֵׁר! הָא תָּנֵי זְעֵירִי: שְׁנֵיהֶם כְּשֵׁרִים. וְתַנָּא דִּידָן? דִּלְמָא גּוּנְדָּלִית חָתִים, וּתְלָתָא אַחַד, וְחַד אַחַד.§

מתני' [ג]שִׁיֵּיר מִקְצָת הַגֵּט וּכְתָבוֹ בַּדַּף הַשֵּׁנִי, וְהָעֵדִים מִלְּמַטָּה — כָּשֵׁר. [ד]חָתְמוּ עֵדִים בְּרֹאשׁ הַדַּף, (א) *מִן הַצַּד, אוֹ מֵאַחֲרָיו, בְּגֵט פָּשׁוּט — פָּסוּל. [ד] הִקִּיף רֹאשׁוֹ שֶׁל זֶה בְּצַד רֹאשׁוֹ שֶׁל זֶה וְהָעֵדִים בָּאֶמְצַע — שְׁנֵיהֶם פְּסוּלִין; [ה]סוֹפוֹ שֶׁל זֶה בְּצַד סוֹפוֹ שֶׁל זֶה וְהָעֵדִים בָּאֶמְצַע, אֵת שֶׁהָעֵדִים נִקְרִין עִמּוֹ — כָּשֵׁר; רֹאשׁוֹ שֶׁל זֶה בְּצַד סוֹפוֹ שֶׁל זֶה וְהָעֵדִים *בָּאֶמְצַע, אֵת שֶׁהָעֵדִים נִקְרִין בְּסוֹפוֹ — כָּשֵׁר. [ו]גֵּט *שֶׁכְּתָבוֹ עִבְרִית וְעֵדָיו יְוָנִית, יְוָנִית וְעֵדָיו עִבְרִי', עֵד אֶחָד עִבְרִי וְעֵד אֶחָד יְוָנִי, (ב) *כָּתַב סוֹפֵר וְעֵד — כָּשֵׁר. *[ז]"אִישׁ פְּלוֹנִי עֵד" — כָּשֵׁר; "בֶּן אִישׁ פְּלוֹנִי עֵד" — כָּשֵׁר; "אִישׁ פְּלוֹנִי בֶּן אִישׁ פְּלוֹנִי" וְלֹא כָּתַב "עֵד" — כָּשֵׁר; *וְכָךְ הָיוּ נְקִיֵּי הַדַּעַת שֶׁבִּירוּשָׁלַיִם עוֹשִׂין. [ח]כָּתַב חֲנִיכָתוֹ וַחֲנִיכָתָהּ — כָּשֵׁר.§

גמ' וְלֵיחוּשׁ דִּלְמָא הָנֵי תְּרֵי גִּיטֵּי הָווּ, וְאִיתְרַמֵּי לֵיהּ זְמַן דְּקַמָּא וְעֵדִים דְּבַתְרָא, וְגַזְיֵיהּ לִזְמַן דְּבַתְרָא וְעֵדִים דְּקַמָּא! א"ר אַבָּא אָמַר רַב: כְּשֶׁיֵּשׁ רֶיוַח מִלְּמַטָּה. וְדִלְמָא זְמַן דְּבַתְרָא מֵיגַז גַּזְיֵיהּ! כִּדְא"ר אַבָּא א"ר: כְּשֶׁיֵּשׁ רֶיוַח מִלְּמַטָּה, הָכָא

וְדִלְמָא בִּשְׁמָא דַּאֲבוּהּ חָתוּם. עַל הַשֵּׁנִי, וְעַל שֶׁנִּיהֶם חָתַם. צָיֵיר כַּוְורָא. בַּחֲתִימַת יָדוֹ, וְלֹא הָיָה כּוֹתֵב שְׁמוֹ. חָרוּתָא. עָנָף שֶׁל דֶּקֶל. מַכּוֹתָא. נֵס שֶׁפּוֹרְשִׂין עָלָיו וִילוֹן שֶׁל סְפִינָה. שֶׁכְּתָבוֹ. כְּתָב שֶׁלּוֹ. וְכִי תֵּימָא כֵּיוָן דְּמוּפְלָג. חֲתִימַת עֵדָיו, שְׁנֵי שִׁיטִּין מִכְּתָבוֹ — אוֹתָן שִׁיטִּין שֶׁחָתְמוּ בָּהֶן הַבָּאִין מִתַּחַת הָרִאשׁוֹן שְׁמוֹת אֲבוֹתֵיהֶן — תּוּ לָא מִיתַּכְשַׁר, דְּתַנְיָא בְּ"גֵט פָּשׁוּט": *הִרְחִיק אֶת הָעֵדִים מִן הַכְּתָב שְׁנֵי שִׁיטִּין — פָּסוּל. וְהָאָמַר חִזְקִיָּה. הָתָם. מִילְאָהוּ. לְאוֹתוֹ אֲוִיר בִּקְרוֹבִים — כָּשֵׁר, דְּלָא קָפְדִינַן אֶלָּא אַאֲוִירָא. וְאַל תִּתְמַהּ, שֶׁהֲרֵי אֲוִיר פּוֹסֵל בִּשְׁלֹשָׁה בְּסוּכָּה, סְכָךְ פָּסוּל פּוֹסֵל בְּאַרְבָּעָה. וְהָתָנֵי זְעֵירִי. בְּהָנָךְ תְּרֵי גִּיטֵּי דְּמַתְנִי': שְׁנֵיהֶם כְּשֵׁרִין. וְתַנָּא דִּידָן. דְּפָסַל אַחֲרוֹן, קָסָבַר: דִּלְמָא גּוּנְדָלִית חֲתוּם הַיְּוָנִים, כְּלוֹמַר שֶׁלֹּא כְּמִנְהָגָם אֶלָּא כְּדֶרֶךְ הָעִבְרִים חָתְמוּ. כּוּלְּהוּ אַחַד. כּוּלָּן עַל רִאשׁוֹן. כָּל שֶׁלֹּא כְּמִנְהָגָן קָרֵי גּוּנְדָּלִית. וְרָאִיתִי בִּתְשׁוּבַת הַגְּאוֹנִים: אָדָם הַמִּשְׁתַּמֵּשׁ בְּיַד הַשְּׂמָאלִית קוֹרִין לוֹ בִּמְקוֹמֵנוּ גּוּנְדָלְיָא, לְפִי שֶׁמְּשַׁנֶּה מִסֵּדֶר הַמִּשְׁתַּמְּשִׁין. וְלִיתַּכְשַׁר הַאי בְּעֵד אֶחָד עִבְרִי וְעֵד אֶחָד יְווֹנִי וְהַאי בְּעֵד אֶחָד עִבְרִי וְעֵד אֶחָד יְווֹנִי גָּרְסִינַן. דִּלְמָא גּוּנְדָּלִית חָתִים. בְּהָנֵי יְוָונִים חָיְישִׁינַן דִּלְמָא גּוּנְדָלִית חָתִים חַד מִינַּיְיהוּ, שֶׁמָּא יְוָנִי הָרִאשׁוֹן חָתַם כְּסֵדֶר הָעִבְרִי, שֶׁחָתַם לְמַעְלָה הֵימֶנּוּ שְׁמוֹ תְּחִלָּה וְאח"כ שֵׁם אָבִיו, וְנִמְצָא שֶׁעַל הַשֵּׁנִי הוּא חָתוּם. וְעִבְרִי שֵׁנִי רוֹאִין שֶׁעַל הַשֵּׁנִי חָתוּם, וְיָוָן אַחֲרוֹן חָתַם כְּמִנְהָגוֹ, וְנִמְצָא שְׁלֹשָׁה עַל הַשֵּׁנִי וְאֵין עַל הָרִאשׁוֹן אֶלָּא אֶחָד. אוֹ שֶׁמָּא יָוָן רִאשׁוֹן כְּדַרְכּוֹ חָתַם, וְיָוָן שֵׁנִי אַחֲרוֹן חָתַם גּוּנְדָּלִית כְּמָה שֶׁרָאָה עִבְרִים חוֹתְמִים, וְנִמְצְאוּ שְׁנֵי הַיְּוָנִים וְעִבְרִי רִאשׁוֹן חֲתוּמִין עַל הָרִאשׁוֹן, וְאֵין עַל גֵּט שֵׁנִי אֶלָּא אֶחָד — הִלְכָּךְ שְׁנֵיהֶם פְּסוּלִין. הַכֹּל פּוֹתְרִין אוֹתָהּ בְּשִׁיטָּה אַחֶרֶת, שֶׁכָּל הָעֵדִים חָתְמוּ כָּל אֶחָד שְׁמוֹ וְשֵׁם אָבִיו בְּשִׁיטָּה אַחַת מִתַּחַת רִאשׁוֹן לַשֵּׁנִי כְּמוֹ שֶׁפֵּירַשְׁתִּי, שְׁנֵי עֵדִים עִבְרִים וּשְׁנֵי עֵדִים יְוָנִים הַשְּׁנוּיִים רִאשׁוֹנָה בַּמִּשְׁנָה. וְאִי אֶפְשָׁר לְיַישְּׁבָהּ כְּלָל, וּמַתְנִיתִין לָא דַּיְיקָא הָכִי — דְּאִ"כ לָא מַשְׁכַּחַתְּ עִבְרִי חָתוּם עַל הַשֵּׁנִי. וּמַתְנִי' מִיפְלַג פַּלְגִינְהוּ עִבְרִי וְיוֹנִי לָזֶה וְעִבְרִי וְיוֹנִי לָזֶה, וּבַגְּמָ' נַמִּי פָּרֵיךְ: וְלִיתַּכְשַׁר הַאי בְּעֵד אֶחָד עִבְרִי וְעֵד אֶחָד יְווֹנִי, וְהַאי בְּעֵד אֶחָד עִבְרִי וְעֵד אֶחָד יְווֹנִי — אַלְמָא כָּל כַּמָּה דְּלָא אָמְרִינַן גּוּנְדָלִית חָתִים, הָוְיָא חֲתִימָה דִּידְהוּ עִבְרִי וְיוֹנִי עַל זֶה וְעִבְרִי וְיוֹנִי עַל זֶה. **מתני'** בַּדַּף הַשֵּׁנִי. שֶׁאֶצְלוֹ, כְּרוֹחַב הַמְּגִילָּה, שֶׁקּוֹרִין בִּלְשׁוֹנֵנוּ קוֹלוֹמ"ל. מִן הַצַּד. בַּגִּלָּיוֹן שֶׁל יָמִין הַגֵּט אוֹ בַּגִּלָּיוֹן הַשְּׂמָאלִי. אוֹ מֵאֲחוֹרָיו. בְּגֵט פָּשׁוּט, שֶׁתִּקְּנוּ עֵדָיו לִהְיוֹת בְּתוֹכוֹ. הִקִּיף. חִיבֵּר זֶה אֵצֶל זֶה, כְּמוֹ: אֵין מַקִּיפִין שְׁתֵּי חָבִיּוֹת (ב"מ דף לב.). שְׁנֵיהֶם פְּסוּלִין. שֶׁאֵין נִקְרִים הַחֲתִימָה לֹא עִם זֶה וְלֹא עִם זֶה. סוֹפוֹ שֶׁל זֶה בְּצַד סוֹפוֹ שֶׁל זֶה אֵת שֶׁהָעֵדִים נִקְרָאִין עִמּוֹ. שֶׁגַּג חֲתִימַת הָעֵדִים כְּלַפָּיו כְּדֶרֶךְ הַחוֹתְמִין — כָּשֵׁר. רֹאשׁוֹ שֶׁל זֶה בְּצַד סוֹפוֹ שֶׁל זֶה אֵת שֶׁהָעֵדִים נִקְרִין בְּסוֹפוֹ. שֶׁגַּג חֲתִימָה כְּלַפֵּי סוֹפוֹ, וְלֹא שֶׁרַגְלֵי חֲתִימָה כְּלַפֵּי רֹאשׁוֹ. וְכָךְ הָיוּ נְקִיֵּי הַדַּעַת. נוֹהֲגִין, שֶׁלָּשׁוֹן קַלָּה, לֹא הָיוּ חוֹתְמִין "עֵד", אֶלָּא: פְּלוֹנִי בֶּן פְּלוֹנִי. חֲנִיכָתוֹ. שֵׁם לְוַאי שֶׁל מִשְׁפָּחָה כּוּלָּהּ. **גמ'** וְנֵיחוּשׁ דִלְמָא תְּרֵי גִיטֵּי הָווּ. הַשִּׁיֵּיר מִקְצָת הַגֵּט וּכְתָבוֹ בַּדַּף הַשֵּׁנִי קָאֵי; דִּלְמָא תְּרֵי גִיטִּין הָווּ שְׁלֵמִים, וְהַשְּׂמָאלִי נִכְתַּב בְּגוֹבְהָהּ שֶׁל מְגִילָּה יוֹתֵר מִן הַיְמִינִי, עַד דְּאִיתְרַמּוּ עֵדִים דִּידֵיהּ, כְּלוֹמַר גְּמָרוֹ שֶׁל *)שֵׁנִי, כְּנֶגֶד הַתְחָלָתוֹ שֶׁל רִאשׁוֹן. זְמַן דְּקַמָּא. הַיְינוּ הַתְחָלָתוֹ, וְעֵדִים דְּבַתְרָא — הַיְינוּ סוֹפוֹ, כְּלוֹמַר שִׁיטּוֹת אַחֲרוֹנוֹת שֶׁהָעֵדִים חֲתוּמִין תַּחְתֵּיהֶן. וְגַזְיֵיהּ לִזְמַן דְּבַתְרָא וְעֵדִים דְּקַמָּא. חָתַךְ סוֹפוֹ שֶׁל רִאשׁוֹן שֶׁהָיָה שֶׁלּוֹ, מִפְּנֵי תְּנָאֵי שֶׁהָיָה בּוֹ, וְחָתַךְ רֹאשׁוֹ שֶׁל שֵׁנִי, וְהִשְׁוָוהוּ לִתְחִלָּתוֹ שֶׁל רִאשׁוֹן, וְכִוֵּון חֲתִיכַת סוֹפוֹ שֶׁל רִאשׁוֹן תֵּיבָה אֵצֶל תֵּיבָה שֶׁל שִׁיּוּר הַשֵּׁנִי, וּמְגָרְשָׁהּ בִּשְׁנֵי חֲלָאֵי גִיטִּין, וְהָעֵדִים לֹא עַל שֶׁלּוֹ חָתְמוּ. כְּשֶׁיֵּשׁ רֶיוַח מִלְּמַטָּה. גִּלָּיוֹן תַּחַת הָרִאשׁוֹן, דְּוַדַּאי לֹא נֶחְתַּךְ מִמֶּנּוּ כְּלוּם, דְּלֹא נִכְתַּב בּוֹ יוֹתֵר. וְדִלְמָא זְמַן דְּבַתְרָא מֵיגַז גַּזְיֵיהּ. שֶׁמָּא הַגֵּט שֶׁלּוֹ נִמְלַךְ מִלְּגָמְרוֹ, וּלְמַעְלָה הֵימֶנּוּ בְּגַלְדּוֹ הָיָה גֵּט אַחֵר כָּתוּב וְחָתוּם, וּכְשֶׁחָזַר וְנִמְלַךְ לְגָרְשָׁהּ — חָתַךְ עֶלְיוֹנוֹ שֶׁל שֵׁנִי, וְכִוֵּון תֵּיבָה אֵצֶל תֵּיבָה לִגְמוֹר גֵּט שֶׁלּוֹ. כְּשֶׁיֵּשׁ

*) פי' דהיינו שורה אחרונה

ודלמא בשמא דאבוה חתים. דיש לנו לתלות ולהכשיר כיון שחתם אביו תחת גט השני. **ודלמא** סימנא שוייה דהא רב צייר כו'. אע"ג דהתם בעו לאפקועי לשמייהו בדיסקי מעיקרא, כדאמר ב"גט פשוט" (ב"ב קסא:) וב"השולח" (לעיל לו.) — הכא יש להכשיר אע"ג דלא אפקע בשטר מעיקרא, כיון שחמו חתום תחת גט הראשון. **דהא** תנן גט שכתבו עברית ועדיו יונית וכו'. אבל מגופיה דמתני' לא מייתי, דקתני: את שהעדים הראשונים נקראים עמו כשר, ולא מפליג בין כתבו שוה לעדיו לאינו שוה — דאיכא לדחויי דבכתבו שוה לעדיו איירי. *‏**עד** אחד עברי ועד אחד יווני באין מתחת זה לתחת זה שניהם פסולין. פירש בקונטרס: על כל גט חתום עברי ויווני. ולפירושו נראה דגרסינן: עד אחד עברי ועד אחד יווני באין מתחת זה לתחת זה, ועד אחד עברי ואחד יווני באין מתחת זה לתחת זה — שניהם פסולים. ובגמ' גרים: וליתכשר האי בעד אחד עברי ועד אחד יווני, והאי בעד אחד עברי ועד אחד יווני. ועל אותן שמפרשים שמיירי שהעדים חותמים כדרכם כל חתימה בשיטה אחת — הקשה בקונטרס: א"כ לא משכחת עברי חתום על השני, ומתני' פלגינהו — עברי ויווני לזה ועברי ויווני לזה! ועוד, דבגמ' פריך: וליתכשר האי בעברי ויווני, והאי בעברי ויווני! ור"ת מפרש: שיש ליישב, שכל חתימה מכוונת בשיטה אחת, ולא גרסינן במתני' אלא: עד אחד עברי ועד אחד יווני, ועד אחד עברי ועד אחד יווני באין מתחת זה לתחת זה. ולא גרסינן: מתחת זה וכו' עד לסוף. ובגמ' נמי לא גרסינן אלא: ולתכשר האי בעד אחד עברי ועד אחד יווני, ותו לא. והכי פירושו: *לא מיבעיא אי לא חיישינן לגונדלית — דאז יש להכשיר שניהם, הראשון בשני עברים והשני בשני יוונים, אלא אפילו חיישינן לגונדלית, ואי אפשר להכשיר שניהם — קמא מיהא ליתכשר בעד אחד עברי [כדרכו], ואחד יווני [גונדלית]. והוה מצי למימר דקמא מיהא ליתכשר בכולהו, דכולהו קיימי עליה, אלא שלא הוצרך להכשיר הראשון אלא בעברי ויווני. ומשני, דתנא דידן דחייש לגונדלית פוסל שניהם, דחייש דלמא חתמו תלתא אחד, וחד אחד — עברי הראשון אקמא, ועברי השני ושני יוונים אשני, וחתם עברי השני גונדלית, או יווני הראשון חתם גונדלית אקמא עם שני עברים, ויווני האחרון אשני. **חתמו** עדים בראש הדף. וא"ת: אמאי איצטריך למתני סיפא הקיף ראשו של זה בצד ראשו של זה דשניהם פסולין? היינו בראש הדף! וי"ל: דאיצטריך למיפסל גגו של עדים כנגד גגו של כתב, למאי דמסקינן בגמ' דלא איירי ברמי כי עיברא, דמהכא לא שמעינן אלא שרגלי חתימת עדים כנגד גג הכתב. אע"פ דהא נמי שמעינן מסיפא — איכא למימר דאיצטריך הך דהכא משום דהוה אמינא: הך דשניהם פסולין היינו משום דכי היכי דלא קיימי אהאי לא קיימי נמי אהאי. אבל הכא, דאין כאן אלא גט א' — א"כ ודאי קיימא עליה חתימה זו. וסיפא דסיפא, דראשו של זה בצד סופו של זה, איצטריך לאשמעינן דלא פסלי מטעם דכי היכי דלא קיימי אהאי לא קיימי אהאי. ולרש"י דגרס מעיקרא: סופו של זה בצד סופו של זה — לא הוה צריך סיפא דסיפא, אלא דכל גווני משמיענו. ויש ספרים דלא גרסי לה, ובגמ' נמי לא מייתי לה. **וניחוש** דלמא תרי גיטי הוו. ולעיל נמי חיישינן לגונדלית ופסיל. אע"ג דלעיל תלינן להכשיר, דפריך: וליתכשר האי כו' — התם משום דאיכא רגלים לדבר שחתם שם אביו תחת הגט השני, אם כן עליו נמי חתם. הכא

...

... מנהגו ועושה מלאכתו בידו השמאלית: **מתני'** שייר מקצת הגט וכתבו בדף השני והעדים ... כתבו העדים בראש הדף מן הצד או מאחוריו בגט פשוט פסול הקיף ראשו של זה בצד ראשו ... באמצע שניהם פסולין ראשו של זה בצד סופו של זה והעדים מלמטה את שהעדים נקראים ב... שכתבו עברית ועדיו יונית יונית ועדיו עברית עד א' עברי ועד א' יוני עד א' יוני ועד א' ע... סופר ועד כשר איש פלוני עד כשר בן איש פלוני עד כשר איש פלוני בן פלוני ולא כתב עד ... נקיי הדעת שבירושלם כותבין כתב חניכתו וחניכתה כשר פי' חלק הגט לשני דפים לרוחב ה... הדף הימני ולא הספיק לכתוב בו כל הגט וכתב מקצתו הנשאר בדף השני השמאלי וחתמו העדים ... ולא אמרינן שאין העדים מעידין אלא על מה שכתוב בדף זה שחתמו תחתיו אלא על כל הגט מעידי... בראש הדף ואח"כ כתבו הגט תחת חתימת העדים פסול שדרך העדים לחתום למטה ומעידין ... למעלה וסתם מתניתין ר' מאיר הוא דאמר עדי חתימה כרתי. או שחתמו העדים מן הצד ש... ימין או בצד שמאל או שחתמו מאחריו של גט והיה גט פשוט פסול דמקושר חותמין העדים מאחו...

...ת הימני והשמאלי אין עליו עדים כלל ומשום זה הוא פסול. עד א' עברי וכו' שניהן פסולין ...יוני נמשכת חתימתן מתחת הימני לשמאל דהיינו שמם תחת הימני ושם אבותם תחת השמאלי ...משכת חתימתן מתחת השמאלי לתחת הימני א' עברי וא' יוני שחתם בשטר ראשונה ראובן בן ...ן תחת הימני בן יעקב תחת השמאלי וכן נפתלי בן דן שהיה יוני והוא חתום דן בן נפתלי ... לשמו נכתב בשיטה שניה דן בן תחת השמאלית ובשיטה שלישית תחת הימני שנמצא עכשיו ... ושם אביו תחת השמאלית ובשיטה הרביעית חתם יוסף בן שמעון שהוא עד עברי וכתב יוסף ...ת גט השמאלית ובן שמעון כתב בסוף שטה החמישית תחת גט הימני (ואשר תחת השמאלית ... אביו תחת הימני) ואשר בן גד יוני שהוא חתום גד בן אשר כתב בשיטה הששית גד בן תחת ...ת השמאלית שנמצא שמו תחת השמאלית ושם אביו תחת הימני ופוסל התנא את שתיהן. ...האי בעד א' עברי ועד א' יוני והאי בעד א' עברי ועד א' יוני דתנן עד א' עברי ועד א' יוני ... תני זעירי שניהן כשרים ותנא דידן דילמא גונדלית חתם חד מינייהו ולא ידעי הי ניהו והוו להו

הָכָא נַמִי – כְּשֶׁיֵּשׁ רֶיוַח מִלְמַעְלָה. וְדִלְמָא אִימְּלוּכֵי אִימְּלִיךְ וְכָתַב! דְּכָתַב "הֲרֵי אַתְּ" מִלְּמַטָּה וּ"מוּתֶּרֶת" מִלְמַעְלָה. וְדִלְמָא אִיתְרְמִי לֵיהּ! כּוּלֵּי הַאי לָא חָיְישִׁינַן. רַב אַשִׁי אָמַר: דִּידִיעָה בֵּיהּ מִתַּחְתָּא דִּמְגִילְּתָא.§ "חָתְמוּ עֵדִים בְּרֹאשׁ הַדַּף" [וכו'].§ אִינִי? וְהָא רַב חָתִים מִן הַצַּד! הָתָם בְּשֶׁגַּגּוֹ כְּלַפֵּי כְּתָב. אֶלָּא הָא דְּקָתָנֵי: הִקִּיף רֹאשׁוֹ שֶׁל זֶה בְּצַד רֹאשׁוֹ שֶׁל זֶה וְהָעֵדִים בָּאֶמְצַע – שְׁנֵיהֶם פְּסוּלִין, וְלֶיחֱזֵי הֵי מִינַּיְיהוּ כְּלַפֵּי כְּתָב וְלִיתַּכְשַׁר! הָתָם דִּרְמֵי לֵיהּ כְּעִיבְרָא. אִי הָכִי, סֵיפָא דְּקָתָנֵי: רֹאשׁוֹ שֶׁל זֶה בְּצַד סוֹפוֹ שֶׁל זֶה וְהָעֵדִים בָּאֶמְצַע, אֶת שֶׁהָעֵדִים נִיקְרִין בְּסוֹפוֹ – כָּשֵׁר; וְאִי דִּרְמֵי כְּעִיבְרָא, לָאו בַּהֲדֵי הַאי מִיקְּרֵי וְלָאו בַּהֲדֵי הַאי מִיקְּרֵי! אֶלָּא, רַב בְּדִיסְקֵי הֲוָה חָתֵים.§ "גֵּט שֶׁכְּתָבוֹ עִבְרִית וכו' כָּתַב סוֹפֵר וְעֵד – כָּשֵׁר".§ *א"ר יִרְמְיָה: חָתַם סוֹפֵר שָׁנִינוּ. א"ר חִסְדָּא: הָא מַנִּי? ר' יוֹסֵי הִיא. הַהִיא כְּתוּבַּת חֲתָנִים דְּאַתְיָא לְקַמֵּיהּ דְּר' אַבָּהוּ, דַּהֲווּ יָדְעִי לֵיהּ לְטוּפְסָא וְלַחֲתִימַת יְדָא דְּחַד סָהֲדָא, סָבַר לְאַכְשׁוּרַהּ, א"ל ר' יִרְמְיָה: חָתַם סוֹפֵר שָׁנִינוּ.§ "כָּתַב חֲנִיכָתוֹ וַחֲנִיכָתָהּ – כָּשֵׁר".§ ת"ר: חֲנִיכַת אָבוֹת בְּגִיטִּין – עַד י' דּוֹרוֹת; רַבִּי שִׁמְעוֹן בֶּן אֶלְעָזָר אוֹמֵר: ג' דּוֹרוֹת – כָּשֵׁר, מִכָּאן וְאֵילָךְ – פָּסוּל. כְּמַאן אָזְלָא הָא דְּא"ר חֲנִינָא: כָּתַב חֲנִיכַת אָבוֹת בְּגִיטִּין עַד ג' דּוֹרוֹת, (דברים ד) כְּמַאן? כְּר"ש ב"א. אָמַר רַב הוּנָא: מַאי קְרָאָה? °"כִּי תוֹלִיד בָּנִים וּבְנֵי בָנִים וְנוֹשַׁנְתֶּם". א"ר יְהוֹשֻׁעַ בֶּן לֵוִי: לֹא חָרְבָה אֶרֶץ יִשְׂרָאֵל עַד שֶׁעָבְדוּ בָּהּ ז' בָּתֵּי דִינִים ע"ז, וְאֵלּוּ הֵן: יָרָבְעָם בֶּן נְבָט, וּבַעְשָׁא בֶּן אֲחִיָּה, וְאַחְאָב בֶּן עָמְרִי, וְיֵהוּא בֶּן נִמְשִׁי, וּפֶקַח בֶּן רְמַלְיָהוּ, וּמְנַחֵם בֶּן גָּדִי, וְהוֹשֵׁעַ (ירמיה טו) בֶּן אֵלָה, שֶׁנֶּאֱמַר: °"אוּמְלְלָה יוֹלֶדֶת הַשִּׁבְעָה נָפְחָה נַפְשָׁהּ בָּאָה שִׁמְשָׁהּ בְּעוֹד יוֹמָם בּוֹשָׁה וְחָפֵרָה". אָמַר רַב אַמִי: *מַאי קְרָאָה? "כִּי תוֹלִיד בָּנִים וּבְנֵי בָנִים". א"ל רַב כָּהֲנָא וְרַב אַסִּי לְרַב: (מ"ב יז) כְּתִיב בֵּיהּ בְּהוֹשֵׁעַ בֶּן אֵלָה: °"וַיַּעַשׂ הָרַע בְּעֵינֵי (שם) ה' רַק לֹא כְּמַלְכֵי יִשְׂרָאֵל", וּכְתִיב: °"עָלָיו עָלָה שַׁלְמַנְאֶסֶר" וגו'! אָמַר לְהוּ: *אוֹתָן *פַּרְדֵּסִיאוֹת שֶׁהוֹשִׁיב יָרָבְעָם עַל הַדְּרָכִים כְּדֵי שֶׁלֹּא יַעֲלוּ יִשְׂרָאֵל לָרֶגֶל – בָּא הוֹשֵׁעַ וּבִיטְּלָן, וְאעפ"כ לֹא עָלוּ יִשְׂרָאֵל לָרֶגֶל, אָמַר הקב"ה: אוֹתָן שָׁנִים שֶׁלֹּא עָלוּ יִשְׂרָאֵל לָרֶגֶל יֵלְכוּ בַּשֶּׁבִי. *אָמַר רַב חִסְדָּא אָמַר מָר עוּקְבָא, וְאָמְרִי לָהּ אָמַר רַב חִסְדָּא [אָמַר רַבִּי יִרְמְיָה:] דָּרַשׁ מָרֵימָר, מַאי (דניאל ט) דִּכְתִיב: °"וַיִּשְׁקוֹד ה' עַל הָרָעָה וַיְבִיאֶהָ עָלֵינוּ כִּי צַדִּיק ה' אֱלֹהֵינוּ"? מִשּׁוּם דְּצַדִּיק ה' אֱלֹהֵינוּ וַיִּשְׁקוֹד ה' עַל הָרָעָה וַיְבִיאֶהָ עָלֵינוּ?! אֶלָּא, צְדָקָה עָשָׂה הַקָּדוֹשׁ בָּרוּךְ הוּא עִם יִשְׂרָאֵל שֶׁהִגְלָה גָּלוּת צִדְקִיָּהוּ וַעֲדַיִין (מ"ב כד) גָּלוּת יְכָנְיָה קַיֶּימֶת, דִּכְתִיב בֵּיהּ בְּגָלוּת יְכָנְיָה: °"הֶחָרָשׁ וְהַמַּסְגֵּר אָלֶף", חָרָשׁ – שֶׁבְּשָׁעָה שֶׁפּוֹתְחִין נַעֲשׂוּ הַכֹּל כְּחֵרְשִׁין, מַסְגֵּר – כֵּיוָן שֶׁסּוֹגְרִין (דברים ד) שׁוּב אֵינָן פּוֹתְחִין, וְכַמָּה? אָלֶף. עוּלָּא אָמַר: שֶׁהִקְדִּים שְׁתֵּי שָׁנִים °לְ"וְנוֹשַׁנְתֶּם".§

אמר

רש"י

כְּשֶׁיֵּשׁ רֶיוַח מִלְמַעְלָה. דְּוַדַּאי לֹא נִכְתַּב בּוֹ יוֹתֵר. וְדִלְמָא אִימְּלוּכֵי אִימְּלִיךְ. מִתְּחִלָּה שֶׁלֹּא לְגָרְשָׁהּ, וַהֲדַר אִימְּלִיךְ לְאַחַר זְמַן לַחֲזוֹר וּלְגוֹמְרוֹ, וְנִמְצָא הָרִאשׁוֹן בָּטֵל. א"נ: ה"ל נִכְתַּב בַּיּוֹם וְנֶחְתַּם לְאַחַר זְמַן, דְּהוֹאִיל וְיֵשׁ רֶיוַח מִלְּמַטָּה – נִרְאִין כֵּן הַדְּבָרִים. הֲרֵי אַתְּ מִלְּמַטָּה וּמוּתֶּרֶת מִלְמַעְלָה. דִּבְתוֹךְ כְּדֵי גְּמַר דִּבּוּר לֵיכָּא לְמֵימַר דְּמִימְלִיךְ, אֶלָּא גּוֹמֵר עַד "לְכָל אָדָם" וְנִמְלַךְ. וְדִלְמָא הָכִי אִיתְרְמִי. שֶׁבְּתוֹךְ כְּדֵי גְּמַר דִּבּוּר חָזַר בּוֹ. רַב אַשִׁי אָמַר. כּוּלְּהוּ קַשְׁיָיתָא בְּהָכִי מִיתָּרְצָן – כְּגוֹן דִּידִיעָה בֵּיהּ מִתַּחְתָּא דִּמְגִילְּתָא, שֶׁנִּיכָּר בָּהּ מְתִיחַת הַקְּלָף סָבִיב כָּל הַגֵּט, שֶׁלֹּא הָיָה בּוֹ קְלָף אֶלָּא זֶה לֹא לְמַעְלָה וְלֹא לְמַטָּה. שֶׁנִּיכָּר סְבִיבוֹת הַקְּלָף שָׁחוֹר וְעַד שֶׁלֹּא נָגַע שָׁם תַּעַר הַגַּלָּבִים, שֶׁדֶּרֶךְ עוֹשֵׂי קְלָפִים שֶׁקּוֹשְׁרִים אֲבָנִים סָבִיב לִמְתּוֹחַ הַקְּלָף וּמַתְחִילִין לְתַקְּנוֹ בְּסָמוּךְ. וּכְשֶׁאֵין רֶיוַח מִלְּמַטָּה עָסְקִינַן, דְּלֵיכָּא לְמִיפְרַךְ אִימְּלוּכֵי אִימְּלִיךְ. בְּשֶׁגַּגּוֹ. שֶׁל חֲתִימָה כְּלַפֵּי כְּתַב הַגֵּט, דְּהָאִי וַדַּאי עַל גֵּט זֶה חָתַם. וּמַתְנִי' בְּשֶׁרַגְלֵי הַחֲתִימָה כְּלַפֵּי כְּתַב הַגֵּט, דְּאִיכָּא לְמֵימַר שֶׁמָּא לְמַעְלָה מֵאוֹתָהּ חֲתִימָה הָיָה כָּתוּב שְׁטָר וְעָלָיו חָתְמוּ הָעֵדִים. לֶיחֱזֵי הֵי מִינַּיְיהוּ. גַּגּוֹ כְּלַפֵּי כְּתָב, וְלִיתַּכְשַׁר, דְּוַדַּאי עָלָיו חָתְמוּ! דְּקס"ד שֶׁהָעֵדִים חוֹתְמִין בְּרוֹחַב הַקְּלָף, כְּסֵדֶר כְּתַב הַגִּיטִּין. דִּרְמוּ לְהוּ כִּי עִיבְרָא. הָעֵדִי' מוּטָּלִין בֵּין שְׁנֵי הַגִּיטִּין כִּבְרִיחַ, רָאשֵׁי שִׁיטוֹת שֶׁל חֲתִימָה מְחַבְּרִין הַגִּיטִּין כִּבְרִיחַ הַדֶּלֶת שֶׁנִּמְשֶׁכֶת בַּאֲוִיר הַפֶּתַח – כָּךְ הֵן נִמְשָׁכִין בֵּין אֲוִיר שְׁנֵי הַגִּיטִּין. אֶלָּא רַב. כִּי חָתִים מִן הַצַּד – לֹא בְּגִיטִּין וְלֹא בִּשְׁטָרוֹת, אֶלָּא בְּדִיסְקֵי, כְּשֶׁהָיָה מַזְמִין אֲנָשִׁים לַדִּין לְפָנָיו וְהַסּוֹפֵר כּוֹתֵב לָהֶם אִיגֶּרֶת הַזְמָנָה בִּשְׁמוֹ, וְהוּא חוֹתֵם פְּעָמִים מִן הַצַּד, וְאֵין הַקְפָּדָה בְּכָךְ. חָתַם סוֹפֵר. עִם עֵד אֶחָד. שָׁנִינוּ. בְּמִשְׁנָתֵנוּ דְּכָשֵׁר, דַּהֲוָה לְהוּ ב' עֵדִים, וְאַשְׁמוּעִי' מַתְנִי' דְּלָא חָיְישִׁינַן לְמֵימַר הַבַּעַל לֹא צִוָּה שֶׁיַּחְתּוֹם הַסּוֹפֵר, אֶלָּא אָמַר לִשְׁנַיִם: "אִמְרוּ לְסוֹפֵר פְּלוֹנִי וְיִכְתּוֹב, וְלִפְלוֹנִי וּפְלוֹנִי וְיַחְתּוֹמוּ", וְחָשׁוּ הָנָךְ שְׁלוּחִין לְכִיסּוּפָא דְּסָפְרָא וְאַחְתְּמוּהוּ – לְהָא לָא חָיְישִׁינַן, כִּדְאוֹקְמִינַן בְּפֶרֶק "מִי שֶׁאֲחָזוֹ" (לעיל עב). הָא מַנִּי ר' יוֹסֵי הִיא. דְּאָמַר: מִילֵּי לָא מִימְסְרָן לְשָׁלִיחַ. דַּהֲווּ יָדְעֵי לְטוּפְסָא. דִּשְׁטָרָא, שֶׁהָיוּ מַכִּירִין כְּתִיבַת הַסּוֹפֵר וַחֲתִימַת עֵד אֶחָד, וְלֹא הָיוּ מַכִּירִין חֲתִימַת הַשֵּׁנִי. עַד י' דּוֹרוֹת. הָוְיָא חֲנִיכָה, שֶׁאִם כְּתָבָהּ בְּגֵט – לָא מִפַּסְלָא, לְמֶיהֱוֵי כְּשִׁינָּה שְׁמוֹ וּשְׁמָהּ. בָּנִים. הַיְינוּ דּוֹר ב'. וּבְנֵי בָנִים. הַיְינוּ דּוֹר ג', וּמִכָּאן וְאֵילָךְ קָרֵי לֵיהּ "וְנוֹשַׁנְתֶּם". ז' בָּתֵּי דִינִין. ז' מִשְׁפָּחוֹת שֶׁל מְלָכִים מִמַּלְכֵי יִשְׂרָאֵל. וְהָנָךְ דְּמַלְכֵי יְהוּדָה לָא חָשֵׁיב, שֶׁהָיוּ בִּימֵיהֶם שֶׁל אֵלּוּ, וְהָוֵי כְּב"ד אֶחָד. הַמֶּלֶךְ וּבְנוֹ וּבֶן בְּנוֹ וְכָל מְלָכִים שֶׁקָּמוּ מִזַּרְעוֹ אַחֲרָיו קָרֵי חַד בֵּית דִּין. שַׁלּוּם בֶּן יָבֵשׁ וּזְכַרְיָה לָא קָחָשֵׁיב, לְפִי שֶׁלֹּא מָלְכוּ שָׁנָה שְׁלֵמָה, וְכֵן זִמְרִי. אֲבָל עָמְרִי אָבִיו שֶׁל אַחְאָב – עַל שֵׁם בֵּית דִּינוֹ שֶׁל אַחְאָב נִקְרָא, וּמִפְּנֵי שֶׁאַחְאָב הִרְשִׁיעַ לַעֲשׂוֹת יוֹתֵר נִקְרָא הַקִּלְקוּל עַל שְׁמוֹ. בִּימֵי הוֹשֵׁעַ בֶּן אֵלָה גָּלוּ עֲשֶׂרֶת הַשְּׁבָטִים, וּמֵהַהִיא שַׁעְתָּא קָרֵי לָהּ חוּרְבָּן דְּהַיְינוּ "אוּמְלְלָה יוֹלֶדֶת הַשִּׁבְעָה" – שֶׁיָּלְדָה שֶׁבַע מִשְׁפָּחוֹת לַע"ז. עָלָיו עָלָה. מִפְּנֵי שֶׁלֹּא הִרְשִׁיעַ כִּשְׁאָר הַמְּלָכִים בָּא הַפּוּרְעָנִיּוֹת בְּיָמָיו? בִּתְמִיָּה. פַּרְדֵּסִיאוֹת. שׁוֹמְרִים. אוֹתָן שָׁנִים שֶׁלֹּא עָלוּ. הוֹאִיל שֶׁאֵין מוֹחֶה בְּיָדָם וְהֵן לֹא עָלוּ – יִגְלוּ וְיֵלְכוּ בַּשֶּׁבִי. וַיִּשְׁקוֹד. וַיְמַהֵר, כְּמוֹ: "כִּי שׁוֹקֵד אֲנִי עַל דְּבָרִי" מְתַרְגְּמִינַן: מוֹחֵי אֲנָא (ירמיה א). גָּלוּת צִדְקִיָּהוּ. חָרְבוֹת יְרוּשָׁלַיִם, שֶׁגָּלוּ כּוּלָּם. גָּלוּת יְכָנְיָה. הוּא יְהוֹיָכִין, קָדְמָה לְגָלוּת צִדְקִיָּהוּ אַחַת עֶשְׂרֵה שָׁנָה. וְזוֹ הִיא צְדָקָה, שֶׁמִּיהֵר וְהֶחֱרִיב בֵּיתוֹ כְּדֵי לְהַגְלוֹת דּוֹרוֹ שֶׁל צִדְקִיָּה לְבָבֶל בְּעוֹד שֶׁחַכְמֵי גָּלוּת יְכָנְיָה קַיָּימִין, שֶׁיְּלַמְּדוּ תּוֹרָה לָאֵלּוּ הַגּוֹלִים אַחֲרֵיהֶם. לְפִי שֶׁרוֹב חַכְמֵי הַתּוֹרָה גָּלוּ עִם יְכָנְיָה, דִּכְתִיב בְּהוּ: "הֶחָרָשׁ וְהַמַּסְגֵּר אָלֶף". כֵּיוָן שֶׁסּוֹגְרִין. הֲלָכָה שֶׁהֵם סְגוּרִים בָּהּ, שֶׁאֵינָם יוֹדְעִים לְהָשִׁיב לְשׁוֹאֲלֵיהֶם – שׁוּב אֵין לָהּ פּוֹתְחִין אֲחֵרִים. עוּלָּא אָמַר. הַיְינוּ צְדָקָה, שֶׁמִּיהֵר לְהָבִיא הָרָעָה לְסוֹף ח' מֵאוֹת וַחֲמִשִּׁים, דְּהַיְינוּ ב' שָׁנִים קוֹדֶם "וְנוֹשַׁנְתֶּם" דְּהִיא בְּגִימַטְרִיָּא ח' מֵאוֹת וַחֲמִשִּׁים וּשְׁתַּיִם. וְאִם שָׁהוּ עַד "וְנוֹשַׁנְתֶּם" – הָיָה מִתְקַיֵּים בָּהֶן "כִּי אָבֹד תֹּאבֵדוּן".

ש"מ

תוספות

הכא נמי כשיש ריוח מלמעלה. מיכן יש להכשיר גיטין ושטרות שאין בהן ריוח כלל, לא למעלה ולא למטה. וכן משמע כולה שמעתין דריש "גט פשוט" (ב"ב דף קסג.). ואמר ה"ר אלחנן: דאפ"ה לא חיישינן שמא יחתוך בעל השטר מן השיטין של מעלה, לפי שהזמן וכל זכות בעל השטר הוא למעלה, ולא יחתוך זכותו. **ודלמא** אימלוכי אימליך. פי' בקונטרס: שביטלו, ושוב אינו יכול לחזור לגרש בו. ואין נראה, °דלר"נ דאמר חוזר ומגרש בו, מאי איכא למימר? ומיהו, אמר ה"ר עזרא הנביא: דלעיל שנגמר הגט – אינו יכול לבטלו, אבל כשלא נכתב כולו – מודה ר"נ דאינו חוזר ומגרש בו. ועוד פי': דה"ל כמו נכתב ביום ונחתם בלילה. ואין נראה, כי העדים ודאי יזהרו שלא יחתמו על שטר מוקדם. ואור"י: דנראה לפרש ודלמא אימלוכי כו' – דשמא התחיל לכתוב הגט לשם איש אחר, ונמלך וסיימו לשם זה, וכגון ששמותיהן שוין, וכר' אלעזר דלא בעי מוכיח מתוכו. א"נ, אפי' כר"מ, ואימליך קודם שם האיש והאשה.

כולי האי לא חיישי'. היינו דוקא לאמליך בין "הרי את" ל"מותרת" לא חיישי', אבל מ"מ בעינן שיהא ריוח למעלה ולמטה. דאי לאו הכי – חיישינן דלמא גייז ליה, ואיתרמי דהוי "הרי את" מלמטה ו"מותרת" למעלה.

אמר רבי ירמיה חתם סופר שנינו. משמע דהלכה כר' ירמיה, מדמייתי מרבי ירמיה ההא עובדא – משמע דהכי קי"ל: חתם סופר ועד כשר בשאר שטרות, וכתב סופר ועד – פסול אפילו בסופר מובהק, ודלא כשמואל דהכשיר כתב סופר מובהק ועד ולכתחילה, אפילו בגיטין. ומ"מ, אין להכשיר חתם סופר ועד בגיטין מכח רבי ירמיה, דהא לכל אמוראי בסוף פ' "התקבל" (לעיל סו:) דמכשרי באומר "אמרו" יש לפסול חתם סופר ועד משום דנפיק מיניה חורבה, כדאמר התם.

*__וכך__ היו נקיי הדעת שבירושלים כותבין. שלא היו כותבין אלא "איש פלוני בן פלוני". ור"ח, וכן ר"ת גרסי: חניכתו וחניכתה – כשר, וכך היו נקיי הדעת שבירושלים כותבין. פירוש: שלא היו כותבין אלא חניכתם וחניכת אבות. דבגמרא לא איירי בחניכת האיש כדהכא, אלא חניכה שהמשפחה נקראת על שמה.

[**מאי** קראה. "כי תוליד" – חד דור, "בנים" – תרי דור, "ובני – תרי דור", "בנים" – תרי דור, הרי ז']. גליון תוס'.

שמע

תוספות רי"ד

אבל גט פשוט צריך שיהו עדיו מתוכו: הקיף ראשו של זה בצד ראשו של זה שסמך שני ראשי הגט זה אצל זה שהתחיל לכתוב גט א' מאמצע המגילה ועד סופה ועוד כתב גט אחר באמצע המגילה ועד סופה השני והעדים חתמו בין שני הראשים שניהם פסולין שאין החתימה עולה לאחד מהם. ראשו של זה בצד סופו של זה והעדים מלמטה את שהעדים נקראין בסופו דהיינו התחתון כשר אבל העליון פסול ולא תימא עדים אתרווייהו מסהדי: כתב הסופר ועד כשר. א"ר ירמיה חתם סופר שנינו. פי' חתם סופר עם עד אחד שנינו דכשר. ואשמעינן מתני' דלא חיישינן שמא הבעל לא צוה שיחתום הסופר אלא אמר לשנים אמרו לסופר פלוני ויכתוב ולפלוני ופלוני ויחתומו וחשו הנך שלוחין לכיסופא דספרא וחתמוהו להא לא חיישינן כדאוקימנא בפ' מי שאחזו דהא מני ר' יוסי היא דאמר מילי לא מימסרן לשליח והבעל בעצמו צריך לומר לסופר לכתוב ולעדים לחתום ולא שישלח להם ע"י שליח הלכך ליכא למיחש להכי: ההוא כתובת חתנים דאתאי לקמיה דר' אבהו דהוה ידע ליה לטופסא דשטרא ולחתימת ידא דחד שהדא. פי' היתה האשה צריכה לקיים חתימות הכתובה והיו מכירים העדים כתיבת טופס השטר שהוא של סופר פלוני וגם חתימת עד אחד. סבר לאכשורה כדתנן כתב הסופר ועד כשר. אלמא כתיבת הסופר כחתימת עד אחד דמיא. א"ל ר' ירמיה חתם סופר שנינו אבל כתיבת השטר לא מהניא מידי. איש פלוני עד כשר. אע"פ שלא כתב פלוני בן פלוני או אם כתב בן איש פלוני עד כשר אע"פ שלא הזכיר שמו או שכתב פלוני בן פלוני ולא כתב עד כשר וכן היו נקיי הדעת שבירושלם כותבין בלשון קצרה ולא היו כותבין עד: כתב חניכתו וחניכתה כשר פי' כגון שכתב אנא ראובן בר פלוני פטרית יתיכי רחל בת פלונית ואותו פלוני אינו לא אביו ולא אביה אלא אחד גדול ממשפחתו שהיו מתיחסין עליו כגון אברהם בן עזרא משה בן עזרא שלא היה שם אביהם עזרא אלא כך היו מתיחסין כולן על שם עזרא גם זה כתב בן פלוני ואותו פלוני לא היה אביו אלא זקן זקנו או יותר רחוק ונתייחס עליו כשר הוא והאי בן לאו דוקא. ולא אמרי' כיון שלא היה שם אביו כך ולא שם אביה כך הוה ליה שינה שמו ושמה והגט פסול. אלא אמרינן דרך בני אדם להתייחס על שם גדול משפחתם ואע"פ שאינו אביו מתייחס על שמו. ת"ר חניכת אבות בגיטין עד עשרה דורות ר' שמעון בן אלעזר אומר עד שלשה דורות כשר מכאן ואילך פסול. פי' ת"ק סבר אע"פ שאותו הגדול שנתייחס עליו הוא רחוק ממנו עשרה דורות כשר הוא ור' שמעון בן אלעזר סבר עד שלשה דורות כשר מכאן ואילך הוה ליה שינה שמו ושמה ופסול. כמאן אזלא הא דא"ר חנינא חניכת אבות בגיטין עד שלשה דורות כמאן כר' שמעון בן אלעזר: אמר רב הונא מאי קראה כי תוליד בנים ובני בנים ונושנתם בארץ פי' אלמא עד שלשה דורות מתיישנים ומשתכחים הראשונים:

מתני'

עין משפט נר מצוה

עג א מיי' פ"ד מהל' גירושין הל' כ סמג עשין נ טוש"ע אה"ע סי' קל סעיף ז:

עד ב מיי' פ"ט שם הל' כז סמג שם טוש"ע שם סעיף יח:

מסורת הש"ס

[לעיל סו: עח.]

[ע' רש"י ות"א ודע שבילקוט לאוהי בנים תרין ובני בנים תרין ונושנתם והושיתם ועשיתם]

הרי כאן שבעה [תענית ל: ב"ב קכא:]

סנהדרין לח.

[שייך למשנה דלעיל פז:]

[גי' הערוך פרוזדאות וע' תענית כח. והוסיף פרוזלאות כו']

גליון הש"ס

תוס' ד"ה ודלמא כו' דלר"נ דאמר חוזר. לעיל דף לב ע"ב:

עה א מיי' פ"ב מהלכות גירושין הל' כ סמג עשין נ טוש"ע אה"ע סי' קלד סעיף ח:
עו ב מיי' שם טוש"ע שם סעיף ח:
עז ג מיי' שם טוש"ע שם סעיף ט:
עח ד מיי' שם טוש"ע שם סעיף ח:
עט ה מיי' שם טוש"ע שם סעיף ח:
פ ו מיי' פכ"ג מהלכות סנהדרין הל' א סמג עשין קז טוש"ע ח"מ סי' כו סעי' א:
פא ז מיי' שם פ"ה הל' ח טוש"ע ח"מ סי' א סעיף ח וטוש"ע אה"ע סי' [illegible] סעי' א:
פב ח מיי' שם הל' ט טוש"ע ח"מ סי' א סעי' א:

בירושלמי איתא: שעשה כמעשה עובד כוכבים כו' שעשו כמעשה ישראל

פג ט מיי' פ"ט מהל' גירושין הל' כב ופי"ז מהל' איסורי ביאה הל' כ סמג עשין מח טוש"ע אה"ע סי' [illegible]:

[וע' היטב תוס' ב"ב מח. ד"ה גט מעושה]

פד י מיי' פ"ט מהלכות גירושין הל' כב ופי"ז מהל' איסורי ביאה הל' כ סמג עשין מח טוש"ע אה"ע סי' ו סעיף ה וסי' מו סעיף ו:

[וע"ע תוס' סנהדרין ב: ד"ה ליבעי וכו']

אָמַר רַב אַחָא בַּר יַעֲקֹב: שְׁמַע מִינַּהּ, "מְהֵרָה" דְּמָרֵי עָלְמָא – תְּמָנֵי מֵאָה וְחַמְשִׁין וְתַרְתֵּי הוּא.§

מתני' *אגֵּט מְעוּשֶּׂה, בְּיִשְׂרָאֵל – כָּשֵׁר, בוּבַגּוֹיִם – פָּסוּל; וּבַגּוֹיִם, גחוֹבְטִין אוֹתוֹ וְאוֹמְרִים לוֹ: עֲשֵׂה מַה שֶּׁיִּשְׂרָאֵל אוֹמְרִים לְךָ (וְכָשֵׁר).§

גמ' אָמַר ר"נ אָמַר שְׁמוּאֵל: גֵּט הַמְעוּשֶּׂה בְּיִשְׂרָאֵל, כַּדִּין – כָּשֵׁר, דשֶׁלֹּא כַּדִּין – פָּסוּל וּפוֹסֵל; הוּבַגּוֹיִם, כַּדִּין – פָּסוּל וּפוֹסֵל, שֶׁלֹּא כַּדִּין – אֲפִי' רֵיחַ הַגֵּט אֵין בּוֹ. מַה נַּפְשָׁךְ? אִי גּוֹיִם בְּנֵי עַשּׂוּיֵי נִינְהוּ, אִיתַּכְשׁוּרֵי נַמִי לִיתַּכְשַׁר! אִי לָאו בְּנֵי עַשּׂוּיֵי נִינְהוּ, מִיפְסָל לָא לִיפְּסֵל! *אָמַר רַב מְשַׁרְשְׁיָא: דְּבַר תּוֹרָה גֵּט מְעוּשֶּׂה בַּגּוֹיִם כָּשֵׁר, וּמַה טַּעַם אָמְרוּ פָּסוּל? שֶׁלֹּא תְּהֵא כָּל אַחַת וְאַחַת הוֹלֶכֶת וְתוֹלָה עַצְמָהּ בְּגוֹי, וּמַפְקַעַת עַצְמָהּ מִיַּד בַּעְלָהּ. אִי הָכִי, שֶׁלֹּא כַּדִּין אֲפִי' רֵיחַ הַגֵּט אֵין בּוֹ?! וְנֶהֱוֵי (א) שֶׁלֹּא כַּדִּין כְּיִשְׂרָאֵל, וּמִפְסִיל נַמִי לִפְסוֹל! אֶלָּא, הָא דְּרַב מְשַׁרְשְׁיָא *בְּדוּתָא הִיא. וְטַעְמָא מַאי? כַּדִּין בְּכַדִּין דְּיִשְׂרָאֵל מִיחֲלַף, שֶׁלֹּא כַּדִּין בְּכַדִּין יִשְׂרָאֵל לָא מִיחֲלַף.§ אַבַּיֵּי אַשְׁכְּחֵיהּ לְרַב יוֹסֵף דְּיָתֵיב וְקָא מְעַשֶּׂה אַגִּיטֵּי, א"ל: וְהָא אֲנַן הֶדְיוֹטוֹת אֲנַן, וְתַנְיָא, *הָיָה ר"ט אוֹמֵר: וכָּל מָקוֹם שֶׁאַתָּה מוֹצֵא אָגוֹרִיאוֹת שֶׁל גּוֹיִם, אע"פ שֶׁדִּינֵיהֶם כְּדִינֵי יִשְׂרָאֵל, אִי אַתָּה רַשַּׁאי לְהִיזָּקֵק לָהֶם, שֶׁנֶּאֱמַר: °"וְאֵלֶּה הַמִּשְׁפָּטִים אֲשֶׁר תָּשִׂים לִפְנֵיהֶם" (שמות כא), "לִפְנֵיהֶם" וְלֹא לִפְנֵי גּוֹיִם, דָּבָר אַחֵר: "לִפְנֵיהֶם" – וְלֹא לִפְנֵי הֶדְיוֹטוֹת! א"ל: יאֲנַן שְׁלִיחוּתַיְיהוּ קָא עָבְדִינַן, מִידֵּי דַּהֲוָה אַהוֹדָאוֹת וְהַלְוָאוֹת. *אִי הָכִי, גְּזֵילוֹת וַחֲבָלוֹת נַמִי! חכִּי עָבְדִינַן שְׁלִיחוּתַיְיהוּ – בְּמִילְּתָא דִּשְׁכִיחָא, בְּמִילְּתָא דְּלָא שְׁכִיחָא – לָא עָבְדִינַן שְׁלִיחוּתַיְיהוּ.§

מתני' טיָצָא שְׁמָהּ בָּעִיר מְקוּדֶּשֶׁת – הֲרֵי זוֹ מְקוּדֶּשֶׁת, מְגוֹרֶשֶׁת – הֲרֵי זוֹ מְגוֹרֶשֶׁת, וּבִלְבַד שֶׁלֹּא יְהֵא שָׁם אֲמַתְלָא. אֵיזוֹ הִיא אֲמַתְלָא? גֵּירֵשׁ אִישׁ פְּלוֹנִי אֶת אִשְׁתּוֹ עַל תְּנַאי, זָרַק לָהּ קִידּוּשֶׁיהָ סָפֵק קָרוֹב לָהּ סָפֵק קָרוֹב לוֹ – זוֹ הִיא אֲמַתְלָא.§

גמ' וְאָסְרִינַן לָהּ אַגַּבְרָא? וְהָא *אָמַר רַב אַשִׁי: כָּל קָלָא דְּבָתַר נִישּׂוּאִין – לָא חָיְישִׁינַן לֵיהּ! יה"ק: יָצָא שְׁמָהּ בָּעִיר מְקוּדֶּשֶׁת, מְקוּדֶּשֶׁת וּמְגוֹרֶשֶׁת – הֲרֵי

רש"י

ש"מ מְהֵרָה דְּמָרֵי עָלְמָא. כְּמִנְיַן "וְנוֹשַׁנְתֶּם", דְּהָא כְּתִיב "כִּי אָבֹד תֹּאבֵדוּן מַהֵר". **מתני'** מְעוּשֶּׂה. בְּחָזְקָה. **גמ'** כַּדִּין. כְּגוֹן הָנָךְ דְּאָמְרִינַן בְּהוּ: יוֹצִיא וְיִתֵּן כְּתוּבָּה, אוֹ שֶׁהָיְתָה אֲסוּרָה לוֹ. פָּסוּל. לְהַתִּירָהּ לִינָּשֵׂא. וּפוֹסֵל. מִן הַכְּהוּנָּה, מִשּׁוּם רֵיחַ הַגֵּט. מַה נַּפְשָׁךְ. דְּקָאָמְרַתְּ בַּגּוֹיִם כַּדִּין פָּסוּל וּפוֹסֵל. אִי גּוֹיִם בְּנֵי עַשּׂוּיֵי. דְּדִין תּוֹרָה נִינְהוּ, לָכוֹף אֶת יִשְׂרָאֵל כַּדִּין. תּוֹלָה עַצְמָהּ בְּגוֹי. שׂוֹכֶרֶת גּוֹי אַנָּס לָכוֹף בַּעְלָהּ לְגָרְשָׁהּ, וּבָאָה עָלָיו בַּעֲקִיפִין. מִיפְסָל נַמִי לִיפָּסֵל. כְּשֶׁלֹּא כַּדִּין דְּיִשְׂרָאֵל, הוֹאִיל וּמִדְּאוֹרַיְיתָא בְּנֵי עַשּׂוּיֵי נִינְהוּ כְּיִשְׂרָאֵל, וְהָא גַּבֵּי יִשְׂרָאֵל אָמְרַתְּ שֶׁלֹּא כַּדִּין פָּסוּל וּפוֹסֵל! בְּדוּתָא הִיא. דְּוַדַּאי לָאו בְּנֵי עַשּׂוּיֵי נִינְהוּ. כַּדִּין. דְּגוֹיִם, גּוֹיִם שֶׁעִישּׂוּהוּ לְהוֹצִיא, וּבְדִין תּוֹרָה אע"ג דְּלָאו גִּיטָּא הוּא – גְּזוּר בֵּיהּ רַבָּנַן לִפְסוֹל בִּכְהוּנָּה, מִשּׁוּם דְּמִיחֲלַף בְּכַדִּין דְּיִשְׂרָאֵל, וְאָתֵי לְמֵימַר יִשְׂרָאֵל נַמִי שֶׁעִישּׂוּהוּ כַּדִּין – לָא פָּסֵיל, וְהַהוּא גִּיטָּא מְעַלְּיָא הוּא. שֶׁלֹּא כַּדִּין. דְּגוֹיִם בְּכַדִּין דְּיִשְׂרָאֵל לָא מִיחֲלַף. וְאִי אָמְרַתְּ מִיחֲלַף בְּשֶׁלֹּא כַּדִּין דְּיִשְׂרָאֵל, וְאָתֵי לְמֵימַר שֶׁלֹּא כַּדִּין דְּיִשְׂרָאֵל נַמִי לָא פָּסֵיל, וַאֲמַרַן לְעֵיל דְּפָסֵיל – הִיא גּוּפָהּ גְּזֵירָה הִיא, אַטּוּ כַּדִּין, וּגְזֵירָה לִגְזֵירָה לָא גָּזְרִינַן. וְקָא מְעַשֶּׂה אַגִּיטֵּי. כּוֹפֶה אִישׁ לְהוֹצִיא אֶת אִשְׁתּוֹ כַּדִּין. הֶדְיוֹטוֹת אֲנַן. שֶׁאֵין מוּמְחִין אֶלָּא סְמוּכִין, דְּמִיקְרוּ "אֱלֹהִים" = דַּיָּינִין, וְאֵין סְמִיכָה בְּח"ל, כִּדְאָמְרִי' בְּפ"ק דְּסַנְהֶדְרִ' (דף יד.). אוֹגְרִיאוֹת. אֲסֵיפוֹת, כְּמוֹ: "אוֹגֵר בַּקַּיִץ" (משלי י). לִפְנֵיהֶם. קָאֵי אַשִּׁבְעִים זְקֵנִים שֶׁעָלוּ עִמּוֹ לָהָר קוֹדֶם מַתַּן תּוֹרָה, כִּדְכְתִיב (שמות כד): "וְאֶל מֹשֶׁה אָמַר עֲלֵה" וגו'. וְאע"פ שֶׁנִּכְתְּבָה פָּרָשָׁה זוֹ לְאַחַר מ"ת – קוֹדֶם מַתַּן תּוֹרָה נֶאֶמְרָה, וְנִבְנָה הַמִּזְבֵּחַ, וְהֶעֱלוּ הָעוֹלָה וְהַשְּׁלָמִים, וּבְאוֹתוֹ דָּם נִכְנְסוּ לַבְּרִית. שְׁלִיחוּתַיְיהוּ. דִּבְנֵי א"י. קָעָבְדִינַן. הֵם נָתְנוּ לָנוּ רְשׁוּת. מִידֵּי דַּהֲוָה. אַדִּינֵי מָמוֹנוֹת דְּהַלְוָאוֹת, דְּעָבְדִינַן שְׁלִיחוּתַיְיהוּ, כִּדְאָמְרִי' בְּסַנְהֶדְ' (דף ג.). אִי הָכִי גְּזֵלוֹת וַחֲבָלוֹת נַמִי. לַעֲבֵיד שְׁלִיחוּתַיְיהוּ, וַאֲנַן אָמְרִינַן בִּשְׁמַעְתָּא קַמַּיְיתָא דְּסַנְהֶדְ' דְּבָעֵינַן ג' מוּמְחִין. מִילְּתָא דִּשְׁכִיחָא. הַלְוָאָה וְכֵן גֵּט. **מתני'** יָצָא שְׁמָהּ בָּעִיר מְקוּדֶּשֶׁת. פְּנוּיָה שֶׁיָּצָא עָלֶיהָ קוֹל: פְּלוֹנִית מִתְקַדֶּשֶׁת הַיּוֹם לִפְלוֹנִי, וְיֵשׁ דְּבָרִים נִרְאִין, כִּדְמְפָרְשִׁי אֲמוֹרָאֵי בַּגְּמָ'. הֲרֵי זוֹ מְקוּדֶּשֶׁת. וְלֹא תִּינָּשֵׂא לְאַחֵר בְּלֹא גֵּט. מְגוֹרֶשֶׁת הֲרֵי זוֹ מְגוֹרֶשֶׁת. קָא סָלְקָא דַּעְתִּין דְּהָכִי קָאָמַר: אֵשֶׁת כֹּהֵן שֶׁיָּצָא עָלֶיהָ קוֹל: פְּלוֹנִית נִתְגָּרְשָׁה הַיּוֹם – הֲרֵי זוֹ מְגוֹרֶשֶׁת, וַאֲסוּרָה לֵישֵׁב עוֹד תַּחְתָּיו. דְּאִילּוּ מְגוֹרֶשֶׁת לְהָקֵל וְלִינָּשֵׂא לַשּׁוּק – לֵיכָּא לְפָרוּשֵׁי, דְּמִשּׁוּם יְצִיאַת קוֹל נִשְׁרֵי אֵשֶׁת אִישׁ לְעָלְמָא? וְהַיְינוּ דְּפָרְכִינַן לָהּ בַּגְּמָרָא: וְאָסְרִי' לָהּ אַגַּבְרָא? עַל בַּעְלָהּ כֹּהֵן. וּבִלְבַד שֶׁלֹּא תְּהֵא שָׁם אֲמַתְלָא. שֶׁלֹּא יְהֵא עִם הַקּוֹל שֶׁל קִידּוּשִׁין אוֹ שֶׁל גֵּירוּשִׁין מָשָׁל וְטַעַם, שֶׁהוּא שׁוֹבֵר אֶת כֹּחַ הַקּוֹל. גֵּירֵשׁ פְּלוֹנִי אֶת אִשְׁתּוֹ עַל תְּנַאי. זֶהוּ שׁוֹבֵר שֶׁל גֵּירוּשִׁין, שֶׁמָּא לֹא נִתְקַיֵּים הַתְּנַאי. זָרַק לָהּ קִידּוּשֶׁיהָ כו'. זֶהוּ אֲמַתְלָא שֶׁל קִידּוּשִׁין, וְהוּא הַדִּין נַמִי אִיפְכָא. **גמ'** וְאָסְרִינַן לָהּ אַגַּבְרָא. בִּתְמִיהָ. וְאַמְּגוֹרֶשֶׁת קָאֵי, אֵשֶׁת כֹּהֵן שֶׁיָּצָא קוֹל שֶׁגֵּירְשָׁהּ בַּעְלָהּ קָתָנֵי מַתְנִי': חָיְישִׁינַן לְקָלָא וְאָסְרִי' עֲלֵי'. וְהָאָמַר רַב אַשִׁי כָּל קָלָא. שֶׁיָּצָא עַל הָאִשָּׁה מִשֶּׁנִּישֵּׂאת, וְלֹא יָצָא עָלֶיהָ קוֹל קוֹדֶם נִישּׂוּאִין. לָא חָיְישִׁינַן לֵיהּ. כְּגוֹן אִם נִשֵּׂאת לְכֹהֵן, וְיָצָא עָלֶיהָ קוֹל שֶׁהָיְתָה זוֹנָה אוֹ גְּרוּשָׁה – לֹא מַפְּקִינַן לָהּ מִינֵּיהּ אֶלָּא בְּעֵדוּת בְּרוּרָה, וְזוֹ נְשׂוּאָה וְעוֹמֶדֶת הִיא. ה"ק כו'. הַאי קוֹל דִּמְגוֹרֶשֶׁת אַרֵישָׁא קָאֵי, אִשָּׁה פְּנוּיָה שֶׁיָּצָא עָלֶיהָ קוֹל מְקוּדֶּשֶׁת – חָיְישִׁינַן לָהּ, וַאֲסוּרָה לִינָּשֵׂא אֶלָּא לְאוֹתוֹ אִישׁ. חָזַר וְיָצָא עָלֶיהָ קוֹל מְגוֹרֶשֶׁת, שֶׁגֵּירְשָׁהּ אוֹתוֹ פְּלוֹנִי שֶׁיָּצָא לָהּ קוֹל קִידּוּשִׁין מִמֶּנּוּ. הֲרֵי

תוספות

שמע מינה מהרה דמרי עלמא תמני מאה וחמשין ותרתי. וא"ת: נהי דמשנכנסו לארץ עד שגלו יש כל כך, מ"מ מאז לא עבדו ע"ז! ועוד הקשה ה"ר אלחנן: ודלמא תאבדו מהר אחר "ונושנתם" קאמר! ואור"י: דמתחילה מיד היו עובדי עבודה זרה, שפסלו של מיכה היה עמהם.

ובגוים חובטין אותו ואומרים לו עשה מה שישראל אומרים לך. אין לפרש דאפי' בענין זה, רוצה לומר דבגוים פסול משום "לפניהם" ולא לפני גוים, אע"פ דהגוים מעשין על פי ישראל – דאין זה לפני גוים, כיון דדייני ישראל מצוים לחובטו. דאטו מומחין עצמן יחבטו אותו, ולא יכלו לצוות להדיוט לחובטו? אלא כמו שפר"ת: והגוים חובטין אותו, שאז כשר בזה הענין. וכן פירש רב יהודאי גאון בהלכות גדולות, דבגוים כשר בזה הענין. וכן איתא בירושלמי דמכילתין, אמר רב: ישראל *שעושה כמעשה גוי – פסול (אפי') באומר "איני זן ואיני מפרנס". תני ר' חייא: גוים שעושין כמעשה ישראל – כשר, אפי' באומר "איני זן ואיני מפרנס". והאי דנקט אפי' [באומר] – דלא מתכשר בגוים שלא ע"פ ישראל, אע"ג דהוי כדין, אמר ר' אסי: מתני' אמרה כן: ובגוים חובטין אותו ואומרי' לו: עשה מה שישראל אומר לך, ולא מה שאנו אומרים לך*.

אלא דרב משרשי' בדותא היא. ב"ח"ה (ב"ב מח. ד"ה דבר) מפורש אמאי מייתי לה הש"ס התם, כיון דבדותא היא.

לפניהם ולא לפני הדיוטות. פי' בקונטרס: דקאי אשבעים זקנים דעלו עם משה, אע"פ שכתובין בסוף פ' "ואלה המשפטים". ור"י אומר דא"האלהים" טובא דכתיבי בפרשה קאי. וכן משמע ב"החובל" (ב"ק פד:) דמ"אלהים" נפקא לן מומחין, דאמר: מ"ש נזקי אדם באדם ונזקי אדם בשור – דאלהים בעינן, וליכא, ואיצטריך קרא ד"לפניהם" (ג) דלענין עישוי בעינן מומחין*.

ולא לפני הדיוטות. תימה: דמשמע דאיירי קרא בכשרים לדון, ואילו בפ"ק דקדושין (דף לה.) ובב"ק (ד' טו.) דרשינן מינה דהשוה הכתוב אשה לאיש לכל דינין שבתורה, ואשה פסולה לדון, דתנן בפ' "בא סימן" (נדה מט:): כל הכשר לדון – כשר להעיד, ואשה פסולה להעיד, כדמוכח ב"החובל" (ב"ק פח.) ובפרק "שבועת העדות" (דף ל.)! וי"ל: דכלל דפרק "בא סימן" באיש איירי, כלומר, כל איש הכשר לדון כשר להעיד. ומדבורה דכתיב בה (שופטים ד) "והיא שופטה את ישראל" – אין ראיה דאשה כשרה לדון, דשמא לא היתה דנה אלא היתה מלמדת להם הדינים. א"נ: שמא קיבלו אותה עליהם משום שכינה. מיהו, בירושלמי דיומא (פ"ו) יש: מעתה דאין אשה מעידה אינה דנה. ואומר ר"י: דקרא משמע ליה דאיירי בכל ענין, בין בדיינין בין בנדונין*).

אי הכי גזלות וחבלות נמי. וא"ת: והא מלינו בכמה מקומות שהיו דנין גזלות וחבלות: ההוא רעיא בפ"ק דבבא מציעא (דף ה.), וההוא גברא דגזל פדנא דתורי דחברי' (ב"ק דף צו:), ובכמה מקומות! וי"ל: דהיו דוחקין אותו ע"י דקבעיה ליה זימנא לא"י. ועוד אור"י: דגזלות ע"י חבלות קאמר, דאין דנין בבבל שחבל בחברו וגזל לו**).

במילתא דשכיחא כו'. כמו בהודאות והלואות. ומה שאנו מקבלים גרים, אע"ג דגר צריך ג' מומחין, כדאמרי' ב"החולץ" (יבמות מו:): משפט כתוב ביה, אור"י: דעבדינן שליחותייהו, דחשיב כשכיחא. וב"החולץ" (גו"ש) נמי משמע שהיו מקבלים גרים בבבל. וא"ת: היכי עבדינן שליחותייהו? והא עכשיו אין מומחין בא"י, ומי יתן לנו רשות! וי"ל: דשליחות דקמאי עבדינן.

והאמר רב אשי כל קלא דבתר נישואין כו'. וא"ת: ולוקמה בתר אירוסין, דחיישינן לרב אשי! וי"ל: דמשמע ליה מתני' אף בתר נישואין. ועוד: דפסקי' לקמן (דף פט:) דאף קלא דבתר אירוסין לא חיישינן.

אכלה

*) וע"ע תוס' ב"ק טו. ד"ה אשר ותוס' שבועות כט: ד"ה שבועות ותוס' יבמות מה: ד"ה מי לא ותוס' נדה נ. ד"ה כל הכשר] **) [וע"ע תוס' ב"ק פד: ד"ה א"נ]

[ב"ב מח.]
[ב"ב מח.]
[ע' מ"ש על הגליון סנהדרין יח.]
[בכתובות פ' ברכות איתא היה ר"מ אומר]
ב"ק פד:
לעיל פא. לקמן פט: יבמות לב.

תוספות רי"ד

מתני' גט מעושה בישראל כשר ובגוים פסול והגוים חובטים אותו ואומרים לו עשה מה שישראל אומרים לך. פי' גט מעושה שכופין אותו בחזקה כגון אלו שכופין אותו להוציא או שהיתה אסורה לו בישראל כשר והוא דאמר רוצה אני כדתנן בערכין בפ' האומר משקלי עלי חייבי עולות ושלמים ממשכנין אותו אע"פ שאינו מתכפר לו עד שיתרצה שנאמר לרצונו כופין אותו עד שיאמר רוצה אני. ואם מסר מודעא אההוא אונסא דקא עבדי ליה צריך לבטולה להההוא מודעא דגרסינן בההוא פרקא אמר רב ששת האי מאן דמסר מודעא אגיטא מודעיה מודעא. פשיטא לא צריכה דעשוה וארצי מהו דתימא בטולי בטליה קמ"ל דא"כ ליתני עד שיתן מאי עד שיאמר עד דמבטיל ליה למודעיה וכן נמי בזביני אע"ג דאמר רב הונא תליוה חבין זביניה זביני אי מסר מודעא עליהו לא הוו זביניה זביני עד דמבטיל ליה למודעא דהכי אמרינן בפ' חזקת הבתים טובי תלה לפפי אדינרא וזבין ליה ארעא חתם רבה בר בר חנה אמודעא ואשקלתא ואמר רב הונא אי לאו מודעא מאן דחתם אאשקלתא שפיר חתם רב הונא לטעמיה דאמר רב הונא תליוה חבין זביניה זביני. ואע"ג דאמר רבה לעיל בההוא פירקא לא כתבי' מודעא אזביני (ד)רב הונא לית ליה דרבה וסבירא ליה דוקא היכא דלא מסר מודעא אההוא אונסא הוא דהוו זביני אבל היכא דמסר עליהו מודעא לא הוו זביני. וכ"כ שם רבינו שמואל ז"ל וקי"ל כרב הונא דלית ליה דרבה דאמר לא כתבי' מודעא אזביני. ובגוים פסול משום דכתיב לפניהם ולא לפני הגוים. אבל גוים חובטין אותו ואומרים לו עשה מה שישראל אומר לך שאע"פ שהן מעשין כיון שעל פי ישראל עושין כשר. א"ר נחמן אמר שמואל גט מעושה בישראל כדין כשר שלא כדין פסול פי' אע"פ שאמר רוצה אני כיון דשלא כדין עישו אותו ואין כאן מצוה לשמוע דברי חכמים לא גמר ויהיב בכל לב ופוסל בתרומה משום ריח הגט. ובגוים כדין פסול ופוסל שלא כדין אפי' ריח הגט אין בו ומתמהינן מה נפשך אי גוים בני עשויי נינהו איתכשורי נמי

אתי לאיחלופי שלא כדין דגוים בכדין דישראל לא אתי לאיחלופי פי' הא דרב משרשיא דאמר דבר תורה אפילו דבגוים כשר ברותא היא אלא מדין תורה הוא פסול וטעמא דמילתא כדאמרינן בפרק חזקת הבתים דהיכא אמרינן גמר ומקנה דוקא בחייבי עולות ושלמים דניחא ליה דתיהוי ליה כפרה וגבי גט נמי דמצוה לשמוע דברי חכמים והלכך גמר ויהיב בכל לב אבל היכא דגוים אנסו ליה ואמר רוצה אני לא גמר ויהיב בכל לב אבל היכא דגוים אומרים לו עשה מה שישראל אומרי' לך מצוה לשמוע דברי חכמים הוא. ומשום הכי בישראל שלא כדין פסול דכיון דשלא כדין הוא אע"ג דאמר רוצה ויהיב בכל לב דהא אין מצוה לשמוע דבריהם ובזביני דאמרינן תליוה וזבין זביניה זביני משום דגמר ומקנה. וכן באשה נמי שנתקדשה באונס שכפוה עד דאמרה רוצה אני אמרי' התם הוא דאגב מתן מעות גמרה וקדישה נפשה. אבל היכא דליכא מתן מעות כגון תליוה ויהיב מתנה אין מתנתו מתנה דהא גבי סיקריקון דליכא מתן מעות אמר שמואל אף בשטר לא קנה והיכא דיהיב זוזי

שמואל

גמי לא לאתכשר אי לאו בני עשויי נינהו ליפסול נמי לא ליפסול. אמר רב משרשיא דבר תורה בגוים נמי כשר ומה טעם אמרו פסול שלא תהא כל אחת ואחת הולכת ותולה עצמה ביד גוי ומפקעת עצמה מיד בעלה. פי' הא דרב משרשיא דבר תורה אפילו בגוים נמי כשר וטעמא דמילתא כדאמרינן בפ' חזקת הבתים דאמר אגב אונסיה גמר ומקנה ואקשינן ליה אי הכי שלא כדין נמי אמאי אפילו ריח הגט אין בו ליהוי מיהת כשלא כדין בישראל פי' כיון דאמרינן אגב אונסיה גמר ומקנה אשתכח דניחא מעליא הוי ונהי דחכמים אמרו דליהוי פסול שלא תינשא בו אבל היאך יוכלו להכשירה לכהונה. ואסיקנא אלא הא משרשיא ברותא היא וטעמא מאי כדין דגוים בכדין דישראל

הגהות הב"ח (א) גמ' ונהוי כשלא כדין בישראל: (ב) תוס' ד"ה לפניהם וכו' לענין עישוי נ"ב עיין סנהדרין דף ב ע"ב תוס' ד"ה ליבעי דמלפניהם משמע ליה מילי דעשוי משום דדרשינן בפ"ק דסנהדרין מאשר תשים אלו כלי הדיינין דשייך בכן שימה ועיין תוס' בפ"ק דב"ק ד' טו:

הֲרֵי זוֹ מְגוֹרֶשֶׁת; מַאי טַעְמָא? קוֹל וְשׁוֹבְרוֹ עִמּוֹ. *אָמַר רָבָא: יָצָא לָהּ שֵׁם מְזַנָּה בָּעִיר – אאֵין חוֹשְׁשִׁין לָהּ; מ"ט? פְּרִיצוּתָא בְּעָלְמָא הוּא דַּחֲזוּ לָהּ. כְּתַנָּאֵי: אָכְלָה בַּשּׁוּק, גִּירְגְּרָה בַּשּׁוּק, הֵנִיקָה בַּשּׁוּק – בְּכוּלָּן ר"מ אוֹמֵר: תֵּצֵא, ר"ע אוֹמֵר: מִשֶּׁיִּשְּׂאוּ וְיִתְּנוּ בָּהּ *מוֹזְרוֹת בַּלְּבָנָה; אָמַר לוֹ רַבִּי יוֹחָנָן בֶּן נוּרִי: א"כ, *לֹא הִנַּחְתָּ בַּת לְאַבְרָהָם אָבִינוּ שֶׁיּוֹשֶׁבֶת תַּחַת בַּעְלָהּ, וְהַתּוֹרָה אָמְרָה: °"כִּי מָצָא בָהּ עֶרְוַת דָּבָר", וּלְהַלָּן הוּא אוֹמֵר: °"עַל פִּי שְׁנַיִם עֵדִים אוֹ עַל פִּי שְׁלֹשָׁה עֵדִים יָקוּם דָּבָר", *מַה לְּהַלָּן דָּבָר בָּרוּר, אַף כָּאן דָּבָר בָּרוּר!§ ת"ר: בבְּעוּלָה – אֵין חוֹשְׁשִׁין לָהּ, (א) נְשׂוּאָה – אֵין חוֹשְׁשִׁין לָהּ, אֲרוּסָה – אֵין חוֹשְׁשִׁין לָהּ, גשֶׁלֹּא לִפְלוֹנִי – אֵין חוֹשְׁשִׁין לָהּ, בְּעִיר אַחֶרֶת – אֵין חוֹשְׁשִׁין לָהּ, מַמְזֶרֶת – אֵין חוֹשְׁשִׁין לָהּ, דשִׁפְחָה – אֵין חוֹשְׁשִׁין לָהּ; ההִקְדִּישׁ פְּלוֹנִי נְכָסָיו, הִפְקִיר פְּלוֹנִי נְכָסָיו – אֵין חוֹשְׁשִׁין לָהֶן. אָמַר עוּלָּא: לֹא שֶׁשָּׁמְעוּ קוֹל הֲבָרָה, אֶלָּא כְּדֵי שֶׁיְּהוּ נֵרוֹת דּוֹלְקוֹת וּמִטּוֹת מוּצָּעוֹת, וּבְנֵי אָדָם נִכְנָסִין וְיוֹצְאִין וְאוֹמְרִים "פְּלוֹנִית מִתְקַדֶּשֶׁת הַיּוֹם". מִתְקַדֶּשֶׁת?! ווְדִלְמָא לָא אִקַּדְּשָׁה! זאֵימָא: "פְּלוֹנִית נִתְקַדְּשָׁה הַיּוֹם". וְכֵן תָּנֵי לֵוִי: לֹא שֶׁיִּשְׁמְעוּ קוֹל הֲבָרָה, אֶלָּא כְּדֵי שֶׁיְּהוּ נֵרוֹת דּוֹלְקוֹת וּמִטּוֹת מוּצָּעוֹת, וְנָשִׁים טוֹוֹת לְאוֹר הַנֵּר וּשְׂמֵחוֹת לָהּ, וְאוֹמְרוֹת "פְּלוֹנִית מִתְקַדֶּשֶׁת הַיּוֹם". מִתְקַדֶּשֶׁת?! וְדִלְמָא לָא אִקַּדְּשָׁה! א"ר פַּפָּא, אֵימָא: "פְּלוֹנִית נִתְקַדְּשָׁה הַיּוֹם". אָמַר רַבָּה בַּר בַּר חָנָה א"ר יוֹחָנָן: לֹא שֶׁשָּׁמְעוּ קוֹל הֲבָרָה, אֶלָּא כְּדֵי שֶׁיְּהוּ נֵרוֹת דּוֹלְקוֹת וּמִטּוֹת מוּצָּעוֹת וּבְנֵי אָדָם נִכְנָסִין וְיוֹצְאִין, אָמְרוּ דָּבָר – זֶה הוּא קוֹל, לֹא אָמְרוּ דָּבָר – זֶהוּ אֲמַתְלָא. לֹא אָמְרוּ?! וְהָא לֹא אָמְרוּ וְלֹא כְּלוּם! לְאַפּוּקֵי מִדְּרַבָּה בַּר רַב הוּנָא, דְּאָמַר: אֲמַתְלָא שֶׁאָמְרוּ – אֲפִי' מִכָּאן וְעַד י' יָמִים, חקמ"ל: לֹא אָמְרוּ הוּא דְּהָוְיָא אֲמַתְלָא, הָא אָמְרוּ – לָא הָוְיָא אֲמַתְלָא. א"ר אַבָּא אָמַר רַב הוּנָא אָמַר רַב: לֹא שֶׁשָּׁמְעוּ קוֹל הֲבָרָה, אֶלָּא כְּדֵי שֶׁיֹּאמְרוּ: פְּלוֹנִי מֵהֵיכָן שָׁמַע? מִפְּלוֹנִי, וּפְלוֹנִי מִפְּלוֹ', וּבוֹדְקִין וְהוֹלְכִין עַד שֶׁמַּגִּיעִין לַדָּבָר הַבָּרוּר. דָּבָר הַבָּרוּר, עֵדוּת מְעַלְּיָיתָא הוּא! אֶלָּא, כִּי אֲתָא רַב שְׁמוּאֵל בַּר יְהוּדָה, א"ר אַבָּא אָמַר רַב הוּנָא אָמַר רַב: לֹא שֶׁשָּׁמְעוּ קוֹל הֲבָרָה, טאֶלָּא כְּדֵי שֶׁיֹּאמְרוּ: פְּלוֹנִי מֵהֵיכָן שָׁמַע? מִפְּלוֹנִי, וּפְלוֹנִי מִפְּלוֹנִי, וְהָלְכוּ לָהֶם לִמְדִינַת הַיָּם. א"ל אַבַּיֵי לְרַב יוֹסֵף: מְבַטְּלִינַן קָלָא אוֹ לָא מְבַטְּלִינַן? א"ל: מִדְּאָמַר רַב חִסְדָּא: עַד שֶׁיִּשְׁמְעוּ מִפִּי הַכְּשֵׁרִים, ש"מ: ימְבַטְּלִינַן קָלָא. א"ל: אַדְּרַבָּה, מִדְּאָמַר רַב שֵׁשֶׁת: אֲפִי' מִפִּי נָשִׁים הָוֵי קוֹל, כש"מ: לָא מְבַטְּלִינַן קָלָא! א"ל: אַתְרָוָותָא נִינְהוּ, בְּסוּרָא מְבַטְּלֵי קָלָא, *בִּנְהַרְדְּעָא לָא מְבַטְּלֵי קָלָא. הַהִיא דִּנְפַק עֲלָהּ קָלָא דְּאִיקַּדְּשָׁה *לְבַר בֵּי רַב, אָתְיֵיהּ רַב חָמָא לַאֲבוּהּ, אֲמַר לֵיהּ: אֵימָא לִי הֵיכִי הֲוָה עוֹבְדָא? אֲמַר לֵיהּ: עַל תְּנַאי קַדֵּישׁ, אַדַּעְתָּא דְּלָא אָזֵיל לְבֵי חוֹזַאי, וַאֲזַל. א"ל: כֵּיוָן דִּבְעִידָּנָא דַּהֲוַאי קָלָא לָא הֲוַאי אֲמַתְלָא, לָאו כֹּל כְּמִינָּךְ דְּמַחְזְקַתְּ אֲמַתְלָא. הַהִיא דִּנְפַק עֲלָהּ קָלָא דְּאִיקַּדְּשָׁה *בַּאֲצִיפָא דְּתוּחְלָא בְּעֵינָא דְּבֵי שִׁיפֵי, שְׁלָחָהּ רַב אִידִי בַּר אָבִין לְקַמֵּיהּ דְּאַבַּיֵי: כִּי הַאי גַּוְונָא מַאי? אֲמַר לֵיהּ: אֲפִי' לְמַאן דְּאָמַר לָא מְבַטְּלִינַן קָלָא, לבְּהָא מְבַטְּלִינַן קָלָא, מֵימַר אָמְרִי: עַיְּינוּ בְּהוּ רַבָּנַן בְּקִידּוּשֵׁיהּ וְלָא הֲוָה בְּהוּ שָׁוֶה פְּרוּטָה.§ הַהִיא דִּנְפַק עֲלָהּ קָלָא דְּאִיקַּדְּשָׁה לְחַד

רש"י

הֲרֵי זוֹ מְגוֹרֶשֶׁת. וּמוּתֶּרֶת לַכֹּל. מַאי טַעְמָא הֲרֵי קוֹל. שֶׁחֲשָׁשְׁנוּ לוֹ תְּחִילָּה – שׁוֹבְרוֹ עִמּוֹ. יָצָא לָהּ קוֹל. לְאִשָּׁה פְּנוּיָה בָּעִיר. שֵׁם מְזַנָּה. לְגוֹי וּלְעֶבֶד שֶׁפּוֹסְלִין אוֹתָהּ מִן הַכְּהוּנָּה. אֵין חוֹשְׁשִׁין לָהּ. לְאוֹסְרָהּ לִכְהוּנָּה. פְּרִיצוּתָא בְּעָלְמָא הוּא דַּחֲזוּ לָהּ. שֶׁשִּׂיחֲקָה בַּשּׁוּק, אוֹ מִיעֵךְ לָהּ בֵּין דַּדֶּיהָ. גִּירְגְּרָה בַּשּׁוּק. הָלְכָה נְטוּיַת גָּרוֹן. מוֹזְרוֹת בַּלְּבָנָה. נָשִׁים הַטּוֹוֹת בַּשּׁוּק לְאוֹר הַלְּבָנָה, וְדַרְכָּן לָשׂוּחַ שִׂיחוֹת בְּטֵלוֹת, וּלְדַבֵּר בַּחֲשׁוּדוֹת שֶׁבָּעִיר. לֹא הִנַּחְתָּ כו'. שֶׁיֵּשׁ אוֹיְבִים מוֹצִיאִים קוֹל בְּחִנָּם, בְּרֶמֶז מוּעָט. בְּעוּלָה. יָצָא עַל בְּתוּלָה בָּעִיר קוֹל בְּעוּלָה. אֵין חוֹשְׁשִׁין לָהּ. לְאוֹסְרָהּ לְכ"ג, דְּדִלְמָא פְּרִיצוּתָא בְּעָלְמָא חֲזוּ לָהּ. דְּהָא דִּתְנַן בְּמַתְנִי' דְּחָיְישִׁינַן לְקָלָא – הַיְינוּ כִּדְאָמְרִי' לְקַמָּן: שֶׁיְּהוּ נֵרוֹת דּוֹלְקוֹת כו' שֶׁהַדְּבָרִים נִיכָּרִים. נְשׂוּאָה. יָצָא עַל פְּנוּיָה קוֹל שֶׁהִיא נְשׂוּאָה זֶה יָמִים, וְאָנוּ מוּחְזָקִים בָּהּ בְּחֶזְקַת שֶׁהִיא פְּנוּיָה. אֵין חוֹשְׁשִׁין לָהּ. דְּקָלָא דְּמַתְנִי' הַיְינוּ שֶׁאוֹמְרִים "הַיּוֹם נִתְקַדְּשָׁה פְּלוֹנִית". אֲרוּסָה. יָצָא עָלֶיהָ קוֹל שֶׁהִיא אֲרוּסָה זֶה יָמִים. שֶׁלֹּא לִפְלוֹנִי. יָצָא עָלֶיהָ קוֹל שֶׁמְּקוּדֶּשֶׁת הַיּוֹם, אֲבָל לֹא הִזְכִּירוּ שְׁמוֹ לוֹמַר "לִפְלוֹנִי", אֶלָּא נִתְקַדְּשָׁה סְתָם – אֵין חוֹשְׁשִׁין לָהּ. בְּעִיר אַחֶרֶת. יָצָא כָּאן קוֹל "פְּלוֹנִית מִתְקַדֶּשֶׁת הַיּוֹם בְּמָקוֹ' פְּלוֹנִי". מַמְזֶרֶת. יָצָא קוֹל שֶׁהִיא מַמְזֶרֶת. הִקְדִּישׁ פְּלוֹנִי נְכָסָיו אֵין חוֹשְׁשִׁין. לֶאֱסוֹר נְכָסָיו עָלָיו. נִתְקַדְּשָׁה הַיּוֹם. בְּהָא הוּא דְּחָשׁוּ רַבָּנַן שֶׁלֹּא תִּינָּשֵׂא, כְּדֵי שֶׁלֹּא יֹאמְרוּ: מַשִּׂיאִין אֵשֶׁת אִישׁ. נֵרוֹת דּוֹלְקוֹת. בַּבַּיִת, כְּדֶרֶךְ הַמִּתְקַדְּשׁוֹת שֶׁנּוֹהֲגִין שִׂמְחָה וְאוֹר נֵר, כִּדְאָמְרִינַן בְּעָלְמָא: אוֹר הַנֵּר בְּבְרוּר חָיִל – מִשְׁתֵּה שָׁם (סנהדרין דף לב.). מִתְקַדֶּשֶׁת. עֲתִידָה לְהִתְקַדֵּשׁ הַיּוֹם. אָמְרוּ דָּבָר. "פְּלוֹנִית נִתְקַדְּשָׁה הַיּוֹם". זֶהוּ קוֹל. שֶׁחוֹשְׁשִׁין לוֹ. זֶהוּ אֲמַתְלָא. שֶׁשּׁוֹבֵר אֶת הַקּוֹל. הָא לָא אָמְרוּ מִידֵּי. לֹא אָמְרוּ "נִתְקַדְּשָׁה" – לָאו קוֹל אִיכָּא וְלָאו אֲמַתְלָא אִיכָּא! לְאַפּוּקֵי כו'. אֲמַתְלָא שֶׁאָמְרוּ בְּמִשְׁנָתֵינוּ, שֶׁשּׁוֹבֵר אֶת הַקּוֹל – וַאֲפִי' לֹא יָצָא עִם הַקּוֹל אֶלָּא לְאַחַר זְמַן יָצָא הָוְיָא אֲמַתְלָא. קמ"ל. הָכָא: לֹא אָמְרוּ דָּבָר – זֶהוּ אֲמַתְלָא, וְהָכִי קָאָמַר: לֹא גָּמְרוּ הַדָּבָר לְהוֹצִיא קוֹל מְקוּיָּים וּמְסוּיָּים, אֶלָּא הוֹצִיאוּ שׁוֹבֵר עִם הַקּוֹל, כְּגוֹן: נִתְקַדְּשָׁה פְּלוֹנִית בְּסָפֵק – הוּא דְּהָוֵי אֲמַתְלָא. אֲבָל אָמְרוּ דָּבָר מְקוּיָּים וּמְסוּיָּים – תּוּ לָא מְהַנְיָא אֲמַתְלָא. מְבַטְּלִינַן קָלָא. שָׁמַעְנוּ קוֹל יוֹצֵא מִפִּי נָשִׁים וְתִינוֹקוֹת – מְשַׁתְּקִין לְהוּ לְבַטּוּלֵי קָלָא, אוֹ לָא מְשַׁתְּקִין לְהוּ? הוֹאִיל וְאָמְרוּ: פְּלוֹנִי שָׁמַע מִפְּלוֹנִי כו', וְלֵיתְנְהוּ דְּלִישַׁיְילִינְהוּ. א"נ: חָזְרוּ אוֹתָן פְּלוֹנִי וּפְלוֹנִי מִמְּדִינַת הַיָּם וְאָמְרוּ: לֹא הָיוּ דְּבָרִים מֵעוֹלָם – מְבַטְּלִינַן אוֹ לָא מְבַטְּלִינַן? מִפִּי כְּשֵׁרִים. שֶׁיֹּאמְרוּ: מִפְּלוֹנִי שָׁמַעְנוּ, וְהוּא הָלַךְ לִמְדִינַת הַיָּם. אַלְמָא, אַקִּילוּ רַבָּנַן בְּמִילְּתָא. וש"מ דְּאִי בְּדִיקְנֵיהּ בָּתַר הָכִי, וְאִשְׁתַּכַּח שִׁקְרָא – מְבַטְּלִינַן לֵיהּ, וּמַכְרִיזִין דְּלָאו קָלָא הוּא, וּמַנְסְבִינַן לָהּ. אַתְרָוָותָא נִינְהוּ. מְקוֹמוֹת חֲלוּקִין בְּמִנְהָגָם. בַּאֲצִיפָא דְּתוּחְלָא. הֵם תְּמָרִים שֶׁלֹּא בִּישְּׁלוּ כָּל צָרְכָּם, וּמַנִּיחִין אוֹתָן בְּחוֹתָלוֹת – כֵּלִים הָעֲשׂוּיִים מִכַּפּוֹת תְּמָרִים וּמִתְבַּשְּׁלִים קְצָת, וּכְשֶׁאוֹכְלִים אוֹתָן נִשְׁאָר מִן הָאוֹכֶל עַל הַגַּרְעִין, שֶׁאֵינוֹ נִפְרָד מִמֶּנּוּ יָפֶה מִפְּנֵי שֶׁאֵינָהּ מְבוּשֶּׁלֶת. וְהַהוּא אוֹכֶל קָרֵי לִיפָא, כִּדְאָמְרִי' בְּ"אֵלּוּ טְרֵפוֹת" (חולין נ.): כִּדְעָיְילָן תְּלָת *קַשְׁיָיתָא בְּלִיפָא בְּדוּחְקָא, וְרָאוּי לְמַאֲכַל בְּהֵמָה. בְּעֵינָא דְּבֵי שִׁיפֵי. עַל הַמַּעְיָין שֶׁל אוֹתוֹ מָקוֹם. מֵימַר אָמְרִי. כְּשֶׁתִּינָּשֵׂא לְאַחֵר, לֹא יֹאמְרוּ: רְאוּ אֵשֶׁת אִישׁ שֶׁנִּישֵּׂאת, דְּמֵימַר אָמְרִי: עִיְּינוּ רַבָּנַן בְּהַהוּא חֲלִיפָא, וְלָא הֲוָה בֵּיהּ שָׁוֶה פְּרוּטָה, דִּסְתָמֵיהּ לָא חָשִׁיב. דְּהָא דְּלָא מְבַטְּלֵי' קָלָא – אֵינוֹ אֶלָּא מִפְּנֵי הַחֲשָׁד, וְהָכָא לֵיכָּא חֲשָׁד. לְחַד

תוספות

אכלה בשוק גירגרה בשוק. אומר רבינו יצחק: דאיירי שפיר בקלא דקודם נישואין, שיצא עליה קול זה ומדברות עליה לעז קודם שנשאת לכהן. א"ל ר' יוחנן בן *ברוקה: א"כ לא הנחת בת לאברהם אבינו יושבת תחת בעלה כהן, שהרי הוא אינו יודע במה שדברו עליה קודם, ומה יש לו לעשות?! **בעולה** אין חוששין לה. פי' בקונט': משום בעולה לכ"ג. ולעיל נמי פי': יצא לה שם מזנה בעיר – כגון שנבעלה לגוי או לעבד, דפוסלין בביאה. וה"נ הוה מצי לפרש חייבי כריתות. ורבינו יצחק אומר: דסתם בעילה דזנות שאין ידוע ממי – פסולה לכהונה, והרי היא בחזקת בעולה לנתין ולממזר, עד שתביא ראיה לדבריה. כדאמרינן בפ"ק דכתובות (דף יד.): דאין אשה בודקת ומזנה. ואפילו לר"ג דאמר: נאמנת – היינו היכא דאמרה "לכשר נבעלתי", אבל היכא דאמרה "לא נבעלתי", או אינה יודעת ממי – אפי' רבן גמליאל מודה. **ארוסה** אין חוששין לה. לא מיבעיא נשואה, דאם אמת היה הדבר – היה מתפרסם. אלא אפילו ארוסה, דאין מתפרסם כל כך – אין חוששין. עד שמגיעין לדבר הברור. מסתמא לא פליג רבי אבא אעולא דלעיל, ואברייתא דלוי. וכן משמע, מדלא קאמר: ורבי אבא אמר. אלא לעיל, דאיכא רגלים לדבר – לא בעינן שיגיע לדבר ברור. אבל הכא, דליכא רגלים לדבר – בעינן שיגיע לדבר ברור. *וקול דלעיל לא שייך אלא בקדושין, והך דהכא שייך בגירושין כמו בקדושין.

מבטלינן קלא או לא מבטלינן. נראה כפירוש שני שבקונטרס: כגון שחזרו פלוני ופלוני ממדינת הים, ואמרו: לא היו דברים מעולם. וכן אמרי' לקמן: אילימא לכי מגליא דקדושין קמאי לאו קדושין – מבטלין קלא. ופירוש ראשון אין נראה. ומייתי ראיה מדאמר רב חסדא: עד שישמעו מפי הכשרים – ש"מ מבטלין קלא, כיון שאין חוששין במהרה לקול. **עד** שישמעו מפי הכשרים כו'. אע"ג דאמר לעיל: ונשים אומרות פלונית נתקדשה – שמא משום דהתם איכא רגלים לדבר. ואית ספרים דגרסי: ובני אדם נכנסים ויוצאין, ולא גרסינן ונשים. **כיון** דבעידנא דהוה קלא לא הוה אמתלא. לישנא משמע דסבר כר' יוחנן, ופליג אדרבה בר רב הונא, דאמר: אמתלא שאמרו – אפילו מיכן ועד עשרה ימים. והלכתא

צד א מיי' פ"י מהל' גירושין הל' ו סמג עשין נ טוש"ע אה"ע סי' יז סעיף נח:

צה ב מיי' שם ופ"ט מהל' אישות הל' כב סמג שם טוש"ע אה"ע סי' ו סעי' ה וסי' מו סעיף א:

צו ג ד מיי' פ"י מהל' גירושין הל' כ סמג שם טוש"ע אה"ע סי' ו סעיף ג וסי' מו סעי' ח:

צז ה מיי' פ"ט מהל' אישות הל' כו סמג עשין מח טוש"ע אה"ע סי' מו סעי' ה:

צח ו מיי' פ"ד שם הל' יג סמג שם טוש"ע אה"ע סי' יז סעיף ב:

צט ז ח מיי' שם ופי"ב מהל' גירושין הל' ד סמג שם טוש"ע שם:

ק ט מיי' פ"ט מהלכות אישות הל' כו סמג עשין מח טוש"ע אה"ע סי' מו סעי' ה:

קא י מיי' וסמג שם טוש"ע שם וסי' לא סעיף ד:

לַחַד מִבְּנֵי פְלָנְיָא, אָמַר רָבָא: אֲפִי' לְמַאן דְּאָמַר לָא מְבַטְּלִינַן קָלָא, בְּהָא מְבַטְּלִינַן קָלָא, מֵימַר אָמְרִי: עַיְּינוּ בְּהוּ רַבָּנַן בְּקִידּוּשֵׁי, וְקִידּוּשֵׁי קָטָן הָווּ. הַהִיא דִּנְפַק עֲלָהּ קָלָא דְּאִיקַּדְּשָׁה לְקָטָן הַנִּרְאֶה כְּגָדוֹל, א"ל רַב מָרְדְּכַי לְרַב אַשִׁי: הֲוָה עוּבְדָא, וְאָמְרוּ: עֲדַיִין לֹא הִגִּיעַ לְפַלְגּוּת רְאוּבֵן, שֶׁנֶּאֱמַר: °"לִפְלַגּוֹת רְאוּבֵן גְּדוֹלִים חִקְרֵי לֵב". § "וּבִלְבַד שֶׁלֹּא (שופטים ה) תְּהֵא שָׁם אֲמַתְלָא". § אָמַר רַבָּה בַּר רַב הוּנָא: אֲמַתְלָא שֶׁאָמְרוּ — אֲפִי' מִכָּאן וְעַד עֲשָׂרָה יָמִים. רַב זְבִיד אָמַר: בִּמְקוֹם אֲמַתְלָא חוֹשְׁשִׁין לַאֲמַתְלָא. אֵיתִיבֵיהּ רַב פַּפָּא לְרַב זְבִיד: וּבִלְבַד שֶׁלֹּא תְּהֵא שָׁם אֲמַתְלָא! א"ל: בִּמְקוֹם אֲמַתְלָא קָאָמַר. א"ל רַב כָּהֲנָא לְרַב פַּפָּא: וְאַתְּ לָא תִּסְבְּרָא? *וְהָתְנַן: אנִתְקַדְּשָׁה וְאח"כ בָּא בַּעְלָהּ — מוּתֶּרֶת לַחֲזוֹר; לָאו מִשּׁוּם דְּאָמְרִי' עַל תְּנַאי קַדֵּישׁ? שָׁאנֵי הָתָם, דְּאָתֵי בַּעַל וְקָא מְעַרְעֵר. אִי הָכִי, נִישֵּׂאת נַמִי! נִישֵּׂאת דַּעֲבָדָה אִיסּוּרָא — קַנְסוּהָ רַבָּנַן, נִתְקַדְּשָׁה דְּלָא עָבְדָה אִיסּוּרָא — לָא קַנְסוּהָ רַבָּנַן. אָמַר רַב אַשִׁי: בכָּל קָלָא דְּלָא אִיתַּחְזַק בְּבֵי דִינָא לָאו קָלָא הוּא. *וְא"ר אַשִׁי: גכָּל קָלָא דְּבָתַר נִישּׂוּאִין לָא חָיְישִׁינַן לֵיהּ; הָא דְּבָתַר אֵירוּסִין חָיְישִׁינַן לֵיהּ. רַב חֲבִיבָא אָמַר: אֲפִילּוּ דְּבָתַר אֵירוּסִין נַמִי לָא חָיְישִׁינַן לֵיהּ. דוְהִלְכְתָא: לָא חָיְישִׁינַן לֵיהּ. אָמַר רַב יִרְמְיָה בַּר אַבָּא, שָׁלְחוּ לֵיהּ מִבֵּי רַב לִשְׁמוּאֵל: יְלַמְּדֵנוּ רַבֵּינוּ, יָצָא עָלֶיהָ קוֹל מֵרִאשׁוֹן, וּבָא אַחֵר וְקִדְּשָׁהּ קִידּוּשֵׁי תוֹרָה, מַהוּ? שְׁלַח לְהוּ: תֵּצֵא, וְהַעֲמִידוּ הַדָּבָר עַל בּוּרְיוֹ וְהוֹדִיעוּנִי. *מַאי ("וְהַעֲמִידוּ הַדָּבָר עַל בּוּרְיוֹ")? אִילֵימָא דְּאִי מִגַּלְיָא מִילְּתָא דְּקִידּוּשֵׁי דְּקַמָּא לָאו קִידּוּשֵׁי מַעַלְיָא נִינְהוּ מְבַטְּלִינַן קָלָא? *וְהָא נְהַרְדְּעָא אַתְרֵי' דִּשְׁמוּאֵל הוּא וְלָא מְבַטְּלִי קָלָא! אֶלָּא, הדְּאִי מִיגַּלְיָא מִילְּתָא דְּקִידּוּשֵׁי קַמָּא קִידּוּשֵׁי מַעַלְיָא נִינְהוּ, לָא צְרִיכָה גֵּט מִשֵּׁנִי. וּפְלִיגָא דְּרַב הוּנָא, דְּאָמַר רַב הוּנָא: ואֵשֶׁת אִישׁ שֶׁפָּשְׁטָה יָדָהּ וְקִיבְּלָה קִידּוּשִׁין מֵאַחֵר — מְקוּדֶּשֶׁת, מִדְּרַב הַמְנוּנָא; *דְּאָמַר רַב הַמְנוּנָא: זהָאִשָּׁה שֶׁאָמְרָה לְבַעְלָהּ "גֵּירַשְׁתַּנִי" — נֶאֱמֶנֶת, חֲזָקָה אֵין אִשָּׁה מְעִיזָּה פָּנֶיהָ בִּפְנֵי בַעְלָהּ. וְאִידָּךְ? חכִּי אִתְּמַר דְּרַב הַמְנוּנָא — בְּפָנָיו, שֶׁלֹּא בְּפָנָיו מְעִיזָּה וּמְעִיזָּה. לֹא מָצְאוּ דָּבָר עַל בּוּרְיוֹ, מַהוּ? א"ר הוּנָא: טמְגָרֵשׁ רִאשׁוֹן וְנוֹשֵׂא שֵׁנִי, יאֲבָל מְגָרֵשׁ שֵׁנִי וְנוֹשֵׂא רִאשׁוֹן — לֹא; מַאי טַעְמָא? אָתֵי לְמֵימַר מַחֲזִיר גְּרוּשָׁתוֹ מִן הָאֵירוּסִין. רַב *שִׁישָׁנָא בְּרֵיהּ דְּרַב אִידִי אָמַר: אַף מְגָרֵשׁ שֵׁנִי וְנוֹשֵׂא רִאשׁוֹן, מֵימַר אָמְרִי: עַיְּינִי רַבָּנַן בְּקִידּוּשֵׁי, וְקִידּוּשֵׁי טָעוּת הֲוָה. יָצָא עָלֶיהָ קוֹל מִזֶּה וּמִזֶּה, מַהוּ? אָמַר רַב פַּפָּא: אַף זוֹ, מְגָרֵשׁ רִאשׁוֹן וְנוֹשֵׂא שֵׁנִי. אַמֵימָר אָמַר: מוּתֶּרֶת לִשְׁנֵיהֶם.

וְהִלְכְתָא

רש"י

לחד מבני פלניא. ולא היו אומרים לאיזה מהם. לקטן. בשנים, שנראה גופו כגדול, והיו מכירין בו. עדיין לא הגיע לפלגות ראובן. כלומר: אין חכמה (*לקטן בשנים וחקרי לב) כדכתיב. גדולים הוא דאית להו חקרי לב, וזה, אע"פ שגופו ארוך – ניכר הוא לבריות במעשיו שהוא קטן בשנים, וכשתינשא לאחר – מימר אמרי: עיינו רבנן בקידושיה, וקטן בשנים הוא. במקום אמתלא חוששין לאמתלא. אפי' אין אמתלא, אלא מקום ופתח יש לדבר שנוכל ללמוד שם אמתלא – חוששין שמא אמתלא פלונית יש לדבר, והקול בטל. ובלבד שלא תהא שם אמתלא. אלמא: אמתלא בהדיא בעינן. הכי גרסינן: א"ל במקום אמתלא קא אמר. ואמתני' קאי האי תירוצא. א"ל רב כהנא לרב פפא ואת לא תסברא. דאם יש פתח למצוא אמתלא – דסמכינן ומנסבינן לה? והתנן: אשה שהלך בעלה למדינת הים, ובא עד אחד ואמר לה "מת בעליך" ונתקדשה – מותרת לחזור לראשון, ואילו גבי ניסת קתני התם: תצא מזה ומזה, ואע"ג דאנוסה היא שהרי ב"ד הורוה לינשא, משום חששא דלא לימרו גירש ראשון ונשא שני, ועכשיו היא חוזרת לו משנישאת. אבל גבי נתקדשה – לא חיישינן להכי. מאי טעמא חוזרת לראשון ולא צריכה גט משני? הרי אין לך יצא שמה בעיר מקודשת גדולה מזו, דודאי ידעו כולם שנתקדשה. לאו משום. דיש כאן מקום אמתלא לסמוך עליו, דכי מהדרי לה לגברא, אמרי: ודאי יש פתח לדבר, שעל תנאי קידשה שני, שאם יבא בעלה שגירשה ממדינת הים – שיהיו קידושיו בטלין. שהיה בעלה חביב לה, אלא לכך גירשה, שלא היה יכול לבא. אלמא, אע"ג דלא יצא אמתלא זה מעולם – סמכינן עליה. שאני. הכא דאתי בעל וקאי, ומימר אמרי: מעולם לא גירשה בעלה, אלא היתה סבורה שמת, ונתקדשה, ואינן קדושין. אי הכי. דלא מסקי אדעתייהו לומר גירש ראשון ונשא שני, ונמצאת אשת איש יוצאה בלא גט. ניסת נמי. אמאי תנן התם: צריכה גט משני ולא תחזור לראשון? הא אתא בעלה וקאי, ולאו נישואין הוו! אלא משום דאתי למימר גירשה זה ונשאה זה, כדאמרי' ביבמות, ובנישואין אין פתח מקום אמתלא לומר: על תנאי נשאה. קנסוה רבנן. דהאי דשריוה בהעדאת עד אחד – משום עיגונא אקילו בה, והיא גופה תידוק במילתא ע"י עוברים ושבים, ותנסיב. והיכא דלא דייקא שפיר – קנסוה, כדאמרינן התם: מתוך חומר שהחמרת עליה בסופה – הקלת עליה בתחילתה. דלא איתחזק בבי דינא. שלא בדקו ב"ד אחריו שלא תהא שמיעת קול הברה. לא חיישינן ליה. אלא א"כ ידעו ב"ד העיר שכך יצא הקול: פלוני מהיכן שמע כו', וגזרו שיחושו לקול זה. דבתר נישואין. ניסת היום, ואח"כ יצא קול שהיום היא נתקדשה לאחר קודם נישואין – לא חיישינן ליה לאוסרה על בעלה, ולא להצריכה גט מבעל הקול, שאם אתה מצריכה גט – נמצאת אוסרה על זה, דמחזקת לקלא, ונמצא זה בועל אשת איש, וקיימא לן: כשם שאסורה לבעל – כך אסורה לבועל. דבתר אירוסין. חיישינן, ומגרש ראשון ונושא שני. לא חיישינן ליה. ואינה צריכה הימנו גט, שלא תתגנה על זה. קידושי תורה. בעדים. והעמידו דבר על בוריו. הוו בודקין אחר הקול להעמיד דבר על אמיתתו, אם אמת הוא או שקר. והודיעוני. עיקרו של דבר. מאי היא. למה הזקיקם להעמיד דבר על בוריו. ובנהרדעא לא מבטלי קלא. כדאמרינן לעיל. מקודשת. וצריכה גט משני. ואידך. שמואל, דאמר: העמידו דבר על בוריו, למימרא דלא בעיא גט משני. כי אתמר דרב המנונא בפניו. דבעל, דאמרה ליה בפניו "גירשתני". אבל קבלת קידושין דרב הונא – לאו בפניו הוא, ולא דמיא לדרב המנונא, וליתא לדרב הונא. ונושא שני. אם ירצה. אתי למימר קא מחזיר גרושתו מן האירוסין. דאמרי: ע"י שגירשה ראשון תחילה – קידשה שני, ועכשיו חוזר ומחזירה. עיינו ביה רבנן. בקידושי שני, ולאו קידושי נינהו, מפני שהיתה מקודשת לראשון. ולא יאמרו שגירשה תחלה, שהכל לא ידעו בגט שהצרכנוה משני. יצא עליה קול מזה. ואח"כ מזה – שלא קידשה שני בפנינו קידושי תורה, אלא קול יצא שקידש אחר הראשון. אף בזו מגרש ראשון. ולא יגרש שני וישא ראשון. ואע"ג דקלא בעלמא הוו נמי הנך קידושי שני – חיישי' דלא לימרו גירש ראשון תחלה וקידשה שני, ועכשיו חוזרת לראשון גרושה שנתארסה.

מותרת

[נ"ל וחקרי לב לקטן בשנים]

יבמות לב.

לעיל פח. וש"נ

ס"א מאי היא אילימא

[לעיל פט.]

יבמות קיז. כתובות כב: נדרים צא. לעיל סד.

[בכרי"ף ובה"ש איתא רב שישא]

תוספות

והלכתא לא חיישינן. ומעשה בא לפני ר"ת באשה אחת שיצא עליה קול אחר נישואיה, שנתקדשה לאחר, והיה אותו האיש שיצא עליו קול בחופתה שנישאת לשני, ואר"ת: שאין צריכה גט מן הראשון, ומותרת לשני. חדא – דקלא דבתר נישואין לא חיישינן, ועוד – דכיון שנתקדשה לזה בפניו – שריא, חזקה אין אשה מעיזה פניה בפניו. וכדרב המנונא קיימא לן, מדפריך מיני' הש"ס בכל דוכתי. ובפ' שני דכתובות (דף כב:) קאמר: לימא דרב המנונא תנאי היא? – לא, דכ"ע אית להו דרב המנונא. ואע"ג דבסוף נדרים (דף צא.) דחי רבה ראיית רב המנונא דמייתי מינה – מ"מ כן הלכה, ורבה נמי אפשר דלפי האמת סובר כרב המנונא.

ובנהרדעא לא מבטלי קלא. אע"ג דהני בי רב דשלחו לשמואל הם תלמידי דרב, ובסורא מבטלי קלא – מ"מ לא הוה מורה להו דלא כנפשיה.

ואידך כי אתמר דרב המנונא ה"מ בפניו. וא"ת: וכי לרב הונא הוי דרב המנונא אפי' שלא בפניו? הא תנן בהדיא בפ"ב דכתובות (דף כב.) דאם יש עדים שהיתה אשת איש–אינהנאמנתלומר"גרושהאני"!וי"ל: דודאי רב המנונא לא איירי אלא בפניו, אבל להחמיר להצריכה גט משני סבר רב המנונא דנאמנת אפילו שלא בפניו. והא דאמר בפרק שני דכתובות (דף כב:): מר סבר שלא בפניו נמי אינה מעיזה – היינו דנאמנת עם מיגו שהיה לה. **אמר** רב הונא מגרש ראשון ונושא שני. אבל במצאו דבר על בוריו – פשיטא לרב הונא דלא יגרש שני וישא ראשון. וכיון דודאי קדשה ראשון ומקודשת נמי לשני לרב הונא, כיון שפשטה ידה וקיבלה – א"כ חיישינן שגירשה ראשון, ואם יגרש שני וישא ראשון – הוה ליה מחזיר גרושתו מן הארוסין. אבל בלא העמידו על בוריו, דאין כי אם קול לקידושי ראשון – הוה אמינא דמותר לשני לגרש, ולישא ראשון, קמ"ל דאפילו הכי לא יגרש שני כו'. **אף** בזה מגרש כו'. אליבא דרב הונא קאמר. וכן אמימר דפסיק הלכתא דמותרת לשניהם – לרב הונא קאמר. ואומר ה"ר אלחנן: דמשמע דהלכה כרב הונא.

והלכתא

תוספות רי"ד

דבר ברור עדות מעליא היא אלא פלוני מהיכן שמע מפלוני ופלוני והלכו להן למדינת הים: אמר רבא יצא לה שם מזנה בעיר אין חוששין לה. פי' שזנתה עם פסולי כהונה. כגון עובד כוכבי' ועבד ונתין וממזר אין חוששין לה לאוסרה לכהן משום זונה דלא חיישינן לקלא עד שיראו דברים הניכרים כדעולא: ת"ר בעולה אין חוששין לה. פי' וכשרה לכהן גדול. נשואה אין חוששין לה חלוצה אין חוששין לה ארוסה אין חוששין לה בעיר אחרת אין חוששין לה שלא לפלוני אין חוששין לה ממזרת אין חוששין לה שפחה אין חוששין לה הקדיש פלוני נכסיו אין חוששין להן. פי' נשואה או ארוסה זה כמה ימים אין חוששין לה דקלא דמתניתין היינו שאומר' היום נתקדשה פלונית. בעיר אחרת שאמרו פלונית נתקדשה היום בעיר פלונית. שלא לפלוני שאמרו נתקדש' סתם אבל לא אמרו למי נתקדשה אין חוששין לקול זה: ההיא דנפק עלה קלא דאיתקדשה לבר בי רב אתייה רב חמא לאבוה א"ל אימא לי אי זי גופא דעובדא היכי הוה. א"ל על תנאי קדיש דלא ליזיל לבי חוזאי ואזל. א"ל כיון דבעידנא דהוה קלא לא הואי אמתלא לאו כל כמינך דמחזקת אמתלא: ובלבד שלא תהא שם אמתלא. אמר רבה בר אבוה אמתלא שאמרו אפילו מכאן ועד עשרה ימים. פי' אמתלא שאמרו במשנתינו ששובר את הקול אפילו לא יצא עם הקול אלא אפי' לאחר זמן יצא הויא אמתלא. ואמר רב אשי כל קלא דלא איתחזק בבי דינא לאו קלא הוא. פי' שלא חזרו ב"ד אחריו שלא תהא שמיעת קול הברה לא חיישינן ליה אלא אם כן ידעו ב"ד העיר שכך יצא הקול פלוני מהיכן שמע כו' וגזרו שיחושו לקול זה: ואמר רב אשי כל קלא דבתר נישואין לא חיישינן לה הא דקמי נישואין חיישינן לה רב חביבא אמר אפילו דבתר אירוסין לא חיישינן לה. והלכתא לא חיישינן לה: אמר רב ירמיה בר אבא שלחו ליה מבי רב לשמואל ילמדנו רבינו יצא עליה קול מראשון ובא שני וקידשה קידושי תורה מהו פי' קידושין בעדים. שלח להו תצא והעמידו דבר על בוריו והודיעוני. מאי והעמידו דבר על בוריו. דאי מגליא מילתא דקידושי ראשון קידושי מעליא נינהו לא צריכה גט משני פי' אע"פ שקידשה השני קידושין גמורים בעדים אי מיגליא מילתא דקידושי דקמא הוו קידושין והקול היה אמיתי תצא מן השני בלא גט. ופליגי דרב הונא דאמר רב הונא אשת איש שפשטה ידה וקבלה קידושין מאחר מקודשת כדרב המנונא דאמר רב המנונא האשה שאמרה לבעלה גירשתני נאמנת חזקה אין אשה מעיזה פניה בפני בעלה. ואידך כי איתמר דרב המנונא בפניו אבל שלא בפניו מעיזה ומעיזה והלכתא כרב המנונא ואין הלכה כרב הונא: לא מצאו דבר על בוריו מהו. אמר רב הונא מגרש ראשון ונושא שני אבל מגרש שני ונושא ראשון לא מ"ט אתו למימר מחזיר גרושתו מן האירוסין. רב שישנא בריה דרבא אמר אף מגרש שני ונושא ראשון מימר אמרי עיינו רבנן בקידושי דראשון דקידושי טעות הוו. יצא עליה קול מזה ומזה מהו. פי' שאין עדים לא לראשון ולא לשני אלא שגם לשני יצא קול עליו אמר רב פפא אף זה מגרש ראשון ונושא שני מדקאמר רב פפא אף זו ש"מ בקמייתא כרב הונא ס"ל וליתא לדרב ששנא.

אמימר

מוּתֶּרֶת לִשְׁנֵיהֶם. כְּלוֹמַר, אַף מְגָרֵשׁ שֵׁנִי וְנוֹשֵׂא רִאשׁוֹן. וַאֲפִי' רַב הוּנָא מוֹדֶה בְּהָא. **מתני'** הִקְדִּיחָה. שָׂרְפָה, אוֹ ע"י אוּר, שֶׁקּוֹרִין אדורשי"ר, אוֹ בְּמֶלַח. כְּמוֹ: "כִּי אֵשׁ קָדְחָה בְאַפִּי" (דברים לב). עֶרְוַת דָּבָר. לְב"ה מַשְׁמַע לְהוּ: אוֹ עֶרְוָה אוֹ שְׁאָר דְּבַר סִרְחוֹן. ר"ע אוֹמֵר. אֲפִי' לֹא מָצָא בָּהּ לֹא עֶרְוָה וְלֹא דָּבָר. **גמ'** מִשּׁוּם דָּבָר תִּנָּשֵׂא. הַיּוֹצֵאת מִבַּעְלָהּ מִפְּנֵי דָּבָר, וְלֹא מִפְּנֵי עֶרְוָה – הוּא דְּקָאָמַר רַחֲמָנָא מוּתֶּרֶת לִינָּשֵׂא לְאַחֵר, כְּדִכְתִיב: "וְהָיְתָה לְאִישׁ אַחֵר", אֲבָל הַיּוֹצֵאת מִשּׁוּם עֶרְוָה – תְּהֵא אֲסוּרָה לַכֹּל. וּב"שׁ הַאי דָּבָר מַאי עָבְדִי לֵיהּ כו'. דְּהָא קְרָא דַּוְקָא בְּעֶרְוָה לְחוּד אַיְירֵי, וְא"כ "עֶרְוָה בְּדָבָר" מִבָּעֵי לֵיהּ, כְּלוֹמַר: עֶרְוָה בְּעֵדִים. אַף כָּאן בְּעֵדִים. בְּרוּרִים, אֵינָהּ נֶאֱסֶרֶת עָלָיו מִשּׁוּם עֶרְוָה אֶלָּא בְּעֵדוּת בְּרוּרָה. וּב"ה. דְּהָא עַל כָּרְחֵינוּ הַאי "דָּבָר" מַפְּקִיתוּ לֵיהּ לְעֵדוּת, כִּדְמְפָרֵשׁ לֵיהּ וְאָזֵיל. מִי כְּתִיב עֶרְוָה בְּדָבָר. דְּמַשְׁמַע: דְּמָצָא בָּהּ עֶרְוָה בְּעֵדִים בְּרוּרִים. *וּב"ה. נַמִּי וַדַּאי מִיבָּעֵי לְהוּ לְהָכִי, לְעִנְיַן לְכוֹפוֹ לְהוֹצִיא, דְּלָא כָּיְיפִינַן לֵיהּ לְהוֹצִיא אֶלָּא בְּעֵדוּת בְּרוּרָה. מִיהוּ, לְהָכִי כְּתִיב "עֶרְוַת דָּבָר" וְלָא כְּתִיב "עֶרְוָה בְּדָבָר", וְלָא כְּתִיב נַמִּי "אוֹ עֶרְוַת אוֹ דָּבָר" – כִּי הֵיכִי דְּלִידְרְשֵׁיהּ בְּתַרְוַיְיהוּ, דְּמִשְׁתַּמַּע עֶרְוָה אוֹ דָּבָר, וּמַשְׁמַע נַמִּי עֶרְוָה בְּדָבָר. כִּי מְשַׁמֵּשׁ בְּאַרְבַּע לְשׁוֹנוֹת. בִּמְקוֹם אַרְבַּע לְשׁוֹנוֹת הַלָּלוּ נִכְתַּב "כִּי" בַּתּוֹרָה. בִּמְקוֹם "אִם", בִּמְקוֹם "פֶּן", בִּמְקוֹם "אֶלָּא", בִּמְקוֹם "אֲשֶׁר". בִּמְקוֹם "אִם" – כְּמוֹ: "כִּי יִמָּצֵא בְקִרְבְּךָ" "כִּי יִקָּרֵא" "כִּי תִרְאֶה חֲמוֹר" "כִּי תִפְגַּע" – כּוּלְּהוּ מַשְׁמַע לִכְשֶׁיֶּאֱרַע, כְּלוֹמַר: אִם יִהְיֶה כָּךְ, וְכֵן רוּבָּן. בִּמְקוֹם "אֶלָּא" – לִסְתּוֹר דָּבָר הָאָמוּר לְמַעְלָה, לוֹמַר: אֵינוֹ כֵּן אֶלָּא כֵּן, כְּמוֹ: "וַיֹּאמֶר לֹא כִּי צָחָקְתְּ" – אֵינוֹ כֵּן כִּדְבָרַיִךְ, אֶלָּא צָחָקְתְּ. וְכֵן "אַל תִּקְפּוֹץ אֶת יָדְךָ כִּי פָתוֹחַ תִּפְתַּח לוֹ" – אֶלָּא פָּתוֹחַ תִּפְתַּח לוֹ, וּכְמוֹ "לֹא כִּי בָרְחוֹב נָלִין" – לֹא נָסוּר אֶל בֵּיתְךָ אֶלָּא בָּרְחוֹב נָלִין, וְכֵן הַרְבֵּה. בִּמְקוֹם "פֶּן" – "כִּי תֹאמַר בִּלְבָבְךָ רַבִּים וגו' לֹא תִירָא מֵהֶם" וגו', אֵין אַתָּה יָכוֹל לְפָרֵשׁ בִּלְשׁוֹן אִם, לוֹמַר: אִם תֹּאמַר בִּלְבָבְךָ וגו' לֹא תִירָא מֵהֶם – הָא אִם לֹא תֹּאמַר תִּירָא מֵהֶם, אֵין זֶה נָכוֹן, וְלֹא בִּלְשׁוֹן "אֶלָּא". אֲבָל נִדְרָשׁ הוּא בִּלְשׁוֹן פֶּן, לוֹמַר: שֶׁלֹּא תֹאמַר כֵּן. וּבִתְמִיָּה נִדְרָשׁ, כְּלוֹמַר: וְכִי תֹאמַר בִּלְבָבְךָ רַבִּים הַגּוֹיִם הָאֵלֶּה וְתִירָא מֵהֶם? וְכֵן: "כִּי תֹאמְרוּ מַה נִּרְדָּף לוֹ" – לְעוֹלָם לֹא תָּשִׁיבוּ אֶל לְבַבְכֶם לוֹמַר מַה נִּרְדָּף לוֹ. וְכֵן כָּל "כִּי" הַסְּמוּכִין לְ"אַף", "אַף כִּי תֹאמַר לֹא תְשׁוּרֶנּוּ" "אַף כִּי אָנֹכִי אֶעֱנֶנּוּ" – כּוּלָּן נִדְרָשִׁין בִּלְשׁוֹן תֵּימָה. הִלְכָּךְ סוֹף *פֵּירוּשׁ מְלַמֶּדְךָ פֶּן תֹּאמַר כֵּן. וְעוֹד מְשַׁמֵּשׁ בִּלְשׁוֹן "דְּהָא", דְּהַיְינוּ "אֲשֶׁר" אוֹ "מִפְּנֵי", כְּלוֹמַר לִיתֵּן טַעַם, לְיַישֵּׁב דָּבָר שֶׁלְּמַעְלָה הֵימֶנּוּ, כְּמוֹ: "לֹא צָחַקְתִּי כִּי יָרֵאָה" – כְּמוֹ: אֲשֶׁר יָרְאָה, כְּלוֹמַר מִפְּנֵי שֶׁיָּרְאָה. וְכֵן "מַדּוּעַ אַתָּה יוֹשֵׁב לְבַדֶּךָ, כִּי יָבֹא אֵלַי הָעָם" – מִפְּנֵי שֶׁבָּא אֵלַי הָעָם, שֶׁהָעָם בָּא אֵלַי. וְכֵן "כִּי זֶה מֹשֶׁה הָאִישׁ" "כִּי אָמַרְתִּי פֶּן תִּגְזֹל אֶת בְּנוֹתֶיךָ" "כִּי אָמַרְתִּי רַק אֵין יִרְאַת אֱלֹהִים" – כּוּלָּן נִדְרָשִׁין כְּמוֹ "אֲשֶׁר" – כְּלוֹמַר: מִפְּנֵי. וְכֵן "כִּי גָוַע אַהֲרֹן", לְפִי הַדְּרָשָׁה שֶׁדְּרָשׁוּהוּ חֲכָמִים שֶׁמִּפְּנֵי גְּוִיעָתוֹ נִסְתַּלֵּק הֶעָנָן. וְכוּלְּהוּ מְתַרְגְּמִינַן לְהוּ "אֲרֵי" – שֶׁלְּשׁוֹן אֲרֵי בַּאֲרַמִּי מִשְׁתַּמֵּשׁ כָּל לְשׁוֹנוֹת "כִּי" בְּעִבְרִי, וְאִם בָּאתָ לְשַׁנּוֹתוֹ – צָרִיךְ אַתָּה לְשַׁנּוֹת כּוּלָּן לְפִי עִנְיָינוֹ. וְכָל "כִּי" הַנִּפְתָּרִים בִּלְשׁוֹן "כַּאֲשֶׁר", כְּמוֹ "וְהָיָה כִּי יְבִיאֲךָ" וְכָל אֵלּוּ שֶׁאֵין אַתָּה יָכוֹל לְפוֹתְרוֹ בִּלְשׁוֹן אִם – דְּהָא וַדַּאי יְבִיאֲךָ, וְכֵן "כִּי תָבוֹאוּ אֶל הָאָרֶץ" "כִּי בָא סוּס פַּרְעֹה" "כִּי תִרְבּוּ וּפְרִיתֶם בָּאָרֶץ" – כּוּלָּן לְשׁוֹן "דְּהָא" הֵן נִפְתָּרִים בְּמִדְרַשׁ סִיפְרָא וְסִיפְרֵי: עֲשֵׂה מִצְוָה זוֹ שֶׁבִּשְׁבִילָהּ תִּכָּנֵס לָאָרֶץ, בִּשְׂכַר שֶׁתִּירַשׁ תִּכְבֹּשׁ, כְּלוֹמַר: מִפְּנֵי שֶׁיְּבִיאֲךָ, וּכְשֶׁתָּבוֹאוּ אֶל הָאָרֶץ אַתֶּם זְקוּקִים לַמִּצְוֹת הַלָּלוּ. וְ"כִי בָא סוּס פַּרְעֹה" וגו' – מִפְּנֵי שֶׁבָּא סוּס פַּרְעֹה וגו', לְפִיכָךְ "וַתִּקַּח מִרְיָם" וגו'. וְכָל (א) כְּגוֹן אֵלּוּ שֶׁאֵין אַתָּה יָכוֹל לְפוֹתְרָן בִּלְשׁוֹן "כַּאֲשֶׁר", וְנִפְתָּרִין בִּלְשׁוֹן "מִפְּנֵי" "כִּי יִהְיֶה לָהֶם דָּבָר" "כִּי יֹאמְרוּ אֲלֵיכֶם בְּנֵיכֶם", כְּמוֹ "כִּי יֹאמְרוּ אֲלֵיכֶם בְּנֵיכֶם" – כּוּלָּן לְשׁוֹן "אִם" הֵם. דְּהָא **מָצָא בָּהּ**. מִפְּנֵי שֶׁמָּצָא בָּהּ, הָא לָאו הָכִי – לֹא יְגָרְשֶׁנָּה. וּב"ה נַמִּי הָכִי מַשְׁמַע לְהוּ לְשׁוֹן "מִפְּנֵי", מִפְּנֵי שֶׁמָּצָא בָּהּ אוֹ עֶרְוָה אוֹ דָּבָר, וְאִם לָאו – לֹא יְגָרְשֶׁנָּה. הִלְכָּךְ "לֹא תִמְצָא חֵן" דְּקָאָמַר קְרָא – הַיְינוּ מִפְּנֵי שֶׁמָּצָא בָּהּ, כִּדְמְפָרֵשׁ בֵּיהּ, וְלֹא מִשּׁוּם חֵן שֶׁל נוֹי. וְר"ע. מְפָרֵשׁ לֵיהּ לְהַאי "כִּי" בִּלְשׁוֹן "אִם", הִלְכָּךְ תְּרֵי מִילֵּי נִינְהוּ: אִם לֹא תִמְצָא חֵן שֶׁל נוֹי בְּעֵינָיו, וְאִם מָצָא בָּהּ עֶרְוַת דָּבָר. **לֹא מָצָא** בָּהּ **לֹא** עֶרְוָה וְלֹא **דָבָר**. לְב"ה, וְגֵירְשָׁהּ. מַהוּ. מִי כָּיְיפִינַן לֵיהּ לְהַחֲזִירָהּ אוֹ לָאו? גַּבֵּי **אוֹנֵס**. הָאוֹנֵס אֶת הַנַּעֲרָה בְּתוּלָה. **לֹא** יוּכַל לְשַׁלְּחָהּ כָּל יָמָיו. וְאָמְרִינַן בְּמַסֶּ' מַכּוֹת (דף טו.): דְּהַאי "כָּל יָמָיו" קְרָא יְתֵירָא הוּא, וּבָא לְלַמֶּדְךָ: לֹא יוּכַל לְשַׁלְּחָהּ, וְאִם שִׁלַּח – לֹא יְהֵא בְּשִׁלּוּחָהּ כָּל יָמָיו, שֶׁבֵּ"ד כּוֹפִין אוֹתוֹ לְהַחֲזִירָהּ. וְאֵינוֹ לוֹקֶה עַל שִׁילּוּחוֹ, שֶׁנִּיתְּקוֹ הַכָּתוּב לַעֲשֵׂה שֶׁל עֲמוֹד וְהַחֲזֵר. מִכְּלָל דִּלְכָל הַמְגָרְשִׁים אֵינָם בַּעֲמוֹד וְהַחֲזֵר, דְּאִי כָּל *מְגָרְשֵׁי נְשׁוֹתֵיהֶן בַּעֲמוֹד וְהַחֲזֵר – לָמָּה לִי לְגַלּוּיֵי בְּהַאי? מַהוּ. יֵשׁ עוֹנֶשׁ בַּדָּבָר אוֹ לֹא. שֶׁהַדֵּעוֹת **בְּמַאֲכָל**. דֵּעוֹת בְּנֵי אָדָם חֲלוּקוֹת בְּאִסְטְנִיסוּת שֶׁל מַאֲכָל וּמִשְׁתֶּה; יֵשׁ שֶׁהוּא אִיסְטְנִיס וְקָץ בְּמַאֲכָל מֵחֲמַת מִיאוּס מוּעָט, וְיֵשׁ שֶׁאֵינוֹ אִיסְטְנִיס כָּל כָּךְ, וְיֵשׁ שֶׁאֵינוֹ אִיסְטְנִיס כְּלָל. כָּךְ דֵּעוֹת בְּנֵי אָדָם חֲלוּקוֹת בִּפְרִיצוּת; יֵשׁ מַקְפִּיד עַל פְּרִיצוּת מוּעָט, וְיֵשׁ שֶׁאֵינוֹ מַקְפִּיד כָּל כָּךְ, וְיֵשׁ שֶׁאֵינוֹ מַקְפִּיד כְּלָל. **פַּפּוּס** בֶּן יְהוּדָה. בַּעְלָהּ שֶׁל מִרְיָם מְגַדְּלָא נְשַׁיָּא הָיָה, וּכְשֶׁיּוֹצֵא מִבֵּיתוֹ לַשּׁוּק נוֹעֵל דֶּלֶת בְּפָנֶיהָ שֶׁלֹּא תְּדַבֵּר לְכָל אָדָם. וּמִדָּה שֶׁאֵינָהּ הוֹגֶנֶת הִיא זוֹ, שֶׁמִּתּוֹךְ כָּךְ אֵיבָה נִכְנֶסֶת בֵּינֵיהֶם, וּמְזַנָּה תַּחְתָּיו. וּפְרוּמָה

תורה אור

א וְהִלְכְתָא: מוּתֶּרֶת לִשְׁנֵיהֶם.§ **מתני'** בֵּית שַׁמַּאי אוֹמְרִים: לֹא יְגָרֵשׁ אָדָם אֶת אִשְׁתּוֹ אֶלָּא אִם כֵּן מָצָא בָהּ דְּבַר עֶרְוָה, שֶׁנֶּאֱמַר: °"כִּי מָצָא בָהּ עֶרְוַת דָּבָר"; וּבֵית הִלֵּל אוֹמְרִים: אֲפִילּוּ הִקְדִּיחָה תַּבְשִׁילוֹ, שֶׁנֶּאֱמַר: "כִּי מָצָא בָהּ עֶרְוַת דָּבָר"; ר' עֲקִיבָא אוֹמֵר: אֲפִי' מָצָא אַחֶרֶת נָאָה הֵימֶנָּה, שֶׁנֶּאֱמַ': °"וְהָיָה אִם לֹא תִמְצָא חֵן בְּעֵינָיו".§ **גמ'** תַּנְיָא, אָמְרוּ בֵּית הִלֵּל לְבֵית שַׁמַּאי: וַהֲלֹא כְּבָר נֶאֱמַר "דָּבָר"! אָמְרוּ לָהֶם ב"ש: וַהֲלֹא כְּבָר נֶאֱמַר "עֶרְוַת"! אָמְרוּ לָהֶם ב"ה: אִם נֶאֱמַר "עֶרְוַת" וְלֹא נֶאֱמַר "דָּבָר", הָיִיתִי אוֹמֵר: מִשּׁוּם עֶרְוָה תֵּצֵא, מִשּׁוּם דָּבָר לֹא תֵצֵא, לְכָךְ נֶאֱמַר "דָּבָר"; וְאִילּוּ נֶאֱמַר "דָּבָר" וְלֹא נֶאֱמַר "עֶרְוַת", הָיִיתִי אוֹמֵר: מִשּׁוּם דָּבָר תִּנָּשֵׂא לְאַחֵר, וּמִשּׁוּם עֶרְוָה לֹא תִנָּשֵׂא לְאַחֵר, לְכָךְ נֶאֱמַר "עֶרְוַת". *וּב"ש הַאי "דָּבָר" מַאי עָבְדִי לֵיהּ? נֶאֱמַר כָּאן "דָּבָר" וְנֶאֱמַר לְהַלָּן "דָּבָר" – °"עַל פִּי שְׁנֵי עֵדִים אוֹ עַל פִּי שְׁלֹשָׁה עֵדִים יָקוּם דָּבָר", *מַה לְהַלָּן בִּשְׁנֵי עֵדִים, אַף כָּאן בבִּשְׁנֵי עֵדִים. וּב"ה: מִי כְּתִיב "עֶרְוָה בְּדָבָר"? וּב"ש: מִי כְּתִיב "אוֹ עֶרְוָה אוֹ דָבָר"? וּב"ה: לְהָכִי כְּתִיב "עֶרְוַת דָּבָר", דְּמַשְׁמַע הָכִי וּמַשְׁמַע הָכִי.§ "ר"ע אוֹמֵר: אֲפִי' מָצָא אַחֶרֶת".§ בְּמַאי קָא מִיפַּלְגִי? בִּדְר"ל, *דְּאָמַר רֵישׁ לָקִישׁ: "כִּי" מְשַׁמֵּשׁ בְּד' לְשׁוֹנוֹת: אִי, דִּלְמָא, אֶלָּא, *דְּהָא; ב"ש סָבְרִי: ["וְהָיָה אִם לֹא תִמְצָא חֵן בְּעֵינָיו] כִּי מָצָא בָהּ עֶרְוַת דָּבָר" – דְּהָא מָצָא בָהּ עֶרְוַת דָּבָר, וְר"ע סָבַר: "כִּי מָצָא בָהּ עֶרְוַת דָּבָר" – אִי נַמִּי מָצָא בָהּ עֶרְוַת דָּבָר. אָמַר לֵיהּ רַב פַּפָּא לְרָבָא: לֹא מָצָא בָהּ לֹא עֶרְוָה וְלֹא דָּבָר, מַהוּ? א"ל, מִדְּגַלֵּי רַחֲמָנָא גַּבֵּי אוֹנֵס: °"לֹא יוּכַל לְשַׁלְּחָהּ כָּל יָמָיו" – *כָּל יָמָיו בַּעֲמוֹד וְהַחֲזֵיר קָאֵי, הָתָם הוּא דְּגַלֵּי רַחֲמָנָא, אֲבָל הָכָא – מַאי דַּעֲבַד עֲבַד. א"ל רַב מְשַׁרְשִׁיָּא לְרָבָא: אִם לִבּוֹ *לְגָרְשָׁהּ וְהִיא יוֹשֶׁבֶת תַּחְתָּיו וּמְשַׁמַּשְׁתּוֹ, מַהוּ? גקָרֵי עֲלֵיהּ: °"אַל תַּחֲרֹשׁ עַל רֵעֲךָ רָעָה וְהוּא יוֹשֵׁב לָבֶטַח אִתָּךְ". תַּנְיָא, *הָיָה רַבִּי מֵאִיר אוֹמֵר: כְּשֵׁם שֶׁהַדֵּעוֹת בְּמַאֲכָל, כָּךְ דֵּעוֹת בְּנָשִׁים; יֵשׁ לְךָ אָדָם שֶׁזְּבוּב נוֹפֵל לְתוֹךְ כּוֹסוֹ וְזוֹרְקוֹ וְאֵינוֹ שׁוֹתֵהוּ, וְזוֹ הִיא מִדַּת פַּפּוּס בֶּן יְהוּדָה, שֶׁהָיָה נוֹעֵל בִּפְנֵי אִשְׁתּוֹ וְיוֹצֵא; וְיֵשׁ לְךָ אָדָם שֶׁזְּבוּב נוֹפֵל לְתוֹךְ כּוֹסוֹ וְזוֹרְקוֹ וְשׁוֹתֵהוּ, וְזוֹ הִיא מִדַּת כָּל אָדָם, שֶׁמְּדַבֶּרֶת עִם אָחִיהָ וּקְרוֹבֶיהָ וּמַנִּיחָהּ; וְיֵשׁ לְךָ אָדָם שֶׁזְּבוּב נוֹפֵל לְתוֹךְ תַּמְחוּי, מוֹצְצוֹ וְאוֹכְלוֹ, זוֹ הִיא מִדַּת אָדָם רַע, שֶׁרוֹאֶה אֶת אִשְׁתּוֹ יוֹצְאָה וְרֹאשָׁהּ פָּרוּעַ, וְטוֹוָה בַּשּׁוּק, וּפְרוּמָה

והלכתא מותרת לשניהם. ומעשה בא לפני ר"ת שיצא על גט אחד קול פסול, ונתנו גט שני מפני הלעז. ולא הצריכה ר"ת להמתין ג' חדשים מזמן גט שני, כיון שהראשון היה כשר, ולא היה גט שני אלא מפני חששא דלעז. והביא ראיה מכאן, דאמרי' הכא דמותרת לשניהם, אע"ג דדמי למחזיר גרושתו מן האירוסין, כיון שאין כאן אלא קול בעלמא – לא החמירו. ואומר ר"י: דאין ראיה, דשאני הכא דהוי קול מזה ומזה, ואין דומה כל כך למחזיר גרושתו מן האירוסין. אבל בקול אחר – יש להחמיר, כדאמרינן לעיל כשלא מצאו דבר על בוריו – שלא יגרש שני וישא ראשון, אע"ג דקידושי ראשון לא הוי אלא קול בעלמא – מ"מ מחמירין משום דקידושי שני קידושי תורה, ודמי טפי למחזיר גרושתו מן האירוסין. **כי** משמש בד' לשונות. מה שפי' בקונט' ד"כי תבא" ו"כי יביאך" ו"כי בא סוס" כולן משמשין בלשון "דהא", דאי אפשר שישמשו במקום "אם" דהא ודאי הביאם הקב"ה לארץ, וכן ודאי כי בא סוס פרעה. ונראה לר"ת: דבחנם דחק, דהרבה "אם" משמשים בלשון זה, כגון "אם תקריב מנחת ביכורים" "אם כסף תלוה" "עד אם כלו לשתות" "אם יהיה היובל לבני ישראל" – כולם הם לשון ודאי. לעיל. **מה** להלן בעדים ברורים כו'. בירושלמי פריך: דאמאי אצטריך קרא ד"לא יוכל בעלה אשר שלחה לשוב לקחתה" תיפוק ליה דבלאו הכי אסור להחזיר סוטתו, כיון שיש עדים! ומשני: לעבור עליו *בב' לאוין]. (ג) בית שמאי סברי [כי] מצא בה ערות דבר דהא מצא בה ערות דבר וגו'. ואית ספרים דגרסי: ב"ה וב"ש. ואור"י: דר"ע סבר כב"ש דאמרי ערות דבר חדא מילתא, דאי תרי מילי נינהו – או ערוה או דבר, למה לי לכתוב "דבר" להקדיחה תבשילו? כיון דכתיב "אם לא תמצא חן בעיניו" דהיינו מצא נאה ממנה מותר לגרשה, ו"ערות" דלאחר תנשא, וה"ה הקדיחה תבשילו. ולפ"ז אתי שפיר הא דנקט בספרים "וב"ש", ולא נקט "וב"ה", לאשמועינן אע"ג דשוין ר"ע וב"ש בדרשא ד"ערות דבר" מ"מ פליגי בהאי. והרב רבי אלחנן מפרש: דר"ע אתי שפיר כב"ה, דאי לאו דאייתר ליה "דבר" להקדיחה תבשילו – לא הוה דריש "כי מצא בה" בלשון "אי נמי".

קב א מיי' פ"ט מהל' איסות הל' כז סמג עשין סח טור ש"ע אה"ע סימן מו סעיף ו:

קג ב מיי' פכ"ד מהל' איסות הל' כד סמג שם טוש"ע אה"ע סי' יא סעיף ב וסי' קטח סעיף ט וע"ש:

קד ג מיי' פ"י מהלכות גירושין הל' כא סמג עשין נ טור ש"ע אה"ע סי' קיט סעיף ב:

[פסחים נג:]

[נ"ל בלאו וכן הוא בהדיא בירושלמי]

תוספות רי"ד

אמימר אמר מותרת לשניהם. ופסיק תלמודא והלכתא מותרת לשניהם: **מתני'** בש"א לא יגרש אדם את אשתו אא"כ מצא בה ערות דבר שנאמר כי מצא בה ערות דבר ובה"א אפילו הקדיחה תבשיל שנאמר כי מצא בה ערות דבר. ר' עקיבא אומר אפי' מצא אחרת נאה הימנה שנא' והיה אם לא תמצא חן בעיניו: א"ל רב פפא לרבא לא מצא בה לא ערוה ולא דבר מהו. א"ל מדגלי רחמנא גבי אונס לא יוכל לשלחה כל ימיו [כל ימיו] בעמוד והחזיר קאי מכלל דהכא מאי דעבד עבד. א"ל רב משרשיא לרבא אם [היה] בלבו לגרשה והיא יושבת תחתיו ומשמשתו מהו קרי עליה אל תחרוש על רעך רעה והוא יושב לבטח אתך. תניא היה ר' מאיר אומר כשם שדעות במאכל כך דעות בנשים יש לך אדם שזבוב נופל לתוך כוסו וזורקו ואינו שותהו זו מדת פפוס בן יהודה שהיה נועל הדלת בפני אשתו ויוצא. ויש לך אדם שזבוב נופל לתוך כוסו וזורקו ושותהו וזוהי מדת כל אדם שרואה את אשתו מדברת עם שכניה ועם קרוביה ומניחה. ויש לך אדם שזבוב נופל בתוך תמחוי שלו ומניחו ומוצצו וזוהי מדת אדם רע שרואה את אשתו יוצאה וטווה בשוק וראשה פרוע

נ"י וב"ש

בס' מ"ד מהפך הגי' דכאן ל"ל וב"ש מי כתיב או ערוה כו'

[לעיל פט. ע"ש]

שבועות מט: ר"ה ג. תענית ט.

[מכות טו. תמורה ה.]

[יבמות לז: ע"ש היטב]

[תוספתא סוטה פ"ה]

הגהות הב"ח

(א) רש"י ד"ה כי וכו' וכל אלו שאין אתה כצ"ל ותיבת כגון נמחק: (ב) תוס' ד"ה ב"ש סברי וכו' נ"ב ס"א ב"ה סברי והיה אם לא תמצא וגו':

נ"ל פסוק

גליון הש"ס

תוס' ד"ה מה להלן וכו' בב' לאוין. קשה לי הוא אל איסור מחזיר גרושתו על איסור סוטה בלא כולל ומוסיף ואומר דהוי גזירת הכתוב מנ"ל זה הא י"ל לצריך קרא להיכא דבלא עדי הזמה והזמנו לעדי הטומאה וצ"ע. וע' רשב"א בתשובה סי' תקנ"ז וצריך לי עיון גדול:

פי' שמגרשה שלא כדת

הגהות מהר"ב רנשבורג

א] תוס' ד"ה מה להלן בעדים ברורים כו' בירושלמי פריך כו' ומשני לעבור עליו בב' לאוין. בלאו כנ"ל וכ"כ בשו"ת פנים מאירות ח"א ססי' ק"ד יעוש"ה וכ"ה בירושלמי:

קה א מיי' פ"י מהלכות גירושין הלכה כב סמג עשין נ טוש"ע אה"ע סימן קיט סעיף ד:
קו ב מיי' שם טוש"ע שם סעיף ה:
קז ג מיי' שם הל' כא טוש"ע שם סעי' ג:
קח ד מיי' שם טוש"ע שם בהג"ה:

עם בני אדם סלקא דעתך. פירש בקונטרס: אם כן רגלים לדבר שזונה היא, ואסורה לו, וחובה לגרשה ולא מצוה. וקשה: דהא טווה בשוק ויוצאה וראשה פרוע נמי חובה לגרשה ולא מצוה, דבעיא היא בסוטה (דף כה.) אי עוברת על דת יהודית מותר לקיימה או לא, ולא איפשיטא. ואמאי לא פריך נמי עלה? ויש לומר: דכיון דבעיא בסוטה לא הויא אלא מדרבנן – קאמר שפיר דמצוה לגרשה, אבל זו – חובה לגרשה מן התורה. ועוד יש לפרש: רוחצת עם בני אדם סלקא דעתך? אפילו אדם רע אינו סובל זה מאשתו, או אפילו קלה שבקלות אינה עושה כן.

הכתוב קראו אחר. מיתוקמא אפילו כבית הלל, וא"ערות" קאי.

הדרן עלך המגרש

ופרומה משני צדדיה, ורוחצת עם בני אדם. עם בני אדם ס"ד? אלא במקום שבני אדם רוחצין. אזו — מצוה מן התורה לגרשה, שנאמר: °"כי מצא בה ערות וגו' ושלחה מביתו והלכה (דברים כד) והיתה לאיש אחר", *הכתוב קראו "אחר", בלומר, שאין זה בן זוגו לראשון, זה הוציא רשעה מביתו וזה הכניס רשעה לתוך ביתו. זכה שני — שלחה, שנאמר: "ושנאה האיש האחרון", ואם לאו — קוברתו, שנאמר: °"או כי ימות האיש (שם) האחרון", כדאי הוא במיתה, שזה הוציא רשעה מביתו וזה הכניס רשעה לתוך ביתו. °"כי (מלאכי ב) שנא שלח" — ר' יהודה אומר: אם שנאתה שלח, ר' יוחנן אומר: *שנאוי המשלח. ולא פליגי: גהא בזוג ראשון, הא בזוג שני; *דאמר ר' אלעזר: דכל המגרש אשתו ראשונה — אפילו מזבח מוריד עליו דמעות, שנאמר: °"וזאת שנית תעשו כסות דמעה את מזבח ה' בכי ואנקה מאין [עוד] פנות אל המנחה ולקחת (שם) רצון מידכם, ואמרתם על מה על כי ה' העיד בינך ובין אשת נעוריך אשר אתה בגדתה בה והיא חברתך ואשת בריתך".§

ופרומה משני צדדיה. אגל אצילי ידיה, כדרך ארמיות שבארפת שבשרן נראה מצדיהן. עם בני אדם סלקא דעתך. א"כ רגלים לדבר שזונה היא, ואסורה לו. במקום שבני אדם רוחצים. והיא נכנסת לעיניהם לאחר יציאתן, כשהן לובשין בגדיהן. כי שנא שלח. פסוק (תורה אור) הוא בנבואת מלאכי. אם שנאת' שלח. כרבי עקיבא. אם שנואה היא לפני המקום שלח. כב"ש. ואית דגרסי: שנוי המשלח. וזו שמעתי: שנוי המשלח לפני המקום, ואפילו לבית הלל, נהי דלא כייפינן שלא להוציא, מיהו שנוי הוא. זוג ראשון. אשת נעורים, ודה משמעי קרא כדכתיב בתריה: "אשת נעוריך", וכתיב: "ונשמרתם ברוחכם ובאשת נעוריך אל יבגוד".

הדרן עלך המגרש

תוספות רי"ד

ופרומה משני צדדיה ורוחצת במקום שבני אדם רוחצין זו מצוה מן התורה לגרשה שנא' כי מצא בה ערות דבר: והלכה והיתה לאיש אחר הכתוב קראו אחר כלומר שאין זה בן זוגו של ראשון זה הוציא רשעה מתוך ביתו וזה הכנים רשעה בתוך ביתו זכה שני שלחה שנאמר ושנאה האיש האחרון ואם לאו קוברתו שנאמר או כי ימות כדאי הוא במיתה שרשעה זו הכנים לתוך ביתו: כי שנא שלח רב יהודה אמר כי אם שנאתה שלח ור' יוחנן אמר שנאוי המשלח ולא פליגי הא בזיווג ראשון הא בזיווג שני דאמר ר' אלעזר כל המגרש אשתו ראשונה אפילו מזבח מוריד עליו דמעות שנאמר וזאת שנית תעשו כסות דמעה את מזבח ה' וגו' עד והיא חברתך ואשת בריתך: סליק פרק המגרש

[סוטה ו.]
ס"ל שנואה היא לפני המקום שלח סנהדרין כב.

הדרן עלך המגרש וסליקא לה מסכת גיטין

סליקא מסכתא דגיטין

The following paragraph is recited three times:

הַדְרָן עֲלָךְ מַסֶּכֶת גִּטִּין וְהַדְרָךְ עֲלָן, דַּעְתָּן עֲלָךְ מַסֶּכֶת גִּטִּין וְדַעְתָּךְ עֲלָן, לָא נִתְנְשֵׁי מִנָּךְ מַסֶּכֶת גִּטִּין וְלָא תִתְנְשֵׁי מִנַּן, לָא בְּעָלְמָא הָדֵין וְלָא בְּעָלְמָא דְּאָתֵי.

יְהִי רָצוֹן מִלְּפָנֶיךָ יהוה אֱלֹהֵינוּ וֵאלֹהֵי אֲבוֹתֵינוּ, שֶׁתְּהֵא תוֹרָתְךָ אֻמָּנוּתֵנוּ בָּעוֹלָם הַזֶּה, וּתְהֵא עִמָּנוּ לָעוֹלָם הַבָּא. חֲנִינָא בַּר פַּפָּא, רָמֵי בַּר פַּפָּא, נַחְמָן בַּר פַּפָּא, אֲחַאי בַּר פַּפָּא, אַבָּא מָרִי בַּר פַּפָּא, רַפְרָם בַּר פַּפָּא, רָכִישׁ בַּר פַּפָּא, סוּרְחָב בַּר פַּפָּא, אַדָּא בַּר פַּפָּא, דָּרוּ בַּר פַּפָּא.

הַעֲרֶב נָא יהוה אֱלֹהֵינוּ אֶת דִּבְרֵי תוֹרָתְךָ בְּפִינוּ וּבְפִי
עַמְּךָ בֵּית יִשְׂרָאֵל, וְנִהְיֶה אֲנַחְנוּ וְצֶאֱצָאֵינוּ (וְצֶאֱצָאֵי
צֶאֱצָאֵינוּ) וְצֶאֱצָאֵי עַמְּךָ בֵּית יִשְׂרָאֵל, כֻּלָּנוּ יוֹדְעֵי
תהלים קיט שְׁמֶךָ וְלוֹמְדֵי תוֹרָתְךָ לִשְׁמָהּ. מֵאֹיְבַי תְּחַכְּמֵנִי מִצְוֺתֶךָ
כִּי לְעוֹלָם הִיא־לִי: יְהִי־לִבִּי תָמִים בְּחֻקֶּיךָ לְמַעַן לֹא
אֵבוֹשׁ: לְעוֹלָם לֹא־אֶשְׁכַּח פִּקּוּדֶיךָ כִּי־בָם חִיִּיתָנִי:
בָּרוּךְ אַתָּה יהוה לַמְּדֵנִי חֻקֶּיךָ: אָמֵן אָמֵן אָמֵן סֶלָה
וָעֶד.

מוֹדִים אֲנַחְנוּ לְפָנֶיךָ יהוה אֱלֹהֵינוּ וֵאלֹהֵי אֲבוֹתֵינוּ
שֶׁשַּׂמְתָּ חֶלְקֵנוּ מִיּוֹשְׁבֵי בֵּית הַמִּדְרָשׁ, וְלֹא שַׂמְתָּ חֶלְקֵנוּ
מִיּוֹשְׁבֵי קְרָנוֹת. שֶׁאָנוּ מַשְׁכִּימִים וְהֵם מַשְׁכִּימִים,
אָנוּ מַשְׁכִּימִים לְדִבְרֵי תוֹרָה, וְהֵם מַשְׁכִּימִים לִדְבָרִים
בְּטֵלִים. אָנוּ עֲמֵלִים וְהֵם עֲמֵלִים, אָנוּ עֲמֵלִים וּמְקַבְּלִים
שָׂכָר, וְהֵם עֲמֵלִים וְאֵינָם מְקַבְּלִים שָׂכָר. אָנוּ רָצִים וְהֵם
רָצִים, אָנוּ רָצִים לְחַיֵּי הָעוֹלָם הַבָּא, וְהֵם רָצִים לִבְאֵר
תהלים נה שַׁחַת, שֶׁנֶּאֱמַר: וְאַתָּה אֱלֹהִים תּוֹרִדֵם לִבְאֵר שַׁחַת
אַנְשֵׁי דָמִים וּמִרְמָה לֹא־יֶחֱצוּ יְמֵיהֶם וַאֲנִי אֶבְטַח־בָּךְ:

יְהִי רָצוֹן מִלְּפָנֶיךָ יהוה אֱלֹהַי, כְּשֵׁם שֶׁעֲזַרְתַּנִי לְסַיֵּם
מַסֶּכֶת גִּטִּין כֵּן תְּעַזְרֵנִי לְהַתְחִיל מַסֶּכְתּוֹת וּסְפָרִים
אֲחֵרִים וּלְסַיְּמָם, לִלְמֹד וּלְלַמֵּד לִשְׁמֹר וְלַעֲשׂוֹת
וּלְקַיֵּם אֶת כָּל דִּבְרֵי תַלְמוּד תּוֹרָתְךָ בְּאַהֲבָה, וּזְכוּת
כָּל הַתַּנָּאִים וְאָמוֹרָאִים וְתַלְמִידֵי חֲכָמִים יַעֲמֹד לִי
וּלְזַרְעִי שֶׁלֹּא תָמוּשׁ הַתּוֹרָה מִפִּי וּמִפִּי זַרְעִי וְזֶרַע זַרְעִי
משלי ו עַד עוֹלָם, וְיִתְקַיֵּם בִּי: בְּהִתְהַלֶּכְךָ תַּנְחֶה אֹתָךְ בְּשָׁכְבְּךָ
משלי ט תִּשְׁמֹר עָלֶיךָ וַהֲקִיצוֹתָ הִיא תְשִׂיחֶךָ: כִּי־בִי יִרְבּוּ יָמֶיךָ
משלי ג וְיוֹסִיפוּ לְּךָ שְׁנוֹת חַיִּים: אֹרֶךְ יָמִים בִּימִינָהּ בִּשְׂמֹאולָהּ
תהלים כט עֹשֶׁר וְכָבוֹד: יהוה עֹז לְעַמּוֹ יִתֵּן יהוה יְבָרֵךְ אֶת־עַמּוֹ
בַשָּׁלוֹם:

The following paragraph is recited three times:

הַדְרָן We shall return to you, tractate *Gittin*, and your glory is upon us. Our thoughts are upon you, tractate *Gittin*, and your thoughts are upon us. We will not be forgotten from you, tractate *Gittin*, and you will not be forgotten from us; neither in this world nor in the World-to-Come.

יְהִי רָצוֹן May it be Your will, Lord our God and God of our ancestors, that Your Torah will be our avocation in this world and will accompany us to the World-to-Come. Ḥanina bar Pappa, Ramei bar Pappa, Naḥman bar Pappa, Aḥai bar Pappa, Abba Mari bar Pappa, Rafram bar Pappa, Rakhish bar Pappa, Surḥav bar Pappa, Adda bar Pappa, Daru bar Pappa.

הַעֲרֶב נָא Please, Lord our God, make the words of Your
Torah sweet in our mouths and in the mouths of Your
people, the house of Israel, so that we, our descendants
(and their descendants), and the descendants of Your
people, the house of Israel, may all know Your name and
study Your Torah for its own sake. Your commandments Psalms 119
make me wiser than my enemies, for they are ever with me. Let my heart be undivided in Your statutes, in order that I may not be put to shame. I will never forget Your precepts, for with them You have quickened me. Blessed are You, O Lord; teach me Your statutes. Amen, Amen, Amen, Selah, Forever.

מוֹדִים We give thanks before You, Lord Our God and
God of our ancestors, that You have placed our lot among those who sit in the study hall and that you have not given us our portion among those who sit idly on street corners. We rise early and they rise early. We rise early to pursue matters of Torah and they rise early to pursue frivolous matters. We toil and they toil. We toil and receive a reward and they toil and do not receive a reward. We run and they run. We run to the life of the World-to-Come and they run to the pit of destruction,
as it is stated: But You, God, will bring them down into Psalms 55
the pit of destruction; men of blood and deceit shall not live out half their days; but as for me, I will trust in You.

יְהִי רָצוֹן May it be Your will, Lord my God, just as you have assisted me in completing tractate *Gittin* so assist me to begin other tractates and books and conclude them to learn and to teach, to observe and to perform, and to fulfill all the teachings of Your Torah with love. And may the merit of all the *tanna'im* and *amora'im* and Torah scholars stand for me and my descendants so that the Torah will not move from my mouth and from the mouths of my descendants and the descendants of my
descendants forever. And may the verse: When you Proverbs 6
walk, it shall lead you, when you lie down, it shall watch
over you; and when you awaken, it shall talk with you
be fulfilled in me. For in the Torah your days shall be Proverbs 9
multiplied, and the years of your life shall be increased.
Length of days is in her right hand; in her left hand are Proverbs 3
riches and honor. May the Lord give strength to His Psalms 29
people; the Lord will bless His people with peace.

The following קדיש *requires the presence of a* מנין.

יִתְגַּדַּל וְיִתְקַדַּשׁ שְׁמֵהּ רַבָּא
בְּעָלְמָא דְּהוּא עָתִיד לְאִתְחַדָּתָא
וּלְאַחֲיָאָה מֵתַיָּא, וּלְאַסָּקָא יָתְהוֹן לְחַיֵּי עָלְמָא
וּלְמִבְנֵא קַרְתָּא דִּירוּשְׁלֵם, וּלְשַׁכְלָלָא הֵיכְלֵהּ בְּגַוַּהּ
וּלְמֶעְקַר פָּלְחָנָא נֻכְרָאָה מֵאַרְעָא
וְלַאֲתָבָא פָּלְחָנָא דִשְׁמַיָּא לְאַתְרֵהּ
וְיַמְלִיךְ קֻדְשָׁא בְּרִיךְ הוּא בְּמַלְכוּתֵהּ וִיקָרֵהּ
(נוסח ספרד: וְיַצְמַח פֻּרְקָנֵהּ וִיקָרֵב מְשִׁיחֵהּ)
בְּחַיֵּיכוֹן וּבְיוֹמֵיכוֹן וּבְחַיֵּי דְכָל בֵּית יִשְׂרָאֵל
בַּעֲגָלָא וּבִזְמַן קָרִיב, וְאִמְרוּ אָמֵן.

יְהֵא שְׁמֵהּ רַבָּא מְבָרַךְ לְעָלַם וּלְעָלְמֵי עָלְמַיָּא.

יִתְבָּרַךְ וְיִשְׁתַּבַּח וְיִתְפָּאַר וְיִתְרוֹמַם וְיִתְנַשֵּׂא
וְיִתְהַדָּר וְיִתְעַלֶּה וְיִתְהַלָּל
שְׁמֵהּ דְּקֻדְשָׁא בְּרִיךְ הוּא
לְעֵלָּא מִן כָּל בִּרְכָתָא
/בעשרת ימי תשובה: לְעֵלָּא לְעֵלָּא מִכָּל בִּרְכָתָא/
וְשִׁירָתָא, תֻּשְׁבְּחָתָא וְנֶחָמָתָא, דַּאֲמִירָן בְּעָלְמָא
וְאִמְרוּ אָמֵן. (קהל: אָמֵן)

עַל יִשְׂרָאֵל וְעַל רַבָּנָן
וְעַל תַּלְמִידֵיהוֹן וְעַל כָּל תַּלְמִידֵי תַלְמִידֵיהוֹן
וְעַל כָּל מָאן דְּעָסְקִין בְּאוֹרַיְתָא
דִּי בְּאַתְרָא (בארץ ישראל: קַדִּישָׁא) הָדֵין, וְדִי בְּכָל אֲתַר וַאֲתַר
יְהֵא לְהוֹן וּלְכוֹן שְׁלָמָא רַבָּא
חִנָּא וְחִסְדָּא, וְרַחֲמֵי, וְחַיֵּי אֲרִיכֵי, וּמְזוֹנֵי רְוִיחֵי
וּפֻרְקָנָא מִן קֳדָם אֲבוּהוֹן דִּי בִשְׁמַיָּא
וְאִמְרוּ אָמֵן.

יְהֵא שְׁלָמָא רַבָּא מִן שְׁמַיָּא
וְחַיִּים (טוֹבִים) עָלֵינוּ וְעַל כָּל יִשְׂרָאֵל
וְאִמְרוּ אָמֵן.

Bow, take three steps back, as if taking leave of the Divine Presence, then bow, first left, then right, then center, while saying:

עֹשֶׂה שָׁלוֹם/ בעשרת ימי תשובה: הַשָּׁלוֹם/ בִּמְרוֹמָיו
הוּא יַעֲשֶׂה בְרַחֲמָיו שָׁלוֹם, עָלֵינוּ וְעַל כָּל יִשְׂרָאֵל
וְאִמְרוּ אָמֵן.

The following Kaddish requires the presence of a minyan.

Magnified and sanctified may His great name be,
in the world that will in future be renewed,
reviving the dead and raising them up to eternal life.
He will rebuild the city of Jerusalem
and in it re-establish His Temple.
He will remove alien worship from the earth
and restore to its place the worship of Heaven.
Then the Holy One, blessed be He,
will reign in His sovereignty and splendor.
May it be in your lifetime and in your days,
(*Nusaḥ Sepharad:* make His salvation flourish,
and hasten His messiah,)
and in the lifetime of all the House of Israel,
swiftly and soon – and say: Amen.

May His great name be blessed for ever and all time.

Blessed and praised,
glorified and exalted,
raised and honored,
uplifted and lauded
be the name of the Holy One,
blessed be He,
beyond any blessing,
song, praise and consolation uttered in the world –
and say: Amen.

To Israel, to the teachers,
their disciples and their disciples' disciples,
and to all who engage in the study of Torah,
in this (*in Israel add:* holy) place or elsewhere,
may there come to them and you great peace,
grace, kindness and compassion,
long life, ample sustenance and deliverance,
from their Father in Heaven –
and say: Amen.

May there be great peace from heaven,
and (good) life for us and all Israel –
and say: Amen.

Bow, take three steps back, as if taking leave of the Divine Presence, then bow, first left, then right, then center, while saying:

May He who makes peace in His high places,
in His compassion make peace for us and all Israel –
and say: Amen.